W9-CJP-735

GUERRILLA TACTICS

For Getting The

LEGAL JOB
OF YOUR DREAMS

Second Edition

By

Kimm Alayne Walton, J.D.

THOMSON
———*———™
WEST

Mat #40544175

Thomson/West have created this publication to provide you with accurate and authoritative information concerning the subject matter covered. However, this publication was not necessarily prepared by persons licensed to practice law in a particular jurisdiction. Thomson/West are not engaged in rendering legal or other professional advice, and this publication is not a substitute for the advice of an attorney. If you require legal or other expert advice, you should seek the services of a competent attorney or other professional.

Copyright © 1995, 1999 The BarBri Group, Inc.
© 2008 Thomson/West
    610 Opperman Drive
    St. Paul, MN 55123
    1–800–313–9378

Printed in the United States of America

ISBN: 978–0–314–17677–6

 TEXT IS PRINTED ON 10% POST CONSUMER RECYCLED PAPER

Quotes

"Life is short. Live it up."
    Nikita Khruschev

"Never never never give up."
    Winston Churchill

"Some of the greatest feats were accomplished by people not smart enough to know they were impossible."
    Doug Larson

"Action will remove the doubt that theory cannot solve."
    Tehyi Hsieh

"I will find a way or make one."
    Seneca

"Life is what we make it, always has been, always will be."
    Grandma Moses

"A person in good health in a Western liberal democracy is, in terms of his objective circumstances, one of the most fortunate human beings ever to have walked the surface of the Earth."
    John Lanchester

"God gave you lips. God gave you teeth. Smile!"
    Andre Benjamin of Outkast

"When the eel on the reef
takes your heel in its teeth
that's a moray."
        For a letter to the editor of Smithsonian Magazzine

"You wouldn't know a classy broad if she took a dump on your head."
    Alec Baldwin in the film "Outside Providence."

*

Dedication

The first edition of this book bore the following dedication:

To my wonderful brother, Keir, who has always given me the greatest gift there is: the belief that anything is possible.

That sentiment is every bit as true as it was ten years ago, when I first wrote it. Keirbo, you're the best.

Since the first *Guerrilla Tactics* came out, the circumstances of my life have changed rather dramatically, and so an addendum to that dedication is appropriate.

I would also like to dedicate this book to my husband Henry. Of all of the men I dated—not that there were many—there's only one I should have married, and I married him. I love you, Lambie.

And finally, to my adorable little son Harry. I ask you: in the absence of visiting law schools with a potty-training three-year-old, when would one ever have the opportunity to say, in the presence of distinguished law school deans, "Harry—I'll bet the dean here wears big boy underpants."

Harry, the worst day with you is a thousand times better than the best day without you ever was. Mommy loves you, Bootsy-Boo.

*

Acknowledgements

Fortunately for you, this book contains not one original thought from me. Instead, it has a cast of thousands. Since the first edition of *Guerrilla Tactics* came out ten years ago, I've had the great fortune of visiting almost every law school in America. Career services people, professors and law firm administrators have been incredibly generous in sharing their wisdom (and favorite anecdotes) with me, and this book reflects what I have learned from them. If you attend a law school (or are with a firm) where any of these people work, I hope you'll seek them out and thank them for contributing, because this book, quite literally, would not have been possible without them.

Sharon Abrahams, McDermott Will & Emery LLP
Lisa Abrams, The University of Chicago Law School
Chasity Adewopo, Indiana University School of Law/Indianapolis
Betsy Armour, Boston University School of Law *emeritus*
Abby Armstrong, Vermont Law School
Susanne Aronowitz, Golden Gate University School of Law
Kathleen Austin, Indiana University School of Law/Bloomington *emeritus*
Mindy Baggish, University of California, Davis School of Law
Jose Bahamonde-Gonzalez, University of Maryland School of Law
Drusilla Bakert, University of Kentucky College of Law
Diane Ballou, Quinnipiac University School of Law *emeritus*
Bill Barrett, Wake Forest University School of Law
Dana Bartocci, Maslon Edelman Borman & Brand LLP
Pat Bass, Mercer University School of Law *emeritus*
Anthony Bastone, Roger Williams University School of Law
Rosemarie Benitez, University of California-Davis School of Law *emeritus*
Margann Bennett, Washburn University School of Law
Susan Benson, University of San Diego School of Law *emeritus*
Erin Binns, Marquette University School of Law
Mary Birmingham, University of Arizona School of Law
Beverly Boone, University of Richmond School of Law *emeritus*
Marjorie Boone, Harvard Law School
Elaine Bourne, Washington University School of Law
Kathleen Brady, Brady and Associates Career Planners, LLP
Carolyn Bregman, Emory University School of Law
Mark Brickson, University of Montana School of Law
Amy Thompson Briggs, Catholic University of America School of Law
    emeritus
Gicine Brignola, Pennsylvania State University The Dickinson School of
    Law
Vickie Brown, Georgia State University College of Law
Kyle Buchanan, University of Oklahoma College of Law

Alexandria Bullaria, Santa Clara University School of Law *emeritus*

Phyllis Burkhard, University of South Carolina School of Law

Joshua Burstein, University of Richmond School of Law

Joanne Casey, Albany Law School of Union University

James Castro-Blanco, St. John's University School of Law *emeritus*

Rosanna Catalano, Florida State University College of Law

Kim Cauthorn, South Texas College of Law *emeritus*

William Chamberlain, Northwestern University School of Law

Angela Chapman, Vanderbilt University Law School

Professor Neil Cohen, University of Tennessee College of Law *emeritus*

Dorothy Commons, Suffolk University Law Scohol

Marcelyn Cox, University of Miami School of Law

Gail Cutter, SLJ Attorney Search

Bernice Davenport, Thomas M. Cooley Law School

Elizabeth Davis, Lewis & Clark College Northwestern Law School

Donna Davis-Gregory, Texas Southern University Thurgood Marshall School of Law

Theresa DeAndrado, Washington University College of Law *emeritus*

Richard DelliVeneri, University of Denver Sturm College of Law

Lisa Dickinson, University of San Francisco School of Law

Lisa Doster, Vanderbilt University Law School

Sheila Driscoll, George Washington University Law School

Suzanne Endrizzi, Fordham University Law School

Alexandra Epsilanty, Syracuse University College of Law

Tracy Evans, Louisiana State University Law Center

Tasha Everman, University of Nebraska College of Law

Brian Keith Faulkner, Campbell University Norman Adrian Wiggins School of Law

Brian Ferrell, Creighton University *emeritus*

Kim Fields, Wake Forest University School of Law

Debra Fink, Case Western Reserve University School of Law *emeritus*

Cathy Fitch, Stetson University College of Law

Courtney Fitzgibbons, Golden Gate University School of Law

Kay Fletcher, Texas Tech University School of Law

Jennifer Flexner, University Tulsa College of Law

Anne-Marie Fulfer, University of Idaho College of Law

Susan Gainen, University of Minnesota Law School

Ian Gallacher, Syracuse University School of Law *emeritus*

Karen Garland, SMU Dedman School of Law

Jayne Geneva, Cleveland State University Cleveland Marshall College of Law

Reginald Green, South Texas College of Law

Sue Willis Green, University of Alabama School of Law *emeritus*

Gary Greener, Southwestern University School of Law

Mary Griffin, Vanderbilt University Law School

Ross Guberman, Legal Writing Pro (www.legalwritingpro.com)

Gretchen Haas, University of Denver Sturm College of Law

Laurel Hajek, John Marshall Law School

Alyssa Hammond, Suffolk University School of Law

Mary Harblin, Syracuse University College of Law *emeritus*

Laurie Hartman, Emory University School of Law

Ken Hayduk, Marquette University Law School *emeritus*

Lou Helmuth, California Western School of Law

Ramsey Henderson, University of Georgia School of Law

Deborah Herman, Catholic University of America Columbus School of Law

Suzanne B. Hill, University of Maryland School of Law

Michelle Hoff, University of Connecticut School of Law

Leslie Hom, Golden Gate University School of Law

Skip Horne, Latham & Watkins, LLP

Kitty Cooney Hoye, University of Notre Dame Law School *emeritus*

Vicky Hubler, Santa Clara University School of Law

Pamela Hyland, University of California, Hastings College of the Law

David James, McGeorge School of Law

Regina Ramsey James, Southern University Law Center

Traci Mundy Jenkins, American University Washington College of Law

Kathy Jernigan, Vanderbilt University Law School

Annette Jones, University of Texas School of Law

Vicky Jordan, University of Tulsa College of Law

Laura Share Kalin, Harvard Law School *emeritus*

Robert Kaplan, William & Mary Law School

Supria Kuppuswamy, Emory University School of Law

Heather Karns, University of Toledo College of Law

Lisa Kellogg, California Western School of Law *emeritus*

Michael Keller, Iindiana University School of Law

Sue Kellerman, University of Nebraska College of Law *emeritus*

Shannon Kelly, Creighton University School of Law

Deanna Coe Kersh, Benesch, Friedlander, Coplan & Aronoff

Natalie Kijurna, Valparaiso University School of Law

Joan King, Brooklyn Law School

Carol Kinser, Oklahoma City University School of Law

Dianna L. Kinsey, University of Arkansas at Little Rock William H. Bowen School of Law

Beth Kirch, University of Georgia School of Law

Cheryl Kitchen, Ohio Northern University Pettit College of Law

Kreig Kitts, Georgia State University College of Law

Nora Klaphake, Maslon Edelman Borman & Brand LLP

Karen Klouda, University of Iowa School of Law

Nancy Krieger, University of Michigan School of Law

Supria Kuppuswamy, Emory University School of Law

Ella Kwisnek, Duquesne University School of Law

Laura Rowe Lane, George Washington University Law School *emeritus*

Linda Laufer, Morgan, Lewis & Bockius LLP

Simone Leavenworth, University of Texas School of Law

Melissa Lennon, Temple University School of Law

Lisa LeSage, Lewis & Clark College Northwestern School of Law

Jay Levine, University of Akron School of Law

Brian Lewis, University of North Carolina School of Law

Helen Long, Boston University School of Law

Merv Loya, University of Oregon School of Law

Angelique Magliulo, Santa Clara University School of Law

Pam Malone, The NALP Foundation

Amy Mallow, MallowSossin LLC

Sandy Mans, Albany Law School at Union University

Hillary Mantis, Fordham University Law School

Steve Marchese, University of Minnesota Law School

Phil Marshall, University of California-Hastings College of the Law

Hope Martin, Mercer University School of Law

Victor Massaglia, University of Minnesota Law School

Sue McAvoy, Emory University School of Law

Debbie McCartney, Albany Law School of Union University *emeritus*

Mike Mendelsohn, St. John's University School of Law *emeritus*

Josie Mitchell, The University of Washington School of Law

Suzanne Mitchell, University of Chicago Law School *emeritus*

Angelique Moliglio, Santa Clara University School of Law

Carol Montgomery, George Washington University Law School

Jessica Natkin, Orrick, Herrington & Sutcliffe, LLP

Mary Obrzut, Northern Illinois University School of Law *emeritus*

Pam Occhipinti, Loyola University New Orleans School of Law

Jacqueline Ortega, University of San Francisco School of Law

Matthew Pascocello, American University Washington College of Law

Frank Patek, Phi Alpha Delta Legal Fraternity

Lisa Patterson, SUNY at Buffalo Law School

Elizabeth Peck, Cornell University School of Law

Jane Reinhardt, Nassau County Legal Services

The Honorable George Perez, Chief Judge of the Tax Court of Minnesota

Gail Peshel, Notre Dame University Law School

Elaine Petrossian, Villanova University School of Law

Andrea Swanner Redding, Lewis & Clark School of Law *emeritus*

Diane Reynolds, Willamette University College of Law

Susan Richey, Franklin Pierce Law Center

Gloria Rivera, St. John's University School of Law *emeritus*

Susan Robinson, Stanford University Law School

Mary Karen Rogers, Suffolk University Law School

Cindy Rold, University of Illinois College of Law *emeritus*

Joann Rothery, University of Tennessee College of Law *emeritus*

Gina Rowsam, Oklahoma City University School of Law

Maureen Provost Ryan, St. John's University School of Law *emeritus*

Karen Sargent, Southern Methodist University Dedman School of Law

Gina Sauer, The Esquire Group

Rachael Schell, Mercer University School of Law

Amy Schwarzenbach, Loyola University-New Orleans School of Law

Ellen Sefton, Florida Coastal School of Law

Tricia Brundo Sharrar, Creighton University School of Law

Carolyn Shaud, Reed Smith LLP

Megan Sheets, Brooklyn Law School

Mary Sheffer, Franklin Pierce Law Center

Beth Sherman, Georgetown University Law Center

Graham Sherr, Loyola Law School/Los Angeles

Ann Skalaski, University of Florida College of Law *emeritus*

Dawn Skopinski, SUNY at Buffalo Law School

David Smith, Georgia State University College of Law

Dawne Smith, St. John's University School of Law

Dorris Smith, Vanderbilt University Law School

Sophie Sparrow, Franklin Pierce Law Center

Linda Spotts, Gray Plant Mooty

Jane Steckbeck, University of Oregon School of Law

Richild Stewart, Cleary Gottlieb Steen & Hamilton LLP

April Stockfleet, Harvard Law School

Vince Thomas, University of St. Thomas School of Law

Amy Thompson, Catholic University School of Law *emeritus*

Jane Thomson, University of California, Davis School of Law

Fred Thrasher, National Association for Law Placement

Jerie Torbeck, Brandeis School of Law, University of Louisville

Marilyn Tucker, Georgetown University Law Center

Karen Jackson Vaughn, Temple University School of Law *emeritus*

Anne Stark Walker, University of Denver Sturm College of Law *Emeritus*

Tony Waller, University of Illinois College of Law

Pavel Wonsowicz, William S. Boyd School of Law at UNLV

LaWanda Ward, Indiana University School of Law/Indianapolis

Matthew Wayman, Santa Clara University School of Law

Ellen Wayne, Columbia University Law School

Mark Weber, Harvard Law School

Elizabeth Wefel, University of St. Thomas School of Law

Susan Kalb Weinberg, University of Michigan Law School *emeritus*

Diane Weinzierl, Case Western Reserve University School of Law *emeritus*

Wendy Werner, Werner & Associates, Career coach and law practice management consultant

Amy T. O. Wiecking, University of Hawai'i at Manoa William S. Richardson School of Law

Pershia Wilkins, Albany Law School of Union University

Abbie Willard, University of Chicago Law School

Tammy Willcox, University of Maine School of Law *emeritus*

Elizabeth Workman, Vanderbilt University Law School

Elizabeth Bergen Zabak, Carlton Fields P.A.

Sari Zimmerman, University of California, Hastings College of the Law

Of those, I must draw special attention to the following Career Services Directors. They are the contributors to the original edition of *Guerrilla Tactics* and, of course, this one as well. Not to put to fine a point on it, but when I first called them, they had *no idea* who I was or what they were contributing to. They took a leap into the great unknown by talking to me, and I truly appreciate it:

Lisa Abrams, The University of Chicago Law School

Betsy Armour, Boston University School of Law *emeritus*

Jose Bahamonde-Gonzalez, University of Maryland School of Law

Drusilla Bakert, University of Kentucky College of Law

Susan Benson, University of San Diego School of Law *emeritus*

Kathleen Brady, Brady and Associates Career Planners, LLP

Amy Thompson Briggs, Catholic University of America School of Law *emeritus*

Gail Cutter, SLJ Attorney Search

Theresa DeAndrado, Washington University College of Law *emeritus*

Annette Jones, University of Texas School of Law

Robert Kaplan, William & Mary Law School

Lisa Kellogg, California Western School of Law

Nancy Krieger, University of Michigan School of Law

Laura Rowe Lane, George Washington University Law School *emeritus*

Linda Laufer, Morgan, Lewis & Bockius LLP

Pam Malone, The NALP Foundation

Sandy Mans, Albany Law School at Union University

Mary Obrzut, Northern Illinois University School of Law *emeritus*

Gail Peshel, Notre Dame University Law School

Andrea Swanner Redding, Lewis & Clark School of Law *emeritus*

Diane Reynolds, Willamette University College of Law

Cindy Rold, University of Illinois College of Law *emeritus*

Maureen Provost Ryan, St. John's University School of Law *emeritus*

Ann Skalaski, University of Florida College of Law *emeritus*

Sophie Sparrow, Franklin Pierce Law Center

Marilyn Tucker, Georgetown University Law Center

Ellen Wayne, Columbia University Law School

Wendy Werner, Werner & Associates, Career coach and law practice management consultant

Tammy Willcox, Uniersity of Maine School of Law *emeritus*

Of the original contributors, I must cite most especially Debra Fink, the Career Services Director at my alma mater, Case Western Reserve. She was the first person I called when I figured out the approach for *Guerrilla Tactics*. I asked her, "What do you think of this idea? I'm thinking of writing a job search book for law students by collecting the wisdom of career services people at law schools . . ." she responded with, "Kimm, I think it's a great idea," and offered her wonderful thoughts and put me onto colleagues of hers.

There is no way to overstate the impact of those original words of encouragement. I shudder to think how my career might have taken a different turn if she had dismissed the idea. I owe her a debt of gratitude I can never adequately repay.

I would also like to thank the following attorneys who shared their stories and insights with me, so that I could share them with you:

Sharif Abdrabbo
Nadia Ahmad
Chris Borsani
Rich Colangelo
Jonathan Dichter
Adam Epstein
Donna Gerson
Margarita Glinets
Charles Goetz
Jack Long
Walter Keane
Linda Markowsky
Randy Matthews
Briant Mildenhall
Alex P. Paul
Victor Ruiz
Michelle Reimer
Joe Scheck
Debra Strauss
Bryan Whitehead
Kristin Waller
John Husain Walker
Steven M. Wells

Shout outs to the thousands of wonderful law students from all over the country who have shared with me their career dreams, fears, and experiences. They are the ones who determined the scope of this new edition, and breathed life into it with their stories of triumph and tribulation. Of those many, many law students, I must cite three in particular who are simply extraordinary, and have inspired me more than I ever inspired them: Jonathan Dichter (Seattle University), Suzanne Hill (SUNY Buffalo), and Chris Borsani (Duquesne).

Not everybody who talked to me would allow their names to appear in print. For all of the law students, attorneys and career counselors who offered their stories and advice but insisted on anonymity, you know who you are, and I thank you.

I would also like to thank my original editor, Stephanie Kartofels Goetz, who was patient beyond reason when this book came in more than two years past deadline. *Two years*. I know she fought more battles in-house on my behalf than she ever told me about, and for that I am—and ideally you are, too—incredibly grateful. My new editor, Staci Herr, shepherded this project through and I am grateful for that. I must also thank freelance editor Sue Koplin who was the first person to read this book cover to cover—phew!

I am also indebted to the legendary Richard Conviser, who originally convinced me to publish with what was then Harcourt Brace.

These acknowledgements would not be complete without a word of thanks to my screenwriting mentor, Stewart Bronfeld, who is like a second father to me. I owe whatever facility I have for telling good stories to his wise counsel.

I would like to mention the librarians at the Wilton Public Library in Wilton, Connecticut, where I wrote much of this book. They provided a very harmonious environment in which to think and write. I am particularly grateful that they were not too diligent in shushing people, so I got the chance to eavesdrop on some really interesting conversations.

Of course I cannot complete these acknowledgements without thanking the two men who make my life wonderful. First, my son and traveling companion, Harry, the most extraordinary child on Earth—matched only by your child(ren), of course.

And finally, my husband Henry, who must be incredibly relieved that he no longer has to hear the words, "No, I *can't* do my share of the housework, because *I'm working on my book.*"

At least, until I start my *next* book . . . ;)

KIMM ALAYNE WALTON
Redding, Connecticut

How to Use This Book

This book is going to change your life. I mean it. The first edition changed a *lot* of lives, and this one's even better. But you have to know how to use it.

You may have noticed that this is a—ahem—weighty little book. You're not going to read the whole thing. My feelings aren't hurt. In fact, I'll tell you how to use it so you have to read as little of it as possible.

It's divided into two parts. The first twelve chapters are for everybody. No matter where you go to school or what your circumstances, they apply to you. Even so, you don't have to read all of those chapters. You can skim the topics in the Table of Contents or Index. You can just dive into the specific topic you want, without having to read the whole chapter. (Of course, you're probably going to want to glance through the "Smart Human Tricks" and "Career Limiting Moves" even if you don't read the text. They're *funny*.)

Because I anticipated you wouldn't read the whole book, you'll sometimes find elements repeated, if I considered them sufficiently important. or instance, the "showing gratitude" element of Chapter 10 on finding jobs through people and activities appears several times in those pages.

Let's turn to the remaining chapters, 13 through 31. They cover special situations. Either a chapter applies to you, or it doesn't. Either you go to a distinguished school, or you go to "Not-Harvard." Either you're a second career student or an evening student . . . or you're not. You're looking for a small firm or a judicial clerkship or a public interest gig, or you aren't. So you'll be able to skip most of *that* and focus on what interests you.

When it comes to the coverage in each chapter, you have to remember that I've lived and breathed this stuff for ten years now. I've heard every question on Earth. The detail level in this book is designed to cover every question I've ever received, every issue I've ever heard about when it comes to law student job searches. As a result, some of the material here will *not* be a revelation to you. You'll read some sections where you will say to yourself, "What *idiot* doesn't know *this*?" Well, this idiot, for one; nothing in this book was obvious to me when *I* was in law school. But you're probably a lot smarter than me. For another thing, you'll know things that other students don't know, and vice versa. So I had to cast a wide net to cover everybody.

Incidentally, as your read through the Smart Human Tricks and Career Limiting Moves, you need to know that I changed all identifying characteristics. So if you think you recognize a story as being yours or about someone you know . . . it's not.

I think that's about it. If you want to contact me, you can e-mail me at jobgoddess@aol.com or go to my website at www.jobgoddess.net. I'd love to hear from you, and I really mean that.

And I *really* hope you enjoy reading this book. I sure loved writing it.

How to Contact the Author

My gosh. Thirteen hundred pages. Haven't you had enough of me?

Perhaps not. If you'd like to share a story or ask a question, I'd love to hear from you. E-mail me at jobgoddess@aol.com or visit my website, www.jobgoddess.net.

*

Table of Contents

*

Chapter One
The Secret to Being Happily Employed for the Rest of Your Life

*"Oh would some power the gift give us,
to see ourselves as others see us."*

From *"To A Louse,"* by Robert Burns

"If you will it . . . it is no dream."

Theodor Herzl

You know more than you think you do.

I stole that line. But at least I stole it from a famous book, the second bestselling book of all time: *"Dr. Spock's Guide to Baby and Child Care."* I would have stolen the opening line from the *top* selling book of all time, but somehow opening any book other than the Bible with the line, *"On the first day God created the Heavens and the Earth"* seemed a little presumptuous.

"You know more than you think you do," however, is strangely apt in the context of nailing a great job. And here's why: as you're going to find out, getting great jobs is not a matter of making radical changes in your life. It's little tweaks here and there in what you say and what you do. Things that will be painless, and will quickly become second nature to you. And because you do these things, you wind up happily employed for life.

For instance, when you stand in line at McDonald's, maybe you don't talk to people around you. But let's say that there was a kindly elderly man standing behind you, shepherding two adorable little tykes. And instead of ignoring them, you make a comment to him about the children. "They're very cute!" you say. It doesn't have to be clever, just a nice observation. And that opens up a little conversation. And you find

1

that the kindly elderly man is, in fact, a judge. "What a coincidence!" you say. "I'm in law school!" And as these conversations go, he asks what you're going to be doing when you get out of school. You've heard *that* once or twice. "Well, I'm not sure yet," you respond. And he invites you to come in and talk to him. And you do, and you wind up with a great job, clerking for a federal judge.

I'm loving it.

And all because you paid one teeny, polite compliment to the guy standing behind you in line at McDonalds. (Incidentally, I'm not making this story up. I never make anything up. I have no original thoughts. It happened just this way to a law student—a student just like you.)

So if you dread the idea of looking for a job, you are in for such a treat! With this book, you're going to learn how to nail great jobs not just now, but for the rest of your life. According to research—which, by the way, means 'I read it somewhere, but I can't remember where'— you'll have at least a dozen jobs after you leave law school. *A dozen.* So I'd hardly be doing you a favour if I got you a job now and then bolted the door shut behind you, would I? So grab the beverage of your choice, sit back, and see just how it is that you're going to be happy with your work, now and forever.

That's a pretty bold claim, and as a result an important question may be rattling around in your head; namely, "Who the heck do you think you are, Kimmbo?" Put a different way: Why should you trust me? Well, it's got nothing to do with my own career, that's for sure. I muddled my way through a so-so college, took the LSAT on a bet, got into a not-Harvard law school, stumbled through that, was pretty sure I'd make a lousy lawyer, and what do you know—every legal employer to whom I applied for a job agreed with me. I graduated without any offers. So clearly it's not my own brilliant success finding jobs that ought to make you sit up and take notice.

But I *am* good at one very important thing: I know how to find smart people and get great advice from them. And that's what I did for this book. Actually, it's what I did for the first edition of *Guerrilla Tactics*. After that, law schools started calling my publisher and asking, 'Does she talk?' and I started going around the country, to eighty or a hundred law schools every year, talking about *Guerrilla Tactics*. I met a bunch more smart and wonderful Career Services folks and legal employers, as well as a ton of very creative law students. I've given the *Guerrilla Tactics* seminar—which summarizes this book—about six hundred times now, and counting. I've answered thousands of questions, at seminars and via e-mail. So although my own legal job search career was marked by leaping boldly from failure to failure, and I may not personally know what I'm talking about, I know what other people who do know what they're talking about, are talking about. And that's what this book is full of.

I get several hundred e-mailed questions from law students every week (you can get in on the fun—my e-mail address is jobgoddess@aol.com), and a good portion of them focus on a magic bullet; that is, the idea that there's some simple secret, some potent words to use on cover letters or resumes that will unlock the door to a great job. We are going to learn a fair number of potent words, but when it comes to magic bullets, well ... there *is* magic to a job search, but it's more like a magic Winnebago. It has everything to do with adhering to a guiding principle which is going to imbue everything we talk about in this book. If you keep this principle in mind in every aspect of your job search, you'll do just great.

In order to explain the principle to you, I'm going to use a hypothetical. Not like the ones you get in law school classes; I can't call on you and humiliate you in front of your classmates, and even if I could, I wouldn't. No, in this hypothetical, you're not going to be a law student any more. You're a lawyer. *I'm* the one who's back in law school, and I want a job from you. So I send you my resume. And on my resume, you see that I'm in the bottom ten percent of my class, and I really haven't done much of anything.

Now barring anything else—and that's a *very* key phrase, 'barring anything else'—are you going to be terribly interested in talking to me, in offering me a job? Probably not. And why is that? It's not because I believe you're typecast by your grades. There's a whole chapter about the grades issue, Chapter 13, entitled "Help! My Grades Stink!" as a matter of fact. Contrary to popular belief, your grades will not determine your career. All the great jobs do *not* go to people in the top ten percent of the class. I don't know if you remember President Bush the Younger's comments to the Yale graduating class when he first became president; he told them, "To those of you graduating with A's, honors and awards, I applaud you; to those of you graduating as C students, I say: You, too, can be President of the United States of America." So my grades aren't the issue, specifically. The problem is this: with what I sent you, my crappy grades and nothing else, you're going to have serious questions about whether I'm going to be able to do the work you want me to do, and on top of that, my *motivation* to do it.

Let's change the facts a bit. Let's say that I'm still at the bottom of my class, but this time when I send you my resume, I don't include my grades at all. Instead, on my resume you see that I've had a couple of jobs in law school; maybe I spent a semester or a summer working for a judge or a prosecutor's office or the Justice Department, or the State Attorney General's office, or something like that. And attached to my resume, I have two glowing letters of reference from those two employers. Are you suddenly going to be more interested in talking to me? *Of course you are.* And why is that? Regardless of what my grades are, two employers you respect have great things to say about my work. And that, after all, is the point of grades, isn't it? To show I can do the work! If I've shown that another way, well, who cares how I skinned that particular cat?

I want to talk for a minute about this specific strategy, because I've seen it work spectacularly well. For a start, you need to know that all kinds of top-notch employers, from federal agencies like the Department of Justice (my favourite employer anywhere, by the way), to state agencies, to local agencies and judges ... they all hire law students. Now a lot of these jobs are volunteer jobs, and I know that the word 'volunteer' is a dirty word in law school. But if you spend even a semester, even part of a summer, doing one of these jobs, and they have great things to say about you—that's often all you need to nail other great jobs. It's an investment in your future, and incidentally you'll truly enjoy what you're doing at the same time. That's a great combination!

The first time I saw this letters-and-resume package idea work was with a lovely young man at Nova Southeastern Law School. What he had done was to put together a pocket folder, with his resume on the left-hand side, and his letters of reference on the right-hand side. Now this guy had bupkes for grades, real bottom-dwellers. But he'd talked his way into a couple of jobs, offering to volunteer at first at law firms, and they wound up paying him—and just loving his work. They wrote letters of reference for him you wouldn't believe, everything this side of 'He walks on water.' I was so impressed by this package of resume and letters. I asked him, 'How has this worked for you?' and he smiled and said, 'I've gotten interviews with every employer I've sent it to.'

A couple of things to note about this strategy. First, don't do this for large law firms. You shouldn't send folders or *anything* other than straight documents to them; they'll make a file for you, and folders, binders and the like just make extra work for them. For everybody else, sure. But not large law firms.

Second, notice how different it is than having a line on your resume that says, 'References available on request.' Never put that on your resume. Why? Because it wastes space. Do you really have references available on request? Well, gee, I hope so. It'd be pretty bad news if an employer asked you, 'Do you have any references?' and you said 'Nope.' What are you? In the federal witness protection program? So they'll assume you have references available on request. Either put the reference contact information on your resume, or leave it off. Or go the extra step and add your reference letters.

Also notice the document placement in the folder. What this student had done, very wisely, was to put his resume on the left hand side and his letters on the right. Why is that? If you have any background in advertising, you know the reason. It's because when you open any magazine, your eye is naturally drawn to the right-hand page first. That's why you see all of the advertising there. Go ahead. Try it, with any magazine. So what you do is to take advantage of people's natural instincts and put what you want them to see *first* on the right hand side. When your resume is, well, not the best thing about you, but your references would eat their way through a roomful of dust to get you to work for them, what they have to say about you gets the place of honour on the right hand side.

So—I've got the same grades, but suddenly based on what I've sent you, I look a whole lot better to you. Let's go back to our basic hypothetical and change the facts again. Let's say that I'm still looking for a job, but this time I don't send you anything. Let's say instead that you've decided that you want to hire a law student, or a new graduate, and just as you're about to look through the five thousand unsolicited resumes that have been e-mailed to you, you get a call from your friend Libby Zbiblenik, who says: "Listen, I know you're looking at hiring a law student. I was just at a bar association function (or a continuing legal education seminar, or conference, or whatever), and I was sitting next to this law student, and she's a ball of fire—if you're going to hire *anybody,* you just have to talk to her first."

Now, I've got a question for you. What's going to make a bigger impact on you? Whatever is in those five thousand unsolicited resumes, or that single phone call from your friend? It's the phone call from your friend, isn't it? You know this instinctively. You know that you pay more attention to people than you do to paper. If we're friends, and I say to you, "I just tried this great new restaurant, *Le Petit Cochon,*" you'll eat there before you try one you find in the Yellow Pages. If I say to you, "I just saw this great new movie," or "I just went to this cool store," or whatever—you'll pay more attention to what I say than you would to an ad.

We're going to spend a substantial amount of time in this book talking about how you make yourself into the person in the phone call, in ways that won't make your skin crawl—but that's not the issue for right now.

For right now, think about what links together the three situations I just gave you. It's *image and message control.* Having spoken with tens of thousands of law students, and receiving advice from hundreds of incredible experts, I'm certain that what controls the opportunities you get is not dependent on your grades, or your school, or your work experience—not directly, not in the way you think. Rather, it's how you *present* yourself, the image you create and the way employers receive your message—*that's* what determines the career you'll have. As Courtney Fitzgibbons at Golden Gate points out, "You're not showing employers the family album. It's a snapshot. And a *great* one, at that—a glamour shot." (Incidentally, this approach doesn't stop once you get your foot in the door. The image you create and the message you send once you have a job will determine the trajectory of your career. But that's a topic for another book. Specifically, *my* book, *What Law School Doesn't Teach You . . . But You Really Need To Know.)*

This is true not just for you but for everybody you know, in every aspect of your life. It doesn't matter what's in people's heads, what they're thinking, how they feel. All that has an impact on you is what they say and what they do. In computerese, it's the "interface." David

Pogue, the tech columnist for *The New York Times,* told a story on this very point in an interview on NPR. He had written a scathing review of Microsoft's Pocket PC, pointing out that it took three or four more steps to accomplish anything than the Palm version. Someone from the Pocket PC group at Microsoft called him, and said, "Do you have any suggestions, other than the interface stuff?" and Pogue responded, "Dude! Interface is *everything.*"

He's right. The interface is the thing. What we're going to be doing for the rest of this book is to talk about every aspect of your image and message, so that we craft the image that gets you the opportunities you want. We'll do it on paper (you know—resumes and cover letters and so on), on "cyber-paper" (e-mails), we'll do it for interviews, and we'll talk about easy, enjoyable ways of getting your message out directly to people, without the filter of paper or e-mail.

What you're going to find is that this is a much easier and more fruitful way of getting jobs. For one thing, it'll make you feel that you're in control of your future. It's too easy, when you create a resume or a cover letter the traditional way, to think of yourself as something of a victim of your credentials, to think that your options are guided as if by the occult hand. What I'm going to show you is that regardless of what you've done up until this moment, there's a way to create the image that'll get you the job—and probably a lot faster than you think. I could tell you a million stories that illustrate this, but I won't wear you out—I'll give you just one.

I remember meeting a student in Nebraska a few years ago. She was a First Year, and she had something in common with a number of students I talk to—she was returning to law school after a long absence from the work force, having raised a family. She had sent out a bunch of resumes over the Christmas Break, and she was just despondent; no positive responses. Zip. Zero. Nada. She desperately wanted to get into Labor Law, and she plaintively wailed, "Why *would* they want me? There's nothing on my resume that would interest them." I told her to take the pressure off herself, and to look at building her resume over the summer, so she'd nail that Labor job in the fall. What I told her to do was to get any experience she wanted, on a volunteer or paid basis, for even part of the summer. But she should make a special point of going to Labor-related CLEs (Continuing Legal Education seminars) whenever she could, and load them onto her resume.

When I returned to her school the following year, she sought me out, a beaming smile on her face. She had gone to CLEs over the summer— *eight* of them, to be exact—and had listed them on her resume, directly below her law school education. She told me that she had walked into a handful of law firms in the Fall, and when she handed over her resume—and they saw all the CLEs she'd taken—they were immediately impressed. One of them made her an offer on the spot, doing exactly what she wanted to do—Labor Law.

Now, notice what happened. Her big gap in experience wasn't an issue any more. Employers weren't focusing on the thing that she *didn't* want them to target. They viewed her as she wanted to be a viewed—as an enthusiastic future labor lawyer. Ah, yes. There are a million more options in that particular bag of tricks, and we'll get into all of them. But at the outset, my point is this: You aren't a victim of things you've done. There's always a way to take simple measures to craft the image that gets you the opportunities you want.

A few threshold matters. First of all, yes, some of this stuff is hopelessly obvious. If your e-mail address is pinkpanties@aol.com, killsformoney@optonline.net, get it off your resume before you send it out. If your phone message at home says, "Whazzup, Dawg, don't know where I am, but I'm probably out partying. Leave me a message"— change it before you put your phone number on your resume. So you'll see some advice in this book that'll make you wrinkle up your face and say, "Geez, doesn't *everybody* know that?" Nope. Stupid mistakes will tank your job search just as easily as not-so-stupid ones, so I'll be pointing out all of them.

Second: I'm not suggesting that you only pay attention to what other people think of you. Your first, *most important* obligation is to figure out what you want. What you *really* want. That's the whole focus of Chapter Two. When I talk about image, I'm talking about how you snag what you want, once you've figured out what your dream is. In fact, when it comes to fathoming your dream job, you should expressly *avoid* thinking about what other people want you to have; follow your own muse. But I'm getting ahead of myself. Image control. It's how you get what you already *know* you want.

Third: The idea of image and message control implies a very important point. A job search is not a confessional. Burn that into your brain. "Control" means you don't say (or write) everything that pops into your head. I'm convinced that when it comes to looking for jobs, the three most dangerous words in the English language are, *"To be honest ..."* because whatever comes next—shouldn't. "To be honest ... I'm not really that interested in working *anywhere*." "To be honest ... I thought law school was boring." "To be honest ... I got fired for stealing."

There are things about you that are not for public consumption. I'll give you an example. I'm a public poop-o-phobe. I know that's not the right word, but I'm not sure there *is* a word for people who are terrified of—well—making Number Two in public toilets. I just can't do it. Or doo-doo it. Now, I know from auditory and olfactory evidence that— ahem—not everybody shares this phobia. Why am I telling you this? By way of telling you that as part of a job search, *I would never tell you this.*

The only things that employers are entitled to know about you—and *should* know about you—are things that impact your work, both your work product and what it's like to work with you. The only things you should *volunteer* are positive things that impact your ability to do the work and work with people. That cuts a pretty broad swath, but it's not all-encompassing. So when you are tempted to disclose something to an employer, ask yourself: Is this Kimmbo's poop-o-phobia? Am I telling something that won't help my chances with this employer? If it's something that's related to doing the job and it's *not* positive, am I putting a positive spin on it? (We go into great detail about exactly how to word 'negatives' in Chapters 9 and 10, about resumes and interviewing.) My point is: you're reading an open book. *You* shouldn't *be* one.

Filtering your thoughts is equally important. I am reminded of a story my brother told me about my five-year-old niece, Hailey. She went with my brother and sister-in-law to her first grown-up dinner party. Hailey was very excited when the hostess told her that they were going to have macaroni and cheese for dinner. Of course, the hostess meant *real* macaroni and cheese—not the neon orange kind out of the box (which comprised all of my food groups in law school). When the hostess put Hailey's plate down in front of her, Hailey screwed up her face, and said, "Yuck! What is *this?* I thought we were having macaroni and cheese!"

My sister-in-law tried in vain to explain to Hailey that this *was* macaroni and cheese. Hailey crossed her arms and refused to eat it. The hostess took it in stride, and as Hailey and her parents were getting ready to leave, the hostess told her, "I'm sorry about the macaroni," and Hailey responded, "You should be."

The grownups all had a good laugh over it. Why? *Because Hailey is five years old, that's why.* My point is this: You aren't five years old. And when you say exactly what you think, it's not so charming. It's also really bad for your career. So when an employer asks you what you know about them, the answer isn't, "Nothing, really." When they ask you why you want to work there, the answer isn't, "I'm not so sure I do." Similarly, the whole purpose of your resume is to show them that you've got the skills to do what they want you to do. It's not an exposé. You put down the truthful stuff that makes you look good.

Now, we'll go over finessing your words. But in the meantime, you get the point: image and message control means just what it says. Control. And that means being aware of how you're coming across, and shaping that image and that message—truthfully—to get the jobs you want.

One more point about image and message control. You may, at this point, be feeling a bit skeevy about the whole idea of controlling your image and message. It seems manipulative. Big-Brotherish. Somehow dishonest. Well, I've got news for you. You've been practicing image and message control your entire life, whether you recognize it or not. If you're still single—I've been married about eight years now—what would happen if you went out on a date with someone for the first time, and they said to you, "Thank God you agreed to go out with me. The last fifty people I asked out turned me down." Not a smart message, is it— even if it's true? And if you're married, you know marriage is the ultimate test of message control. When I say to my husband, "Honey, do you think I'm putting on weight?" What does he say to me? "Well, how do you feel? Are your clothes getting tight?" Now, why does he do that? Presumably because he loves me and wants me to be happy—which is why he doesn't say, "Geez, it's about time you noticed you look like a manatee."

Image and message control. It's not dishonest; it's about exhibiting different aspects of yourself in different situations. As Boston University's Helen Long points out, "You don't have just one dimension." Image and message control is something you do naturally, perhaps without even realizing it. All I'm going to do in this book is teach you how to use it to get great jobs.

By the way, you see smart examples of image and message control all the time. For instance, I saw a story in *The New York Times* about when Rudolph Giuliani became mayor of New York. He realized that even though crime was declining in the city, people's fears were being stoked by the relentless tabloid and television coverage of the day's most grisly crime. No matter how much the felony rate dropped, in a city of seven million there would always be at least one crime scene for a live shot at the top of the 11 o'clock news.

So Giuliani told the police to stop giving out details of daily crime in time for reporters' deadlines, a policy that prompted outrage from the press but not many complaints from the public. With the lessening of the daily media barrage, New Yorkers began to be less scared and more realistic about the risks on their streets. In other words: the risks were what they'd always been, but people's image of them changed.

Another example: Poker. Texas Hold 'Em. The kind that's hyper popular on cable television. In an interview with one of the top-ranked players, he made a point of saying that "chip control" is crucial to winning; that is, creating the *image* that you're a pro by the way you manipulate your stack of chips at the table. If you watch these players, they can do amazing tricks of prestidigitation with their chips. It's intimidating to less-chip-savvy players. And it's meant to be. It's part of the image.

Yet another example, from an unlikely source. Holiday Inn Expresses, the hotels with the cinnamon rolls. (I don't want to imply anything about the quality of travel I enjoy ... but I guess I just did.) They apparently had a terrible problem with guests stealing stuff. *Every* hotel suffers from this problem; people take everything that's not nailed down, and many things that *are*. Anyway, on a recent stay I noticed a little sign in the bathroom, and it said essentially, "Like our amenities? Take them with you! You don't have to ask at the front desk. Simply take what you want and we'll add it to your room charge." And then it had a list of prices for everything from washcloths to towels to irons and clock radios.

Now, I ask you: how brilliant is *that?* Instead of trying fruitlessly to keep people's sticky fingers off the goods, they turned it around and said, welcome to the Hotel Store in your room. All of a sudden, you're not a thief. You're a customer.

The *actual* message is somewhat different, isn't it? It says: *If you take it, you pay for it.* But how much *nicer* is it to say it the way they say it? How much *smarter?*

Image. Image. Image.

Incidentally, using image and message control to get the job of your dreams does *not* mean doing things that make your skin crawl. I know what you're thinking: she's going to make me do stuff I hate. No I'm not! What I *am* going to do is to teach you how to think strategically; so that you do things you enjoy that coincidentally get you the opportunities you want. I read a quote that said, "You are as successful as other people want you to be." As we'll see, much of what we'll discuss in this book will position you to tap into the font of natural human kindness and willingness to offer advice.

Here's a story that proves the point. Female law student, first year at a law school in Florida. She's seriously interested in getting into International Law. The problem? Law school hasn't been the Happy House when it comes to grades. Her undergrad credentials? Not much better. So she knows her credentials aren't going to get her what she wants. But she does a few very smart things.

The first one: She keeps her eye on the local newspapers to see when there's anything related to International Law coming to town. She sees that there's going to be a meeting of the Organization of American States coming to the city where she goes to school. Armed with that, she does another really smart thing: she finds out who's organizing the meeting, gives them a call, and volunteers to help out. (Every event needs volunteers—whether you're giving people rides from the airport, touring them around the city or around campus, pouring the punch, handing out name tags, summarizing the proceedings—there's always a way to volunteer.) She winds up acting as a gopher for the person organizing the meeting.

In this capacity, she meets a ton of people, and she does smart thing number three: she works into every conversation her interest in International Law. One of the people she meets tells her, "I can help you get to Washington for the summer. How would you like to work at the White House?" Well, I think we can all agree that having the White House on your resume as a 1L summer job is da bomb.

While she's at the White House, she again works into every conversation her interest in International work. One of the people she meets there says, "How would you like to spend next summer working at the U.S. Embassy in Barbados?"

Not a bad way to start your career in International Law, wouldn't you say? The takeaway here: Note that she didn't get there with her grades—they weren't remarkable. It wasn't her connections—she didn't have those either. She did smart things that put her in a position to get the opportunities to get what she wanted.

And I'm going to teach you how to do exactly the same thing.

Now in order to know what kind of image you need to form, it's important to know what employers want from you. When you strip away all the extrania, there are really only two things employers want, and every aspect of your job search is going to focus on one of them. The first one is obvious: they need to know that you can do the work. That's the function of your resume, although your resume can show other things, as well—we'll talk all about that in the resume chapter, Chapter 8. And there are lots of ways *outside* your resume, and certainly outside of your grades, to show them you can do the work. We'll talk about those in Chapter 8, as well.

The other thing employers want from you is not so obvious, but it's just as important. *They want to know that they like you and want to work with you.* The dirty little secret of job search is this: If you give them an opportunity to know you and like you, they will often convince themselves you can do the work. That's how important this element is. Now, normally when we talk about meeting employers, we think about interviews. We'll cover those in Chapter 9. But there are lots of other ways to skin that particular cat, and we'll spend Chapter 10 discussing those. The bottom line is this: You aren't a resume. You're a living, breathing, dynamic, interesting human being, and the best way to get great jobs is to give employers the opportunity to see *you*—not a stinking piece of paper, not an e-mail.

One more thing before we get started. Everything in this book is useless to you if you don't do anything with it. I write movie scripts for a hobby, and I'm not in the habit of quoting from them. Which means, of course, that I'm about to do exactly that. In one of my scripts, a woman's been stuck in a miserable job for twenty years, working as the bookkeeper at a wire factory. There's nothing wrong with that job, but it's not her dream. And she's asked, "How did you ever wind up doing *this* for twenty years?" and she responds, "I didn't do it for twenty years—I just never did anything about it *today,* and it turned into twenty years."

Don't let that happen to you. Not the wire factory job; the "not doing anything" part. Resolve to do something, anything, for your job search, every day—whether it's researching an employer, contacting an alum, talking to career services, asking a friend if they know someone who does something you'd like to do. *Something.* It's amazing how those "little somethings" will build into something big. I met a law student at one school who'd just published a novel, that he wrote as a *first year law student.* Can you imagine? All of his friends were flabbergasted (as was I) that he had the time, as a First Year, to bang out a novel. I asked him how he did it, and he said, "When everybody else left the library every night, I hung around for an extra half hour and worked on my book." That was it. Half an hour every day, time that most of us wouldn't even miss.

So do the little things every day. Don't wait for a huge block of time when you'll "do it all," because that block of time will never come. I could give you that hoary piece of advice about every journey of a thousand miles beginning with a single step ... hmm. I guess I just did.

But enough of this introductory stuff. You understand image and message control. You know where we're going. Let's get started!

Chapter Two

Figuring Out What the Heck the Job of Your Dreams Is

"When I was a teenager I wanted to write the Great American Novel. But then I realized I didn't even want to read *the Great American Novel."*

    Ray Romano

"What if the hokey-pokey really is what it's all about?"

    Unknown

"I'll tell you what I want, what I really really want,

    I wanna–huh!

    I wanna–huh!

    I wanna–huh!

    I wanna–huh!

    I wanna really really really wanna zig-a-zig ... ahhh."

    The Spice Girls, "Wannabe"

"What would Scooby Do?"

    From the theme to the cartoon "Scooby Doo"

"Here's my passion: Genital mutilation."

That's how a student introduced himself to me after one of my Guerrilla Tactics seminars at a prestigious East Coast law school. As you might imagine, he caught my attention immediately. "Genital mutilation" and "passion" are not two terms I'd ever heard together in the same sentence.

Before my imagination had a chance to run wild, he explained further that he believed that circumcising baby boys mutilates them. He spoke on about it, very excitedly, handing me all kinds of brochures on the topic. This guy was obviously living the hard hats vs. anteaters' debate!

After a couple of minutes of animated advocacy, he said, "Everybody tells me that I have to shut up about genital mutilation in job interviews. But here's my question for you. I've found only two lawyers in America who focus on this issue. Do you think I should work for one of them?"

Without even a moment's hesitation, I told him, "I don't think you should bother applying to anybody else."

Sometimes my Job Goddess gig is cake.

Odds are you aren't into genital mutilation. I'm mentioning this very enthusiastic guy to you for one simple reason: He's very, very lucky. He knows exactly what he wants, and once you figure that out, you're a huge leap toward getting it.

The vast majority of the students I meet don't have that luxury. Gosh knows I didn't as a student. On the children's show "Pinky Dinky Doo," Pinky has a "what you're good at" box. You say your name, turn the crank, and out pops your talent. If only it were that easy! For most of us, the question of "What am I going to do when I grow up?" is excruciating, and for many, many people it's never answered entirely to their satisfaction. I've talked with many a law student with graying temples about this very issue, and either they're well into their forties and fifties, or they're twenty-two year olds who've lived a very hard life.

By the way, don't be intimidated when you hear classmates braggin' on how they know exactly what they want to do. Maybe they're well-informed, and it's a good choice. But maybe they're delusional. Either the job isn't what they think it is, or they're whacked about what they really like or what they're good at (read: 99% of the contestants on *American Idol*).

In this chapter we'll shake off some of the myths and obstacles involved with figuring out your dream job, and get you on your way to something you'll really enjoy. Simply put, I can't help you get what you want—nobody can—if you don't know what it is.

I'm going to start you off with overcoming the thirty-four obstacles to making a great decision. It's just as important, by the way, to wipe away the cobwebs and rid yourself of these delusions as it is to taking positive steps toward making a decision. I've found in many cases that students really have a much better idea of what they want than they think they do, but something—or somebody—is stopping them from acknowledging it.

With those hurdles overcome, we'll do some strategerizing, to quote George Bush the Younger, about nailing what your dream job is. I know what you're thinking: there's going to be some of that gross touchy-feely-what-does-my-inner-child-want stuff. Wellllll ... kinda. I know that as a law student what you really want is a series of black-and-white questions—multiple choice even?—that'll spit out your dream job. You won't get that here (and by the way, anyone who tells you they can give you that is yanking your chain). But we'll zero in on the kinds of traits any job has to have to make you happy. Finally, we'll talk about how to get yourself "unstuck" if, after all of this, you still can't decide.

Let's get started!

A.   THE 34 BIGGEST MISTAKES LAW STUDENTS MAKE IN DETERMINING THEIR DREAM JOB

1.   REMEMBER YOUR <u>REAL</u> GOAL: IT'S NOT FINDING A PARTICULAR JOB. IT'S LIVING A HAPPY LIFE

That's what we're talking about, really, isn't it? Not so much the job you take, but the life you live, and making it the happiest one it can possibly be. They say there are three keys to happiness: something to do, someone to love, and something to hope for. Your work is only one of those (or maybe two, if you include at least in part the "something to hope for").

The jobs that will contribute the most to your happiness will reflect your talents, motivations, and values. They will employ skills you enjoy using. They will give you the chance to work with people whose company you like.

There's been a great deal of research in the last few years in the area of "positive psychology"—that is, the study of happiness as opposed to psychological disorders. It's developed some very interesting and simple conclusions. Firstly, a large part of your happiness comes from your natural happiness "set point"—that is, your predisposition to view the glass as half empty or half full. When you look at the people you know and think about how happy they are, you know that some of them tend to naturally be happier than others. There's a great story about this. I wish I could remember it. But I *do* remember the punch line. Basically there are these two boys, one of them miserable and the other one, happy. Their parents give the miserable one a pony and the happy one a room filled with manure. The miserable one isn't happy with the pony, but when the parents look in on the other boy in the room full of s**t, he's happily digging through it. Incredulous, they ask him how he can possibly be happy. He says, "With all of this manure, there must be a pony in here somewhere." Not exactly a side-splitter, but you get the point!

Interestingly enough, the one element of happiness over which you have control is voluntary work. The more connected we feel with other people, the happier we are. It's not surprising, then, that public interest jobs typically result in so much satisfaction!

Another element of happiness is the sense of control we feel over our lives. Autonomy, whether you recognize it or not, plays a huge role in your job satisfaction. Again, people who work in jobs with greater autonomy, like small law firms, tend to be happiest. In fact, study after study reveals that the happiest lawyers in private practice are those who work in the smallest law firms.

Finally, it's easy to be deceived by the importance of money. This is America, after all! Studies show that making more money does, in fact, make people happier ... but above $50,000 a year, it doesn't matter. If you think money (or fame, for that matter) makes people happier, you need to watch more biographies on A & E. It turns out that people always believe that $10,000 more would make them happier. It doesn't—because it's always the next $10,000 that matters!

Money, autonomy, "voluntariness"—those are all parts of the puzzle. In topics B and C in this chapter, we'll talk about figuring out your talents, motivations and skills and values and fashioning a happy life from them ... of which your work is just a part!

2. DON'T MAKE YOURSELF CRAZY WITH THIS DECISION. EVEN IF YOU MAKE A MISTAKE, YOU CAN ALWAYS "RIGHT THE SHIP"

You can drive yourself to distraction trying to choose a career. Part of the problem is that damned Internet. Knowing that there are millions of jobs out there—with 30,000 + different job titles, by the way—can convince you that a) there has to be a "perfect" job for you, and b) no matter what you choose, there's something better.

Here's the truth. There's no perfect job for you, any more than there's a "perfect" mate for you. You'll find a job—and a mate, for that matter—that will have most of the things you like and the absolute minimum of things you don't. You'll find that job by gathering all of the information you can right now, about yourself and about the jobs that are out there—we'll go over your strategy detail by detail in this chapter—and you'll go for what looks best. You'll still keep your eyes open. As you go after your choice, you may find something else you like even more. OK. Go for that instead. Or you may get the job, and it'll suit you for a while, but you'll *still* keep your eyes open, and when you see something better, you'll switch jobs. If you have a goal that requires intermediate steps, like an in-house counsel gig at a major company or being President of the United States, you'll learn what other people have done to get there, and adjust your course accordingly; again, reexamining your goal as you progress to make sure it's still what you really want. This ongoing information-gathering process—living with your eyes wide open, being a fully-participating member of the human race—is the recipe for a happy life.

Here's a little secret. The happiest people I know don't have "life plans." They do exactly what I've just described. They know something about themselves, they gather information, they make a decision knowing it may not be perfect, and they change course when something better comes along.

If you make a mistake—oops! You make a change. One law school graduate went to a very large law firm, and just hated it. "I was a chimp," he said. He went to a small firm doing insurance defense litigation—and hated that, too. Then he went into law school administration, and *loved* it—he got a chance to teach a class or two, and had the time to pursue a favourite hobby—acting in musical theater. (By the way, we talk about law school administration jobs in the "I Want To Be A Not—Lawyer" chapter, Chapter 31.)

So take it easy on yourself. There's no way you can make a fatal mistake—because your career decisions are always reversible.

3. DON'T BELIEVE THAT YOUR DREAM JOB WILL SATISFY ALL OF YOUR NEEDS. UNREALISTIC EXPECTATIONS CAN KILL ANY GREAT JOB ... BECAUSE EVERY JOB, EVEN A DREAM JOB, REQUIRES SACRIFICES

It's impossible to be happy with any job if you think the job is going to give you everything you want—just as it's impossible to find a spouse if you demand that the other person be perfect. Career wise, there are many great jobs. There are no *perfect* jobs. It's true of every aspect of your life. Having a baby? The best gig in the world. But its downsides are neatly summarized with the words "rectal thermometer."

So part of figuring out what you want is figuring out what you'll put up with to get it.

For instance, let's say you want a lot of variety in what you do, that you get bored easily. The kinds of jobs that spring to mind immediately would be working in a prosecutor's office or a state attorney general's office, where you get a lot of variety. A small practice in a small town is also a place where you'll handle all kinds of work, a kind of one-stop shop, where you'll close on a person's real estate for them, handle their divorce, and represent them on a criminal charge—presumably not all at the same time. In those kinds of jobs, by and large you'll also work reasonable hours. Another positive. But are you going to pile up the dead presidents, make the mad cheese? No, not at first, anyway. Are you going to travel a lot for work? Not likely.

Or let's say you want to work at a large, prestigious law firm, rake in the semolians, and you want reasonable hours. Bwahahaha. While you may negotiate for part-time work (read: forty hours a week) at a large firm after you've impressed them and built up some leverage, you'll make yourself miserable if you think you can avoid long hours for big pay at a big firm. (It just doesn't make economic sense—when you're selling your time, the only way to make big money is to work long hours.)

Let's take another one. Let's say you love to write, and you want to be in court, you want to be a litigator. As SLJ Attorney Search's Gail Cutter points out, the litigation job isn't likely to satisfy your creative writing bent. You'd have to consider the writing a hobby ... and there's nothing wrong with that.

I could go on. Autonomy? Breaking out on your own so that you have total autonomy will mean a commensurate lack of security. Travel? If you have a job that requires a lot of travel, you'll miss a lot at home. I remember talking to one law student, who was thinking of designing video games instead of practicing law. He asked me, "Won't the other game designers resent working with a lawyer?" and I said, "You won't be a lawyer. If you take your degree and design video games, you're a video game designer." An alternative career means giving up the sobriquet "lawyer," and the prestige often associated with it.

Part of what makes choosing a career so difficult is that by opening one door, you are necessarily shutting others. While you're a student, you have the great luxury of being a potential "anything." You haven't had to make a choice. Nobody can criticize your decision because you haven't made one. But once you're done with school, that phase of your life is over. If you're going to be a lawyer you're not going to be an astronaut (not in the short term, anyway). If you're going to be a movie star, you're not going to be President of the United—oops. Not unless you're Ronald Reagan, anyway.

So being a grownup is tough. Shedding expectations is tough, as well. After all, you came to law school to maximize your career happiness quotient. And you're going to do that. But the fact is, the fewer expectations you can attach to your immediate job goal, the more likely you'll attain it. In every single aspect of your life, expectations are everything.

You see this all the time. Disney World, for instance, is reputed to put up signs at their rides saying "The wait is 30 minutes from here," knowing that it's only 25 minutes, so that people are pleased when they get to the ride five minutes earlier than anticipated.

Another setting where you see the dark side of expectations is in television ratings, specifically the different expectations between network and cable viewership. In one week in April of 2002, *The Osbournes* on MTV was watched by six million viewers. The *New York Daily News* called it "White hot" and Ozzy Osbourne requested a multimillion dollar raise.

That very same week, the show *Ally McBeal*, on network TV, was watched by 8.1 million viewers, which the *Daily News* called "Nothing spectacular ... sluggish ratings." That day, *Once and Again*—another network show—had its finale, and the *Daily News* said it did "Absolutely zilcho in the ratings department ... with a measly 7.7 million viewers to go out with a whimper."

Notice those numbers? Six million means Ozzy Osbourne rocks. Whereas two million *more* viewers for Ally McBeal makes it a snooze! What's going on? *Expectations.*

I see this happen to law students and new graduates all the time. When I was on honeymoon in French Polynesia in 1999, I ran into a recent law school graduate while we were taking a photo safari on the island of Moorea. It turns out that he worked at a firm that appears in my book *America's Greatest Places To Work With A Law Degree*. He leaned over to me and said, "I have to tell you, Kimm, it's not that great. They often make us work until 6:30 at night."

I couldn't believe what I was hearing. Here's this guy, and within six months of graduation, he's on a vacation that I'd saved up for years to take as my honeymoon. Having been on the job for half a year, he obviously had at least two weeks of vacation, because you don't hop over to Tahiti for a long weekend—it's too damned far away. And on top of that—6:30? I knew this guy was pulling down six figures, and as I've pointed out before, in the practice of law, you're selling time and that means the more you make, the more hours you have to expect to work. 6:30 in that context is very, very reasonable. No wonder this outfit made it into *America's Greatest Places!*

But you see what had happened. He'd obviously convinced himself that he shouldn't be working beyond five o'clock. Now, there are many legal jobs that will allow you to do that on a regular basis. Working in a large law firm isn't one of them!

What would you be wise to expect? A job that maximizes what you like and minimizes what you don't. Working with people you like. Doing work that's consistent with your values, talents and motivations. But a job will *always* have aspects that don't appeal to you. *Always.* To tell you the truth, it's a lot like choosing a spouse. As my father always told me, "Look for someone who's 90% of what you want. That's the most you can expect. The rest of the relationship is figuring out whether you can put up with that other 10%."

As is true in so many other aspects of your job search—we'll be talking about it all the way through this book—make an effort to talk to people about what they do, and be sure to ask them: "What would you change about your job if you could?" Listen to the down sides as well as the positives, to keep yourself conscious of the fact that when you get some things, you give up others—and being happy with your job is ultimately being satisfied with both.

4. DON'T BE INFLUENCED BY YOUR GRADES OR YOUR SCHOOL

Law school can mess with your mind in a big way. You came to law school a confident person, and now . . . yikes. I've heard all kinds of downers. A student at a California school wanted international law, specifically the State Department. Everyone he mentioned this to scoffed at his idea, some of them telling him straight out, "Forget it. You have to go to Harvard to get in." At another school, a guy who'd been a chemistry major in undergrad wanted to take that technical background and go into Intellectual Property, a logical choice. A professor had told him, "If you're not in the top ten percent of the class—forget it."

He wasn't in the top ten percent of the class.

I'm not going to kid you into thinking that life isn't easier finding a job if you're #1 in the class at Harvard Law School than if you're . . .

well, the kind of law student I was, for example, with OK grades at an OK law school.

But when you're trying to figure out what your dream job is, you have to set that thought aside, and here's why: I'll guarantee you that no matter what your grades are like, or where you go to school, you can get more jobs than you think you can. The State Department, IP Law—please. Of *course* they've hired students from schools other than Harvard, below the top ten percent of the class!

There's a simple way to verify this. Let's say that you want to work at a large, prestigious law firm. I get e-mails all the time from students who say, "They won't even look at students from my school." Really? Well, go to alumni services and find out if any student from your school has ever worked at a large, prestigious law firm. The answer is yes—no matter where you go.

Now, with any particular law firm, it may well be that your school is an issue. But translated, all that really means is: "We want you to show us more." All right. If it's a firm some distance from your law school, the issue is probably just that they don't *know* anything about your law school. It's ignorance, not disdain. They're not dissing your school. You lean on your Career Services Director in that case, and have them send the employer information about your school … and you convince them that you're serious about being in that city (see Chapter 17 for Out–Of–Town Job Searches). Or maybe it's a firm that *is* familiar with your school, and they just don't hire anyone from there. That's very, very, *exceptionally* rare. But just for giggles, let's go with the premise. What do you do? You take an intermediate step, that's all. An "apprenticeship," if you will. You go to a smaller firm to prove your chops. Or the state attorney general's office. Or the prosecutor's office. Or you go to a state court clerkship, move on to a federal court clerkship, and I promise you they'll look at you differently.

I could go on and on about this, but here's my point: when you're trying to zero in on a dream job, don't eliminate classes of jobs just because you think your grades or your school disqualify you. We'll talk strategy once you have a dream in mind!

5. DON'T PUT PRESSURE ON YOURSELF TO MAKE A DECISION RIGHT THIS MINUTE

If my student correspondents are any indication—and they are—there is unbelievable pressure in law school to know <u>exactly</u> what you want to do with your degree when you get out. The pressure starts the moment you tell people you want to go to law school, and gets excruciatingly more pressing as you approach graduation. (April is my busiest month for e-mail, because that's when I get the 'I'm-graduating-next-month-help!' e-mails.)

Now, I'm not pretending that April of graduation year isn't a bit—hmm—late to start thinking about these things, but I've got a whole chapter devoted to that issue (Chapter 29). But I often get this question from 1Ls and 2Ls, and I know where the pressure on them largely comes from: other people. After all, when people are constantly asking you: "So what are you going to do when you get out? So what are you going to do when you get out? So what are you going to do when you get out?" Like some freaking mynah bird, you start thinking to yourself, "Hmm. I guess I'm supposed to <u>know</u>."

To that I say: No, you're not. There may have been nothing in your life to this point that gives you that knowledge, especially if you went straight from college to law school and you've always had the 'you-want-fries-with-that' category of jobs. Why <u>would</u> you know? Maybe you went to law school thinking law school would <u>tell</u> you that. Maybe you've had six careers before law school and you just aren't good at making this kind of decision. Whatever the situation is, I'd tell you: don't pressure yourself into making a decision right now.

In fact, take the whole issue out of the realm of making a decision and recharacterize it this way: You're learning what's out there. You're learning about what you're good at, what will make you happy at work. No pressure. You're just going to learn about what people do, as though you were researching it for a class project, or for your best friend. What does this do? It lets you relax a bit and enables you to take in lots of information, which is the best way to make the decision in the first place. You aren't looking at every specialty as though you were looking for a spouse because you have to be married right now.

You may be thinking, "Well, that's great, Kimmbo, but what do I <u>say</u> when people ask me what I want to do?" Good question, since that's where a lot of the pressure to make a decision comes from in the first place. The way you deal with that question is to deflect it, in a particularly useful way. When someone asks you what you're going to do when you get out of school, say, "That's a question I'm spending a lot of time researching. How did you decide what <u>you</u> wanted to do?" What does this accomplish? Well, it doesn't make you sound like a slacker, because it's got that 'researching' word in it. And on top of that, it might actually give you some useful guidance, because the 'questioner's' answer may give you some insights into your own decision. "I knew this about myself ..." "I talked to somebody who ..." Or you'll find out that they were more clueless than you could *ever* be. "I took the first thing that paid the bills ..." "I dunno, I just fell into it ..." Either way, you've deflected the issue—and that's exactly what you wanted to do.

6. THINK ABOUT WHAT YOU WANT TO DO, THE LIFE YOU WANT TO LIVE ... NOT THE EMPLOYER YOU WANT TO WORK FOR

When you're trying to hone in on what will make you happy, it's important to focus on what counts: the activities with which you fill your day, what's important to you, the people you work with, and the people you serve.

In Topic B, "The internal part," we'll uncover this. Why is it so important? First, it will expand your options. If you think about what you like to do, how you want to fill your day, you will find that there are many more settings in which your ideal days are spent than if you focus on a particular position. Secondly, you may find that employers you consider dream employers don't give you the life you really want.

Let's pretend for a moment that you have a family, and spending time with your family is one of your core values. And let's say that one of the most rewarding things you've done was a clinical program in which you helped small business people.

And let's say that you've had it in your mind that you want to go to a large firm, because ... well, who doesn't? And you figure you'll do transactional work because that involves working with businesses.

But let's take a look at that job. Big law firms—with big paychecks—work you long hours. When all you're selling is time, the more you make, the more you work. That's it. And small businesses? Ha ha. They can't afford large law firms. As one associate at a large firm commented, "When you work here you shift money around between rich people."

In other words: the two most important elements of your "happy job"—spending time with your family and helping small businesspeople—will expressly not be satisfied by a large law firm job.

So when you think about what you want to do, Job #1 is to strip away titles and focus on the life you want to live, and what the elements of that life are. Values, motivations, talents ... once you have those elements in hand, then you can look at settings that will satisfy you!

There's a concrete example of this that strikes very close to home for me. My great friend Laura has a three year old son, Max. She's in the throes of a divorce. She is absolutely devoted to Max; he's the most important thing in her life by far. She spends lots of time with him, and takes him to her parents' place in Cape Cod every summer for two months.

Laura has been a full-time mom since Max's birth. Before that, she was in financial services, specifically as a compensation consultant. (She also worked at Priceline.com before it went public, and on paper, for a few weeks at least, she was worth $50 million ... then, poof! But I digress.)

Now, although she'll get child support and alimony in the divorce, she'll have to get a paying gig. She's flirted with the idea of returning to financial services, but ... here are the realities of that job. To commute into New York, where those jobs are, from our homes in Connecticut takes an hour and a half each way. Financial services pays well—exceptionally well—but it also requires notoriously long hours, a good twelve a day. And vacations? The standard week or two to start.

So—if she returns to financial services—what's her life like? It requires an au pair or nanny for a start, since she'd have to leave for work before Max gets up, and he'd be asleep on her return. There goes about $40,000 in pre-tax dollars from her salary. On top of that, no summers on Cape Cod. All around, a major sacrifice.

I suggested she consider teaching. Teachers are greatly sought-after where we live. The pay is damn good, $60,000 to start, bennies are outstanding, hours are reasonable, and she'd get summers off ... just like Max will. It means 33 hours of grad school credits to get certified, but by talking with people who work at the local university she found that if she works there ten hours a week, the tuition is free. She likes kids, and there are subjects she'd love to teach. Will she make the same dough she'd have raked in in financial services? Nope. But remember: there are no perfect jobs. Only ones that offer you more of what you like, and less of what you don't. So a teacher she's going to be!

The key: looking at the life you want to live ... not just the job you want to do.

7. DON'T BE INFLUENCED BY WHAT OTHER PEOPLE (OR YOU YOURSELF) MAKE YOU FEEL YOU *OUGHT* TO WANT

It's terrifyingly simple to work the mental alchemy of turning "I know I *ought* to want ..." into "I want." I see this happen all the time. 1Ls come to school with all kinds of interesting ideas about what they want to do, and by the Fall of Second Year—everybody wants to work at a large firm. It's like salmon spawning. Do they really all want that job? Of course not. But what happens is that everybody learns that large law firms pay the mad cheez from the get-go.

The fact that we use the word "top" instead of "large" when we talk about big law firms doesn't help either, with its connotation of quality rather than merely size. Your "top" law firm may well consist of three lawyers!

Then you have the fact that large law firms are the ones who largely comprise fall recruiting programs, and so everybody who's visibly interviewing is interviewing with them. Add to that the prestige, and you've got a recipe for bad decision making.

Parental pressure is equally harmful. Every student who has ever been convinced an alternative career is for them immediately evokes an image in their minds of their parents, devastated by the news that Junior isn't going to be a lawyer after all. As Minnesota's Susan Gainen puts it, it's too easy to succumb to the pressure of "Our Susan the lawyer." But again: your parents aren't going to live your life for you. No matter how much they've done for you, how much of your education they've funded, they ultimately want you to be happy (no matter how well disguised that desire can sometimes seem!). They may feel that with their greater experience, they know better than you what will make you happy. A Career Services Director told me about her own experience. She'd done very well in law school and was pursued by several large law firms. She had a nagging (and ultimately accurate) feeling that she wouldn't enjoy large firm practice, and she talked about her doubts with her father. He was dumbfounded. "Don't tell me you can't be happy on a *hundred thousand* dollars a year!" he thundered. She said, "I realized that he thought I was crazy. Here was a man who'd immigrated to

America, often worked several jobs to support his family, and here *I* was, saying I wasn't sure I could be happy on more money than he'd ever made." You can see his point but you can also see how that can lead to a life of unhappiness. While it's undeniably true that finances are a leavening aspect of your career—you do, ultimately, have to pay the bills—what we're talking about here is the threshold question of figuring out what you want to do.

Hear out your loved ones, consider their opinions, but ultimately remember: you've got to live your life on a day to day basis, and if you want a job that pays less, that doesn't merit the letters "Esq." after your name—so be it.

The pressure to conform to other people's expectations is also severe if you happen to have great grades or go to a distinguished school. The best example of this I ever saw was when I spoke at one of the country's premier law schools. After my talk, students hung around to chat and ask questions, and I noticed one guy who was kind of hanging toward the back of the pack. That's always the person with the most interesting question! When everyone else had left, he nervously approached me and said, "I think there must be something wrong with me, with what I want, because Career Services won't talk to me. I go in there and ask them about it, and it's like—they pretend I didn't say anything. I just—I think I must be crazy."

Naturally at this point I was dying to hear what the heck his dream was, and after a bit of nervous lip-biting, he whispered: "I think I want to be a personal injury lawyer."

"Are you kidding? There's <u>nothing</u> wrong with you!" I immediately reassured him. And at virtually any other law school in the country he'd have a wealth of information at his fingertips, and a whole bunch of alums to talk to, as well. But at <u>his</u> school—well, PI is not the order of the moment. Or the century. They all go to large law firms, or federal court clerkships, or jobs of that ilk. I doubt that there's a single PI lawyer in the history of the school—until this particular young man! I told him he could very well enjoy PI immensely, and on top of that, he'd likely be the wealthiest person in his class!

Whatever decision you make, there's always someone to knock it down. When career counselor Amy Mallow's husband moved cross-country to set up a solo practice, people told her, "Do you think that's *smart?*" Gee, thanks! (It *was* smart, by the way.) Remember: You're the only one who's got to live your life. Take other people's advice—but remember that the decision is ultimately yours alone!

8.   BE SKEPTICAL WHEN YOU READ (OR SEE) PEOPLE WHO HAVE WHAT SEEMS TO BE "THE PERFECT JOB"

When it comes to figuring out your dream job, the media is not entirely your friend. You'll often read profiles of people who are described as 'having it all.' In fact you may be saying to yourself, "Wait a second, Kimmbo. I read about all kinds of people in newspapers, I see them on TV, who have perfect jobs.'' Well, I read and see those things, too. One that particularly stands out for me—I think it was in the *Wall Street Journal*—was this babe who went on and on about how she successfully managed to 'have it all,' a satisfying family life and a high-powered career. If I remember it right, she was a top exec at a credit card company, and she was jawboning about how she gets up at four in the morning, works for a couple of hours at home, has breakfast with her three kids and gets them off to school, goes to the office and conducts glamorous deals all day, goes home for dinner with the kids and reads them a night-night story, and works until midnight at home.

I may be wrong about her being an executive at a credit card company, but I'll tell you one thing she is: A lyin' sack of pony loaf. Nobody has it all. Nobody. If you think you know people who do, you don't know them well enough to know what they've given up.

When you read about people in the newspaper or see them on TV, remember: they're telling you what they want you to hear. If the theme of the piece is how they live a perfect life, they're unlikely to tell you the warty aspects of their lives. And there's always the possibility that regardless of what they actually said, their words were edited into something else.

Remember: when you read about someone or see them on TV, you aren't following them around or living in their head. So for gosh sakes if you want to be happy, don't tell yourself that there are people whose jobs are completely fulfilling to them in every possible way, because every job has aspects that are less than fun. Every one.

I have a friend who was an extra in *"The Stepford Wives."* She was talking about life on the set, and she said, "I always wanted to be a movie star until I actually saw what they do. They sit around for hours and hours and hours in between filming, looking completely fed up. It seems glamorous but it was really, really boring. I could never do it." Add to that the constant, excruciating pressure of paparazzi, the humiliation of bad reviews, having your missteps splashed on the cover of the *New York Post* . . . so, yeah, sure, being a movie star is undeniably not a bad gig—but it isn't a perfect one.

As an aside, a lot of what we think we know is wrong, because a movie, TV show, or article has misled us. You probably believe, for instance, that lemmings are suicidal, throwing themselves off cliffs in droves. Do you know where that comes from? A 1958 Oscar-winning documentary called *Wild Wilderness*. The filmmakers knew lemmings like to jump into rough water together, but that fact alone lacked dramatic tension. So they herded the unsuspecting lemmings toward the edge of a cliff, filmed their plunge into the river, and added later a narration about "suicide." Lemmings are actually perfectly well-adjusted. The mass suicide thing is a media fantasy.

Back to jobs. Don't weigh down your dreams with unrealistic expectations based on what you see in the media. Articles about what people do are often a great jumping-off point for identifying jobs you might like.

But whatever those articles say, there's no perfect job. The best and only thing you can demand of your career is that the good things outweigh the bad things—far outweigh them. And that's perfectly attainable!

9. Don't Freak Yourself Out by Believing You're Making a Lifetime Decision. It's All Right to Be Fickle

I hear this "lifetime decision" advice from law professors and deans all the time. In stentorian tones, they say, "Be careful about that first job. It'll typecast you for life." As though it's an albatross around your neck. The Scarlet Letter. You'll be the star-bellied sneetch.

For gosh sakes—it's just a *job*. It won't determine the trajectory of your career if you don't want it to! As Richmond's Josh Burstein points out, "It's not a lifetime decision!"

I've mentioned before that on average, when you get out of law school you'll have more than a dozen jobs. Virtually nobody stays in their first job for more than two or three or five years. The most you can expect of yourself is to gather all the information you can right now, make the best decision you can with what you know, and then keep your eyes open, making a change when you find something you like even more. Every happy person I know operates exactly that way, and I'm convinced that you will, too.

I just laugh and laugh when I hear people talking about a lifetime plan. This was brought home to me last summer when my father received an honorary degree from his alma mater, the University of Nottingham in England. He gave the commencement address, and I sat in the audience listening to him talk about how important it is to have a lifetime plan, how "you can't succeed without it." I looked around and noticed this auditorium full of students nodding earnestly as he spoke. At the reception afterwards, I took Dad aside and said, "Gee, Dad, I have a question for you about that lifetime plan. When you graduated from here, did you have it in your mind that you would be a professor for a while, then you'd become CEO of a biotech company, then you'd go into venture capital?" (That is, in fact, the career he's had.)

He responded, "Of course not!"

I said, "Then why did you tell the students they have to have a lifetime plan?"

Without a moment's hesitation, he responded, "Because it's graduation. You have to say that kind of thing."

You don't have to take my word for lifetime plans not being the way people really operate, by the way. If you read profiles of people who've been successful in just about anything, if you ignore what they say and look at what they've done, you'll see that they've typically jumped at new opportunities that came into view. They adjusted course as their goals and circumstances changed and their knowledge base expanded. That's the way just about everybody does it. You give yourself a break when you don't try and map out your life from the vantage point of "right this minute." Put yourself to task making the best decision you can right now . . . and trust that you'll use the same wisdom in making choices down the road!

10.   DON'T BE TOO INFLUENCED BY "KEEPING YOUR OPTIONS OPEN"

When you start law school, and have a little exposure to different jobs and specialties, it makes sense to keep a broad outlook (unless you're fortunate enough to know what you want, and you've had enough exposure to it to know your image of it is accurate). I often tell 1Ls that a great "starter" job for the summer is to work as a clerk for a trial-level judge, a prosecutor's office, or a public defender's office. Small firms are also good. Anything that gets you practical experience, and certainly in the case of judges, prosecutors and public defenders' offices, let you see the law "in action."

But as you get closer to graduation, if you identify what you really like, go for it—not what you think will leave you open to the most jobs in future. You can "leave your options open" your whole life and never be happy, because you're constantly focused on "what's next."

Of course, there are exceptions to this that we'll discuss. Sometimes your dream job has a "prerequisite"; that is, it requires some experience, as most corporate in-house counsels' jobs do. Or you need to do something that's not your first choice coming out of the gate because your credentials won't get you what you want right away. Or you want to wipe out a bunch of debt with a high-paying job before you take the job you really want (although that's fraught with danger, because it's easy to get addicted to a big paycheck). Or maybe you just want to buy time to make a decision, so you take a short-term job to give yourself time to figure it out. But the point remains: you can't put off your decision forever.

As Harvard's Mark Weber points out, "You can't forever choose the job that leaves you the most options. You came to law school to do something you enjoy. Think more about the job that will accomplish that and less about what you'll be able to do with that credential later on."

The fact is, there's always an opportunity to change your mind later on, no matter what you decide to do. Although career changes once you're out of school are beyond the scope of this book—for pity's sake, something has to be—by way of a thumbnail sketch, when you want to change jobs, you start acting "as if." You take CLEs on the new specialty, you talk to alums from school that practice in that specialty, and you take part in appropriate bar activities. In other words, you do much of what you'd do to find a job the first time around!

But I digress. The key point here is: as soon as you identify what you want, go for it. Worry about what you'll do next when it strikes you that you want a change—and trust that, in the words of the legendary Hollywood producer Sam Goldwyn, you'll burn that bridge when you get to it!

11. REMEMBER: YOU HAVE TO DO SOMETHING. AND IF YOU DON'T DECIDE FOR YOURSELF—THE DECISION WILL BE MADE FOR YOU

Here's a headline for you. Time marches on. Law school <u>will</u> come to an end.

You will do something, because the rest of your life isn't going to be a vacuum. It'll be filled with some kind of activity. If you don't opt for some kind of target, you'll drift aimlessly . . . and probably unhappily. As Tennessee's Joann Rothery puts it, "If you don't choose a piece of fruit from the tree, it all falls and rots."

If you're having a tough time deciding what you want to do and you're procrastinating as a result—I'm down with that. Heck, my prime motivation for going to law school in the first place was to put off working for another three years. One of the tremendous benefits of school is that it gives you that luxury. But it's a limited time offer.

If you're stuck, give the rest of this chapter a chance to help you. Solicit the help of Career Services at school. They're *there* to help you make decisions like this.

Remember: You can always change your mind, and your choice will never be perfect. But <u>make one</u>. The alternative is a lot worse!

12. KEEP AN OPEN MIND ABOUT SPECIALTIES AND SETTINGS YOU THINK SOUND ICKY

This is an offshoot of the idea that you should focus on the life you want to live, the job you want to do, rather than what you want to be. You may well sweep aside jobs that would make you very, very happy.

Two examples come immediately to mind. I've always thought that bankruptcy would be a miserable specialty to practice. Bankruptcy, after all, is the death of a dream. You'd be dealing with people at the very nadir of their existence. What a bummer!

Well, it just goes to show that the Job Goddess can be an idiot. My eyes were opened by a law school graduate from Chicago who'd really traveled a bumpy road. Exceptionally bright but personally troubled, he'd been out of law school for ten years drifting aimlessly from job to job, holding them for no more than a few months at a time. He'd gotten it into his head that the only "real" job was working at a mega firm in Chicago, which with his academic background and work history was an extreme long shot. He trolled job postings from his school every day, and one that lingered for a while was a small personal bankruptcy firm in a small town some hundred miles from his law school. Out of desperation more than anything else, he applied for it—and got it.

Totally unwittingly, he'd stumbled into his dream job. As he reported, "I'm a hero to these people. By the time they come to me, they've been hassled by creditors every night. They're convinced they're going to lose everything. They're at the end of their rope. Then I go to court for them, and I come out and tell them, 'Good news. You get to keep your house, you get to keep your car.' They weep, they hug me, and they have hope."

On top of that, the job kept him so busy that he didn't have time to focus on the voices in his head—a real benefit for this particular guy.

"An exciting, fulfilling job" and "personal bankruptcy" are not two phrases I thought I'd ever see together. But it proves my point: Think of the aspects of work that are valuable to you, not the title!

Another example: Small law firms. Studies suggest that the happiest lawyers practice in the smallest law firms. You may have already dismissed small firms for a bunch of reasons. But the fact is, they offer lots of variety, reasonable hours, lots of responsibility, direct client contact—all desirable elements for most people.

So if you've already written off broad swaths of career possibilities without knowing much (or anything) about them—put them back on your list!

13. DON'T LET THE NAMES OF SPECIALTIES MISLEAD YOU AS TO WHAT THEY'RE LIKE ... ESPECIALLY THE "GLAMOUR" JOBS IN SPORTS, ENTERTAINMENT AND INTERNATIONAL LAW

Names can be misleading. A friend of mine frequently gets calls from people intending to call the White House; her cell phone number is apparently close to the President's. Her voice mail messages are hilarious. Whenever there's an opening for a cabinet position—say, Secretary of State—she'll get phone calls from people applying for the job, talking about *their typing speed*—clearly confused by the title "Secretary"!

"Secretary" isn't the only misleading title. Entertainment, sports, and international law—I get more e-mails about those three specialties than any other. (They've even got their own chapter, Chapter 24.) Every career counselor at every law school in America has the same experience. And they all say the same thing: Look at what the job really <u>is</u> before you set your sights on it!

Lisa Dickinson of the University of San Francisco comments, "When students tell me they want a specialty like International Law, I ask: 'What does that life look like to you? When you imagine yourself doing it, what do you see?' After all, a lot of International Law is done sitting in an office in New York or Los Angeles, not jetting off to London or Paris for a week. I'm trying to find out if it's a dream job ... or a fantasy!"

A partner in International Law at one of the country's most prestigious firms echoes that sentiment: "International Law has glamorous aspects to it. Yeah, I was a frequent flyer on Concorde. But I was going to London to sit in a meeting room. Or Munich. Or Stockholm. Every city looks pretty much the same when you're looking at the inside of airport conference rooms."

Sports law is largely contracts law. Entertainment law—surprise surprise. Same thing. International Law doesn't mean exotic international travel (not most of the time, anyway!). As one counselor explained it to me, "Whenever a student asks me about sports or entertainment law, I immediately ask them, 'How do you like contracts?' They'll often say 'Ugh!' but that's what those jobs are!''

Here's the thing. It's dangerous to assume that because you like the output of an industry that you'll like being in it. Liking hot dogs doesn't mean you'll enjoy making them. Being a football fan doesn't mean you'll love working in Sports Law. Liking movies or wanting to hang with celebrities doesn't mean you'll like Entertainment Law. Liking to travel means you should get a job with vacation time, where you can travel for fun!

Now, having said that, I'm not suggesting that setting is unimportant in choosing a dream job; it's a sizable element. But don't confuse the setting with the legal specialty! Which leads naturally to . . .

14.   Realize That if a Particular Setting—Like Entertainment or Sports—Appeals to You, There Will Be Tons of "Hidden" Jobs Associated With It

It's very easy to think that if you like a particular setting, then there's only one route to getting into it. Take sports or entertainment, the two specialties about which I get questioned the most often. There are many, many ways to be in a sports or entertainment environment without technically practicing sports or entertainment law. For instance, as Susan Gainen points out, "Something very few people realize is that Insurance Law can actually be a very sexy specialty. That's because for every sports deal, for every entertainment deal, there has to be an insurance lawyer at the table. It's a crucial part of the package. Every sporting event, every facility needs insurance. Every sports figure needs worker's comp." Now, if anyone ever told you that *insurance* would be your route to a glamorous career, you wouldn't have believed them, right?

The "hidden jobs" thing can sweep in nontraditional jobs, as well. There was one student at a Texas law school who told me she wanted "hospitality law" but she wasn't entirely clear on what it was. She'd majored in hospitality in college, worked two years in a public-interest oriented counseling job, and talked with someone in Human Resources at a Hilton Hotel and thought the hospitality law thing sounded good. But as a *lawyer,* what would she do? Contracts, slip and falls, the management side of EEOC cases, real estate. If she liked the people side of it—which with her counseling background was clearly true—hotel management would suit her better, and with her combination of credentials, it was a good fit.

Remember that there are lawyers in every setting. Zoos need risk management people—a great job with a law background. Fashion. Wineries. You name it. There are legal and law related jobs in every industry! In fact, one terrific job is working for an industry's trade association. You get to travel a bit, there's a teaching aspect, and you get to look at industry-wide issues. It's a sweet gig! (We talk more about alternative jobs in Chapter 31, "I Want To Be A Not—Lawyer.)

In fact, even in so-called "traditional" settings, there are hidden jobs. For instance, take large law firms. Whether or not you like the long hours of an associate, you may like the setting. One student told me about her experience at a large firm before she started law school. She asked junior associates if they liked their work, and they'd shrug and say, "It's a job." She said, "They worked from 6:30 in the morning until 11 at night. That's not for me. But there are so many other jobs at large firms. Training. Recruiting. Marketing. A law degree is good for all of those. I loved the firm. I just didn't want to be an associate. I want one of those *other* jobs!"

You see the point. If the setting is the most important element to you, focus on that—and broaden your options by looking at all of the different kinds of jobs that can get you into that setting.

15. DON'T BE SEDUCED BY THE NAME ON THE DOOR OR THE PAYCHECK

I'm probably not the best person to give you this advice, because this is precisely the trap I fell into in law school. I ignored what little I knew about myself, I remained deliberately ignorant about the realities of the job, and took a clerkship after Second Year with the largest law firm that would hire me, one of the biggest ones in the country . . . which of course paid mad cheez.

What a mistake. I couldn't have been more laughably ill-suited for a job than if I'd tried to join an NBA team (I'm 5'1"). They hated me and I was miserable, crying in the john every day at lunch time.

What did I do? And what am I begging you not to do? I allowed myself to be seduced by the prestige, by the dough. Having gone to an OK law school, the idea of working for a law firm whose very name cloaked me with intelligence, prestige and success was an irresistible lure. It made me ignore the fact that I'm frivolous and thoroughly incapable of leaving my emotions at the door—an absolute prerequisite for practicing at a large firm. Even a cursory talk with anyone who'd practiced at a large law firm would have told me it was just wrong, wrong, wrong for me to go there.

And, yes, for a summer my parents were really proud. People I met at parties viewed me with instant respect when they heard where I worked.

But you know what? That's not your life. Telling people where you work isn't living it day to day. And that paycheck? If you do something you don't believe in it'll turn to ashes in your hands. You'll resent it and you'll blow the money because you feel you deserve it for doing something you hate. You'll get used to a level of luxury you just can't break away from; it's like an addiction. I see this happen all the time. A partner at one huge Chicago law firm commented sadly, "I've been here for thirty years. I've hated it for the last twenty-seven." A 25-year partner at another law firm was asked by a law student, "What's kept you here all that time?" and the partner responded, "Inertia."

The money trap isn't confined to law, of course. When I wrote *America's Greatest Places To Work With A Law Degree,* I interviewed law school graduates who went into investment banking, a career simply dripping in doubloons and pieces of eight. I'll never forget how one of them described his job: "It's 364 days of pain, and a bonus check."

Now I'm not indicting large law firms or any other financially gifted employer, because you might love the life. And the money? If you do something you enjoy that coincidentally stacks up the dead presidents . . . that's the best of all possible worlds. It could well be you'd hate to clerk for a judge or work for a prosecutor's office or public defender's office or at a small law firm. But I speak from experience, mine and that of thousands of law students with whom I've spoken, when I tell you that you're far more likely to ignore your gut when there's prestige and money on the line. Please give more than a passing thought to what you're like, what you like to do, and talk to people in the jobs you think you want before you pursue those opportunities!

16. A Stepping Stone Is a Good Start. Look at Where Your First Job Can Lead You

When you've slogged through three years of law school it's very easy to think, "I want what I want *right now.*" You're vastly more educated than most people, you probably have a lot more student loan debt, and you deserve it—right?

Well . . . that's dangerous thinking. Because there are an awful lot of sweet gigs that require "prerequisites" after law school. For those, think of your first job as an apprenticeship, a stepping stone.

On top of that, I've mentioned to you before that you're likely to have at least a dozen different jobs in your career. That first job? It's hardly the place you'll stay for a lifetime. You'll likely be there for no more than a few years. Just choose something that leads you in the direction you want to go, if your specific dream job doesn't fall in your lap right away.

One of the major assets of starting with a large law firm is that they pave the way for other possibilities. At least fifty percent of large law firm associates leave within five years. While some grads join large firms with it in mind that they'll strive for partnership, there's nothing that says that's the only reason to join a large firm. One Ivy League student told me that she had no intention of staying with a large firm for longer than three years. She wanted to pay off some major debt and then move onto something she'd enjoy. She had three offers in hand, and her favourite professor told her to take the "prestige" job among the three. She responded, "I'm going to do this for three years and leave, so I'm going to the highest bidder." One of the firms paid $9,000 a year more than the other two, so she took it. While I'd caution you about following her example—if you take a job you actively hate, three years will be a long, long time—there's some validity to her reasoning. As the recruiting coordinator at one large firm commented, "Firms like ours are great places to pay off your bills. You have a lot of flexibility when you leave. Those are major assets."

Politics is another example where your first job can act as a great stepping stone. If you look at the background of many successful politicians, you'll find a stint in the prosecutor's office. There's no reason to reinvent the wheel when you try to figure a career path; if it's worked before, it can work for you. In addition, people tend to really enjoy working at DA's offices, so you'll have a double benefit: career enhancement and enjoyment in the meantime!

While we're talking about politics, when you're looking at your first job as a jumping-off point it's important to consider where you want to wind up geographically. A student I talked to in upstate New York wanted to get into politics back home in Texas, but in the meantime wanted to see "what's out there" in New York State. Since you can seek "what's out there" anywhere in the country, it makes sense to do it where you want to spend the bulk of your career—especially if it's location-specific, as politics is. You want to build a reputation, a political base, where you intend to run for office!

Your first job can also be a stepping stone to an alternative career. One student told me she ultimately wanted to be a novelist, and wanted to take a job that would propel her in that direction. I know I sound like a one-trick pony here, but again I recommended the prosecutor's office. Look how many best-selling novelists got their start there! Lisa Scottoline is one who comes to mind. Seeing "crime in action" is a great way to spur your imagination.

Your first job can also remove the "sting" from poor law school credentials. It may well be that your grades are a stumbling block to getting the job you want straight out of law school (I address ways to overcome this in great detail in the chapter "Help! My Grades Stink!") The point is, if law school didn't showcase your genius, your first job may well do so—and set you up for your dream gig!

There are also jobs that expressly require a "prerequisite" job. For instance, working for the Department of Justice—a fabulous, fabulous job—typically requires two years' of work experience (unless you get into the Honors Program, which takes you directly out of law school). In-house counsel's offices? Same deal. Most corporate counsel jobs require some experience.

Now of course there are always exceptions. If you work for a U.S. Attorney's Office during law school, even as a volunteer, and you do a phenomenal job, they might make an exception for you. In-house counsel's offices that are huge, with hundreds of lawyers, can train you just as a law firm would, so they, too, take "newbies." But usually, experience is a prerequisite.

"But Kimmbo," you may be saying, "What kind of experience do I get? How do I know what I'm supposed to do *first?*" Easy, Weed Hopper. Go to Martindale–Hubbell (www.martindale.com), your school's alumni directory, or any other lawyer database, look at lawyers who do what you want to do ... and look at how they got there. There are a bunch of ways to get into any particular job. Look and see what other people have done to get where you want to go. You may even want to contact them and ask their advice about what you want to do! You can say something as simple as, "My dream is to do what you do. Here's my situation. I'm a student at X and I've done X and X. I'd be so grateful for your advice about what I should be doing, what I should be reading, what activities I should take part in to position myself to do what you do."

The fact is, there are many, many jobs that naturally lead to other positions. State Attorney's Generals Offices are a great entré to specialties in private practice. Judicial clerkships are a fabulous springboard into just about any practice area. Developing a specialty at a firm can set you up to have a practice of your own. So don't look at your first job as a be all and end all—look where it can lead!

* * * SMART HUMAN TRICK * * *

Female law student, last in her law school class. Her dream is to be in-house counsel at a large insurance company. Even with better grades, that could not be her first job. She takes something insurance-related that she can get ... working for her state's department of insurance. In that role she liaises with small in-state insurance companies. After less than two years on the job, one of them asks her to come in-house. This isn't her dream—she wants a large company—but it's a good step. She takes it. What they don't tell her is that when they bring her in, they are planning to merge with one of the largest insurance companies in America. Within two years of graduating last in her law school class, she's assistant general counsel at one of the largest insurance companies in the country—pulling down in excess of a half million dollars a year.

* * * SMART HUMAN TRICK * * *

Female law student, lousy grades, graduates from school in the Pacific Northwest. She is interested in work involving children's issues, and takes the only job she can get, working for the state's department of child support. It has a serious downside in that it doesn't pay well at all. However, within a year or two of working with the program, the state decides to privatize it. Suddenly, because this woman is one of only two people who know how the system works, she is in the catbird seat. The state needs her and they know it. She negotiates a 25% raise, three weeks' vacation to start, and a contractual guarantee of no more than forty hours per week.

17. RECOGNIZE THAT THE PEOPLE YOU WORK WITH AND THE SETTING IN WHICH YOU WORK ARE AT LEAST AS IMPORTANT TO YOUR HAPPINESS AS THE SPECIALTY YOU CHOOSE

This sounds counterintuitive, but it's not. Studies have shown over and over again that the actual intellectual content of what you do is not the prime element in your job satisfaction. That's why when it comes to choosing a target, thinking about the kind of people you want to work with and the setting in which you want to work are so important (we'll cover all of that in Topic B, below). As Seattle career expert Karen Somerville describes it, "The environment in which you work is at least as important, if not more important, than the type of substantive work you will do: location, physical space, people, and culture."

A favourite story of mine illustrates this point perfectly. The Career Services Director at one prestigious school got a call one morning from a grad at a very large law firm. "I just wanted to tell you," this grad trilled delightedly, "How much I love this firm! The people I work with are amazing. You turned me on to this place, and I just wanted to thank you!"

In the early afternoon, the Career Services Director got another call from another grad, ironically working at the same firm. She was whispering. "Listen—you've got to get me out of here!" she pleaded. "This is *awful*. I hate it. The people are such unbelievable a**holes. I can't stand it one more day."

As it turns out, the two grads were in two different departments, on two different floors of this particular firm. Each department functioned pretty much like its own law firm—with obviously different cultures! So remember: the substantive content of your work isn't irrelevant, but it's not the most important feature, either!

18.   DON'T BE INFLUENCED BY WHAT YOUR CLASSMATES ALL SEEM TO WANT

I've visited law schools where student after student will tell me they want to work for the same prestigious employer. The likelihood that all of these students genuinely want the identical gig is very slim. What's happening here? What I call "dream cloning." Someone with an alpha dog personality may genuinely want that job, and they are so persuasive talking about it that they convince their classmates, "Gee, I want that, too!" Especially if the job pays very well and the employer is well-known, the self-delusion is easy to fall into.

The trap, of course, is that there's no one-size-fits-all dream job. The job that will make your best friend deliriously happy may leave you miserable. It's important to go through this chapter, and do your "internal" and "market" research before you settle on a dream!

19.   WATCH OUT FOR YOUR FRIENDS' DESCRIPTIONS OF JOBS

When you tell your classmates what you want to do and they say, "Oh, that's *great*," or "Ugh! That job sucks!" be sure to determine the basis of their advice before you put too much weight on it. If they've worked in that setting—great. Ask them more about it and why they feel about it as they do. If not ... proceed accordingly.

This was brought home to me in a conversation with a law student here in my home state of Connecticut. This student had done a really good job of figuring out what kind of person she was and the setting that would make her happy. "I like a lot of variety, I get bored easily, I don't want to work long hours ..." and she asked what kinds of jobs she ought to be pursuing. Right away I asked her, "Have you considered the State's Attorney's Office?" (the Connecticut equivalent of a District Attorney). She said, "No. I had a friend who said it's a crappy job." I asked her if her friend had worked at a State's Attorney's Office, and she said, "No," and I said, "Well—has your friend lived before?" She saw immediately what I was getting at and we both laughed. She had eliminated from consideration a whole category of jobs based on an off-hand comment from someone who knew nothing about it!

A student at another school had a similar experience. In her mid-forties, she'd gone back to law school to go into public interest, and had set her sights on Legal Aid. Her classmates told her, "Don't bother. You can only work for another fifteen years. They won't take you." Oh, *really?* For one thing, Legal Aid doesn't discriminate. For another, second career people get hired all the time in all kinds of jobs ... at every age! (For Second Career Students, see Chapter 22.)

So—research is great. Gather all the tidbits you can. But be sure you know what that advice is based on—especially if you're going to write off a job because of it!

20.   BE AS MISERLY AS YOU CAN WITH THE MONEY YOU THINK YOU NEED IN YOUR FIRST JOB. IT'LL OPEN UP THE WORLD FOR YOU

It's simple math: the less money you have to make, the more options you'll have. I know, I know, student loans. But there are all kinds of ways to consolidate and economize to make those monthly payments bearable.

Or, maybe it's not student loans you've got on your mind. You might be thinking, I've sacrificed enough. I've eaten so much Kraft Macaroni & Cheese my skin is turning orange. It's time for me to be able to enjoy some luxuries.

I'm down with all of that. But my central point stands: The less money you can get by on for a little while, the greater your options.

I remember one student in particular when it comes to the "money" issue. His Career Services Director had called me in advance of visiting his school, and asked me a special favour: This student desperately wanted to talk to me, and he wasn't going to be able to come to my Guerrilla Tactics seminar at school. He asked if he might pick me up at the airport and give me a ride to school, and talk to me then. Well, why the heck not? I said, "Sure." The Career Services Director told me the basic outline of this guy's issue: He was about two thousand miles from home, his home town was in a perpetual economic slump, and he was terribly concerned about getting a job there.

With that in mind, I flew in and met this student. Charming young guy, worried terribly about his long-distance job search as well as finding a job that would pay well enough to support him. I offered whatever bromides came to mind, as we walked toward the parking lot.

Then I saw his wheels.

This guy had a brand new, *very* expensive sports car. The kind of car I only dream about owning. Honestly, a real beauty. The rest of our conversation is a blur to me. All I could think of was: *"If this guy sold this car and bought some basic transportation, he could support himself for two years, if he needed to, while he pursued his dream job."* It didn't look like it, but this car was his prison. It was going to hamstring him in pursuing what he really wanted!

A student from an Illinois school e-mailed me and asked the question straight out: "Do I take the low-paying satisfying job? Or do I take the big check?" My advice, predictably enough, was along the lines of "Take the low pay now. If you take the big check, you'll start taking the dough for granted and develop expensive habits. If you then chuck it, you'll be even more miserable because you won't want to chuck the bennies. Once you have a certain new experience, you need to keep on having more of it to sustain happiness. So the thing to do is to avoid that treadmill all together. If you want manicures, get a side business that involves other passions: yoga instructor, caterer, and businesses with low start-up costs." (You can find them at www.entrepreneur.com, by the way.)

You already know that I created the study aid series *Law In A Flash*—the funny flashcards in the yellow boxes. It was my first real gig after law school. I've also mentioned that it took me three years before any law school bookstore in the country was willing to try it out. Those three years? They defined *lean*. I lived in my parents' basement, I drove a clunker I inherited from my father's secretary, I did odd jobs to plump up my pay ... which totaled about $20,000 for all three years combined ... and most of *that* went to pay student loans. No vacations. No new clothes. No dining out. Nada.

But, I was pursuing my *dream*. Sure, I lusted after new cars and clothes and exotic vacations. I wanted to eat out. I'm not *that* much of a freak. But, I simply couldn't have pursued that dream if I'd insisted on a handsome salary. My investors needed to see that I was willing to sacrifice. And I was.

I'm not suggesting that you, too, have to go on the Alpo-and-tap-water diet to pursue your dreams. You may have a family already, you may just be interested in a higher standard of luxury than I was (other than sleeping on a bed of nails, it'd be hard to imagine a *lower* standard). But you see my point. If you're willing to forego maximum buckage up front in your career, you maximize your options. Alternative careers, public interest jobs, a practice or business of your own ... they all become possibilities.

Notice that I'm not saying you have to sacrifice *forever*. Just in the short term. Virtually every job winds up paying well within a very few years after law school. Government jobs, small law firms, their salaries jump as though they're spring-loaded. So if you bite the bullet now, you won't have to chew ice for a hobby for very long—and you'll have the luxury of choosing a job you truly love.

21. BE AWARE THAT 'I'LL DO ANYTHING' DOESN'T SOUND GOOD TO EMPLOYERS

I know many, many students who deliberately *avoid* choosing a goal, even an immediate one, thinking they'll improve their marketability by stating a willingness to do "anything."

There are two problems with this. For a start, it's not true. No matter how many things you'd be willing to do, you *know* there are things that will make you miserable. I remember visiting one law school where a 3L came up to me and said, "I'm desperate. I'll do anything. I don't care what it is. I like everything." A classmate of his, standing nearby, said "Hey—I heard the magistrate is looking for clerks. Why don't you apply there?" This guy, without a moment's hesitation, said, "No way! I heard when you work for him all you do is research."

Well! *There's* a valuable piece of information! He wasn't into any job with a strong research component—he didn't "like everything," because *nobody* does! If you did somehow stumble into a job that makes your skin crawl, you wouldn't last a week. So be realistic, and admit that there *are* things you prefer. It won't hurt your job search. In fact, it will ironically enhance it, because employers will feel you've honestly assessed what you want and what you're good at, and targeted them as a result.

That may seem hard to believe. But employers tell me all the time that when they hear law students say "I'll do anything," it means one of two things: they've done no self-assessment or they're desperate. Neither one is appealing. An employer wants to hear you say, "I want to work for you, because I know this about you, this is how I am, and this is how I can help you." That takes self-awareness and market-awareness—the two factors we'll be covering in this chapter!

22. IGNORE WHAT YOU DREAMED OF DOING WHEN YOU WERE A KID

OK. Don't ignore it *entirely*. But take it with a large grain of salt. Because the fact is, no matter how extraordinary a kid you were—and I'm sure you were one in a million—your knowledge base of jobs was limited.

I know this because of my three-year-old son Harry. Among his many books he has a Dora the Explorer book on careers. What's in it? The usual suspects. Teacher. Doctor. Firefighter. Hmm. I've looked and looked and Dora doesn't have a "utilities lawyer" option. No "consultant." No "M & A expert." At a Bob Evans Restaurant in Indiana, he got a kid's placemat with six occupations on it: teacher, farmer, police officer, firefighter, construction worker, and non-profit executive director. Just kidding about that last one. You get the point.

Similarly, my niece Emily, when she was in kindergarten, came home one day and announced that she wanted to be a dolphin trainer. Then she had a few friends over, and they, too, all announced they wanted to be dolphin trainers. Had they all taken the Myers–Briggs Type Indicator test at school to determine they'd all enjoy being marine biologists? Of course not. A dolphin trainer had visited their school that day, and boom—that's what all the kids wanted. Now, I'm sure being a dolphin trainer is an awesome job, and that both people in the United States who do it are very happy, but come on—with Emily and her friends, what jobs did they *know* about? They all wanted the only good job they'd heard about—dolphin trainer.

Statistics show that 50% of high school students want to be President of the United States. Whatever else it is, it's the most visible job in America. As a kid, I'm fairly certain I wanted to be a fashion designer. Then an actress. The fact I have no fashion sense and have laughably poor acting skills? Not obvious to me then. Nor were the thousands of jobs that are out there.

So, when you're trying to nail down a goal, analyzing what you wanted as a child, to the extent it tells you something about yourself, is useful. But you have a lot more information at your fingertips now than you did then—and you'll make a much better decision as a result!

23. KEEP YOUR EYES OPEN EVEN AFTER YOU MAKE A CHOICE ... BECAUSE YOU NEVER KNOW WHERE YOUR DREAM JOB WILL SHOW UP

As Sue Gainen points out, "Most happy people could never have predicted in law school what they're doing now—they didn't even know it existed." The fact is, you don't know when today will present you with a great opportunity. You have to stay connected with people, interested in what's going on around you, and actively involved in hobbies that interest you. Challenge yourself to try new things, take new classes.

I am reminded of the experience of Julia Child, the legendary chef. She didn't take her first cooking lesson until she was *thirty-seven years old*. In that first class, as recounted in the book *Julie and Julia*, she roasted pigeons. She was immediately hooked on cooking. She went home, and roasted pigeons that very night for her husband, Paul. He sat in the kitchen keeping her company while she cooked. As he sat, he dashed off a letter to his brother, Charles. He wrote, *"If you could see Julie stuffing pepper and lard up the a**hole of a dead pigeon, you'd realize how profoundly affected she's been already."*

The actor Brad Pitt had a similar poetic experience. As reported in *Newsweek*, one of Pitt's early jobs was acting as a stripper's caddy. In 1986, he had a job driving strippers around to bachelor parties and gigs like that, where he would collect the money, play the "bad Prince tapes" and catch the girls' clothes. It was a depressing job. After two months, he was on the brink of quitting. He went to his boss, who said, "Listen. I've got this one last gig tonight." Pitt did it, and the stripper—whom he'd never met before—was in an acting class taught by famed acting coach Roy London. Pitt went to check it out and "It really set me on my path." He commented, "Strippers changed my life!"

The fact is, you never know when lightning will strike. I've seen this happen over and over again. Three stories that stand out in my mind:

- Elite law school graduate, goes to a law firm in the Pacific Northwest. He's moderately happy. He volunteers as a fireman in his spare time. He loves *that* job so much that he dumps the firm and becomes a full-time fireman.

- Graduate from a Florida law school, practices law for several years before she volunteers at a local children's hospital. She loves that so much that she quits her practice, goes to medical school and becomes a pediatrician.

- A student I talked to at a distinguished West Coast law school decided one morning that she wanted to work for Mother Theresa. She loaded up a backpack, worked her way to Calcutta, showed up, watched Mother Theresa, and gave what she had to give. It was exactly what she'd envisioned it would be. She didn't come back.

My law school roommate is another great example of this principle. Pat, or "Crazy Pat" as many people called her, is one of the most colorful people I've ever met. She routinely woke up five minutes before our first class in the morning, ran her hands through her hair, and often went to school in her pajamas. She went on a summer abroad program to France, slept on the Riviera—literally on the beach—the night she got there, next to her backpack containing her books. Overnight the backpack was stolen ... and she never bothered to replace the books.

In fact, to my knowledge Pat never once cracked a book the whole time we lived together. Her grades were predictably awful. Once, in Con Law, the professor called on her to give the rule of law from a case, and she miraculously came up with the right answer. Of course, it was because she had the Gilbert's Outline open on her lap! At the end of the semester, she went to him to argue her grade in Con Law, saying, "What about my class participation? I gave the right answer that time. Don't I get credit for that?" And he responded, "All right, all right, D! D minus! What's the difference?"

So now you know Pat. Here's what happened to her. When we were just about to graduate, she was hanging out at some bar and met a Libyan guy. They got married a couple of months later. Well, it turns out that all of her husband's friends were having a heck of a time moving to the U.S. from Libya. Read: They all needed an immigration lawyer. Pat told me, "I figured, I'm not doing anything else. These are nice guys. I can help them out." So she opened an immigration practice, and was immediately busy—doing work she actually enjoyed.

So when she went to that bar that fateful day, love isn't the only thing that walked through that door. Opportunity did, as well!

This idea of inspiration "in the air" is true in every aspect of life. If you read anything about inventors and artists, you see that they, too, have no idea where inspiration will strike. A few examples:

- Jack Kilby, who invented the microchip, hadn't worked at Texas Instruments long enough to merit a vacation during the company's summer shutdown. So he was alone and working on borrowed equipment when, on July 24, 1958, he came up with an idea he jotted in his notebook: "The following circuit elements could be made on a single slice, resistors, capacitor, distributed capacitor, transistor"—i.e., a microchip. And he came up with it because he wasn't entitled to a day off!

- Beatrix Potter didn't set out to write the legendary Peter Rabbit books. She just told a story in a letter to a bedridden child. A publisher saw the letter and encouraged her to write books.

- Leo Szilard, who discovered nuclear fission, was struck by the idea when he noticed a sequence of traffic lights turning green while walking in London.

- Phil Knight came up with the famous waffle design of Nike shoes while gazing at his wife's open waffle iron.

So, as Chicago's Abbie Willard says, "Keep yourself open to the Universe." You never know where your great job will come from!

24. RECOGNIZE THAT YOU'RE ALLOWED TO HAVE HOBBIES THAT FULFILL YOU!

You can take a lot of pressure off the "dream job" decision if you break out the specific things you're looking for, and allocate some of them to your private life. Having a vocation doesn't stop you from having *avocations* as well. It may be that at some point your avocation turns into your vocation—and that's fine! But in the short term, recognize that a reason you may be having a hard time making a decision over the job to pursue is that you're looking at multiple goals irreconcilable into a single job.

I remember talking with a charming student at the University of Tennessee who said, "I want to combine singing and law." Unless you want to be a judge who sings his verdicts—and thereby makes plentiful appearances in the media—those are two goals that just don't mesh. Now, is it possible to have a legal career and sing, as well? Sure. Gina Sauer, former Career Services Director at William Mitchell Law School and now a consultant with The Esquire Group, is also the lead singer in two bands!

It's often the case that working at a large firm is made that much more attractive by feeding one's soul with pro bono work. An associate at one large firm in Los Angeles had a jones for public interest, which she satisfied by creating wills for AIDS sufferers in hospices.

Acknowledging the existence of your free time can have a dramatic impact on the career you choose. For instance, let's say that you want to practice International Law because you love the idea of travel. Well, I've pointed out before that a lot of International Law doesn't involve travel, and even when it does, it's not generally *fun* travel. When the Ambassador to Australia spoke at UC Hastings, she pointed out that many law students who want international law actually want foreign travel. So what do you do? You take a job that provides you with decent vacations, and during those vacations, you go everywhere in the world you want to visit. Your time will be your own, and you can go from dawn to dusk and beyond exploring everything that tempts you … without having to worry about work!

In fact, throughout your career, consider taking "fantasy camp" vacations, where you get to live a life very different than your own … at least for a few days. The possibilities are endless. "Cowgirl 101" at the National Cowgirl Museum and Hall of Fame (www.cowgirl.net). Rock and Roll Fantasy Camp (www.rockandrollfantasycamp.com). Space Camp in Huntsville, Alabama at the U.S. Space and Rocket Center (www.space camp.com). NASCAR's "Pit Crew U." Baseball umpire camp. Disney U. at Disney World. Tinker. Tailor. Candlestick maker. You name it. You can find them all at www.grownupcamps.com. You never know when pursuing a wacky long weekend will make a switch will flip in your head, making you think, "Gee—I like this a lot better than my *real* job." People have been known to make radical career changes based on their experience at fantasy camps. Even if you don't make the leap—it gives you a few days "out of your skin" to get a fresh perspective on your life!

Perhaps the most successful "hobbyist" of all time was a patent clerk at the turn of the twentieth century. He had a few free hours, and with that spare time, in 1905, he wrote four papers.

Those papers changed the foundation of physics. One of them laid the foundation for quantum theory … and won him the Nobel Prize. Another of them modified "the theory of space and time"—the theory of relativity. Yep. It was Albert Einstein.

And that wasn't his paid gig. It was his *hobby*.

So remember: you have a combination of work time and free time, and make sure you allocate both of them to accomplish your dreams!

Law professor by day … **Dixie Chicks tour blogger by night.**

Talk about a wild hobby! Junichi Semitsu is a law professor at the University of San Diego School of Law … but he spent the summer of 2006 touring with the Dixie Chicks as their official blogger.

How did he become one of the first "embedded bloggers" in the music industry? As reported in *The Washington Post,* he had his own politics and pop culture blog as a hobby, Poplicks.com. An economics major undergrad and briefly an attorney before turning to teaching, he had no journalism training. MSN (who partnered with the Dixie Chicks' record label to fund the blog) contacted him and asked for writing samples. He thought it was a joke, that perhaps he was being "Punk'd" by friends.

He was MSN's second choice for the job. The front runner had a personality clash with the Dixie Chicks, which left Semitsu with the job.

He traveled with the Chicks throughout the summer, posting a "behind the scenes" view of the tour on a frequent (albeit not daily) basis. And when he returned to school, he no doubt won the "So what did you do this summer?" contest, hands down!

25. IF YOUR DREAM JOB DOESN'T INVOLVE YOUR LAW DEGREE, SO BE IT

There are three basic kinds of jobs. Jobs where your law degree is a necessity. You know—a job like, say, "lawyer." Then there are jobs where your degree is really, really useful but not necessary. Real estate development, government relations expert, jury consultant, there are a million of 'em.

Then there's that enormous third category, where your law degree is irrelevant. Suitcase-holder on "Deal or No Deal." Host of "Meet The Press." Rapper. Baseball manager. Juggler. Custom cake decorator. Those are all jobs that law school graduates have held down. There are law school graduates lurking virtually everywhere!

My point? So what if your dream job doesn't require a law degree? There's no extra credit when you die for having used your degree, you know. God isn't going to say, "You had a career that used your degree? Great! You get an extra angel wing!" or whatever God might do for the particularly righteous.

Now, you can argue that you've wasted your money if you don't take a job that uses your degree. That you'll disappoint everybody if you don't. But I'd argue: you went to law school for one reason and one reason alone, and that's to make yourself happy. If you wanted to be miserable, you could have dropped out of high school. I'd consider it your duty to figure out what makes you happy, and pursue it . . . regardless of whether it makes "good use" of your degree.

What's the alternative? Take a job that makes you miserable just so you can say your J.D. was necessary? What do you care? I get that all the time, you know. "What a shame," people will say. "You wasted your degree." Now I'd say that writing *Law In A Flash* and being the Job Goddess are pretty good uses of my law degree, but hey. Everybody is entitled to an opinion. It's just that when it comes to my career, my opinion is the only one that counts. And when it comes to your career . . . well!

If you must have a retort for people who lay the "tsk tsk" attitude on you, you can point out that a law degree is always valuable. That is absolutely true. Whether you're running your own business, negotiating your own contracts, or just being a savvy consumer, your law degree will always be an asset. In every setting, people will take you more seriously because you've got a law degree. Whenever I, as a consumer, have an issue with a company—it's not very often—and they try to jerk me around, out comes my law degree. The fact is, with a J.D. you'll never be bent over the proverbial table. If your job doesn't require a law degree? All right. It's still an asset.

Heck, you may discover down the road that you want to practice law after all. While it's unquestionably easier to break in to practice straight out of school, I've talked with literally dozens of people who did something else for years, and then jumped back into practicing law. It's definitely do-able. So if you don't want to use your law degree for the foreseeable future, if you've done all of the "internal" analysis and "market" analysis called for in this chapter and you're sure that you want to be a hot air balloon operator, a beekeeper, a modern day *Le Petomaine*—go for it!

26. Don't Reject Yourself From Your Dream Job

We do it almost without thinking about it; we're sure that either a specialty is so narrow that there are virtually no jobs available, or we figure our grades will keep us out of it.

I see this happen at law schools all over America. Students will come to talk to me, and they'll say, "I can't choose between these two specialties." Often what's really going on is that they *really* want one of those specialties, but the other one is a lot easier to get.

I remember one student in particular who was torn between litigation in the Midwest or practicing Native American Law. It was absolutely obvious from the way he talked that he really wanted Native American Law, but he didn't think he could get it . . . so he convinced himself that he was equally interested in the much-easier-to-obtain litigation job.

I asked him about how he'd become interested in Native American Law, and he said he'd taken a class that he'd aced, and the professor had really inspired him. I asked, "Did you tell the professor that?" and he said he hadn't. I told him, "Well, that's where you start. Tell the professor, 'You inspired me. This is what I want to do with my life.' Ask him what you should do. Do a PSLawNet volunteer project involving Native Americans. Contact every expert you can track down on line and ask their advice." By the time we were finished talking, there were dozens of items on his "to-do" list in pursuing a job in Native American Law. He was *so* excited about it!

It's too easy to pursue the "bird in hand" option . . . even if you don't really want it. The comfort of an offer, a guaranteed paycheck, not having to tell people we're unemployed. The advice we get from authority figures sure doesn't help. I hear some of the crappiest advice come from the mouths of administrators who ought to know better. I talked to the dean at one law school who told me about a student he'd advised. She had an offer from her summer employer, but she didn't want it. He told her, "Wait just a moment. What do you want that they didn't give you? Did they train you? Did they seem concerned with you?" She said yes, and he told her, "Then take it . . . *all law firms are the same* [my emphasis]." Can you *imagine?* With advice like *that* in the air, no wonder we give up in a hurry! The prospect of reaching for something that's a stretch ... we tend to dismiss it without having even *tried!*

There was a student I talked to in Washington, DC who had a friend who could get her into a firm in Arizona. The problem was, she wanted Civil Rights or Environmental work in DC. "It's my dream," she said forlornly. So ... turn down the Arizona gig and give your dream a try! Why else are you in law school in the *first* place if not to make your dreams come true—or at least take a stab at them? If you don't try, you're *guaranteed* to get something you don't really want!

Another student, this one in New York City, had a buddy who could get him into the trust department at a major bank. The problem was, he was really jonesing for the recording industry. He asked, "Should I just take the bank job for a year to pay off debts?" Now, I could tell from the way he was talking to me that he was *begging* me to tell him to turn down the banking gig. So I said, "Join Lawyers for the Arts, look for internships in entertainment, talk to everyone who'll talk to you"—in other words, everything in Chapter 24 on Glamour Careers—"*then* revisit the banking offer." Even if he wound up taking the banking job, he'd at least have the contacts in place, the activities nailed down, to keep that dream alive. But ... Holy Crow. Dreams are great. Don't nip them in the bud!

It may also be true that you've "rejected yourself" because you face some special challenges. I remember a student at a southern school who had a disability related to writing. She also had ADHD. She had been a DJ for a year before law school, and really enjoyed working with people. Other students had told her, "You'll never get a job." B.S.! As it turns out, her Career Services Director had just had an employer call her looking for potential hires, and said, "At our firm, we don't do any research. We only counsel, negotiate, tell juries stories. If we have to research or do briefs, we subcontract that out. All we care about is how good people are with people." Well! That job had this student's name all over it!

Whatever you *can't* do, there's a job that'll suit what you *can* do. A disability is the equivalent of something you don't want to do. It's not fatal. Nor are grades, nor your school, nor anything else.

So don't dismiss your dream out of hand because you're afraid of rejection. We'll be talking throughout this book about hundreds of ways to break into just about anything you can think of. When you're figuring out your dream, isolate your passion—and leave the strategy for later on!

27. EXPECT THAT YOUR DREAMS WILL CHANGE OVER TIME. YOUR DREAM JOB TODAY WON'T SUIT YOU YEARS FROM NOW ... AND THAT'S OK!

Your life changes. Your circumstances change. Your idea of a dream job will necessarily change throughout your career. There's nothing wrong with that, and just because you choose something that won't sustain you to retirement, it doesn't mean it's a bad fit for right now!

Let's say that you're single. You don't have any kids. Well, a job that involves long hours, or low pay, or tons of travel—those are all possibilities for you because you don't have a bunch of responsibilities weighing on you. But let's say that five years from now, you meet Mr./Ms. Right, get married, and the two of you squeeze out a couple of pups. Suddenly the long hours, the low pay, the extensive travel ... they don't fit your lifestyle any more. But that doesn't mean they were a bad choice at the outset!

It may well be that your initial dream job just gets old. Anything, no matter how exciting at the outset, can become routine. I talked to one assistant DA in Texas who worked in the appellate division of the DA's office, handling writs of habeas corpus. She loved it for five years, and then—poof. It got boring. So, she left.

Another possibility is that you chug along happily in a job until the job itself changes ... or its negatives become more pronounced. One student took a job at a large law firm, even though it wasn't particularly in-line with his values. He was down with it until one day when Ferdinand Marcos, the former Philippine dictator, walked in as a new client. This guy said, "I looked at him and thought, 'This is Evil personified. I can't do this.' So I quit." But again—it doesn't mean it was the wrong choice in the first place.

As Sue Gainen points out about your career, "It's not for life. It's like Baskin Robbins. You choose a flavour, go back next week, and choose another flavour."

28. REALIZE THAT LIKING A SUBJECT IN SCHOOL DOESN'T NECESSARILY MEAN YOU'LL LIKE THE PRACTICE ... AND VICE VERSA

Law school classes, being by and large theoretical discussions of appellate cases, don't tell you if you'll like those subjects as practice areas. (Clinical programs and externships, on the other hand, are *unbeatable* ways to figure out if you'll like a practice area—because they're practical rather than theoretical.) Law school classes are a good jumping-off point, but that's about it.

Of course, job satisfaction does have an intellectual component, and depending on the job, it can be a significant factor. If you go to work with a large firm or work for a judge, you better love intellectual problem solving, because you'll be doing a lot of it!

But for many jobs, law school classes aren't reflective of the real world. Liking Property class doesn't mean you'll love real estate. Domestic relations class and representing people getting divorces could hardly be more different. International Law and international practice? Night and day.

For one thing, in law school classes you're a third party observer of disputes. In real life, unless you're a judge or other objective arbiter, you're a zealous advocate of one side or the other. *Very* different emotional beast!

Also, unless you have a research intensive job, like being an appellate court clerk, the people you work with and represent and the setting in which you work will have a far greater impact on your satisfaction.

It's actually very likely that you'll wind up practicing something that you didn't, and perhaps couldn't, take in law school. Many practice areas just don't have law school classes devoted to them, and even ones that do—practice areas you may really enjoy—might not have flipped your switch enough to take the class in law school.

So, what classes give you a starting point. If you love a subject, go to the professor—unless that makes your blood turn cold—and say, "I love this class. What kind of jobs/practices do you think I should consider that would incorporate it?" You can ask the same advice of counselors at the Career Services Office.

You see my point. Take your reaction to classes with a grain of salt!

29. REALIZE THAT THE SAME SPECIALTIES IN DIFFERENT SETTINGS CAN BE VERY DIFFERENT JOBS

It's a *big* mistake to believe that because one specialty at one employer appeals to you—or the subject itself is something you enjoyed in school—that it will be similarly appealing everywhere you find it.

Take litigation. Maybe you loved your Trial Practice class at school—who doesn't?—but it's a mistake to think you'll love litigation *everywhere*. That class reflects a practice where you get tons of courtroom exposure. Now, you *would* get that at a prosecutor's office, public defender's office, in the JAG Corps, or in a small litigation practice. But at a large law firm? The hiring partner at one very large law firm told me, "I have to try hard not to laugh out loud when students tell me they want to join our litigation practice because they love being in the courtroom. The cases we litigate mean they'll be researching for years before they get to argue even a motion in court! It just tells me they don't understand the nature of our practice. And also that they won't like it."

Bankruptcy is another one. I've mentioned the practice of personal bankruptcy earlier in this section, where there is lots of personal contact with people whose lives are in turmoil. Bankruptcy law like that is exclusively practiced by small firms. When large firms have bankruptcy practices, they are very different. As one bankruptcy lawyer at a large firm describes it, "When we litigate, we're not talking about anybody's personal assets being at stake. Usually it's very wealthy people, doctors, say, who've all made back their investments in the business long since. We're just fighting over what's left. It's like a chess game: are we going to win or is the other side going to win?" Same specialty—but *very* different life!

Environmental law is another one. The Career Services Director at one law school told me about a student who had been an environmental engineer before law school and wanted to pursue environmental law at a large law firm. She immediately asked him, "Do you want to advocate on behalf of the environment?" He said "Yes," and she responded, "Then you don't want a large firm. Look at Energy Law in the Attorney General's Office of consumer protection. You start with rate cases, then you represent the little guy against huge utilities. It's complex, highly paid, and you get to be the 'White Knight.'" In other words—*exactly* what he dreamed of when he thought of Environmental Law!

So be aware of the crucial role that *setting* plays in determining the nature of a job—and factor that in as you make your short-term career goals.

30. Recognize That Your Dream Job May Be Something You've Already Been Exposed to . . . You Just Haven't Realized It Yet!

In Topic B, we'll go into detail figuring out what you're like so that we can nail down a great job for you. A large part of that is creating a "life resume" of things you've done to see where you've excelled and been happy . . . and where you haven't.

In doing so, it may jump out to you that you've worked with or otherwise been affiliated with someone whose job you'd love.

I'll give you an example. At one Midwestern law school, I met a student who'd helped his mom create an eyeglass business, grow it, and sell it to Pearle Vision Center. He was toying with the idea of getting into franchising. As we chatted about it, it became obvious that he was sort of fuzzy on what franchising was. Suddenly he said, "You know what I really want? There was a guy in Chicago who helped Mom and me negotiate and sell our business to Pearle. I'd *love* to do that." So of course I told him, "Tell that guy what you just told me—and ask for advice about what his work is like and how to break into it. He'll be so flattered!"

Odds are you don't have an eyeglass business. But if you look at everything you've done, there may well be someone who has a gig you'd like. Seek them out and learn more about what they do. It may be your dream job . . . or lead you to it!

31. Recognize That There's No Law That Says You Have to Finish Law School if You Start It . . . and That You Can't Take a Break From It if There's Some Other Goal Burning You up

I sometimes meet students who came to law school as a back-up. Their real goal is to be a singer, or an actor, or they've got another dream. In those cases, what's probably going on is that somebody's told them, "Your dream is a long shot. Law school is sensible. Go get your degree first." So they did the sensible thing. *Sensible.*

The problem is, nobody told their heart that. I'll hear, "I'm really dying to go to New York and be on Broadway . . ." They're *physically* in law school, but *mentally* . . .

The advice I always give is the same: Give yourself a year off from law school, with a firm plan in mind to come back if things don't work out. Then go and pursue that dream. You'll *still* have the "sensible thing" in your back pocket, but you'll satisfy whatever jones you have in the meantime.

During that year off, pursue that dream with everything you've got. A year is a fair amount of time to figure out which path you should take. If the reality doesn't fit with the dream you'd had in your head, you'll come back to law school with a renewed sense of purpose, and be able to look at all of the myriad possibilities your law degree brings you with fresh eyes.

The fact is, law school is expensive and time-consuming. It's challenging. It's not the place to be if your heart's not in it. A year off *now* to figure out what you really want is a great investment in yourself.

32. Look at What You're Terrified of Telling Employers as a Possible Source of a Great Job

I have talked with many law students, all over the country, who had something in their background that they were horrified to raise with employers ... or that employers might find out about. Prison. Drug addiction. Lawsuits against former employers. Sexual harassment claims. You name it.

In so many of these cases, it turned out that what the student thought was a serious handicap was *actually* entré to a job they'd love!

For instance, one student I talked with in Texas was a recovering drug addict, and was all tied up in knots about explaining his stints in rehab to potential employers. I asked him what he wanted to do, and he said, "I don't know, work for a law firm, I guess." I said, no—what do you want to *do?* He actually liked the idea of helping people who were going through what he'd gone through. I asked him, "Then why not go for a public interest job where you can *do* that? Your background won't be a hindrance there—it'll show why you can empathize with your clients and why you're motivated to help them." This formerly apathetic guy lit up like a Christmas tree at the prospect!

Another opportunity-in-disguise situation involved a student from Michigan who'd sued her former employer over a workers' comp claim. The lawsuit had taken her *four years* before she prevailed. She wondered how to address it with employers, knowing it could be viewed as a strong negative. I asked her, "How did you enjoy working on your own case?" She absolutely loved it. I said, "Then why not go into workers' comp yourself—representing other people in your situation?" I told her she could ask her own attorney for advice and leads. She just *loved* it. And again—her background wouldn't be a negative!

So don't be so sure that whatever you're hiding in your closet is a skeleton. It might be a dream job in disguise!

33. **If People Keep Telling You "That Job Is *Perfect* For You," or "You'll *Hate* That Job," Don't Take Them at Their Word. Ask Them *Why***

I've told you that your dreams are your own, and to be wary of what others want for you. That's true. But if you keep hearing the same "job riffs" from people who care about you ... maybe they see something in you that you don't see in yourself. See what's behind their opinions before you dismiss their advice!

I am reminded of a woman I met at one southern law school. She was very meek, delicate, and came to tears easily. She said she wanted to litigate—specifically, she wanted to be a prosecutor—and that everyone told her, "You don't want that!" I told her to talk to a few prosecutors, to find them through her Career Services Office, and maybe sit in on a few court cases to see what it was really like. It was reasonably obvious to me that she'd come to the conclusion herself that litigation would be a struggle for her and probably make her miserable as a result—but also that she'd be better off figuring that out for herself. The cautions from her family and friends would have been best addressed by her asking "Why do you say that?" If the foundations of people's opinions are sound, they're worth paying attention to!

34. **Remember That What Makes You Uniquely *You* May Make You a Crappy Lawyer ... But a Wonderful "Something Else"**

I've been privileged to meet many thousands of wonderful law students, many of whom I think would make truly excellent lawyers. But there are those few with just great personalities, smart, quick—who just shouldn't ever, *ever* be lawyers.

Maybe you're one of them.

If you are a nonconformist, if you're creative, if you like to dwell on the "lighter side" of life, think about it: law is a serious business. It accommodates a lot of personalities, but if you're just incapable of acting responsibly—you'd *always* be swimming upstream as a lawyer.

The most glaring example of this I've seen so far is a student in Boston. In his correspondence packet for prospective employers—he was targeting medium and large law firms—he had a sample cover letter. It was fashioned like a ransom note, with letters and words cut out of magazines, reading "Hire me or the puppy gets it"—with a picture of Snoopy with a gun aimed at his head.

He also included in his packet a pre-written fill-in-the-blank rejection letter for the employer, disguised as a Mad Libs. It read, "I'll save you some time and pre-write my own rejection letter. Dear [his name]: I am very ___(emotion)___ to inform you that we will not be offering you an interview. While ___(noun)___, your credentials suggest that you are ___(adjective)___ ___(noun)___ ..." and so on.

My jaw dropped. This guy was *oozing* creativity—but not in a way that any legal employer would appreciate! (And for those employers who responded positively to his humor—I knew there'd be some—they'd believe he'd never be happy as a lawyer.)

You see my point. A dream job is one that doesn't require you to hide your light under a bushel!

B.   FINDING OUT WHAT YOU REALLY WANT . . .

"You never find yourself until you face the truth"—

Pearl Bailey

With the myths and cobwebs of job searches cleared from your mind, we've got some work to do. In this section, we'll do "internal" and "external" tasks. The "internal" piece is figuring out what you're like, so we can determine what *you'll* like. The "external" piece involves doing what you can to figure out what's out there. Let's go!

1.   THE "INTERNAL" PIECE. YOU CAN'T AVOID IT . . . SO BITE THE BULLET AND READ THIS!

I know, I know. If you liked the idea of navel-gazing, you wouldn't have gone to law school. It's not intellectual. It's not cut-and-dried. In law school, you analyze elements and come to a conclusion. As St. John's' Maureen Provost Ryan says, "Law students like action, results, and formulas. Soul searching is *not* a strong suit for them."

You may cringe at the thought of answering touchy-feely questions, and you may be tempted to skip over this section, and go right to the "Market Analysis." Or even worse, skip the rest of this chapter entirely. But I *implore* you not to do that, because you simply can't find a dream job—all of the guerrilla tactics in the world won't help you—if you don't understand yourself first. A few hours of doing this kind of self-analysis can save you years of misery.

The simple fact is, there's no one perfect job that suits everybody. It's kind of like food. For a giggle sometime, visit the web site www. allrecipes.com. (As a devoted foodie, it's one of my favourite places on the web.) My favourite part is the reviews of recipes; people post their recipes and then other people who try them offer what they think of those recipes. No matter how wildly popular a recipe is—there may be hundreds of raves—there will be someone who gives it a thumbs down, saying "I don't understand the fuss, this didn't work for me." Why is that? Because people have different tastes. I personally love Marmite, a fermented yeast spread I grew up eating in England (you can actually buy it in grocery stores in the U.S. now). One of the greatest things about Marmite is that it never goes bad; I've had a jar in the fridge for five years with no noticeable diminution in flavor or quality. You'd probably *hate* Marmite—most people do. We just like different things . . . and there's nothing wrong with that.

Work is the same. You don't have the same personality and goals as your parents or friends or classmates. Different jobs will make you happy. That's what employers mean when they talk about the "fit" between them and you. It's not just a matter of whether you can technically do the work; it's so much more than that. Whether your personality and goals mesh with the employer ... that's vitally important. If they're hard partiers and you're not—if alcohol is a big part of every lunch and Happy Hour—you'll hate it there. If you're family-oriented and they consider anyone who works less than eighty hours a "wimp," honestly—you don't want the job. You have to know what you're like and what you want if you expect to be happy at work.

The most glaring example of this was a student I met at a school in the Pacific Northwest. After I finished the *Guerrilla Tactics* seminar, she waited with a bunch of students to talk to me. She was hanging back from the crowd, and when I asked her what she wanted to talk about, she shyly looked around and said she'd prefer to talk to me alone. So, I finished up with everyone else, and asked her, "OK—what's up?" She twirled her hair in her fingers as she looked at the ground, and whispered, "I didn't want anybody else to hear what I want.

"I want to be ... President of the United States."

Now, I don't know how much you've read about the childhood of presidents, but you know from the presidential campaigns you've seen that it requires a personality that shouts from rooftops. It's a dream that has to be shared with not just everyone you know, but three hundred million other people, as well. If you're the kind of person who's too nervous to tell your classmates what you want, there are a bunch of jobs that you'll enjoy and be good at ... but President of the United States isn't one of them!

The comedian/movie star Will Ferrell is a great example of the importance of understanding yourself in figuring out your dream job. He was a sports-information (journalism) major at USC. At that time, the football Rams were still in Southern California, and being coached by John Robinson. One of Ferrell's professors told the class, "Someone needs to go interview John Robinson." Ferrell thought, "Oh, it's going to be a lot of work. I'll have to lug the camera ..." He caught himself and thought, "That's not the right instinct. That's when I realized, 'Oh, I like *playing* Chevy Chase playing a journalist, I don't like *being* a real journalist.'"

It seems fairly obvious, doesn't it? Shouldn't we all have a moment like Will Ferrell's? In fact, at this point you might be thinking, "What kind of idiots don't know what they themselves are like?" Gulp. I'm one of them. Or more appropriately, I *was* one when I was in law school.

As I've mentioned before, as a 2L, I did what a lot of law students do: I accepted a summer offer with the biggest, most prestigious firm that would hire me. You'd recognize the name immediately. Did I pay any attention to what the job would be like? Did I know anything about myself? Nope. I figured if everybody wanted it, it must be the best job.

Not for me, it wasn't. The job required somebody who had great powers of concentration, loved to research, and was capable of leaving their emotions at the door. As it turns out, I possess none of those qualities. Had I done more research into the job and done some of the work *you're* going to do in this section, I might have avoided what I call my "summer of pain." I wouldn't wish it on you. Nobody who cares about you would. So, do yourself a favor and do a bit of soul-searching.

It's the most valuable possible way to spend your job searching time.

If you're at all worried about doing this self-analysis, it may be because you're worried that what you'll discover is not the way you've liked to picture yourself. Maybe it will tell you that pursuing a job at a large law firm, the big prestige job, isn't for you. A career counselor at one New York school told me that one of her toughest jobs was convincing students that the self-assessment tests she administered were accurate. She said, "If they take a test that suggests that they're introverted, they're very upset. They don't want to be introverts, they want to be extraverts. But the tests don't lie." The fact is, if a job requires a glad-hander and you prefer a quiet conversation, you just won't be happy. You are what you are. And if a few self-analysis quizzes help you figure that out—that's a *great* use of your time!

When you're done with this section, you should wind up with a pretty good snapshot of what you're like, and the elements that will make you happy at work. Write it down. Hang on to that information.

As you go through the rest of the activities in this book, as you meet people and talk to them about their jobs, as you read about what's out there, refer back to your list and see if the workplaces you're learning about fit your talents, motivations, values and goals. See if the people at your potential workplace have the same values as you. Identify if the same kinds of things that are important to you seem important to them, as well. See if the nature of the work they do comports with the factors that are important to you. If the job doesn't meet these criteria, then it's not your dream job!

There are three basic questions to ask in this "internal" analysis, according to Deborah Arron in the classic "What Can You Do With A Law Degree?" They are:

Who am I?

What do I want?

What am I willing to give up to get what I want?

We'll go into some detail about answering these three questions, so that you'll wind up with a great framework for learning, in concrete terms, more about exactly what you'll enjoy doing with your life. Let's take a look at each of those questions in turn.

A. WHO AM I?

That question makes you want to barf, right? What the hell does it mean? Well, for our purposes here, it's pretty straightforward.

We're trying to get at four elements: Your talents, skills, interests, and values & motivations (the last two count as one). In doing this, we'll also be determining an important sub-issue, namely: What do you have to offer an employer?

By way of getting at those talents, skills, interests, values & motivations, we'll use a couple of tools. They both require a bit of work. Sorry about that, but it's unavoidable.

1. WRITE DOWN A BASIC "LIFE RESUME"

This isn't a resume for an employer, but you can use your resume as a starting point. I want it to be more basic. School—high school (if it's not in the too-distant past), college, any other grad school you've attended. Each job you've had. Volunteer activities. Clubs and organizations you've belonged to. If you have children, parenthood counts. Hobbies. We'll call each of these "activities."

Now, write them down across the top of a sheet of paper, giving each one a column. (You can turn a sheet of paper on its side, or heck, use more than one sheet if you need to.)

Please note: If you've been out of undergrad for a while, please check Chapter 22 for Second Career Students for a more "grown up" version of this exercise.

For each activity, note the following:

- Any accomplishments that spring to mind, no matter how trivial you think they'd be viewed by others.
- What did you like most about the activity? Even if it's "chatting at the water cooler," write it down!
- What did you dislike the most about the activity? A function, a certain type of person, hours, anything at all.
- What kinds of functions came easily to you? What did people tend to turn to you to accomplish quickly?
- What was a struggle for you to accomplish?
- Have you enjoyed any form of selling in your activities? Whether fundraising, soliciting new members, or any other form of selling?
- If the activities involved intellectual challenges or puzzles, did you enjoy that?
- What skills did you learn and/or utilize? (e.g., as a summer law clerk, research, writing, organization, communicating with clients)
- Which skills did you enjoy using? (with the summer clerk example, for instance, writing and communication)
- Which skills did you dislike using? (in the summer clerk example, for instance, research)

- Did you get external recognition from peers or authority figures? If so, was it necessary for your sense of accomplishment?

- In situations where either is possible, have you tended to lead or follow? Are you generally the "ringleader"?

- Have you enjoyed situations where your role is structured, or have you preferred to "do your own thing"?

- Think about the people you've been involved with in these activities. What are the characteristics of the people you enjoyed the most? Disliked the most? Did you hang with the Type—A personalities, the go-getters? Or were your homeys the laid-back, chill-out types?

- In the case of jobs—look at why you left. Did you get fired? If so, why? If you grew to dislike it and left, why? If you left to go to school—what did you miss the most about it (if anything)?

- What kinds of hours did you put in (with work, or school and studying)? Don't forget to include commuting time. If the hours were long, were you OK with that?

- In classes you've taken, in high school (if it's not too far back!), college and law school, when did you shine? What classes did you dislike the most, and what did you dislike about them?

- For paying jobs, to what extent did you take a job that paid a lot just for the dough, as opposed to your enjoyment? If you took the big dollars, how did you feel about the job?

- What elements of your activities have you procrastinated to avoid doing?

- Looking at the activities overall—time flies for you when you've done . . . what?

This very basic exercise will help you ascertain your talents, skills, and values and motivations. Look for patterns. Consider having a friend look it over for you to see the patterns that elude you.

Your talents are those things that come naturally to you, what you have a "flare" for. It's easy to overlook your talents because you may believe that if something comes easily to you, it comes easily to everybody so it's meaningless. I'll give you an example. It's always been a snap for me to write advertising copy. I've handled the promotion for every club I ever belonged to, for every business I've ever owned (and every book I've ever written). It's so easy for me that I've always ignored it when I've thought about what my talents are. I felt silly mentioning it. Don't you make that mistake! Make special note of *anything* you naturally do well. Maybe you are naturally decisive, empathetic, a great problem-solver, a born public speaker, the "class clown." You might always assume the role of peace maker, leader, or rabble-rouser. Maybe you write well, so you're the one who always handles the newsletter, or you worked on the school paper, or you have a blog that's widely admired. The scope is endless. But honing in on what you naturally do well is a good insight into jobs you will enjoy.

Skills are a different animal. As Seattle career consultant Karen Summerville points out, **skills and talents are not the same thing, and it's important to distinguish them. In a nutshell, talents are natural; skills are acquired.** It's possible to become highly adept at tasks you don't really enjoy, to develop expertise in specialties that give you little satisfaction. So the most important feature of distinguishing skills and talents is to check to make sure that the skills you've developed are ones that you look forward to utilizing in future jobs. If not—well, you're in law school to reinvent yourself! It's always possible to acquire new skills through classes, volunteer projects, and part-time jobs.

Values and motivations are the most amorphous elements of self-analysis. **Values and motivations are the nonsubstance-oriented elements that create job satisfaction for you—** things like recognition, autonomy, variety, intellectual challenge, helping others.

The reason I had you do your jobs-clubs-school exercise is that I don't think it's possible to get at your values and motivations in the absence of an honest look at what you've done. While it's entirely possible that you're striving to do something important to you that you've never done before, the elements of your life so far nonetheless provide valuable insight into what you're like.

With your "life resume" in hand, take a look at this list and determine the values that mean the most. Cross out the ones that don't matter to you. Look and see how many are remaining. (This list is adapted from "What Can You Do With A Law Degree?" and the University of San Francisco "Legal Career Decision Making Process" Handout):

___ Achievement, accomplishment

___ Action, adventure, fast-paced environment

___ Aesthetics, appreciation of beauty

___ Autonomy, the freedom to make your own choices

___ Competition, winning

___ Creativity and self-expression, generating new ideas

___ Peace of mind, low stress

___ Being genuinely yourself with others

_____ Sense of humor, wit

_____ Intellectual challenges, learning new things

_____ Treating others fairly, wanting equity for them

_____ Knowledge, seeking truth or information

_____ Love and family, affection, intimacy

_____ Loyalty, allegiance to a person, group or cause

_____ Integrity, morality, following standards of honor

_____ Nature, appreciating the natural world

_____ Pleasure, fun, enjoyment

_____ Influence, power to get things done

_____ Recognition

_____ Religious conviction

_____ Security

_____ Helping others, serving a cause

_____ Skill, being good at something

_____ Tangible results of effort

_____ Variety in terms of number and type of experience

_____ Wealth, ample money for things you want

_____ Wisdom, insight, judgment

_____ Productivity at work

_____ Leisure, lots of time off

_____ Opportunities to travel

You might have a lot of items left on your list. Now, the hard part: hone it down to five or six things you absolutely could not live without. They reflect your core values and motivations.

Keep a list of these values and motivations as you go through your job search. When you talk with counselors in the Career Services Office at school, tell them what's important to you. When you go on information interviews, ask people the questions that get at what values are reflected in the work they do. I'm not sure it's particularly useful to ask people what their values are—I'm not sure any of us can reel them off, off the top of our heads, with anything approaching accuracy—but you can ask the questions that get at that (I go over them in detail in just a few pages when we talk about informational interviewing, topic d.4.e, "Have questions ready.").

There is no getting around the fact that your dream job _must_ reflect your values and satisfy your motivations. That's why it's so important to figure out what they are!

This came home to me in chatting with a student at one school whose dream job was to work at the prosecutor's office—a great gig. They didn't have any openings, and she had gotten advice from professors to do defense work in the meantime to get courtroom exposure. She told me, "I just don't know if I can do it. My husband was a police officer, and he was killed in the line of duty." OMG. Of *course* she'd be miserable doing defense work—it couldn't be more out of line with her values!

I talked to another student who had figured out that the most important feature of any job for her was variety. She got bored easily and needed lots on her plate. With that in mind, she accepted a job with the state general counsel's office of mental health, and worked there for two years in law school. She said, "I'd never have chosen a specialty like mental health, but I've gotten to do *everything*. Probate, litigation, counseling, the variety is tremendous." By following her muse—variety—she was sure to find jobs she enjoyed!

So we've covered talents, skills, motivations and values. In terms of figuring out the "real you," that leaves us with interests. While what you've done by way of jobs, clubs, volunteer activities and school choices are relevant, there are some more questions to ask to unearth your interests. Answering these questions will help address the nature and intellectual content of jobs you'll enjoy:

- Go through the Sunday paper. Which articles do you read?
- What kinds of magazines do you read?
- What kinds of blogs do you routinely check out?
- What kinds of subjects in books draw your attention?
- When you talk to your friends about substantive issues, what do you like to talk about?
- What kind of television programs do you watch? What do you TiVO?
- Do you have many different interests that change over time? Or do you focus on one field and delve into it at great depth?

Take into account that no single job is likely to encompass *every* subject that interests you. You're allowed to have hobbies too, you know. But since your job will take up the lion's share of your waking hours, it should be something that engages you intellectually.

2. A SIMPLE "HOW-MANY-HOURS-DO-YOU-WANT-TO-PUT-IN?" EXERCISE

I've pointed out that your starting pay at a private law firm is directly related to the hours you will be required to put in. If you're like most law students I know, it's easy to delude yourself about the amount of time you're willing to devote to the office.

Here's a simple exercise to help you figure it out. Keep track of what you do, in fifteen minute increments, for a few days. You don't need excruciating detail—the details of your bathroom habits don't require diarizing—but the key is, the time you spend on schoolwork and homework. *Really* homework, I mean—trolling the internet, IM'ing, chatting with friends at the library—that ain't work. Keep track of the real work portion of your day. How many hours does it add up to?

You can, of course, massage your background to figure out your sensitivity to long hours. As one career counselor pointed out to me, "If you were the kind of student who skated through undergrad without doing much homework, you're not going to suddenly morph into the person who enjoys a seventy-hour work week."

Incidentally, as part of this exercise it's important to take commuting time into account. It may well be that you've always lived close to school; in college and law school you may even have had on-campus digs. But commutes *count*. You don't know how wonderful a ten-minute commute is until, well, you've had a ten-minute commute. In my part of the country—Fairfield County, Connecticut—virtually everybody commutes into Manhattan to work. From my town to Wall Street is a *two-hour commute ... each way!* That adds *four hours* to the average workday; even people who put in eight hours at the office are away from home from seven to seven! A quick commute is one of the factors that leads to satisfaction for people who work in smaller towns. It really counts!

So look at your background and your life now, and be *honest* with yourself about how much time you're willing to dedicate to work. There are scads of awesome jobs that don't require long hours. Be careful about convincing yourself that you're alright with burning the midnight oil if you've never done it before and you're not doing it now.

3. SELF-ASSESSMENT TESTS THAT HELP YOU DISCOVER WHAT YOU'RE REALLY LIKE ...

I've never been a great fan of self-assessment tests. But an awful lot of people are, so it's entirely possible that Kimmbo is talking through her hat. There are essentially three views on these tests:

1. They're invaluable.

2. They're worthless.

3. They're useful in figuring out how to interact with people once you've got a job, but they're not hyper-useful in figuring out which kind of job you ought to seek.

So the least risk alternative is to take at least one self-assessment test, because there's a good chance they'll be useful to you. At the very least you'll learn more about yourself, and that's fun.

The most popular self-assessment test, hands-down, is the Myers—Briggs Type Indicator, a very large true-false test. I've taken it myself and I have to admit, it's scarily accurate.

In a nutshell, Myers—Briggs proposes that everybody fits into one of sixteen personality "types." It figures out your motivations and what energizes you and as a result ideally helps you seek a job that's harmonious with those qualities.

The sixteen types are derived from four personality "dimensions." For each of these dimensions, you tend more toward one of the extremes than the other. The four dimensions are:

Extraversion (E)—Introversion (I)

Sensing (S)—Intuition (N)

Thinking (T)—Feeling (F)

Judging (J)—Perceiving (P)

If you take every combination of four different dimension, that's where you get the sixteen types.

Interestingly, these terms don't mean what most of us think they do. And everybody has at least a little of each dimension in their personality. (The following descriptions of the dimensions are adapted from the book "Do What You Are," a do-it-yourself Myers—Briggs test that's really excellent.)

The Extraversion/Introversion dimension determines how you interact with the world. Extraverts (Es) are energized by being around others, like being the center of attention, are an "open book," talk more than listen. Introverts (Is) are energized by spending time alone, don't like the limelight, like to share personal information with just a few people, listen more than talk.

The Sensing/Intuition dimension addresses the information you notice. Sensors (Ss) trust what is concrete, what they can gather through their five senses, want to know exactly what's going on in a situation, focus on what *is*. Intuitives (Ns) look "between the lines," value imagination, trust hunches, focus on what *could* be.

The Thinking/Feeling dimension looks at how you make decisions and form conclusions. Thinkers (Ts) are logical, objective, analytical decision makers, unbothered by unpleasant conclusions, value truth over fact, are motivated by a desire to achieve and accomplish. Feelers (Fs) are powered by empathy and compassion, consider fact important, and are motivated by desire to be appreciated.

The Judging/Perceiving dimension tests your desire for structure or spontaneity. Judgers (Js) like finishing projects, prefer things orderly and like structure, like making decisions, have a work ethic. Note that judgers are not "judgmental," they just like having issues resolved. Perceivers (Ps) like starting projects, prefer spontaneity and flexibility, like perceiving options, have a "play ethic" (play now, finish the job later).

Now what I've just done is reduced Myers–Briggs to the point of absurdity. There's a lot more to it than that. But my descriptions give you a very basic idea of the four dimensions.

When you take the Myers–Briggs test, you wind up with a four-letter "type," one letter for each of the four dimensions. It's important to recognize what this "type" does for you. As Cornell's Elizabeth Peck points out, "Myers–Briggs really helps you conceptualize and understand things you really already know about yourself. It doesn't predict behavior. But it does help you figure out where you'll be the happiest and most comfortable."

She offers the following example. "Say that you have a 'feeling' preference, so you tend to like to work with values, you're empathetic, and you step into the shoes of the person you're trying to help. It will be very important to you to find work that's in line with your values. But if you're a 'thinker'—you're on the other end of that particular preference—you can think logically and be emotionally detached. You can take positions that you don't personally agree with."

Now, how does this translate into a job search? As Liz Peck points out, "Myers–Briggs *shouldn't* be used to tell you what you *can't* do! What it will tell you is what challenges you might face in a given work environment. For instance, if you have a 'feeling' preference, you'd want to think about what working in a large law firm would mean for you. You might not do a lot that's in line with your values. But you could temper that with pro bono work, extracurriculars. You'd need to think about how you'd feel being a fish out of water."

While I hate to bring up my miserable summer clerkship yet again, there's no question that taking Myers–Briggs ahead of time could have averted disaster for me. As a 'feeler' rather than a 'thinker,' I was unable to leave my feelings at the door and do my job with an objective, analytical eye. That's absolutely necessary in a large firm. So, knowing a little bit about myself might have saved me from making a big mistake. (Or not. I think my head would still have been turned by the enormous paycheck.)

While I've focused on Myers–Briggs here, it's far from the only personality test you can take. There are hundreds of them. I've heard rave reviews regarding the Holland Code, which gives you one of six personality types (the Bureau of Labor Statistics breaks down jobs that way). Some people are fans of the Strong Interest

Inventory. And on-line there are a ton of tests you can take. I've listed some on-line resources in Appendix A at the end of this chapter.

Is it worth taking a bit of time to get to know yourself through these tests? Sure. Why not? They're fun. They're interesting. They're more accurate than having your tea leaves read or your astrological chart analyzed. And if they help you even a little bit in figuring out what you'd be happiest doing ... they're worth it!

B. WHAT DO I WANT?

The quizzes you just took should give you insight into what you want: The kind of people you want to work with and for, the setting and location, the hours and money you're willing to tolerate, the intellectual content, the general contours of your work life. At this point, notice that you're looking at the qualities a dream job would have—not the name of the employer or the title the job might carry.

C. WHAT AM I WILLING TO GIVE UP TO GET WHAT I WANT?

I know what you're thinking. "What do you mean ... *give up?*" There's no getting around the fact that every job in the world involves compromise. You get some of what you want ... but not all of it. It's vitally important that you get in touch with what you're willing to give up!

The two basic conflicts for lawyers are money versus meaning, and work versus family. Let's take a look at each of them.

1. MONEY VS. MEANING

I've warned you before—don't overvalue a big paycheck! Studies show that enough is never enough. I talked with the Chairman of a sizable public company, someone who routinely works with investment bankers. Investment bankers, as you know, make mucho dineros, and investment banking is a career you can break into with a law degree. I asked him if he thought the investment bankers were happy, if they enjoyed their jobs. He thought about it for a moment before he said, "No. They're like dogs at a banquet. No matter what they eat, they want more."

If you take a job that is meaningless to you just to pursue the big money, money had better mean *everything* to you. As Orson Welles said in *Citizen Kane,* "It's not hard to make a lot of money ... if money is all you want."

I remember talking with one student in particular. He was under great pressure from his uncle to join the uncle's law practice. The uncle was drowning in work, and was pulling in $60,000 a week—a *week*—and wanted to cut his nephew in on the action. The stumbling block? The uncle was doing criminal defense work, representing Colombian drug lords. This student said to me, "The money's unbelievable, but ... I just don't think I can do it." Can you blame him? And if you *can* ... then I've found a specialty for you.

2. MONEY VS. PRIVATE LIFE

If you have a family—how much time are you willing to spend away from them, including weekends? Whether you have a family or not—how much time are you willing to devote to your work? I talked with the junior associate at one large firm, where her department manager sat everyone down to determine who was going to work weekends for a few weeks. He asked for a show of hands to show which associates were married, who had children, saying they shouldn't have to come in for the extra work. This particular associate raised her hand, and asked plaintively, "How are we ever supposed to be *not* single if we have to work weekends?"

It's impossible to get *anything* without giving something up, and analyzing *specifically* what you're willing to give up will go a long way toward guiding you to a dream job. (This is especially true if you think you want to work for a large law firm, because the lure of money and prestige leads many law students to believe they're willing to give up quality-of-life elements that they aren't, in fact, willing to sacrifice. For more on large law firms, see Chapter 23.)

2. THE MARKET RESEARCH. WHAT'S OUT THERE? WHAT'S IT LIKE?

You can't choose a target without having some idea about what's available. Career Counselor Wendy Werner points out that the problem most people have opting for jobs is limited information. Of course, it's not a lack of choices "out there" that's a problem. If anything, it's just the opposite. It's the paradox of choice: having too much available can paralyze you into not making a decision at all. It's like internet dating. No matter how cool the person you're e-mailing is, you think ... gee, who *else* is out there? When it comes to jobs, there are in excess of a hundred specialties, hundreds of settings, alternative careers ... how can you possibly get to know them *all*?

You can't. Nobody can. Your goal should be to gather all of the information you can about what's out there before you narrow your choices. Because you've done the "internal research" first, as you learn about specialties and settings you'll be able to view them through the lens of, "What will make me happy, based on what I'm like and what I want to do with my life?" Your search won't be perfect, because it *can't* be. But it'll be damned good.

This research is *so* important. Without it, you can make some howlingly bad career choices, no matter how well you know yourself. I am reminded of the story of Robert Reed, the actor who played the dad on "The Brady Bunch." You know. Mike. He'd apparently been a serious actor before the show, and he was just disgusted with what he viewed as the inanity of the Brady scripts. He'd take Shakespearean plays to the show's producer, and ask "Why aren't we doing scripts like *this?*" Now, where was this guy's freaking *head?* Did he ever *look* at the show's premise before he took the job? "Here's the story . . . of a man named Brady . . ." There's nothing wrong with wanting to be a Shakespearean actor. Just don't take a role on a sitcom!

A similar story that comes to mind involves Bobby Harrison, the ornithologist who rediscovered the ivory-billed woodpecker. An escapee from academia, he commented, "I found that if I don't have to see students and I don't have to go to class, I love teaching."

So you can't be happy with a job you don't research up front.

What we'll do first is funnel the world of options down to three or four with some basic detective work. Of course, if at any point you have a poetic experience and your dream job becomes obvious to you . . . great! Use the rest of this book to go for it! If, however, that doesn't happen, you'll take those three or four best options, and research those in more depth to identify a target. Now remember: If as you research you change your mind—in fact, if you change your mind at any time based on what you learn—that's all right. The fact that you're learning and that's what's changing your options is a positive; you're taking the initiative, and you'll always be happier as a result. As Benjamin Disraeli said, action is not happiness, but there is no happiness without action.

So let's get going!

A. HOW TO CONDUCT THE "INITIAL ELIMINATION ROUND"

Keeping as open a mind as possible, take advantage of these resources in identifying your initial three or four targets:

1. CAREER SERVICES PANELS AND SPEAKERS

At most law schools, the Career Services Office offers a wealth of presentations about careers, speakers, panels, "Day In The Life" programs, brown-bag lunches with lawyers, you name it. Go to as many of them as you can. (Some schools will even bribe you to attend—I've known students who've won iPods for going to every CSO presentation for a year!) If you're like so many students I've met, you'll find that one of these panelists or speakers will open your eyes to a practice you might never have considered!

2. TALK TO COUNSELORS IN THE CAREER SERVICES OFFICE

Tell them "If I'm looking for the features X and X and X in a career [the results of your 'internal research,'] what specialties/settings should I be considering?" The underutilization of Career Services at most schools I visit is a crying shame. They know so, so many people and have so many good ideas for you. Tap into all that knowledge!

3. LOOK AT CLE OFFERINGS LOCALLY

CLEs are continuing legal education classes that practitioners have to attend to maintain their licenses to practice law. As a student, you can typically get in for free on scholarship. You'll find the offerings on your local bar association web site, your Career Services Office's web site, and you can also find them from the Practicing Law Institute (which gives them nationwide) at www.pli.edu. See if the topics are of interest, and if they are, go to the CLE—they're typically pretty short—and be blunt with people around you during breaks. "I'm still in school, I'm trying to figure out what to do with my degree ... what do you like about this?" Listen to what they say and see how it meshes with what you know about yourself and what you want!

You can also take part in live chats with lawyers on-line; check out what's available at http://community.lawyers.com/chat/list.asp.

4. ATTEND BAR ASSOCIATION MEETINGS LOCALLY

Local bar association practice sections usually hold monthly meetings with an educational component and an opportunity to chat. It costs a pittance to join the bar association as a law student, and hearing people talk about what they do is the best way to help figure out what you want.

5. SKIM BAR ASSOCIATION PUBLICATIONS AND SPECIALTY PUBLICATIONS

Look at profiles of attorneys in publications like *The National Law Journal* and *American Lawyer*. Some cities also have their own bar journals, like *The New York Bar Journal*. See if the lives they describe sound good to you.

6. TAKE ADVANTAGE OF YOUR LAW SCHOOL'S MENTORING PROGRAM, IF IT HAS ONE (YOUR LOCAL BAR ASSOCIATION MAY ALSO HAVE A MENTORING PROGRAM)

There are practicing lawyers just chomping at the bit to give you advice. Tell them the parameters of the life you want to live, and see what they advise you to consider.

7. GO ON-LINE TO ONE OF THE MEGA-JOB SITES—MONSTER, CAREERBUILDER, AND SO FORTH—AND JUST SCROLL THROUGH THE JOBS THAT ARE "OUT THERE," TO SEE WHAT CATCHES YOUR EYE

8. LOOK AT PUBLICATIONS THAT WILL SCOOT YOU THROUGH A BUNCH OF JOBS IN A HURRY

Of course I have to recommend my own "America's Greatest Places To Work With A Law Degree." But there are other unbeatable resources as well, particularly Lisa Abrams' "The Official Guide To Legal Specialties." There are the Vault guides to various specialties. For alternate careers, check out Chapter X and take a look at Debra Arron's classic "What You Can Do With A Law Degree."

9. If You Were Inspired by a Law School Class, Talk to the Professor and Ask for Ideas About Practice Areas That Incorporate the Substance of the Class

While it's true that practicing law is very different than what you find in law school, it can be a good starting point—especially if you were really intrigued with the subject.

10. As Sue Gainen Advises, "Read the Newspapers and *Think*." She Points Out That the Jobs of the Future Don't Exist Now

She explains, "Cleaning up space junk for cell phone satellites, space travel. That will involve contracts, treaties, negotiating skills. Also—infrastructure. The infrastructure is falling apart, and replacing it will involve all kinds of legal aspects. You can position yourself for careers that don't exist right now—but *will* exist in your career."

B. When it Comes to Money, Make Sure You're Comparing Apples to Apples

As you learn about jobs, don't eliminate any because of money without taking into account the following:

1. Many Jobs That Start Out With a Low Salary Ramp up in Pay Very, Very Quickly

It's common to think that large law firms are the only setting in which you can make big dough. Not true! As the National Association of Law Placement discovered, within five years of graduation, the difference in pay between large firms and small firms is *ten percent*. That's *all*. Because while large law firms start out paying a lot more, salaries there suffer from "compression"— that is, they basically flat line for a while. At small firms, on the other hand, your pay tends to jump rapidly.

The same is true for government jobs. The pay gets relatively handsome relatively quickly. So don't pay attention just to the "opening bid." Look at what jobs pay within two, three, five years. You'll often be pleasantly surprised!

2. Take Into Account the Dramatic Effect of Geography. Cost of Living Can Make an Enormous Impact on the Quality of Your Life

I visit about seventy cities a year, and I always pick up local real estate books along the way. I bring them home and when I have friends over to dinner, we look them over. We laugh. We cry. You wouldn't *believe* what some people pay to live. As I write this, even a modest one bedroom apartment in New York City will run you a million bucks. A *million*. In the Midwest you can get the same joint for a quarter of that price.

While employers with offices in many cities will often pay a "cost of living" bonus for expensive cities, it doesn't make up the difference. It costs *at least* twice as much to live in New York or San Francisco than it does in—well, "normally priced" places.

Living in a less "financially challenged" city can make a dramatic impact on the life you live, from the size of your house to the activities and vacations you can take part in because you're spending so much less money. Remember to take that into account when you do your financial calculations!

3. LOOK AT THE POSSIBILITY OF PAY "PERKS," LIKE LOAN REPAYMENT PROGRAMS

For instance, some federal agencies have a student loan repayment program (with limits, of course!).

Some law schools supplement the salaries of students who go into public interest jobs. Check with your Career Services Office to see what other kinds of programs might be available to you.

4. MAKE SURE THAT YOU'RE CALCULATING ALL OF THE ELEMENTS THAT GO INTO COMPENSATION

It may be that you go to a small firm where you get a salary as well as a portion of the business you bring in. That can make a *huge* difference in your compensation—and the fact that you've got control over it is an element of job satisfaction by itself.

Or take the JAG Corps (a great job, by the way). As Thomas Feiter pointed out in a 2006 article in the University of San Diego Law School newspaper, there's much more that goes into military compensation than just the salary. Six months into the JAG program, the base pay is $39,000. If you looked at that by itself, you might turn up your nose at it. Here's what you'd be missing:

There's a base housing allowance (it varies geographically, but in San Diego, it's $22,000);

There's a base allowance for subsistence (again it varies geographically; for San Diego, it's $2,200).

You'd also want to consider that the base housing and subsistence allowances are not taxable. Assuming a 25% tax bracket, those turn into almost $32,000. When you add that to the base pay, you're at $71,000!

Even that $71,000 figure doesn't take into account the loan repayment bonuses for officers, as well as signing bonuses for subsequent terms; for instance, the Marine JAG Corps has a $50,000 bonus if you sign for a second four-year term; the Army JAG pays $25,000 for the first two years, $25,000 for the second two years, and $10,000 after four years in bonuses.

And beyond the money, there's thirty days of paid vacations every year and full benefits. (To see a full run-down of these figures on-line, see on-line resources in Appendix A at the end of this chapter, and check the military websites.)

C. WITH THE SPECIALTIES AND SETTINGS THAT INTRIGUE YOU, KEEP NOTES ON THEM

Put the name of the specialty/setting on the left, and have two columns: "Positives" for what appeals to you, and "Negatives" for what doesn't.

If a job just jumps out at you as a dream job—great! Stop your "winnowing down" and focus on it.

Otherwise, cut your list to three or four targets. Remember— these are just preliminary targets. You may change the list as you narrow down your choices from here.

D. TIME TO GET THE DOWN-LOW FROM THE HORSE'S MOUTH . . .

Or the horses' *mouths,* more appropriately. Once you've got three or four choices, you're going to find real, live people to talk to. This is going to kill two birds with one stone. Not only will it help you figure out a first job "target," it will give you contacts to return to in helping you get your foot in the door.

The reason I implore you to consider "fresh meat" in honing your choice is that talking to people doing what you think you want to do is simply the best way to figure out if you'll like it. As Daniel Hill says in his phenomenal book "Stumbling Onto Happiness"—I implore you to read it—the only reliable way to figure out if something will make you happy is to talk to people who are doing it.

1. HOW DO YOU FIND "INFORMATION TARGETS"?

a. The way you honed in on what they do is one fertile source.

If you went to a bar association event or CLE or CSO-sponsored event and saw them, or you read about them in a newspaper or on a web site or anywhere else, following up with them is a logical—and flattering—way to learn more.

b. Ask at the Career Services Office for the names of alums who do the things you think sound interesting and are willing to chat with law students.

Don't worry about being a pest. Law school alums are always lamenting the fact that students don't lean on them *enough.*

c. Ask at the local bar association for people to talk to in specialties that potentially float your boat.

Again—you're not being a pest. People at bar associations are always telling me they wish law students would contact them more.

d. If your jumping-off point of interest was a class you took in school, tell the professor you'd like to talk to people who practice what the professor preaches.

2. IDEALLY, BEFORE YOU CHOOSE AN INITIAL TARGET, PLAN ON TALKING TO AT LEAST THREE PEOPLE WHO DO IT

That's right—at least three. If that sounds like a lot, look at the enormity of the decision you're making. Isn't your personal happiness, at least for the foreseeable future, worth this paltry time investment? It'll take you less time than a one-credit class. If you didn't do the footwork and wound up a year after law school with a miserable job, wouldn't you look back and think that fifteen-minutes-per-person would have been a *really* smart strategy? Of course you would. So bite the bullet and *do it*.

Why three people? Because you minimize the odds that you'll get a false positive or negative. People's experiences are idiosyncratic. Maybe one person is having a bad day, or just got unusually great news. Their feelings about their work will be predictably biased. Or one person may have a very different personality than you. But with three points of view, you're more likely to get a realistic snapshot of what the job is like.

3. MAKE SURE YOUR TARGETS HAVE JOBS WITH THE MAJOR "ATTRIBUTES" THAT YOU'RE CONSIDERING

Make sure that your targets are all in the setting that interests you, ideally the city you want, and again ideally practicing in the specialty that you think sounds intriguing. Specialties may not be that important, depending on the nature of your potential targets. For instance, being a judicial clerk is largely setting specific (except for "specialty" courts, like the Court of Special Claims in Washington); the big difference is whether you go to a trial court or an appellate court, so you'd target your clerks appropriately.

Also—target junior people if you can. The perspective of a name partner at a firm, twenty-five years out of law school, would undoubtedly include some valuable pearls of wisdom but wouldn't help too much with helping you figure out what an entry-level position is like.

4. CONTACTING YOUR "INFORMATIONAL INTERVIEW" TARGETS

When you're contacting people for information, you're asking for a favor. That can be intimidating. It's important to remember that people by and large are hard-wired to be helpful. People like to feel like experts, they like to offer advice ... if they are approached correctly!

There are four important points to remember:

* You don't want to "surprise" your informational interview targets.

Let them know what you're contacting them about *before* you speak with them. Either a voice mail or e-mail will do. I prefer voice mail just because it's impossible to ignore; people can (and do) ignore e-mails from people they don't know until they take care of all of their "business" e-mails.

* If you do leave a voice mail, make sure you leave it at a time when the person won't be at the office— early in the morning or late at night.

* If you send an e-mail, make the message line something about how you found them.

"X told me to contact you" (if you had an intermediary recommend them); "I saw you speak at X law school," "I read about you in X publication. I respect what you do, and I have a quick question . . ."

* Drench your communications in gratefulness.

While people generally like to be helpful, there's no question that they don't *have* to be. Whether they're just answering your e-mail, talking to you over the phone for even a few minutes, or meeting you for coffee or lunch, they're taking time away from their lives to help you. Be sure that you thank them profusely, and send a thank you note afterwards.

a. What about the content of your message?

In your voice mail or e-mail message, you're in general going to tell them who you are ("Hello, I'm . . . I am a 1L/2L/3L at X"); here's how I found you; I've put a lot of research into figuring out what I want to do with my degree, but I'm not sure yet; something about your background that is interesting/relevant ("I think I might like your kind of international practice because I loved my two years in the Peace Corps in Namibia"); I'd appreciate ten minutes of your advice (give a definite time limit, so they aren't scared you'll take up a whole morning or afternoon) at your convenience. I'm available (as big a time block over a few days as you can muster)."

Make your message brief and again, drench it in gratefulness: "I can't tell you how much it would mean to me to receive your advice," or something like it that suits your style.

b. If you choose the voice-mail route, have a few basic questions ready if by chance you reach the person instead of their voice mail.

You may call at 6 in the morning figuring they'd never be at work, and—hello! There they are. They may say to you, "Let's just talk right now." Wha . . . wha . . . wha . . . you've got to have questions ready! On the next page or so I give you a basic list of questions you can have in front of you when you call.

c. While a conversation by phone or in person is optimal, *take what you can get.*

If the "target" insists they're too busy to talk and asks that you e-mail your questions, then do so. A partner at one law firm told me about a student who contacted her, asking for some advice, and asking for a phone conversation. The partner e-mailed her back, and said she didn't have time for a conversation but that she would be happy to answer questions by e-mail. The student e-mailed back, "It would be difficult for me to put my questions into an e-mail. I really want to talk to you." They conducted this back-and-forth a few times, with the student continuing to insist on a phone conversation. Needless to say, the partner got angrier and angrier. "I finally just directed this student to a few articles and books that I thought she'd find helpful, and I wished her luck. PS: I never heard back from her."

People generally will give you a few minutes, but if they just can't ... accept it, take whatever they'll give you, and say thanks!

d. If the person can't/won't talk to you or give you advice, thank them anyway.

People inhabit in their own little universes. You and I certainly do. That's healthy. Maybe some of the people you contact are preoccupied, or maybe they're truly extraordinarily busy, or maybe they never got your message because they've gone into the Federal Witness Protection Program. The point is: don't assume that someone who doesn't help you right now is a jerk.

The legal community is small. You don't know when you'll run into (or even work with) them. Say "Thank you anyway" and leave it at that. Don't make an enemy with a snide comment. It's not worth it.

5. CONDUCTING YOUR "INFORMATIONAL INTERVIEW"

a. If they do agree to talk to you, research them as much as possible ahead of time.

Don't waste their time by asking them questions about their background that you could easily have found out ahead of time. Don't make yourself crazy, but googling them, looking at their profile on their employer's web site, doing a Westlaw or Lexis/Nexis search, asking at the Career Services Office (if it's an alum or speaker at school) makes sense. And if you heard the person speak, you probably learned all you need to know from their speech.

b. Have questions ready when you talk to them.

While your questions will vary depending on your research, they'll fall along the lines of:

- What do you like about what you do?
- How did you choose it?
- What would you change about it if you could?
- What do you wish you knew when you started?
- If you were me . . . what would be the most important questions to ask someone like you?
- How did you get into what you do?
- If you were going to do something else in the future . . . what would your job now prepare you to do then?
- What's a typical day/week like for you?

And if the job sounds good to you, tell them they've inspired you! And ask . . .

- What organizations should I join, what should I be doing to break in?

You'll think of many more questions, and the conversations you have will lead you in different directions. Remember: What you're trying to get at is whether or not this is a job that will make you happy. Listen carefully to whether the people you'd work with, the intellectual content of the job, the work/life balance, the talents, skills and values involved, are elements that appeal to you.

If the person is negative about their job, don't take that as a dead end on the specialty. Maybe they're having a bad day or maybe their happiness "set point" is just naturally low. You know. They're a miserable troll by nature. Try to pin the source of the dissatisfaction and consider it accordingly. A student at a California law school told me that "A lot of people I talk to are miserable, they hate their jobs, and they get mad at me when I do what comes naturally, and try to cheer them up, 'Oh, it's not that bad.'" I suggested instead asking, "What's different about what you do than you thought it would be?" That way, you lend a sympathetic ear *and* you learn valuable tips about what to avoid in *your* job search!

c. Thank you, thank you, thank you.

Thank them for their advice. And follow up with a thank you note. Not only is it what we English people call "good form," but it primes the pump for asking for further advice. If it turns out that you want a job like the interviewer's, they may continue to be a great resource . . . if you're appropriately grateful.

6. Once You've Talked to Your Informational Interviewers, Look Over What You've Learned

As you spoke with them, you undoubtedly heard elements that appealed to you, and others that didn't. You probably started focusing in on one target as you learned more. If not, and you still have a couple that appeal to you equally, there's no shame in pursuing two different kinds of jobs, say, in two different specialties. (I've talked with students who've pursued even more than that, but it becomes difficult to juggle them!) Go ahead and come up with two different versions of your resume, customize your cover letters appropriately, and remember that in interviews you'll answer questions focusing on that particular specialty/setting/type of job, without mentioning your other focus. (I address all of those topics in the resume, correspondence and interview chapters.) What you'll probably find if you pursue more than one type of job is that as you interview, one of them will become more attractive to you than the other. That's great! If it doesn't, then take the best opportunity you get. Either way, with the work you've done on getting to know yourself, what you want, and researching what's out there . . . your career is off to a fabulous start!

E. Make Every Effort Possible to Get "Eyewitness" or "Hands on" Experience Before You Finalize Your Choice

No matter what other people tell you, there's nothing like seeing and doing things for yourself. The most vivid example of this in my own experience has to do with those safety videos some airlines run. You've seen them; where they say, "In the event of a loss of cabin pressure, an oxygen mask will drop from the compartment above you . . ." Everything is very calm. You see people reading the newspaper, the mask comes down, and they put the newspaper on their lap, merrily take the oxygen mask, and strap it on.

Yeah . . . rrrright. I was on a flight once where the oxygen masks came down. You know what *really* happens? Everybody starts screaming so frantically that *nobody* puts them on—let alone calmly straps them on and "breathes normally." (It turns out that the masks came down by mistake; we were flying through a wicked thunderstorm that apparently triggered the masks.)

So—living through something and hearing about it are often very different!

There are several ways to take a nibble at what you think you want before plunging in:

1. **Clinical programs/externships at school.**

2. **PSLawNet projects** (at www.pslawnet.org). These projects are broadly "public interest" oriented; that is, they include all kinds of government jobs. They take as little as a fifty-hour commitment, so you can fit one into a week's school vacation. They are outstanding snapshots of what a job is like, and on top of that, they're great resume fodder.

3. **A "vocation vacation."** Offer to volunteer for any particular kind of employer that appeals to you, for a day, two days, a week. There is an organization called "vocation vacations" that sets up these kinds of gigs, but there is no reason in the world you can't do it for yourself; many, many employers can use an extra set of hands, even briefly. Contact your local bar association (or the trade association for any other industry that interests you), tell them you're a student, and ask for likely targets.

4. **Shadow anyone whose job interests you.**

    You follow them around for a day or so, getting an idea of what living their life is like. Contact the local bar association (or a trade association if the industry that interests you is not law), tell them you're a student, and ask for people to contact.

    My favourite shadowing story ever is this one: President Reagan offered Howard Baker a seat on the Supreme Court. Baker shadowed Justice Potter Stewart for a day to get an idea of what the life was like ... and then turned it down!

C. WHEN YOU JUST CAN'T DECIDE ... HOW TO GET UNSTUCK

So. Here we are. You've done whatever soul searching you're willing to do. You've thought about specialties and perhaps alternatives. You've considered settings you might want to work in.

And you're stuck. You just don't know what the heck you want.

OK. For a start, I'm not going to make you feel guilty about it. I didn't know what I wanted until after graduation, and I didn't even start seriously thinking about it until then, either. (I'm not recommending that approach, by the way.)

What I'll do here is to go through a few possible sources of what's bugging you. Maybe if you read them you'll recognize yourself, and it'll help you get unstuck. If you're still stuck, we'll talk about a few strategies—one of them radical—for jolting you out of your quandary.

1. SO ... WHY ARE YOU STUCK?

A. NOTHING HAS "TOUCHED YOUR SOUL"

I don't think I'm breaking any new ground when I tell you that the jobs you see the most at school are generally the least "soulful." It may well be that you came to law school to change the world, and when you think about corporate, or real estate, or litigation ... ugh. You just can't get your mind—or your heart—around it.

I've got a simple fix for you. Do a short, volunteer public interest project. Ask at Career Services or visit the PSLawNet web site for ideas, or check out Chapter 26 on Public Interest Careers.

Maybe you're worried about the money thing. There are a million ways to shore up your finances, which again I talk about in the Public Interest Chapter. Or you may think that public interest jobs lack the prestige you want. I'd say: Don't kid yourself. You're not looking at practice from the inside. Directors of public interest organizations tell me that they get calls from junior associates at large law firms *all the time* begging for work. One public interest lawyer I talked with said that he quit his firm *the day before* he was to make partner. While people outwardly took the "he's crazy!" attitude, he told me, "The partners all called me quietly and said they wished they had the guts to do what I'd done."

So even if you think that you've got no interest in public interest work, for *any* reason, I'd encourage you to give it at least a quick look. That's because so many, many students find it so rewarding. I spoke at a Women's Law Society conference, where one of the other speakers, Irene Lieberman, represented the Tejiri Project, this really amazing organization that aids refugee women. She said, "Help one refugee woman and it will transform your life. You'll never wonder why you went to law school." The possibility that a brief project will be a transforming experience for *you* makes it worth a try.

B. You Don't Want to Make a Decision at All

It may be that you just don't want to—for lack of a better term— grow up. You're in good company. Law school career counselors all over the country report that there are many students who don't want to grow up. "Some people just don't want to deal with life, to grow up and find a job," one of them told me. Another said, "Some law students don't even recognize it on a conscious level—they just don't want to have to deal with the idea of getting a job." Lisa Abrams goes even further: "Many people go to school to *avoid* thinking about what to do with their lives!" She herself was an English major, and felt that society pushed her into law school!

So the reason you may be stuck is that you either consciously or subconsciously don't want to think about what you'll do when school's over. You may not want to be Peter Pan and go and live with the fairies, but you sure don't want to grow up. I'm down with that. I was you. Thinking about what I wanted to do with my law degree was the last thing I wanted to do as a student.

But remember: the alternative to making a choice is a *lot* worse. Time passes, graduation comes, and then ... you've got to do *something*. If you don't opt for some goal, if you don't take an active role in deciding what you want, the people who *are* willing to do that will snap up all the good jobs, and you'll be left with a bow-wow because you didn't want to step up the plate and take a swing.

This isn't denying the validity of your feelings. There are a million reasons to be reluctant to make a decision. One is that it's finally and irrefutably waving goodbye to your childhood. The idea of being an adult with responsibilities is *scary,* but once you've got a graduate degree, you really can't put it off much longer. Sure, there are LLMs and other graduate degrees, but they'll come to an end, too.

I'll make it a lot easier for you to choose a target. Remind yourself of the truth: namely, you're not making a lifetime decision. You're not choosing Mr. or Ms. Right ... you're choosing Mr. or Ms. Right Now. Tell yourself that you're just making a decision for a couple of years, maybe the equivalent of another graduate degree. Then you'll reevaluate your choice. Maybe you will go back to school. Maybe you'll become a professor so you can come back to school permanently! But tell yourself: This isn't forever. I'm just figuring out what I'll enjoy for now.

Frankly, happy professionals are always reevaluating their situation, keeping their eyes open, seeing if there's something better out there. Happy people move around. So if the idea of an adult "lifetime commitment" scares you, you can perfectly honestly tell yourself: you're not making one!

C. YOU'RE AFRAID OF BEING CRITICIZED FOR YOUR CHOICE

You may have a pretty good idea of what you like ... but you cringe at the howls of derision you anticipate from your friends and family if you admit what it is. This may be particularly true if what you want to do doesn't bring in tons of dough, or it's an alternative career that doesn't—gasp—utilize your law degree.

But it doesn't have to be a low-paying or alternative career to leave you afraid to admit what you want. To tell you the truth, no matter *what* you decide you want, there will be people who will sneer and say, "You want *that?*" Charming trait, that, sneering at other people's choices. But everybody's been a victim of it.

When I got out of law school and started *Law In A Flash,* it was a very small company. We had four employees, total. So everybody—including me, president of the company—wound up answering the phone and taking student orders. Once in a while in these conversations, students would remark that I seemed "very familiar" with law school, and asked if I had a law degree. When I admitted I did—without telling them I was president of the company—they'd sometimes say, "And you're answering the phone, taking orders for flash cards? I don't mean to sound cruel ..." Maybe not. But you can imagine ... if I *had* been an order taker and nothing else, I'd have had a steady stream of criticism for my career choice!

I would argue, no matter what you feel you really want to do, that it's best to bite the bullet and admit it. For one thing, people will have whatever reaction they have, once. After that, the "shock value" is gone. They're not going to continually say to you, "I can't believe you want to ..."

For another thing, there is absolutely nothing wrong with addressing the issue directly, and saying, "I don't expect you to agree with my choice, and I understand that it wouldn't be yours. That's OK." You're the one who gets to make your own choices. If people who care about you have valid concerns, listen to them, but remember: the choice is ultimately yours. You're the only one who has to live your life on a day to day basis, and if you want something off the beaten path, so be it. You're the only one you ultimately have to answer to.

Furthermore, don't discount the possibility that people are criticizing your choice because they're secretly envious that you have the nerve to follow your muse. People's motivations aren't always obvious; they may be criticizing your choice because of envy, not disdain.

The bottom line: Admit what you want. Pursue your dream. If people give you a hard time about it, cut them out of your life until they come around. People who truly care about you will come to accept your decision!

D. You Don't Want to Do Anything

Maybe nothing particularly appeals to you because you'd frankly rather do . . . nothing.

You're not alone. Law school career counselors report to me that the reason a number of law students have a hard time making career choices is because "They're lazy. They don't want to do anything."

Maybe you're the one whose favourite class in school was recess. Maybe you live for vacations. You're not alone. But unless you're a trust fund baby or a lottery winner, you're going to have to do something to feed at least one mouth . . . yours!

Now, I'm not suggesting that you have to drink the long hours Kool—Aid. There are plenty of jobs that have reasonable hours, and others that involve long vacations (read: teaching). You may not make a huge amount of dough, you won't have a high-powered career, but if your free time is your motivator, that's something you have to accept.

Or you may prefer to do contract work or temp jobs, where you have short assignments and time in between. So if you want to trek to Nepal for a few weeks, you can work a temp or contract assignment, save up some money, and take off. In other words, you can be episodically lazy.

The key is: while you can't idle away the rest of your life, you *can* take low-stress, leisure-intensive jobs.

E. You're Afraid to Make a Mistake

Let's face it: by the time you get a law degree, you've invested a lot in your career. You could have dropped out of high school and worked northbound, but you didn't. You graduated. You went to college. You went to grad school. Haven't you done these things to "insulate" yourself from making a mistake with your career?

Well, I've got great news for you. You *can't* make a mistake. I take that back. You *can* make a mistake, but you can't make a lifetime, career-ending mistake by choosing the wrong initial job. I don't care how much energy you put into getting a particular job, if you get there, and the first day you realize the job is whack . . . all right. You make a change. I've told you before that on average, law school graduates have twelve or more jobs in their career. What does that mean? At least eleven of those jobs didn't cut it at some point!

So let's say that worse comes to worst and your first job is a dog. You take part in bar activities, go to CLEs in other specialties, you keep your eyes open for something you'll enjoy more. The CLEs give you something on your resume in other specialties, as well as contacts to help you break in. There's *always* a way to make a change out of something you hate into something you love. The experience of a law student in Texas is illustrative of how you get out of it. She took a job researching oil and gas leases, which apparently is not the most thrilling gig on the planet. But she had crappy grades, and believed it was all she could get. So she did it, and she did a good job of it, but—knowing it wasn't going to be her lifetime appointment!—she started going to local bar functions just to see what was out there. She met a guy who was running for District Attorney. She thought he'd be a great DA, and volunteered on his campaign. She helped him out a lot, he got elected DA, and he called and asked her to be his civil division chief.

At worst, choosing a job that doesn't ultimate suit you gives you a valuable piece of information: qualities of jobs you should avoid in the future. When you break down what you like and don't like about any job you take, you've got ammunition for making a better decision next time around!

F. THE THOUGHT OF STARTING AT THE BOTTOM OF *ANYTHING* APPEALS YOU

Especially if you have great grades and/or a degree from a distinguished law school, the idea of working your way into a dream job might make your skin crawl. Heck, you don't need great credentials to feel that way! There are many great jobs—general counsel for a corporation, judgeships, for instance—that you can't get right away. The idea of toadying for a few years as you climb the ladder might insult your vision of yourself.

One Career Services Director told me a story about a guy who got a clerkship at a law firm for the summer, and in the first week, as all of the clerks were shown the copy room and how to work the fax machines, he walked out in a huff, saying that he had *no* intention of making any copies, so he wasn't going to learn to work the machine. Needless to say, word of that kind of behavior spreads like wildfire.

He didn't have to worry about working a copy machine anymore. Or anything else at the firm, for that matter . . .

The cold reality is that no matter what you've accomplished in law school, in the eyes of the working world, you haven't accomplished anything yet. You are pure potential. That's terrific, but if you have the attitude that you won't prove yourself at work—if you won't, in the words of the old saying, "pay your dues"—nobody will sympathize with you. Every single person with whom you interview "paid their dues," and they'll resent it if you project a refusal to do the same!

Of course, there's always a way to avoid working your way up. It's to start at the top . . . of your own gig. Nothing in the world stops you from starting your own solo practice, partnership, or business of any kind. A law degree is a great credential for getting your own show started. I ought to know. I started *Law In A Flash* on the basis of my law degree. I didn't "start at the bottom" in a traditional sense, but when you run your own company, it's a lot of work, and a lot of that work is "beneath the dignity" of a law school graduate. So, sure, if starting at the bottom is anathema to you, you can start your own shop and avoid it. But if you're going to work for anyone else . . . paying your dues is part of the package.

G. You're Afraid of Admitting What You Want, for Fear You Might Not Get It

One of the scariest things in the world is to admit that you want something you might not be able to get—at least, not right away. Because on top of disappointment, you've got humiliation—you staked a claim to what you wanted, and it didn't happen. That leaves you open to ridicule.

I'm hoping against hope that this isn't true for you. Dreams are wonderful. They're part of what makes life worth living. And people who *have* them are a joy to be around. When students come to talk to me after my *Guerrilla Tactics* seminars at law schools, the ones who have dreams, no matter how outlandish, are the most delightful company. I've talked strategy for hours with some of them!

So, if there's a little voice inside of you telling you what you really want, I'm *begging* you—give it a hearing! There's *always* a way to make it happen, as the rest of this book will prove to you.

You know, I'll bet your dream isn't so ridiculous after all. I'll bet it's not as unattainable as you think it is, either. (It's certainly no more unattainable than my secret dream. I want to win an Academy Award for Best Original Screenplay. There. I told you. And you know something? It wasn't so tough.)

2. How to Get Unstuck: Plan A

Perhaps nothing I've said here helps you. Or maybe there's another reason you're stuck. Whatever the case, beat a hasty path to your Career

Services Office and talk with a counselor. Tell them the truth. "I'm stuck. I need help. I have no idea what I want to do." Trust me, going through that door and *saying* that puts you *way* closer to figuring out what you want to do. Most Career Services people have a background in counseling. They live to help you, with all kinds of tests and resources that are way beyond the scope of this book. So make them happy. Give them a chance to help you!

3.   HOW TO GET UNSTUCK: PLAN B

If you just can't make a decision about a goal, at least for the short-term, there's nothing that stops you from putting off the decision by taking temporary gigs. Whether it's temp work or contract work—where you work on a project by project basis for law firms—it'll give you time to make a decision. It'll give you a chance to gather more information and see what's out there, and settle whatever doubts you have about choosing a goal. You'll talk to people, see the components of jobs, and see the benefits and downsides of all kinds of work. So you didn't have a goal in mind when you left law school? That's all right. You wouldn't be the first one to take a bit more "seasoning" to figure it out!

4.   HOW TO GET UNSTUCK: THE RADICAL ALTERNATIVE

Maybe nothing in this chapter has helped you. Maybe all the soul searching, all the talking you can possibly tolerate hasn't made a difference. You wouldn't be the first person I've talked to to be completely dispirited with law school, totally at sea. I've got a radical alternative for you.

Leave law school.

That's right. Unless you're a 3L and pretty close to the end of school anyway, go. Leave. Scram. At least for now. You know why? Because you're in a rut, and by staying in law school right now you're either (a) wasting money, (b) piling up debt, and on top of that you're (c) wasting time.

Now, what are the downsides of doing this? One is that you'll have a lot of 'splaining to do with people you care about. You might feel as though you're letting them down. Now this is going to sound hackneyed, but if they really care about *you,* they'll understand. *Nobody* who truly cares about you would want you to be unhappy. And remember—you're not saying you're going to stay away from school *permanently.* You're just taking a break while you decide what it is that you're going to do with this darned degree.

You may also worry how it will look to future employers if you take time off from school. Will you seem like a wimp and a quitter? No—in fact, just the opposite! Think about it from the perspective of an employer. Let's say you take time off, decide what you want to do with your law degree, and come back with a renewed sense of purpose. You'll be able to look interviewers in the eye and say, "I didn't know what I wanted, but I took a year off, and that gave me perspective to be able to say for certain that I want to do the kind of work you do." Trust me—you'll shine!

Now, this isn't to say that you should take a year off and sit around watching soap operas and eating Cheet-ohs. As William & Mary's Rob Kaplan points out, "You've got to use your sabbatical in a productive way. Get a sense of what you want to accomplish." Speak with practitioners, do some informational interviewing, and see more of what's out there. Do some traveling, if that helps clear your head. I talked with a student at Berkeley toying with the idea of taking a year off to spend a few months in each of three specialties to try and nail down his dream. Great!

On a visit to another school, a student told me she needed to clear her head for a few months, maybe go on a retreat. Another student standing nearby piped up, "What kind of retreat?" She said, "I don't know—a Buddhist temple, something like that." He said, "A partner at the firm I clerked for this summer is a big believer in that. He took several months at a Buddhist temple and highly recommends it. You should talk to him." No matter how you choose to find your career answers—you obviously won't find something that a successful attorney hasn't tried first!

Consider doing some shadowing of different kinds of professionals to help you see what their jobs are really like. If it's in other industries—that's fine, too. Do whatever it takes to help you decide. And if after a semester or a year you decide that you really don't want the law after all, then you've saved yourself all of the time and money completing a degree that you really don't want!

D.   FAQs ABOUT DREAM JOBS

What's wrong with making big money for a few years and then doing what I really want?

There are at least two problems with it. Neither one of them may be "deal killers" for you, but they're worth thinking about.

First of all, not to be morbid, but how much of your life are you willing to sacrifice to what you *don't* want to do? You may live to be a hundred and twenty, in which case, the two or three or five years you spend with your nose to the grindstone will seem a pittance.

Or maybe you won't.

I am reminded of a story the mother of a former boyfriend told me. She had gone on a cruise, where a very fit woman turned down every fattening dessert. And trust me, on cruises, food is not a spectator sport. It turns out that this woman died in a car accident a week after the cruise was over. My boyfriend's mother said triumphantly, "You see? What was the point of turning down those desserts?" Well . . . I think we can all see the point of turning them down. But in a larger sense—no pun intended—nobody knows what their future holds, or how much of it they've got. You're the only one who can decide how much time you want to sacrifice to something you don't want to do.

A second problem is that once you get addicted to a certain level of pay, it's very hard to backpedal. You develop expensive habits that become a fabric of your life. You buy new cars, take on an expensive mortgage, and get your family used to perks that are hard to yank away. Unless you've got superhuman self-control and really pay off your debts, you'll find that that brief stint pulling in the big money turns into an entire career . . . a career that you didn't really want in the first place. It is much, much easier to start out making less money and then make more, rather than the other way around.

Having said all of this . . . do I know people who've successfully moved from high-paying jobs into low-paying ones? Absolutely. You probably do, too. So, it's not impossible. It's just difficult.

How long do I hold out for my dream job before I settle for something else?

There are a couple of aspects to this.

One is that you never really have to give up a dream. That's entirely voluntary. Even if you take another job right now, there's nothing that says you can't move into something you really want. I've told you before that you're likely to have at least a dozen jobs when you leave law school. What if that dream job is job number 2, or 3, or 5? A dream delayed can be . . . delicious. You just do what I've taught you to do: take a job and keep active, keep your eyes open for other opportunities. You never know when the opening you want will present itself to you.

The other aspect of the "holding out for a dream" issue is determining what I call your "threshold of pain." This depends on your circumstances, including your financial obligations and your stubbornness, among others.

I've told you before that I created *Law In A Flash,* the flash cards. You know. The funny ones in the yellow boxes. I lived in my parents' basement for three years after law school getting *Law In A Flash* off the ground. Now, I had a few things going for me. For one thing, I was five hundred miles away from law school, from my friends, from anyone I knew—so I didn't have anybody to tell me I was crazy. I had fairly handle-able law school debt; I'd worked during school to keep it under control. I didn't have a house of my own or a family to support, and I didn't have any expensive hobbies. Also, I didn't have any employers beating down my door to have me work for them; I got rejected from pretty much every job I ever applied for. On top of that, I was absolutely convinced that *Law In A Flash* was a great idea. Every time a law school bookstore turned it down—as they did for three solid years before any one of them would try it—I just became more convinced that I was right.

In short: my "threshold of pain" was very, very high. You're the only one who can determine what your "threshold of pain" is. I'd suggest that it's probably higher than you think it is. But everybody reaches a point where they say, "You know, this might work, but not right now in my life." There's nothing to say that had I taken another job, I couldn't have gotten *Law In A Flash* off the ground in my off-hours. The three years was a long time when I was living it. Had it turned into five or ten, I think there would have been a clinical psychiatric diagnosis for me.

The fact is, there are any number of routes into every kind of gig you can imagine. Taking a job that's enjoyable, albeit not your dream ... there's no shame in that. You might grow to love it ... or find something else that you like even more!

*

Appendix A
On-line Resources

Learn more about industries/companies:

    On-line discussion groups:

        www.topica.com

Internships:

    www.rileysguide.com/intern.html

Career information portals: (from "Princeton Review Guide to Careers")

    www.myjobsearch.com

    www.rileyguide.com

    www.acinet.org

    www.jobstar.org

Figuring out how your personality meshes with any particular career:

    Princeton Review:

        www.review.com/career (TPR career quiz)

    From Career City:

        www.careercity.com

    From the *Wall Street Journal*:

        www.careerjournal.com

    From Wet Feet:

        www.wetfeet.com

    From the American Bar Association:

        www.abanet.org/careercounsel/

Americorps for a year after school:

    www.cns.gov

*

Appendix B
Specialties ... What's Out There?

The short answer is: nobody can tell you. It's like fractal geometry. The closer you look, the more you realize the answer is infinite. There are lawyers who practice Dog Law. Lawyers who represent Korean grocery stores. And as we learned at the opening of this chapter, lawyers who focus on Male Circumcision Law (a highly-respected one actually works with a firm where one of the names in the firm's title is "Johnson." I just had to tell you that.).

However, what I've done here is to give you a list of more than a hundred legal specialties. I haven't given you a description of them, because that's a book in itself. Any one specialty may be practiced in such a broad variety of settings that it's impossible to give it a thumbnail sketch; criminal law is very different if you're a prosecutor rather than a public defender or a white-collar-criminal defense lawyer. Litigation is very different at the Justice Department than it is at a large law firm. However, there's a lot out there to help you. You can learn more about the more significant specialties from other resources, both in book form (like Lisa Abrams' "Official Guide to Legal Specialties") and the Vault Guides, and on-line (see On–Line Resources in Appendix A).

Administrative

Admiralty

Agriculture

Alternative Dispute Resolution

Appellate Practice

Antitrust/Trade Regulation

Art

Aviation/Space

Banking

Bankruptcy

Business

Civil Rights

Collection

Communications

Commercial

Computer

Condemnation

Construction

Consumer

Contracts

Constitutional

Copyright

Corporate

Creditors' Rights

Criminal Defense

Criminal Prosecution

Crime, White Collar

Customs

Defamation/First Amendment Law

Disability Rights

Discrimination

Domestic Violence

Education

Elder Law

Eminent Domain

Employee Benefits and Executive Compensation

Employment

Energy

Entertainment

Environmental

ERISA/Pension

Family

Fidelity & Surety

Finance

Forest Products

Franchise

Gay & Lesbian Rights

Government Contracts

Health

Homelessness

Housing

Human Rights

Immigration

Import/Export

Insurance

Intellectual Property

International

Juvenile

Labor and Employment

Landlord/Tenant

Land Use

Legal Aid and Public Interest

Libel

Literary Property

Litigation

Maritime

Media

Medical Malpractice

Mental Health

Mergers/Acquisitions

Migrants/Farm Workers

Military (JAG Corps)

Mining

Municipal

Municipal Bonds

National Security

Native American

Natural Resources

Negligence

Oil & Gas

Patent

Pharmaceutical

Personal Injury

Poverty

Prison/Death Penalty

Probate

Products Liability

Professional Liability

Public Utilities

Real Estate

Redevelopment

Regulatory

Reorganization

Railroad

Securities

Sports

Social Security

Tax

Tax Exempt Financing

Trademarks

Tort Defense

Toxic Tort

Trade Regulation

Transportation

Trusts and Estates

Unfair Competition

Venture Capital

Veterans' Rights

Water

Welfare

Whistleblowers

Women's Rights

Workers' Compensation

Zoning

Adapted from "Career Options," Northwestern School of Law of Lewis and Clark College.

Appendix C
Private
Firms, Government,
Corporations and More
... Common
Career Settings for
Law School Graduates

The following descriptions give you a basic snapshot of the most common settings for practicing law. This is, by necessity, just a quick glimpse. To learn more, you really should talk with your Career Services Director, and any alumni or practitioners you contact through your Career Services Office or on your own.

1. LAW FIRMS

See also: Large Law Firms (Chapter 23), Small Law Firms (Chapter 18), Solo Practice (Chapter 19).

A law firm is basically a for-profit business, with partners as co-owners and associates as employees. They generate income by cultivating and satisfying clients and maintaining and improving the quality of service they provide, while reducing their costs, which includes overhead like associate salaries!

When you work for a law firm, you typically start as an "associate," which means that you do work on a salary basis. After that, with luck, skill, and savvy, you move on to partner, where you actually go out and solicit clients (and in that way generate income) and you get a share of the partnership's profits. (The associate-to-partner track isn't the only way to operate in a law firm; especially in large firms, there are nonpartnership-track job possibilities as a staff or contract attorney. We talk about these a lot more in the chapter on large law firms, Chapter 23.)

By way of size, firms go all the way from mega firms with more than a thousand attorneys, down to simple partnerships. In fact, most lawyers practice in firms with fewer than ten lawyers, but since they don't get as much press as the giant firms, it sometimes doesn't seem that way. If a firm has over a hundred lawyers, it will typically have a lot of different practice areas, so that one client can work with many lawyers in different departments, typically in different cities, depending on what the client's needs are.

There are two different basic types of firms: client-driven or substantively-oriented. Client-driven firms handle clients' needs on demand, no matter what they are—mergers, dissolutions, acquisitions, bankruptcies, labor, estate planning, real estate, divorces, you name it. Substantively-oriented or "boutique" firms specialize in a specific field—like labor arbitration, or criminal defense, or education board representation, municipal bond work, oil and gas rights—you name the specific field and there are boutique firms who focus on it!

Law firms also vary in terms of how rigidly structured they are. For firms with more than a hundred lawyers, there are typically structured departments—for instance, a litigation department, a labor department, a trusts and estates department, and a tax department. In these firms, it's typically very difficult to move between departments, once you're assigned to one. For firms with fewer than a hundred lawyers, associates can typically rotate through several departments before choosing one.

Firms also vary in the types of clients they serve. Very large firms typically have as clients medium to large corporations and their executive boards and managers, as well as government offices and institutions. Smaller, general-practice (as opposed to boutique) firms typically serve smaller businesses, as well as individuals.

The atmosphere of any particular firm is unique, and so only the broadest generalizations are possible about what new associates are likely to face. (In Chapter 10 on the Birds and Bees of Great Jobs, and in Chapter 23 on large firms, I'll tell you exactly how to go about finding out what it's like to work at any law firm, regardless of size.) However, in a very large firm, for the first couple of years, you'll typically handle research on a very large case, so that you'll be exposed only to a small slice of the total business of any one case. Small firms vary, although because you're a larger part of the staff of a small firm, you'll typically get more responsibility. While large firms tend to be very institutionalized and structured, small firms vary. Some are hard-driving and results-oriented, and others are more collegial. They also differ greatly in management responsibility and power of junior associates.

By the way, the purpose of summer jobs differs between large and small firms, as well.

For firms with more than fifty lawyers: They'll typically have a summer associate program, whose main purpose is to lure top students in the hope they'll accept permanent offers when they graduate. So the aim isn't primarily to get work done! This explains the wining and dining and sky-high salaries you associate with these summer programs, where permanent associates often refer to the lucky recipients as "summer partners."

For firms with fewer than fifty lawyers: They'll typically hire clerks year-round because they legitimately have work they need to get done, but the work doesn't require full-time lawyers or support staff. These clerkships typically pay on an hourly basis, and the experience you get varies on the work they need done. When it comes to permanent job opportunities, they may or may not exist. But compared to large firms, there are some advantages. One is that since there are fewer layers of "management," you'll have more of a chance to work with senior partners, and since the work is less complex, you'll get a better overall picture of how cases and clients are handled. You may even get client contact virtually immediately, a real source of satisfaction to many people. In addition, jobs with smaller firms tend to be easier to get. While I'll tell you in Chapter 23 on large firms how to get into a large firm if you don't have top grades, the biggest firms typically only take students who are at the top of their class and/or from a distinguished law school.

2.   SOLO PRACTICE

See also: Chapter 19 on solo practice

Hard as it is to believe, 40% of practicing lawyers are sole practitioners!

There are a couple of ways to get into solo practice. One is to hang out your own shingle and develop your own clients and practice from scratch. That's very tough to do unless you have a prior career or some other built-in route to developing clients. For instance, one Career Services Director told me about three students who were detectives. When they graduated, they set up a practice of their own. They continued to work nights as detectives, and spent their days as civil lawyers (so as not to create a conflict with their criminal work). As their practice picked up, they cut down their detecting hours. So you see my point: It helps to have an avenue for quick client development if you want to go into practice for yourself right away.

Another way to enter sole practice is to go into an office-sharing arrangement with another practicing attorney, who may subcontract work to you. If you want to hang out your own shingle, it certainly pays to either have a career before law school to use as a client base, or get some experience with another firm before striking out on your own.

Sole practice typically attracts experienced lawyers who are not team-oriented and are more entrepreneurial. It's more financially risky than firm practice, but "being your own boss" is potentially more rewarding as well!

3.   GOVERNMENT

See Appendix D below, "Great Government Gigs Not To Be Overlooked."

4. ADMINISTRATIVE AGENCIES

See also Appendix D below, "Great Government Gigs Not To Be Overlooked."

Not many students think of administrative agencies as a career goal, but they're a great way to learn a specialty. You spend your time creating policy and gaining contacts that you can transfer to your own practice afterwards, or to law firm practice, or a corporation. (Incidentally, this is a great "back door" way to get into a large or boutique firm if your grades wouldn't get you in the front door!)

If you go to an administrative agency, be prepared to contend with a fair amount of bureaucracy. You won't last long if you're entrepreneurial. And also be prepared to make a time commitment to the job—sometimes there's a contractually-minimum four-year stint. You're more likely to get hired or advance if you're geographically flexible, since it's easier to get a job offer for a rural area. However, don't be too quick to dismiss a job in "the boonies." For instance, for federal administrative agencies, where wages are fixed, your money will go a lot further out in the country than it would in a big city. (State wages vary by state.) Also, there is always the possibility of a transfer to another place further down the road.

5. THE JUDICIARY

See also: Judicial Clerkships, Chapter 25.

As you might imagine, lawyers are found everywhere in the judiciary, as judges, magistrates, referees, clerks and prosecutors.

JUDGES

Obviously you're not likely to start your legal career as a judge! The best way to learn about being a judge is to spend time as a judicial clerk. It's sometimes a nonpaying job (especially at low-level courts), but the benefits are great: you get direct contact with judges, you get to attend trials, research actual cases, draft orders and opinions, and gain insight into the workings of courts and judicial decision-making. The icing on the cake is that you get a judge as a mentor and a reference, and that's tough to beat.

What kinds of judges are there? In the federal system, there are district court (trial-level) judges, appellate (Circuit court) judges, and Supreme Court Justices. There are also specialized courts, including bankruptcy, tax, claims, and international trade. Federal court judges are appointed by the President, and don't need to have prior judicial experience. (However, as a new graduate, don't plan on getting a federal court nomination unless you have some particularly compelling blackmail Polaroids of the President.)

The structure of state court systems vary by state. They typically have the same three levels as the federal system: trial, appellate, and "ultimate," as well as special courts like probate, juvenile, and domestic relations. Most state judges are elected.

JUDICIAL CLERKS

A judicial clerk isn't a clerk in the way you typically think of a clerk, that is, as a summer associate for a firm. Instead, judicial clerks are law school graduates, typically straight from school. They act as a judge's right hand person for either a set term (one to three years, typically), or permanently. Most clerks do a lot of research and analysis for the judge, and present it orally or in writing to the judge. At the trial level, clerks handle administrative tasks for the judge, as well.

A judicial clerkship is considered an honor, especially for federal judges, so the competition is intense. Grades are typically important, although if you make contacts effectively, as I'll teach you in Chapter 10 on The Birds and Bees of Great Jobs, they can be somewhat circumvented. Check with your Career Services office for deadlines on applying; they change every so often, but you always have to think ahead; don't put it off until April of Third Year.

A great way to learn more about judicial clerkships is to find out from your Career Services Office which of your professors had judicial clerkships, and talk with those professors directly. (A judicial clerkship is a common experience for law professors.)

MAGISTRATES AND REFEREES

As a magistrate or referee you reign over court proceedings and have decision-making capabilities, although not as extensively as judges. Many magistrates and referees also have externs and clerks, as judges do.

PROSECUTORS

Prosecutors work on the federal, state, county and city level. Depending on where they work, they go by a variety of names. For instance, U.S. Attorneys are federal prosecutors, Attorneys General are state prosecutors (as well as being the title for the head of the U.S. Department of Justice), and then there are district attorneys, prosecuting attorneys, and so on.

Being a prosecutor has a number of benefits. For one thing, it's a great place to get experience in criminal or civil trial work. Prosecutors' offices are known for offering early responsibility, and a very fast-paced environment.

Most prosecutors' offices hire students as volunteers or in paying jobs. Except for the U.S. Attorney's Office, they also hire new graduates. If you're interested in long-term job potential, politics plays a big part. Prosecutors are generally either elected, or appointed by the chief elected figure in the jurisdiction.

As with administrative agencies, it's generally easier to get a job in a rural area and plan on moving to a higher court or a big city later on, because the competition is pretty strong for those jobs.

6. LEGISLATURE

See Appendix D, Below, "Great Government Gigs Not To Be Overlooked."

7. THE MILITARY

See below, Appendix D, "Great Government Gigs Not To Be Overlooked."

8. PUBLIC INTEREST ORGANIZATIONS

See also Chapter 26 on Public Interest.

While "public interest" is a loose concept—it sometimes even sweeps in lawyers in any kind of government job, the thought being that the government works in the public's interest (no snickering, please)—but a more commonly accepted definition of a public interest lawyer is one who helps individuals and groups who lack equal access to the legal system due to some type of disadvantage or disenfranchisement, whether economic, environmental, societal or otherwise.

Unlike attorneys in private practice, public interest attorneys do not pick their cases or design their practices based on financial considerations. This often (although not always) results in comparatively low salaries and limited support staff and resources. However, public interest jobs are rich in "psychic income": opportunities to express one's political and social interests professionally as well as personally, increased client contact, a casual work environment, and the ability to impact the community.

Depending on the public interest organization, law school grades are less emphasized in the hiring process than a demonstrated interest and commitment to public interest. Volunteering first is often the key to getting your foot in the door. Competition for jobs in this arena can be intense due to budget constraints.

LEGAL SERVICES

Legal Services Offices are non-profit organizations that provide free representation to indigent clients in civil proceedings. The predominant legal aid issues are housing, government benefits, domestic violence, and immigration law. Some organizations focus on a particular client community while others will focus on a particular legal area. The majority of the work in legal services involves direct services to individual clients, but some organizations also handle some impact litigation and community education.

PUBLIC INTEREST LITIGATION ORGANIZATIONS

Public interest litigation organizations specialize in class action and impact litigation. Most are non-profit organizations. Examples of public interest litigation firms include Public Advocates, ACLU, Legal Defense Fund, Natural Resources Defense Council, and Environmental Defense Fund.

PUBLIC INTEREST RESEARCH GROUPS

Public interest research groups (PIRGs) are public interest advocacy organizations that concentrate their efforts on the direct impact of policy through lobbying and research analysis rather than litigation. PIRG attorneys usually have a strong community base to function successfully. Much of their effort goes into coordinating campaigns to develop community support and education for particular issues of concern and relevance in that community.

PUBLIC INTEREST LAW FIRMS

Private public interest law firms are often small firms with attorneys who have a common interest in a particular cause, policy or population. These lawyers devote a substantial portion of their practices to those causes, policies or populations, regardless of the extent they are paid for their work. These types of firms often focus on issues such as unlawful discrimination (race, age, gender and sexual orientation) and immigration. Lawyers at these firms may devote some portion of their work to other more traditional types of practice to support their public interest work, but the cause-related work generally takes precedence.

(Adapted from "Exploring Legal Employers," Santa Clara University School of Law.)

9. CORPORATIONS

See also Chapter 31, "I Want To Be A Not—Lawyer," for corporate opportunities outside of the general counsel's office.

Corporations offer a treasure chest of opportunities to use your law degree. The traditional setting is the corporate counsel's office, but law school graduates also work in many other areas, including government relations, investor relations, business development ... virtually everywhere in corporations.

It's comparatively easier to get a job with a corporation as an intern than it is as a new graduate. Some corporations offer summer internships. Of these, some are in the legal department, on things like purchase/sale agreements and employee contract negotiations. Others involve work in areas specific to the corporation's products or services, like patent applications, trust and estate planning, and regulatory compliance. They may also involve work in tax, personnel, and risk management.

Permanent opportunities depend on the size of the corporation. Most companies hire only experienced attorneys from law firms, because they typically need substantive expertise and the ability to understand and control law firms' functions and costs in dealing with corporate clients, and that only comes with law firm experience. But very large companies often have legal departments with several hundred attorneys, the equivalent of a large law firm. They do hire new graduates. Also, very, very small companies and start-ups will often hire new graduates, expecting them to wear other "hats" as well as simply "corporate counsel."

There are real benefits to working for a corporation instead of a law firm. They are summarized simply: rain-making and billable hours. Corporate attorneys do not have to solicit business; they have one client, the corporation. As in-house counsel you may have to sell your ideas and recommendations to higher-ups, but you don't have to woo clients the way private attorneys do. Furthermore, corporate attorneys do not have to keep track of their time in ten-minute increments as attorneys at firms do. The hours also tend to be more relaxed than private practice, although this isn't always true. A potential downside is that some attorneys find that working in-house makes their skills less transferable than working in a law firm would.

10. FELLOWSHIPS AND GRANTS

Fellowships are short-term post-graduate gigs. Many are established programs; others involve creating your own position. You can get funding for the "self-created" positions from a number of sources, including the very well-known "Skadden Fellowships," Equal Justice Works Fellowships, and grants from foundations and like organizations.

Many fellowships, particularly those devoted to public interest issues, offer you the opportunity to do a significant project under the tutelage of an expert in the field. Some fellowships also give you the chance to get a graduate degree.

Great resources for fellowship information include the Equal Justice Works Post—Graduate Fellowships Guide (you can find it at Career Services), and the Yale Fellowship Opportunities Guide (also at Career Services).

11. ACADEMIC INSTITUTIONS

So ... three years just isn't enough law school for you? You want *more?* All right. There are lots of great jobs in academia, aside from the obvious "law professor" position. I go over them in some detail in Chapter 31, "I Want To Be A Not—Lawyer."

12. ALTERNATIVE CAREERS

Whether legally-related or not, from law librarians to custom cake decorators, many students use their degree to be not-lawyers. I cover a whole bunch of these in Chapter 31 "I Want To Be A Not—Lawyer."

Appendix D
Great Government Gigs Not to Be Overlooked

The Federal Government is the largest legal employer in the world, by a long shot. On top of the federal government, there are opportunities at every other level of government as well—state, county, and local. I've given these jobs special attention in this appendix for two reasons: students tend to disdain working for the government ... and I've talked with tons and tons of happy government lawyers. It's an area you should definitely consider!

Government jobs have a lot going for them. They give you great hands-on experience right away. While the hours vary, they tend to be more livable than law firms, certainly large law firms. You don't have to solicit clients, as you would sooner or later with a law firm. And while the pay is not as high as it is for some private employers, it ramps up fairly quickly and becomes quite handsome within a very few years. On top of that, government work is a great stepping stone into myriad private opportunities. While some attorneys stay with the government for their entire careers, others use their government stint as a springboard into all kinds of exciting private jobs. (It's also possible to move the other way, of course, and take private experience into a government position.)

Let's take a look at government jobs at every level, federal, state and local. (We won't be discussing one other major option, the Judiciary—we do that in Chapter 25.)

A. FEDERAL GOVERNMENT

The federal government is composed of hundreds of departments, agencies, commissions, and boards. Almost all hire lawyers in some capacity, and many hire law students during the summers and academic year.

When it comes to specialties—if you can name it, the federal government probably has it (see Topic B, below, for a listing of the specialties available in different government departments).

Attorney positions in the federal government are in what's called the "excepted service," typically under an appointment called "Schedule A." By being in the excepted service, attorney positions are not covered by regular civil service hiring procedures. Agencies may hire for attorney positions directly without conducting examinations or utilizing the U.S. Office of Personnel Management (OPM) for lists of eligible applicants.

Virtually all federal agencies have attorney positions, with many requiring specializations. Because of this, agencies are responsible for setting qualification requirements for attorney positions. Generally, a JD degree and membership in a state bar are required. The entry-level grade is usually GS-11, but those with experience may qualify for higher grades.

USAJOBS (www.usajobs.opm.gov), the federal government's employment information system, provides worldwide job vacancy information, employment information fact sheets, job applications and forms, and has online resume development and electronic application capabilities. Experienced attorneys can apply for positions online. It's a good idea to both search the USAJOBS website and to explore individual agencies directly. As is true for every job, you can also network your way in; students often underestimate the value of having someone who already works in an agency "rooting" for them. Find out from your Career Services Office if there are upperclassmen who have worked with federal agencies, or alums who are there now. Contact them for advice and leads.

1. LAW STUDENT AND ENTRY–LEVEL HIRING

There are tons of opportunities for law students in the federal government, internships and clerkships that are available starting the summer after First Year. Most federal agencies actively advertise at law schools and recruit via job search websites to fill both summer and academic year positions. However, when you find that a particular agency of interest to you has not advertised an opening, go ahead and contact that agency directly to inquire about the availability of positions.

a. HONORS PROGRAMS

Students in their third or final year of law school as well as completing either LL.M. degrees or judicial clerkships are typically eligible to apply for entry-level attorney positions with federal agencies. Most often called Honors Programs, these recruitment initiatives are the most common way that entry-level attorneys may enter certain departments and agencies of the federal government. Honors programs often combine on-the-job training, professional development workshops, and mentoring to acclimate new attorneys to the practice of law within the employing agency. Recruiting and interviewing for most honors programs is typically conducted between

September and December of a student's final academic year, and the selection process is completed by the spring of each academic year.

The application deadlines and processes vary from agency to agency so it is wise to consult the employment guides listed below or to review an agency's website for the most current information. Many require that you submit a resume, cover letter, application form (often online) and a writing sample. One exception to that practice is that the Department of Justice has made its prestigious Attorney General's Honors Program and its Summer Law Intern Program application processes entirely paperless. Students must apply online at the DOJ website by mid-September. The website address is: www. usdoj.gov/oarm/

Resources to help you learn about federal agencies and their recruiting programs include:

1. *Federal Legal Employment Opportunities Guide*

This guide gives you descriptions of the mission and responsibilities of federal agencies and their major departments. It outlines different points of entry for law students and attorneys, including hiring projections and salary and benefits information. It's updated yearly. You can find it on-line at (www.nalp.org). It is published by the National Association of Law Placement in cooperation with the Partnership for Public Service.

2. *The Government Honors and Internship Handbook*

This handbook provides profiles of the recruiting programs at federal agencies and gives you the skinny on the application process for internships available both summer and academic year, as well as attorney positions available post-graduation. The handbook is available only to students at schools that pay a subscription fee (check with your Career Services Office for availability; most schools subscribe). It is published and updated by the University of Arizona Law School.

3. Agencies that commonly hire students and new graduates include:

U.S. Army Corps of Engineers

Central Intelligence Agency

Department of Commerce

Commission on Civil Rights

Commodity Futures Trading Commission

Comptroller of the Currency

Corporation for National & Community Service

Department of Defense

Department of Energy

Environmental Protection Agency

Equal Employment Opportunity Commission

Export—Import Bank of the United States

Federal Communications Commission

Federal Emergency Management Agency

Federal Trade Commission

Federal Labor Relations Board

Federal Reserve Board

General Accounting Office

Department of Housing and Urban Development

Department of the Interior

Internal Revenue Service

Department of Justice

Department of Labor

Legal Services Corporation

National Labor Relations Board

Nuclear Regulatory Commission

Overseas Private Investment Corporation

Pension Benefit Guaranty Corporation

Presidential Management Internship Program

Securities and Exchange Commission

Small Business Administration

Smithsonian Institution

State Department

Trade and Development Agency

Department of Transportation

Treasury Department

US Agency for International Development

US Postal Service

Veterans Affairs

(For links, see www.firstgov.gov/index.shtml)

b. PRESIDENTIAL MANAGEMENT FELLOWSHIP PROGRAM (PMF)

PMF provides law students a prestigious, unique, alternative point of entry into the federal government. Being chosen for PMF is an honor to you and a real feather in your law school's cap, as well. It's a two-year, policy-oriented fellowships both for new graduates and experienced attorneys. It's aimed at people who are interested in analysis and public policy positions. It gives you the chance to work with a particular federal agency (you interview with the ones that interest you).

There are two tracks: One is available to law students completing their final year of school, with the idea of grooming them for upper level management positions in the federal government. The second is for experienced lawyers who'll use their expertise to assume higher level management positions.

Here's how you apply. In the fall of your last year in school, you fill out an on-line application form. You also need to be nominated by a school official (see your Career Services Office for the appropriate person). PMF then selects the applicants who will participate in a structured one-day screening process, called an "assessment center." That takes place in January or February. During that day, you engage in role playing, group interviews, and written and verbal exercises. It is a *great* advantage to you to talk with the Career Services Office to find alums that have been through the PMF application process before, for advice on specific questions and activities to anticipate!

From this competition, finalists are chosen and notified in March. They are then invited to participate in a job fair in early April where they get to interview with agencies to find a match for their specific interests. Many finalists get a jump-start on the competition by proactively contacting agencies to interview and possibly nail a fellowship in advance of the job fair.

Fellows may be appointed between the GS–9, 11 or 12 levels and Senior Fellows (with experience) enter at either the GS–13, 14 or 15 levels.

During the program, PMFs may work on assignments involving domestic or international issues, technology, science, criminal justice, health, financial management and many others. Each fellow will have an individual development plan approved by the agency's executive resources board that focuses on managing in the fellow's area of expertise. Fellows also get an annual performance evaluation to assess their progress.

Many PMFs go on to permanent jobs in their agency when the fellowship is over, both as attorneys and in law-related positions. Others have moved on to other agencies at the end of the program.

To research the PMF Program on-line, visit (www.pmf.opm.gov/).

c. ADMINISTRATIVE LAW CLERKSHIP

See also: Chapter 25 on Judicial Clerkships.

There are more than 1,300 Administrative Law Judges (ALJs) in the federal government, with the Social Security Administration having the largest number. Some ALJs hire recent law school graduates for clerkships. These are typically one to two-year positions with duties parallel to those of a judicial law clerk. The availability of these clerkships varies year to year; the *Federal Yellow Book* (available at your Career Services Office) identifies the names of ALJs or hiring personnel in each Office. Online, you can check out the Federal Administrative Law Judges Conference website (www.falcj.org).

Agencies with offices of Administrative Law Judges include:

Agriculture Department

Commodity Futures Trading Commission

Department of Education

Environmental Protection Agency

Federal Communications Commission

Federal Regulatory Commission

Federal Labor Relations Board

Federal Maritime Commission

Federal Mine Safety & Health Review Commission

Federal Trade Commission

Department Appeals Board, Department of Health and Human Services

Food and Drug Administration, Department of Health and Human Services

Department of Housing and Urban Development

Interior Department

International Trade Commission

Drug Enforcement Administration, Department of Justice

Executive Office for Immigration Review, Department of Justice

Labor Department

Merit Systems Protection Board

National Labor Relations Board

National Transportation Safety Board

Occupational Safety & Health Review Commission

Office of Financial Institution Adjudication

Securities & Exchange Commission

Small Business Administration

Social Security Administration

Department of Transportation, Office of the Secretary

Department of Transportation, Office of the Coast Guard

US Postal Service

d. CONGRESS ... WORKING "ON THE HILL"

The glamour and excitement of working "on the Hill" attracts many law students. The primary points of entry for an attorney on the Hill are as a legislative assistant or legislative Director of a particular Congressperson, as a legal staff member of a congressional committee, and as legislative counsel within the Senate or House Office of Legislative Counsel. Political caucuses also hire staff attorneys; the Democratic Study Group and Republican Study Group hire lawyers as policy analysts. The American Law Division of the Congressional Research Service is an option particularly attractive to people interested in research and policy analysis.

There are also a number of private organizations that function in a lobbying or watchdog capacity which hire attorneys. Those jobs, in turn, offer lots of visibility in congressional and political circles. Those groups include organizations like Common Cause and Public Citizen as well as organizations that represent any number of particular interests.

As is true of many jobs outside of government, your best way in is through who you know, and who you *get* to know ... the focus of Chapter 10 on the Birds and Bees of Great Jobs. Professional positions "on the Hill" are seldom advertised through traditional means, so people are virtually your only way in too many jobs. This isn't a negative! Volunteering on political campaigns is a great way to get to know people. Also, internships in the offices of congress people—often volunteer—give you a tremendous advantage. And, of course, ask everyone you know for people you may talk to for advice and help.

You could also apply to a Congressperson who deals with a field of law in which you have a strong interest and/or expertise. Read the Congressional Record, debates, and legislation the Congressperson is involved with, as well as bills and articles (s)he supported and/or introduced. If you apply this way, don't just wait for a response; follow up (I talk all about this in Chapter 7 on correspondence). Persistence pays!

Note that there is no formal "hiring season" for Congress. Jobs open up regularly. Offices rarely take much time interviewing; instead, they rely on the 'who you know' network (which is why it is so crucial to volunteer on campaigns, intern, get to know people any other way you can). By way of credentials, academic requirements vary from office to office. In general, offices are more interested in issues like your ties to the congressional district, your familiarity with the Members' or committee's issues, or more importantly, your relevant experience in the legislative process.

Working on the Hill, apart from being an exciting job itself, sets you up for great opportunities in the future; for instance, if you work with a Congressperson, you'll have the chance to network with law firms, trade associations, and corporations. You may need to explain your experience to employers outside of the DC area, but it's unquestionably a great background for future jobs.

On-line resources include "Roll Call," a twice-weekly periodical with news and commentary about activities on the Hill. You'll find it at www.rollcall.com. It has employment listings for available positions at Hill offices (www.rc.jobs.com). The Senate Employment Bulletin, published weekly, advertises staff vacancies in Senate offices. You can find it on-line at www.senate.gov/employment, or listen to listings by phone at 202–228–JOBS. Other useful websites include the Congressional Research Service (www.loc.gov/crsinfo/), the publication "The Influence: The Business of Lobbying" (www.influence.biz), and a subscription-only site available through most Career Services Office, called Opportunities in Public Affairs (www.opajobs.com).

B. SPECIALTIES AVAILABLE IN FEDERAL GOVERNMENT DEPARTMENTS

I've mentioned before that if you can imagine a specialty, you can practice it with the federal government. If you've got a particular focus, this list will help you target appropriate federal government departments. The key to the department abbreviations is at the end of the list. (List courtesy of the Catholic University Columbus School of Law).

Administrative Law: AFJAG, AJAG, COMM, COC, FTC, DOI, DOJ, NJAG, ITC, EPA, FCC, DOL, VA, EEOC, NTSB, DOA, MCJAG, EDUC, FERC, HHS, HUD, DOI, FLRA

Aviation/Admiralty: AFJAG, DOJ, NOGC, NJAG, DOT, NTSB

ADR/Arbitration: DOJ, DOE, FERC

AIDS/HIV: DOJ, HHS

Antitrust & Trade Regulation: COC, FTC, DOJ, COMM

Appellate Practice: DOJ, AFJAG, AJAG, NJAG, MCJAG, EDUC

Banking: CIA, COC, FDIC, DOJ, TREAS, FED, EIB, NCUA

Bankruptcy: DOJ, IRS

Business (Torts, Litigation): ITC, DOJ

Children, Youth: DOJ, EDUC, HHS

Civil Litigation: CIA, DOJ, USAO, NJAG, ARJAG, MCJAG, EDUC

Civil Rights: DOA, EPA, FBI, HHS, DOJ, DOA, HUD, CCR, EEOC, EDUC

Complex Litigation: DOJ

Commercial: COMM, FDIC, DOJ

Communications: FCC, BBG

Computer Crime/Cyber Crime: FBI, CIA, DOJ

Constitutional Law: DOJ

Construction: DOJ

Consumer Protection: COC, FTC, DOJ, NJAG, DOA, HUD, FED

Contracts: COMM, CIA, GAO, DOJ, DOL, MCJAD, SBA

Copyrights & Trademark/Patent: COMM, CIA, EPA, FBI, HHS, DOJ, VA

Corporation/Corporate Law: CIA, COC, FDIC, DOJ

Criminal Law: AFJAG, AJAG, CIA, FBI, DOJ, USAO, MCJAD, NJAG, IRS, EPA

Customs/Trade: DOA, ITC, DOJ, FTC, COMM, TREAS, CUST, CSA

Death Penalty: DOJ

Disability/Mental Health: DOJ, EDUC, DOL, VA, SSA

Domestic Violence: DOJ

Education: DOJ, EDUC

Employee Benefits: GAO, DOJ, DOL, OPM, PBGC

Employment Law: AFJAG, AJAG, GAO, DOJ, DOL, NOGC, FAA, EEOC, NJAG, MCJAG, OPM

Energy: DOI, DOJ, DOE, NSF, NRC

Environmental: AFJAG, AJAG, COMM, EPA, DOI, DOJ, MCJAD, NOGC, NJAG, FAA, DOD, DOE, DOI, DOT, NRC

Federal Employees: DOJ, GSA, OPM, OSC

Freedom of Information Act: DOJ

Gaming: DOJ

Government Contracts: AFJAG, AJAG, DOJ, NOGC, NJAG, MCJAG, DOE, GSA, NASA, SBA

Grant Law: DOJ

Health/Medical: HHS, DOJ, VA

Healthcare: HHS, DOJ, VA

Housing: DOJ, HUD, VA

Immigration & Naturalization: CIA, DOJ

Indian: DOI, DOJ, DOI

Insurance: DOJ

Intellectual Property: CIA, DOJ, NOGC, USPTO, COMM, DOE

Intelligence/Counterterrorism/National Security: CIA, FBI, DOJ, DOD, DOE, TREAS, USSS, FEMA, DHS, CUST

International: DOA, AFJAG, AJAG, COMM, CIA, EPA, FBI, DOJ, MCJAG, NJAG, FAA, DOS, TREAS, ITC, DOD, EIB, DOT, FCC

International Transactions: CIA, ITC, DOJ, DOS, TREAS, COMM, EIB

Internet/Electronic Commerce: DOJ, COMM

International Human Rights: DOJ, DOS, USAID

Juvenile: DOJ, EDUC

Labor: COMM, DOJ, DOL, MCJAG, NLRB, FAA, FLRA

Legal Services/In House: AFJAG, AJAG, DOE, COC, DOJ, DOS, IRS

Legislation: DOA, COMM, CIA, COC, FDIC, DOJ, FAA

Litigation: AFJAG, AJAG, COMM, CFTC, COC, DOJ, NLRB, NOGC, FAA, IRS, OPM, HHS, EIB, HUD, DOT, VA, NSF, TREAS, FDIC, EDUC, DOE, FERC, HHS, USAID

Malpractice: DOJ

Maritime: DOT, FMC

Military: AFJAG, AJAG, DOJ, NJAG, MCJAG, USCG

National Resources: DOA, COMM, DOI, DOJ, NRC

Personal Injury: DOJ

Physician Representation: DOJ

Police Misconduct: DOJ

Prisoners' Rights: DOJ

Product Liability: DOJ

Professional Disciplinary Proceedings: DOJ

Public Benefits: DOJ

Racial/Ethnic Justice: DOJ

Real Estate: DOJ, NJAG

Regulation: DOA, COMM, CFTC, COC, DOJ, SEC, FAA, DOE, DOI

Securities: COC, DOJ, SEC, TREAS, CFTC

Social Security/Disability: DOJ, EDUC, VA, SSA

State and Local: DOJ

Tax: AFJAG, AJAG, CIA, DOJ, NJAG, IRS, TREAS

Telecommunications: COMM, FCC, DOJ, FERC

Torts: MCJAG, HHS, NJAG

Transportation: DOJ, NOGC, NTSB

Trial Practice: DOJ, NLRB

Veterans: DOJ, VA, OSC

Voting Rights: DOJ

Whistleblower Protection: OSC

Women's Issues: DOJ

Workers' Compensation: GAO, DOJ, DOL, OPM

Key to Chart:

AFJAG = Department of the Air Force, Judge Advocate General's Corps

AJAG = Department of the Army, Judge Advocate General's Corps

BBG = Broadcasting Board of Governors

CCR = Commission on Civil Rights

CFTC = Commodity Futures Trading Commission

CIA = Central Intelligence Agency

COC = Comptroller of the Currency

COMM = Department of Commerce

CSA = Court Services and Offender Supervision Agency

CUST = Customs

DHS = Department of Homeland Security

DOA = Department of Agriculture

DOD = Department of Defense

DOE = Department of Energy

DOI = Department of the Interior

DOJ = Department of Justice

DOL = Department of Labor

DOS = Department of State

DOT = Department of Transportation

EDUC = Department of Education

EIB = Export/Import Bank of America

EPA = Environmental Protection Agency

FAA = Department of Transportation, Federal Aviation Administration

FBI = Federal Bureau of Investigation

FCC = Federal Communications Commission

FDIC = Federal Deposit Insurance Corporation

FED = Federal Reserve Board

FEMA = Federal Emergency Management Administration

FERC = Federal Election Regulatory Commission

FLRA = Federal Labor Relations Authority

FMC = Federal Maritime Commission

FTC = Federal Trade Commission

GAO = General Accounting Office

GSA = General Services Administration

HHS = Department of Health and Human Services

HUD = Department of Housing and Urban Development

IRS = Department of the Treasury, Internal Revenue Service

ITC = International Trade Commission

MCJAG = Marine Corps Judge Advocate General's Corps

NASA = National Aeronautics and Space Administration

NCUA = National Credit Union Administration

NJAG = Department of the Navy, Judge Advocate General's Corps

NLRB = National Labor Relations Board

NRC = Nuclear Regulatory Commission

NSF = National Science Foundation

NTSB = National Transportation Safety Board

NOGC = Department of the Navy, Office of the General Counsel

OPM = Office of Personnel Management

OSC = Office of Special Counsel

PBGC = Pension Benefit Guarantee Commission

SBA = Small Business Administration

SEC = Securities and Exchange Commission

SSA = Social Security Administration

TREAS = Department of the Treasury, Office of the General Counsel

USAID = U.S. Agency for International Development

USAO = U.S. Attorney's Offices

USCG = U.S. Coast Guard

USPS = U.S. Postal Service

USPTO = U.S. Patent and Trademark Office

USSS = U.S Secret Service

VA = Veterans' Administration

This list courtesy of The Catholic University of America Columbus School of Law.

C. THE MILITARY

Each branch of the military has a department called the "Judge Advocate General's Corps" or "JAG Corps." The JAG Corps gives you immediate responsibility in a practice that ranges from criminal law to international law. As a JAG lawyer, your practice may take you to any of the fifty states or almost any country in the world.

Attorneys in JAG Corps usually start their career in the general practice of law. Initial legal training in the military is fast-paced and demanding, and the opportunity to litigate comes quickly after training. To become a member of the JAG Corps, you must enter active duty in one of these branches. There are also civilian legal positions in the offices of general counsel for the branches of the armed services.

Because of the way that military courts-martial have appeared in movies like *"A Few Good Men,"* when people think of military justice they think of JAG Corps attorneys as prosecuting or defending soldiers charged with violating the Uniform Code of Military Justice. However, as a member of the JAG Corps, your practice involves not only representing officers and enlisted men and women in matters of military justice, but it sometimes also involves representing and assisting soldiers and military dependents in other types of matters. You may also get involved with:

- Becoming a claims attorney (in which case you investigate and settle claims for damage by or to government property, or for injury to people who receive medical care from the military);

- Becoming a legal assistance attorney (where you counsel soldiers and their families with respect to all matters other than military justice, such as taxes, trusts and estates, and family law);

- Becoming an administrative law attorney (where you handle many diverse matters involving things like labor law, contract law, environmental law, the Freedom of Information Act, the Privacy Act, access to military installations, or interpreting military regulations).

If you are in the Army or Air Force JAG Corps, you may try cases before the Armed Services Board of Contract Appeals. (In the Navy, this kind of work is done by civilian civil service attorneys.)

On-line resources are a great place to learn more about JAG Corps opportunities. They include:

Department of Defense federal web locator (with links to military websites): www.infoctr.edu/fwl/

Army Judge Advocate General Corps: www.jagcnet.army.mil/

Navy Judge Advocate General Corps: www.jag.navy.mil/

Air Force Judge Advocate General Corps: http://www.hqja.jag.af.mil/

Marine Judge Advocate General Corps: http://sja.hqmc.usmc.mil/

U.S. Coast Guard Legal Division: http://uscg.mil/legal/

D. STATE AND LOCAL GOVERNMENT

Students often overlook state and local governments as a source of legal jobs, and that's a cryin' shame. There are tons of opportunities at every level. Almost every state, county, and city employs attorneys to handle legal issues related to housing, labor and employment, tax, public utilities, health care, education, and child welfare, among others. The primary state employer of lawyers is the Attorney General/Department of Justice; numerous other agencies employ attorneys, including state departments of agriculture, education, employment, environmental quality, treasury, and the like.

Then, of course, there are county and city attorneys' offices, as well as prosecutors (called "District Attorneys" in some states, and "State's Attorneys" in others), public defenders, Legal Aid Bureaus, and more.

Some city attorneys' offices are huge; for large cities, they can employ hundreds of lawyers, rivaling the largest law firms in the country.

Most state and local government legal employers do not interview on campus. They also do not hire on a regular calendar basis; they hire on the basis of determined need. On top of that, the positions tend not to be advertised. As is true in so many private employer situations, Chapter 10 on The Birds and Bees of Great Jobs is a vital resource for identifying and nailing these positions.

Online resources include:

Comprehensive links to state and local government websites: www.statelocalgov.net

Links to DA and SA websites around the country: www.prosecutor.info

Legal Aid and Public Defender jobs nationwide: www.nlada.org/Jobs

For links to helpful websites for state and local positions: www.law.gwu.edu/cdo

Appendix E
Other Resources

Just can't get enough, eh? Here are other resources to check out:

Lisa Abrams' popular book "The Official Guide To Legal Specialties"

The Vault Guides to various specialties

Deborah Arron's classic "What Can You Do With A Law Degree?"

Patricia Comeford and Gina Sauer's accessible and comforting book "Lessons from a Headhunter ... with Heart" (particularly for second career students)

Shout-outs for materials excerpted in this chapter: University of San Francisco School of Law, Duquesne University School of Law, Northwestern School of Law of Lewis and Clark College, Santa Clara University School of Law, Catholic University Columbus School of Law, George Washington University Law School, New England School of Law.

Chapter Three
Getting the Most Out of Your Career Services Office

What if I told you I was going to give you the services of a private career counselor, for free. Something that would cost you thousands of dollars if you went out and bought it yourself. Would you say, "Thanks anyway, Kimmbo. I'll pass." Of course not. You'd kiss me!

Whether your school calls it the Career Services Office, the Career Development Office, the Professional Development Office, Placement—it's generally the most useful and least utilized office on campus. That's a crime. Everything I know I've learned from Career Services people. So if you like this book, trust me—you'll love your Career Services Office!

Let's talk about exactly how you can squeeze the most benefit out of Career Services. But first, let's talk about . . .

A. DANGEROUS MYTHS ABOUT CAREER SERVICES

1. "THEY ONLY HELP THE TOP 10%"

I hear this at almost every law school in America except, perhaps, Harvard. I joke about it whenever I give the *Guerrilla Tactics* seminar at schools. Every Career Services person bemoans this misconception. "Most of the work we do isn't with the top 10%, because they don't *need* it. It's the other 90% of the class who need us," says Willamette's Diane Reynolds. Lisa Abrams adds, "Most students don't realize it, but we identify with students who aren't in the top 10% of the class—because *we* weren't in the top 10% of *our* law school classes, either!"

The top 10% thing has an obvious source: On-campus interviews. At most law schools, the students chosen for on-campus interviews are in that elite decile. It varies from school to school—at some distinguished schools almost every student gets on-campus interviews, while at others I've visited, the portion of students that interview on-campus is "that guy"—but 10% is the average.

114

Now, do you suppose this is the fault of *Career Services?* Do you imagine that they're on the phone with employers saying, "What? You want to interview students in the *bottom* half of the class? I absolutely *forbid* it! We have some fine Law Review students . . ."

Of course not. It's employer-driven. Every Career Services person I know would *love* for every student to get on-campus interviews, and they strive mightily to get employers to look out of their "comfort zone."

But you know what? The hell with on-campus interviews. They're a vastly overrated way to get a job. They certainly don't help you develop the job search skills you'll use for the rest of your life, for the dozen or so jobs you'll have in your career. Career Services can help you in every other way—determining what your dream job is, turning you on to alums and other lawyers who can help you, polishing your written package . . . the list goes on and on.

The top 10% conception is a myth. And if it keeps you out of the Career Services Office, it's a dangerous myth. Don't believe it!

2.   "With All I'm Paying for Tuition, They Owe Me a Job"

As Santa Clara's Matthew Wayman points out, "That's not an unfair perception. They pay *a lot* of money." If you're at a private school and paying, oh, the income of an average American family in tuition, it's fair to expect that you ought to get a job out of it . . .

Right?

The reality is, nobody other than you can get you a job. The Career Services Office can help you. Help you *a lot*. From information to strategy to contacts to cover letter and resume polishing, they can be the difference in your getting a job you enjoy. But they can't force anyone to hire you, nor can they guarantee you that your credentials will get you any particular job. They can't sit on your lap in an interview room and say, "Excuse me, Interviewer, what (s)he *meant* to say was . . ."

They also work in ways you can't see to help make sure you get a job. A large part of Career Services Directors' duties involve marketing law schools to employers. I know Directors who routinely travel the country persuading employers to consider their students. They routinely meet with local employers to keep their finger on the pulse of local hiring, and to ferret out opportunities for you. If you look at on-campus interviews and job postings as capital, every new employer who interviews on-campus or posts a job represents the sweat equity of your Career Services Director.

The fact is, your Career Services Office would *love* to have a "magic drawer" of jobs, where they'd pull out a slip of paper with your employer's name on it . . . no effort at all. But that magic drawer doesn't exist. They do their best, and in Topic B, we talk about all the ways you can help them help you!

3.   "THEY CAN'T GIVE ME ANYTHING I CAN'T FIND ON-LINE"

That damned Internet. It's true that it's a research treasure chest. But when it comes to giving you tailored advice about activities that can help you, at your school and in the community where you want to work, about alums who'll talk to you, about employers you personally should consider ... the Internet can't help you.

Your Career Services Office has a wealth of knowledge that can mean the difference between getting an offer and getting rejected over and over and over again. There's no question that the live, real-time advice they can give you is better than anything you can find anywhere else. Use them!

4.   NO MATTER *WHAT* YOU'VE HEARD, NO CAREER SERVICES PERSON *ANYWHERE* HAS EVER TOLD A STUDENT THAT THEY WERE *UNEMPLOYABLE*

When I visit law schools, I will periodically run into students who will swear up and down that people at the CSO told them they were unemployable. I met one student at a law school down South who walked up to me and huffily declared, loudly and in front of several of her classmates, "The Career Services Director told me straight out that I will *never* find a job." She went on to show me a list of the fifty-four characteristics she did not want in a job: "No long hours, no socializing with other members of the firm, no xeroxing or faxing, no dogs in the office ..." it was amazing. Now, I would never call a student unemployable, because I don't think such a person exists.

But she was tiptoeing on the ragged edge ...

Of course I went straight to her Career Services Director afterwards, and asked, "Did you tell X that she's unemployable?" The Career Services Director rolled her eyes, and said, "Of course not. I give her lists and lists of alums to talk to, but she doesn't want to do that. I wish I could get her on-campus interviews, but she doesn't have the grades for that." So in other words: this student wasn't eligible for on-campus interviews at her school, the Career Services Director had told her *that,* and the student converted that into her mind into "I'm unemployable."

If you have a classmate who swears the CSO told him/her that (s)he could never get a job, you've got a classmate who has serious communications issues. It's just not true. Every student is employable. More importantly, *every* student can be helped by the CSO. Don't believe anything you hear otherwise!

B.   EIGHTEEN GREAT WAYS TO GET THE MOST OUT OF CAREER SERVICES

1.   WOODY ALLEN SAID 80% OF LIFE IS SHOWING UP, SO: SHOW UP!

When I visit law schools to give the *Guerrilla Tactics* seminar, I usually need to ask directions to the Career Services Office. It's often amazing how many students I approach who'll tell me, "I'm not sure," "I think it's in the basement," "Maybe that way. No. That way ..."

No matter what Career Services can do for you, if you don't go there, they can't do *anything* for you! Even if you think they only "help the top 10%," even if your best friend tells you "They told me I was unemployable," (which has never, ever, ever really happened), go there *anyway* and see what they can do for you. Just say hello. Many a Career Services Director has sadly told me of the experience of being at graduation, and seeing faces they've never seen before. You could be passing up a dream gig if you don't give the CSO a chance to help you. Go!

2. IT'S NEVER TOO EARLY IN YOUR JOB SEARCH PROCESS TO ASK FOR HELP (BEGINNING NOVEMBER 1 OF YOUR FIRST YEAR. BEFORE THAT, IT *IS* TOO EARLY.) SEEK THEIR ADVICE EVEN IF IT'S TO SAY, "I DON'T HAVE ANY IDEA WHAT I WANT TO DO WITH MY DEGREE"

There's no magic door you walk through when the CSO suddenly becomes useful to you, you know. From figuring out what classes will be useful to you, turning you on to activities both in-school and in the legal community that will help you, to internships, clerkships, you name it ... let the CSO be your partner in charting your career.

When you're trying to figure out your target, they brainstorm with you about the kinds of jobs you might like, bringing up employers you might never have found any other way. They can help you with self-assessment tests that figure out what you're like, and what you'd like to do. While your career is still just a glimmer in your eye, let them help you!

The November 1 of 1L starting date, by the way, isn't the creation of your CSO. It's their membership in the National Association of Law Placement (NALP) that's the culprit. NALP rules require that the CSO not have any contact with you until you've reached November 1 of your First Year, with the idea in mind that you should be focused on your schoolwork before that.

Recognize what that November 1 date means, by the way. It doesn't mean that you can't research or contact employers yourself, or take part in any activities, or go to any CSO-sponsored panels or presentations; I speak before November 1 at a lot of schools and many students in the audience are 1Ls. They won't throw you out of the CSO library if you show up. It's just that the CSO can't *officially* talk to you, that's all.

3. GO TO CAREER SERVICES PANELS AND SPEECHES

If your law school is like most schools, your CSO puts on a staggering array of presentations. From "brown bag" informal lunches with practitioners to speakers to panels to workshops to Career Days and Job Fairs to—ahem—the *Guerrilla Tactics* seminar from the Job Goddess herself, there might be something going on seemingly all the time.

They don't do all this for their own edification, you know. It's for you. From helping you to figure out what you want to do by hearing about other people's experiences to making valuable contacts, I can't encourage you enough to attend as many of these functions as you can. I've talked with students who've gotten their foot in the door with the most amazing employers just because they attended a CSO presentation. I talked with one student at a Boston law school who actually nailed a clerkship with the Israeli Supreme Court because he went to see an Israeli Supreme Court justice speak, and sent her a thank you letter, which led to correspondence . . . and a phenomenal summer job!

I've talked with many other students who found *other* students to help them by attending CSO presentations. When I give the *Guerrilla Tactics* seminar at schools, there'll always be students who hang around afterwards to chat (that's my favourite part). They'll talk to each other, and inevitably there will be students who'll hear a classmate's dream and say, "You should talk to my father . . ." "You should contact my friend . . ." and it's all because the setting brought out the conversation.

But it all starts with going to those presentations. As I've said before: Go!

4.   HAVE CAREER SERVICES COUNSELORS REVIEW YOUR WRITTEN MATERIALS, RESUMES AND CORRESPONDENCE, BEFORE YOU SEND THEM OUT

Don't send out *any* cover letter or resume until you've given it to a counselor at the CSO. Don't be coy. They've seen it all, and the more pairs of eyes you have reviewing and proofing your work, the better off you are. Whether it's the tone, the way you "pitch" yourself, or even typos, they'll pick up a lot that you'd never notice alone.

In Chapters 7 and 8 we go into excruciating detail about correspondence and resumes. But as much as I'd love to, I can't review what you come up with to see if you got it right. Your Career Services counselors *can*. Take advantage of that!

5.   READ THEIR E-MAILS

You probably get a bunch of e-mail from Career Services. And when you're pressed for time, you've got your studies, your friends, your life . . . you may be tempted to ignore those e-mails.

Don't!

Whether they're telling you about an on-campus function or notifying you of activities or job postings that may be of interest to you in particular, it's worth taking a quick glance to see what they're telling you.

I can't tell you how many times I speak at law schools, only to have students stop me in hallways afterwards and say, "I didn't know you were going to be here!" In other words: *they didn't read that e-mail.*

It takes ten seconds to skim an e-mail. Make sure you don't ignore what the CSO sends you.

6. DON'T PUT THE CSO IN A *HORRIBLE* POSITION BY IGNORING EMPLOYER DEADLINES

Whether it's a "resume drop" for an employer or an application "drop-dead" date, make sure you get your materials in on time. Every CSO in the country has had the experience of a student showing up a couple of days after the deadline, and insisting that their materials be forwarded.

You can see why this puts your CSO in a dreadful position. They very much want you to get the jobs you want. But at the same time, deadlines are a fact of working life. It may well be that no matter how much the CSO personnel plead your case with an employer, they just won't accept late materials.

When you get out of school and start a job, you'll find that deadlines are crucially important to your employer. Whether it's turning in work to your supervisor or depositing motions and other documents with the court, you can't ignore deadlines imposed on you by others. So get into a very valuable habit now, and heed deadlines!

If you do as I advise in Chapter 7 on Correspondence, you'll already have a calendar handy. Make notes of CSO deadlines on it for jobs you want to pursue. That way, you'll never turn your materials in late.

7. YOU ARE THE NATURAL OBJECT OF BOUNTY FOR ALUMS FROM YOUR LAW SCHOOL. ASK THE CAREER SERVICES OFFICE TO PUT YOU ON TO HELPFUL ALUMS AND MENTORS

In Chapter 8 we deal with the issue of reaching out to people to snare great jobs. If the idea of making personal contacts yourself makes you cringe, then take heart. Your Career Services Office to the rescue! As William and Mary's Rob Kaplan points out, "Career Services Directors are a kind of chamber of commerce for the law school—their primary function is to market students to employers." In the process, they meet and maintain a network of *innumerable* alumni and practitioners. So if you tell them what you want, they'll undoubtedly be able to put you on to somebody who can help you!

8. USE THE CAREER SERVICES OFFICE LIBRARY—ESPECIALLY FOR MATERIALS UNIQUE TO YOUR SCHOOL

Your CSO library is a virtual Aladdin's cave of useful materials. You may well be reading this book at the CSO library, in which case . . . buy your own, dammit!

Just kidding.

Ahem. The point I was trying to make is this: Research is crucial at so many junctures during your job search—from self-assessment tests to finding out what's "out there" to getting the basic information about specific employers in preparation for interviews. Your CSO will have books, videos, on-line resources, you name it, to help you at every turn.

Even more valuable are the "custom" binders I've seen at many law schools, where the CSO surveys students and graduates about their work experiences. You'll often find binders of these surveys, and they're fantastic; the inside skinny on all kinds of jobs, as well as the names of people who would make great "informal mentors." Take advantage of these unique resources!

9. GET THE "INSIDE SKINNY" ON EMPLOYERS ... *AND RESPECT THE CONFIDENTIALITY OF WHAT YOU HEAR.* DON'T RAT OUT THE CSO!

The information you can get from books, directories and on-line databases, message boards and chat rooms only go so far. If you really want the scuttlebutt on employers, ask at the CSO. They keep their ear to the ground, and hear all *kinds* of gossip—and if they don't know the juicy stuff about a particular employer, they probably know somebody who *does.* That kind of information can go a long way toward helping you assess if you really want to pursue a job with a particular employer, what to highlight on your resume, what to bring up—or avoid—in an interview.

By the way, when it comes to using what you hear, *protect your sources.* Especially for information that is—ahem—south of complimentary, don't *ever, ever* say to an employer, "At the CSO they told me that you're having financial troubles." Their ability to gather information depends on staying in the good graces of employers. If you trash their reputation, you've cut off opportunities for your classmates, and hurt people who were only trying to help you. You also make yourself look indiscreet.

So play your cards close to your chest. If you mention "I've heard ..." and an employer asks, "Where did you hear that?" Just shrug and say, "The grapevine." Don't ever give your sources away for negative information.

For positives, on the other hand, *always* attribute the source! "They told me at Career Services that you had a great X practice ..." You'll stoke the engine for students who come after you. *Every* employer likes honest flattery. It'll make you look good ... and reflect well on your CSO, and your school!

10. CHECK JOB LISTINGS FROM THE CAREER SERVICES OFFICE *EVERY DAY.* OK. TWICE A WEEK, AT LEAST

At every law school I visit, there will be students who've nailed phenomenal, unusual summer jobs. Entertainment jobs. Sports jobs. Unique opportunities in all kinds of desirable specialties. While they usually get these jobs through self-initiated contact with employers, there are always students who got their job the old fashioned way: through a posting at Career Services. I'll ask, "How did you *get* that?" and they'll shrug and say, "I looked on-line at job postings from the school, and there it was."

Believe it or not, your CSO *does* get postings for amazing opportunities. If you don't think so, it's because you don't check the job postings often enough! The really fly jobs aren't going to hang around on-line for a week or two.

So check job postings at least twice a week, if not every day, to make sure you don't miss anything awesome!

11.   Do Mock Interviews

Interviewing is like that old joke about the New York tourist asking, "How do I get to Carnegie Hall?" The response: "Practice, practice, practice."

Practice is the way you get good at interviewing. All of the prep work, all of the theoretical advice about how to conduct yourself—as we talk about in great detail in Chapter 8–won't help you if you don't put it to work.

Every CSO in the country does mock interviews, so that you can hone your skills in a setting with no real-world consequences. Many videotape their mock interviews so you can see how you come off. Some even bring in real practitioners to do mock interviews—and some students have gotten jobs as a result of these mock interviews, with the interviewer saying afterwards, "You did a great job. Send me your resume!" Maine's Tammy Willcox had a student who showed up for a mock interview with a local practitioner, and they wound up getting married!

Even if you don't wind up with a spouse, you *will* be able to smooth over any "rough patches" in your interviewing style. When students have told me about being rejected after numerous interviews, I can bet dollars to doughnuts that there's a simple hitch in their interviewing that needs repair. Mock interviews can save you from that fate, before you set foot into real interview for the first time!

12.   When You Suffer Setbacks, Don't Suffer Alone. Go to the CSO for a Shoulder to Cry on

Every law student faces setbacks in their job search. If you think you know classmates who don't ... trust me. They do.

It's easy to exile yourself in Loserville when your job search isn't going your way. I had classmates at law school who actually papered the walls of their apartments with *rejection letters*. What a great way to boost your ego, eh?

The fact is, they call them career *counselors* for a reason. Counseling is the primary function of the folks at your CSO. Part of their job is providing comfort; that's why you'll always notice a box of Kleenex on their desks! There's no question that sharing your feelings and concerns with a "sympathetic ear" will make you feel better. If you need it, reach out for it. "Don't worry," says Georgetown's Marilyn Tucker. "We're used to it!"

13. LOOKING OUT-OF-TOWN? HAVE THE CSO GET YOU "RECIPROCITY" WITH A LAW SCHOOL IN THE CITY YOU'RE TARGETING

When you're looking for jobs in another city, wouldn't it be great to be able to utilize a Career Services Office *there?* Well, great news. That's usually possible, via what's called "reciprocity."

Rules on reciprocity vary from school to school. Most will at the very least let you look at their job listings and use their materials. Remember: When they *do* let you do this, a show of gratefulness is always wise. It reflects well on both you and your school.

By the way, you don't get reciprocity on your own; your Career Services Office has to request it on your behalf. They'll be able to tell you the policies of schools in cities you're targeting ... and while you're there, ask for what else you ought to be doing to get a job out-of-town!

14. MAKE SURE THE CSO HAS AN UP-TO-DATE RESUME FROM YOU

As UConn's Michelle Hoff advises, "It's a good idea to have an up-to-date resume at Career Services. Make sure your profile is current." Why? Because Career Services Offices often get calls from lawyers who say "I need resumes *today.*" It doesn't matter how perfect you are for a job if people at the CSO can't track you down and get your resume from you!

So make sure the CSO has your resume along with guidelines from you on the kinds of jobs you're looking for. They'll be able to keep an eye out for opportunities you'll enjoy.

15. LET THEM KNOW ABOUT ANY SPECIAL SKILLS YOU HAVE

I'm not talking about the tie-a-knot-in-a-cherry-stem-with-your-tongue variety (although I can, in fact, do that). I'm talking about skills of interest to employers. If you have exceptional computer skills, you speak a foreign language, you've got Top Secret security clearance, you have other professional certifications (like a CPA), you can leap tall buildings with a single bound ... let the CSO know about it! *Many* times job openings will come in to the CSO that call for special skills, and if no one there knows what you can do, they can't tap you for those jobs. So don't be modest; if you've got something out-of-the-ordinary to offer, let the CSO know about it!

16. MAKE SURE THE CSO KNOWS YOU'RE LOOKING FOR A JOB—AND WHAT KIND OF JOB YOU'RE SEEKING

Many students mistakenly believe that if they don't say anything, everybody will *assume* they're looking for a job. Wrong! The assumption is just the opposite: If you don't tell people you're looking for a job, they'll assume you *aren't* looking. And that means that if they get any good leads for you, they won't tell you about them!

There's no shame in admitting you're looking. I've told you before that more than half of law students graduate without a job in hand. The vast majority of students don't get jobs through on-campus interviews. So swallow your pride and tell people at the CSO what you want, so they can help you find it!

17. RECOGNIZE THE LIMITS OF WHAT THE CSO CAN DO—THEY'RE YOUR SHERPA. YOU STILL HAVE TO CLIMB THE MOUNTAIN

There's a reason they don't call it the "placement" office anymore, you know. As I hear from law school Career Services people all over the country, they can't *place* you in a job—much as they'd like to! Franklin Pierce's Sophie Sparrow says that students often walk up to her saying, "So where's my job?" to which she responds, "I don't know. Where is it?" Maine's Tammy Willcox adds, "Some students have this misconception that I'm going to be this matronly woman who's going to feed them candy. No! I'm here to help students get jobs!" Washington's Teresa DeAndrado says, "It's a *partnership* between Career Services and the students."

So you shouldn't treat your Career Services Office as executive headhunters; they're simply not that. That may anger or upset you, but as Notre Dame's Gail Peshel points out, it's ultimately good for you that they *don't* do that. "Some students think that they'll just walk in and get a list of employers who will hire them. Instead, we *teach* them how to find a job. That makes them happier in the long run, because even if someone *would* automatically hire them, that employer might make them *miserable!*" Ultimately, an employer is going to hire *you*. It'll be you, alone, in the interview room. And it'll be you, alone, performing that job. Career Services can lead you to the door, but they can't go in with you!

So whether it's providing speakers and panels and workshops, doing letter and resume reviews, mock interviews, letting you know about job openings and giving you the names of employers and alums to contact for advice—phew! Career Services can "carry your career bags" for you. But you've still got to make the trip yourself!

18. DON'T LET YOUR PARENTS CALL CAREER SERVICES ON YOUR BEHALF . . . AND FOR GOSH SAKES, DON'T *ASK* THEM TO!

Career Services Counselors call parents who phone on their children's behalf "helicopter parents"—the hover over you. As one Career Services Director points out, "It's totally unprofessional. *You're* the one who's going to be a lawyer. I don't care who's paying your tuition. You wouldn't have your parents call a judge and say, 'Why did you rule against my child?' Don't do it to Career Services, either! It'll hurt your image. Just talk about your own issues directly. Don't have your parents plead your case."

19. IF YOU'VE GOT A BEEF WITH THE CSO, TALK WITH THE DIRECTOR PERSONALLY

No trashing them in blogs. No mass e-mails. No poison pen editorials in the school newspaper. Talk to them, and be polite. No berating them, no snippy e-mails (which can easily be forwarded to anybody at all).

Now before you say, "Hey, Kimmbo, you've drunk the CSO Kool–Aid," let me explain why I'm telling you this.

A. WHATEVER YOU THINK—THAT THE CSO ISN'T DOING ENOUGH TO BRING EMPLOYERS TO ON CAMPUS, THAT THEY'RE NOT PROMOTING THE BOTTOM HALF OF THE CLASS, THAT THEY'RE NOT CUTTING YOU IN CERTAIN JOB FAIRS—YOU NEED TO KNOW THAT THEY'RE ON THE SAME SIDE AS YOU

They *want* you to be employed, and if they had their choice, every employer in America would come to your campus and make an offer to everyone in the class, regardless of their grades. But on this planet, your CSO can only do so much.

I have never seen a CSO at any school I've visited—and that's almost all of them—that didn't market the snot out of their students to every employer who would listen. They can't blackmail employers into coming on campus, or accepting resumes. They do everything short of that. As one Career Services Director points out, "I get questions all the time about Career Fairs, and how come we're not going to this one, or that one. I point out that a lot of them are by invitation only. Trust me, I do everything I can to get our students into every one they want. But when I can't do that, I find out which employers will be there, and I reach out to them individually on behalf of our students. At least when students ask me about these fairs, I can tell them that."

And if you have ideas for how Career Services might do better, trust me—they really *want* to hear from you! As Santa Clara's Matt Wayans says, "When students say they're not happy with what we're doing, I tell them, 'Come in and let's talk about what else we can do.'"

B. ADDRESSING ISSUES WITH PEOPLE DIRECTLY—RATHER THAN HUMILIATING THEM—IS A SMART STRATEGY FOR YOUR CAREER

I'm getting a little ahead of myself here by talking about how you become a superstar at work. That's the focus of my book, "What Law School Doesn't Teach You." Suffice it to say that you'll do your reputation a favour if people believe that you're a stand-up person, that you address grievances directly with the person/people you feel have wronged you. People will respect you and want to work with you. So develop that trait while you're still in school. It will serve you well forever.

C. REMEMBER THAT YOUR CLASSMATES TODAY WILL BE YOUR COLLEAGUES TOMORROW

Trashing the CSO, whining loudly about how they haven't gotten you a job, may get you kudos and understanding nods from your classmates now ... but when they look back years from now, they're not going to remember you favourably. They may then be in a position to hire you or throw work your way. You want them to think of you as a smart person with good judgment. Conducting a CSO witch hunt doesn't create that image for you!

Quietly commiserating with friends about your job hunt—absolutely. There's camaraderie in sharing disappointments. But remember that you're not just creating an image with employers; you're doing it with classmates, as well.

d. You Don't Want Grudging Help From Your CSO. You Want Them to Be Genuinely Enthusiastic About You

If you make the CSO look bad, sure, they'll outwardly help you. But let's be honest: put yourself in their shoes and ask yourself, how much would you do for someone who makes you look bad? You'd do the bare minimum. You wouldn't go out of your way to be helpful. It's not revenge; it's human nature. They're duty-bound to inform you of opportunities that are sent to your school, but realistically, how much will they go out of their way for you if you diss them?

Make human nature work *for* you, not *against* you! If you're frustrated, by all means go to the CSO and *say so*. Make an appointment with your Career Services Director and pour out all of your job search frustrations. Ask for help. I'm not telling you to be stoic. But if you're direct and honest about how you feel, and you let the CSO work *with* you, I promise good things will result!

Chapter Four
The Most Important Element of Your Image

(Psst: It's Not Your School, Your Grades, or Your Work Experience)

The most important element of your image. What could it be? Great grades? Nope. Law Review? Sorry. Phenomenal work experience? Doesn't hurt ... but that's not it.

We're going to get to it in a minute, through a little role playing.

Here's the set up. You're a legal employer. I'm a law student. I send you a letter that reads:

> *Dear Hiring Partner,*
>
> *I am currently a law student. I'd like to start my career with you, because I believe that by working for you, I will learn how to deal with clients. I will learn how to behave in court. I will hone my research skills. I ... I ... I ...*

Now—what's the problem with my letter? Do you care about me? No, of course not. You probably assume that working for you would be a *great* gig for me! This highlights an important point to remember. Namely: Employers don't care about you. You can *make* them care about you, but only if you do this: *Show them how what you bring to the table will help them accomplish what <u>they</u> want.* The focus in every aspect of your job search—letters, resumes, interviews, all the things we'll be discussing in detail in this book—should be on the employer and what you can do for them. That's all they care about.

By the way, this is true in every aspect of your life. When you get offers in the mail, do they say, "Please buy this product so we can vacation in the Caribbean"? When you go to the grocery store to buy cereal, do the boxes say, "Eat this so we can retire rich!"? Of course not. Because you don't care. You want to know what's in it for you, and that's what advertisers and marketers try to give you.

So when you're looking for a job, the shoe is on the other foot. What's in it for the employer? That's why it's so crucial to show in letters that you've researched the employer, you know what they're about and you've thought about how you fit in. That research can include the employer's web site (easy), talking to your Career Services Office about what this kind of employer looks for (better), talking with classmates or upperclassmen who've worked at this employer or employers like it (great). We'll go into this in more detail when we talk about cover letters in Chapter 7, but for now, you see the point: the focus is on what you bring to the table for the employer.

Now, you may be thinking what I would have thought when I was in law school: "That's all well and good—but what exactly *do* I bring to the table?" Regardless of what other qualities you offer, there is one trait you are capable of exhibiting, regardless of your credentials or background, and it's *crucial* to your job search success: *Enthusiasm*. That's it. Enthusiasm. Everything about your job search should exude, "This is a job I really want."

I know what you're thinking. Enthusiasm. Rah freakin' rah. Who wants the yappy little lap dog around, right? Butt kisser. Brown noser.

But when I say enthusiasm, I'm not talking about having the drink-the-Koolaid frozen smile, the oleaginous fake heartiness, the "Yes man" persona. It's what enthusiasm motivates you to *do* and *say*. When you're enthusiastic about an employer, you'll find out all you can about them before you send them your resume or interview with them. You'll ask questions. You'll go to events where you can see and talk with them. You'll pay compliments, *heartfelt* compliments ("I'm really impressed that you . . .")

Students have occasionally asked me, "OK, so enthusiasm is important. How do I fake it?" Easy.

You *don't*.

In other words: You don't pursue employers you're not enthusiastic about! If you find yourself trying to djinny up any oomph for employers you're pursuing, you're jumping the gun. You need to take a step back to Chapter 2 and figure out what you want to do. Once you've done *that*, your enthusiasm for employers you approach will be genuine.

Or let's take a more difficult case. Let's say you're about to graduate, or even that you've already graduated, and you feel desperate. You'll "take anything" to pay the bills. How do you generate enthusiasm *then?* It's all in what you tell yourself. You can say, "Whichever job I take, this employer is giving me my first chance. My career could go anywhere from here. I'll learn skills I don't have now, and who knows, I might turn out to really enjoy it. Even if I don't, if I do my best at this, opportunities I can't imagine now will open up for me." All of that is absolutely true, by the way. And there's your motivation to take a genuine interest in the employers you pursue.

Another thing that gives enthusiasm a bad rap is a dangerous myth about job searches. Everybody's heard that the best way to get a job is to pretend you don't want one. "You know how he got that job? He pretended he didn't want it." Oh ... *really*? Here's the truth: playing hard to get works when you date. It doesn't work when you're looking for your first "real" job. Show them you really want it. Even the very words, "I know I don't have any experience doing what you do, but this is a job I really want, and I will work hard to reward your confidence in me" can work like magic.

I have talked with hundreds of employers, and what I hear *to a person* is that when they have to make tough calls about who to hire—and trust me, they *always* have to make tough calls about who to hire—they'll choose the person who seems to want the job more. Who's more *enthusiastic* about it. They know that that genuine interest will buoy the student in the steep learning curve that becoming a lawyer entails. (And PS: Even once you *have* a job, enthusiasm counts. When employers are faced with a layoff, they'll often choose the most apathetic associates. "She just didn't seem interested" will be their justification.)

Now, there *will* be times, later on in your career, when 'playing hard to get' in the job hunt makes sense. Two principal ones spring to mind: When an employer or headhunter solicits you, or the job you're talking about is at a very high level. Even under those circumstances, you'd want to be careful to suggest that you're very interested in the job, but ... and then negotiate yourself a great package. But I tell you all of this cautiously, because at the beginning of your career, that's not the attitude you want to adopt.

I hear stories all the time that illuminate the importance of enthusiasm. One prosecutor I talked to stressed its importance at job fairs. He said, "When I work tables at job fairs, I might as well be radioactive. Students will sneak up to the table, grab a brochure, and run away. I'm only there because I want to talk to them! They don't have to be witty. They don't have to come up with a quote I'll always remember. All they have to do is ask me, 'What's your job like'? Just take an interest. I'll take it from there."

* * * SMART HUMAN TRICK * * *

Law student in Minnesota. His dream job was to get into the Navy JAG—a fantastic job. He applied for an on-campus interview with Navy JAG, and didn't get it. Undeterred, he did something we'll talk about later in the book—he sat outside the interview room for a couple of hours, so that every time the Navy JAG recruiter came out to retrieve the next interviewee, he'd see this particular student. After this happened a couple of times, the JAG recruiter asked him, "Are you here to see me?" The student responded, "I'm dying to get into Navy JAG, but I didn't get an on-campus interview. I was hoping you might have a few extra minutes to talk to me." The JAG recruiter, impressed, said, "Sure, hang around—we can chat after the interviews are done." When the student got in to talk to the interviewer, he asked, among other things: "Would it be all right if I came down to your office and shadowed you for a day?" (Many employers will allow you to do this; check with Career Services at school or your local bar association.) The JAG recruiter said, "Sure." So the student trundled down and met everyone in the office, all of whom encouraged him to apply for his commission. He did so—and got rejected. On the day the rejection arrived, he got a call from the recruiter, who asked if he'd heard about his commission. He said, dejectedly, "Yeah—I got rejected." The recruiter responded brightly, "Oh, don't worry about that. We all got rejected the first time around. Apply again in three months." He did so, and got accepted.

Now—what did Navy JAG guy *have*, other than raw enthusiasm? He didn't even have the paper credit to get an on-campus interview, let alone a commission. But he wanted it badly, and conveyed that to the interviewer—and that counts for a lot. Because if you convey enthusiasm, it tells the employer: "I'll work hard to learn everything I need to learn, to do a great job for you." And that's the most important thing they need to know about you!

* * * SMART HUMAN TRICK * * *

New law school graduate. He has trouble nailing a law-related job, and to pay the bills in the meantime, he takes a job working the cash register at Wal Mart.

Rather than let his disappointment show, he makes a point of talking with everybody who comes through his register line. One regular customer is a guy who turns out to be a lawyer—a lawyer who happens to be running for State Attorney General.

The graduate thinks the lawyer is a great guy and would make an outstanding Attorney General. He volunteers on his campaign for Attorney General, devoting much of his spare time to it.

The guy gets elected ... and names Mr. Wal Mart the Special Assistant to the Attorney General.

Chapter Five
Overcoming Rejection . . . and Turning It Into Job Opportunities

"What is to give light must endure burning."

   Viktor Frankl

"Without the wind in my face, I would not have been able to fly."

   Arthur Ashe

"If you're not failing, you're not taking enough chances."

   Mark Burnett

"Never never never give up."

   Winston Churchill

"Being defeated is only a temporary condition. Giving up makes it permanent."

   Marilyn vos Savant

"A kick in the ass is also a step forward."

      Quentin Tarantino

"You only hit a great shot when the other player forces you to hit a great shot."

      Martina Navratilova

An exchange between Vince Armstrong (as Dodgeball player Peter LeFleur) and bicycling legend Lance Armstrong (as himself) in the hilarious movie "DodgeBall," in a scene just after LeFleur has betrayed his teammates, and quit the team the night before the finals of the National Dodgeball Championship.

   LeFleur is sitting alone at a bar when Armstrong walks up and recognizes him:

   "Aren't you Peter LeFleur?"

   "Lance Armstrong?"

"... I'm a big fan of yours...I've been watching the DodgeBall tournament. Good luck ... I'm pulling for you ..."

"Actually, I decided to quit."

"Quit? Once I was thinking about quitting, when I was diagnosed with brain, lung and testicular cancer ... all at the same time. But with the love and support of my friends and family I got back on the bike and I won the Tour de France five times in a row. But I'm sure you have a good reason to quit. Hey, what are you dying from that's keeping you from the finals?"

"Right now it feels a little bit like ... shame."

"I guess if a person never quit when the going got tough, they wouldn't have anything to regret for the rest of their life. Good luck to you, Peter. I'm sure this decision won't haunt you forever."

"When you're going through hell ... keep going!"

Unknown

"Resentment is like taking poison and waiting for the other person to die."

Malachy McCourt

Let's say I sat you down and said to you, "No matter what you've done to look for a job, starting today, if you send out a hundred and fifty letters"—or make a hundred and fifty phone calls, or go to a hundred and fifty CLEs—"On the hundred and fifty-first, I *guarantee* you'll get a job you like," would you do it?

Of course you would. You'd do it because you'd *know* that when you get to number one hundred and fifty-one, you'd have an offer.

Well, I can make you that guarantee.

It's just that I don't know the number. It might be *one*. It might be the very next thing you do.

The fact is, you're not unemployable. I've met tens of thousands of law students and I've never met *one* who was unemployable. Your obituary is not going to read, "(S)he graduated from law school, and ... that was it." Every law student who ever *lived* got a job.

But in the meantime, when you don't have one ... it sucks. When you're sending out resumes or signing up for on-campus interviews or responding to job postings or *whatever* you're doing and you're not getting anything, it blows. (Isn't it ironic that "suck" and "blow" mean the same thing?)

What I'm going to do in this chapter is to talk about this very important topic of rejection. Job search books rarely talk about it, and I think that's a *huge* mistake. Because the fact is, no matter how great you are—and I'm sure you *are* great—no matter how wonderful your credentials are, no matter how well you interview, you *are* going to get rejected. It's a necessary part of the job search process.

All the great advice in the world can't protect you from at least *some* rejection. I read somewhere that a typical job search looks like this:

No no no no no no no no no no no no no no no no no no no no

No no no no no no no no no no no no no no no no no no no no

No no no no no no no no no no no no no no no no no no no YES.

You've *got* to go through those "no's" to get to that "yes"!

The way you handle rejection *in the meantime* can make all the difference in how long your job search lasts ... and the kind of job you wind up with.

The simple truth is that the fear of rejection can paralyze you. In psychology-speak, it attacks your "self-efficacy"—the sense that you can succeed at a specific task and at life in general. I've seen this happen all over the country. Otherwise competent, fully-functioning law students are reduced to a quivering bowl of jelly at the prospect of one more employer telling them *no*. What happens in this situation? You feel like a fire plug at a dog show. You start aiming too low. You give up on your dream. Working Northbound starts sounding good. Or you wear a metaphorical "Kick me" sign, such that employers shy away from you. They may not be able to put their finger on what's wrong ... but it's *something*. It's what Oklahoma City University's Gina Rowsam calls "the internal cloud of rejection." And it makes employers turn you down.

Or maybe, just maybe ... you stop doing anything at all.

I can't tell you how many students I've talked to whose *sole problem* was that they couldn't put rejection in perspective. I remember one student in particular. I was speaking in Seattle, and I watched students filing in. One student particularly caught my attention. She was so *mad*. You could just see it. She was radiating anger. She was the kind of person who drinks scotch and eats the glass afterwards.

As I gave the seminar, I kept an eye on her. She didn't get any happier. I thought, "Boy, I can't wait to get to the question and answer session—because I don't know what she's going to ask, but it'll be something good." Sure enough, I was hardly done talking when her hand shot up. "Well, Kimmbo," she snarled, "It's easy for you to say that anybody can get a job. Well, I can't."

"Why not?" I asked.

"Because I have a gap on my resume."

Well, *there's* something I've never heard before ... except maybe five or ten thousand times. You name it: People taking time off from school or work to reconsider a career in law, raise a family, hitchhike around the country, or take off to Tibet with a yak and a mystic to find themselves. So I'm thinking: If this gap on your resume is stopping you from getting a job, let's at least make it interesting. Like an alien abduction.

So I asked: "Why the gap?"

"I was sick for a year, and I missed a year of law school."

Bummer, but not unheard of; it shouldn't have stopped her from getting a job. I asked, innocently: "Are you better now?"

"Yes, but it doesn't matter! I can't get a job!"

Gee—I wonder why? The gap on her resume—or the chip on her shoulder the size of Mount Rushmore?

Remember: employers don't care about you. They don't care how upset you are about rejections you've received. All they want to see is what you bring to the table for them. It's an image you *control*. Don't let them see anything else!

Now you may be thinking, "Not *everybody* gets rejected, Kimmbo. If I went to a better school/if my grades were better/if I was on Law Review ..."

Rrrrright. If you think that there are people who don't get rejected, you don't know them well enough to know what their rejections are. Students who go to phenomenal law schools get some rejections. Students who are #1 in the class get rejected. In major league baseball, players who fail seven out of ten times they step up to the plate are Hall of Famers. Venture capitalists that pick one out of ten companies correctly are great successes. At Hallmark, people who write Shoebox greeting cards expect four out of five of their ideas to get rejected. No matter how great the advice in this book is, *you'll* get rejected.

Now, you hear a lot of heartwarming stories about people overcoming rejection. Famous stories. (I've got a lot of them in the Appendix at the end of this chapter, and they really are very satisfying.) I've even got one of my own. As I have mentioned in several sections of this book, I created the study aid called *Law In A Flash,* the flash cards in the yellow boxes. They're one of the most popular legal study aids in the country. I wrote every one of those cards, thousands in all. But that's not the part that's relevant here. The thing I want to tell you about *Law In A Flash* is that for the first three years we tried to get it into law school bookstores, *not one store in America would buy it*. The rejections were pretty comical. "Law students have no sense of humor." "It's juvenile." Three years of nothing but rejection, before even one law school bookstore took a chance on it. But once they gave it a chance ... well, the rest is history. Law students have spent tens of millions of dollars on those flash cards.

Much as I love to tell that story, there's a big problem with it, and every other story you hear about overcoming rejection. You hear about them only in *retrospect*. They're only heartwarming when the pot of gold at the end of the rainbow has already been found. While you're suffering through rejection, you've got to take it as a matter of faith that the pot of gold is there. Trust me, when I was at month 34 of *Law In A Flash* rejections, pretty much everybody was questioning whether those stupid flash cards were such a good idea after all.

I promise you that if you do the things I tell you to do throughout this book, you will be happily employed, and it will happen sooner rather than later. I *promise*. In the meantime, I want to tell you a few things to keep in mind that will make rejection much easier to bear, now and for the rest of your life.

1. DON'T HORRIBILIZE REJECTION. YOU HAVE NO IDEA HOW CLOSE YOU MIGHT HAVE BEEN TO GETTING THE JOB

When you get rejected, don't assume that the employer hated you. Don't assume there's something wrong with you. Don't assume that since they looked at your resume or interviewed you, they've fashioned a voodoo doll out of you, and they're sticking pins in it behind you back. They're not! When you get rejected, you might have been "thisclose" to getting the job.

Any employer who's honest with you will tell you that hiring is a crapshoot. They make the best decision they can, knowing inevitably that there are a lot of great people out there that they didn't interview—perhaps someone far better for the job. Like, of course, you.

When you get rejected, remember this: All rejection says is that at one moment in time, for some reason—and it's probably a reason entirely out of your control—you didn't show this particular employer what they needed to see in order to make you an offer. As Maslon's Nora Klaphake says, "You can be just great, but there's just one other person with a more useful background than you." Rejection is not etched in stone. It has no predictive value. Because you've been rejected once or twice or a hundred times before, it doesn't mean you'll be rejected again. At some point, you're going to do something—whether it's responding to a posting or talking to someone at a bar association event or taking a continuing ed class—that's going to lead to a job you love. The point is: you don't know when the very next thing you do will turn into a job opportunity.

* * * SMART HUMAN TRICK * * *

From a recent graduate in Georgia:

"The job I have I like to call "#153" ... this is because it was in fact the one hundred and fifty-third job I had applied for, and the only one from which I got a decent offer. The career services office at school even had a contest for the most rejection letters—which I won by a longshot—and I got a $500 gift certificate toward Bar/Bri!

As a 2L I sent out a ton of letters. That didn't work. I went to a social thing in our town and met one of the partners at the firm. I got a summer job with the mutual understanding that there were no long term possibilities there. By the second month of hard work there I had a standing offer to come back after school as a permanent associate.

This firm couldn't be a more perfect fit for me. AND I'm making more salary-wise than even some of my friends working twice as long a week in big Atlanta firms!"

2. Is There a Job Lurking in That Rejection ...?

Rejection doesn't necessarily mean "no." It's not a guillotine. It doesn't mean you'll <u>never</u> get any job or even this particular job. It just says that at this one moment in time, for some reason—and it might be a reason entirely out of your control—you didn't show this employer what they needed to see in order to make you an offer. That's all. It has *no* predictive value!

Let's talk about all the different ways it can lead to a "yes."

a. The Magic Words That Turn a Rejection Into Job Possibilities: "If Your Needs Change ..."

I've talked with tons of law students who've actually gotten the job of their dreams <u>after</u> they were rejected from it because instead of drowning their sorrows in happy hour, they contacted the employer again and said, "I'm disappointed I'm not going to be working with you now, but *if your needs change*"—that's a magic phrase, because employers' needs do change; people don't show up, they don't work out, budgets open up, more business comes in, people get abducted by aliens—"if your needs change, I hope you'll reconsider me." And sometimes they do get reconsidered, and they do get those jobs.

It's very important to remember that if you try this strategy, you use the right tone in recontacting the employer. What you're striving for, as in every aspect of your job search, is humble confidence. You don't want to badmouth the employer—"That was a really stupid decision and you'll all be sorry, very sorry!" And you don't want to be a low-self-esteem poster child. "I know you don't want me. Nobody wants me. I think I'll eat worms." Be matter-of-fact and friendly. In other words: Be the kind of person you'd want to work with. The feeling you want to engender is, "Gee, maybe we made a mistake about him/her," not, "Thank God we dodged <u>that</u> bullet."

* * * SMART HUMAN TRICK * * *

Third Year student in Florida. He's one of two finalists for a job he really wants. The other candidate gets the job. He writes a letter to the employer, saying, "I am disappointed I'm not going to be working with you, but I understand your decision. I want you to know that I'm still very interested in your firm, and the sense that I would be a good "fit" was only enhanced during my interviews there. If your needs change, I hope you will reconsider me."

The employer was so impressed with his gracious letter, they *created* a job for him!

* * * SMART HUMAN TRICK * * *

Law student in the Pacific Northwest. He applied for a summer job at the Department of Justice in Washington, DC—that's a phenomenal job, by the way—anyway, he applied through standard means and he got a standard-form rejection. The rejection said, "Thank you very much for applying to the Department of Justice. We don't need anybody with your credentials at this time." He wrote back to the person who sent him the letter, and said, "I appreciate that you don't need anybody like me at this time. But I'll tell you what I'm going to do. When Spring Break comes around, I'm going to get in my car and drive to Washington. I'm going to send you postcards along the way, so you'll know when to expect me. Perhaps by the time I get there, your needs will have changed." And he actually did this. When Spring Break came around, he got in his car on the West Coast, and drove across the country, sending postcards from every stop along the way—Yosemite, Mount Rushmore, the Gateway to the West. By the time he got to the Justice Department, everybody in this particular division had heard about him. The lawyer in question had the postcards pinned up next to his desk. They had balloons. When the student pulled up, the lawyer greeted him with, "Well, you have driven over three thousand miles. I suppose the least I can do is interview you." And needless to say, he got the job.

* * * SMART HUMAN TRICK * * *

College senior, getting ready to enter law school in the fall. For the summer before law school, he wanted to work in Washington.

He applied for a bunch of internships in DC, did everything he had to do, including getting a recommendation from his congressman. One hitch: his school forgot to send his transcript! By the time he discovered this, the deadlines had all passed two days earlier. He called the White House, frantic, and begged to be able to send in his transcript late. The woman who answered his call said, "Honey, I got 5,000 complete applications her. I can't make an exception for you—I'd have to do it for everyone."

He was dejected. His faculty advisor said, "Listen—send out another round of letters anyway." One of the internships he applied for was at the Supreme Court. It turns out that the day his new letter arrived, the guy who had previously accepted the internship backed out of it. He got a call at home saying, "We just got your letter. When can you start?"

So he spent the summer before he started law school working for the Curator of the U.S. Supreme Court, where he got to meet the justices, played hoops on the "highest [basketball] court in the land," and spent time at the White House.

* * * SMART HUMAN TRICK * * *

One of the best letters I've ever received is from a young man named Steven Wells. I'll let him speak for himself:

"I moved from California to Nashville so my wife and I could be closer to family. My in-laws knew of a job opening. I needed to retake the bar exam because I wasn't licensed in Tennessee, but this job involved largely federal law, so that would not be a problem. I got the job.

I left that job because it was not what I'd been led to believe it was. The practice was not very challenging, the pay was poor, the trial practice I had been told existed did not, and this fellow planned on remaining several more years (it was a solo practice, and my in-laws had believed he would be retiring within about a year of my arrival). As a result, I decided that I was going to do what I love to do: litigate. So, even though no job prospects were on the horizon and I had not passed the Tennessee bar, I quit. I began printing between 25 and 30 resumes a day and hand-delivering them to the hiring partners at various law firms.

I wound up at one law firm and the receptionist really helped me. She made sure that my resume made it to a name partner and encouraged me to return. The next time I returned, she told me that they had hired a new attorney, but she thought they might be looking for someone else because of how busy they were. I returned a third and fourth time to find the name partner gone each time. The fifth time I returned, she took my resume in to the name partner and I heard him say (he was in the conference room right by the entrance) "Is this the young man who's returned here so many times?" I got to speak to the name partner and we talked for over an hour. He told me that one attorney had just resigned and would be leaving shortly, but they really needed someone with several years' experience, so he would forward my resume to the people that did the hiring because he was not involved in the day-to-day practice of law, but rather he administered law firm business.

I met with the hiring partners (there were two) and they grilled me for over two and a half hours. When I say 'grilled,' I truly mean it. This was an extremely stressful interview, and I believe I handled myself well. I read the biographies of the attorneys in Martindale–Hubbell, but I could find no other information, despite all of my searching. It did reveal that one person with whom I would interview (I'll call him Fred Bloggs) was a philosophy major. About halfway through the interview, the other fellow asked why I would major in philosophy. I gave some interview answer, and then turned to Fred and stated that I believed he also majored in philosophy. I found out later that this really impressed the two of them.

*I had been practicing my "Miss Americas" [answers to questions
you know you'll get], and they did ask me many of them: Tell me about
yourself, what are your strengths, etc. I had practiced them so many
times I had them down cold, but I did not give that impression. One of
the personal aspects I gave in my answer to 'tell me about yourself' is
that I have some moxie, for lack of a better term. I do not like to let my
fears get the best of me and so, because I am claustrophobic, I took up
caving in college.*

*After I answered the question, I turned it around to them and
asked, "Is that what you are looking for?" They seemed to have liked
that answer, and we established a real rapport. I was well prepared for
the question of why I left my previous job, because I had only been there
for a few months. Employers are obviously not looking forward to a
potential employee who might leave after a few months. This firm is a
strongly litigation-oriented firm, so I told them that I took that job
because I had been told that there was a lot of litigation and that after
six months that trial practice was just not there.*

*That was on a Thursday, and they said they would let me know
their decision within a couple of weeks. The next Monday, they wanted
me to come in and talk to them. I wasn't eager to do so because I had
been walking around downtown Nashville on a really hot, humid day,
and my face was quite red, my shirt was extremely wrinkled, and I had
lost my top button. Nonetheless, I went back to see them and they
wanted to have another interview, this time with the office manager
there. She'd been with the firm for over 25 years and they wanted to
explain their way of doing things and give me an opportunity to ask any
questions I hadn't asked previously. I met with them for over two hours
again this time, and they offered me the job. They told me that I "was
not what we were looking for," they really wanted someone with several
years' experience, but my persistence and motivation spoke well of me
and thus they wanted me on board. Fred also told me later that I
reacted very well to the stress of the interview and told me that if you
can't interview, you can't try a case.*

*I have been with the firm for about a month now, and I've already
tried a small case of my own. I won!*

I absolutely love this job!"

B. IF YOU FEEL YOU REALLY HIT IT OFF WITH THE EMPLOYER (OR SOME OF THE PEOPLE WITH WHOM YOU INTERVIEWED) BUT YOU DIDN'T GET AN OFFER ... THEY JUST MIGHT BE THE KEY TO A GREAT JOB SOMEWHERE ELSE. TURN THE REJECTION INTO AN INFORMATIONAL INTERVIEW

Here's the situation. If you haven't faced it yet, you will. You go
on an interview with an employer, and you talk with several people in
a row. In a law firm, that's typically a callback interview (that is, the
interview after an initial, screening interview). You really hit it off
with at least one or two of them, and you leave the interview feeling
really good. You just *know* you're going to get this job! And then ...
you get rejected. And what happens? Those people you loved thirty
seconds ago? Now how do you feel about them? They misled you!

They made you feel as though they liked you! You want them to die a slow, painful death, right?

Mistake! Getting rejected in that situation doesn't mean that your instincts are all wrong, that you thought you got along with people who really didn't like you. They may be just as disappointed that you didn't get the job as *you* are. They may have lobbied hard for you. Here's what you do: Get in touch with (either by e-mail or voice mail) the person you really hit it off with, and say this: "I'm disappointed I'm not going to be working with you, but I really enjoyed talking with you and I respect your advice. Can you suggest to me other people I should be talking to, other things I should be doing?" Then call and talk to them "live."

Here's why this works. You can be sure that anybody who does what you want to do knows a bunch of other people who do the same thing. I know lots of law students who've gotten great jobs through people they got along with, who just happened to work with employers who rejected them!

* * * SMART HUMAN TRICK * * *

Female student, Midwestern law school. She interviews with a family court commission. The interview goes extremely well, but she didn't get the job. She calls back to follow up, and asks what she might do to improve her chances in the future. The interviewer tells her, "You were great, it's just that somebody else had fifteen years' worth of mediation experience."

Four months later, the interviewer calls her out of the blue, and says, "If you're still available I know another commissioner who needs help. I raved about you. Are you interested?"

She got the job.

c. If They Say 'Keep in Touch With Us' or 'Contact Us Again Next Year' or Something Like That, Then *Do It*.

Students often ask me, 'Well, gee, aren't they just being polite?' Nope! Trust me. They don't feel the need to be polite. If someone doesn't want you to contact them again, they can say 'Thanks and good luck!' and leave it at that. If they invite further action, *take it.*

How do you keep in touch? Do you send them an e-mail every few months saying, 'Do you want me yet'? Not exactly.

You *do* want to make sure you contact them every few months, but here's what to do. For a start, notify them every time you have a change in status: When you get new grades (if they're good), if you get new clinical, externship, or other experience, volunteer or paid, if someone else makes you an offer (nothing makes you as desirable as someone else wanting you—it's just like dating).

There's also nothing wrong with sending a card every few months talking about what you're doing, and reiterating your interest in working for them: 'I just wanted to let you know that I'm still very interested in working with you, and I hope you'll keep me in mind if and when something opens up.'

My favourite strategy for keeping in touch, however, goes along with the idea of keeping your focus on the employer—not you—throughout your job search. Here's what you do. When you're casually reading the paper, magazines, whatever professional publications you peruse, keep an eye out for references to the employer, your contact(s) there, or hobbies and interests you know your contacts have. Google them. And when anything shows up, clip, copy or download it, and send it to the employer—with a note attached, saying "I thought you might find this interesting . . ." and reiterating your interest in working for them.

So, for instance, let's say you see in the paper a little blurb about the employer winning a big lawsuit, or lassoing a new client—any news bit. Or let's say that you know your contact there is particularly interested in Egypt, and you see in the newspaper that there's going to be an exhibit at the local museum about the pharaohs. Send it! An obvious no-no here is to avoid sending anything embarrassing to the employer. I spoke with one student who was researching an employer and found that one of the partners had just been disbarred for defrauding a client. Yipes! No need to remind them of *that!*

d. If They Say, "No, Thanks, But You Should Contact X At X"— Do It!

Sometimes an employer, in rejecting you, will put you on to another employer. It's easy to think that if *they* don't want you, why should you contact their *friends?* Are they serious?

In a word: Yep. When someone puts you on to someone else, they are implicitly putting their reputation on the line for you. If I tell you to give someone a call, you're going to call them and say, "Kimm Walton told me to contact you." That means that I'm willing to stake my reputation that you're not going to embarrass me. *Nobody's* going to do that lightly, so when people make you that offer: "Give so-and-so a call"—do it!

As American's Traci Jenkins says, "They're not just being polite! No one has to offer help or advice. They can just say 'Thank you and good luck'—if they offer more, take it . . . and thank them!"

That "thank you" part is extremely important. When someone puts you on to someone else, they've become a contact, and they should be treated the same way. As we go into in Chapter 10, you need to keep them up-to-date on your success with people they put you on to, and thank them frequently. Even if they haven't made you an offer, they've done you a *big* favour.

E. "NOT NOW" DOESN'T MEAN "NOT EVER." PERSISTENCE PAYS OFF!

Remember, when you're applying for jobs, you're asking employers to consider you in one small sliver of time. It may well be that jobs open up *outside* of that time frame . . . or it might be that in being persistent, in trying again and again, you show employers a quality they really respect.

I've heard tons of stories about this. I talked to a student at one law school who was just dying to work for an airline's in-house counsel's office. He tried every week for six months, calling the general counsel's secretary and pleading his case. He was polite, friendly . . . but determined. Finally after six months, on one of his Friday phone calls, she said, "All right . . . come on in." He wound up with the job.

A famous story along these lines involves David Falk, Michael Jordan's sports agent. When he graduated from law school he contacted ProServ, a blue-chip firm representing athletes. He got rejected. He called *every day* for a month after that . . . and got the job.

* * * SMART HUMAN TRICK * * *

A 1L at a Southern school set his sights on one particular firm. He contacted them, and they told him, "Sorry. We don't take summer clerks." They let him talk to a couple of associates, but that was it. He cooled his heels for a year, and then applied again during his Second year. Same response; no luck. He gets to Third year. Now he's waited two years for this firm, with no success. They weren't doing on-campus interviewing, and hadn't put up any job notices. But he contacted them again anyway. He didn't have a stellar record—no great job experience, no top grades. But they made him an offer anyway . . . because they said they admired his persistence!

* * * SMART HUMAN TRICK * * *

A 3L at a Northeastern school had her heart set on a particular small firm. She went on other interviews, but nothing interested her except this firm, and they wouldn't bite. She graduated without a job. And in fact, she was unemployed for *thirteen months* after graduation, all the while politely—but persistently—staying in contact with this one firm. They hemmed and hawed, and she finally said, "I'm so confident this is the right match that I'm willing to volunteer for a month, for free, to prove it." She got the offer!

* * * SMART HUMAN TRICK * * *

Law student on the East Coast whose dream is to work for the DA's office. He tries, starting as a 1L, with no success. He gets a chance to meet the District Attorney at a bar association function, and states his interest in working for him. The DA tells him to "Give me a call." He calls ... nothing.

After that, every three months, he'd call. "Hi. It's me again. Anything open up?" The DA's response would be, "Nope. But call me back."

He did. Every three months ... for *four and a half years.* Finally, the DA said, "Yep. Come on in."

Needless to say ... he got the job.

These are pretty extreme stories, to be sure. And there's definitely a point at which persistence becomes stalking. As a rule of thumb, you want to stop pursuing an employer when they take out a restraining order on you ... or when their tone turns nasty, whichever comes first. You want to be polite, cheery, and determined ... but recognize that even if a particular job doesn't pan out now, it may at some point down the road. Or you may find something else along the way that you like just as much!

3. WHEN YOU GET REJECTIONS, DON'T IMBUE EMPLOYERS WITH MAGIC POWERS THEY DON'T HAVE

When you get rejected, it's way too easy to attribute magical powers of insight to employers. You think: When they rejected you, it's because with their magic superhero laser vision they looked into your soul, and that showed them that you're simply not good enough.

Don't kid yourself. Remember: employers don't have a crystal ball. They're operating by analogy: Because you did X in the past, you'll do Y in the future. On top of that, they are going on the basis of very skimpy information when they make hiring decisions. A stinking resume. A twenty-minute interview. You are a much more interesting, complex, dynamic human being than you can get across in the hiring process. Don't give employers the power to convince you that you can't get a job, because they don't have that power over you if you don't give it to them. Don't give it to them!

You'd be just horrified if you knew how little attention some employers pay to the correspondence they get. I've talked with more than one Career Services Director who sent student resumes to an employer, along with a transmittal letter saying "Here are the resumes of our students ..." only to *themselves* get a rejection letter from the employer! At one Georgia law school a firm sent rejections to *five* non-applying students!

So don't suffuse rejections with importance. Employers aren't paying as much attention as *you* are.

4. DON'T LOOK TO EMPLOYERS TO VALIDATE YOU

You may be looking for an employer to put the imprimatur of approval on your career choice, so you can say to yourself and everyone else, "See? I was *right* to do this!"

In a word: Don't. Your law degree is valuable for a million reasons, no matter what you do with it. Don't look to others for validation. As the actress Doris Roberts says, "I fear rejection like anyone, but I say to myself, 'What can they do to me?' If I go to an audition, before I put my hand on that doorknob I say to myself, 'I'm not here to be validated. I'm here to get a job.' "

5. A REJECTION THAT'S REALLY RUDE IS NOT A REFLECTION ON *YOU*. IT'S A REFLECTION ON *THEM*

Excuse me while I climb up onto my soapbox.

There.

I think employers who are rude to law student applicants are *morons*. I've told you many times that the legal community is small, and it's important not to burn bridges. Well, it's important for *employers,* too, but they sometimes seem to forget that. What's wrong with a gracious note thanking you for applying, and wishing you luck with your career, hmm?

Apparently being even civil is too much of a burden for some employers. I've heard all manner of rude rejections. It particularly hurts when you've gone through several rounds of interviews with an employer, and *then* they reject you badly. One law student on the West Coast told me about an employer with whom she'd interviewed in Nevada. She'd flown out and spoken for two hours with each of three lawyers at the firm. After she got home, she didn't hear anything for a month. She left a voice mail for one of the lawyers, asking when she might expect to hear something. No response. She said, "I don't even mind the rejection as much as the fact that I didn't hear *anything.* Couldn't they tell me no? Didn't I deserve a response?" *Of course* she did!

When an employer rejects you rudely, remember three things: First, it's not about you. It's about *them.* Second, remember that you'll have many chances to prove them wrong. Go on and be a brilliant success. That's the way to make them feel stupid about the way they treated you. And finally: Resolve that when you're a lawyer, you'll never, *ever* treat a law student that way!

6. VENT APPROPRIATELY

Let's face it. Rejection stinks on ice. When you get rejected, I'm not suggesting that you just plaster on a fake smile and soldier on uninterrupted. It's important to vent. But it's even more important to vent *appropriately.* Remember, it's not *every* employer who rejected you. And they didn't reject *you.* They rejected whatever you showed them, be it a letter, a resume, twenty minutes of what you showed them in an interview.

So, go ahead and vent. Toss back a cold one with friends. Call a buddy and bitch all you want. (Do *not,* however, memorialize your feelings about the employer in an e-mail, an IM, or on your blog, website, at autoadmit.com, or any social networking site. That stuff lives forever, and you don't want it to.) You know what Abraham Lincoln did when people did something nasty to him (and let's face it, a lot of people did)? He would write them a truly angry letter, unloading everything he thought of them. But he never *sent* those letters. He put them in a drawer. The whole therapy was in the writing.

It's important to remember that circumstances—and people—change. You never know when people will show up in your life again. The employer who rejects you today may be your colleague down the road . . . and you don't want their lasting memory of you to be an e-mail reading, "Oh, yeah? Well f* * * you!"

Abe Lincoln once again provides a useful example. When he didn't get the U.S. Senate nomination in 1855, his wife, Mary, bitterly resented the politicians who hadn't backed him. Lincoln didn't. He wrote to one of them, Norman Judd, the leader of a small Democratic group, and said he didn't hold Judd's lack of support against him. Later, guess who nominated Lincoln for President? That's right. Norman Judd.

No matter how crappy employers are to you, rise above it. At most a gracious note, "While of course I'm disappointed I won't be working with you, I respect your decision, perhaps we'll have a chance to work together in future . . ." something along those lines, in your own words, should be your parting shot—if you need a parting shot at all.

7. WHAT YOU TELL YOURSELF ABOUT EMPLOYERS AFTER YOU'RE REJECTED IS REALLY, REALLY IMPORTANT. IN SHORT: GET OVER IT AND GET ON WITH IT

As is true in every aspect of your life, the way you characterize something determines how you feel about it. What makes "Look at the bright side" such difficult advice, however, is that it's not natural to do that! As Jonatan Haidt, author of "The Happiness Hypothesis," points out, we are "hard wired to emphasize the negative. Bad is stronger than good. Responses to threats and unpleasantness are faster, stronger, and harder to inhibit than responses to opportunities and pleasures." It's difficult. But it's *necessary*.

In one of the opening quotes to this chapter, I quoted Lance Armstrong in "DodgeBall." As he said there, he was diagnosed with lung, brain and testicular cancer simultaneously. Most people would feel, understandably enough, hopeless. Not him. He said, "Cancer chose the wrong body to invade."

What an amazing attitude. Similarly, Thomas Edison knew how to frame adversity. He wanted to create a viable store battery. He failed 10,000 times. When ridiculed, he said, "Why, I haven't failed. I've just found 10,000 ways that don't work."

A less familiar example is Alan Newton, a man who was released from prison in 2006 after spending twenty years wrongfully imprisoned for rape. If there ever were grounds to be angry, that would be it. He said, "I let go of the anger. It wasn't doing me any good."

For gosh sakes, you can certainly muster some positive self-talk about job rejections! You can't control the first thought that pops into your head ... but you can reconfigure it immediately into something useful. When you get rejected, you might think, "Great. Nobody loves me. Everybody hates me. I think I'll eat worms." But you can *tell* yourself, "OK. These rejections suck. I didn't want them. But I *will* get a job. There are plenty of ways to find employers, and all I need is one job. No matter what hasn't worked for me ... something *will*."

You might be thinking self-talk is goofy. There is a lot of happy talk that's useless, cat-poster philosophy. "You can be anything you want to be." Oh, really? I want to play for the NBA. I'm a middle-aged, 5'1" woman. I don't *think* so! But there is a lot of valuable self-talk, specifically targeted at situations that face you, and it *does* work. Try it!

A. Keep Rejection In Perspective. It's Just *Words*

Being told 'no' is never pleasant. But don't roll it over and over in your mind and turn it into something it's not. Next time you get a rejection letter, take a good look at yourself in the mirror. You're not cut or bruised. It's just words, for gosh sakes. Sometimes it's really *mean* words, but still, just words. As I stated earlier, I know students who paper their walls with rejection letters. I guess there's some masochistic humor in it, but really—are you going to have an easier time projecting enthusiasm when you wake up every day reminding yourself of the less-than-happy aspects of your life? Do you have pictures of your former romantic partners on your refrigerator door, as well?

When you get rejected, do what you can to forget about it as soon as possible. Do *something* every day. As Theodore Roosevelt said, "Black care (depression) rarely sits behind a rider whose pace is fast enough."

Try one or more of the hundreds of things in Chapter 10 that will get you on the road to a job. Doing nothing creates anxiety; it makes you feel you have no choices. In fact, psychologists say that behavior change often precedes and causes attitude change. Even if you *think* nothing will work, try anyway. And remember: no matter what, you're going to get a job. *Everybody* gets a job. This is a temporary hiccup on your career path. That's all.

B. Avoid Conducting a Post Mortem on Rejections by Demanding Reasons From Employers. And if You Do it Anyway ... Be Very, Very Careful.

One of the most frequent questions I get is, "Can I call an employer and ask them why they rejected me?" Of course, I can't throw myself in your path and stop you from reaching for the phone. *But most of the time—I would if I could.*

Here's why. Put yourself in the shoes of the employer getting a "Why did you reject me?" call from a student. It's highly unlikely you're going to say anything terribly meaningful. And you're *really* going to resent being put on the spot. Even if those both weren't true, look at who you're talking to: a future lawyer. You're hardly going to say anything that could be the basis for a lawsuit, even a frivolous one! "We've hired enough minorities already," "We never hire young married women, they just quit when they have kids," "You're just too old." No! You'll look for some bromide like, "It was a really tough decision," "We really liked you, but ..." or even more likely, no response at all.

This isn't to say that it *never* works. There's no job search strategy, no matter how unbelievably lame, that fails to work in every single situation. Having "tanning" on your resume as a hobby would probably attract one in a million employers. I have talked with a tiny handful of students who actually learned something useful in contacting an employer who rejected them, but you know what? It was never about them and how they interviewed, or what was on their resume. Inevitably, it was "We liked you, but someone applied for the job with a whole lot more relevant experience," or something like that.

Having said that, if you continually apply for jobs that your credentials say ought to be coming your way, there's something else going on. There's something in your letter, your resume, your interviewing, or your party patter. I'll bet you dollars to doughnuts that it's a simple issue, and a quick fix. The best way to figure it out is to talk to Career Services at school, and ask for a letter/resume review and/or a mock interview. It's a time-effective way to get your career back on track, without wondering after every interview why you didn't get the job.

c. DON'T GENERALIZE A FEW EMPLOYERS WHO REJECT YOU INTO THE ENTIRE LEGAL MARKET

I have spoken with many students who'll tell me dejectedly, "Nothing works. I can't get a job." I'll ask if they got a list of people to talk to from Career Services. They'll generally reply, "Yeah. That didn't work."

When I delve a little further, let me tell you the general pattern of what I hear:

1. Student goes to Career Services, states an interest, and gets a list of fifteen alums to talk to.

2. Student goes home, e-mails three of the alums, asking for advice.

3. One of the alums doesn't respond. A second one responds that he's too busy to talk right now. A third offers an informational interview.

4. Student goes to the informational interview. It generates some insights but no job interviews or offers.

5. Ergo ... nothing works.

Notice the "telescoping" that happens here? In point of fact, this student hasn't been rejected by *anybody*. It's too easy to be dispirited! As Suffolk's Alyssa Hammond points out, "Don't be put off by a failed response to one e-mail. Be persistent. People are busy!"

There was a student in Chicago who was reduced to tears by rejection. She was just lovely and I felt so bad for her. She was dying to do litigation. She'd leaned on her summer employer, a judge, to help, but it hadn't worked. She moaned, "Nobody takes me seriously. Everybody tries to convince me to do transactional work." *Nobody. Everybody.* Whenever I hear those words, my antennae go up. I asked her, "When you say 'everybody,' who do you mean?" It turns out she'd had two informal lunches with two lawyers her judge had put her onto, and they hadn't been encouraging. *Two people.* Hardly *everybody!*

Another student, this one on the West Coast, nailed thirty on-campus interviews with large law firms. He went to eight of them, and got no call-backs. He cancelled the rest. "They're just wasting my time," he said. No question of what he'd done wrong in the interviews, how he could improve. Just a complete write-off of twenty-two employers who *wanted* to talk to him!

In Chapter 10, we talk all about the hundreds of things you can do to get your foot in the door practically anywhere. Don't let one, or two, or a handful of "No's" deter you from pursuing what you want!

D. Don't Reject Yourself

Don't let a couple, or even a bunch, of rejections make you denigrate yourself and what you have to offer. As Gina Rowsam points out, "Without even realizing it, many students talk themselves right out of an opportunity before they even have a chance to give it a good try. They say things to themselves and to others like, 'Why would they want me, I haven't done ... fill in the blank?' They don't do this once or twice, but chronically and repeatedly. It keeps them in a position of not being able to put their best foot forward. When they do have the good fortune of getting an interview, they can't take advantage of it. I tell them: study the business practices of commissioned sales folks and see how *they* handle rejection. They learn not to take it personally, but to see it as part of the process that will get them to the ultimate 'Yes.' "

8. Don't Overlook *Practical* Reasons for Rejections

Let's say that you call me and tell me that you're having a dinner party, everybody's bringing a dish, and my assignment is Fettuccine Alfredo. In case you're not familiar with this Italian classic, it consists of butter, heavy cream, and parmesan cheese—which is why it is euphemistically known as a "heart attack on a plate"—and, obviously, fettuccine. Let's say that I show up at your house with a covered dish, and I say, "By the way—I had everything but the fettuccine. I hope you don't mind." Unless you want bland cheese soup, you *do* mind. Fettuccine is a crucial element of the recipe!

Sometimes, when you get rejected, it's because there's something crucial that the employer just can't live without. It's not all about personality fit, you know. If an employer has needs you just can't meet—professional needs, that is—you just can't blame them for rejecting you. If they need a full-time associate for a huge case they're working on right now and you won't be graduating for another six months, that's not the job for you. If they need help in their Schenectady office and you want to live in Indianapolis, that's a problem. If they have a Korean immigrant clientele who are largely non-English-speaking, if you can't speak Korean, you won't be their particular bomb.

There was a student I talked with in Alabama who was dying to work at one particular small firm in town, part-time while he was in school. They wanted five mornings a week, and he could only manage two with his class schedule. He talked to an old clerk there who said they like to have a warm body there in the mornings to run over to the courthouse if need be. He was frustrated that he wasn't getting the job, but really . . . you can understand the employer's point. If in some fundamental way you don't match their requirements, it doesn't mean you won't be a brilliant lawyer, it's just that that particular job isn't the right one for you, right now.

This isn't to say you shouldn't reach for jobs beyond your current "skill set." As I talk about in Chapter 7 on Correspondence, you *should* respond to postings for jobs whose requirements you don't precisely fit, because you don't know whether the "perfect candidate" will apply. But by the same token you can't be angry if you don't *get* those jobs, because it may not be obvious which requirements the employer can't live without.

9.   NOT GETTING A JOB THROUGH ON-CAMPUS INTERVIEWS IS MEANINGLESS

It breaks my heart to see how many students come up empty-handed at the end of on-campus interview season and figure . . . that's it. "I'm unemployable." It can *hammer* your self-respect.

Don't let that happen. OCI season is a tiny fraction of what's "out there." It represents the tiny minority of employers large and institutional enough to know how many people they're going to need far in advance—*and* can spare the personnel necessary to participate in the interview process. On top of that, not every employer in that category will visit every school. The fact is, the job you'll love is unlikely to come to school to find you. And even if it *does,* the best thing about you might not be your resume . . . and that's all OCI employers get to see when they make a decision about interviewing you!

Chapter 10 has hundreds of OCI "work-arounds," ways to get to employers through ways other than on-campus interviews. Ironically, career experts agree that if you have to work a little harder to find a job, you're more likely to ultimately wind up with something you love than if a job fell into your lap via OCI. The extra thought you have to put into researching and contacting employers means you'll make better choices. So take heart if OCI doesn't pan out!

* * * SMART HUMAN TRICK * * *

Second career student with a background in Human Resources. She is rejected by every OCI employer. She contacts employment groups at some of these large law firms directly, explaining why her background would be perfect for them.

She winds up with three interviews ... and three offers.

10. THE HIDDEN BENEFITS OF REJECTION

Benefits, you say? What could possibly be helpful about rejection? There are a bunch of things that may not be obvious to you when you're opening that 'Thanks-but-no-thanks' letter!

A. MANY TIMES, YOU'LL GET REJECTED FROM JOBS YOU WOULD HAVE HATED

Give employers at least the benefit of the doubt when it comes to figuring out 'fit.' I know that sounds like bizspeak, but the fact is, they know the personalities at the office and you don't. If they're all major partiers and you're a quiet intellectual, you could be right in every skills-based way—but you'd hate the environment. If they play bridge for fun and you smash beer cans against your forehead and belch the alphabet, you wouldn't be any happier with them than they would be with you. And maybe, just maybe, they figured that out before you.

Your personality will make some jobs great for you, and some unbearable. It's true of everyone. I'm reminded of the Enron trial—the trial of Ken Lay and Jeffrey Skilling. In *The New York Times,* Jamie Wareham, global head of litigation for the law firm Paul, Hastings, commented that CEOs make difficult witnesses for their lawyers, because the same qualities of toughness, charisma and confidence that propelled them to the top translate poorly in the courtroom. "They tend to have an unwillingness or inability to reflect self-doubt. Companies that are led well are not led well by people who in public express self-doubt. But juries like that. They want to see that doubt, that humility." Lay and Skilling couldn't project it, and they were both convicted. So what made them great CEOs made them *lousy* witnesses.

I talked with a student in Oregon who had done some volunteer work where she helped victims of domestic violence. She really wanted a judicial clerkship, and she'd just interviewed with a female judge. "I got a rejection, and I'm really bumming about it," she said. It turns out that in the interview, the judge took a look at her resume and scoffed at her domestic violence experience. "It's usually the woman doing the hitting anyway," said the judge. The student responded, "I'd respectfully disagree with you on that, Your Honor," and she said after that, "We just didn't hit it off." I asked her if she believed in the work she'd done on domestic violence, and she said she really had. So I asked, "Do you really think you'd have enjoyed working for this particular judge ... no matter how much you want a judicial clerkship?" Remember, when you work for a judge, you're working in pretty close quarters. It's not like you can avoid them. When she ruminated on it, she realized she really wouldn't have liked it. And when you don't get jobs you would have hated ... that's the Universe working out just fine!

B. REJECTION FORCES YOU TO HONE YOUR JOB SEARCH SKILLS

Now, you may be thinking, 'I'd rather not get the rejections and leave my skills unhoned, thank you very much.' But the fact is, you're going to have at least a dozen different jobs when you leave law school. Even if somebody dropped a job in your lap through on-campus interviews while you're in school, once you graduate, that OCI option is over. When you're ready for job number two, you can't call Career Services, rub your hands together in anticipation, and say, 'Alrighty then! When does OCI start?' The skills you're learning in this book are ones that you're going to use to nail great opportunities for a lifetime. You'll follow the advice in this book, zeroing in on activities and approaches that work for you, and winnowing out ones that don't. The sooner your job search skills are in tip-top shape, the better opportunities you'll have—for the rest of your life.

C. REJECTION OPENS YOU TO OPPORTUNITIES YOU WOULDN'T HAVE HAD OTHERWISE

The great Abbie Willard, of the University of Chicago Law School, calls this 'opening yourself to the Universe.' When you're facing a pile of rejections and a future entirely populated by Kraft Macaroni and Cheese, that may seem like cold comfort, but it shouldn't. The fact is, if you're tied down to a job, you're doing that job. What you might have become is put off, at least for now, because you're busy. When you're unemployed—aaah. Who knows what's in store for you?

By way of personal example—which I'm inevitably going to use again in this book—I experienced exactly this phenomenon when I graduated from law school. I was unemployed, and promptly moved into a room in my parents' basement. I went on whatever interviews I got, and was roundly rejected by all of them. I delivered meals to invalids, waited tables, scratched out the dough I could. I took on whatever temporary writing projects came my way. It was around that time that I started thinking, if you like to write, how about writing ... study aids? I came up with *Law In A Flash*. The only reason I'm mentioning *Law In A Flash* again is to show that if I'd gotten an offer from my summer employer, if *anybody, anybody* had made me an offer third year ... *Law In A Flash* never would have existed. I wouldn't have had the motivation to create it because I'd have been gainfully employed.

This same experience has happened to a bunch of people. Not *Law In a Flash* specifically, of course, but the same kind of thing. Mark Cuban, the fabulously successful businessman and 'out-there' owner of the Dallas Mavericks, owned a bar when he was going to college at Indiana/Bloomington. It failed. As he says now, 'If that bar had worked out better, I'd be tending bar now.'

Or take Supreme Court Justice Ruth Bader Ginsberg. She wanted to be a diva. When asked if she'd trade it all in for that dream, she said, "As I get older I realize I couldn't be a diva into my 60s, 70s, 80s—but law is something you can do forever. So as I get older law looks better and better."

The fact is, early rejection gives you the opportunity to create your own Horatio Alger story. Early success is no gift. If you don't believe me, you haven't seen enough *Diff'rent Strokes* reunion specials. Every VH1 "Behind the Scenes" story has the same arc: early success, tons of money, decline into drug use and a tragic traffic accident. David O. Selznick was ruined by having one of his early movies happen to be "Gone With The Wind." He spent the rest of his life trying to recreate it. He made a bunch of movies that by any other measure would have been a great achievement ... but they weren't "Gone With The Wind." I read a great book called "The Jock's Itch" about professional athletes, and how life is so difficult for them when their careers are over, at a time in life when most of us are just getting revved up. Believe me, it's nothing to be envied.

11. There Are Certain Jobs You Can *Only* Get by Tolerating Gobs of Rejection—and They Tend to Be the Most Glamorous Jobs

If you're interested in a job in sports or entertainment—and judging from my e-mails, there's a strong possibility you are—anybody will tell you that you have to be 'persistent.' Persistence is a code word for soldiering on in the face of ongoing rejection. It means you have to put up with rejection, often over and over and over again. I talk all about nailing those jobs later in this book, but the point I want to make here is that if you want a job that everyone else you know also wants, then that means you're going to have to outlast them. Just like *Survivor*. When you're after something ultra-competitive, put rejections in perspective by keeping your eye on the prize.

12. If You're Seriously Bummed Out, Take a Vacation From Job Searching. Gather Information and Do Things That Make You Feel Good About Yourself and Your Prospects

In Chapter 10, we talk about dozens of activities that aren't overtly job seeking. Informational interviews, attending bar association functions and CLEs, and dozens more ... they all position you to get valuable advice and insights, without ever asking for a job or risk being rejected.

When you're licking your rejection wounds, these kinds of activities are a great way to stay connected without putting yourself in a vulnerable position. So consider taking a month, ramping back on your search, and doing some of those activities. You might nail a great job without even trying!

13. THE ONLY WAY TO GET REVENGE ON EMPLOYERS WHO REJECT YOU IS TO GO ON AND SUCCEED *IN SPITE OF THEIR REJECTION*

Trust me, I understand rejection. I've been rejected a million times. As I stated earlier, my dream is to win an Oscar for Best Original Screenplay. I've written about twenty movie scripts pursuing that dream. But I've learned something interesting: People who win my Oscar tend to do a lot better when they can actually convince a movie studio to make a movie out of one of their scripts. I've found that's a lot more difficult than actually *writing* a movie script!

The first time I ever sent a script to Hollywood, well—it was my first script, of course. The ink was hardly dry, and I had it in an envelope on its way to an agent in Los Angeles. Man, I was *ready*. I could see myself at the premiere. I envisioned the Oscars. I'm in a slinky outfit, thanking the members of the Academy. I had my speech written.

Well, I got that script back a week later in an envelope, with a note attached to it. I'll never forget what the note said:

> *Dear Miss Walton,*
>
> *Enclosed please find your script. I was not sufficiently enthralled to read past page ten. (It was a 120–page script.)*
>
> *However, I encourage you to send your script to other agents, because I'm confident you'll find somebody whose standards are considerably lower than mine.*

Aarrghh! My family had to hide sharp objects from me for about a month after that. It's been years, and I'm still sending out scripts. Why? *Because I want to win an Oscar.* And if I *stop* sending out my scripts, what's the only outcome I'm guaranteeing? That I'm never going to win, right? If I keep sending them out, maybe . . .

I don't care what job you want. I don't care about your grades, where you go to school, the job market. I don't care how many people tell you you can't get that job. You'll have that job long before I win my Oscar. Why? Because ultimately, there are only two things you can do with rejection, aren't there? You can accept it. You can believe it. You can internalize it, and you can quit looking, sit at home, drink beer, eat cheese puffs, and watch reality shows for the rest of your life. Nobody will stop you.

But is that what you *want*? Do you want employers to hear about you later on, that you gave up on yourself, and have them react, 'Phew! Thank God we avoided *that* loser!' No! You want them to think, 'We rejected *that* student? What were we *thinking?*'

So acknowledge outright what you know in your heart of hearts is true: There's not just one job that's going to make you happy. No one employer controls your future. There are hundreds of jobs that'll make you happy, and there are hundreds of ways to get those jobs—we'll be talking about all of them. And the *only* way to get revenge on employers who reject you is to go on and live that happy life. That *is* within your control.

I went to law school at Case Western in Cleveland. When I was a Second Year, I nailed down a summer job with a relatively large law firm; they had twenty-two summer clerks. At the end of the summer, they extended offers of permanent employment to twenty-one of the twenty-two.

I was number twenty-two.

Yeah, that came up in interviews once in a while after that. It came up with my parents every night over the dinner table for the next five years. But in the mysterious way the Lord works, guess which American law firm does not appear in my book, *America's Greatest Places To Work With A Law Degree?* Bwa ha ha ha ha! Now to be perfectly fair, I did talk to associates there who hated it—so I didn't besmirch my integrity by not including them. But you see my point: Rejection does not define your career unless you allow it to.

Who knows what fate has in store for you? I guarantee you it's not a lifetime of rejection. It's just a necessary bump in the road. Get over it— and get on with it!

*

Behind Every Great Success Lies Failure

She graduated number three in her class at Stanford Law School. The only job she was offered upon graduation? Legal secretary.

You know her as ...

Former Supreme Court Justice Sandra Day O'Connor.

He was cut from his ninth grade basketball team.

You know him as ...

Legendary basketball player Michael Jordan.

He was told that his sitcom scored so poorly on audience tests that the network would not pick it up.

You know him as ...

Jerry Seinfeld, and the show: *Seinfeld*.

He was rejected by the first twenty-seven publishers he approached.

You know him as ...

Dr. Seuss, who sold more than 100 million books in 20 languages.

He was almost fired from his first job, at J.C. Penney, because his bosses felt "He doesn't belong in retail."

You know him as ...

Sam Walton, founder of Wal Mart.

When she first went to New York in search of acting jobs, she was told she was too shy ever to make it as an actress.

You know her as ...

Lucille Ball.

Her early bosses at CNN said: "Get her off the air!"

You know her as ...

Katie Couric.

He struck out in his first thirteen at-bats in major league baseball. He requested that his manager send him back down to the minors. His manager refused.

You know him as . . .

Willie Mays.

He failed in business in 1831. He was defeated when he ran for the legislature in 1832. He failed in *another* business in 1833. He was elected to the legislature in 1834, but suffered an immediate personal setback when his sweetheart died in 1835. He had a nervous breakdown in 1836. He was defeated for Speaker in 1838, for Elector in 1840, for Land Officer in 1843. He was elected to Congress in 1846, but defeated when he ran for reelection in 1848. He was defeated for Vice President in 1856, and defeated for the Senate in 1858.

You know him as . . .

Abraham Lincoln, elected President of the United States in 1860.

This show received the lowest test audience score in the history of the BBC.

You know it as . . .

The multiple Emmy winner *The Office.*

She was a failure as a newswoman at a television station in Baltimore, the assessment being that she was considered too passionate and emotional for the role.

You know her as . . .

Oprah Winfrey.

He dropped out of Juilliard to play saxophone in a swing band. While technically proficient, he had difficulty with the bebop improvisations the band played. When a genius sax player joined the band, he realized that "You either have it or you don't . . . so I decided that, if that was as far as I could go, I was in the wrong profession." So he quit the band and went to business school.

You know him as . . .

Former Fed Chairman Alan Greenspan.

He was a movie producer and director. His first movie after World War II performed so badly at the box office that he had to sell his movie studio.

You know him as . . .

Frank Capra, and the movie: *"It's a Wonderful Life."*

Her first movie appearance was in *A Certain Sacrifice,* an awful 8–mm student film where her most memorable line was "I'm a do-do girl, and I'm looking for my do-do boy."

You know her as . . .

Madonna.

An out-of-work architect named Alfred Botts created a game he called "Criss–Cross" to support his family. He showed it to toy companies, who condemned it as "too intellectual" and said it had no potential.

After regaining his job as an architect, it was seventeen years before he and a friend started manufacturing the game themselves. For four years, the game eked out barely enough to support the friend. Suddenly sales bloomed.

It became the second-best selling game in history.

You know it as ...

Scrabble.

He was a television producer. While producing a show in the early 1960s, he came up with an idea that he pitched to MGM Studios. They turned it down. Desilu bought it and sold the idea to NBC, which financed a pilot. NBC saw it, and rejected it. They financed another pilot, and bought the show.

You know the producer as ...

Gene Roddenberry, and the show: *Star Trek*.

He came up with the idea for a detective series. He sent the first story to a publisher.

It was returned unread.

He sent it to a third, fourth, and fifth publisher.

It was rejected each time.

Finally, a publisher agreed to publish it in a Christmas magazine.

It was read and quickly forgotten.

A pirated version of the story was published in a magazine called *Lippencott*. The wife of the publisher read it and liked it.

It wasn't until five years later that a story called "The Scandal in Bohemia" was published in *Strand Magazine,* establishing the author's reputation.

You know him as ...

Arthur Conan Doyle, and his detective: Sherlock Holmes.

He couldn't attract girls as a young man. "As a high school student I had crushes on several attractive girls who either didn't know I existed or didn't care I existed. It occurred to me: What if I was real terrific? What if I had something special going for me, like jumping over buildings or throwing cars around? Then maybe they would notice me." This gave him the idea for a superhero.

You know the superhero as ...

Superman. And his co-creator: Jerry Siegel.

In the 1950s, a story book artist drew up a draft of a children's story about horses. The problem: He couldn't draw horses. He tried other animals, but they didn't fit the title of his story. Finally, eight years later, he settled on "Things," and dumped the horses in favor of monsters.

You know him as . . .

Maurice Sendak, and the book, the classic children's tale "Where the Wild Things Are."

As an anti-smoking fanatic, he marketed a peppermint-flavored candy as a cigarette substitute in Europe. He brought it to the U.S. in the 1950s, and it bombed. He took it off the market and reintroduced it as a children's toy, with cartoon heads and fruity flavors.

You know it as . . .

Pez, and its inventor, Eduard Haas.

In 1977 a starving London band was scheduled to open for a punk band in Paris. They loaded their gear into a car and took a ferry to France. It turns out there was no gig, no one came to see them, and they wound up the evening in a funk. They had no money, and they'd come to Paris for nothing.

As they drove around the city that night, their car broke down.

Their lead singer figured that as long as he had to walk, he might as well take a stroll through Paris's infamous red-light district. As he looked at the prostitutes he imagined what it might feel like to be in love with one of them. He translated the experience into a song.

You know him as . . .

Sting. The song was *Roxanne*. It became the first big New Wave hit and established his band, The Police.

He tried out for his high school glee club, and was turned down on the grounds "He couldn't sing well enough."

You know him as . . .

Elvis Presley.

This British band auditioned for a British recording label . . . which turned them down. So did the next several labels they approached. They finally got a recording contract. Their first three singles, hits in England, were denied issue by an American label on the grounds that no British act had ever succeeded in America. Finally, a small label was pressured into releasing the singles in order to get the rights to another performer's music.

That same year, another label tried to promote another of the band's songs in the U.S., and couldn't get airplay. The song was played on Dick Clark's wildly successful "American Bandstand" show, and received laughter and scorn.

You know the band as . . .

The Beatles, and the song that got dissed on "American Bandstand" ... the classic "She Loves You."

A success on Broadway, he ventured West for a screen test. The assessment: "Can't act. Can't sing. Slightly bald. Can dance a little."

You know him as ...

Fred Astaire.

As an unknown director working on a low-budget movie in the early 1970s, he approached Universal Studios to see if they were interested in a film idea of his. They turned him down. Another studio financed it. In the first screening, the studio's executives hated it. Some fell asleep. Others didn't understand it at all.

You know the movie as ...

Star Wars, and its creator: George Lucas.

In the 1960s, she came up with the idea of an educational TV show for pre-schoolers. She took her idea to NBC, ABC, and CBS, all of whom considered it too risky and refused to take it on. She wound up at PBS.

You know the show as ...

Sesame Street, and its creator: Joan Ganz Cooney.

When he found himself out of work after the stock market crash in 1929, to kill time he invented a game involving money for players to invest or speculate with. He made it himself and sold it to friends. He started getting orders for it, and to help with distribution, he took it to the game company Parker Brothers. They turned him down cold.

Among a list of 54 weak points that made the game unsalable, they deemed it too long to play and too complicated.

So he distributed the game on his own. He convinced two large East Coast toy stores to stock it. It quickly sold out. Parker Brothers reconsidered. They took it on.

You know the game as ...

Monopoly, the best-selling game in history, and its creator: Charles Darrow.

He was cut from his high school baseball team ... which made him realize he'd never attract girls with his athletic prowess. He started to write poems instead.

You know him as ...

U.S. Poet Laureate Donald Hall.

This comedy duo debuted at Atlantic City's 500 Club in 1946. Their first show was a resounding dud. They retreated to their dressing room, where one of them grabbed a greasy dressing room sandwich bag and on it wrote "routines" for their second show.

The second show was a smash hit.

You know them as ...

Dean Martin and Jerry Lewis.

He was rejected by 26 publishers before found one willing to take him on.

You know him as . . .

Best-selling author James Patterson.

He failed miserably at running a general store, cutting and selling ice, raising potatoes, and farming, before he found success in the military.

You know him as . . .

Ulysses S. Grant.

She had a great singing voice and wanted to be a diva. When that didn't work out, she turned to law.

You know her as . . .

Supreme Court Justice Ruth Bader Ginsburg.

He got injured in high school and couldn't pursue his first love, wrestling, so he tried acting.

You know him as . . .

Tom Cruise.

He took his invention to Western Union and offered to sell it to them for $100,000. They turned him down.

You know him as . . . .

Alexander Graham Bell, and his invention: the telephone.

He failed the college entrance exam at MIT.

He went on to invent the microchip, as well as the handheld calculator, the iPod, sportscast replays, microwave ovens, CAT scans, and much more.

You know him as . . .

Nobel Prize Winner Jack Kilby.

He was fired as the fifth lead on the sitcom "News Radio," which freed him up to work on a sitcom of his own.

You know him as . . .

Ray Romano, and the show: *Everybody Loves Raymond*.

Poor health kept him from sitting for exams at a nearby lycee, and also kept him out of the military. Recovering from physical collapse at the age of 20, his mom gave him a box of paints. He went on to fail as an art student.

You know him as . . .

Henri Matisse.

Before his show debuted on the BBC, the head of light entertainment at the network told the show's director, "Look, you've got to do something about this show. It just isn't funny."

You know the show as ...

Monty Python's Flying Circus, and its director, Ian MacNaughton.

As an eighteen-year-old fashion model, she came down with arthritis, was bed bound for two years, and was told she'd never walk again. Her modeling career died as a result.

You know her as ...

Lucille Ball.

In 2001, producers of a successful British TV show approached American television networks, hoping to replicate their success here.

ABC turned the show down.

NBC passed on it in a meeting.

CBS rejected it in a phone call.

WPN said no.

MTV wasn't interested.

Fox was tepid and said it had no budget left for the show.

The show became an even bigger hit in England. The producers went back to ABC with this success.

ABC passed on it again.

The daughter of the owner of Fox saw the show in England and loved it. She told her father about it and begged him to buy it.

He did.

You know the show as ...

American Idol.

ABC turned this show down twice. The producer turned to Fox, which picked it up.

You know the show as ...

Survivor.

He was voted "Least Likely To Succeed" in high school.

You know him as ...

Robin Williams.

An actress, she was dropped by her studio after a one-year contract because the studio chief didn't think she was attractive enough.

You know her as ...

Marilyn Monroe.

His first novel was rejected by sixteen agents and twelve publishers.

You know him as ...

John Grisham, and the novel, "A Time To Kill."

An artist, he started a commercial art business with a friend. Unsuccessful in attracting clients, it went bust. Two years later, he started another business, producing cartoons. That business failed within a year. He went to Los Angeles and tried to get a job directing movies. Every studio in town rejected him.

You know him as . . .

Walt Disney.

He was voted by his high school classmates as "Most likely to end up in the electric chair."

You know him as . . .

Sylvester Stallone.

As a high school student, his cartoons were rejected by the yearbook staff.

You know him as . . .

Charles Schulz, the creator of the "Peanuts" comic strip.

Under his real name, Pal, he was an unruly dog who was rejected in his first screen test. He finally got a job as an understudy for a star, and only got his big break when the star refused to swim in a river.

You know him as . . .

Lassie.

He got socked with a $40 late fee on a rental video. He was so angry about it, he resolved to do something about it.

You know him as . . .

Reed Hastings, the founder of *Netflix*.

Chapter Six
Detective Work:
The Prerequisite to
Every Employer Contact,
From Cover Letters
to Interviews

"If we knew what we were doing, it wouldn't be called research."

    Albert Einstein

Related topics:

Figuring out which employers you'd like to work for: Chapter 2, "Figuring Out What The Heck Your Dream Job Is," and Chapter 10, "Birds and Bees," Topic D on "Informational Interviews"

On-line resources: Chapter 11, "What the Internet Can—and Can't—Do For You."

Researching interviewers: Chapter 9, "Interviews."

Researching small firms: Chapter 18, "Off the Radar Screen."

Researching non-traditional employers: Chapter 31, "I Want To Be A Not–Lawyer."

You go to your mailbox, and you find you have a letter. You open it, and it reads:

> *I love you. I want to spend the rest of my life with you. Will you marry me?*

You're touched and flattered. But then ... you look back at the envelope, and notice that it's addressed to "Occupant." Kind of changes your feelings about the proposal, doesn't it?

Well, when you contact employers blindly—like, oh, just wild speculation here, by sending out a five-hundred-piece mass mailer—that's just what you're doing. You're asking them to invest tens of thousands of dollars in training you, and you haven't bothered to find out one thing about them, other than their address. You haven't told them what you can do for them. You *couldn't* have, otherwise it wouldn't be a mass mailer.

"So what, Kimmbo?" you're saying. "If my resume is impressive enough, who cares what my letter looks like?" Ha ha! The simple answer is, it doesn't matter how good your resume looks, if the employer feels you're not serious about working for them. They don't want to know that you want *any* job, no matter how skilled you are. They want to feel that you want *them*. And anyway, it's impossible to devise a truly perfect resume without knowing something about your target employers, so that you can arrange, expand and contract your entries accordingly.

There's another great reason to research employers before you have contact with them, whether by letter or in an interview. And it's this: If you *don't*, you may wind up with interviews with employers you have no interest in working for. When that happens, you just can't manufacture enthusiasm. Now you might be saying, "It doesn't matter what job I get. I just want a job." No, you don't. There are plenty of jobs you wouldn't take.

This was brought home to me by a law student in Georgia. She told me a hilarious story about the hazards of mass mailers. She was looking for jobs in Florida, and sent out a huge mass mailer in search of same, contacting employers she found on the web. She got an interview with a lobbying outfit, and she told me, "You know Save the Manatees? Well, these guys were essentially 'Kill the Manatees.'" She went on to explain that they represented boat propeller manufacturers, who were interested in fighting legislation designed to curb boating in an effort to protect manatees, hence: Kill the Manatees. I asked her how it went, and she said, "My skin was crawling the whole time. I just couldn't ever in my lifetime on Planet Earth work with these guys. They were creepy. I swore to myself right there: no more mass mailers!"

So—research! The Boy Scout motto, "Be Prepared," is particularly apropos for job searches. It's not very time-consuming to come up with really useful information ... as we're about to find out.

* * * CAREER LIMITING MOVE * * *

Female law student, interviews with a firm that does insurance defense work. When the interviewer asks why she wants the job, she responds, "I like the idea of defending insurance companies."

The interviewer comments subsequently, "I was incredulous. She had *no clue* what we do. I explained to her that insurance defense means you stand in the shoes of the insurance company, arguing why they shouldn't be liable. She looked at me and said, 'Oops.'"

So, you got the message: Research counts. What do you *most* want to know? While there are lots of bits of intelligence that are useful, there are four basic categories you need:

- Hard facts about the firm—specialties, offices, and the like—that will lose you an opportunity if you *don't* know them.

- Any particular skills or traits the employer prizes in law students. You'll want to key your cover letter to focus on any match between what they're looking for and what you've got. You'll want your resume to focus on experiences and achievements that reflect on what they want. And in interviews, you'll want your "tell me about yourself" answer to focus on skills and traits the employer seeks.

- Tidbits on anything the firm is particularly proud of, which translates into something that would earn you brownie points if you mention it in your letter/interview.

- The "personality" of the employer; what it's like to work there, and how (and if) you'll fit in.

How do you do it? That's what we'll talk about for the rest of this chapter. It's important to remember at the outset that we're talking about researching employers you've already identified; if you're looking for employers, you want to go to the "Internet" chapter, chapter 11, and the "Birds and Bees" chapter, Chapter 10, where you'll learn how to find them.

A. TWO BASIC PREMISES UNDERLYING THE ADVICE IN THIS CHAPTER

The first premise: I'm going to give you a pecking order of research, going from the most accessible and most basic to the more 'advanced.' I'll give you a sneak peek here by telling you that the more advanced methods require that you talk to people familiar with an employer, either by phone (which works) or in person (which works even better). The 'relative desirability' of these methods is based on this premise:

> People will tell you better information than they'll write to you, and they'll tell you better information in person than they will over the phone.

It's strategic, and it's also human nature. When someone writes you something, for instance by e-mail, they have *no clue* where their words will wind up. That makes most people reticent. As Thomas Cooley's Bernice Davenport says, "In writing, people will be honest with you, but they won't be candid."

When you talk with someone, especially in person, they'll relax more. As you might imagine I talk to people all the time in the course of writing books, and they tell me the most unbelievable things, items I could *never* publish. I guarantee you they'd never say these things in e-mail, but when you're chatting . . . you never know.

In-person talks are better than phone talks, because people relax more when they can gather non-verbal information about you. Research suggests that up to 90% of communication is non-verbal. If a person can see you when they talk to you, they'll be able to judge from your demeanor what they should say.

Furthermore, people will be more candid away from the office than they will at work. Bernice Davenport points out that "If you talk to someone at their office, they're going to be more circumspect for fear of being overheard. Talk to them *outside* the office." So if it's possible, offer to meet them for coffee (or a beer) outside of work, or at least talk to them by phone when they're away from the office. You'll get a more honest assessment of employers.

The second premise underlying the advice in this chapter is this:

Personal accounts are more desirable than published sources, on-line or in print.

That may seem like a strange statement coming from an author, but the fact is, you want to get personalized information wherever you can. Published sources are a great start. The Internet? A wealth of information. But it can only get you so far.

There are two reasons for this. One is that when people talk to authors or compilers, they're going to be careful about what they say. The only way I got people to be candid with me in this book was to promise them anonymity for their "spicier" or negative advice.

The other reason is this. As many experts pointed out to me, the information that's gleaned from surveys and compilations tends to be skewed. There's a built-in 'contributor bias.' You can easily figure out why if you harken back for a moment to your college statistics class. Remember the Poisson distribution? The bell-shaped curve? That most items in any population tend toward the "mean," or the middle? That's the way it is with jobs. Most people are okay with what they do. On the fringes—the three standard deviations away from the middle—you have the people who just hate it or simply adore it. It's the people further away from the center who are most motivated to blab; they've got a rooting interest in getting their point of view out. When they get surveys, they'll say, "People really need to know what it's like here, how great/terrible it is." The people in the middle aren't so tempted to respond, to tell the world, "Hey! My job is pretty all right!"

How To Lie With Statistics is an ancient book but as relevant today as it was when it was published. One of its basic tenets is, when you read a survey you have to ask yourself, "Why would a person be motivated to respond to this survey?" One of the examples they use is a survey reflecting the average salary of Yale graduates, which was unbelievably high (you can tell how old the book is in that "unbelievably high" was twenty-five grand a year!). As the book points out, ask how that survey must have been conducted. They sent surveys to Yale grads, and who would be most likely to respond? The grads making the most money. The homeless pencil-sellers probably weren't going to answer. So the result would naturally tend to be skewed on the high end.

None of this is to say you should avoid surveys and published sources. For gosh sakes I've written a lot of them. But when you read surveys or see published resources talking about employers, keep in mind the motivation of the contributors.

B.   THE "PECKING ORDER" OF RESEARCH

We're going to go over a lot of resources here, and you're unlikely to use all of them for every employer that interests you. If you go to a distinguished law school (see Chapter 16) or you're at the top of your class—congratulations, by the way—and you have a ton of on-campus interviews as a result, there just isn't the time to conduct a body-cavity search on every employer with whom you'll interview.

Nonetheless—research is an *absolute necessity* no matter how many interviews you have, and no matter how good you look on paper. Employers want to feel you genuinely want them no matter how good you are ... so do as much research as you can for every employer.

If you aren't "credentially gifted"—which is the vast majority of us, by the way—the more research you do, before you send letters or interview, the better off you are. You have no idea when the next item you dig up about an employer will be your key to getting your foot in the door.

Here's the pecking order:

Bottom rung: Basic Internet research. You just can't avoid it. The employer's web site, Google, and for large law firms, their NALP form. If an employer catches you ignorant of a fact about them that you could easily have found on-line, it'll torpedo your chances with them.

Second rung: A quick visit to Career Services for "hum-int" 1.0. That's CIA-speak for "Human Intelligence." The inside skinny from Career Services Counselors and bindered reviews by students who've worked for employers you're targeting.

Third rung: Internet Research 2.0. Still "objective," it just takes a little more time to find out a lot more information using sources like Lexis/Nexis and Westlaw.

Fourth rung: Published resources, either purchased or "rented" at your Career Services Office at school.

Top rung: Advanced "humint." The very best thing you can do. Seek out people who know about the employers you're targeting for either phone or face-to-face advice about those employers.

Optional rung: Internet research 3.0, to be conducted with your b.s.-o-meter turned firmly "on." You'll have to have your "b.s." filter in place, because the information here is unfiltered; blogs and social networking sites. You don't know who's posting it and you can't judge their demeanor. But it's useful to see.

1.   BOTTOM RUNG: BASIC INTERNET RESEARCH

Well, duh. It's so-o-o easy.

A.   YOUR FIRST STOP SHOULD BE THE EMPLOYER'S WEB SITE. DOUBLE DUH!

If you're going to do any research at all, the employer's web site is the logical place to start. Employers large and small have them, of course. Many employers say that *if you ask a question in an interview whose answer you could have found easily on their web site, they won't hire you.* That's how important it is to visit the employer's website! On top of that, many students tell me they've had experiences where the interviewer isn't familiar with the web site, and the student teaches *them* something about the employer that they didn't know. Sweet!

What you want to find out from the employer's web site:

1.   Their "basic statistics"—how many lawyers, their specialties, their offices.

This is absolutely crucial. You have no idea how many students have told me they've blown an interview by saying that they wanted to be in the "Miami Office" of a firm with no Miami office, that they were interested in the Tax Department of a firm with no tax practice, that they were interested in a large firm in an interview with a twenty-person outfit.

While you're at it, check and see how many attorneys practice in any given specialty. One of the problems with the Martindale/Hubbell listing of specialties (see below) is that law firms have a tendency to take a kitchen sink approach to specialties, listing everything they've done in the last decade, even if their only exposure to the specialty is that one of their lawyers had one case that touched on it five years ago. It's not really a specialty for them, and they're not hiring lawyers in that specialty. The only relevance specialties have for *you* is whether they're going to hire anybody to do it—so the web site is a better source, especially if it shows that the specialty is vibrant and growing.

* * * CAREER LIMITING MOVE * * *

Law student in Oklahoma. He gets out of First Year in a very enviable position: Number One in his class. He waltzes into law school Second Year, confident that every employer who visits his campus will want him.

He's right. They all want to talk to him. The very first employer to visit his campus: a very large, very prestigious law firm from

Kansas City. He walks into the interview *very* confident—he's #1 in his class! He's the man!

The first question the interviewer asks him: "So . . . what do you know about our firm?"

The student gulps. "Well . . . I know you're in Kansas."

The interviewer stands up, holds out his hand to shake hands, and says, "Thanks for coming.

"We're in Kansas City . . . Missouri."

2. Press releases.

Look and see what makes them proud, what's new. Maybe they've taken on a new client, won a big case, opened a new office or announced an open house. These all provide fodder for interview questions you can ask, casual comments you can make to show that you're interested in them. And the announcement of an open house— if it's a firm you want, go! Nothing shows your enthusiasm more . . . and casual contact with attorneys can give you a serious edge over the competition.

3. Attorney profiles.

If you're sending correspondence to a particular lawyer or have an interview with a specific attorney there, you have to read their profile. Look and see where they're from, where they went to college and law school, what their extracurriculars were, their career path since law school. Look at the hobbies they mention.

You particularly want to see what you have in common. People like to work with people like them, so those commonalities are important. An attorney's profile can also provide a great ice breaker: "I'm curious . . . how did you get interested in sky diving?"

If you're researching an employer and you haven't chosen a contact "target," attorney profiles will help you identify him/her. Look again for points of commonality: law school, a college major, an undergrad school, perhaps a career before law school or an important extracurricular (a club or society or fraternity/sorority).

4. CLEs offered/speaking engagements by attorneys at the employer.

A great "side door" into an employer is attending a speaking engagement by one of the attorneys. CLEs—Continuing Legal Education seminars, which I rave about throughout this book—are often taught by lawyers at firms. If you go, and make a point of introducing yourself during a break or afterwards as someone who's interviewing with/interested in working with the firm—trust me, you will *really* stand out!

5. Blogs by associates.

Some employers have firm-sanctioned blogs by associates. Now, you may be wondering: how useful can these blogs *be* if the firm knows about them? Point well taken. But whether it's the party line or not, if a firm goes to the trouble of posting blogs, you ought to read them. You're likely to get some useful insights into life there, and you'd be well-advised to mention that you read them.

6.   Overall tone.

While you're at the employer's web site, get a feel for how they view themselves with the kind of language they use. Are they formal and hard-driving? Are the lawyers presented in such a way as to make them seem friendly and approachable, or are they made to seem more aloof? Counseling oriented? Tailor your approach, both on paper and in person, accordingly. For instance, if you see on their opening page a headline reading: "Anyone can represent you in your DUI. We'll make you feel good about it ..." you know that the firm is interested in counseling skills, and those are what you'd want to accentuate in contacting them. If they brag about hiring the "best and brightest" law students, you'll pull out credentials that say that about you. If they say, "We help dads maintain their parental rights," you know whom you'd need to show an interest in helping.

The web site may also tell you about the employer's summer clerkship program (if that's what you're interviewing for), and that can give you the basis for good questions during the interview. For instance, as Marilyn Tucker points out, if a firm says that summer interns work in three areas, you can ask whether you get to choose those areas or not.

The web site may also mention clients. Is there a wide client base, or is the firm dependent on one or two large clients? If it relies on a client or two then you'll want to research those clients, as well, because the fortunes of the firm depend on the fortunes of those clients. For instance, let's say you research the *Wall Street Journal* and find that the single large client of the firm you're interviewing with is on the block, and it's going to be moving far away. That doesn't bode well for your potential employer, does it?

So squeeze from the employer's web site all the information you can!

B.   IF THE EMPLOYER'S WEB SITE DOES NOT HAVE ATTORNEY PROFILES, GO TO MARTINDALE HUBBELL

The granddaddy of research tools, "MarHub" has a brief profile of virtually every practicing attorney in America. Absolutely crucial for finding out about the backgrounds of people you intend to write to or meet. MarHub is in (voluminous) hard copy at your Career Services Office at school, in virtually every public library, and on-line at www. martindale.com.

A caveat: Don't choose specialties based on MarHub. Firms have been known to list practice areas as 'specialties' when they may have had one partner handle a case tangentially related to the specialty, five years ago. No personnel, no plans to expand: and if you state it as a goal in a cover letter/interview, no possibility that you'll get an offer!

C.   FOR LARGE LAW FIRMS ONLY, CHECK THE FIRM'S "NALP" FORM

NALP stands for the National Association of Law Placement. The NALP Directory, which is on-line at www.nalpdirectory.com or in hard copy at your Career Services Office, compiles detailed information about large law firms all over the country. Law firms take a *lot* of time compiling their NALP entries. The NALP directory goes beyond information most employers include on their web sites, including the number of lawyers in each area, projected hiring needs, diversity information, and more.

D.   GOOGLE

See where else the employer shows up. Have they been in the news? Anything cutting edge that will impact your cover letter/resume/interview?

E.   FIND OUT IF THE EMPLOYER IS IN DISCIPLINARY TROUBLE . . .

Bernice Davenport advises you to check and see whether your target employer faces disciplinary action by the bar association. "Every state's bar association lists this information on their web site; for ours, it's www.michbar.org/professional/disciplinary.cfm."

2.   SECOND RUNG: A QUICK VISIT TO CAREER SERVICES FOR BASIC 'HUMINT' . . .

As I mentioned before, 'Humint' is CIA-speak for "human intelligence." It's the very most valuable kind of information.

If you've got time for only one more thing beyond the employer's web site, Google and NALP, stop by your Career Services Office for two things:

A.   ASK IF ANY OF THE COUNSELORS KNOW ANYTHING ABOUT THE EMPLOYER

Career Services Counselors are employer gossip vacuum cleaners. They talk to employers all the time, as well as alums and students who work for all kinds of employers. It's very likely that someone at your Career Services Office will know something useful about employers you're targeting.

There is a *huge* caution with this source. Namely: You cannot repeat *anything* negative that you hear!

Never, *ever* say something to an employer like, "My Career Services Director, Neva Aggin, said she heard there was some hooky-dooky going on with your escrow accounts, and that you're the subject of a criminal investigation . . ." or "I heard at Career Services that you stopped offering a buffet for on-campus interviews, and you want to serve chips and salsa. They said you were probably having financial trouble.''

Remember: the only way your Career Services Office can provide excellent skinny is by keeping their network of contacts alive. You're going to squash that network like a bug if you repeat negatives. On top of that, you're showing that you can't be discreet, and that's a really bad quality for a lawyer.

By the same token, if you hear something glowing from Career Services, share it—and attribute it. Honest flattery is a very effective weapon, and repeating what someone else has said purges any possible butt-kissing taint. "My Career Services Director, Greta Jobb, told me that your firm is the best place to work to get immediate courtroom experience . . .''

B. CHECK TO SEE IF THE OFFICE COMPILES REVIEWS BY SUMMER ASSOCIATES/CLERKS AT EMPLOYERS YOU'RE TARGETING

Most Career Services Offices have binders of employer reviews filled out by other students. These are great resources, and worth a quick look when you're researching employers. You'll learn what it's like to work for a particular employer, and you'll often gain insights into what to stress about yourself in the application process.

One great advantage to them is their exclusivity; students at other schools can't access them.

We'll revisit these binders shortly, when we talk about more advanced 'humint.'

3. THIRD RUNG: INTERNET RESEARCH 2.0

It's not that this is more difficult, it just takes a little more time. With virtually no time, you go to the employer's web site and Google them. With even a few minutes more . . .

A. LEXIS/NEXIS AND/OR WESTLAW.

1. LEXIS/NEXIS

a. Basic information about employers:

Some of the information you can find mirrors what you'll learn in employer web sites: size of firm, practice areas, biographies of lawyers there.

Your portal is www.lawschool.lexis.com/career/index.html. Choose "job hunting sources." You'll find basic information about employers in resources that include the Martindale–Hubbell Law Directory, NALP Judicial Clerkship Directory, Public Interest Employer Directory, and the National Directory of Legal Aid and Defender Offices.

b. Current events affecting an employer, mentioning the employer or a particular interviewer, as well as cases the

attorney/firm has been involved with and clients they've represented:

Choose "News" from the "Source" page after signing in with your ID.

c.   Check "Courtlink Strategic Profiles." "You'll find charts of the types of cases particular law firms take on, the clients they work for, and where they litigate," advises Georgia State Reference Librarian Kreig Kitts.

d.   "Get the latest headlines from the local legal newspaper for any city you're targeting e-mailed to you regularly," says Kreig Kitts. "You can also do this through Westlaw."

2.   WESTLAW

a.   Basic information about employers:

Go to www.lawschool.westlaw.com and click on the career link in the left frame of any lawschool.westlaw.com page. Some sources available include:

- Legal Support Systems Employers Directory Database (EMPL–DIR)—a directory offering information on large and medium size law firms

- West Legal Directory (WLD)—a directory of both domestic and international attorneys

- NALP Directory of Legal Employers

- West Legal Directory of Judges

- West Directory of Judicial Clerkships

- Directory of Corporate Counsel

- Directory of Bankruptcy Attorneys

- Almanac of the Federal Judiciary Database

- FindLaw Careers (information about firms)

b.   Current events affecting an employer, mentioning the employer or a particular interviewer, as well as cases the attorney/firm has been involved with and clients they've represented.

For current events impacting the employer, check WestNews (for access to thousands of domestic and foreign newspapers, magazines and trade journals).

For cases an attorney has been involved with, choose the "Case Law" database for the jurisdiction where the attorney practices, and then click on the "Fields" link and type the attorney's name in the "attorney field."

4. FOURTH RUNG: PUBLISHED RESOURCES EITHER PURCHASED OR 'RENTED' AT YOUR CAREER SERVICES OFFICE AT SCHOOL (AND ALSO ON-LINE)

There are two kinds of materials covered here: Employer-generated materials, and "compilation" materials.

A. EMPLOYER-GENERATED MATERIALS

Namely, employer brochures. These are fading in importance as research tools with the advent of the internet and web sites. But employers spend a lo-o-o-ot of money on these things, so look for them.

"Compilation" materials: These are materials based on surveys by independent publishers.

1. AMERICAN LAWYER SURVEYS OF SUMMER ASSOCIATES AND MID-LEVEL ASSOCIATES

Every year in October, American Lawyer publishes rankings of large law firms based on surveys of summer associates and mid-level associates. Unlike most surveys, the American Lawyer gets a very high response rate. And as you'd expect from American Lawyer, the coverage and comments are lively and a really fun read.

As you read the American Lawyer surveys, it's important to look at specific comments and to take the ranking number *itself* with a grain of salt. Here's why: there's a respondent bias that reflects an employer's *past* ranking. As the recruiting coordinator at one prestigious law firm describes it, "Student expectations rise and fall on the American Lawyer rankings. If you're #1, students come in with such lofty expectations that you can't possibly live up to them. So they downgrade your program. With more realistic expectations, new students come in and are blown away, so they upgrade you. You've got the same program. It's the expectations that change."

That being said, if an employer does well in the survey, it's fine to mention in your materials and interviews; employers are very proud of it. If they don't do well . . . leave it alone!

2. VAULT REPORTS

Vault is the leading source for survey-based insight on employers; you can also find some of their materials on-line at www.vault.com. You get access to the vast array of materials through Westlaw, www.lawschool.westlaw.com.

Vault has guides on every major city, on large law firms, specialties—they hack up the legal market in just about every way. No matter who you're targeting, if they're a large-ish employer, Vault will cover them.

As is generally true of compilation materials, remember that the image of an employer depends on the people who offered information, which may or may not reflect what *your* experience would be. But it's very useful to see, and if an employer is favourably reviewed, go ahead and mention it in your pitch to employers and in your interviews. If the employer doesn't fare so well, don't mention it.

3.   AMERICA'S GREATEST PLACES TO WORK WITH A LAW DEGREE

Talk about shameless self-promotion! That's my book. It lists hundreds of places that alums report back to Career Services Directors as great places to work. You'll only find positives about the employers who appear in it. It's definitely worth checking out whether the firm or company or agency with whom you're interviewing appears in the book, because if they do, you should mention it in the interview. They're all very proud of it!

(Incidentally, *America's Greatest Places* is representative of the 'contributor bias' I mentioned at the beginning of this chapter; I found the employers by surveying law school personnel for reports back from happy graduates. Not every law school responded, and obviously the ones who *did* didn't know *every* happy alum. So it's a useful resource . . . but not a dispositive one!)

5.   TOP RUNG: ADVANCED 'HUMINT.' THE BEST THING YOU CAN DO

I should say: best, and most time-consuming. But the fact is, what you want more than anything else in the world, perhaps without realizing it, is a flesh-and-blood take on the employer in question. This is the Holy Grail of research.

You can ask all kinds of questions. While we go into this in detail in Chapter 10 when we talk about informational interviewing, you can seek:

- Tidbits about the work environment; what's it like there?
- What impresses the employer;
- What they look for in new/summer associates;
- The kinds of things that really piss them off;
- Things they like to hear in interviews and what you should avoid saying;
- What kinds of demands they put on the people who work there;
- What their prospects are like, whether they're confident or fearful about the future.

In a nutshell, you want *gossip*. It's a little more work to find the inside skinny, but the insights you'll get are often irreplaceable.

I talked to a female student at one school who was looking at working part-time for a sole practitioner in town. He did patent work, and she thought the work sounded exciting, his client list was phenomenal, the pay was really good—and she thought their initial phone contact went very well. He invited her in for an interview. Before she went on the interview, a classmate of hers pulled her aside in a hallway, and said, (all names are made up, by the way), "Marty told me you're interviewing with Phil Snotgrass. Be careful. He plows through female clerks. He's a real scumbag. What he does isn't technically sexual harassment, but . . . he's creepy. Talk to Wanda Newgig before you take that job—she used to work for him." Wanda confirmed everything the classmate had told her, and needless to say—she didn't pursue the job.

A caveat: use judgment about what you hear. Consider the source. Personalities can clash; someone else might not get along with an employer you'd really like. The person you're talking to might have an agenda that's not obvious. And be careful about law school myths: large firms are the only ones with sophisticated work. You can't make a lot of money working for a small firm or the government. There are employers who belie every stereotype. That's why research is so important: you want to know what individual employers are really like!

Where do you find the ultimate inside skinny? **Your Career Services Office is your best start**. I've already told you to ask them for their own scoop; they're the repository of all the collected job wisdom at school, and they're virtually certain to have insights that will be valuable to you.

On top of that, they'll be able to put you onto three other sources of good inside dirt: Alums and upperclassmen who've worked for an employer (or still do), and other students who've interviewed there.

Let's talk about those sources, and others.

A. ALUMS/UPPER CLASSMEN WHO'VE WORKED FOR THE EMPLOYER (OR STILL DO)

If the job in question is one you really want, it's worth asking Career Services for the names of alums and/or upper classmen who've worked there (or are working there currently). Give them a call—or e-mail them first, letting them know you'll call—and say something like, "I'm going to be interviewing with Banger & Masch. I'd really like to work there and I'd truly appreciate your advice." Mention the name of your Career Services Director/Counselor in the message line of your e-mail, so that when you call they're prepared for you. Once you're talking to them, take a lead from their tone, and ask for more as appropriate: ask them what they like(d) about working there, what they'd change if they could, what they wish they'd known ahead of time, what advice they have for interviewing there, tidbits about the interviewer. And remember: if they still work there, try to schedule a chat with them outside of working hours, so that they won't feel constrained by the possibility colleagues will hear what they say.

There is a hidden benefit to talking with current and former employees: Employers often ask the opinions of these people in making decisions about whom to interview and hire. As one Career Services Director told me, "They'll often hand a list of applicants to a 3L, and say, 'Do you know any of these people?' " So making yourself a known quantity to a current/former worker can give you a real edge.

Also, keep in mind that if they still work there, they will (hopefully) be loyal to the employer, so you can't ask them everything you'd ask Career Services. You have to avoid asking anything that reflects badly on you or might embarrass them, questions like "Do they make you burn the midnight oil?" or "How much do they pay?" But if you ask the more general questions I suggested in the last paragraph, you'll learn lots of valuable insights about the firm. And apart from getting great information, you'll be demonstrating your enthusiasm for the job just by talking to them!

B. OTHER STUDENTS WHO'VE INTERVIEWED WITH THE EMPLOYER

You can find out who they are from Career Services. Schools differ in terms of competitiveness when it comes to interviewing. At some schools, it's perfectly normal to ask other students who've interviewed with the same place, "What was the interviewer's style? Is there anything I should bring up? Or avoid?" At other schools, the competition is cutthroat and you wouldn't learn anything useful this way. It's worth asking around, anyway.

Incidentally, when the shoe is on the other foot, and a classmate is asking *you* for insights, provide them generously. It's easy to overlook the fact that your classmates are your colleagues for life. Establishing good karma while you're still in school is a wise idea. So be as generous with other people as you'd want them to be with you!

C. ADJUNCT PROFESSORS WHO ARE PRACTICING ATTORNEYS

As Bernice Davenport points out, "Adjunct professors who practice law are usually plugged into the community, and can give you valuable information." If you're not sure which of your profs are adjuncts, check at Career Services to see whom to approach.

D. LOCAL ATTORNEYS YOU KNOW

Maybe you've worked for a lawyer in town, or you volunteer at the bar association, or you've met local lawyers at alumni events or CLEs. Maybe they're even friends of the family. Whatever the reason you know them, lean on them for information about employers with whom you interview. Law is a small, tightly-knit community—it's very likely that lawyers you know will be familiar with employers you're targeting, and might be able to provide you with useful skinny.

E. FOR EMPLOYERS WHO ARE LITIGATORS, CHECK WITH CAREER SERVICES FOR UPPERCLASSMEN/ALUMS WHO CLERK FOR TRIAL-LEVEL JUDGES IN TOWN

One of the benefits of being a trial court judicial clerk is that you get to see litigators in their "natural habitat." Tap into that font of wisdom by seeking out those clerks. Find out who they are from

Career Services and call or e-mail them with a request for information about the employer: "I'm interested in X and I am wondering if you're familiar with them. If you know anything can you share that information with me?" They may be able to clue you in to the quality of the attorney's work and their general reputation in the legal community.

6. OPTIONAL RUNG: INTERNET RESEARCH 3.0, WITH YOUR B.S.-O-METER SET FIRMLY "ON"

What we're talking about here is the "unfiltered" kind of information you get from blogs, MySpace and FaceBook profiles, and any other social networking sites.

A. BLOGS

He-e-e-re's the problem. When you have self-selecting, unedited material—and this is true of any kind of evaluation, review or essay, on the Internet or not—ask yourself this basic question: *why is this person saying this?* Because it's unedited, no one else has had a moderating influence on it, which is both good and bad. It's good in the sense it might be more honest. But it's also lobbying for *some* point of view, so it's not necessary more accurate.

When you read blogs, remember: most people don't blog. People who *do* blog don't do it because they feel just OK about their subject matter. They don't sit down and say, "My life's OK. I'm fine with school/work/life. I think I'll write about it." They're either really into it or really hate it, and it's usually the latter. Studies have actually shown that we are more likely to connect with other people through shared *dislikes* than likes.

So if you read a blog about a particular employer, or by a particular attorney, remember: the person in question has some sort of bias, and it's hyper-important to remember that as you read what they say.

B. MYSPACE, FACEBOOK, AND OTHER SOCIAL NETWORKING PROFILES ... *WITH A CRUCIAL CAVEAT*

Who could resist the temptation to see if an employer/interviewer has a MySpace profile? It can't help to look, but proceed with caution.

When it comes to MySpace, FaceBook, or other social networking profiles, keep in mind: what audience did this person have in mind when they wrote this? How were they trying to make you think about them? If you read profiles of attorneys at firms you want to work for, take into account that they're probably not intending for *you* to read their profile. It's for their friends. It may give you useful insights into them and their employer, but even if it does, here's what you absolutely *must* remember when you read an attorney's social networking profile ... **unless it's got a painfully obvious "professional" slant, you can't mention that you've read it!!**

I can't tell you how many students have trashed their job chances with an employer by mentioning inappropriate material in attorney's MySpace profile. You may ask yourself, "Well, if they didn't want me to read it, why did they *post* it?" Good question, Weed Hopper. I'm not saying *their* judgment is great. But they've already got a job. You don't. If you find out the attorney you're about to interview with fronts a transvestite lounge band, *keep it to yourself!*

* * * CAREER LIMITING MOVE * * *

On-campus interview. The student and interviewer are just getting acquainted.

Student: "So—how was the bachelor party in Vegas?"

Interview over.

c. "LEGAL GOSSIP" SITES, LIKE WWW.JUDGED.COM, WWW.AUTOADMIT. COM, AND WWW.GREEDYASSOCIATES.COM

You've probably already visited these; while they have links to all kinds of other useful resources, they're best known for posts from "insiders" at employers. While I find them a bit difficult to navigate, you're cleverer than me, and you may not. The posts often include very useful information on everything from culture to salaries to guidance on breaking into a particular employer. Check them out!

C. WHAT IF YOU TRY TO RESEARCH AN EMPLOYER . . . AND COME UP EMPTY?

Sometimes you might stumble across an employer about whom it's just impossible to learn anything. Typically we're talking about small, out-of-town law firms. They don't have a web site, and you can't find anyone who knows anything about them.

You can try even more exotic resources:

- The local Yellow Pages (which you can find on-line). Lawyers sometimes have display ads that disclose a fair amount of information about their practice;

- The local bar association for the city where the employer is located, asking the head of the section covering the employer's specialty if they know about the firm (or the head of the small firm practice section, if you don't know the specialty);

- The Career Services Office of the law school in or nearest the city where the employer is located (get "reciprocity" from your Career Services office to talk to that school's office and use their resources);

- Dial for info: take the bold move of calling the firm, and asking the receptionist (or whoever answers the phone) for some information, pleading your case politely.

Now, if none of these sources work, it may be time to question whether the employer is in the federal Witness Protection Program. Ha ha. Just kidding. But if nothing works—if you got their name from the yellow pages and that's all you know—Harvard's Marjorie Boone suggests that you tell them what you did to find out about them, and that you came up empty. The fact that you made such a great effort says a lot that's good about your diligence, even though you didn't come to the table with any tangible results!

D. RESEARCHING COMPANIES

If you're looking at a corporate employer rather than a law firm or government agency, in some ways your research is the same:

- The company's web site;
- Career Services, to see if any alums have worked there (or still do).

But there are other sources you can use, as well. Try:

- Contact salesmen for the company and get them to send you the information that goes to potential customers;
- The major job search web sites, for links to corporations;
- Trade association publications and web sites, to ensure that you are familiar with the industry (you can find trade associations for virtually every industry at Career Services or a public library, in the Yellow Book of Trade Associations);
- Hoovers.com, which has voluminous information about companies, as well as http://www.businessweek.com (look for "first jobs"), www.forbes.com (for large private companies), and www.fortune.com.
- The resources in Chapter 11, on the Internet.

E. HOW TO BE UP-TO-DATE ON "HOT" LEGAL TOPICS IN THE EMPLOYER'S GEOGRAPHIC LOCATION OR AREA OF PRACTICE

1. FOR UPDATES IN LAW AND A SPECIALTY IN PARTICULAR, THERE ARE SOME REALLY USEFUL WEBSITES

Try: www.law.com, www.lawfuel.com, www.jurist.law.pitt.edu. You can also keep up with legal news with Westlaw easily, using www.lawschool.westlaw.com:

- Wall Street Journal (WSJ) "Legal Beat" column—Access WSJ and search for "legal beat"
- New York Times (NYT): The search IN (law legal) brings up only articles with a legal slant.

(for a lot more of these general websites, check the Internet chapter, Chapter 11).

2. READ THE LEGAL PRESS IN THAT CITY OR LOCALE

If you're not game for reading hard copy, most newspapers are available on-line. That's particularly useful if you're engaging in an out-of-town job search.

3. SEE WHAT ISSUES CLIENTS ASK LAWYERS ABOUT, IN A VARIETY OF SPECIALTIES

The website www.lawguru.com has a neat feature. Lawguru offers free answers and legal advice from attorneys. Look at the Q & A database to see what people ask in various specialties.

F. FINDING SALARY INFORMATION FOR LEGAL EMPLOYERS OF ALL SIZES IN ALL LOCATIONS . . .

Most law students aren't familiar with a really tremendous resource for salary information. NALP compiles statistics for legal employers nationwide, based on:

- Location
- Small, medium and large firms
- New associates, as well as 2–3–4–5 years out.

The statistics provide a range applicable to employers of any given size and location. So if you're looking at small firms in Barnyard City, you might find that the firms there start new associates at between $35,000–45,000.

You'll find the statistics on-line at www.nalp.org, as well as at your Career Services Office.

For governmental employers, check the agency's web site for the starting "G" rating for new attorneys. You'll find on-line the current starting pay for each level. (An important note: As I've stated before, government salaries don't start out at an exciting level, but they rise pretty fast. Lawyers I've talked to tend to love government jobs, so don't let the starting dough be your deciding factor!)

For alternative careers, check salaries.com for a run-down of what to expect from a huge variety of jobs.

Shout-out to Suzanne Hill, Career Services Director at the University of Maryland School of Law, for her help with this chapter.

Chapter Seven
Correspondence: Making Your Letters (and E–Mails) to Potential Employers *Sing!*

Related topics: Keeping up with lawyers who say "Keep in Touch"—Chapter Ten

Transcripts—Chapter Eight

Following up after an interview—Chapter Nine

Thank you notes—Chapters Nine and Ten

"Cold e-mailing" employers—Chapter Ten, Topic D(3)(a)

The right cover letter can work all kinds of magic. It can make an employer sit up and notice you, in a way your naked resume never could. It can explain away sins on your resume that might otherwise be job-killers. It can even take the place of a resume, in extreme circumstances.

And, of course, at the other end of the spectrum, a cover letter can make you the laughingstock of the legal community ... if you thought the only important thing about a cover letter was to be 'memorable.' But of course Auntie Kimmbo is not going to let that happen to you! We're going to learn to write cover letters that get your foot in the door, and that's exactly what you want your letters to do.

Where do we start? With something that you're not expecting. We're going to talk about letters *I* write. Relax—I'm only doing it to make the most important point there is to make about cover letters.

Since you're reading this, you've already divined that I'm a writer. When writers send letters to publishers to see if they'd be interested in publishing something, those letters are called "query letters." (Perhaps you're beginning to see the analogy here, since the letters you send will also be designed to pique someone's interest in something—namely, meeting with you. Although the goal is different, the principles are exactly the same.)

Anyway, back to query letters. Now, publishers get a kajillion query letters, and so the sole purpose of query letters is to try and get them to nibble, and take a look at a manuscript.

So let's say that I've got a book that I want to get published. Truth be told, I've *always* got a book that I want to get published. Let's say that the book is a funny book about dating. And let's say that I do some research and find out exactly who would be the perfect publisher for this book, based on other books they publish. I find out the name of the acquisitions editor at that publisher—that is, the person who decides which books to publish. Let's say it's Muggo Doodleberry. I sit down at my trusty computer, and I start to bang out a letter:

> *Dear Mr. Doodleberry,*
>
> *I have been a writer since I graduated from the Case Western Reserve University School of Law. I have an extensive list of writing credits, starting with a book I wrote about investing in biotechnology, followed by a series of legal study aids called "Law In A Flash," as well as some travel articles and some film scripts. I have also written several books about job searching, including "Guerrilla Tactics for Getting the Legal Job of Your Dreams," "America's Greatest Places To Work With The Law Degree," "The Best of the Job Goddess," and "What Law School Doesn't Teach You."*
>
> *I am interested in publishing a humorous book about dating in order to break into the general trade market. Pursuant thereto, I would like to send you a manuscript . . .*

Asleep yet? I would be, and so would Muggo Doodleberry. This letter commits the cardinal sin of letter-writing, and the sin applies equally to letters to legal employers as it does to publishing houses. It's this: *It's not about you. It's about* them. Do publishers I write to really care about what *I* want? Of course not. They don't give a damn about me. They care about what I've done to the extent that it answers the question, 'What have you done that generates skills and enthusiasm for what we do?': *What's in it for them?* I'm telling you this at the beginning of this chapter, because there's nothing more important I can tell you about letter writing than this:

> *The entire focus of every letter you write to any prospective employer is this: What's in it for them? What can you bring to the table for them? Why should they want to meet you?* **That's the only thing that matters.**

As Suffolk's Alyssa Hammond puts it, your cover letter should show enthusiasm and answer the question "why": "Why this specialty, this firm, why would you be useful?"

And that, in and of itself, tells you why the classic cover letter is just so incredibly bad:

> *Dear Hiring Partner,*
> *Enclosed please find my resume for your consideration.*
> *Sincerely,*

I'm *begging* you not to send that letter! But if sending the kind I'm talking about—the kind that will make employers think, Gee, we've got to meet this student!—sounds intimidating, don't worry: I'm going to show you exactly how to focus your letters appropriately, even if you're thinking: "How the heck should I know what they want? And even if I do know—what the heck *do* I have that *they'll* want?" You know me better than that. I'm going to teach you everything you need to know.

By way of example, let's take a look at how I might rewrite my letter to Muggo Doodleberry, so he doesn't think I'm an insufferable stiff:

> *Dear Mr. Doodleberry,*
>
> *If Henry the Eighth wrote himself a singles ad, how would it start? "Male, divorced, widowed, widowed, divorced, widowed . . ."*
>
> *How could a guy blow it at the very beginning of a blind date? How about exclaiming, "My mom has that very same dress"?*
>
> *How would you define a dating service? Perhaps as "Paying someone else to introduce you to the kind of person they couldn't pay you to date"?*
>
> *These are some of the bits from a book you may be interested in publishing under your Peacock imprint. I've tentatively titled it "Dating 101," and I'd like to submit it to you because I think it would fit well with the humor books you already publish, like "The Worst Ideas of the Best Thinkers" and "My Car and Welcome To It." It's about the same length as those books, it's targeted to the same audience, and I like to think it's just as funny!*
>
> *"Dating 101" features . . .*

. . . and so on. Now, put yourself in Muggo Doodleberry's shoes. If you got that letter, would you be enticed into seeing the manuscript? Absolutely. Because that letter is laser-focused on just one thing: *Saying what's necessary to make him want to see my manuscript.* It's clear from the very start what's in it for him: the opportunity to get his hands on a funny book.

This isn't to say that great cover letters don't say anything about you. Of course, they have to. When it comes to query letters, publishers do want to know what else you've published, so they have some assurance that you won't be sending them pure birdcage liner. But that's the icing on the cake, and that's why it goes further down in cover letters. I'm getting away from my central thesis, which is: never forget who your audience is. And never forget their entire motivation as they read anything you send them: *What's in it for them?* As Washington's Josie Mitchell advises, "When an employer receives an application from a student, the first question they'll ask themselves is, 'Why should we interview this person?' Distinguish yourself from the hundreds of other law students who will apply to that firm. If you can't distinguish yourself through grades, do it in another way—law school activities, diverse life experiences, *something.*"

If you stopped reading this chapter right now and went away with that one simple message in mind, your letters to legal employers would be a thousand percent better than the ones your uninformed classmates will send. But of course we're going to go into a lot more detail than *that*. I'm going to show you, in detail, how to write letters that will guarantee a response. I'll show you exactly what your letters should do, and what they shouldn't do. In short: I'll show you how to make the most of every letter you write!

Here's what we'll do, in order:

- We'll talk about the three basic types of letters you can send to employers, and that's where we'll talk about the seven magic words that guarantee a response;

- Then, we'll take a look at content. We'll dissect the three elements of your letter: the opening, the 'middle part,' and the closing; and we'll talk about all kinds of issues you might want to address in your letter, including out-of-town job search issues, "mommy" issues, and many more;

- We'll go over a "perfect cover letter" checklist, where we'll talk about vital style issues;

- We'll float the idea of sending letters *without* resumes—heresy!—when your résumé's got issues you'd be better off discussing in person;

- We'll go through choosing a great writing sample—and whipping up a killer writing sample in a hurry if you don't have one already;

- We'll discuss the special issues involving corresponding with small employers;

- We'll talk about follow-up calls after you send your letters. I know that's not really a correspondence issue, but where else would I put this advice, hmm?

- We'll go through how you respond to job ads;

- And finally, we'll discuss the 21ˢᵗ century issue of e-mail correspondence.

I want to warn you up front that this is going to be a bit of work. Students often agonize for hours over their resumes, and then dash off a lackluster cover letter in a few minutes. Because the cover letter is the first thing employers see when they get your materials, it's *at least* as important as your resume. So don't get frustrated if it takes a little more time than you anticipated.

With that little introduction in mind, let's get started!

A. DETECTIVE WORK: YOU CAN'T WRITE A LETTER WITHOUT UNDERSTANDING YOUR QUARRY

Simply put, the more you know about the employer, the better cover letters you'll write. In fact, the better resumes you'll craft, the better interviews you'll conduct ... you can't escape research! That's why I wrote a whole chapter about it, Chapter 6.

Depending on how much you want the job, the amount of research you do before you send a letter will vary. I'd encourage you to do as much as you can, but at the *very* least, and I mean as an *absolute floor*, you *have* to:

- Visit the employer's web site and go through it carefully. Make sure that the employer actually has an office in the city where you want to wind up; that they practice the specialty you state an interest in (if you state one); that the tone/content of your letter matches any hints you get on the web site (for instance, if they pride themselves on the quality of the research they do, your letter better mention your excellent research skills, and have back up to prove it).

- Read the blog(s) of anyone at the employer.

- Google the employer.

- Check to see if the employer is mentioned on Lexis/Nexis or Westlaw.

- Get the name of a person to whom to send your letter; no "Dear Hiring Partner" or "Dear Recruiting Coordinator" or "Dear Office Manager." If the web site doesn't give you that, call and ask for the name of someone to whom to send your materials. If they won't give you that, just choose a name from the firm's letterhead.

- If the addressee is a lawyer, look at their profile on the employer's web site or in Martindale–Hubbell (martindale.com) to learn about their background.

- Check at Career Services for any useful information about the employer, whether in published materials or in binders of upperclassmen/alum experiences there. Ideally you want "humint"—

human intelligence—from Career Services Counselors and/or alums and upperclassmen, but that's a time issue.

As I say, there's lots more you can do. But this list gives you the very basics.

B. KEEPING TRACK OF YOUR CORRESPONDENCE FROM THE START . . .

You may wind up sending out quite a few letters. It's *very* important that you keep accurate track of them, so that you know your targets and you follow up appropriately. If you do it on the computer, use a spreadsheet so that you can easily alphabetize the employers you contact. Whether you do it in "hard copy" or on the computer, you'll want to keep track of the same information about your targets. To make it easy for you, I've provided a handy worksheet in Appendix A at the end of this chapter.

C. THE THREE BASIC TYPES OF LETTERS TO POTENTIAL LEGAL EMPLOYERS . . . INCLUDING THE SEVEN MAGIC WORDS THAT ENSURE A RESPONSE!

Every letter you send an employer when you're seeking a job with them falls into one of three basic categories:

- A personal letter, in the sense that you've either met the person you're writing to, or—as is more likely the case—you know somebody they know, and that somebody told you to write to them.

- A so-called "targeted" mailer, where you heavily research no more than a handful of legal employers at a time, and send them distinctive letters.

- The old law school chestnut, the mass mailer—or more modernly, the e-mail mass mailer—where you send hundreds of the same letter/e-mail to legal employers, changing only the name and address on each letter.

Let's go over each of them separately.

1. "PERSONAL" LETTERS THAT YOU SEND EITHER TO PEOPLE YOU'VE MET OR TO THOSE YOU'VE MET THROUGH A MUTUAL ACQUAINTANCE

The very best, the very strongest, and the most powerful letter you can send to any prospective legal employer starts with these seven words:

> *[Mutual acquaintance] recommended that I contact you* . . .

If you can start every letter you write with the name of someone your addressee knows, I *promise* you will always get a response to your letters. *Every time*. In fact, for some attorneys, it's the only way they'll bother reading your letter. I talked with one student who'd summer clerked at a lobbying firm in DC. One of her tasks was to read correspondence. There were hundreds and hundreds of letters from law students seeking jobs. She asked her employer what to do with them. He responded, "If they mention people we know, bring them in for an interview. If they don't—chuck them." That's an extreme example, but it proves the point: those are seven powerful words!

Now, you may be thinking to yourself, "Well, that's all well and good, Kimmbo. But how the heck am I supposed to find a mutual acquaintance for every job I want?" That's the whole point of Chapter 10, "The Birds and Bees of Great Jobs."

If you do the things I suggest there, you should be able to find a mutual acquaintance for virtually every job on the planet. Or at least, you'll find a mutual acquaintance for an informational interview, and through a series of referrals, you'll find *somebody* who knows someone you want to contact. So the simple fact is, yes, it may take a bit of work to be able to say, "[Mutual acquaintance] recommended that I contact you." But remember: people trust people more than they trust paper. Therefore, if using this opening to a letter ensures you'll get a response, that should be enough to convince you that it's worth the effort!

You may be wondering what ought to go in the letter *after* that first, magical phrase. You'll find exactly that in the section that talks about the content of letters, Topic D, below.

But first, let's talk about the other two basic types of letters.

2.   "TARGETED" MAILERS—DISTINCTIVE LETTERS SENT TO A HANDFUL OF CAREFULLY CHOSEN POTENTIAL EMPLOYERS AT A TIME

Now, it may well be that despite your most diligent efforts, you just can't come up with a mutual acquaintance whose name can open your letter to a potential employer. What do you do in that situation? The next best thing—a targeted mailer. It's not nearly as desirable as a "So-and-so told me to contact you ..." letter, but it'll do in a pinch.

Your first task in sending targeted mailers is to research the employer. I told you in Topic A about your "entry level" research; Chapter 6 gives you much more. Then you send the employer a letter redolent with that research. Redolent. What a great word. You show them how, based on what you've learned about them, you have skills they'll be able to put to use.

Now, I'll go into much more detail as to what to put in the guts of your letter in Topic D, below. My only intent here is to introduce you to targeted mailings as a type of letter you can send to employers—and to tell you that they're worth sending!

3.   MASS MAILERS

The *bete noire* of job search strategies. Everybody has—or knows—stories about mass mailers. And they're almost always bad.

You know what a mass mailer is. The time-honored law student tradition of generating hundreds of employer names from directories, databases, whatever, doing a mail merge, and spitting out hundreds of identical letters. You've probably seen the kind of letter I'm talking about. They're generally dreadful, along the lines of this one, sent to a law school administrator:

> *To whom it may concern,*
>
> *I am interested in working for a university. If you have any positions available, please let me know.*

Honestly, now. If you were in the shoes of the administrator, how motivated would *you* be to do anything with this letter? The person who sent it might be the most charming, hard-working, talented guy on Earth—*but this letter doesn't tell you that!*

In the first edition of GT, I gave mass mailers a thumbs-down, based on all of the expert advice that I heard. I'm older and wiser now, and I've talked to a bunch more people, and ... I still feel the same way. *Mostly.* **Let's talk about the problems with mass mailers first:**

- **The vast majority of the time, they just don't work.** The statistics on mass mailers hover around a 1% success rate, success in this context being getting an interview. And that ain't success in my book. 2–3% is considered unbelievably good. Why are the stats so bad? Well, for a start, remember what I told you at the beginning of this chapter: No employer wants to feel like just another name on a list. "Occupant." And there's no way to make them feel any other way with a mass mailer. What you're essentially saying to an employer is, I'm going to throw whatever I've got on the front porch and see if the cat will lick it up. (That's from *Twelve Angry Men,* by the way, if you're wondering about the weird analogy.) Employers don't like going through that kind of work; and they want to feel you want them, not just "any job."

- **The scant positive responses you *do* get may well be from employers who make your skin crawl.** Remember the story I told in Chapter 6 about the 'kill the manatees' employer? A mass mailer inherently means that you haven't researched the employers, and therefore can't have a great insight into whether you'll like what they do. Remember: this book is about finding your *dream* job, not *any crappy* job. A mass mailer can lead you down a lot of dry holes!

- **Mass mailers mislead you into feeling as though you've done something concrete to find a job.** There's no question that there's a heft to a box of 500 letters, and the busywork associated with putting such a mailer together makes you feel like you've really accomplished something worthwhile. Even if you've e-mailed a mass-mailer, you *still* feel like, wow, there are five hundred little packages of me zipping their way to employers all over the Internet. Yippee!

Don't pop that champagne cork just yet. It only *feels* like you've done something. As Gail Cutter points out, "You're much better off with 10 really targeted letters than a hundred nontargeted ones."

- **They'll have a severely dampening effect on your mood.** Here's what'll happen. You'll hear from a pathetic few of the employers you contacted. Most of those responses will be rejections. What's perhaps even worse is that a whole ton of employers won't respond at all. You'll be waiting and waiting, thinking they're sure to get back to you . . . until you get that sinking feeling that you're not going to hear anything at all. I see that happen all the time. Students walk up to me looking as though they've been sucker-punched, and they'll say something like, "I sent out two hundred letters, and only twelve of them even bothered to get back to me. I can't believe how rude employers are!" They're only "rude" in the sense that you're rude when you don't respond to unsolicited fourth class mail (or what you probably call junk mail). Regardless, it really gives you a case of the red-butt. You feel humiliated. Ugh! I don't *want* that for you! Looking for a job really requires you to have your game-face on, and that's so much harder when you feel like hundreds and hundreds of employers don't want you. It's not that they don't want *you*—they just didn't see the you they wanted in that crappy mass-mailer, that's all. The misery is so totally unnecessary!

So that's what's bad about mass mailers. **There are a few situations where mass mailers make sense, a couple of positives that are worth mentioning.**

- **You've got killer credentials.**

OK. If you're the president of the Harvard Law Review, yes, you can scrawl your resume on a brown paper bag with a crayon, send it all over the place, and you'll get lots of interviews. If you've got lots of relevant experience in an area—ditto. But you're still better off with targeted letters, because employers still want to see that you're particularly interested in *them*—because if they don't think you're going to accept an offer if they make you one, they won't take one step in your direction, even if it just means interviewing you.

- **A terrible response rate still means that, yes, they do work once in a while.** And the more robust the job market, the better they work (although they never, ever, ever work well). After all, as St. John's' Gloria Rivera points out, "All you need is one job." While a positive response from an employer only means you've got your foot in the door for an interview, and there's still work to do in nailing an offer, we're not talking about hunting for Easter eggs, or collecting shrunken heads. You're not a whale that needs tons of krill, just one little shred—or whatever unit krill happens to come in. So if sending two hundred letters results in you getting an interview, that's an interview you didn't have otherwise. And that's not nothing.

- **You are capable of—and willing to—use the "lottery" mind-set if you send out a mass mailer.** What do I mean? Well, when you buy a lottery ticket, you don't assume you're going to win. And if you buy Connecticut lottery tickets, you're definitely not going to win—because *I* am. Ha ha. Seriously, if you view your mass mailer as a one-in-a-million, if it comes through, great, and if it doesn't, eh, kind of a proposition—you've got the right attitude for a mass mailer. The reason mass mailers are such ego crushers is that it's very, very difficult to have that kind of focus.

- **You do lots of other things *as well*.** If your mass mailer is part of a multi-theater assault on a job, I'm not going to talk you out of it. The problem with mass mailers often comes from the fact that it's the *only* thing a lot of people do. I was on an airplane once, talking about finding jobs (no surprise there), when a guy in the row in front of me turned around and said, "Well, I can't find a job, no matter *what* I do." I asked, naturally enough, "So what are you doing?" and he told me "Everything—I've posted three hundred resumes on-line"—the cyber equivalent of a mass mailer, but even worse. What he'd done to look for a job was just the opposite of what he thought.

So the ideal solution—if you're intent on sending a mass mailer—is to do a lot of other, much-higher-return activities as well. At the very least, send at least some of the other two types of letters, as well—the personal kind and the targeted mailer—if for no other reason than to prove to yourself that they're so much more worthwhile!

4. DON'T BE INTIMIDATED BY PERSONALIZING LETTERS. IT'S NOT *THAT* MUCH WORK

You may be tempted to send out a mass mailer because you figure, it's going to take me *forever* to personalize letters. No, it won't. You're often talking about changing three lines or so. What you'll do when you start writing your letters is to see that there are sections that you can lift whole from one letter to the next. For instance, if you're targeting a certain kind of practice—small general practice firms in the same city—really all that's going to change for each firm is a line or two about what they do that you glean from their web site, Lexis/Nexis, Career Services, whatever.

You may want to come up with three or four "templates" for personalizing letters to specific employers. For instance, you can have one for the employers you found through a mutual contact; one for firms emphasizing your geographic ties ("I am anxious to join family and friends in Empire Falls"); another featuring your undergrad major prominently; and another for a specific type of employer (e.g., small general practice firms). Again, you'll modify these for each employer to include something specific that attracts you to them, but you won't be starting from scratch with every letter.

The bottom line is this: don't overlook what'll really make your correspondence shine for want of time. It's not as time consuming as it seems!

5.   DON'T PAY A SERVICE TO SEND OUT "MASS MAILERS" FOR YOU

You may be tempted to pay a service to "customize" letters (read: change the employer's name) for you and send them out to hundreds of employers. If I could, I would throw myself on your checkbook and stop you from sending that check!

Services like this prey on the idea that they'll save you time, that sending letters to employers is a time-wasting P in the A. *Really?* Trust me. Employers can smell a mass-mailer a mile away, and their attitude is, if you didn't care enough to send them a personalized letter, they don't care enough to offer an interview.

Sure, there are students who will get jobs that way. I've already told you that mass mailers work once in a great while. Those students who get jobs through these letter-sending services could have sent out their own mass mailers with *exactly* the same results, and saved themselves the dough.

I saw an ad for one of these services, and the cover letter it featured was from a Harvard student, on Law Review, with a technical background in the same specialty he wanted to practice. *Trust me. If you've got those credentials ... you don't need no stinkin' letter-sending service to get you a job.*

So take the money and blow it on something for yourself. Send your own letters. It's *so* worth it.

D.   CONTENT: DECIDING WHAT GOES IN THE LETTERS YOU SEND

What ought to go in the letters you send? (I'm talking, of course, about the two you really should be sending—the personalized letters and the targeted mailers.) What I'll do here is discuss two principal issues:

- The format of your letters, including the elements to include in them; and
- The style of your letters.
- OK. One "bonus" issue: what to send with your letters to make them *really* stand out.

Now if you've flipped ahead a few pages, you may notice that there seems to be something missing; that is, complete sample letters. Before you say to yourself "What a gyp!" let me explain why I didn't include them. I'd be doing you a huge disservice if I *did*. No matter how much I begged you, I know what you'd do, because the temptation would be too great: you'd copy sample letters word-for-word, and send them out chock-a-block to legal employers. I don't want you to do that, for two very good reasons.

One is that the whole basis of this approach is to personalize your letters to the greatest extent possible. By its very nature, any letter I'd give you couldn't accomplish that. Instead, I'll be showing you, sentence by sentence, how to construct great letters for yourself.

The other reason is that canned letters make a horrible impression on legal employers. I promise you, if you copy a letter out of any book, employers you send it to will recognize it as being identical to a bunch of others they've received. Suffice it to say that doesn't reflect well on you!

So what I'm going to do here instead is to go through your entire letter, explaining everything it ought to contain. With my guidance and a bit of thought, you'll be able to come up with letters much better than you'd find in any book!

With that in mind—let's get started!

1. THE FORMAT FOR YOUR LETTERS

What I'm going to give you here is a **basic, three-part format for your letters.** It gives you a good, solid framework for setting up your letters. In a nutshell, here are the three questions the parts answer, in order:

- **Why should the reader bother reading the rest of your letter?**
- **Why should they meet you?**
- **What do you want to happen next?**

That's it. Now, we're going to go through these in a lot more detail, but don't ever take your eye off the ball: those three basic goals are all you need to accomplish in your cover letter.

Let's take a look at them individually.

A. THE FIRST PARAGRAPH OF YOUR LETTER: WHY SHOULD THE READER BOTHER READING ANYMORE?

What you'll accomplish in this first paragraph is to give your reader some hook, some reason for going on. And what that's going to boil down to is the *why* of your letter; that is, why did you write?

Specifically, your first paragraph should include:

- **What the catalyst for your letter was, be it a recommendation from a mutual acquaintance (the best), or something about the employer that struck you in particular. Show knowledge of the employer's practice area, ties to the community, or anything else that lifts your letter from the realm of mass mailer.**

A student at one school, interested in a judicial clerkship, found that one judge had been very involved in a law school organization that the student himself was heavily into. The student mentioned the organization toward the top of his letter, ("I learned that you were also . . .") and got the interview as a result.

- **Who you are, if you don't include it in the first sentence;**
- **What you want (e.g., an interview, a summer associate-ship, a permanent position).**

That's it. With three sentences or so, you should be done.

1. Someone Suggested You Contact Them

As we've discussed, this is the very best kind of letter to send, and it starts with the very best opening:

[Mutual acquaintance] recommended that I contact you ...

Well, you can see how that fits my criteria here. What that does is to make your reader say, "Hmm. I know mutual acquaintance, and if (s)he thinks I ought to pay attention to this person, I will."

The rest of that sentence, by the way, will be the "because"—that is, why did the mutual acquaintance suggest you contact this person? There are a bunch of reasons:

"... regarding a summer clerkship position with this firm."

"because we share a mutual interest in ..."

"because (s)he felt my background in X would be useful to you ..."

"because (s)he thought my skills in X might make me a good candidate for an X position with you."

"because I have blackmail Polaroids of [mutual acquaintance] which I will post on the Internet if she doesn't help find me a job."

Just kidding.

Let's look at a few examples of first paragraphs with a "mutual acquaintance" or other personal connection:

Booboo Meerschaum of Pipe, Cleaner and Toadstool recommended that I contact you. As a temporary legal clerk, I recently completed some tax work for Mr. Meerschaum. Since he was pleased with my work and familiar with your needs, he indicated that you might be interested in meeting with me to review my background and how it might fit with your plans for either this summer or next year.

Here's another one:

Babaloo Beestung, director of the Career Services Office of Case Western Reserve University School of Law, recommended that I contact you, as I have a technical and regulatory background in which you may be particularly interested. I would like very much to have the opportunity to work for you as a summer clerk, and thereafter on a part-time basis if possible, after my first year of law school.

And yet another one:

While discussing career opportunities in the Midwest with Professor Lara Croft, she drew my attention to your firm and recommended that I contact you directly. Professor Croft mentioned that you and two other partners at Stealth, Sneak & Spie graduated from

Cloakndagger Law School, from which I also received my J.D. last year. I understand too that your firm represents Chicago's largest local employers—Chicago Large, Chicago Larger, and Chicago Largest—and has a growing labor relations practice, in which I am very interested.

Here's one renewing a personal connection:

You may recall that we met last year at the annual Lawlapalooza International Law Conference in Seattle, at which you were the keynote speaker. I was there reporting on the event for the Midnight Oil Law School Newspaper, *and we had the opportunity to speak at the reception following the general membership meeting.*

* * * SOMETIMES THE BEST OF INTENTIONS ... * * *

One law student was introduced to Clarence Thomas by a mutual friend, at a cocktail party, a year before Thomas was elevated to the Supreme Court.

When Thomas got the Supreme Court nomination—and before his highly contentious Senate confirmation hearing—the student wrote to Thomas to offer his congratulations and state his interest in a clerkship.

He wrote: *"You may remember me. We were introduced last year by a mutual friend, Anita Hill."*

2. YOU FOUND THEM ON YOUR OWN, AND THEY HAVEN'T POSTED A JOB OPENING

What if you're sending a targeted mailing? *Ideally,* **you'll be able to draw on something you learned in your research as a means of leading off your letter.** For instance:

I was fascinated to read your profile in the September issue of the Northern Moose County Bar Journal. In it, you described your firm as being on the cutting edge of biotech patent law. As a second year law student at Case Western Reserve, I have a strong, demonstrated interest in patent law, and would welcome the opportunity to work with you as a part-time or summer associate, as your needs require.

Or this one:

Susan Amullmahay, a former summer clerk at your firm, described your firm to me as a dynamic environment for learning about criminal defense work—and I found upon further research that she's not the only one who thinks so! As a first year law student at Case Western Reserve with a strong interest in criminal law, I would be very interested in pursuing possible job opportunities with you.

Or this one:

I read with great interest your article in last month's Dog Law Journal *on the "one bite" rule. As a Second Year student at Case Western Reserve University, I have begun to focus on Dog Law as my specialty, and I would like to spend next summer getting practical experience in this area by clerking for a firm like yours.*

Or this one:

> *I was very interested to read a recent article in the La Jolla Examiner about your representation of the Humpty Dumpty Diner. Upon further research, I learned that your firm gears its civil practice toward small businesses. I am particularly interested in this kind of practice, and would like to pursue an associate position with your firm should one arise. I will be relocating to La Jolla in September to rejoin close family who have moved to the area.*

Here's one stating an interest in a particular practice area:

> *As a graduating law student, I am writing to express my interest in a position with Grumpy, Sleepy and Dopey. I am seeking a position with a medium-sized firm with a strong litigation section. I am particularly interested in construction litigation, and I understand that your firm has an excellent reputation in this field.*

Here's one that shows off research into the employer:

> *As a first year law student at Fred's Night YMCA Law School, I would like very much to have the opportunity to work with your firm as a summer associate. I understand from speaking to Herman Munster and Uncle Fester, students who have worked at Spectre and Coffin, and from research, that your firm is engaged in a wide ranging, general practice and that summer and permanent associate assignments are arranged so as to give a solid introduction to several areas. Because I am undecided regarding a specialty, I am very interested in the experience that your firm has to offer.*

Clearly, it takes some work and some research to be able to come up with openings like that. And that's just the point! What you're doing with a personal letter or targeted mailing is to make the employer feel unique, and in doing so, you're distancing yourself from the competition.

3.   YOU'RE RESPONDING TO A JOB POSTING OR AD

I cover "letter openers" responding to job ads when we talk about job ads in general, under Topic H.

B.   THE 'MIDDLE PART' OF YOUR LETTER: WHY SHOULD YOUR READER MEET YOU?

The middle part of your letter—between the first paragraph and the closing—is what I'll imaginatively call "the middle part of your letter." It's where you wheel in your big guns. Simply put, **you bring in the specific things about yourself and your background that will make the reader think, "Gee, I really ought to give this person a chance!"**

What you'll want to do here is to **skim your background, and choose the two or three things about you that will be of most use to the employer.** That's the benefit of researching the employer before you write a letter to them—it helps separate personalized letters from mass mailers!

You can highlight a huge variety of things, including:

- High grades or classes relevant to the employer;
- Work experience relevant to the employer's practice;
- A demonstrated enthusiasm for working with a particular issue or population relevant to the employer;
- CLEs you've taken or conferences you've attended related to the firm's work;
- Research or specific interests relevant to the employer's work;
- "Non-law-related" skills transferable to the employer (e.g., self-starter, with backup facts proving it!)
- If the geography isn't obvious, your reason for wanting to work in the employer's city.

Remember: You're not confined to your resume. Saying you're interested in a location because you lived there through high school would be very useful information for the employer. Or the fact that you want to work with children because your father is a social worker who sparked your interest in children's issues, or you got interested in workers' comp because your father was denied a worker's comp claim and you followed his lawsuit closely. Whatever it is, it can make your candidacy more vibrant.

1. Do's and Don'ts in the Middle Part

a. Don't Undervalue Qualities That Employers Treasure— and Most Students Overlook!

Every employer—and I mean *every one*—appreciates a few key qualities in law students. They are **a proven ability to work hard, the value of volunteer experience, and enthusiasm for what the employer does.** But I talk with law students *all the time* who brush off evidence of these in cover letters and resumes, saying "Oh, they won't care about *that.*" Ah, yes—but they do!

Here are a few things to watch out for—

1. How much of your undergraduate education did you fund? If you worked quite a few hours a week and/or summers to pay your way—as I did—*be sure* to mention this, and the percentage of your education you covered. It indicates your willingness to work hard, and that's *always* a positive!

2. Have you done any volunteer work?

I don't care if you candy-striped, tutored, worked on Habitat for Humanity, helped at the animal shelter, whatever it is—for gosh sakes, look at what it says about you: your ability to deal with people, your willingness to reach out to the community, which translates for private employers—especially small law firms—to your potential as a rainmaker.

3. Any activity in which you've taken part that relates to your desire to learn more about what the employer does.

If you haven't done so already, join the bar association in the state where you intend to practice (or several, if you aren't sure yet—it's dirt cheap while you're in school), and go to local bar association functions focused on practice areas/employers for whom you'd like to work. Go to a CLE or two or more in specialties they practice. Join the relevant club at school—that's an obvious one. You'll be able to mention this casually in a cover letter, and it looks *awesome*. "I was interested to learn at Kitty Katzman's CLE given by the Practicing Law Institute last week that animal rights lawyers are concerned about . . ."

b. Don't parrot your resume!

The middle part of your letter shouldn't be a mere rehash of your resume. As William & Mary's Rob Kaplan points out, "When you put in letter form what's on your resume, you're showing the recipient the same information twice. They don't need that."

The middle part of your letter has to elaborate on specific elements of your resume (and non-resume experiences), by showing how your specific experiences translate into transferable skills which will be of use to this particular employer. You'll show why what you learned from what you've done can be useful to the employer.

As Rob Kaplan says, "You have to first sit down and decide what two or three points you want to make about yourself in the letter. If you have strong client relation skills, that's a topic sentence. And then as support for that, pull different things from your background that support that proposition. Maybe something from law school, like success in a client counseling competition, and then something from a summer job, like being a counselor at a camp. It's very important to do some self-assessment first, and find what supports the contentions you make. You can't just say, 'I did this job, and here's what I did there, and I did this job, and here's what I did there.' "

So don't just have your cover letter mirror your resume. Show why what you've learned will be useful to this particular employer!

c. Do include information about where your strengths came from, even if—especially if—it's unusual.

If your interest in an employer or your particular skills of use to them are unconventional—that just makes your letter more interesting! For instance, if your father is a doctor and you're interested in med mal, you might mention in the middle part of your letter, "Having spent many summers helping my father in his medical practice, I developed a first-hand understanding of issues related to medical malpractice.''

By way of another example, there was one student who was very interested in working for Legal Aid. His problem was that as a middle-class, suburban white kid, there was nothing to suggest that he'd have any rapport whatsoever with the clients he'd have at Legal Aid. But as it turns out, he worked as a trash collector during the summer after First Year, and his 'beat' was a low-income neighborhood. He developed a rapport with people in the neighborhood, and learned a lot about a way of life he'd had no exposure to previously. When he applied for a summer clerkship with Legal Aid for the summer after Second Year, that experience was a real plus—and made for a fascinating cover letter!

Another student wanted to work for a charity raising money for kidney research. This very unusual interest stemmed from the fact that four of his relatives had suffered terribly from kidney disease. What better motivation could there be for wanting to work for a kidney foundation—and how compelling would his letter be *without* it?

Yet another student was particularly interested in getting into a domestic relations practice, and she brought to the table unique experience and insight: She had been divorced twice, and had represented herself successfully both times! Now, tell me: if you were a divorce lawyer, wouldn't you want this particular student as a clerk or associate?

The most extreme example of this—which you'll see again in Chapter 8 on resumes—is a student who wondered how to handle the fact that he'd spent several years in prison before he attended law school. Now while in most circumstances this would be a real negative, he had a particularly fortuitous goal: He wanted to be a prisoners' rights advocate. Who could possibly have greater sympathy for prisoners—and understand the issues facing them—better than someone who'd been a prisoner himself?

When you're talking about these kinds of situations, you're talking about ones where you tiptoe on the edge of TMI—too much information. We talk about that very issue slightly below, in item (k). So, if you're going to include an offbeat paragraph like this, I implore you to run it by your Career Services Director first, to make sure you won't turn off employers more than intrigue them. (Or, of course, you can always e-mail me: jobgoddess@aol.com.)

d. When you say what you're good at, back it up! In other words, don't just tell them: *show* them!

If you've taken a Contracts class yet, you're familiar with the term 'puffery'—that is, inflated claims in ads that can't be pinned on the advertiser. 'The best car money can buy!' That kind of thing. Best, most popular, finest . . . how do you prove them? In a cover letter, it's easy to think the same principle applies. How do you quantify 'hard working,' 'smart,' 'great researcher,' 'enthusiastic'?

Well . . . cover letters ain't Contracts class. And puffery won't help you. If you claim in a cover letter that you're hard working, yet your resume shows crappy grades, no extracurriculars, and no other 'outside distractions' like a job or a family, you're not hard working—you're delusional.

So **when you say what you're good at, provide the proof!** As Albany's Sandy Mans points out, "If you're going to say, 'I'm a great writer, a good researcher, and a hard worker,' you have to back it up! *Show* that you're a hard worker by pointing out that you've juggled several jobs, or worked without supervision, or whatever."

Rob Kaplan offers a simple trick for determining if you've written your second paragraph correctly. That is, check for the word 'because.' If you're going to say you've got strong research skills, you have to provide the 'because'; for instance, because you spent a semester working as a research assistant for Professor Werbezerk.

Or let's say you're applying for a government job. You want to stress your long-standing commitment to the area of law practiced by the department or agency, as evidenced by certain undergrad and law school courses you've taken, internships, research projects, bar association activities, conferences you've attended, and the like.

Now, you may be tempted to bring in every single example you can think of to back up any contention you make. Don't fall into that trap! Two or three features, and an experience or two to support each of them, is all you need.

So the key here is: be sure to back up everything you say with evidence.

Here's an example that makes the point beautifully:

My research shows that you seek superb academic credentials and work experience. I completed my B.A. in Comparative Literature from the University of California at Berkeley in two years with high honors. Then at the [law school] I was the Assistant Editor-in-Chief of the [state] Journal of International Law as well as recipient of the distinguished [name] fellowship. My work for the Volunteer Income Tax Assistance program earned me Pro Bono accolades. Furthermore, my experience in print and broadcast journalism has taught me to work well with deadline constraints and in high pressure situations.

e. Make sure your letter shows you've researched the employer.

Remember, the thing that distinguishes a personal or targeted letter from a mass mailer is the fact that you put information about the employer in your cover letter. It's not enough that you've gone to the trouble of researching the employer—you have to show evidence of that in your cover letter. *Communicate* that you know what they do!

I've told you a couple of times the basic research you have to do, including visiting the employer's web page, googling them, looking on Lexis/Nexis to see if they've been in the news, checking at Career Services. You can do much more, as Chapter 6 on Research suggests, but you've got to do *some* base level of research to write great letters.

What if you try to research an employer, and come up empty? It's getting increasingly rare, but it can happen. Small employers may not have a web site. You can try the Chamber of Commerce or bar association in the employer's city for information, but if you still come up empty, what do you do? Go ahead and acknowledge it in your letter, at the same time briefly summarizing what you did to find out about them. As Debra Fink says, "If you admit that you've tried to research the employer and haven't come up with anything, you've shown initiative!" That's a very positive trait, and it will put you in a good light with the employer.

Show, and support, your interest in the city where the employer is located.

We talk about out-of-town job searches in Chapter 17, so here I'm just going to go over a few special points to remember for your cover letter.

You'll want to explain why it is that you're interested in moving to wherever the employer is located.

When it comes to providing that reason, a few caveats:

- Unless you're talking about a fellowship, clerkship or any other job with a defined one or two year term, your reason has to indicate that you intend to settle in that city for the foreseeable future. Remember the issue for out-of-town employers: They need to know that if they make you an offer, you'll take it. And if you take it, you'll stay for at least a while. So it has to be something with a little more gravitas than "Yo, Dude, I spent Spring Break there and your town rocked!"

- Being interested in a practice area that is specific to—or thriving in—a particular city is a good reason. In other words, you aren't married to the city, but you're so married to the practice area/type of employer that your odds of staying with the job seem good. For instance, if you're interested in International Law, specifically focusing on the Pacific Rim, and you go to school in the Midwest, a desire to work on the West Coast is altogether believable. Or if you're particularly interested in patent work, a desire to live in Silicon Valley or work at the Patent Office in DC makes sense—regardless of how much you're attached to the neighborhood (both areas are pretty awesome, by the way).

The practice doesn't have to be unique to the city. You can always say that you're particularly interested in a practice area and, having researched it, you found that a city with great growth potential in that practice area is the one where the employer is located (and of course it's a practice area of theirs!).

• Personal reasons are good, but have to be worded carefully.

In a nutshell: Following parents or close friends works fine.

Following a spouse, fiancé(e) or boyfriend/girlfriend is more problematic. If you are the "trailing spouse," you have two choices: Either be certain that you stress in your letter that your spouse is going to be employed in that city permanently (which, in career terms, means 'for the foreseeable future'). Or, make the sentence more general in your letter, and substitute 'family' for 'spouse,' saying something like you have family who have recently moved to the city or are about to do so. Having said that, if your spouse will *not* be there for the foreseeable future—for instance, they're in the military, or they're in residency after med school, or they're on sabbatical—I'd strongly encourage you to do one of two things: don't apply for permanent jobs, or be honest about it in your letters to permanent employers.

The cut-off among experts seems to be two years: that is, the 'foreseeable future' is anything over two years. For two years or less, don't apply for permanent jobs, or be honest. If it's more than two years, as one Career Services Director points out, "Lots of things can change in that time. Your spouse might change his or her mind. Or, God forbid, you might be divorced."

So it seems to be "fair dinkum" to apply for any job without saying anything about your plans if you'll be there for at least two years.

This is controversial advice; some career experts will tell you to shut up about it all together. But remember this: there are great, short-term jobs you can get all over America. Judicial clerkships and fellowships are at the top of that list. Furthermore, telling a law firm "I will be there for two years" is not the negative you might assume that it is: it means they don't have to make a decision about keeping you on long-term or making you a partner. The point is: be honest!

The situation is different with a "non-spousal" significant other, a boyfriend or girlfriend.

You can say you're joining friends in the city, which of course, you are—it's just a friend with benefits. Ar ar ar. Or, even better, you can generate an independent interest in the city, either its growth prospects in an area that interests you, or its other attributes that are desirable to you, whatever. And you can put that in your letter.

There are two reasons for not being completely open with employers in this situation. For a start, if you're engaged it may well be that an employer will be nervous that if your relationship goes up in flames before you tie the knot, so will your desire to work in their city. A boyfriend/girlfriend relationship is even further down the food chain of permanence. Furthermore, if you're a woman, suggesting an impending marriage will raise the specter of you'll-just-have-a-baby-and-quit, and why go there if you don't have to—particularly in a cover letter?

So say you're joining friends or pursuing a career goal. That's all the employer needs to know!

g. If you're stuck in terms of getting your personality across, go back and reread the personal essays on your law school applications.

Illinois' Cindy Rold recommends reading the personal essays that got you into law school in the first place. "As you read them, ask yourself: What from this essay, about who I truly am, can be captured in a letter to get my personality across?" It's *very* important to communicate that you're a "living, breathing person!" You're not just a collection of experiences. So, if you find your letter's a snooze, dig out your old entrance essays, and use them to add some sparkle to your letters!

h. If you're writing to a grades-conscious employer (read: large law firms) and your grades aren't top-notch, explain your grades in your cover letter—but *only* do this if you're *positive* the employer is a grade fanatic!

Man, talk about a high-risk piece of advice! Here's why: since a cover letter is a marketing piece, technically speaking you should only be highlighting positives about yourself—and making excuses for bad grades is *not* a positive.

Having said that, there are employers for whom it makes sense to violate this rule, just because you *know* they're credential hounds. Specifically: Large, prestigious law firms. Now I spend all of Chapter 23 talking about how to get your foot in the door at a large firm if the god of grades hasn't smiled on you, and frankly writing them a letter isn't the way to do it. But if for some reason that's the approach you take, and you're not lingering at the top of your class, then you *should* say something about your grades in your cover letter. As Benesch Friedlander's Deanna Coe Kursh says, "Don't assume the employer won't notice that your grades aren't on your resume. You need to volunteer information, to show that you recognize the problem." For instance, there's the old chestnut of a strong upward trend in grades. They don't care what you *did;* they care what you're *capable* of doing. So if you bombed in your first semester of law school but you've had a four-o ever since, definitely mention that in your cover letter. Or if you've got great job experience that compensates for your grades, by all means highlight it. Blackmail Polaroids, you say? Well. Proceed at your own risk.

It's worth restating: I'm imploring you not to send a letter to large, prestigious law firms unless you have a "grade substitute," as we discuss in Chapter 13. Just don't send letters pretending they won't notice your grades. Trust me, they will. I don't want you to waste time on pursuits that will only bum you out. I want you to do things that nail the job you want, as quickly as possible!

i.   It's a letter, not a timeline. Open with your most relevant skills.

As Rob Kaplan points out, it's a huge temptation to just go through your resume, pick out things you've done, and list them in your cover letter in chronological order. But that's not helpful to the employer. You want to take what reporters call an "inverted pyramid" approach, starting with the strength that will be most important to the employer, and proceeding in order of lessening importance after that. If you've got great grades, you lead with that. If your writing skill is the asset of most interest to the employer, that'll be there front and center, as well, followed by support for it—and it doesn't matter whether your writing skill is proven by your most recent job, because you're not listing your experience chronologically!

So make sure that your letter is structured with your "best foot forward"—not "first things first"!

j.   Don't focus on what you don't have!

One of the most dangerous words in cover letters is: "Although." If you're using 'although,' it means you're focusing on negatives, not positives. And as Rob Kaplan advises, "A cover letter is a *marketing* piece. Firms want to see how you market yourself. What are your instincts?" And that's why it's so important *not* to use 'although,' not to be apologetic! Career Counselor Kathleen Brady adds, "Focusing on what you don't have is not useful. Mentioning your art history major isn't a plus unless you're writing to a firm that represents museums."

Rob Kaplan goes on to offer the wording that often appears in cover letters: " 'Although I've never worked in a firm,' or 'Although I've never taken Criminal Law ...' and that's wrong. You're selling a product! When you go to buy a car, the salesman won't say, 'I should tell you up front that this car only gets 18 miles to the gallon.' Instead, they'll sell positives, and they only offer negatives if asked about them. Don't worry; you'll have opportunities to explain away your negatives. But don't do it in a cover letter—even though you'll find that with your law school training, you'll be tempted to find leaks, holes, and gaps in arguments, and address those."

Remember that your cover letter is designed to give the employer reasons *to* interview you, not excuses to *avoid* interviewing you. Stick with your positives!

* * * CAREER LIMITING MOVE * * *

From a law student to a law firm:

"Enclosed please find my resume. As you can see, there's not much to it . . .

. . . so now you have my resume. God knows what you're going to do with it."

* * * CAREER LIMITING MOVE * * *

From a law student letter to an employer:

"My academic performance is exceptional. Although my grades have only been slightly higher than average, it must be emphasized that these grades were earned at the top educational institutions in the world. In addition, it should be noted that in both my undergraduate and graduate studies, my grades have shown steady improvement. For example, last semester I earned a 3.54 at [name of law school], putting me in the top 15% of my class. In addition, it should be noted that I take education very seriously, "learning for the sake of knowledge," rather than for the sake of grades. It should be noted on my transcript a staunch refusal to take any "fluff" courses.

k.   Beware of TMI.

Too Much Information. You want your cover letter to reveal you as a living, breathing, vibrant person. But . . . there's a limit to what you disclose.

Here's the situation: You've been through something that was a life-altering event. It explains a great deal about you and how you look at life, how strong and resilient you are, why you have a passion for a particular city/specialty/the practice of law. If you want to share it with employers in cover letters, I would *urge* you to run your letter past your Career Services Director first. And I'll tell you why: It's important to remember that employers don't know you. They don't have a frame of reference for what you tell them; all they have is this little piece of paper in front of them. And something that might be perfectly appropriate to share with people in person, or after you've known them for a little while, can be jarring in a letter from a stranger.

I'll give you a personal example of what I'm talking about. When I was a kid, my mother became seriously mentally ill. She was dangerous to be around, and attempted suicide a dozen times before she finally killed herself when I was ten years old. You know me pretty well because you've been reading this book, but nonetheless—that was along the lines of a shocking revelation, wouldn't you agree? Can you imagine how much *more* shocking it would be if I mentioned it to you *in a cover letter?* If I said something like, "Overcoming my mother's suicide made me a stronger person ..." and so on? Maybe it *did*—but it's just, well, it's just too much information in a cover letter.

Let's take a couple of student examples to further plumb the distinction I'm talking about. On the "thumbs up" side is a student I've mentioned before, who wanted to go into domestic relations. She mentioned in her cover letters that she got interested in family law because "of my two divorces, in which I represented myself: with great success!" It was a big hit, and got her foot in the door at several desirable employers.

Another positive example is the situation where a personal experience got you interested in a particular specialty. One student had a grandfather who died as a result of a botched operation. His family sued the doctor, he followed the lawsuit closely, and it got him interested in plaintiff's side med mal. There's nothing wrong with mentioning that in a cover letter.

Similar theme, different situation: A student at a school in Arizona was a mom interested in doing criminal defense work. What got her interested in it? "My husband is in jail. I learned a *lot* watching his trial every day."

You can see what ties together these examples: they weave a personal experience in with interest and familiarity with a particular practice.

On the flip side of that was a student in California, a lovely young woman who introduced herself to me with a rather interesting conversational opener: "I have a plate in my head!" When I tell you there's no way you would ever have known this by looking at her, I'm understating it: she was a real hottie, and seemed perfectly fine. She went on to explain that as a senior in college she had been in a car accident and flown through the front window. Her injuries had required the implantation of a plate in her head, and left her with no memory of high school or college.

I complimented her on her remarkable recovery, and she went on to tell me that her physical therapy had been very demanding, and that—you probably saw this coming—she had been advised to open her letters with a sympathy play, to say "I have a head injury." I asked her what kind of success she'd had with these letters—after all, there's no such thing as a bad strategy if it works!—and she hadn't had any luck. An opener to someone who has no idea who you are? It's not the right place. If she was in an interview and things were going well—maybe. After she started a job, and out for lunch with colleagues—absolutely. It's the *context* that determines how a revelation will play.

Another example is also fairly common: students who've lost a tremendous amount of weight. There's no question that taking off, and keeping off, significant tonnage says remarkable things about personal discipline, determination, and so on—but it's not "cover letter ready." In an interview, on the job—OK. Just not in a letter.

As the weight loss example particularly highlights, experiences that fall under "TMI" also tend to have another quality that makes them questionable cover letter content: They tend to speak only tangentially to what you have to offer an employer. Strength, resilience, determination, those are all terrific traits—but when you figure that what employers want to see tend to be qualities like hard working, affinity for and experience in a particular specialty or setting, writing ability, counseling ability, a talent for attracting business—you can see that these kinds of experiences are not the best choices.

By the way, a simple test to see if you're disclosing too much is to look at the length of your cover letter. Students send me their cover letters all the time, and I've never seen a TMI letter from a student that ran less than two full pages. There's no real reason for a cover letter to run more than one. If yours way overshoots that . . . check for TMI.

l. If you're a woman with children, consider mentioning that in your cover letter.

I can hear you shrieking: *"Have you lost your mind, Kimmbo?"* Nope. But I know that a lot of people will advise you to hide the kids like, I don't know, nutty Aunt Hattie living in the castle tower. I think that's a big mistake, and a lot of smart people agree with me. And in your heart of hearts, you agree with me, too.

Here's the thinking:

- If you've already had kids, you've *proven* the main thing that concerns employers: you can balance work (in your case, school) with family. That's a tremendous benefit.

- Because you've already had children, you obviously aren't going to quit your job to get married and have children. I realize that employers can't legally ask you about your marital/parental status (of course they often do), but their legitimate concern is this: are they going to put a lot of money into training you, only to have you quit to have kids before they've earned back their investment? I know that sounds cold, but them's the facts. If you've already had children, clearly you aren't quitting to stay home with them. You've answered the question that's on their minds even if they don't ask it.

- Having children will help explain why you don't have an extracurricular-heavy resume. Almost, every dual-duty mom-and-law-student with whom I've ever spoken has a "lighter" resume; that is, there aren't a lot of school-related extracurriculars because there's a living, breathing, albeit unmentioned "extracurricular," who needs motherly attention. If you don't mention *anywhere* that you have kids, employers will fill in the blanks themselves: are you lazy? Do you drink heavily? Are you particularly inefficient with your homework? Trust me, having a family is highly preferable to any of those!

- It'll eliminate you from consideration by employers who are horrified that you have children, that's true. In other words: Employers you would hate to work for won't hire you. I think that's the Universe working out, don't you? If you get an emergency call from your kid's school because junior has a spiking fever and your employer is furious about this—where are your priorities? You want to work for employers—and trust me, there are lots of them—whose values are yours.

I think the corker is this: If you do get a job with a certain employer, sooner rather than later they're going to realize that you have kids. It might not be that you show up at the office with oatmeal on your lapel, but it'll happen. And if the subject of your children has never, ever come up before that—well, it seems a little off-putting, don't you think? What else are you hiding? So don't make it a secret. Use it to show your strengths, which are, on top of anything else, the proven ability to juggle lots of responsibilities, and a solid connection with the community (you wouldn't be the first person to get a new client via another kid's dad on your kid's soccer team).

m. "Spinning" a prior job you hated in your cover letter.

Remember: Your skills are *always* transferable. While we talk about this at length in the "Second Careers" chapter, it's worth noting here that whatever you've done before is somehow useful to employers you target—but you've got to make that plain to them! Sue Gainen provides the following excellent examples.

Let's say that you're applying to the Prosecutor's office, and you've previously worked at the Public Defender's office. You might say something like, "Although my school-year clerking experience is in a public defender's office, the criminal law practice skills I have acquired should easily transfer to a prosecution setting ... I respect and admire the lawyers I worked with, but it is clear to me that my interests and instincts are better suited to prosecution."

Or let's say you've done family law and you want commercial litigation. You might say, "My school-year clerking has been in a busy family law practice. The client service, research and file management skills that I acquired should easily transfer to a more general commercial litigation practice ... After working with extremely dedicated and talented lawyers who will remain excellent role models, it is clear to me that my interests and skills are more suited to a general commercial practice."

2. EXAMPLES OF MIDDLE PARTS

Here's one, from a 2L with legal experience and average grades, looking for a job at a small firm with an employment discrimination practice:

With my work experience and coursework in employment discrimination, I believe I have the skills and knowledge to contribute to your practice. Last summer at the Ohio State Division of Human Rights, I assisted attorneys and investigators in researching complaints and law. I interviewed complainants, wrote substantive memoranda, and drafted pleadings. Since the office was short-staffed due to state budget cuts, I was given increased responsibility during my ten weeks there. The class on Employment Discrimination that I took last Spring helped to prepare me for my work last summer, and it is something I would continue to draw upon in working for you this summer.

Here's one, in a letter from a 3L seeking a permanent associate position at a medium-sized firm:

In the course of researching your firm, I learned that you look for associates with strong legal and analytical skills, and a strong work ethic. I believe my background exhibits all three. For example, while attending college I was simultaneously employed full-time for Ford Motor Company between the hours of 11:30 p.m. and 7:30 a.m., and yet graduated in four years with honors. And my legal and analytical skills were sharpened in a recent externship with the Honorable George Lowrey, United States Magistrate, Central District of Ohio, where I gained extensive hands-on experience with many kinds of cases, and analyzed a wide variety of legal issues.

Here's another one, for a summer clerkship with a small firm:

I understand that you seek out summer clerks who are self-starters. That describes my legal background perfectly. My last summer was spent with Lawson Wills, a sole practitioner in Covington. As he was running for state office, I was given unusual independence in structuring and completing the tasks that were assigned to me. I produced work that was praised and used almost without revision. I was able to prove to him and myself, my self-reliance and organizational, research, analytical, and writing abilities. I would bring these same qualities to work for you.

Here's one from a 3L seeking a permanent associateship with a medium-sized firm with a strong construction litigation practice:

I have a strong academic background and experience in the types of cases handled by your firm. During an externship for Judge Crater, I researched various issues regarding construction law and civil litigation. I also drafted several bench memoranda and orders for the judge.

This past summer I worked as a summer associate in the professional liability section of a large Detroit law firm. As a summer associate I performed research, wrote memoranda, and prepared pleadings on behalf of engineers and architects in cases involving various construction issues.

Now, at this point, if you don't have much (if any) legal experience to date, you may be getting depressed. Don't! Remember, what you're doing is bringing skills to the table that will be useful to your employer, and if you look closely at the examples I've just given you, they mention things that aren't law-related. You may even want to address your lack of experience straight out in a sentence or so; that's what I did when I was a law student. I used to have a section in the middle paragraph of my letters that read:

I wish I could tell you that I'd clerked for a U.S. Supreme Court Justice, or competed in the Olympics, or started a Fortune 500 company. I can't do that, because I haven't. But what I lack in experience, I make up for in my willingness to work hard for you. I worked full-time to put myself through college, often waiting tables thirty hours a week while carrying a full course load at school. I would love to work for you, and I promise your confidence in me would be rewarded with loyalty, dedication, and hard work.

Frankly, they ate up that kind of stuff, and if you don't have a lot of experience yourself, it could work for you, too (but do us both a favour: don't copy it word for word. Employers read this book too, you know—and nothing is more off-putting than plagiarized enthusiasm!)

Here's another one, from a 1L with no legal experience, looking at a law firm with a banking practice:

My experience working as a teller and in the administrative offices of the Hostile Takeover Bank will help me in making the transition to working this summer in banking law. I understand the basic business practices of banking and will draw upon this knowledge base to perform the tasks assigned to me as a summer law clerk.

Furthermore, my law school classes also prepared me well for a summer law clerk position. I recognize that strong legal research and writing skills are what legal employers like you seek in a candidate. [Law School's] first year program provides excellent training in legal research and writing. As a student in the year-long course entitled "Law Firm" I am writing legal memoranda, conducting research, and drafting contracts and pleadings.

Here's one from a 1L with some experience before law school, applying for a job with a legal department at a hospital:

As the enclosed resume indicates, I was an admissions group coordinator at General Hospital until I entered law school. This was the last of three progressively responsible positions I held at the hospital. My experience with such exacting professional standards contributed directly to my success in law school and I am eager to have the opportunity to learn about the corporate legal aspect of hospital administration. In addition, my familiarity with the hospital should limit the amount of training that I require and permit me to quickly contribute to your department.

Here's one from a 1L to a small firm with a strong corporate and commercial law practice:

You may find my background and credentials to be of particular interest. Although I have attended school continuously, I have developed business acumen through operating my own seasonal service company, which has employed up to five people each summer for the past three years. I was able to put into practice the theoretical education I received as an undergraduate business major. The sale of this business this year has enabled me to finance a significant portion of my law school expenses. This school year, I have worked with a small partnership, which helped me to decide that my interests and talents could best be utilized in a small, business-oriented firm like [name of firm].

Here's one from a 1L with no legal experience, undecided about what he wants to do, to a firm with a wide-ranging general practice:

I understand that [name of firm] is noted for community leadership. As the enclosed resume demonstrates, I have considerable experience in peer leadership through volunteer and organizational activities. This has helped me substantially in law school and should prove to be a continuing asset in my career with a firm like yours. Through receiving professional instruction and intense experience in crisis management as a Resident Assistant Director in college, for example, I was able to compete successfully in the law school's Client Counseling Competition, where a partner and I placed second among six teams. The academic success of my first semester in law school can be attributed partly to the skills that I have developed in managing the often-competing demands of school and other duties. As a result, I believe that my summer with your firm would prove beneficial to both of us.

So—the middle part of your letter is the one that answers the question: why should they meet you? That only leaves one more paragraph . . .

c. THE CLOSING PART OF YOUR LETTER: WHAT DO YOU WANT TO HAPPEN NEXT?

Here it is—the call to action. **It's where you state what you're going to do, and what you want the recipient to do.** This is really pretty simple stuff; a few examples will get across exactly what I'm talking about. You'll notice a general pattern in them:

- **You're grateful to be considered;**
- **You ask directly for an interview;**
- **You state how the employer should contact you;**
- **You say when you're available; and**
- **Either you say you're going to follow up, or you don't.**

"Wait a second, Kimmbo," I hear you saying. "Which is it—do I tell them I'll call, or not?"

Wellll ... that's an open question. Experts disagree. Some people will tell you that it sounds pushy if you say you'll call; you'll be a pest. Others say that it's impressive, it shows initiative and enthusiasm. Of course, the $64,000 question is: how are you supposed to know what your recipient will think? It's a roll of the dice, unless, of course, you're writing to someone because you were told to do so by a contact; you remember, my favourite kind of letter, that starts with the words "So and so recommended that I contact you ..." in that case, ask "So and so" whether you should say you'll call. And if *they* don't know ... well. You're back to rolling the dice.

One thing on which all experts agree, however, is that if you say you'll follow up—do it! Why? As Notre Dame's Gail Peshel says, "If you say you'll call, some firms, especially smaller ones, will set aside your letter and not respond, assuming you're going to call."

Let's take a look at a few examples.

Here's one for an out-of-town interview possibility:

I would appreciate the opportunity to meet with you and discuss the possibility of a summer position. I will be returning to Cincinnati just before Columbus Day weekend. I will contact you when I arrive, if I have not heard from you before that time and, if appropriate, arrange a time that will be convenient. Thank you for your consideration.

Or:

If my experience and background meet you requirements for a new associate, please contact me at the address, e-mail address, or telephone number listed above. I will be available to interview in Detroit throughout the winter/spring semester. Thank you for your consideration.

Or:

I look forward to hearing from you to arrange a personal meeting. You can reach me at the phone number, e-mail address, and address listed above. Thank you, in advance, for your consideration.

Or:

I would appreciate the opportunity to discuss how my background may fit your needs. I look forward to hearing from you. Thank you for your consideration.

Or:

I would welcome the opportunity to meet with you at your convenience, either at your office or before the workday. You may reach me at the above address, e-mail address and phone number to arrange a meeting, if appropriate. Thank you for your consideration.

Or:

I would very much welcome the opportunity to meet with you personally should you have an appropriate opening. I can be reached at the telephone number or address above, and can arrange an appointment at most any time that is convenient to you. Thank you for your consideration.

* * * CAREER LIMITING MOVE * * *

"... I need an acceptable job offer.[1]

2. WHAT GOES *WITH* YOUR COVER LETTERS? A KILLER TIP TO MAKE YOURSELF STAND OUT ...

Typically your cover letters will go out with only one additional document: your resume. Don't weigh down employers with lots of extraneous material, because a) they're busy, and b) they won't read it.

However ...

There are a couple of situations where you might want to send out more.

A. AN ARTICLE YOU'VE WRITTEN *DIRECTLY RELEVANT* TO THE EMPLOYER'S PRACTICE

Let's say that you do as I advise in Topic G(14), below, and write an article about an issue *directly pertinent* to the employer's practice, for, say, a bar association publication or website. *Because it will engage the employer substantively,* it's a wise thing to send. It proves not just your ability to write but your enthusiasm for what they do, and your awareness of the issues they face. If you send along such an article, you'd add a "P.S." to your letter to draw attention to it. (Studies show that people pay special attention to what's in a "P.S.")

B. OUTSTANDING REFERENCE LETTERS

Consider sending along stellar letters of recommendation from prior legal employers. I mentioned this way back in Chapter 1 as a tactic I've seen work brilliantly well for some law students I've met around the country. A super reference letter can make an otherwise diffident employer sit up and pay attention.

Here's what you need to know before you try this tactic:

(1) **The letters have to be *stellar,* complimenting the quality of your work and anything else that the employer really appreciated about you**: excellent research skills, hard work, ability to deal with people and/or a specific population, efficiency, creative problem-solving, ability to work without close supervision, *whatever* it is. (The more the letters reflect the qualities your "target employers" want, the better off you are.) The letters can't be just OK. "Well, he didn't drool on himself" or "I could have done a lot worse" won't help you.

---

1. An "acceptable job offer" includes a base salary of at least $70,000.00 per year, a "sign on" or "relocation" bonus of at least $5,000.00, an "end of year" or "Christmas" bonus of at least $5,000.00, a firm "401K" which offers a firm match of at least 50% of voluntary salary deductions of at least 6% taken by its associates, a firm-wide medical plan, including major medical, dental and optical, and a firm-wide life insurance policy or accidental death and dismemberment policy. Also, note that an increase in base salary is an acceptable alternative to any or all of the benefits enumerated in this footnote.

(2) **Offer to write your reference letters yourself.**

Writing references letters is work. Make it easy on your references by offering to write the letters yourself. Not only will you be helping them, but this is one way you can be sure that your reference letters highlight the skills and qualities you want to showcase.

If you feel uncomfortable with this idea, Michelle Hoff encourages you to go to your Career Services Office and "Tell them what you've done. They'll help you write your reference letters. We do it all the time."

Please remember: Offering to write your own reference letters is great. Writing them without telling the reference about them is not!

(3) **You have to let the prior employer know what you're doing, and get their OK.**

Whenever someone writes a reference letter for you, you're leaving them open to phone calls and e-mails from prospective employers asking about you. *Whenever* you send out correspondence mentioning your reference's name, let them know the employers you're contacting, so they won't be caught off-guard.

(4) **For employers other than large law firms, consider sending your letter and references in a two-pocket folder.**

What you do is to put your letter (with your resume behind it) in the left-hand pocket and your letters of reference in the right-hand pocket. This way, when your targets open the folder, they see the letters of reference *first*—people instinctively look to the right-hand side before they look to the left. You want them to form their first impression of you from those brilliant letters!

If you're sending your materials to the recruiting coordinator or hiring partner of a large law firm, however, bag the folder, and here's why: they'll have a specific protocol for handling student correspondence, and they'll immediately ditch your folder. It adds more work for them, and it doesn't do you any good. So in that circumstance: don't use the folder.

But for other correspondence ... consider trying it. It's worked for a lot of other students. It could work for you, too!

E.   THE PERFECT COVER LETTER CHECKLIST. IT'S NOT JUST WHAT YOU SAY ... IT'S THE WAY YOU SAY IT

And the way it looks, by the way. In this section, we'll make sure that your letters don't get tripped up with ancillary issues of style—and judgment.

1. THERE'S ONLY ONE COLOR FOR COVER LETTERS . . .

White, dagnabbit. *Legally Blonde* was a *comedy,* not a documentary. Not beige, not blue, not green, and nothing neon. Use the same paper—the same white paper—you use on your resume, and the same type font. And it doesn't have to have a heavy rag content. They're going to read it, not wash it.

2. STANDARD LETTER FORMAT, *ANY* STANDARD LETTER FORMAT, IS FINE

What you're aiming for is the recipient not to notice the format of your letter, or a funny font. You want them to focus on what you've got to say. So whether you indent your paragraphs or skip a space between them, or put your name and address on the right margin or the left, it doesn't matter, as long as it looks professional. (For a sample format, see Appendix B.)

* * * CAREER LIMITING MOVE * * *

One law student chose a highly unusual letter format: namely, a ransom note. He cut letters out of magazines, and spelled out his cover letter, in its entirety: "Hire me or the dog gets it"—and had a photo of Snoopy pasted to the page, with a hand holding a pistol aimed at its head.

3. GET THE EMPLOYER'S NAME *LETTER—AND COMMA—PERFECT!*

Go to the employer's web site and copy down their name *letter for letter, comma for comma.* And put it *in its entirety* in your letter's "header" (right before the "Dear___" line) and on the envelope.

So if the law firm is "Grumpy, Dopey, Sleepy, Doc, Smiley, Bashful and Happy," don't write "Grumpy, Dopey," and leave it at that. And pay attention to those commas. Someone told me once that leaving out commas in a law firm name is supposed to show that they're all equals. Go figure. But as the line from *To Kill A Mockingbird* goes, if they want to pour syrup on the table cloth and eat it, they can. It doesn't matter if the employer wants to be addressed as She–Rah Goddess of the Universe. Call them what they want to be called, and get it *letter perfect.*

4. NO TYPOS, GRAMMAR, SPELLING, OR PUNCTUATION MISTAKES. "DEVOTED DAUGHTER, BELOVED AUNT . . ."

Do you recognize that line? If you do, you're a fan of *Curb Your Enthusiasm.* The reason I mention that line is that it was the focus of an episode where Larry, the main character, was responsible for getting his wife's aunt's obituary in the newspaper. It was supposed to read "Devoted daughter, beloved aunt . . ." except the "a" in aunt appeared in the paper as a "c"!

Remember, when an employer is looking at your cover letter, the only 'in-hand' evidence they have of the quality of your work and your attention to detail is that letter. Deanna Coe Kursh points out that

"Your readers' clients have to have confidence in you, and they won't if you can't even present yourself perfectly in a cover letter."

Does this seem obvious? Sure—but the reason I'm telling you is twofold: Number one, it happens all the time. Every hiring person at every law firm in America can tell legions of stories about letters with typos they've received. And when they see spelling and grammar errors *they ditch the letters*. That's it. No matter how much you have to offer— and let's face it, you *do* have a lot to offer—they'll never consider you if your letter displays typos and grammar mistakes.

Furthermore, you can't proofread your own stuff. I know what you'll be tempted to do: glance over your letters before you send them out, and leave it at that. Don't! You're too familiar with what you write, so you read what you *think* is there. I know this from vast personal experience. I'll hand in pieces to be published, convinced that they're in great shape, only to get back a marked-up manuscript with the most basic mistakes I've overlooked.

Spell-checking is similarly flawed, because it doesn't pick up words that are used incorrectly (like "their" when you meant "there."). This can entirely change the meaning of what you write.

I was reading a job search book recently, which included the following passage about informational interviewing: "Once you've ... learned about your contact's current job ... broaden your questions to illicit information about her employer and the industry as a whole." No matter how well you get along with an interviewer, it's probably not a good idea to ask if her boss flashes people in the park. Nor is it what the author meant to say!

* * * SPELL–CHECKING GONE MAD * * *

Law students aren't the only ones with spell checking issues. It happens to practicing lawyers, as well.

In early 2006 a story hit the media about a California lawyer representing a former judge who'd been convicted of fixing traffic tickets. In an opening brief to the appellate court, the lawyer used the term "sua sponte"—which as you Latin scholars know means "on its own motion"—six times.

Or at least ... he *meant* to.

His spell-checking program replaced each of the "sua sponte"'s with "sea sponge," "sua sponte" apparently not being part of the spell-checking function's vocabulary.

He didn't proofread the brief before he submitted it.

So the court received a brief with sentences like: "An appropriate instruction limiting the judge's criminal liability in such a prosecution must be given sea sponge explaining that certain acts or omissions by themselves are not sufficient to support a conviction." And:

"It is well settled that a trial court must instruct sea sponge on any defense, including a mistake of fact defense."

If you have to proofread your letter yourself, read it backwards, because then the individual words stand out; you're not reading for context. It won't pick up grammar errors, but spelling mistakes will jump out.

Grammar mistakes can also make you look goofy. Put yourself in the shoes not so much of an employer, but of a client—because that's how employers will look at you. What would happen if you got a letter from your lawyer—the person who's safeguarding your property if not your liberty—that read, "I think we'll do good if we go to court, they're claim don't have any merits." If you're not confident of your grammar skills, take the simple precaution of showing your letters to the folks at Career Services before you send them out. They'll be happy to go over them for you.

(In following examples, emphases are mine.)

* * * CAREER LIMITING MOVE * * *

One student sent out a letter, heralding his experience at the prosecutor's office, where he "researched issues that will go down in the *anals* of criminal law."

* * * CAREER LIMITING MOVE * * *

A student had to reschedule a law firm interview, and wrote a very polite letter asking for a different time. He finished by apologizing and saying, "I hope this rescheduling does not cause you any *incontinence*."

* * * CAREER LIMITING MOVE * * *

A line in one student's cover letter: "Test scores reveal that I have a *jenius* I.Q."

* * * CAREER LIMITING MOVE * * *

A student, trying to highlight her people skills, intended to say that she was an excellent "glad hander." In her letter, it translated as *"gland-handler."*

* * * CAREER LIMITING MOVE * * *

To an employer in Macon, Georgia: "I've long wanted to live and work in *Maconga*."

* * * CAREER LIMITING MOVE * * *

In a letter to the National Deaf Society: "I am interested in working for the National *Death* Society."

* * * CAREER LIMITING MOVE * * *

Describing her summer clerkship, one student wrote that "I learned everything there is to know about the prosecutor's *roll.*"

* * * CAREER LIMITING MOVE * * *

A student emphasized his enthusiasm for the employer's mission by lauding "the *impotant* work you do."

5. **"DEAR MR. REBOZO" BETTER GO TO A MALE NAMED REBOZO! GET ALL OF YOUR RECIPIENT'S INFORMATION DOWN *PERFECTLY***

Get the information about your recipient wrong, even slightly, and to borrow a baseball analogy—you're out!

If you aren't sure of the spelling of their name, go to the employer's web site to check it, or try Martindale Hubbell (www.martindale.com), or call the employer's office, and ask to have the recipient's name and the employer's name spelled for you over the phone; you don't have to give your name or the reason for your call, other than to say you're sending correspondence. Don't be embarrassed about making this call; it's a far better to *check* than to risk getting it wrong—and losing any chance of getting a job there!

Similarly, make sure you've got the person's gender straight. I can't tell you how many times I've received letters addressed to "Mr. Walton"—I guess "Kimm" is one of those names that could go either way—but I'm not a "Mr." (I should tell you, however, that I am not insulted by that, and actually have a response that I put in the "P.S." in responses, namely: "Incidentally, it's "Ms." Walton, not "Mr."—but if you had to make that mistake, I'm glad you did it on the basis of a name, and not a personal meeting!")

Another *very* common mistake in correspondence is to have the letter addressed to one person, and the envelope addressed to someone else. I know, I know, you're saying, "Geez, Kimmbo—what am I? A *complete idiot?*" No, of course not, but I should point out to you that fully a third of the application letters I've ever received were *addressed to the wrong person.* That is, the name and address on the envelope were mine, but the letter inside was addressed to someone else. Or the name and address at the top of the letter didn't match the salutation (Dear So-and-so) line. The worst thing about a letter like this is that it means you've alienated *two* possible employers—because you can't mess up one letter like this, you're messing up at least two at a time. So, no matter how much time you spend making contacts, or researching, or putting together a kick-butt resume, it just doesn't matter if you screw up and send mismatched letters, or misspell the recipient's name or address.

How do you avoid this? Glance over your letters *as* you're putting them in the envelopes. Check the name and address and salutation line, and make sure the name on the letter matches the one on the envelope. That's all it takes!

* * * CAREER LIMITING MOVE * * *

Law student, in an interview with a large firm in Los Angeles. We'll call the law firm Stars & Stripes. Student asks the interviewer, "What phrase do you think describes what's best about your firm?" The interviewer thinks about it for a moment and responds, and follows up by asking, "All right—what phrase do you think describes what's best about *you*?" The law student pauses a moment, and says, "I'm sure I'll come up with one—I'll send it to you."

The interviewer goes back to his office at Stars & Stripes, and sure enough, two days later he receives a letter from the law student. The student says how much he enjoyed the interview and says, "By the way, I thought of a phrase that describes what's best about me: my attention to detail. That's what would make me so valuable to Hammer & Sickle"—another large law firm in Los Angeles.

* * * CAREER LIMITING MOVE * * *

Student sends a cover letter to a lawyer named Marvin O. Laughlin. The letter, however, is addressed to "Marvin O'Laughlin" ... same letters—very different name!

* * * CAREER LIMITING MOVE * * *

Letter to District Attorney's office, saying "and that is why I believe I would be a valuable addition to the Public Defender's office."

6. PROOFREAD FOR CONNOTATIONS AND DOUBLE ENTENDRES

Sometimes it's not the spelling or grammar that's a problem; it's an unintended meaning. Put your letter aside for a few hours and read it again, to see if it means what you want it to mean. Even better, give it to a friend or a counselor at Career Services; they'll spot the flaws you might overlook.

* * * CAREER LIMITING MOVE * * *

Female law student, sending a letter to a lawyer seeking an informational interview, says, "My friend X says you are a large firm lawyer, and that's what I want." (As opposed to ...)

* * * CAREER LIMITING MOVE * * *

Second career student, intending to show employer that his work experience makes him the perfect candidate: "I have a package you just have to see."

7. MAKE SURE THE TONE IS LIKE BABY BEAR'S PORRIDGE: JUST RIGHT. NOT TOO POMPOUS, NOT TOO CASUAL

The tone of your letter should reflect *you*. That's why I can't write them for you. If you're serious, if you're light-hearted, let the tone reflect your personality.

In the interviewing chapter, I tell you the story about a law student who went on a few too many practice interviews at a job fair, such that when she got to the interview for the job she really wanted, she hyperventilated and couldn't talk . . . for the entire twenty minutes. She wanted to know how to follow up with the employer, and one of her classmates recommended that she write a letter saying, "You've seen me at my worst; I'd like to show you my best." That's a great line, and it would have fit the person who said it. The problem was this was a very serious student; it would have misled the employer about her nature.

Employers have told me about situations where they read a cover letter fully expecting one kind of person, and somebody else entirely walks through the door. It's jarring, and it makes them wonder: Who exactly *wrote* that letter?

At the same time, the tone has to avoid being too pompous or casual. I've seen letters—more often e-mails, actually—to employers, with the opening line "How are you doing?" Too casual. At the other end of the scale, a student at one school had a cover letter that opened with the line, "I penned this letter to you in pursuance of the goal of becoming an associate at your firm." Yikes!

These kinds of problems are easily avoided with a visit to Career Services. Even if you fall into one of these traps, when they're pointed out to you it'll never happen again.

8. DON'T SEND THEM TOO MUCH OF A GOOD THING!

As Texas' Annette Jones points out, "Some students think 'the more, the merrier.' When it comes to correspondence, they should be thinking, 'more is less.'"

What *shouldn't* you include? Annette Jones offers examples:

- Fitness reports from the military
- Copies of award certificates
- Published short stories
- Entire books and magazines with your byline buried on page 27
- Poetry
- Copies of personal statements from law school applications

One recruiting coordinator told me about a student who had googled herself, and included along with her letter and resume *an entire, downloaded file of every mention of her on the Internet!* I mean, every time her name appeared. Let's face it: googling yourself is a gas. But it's a hobby—not a job search tool.

Another student, interested in Sports Law, had been a creative writing major. He wanted to send employers a short story he'd written along with his cover letter and resume. The fact that he wrote short stories is great for the "Hobbies" section of his resume (along with whether the stories had been published or won any prizes), and it's fine fodder for an interview ... but as part of an application package? Put yourself in the shoes of a Sports lawyer. You get a letter from a student with a story, "The Christmas Surprise." You'd be confused.

Of course, there are exceptions where sending additional material is appropriate. Even in the Sports Law short story setting, if the short story in question was about baseball and the lawyer in question represents baseball players, maybe. And if you've done as I suggest in the Birds and Bees chapter and written a short piece about an issue in the specialty—absolutely. Send it! But you can see how far down the spectrum this is from sending an unrelated article or a book.

The watchword here is: Entice employers—don't suffocate them. A short, dynamic letter. A brilliant resume (we'll talk about writing exactly that in the next chapter). *Perhaps* glowing recommendation letters. And that's it!

9. THE WORDS THAT FOLLOW "DEAR" SHOULD BE A NAME—NOT "HIRING PARTNER." THE ONLY EXCEPTION: A JOB AD OR POSTING, WHICH GIVES YOU A TITLE RATHER THAN A NAME

I have a question for you. What would happen if you received a letter in the mail, and you opened it, and you read the following:

> *I love you. I want to spend the rest of my life with you. Will you marry me?*

And you took a look back at the envelope, and noticed that it was addressed to:

> *Occupant.*

Gee—sort of deflates the message, doesn't it?

Well, the same thing applies if you send letters addressed to "Dear Hiring Partner" or even worse, "To Whom It May Concern." You're asking an employer to invest in you, train you, take their hard-earned cheese and take a risk on you. The *least* you could do is find the name of a flesh-and-blood person to address your letter to!

Now, obviously, if you're responding to a "blind" job ad, you can't name names (we discuss job ads pretty soon. But otherwise: *Always* get a name. If necessary, call the employer's office, and—with a smile on your face—say you're sending correspondence to the person in charge of hiring, and you want to make sure you have the correct name. You could also check with the employer's web site for guidance, or your Career Services Office. The point is: Personalize your correspondence!

10. MAKE SURE YOU SHOW IN YOUR LETTER THAT YOU KNOW WHAT THEY DO! IF YOUR LETTER MENTIONS A SPECIALTY, MAKE SURE THEY ACTUALLY *HAVE* THAT SPECIALTY

Of course, this is yet another swipe at mass mailers, where by their very nature you can't acknowledge what any individual employer does. I've spanked you plenty in this chapter with the importance of research. Showing the fruits of that research in your cover letter is flattering and gratifying to employers, and it makes them feel unique—and that's exactly how you want them to feel!

Sorry to say, some letters make a worse mistake than failing to discuss the employer's practice. Some letters talk about it, and get it *wrong*. "I'm particularly interested in your family law practice" is not going to resound with a firm that doesn't practice family law. You'd be horrified to know how often this happens!

By the way, it doesn't much matter what the source of your information is. You're golden with any sentence that starts:

"While researching your website/ NALP form I saw that you ..."

"My Career Services Director, Anne Frank, told me that you ..."

"In speaking with your former summer clerk, Sylvan Glenn, I learned that you ..."

"In your profile in *America's Greatest Places To Work With A Law Degree,* I noticed that you ..." (Sorry. Shameless self-serving plug for one of my *other* books.)

Incidentally, if it's the setting you want and not a particular specialty—a large law firm, or a small, civil practice, for instance—go ahead and say that without confining yourself to a specialty.

* * * CAREER LIMITING MOVE * * *

Law student takes his cover letter to Career Services for review. His letter includes a line saying, "As you can see, most of my experience is in Admiralty, which I would like to practice."

Career counselor: "Do they have an Admiralty practice?"

Law student: "No."

11. DON'T LET YOUR PRIDE GET IN THE WAY OF MENTIONING OBVIOUS HOOKS!

Gosh, this happens *all the time.* I talk to students who'll sheepishly say, "Well, my uncle *is* a federal judge/mother works at the court house/friend's father is a partner at a law firm/aunt knows the hiring partner at ..." and follow up by saying, "But I don't want to *use* that!" Oh, for gosh sakes, swallow your pride and say, "[Mutual acquaintance] recommended that I contact you"! As Sophie Sparrow advises, "Always mention obvious hooks *first*. The job search process can be tough and demoralizing. Don't let that overshadow what you naturally *know*— which is that it helps to mention an obvious connection!"

12. CONFIDENCE IS GREAT ... ARROGANCE IS NOT!

This is a major problem, and a common one. It's easy to slip over the line from confidence into cockiness. But it's an important barrier to heed, because there's the world of difference between saying "I would prefer litigation, but I would *consider* ..." and "I would prefer litigation, but *I would be pleased to be considered for* ..." The second choice strikes the appropriate note. As Maine's Tammy Willcox says, "The tone you want to approximate is humble, yet secure." Gail Cutter adds that "Wording like 'I was fortunate enough to work for a federal judge,' or 'I was lucky to have the opportunity to take charge of client matters'" sounds less pushy.

So—what kinds of lines do you want to avoid? Anything that sounds like these actual lines from student cover letters:

- *"I'm confident that I will be an incredible asset to your firm."*
- *"I'm going to bust my ass for you."*
- *"I'd be perfect for you because ..."* (The problem here is that you're drawing a conclusion for them; you're better off saying, "I have strong skills because ..." and then explaining the source of your skills, letting the reader draw the conclusion you'd be perfect for them!)

It is very, very difficult to spot arrogance in your own letters. Do yourself a favour and shoot them over to Career Services before you send them out, to make sure that you're tooting your own horn—without deafening people in the process!

* * * CAREER LIMITING MOVE * * *

"Dear Mr. [name]:

You are not going to get many applicants like me. I advise you to examine my credentials carefully. I guarantee you will be pleased I applied."

* * * CAREER LIMITING MOVE * * *

Law student with stellar credentials. He writes letters to employers heralding his achievements, concluding by saying: "... and I don't disappoint."

13.   NO LIES!!

I know you're not a liar. But I also know the temptation when you're faced with a blank page, cognizant of the fact that what you *say* on that page can get your foot in the door at a dream employer. So, is there really a problem with a little white lie, something they'll never catch, and something that makes you look a lot better ...?

Stop! Don't do it! It's not a moral judgment, but the fact is you're *far* more likely to be caught than you think. You wouldn't believe the obscure lies I've heard coming to light. And the results are *devastating*. I can help you overcome all kinds of shortcomings, but when you're caught in a lie—nothing can help you. (Incidentally, every few months you'll see this come up in the news. Someone will have been on the job for months or years, and then it turns out that they lied in their application materials, typically a letter or resume where they've claimed a degree where they only had course work—and they're bounced out. Lying is really, really bad in job searches.)

* * * CAREER LIMITING MOVE * * *

Student writes a letter to a large California law firm saying, "My husband has accepted employment in your area so I'm interested in pursuing a job there." As it turns out, this student sent this *very same letter* to law firms in several different cities, not realizing that they were all part of the same law firm going under separate names, and that every application letter was logged on to a computer. When they called the student on this lie, she stumbled and said her husband was *thinking* about accepting a job in each one of the cities! It didn't help. Her credibility was ruined with the employer.

So—don't lie! Taking into account all of the advice in this chapter, make the most of the experience you have (and if you don't have that experience, look at the resume chapter for advice about things to "beef up" your experience file in a hurry). The bottom line on lying is this: you just don't have to do it to nail a great job.

14. ZZZZZZ . . .

Remember how I started this chapter: By pointing out the importance of sounding enthusiastic, interested, and upbeat. As Lisa Abrams says, "Cover letters are more important than resumes. Make sure they're not boring!"

Perform this simple test: Once you've written your letter, put it aside for a few hours and do something else. Then pick it up and look at it with fresh eyes. Put yourself in the shoes of an employer receiving the letter, not knowing anything else about you. Ask: Does this letter pique your interest? Does this person seem like someone you'd want to work with, someone you'd want to have representing you to your clients? If the answer isn't "yes" on all counts, tweak it until it is!

* * * SMART HUMAN TRICK * * *

Student applying for a judicial clerkship to a judge known for his sense of humor. Across the top of her letter, she writes in big hand lettering, "THIS IS NOT FROM A HARVARD LAW REVIEW STUDENT."

The judge loved it, and hired her.

15. THE MOST DANGEROUS WORDS IN THE ENGLISH LANGUAGE: "ALL THAT COUNTS IS THAT THEY REMEMBER YOU . . ."

The importance of making your letters memorable may tempt you to voyage into the cute or avant-garde. I warn you not to, not because I have a problem with things that are either cute or avant-garde—but it doesn't matter what I personally like. The profession you're looking at, law, is conservative. As Rob Kaplan comments, "Some people just try too hard to stand out!" Georgia's Beth Kirch adds, "You don't want yours to be the letter they put up on the bulletin board."

Every hiring person has a ton of stories along these lines, and, frankly, I applaud the creativity and imagination that went into these letters—although you'll immediately see why they're not appropriate. At least, not for lawyers. These kinds of approaches would work *great* in professions where this kind of creativity is highly prized: Advertising, marketing, public relations. But fairly traditional lawyers will not trust their clients to students who take approaches like this:

* * *CAREER LIMITING MOVES* * *

- A student sent a cover letter in the form of a personal ad to employers:

  SWM, in search of perfect law firm for long-term commitment. Me: Hard working and curious. You: Interested in hooking up? Call . . .

- One student set up her cover letter like a pre-written rejection letter for the employer to fill out, "Mad Libs" style: "I am very (emotion) to inform you that we will not be offering you an interview . . . ''

- Another student sent her letter encased in a basketball shoe, and started her letter by saying, "At least I know I got my foot in the door!

- One student cut letters out of magazines, and sent a "ransom-style" cover letter to employers, with a picture of Snoopy with a gun to his head. The entire letter read: "Hire me or the dog gets it."

- A student sent his resume wrapped around a ball, saying "Now the ball is in your court."

- Another student had pencils printed to read "I'm on Law Review," followed by his name and phone number.

- One student had his cover letter and resume disguised as a subpoena, and delivered to the hiring partner at a law firm where he wanted to work.

- A student had a four-color resume and cover letter, with artwork and testimonials about her on the back.

- One student sent a cover letter and resume to a law firm, filling the envelope with confetti in order to stand out. The day it arrived at the firm, the firm had just had the office professionally cleaned in preparation for an important presentation. When the lawyer opened this particular envelope, the confetti sprayed everywhere.

- Students have been known to shrink their resumes and cover letters and affix them to wine bottles, like wine labels.

- In a real miniaturization effort, students have had their resumes printed on matchbook covers, and sent them to employers.

- One student had a five paragraph letter, and each paragraph strategically started with a letter of the word "READY." The first paragraph started with an "R," the second with an "E," and so on. The letter wound up with the statement, "Yes, Mr. So-and-so, I am R = reliable, E = enthusiastic ..." and all the way to "Y = yearning to learn! In short—I'm READY."

One student sent a brochure with her name on the diagonal, and a screaming headline reading, "Why you should hire ROWENA BLOTZ."

* * * CAREER LIMITING MOVE * * *

IN THE LAW SCHOOL OF_____,

IN AND FOR_____, _____.

[Student's name]

       Plaintiff(s)

Vs.

The legal system in general, specifically

Mid-size to large law firms with a need for

Hard-working competent trial lawyers

       Defendant(s)

PLAINTIFF'S FIRST REQUEST FOR AN INTERVIEW

Plaintiff argues that he is qualified to be offered an interview for the following reasons:

1. I am an extremely competent and hard-working individual. My favorite quote is taken from Ayn Rand's *Atlas Shrugged:* "The code of competence is the only system of morality and a gold standard." I do everything to the best of my ability and I am not shy or nervous about asking for assistance when necessary. I believe in doing as thorough a job as possible before seeking help, but I also understand that 'time is money' and that 'there is no need to reinvent the wheel.'

2. I am very ambitious. From the moment I enter a law firm and begin my legal career, all my thoughts will be focused on what needs to be accomplished to make partner. I have no desire to return to academia, write a book, or do anything less mentally challenging and time consuming than the practice of law. There is no (read: zero, zilch, nil, nada) chance that I will be "burned out" in a couple of years.

* * * CAREER LIMITING MOVE * * *

In a letter to a firm:

"The difficult thing about resumes and mailings is that they are much like pointing to an unknown smiling face in the crowd and singing the virtues of the stranger. You may see the person smiling, and you may see them waving to grab your attention, but that is not really an indicator of how well they can perform. The trick is, of course, to take the person aside, shake their hand and try to get a reading on what makes them tick.

I am a rather nondescript individual—nothing extraordinary to look at. I look like any number of faceless students that are turned out by the law school every year. Just to look at me you would not think anything special. So what makes me so special? What makes me tick?

It is no big mystery what makes me tick—I live to serve ... I want nothing more than to be put to work—hard work—and to get some real-life experience in the legal field.''

* * * CAREER LIMITING MOVE * * *

From a law student letter to an employer:

I am utterly unconcerned with having any sort of personal life outside of the office. I would work 100 hours a week, 52 weeks a year if required. I do not feel that collecting fees for 3000 hours of work (not merely 'billing' but 'collecting') my first year would be unreasonable, so long as the work is available. While I have no interest in 'face time,' that is sitting around the office doing something just because everybody else is there, so long as there are pressing client demands and money to be made, I will work nights, holidays, vacations, whatever. If my mother's funeral was the date of a key deposition, I would do the eulogy via teleconference after the deposition. If my wedding was on the date of a key trial, the wedding would be postponed. If the wife to be did not like it, I would inform her that work comes before EVERYTHING ELSE and that if she does not like this, she is free to find a competing husband. Please understand that if I do not see the light of day ... for the next 30 years, if I have to eat all meals in the office or even sleep in the office, I would accept that opportunity with open arms and with a big smile on my face.

16. IT'S NOT ABOUT WHAT'S IN IT FOR *YOU* ...

Of course, that's *exactly* what it's about. That's why you're reading this book! But remember: We're talking about we show to employers.

By the way, focusing on you is an easy trap to fall into, because you see examples that make exactly this mistake all the time in books on writing cover letters. The wording I'm begging you to avoid runs along these lines:

- "Working for you would give me a great opportunity to use my history degree."

- "Being associated with your firm would give me the chance to get familiar with San Francisco, which is something I've always wanted to do."

- "I have always been a sports fan and so would be very interested in joining your Sports Law Department."

You see the pattern: "Me, me, me." As Wendy Werner points out, "You have to appeal to what the *employer* needs." San Diego's Susan Benson frames it as the "I" problem, saying, "Don't mention 'I.' As in, 'I want to work for you because it'll give me this opportunity, blah blah, blah.'"

What you want to do is to artfully weave what you want into what you offer the employer. As Susan Benson puts it, "You should be very specific about what you're bringing to the table. So if you say, 'Your firm does this kind of work, and my background includes drafting documents related to it,' it's clear that you will be pursuing something you want because you're using talents you've developed. But you haven't framed it in terms of, 'Working for you will do X for me.'" And that's what you want to avoid!

* * * CAREER LIMITING MOVE * * *

Final paragraph of a very short cover letter to an East Coast law firm: "Working for you for a year will let me do what I really want: Take a cross-country trip on my hog with my girlfriend."

17.   YOUR LETTER DOESN'T HAVE TO GO WITH A RESUME

In Topic E below, I talk about solving resume issues by sending a letter without a resume. But that's not the only situation where a "Naked cover letter" makes sense. The *Wall Street Journal* suggests that you consider sending a letter by FedEx, and follow up with a resume. It's one of those things that so few people do; it'll stand out—if you've got a compelling, well-crafted letter.

Of course—it's wicked expensive to do this. Save this tactic for jobs at the very top of your wish list!

18.   THERE'S NO SUCH THING AS QUALIFIED ENTHUSIASM

The subtext of your cover letters should be, "Working for you is what I really want. I know you will have to invest in me to train me. I appreciate that. Talk to me, give me a chance to prove myself, and you won't be sorry."

So there's no hemming and hawing in your enthusiasm!

Even if you're looking at different kinds of employers in different cities, you have to make each of them feel as though they're at the top of your list.

* * * CAREER LIMITING MOVE * * *

Cover letter to a union employer: "Although my personal sentiments are more management-oriented, I could work for a union."

19. BE BRIEF!

Golden Gate's Courtney Fitzgibbons has a great line about cover letters: "Employers want a snap shot—not a photo album! Give them the opportunity to ask you for more." Beth Kirch points out that lawyers are busy. A letter that's too long will bury your key points and/or give employers the impression that you're desperate.

There's rarely a reason to go beyond one page for a cover letter; if yours gets to two full pages or more—edit!

20. CONSIDER SENDING YOUR CORRESPONDENCE IN A 9x12″ ENVELOPE

Ordinarily, you'd send your documents in a regular #10 business envelope. However, Iowa's Karen Klouda suggests considering large envelopes instead, so that your correspondence lies unfolded, because "It creates a better visual impression that way."

21. DON'T LET YOUR LETTERS GO TO EMPLOYERS WITHOUT LETTING SOMEONE ELSE SEE THEM FIRST

Almost every flaw on this list can be avoided by letting another pair of eyes—that is, a pair of eyes attached to someone who cares about you—see your letters before you send them out. Whether it's a counselor at your Career Services Office or a trusted mentor, let someone review it for you. They'll spot both style and substance errors you might have missed . . . and point out where you can shine even more!

F. WHO TO SEND YOUR LETTERS *TO*

Students often ask me which person to contact at any given employer. Interestingly enough, it's probably not the first person you'd consider—namely, the hiring partner or recruiting coordinator!

Here are a few guidelines:

1. IF YOUR CREDENTIALS ARE STELLAR, SEND YOUR LETTER TO ANYBODY YOU WANT. IN FACT, WRAP YOUR RESUME AROUND A ROCK AND THROW IT THROUGH THE WINDOW

Just kidding. The point is, if you look great on paper, send your letter to the hiring partner at a firm, or the recruiting coordinator; at a company, to the general counsel; at a small to medium-sized firm, any name partner.

2. IF YOUR CREDENTIALS ARE LESS-THAN-STELLAR ... *AVOID* SENDING LETTERS TO "GATEKEEPERS" LIKE RECRUITING COORDINATORS. FOCUS ON PEOPLE WITH THE POWER TO HIRE YOU

"But wait a minute," you're thinking. "Isn't that what recruiting coordinators do?" Well, partially, sure—but that's why you want to avoid them whenever you can. As St. Johns' Maureen Provost Ryan points out, "Recruiting people get resumes all the time," so they're going to be less likely to pay as much attention to each one they receive—namely, yours. Instead, she suggests, send letters to lawyers with the power to hire you, who will see the possibilities in you—and who, coincidentally, receive far fewer letters and so are more likely to pay attention to the ones they *do* receive. So for instance, if you want to practice in the environmental law division of a law firm, find out who runs that division (either through the employer's web site or a phone call), and write directly to *them*. (At worst, they'll forward your materials to the recruiting coordinator or hiring partner—so you haven't lost anything!)

3. CHOOSE A PERSON WITH WHOM YOU SHARE SOMETHING IN COMMON. THIS IS TRUE AT FIRMS, GOVERNMENT AGENCIES, COMPANIES . . . YOU NAME IT

Who are we talking about here? The possibilities:

- An alum from your law school who works there;
- Someone who went to your undergrad school;
- Someone who shares something "non-academic" with you, like membership in an organization, an ethnic background, a language skill, a "second career" person, a part-timer with mom duties, a Peace Corps experience or other pre-law-school career, a military background.

Basically what you're doing here is to operate on the notion that people like to work with people with whom they share commonalities. Put yourself in the shoes of your letter recipient. You'd be more likely to help someone who taught school in Americorps as you did, or went to your beloved alma mater, than somebody who just contacted you "cold."

4. AT A SMALL LAW FIRM, CALL AND ASK FOR THE APPROPRIATE RECIPIENT, AND IF THAT DOESN'T WORK, CLOSE YOUR EYES, POINT, AND PICK A NAME

You may not have anything in common with anyone at a small employer, particularly if it's out-of-town. Go ahead and call the office and ask very pleasantly who your correspondence should be addressed to. If they're not helpful, just pick a name of a lawyer there.

G. THE "NAKED" COVER LETTER: A SOLUTION FOR RESUMES WITH *BIG* ISSUES . . .

Query: Does your letter *have* to travel with a resume? We always think of them that way, like salsa and chips, don't we? But of course there's no law that says your correspondence *has* to include a resume. Here's the bottom line: I don't think there's anything you can't explain in person, and once an employer has *seen* you, and feels comfortable that you're not a drooling troll, they'll be able to put what you have to tell them in perspective. *But you have to get an interview in order for that to happen.* With that in mind, I can think of several situations where you're better off without sending a resume. They include:

- You've been out of the job market for a long time. You know—raising children.

- You have a "Shanghai Surprise" on your resume—that is, something that *looks* OK, but doesn't bear investigation without your explanation first. For instance, let's say you sued your prior employer. A potential employer receiving your resume could easily call that employer to ask about you before contacting you. Yikes! You want to get your explanation in *first*.

- You have extensive experience in another field (or other fields), which makes your resume voluminous.

- You have a gap of any length on your resume, due to—let me think of all of the ones I've heard—prison, mental hospitals, meditating, living off a trust fund—you name it.

- Your resume is heavily 'skewed' in a way that won't help your job search now. For instance: You have a lot of political experience with the Democrats, and the city and practice area you're looking at is heavily Republican. Or you've changed position on an important issue that will affect your job search. There was a young man in Georgia who exemplifies this: He'd been a Right-To-Life lobbyist, and now wanted to work on the same issue, but as a Pro Choice advocate.

- Anything on your resume that takes so much explaining that it obscures what you have to offer.

In these situations, a resume may hurt you more than help you (although it's always worth looking at the Resume chapter, Chapter 8, which features a whole lot of 'quick fixes' for even the most problematic resume).

If you decide to send a letter rather than a resume, you've got a number of advantages; mostly, you can use the second paragraph to 'spin' the positives in your background, how your best qualities can help the employer, and offer evidence of your research, without having to worry about an employer focusing on any negatives. On top of that, you don't have to worry about your letter being separated from your resume, and having your resume forwarded to a hiring person (which often happens at large employers).

Incidentally, remember that what we're talking about here are letters seeking jobs—not informational interviews, which we discuss in Chapter 10. If you're simply making contact for the purpose of seeking advice (e.g., with an alum recommended by your Career Services Director), you can offer to send a resume, but don't include one; it smacks too much of "I want you to give me a job," and that's not the purpose of communiqués like that.

So we're focusing on job search letters where you would, traditionally, expect to send a resume. If you *do* decide to send letters without resumes, take heed of the following:

- Make sure that your contact information appears in its entirety on your letter.

- The fact that you're not including a resume doesn't mean you can wax on and on in your letter; keep it as short as you can, preferably to one page.

- Be sure to carry your resume with you when your letters result in interviews. *Any* resume is all right *if you're there to explain it.*

Now—will *everybody* you talk to agree with the idea of sending letters without resumes? Nope. It's not traditional. But who cares? I've seen it work for lots of students with non-traditional issues on their resumes. And if you fit that profile—I'll bet it'll work for you, too!

H.   KILLER WRITING SAMPLES (AND HOW TO WHIP ONE UP IN A HURRY IF YOU DON'T ALREADY HAVE A GOOD CANDIDATE)

Inevitably, at some point in your job search process you're going to need a writing sample. It's not something you send with your cover letter, unless you're responding to a job listing that requests one, or you've already spoken with the employer and they've requested a writing sample.

But since it *is* part of your correspondence, let's talk about what your writing sample ought to look like. As you'll see, a lot of what I'm going to tell you here reflects advice I gave you about cover letters.

1.   STYLE ISSUES

- Regular white paper. Photocopy paper is fine; it doesn't have to match your resume and cover letter.

- Easy-to-read font.

- 12–point typeface, no smaller.

- No notebooks or binders; the employer will put a copy of your writing sample in your file, and notebooks and binders slow them down.

- If the writing sample in question is customarily bound—like a law review or journal piece or an appellate brief—leave the document in that form when you send it to employers.

- Put your name, address, phone number and e-mail address on the front of your writing sample, in case it gets separated from the rest of your materials.

2. DON'T BLOVIATE. MAKE SURE IT'S CLEAR, CONCISE, AND FREE OF "LEGALESE"

Remember, if you go to work for an employer, they're going to be reading a *lot* of your stuff. They want to believe you're going to make their lives easier. Clear, concise writing does that.

Tighten up your writing sample so that an employer thinks, "Gee, I wouldn't mind reading more from *this* student." If you feel you need help, ask for it from your writing instructors at school.

Another great resource for writing tips is Ross Guberman's *Legal Writing Pro*. Ross is not only wicked smart, funny, and handsome, but he has great advice for anyone doing legal writing—like you. He does very expensive writing seminars for elite law firms all over the country, but he also gives away a lot of great advice on his web site, (www.legal writingpro.com). Check it out!

3. IF THE WRITING SAMPLE IS AN "AWARD WINNER," *FOR GOSH SAKES SAY SO!*

As Sue Gainen points out, "If your writing sample won Legal Writing Honors, was named 'Best Brief,' was used as the model brief for the judges who heard your oral argument or won you a position on a journal or moot court, don't hesitate to let employers know. Note this on your resume, and **make a notation directly on the writing sample**. Highlight it. This is not bragging, but simply letting employers know something very, very important about you and your skills and abilities."

4. BIGGER ISN'T BETTER—AT LEAST WHEN IT COMES TO WRITING SAMPLES

. . .

You may be very proud of your hundred-page thesis, your Law Review Note, your novel . . . but it's too much to foist on a prospective employer. Instead, pick out **ten pages *max***. If that means you're excerpting something you've written that's perfectly fine. You can include an introductory paragraph if necessary to place the snippet in context.

Remember: the point is to show the employer that you can write. Unless the topic is one that is related to what they do and will as a result engage them substantively, you'll wear 'em out if you offer up more than ten or so pages.

5. MAKE SHER ITS PERFIKT

As is true of every written word an employer sees from you—letters, e-mails, resumes, you name it, writing samples must be letter perfect. No typos, no grammar mistakes. They're the kiss of death.

Remember: you can't proofread your own stuff. You know it too well. And spell-checkers miss inappropriate words. So have another set of eyes look it over for you.

6. MAKE SURE IT'S RECENT

If you're a 3L, your brief for your 1L writing class is probably not going to do you a favour; it doesn't reflect your current skills. Employers want to know what you can do for them, and that means what you can do *now*.

Incidentally, **it's *always* wise to go back and revise and re-edit your own writing.** As Billy Wilder once said, "Writing is rewriting." No matter how good a writer you were when you wrote the piece, you're better *now*.

7. MAKE SURE IT'S APPROPRIATELY "BLUE BOOKED"

Aah, yes. I remember those sylvan days in law school, whiling away the hours wondering whether the underline goes under the quotation marks in a cite for a . . .

Aarrrghhh! Sorry. The Blue Book. Ugh. What a nightmare. But you've *got* to pay attention to it on your writing sample! If you have legal citations on it, make sure they are appropriate. If you have any doubts, contact your Legal Writing department at school and solicit their help.

8. IF UNDERSTANDING THE CONTEXT IS NECESSARY TO APPRECIATE THE DOCUMENT, ADD ONE OR TWO SENTENCES AT THE TOP OF THE FIRST PAGE

This usually isn't necessary; most writing samples are self-explanatory.

9. IF YOU WROTE THE DOCUMENT AS PART OF A JOB, *MAKE SURE YOU REDACT ALL CONFIDENTIAL AND "IDENTIFYING" INFORMATION BEFORE YOU SEND IT OUT*

This is so desperately important that if you're going to send a memo, brief, motion, *whatever* you wrote for an employer, *check with your Career Services Office first* to ensure that you've appropriately blacked out confidential or sensitive information. Insert fictitious names as replacements; they should be generic, like "Plaintiff" and "Defendant." If the deleted material interrupts the flow of the document, add something fictitious—clearly marked as such—to make it read well. Remember: you want to make the employer's life *easy*.

Revealing confidential information is one of the very worst things you can do. *Please* don't fall into that trap!

* * * CAREER LIMITING MOVE * * *

Law student works for a law firm during the school year. He applies to other litigators for a summer job. One of them asks for a writing sample. He provides a brief he wrote for his school year employer. He doesn't bother to remove any names or identifying marks.

It turns out that the firm requesting the sample represents a client on the opposite side of the issue the student wrote about. Needless to say, they love the writing sample ... but he doesn't get the job.

10.   HOW MUCH OF IT HAS TO BE ... YOURS?

Let's face it. Almost nothing you write goes through your hands and no one else's. Papers for class come back with suggestions from the professor. Articles for newspapers and magazines are edited. Editors edit the snot out of Law Review notes. If you are a judicial clerk, your judge will change what you write. So ... when it comes to writing samples, what's yours—and what's not? This is an important question, because the whole point of a writing sample is to reflect *your* work!

Here are the basic rules:

- For class papers, incorporate all of the suggestions made by the teacher. Don't send a copy with the teacher's remarks still present; incorporate the suggestions and send a clean copy.

- If you've worked for a judge, an opinion you drafted for the judge is not yours, no matter how much of it you wrote. You can't use it. (Documents you wrote for the judge can be used, because those *are* yours—but *ask the judge's permission before you use* anything *you wrote as part of your externship*.)

- Any time you didn't write an entire document—you wrote documents for a supervising attorney at a firm, agency or company, or you were part of a moot court team that wrote a brief—you can either use the "strike through" function on your computer to strike what you didn't write, physically "X" it out, or use the " **** " symbol to show deletions for sections you didn't write. The only thing the employer wants to see is *your* work. As McGeorge's Dave James points out, "The last thing you want to do is to take time during an interview pointing out who did what. Wasting time makes you seem unprepared."

- If you wrote a pleading for a firm or clinic where you were given a "boiler plate shell" from which to start, Dave James insists that "You must explain what is original work."

- If you worked with other clerks in an office to generate a document, you need to include an explanatory note. When he was Assistant City Attorney in San Diego, Dave James reports that he "received writing samples with whole sections in common from students who clerked in the same office." Employers want to see what *you* can do, not anybody else!

11.   IF YOU'VE GOT CHOICES OVER WHAT YOU CAN USE, HERE'S HOW YOU CHOOSE

If you're a 1L, you're likely to be limited to what you did in your writing class, a memo or a brief. That's perfectly fine. But if you're an upper class student and you've had a bit of experience, as well as other classes in which to draft documents, how do you pick? Dave James reminds you that "The purpose of a writing sample is to convince the employer that the student can do the kind of writing the employer's attorneys do." Here's a good-and-not-so-good list:

a. If you have several appropriate writing sample candidates, ask the employer what they'd most like to see!

b. A "real world" document that reflects the employer's practice (e.g., a pleading, a memo supporting a motion for a litigation firm; a research memo for a transactional firm), that you drafted as part of an externship or clerkship. You might also consider taking a CLE that teaches drafting skills for a certain type of document, and write one as a part of that (or adjunct to it).

c. Still really good: a paper that simulates a real problem, like a moot court brief or a document prepared for a trial practice-type class.

d. Good to show that you can write well and that you're hip to the issues the employer faces: An article you draft for a bar association publication relevant to the employer's practice, as described in #13, below.

e. Good only in limited circumstances: A law journal note or article tends to be a good choice for judicial clerkships, because they show sophisticated legal analysis. They're generally considered not so great for most private employers, because they reflect neither the style you employ in practice nor are they written under the time constraints of legal practice. Also, journal pieces tend to be edited to death, so they may bear little resemblance to your original work.

12. MAKE SURE IT'S "PROFESSIONAL"—NO INAPPROPRIATE CONTENT!

Stuff that's riotously funny to you—and me, probably—is totally out of place in a writing sample. Remember: employers are concerned about whether you can be trusted with their "customers"—people who are placing their property, and perhaps liberty, in the hands of their lawyer. If you get that job, "their lawyer" includes *you*. It's a big leap of faith for employers, and it requires that they implicitly trust your judgment. Sending them an appropriately professional writing sample is part of that good-judgment image you create. So be careful about content!

* * * CAREER LIMITING MOVE * * *

Law student, interviewing widely, getting slammed by every employer to whom he sent a writing sample. His Career Services Director asked to see the writing sample, and found, to her horror, what the problem was.

In a footnote, he made a particularly rude penis joke.

13. TAILOR THE WRITING SAMPLE TO THE EMPLOYER, IF YOU CAN

The absolute best writing samples kill two birds with one stone: they don't just show the employer that you can write. *They prove your enthusiasm for the employer's practice area.* So, to the extent you can, make sure your writing sample addresses a topic of interest to the person who's reading it. I realize that time constraints may mean you've got to send something you wrote for your school's First Year writing class, but if you can avoid that, all the better.

At this point, you may be slumped over in your chair, saying, "But Kimmbo, all I *have* is my brief from First Year," take heart. If it's all you've got time for, send it. Make sure it's letter and grammar perfect, and doesn't have any rude penis jokes in the footnotes.

But just for giggles, let's talk about . . .

14. CREATING AN ABSOLUTELY FABULOUS WRITING SAMPLE *RIGHT NOW*

If you can squeeze out a bit of time spread over a couple of weeks, you can generate a killer writing sample. As we'll see here, when it comes to writing samples, you're not a victim of what you've already done, you know. It doesn't have to be something from a class you've taken, or a clip from a Law Review note. Remember what it's supposed to accomplish: showing you can write, and, ideally, engaging the recipient substantively. Those are both easily accomplished, much faster than you think. You have two options:

A. A PIECE FOR A LAW-RELATED PUBLICATION

What I'm going to do is premised on something you probably don't know: virtually every law-related publication in the world—outside of Law Reviews and scholarly journals, which professors fight over like raw meat—is crying out for content. Bar association publications at every level, specialty publications, alumni publications, specialty newspapers, law-related web sites like lawfuel/.com—they all need content.

Here's where you fit in: You go to Career Services, and ask for the name of an alum that practices in a specialty (or city) where you want to practice. And you contact that alum with a very enticing question. You ask, "What issue would you like to read more about?" Now, when a practitioner hears those words, here's what they're really hearing: "Free research." When they tell you the issue, you get on-line, research it for a few hours, figure out the current status of that issue, and write up a one-or-two page piece about it. It'll take you very little time, I promise you.

Then you contact the editor of one of the above-mentioned publications/web sites, and say, "I understand your members/readers are interested in this issue . . ." and offer your piece. I *promise* you that one of these publications/websites will take it. Even if you decide *not* to submit it, you've *still* got a killer writing sample, because it doesn't just prove you can write: it proves your enthusiasm for what you want to do. And the beauty of it is—or, I should say, *more* of the beauty of it is that you can generate a few of these for different kinds of employers, if you're interested in different areas.

Incidentally, contacting alums of your school is only one way to generate ideas. If you read the newspapers or listen to the news frequently, you'll find that legal issues pop up all the time. Those are also fertile grounds for ideas. And, oh, you'll think of others. You're clever. My point is this: if you don't already have one, a great writing sample is just a few well-spent hours away!

B. A "Practice" Document Created as Part of a CLE Course

Given enough time, you can take a law school clinic and draft legal documents as a part of that. Those documents make excellent writing samples.

But what if your "writing campaign" to employers won't wait? You can always try and take a writing-oriented CLE near school. I've talked about CLEs throughout this book; Continuing Legal Education classes that practicing lawyers have to take. Some of them involve hands-on writing practice for different kinds of legal documents. Go on-line or ask at Career Services or the local bar association about any CLEs being offered in your area, and see if any offer writing practice. If they do, there's your chance to generate a quick, relevant writing sample! (Of course, if they give you a template from which to work, you *have* to make that plain when you send out your writing sample, because employers need to see what you've written—not what's been provided for you.)

I. SMALL FIRM CORRESPONDENCE: A SPECIAL APPROACH FOR A PARTICULAR AUDIENCE

. . .

For a start, if you're looking at small firms, you should be looking at Chapter 18, where we talk about it in detail. When it comes to correspondence, if you're targeting small firms, I don't mean to suggest that everything else in this chapter doesn't count: researching the employer first, showing enthusiasm, and so on. But the fact is, small firms are a special breed when it comes to correspondence. Let's talk about what's different.

1. A Writing Campaign, by *Itself*, Is a Long Shot

Think, for a moment, about what goes on a small law firm. You've got maybe a couple of partners, a few associates, all focused on their work. They don't have lots of levels on the org chart, or a large, administrative staff. In other words: handling student correspondence isn't part of their routine. They just don't hire often enough to justify an entrenched bureaucracy. What does this mean? It means that a letter-writing campaign to small employers is unlikely to work. You've rolled the dice that they'll need somebody at the moment they get your correspondence.

You can greatly improve your success with small firms by looking at Chapter 18. On top of that, make a point of checking your law school's on-line job listings on a frequent basis, at least twice a week. Because small firm hiring is unpredictable, you have to check frequently to ensure that you'll spot opportunities when they arise. On top of that, be willing to do everything that I suggest in the chapter on making contact in general, Chapter 10. They're much more fruitful than writing letters—especially with small firms!

2. SINCE RESEARCH IS MORE DIFFICULT, YOU NEED TO HIGHLIGHT SKILLS COMMON TO MOST SMALL FIRM ASSOCIATES

Web sites, Martindale—Hubbell, brochures, NALP forms—the avenues for researching large employers don't exist for small firms. When you write letters, that's a real handicap! But if you put yourself in the shoes of a small employer, you can imagine the kinds of qualities you'd be looking for in a student, things like:

- Self-starter. In a small office, nobody has the time to spend a lot of time supervising you. So self-management is an important skill.

- Connection to the community. In a small law firm, you'll be expected to become a participating member in the community—and ideally a revenue generator!—much more quickly than you would at a large firm. So, show your connection to the community, or alternatively, if you've lived in a few places, your ability to adapt quickly in a new environment.

- Ability to deal with people. Experience you've had dealing with people—from teaching to waiting tables to customer service of any kind—is a necessity, because you'll be dealing with clients much sooner rather than later.

3. A NAMED ADDRESSEE INSTEAD OF "RECRUITING COORDINATOR" IS A MUST!

Addressing a letter to a small firm using "Recruiting Coordinator" is a real no-no, and here's why: It doesn't just show that you didn't try to find a name to write to, it also shows that you didn't realize that small firms don't have the 'critical mass' necessary to even *hire* a recruiting coordinator. (When you're 'recruiting' a person here and there, it wouldn't be a very taxing job!)

Instead, the first choice would be this: Get on the phone, explain very nicely to the person who answers the phone that you'd like to send some correspondence regarding a potential summer/part-time job, and you want to make sure you send it to the right person. If you hear 'We don't need anybody' say, 'I understand. It's not for right now. Who should I write to?'—and make sure you get the right spelling of the attorney's name!

If a phone call turns up nothing, then turn to the trusty Yellow Pages. Pick a name, any name, at the firm. Look at it this way: If you're talking about a law firm with only two partners, your odds of writing to the one who does the hiring is fifty-fifty.

4. FOLLOWING UP WITH SMALL FIRMS

Call the employer about a week to ten days after you send your materials. However, don't ask them if they received your package! As Wendy Werner points out, "If you call a small firm and ask, 'Did you receive my materials?' you'll drive them *crazy*. You're probably talking to an overworked lawyer who as a desk piled high with files and papers. Expecting them to look through all that just tells them you don't know that." Instead, Wendy suggests that you "**Call and say you sent some materials to them a week or two ago in search of a job, and ask if they remember receiving them, or you can send them again**." In other words: Don't increase their workload by expecting them to find your paperwork. Making their life easier will make you look very good indeed!

J. RESPONDING TO JOB ADS

There are two kinds of job ads: the kind that mentions the name of the employer, and the kind that, duh, doesn't (so-called "blind" ads). If a job ad mentions who the employer is, then you do everything you'd do for any other kind of employer letter: the research, tailoring your resume (we'll cover that in the next chapter), and so on.

Blind ads are the real challenge. How can you possibly tailor a letter if you're not sure who's getting it? Here's how you handle this situation:

1. THE SALUTATION

The ad is likely to give a title instead of a name ("Recruiting Coordinator," "Hiring Manager"). That's the title you put above the address, and then you write, "Dear Sir or Madam:". Don't assume that it's either a man or a woman, and "Dear Sir or Madam" sounds better than "To Whom It May Concern."

2. THE OPENING

Take into account the fact that a lot of people may be responding to the same ad. Most of them will say something like, "I am writing in response to your ad for ..." or "Enclosed please find my resume in response to your ad for ..."

You can do better than that. *Make it interesting!* That's not so easy to do when you're responding to an ad, but you can *always* inject enthusiasm into your response:

> *I was excited to see your advertisement for a summer clerkship. I am extremely interested in Environmental Law.*

What it lacks in personalization, it makes up for in enthusiasm. "I am pleased to submit my resume to you in light of your need for ..." or "I was very pleased to see your advertisement in the *New Fredonia Lawyer's Weekly* ..." is a bit more zippy, 'zippy' being a good quality in this context!

Incidentally—*always* identify the ad to which you're responding. They may be running more than one!

3. THE MIDDLE PART

Remember, this is where you weave together what you know they want, and what you bring to the table. **What you want to do is dissect that ad, and mirror (not repeat) it in your letter, weaving in what you offer**.

Here's an example, from a 2L, responding to an ad for a civil rights litigation practice:

> *Your job description attracted me because I have a strong background in civil litigation and an interest in civil rights issues. I recently participated in a Trial Moot Court Competition and completed a Trial Tactics course. The class provided extensive motion, hearing and discovery practice, while the competition offered practice in opening and closing statements and direct and cross-examination techniques. In addition to my coursework, I am currently participating in my law school's Civil Justice Clinic. This program enables me to counsel clients and to appear in court, with the supervision of an attorney.*

4. IF YOU DON'T HAVE ALL OF WHAT THEY WANT ... ANSWER THE AD ANYWAY!

This little tidbit doesn't technically belong here—we're just talking about correspondence—but you need to hear it more than once. Namely: Don't shy away from answering ads for jobs just because you don't have all of the qualifications they're looking for. Here's why: When employers write up an ad, they're talking about their 'dream' employee. *That person may well not apply for the job!* So don't convince yourself not to apply because you don't have every single qualification they request. On top of that, you don't know how they're ranking those qualifications: some of them are clearly more important than others. You may well qualify in every important respect!

Incidentally, if you don't have the right experience, don't draw attention to that in your letter. "I know you're looking for 2–3 years' experience. I don't have that, but ..." Just talk about why you *are* qualified, how you *can* help them. What you're doing is offering a substitute for any lacking requirement. For instance, in the 2–3 years' experience, "My clerkship with the Law Office of Humpty Dumpty and my clinic experience representing ..."

When it comes to finding "substitute" experience, don't overlook the value of CLEs. In Chapter 10 I talk about the importance of attending CLEs while you're still in school. Let's say that you've gone to eight of them on Real Estate Law, which is what you want to practice. And you see an ad seeking someone with a year's worth of practice under their belt. Well, in responding to the ad, you could say, "I have attended eight CLEs on Real Estate Law in the last few months, which have made me very familiar with the practice of real estate law in our community. The CLEs have also given me the opportunity to meet many local practitioners and learn about the issues facing real estate lawyers here."

Now, you may be thinking, "Who's going to fall for that? It's not a year's worth of practice!" Well, Weed Hopper, employers *have* fallen for it, and here's why: If you go to a bunch of CLEs, you *are* familiar with the issues in the field, you may have learned some practical skills, and you *do* know people. And that covers a lot of the ground that a year's worth of practice would give you!

So the bottom line is: Even if you don't have what they're technically asking for—answer the ad anyway.

5. BE JUDICIOUS ABOUT RESPONDING TO ADS FOR POSITIONS YOU DON'T REALLY WANT

Here's the situation. You see an ad for a job, and either the money or the hours aren't what you want. It's an employer or a practice area that appeals to you, but . . .

What do you do? *Maybe* you respond.

Here's the quandary. If you respond to an ad the employer will rightfully assume you're game for the gig as described. If you flat-out *aren't,* you're wasting your time and theirs. One Seattle firm put out an ad reading "Small criminal defense firm, looking for work-study intern." One of the lawyers reports, "The first three resumes we got were from graduates. I called each of them and said, 'We're looking to pay $8 a week for a work-study intern. Still interested?' All three said a resounding 'No!' If they'd been game for the experience, we would have considered them. But as it was, why respond to a posting looking for a work-study intern if you aren't willing to take it?"

But the other side of the coin is this: a posting by an employer suggests they need help. You're not behind the eight-ball if you acknowledge what they're offering but try for more. "I see you're looking for a work-study intern. I'm a new graduate, but I think my experience and skills might be useful to you . . ." or "I'd like to take you out for a cup of coffee, even if we don't work together now, and get your advice about what I should be doing . . ." In other words: Make the job posting into the opportunity to make a potentially valuable contact.

6. RESPOND AS QUICKLY AS POSSIBLE. THERE'S NO RULE THAT SAYS EMPLOYERS HAVE TO WAIT UNTIL ALL APPLICATIONS COME IN BEFORE MAKING A DECISION

I've told you elsewhere to check your CSO's job postings as often as possible. When a job you really want shows up, get your application in *as soon as possible.* As Attorney Nadia Ahmad points out, "Time is of the essence." So e-mail or fax your application rather than sending it (if the employer doesn't specify a means of response). Better yet, consider ...

7. IF POSSIBLE, DROP OFF YOUR APPLICATION IN PERSON. IT WILL *REALLY* MAKE YOU STAND OUT!

I've mentioned before that in the "hierarchy of memorability," you are least memorable on paper, more memorable on the phone, and most memorable in person. You want to move up that hierarchy whenever possible!

So in the case of a job ad where the employer is identified, try and drop off your credentials in person. Dress professionally, and use your most winning smile. It can make a big difference

* * * SMART HUMAN TRICK * * *

Student responding to a job posting. He calls the employer and says he wants to bring in his credentials, adding that he hoped they could chat. Every other student mails in their applications.

As the employer reports, "He got the job because he stood out. He had 'seykhl.' " (The Yiddish word for "common sense.")

* * * SMART HUMAN TRICK * * *

My all-time favourite "job ad" story comes from a non-legal source: Will Shortz, the crossword puzzle guru of *The New York Times* (I dated him once upon a time, BTW, in the department of useless trivia.)

Will made up his own college major, "Enigmatology," essentially studying games and puzzles. He saw a blind ad for an assistant editor for a game-oriented magazine. Positive that the magazine in question was *Games Magazine*—a fantastic magazine, if you've never seen it— he bypassed the ad and went to the *Games Magazine* offices, saying, "I know you placed this ad. I want this job and here's why you should hire me." The rather nonplussed receptionist responded, "That's not our ad. But they should talk to you."

He got the job. And, as they say, the rest is history.

K. FOLLOW-UP CALLS

1. WHEN YOU'VE RESPONDED TO A JOB POSTING OR AD ...

Following up shows your enthusiasm and interest in the job. Here's how to handle it for maximum effect.

A. TIMING: A WEEK TO TEN DAYS AFTER THE DEADLINE

As Sue Gainen suggests, "Call a week to ten days after the deadline." That's a phone call—not an e-mail! And it's a week to ten days after the *deadline,* not after you *applied.*

B. Who to Call

At a small to medium firm, Sue Gainen recommends that you **call the assistant to the person to whom you applied.** "If you are politely curious and nice, she (most likely) might give you a sense of how huge the stack of resumes is, where the firm is in the hiring process."

C. What to Say

After stating your name, year (1L/2L/3L) in school, and that you applied for the job, tell them you're very interested in the job—enthusiasm is always a plus!—and ask, **"Where are you in the hiring process?"** As Sue Gainen advises, "You want to get a sense of the employer's timeline. Are they starting to interview? Will the process be delayed because the managing partner is in a trial?"

Incidentally, you don't have to ask the old chestnut, "Did you receive my application?"

* * * SMART HUMAN TRICK * * *

Law student responds to a job ad and sends in her letter and resume. She calls to follow up, and the employer says, exasperated, "I've got a huge stack of resumes on my desk. I haven't had a chance to look at any of them." She responds brightly, "Why don't I just fax my resume to you? I don't expect you to find it among all of those other ones." She does so.

And gets the job.

D. You Can Leave a Message, But It's Not the *Best* Approach

A voice mail message with a request for information about where they are in the hiring process is acceptable. Sue Gainen reminds you to "Speak slowly and repeat your phone number." At least a message conveys your interest in the job.

A conversation with a live person is better, because it makes you more memorable, proves your conversational skills, and can convince the employer to bring you in for an interview if they wouldn't have otherwise. But a voice-mail is better than nothing. In fact, you can do both: you can leave a voice-mail saying you'll call back to check up on the status of the hiring process.

E. If the Ad Says, "No Phone Calls or E-Mails. We'll Let You Know if We're Interested . . ."

They're not just lazy, by the way. As Hastings' Sari Zimmerman points out, "They generally put that in ads if they've been burned in the past by the 'stalker candidate.'" Wake Forest's Kim Fields adds that "Oftentimes, when small firms post such positions and include the 'No phone calls' instruction, they just don't have a recruiting person to handle details and filter the calls."

But the fact is, a "no phone calls" prohibition leaves you between the Scylla and Charybdis. You don't want to piss them off by ignoring their instructions. On the other hand, if they don't call you, you don't have a chance, and if you call, you *might* have a chance. It's the least-risk alternative.

Here's a way to cut the Gordian knot. Call when you *know* they won't be there, and leave a voice-mail message saying, "I'm [your name, year in school, name of law school]. I responded to your ad in [source] for a [position]. I just wanted to call and leave you a message to let you know how interested I am in the position, and I hope very much that we can meet for an interview ..." or something along those lines, showing your enthusiasm. Because you didn't call during business hours, you weren't a "pest." But you *did* get across your enthusiasm for the job. So there!

* * * CAREER LIMITING MOVE * * *

The Career Services Director at one law school tried to set up a really sexy externship with an entertainment company. She put out a job posting, and received fifty resumes from students interested. She told the students who responded, "I've sent your resume on to [employer]. Please do not follow up with them. They are in the middle of an acquisition and expressly told me they did not want to address the externship until the acquisition is complete. I'll let you know when I receive more guidance from them."

One of her students got impatient, called the woman doing the hiring [we'll call her Mary], and sent her flowers along with a note that read, "Mary—I'm your man."

Not only didn't he get the job ... the company refused to hire *anybody* from his school as a result of his actions.

2. WHEN YOU'VE SENT LETTERS "UNSOLICITED"

OK. You've dropped your personalized, interesting, well-researched letters in the mailbox (or e-mailed them). Now what? Eat Cheet-ohs and watch soap operas, waiting for responses? You know Auntie Kimmbo better than that.

No, if you don't hear anything within seven to ten days, it's time to follow up. And that means—odds bodkins!—making some phone calls.

You need to know up front that when you're calling employers you've sent letters to, you're facing a situation where you can expect a fair amount of rejection. It's not you. It's the process. The odds that you're going to contact an employer by letter at the exact moment they're thinking of hiring someone ... well, you see what I mean. Handling rejection is such an important element of a successful job search that I devoted a whole chapter, Chapter 5, to that very subject. Remember: It's not an Easter Egg hunt. You don't win by collecting a *lot* of offers. You win by snatching *one* job offer from an employer you really want. You just don't know which follow-up phone call is going to hit pay dirt.

It could be the *very next call you make.*

Anyway, I'm going to make things easy for you. I know that the thought of talking to strangers makes the cold hand of fear clutch your heart. So we're not going to have you calling the people you wrote to and saying, "Well, you gonna hire me or what?" Instead, all you're going to do—at least at the outset—is to check *ostensibly* to see if they received your letter. And remember, you want to give them a week to ten days before you call—that way, they'll have had a chance to get your letter, but it won't be a distant memory.

Incidentally, if you're still "phone-shy" about this, keep this in mind: A follow-up call can often turn an also-ran into a winner, and here's why. Showing that you've got the initiative, enthusiasm and cojones to call them *by itself* says good things about you, your ability and willingness to deal with people. Those are great qualities!

Let's run through the scenarios you might expect when you call.

YOUR OPENING:

Make it simple. "Hi. I'm Kimm Walton, a 1L at Case Western. I sent you my resume last week. I wanted to make sure you received it."

The response you receive determines if it makes sense to ask for more.

RESPONSE #1:

"Absolutely! You're the law student we've been dreaming about. When can you start?"

Hey—it *could* happen!

RESPONSE #2:

An enthusiastic "Yes—your letter was very interesting."

YOU ANSWER: "I'm glad you thought so. I'm wondering if I might be able to schedule an interview."

Because they liked what you had to say, it makes sense to ask for more!

RESPONSE #3:

A nonchalant, "Yes, we did."

YOU ANSWER: Something encouraging, like, "Good. I'm wondering if you might need any other materials from me—a writing sample . . ."

RESPONSE #4:

"I don't know."

YOU ANSWER: *Not* with what you're tempted to say, which is something like, "Thanks a lot, Butthead." What you say—politely—is, "All right. I'll resend them today. I want to make sure I'm sending them to the right person ..." and recheck the name of the recipient.

RESPONSE #5:

"We don't have anything right now. Can we keep your resume on file?"

YOU ANSWER: Absolutely! Students often ask me, "Do they mean it when they say that?" Sure they do. They don't *have* to say it. What you'll want to do, however, is to contact "hot prospects" every few months to reiterate your interest in working for them; keep your potential candidacy "alive" if you haven't found anything in the meantime. Remember: For every legal employer other than the largest, most institutional ones, there's no hiring timeline. Timing is everything. So keep in touch with them!

RESPONSE #6:

The "thanks but no thanks" answer, which can take several forms:

"We don't have anything."

"We really liked your resume, but we just don't have anything right now."

"We've cut way back on our summer program. Why don't you call us next year."

YOU ANSWER: It depends on the tone.

Let's say that they don't hang up, and they're not mean about it, they're just stating a fact, and they do it with a friendly tone. What you do in that situation is to *try—politely—to get* something. For instance, you can ask them, "I'm really interested in breaking into X practice area in X city. Is there anyone else you think I should contact?" "Do you know of any other firms doing work like yours who might be looking?"

If the tone is friendly, you can also turn a job application into a request for an informational interview. You can say, "I appreciate that. I really am interested in practicing X in X city. I'm wondering if I might meet you for a fifteen minute informational interview, at your convenience, to get your feedback on what I ought to be doing to further that goal. I would really appreciate it." Or, "I'm going to be in town anyway, and I'd like to find out as much as I can about the legal market in X city. Could you possibly spare me ten minutes next Thursday morning? I'd really appreciate it."

On the other hand, it may be that they hang up as soon as they say it. Alright-y then! You obviously don't have to answer this—what you *do* is to cross them off your list, at least for now. And remember: Hiring needs change, everybody has a crabby day, and not everybody at an employer mirrors the person who answers the phone. So don't hold it against them *forever*.

Don't forget: in every situation except the immediate hang-up, the door is still open. If they don't tell you anything definitive over the phone, it doesn't mean you *won't* be called for an interview; it may legitimately mean that they got your letter but haven't read it yet.

The bottom line is, firing off your letters doesn't mean your work is done. Always call within two weeks to follow up!

* * * SMART HUMAN TRICK * * *

Law student sends a targeted mailer to a few employers, and then makes follow-up calls to schedule interviews. One of the firms she calls tells her they hadn't received her resume, and they thought they lost it. They go ahead and schedule an interview with her anyway.

After the interview, the student goes back through her correspondence ... and realizes that she hadn't written to them in the first place.

Incidentally—she gets the job.

L.   E-MAIL CORRESPONDENCE: *PLUS ÇA CHANGE* ...

For "cold e-mailing employers," see Chapter 10, Topic D(3)(a)

"Plus ça change ..." It's the beginning of a French phrase which reads in its entirety, "Plus ça change, plus ça le meme chose," meaning "The more things change, the more they stay the same." I'm telling you this, apart from showing off my high school French, to highlight the idea that e-mail correspondence is in almost every respect the same as regular snail-mail correspondence. In fact, one of the big mistakes students make in e-mail correspondence is to assume that it's different.

Here's what you need to know about e-mailing employers:

1.   MAKE SURE YOUR E-MAIL ADDRESS SOUNDS PROFESSIONAL. YOU MAY BE A "SEXYLAWSTUDENT," BUT YOUR E-MAIL ADDRESS SHOULDN'T BE

2.   MAKE YOUR SIGNATURE BLOCK LOOK PROFESSIONAL

Sue Gainen recommends that you program your signature block to include your name, address, phone and e-mail. *If you have a professionally-oriented blog (see Chapter 11 on The Internet), you can include that, too.* If your blog is meant for the amusement of your friends, Golden Gate's Susanne Aronowitz advises you to leave it off your signature block. "Even if it's password protected, don't draw employer attention to it by including it," she says.

3. IF YOU WORK, DON'T USE A WORK E-MAIL ADDRESS FOR CORRESPONDENCE WITH EMPLOYERS

Or anyone else, for that matter. They might not be pissed if you answer job ads, visit chat rooms or order stuff on-line . . . but they might be. They can, and perhaps do, read your e-mails from your work account. Fifty percent of employers do. So use your school account to correspond with employers, or set up a separate one for the purpose.

4. BE CAREFUL ABOUT THE "SUBJECT" LINE . . .

I heard a lot of funny responses when I asked experts about subject lines for e-mails: "Read this, Dammit! . . . but perhaps that's a bit of a career-ender." "I'm standing on a ledge until my resume's considered." You get the general impression that e-mailing employers is generally not a favoured way to break the ice!

But there are, of course, good subject lines for your initial pitch.

Obviously, the best subject line reflects the best opening line of a letter to an employer: *So-and-so recommended that I contact you.* Or, *I read your article in the Post.* Or, *I read the profile of you in the Bar Journal.*

If you're responding to a job ad, Wendy Werner recommends that you make your subject line "absolutely clear. 'XYZ Firm Associate Application.' 'Response to XYZ firm ad.' I typically ask people to put it in the subject line when they are responding to a position that I am recruiting for. When you're scrolling through a bunch of e-mails quickly, if there is some cute subject line, and it doesn't reference a job ad, and it includes an attachment, I would assume it's spam and just delete it. It's really not the place to be clever."

If you've researched an employer and you find you've got all of the qualifications they're looking for, Sue Gainen recommends that you fit them into the subject line, for instance: "2nd year attorney with strong litigation experience," "2nd year law student with computer engineering Ph.D.," "Multi-lingual 2nd year attorney with venture capital experience."

You've noticed that these examples involve unique backgrounds and work experiences. For a run-of-the-mill targeted mailer, experts agree that you're best off not doing an e-mail campaign; rather, send your stuff via snail-mail. If you're soliciting *advice*—which leads to jobs—e-mail can work. We cover that in "Cold e-mailing employers," Chapter 10, Topic D(3)(a).

And remember: **Don't leave the subject line blank.** Because it offers the recipient *no* information, it smacks of spam.

5. ATTACH YOUR RESUME IN A FORMAT YOU KNOW CAN BE OPENED BY THE EMPLOYER (LIKE A WORD FILE)

Truth be told, there's no absolutely universal way to ensure that employers will be able to open any attachment you send them. But Word and PDF files are pretty darn close. Sue Gainen recommends that you send a PDF with Word as a back-up, just as insurance. Minnesota's Vic Massaglia offers that you should also send your documents via snail mail, to be absolutely sure that the employer can see what you want them to see. North Carolina's Brian Lewis agrees, pointing out that the recipient may well open up your document on their Blackberry. The resume that looks so good on a large screen won't look all that impressive on a Blackberry. The hard copy back-up avoids that problem.

The key here is: don't run the risk that an employer won't be able to see the resume you've so carefully crafted—because if they can't open it, they won't contact you and let you know. It's a rejection you don't deserve!

6. IF YOU ARE E-MAILING YOUR RESUME IN SEARCH OF A JOB, YOU STILL NEED A COVER LETTER

If you're applying for a job, your e-mailed resume requires a cover letter just like a snail-mailed resume would. The format, the tone, everything has to be the same as the letters we've talked about throughout this chapter.

Sue Gainen recommends that you attach your cover letter to the e-mail just as you do your resume. Why? "The letter may be passed around, and photocopied e-mail looks unprofessional."

In the e-mail itself, you convey enough about yourself so that you can be contacted even without the attachment, something like:

Dear X:

[If you found them through a contact, mention that first: "So and so recommended that I contact you." If not, just lead with the next sentence . . .]

I am a 1L/2L/3L at __ law school applying for a [type of job] with your law firm.

I have attached my cover letter and resume to this email. If you have questions, you have difficulty opening the attachments or you need more information, please contact me at the phone number or email address listed below.

I look forward to hearing from you.

Your name

Address

Phone

Email address

7. DON'T GET CAUGHT BY THE DEVIL IN THE "CC"

If you are sending a "mass e-mail" to employers, *for gosh sakes don't leave an 'e-mail trail' of everyone who's receiving it!* No employer wants to feel like a name on a list. You're hitting them over the head with it if you let them see all the dozens of other people who got the same pitch.

* * * CAREER LIMITING MOVE * * *

Law student in the Midwest e-mails his resume to two hundred employers in fifteen states. Each e-mail says, "You are my #1 choice."

The problem? Instead of hitting "bcc," he hit "cc" ... so every "#1" employer who received it saw the other 199 "#1's," as well.

* * * CAREER LIMITING MOVE * * *

Summer associate at a prestigious New York law firm. He intends to e-mail a friend, but accidentally pushes "cc" and copies the e-mail to everyone at the firm ... including the hiring partner.

The e-mail read:

'I'm busy doing jack s**t. Went to a nice 2hr sushi lunch today at Sushi Zen. Nice place. Spent the rest of the day typing emails and bulls****ing with people. Unfortunately, I actually have some work to do. I'm on som corp finance deal, under the global head of corp finance, which means I should really peruse these materials and not be a f***up.'

Incidentally, the e-mail didn't die at the firm. It made it into *The New York Lawyer.*

By the same token, if you are sending an e-mail to one attorney at a law firm, don't "cc" all of the other attorneys at the firm. Correspond with attorneys individually.

8. REMEMBER THAT E-MAIL ISN'T NUANCED. ALL YOU'VE GOT ARE THE WORDS ON THE SCREEN. REREAD BEFORE YOU PUSH "SEND" TO MAKE SURE YOUR MESSAGE SAYS WHAT YOU WANT IT TO SAY

Rosanne Barr does a funny bit in her stand-up act. She's talking about sex, and she says that she tells her husband, while they're getting their swerve on, "Oh, you manly man you. Oh, stop. I just can't take it. You're the best." And so on. Now, on paper, that's vaguely pornographic—right? The humour is in the way she says it. She's chewing gum, examining her manicure, speaking in a bored monotone and rolling her eyes. In short: It's really funny. *But you don't get that from the words themselves.*

That's the problem with e-mail. Tone of voice, demeanor … it's all lost in e-mail. The 90% of communication that's non-verbal is chucked out the window. So be *very* careful about what you say. Humor—especially sarcasm—doesn't translate well in e-mail. So be sure to reread your e-mails before you send them, checking with a fresh eye to make sure they say what you want them to say.

* * * CAREER LIMITING MOVE * * *

Law student, 2L in California with mediocre grades, had been on two interviews with a law firm. He had a good relationship building experience with the lawyers there. He got a call from the firm requesting a transcript. He e-mailed it to them, opening with the line, "Are you looking for a reason to reject me?"

The employer reports, "We had really liked him. Reading that turned us right off."

9. E-MAIL IS CASUAL. YOUR GRAMMAR AND WORDING SHOULDN'T BE

E-mail smacks of casual contact. And that can lead you to be more lax in your approach. Don't succumb to that temptation! Everything we've talked about, in terms of research, opening, middle part, closing, tone, and *particularly* perfection in terms of grammar and spelling—they all still apply. As Indiana's Michael Keller points out, "Remember the recipient. You can't use phraseology in an e-mail to an employer that you'd use in a note to a friend. You can't, for instance, say 'Ditto.'"

Similarly, no emoticons, and BTW, no text-messaging acronyms. And even if it's an e-mail, you can't open contact with the hiring partner of a law firm with the line "How's it hanging?"

* * * CAREER LIMITING MOVE * * *

Law student in Florida goes on a call-back interview with an employer. She talks to several lawyers.

By way of a thank-you, she sends the same e-mail to all of them, with the greeting:

"Hey Gang."

10. DON'T WRITE IN ALL CAPS (IT'S HARD TO READ AND IT IMPLIES SHOUTING), NOR IN ALL LOWER CASE (IT'S BAD GRAMMAR AND IT'S DISTRACTING)

11. BE BRIEF!

This is especially important for people you don't know. Assume that the lawyers you're e-mailing are very busy. Whether you're asking for advice or applying for a job, be concise. As one employer puts it, "I just don't have time to read 'stream of consciousness' e-mails from students. I'm willing to help, but get to the point."

12. IF YOU RESPOND TO AN E-MAIL FROM AN ATTORNEY, USE THE "COPY" FEATURE SO THEY CAN SEE WHAT THEY WROTE TO YOU

13. JUST BECAUSE THEY GOT IT IMMEDIATELY, DOESN'T MEAN THEY'LL RESPOND IMMEDIATELY

E-mail screams "right now." And when you e-mail your friends, you tend to get a response right away. But put yourself in the shoes of an employer: you're at work, you've got a mountain of stuff to do, you want to get home to your family, or to the bar with your friends, or whatever. E-mails that you get from people looking for job advice—you'll respond to them, but they won't be at the top of your list of things to do.

So when you contact employers via e-mail, you want to wait the requisite week to ten days before you contact them to follow up (see "Follow–Ups," above). And if they haven't had a look at your e-mail, offer to snail mail your materials as well!

14. WHILE YOU SHOULDN'T EXPECT THEM TO RESPOND TO YOU IMMEDIATELY, BE SURE YOU RESPOND TO *THEM* IMMEDIATELY

Try to get back to employers the same day, "Within 24 hours at the latest," advises Brooklyn's Joan King.

15. WHEN YOU ARE GOING OUT OF TOWN, PROGRAM AN "I'M AWAY" REPLY TO YOUR E-MAIL

16. DON'T "OVER ASK"

When you e-mail attorneys, be careful about what you ask for. If you're doing anything other than applying for a job, ask questions that can be answered briefly, *or* request an informational interview (we cover those in detail in Chapter 10, Topic D. You may be a fast keyboarder but your attorney correspondent might not be. You don't want to tax their goodwill by asking them questions like, "I'm about to graduate. What should I do next?" Furthermore, as North Carolina's Brian Lewis points out, "your 'one quick question', the one that took only a minute for you to type out in your e-mail, may require an answer that would take the recipient thirty minutes to type in response. The risk is that you'll seem not to understand the demands of a busy law practice."

On top of that, in order to get more than rudimentary advice, the person whose help you're soliciting must be motivated to help you; they have to be "invested" in you, to know you even a little bit. E-mail is great for a quick question or as a means of opening the conversation, but it can't embody your entire relationship if you expect any significant help.

* * * CAREER LIMITING MOVE * * *

Law student's e-mail to an alum:

Dear X,

I am a 3L at [alum's law school]. I found your name in the alumnae database at Career Services.

Attached you will find my resume. Please circulate it to anyone you know who may be hiring.

Thank you.

* * *E–MAIL NOT TO SEND* * *

This is an actual e-mail between a student and alum (all relevant names have been changed):

Dear Mr. Bologna:

I am about to graduate from the Loudmouth College of Law. I would like to work in California if possible. If you have any suggestions for me about possibly finding a job somewhere in California would you you please respond. Thank you.

Sincerely,

Lillian Purplepurse

And the response:

1. I would be more than happy to help you and meet with you if you are in Los Angeles, however, I have the following suggestions:

2. If you are going to send e-mails, spend as much time on the e-mail as you would a cover letter to a firm (i.e, indicate who you are, where you are from, why you want to work in California, what type of law you want to practice, why a firm should look at you, why you are contacting this firm, and so on);

3. Attach your resume to the e-mail; (Note: the alum assumed the student was applying for a job; in fact, the student was only seeking an informational interview, but the e-mail didn't make that clear. A request for an information interview without a resume is appropriate.);

4. From your e-mail, I have no clue if you want to practice litigation or transactional work, or if there is any particular area of the law that you find interesting;

5. You must be assertive and portray a sense of direction in your e-mail, not "I would like to work in California if *possible*" and "suggestions for me about *possibly* finding a job *somewhere* in California."

6. Target one or two people in a firm and make your e-mail to that individual or those individuals (do not send e-mails to everyone in a firm); and

7. MAKE SURE THAT THERE ARE NO MISTAKES IN YOUR E–MAIL (e.g., "you you")!

17. NEVER, *EVER* SEND NEGATIVE, SNIPPY E-MAILS TO EMPLOYERS

It may well be that an employer is rude to you, or doesn't respond to your application, or interviews you and never contacts you again. It doesn't matter what the provocation is—*never, ever send them a nasty e-mail!* Prove them wrong by making a success of yourself, so that they'll be sorry they didn't hire you. A snippy little e-mail does nothing for your image. If you need to blow off steam, that's why you've got friends. That's why there's beer. Remember: e-mails live forever, even after they've been deleted. Don't memorialize yourself in a negative way.

Incidentally—and this is a really useful technique to remember in communication situations outside of e-mail, as well—a great way to treat people who are nasty to you is to be *obsequiously, oleaginously* nice to them. It's much more effective. After all, if your goal is to make someone feel bad about treating you badly, the way to do it is to show them how nice you are. If you're a jerk to them, they'll feel perfectly justified in mistreating you.

18. DON'T IM EMPLOYERS!

Gosh, *whatever* you do, don't instant message any employer! You'll make them *crazy.* Yes, it will get their attention. So would a brick through their windshield, and they'll respond just as favorably.

If a lawyer is on-line at the office, (s)he's probably researching, contacting a colleague, responding to professional e-mails. Oh, all right, there's a chance there's a little ego-googling and web surfing going on, but you can't take that risk. It's *their* time. You want to show respect for it, by letting them respond to you at their leisure.

19. NEVER, EVER INCLUDE EMPLOYERS IN YOUR CHAIN MAIL AND JOKE LIST

20. MASS MAILERS ARE JUST AS EVIL—EVEN *MORE* EVIL—ON-LINE THAN THEY ARE BY MAIL

The problem with mass mailers—that their lack of personalization bespeaks a certain laziness in looking for a job—is magnified when it comes to e-mails. Heck, if you're e-mailing hundreds of employers, you didn't even have to stick stamps on envelopes and haul them to the post office—you just hit "Send."

Employers are just like you, in the sense that they want to feel unique—and uniquely wanted. Spending the time to research and contact ten employers will get you a better response than fifty times as many "mass-mailed" letters!

* * * CAREER LIMITING MOVE * * *

Law student sends a mass e-mailer to dozens of employers. Instead of sending them individually, the student sends them so that *all* of the recipients show up on each e-mail. "It was interesting seeing who else he wrote to," said one recipient. "But it didn't exactly make us feel unique."

Appendix A
Correspondence Contact Worksheet

PROSPECTIVE EMPLOYER CONTACT SHEET

<u>Employer</u>

Firm Name _____ Telephone No. _____

Address _____ Fax No. _____

_____ Email _____

Referred by _____ Date of First Contact _____

<u>Contacts</u>

Name	Title	Phone	Info.

Notes: _____
_____
_____
_____

PROSPECTIVE EMPLOYER CONTACT HISTORY

Contact (Date/Time)	Mode (Ph./letter/email)	What Occurred	Follow up req'd (date/action)	Follow up done

Courtesy of Duquesne University School of Law.

*

Appendix B
Cover Letter Formats
In A Nutshell

This "format letter" summarizes paragraph by paragraph many of the points we discussed in this chapter. Not all of them, mind you—you're not off the hook!—but it's a good recap.

Your name

Your City, State, Zip Code

Your e-mail address *(appropriate, please!)*

Date

Contact Name (Mr./Ms. *Name,* not 'Hiring Partner')

Name of organization/firm (with all appropriate punctuation)

Street Address

City, State, Zip Code

Dear Mr./Ms. (Last Name):

Opening paragraph: If you have been referred to this employer by someone, your letter should begin with that person's name, and that (s)he recommended that you write. State the reason for the letter, the position you are applying for and, if applicable, the source from which you learned of the opening. If you met the attorney previously, reintroduce yourself (e.g., It was a pleasure meeting you at the Paintball Splat-a-thon at the State Park last September). State your reason for applying and compliment the employer in doing so. Include the law school you attend and your status (1L/2L/3L/graduate). If you are applying to a city where you have no easily recognizable ties, make sure you state why you are looking in city "X."

Middle part: Sell yourself. You need to answer the fundamental question, "What can you do for the employer?" Supplement, don't replicate, what's on your resume. Point out anything in your work or volunteer experience that makes you especially qualified for the position. This is your chance to amplify any particularly good grade in the field of law that the firm practices. Be sure to mention relevant skills not on your resume (e.g., ability to work well under deadline pressure, skill dealing with people, hard-working—*with back up*.) Once you have some legal experience, this should be the focus of your middle paragraph(s), with a particular emphasis on the skills transferable to the employer you're writing to (whether researching, writing, counseling, or dealing with a particular specialty or population). If your experience in non-legal, be sure to explain how your skill set can easily be translated to this job. If you are responding to a posting or ad, use terms or words used for the job description so that you sound like the person they are looking for.

Tell why you are interested in working for this employer, and specify your interests in this type of work.

Closing: Anticipate a positive response. Indicate your flexibility for interview time and place, without saying you are "available anytime." If the employer is in another city and you will be there at some time specific, say so. If you are going to call to follow up, this is the place to tell the reader that, and to say that you will contact his/her office shortly to arrange for an interview. Thank the employer in advance for consideration of your application.

Very truly yours,/Sincerely,

Your full name

Enclosure (*for one enclosed document, like a resume*)

Or

Enclosures (*for two or more enclosed documents, in case the employer requested something like a writing sample or transcript*)

(Adapted from the Syracuse University College of Law Job Search Guide and The Florida State University College of Law Career Development Handbook)

Appendix C
Helpful Phrases for Each Section of Your Cover Letter

Customizing cover letters doesn't mean you have to work from scratch. Here are some phrases that may be of use to you in crafting letters unique to each employer you contact. If you and your friends are really pushed for entertainment, you can always use these as Mad Libs, filling in the descriptions as you see fit.

1. Opening paragraph:
   - [Name of contact] recommended that I contact you regarding _____;
   - As a 1L/2L/3L student at [school] interested in_____ ...;
   - With a background in _____ I am seeking opportunities to _____;
   - I am interested in applying for [position] with your (firm/agency/company) because of (type of practice, ties to geographic location, reputation, etc.);
   - I am applying for a position as _____ (part-time clerk, summer associate, judicial clerk, associate, etc.);
   - I graduate in [month, year] and intend to return to _____ to begin my legal career;
   - We met at the [conference, CLE, bar association meeting] in [month].
   - My interest in [specialty] prompted me to contact you.
   - My primary interests are _____ and _____ law.
   - I was fascinated to read about your firm's [specialty] practice in the [issue, publication].

2. "Middle part":
   - I can offer your firm specific [experiences, courses] in _____.

261

- My background in _____ might be of particular interest to you.
- I am currently _____ and anticipate _____.
- The position that [you listed, advertised, we discussed] would make use of my background in _____.
- Prior to law school I spent _____ years as _____.
- My work at _____ strengthened my _____ skills.
- I developed strong _____ skills at _____ (college, prior job).
- As [position in organization] I gained experience in _____.
- I have been fortunate to gain extensive experience as _____.
- My experience working for _____ has strengthened my interest in _____.
- I can offer your firm _____.
- Your [firm's/agency's/company's] efforts [in the area of _____] are attractive to me in light of my [skills/background/experience] . . .
- As you can see from my background, I have concentrated on obtaining experience in [field/area/industry] with my ultimate objective to obtain a position in [specific industry/field] . . .
- My academic achievements demonstrate that I produce quality work, work hard and am dedicated to what I am doing. My GPA places me in top [high ranking!] of my class . . .

3. Closing paragraph:
    - I would appreciate the opportunity to meet with you to discuss my qualifications.
    - I am available for an interview at your convenience.
    - I will be in _____ between _____ and hope to have the opportunity to meet with you at that time.
    - I can arrange to visit [city] should you wish to discuss my qualifications further.
    - I appreciate you taking the time to review my resume. I will call your office to see if we can possibly set up a time to meet.
    - Thank you for taking the time to review my qualifications. I look forward to talking with you soon.
    - I can be contacted at _____ and look forward to hearing from you soon.
    - I will contact you on _____ to arrange a time when we can meet.
    - I would be happy to discuss arrangements for an interview.

Adapted from the University of Georgia School of Law, New England School of Law and Gonzaga Law School.

Appendix D
Cover Letters *Not* to Send!

We've talked an awful lot in this chapter about how to write your cover letters. Let's take a look at a couple of please-don't-send-this letters!

Kimm Walton

10 Giles Road

Chagrin Falls, Ohio 44022

Phone number[1]

thonggirl@optonline.net[2]

April 1, 2009

Hiring Attorney[3]
Macon, Lotsa & Moolah
San Francisco, CA 98765

Dear Sir or Madam,[4]

How are you doing?[5] I am a second year student at Joe's Drive–Thru Law School, and I am seeking a position with your firm for this summer. I am writing to your firm because of its excellent reputation and its location in San Francisco. I've always wanted to live in San Francisco because it has so much to offer—sports, culture, history—but I don't need to tall[6] you that because you obviously made the wise choice to live there yourself![7]

I plan to be a litigator when I graduate, and working for your firm would help me to develop strong research and writing skills.[8] In addition, I would like to be able to gain exposure to other practice areas, and because your firm has several departments, I would be able to rotate among them.[9]

As my resume shows, I received good grades in Criminal Law[10] and Contracts, and I am nearly in the top half of my class.[11] I am a hard worker and I work well under pressure.[12] I would be a good addition to your firm.[13]

I have attached my resume for your review. I am available anytime for an interview.[14] Give me a call. You won't be disappointed![15]

Sincerely,

Kimm Walton

1. Before you send letters, be sure to check your voice-mail message and make sure it sounds professional. "Yo, Dude, leave me a message!" won't impress employers!

2. OMG, don't even think about it. yourname@emailservice is the best option.

3. Get a name, *unless* it's a job ad and you're not provided one. Otherwise, check the employer's web site, call, whatever—get a name!

4. Unless you're writing to a hermaphrodite, it's one or the other ... and anyway, it's a *name* (unless you're responding to a "blind" job ad *with no contact name*).

5. Too casual! This is a professional letter.

6. Typo! Remember: a cover letter is your first "work product" for an employer, and you're showing you don't have attention for detail.

7. While it's always a good idea to let an employer know that you're interested in the city where they're located, remember that this is a professional letter—avoid being too familiar ("I don't need to tell you that ...")

8. It goes without saying that working there would be great for you. They need to know ... what's in it for *them*?

9. How do you know that you can rotate? Refer to the research (web, upperclassmen or alums, Career Services) that you did on the firm.

10. Is this relevant to the employer? If it is a civil litigation firm, for instance, your Criminal Law grade doesn't matter to them.

11. "Nearly the top half" isn't strong enough to mention in a letter. You want your *best* qualities on display.

12. Objection—lack of foundation! What shows that you are a hard worker and work well under pressure? Give examples.

Kimm Alayne Walton

39 Old Oak Road

King's Norton, Massachusetts 06106

Phone Number

E-mail address

Date

Dora Explorer

Recruitment Coordinator

Comb, Heller & Highwater

Address

City, State, Zip

Dear Mr. Explorer,[1]

I am contacting you about a possible associate position. I am completing my first year at Headcase Law School,[2] and I have attached my resume for your consideration.

Although I have no legal experience,[3] I have spent the last ten years in business management. I have developed strong skills in customer service and as Assistant Manager, my Ecoli Pizza outlet was the most profitable pizza restaurant in Cuyahoga County for three months in a row.[4] I'm sure that you're[5] company[6] can use someone with my drive and motivation.[7]

In addition I have excellent writing skills as evidenced,[8] by my receiving one of the highest grades in my section of Legal Process. You can be assured that I can hit the ground running.[9]

I welcome the opportunity to interview with your firm. I will call you within the next two weeks to arrange a time for an interview.

Sincerely,

Kimm Alayne Walton

1. Note that it's *Dora* Explorer ... so the salutation should read "Ms."
2. As a 1L you'd be looking for an associate position? You must mean summer associate or law clerk.
3. Don't lead with a negative!
4. While business management skills are definitely transferable to law practice, it's not done here.
5. Typo!

6. It's not a company, it's a law firm. Along with the general tone of this letter and a failure to state why you want to work for this particular firm or to suggest any research into it, this screams "mass mailer."

7. You can't assume your reader will "fill in the blanks." You have to back up what you say you have. What shows you have drive and motivation? Have you worked at the Ecoli Pizza Parlor long hours while going to school full-time? Be specific.

8. Grammar mistake—no comma here. Ironic that it appears in a discussion of writing skills . . .

9. Don't be colloquial. What's meant by "hit the ground running"? Are you a self-starter? Do you work well without supervision? Give examples.

Adapted from University of the Pacific McGeorge School of Law "Guide to Letter Writing."

Shout-outs for materials excerpted in this chapter to: *Duquesne, Syracuse, University of Georgia, Catholic University, University of the Pacific McGeorge, University of Minnesota, New England, Florida State University, The University of Iowa.*

Chapter Eight
Resumes: Squashing Three-Dimensional You Onto Two-Dimensional Paper

RELATED TOPICS:

In this chapter, I'll show you how to create killer resumes. We'll make your experience, no matter how skimpy or vast it is, absolutely shine. And we'll learn something very important: you're not a victim of what you've done. We'll learn how to "pimp your resume" with a lot of quick fixes that'll make you look *awesome*.

This isn't to say that we'll ever come up with a resume that captures everything wonderful about you. It's not possible, because the best thing about you is *you*—not some stinking piece of paper, no matter how well-crafted it is. I've heard so many stories from students who sent employers resumes to no avail, only to meet them at a bar association function or conference or CLE and get an interview. It's because three-dimensional you can never adequately be confined to two dimensions, and it's why I hit you over the head so vehemently, in Chapter 10, to get you to do things that let people see you *before* they see your resume!

But the fact is, you do need resumes for job postings, on-campus interviews, targeted mailers, and the like. So let's talk about ones that address the *raison d'etre* for resumes: getting you an interview.

A. THE GUIDING RESUME PRINCIPAL: FOCUSING ON WHAT YOUR RESUME IS SUPPOSED TO *DO*

About five years ago, I noticed a hand-written ad posted on the message board at my YMCA. I was so struck by it that I wrote it down.

Here it is:

> *"A great classic car at a very reasonable price. 1980 Dodge Aspen 4–door sedan in good mechanical condition, with super clean body and interior. Last of the extra-reliable rear wheel drive Chrysler line with many extra options, automatic, air, rear window defroster, etc. and only 55,000 original miles on the fabulous long-lasting extra-durable 225 cubic inch slant–6 engine.*
>
> *Asking only $687–call 555–8589 late afternoons and early evenings."*

I am not in the habit of writing down used car ads. But *look* at this one! Have you ever seen a car described so lovingly, so convincingly? Doesn't the owner make it sound wonderful? Compare this with what you'd expect to see:

> *" '80 Dodge Aspen. Automatic. 55K miles. $687."*

Same car, but this meager blurb evokes a *very different* picture!

You've probably already divined why I'm describing this to you. When you send out your resumes, wording *counts*. Descriptions *count*. When you're sending employers resumes, you're selling something—your services—just the way vendors sell products and services in the United States every day. They focus on their audience, and word their "pitch" accordingly. This came home to me directly when I created *Law In A Flash,* the flash cards. We floundered for a few years without selling any of the damn cards at all. I came up with all kinds of advertising slogans. They were mostly pretty lame ... until I dreamed up one that stuck: *Better Grades. Less Work.* We pasted that on brochures, posters, boxes, and suddenly sales took off like a rocket.

You see stories like this in the media all the time. I saw one just yesterday, about a book called *Compact Classics*. It was launched a few years ago, and bombed. The publisher recalled it and changed the name to *The Great American Bathroom Book,* and it sold a million copies.

I'm not suggesting that you work the word "bathroom" into your resume, but you see my point. The way you word your experiences, the "verbal snapshot" you give employers, can make the difference between an interview, offer ... and the circular file.

So our most important lesson on resumes is the very first one:

Your resume is not an obituary. It's not a tribute to things you've done.

> *It's a marketing piece.*

Your resume's only relevance is this:

> *It shows employers what you can do for them based on what you've done, whether law-related or not, part-time or full-time, volunteer or paid.*

What does that tell you? For a start, you're not a victim of your grades or your work experience. You can *always* pull useful skills and qualities from what you've done with your life so far. We'll even talk about things you can do in a hurry to "pimp" your resume.

For another, your resume's marketing status shows how important it is to remember your audience, and rearrange, expand or contract your descriptions of various elements of your background accordingly. If you have civil and criminal law experience, you include more about the criminal work for a Federal Public Defender than a large law firm.

One of the most memorable questions I've ever received was from a student who told me he'd spent several years in prison before law school. Hey—it happens. On his resume, he talked about the jobs he had while he was in prison ... without mentioning where he was when he did them! A really smart idea, by the way. But he wondered if this was the best way to handle it. The last part of his question made the answer easy: "By the way, when I get out of law school, I want to be a prisoners' rights advocate." All of a sudden, what would be a tremendous negative for most employers is suddenly kind of a positive! After all, who's going to understand the problems of prisoners, and be motivated to help them out, more than someone who *was* one himself? I encouraged him to mention his prison background on his resume for just that reason!

I trust you don't have a prison record, but you see my point. If you're looking for different kinds of jobs in different locations, you'll want to have a "wardrobe" of resumes. We'll talk about exactly how to do that.

1.   YOUR TOOL KIT—A QUICK OVERVIEW

Let's talk from the outset about the possible sections of your resume, and how you'll use them. Note that **there are only four that *must* appear: the heading, education, experience, and hobbies/interests**. You'll pick and choose from the rest, depending on your background and the employer(s) you're targeting.

"Heading" Information:

> **Name**: Include nickname in parenthesis *only* if your name is difficult to pronounce.
>
> **Address**: Current address. Also include permanent address for employers in your "home" area.
>
> **Phone**: Use the phone at which you are most accessible. That's likely to be your cell phone. Check the message to make sure it's "professional" sounding.
>
> **E-mail**: Professional-sounding *only*.

Education:

Start with law school.

School name (formal, not abbreviated), city, state.

Graduation date, anticipated (if you're still in school), or actual (if you're out).

GPA *if appropriate*. Depending on the school, you will state it only if you are between the top 10% and top half of the class.

Class Rank *if appropriate*. Useful if you are both toward the top of the class *and* your school does not use grade inflation, such that your grades don't immediately impress employers with how well you're doing.

Selected class performance *if appropriate* (namely, your grades overall aren't great but you've done extremely well in classes related to the employer).

Honors and Awards

Activities *gauged to the employer.*

Publications *or can receive their own section.*

Additional Legal Education:

If you have taken CLEs, which I <u>beg</u> you to do.

Undergraduate Education:

Listed in the same way as law school.

High School:

Only to show geographic ties *or* stellar (e.g., valedictorian) performance.

Experience:

Paid work both legal and non-law-related, work study, volunteer work, and clinical programs.

Can be listed as one section, or separated in several sections, as appropriate. Note that if you call a section "Employment" it can *only* include *paid* work.

For instance:

Related Experience/Other Experience

Legal Experience/Other Experience

Employment/Other Experience

Legal Experience/Business Employment

Employment/Volunteer Experience *for public interest jobs*

In each section, list experiences in reverse chronological order. Alternatively, in a "functional" resume, work is grouped by type of experience; useful if you have tons of experience or you've been a job-hopper or your resume has significant gaps.

Publications:

For *any* publications, including Law Review and Law Journal notes, bar association publications, *anything at all.*

School-related publications can also be included under law school heading.

Can include unpublished works if you title it "Writing Experience."

Skills:

Primarily for languages and computer skills. Can also include other licenses (CPA, MD, RN).

Language(s):

If languages are important to the target employer(s) *or* comprise your only skill; otherwise, include in "Skills" section.

Research Projects:

If relevant to employer. Otherwise, can appear under appropriate Experience or Education heading.

Licenses:

To highlight licenses that can otherwise appear in the Skills section: CPA, MD, and so on.

Professional Affiliations:

Must useful if you've already passed the Bar Exam, but can also be used for other affiliations.

Military Experience:

Can appear under "Experience" or "Employment," but can be highlighted in its own section, particularly useful for employers who give preference to veterans and/or have a military background of their own.

Volunteer Experience/Community Service:

To highlight your non-paid contributions. Particularly important for public interest employers.

Hobbies/interests:

Include those that accomplish one of the following goals:

- Hobbies that suggest future rainmaking potential.
- Hobbies that reflect activities the employer or a significant client takes part in.
- Hobbies that reflect positive personal characteristics, like self-discipline, leadership, teamwork.
- "Brainiac" hobbies.
- Hobbies in which you've excelled.
- Hobbies that reflect community service.
- Hobbies and interests that provide conversational fodder.

Other Information:

A "catch-all" for relevant information, including:

- Connection to geographic area if it's not otherwise obvious from your address/law school.

- The reason for your interest in what the employer does, if it's not otherwise obvious from your activities/experience.

- Outstanding performances in activities/schooling that doesn't otherwise appear on your resume (e.g., high school valedictorian, sports achievements).

- If you are a woman, the fact that you attended school while raising children. *This is highly controversial.*

- Unusual and intriguing elements of your background which do not rise to the level of a hobby/interest (e.g., spent six weeks on a survival course in Tasmania, exotic travels, appearing on a game or reality show ... anything that would make interesting and appropriate interview fodder).

2. MAKING THE MOST OF WHAT YOU'VE GOT: REWORDING YOUR RESUME FOR MAXIMUM EFFECT

When an employer receives your resume, you know how much time they'll give it? *Between 30 and 90 seconds.* That's it. They're going to skim it, and if they see something that interests them, *then* they'll cycle back and go into more detail. The takeaway: You've got to make that sucker *pop* if you expect an employer to bring you in for an interview!

In those brief seconds, this is what's going through the employer's mind, as stated in *The National Business Employment Weekly*:

- Address my needs and priorities, not your wishes and aspirations;

- Don't tax my patience;

- Don't tax my credulity;

- Give me the information I want, and *only* the information I want, in a sequence that lets me make a snap judgment about you.

With that in mind, we're going to look at your resume as real estate. The prime real estate is toward the top; that's where employers look first. So you'll want to make sure that your resume features the information most relevant to the employer in the top third or so, with information of decreasing importance as you venture down the page. Information that's not relevant or, even worse, harmful to you *shouldn't appear at all*. The real estate of your resume is too valuable to waste on anything that won't help get your foot in the door.

Beyond real estate, what are employers doing when they look at a resume? Consciously or not, they're operating by way of analogy—you remember, like on the old SATs. They'll be saying to themselves, "Because you did this in context A, it says this about your ability to perform in context B—namely, working for us." Put another way, they're looking for *transferable skills*. Skills you've picked up elsewhere, talents you're born with, and the enthusiasm you manifest are all part of the equation.

Let's look at an example. You're the employer, you practice Space Law. And you get the following resume from a law student (in pertinent part):

James T. Kirk
1 Wrathokhan Road
Enterprise, USA
(888) 555–5555
spaceyboy@optonline.net

EDUCATION   Federation School of Law
JD expected 2 * * *
GPA: 3.02   Class Rank: 55/168

Tribble University
BA 2 * * *
Major: Physics   Minor: Music

ACTIVITIES   Space Law Club
Phi Alpha Delta Law Fraternity

EXPERIENCE   Professor Spock
Research Asstisant, 2 * * *-* school year.
Law Firm of Bones & Scott
Summer 2 * * *
Researched issues and wrote memos.
Piggly Wiggly Grocery Store
Summers 2 * * * -*
Packed meat for display and sale.

What's wrong with Jimbo's resume?

Well, for a start, the only thing on the whole resume related to what you do is the Space Law Club. That's not bad, but you don't have any idea whether he's the founder, an active member . . . or whether he came to the first meeting, signed up, and never showed up again. Yippee. ('Naked' club memberships are OK by themselves, but if you've done more, it shows employers good things about you. Show it off.)

On top of that, look at his experience. Two items may be really useful to you: Professor Spock and Bones & Scott. But again: what do you learn about Kirk from them? Not much. Did he sell you on what he learned substantively, the skills he picked up in these jobs? No!

Furthermore, look at the relative space given to his legal jobs and his non-legal job at the Piggly Wiggly. His law firm experience gets five descriptive words: *Researched issues and wrote memos*. His non-legal experience gets *six* words: *Packed meat for display and sale*. (A student showed me that on his resume, and I've always used it because I like it so much.) There's nothing wrong with packing meat, of course. But does it really deserve more space on a resume than legal experience—when the target is a legal employer? No!

Cycling back up to the top of his resume, check out the e-mail address. "Spaceyboy"? Do you want to trust your money, your livelihood, your liberty to *Spaceyboy?* If you've got a cute or naughty e-mail address, get a professional-sounding one as well, and use it for employers!

Finally, the resume has a typo—He was a research *assistant* for Professor Spock. Employers have a Freudian thing going on with typos on resumes; they figure if you can't get this very important document right, what happens to their detail-oriented work? Remember, your resume is the *first* example of your work product an employer is likely to see. Before you send any resume to any employer, have another set of eyes review it for you; ideally, a counselor in your Career Services Office at school. You just can't proofread your own stuff; you're too familiar with it, so you overlook obvious mistakes.

Let's say James thought the better of it before he sent you this resume, and instead, this is the one you got:

James T. Kirk
1 Wrathokhan Road
Enterprise, USA
(888) 555–5555
jtkirk@federationsol.edu

EDUCATION   Federation School of Law
JD expected 2 * * *
GPA: 3.02   Class Rank: 55/168
    Space Law: A–
Activities:
    Space Law Club
        Seek out and contact new speakers for the club's monthly meetings.
        Edit the club's web site, featuring articles of interest drawn from scholarly and popular publications.
    Phi Alpha Delta Law Fraternity
        Organized "Meet the Lawyer" Day, bringing students together with practitioners in forty legal specialties.
        Event was attended by four hundred law students.

Tribble University
BA 2 * * *
Major: Physics   Minor: Film
    Financed 60% of undergraduate expenses through summer and part-time employment.

ADDITIONAL LEGAL EDUCATION	"Space: The Final Legal Frontier," Continuing Legal Education Program, September 2 * * *, offered by the Space Law Institute. Learned to draft complaints related to fallen satellite parts.
	"Space Can't Take It Any Longer!—Legal Issues Involving Space 'Junk'," Continuing Legal Education Program, September 2 * * *, offered by State Bar Association.
	"Private Space Flights, Disclaimers and Liability Issues," Continuing Legal Education Program, October 2 * * *, offered by Vulcan & Vulcan.
	"Space Law: Where Is It Going?" Continuing Legal Education Program, October 2 * * *, offered by Space Law Institute.
LEGAL EXPERIENCE	Professor Spock
	Research Assistant, 2 * * * -* school year. Researched issues involving cloning for upcoming textbook on patent law. Used LEXIS/NEXIS and Westlaw databases on a daily basis.
	Law Firm of Bones & Scott (Four-person patent law firm) Summer 2 * * *
	Interviewed clients, researched issues and wrote memoranda involving the patentability of inventions, performed patent searches.
OTHER EXPERIENCE	Piggly Wiggly Grocery Store Summers 2 * * * -* Packed meat for display and sale. Named "Employee Of The Month" seven times.
HOBBIES	Geocaching, reading science fiction novels

What did you notice immediately? That I just couldn't give up the "Packed meat for display and sale" line, right? But on top of that, you probably noticed that this version is replete with all of the things that are important to you. By expounding on what Kirk has done, the resume is now crammed with key words related to Space Law. Even if Kirk's resume is scanned or submitted electronically, it will be impressive because a key word search will pick up so many relevant terms.

Also, take the "Additional Legal Education" section, which you probably noticed right away. For one thing, it's in "prime real estate" on the page—just above the middle, where people naturally look first. It's human nature. On top of that, it takes up a bit of space. It takes up almost four times as much room as the "packed meat for display and sale" entry. *And that's good, because it's at least four times as important!*

We'll be coming back to the idea of taking CLEs—continuing legal education classes—over and over in this book. I'm putting it here at the beginning of the resume chapter, because it's in resumes that I think it's truly a killer idea, most of all because it's not something you have to have done *already*—you can start taking CLEs *today* to make your resume shine. You see what I mean when I say you're not a prisoner of what you've done? Taking CLEs screams "enthusiasm" and "initiative" to employers. They show that you're on top of issues facing practitioners. The names and descriptions of CLEs contain tons of key words. Oh, they're just wonderful in so many ways!

CLEs work particularly well if you've got a resume that's heavily loaded with experience that's not relevant to what you want to do. You can minimize that experience—by, say, putting it in narrative format in a paragraph and moving it further down on your resume—and slotting in the CLEs above it. It's the real estate idea; you may have taken ten years doing something else and two months taking CLEs, *but the CLEs get a more prominent role on your resume.*

I'll wax rhapsodic about CLEs elsewhere, but let's move on to other elements of James Kirk's resume. You also notice that he:

- Has a professional-sounding e-mail address.

- Pulls out relevant grades. If you've got OK grades overall but great grades in classes related to what the employer does, highlight them!

- Goes into detail about what he does for the Space Law Club and Phi Alpha Delta. He's not sitting around with his thumbs you-know-where and attending club Happy Hours. He's reaching out to the community, keeping up with issues in the field—in other words, his initiative bespeaks the ability to communicate well, potentially bring in business, and stay on top of current issues facing the specialty.

- Tells more about his relevant work experience, showing exactly the skills he picked up and exhibited.

- Separates his legal experience from his other experience—"packed meat for display and sale," I just can never say that enough—to bring attention to it. The legal experience, not the meat.

- Talks about how much of his own education he financed. It doesn't much matter what kind of work you do—as long as it's not illegal!—if you show you've picked up some of the cost of your own education yourself. That self-reliance trait is a real plus for employers.

- Has a hobbies section. This is mildly controversial; some employers say hobbies have no place on resumes. *However,* I've talked with lots of law students who got interviews just because they had something interesting in the hobbies section of their resume. On top of that, most employers enjoy having a "third dimension" to talk about with you, besides school and work. On balance, I'd strongly encourage you to include hobbies and interests on your resume!

- Is *letter perfect.* No typos!

We're going to revisit many of these ideas throughout this chapter, but I wanted to start you off with a basic introduction to the approach we'll take. Simply put: We'll turn your resume into a fantastic marketing piece. Let's get started!

B.   Creating "Brain-Dump" Resume Work-sheets: Identifying the Ore From Which You'll Mine Your Perfect Resumes

1.   An Opening Exercise to Get You Into "Resume Think"

"An *exercise,* Kimmbo?" you're saying to yourself. "I don't need no stinkin' exercise. I want to write my resume!" All right, all right, we'll get to that in a minute. This exercise will ensure that the resumes you write tell employers what you want them to hear.

We'll start with a list of skills and qualities. These are, not coincidentally, the elements that are most often cited as comprising the "ideal lawyer" (adapted from the ABA's "Creating the Ideal Lawyer," by Ruthe Catolico Ashley, among other sources).

Qualities of an ideal lawyer:

Energy (hard worker)

Follow-through

Ability to juggle multiple tasks and prioritize

Ability to pick up new information quickly

Ability to deal with time pressures and tight deadlines

Team player

Initiative

Motivation

Creativity/Imagination/Inventiveness

Self-confidence

Flexibility

Intelligence

Persuasiveness

Persistence

Attention to detail

Willingness to accept responsibility

Ability to handle stress

Goal-orientation

Enthusiasm

Skills of an ideal lawyer:

Problem solving

Legal analysis and reasoning

Legal research

Factual investigation

Communication (written and verbal)

Counseling

Negotiation

Organization and management of legal work (office procedures)

Recognizing and resolving ethical dilemmas

Pick five of them that you think fit you, and put a check mark next to them. They probably won't be the only five, but just pick five.

What I want you to do with the five terms you've chosen is to write them down using the spaces on the next page. And you can see from the additional lines on those pages what I want you to do next: Think of *specific experiences* that *prove* that those terms apply to you. The important thing here is to remember to draw from *all* of your experiences, school classes and activities, legal or not, paid or volunteer, part-time or full-time. *Everything.*

Incidentally, it's important for you to remember, in doing this little exercise, to relate your experience at the level that makes it relevant to lawyers who aren't familiar with your old job(s). Particularly if you've had 'real' jobs before law school, you may be tempted to be terse about your experience: 'social worker', 'retail sales manager,' 'stock broker.' Don't assume lawyers will make inferences about what skills you bring from other jobs!

By way of example, one student used his computer skills during a summer job to help a company computerize its inventory control and billing and that kind of thing. He had to analyze the existing system the company used, identify its problems, research computer programs, and present and sell his solutions to the firm owners. Then he had to set up the systems once they were bought, customize the computer applications, and train all the staff. He beat the schedule the owners had set up for him, and trained the staff with no significant problems. Now, all of these functions he performed would be useful in a law firm, above and beyond his considerable computer skills. But instead of focusing on these transferable skills, he had simply written on his resume that he helped in a computerization! If all you list on your resume are job titles and a brief list of duties, you can't assume that a potential employer will be able to make the leap and figure out what your transferable skills are. It's up to *you* to show what you bring to the table based on what you've already done!

Term #1: _____

    Specific experience(s) I've had which prove this term applies to me:

Term #2: _____

    Specific experience (s) I've had which prove this term applies to me:

Term #3: _____

    Specific experience (s) I've had which prove this term applies to me:

Term #4: _____

    Specific experience (s) I've had which prove this term applies to me:

Term #5: _____

    Specific experience (s) I've had which prove this term applies to me:

Now, look over what you've written. See what an impressive resume you're going to be able to write? You can see that with the descriptions you've given, there's *no question* about whether the terms you chose apply to you. An employer wouldn't have to fill in the blanks to figure out whether you have those traits they're looking for. And best of all, you're doing it in the most persuasive way possible; *you're showing them, not telling them.* You're laying out the evidence and letting them draw unavoidable conclusions. And that's why you're going to have a killer resume!

2.   "BRAIN DUMP" RESUME WORKSHEETS: LISTING EVERYTHING YOU'VE EVER DONE IN A DOCUMENT NO EMPLOYER WILL EVER SEE

Now that you see how things you've done translate into things you can do for employers in the future—it's time to get down to brass tacks, and look at *everything* you've done. This is a two-pronged process.

First, I'm going to take you through your background, and we'll figure out the "universe" of things to choose from when you actually write your resume. I call that your 'brain dump' resume, because on it you're disgorging everything you've ever done, every volunteer experience you've had, all of your post-high-school education, every club you've ever belonged to, every role you've ever played in anything you've ever touched. But nobody's going to see it! I talk to so many students who share the same delusion that I had in law school: that if I just wrote down every damn thing I'd ever done, some employer would look at my resume, mine it for the gems, and say, "Aha! Here's why Kimm's our perfect employee!" It doesn't happen that way. Employers spend a few seconds scanning resumes, and either they see what they want and they go on reading—or they don't.

What we're going to do is to take the raw material of your 'brain dump' resume and put it into 'marketing' form, so that employers see you as you want to be seen.

Let's get started!

A.   GETTING DOWN ON PAPER EVERYTHING YOU'VE DONE, HOW WELL YOU'VE DONE IT ... AND WHAT IT SAYS ABOUT WHAT YOU *CAN* DO

We're going to go through your post-high school background, and dissect what you've done, focusing particularly on two things: how you stood out and what you learned that can be transferred to your work for future employers. Consult the "Ideal Lawyer" qualities we just discussed in our resume exercise to inspire you.

Note two important points as you do this. First, not every legal employer will weigh these skills and qualities equally; a large law firm won't be so concerned with your factual investigation skills, while a prosecutor's office will likely be less concerned with your legal research skills. But as an overall matter, these are the kinds of skills and qualities you want your background to illuminate.

Second, note that even if you have not one *minute* of legal experience, virtually anything you've done can contribute to one of these skills or qualities. If you were promoted in a job that normally has a high turnover rate—you became head cashier at a big box store where most people leave after a few months—that's an accomplishment that speaks to your communication and motivation.

1. EDUCATION

a. Law School—Your Most Important Resume Feature.

For any legal employer, your most important resume item will be your law school career. (If you're looking at a non-traditional job, that may not be true; for alternative careers, look at Chapter 31.)

Even if you've got an extensive prior career, it's going to be your law school information that will draw a legal employer's attention first. Normally, it'll be the first thing on your resume, under your name and address.

We're going to use a "Law School Resume Worksheet" as a guide. I'm giving you detailed descriptions of what you ought to include in each section. By way of a general comment, you can see that what goes on in the *left* column shows what you've done; the *right* column shows what you've accomplished and how you've distinguished yourself from the crowd. Don't be modest. Toot your own horn to the greatest extent possible!

Nuts & Bolts:

School Name:

Location (city and state):

Expected graduation date (if
you're still in school) and actual graduation
date (if you aren't):

Co- and extra-curriculars:
*Law Reviews – duh! – journals, moot court,
mock trial, clinics, student bar association, law
fraternities, client counseling/advocacy/
negotiation competitions, fund raisers, clubs,
everything. Every damn thing you've signed your
name to under the auspices of the law school.*

Additional Legal Education (CLEs):
*Write down what each CLE was about and how
many hours it was.*

What Makes Me Stand Out:

GPA:
*In addition to your GPA, you want to have your
transcript on hand. Relax! It's not going on your
resume! But we might mine it for useful tidbits.
As a 1L, if it's second semester, there's your first
semester GPA if you have it. Also, if you are an
upperclassman, list your GPA for each
completed year of law school, and the first
semester of this year if you're in the second
semester.
Unless you are toward the top of the class, list
any classes in which you've done particularly
well.*

Class Rank: of
*Along with your current rank, if you are an
upperclassman, include your rank for prior
year(s). If you are a 1L, include your class rank
for first semester, if your school calculates them.*

Scholarships, academic awards, honors:
*Be sure to offer details! Include how much of
your tuition was covered by scholarships, how
the scholarships were awarded, and the details
necessary to understand any other academic
award or honor. "Full-tuition scholarship
awarded to five class members each year";
"Won essay contest on X topic to qualify for a
$5,000 annual scholarship"; "Award given to
outstanding student in Tort Law every year."*

What I did, started, improved, or anything
else that distinguishes me from anyone else
doing the same activity:

*For instance: publications in law
reviews/journals, editorial positions on same, if
you were selected for teams, moot court or mock
trial ranking, offices held in clubs and SBA,
results of competitions if you did well, anything
you did in clubs other than joining, for instance:
Did you found the sports law club? Did you
solicit speakers? Did you write for the club's
newsletter or develop/maintain its web site?*

*Write down a brief description of what you
learned. For instance: "Learned how to take
depositions in medical malpractice cases."*

There! Now you have the basics. Take a sheet of lined paper
and copy onto it everything on the worksheet that appears
in bold print. You know—the basics. Go ahead and fill it in.
Remember: This is not the place to be terse. Go into
excruciating detail about everything you've done (and are
doing) in law school. We'll deal with editing it down shortly.

b.   **Undergraduate School.**

Pop quiz: Guess what we're going to do now? Tha-a-a-at's
right: exactly the same worksheet you just did for law
school. The only difference is that your "expected graduation date" will turn into "graduation date," and you won't

have a CLE section—unless you were an incredibly motivated and forward-thinking college student!

Furthermore, your Co- and extra-curriculars will probably be slightly different. Be sure to include sports, fraternities/sororities, student government, journals, and student organizations.

c.   Any other graduate school.

If you're a 'serial student,' and you've got an MBA, Ph.D., MD, or any other kind of degree—go ahead and make up a worksheet for that/those, as well.

d.   Ancient history: high school and earlier ...

Ordinarily you don't want to mention any experience further back than college. *However,* if your high school performance was stellar *or* your high school has a national reputation *or* the location of your high school gives you a geographic tie to the employers you're targeting, it can be included.

Include the name of the school, city, state, and year of graduation, and the information that makes it relevant if appropriate.

* * * CAREER LIMITING MOVE * * *

Student at a law school in the Southwest, in her 40s, includes on her resume: "You may order copies of my report cards as far back as you wish. My teachers always reported that I was one of the best students at Wabash Elementary School, Hathaway Middle School, and Brown High School."

2.   NONACADEMIC EXPERIENCE: WHAT HAVE YOU DONE, HOW WELL HAVE YOU DONE IT, AND WHAT DOES IT SAY ABOUT WHAT YOU CAN DO?

Once you've completed your academic worksheets, it's time to turn your attention to your nonacademic experience.

This will include every job you've ever had, law-related or not, full-time or part-time, summer or permanent, volunteer, work study or paid.

Here's a worksheet to use. Copy one for every job you've had.

Employer Resume Worksheet

Nuts & Bolts:	What Made Me Stand Out:
	*Accomplishments
Employer Name:	*Transferable skills learned or
	sharpened by tasks and duties
Location (City and State):	

Job Title(s) (Reverse Chronological Order if more than one):

Dates of Employment (Months
and Years):

Tasks and Duties (in as much detail as you can muster, including
quantifiables—numbers and
ranges where possible)

As you can see, this worksheet is very similar to the academic
ones you just filled out: the left hand side focuses on nuts and
bolts, like tasks and duties. The right-hand side focuses on accomplishments and transferable skills.

Don't worry about phrasing; you're just getting down on paper
as much as you can right now. We'll get into specific wording
when we get to formulating your resume.

a. The left-hand column: Nuts and bolts.

In this column, you include tasks and duties in detail,
and you quantify them to the extent possible.

To aid your memory, look back at the list of skills and
qualities that make an ideal lawyer, and wrack your brain
for tasks and duties you performed that speak to those
skills and qualities.

For **law-related jobs,** use appropriate legal terminology and talk about the specific types of specialties/issues you
researched and documents you drafted. List every practice
or substantive area in which you have experience. List
every other task you performed, from interviewing to sitting in on negotiations/trials to anything you did involving
the courthouse. Include also any office tasks, like organizing files.

Needless to say, legal employers are most interested in
your familiarity with an area of law and experience in a
legal setting!

On top of that, as William & Mary's Rob Kaplan says,
"It's important to quantify."

For instance, instead of writing "wrote memoranda," jot
down the topics you covered. Count the number of trials
you attended, the briefs you wrote—every single thing you
can think of. If you just say you "attended trials," it could
be 2–or 200. Be as specific as you can!

For **non-legal work,** whether full-time, part-time, summer or during the school year, *no matter how menial you consider the position,* be just as detailed.

It's important not to minimize *any* job you've had. Remember that even the most so-called menial job can often give you skills vital to being a good lawyer! For instance, let's say you were a clerk in a retail store. Were you responsible for sales and cash registers? Did you supervise other people, and if so, how many? Did you open and/or close the store? Did you handle customer complaints? Did you have a lot of supervision or did you work independently? Be specific!

One student in California had sold pest control systems door-to-door, and said it got a great reaction from legal employers. He said, "I learned everything there is to know about dealing with people, down to the details. Like not looking someone in the eye for a second when you meet them . . . give them a chance to check you out, *then* look them in the eye. Where else could I have learned *that*?"

Another student was a car salesman before law school. He said that legal employers responded very positively to it, saying, "If you can sell cars, you can sell anything"—like legal services to potential clients! A student who'd sold vacuum cleaners door-to-door got the same reaction.

* * * SMART HUMAN TRICK * * *

Law student in the South, in an interview with a law firm. The interviewer asks her, "Do you have any retail in your background?" She said, "Well, um, yes . . . Sears." She was embarrassed about it and had left it off her resume as a result.

The interviewer said, "Are you kidding? Selling is the biggest part of law. Working with people. I did it myself to pay for school. It's nothing to be embarrassed about!"

So don't undervalue your work experience, even if you don't think it's particularly dignified!

At this point you're probably thinking, "OK, Kimmbo, you've beaten that left-hand column to death. What's left for the right-hand side?" Let's talk about that right now.

b. **The right-hand column. What distinguishes you? What did you learn that you can use elsewhere?**

As the worksheet heading "What Made Me Stand Out" suggests, in the right-hand column put the accomplishments that spring from the duties in the left-hand column. Ask yourself: How *well* did you do those things in the left-hand column? This is crucial, because remember, employers, both legal and non-law-related, aren't looking for employees with the exact background for the job. Rather, they're looking for people with the potential to learn and excel. How well you've done what you've done tells them that.

Accomplishments tend to fall in these general categories:

- You brought in money (sales, fundraisers);
- You improved productivity or safety;
- You solved problems;
- You created new procedures;
- You saved your employer money;
- You came out on top in competitive rankings;
- You received laudatory quotes from performance evaluations;
- You were given increased responsibility;
- You received compliments from customers;
- You lasted in a job with high turnover;
- You were published in industry or company publications;
- You handled a heavier client/customer load than others;
- You were reliable;
- Being *part* of an accomplishment counts, too. If you worked with others to do something noteworthy, write it down!

For **transferable skills,** look back at the "Ideal Lawyer" list of qualities and skills earlier in this chapter, and see how what you did relates to those. Trust me: you'll find a lot. I talked with one student in Wisconsin who'd been a manager of a very prestigious hotel for several years prior to law school. She said, "I can't figure out what I have to offer. All I did was customer service and problem solving." In other words: exactly what lawyers do! If you say about any job that you worked with clients, solved customer problems, juggled multiple projects ... there are infinite ways what you did at a prior job can translate into useful skills in a legal setting. Writing down what you did with an eye toward what legal employers look for lets them see just how valuable you are.

Incidentally, don't even *think* about skipping over your volunteer experiences!

Maybe you volunteered during undergrad for course credits, you volunteered for personal reasons, you worked a hotline for four hours a week for a semester or two, you taught adults to read, or you did what I've done and volunteered on political campaigns or volunteered at a summer camp. Or maybe you've taken my advice in Chapter 10 and you've volunteered with the local bar association or as an extern for a local judge or you've done projects for PSLawNet.

Regardless of why or when you did it, give each volunteer experience its own worksheet. In the left-hand column, be just as specific about what you did as you were for your law-related and non-law-related jobs: list specific tasks you performed, and quantify your experience.

For instance, if you volunteered on a presidential campaign, instead of just saying that by itself, offer specifics: "Worked from 5 a.m. to 10 a.m. every day contacting radio stations with taped feeds of the campaign; did telephone canvassing of over 1,000 residences for voting preferences; went door-to-door in ten neighborhoods, hanging door tags with candidate information; helped to organize fundraisers, by working as liaison with hotel and catering staff; acted as local liaison with reporters traveling with the candidate." This wouldn't all appear on your resume, but remember: you're just listing the "ore" from which you'll mine your resumes!

In the right-hand column, just as you did for your paying gigs, you'll focus on accomplishments and transferable skills. Of course, when it's a volunteer experience, your accomplishments are likely to be somewhat different than for paid jobs. They might include:

- Succeeding in a competitive selection process;
- Bringing attention to a cause (for instance by writing brochures/articles);
- Raising money for a cause;
- Being offered more responsibility;
- Being invited to volunteer for another semester/summer/year;
- Winning awards;
- Receiving positive reviews and/or comments on your work;
- Being offered a paid position.
- Learning relevant skills.

Also, be sure to note how much time you devoted to the volunteer position. Being willing to volunteer time translates directly to the ability to bring in business as a lawyer, because so much business comes from community involvement.

By way of an example, let's use the political campaign again. Maybe you appeared on the local evening news because of your work with the candidate. Maybe you were invited to stay on and take a paying job with the campaign. Those are noteworthy. Your transferable skills from the experience would include your ability to communicate with a variety of people, which you'd convey by way of talking about communicating with journalists, campaign personnel and constituents.

It may well be that the right-hand column of your volunteering worksheets are skimpy; in other words, there isn't a lot that made you "stand out" in your volunteer work. *It doesn't matter.* The very fact that you volunteered at all is impressive to employers. It shows you're willing to reach beyond your peer group and communicate effectively with others, and you'll tend to be more aware of others, as well. The maturity and perspective you gain from volunteering are *very* marketable achievements. These all say that you've got the skills to reach out to clients and prospective clients, and legal employers obviously love that!

In fact, if you're interested in public interest work, a record of public service is *critically* important—a make-or-break resume element. And if you've done law-related volunteering—like PSLawNet—you've got legal skills to transfer as well—that's icing on the cake!

3. HOBBIES, INTERESTS, SPECIAL SKILLS, PUBLICATIONS, "OTHER INFORMATION" AND UNUSUAL ELEMENTS OF YOUR BACKGROUND BEFORE COLLEGE: WHAT MAKES YOU A LIVING, BREATHING PERSON!

Finally, we're approaching the finish line with these blasted worksheets! This is the last of your fact-collecting.

You need one sheet of paper for all four of these, because unless you've lived several lifetimes, you don't need more than a page to list your hobbies, special skills, "other information," and unusual elements of your background.

What these categories have in common is that they each say a lot about you—but they don't fit anywhere else on your resume.

Since you're fact-gathering here, please be liberal in what you write. Don't think, for now, about how this information will appear to an employer; we'll get to that soon enough!

What kinds of things should you include?

a. Hobbies and interests—anything, anything, anything!

Your hobbies may cut a broader swath than you think. Write down:

- Something you do now given the chance;
- Something you did before law school but don't have time/money for now;
- Something you're learning to do;
- Something you've done once or twice but intend to do more of when you've got the time/money.

Among the more common ones:

- Sports, be it golf, (the ultimate lawyer hobby), tennis, swimming, windsurfing, sailing, yacht racing, scuba diving. Team sports, from softball to cricket to paintball.
- Also, remember to include whether or not you've stood out in a particular sport. An Olympic medal? Why, sure, I wouldn't leave that out. But any award of any kind should be included.
- Music—be it playing classical piano, dancing (and be specific about the type—hip-hop, swing, ballroom), opera or musical comedy buff.
- Acting or taking part in community theater productions in any other capacity
- Travel—be specific about the places!
- Reading—what kinds of books?
- Movies—what kinds of movies?
- Surfing the web—what kinds of sites?
- A blog or web page of your own.
- Anything else: I've seen them all, from champion pie baker, to private pilot, hunting, wine connoisseur, to reading (be specific as to type of book you prefer), knitting, quilting, taxidermy, body piercing, tattooing, body building, Trekkie, Buffy the Vampire Slayer fan. (I didn't say these would actually appear on your resume—I'm saying you should write them down!)

b. Special skills:

These are skills that would be useful to employers. The general categories I'd focus on here would be:

- Computer proficiency: whether it's web-related (like formulating web pages) or related to a specific program (e.g., LEXIS or Westlaw).

- Language proficiency, and be specific: are you fluent? Can you speak but not read it, or vice versa? Are you "conversational?"

- Licenses and professional affiliations. If you've passed the Bar, of course put that first! If you have a real estate license, CPA, you name it, list it. (On your resume, you may have a separate section for licenses/professional affiliations.)

- Security clearances. If you have them, absolutely include them. I talked with a student in Philadelphia with top secret State Department clearance. Even if the employers you're targeting now have nothing more secret than a handshake, they'll respect the background checks you've been through.

c. Publications.

If you've written anything at all, write it down! Not just law-related publications but non-law ones, as well. If you've written articles/stories/books that haven't been published, write them down as well; you may wind up including them in a section of your resume called "Writing Experience."

d. "Other information"

Here, you'll include **anything that will help the employer choose to talk to *you* as opposed to anyone else**. Put yourself in the shoes of the employers you intend to target, pretend that all you've got is a piece of paper by which to evaluate a person, and ask yourself: what else about this person would make me want to interview them?

The general types of information you'd include here would fall into four categories:

1. Information That Ties You to the Employer's Location

Let's say you're applying for a job out-of-town, and nothing on your resume—your law school or college or permanent address—suggests your connection to the community, but you happened to have grown up there or have a lot of family members there. I'd include that under "other information." Why? Although you could mention it in a cover letter—and should—it's possible that your cover letter and resume will get separated, and you want everyone who sees your resume to understand why you want to be in that particular city.

2. You've Done Something Fascinating That Doesn't Rise to the Level Of A Hobby

A hobby suggests something that you've done more than once—or intend to do again. But perhaps you've done something amazing that's a once in a lifetime feat. For instance, maybe you skydived onto the North Pole, or climbed Mount Kilimanjaro, or hang-glided off Sugarloaf Mountain, or flew a decommissioned MiG fighter. (I mention those because my father's actually done all of them.) They would make great interview fodder and they speak well of your courage . . . so write them down!

3.   Accomplishments That Don't Fit Any Traditional Resume Category.

One student spearheaded the financing for a Martin Luther King, Jr. statue at his undergrad school in Texas, convincing the state legislature to pay for it. Quite an accomplishment, albeit not one that fits a traditional resume category. But because it says so much about his determination, initiative, ability to communicate . . . it clearly is resume material!

There are many others, of course . . .

Maybe you made it to the Little League World Series. Maybe you were on a game show. One student made it onto "Jeopardy"—an excellent resume item because it's not just interesting to be on TV . . . it bespeaks great intelligence!

Or maybe you were involved with a reality show. I've talked with students who were chosen for MTV's The Real World, Fear Factor . . . you name it. Unusual accomplishments, but worth writing down. (Of course, judgment is necessary. There's a big difference between being on "Who Wants To *Be* A Millionaire" . . . and "Who Wants To *Marry* A Millionaire.")

It's not just accomplishments that merit inclusion on your worksheet, and ultimately your resume. "Near misses" can be worthy of mention, as well. One student, for instance, made it to the finals of tryouts to be a Disney character at Disneyworld. If you don't know anything about that whole character gig, it's a grueling process to get your foot in the . . . costume. *Almost* accomplishing something can make you stand out, as well!

4.   Something About You That Speaks to Your Enthusiasm for the Employer's work.

For instance, one student was particularly interested in working in non-profits involving kidney research because four members of his family suffered from kidney disease. Now, that's not something that would fit anywhere else on his resume—but it's clearly indicates his sincere enthusiasm for working to help conquer the disease, as opposed to simply finding a job "to pay the bills"!

5.   Motherhood

Another possibility for the "other information" section covers moms. If you're a woman with children, going to law school has proven that you can juggle family and career. This is *very* controversial, but it makes sense for a lot of reasons. As Texas Tech's Kay Fletcher points out, "If you've got kids, you've proven you can balance motherhood with other duties!" On top of that, it will explain why your extracurriculars are kind of skimpy. Why have employers think you're lazy, when you're actually holding down the world's most important job?

There is a school of thought that says you *never* mention children, that there are employers who will immediately eliminate you from consideration if you have children. I'd respond: You *do* have children, and if they're anti-kid, don't you want to know that up front? How will they react when you need to rearrange your schedule to take an hour to see your kid be the tooth in the school play? So you wouldn't wind up getting jobs that would make you miserable. What's wrong with that?

e. Unusual elements of your background before college.

In this section—which may provide content on your resume under the "Other Information" heading—you include information about yourself before college.

One problem with formulating a resume is the issue of how far you go back. The rule of thumb in grad school and beyond is, only college—*unless* there's something before that worth mentioning. The focus in this section is items that say positive things about:

- your ability to adapt
- your worldliness
- your creativity
- your determination and discipline
- your leadership
- your communication skills
- your interest in what the employer does

Now, most of us won't have anything to put in this section, and you can write a killer resume without it. But maybe you *do* have things that are worthy of inclusion.

For instance, did you spend a great deal of time living abroad? A friend of mine spent a year off high school because her father was on sabbatical. The family built a boat, which they sailed from San Francisco to Australia.

Now that's unusual! A law student in New York had ridden the Orient Express from end to end. Cool beans!

Of the thousands of law students I've met, I've heard a vast array of "early" accomplishments that merit inclusion on a resume. Did you win awards in high school on a very high level, like being chosen as the only one from your school or community to attend a mock U.N.? Did you make it to the National Spelling Bee? Did you appear in Burger King ads as a child? Did you organize and run something unusual, like a tutoring service in your community for new immigrants? Did you have a remarkable sports achievement? Again, the Olympics—yeah, I'd include that, even if it goes all the way back to high school.

4. Your "Brain Dump" Resume Is An Organic, Ongoing Process

Don't discard your "brain dump" resume worksheets as soon as you've gotten a job. Hang on to it in a file folder. Every time you join an association or organization, you get a new job, you start a new hobby—add it to your "brain dump" resume worksheets.

When you're on the job, get into the habit, every Friday, of taking a few minutes to write down, in detail, what you worked on during the week. That way, you'll have the raw material to formulate a perfect resume for your *next* job!

C.   FORMULATING YOUR PERFECT RESUME(S) WITH THE INFORMATION FROM YOUR WORKSHEETS

Now you've got a bunch of worksheets in hand, including:

Law School

Undergraduate School

Law–Related Employment (One for each employer)

Non–Law–Related Employment (One for each employer)

Hobbies, Interests, Special Skills, "Other Information," and Unusual Elements of Your Background Before College.

Phew! From those, we're going to mine the gems that go into your resumes.

Now, notice I said *resumes*, not *resume*. One of the biggest mistakes I've seen law students make is to assume that they're writing one resume, and that's it. In fact, that's probably *not* it. Yes, if you're talking about on-campus employers and/or you're looking only at a particular type of employer in a given city—mid-sized law firms in Cleveland, for instance—one resume is likely to do just fine.

But if you're looking for different kinds of jobs in different cities, you're going to have a wardrobe of resumes. That's why God invented word processing! Your resume for a large law firm in New York City is going to be very different from a small law firm in a rural area, a public interest job, or a nontraditional job. In each situation, you'll want to rearrange your resume as necessary so that the information about you that's most important to the employer appears higher up on your resume. You'll go into more detail about jobs relevant to the employer, and diminish others accordingly. In Section G later in this chapter. I take you through an exercise in doing this, taking the same credentials and "refashioning" them for different types of employers.

You see my point: don't be married to one particular resume. Keep your worksheets handy and up-to-date, so that you have a wealth of material on which to draw for any new resume you need to write.

Let's talk about what goes on that resume.

1. STYLE ISSUES

Paper: White. Most experts say you can use cream or gray as well. But here's the thing. Your resumes, cover letters, reference page (if you have it), any other supplemental materials and envelopes have to be the same colour. On top of that, employers have to be able to reproduce your resume—sometimes several times—without the content becoming muddy or unreadable. On top of *that,* larger employers might want to scan your resume, and scanners most easily handle white paper.

The capper is that there has *never* been an employer—never—who made a decision on a candidate because of the paper on which their materials were printed. *Never.*

Since white is universal and ubiquitous, use it. 20–lb bond, for everything.

Type font: Just one. If you use more than one, your resume starts looking like a ransom note.

Font choices:

Sans serif: Arial, Century Gothic, Helvetica.

Serif: Book Antiqua, Century Schoolbook, Garamond, Times New Roman.

Avoid Courier. It looks typewritten.

Size matters: The body of your resume should be between 10–12 points. Your name goes two points larger than the body of the resume. You can also make headings stand out by making them a point bigger than the text underneath them.

Highlighting section headings and subheads:

ALL CAPS

Underlines

Italics

Boldface

Larger fonts.

The guiding principle is to offer distinctive format cues to make it easy for the employer to scan the page.

Orientation: Vertical, just like the page you're reading now. No diagonals, bi-folds, "pleadings" set-ups, brochures. They all scream to employers that you're trying to stand out by way of stunts instead of your merits.

* * * CAREER LIMITING MOVE * * *

Law student puts his resume in the form of a train going down a track, with the words meandering around the page like a model train layout. At major junctures in his career—like college graduation—the little model train engine on the resume has a voice balloon over it that reads "toot toot."

Margins: Ideally an inch all around, no less than three-quarters of an inch on sides, ½" top and bottom. A busy resume doesn't improve your image. On top of that, if it's copied, margins any smaller can result in words being cut off.

* * * CAREER LIMITING MOVE * * *

Female law student has a "Personal Interests" section at the bottom of her very crowded resume. Among the interests listed are "State Fair award-winning quilter and rug hooker." The first line breaks after the word "and," but because her left-margin is narrow, when an employer photocopies her resume the word "rug" is cut off, so that the entry reads: "State Fair award-winning quilter and hooker."

Abbreviations: Be consistent. If you use "J.D." for your law degree, then use "B.S." or "B.A." for your undergrad degree. Similarly, "Juris Doctor" means you use "Bachelor of Arts." Also be consistent with months: January, September or Jan., Sept.

Dates: Don't emphasize them. Put them at the right margin or at the end of the job description. Use full names of months or abbreviations, but no numbers. January–April 2005 is easier to read than 1/05–4/05. You can also use seasons: Summer 2003 or Summers and Holidays 2002–2004 or Winter Break 2006.

Examples:

Marx, Marx, Marx and Marx. (Six-attorney civil and criminal practice.) Helped negotiate settlements of battery charges for pie-throwing incidents. (Sept. 20**-Apr. 20**)

Hearst & Welles Properties, San Simeon, California

Property maintenance technician

Landscaped, painted and did carpentry in construction and maintenance of rental properties. September 2001–June 2002 (Part time) and June 1998–September 1998 (Full time)

Length: One page if you haven't done a ton. Two pages if you have. Don't sacrifice content for the sake of producing a one-page resume. If you genuinely have two pages of relevant material, use it.

No more than two pages for legal employers; for alternative employers, curriculum vitae can be longer, but we'll talk about that in Chapter 31 on Alternative Careers.

Number of sections: Don't go crazy. You don't want your resume to look like the Yellow Pages, with a bunch of little headings. Limit sections to five or six, tops. Pick the ones that best highlight what you bring to the table for your target employers, and change them for different kinds of employers as appropriate.

Headers on additional pages: If you have more than one page, have name and address on every page in case pages get separated.

Attaching pages together: If you have a multi-page resume, use paper clips instead of staples to attach them. Employers often photocopy or scan your resume, and that requires that staples be removed. It's an extra step that makes them crazy.

No puffery. Lawyers don't like to have their chains yanked. "Exceptional interpersonal skills," "Excellent communicator," "Effective manager"—no. Instead, state what you did that *proves* the personality trait/skill you want to convey. Let results speak for you. "Was asked to represent the law school by speaking to groups of as many as 120 admitted students" *proves* your communication skills.

Set-up: Choose any of the formats in Appendix B at the end of this chapter, or choose one your Career Services Office gives you.

All originals: Don't photocopy your resume. It looks crappy and if the employer recopies it, it looks *really* crappy. Print each copy fresh.

2.   FOCUS ISSUES: THE "IDEAL LAWYER" QUALITIES AND THE ELEMENTS PARTICULAR TO YOUR TARGET EMPLOYER

As you formulate *every* element of your resume, from your education to your experience to your hobbies, you need to be aware not just of what legal employers in general want ... but what your particular target employers will want to see in people they hire. You will determine this for yourself as you research your target employers, visiting their websites, reading about them, talking to Career Services about them, consulting upperclassmen and alums and so on. But as a rule of thumb, you can pretty much guarantee:

- Every employer to whom you apply for a permanent job will want to see evidence of your commitment to their geographic area.

- Large law firms are interested in three things: grades, grades, and grades. This is only marginally facetious! They want proof of *killer* research and writing skills (See also Chapter 23 on large firms for "work-arounds.")

- Prosecutors want to see evidence of advocacy skills.

- Small firms want to see community involvement and "people skills." (See also Chapter 18 on small firms.)

- Public interest employers want to see evidence of your commitment to the cause. As one public defender describes it, "I want to see what your life experience is. In my job you've got to relate to clients, to victims, to jurors, to witnesses. What you've done in your life is more important to me than great grades."

Note that these are threads that should run throughout your resume. For instance, if you were applying for a job in a prosecutor's office in Colorado—I wouldn't blame you, by the way—maybe you'd get a cell phone with the appropriate area code, to go in your "header" information. In your law school section, you'd highlight your advocacy experience, maybe moot court if you have it, and advocacy competitions. If you did litigation-oriented CLEs, you'd highlight those. For undergrad, if you did debate, you'd draw attention to that, listing it first among your activities. If you've had jobs where you had to think quickly on your feet, you'd make a point of saying what they were. If you were to apply to the prosecutor's office in a place like Boulder, where outdoor sports are so popular, it would make sense to include energetic outdoor hobbies like mountain biking or hiking, which are so popular there (as long as, of course, you actually *do* them). Or if you heard that the office you're applying to has a softball team and you know how to play, you'd include that.

Of course, those aren't the only things you'd mention ... but you'd make a point of going into more detail about them and leading off with them, because they're what your target employer will want to see!

I could go on and on, but you see my point: Keep not just "generic" lawyer qualities and skills in mind when you formulate resumes for target employers ... find out and focus on the particular skills and qualities your target employers want to see in you!

3. HEADER INFORMATION: NAME, ADDRESS, E-MAIL ADDRESS AND PHONE NUMBER

Hey, I didn't say every word I wrote would be a revelation, did I? Name, address, phone number and e-mail address goes on every resume. Duh. But there are a couple of things to remember ...

- **If your current address and permanent address are different,** include the current address by itself *unless* your permanent address *makes you geographically attractive* to your target employer(s). So if you go to school in Cleveland and you plan to target employers in your home town in Connecticut, list your permanent address as well as your current one.

- **If you've found your name is difficult for people to pronounce,** include a nickname or phonetic pronunciation. For instance:

Ramshavandrian (Rami) Ramashandran

I should tell you that this is controversial. I had a student challenge me once on it, in a sneaky way—he told me his real name, and then said, "But I go by 'Nick' in this country. Do you think I should put 'Nick' on my resume?" I told him if he felt comfortable with it, he should, and then he jumped all over me, saying "Are you telling me not to be myself?" No, no, of course not. As with any other bit of career advice you'll ever get from anybody, if you're dead set on something, go ahead and do it. If it alienates employers you otherwise might have enjoyed working with, that's just the way it is. It's your call. But if you don't feel so strongly about it, remember: you're trying to make things easy for employers—and helping them to pronounce your name definitely does that!

- **If you're looking for an out-of-town job, consider getting a cell phone with that city's area code.** Gosh, isn't this clever? It creates the impression of a local connection, on a very basic level. I wish I could tell you I came up with it, but again, it's a law student invention—and a very wise one!

- **About that phone number: Check your answering machine message before your resume goes out.** Remember, employers are going to be judging your professionalism from moment one. If your answering machine message is "Yo, Dawg, don't know where I am, but I'm probably out partying . . ." there goes the professional image!

    Also, check for background noises on your message. Albany's Pershia Wilkins notes that "Employers react badly if they call and your answering machine message has loud music playing in the background."

- **Make sure your e-mail address is neutral.** Spankboy@aol.com? Naughtygirl@msn.com? Killsformoney@optonline.net? Major stoner@yahoo.com? I don't think so.

- **Don't use the word "Resume" as a heading**. Just start with your name.

4. ACADEMIC STUFF

Haul out those law school, undergrad school, and other grad school worksheets—because this is where you're going to start using them.

Your academic information goes first on your resume. This is true as long as you are still in school or less than two years out, and you're looking for a law-related job (for non-traditional careers, go to Chapter

31). And it's true even if you had a long career before law school. Why? Because you're looking at legal employers, and they'll be most interested in your legal education.

What goes in this academic section? Let's see . . .

A. LAW SCHOOL

It probably goes without saying that law school goes first!

* * * CAREER LIMITING MOVE * * *

Law student, with a substantial career before law school, takes his resume into his Career Services Office, and leaves it for review. The counselor who looks it over is stunned to see that the law student has made no mention of the law school. She calls him and says, "There's a mistake on your resume. You forgot to mention the school." He responds casually, "That's not a mistake. I got that resume professionally written before I started law school. I spent lots of money getting it printed. I don't want to waste it. Anyway, every employer I'm going to send it to will know I'm in law school."

1. LAW SCHOOL GEOGRAPHICAL INFORMATION

Put down the name, city and state of your law school. It's best not to use abbreviations on your resume, so write out the name of your school, even if everybody in the world knows it by its 'nickname.' For instance, USC would be the University of Southern California School of Law, Los Angeles, California.

2. GRADUATION INFORMATION

Put down the year and either the month or season (Spring, Fall) of your actual or anticipated graduation. There are a few ways to put down your graduation date. For example:

- J.D. expected Year X

- Candidate for J.D. expected Year X

- Expected graduation date Year X.

Don't lose any sleep over this one. They're all fine. The only important thing to get across is that you haven't yet graduated (if, in fact, that's the case).

3. IF YOU'RE A VISITING OR TRANSFER STUDENT . . .

a. For visiting students:

List your primary school first, and then your "visitation":

Harvard Law School, Visiting Student, 20**–20**.

b. For transfer students:

Lead with the school from which you'll graduate. Then list the school from which you transferred and the dates of your tenure there.

List GPA/class rank, awards, honors, activities, and so forth under the appropriate school.

4. GPA AND CLASS RANK

Sigh. It's all been so simple up to now, hasn't it? Now we hit our first speed bump. The issue of whether to put your GPA and class rank on your resume, assuming they aren't stellar, is an issue many law students grapple with. I get e-mails about it dozens of times a week. To add to the confusion, there's no consistency among Career Services professionals about where the cut-off is; it varies from school to school.

Employers will tell you that they want to see your grades no matter how bad they are. Ha ha! As San Diego's Susan Benson points out, "If employers are going to ding you if your grades are low, then you shouldn't mention low grades, *regardless* of what they say they want!"

And you've probably heard the old chestnut that you should put your grades down, because if you don't, employers will assume your grades are much worse than they really are. But the fact is, there *is* a cut-off where putting your grades down will hurt you more than help you. It's usually between the top third and top half of the class. If you're close to that cut-off point, it's worth visiting your Career Services Office to find out what their advice for your particular school is; they'll know how employers in the area react to grades from your school.

If your grades are really bumming you out, you should definitely read Chapter 13, called 'Help! My Grades Stink!' Your grades won't torpedo your career. You just have to be clever about the way you work with them, and around them.

When it comes to grades of any kind on your resume, here's what you need to know:

a. Don't 'round up' your GPA. Take it to the precise decimal point that's customary at your school. Linda Spotts of Minneapolis' wonderful firm Gray, Plant, Mooty says "We see resumes all the time, and we *know* how percentiles work at the different schools. At any one school the difference of .01 can cover twenty percent of the class. If a student's going to lie to us about something as simple as that, we just can't consider them." As with just about every possible thing you could lie about on your resume—don't do it!

b. If you have 'Jekyll and Hyde' grades—one great year (or semester) and one bad year (or semester)—use the psychology of advertising to your advantage.

This fabulous piece of advice comes from Kathleen Brady. As she points out, "**Anyone looking at your resume is going to look down the left hand side first**, and when it comes to grades, the first one they see is the only one they're likely to notice—and remember." So let's say that you had a 3.5 out of 4.0 as a 1L, a 2.5 as a 2L, and a 3.1 overall. Here's how you'd set them up on your resume:

3.5/4.0 First Year   2.5/4.0 Second Year   3.1/4.0 Overall

Now—are you going to have to explain the drop second year in interviews? Sure. But it certainly shows that you are capable of doing excellent academic work, and that's more important.

c. If your school grades on a traditional curve—in other words, it's bucked the trend of awarding at least a B+ to anybody who isn't the missing link—make sure to include your class rank *first*, and perhaps *exclusively*.

To tell you the truth, law schools should go back to a real curve. If everybody in the class has a 3.5 average, it's just meaningless. Unless, of course, *you* have a 3.5, in which case—bravo! But seriously—if your school grades on a traditional C curve, the initial impact of that GPA on an employer can hurt you. So put up front what helps you the most: your class rank, which is impervious to the curve. If you put your GPA at all, I'd also consider doing what students at some 'traditional curve' schools do, and include a letter from their Career Services Director or Law School Dean explaining the school's grading policy.

d. For both GPA and class rank, you may include *only* your *official* numbers. If your school doesn't calculate class rank, you can't estimate it on your resume. (In a cover letter, you *can* say what you'd estimate it to be.) Employers will assume that they can call your school to verify your GPA and class rank, and if you've djinnied it up by yourself, you'll be in serious trouble.

e. If you don't put your grades and class rank, you have to put *something* down about your academic performance. Best food forward!

1. If you've got a strong upward trend in your grades, highlight that.

You know, this happens to an awful lot of law students. You get to law school, it's intimidating, the whole 100%-final-exam format freaks you out—and your first year grades are depressing. But then you get the hang of the law school exam thing, and second year—well, hello! *Now* we're talking. I see it all the time. What do you do? Well, you remember that what truly matters is what you're capable of doing—not what you did when you got to law school, before you figured things out. So you highlight your great grades by putting them first:

Either: 2nd year GPA: 3.5/4.0, 20th out of 250

1st year GPA: 2.5/4.0, 170th out of 250

Overall GPA: 3.1/4.0, 90th out of 250

You could also use the "Jekyll and Hyde" format we discussed above, if you've got enough space across the page. But you see the point: The first thing employers get to see is what you want them to see: your strong academic performance!

2. If you do better on 'paper' courses than 'exam' courses, highlight that in your resume.

Everybody knows that law school exams are a horse dung way of testing knowledge. (Research shows, incidentally, that the best way to ensure long-term retention of information is to give weekly quizzes.) As we'll discuss in the interview chapter, one way to lightheartedly address low grades in interviews is to say, "I don't do so well in blue books—so if you're intending for me to do my work with two-hour deadlines, in a closed book exam format, I'm probably not the right person for the job"—followed of course by why you *are* the right person for the job!

On your resume, you can employ this same technique by pointing out how well you do in classes where you had to turn in a paper as opposed to taking an exam, as long as you did really well on the papers compared to the exams. After all, papers are much more analogous to what you'll have to do at work, at least if you go to a research-heavy job—and that's why it helps you on your resume.

3. Put down individual class grades, *if* the classes relate to the employer's practice, *and* you did really well in those classes (even if your overall GPA isn't so hot).

SLJ Attorney Search's Gail Cutter suggests adding a line to your resume that says "Relevant Course Work," and putting down any stellar grades relevant to the employer. For instance, if you apply to a med mal firm and you got an A- in medical malpractice class at school even though you're in the bottom half of the class—highlight that grade on your resume! (In fact, no matter where you are in the class, you'd highlight a performance like that.)

Or let's say you're applying to the DA's office, and you got an A in Crim Pro. On your resume it goes! I could go on and on—an A in Trial Tactics if you're applying to a litigation practice. Yadda Yadda Yadda. But you see the point. If you're good at what an employer does, it doesn't matter so much if you ain't so great at what they *don't* do.

Incidentally, this highlights once again that you'll need more than one resume. But you were going to anyway, right? So individual class grades are one more thing to tailor to the nature of the employer.

4. If all of your law school grades chomp, put down your undergrad grades (assuming *they're* good).

As St. John's' Maureen Provost Ryan suggests, "One semester of law school won't capture someone as accurately as four years of undergrad will!" So if your college grades are great, put them down!

5. Remember, grades aren't even *close* to everything.

If this whole subject of grades depresses you, don't let it. As I've pointed out time and again in this book (and cover exclusively in Chapter 13), bad grades will not stop you from having a wonderful career. There are very few employers who are terribly grades conscious. It just seems like all of them are, because the ones who interview on campus tend to be the 'grade hogs.' As Gail Peshel points out, "Smaller employers are more concerned with whether you'll stay or leave—geographic ties and rainmaking skills are much more important to them than grades are!" And Sophie Sparrow points out, "Sell what you've got. If it's great experience—sell that. If you've got a great personality—make contacts to get your foot in the door. Consider the whole picture of you. People who don't do well in school can be stellar!" Keep this whole discussion of grades on your resume in perspective. All we're talking about now is how you show yourself off to best advantage on a stinking piece of paper, and you *know* I don't consider your resume the lynchpin of your job search by any stretch of the imagination. If you don't have grades, make up for it some other way—with great experience or by making contacts to skirt the whole credentials problem from the word go. All you're doing here is thinking of how to best present your academics. Get that out of the way, and then forge ahead!

* * * CAREER LIMITING MOVE * * *

On a new graduate's resume:

"Graduated in the top 85% of my class."

5. AWARDS, HONORS AND SCHOLARSHIPS

Time to pat yourself on the back! Go through your law school worksheet and pull out any awards, honors and scholarships you've received. In your case, that may take a little time. For me ... well, I would have zipped right on to the next section!

Ahem. Let's talk about how you word awards, honors and scholarships on your resume. Simply put, you want to put just enough down so that anyone reading your resume will understand the nature of the prize and what you did to receive it.

For instance:

"James Fordham Scholar: Three-time honoree for outstanding academic achievement."

"AmJur Award for highest score in Torts."

"Dean's List for maintaining at least a 3.5 average, two semesters."

For Dean's List, unless you made it every semester, you must say how many times you were on it.

How about scholarships? They reflect wonderfully well on you, and should always be mentioned on your resume if you're lucky enough to have them.

For full tuition scholarships, you'll want to highlight for the employer how you were chosen. A short descriptive phrase will help. Try including information like this:

"Full Tuition Scholarship: Awarded and renewable on the basis of grades; one of X distributed to incoming class."

For partial scholarships awarded on the basis of grades, you'll want to include the same kind of language. If additional factors like residential or ethnic background are involved, mention that. And you may find out during the year that your scholarship has a donor name. If so, include it. If not, such a scholarship is known simply as an "Academic Scholarship," and that's what you put on your resume. List it like this:

"Academic Scholarship: partial tuition paid."

"Partial Academic Scholarship: renewable for three years."

"President's Scholar—full tuition waiver for academic excellence."

Incidentally, **don't mislead employers about the nature of scholarships.** I'm embarrassed to admit that I did this. I had a full scholarship undergrad because my scientist father had a laboratory at school. I put "Full Scholarship" on my resume, knowing full well employers would interpret that as an academic scholarship, rather than a "Daddy's Little Girl" free ride. Employers smoked me out immediately, and of course asked, "So how *were* your grades?" "As a matter of fact, they sucked." I didn't say that, but it was a stupid resume idea anyway. No lies—nothing misleading!

If you already graduated and it was "with honors" (e.g., cum laude), the honor goes after the degree received, *not* in the honors section.

For instance:

Toejam School of Law, J.D. awarded 2* * * *cum laude*

6.   HONORS AND ACTIVITIES CAN BE LISTED SEPARATELY OR TOGETHER, YOUR CHOICE

If you call it "Honors and Activities," start with honors first (academic awards and the like) followed by activities in descending order of importance to target employers and significance of your involvement.

7. JOURNALS

Many, if not most, legal employers highly prize writing ability, and that's why experience on legal journals in law school is so valuable. Be it the *sine qua non* experience of Law Review or any other journal, be sure to highlight your experience on your resume. Here are some things to keep in mind about how you present your experience:

- If you haven't done it yet, say so on your resume:

International Law Journal invitee, 20**–20** school year.

- **If you had a writing contribution, include the topic you wrote about on your resume—as long as it is not highly controversial.** However, keep in mind that if you write down your topic and the employer knows something about it, you may find yourself spending your entire interview discussing it—so make sure you bone up on what you wrote before you go on such an interview!

  If your topic *is* highly controversial—charged for political or other reasons—then be vague about it on your resume. By way of example, I wrote my Law Review note about legal liability for sexually transmitted diseases. I read an article about it in *Newsweek,* and it seemed pretty racy, so . . . I could go into more detail, but you see the problem: you just shouldn't have that wording on your resume! Instead, euphemize it; in my case, a vague reference to emerging Tort issues would suffice.

- **If your piece has been chosen for publication, list it appropriately:**

  Title (in blue book form), with a notation like "publication pending" or "will be published in Spring 20** edition."

- **If you have/had any editorial/managerial role, be sure to highlight the skills you employ(ed).** For instance, as an editor, you'd select, supervise, and advise other student contributors. This highlights your leadership, management, and critical analysis skills in a legal setting, as well as your ability to delegate and oversee work. If you acted as a solicitations editor, you'd have significant managerial duties as well, including developing topics and soliciting prospective authors from the legal community. These skills involve creative and organizational thinking from the viewpoint of marketing, a *very* valuable skill for lawyers in private practice!

- **If the employer is not 'research-oriented,' don't list your journal experience first.** We've already talked to death about researching employers. If you know from your research that the employer you're contacting is people-oriented—for instance, this is very true at some prosecutors' offices and some small law firms, who consider everyone who works for them to be a counselor, not a researcher—then put down your 'people-oriented' law school activities first, like moot court, client counseling, those kinds of things. Remember: It's a marketing piece. Market first what they most want to see!

a. Law Review.

Here it is—the golden law school credential. The Great Leveler. You can go to Fred's Night YMCA Law School, but if you're on Law Review ... aaah. You're *it*, baby. I remember an old ad for Chivas Regal. It had these two gorgeous babes jogging, and one of them is saying to the other, "He's on Law Review—and he drinks Chivas." Yep. Law Review sticks with you for life. When I meet new people—largely my parents' friends, that is—who hear that I went to law school, the first question they'll *inevitably* ask me is, "Were you on Law Review?" So, yeah, it's a good thing to have.

Which is only fair, because when you think about it, actually *doing* Law Review kind of blows. Nobody else will tell you that, but if you're on it, you kind of know it's true. Gee, not that spending hours talking about whether the period in the citation goes inside or outside of the quotation marks isn't *fascinating*, mind you. I had a professor who told me once that when he submitted law review articles, he always made sure to have one paragraph that was all bad, grammar, citations, you name it. "They just love that stuff," he said. So, really. It's not the most wonderful experience in the world ...

But it sure does look good on paper!

Here's how to address it on your resume:

- **Because of its selectivity, Law Review is considered an 'Honor,' not an 'Activity.'**

- **If you've been selected for Law Review but you haven't done it yet** ... well, let me congratulate you. And, hey, ignore all that stuff I said about how it's not much fun. Here's how you list it:

"Case Western Reserve Law Review Invitee, 20**–20**."

or

"Case Western Reserve Law Review, Year X–Year Y."

- **Don't state how you were chosen.** At most law schools, you can get on Law Review either by grades or by a writing competition. If you graded on, it'll be obvious from your grades. And if you wrote on, don't draw attention to the fact that you're not at the top of the class. The fact that you're on Law Review is all that counts!

- **If your law review duties are not obvious from your job title, describe them briefly.** For instance:

  "Case Western Reserve Law Review; Articles Editor. Full editorial and verification responsibility for three articles to be published Spring, Year X. Supervised six associates."

b. Other Journals

Since journals other than Law Review vary from school to school, you'll want to explain other journals in more detail. For instance, explain whether the journal is student-run, whether it's a scholarly publication, or exactly what the heck it is. As with Law Review, you'll want to refer to your own specific contribution(s). For instance:

  "Case Western Reserve Journal of Phlegm Reclamation Law; Business Editor. Full responsibility for $18,000 annual budget of student-run scholarly publication. Negotiate contracts with publishers and reprinters; manage web site; arrange copyrighting; sell subscriptions."

As is true with Law Review, if you've been selected for a journal but haven't undertaken the activity yet, state that on your resume. "Case Western Reserve Journal of Phlegm Reclamation Law, Year X–Year Y."

8.   Theses and Papers

Include the subhead "Thesis" or "Paper" and include the title in italics—or include it in a separate "Publications" section, if you use one.

9.   Moot Court Competitions

Moot Court is really important to employers, for two reasons: It shows your ability to research and analyze points of law, and it shows your ability to express yourself persuasively, both orally and in writing. Beyond that, it's the best indicator of how you stack up against your classmates in a non-exam setting.

Make sure to describe both how you were selected *and* your results, if your results are good. For instance:

  "National Moot Court Team. Selected for team after ranking among top six oral and written advocates out of 75 participants in intramural competition."

  "National Appellate Advocacy Team: One of six students chosen."

If you've been selected for moot court but you haven't taken part in it yet, try wording it something like this:

  "Appellate Advocacy Program, Year X–Year Y."

Please note that you can only include this line if you're *definitely* going to be taking part in moot court in the Fall, not if you're *likely* to, or are going to try out for it.

10. MOCK TRIAL COMPETITION

Legal employers like to see mock trial experience on your resume, because it shows you've developed your advocacy skills and, in particular, your spontaneous courtroom skills, in a start-to-finish trial situation. The ability to think quickly on your feet is useful to *every* lawyer.

On your resume, talk about the time you invested in mock trial and your results (if they were good). For instance:

"National Mock Trial Competition: Ranked 12th out of top 22 teams in the United States, after winning regional competition against 25 teams. Preparation and participation involved over 100 hours per semester, without course credit."

11. CLIENT COUNSELING COMPETITION

If you do well in the client counseling competition, this will draw an employer's interest because it's a harbinger of your effectiveness in working with clients. Since this is the one activity in which First Years tend to excel, it often stands alone on 1L resumes. If that's the case with you, try to compose a sentence or two that will really attract a potential employer, like this:

"Client Counseling Competition: Ranked third of 48 teams in intramural competition. Judged by visiting attorneys and psychologists on the basis of ability to advise, counsel, and elicit information from clients in a mock counseling situation."

12. LAW SCHOOL CLINICS

Clinics look great to employers for a bunch of reasons. For a start, clinics give you a chance to apply theory to real life situations, and to handle clients, and to budget your time—and they also give you a chance to get basic mistakes out of your system in a uniquely structured environment, designed as much to educate you as to provide client care. Especially if your grades aren't awesome, a law school clinic can give you the ammunition to show why employers should hire you!

As a result, definitely state the scope of your activities and responsibilities in any clinics you take part in, whether voluntarily or as part of a clinic program required by your school. Word it something like this:

"Law School Clinic, Intern: Served as legal counsel in seven civil cases over full academic year. Conducted client interviews, witness identification and preparation; researched and wrote memoranda, briefs, and motions for each of the seven cases; represented three clients in trial under supervision of Clinic lawyers. Gained direct experience in client contact, case development, pretrial and trial procedures, and law practice management."

13. STUDENT ASSOCIATIONS AND FRATERNITIES

There are more student associations than you could shake a proverbial stick at. We can't talk about all of them—but I can give you ideas on how to cover them on your resume, focusing in every case on your accomplishments with the organization in question.

a. Student Bar Association.

Whether you were elected or appointed to the Student Bar Association, you'll probably be called on to represent and "sell" the school at various functions. What does this say to legal employers, particularly private firms, keeping in mind that they're always looking to attract new clients and keep current ones? *Rainmaking potential*—that's what it says. On top of that, many SBA officers also become involved in counseling and mediation, which provide direct evidence of an ability to do the same with clients. So when you present your SBA experience on your resume, be sure to focus on the *marketability* of what you've done. Here are a couple of examples:

> "Student Bar Association: Chairperson, Curriculum Committee. Targeted and recommended new international law course and clinical program to faculty, which will commence in the Year X school year, in response to student/faculty survey to identify curriculum gap."

> "Student Bar Association, Cuyahoga County Bar Association Liaison: Regularly attended bar association meetings and expressed student concerns on various issues. Attracted over 50 new members through first on-campus recruitment in over ten years."

b. Other Student Associations.

Your commitment to any student association is a plus to legal employers. Again, like the Student Bar Association, you should be specific as to what you accomplished. If you have trouble with this, focus on the fact that many student associations sponsor activities and this is a good chance to show your organizational, leadership, and oral skills. Here are a couple of examples:

> *"Black Law Students Association, Midwest Recruitment Conference Volunteer: Manned student and employer check-in booths. Recruited and supervised 10 students in preparing resume binders."*

> "Environmental Law Students Association; Chairperson, Speaker Committee: Solicited several national speakers, generating press coverage. Events attracted greatest per-event attendance of all student groups."

While it's obvious that public interest employers will be interested in your associational activities, those aren't the only employers who will find them attractive. However, for employers outside of public interest, be very sure that your description of your activities focuses on the transferable skills you learned. Here's an example:

> *"Student Public Interest Law Fellowship, Board Member: Helped to raise awareness among law students and lawyers of employment opportunities. With fellow students, raised $13,000 during one year and $19,000 during the next year for student internships."*

c. Fraternities

Joining law fraternities can help you in a couple of ways. First of all, if you have any kind of leadership role—and they aren't hard to come by—you've got transferable skills to show off to legal employers. Secondly, to alumni members of the fraternity, your membership will catch their eye on your resume. I know that the alumni members of my fraternity, Phi Alpha Delta (I implore you to join—you can find it on-line at www.pad.org), really do pay attention to student members. Anyway, more on that in Chapter 10 on activities. Here, we're concerned about your resume.

If you play a leadership role, flesh out what you did. Here's an example:

> "Phi Alpha Delta Law Fraternity: Active in tenants' rights issue which involved representing tenants through the media, letters, and a court appearance."

If your title in the fraternity doesn't make your role immediately obvious, explain it. For instance, if the liaison officer in your national fraternity is called a "tribune," you'll want to explain that in the description of your role.

> Even if all you did was join a fraternity and attend social events, be prepared to talk about the fraternity in interviews. One judge I know makes a point of asking student members of his fraternity the name of their local chapter—just to see if they're truly involved in it or not!

14. STUDY ABROAD PROGRAMS

Woo-hoo! Par-tay! Ahem. Sorry. I know you did it for the credit.

How do you list a Study Abroad Program on your resume?

It depends whether or not you want to do international work.

If you *do,* then for your target employers, have a "Foreign Study" section directly below your law school education, and put your study abroad program there.

If you're not into international law as a career, it's *still* worth mentioning on your resume, because it's such an interesting interview item. If you got credit for it from your law school, it's not a separate school entry. List it as a law school activity, stating where and when you studied. (If you got credit from the other school, then list it as a separate graduate school.)

15. BAR ASSOCIATION STUDENT MEMBERSHIPS

If you join the bar association as a student, and I *implore* you to do so, it is listed as a law school activity. Be specific about any sections you've joined (if relevant to target employers) and activities you've taken part in.

If you're a 1L and/or you have a skimpy resume, bar association activities can be listed under "Experience" on your resume.

If you've passed the bar—props to you, Sport!—list it in your "Licenses" section.

B. OTHER LEGAL EDUCATION—IF YOU'VE TAKEN MY ADVICE ABOUT TAKING CLEs . . .

And if you *haven't* taken my advice—who's nailing your feet to the ground? For gosh sakes, especially if your grades aren't awesome, get a few CLEs on your resume to make yourself stand out. I address them in excruciating detail in the Birds and Bees, Chapter 10. If you do go to a few—**they go directly under your law school education**, in prime real estate on your resume—because they deserve it!

List CLEs under the heading "Other Legal Education," just as prominent as your "Legal Education" section. Include the name of the CLE, who gave it, how many hours it was, and any other descriptive information necessary to explain what you learned.

This is one area where you will tailor your resume depending on the employers you're writing to. Include only the CLEs relevant to the particular employer. If you've taken CLEs on three different specialties—say, domestic relations, tax and environmental—show *only* the CLEs in the employer's specialty in resumes they get. More general CLEs—like ones on ethics—can go on every resume. Remember: the point of CLEs is to prove your enthusiasm for what an employer does and show familiarity with their particular practice. So edit your CLEs accordingly!

C. OTHER GRADUATE DEGREES

I've talked to law students who have some of the most remarkable educational backgrounds. Ph.D.s, MDs, RNs, MBAs—gee, all the letters you can think of, in so many combinations.

If you have an additional graduate degree, list its nuts and bolts exactly as you did your law degree: name of school, location, graduation date, GPA/class rank (if they were good). Placement and detail on your resume depend on its relevance to the employers you're targeting. If you're going into a field related to both your law degree and your other degree—for instance, you want to be in real estate development or work in a corporation, and you have an MBA—then you'll highlight both accordingly. For your additional degree, you'll highlight any significant accomplishments and relevant activities/classes, just as you would for your law degree. Same if you want to work at a museum and you have a Ph.D. in art history, or you want to go into med mal and you have an MD or RN.

If your desired job is *not* related to your 'other' degree, then drop it down on your resume, and cover it very briefly. Education is always a great thing, but you don't particularly want employers questioning, before they meet you, why you went for a degree that's not useful to them. I'm not saying you should delete it; just don't put it near the top, where it'll be noticed immediately.

If you have part of a graduate degree—that is, you've taken coursework toward another graduate degree but didn't actually receive the degree—**don't make the wording on your resume mislead the employer into thinking you've got that degree!** I know I keep harassing you about not lying on your resume, but really—you read the newspaper. You see how people get bounced out of jobs—really prestigious jobs, like college deans and sports directors—when a lie about their credentials on their resume is smoked out, even if it's been years since they got the job and even if they've done really well in the position. It's just not worth the risk.

Here's how to word it:

> University of Transylvania, Slogolz, Transylvania.
>
> Completed fifteen credits toward MBA, including courses in ...

And mention the classes most relevant to the employer who's receiving this particular version of your resume.

If you only took a couple of graduate classes toward another degree, and the courses aren't relevant to employers in which you're interested, I'd leave them off your resume all together. Use the space for things that'll help you more!

D. **UNDERGRADUATE SCHOOL**

The "identifying" information for undergrad will be the same as law school: The formal name of your school (it's Massachusetts Institute of Technology, not MIT), city, state, and graduation date.

If you graduated with honors, they go in italics and all lower case, as follows:

> Krusty Klown College, Springfield, Nostate, B.S. 20** *magna cum laude*

The amount of space you dedicate to your undergraduate experience depends on two things: What else you've got (if you have extensive law school and law-related experiences as an upper class student, you minimize your college listing; as a 1L, it'll probably be quite prominent), **and how relevant it is to what you want to do.** For instance, if you want to go into environmental work and you were a geology major, or you want to go into intellectual property and you were a mechanical engineering major (like my husband), your college experience will get commensurate space on your resume.

If you received awards or honors, include them. Remember, by the way, that being selected for an athletic team should be listed as an honor (e.g., varsity field hockey). Also, if you received an academic scholarship, include information about how you got it.

If you were on the Dean's List, you have to state how often you made it: e.g., "Dean's List, six semesters."

You can also include minors and assistantships.

By way of activities, include those that indicate:

- **Leadership ability (student government, organizations);**
- **Public speaking skills (e.g., debate);**
- **Research and writing skills;**
- **Interest/skills related to the employer's focus;**
- **Athletic participation;**
- **Community involvement.**

Be sure to focus on transferable skills. If you were secretary of the Soccer Club, and that involved taking meeting notes and writing articles for the newsletter, say so. Those illustrate your listening, interviewing, and writing skills.

If you have a lot of undergrad activities, only list those most significant or of greatest interest to your target employer(s).

If you did a study abroad program, it's not a separate school *if* your undergrad school gave you credit for it. List it as an activity, with a brief description—unless you want to go into international law, in which case you should list it in a separate section on your resume called "Foreign Study."

If you did a thesis or paper, have a subhead saying so and include the title in italics. (If you use a "Publications" section on your resume, you can put it there instead.)

If you went to more than one school, you only need to state which school gave you your degree.

5. EXPERIENCE, PAID AND UNPAID, PART-TIME, FULL-TIME, LAW RELATED
        OR NOT . . . ALL OF IT!

This is probably the section of your resume that will take you the most time, especially if you've held down full-time jobs before law school.

(And if that's the case, by the way, be sure to look at Chapter 22, on second-career students.)

Let's start by talking about how you ought to present any job you've had.

A. USING YOUR WORKSHEET INFORMATION TO FORMULATE JOB DESCRIPTIONS ON YOUR RESUME

1. IDENTIFYING INFORMATION

a. For legal employers, whether your work was paid or volunteer:

List the employer's name, city and state, your job title, and dates of employment. Unless your employer is very likely to be known to your target audience (e.g., it's the Environmental Protection Agency, or an enormous law firm in or near your target city), include a line briefly describing the employer to help potential employers put your experience in context with their own needs.

For instance, you can describe a firm this way:

"O'Pea and Anthony: Springfield, Ohio. Seven-attorney firm with general civil practice."

If you worked on a volunteer basis, *don't mention it* unless *your resume is going to public interest employers, where you'll have a separate "Volunteer Experience" section* (we discuss this below).

b. For Non–Law Related Employers, whether your work was paid or volunteer: Same identifying information as legal employers: **employer's name, city and state, your job title, and dates of employment.** If the name of the employer doesn't give it away (Hathaway Brown School, General Hospital), or the employer is not well known, add a *very brief* description of the organization after city and state.

c. If you worked on a volunteer basis, don't mention it *unless* your resume is going to public interest employers, in which case you'll have a separate "Volunteer Experience" section (as we discuss below).

d. In deciding whether you lead with the employer's name or your position, consider which is most impressive or likely to catch an employer's eye. Whichever you decide, use the same order for each experience.

e. Organizing header information:

As a rule of thumb, **the most relevant and significant information goes on the left,** where the employer looks first. Reserve that for the name of the employer and your job title.

Less significant information goes on the right: for instance, dates of employment and the geographic location of the employer.

2. **DESCRIBING YOUR WORK: START WITH VERBS AND RESULTS!**

a. **Don't write in complete sentences. Instead, use phrases that start with verbs.**

Instead of: *"I researched issues relating to shredding e-mails in SEC investigations"*

Use: *"Researched issues relating to shredding e-mails in SEC investigations"*

b. **Don't use introductory phrases. Jump right in with what you *did*.**

Don't say *"Responsibilities included shredding e-mail documents in an SEC investigation."*

Say: *"Shredded documents in an SEC investigation."*

Just kidding. You get the point.

Don't say *"Was given the task of conceiving and executing a new filing system for two-person law firm."*

Say: *"Conceived and executed new filing system for two-person law firm."*

Don't say *"My duties included ..." "As the tax clerk I ..."*

c. **Use current tense for jobs you have now, and past tense for former jobs.**

For a current job: *"Purge hard drive of incriminating e-mails."*

For a prior job: *"Purged hard drive of incriminating e-mails."*

d. **For gosh sakes, don't refer to yourself in the third person!**

"Found himself rewarded with increased responsibility."

"Discovered herself under investigation by the SEC."

Where's my barf bag?

e. **Use quantifiers to state *specifics*.**

"Supervised seven people" sounds better than *"Supervisor."*

"Increased sales 25%" is better than *"Increased sales."*

f. **Remove "a," "an" and "the" to keep descriptions concise and readable.**

Don't say *"Was an intern for the SEC Office in Atlanta ..."*

Say: *"Interned in the Atlanta SEC Office."*

g. **Avoid redundancy between your job title and description.**

As Hastings' Phil Marshall advises, "Don't tell me what you've already told me, or what a reasonable person would've figured out independently. If your job title was 'Judicial Extern to Judge Lawless,' you don't need to start your job description with 'served as judicial extern to Judge Lawless.' Just tell me the types of incredible research and writing you did for her."

h. **Refer back to the qualities and skills of an ideal lawyer list earlier in this chapter as you word your experiences, to make sure they "sing" to lawyers.**

Make sure that every entry includes information that either illustrates your capacity for job performance, proves your commitment to the geographic area, and conveys genuine interest in or knowledge of the employer and the employer's focus, or distinguishes you from other potential candidates.

i. **Avoid editing descriptions so severely that they don't make sense to your target employers.**

I've seen resumes with entries like "Selected for LDP Program," "Chosen Honorary Fordanite," and so on. They may be *great* honors, but who the hell, outside of an LDP Fordanite, would *know* that? "Department of Commerce: Evaluated enumerators" may be meaningful to you, but I don't get it.

Make it easy for employers to see why your experiences and accomplishments make you the perfect candidate!

j. **Try to use "action verbs" to start your descriptions, to highlight your accomplishments.**

Here's a list of action verbs and skills to include wherever appropriate (courtesy of New England School of Law):

Accelerated	Assumed
Accomplished	Assured
Accounted for	Authored
Achieved	Bolstered
Administered	Briefed
Advised	Brought
Aided	Built
Analyzed	Calculated
Anticipated	Catalogued
Appraised	Caused
Approved	Chaired
Acquired	Changed
Arbitrated	Checked
Argued	Clarified
Arranged	Classified
Assessed	Closed
Assisted	Combined

Communicated
Compared
Completed
Composed
Conceived
Concluded
Conducted
Constructed
Consulted
Contracted
Controlled
Converted
Convinced
Coordinated
Corrected
Correlated
Counseled
Crafted
Created
Critiqued
Dealt
Debated
Decided
Defined
Delegated
Delivered
Demonstrated
Designed
Detailed
Determined
Developed
Devised
Diminished
Directed
Discovered
Distributed
Drafted
Earned
Effected
Enlarged
Engineered
Established
Evaluated
Executed
Expanded
Experienced
Foresaw
Formed
Formulated
Generated
Governed
Grouped
Guided

Improved
Implemented
Increased
Initiated
Inspired
Installed
Integrated
Interviewed
Invented
Investigated
Justified
Keynoted
Led
Litigated
Managed
Maintained
Mediated
Moderated
Motivated
Negotiated
Operated
Originated
Organized
Performed
Planned
Promoted
Provided
Recruited
Saved
Wrote

And skill words:

Act on
Clarify
Conceptualize
Cooperate
Counsel
Delegate
Disseminate information
Edit
Establish priorities
Facilitate
Identify issues
Implement
Improvise
Innovate
Integrate
Interpret legal language
Interview clients
Negotiate
Operate
Present

Prioritize

Process

Proofread

Resolve

Speak persuasively

Summarize

Synthesize information

Troubleshoot

Of course, you aren't going to want to use *all* of these words in one resume! Here are a few examples:

"Wrote memoranda on . . ."

"Researched cases for . . ."

"Processed estates . . ."

"Assisted at trials . . ."

"Drafted briefs . . ."

"Prepared testimony . . ."

"Buried evidence . . ." Just kidding.

And to accentuate your accomplishments, it helps to start sentences with the results of your efforts. Here's an example:

"Reduced overtime 23% while increasing productivity, by cross-training all staff. Virtually eliminated downtime through equitable task distribution."

3.   FIGURING OUT WHAT TO INCLUDE ABOUT EACH EXPERIENCE

As you go through your worksheets, remember: **Employers want to see how you stood out in prior jobs, the transferable skills and qualities you bring to them. You don't want your experiences to say what you did, but rather what doing them says about *you*—and what you're capable of doing in the future.**

Instead of:

Driveway Sealer, S & S Driveway Sealing, Cleveland, Ohio

Painted houses with a friend. Summers, 2004, 2005.

Consider this:

S & S Driveway Sealing, Cleveland, Ohio

Owner: Founded driveway sealing business with a friend. Negotiated fees with customers and developed an application method that reduced application time by 40%. Second summer profit increased 300% over first summer profit. Summers 2004, 2005.

With that in mind, let's look at how you choose the information from your worksheets that goes onto your resume.

● **Accomplishments:**

This is the highest level of description that you can relate to an employer. It's the one that truly highlights your successes. Here are a few examples:

"Began as volunteer; hired and subsequently promoted on basis of performance."

"After brief training period, handled heavy caseload with minimal supervision."

"Developed new chemical process which received patent."

"General Litigation Paralegal: In addition to customary duties, performed legal research and drafted briefs, which were largely accepted with very little revision. Assessed computerized documentation systems and recommended package which was purchased."

"Undertook five-year mission to explore new worlds and new galaxies. Boldly went where no one had gone before." (Thank you, Captain Kirk.)

Note that if you worked as part of a team to accomplish something, you have to state that in your description.

"Along with another intern . . ."

"Member of three-person team that . . ."

"Contributed X to Y project . . ."

- **Quantifiers:**

Numbers and percentages jump out on resumes, and they're particularly helpful in terms of providing evidence of accomplishments. So use them if you have them! Here are a few examples:

"Employed up to thirty hours per week on third shift while attending school full-time. On Dean's List six of eight semesters."

"Managed caseload of 25 clients."

"Increased productivity by 10%."

"Founded company with two fellow engineers. Built $5,000 investment into $2.5 million annual gross revenues within five years."

"Upon withdrawal from college, founded software company. Within ten years, became richest man in the world."

- **Skills gained on the job, abilities sharpened because of it:** These are valuable to employers, *particularly* law-related skills and abilities.

Be *specific* about what you did and what you learned:

"Punt, Passe and Kique (five-attorney firm). Summer intern 20**. Researched topics including higher education, labor and employment, bankruptcy, and sports and environmental law. Summarized research findings in memoranda. Researched and wrote trial briefs. Prepared material for CLE presentation on drafting sports contracts. Reviewed sports and entertainment contracts. Observed depositions, arbitrations, and mediations."

"Patent clerk: Reviewed over 5,000 patent applications, which sharpened analytical skills. As a result, in spare time, wrote the Theory of Relativity."

If you've worked with a particular body of court rules, administrative practices or particular kinds of transactions, detail it.

Instead of: *"Drafted pleadings,"*

Say: *"Drafted motions to dismiss and motions in limine."*

Instead of: *"Reviewed documents,"*

Say: *"Assessed and analyzed purchase and sale contracts, balance sheets, profit/loss and income statements."*

Detail substantive areas with which you're familiar, being sure to use "terms of art" related to practice areas you worked in, e.g., reasonable cause, sentencing, suppression. *Always* include the name of the specialty and not just the particular issues you learned about, so that when an employer does a "key word" search of your resume that/those specialty area(s) will jump out.

Instead of: *"Researched employment law issues,"*

Say: *"Researched numerous employment law issues including wrongful termination, wage and hour disputes, and gender discrimination."*

Instead of: *"Answered calls from constituents,"*

Say: *"Assisted constituents with various matters including social security benefits, access to public information and analysis of pending legislation."*

Be sure to include your professional contact with different kinds of people. Lawyers have to be comfortable communicating with various constituencies. Highlight the different ones you've dealt with:

"Interviewed clients respecting strengths and weaknesses of cases, analyzed expert witness depositions, and negotiated financial settlement with SSI caseworkers."

- **Anything else that makes you stand out to legal employers.**

Use the opportunity to highlight:

- **how many hours you worked (if you worked more than one job, or worked while you went to school);**

- **how much of your education you helped to fund; and**

- **any activity that put you in close contact with lawyers, or had you performing duties that reflect on what you'd do as a lawyer**—like negotiating contracts or disputes, or being an expert witness, or participating in judicial boards for undergrad fraternities or student governments.

4. FOR NON-LEGAL EMPLOYERS, REMEMBER TO FOCUS ON THE NEEDS OF LEGAL EMPLOYERS: STATE YOUR EXPERIENCE BY WAY OF SHOWING THE TRANSFERABLE SKILLS IT GIVES YOU

I keep referring to that blasted "ideal lawyer" list earlier in this chapter, but that's what you want to use to "legalize" your experience.

By way of example, one student had sent out a whole raft of resumes with no success; when she showed it to me, it was obvious why this was happening. She had worked at a phone company for eight years before attending law school, and her resume listed her job titles without really talking about what she'd done in each job. It turns out that as we talked, she rattled off a whole bunch of things she'd done that legal employers would just eat up; she'd taught classes, made all kinds of presentations, she'd negotiated contracts with vendors, she'd worked in customer service handling complaints. When she took these experiences and bullet-pointed them on her resume, she instantly drew attention from employers; she had a job in no time.

In describing your non-law-related experiences, don't list every duty you performed. Focus on your most significant responsibilities and those of interest to your target employers. Be sure to translate your duties into relevant transferable skills!

(For a detailed discussion of handling "Second Career" resumes, see Chapter 22.)

Maybe you haven't had a few years of experience before law school. I sure didn't, and most law students don't. And you may be thinking, "Does that job behind the cash register at Wal–Mart really do anything for me?" Of course it does! At its most basic, non-law-related employment shows any employer that you *get it*. You understand the meaning of work. You get the idea of showing up on a regular basis, following orders, structuring your life around the needs and schedule of the employer. It proves you're willing to do what you need to do to pay tuition or the rent or just build up some spending money to blow on what you want.

On top of that, I can't think of one job—not one—that doesn't have some skill that's transferable to a law-related job ... and I know about lotsa jobs. It's because law-related jobs have so many facets, from dealing with people to digging up information to analyzing fact patterns and cases. So don't undervalue your work experience. Make sure your descriptions focus on those transferable skills that lawyers want, regardless of what the job was!

"As shop foreman in a union environment, developed ability to vary communication style to suit audience, from Ph.D. chemists to assembly workers. Received formal training in grievance procedures, negotiation techniques and anger diffusion."

"Bartender. Worked full time to finance law school education while developing supervisory and interpersonal skills."

"Journalist; developed quick, concise writing style under strict time constraints. Approach emphasized fact-gathering and distillation, and multiple angles in stories ranging from local public health crisis to international stock market trends."

"Admissions Office Assistant: Required to work with little direct supervision; noted for accuracy, even in repetitive tasks, speed, and attention to detail. Received two merit raises in six months."

5.   DON'T UNDERESTIMATE THE VALUE OF VOLUNTEER WORK! DESCRIBE IT JUST AS YOU'D DESCRIBE A PAID POSITION

No matter what kind of volunteering you've done, it deserves mention on your resume!

Lift the accomplishments from your worksheets, being sure to add how much time you devoted to volunteering.

Furthermore:

If it's law-related, remember: legal experience is legal experience. Students often tell me, 'Well, I didn't get paid for it," as though that somehow diminishes the value of the experience. Not at all! As Northern Illinois' Mary Obrzut points out, "It doesn't matter to employers if the work was volunteer or paid. Include it!" So whether it's for the local bar association, or a judge as a volunteer extern, or for a federal or state or local agency or PSLawNet–go into detail about it on your resume.

If it's non-law-related volunteer work, again: show it off! While the rest of us were sitting around eating cheese puffs and surfing the web, you were giving back. Get the props you deserve by showcasing it on your resume.

As Illinois' Tony Waller points out, "Students don't realize that community involvement is a good source of revenue for employers. Lawyers don't get their clients by scattering business cards on Main Street. It's from being on the board of the YMCA and having another board member say, 'Hey, I just shot my wife and buried the gun. Am I in trouble?' "

Your volunteering activities may have given you a level of responsibility or results that tell prospective employers a lot more about your potential than any paid job you've had. After all, just because you didn't work for pay doesn't mean the work was any easier or the results were any less indicative of your abilities.

Use the same approach to describe your unpaid work as you've used for your paid work, focusing particularly on accomplishments. Here are a couple of examples:

"Amigos de las Americas: Community volunteer in Ecuadorian village for international volunteer health organization; summer, Year X. Introduced modern sanitation methods to village of 220 people in successful effort to stem further typhoid outbreaks. Spoke exclusively in Spanish."

"Big Brothers/Big Sisters of Fairfield County: Helped one little sister through family transition over two-year period. Raised $450 and coordinated weekend camping trips involving 24 big and little sisters, which was reported in national newsletter."

6.   FOR LEGAL EMPLOYERS, IF YOU RECEIVED AN OFFER OF PERMANENT EMPLOYMENT FROM A PRIOR SUMMER EMPLOYER, MENTION IT AT THE END OF THE JOB DESCRIPTION

Just say:

"Received offer of permanent employment."

Or:

"Offer extended."

Be aware that if you do this, you have to have let the prior employer know that you aren't accepting their offer *first,* and you have to know what they'll say about it before you send your resume out. Also, you have to be prepared to discuss your reasons for turning down the offer when you interview. We talk all about that when we discuss interviews in Chapter 9.

7. ANY WORK THAT YOU HAVE PERFORMED FOR LAW SCHOOL PROFESSORS SHOULD BE INCLUDED IN THE LAW-RELATED WORK SECTION OF YOUR RESUME

Structure your descriptions the same way you've done all of your other employment experience. If you're not sure of how to title or describe your work, ask the professor! However, a typical entry would look something like this:

"Professor Shemp Stooge, Nyuck–Nyuck School of Law, Legal Research Assistant, Summer, Year X. Researched 'Negligence Cases Based on Pie Fights in Pennsylvania, 1976–2006.' Utilized LEXIS and Westlaw databases daily; taught database research methods to three research assistants. Drafted two sections of article for publication."

8. DON'T INCLUDE SALARY INFORMATION, YOUR REASON FOR LEAVING JOBS, OR STREET ADDRESSES OF EMPLOYERS

9. DO *NOT* IMPLY THAT YOU PRACTICED LAW *UNLESS* YOU'VE PASSED THE BAR OR HAVE A SPECIAL DESIGNATION IN YOUR JURISDICTION!

This is a common and serious mistake; you can't as a law student counsel clients or represent them in court *by yourself* . . . so choose your action words carefully! You can't "advise clients," "represent the state," "counsel immigrants" on legal matters. You can inform, explain, and describe legal matters. Otherwise, mention supervision, such as:

"Case intake and evaluation (under attorney supervision)."

10. FOR WORK YOU HAVEN'T STARTED YET . . .

If you've accepted an offer for a temporary position, word it something like "Selected for . . ." as in:

"Selected for Legal Aid Foundation Internship, Winter Break 20**–20**."

11. REMEMBER THAT EXPERIENCE DESCRIPTIONS ARE *FLEXIBLE.* YOU'LL EXPAND AND CONTRACT THEM ACCORDING TO THE EMPLOYERS YOU TARGET

We started this chapter by talking about the importance of focusing on the needs of employers in formulating your resume. In

Section G below, we talk about how to rearrange and adjust descriptions depending on the nature of the employer who'll receive your resume.

You'll use the longest descriptions for the work experiences most critical to your target employers. Employers assume that the longer the description, the more important you consider the experience.

Conversely, you play experiences down by simply listing them or sharply abbreviating their descriptions.

So the descriptions you created here—they're not engraved in stone. You'll be looking at them with a critical eye once you've put together your entire resume, to see if they need adjustments!

B. ORGANIZING THE EXPERIENCE SECTION(S) OF YOUR RESUME.

Once you've described each of your experiences, it's time to organize the experience section(s) of your resume.

Most resumes you see use a simple, reverse chronological format to organize experience; that is, they start with the most recent experience, and work backwards. Under each specific job, the details for that job are presented.

That may or may not work for you, depending on what kinds of experiences you've had.

Let's talk about the options:

1. CALLING A SECTION "EXPERIENCE" INSTEAD OF "EMPLOYMENT" GIVES YOU THE OPTION OF INCLUDING MANY NON-PAYING EXPERIENCES

Using the "Experience" heading instead of "Employment" gives you tremendous flexibility in highlighting *everything* you've done that gives you transferable skills relevant to your target employer(s).

Under "Experience," you can include:

- Full-time or part-time work, including work-study;
- Part-time or full-time positions;
- Field placement internships;
- Research assistant positions;
- Volunteer activities;
- Civic activities;
- Workshops or practicums with actual work involved.

Particularly if your work experience is meager and/or you don't have a lot of paid experience that's relevant to your target employers and/or most of what you *do* have is unpaid, this gives you a *lot* more to work with!

2. **IF YOU ARE TARGETING LEGAL EMPLOYERS OTHER THAN PUBLIC INTEREST EMPLOYERS** . . .

a. **If you have little professional experience before law school**—that's most of us—**then a reverse chronological format works fine.**

You'll include both paid and volunteer experience. So you'll have:

> Most recent experience, description.
>
> Second most recent experience, description.
>
> Third most recent experience, description.

b. **If you've had both legal and non-law-related experience, list your legal experience and other experience in two separate sections. In each section, list your experience in reverse chronological format.**

Your two headings will be something like:

> Related Experience/Other Experience
>
> Legal Experience/Professional (or Business) Experience
>
> Legal Experience/Other Employment

If you've got tons of non-law-related work experience, see #4, below.

c. **If you have military experience, you can incorporate it into your "Other Experience" or give it its own section.**

Employers tend to view military experience very favourably. As a result, you may want to highlight it by giving it its own section, titled—remarkably enough—"Military Experience."

You'll list your serviced with inclusive dates, then list assignments underneath in reverse chronological order.

Be sure to include:

- Medals you received;
- Your rank at time of discharge.

3. **IF YOU ARE TARGETING PUBLIC INTEREST EMPLOYERS** . . .

All the rules I just told you about not mentioning the volunteer status of your work are out the window. **You want to draw special attention to the fact that you've donated your time. So take all of your volunteer experience, law-related or not, and put it in a section titled "Volunteer Experience" or "Community Service."** You can have subsections for law-related and non-law related volunteer experiences within that section.

In this instance, you'll call your paid experience "Employment," to distinguish it from your volunteer experience.

4. IF YOU'RE TARGETING NON-TRADITIONAL EMPLOYERS, YOU'LL PUSH TO THE FOREFRONT THE EXPERIENCE YOU'VE HAD THAT'S RELEVANT TO THEM. WE GO OVER THIS ON DETAIL IN THE ALTERNATIVE CAREERS CHAPTER, CHAPTER 31

5. IF YOU HAVE A GREAT DEAL OF NON-LAW-RELATED WORK EXPERIENCE AND/OR MANY DIFFERENT JOBS OF SHORT DURATION, AND/OR A SIGNIFICANT CHRONOLOGICAL GAP, CONSIDER A "FUNCTIONAL" RESUME OR COMBINATION "FUNCTIONAL/CHRONOLOGICAL" RESUME

Chronological resumes don't highlight skills from many experiences. That's where the functional resume comes in. It focuses on transferable skills, rather than on job titles and employers.

While we talk a lot more about this in Chapter 22 on "Second Careers," here are the basics.

In a functional resume, positions are listed by function or skill, with titles like:

> "Research and writing activities"
>
> "Writing activities"
>
> "Negotiation"
>
> "Oral Advocacy"
>
> "Management"
>
> "Public Speaking"
>
> "Contract Writing"
>
> . . . and so on.

You describe what you've done in different positions within each functional area, without regard to chronological sequence, focusing concrete examples on your use of the titled skills.

For instance, for writing, you might have written movie reviews for a newspaper, research papers for a scientific publisher, freelance briefs for small law firms, and travel articles for magazines.

Your writing ability is powerfully proven listed together like this (leading off, of course, with the brief-writing experience!); it would be diffused in a chronological resume.

If you're wondering why everyone doesn't use a functional resume, there's a simple reason: Employers aren't fond of them. Employers are used to—and like to see—reverse chronological resumes that let them see in a snap the jobs you've had. But the fact is, if your experience is such that a functional resume addresses the employer's needs better, then use it!

You can see an example of a functional resume in Resume #6, in Appendix B at the end of this chapter.

A combination resume, as the name suggests, is part functional and part reverse chronological. Most of it is in traditional reverse chronological format, with one or two functional sections to highlight relevant skill(s). This can work for you if you have some legal experience (that goes in reverse chronological order), and a variety of non-legal experiences that, taken together, give you a couple of valuable transferable skills. You put the transferable skills in functional sections.

6. Publications Section.

Publishing says great things about you to legal employers because research and writing are such key skills for most new lawyers.

Here's what you need to know if you include a publications section on your resume:

- **Call it "Writing Experience" if you want to include unpublished papers and articles;**
- **Include all relevant publications.** Use blue book form for legal journal publications. Otherwise, list the article name, the publication it appeared in, and a brief description of it if the name is not self-explanatory;
- **If you are scheduled for publication, include the title with a notation** like *"Publication pending"* or *"will be published in Spring 20** edition."*
- **If your only publication is under the auspices of law school or undergrad—a journal piece or thesis—you can list it under the appropriate school or highlight in this section;**
- **If your publications are extensive, you can have a separate "publications" page,** attached to your main resume with a paper clip.

7. Licenses Section

If you have licenses that are relevant to your target employer(s), highlight them in a separate "Licenses" section.

They can include, among others:

- Bar memberships. Well, duh.
- CPA
- Real Estate License/Broker
- Computer certifications
- Psychologist
- Teacher
- International Association of Mechanical Engineers

8. PROFESSIONAL ASSOCIATIONS SECTION

If relevant to the employer, highlight professional association memberships in their own section.

9. SKILLS SECTION

Traditionally this section is used for computer skills, languages, licenses and professional affiliations, and security clearances. As you've already noticed, any or all of these can be given their own sections *if* they are relevant to your target employers!

Computer skills:

LEXIS and Westlaw are obviously the prime candidates. Opinion among experts is split: Some say all employers expect students to know them, so there's no point in mentioning them; others say, not so fast, Roscoe, employers may *not* know that. To cut the Gordian knot you may want to include your LEXIS/Westlaw skills for employers who aren't deluged with resumes, and leave them off for ones who *are* (like large law firms and government agencies).

Don't include word processing programs and for gosh sakes don't mention that you're a "touch typist," unless you're applying for a secretarial job!

b. Languages:

Be *specific* about your proficiency. Use language like:

- Fluent in . . .
- Proficient in . . .
- Conversant in . . .
- Working knowledge of . . .
- Can read . . .

I can't emphasize this strongly enough. Employers will *rely* on your representation of your language skill; if you just put "French" or "Tagalog," they will expect you to be able to translate documents and speak with clients in that language. So don't mislead . . . even a little bit!

10. HOBBIES AND INTERESTS SECTION

We're stepping into mildly controversial territory here. There are certainly employers who'll say, "Who the hell cares about hobbies?" "Personal interests have no place on a resume," "If I'm hiring you for a serious job, I don't want to see something frivolous on your resume," and so on. But they're in the distinct minority.

The vast majority of employers will tell you that showing hobbies and interests on your resume gives you that vital "third dimension"—you're not all-work-and-no-play. On top of that, it gives interviewers something to talk about with you outside of work, and trust me, they ree-e-eally want that! As Michigan's Nancy Krieger points out, "When you have an interviewer who's talked to twenty students, their only salvation is the hobby column on your resume."

I can't tell you how many employers have told me that it was something in the hobbies and interests section of a student's resume that encouraged them to bring the student in for an interview in the first place. So if you ask me, that all adds up to: Include your interests and hobbies on your resume!

* * * SMART HUMAN TRICK * * *

West Coast interviewer, spending the day at an Ivy League law school. He's so bored with talking about Law Review and law school in general that he's having a hard time staying awake.

Late in the day, a student walks in, and the interviewer glances at the student's resume to notice that under "Hobbies and Interests" he has listed, "I can do perfect imitations of both Elvises—Costello and Presley." Instantly intrigued, the interviewer asks, "Is this true?" The student says that it is, and the interviewer says, "Well—let's see them!" The interviewer says, "Would you believe it—this guy got up and did absolutely flawless imitations of both Elvises!"

He was the only student all day to get a call back interview.

* * * SMART HUMAN TRICK * * *

Trial court judge, reviewing resumes of potential clerks. He notices that the hobby listed on one student's resume is "Northern Italian cooking." The judge reports, "This one entry on his resume made me interview him. He might have been acceptable otherwise, but he did not stand out. I am embarrassed to admit to you that his interest in Northern Italian cooking made me think, 'If I hire this person, maybe he will make dinner for me and the other clerks.' "

The student didn't just get the interview—he got the job.

* * * SMART HUMAN TRICK * * *

Lawyer interviewing a student in an on-campus interview. Lawyer notices "Dollar bill origami" as a hobby on the student's resume. When the lawyer asks about it, the student says, "I can make elaborate animals out of dollar bills. Got a dollar? I'll show you."

The lawyer gives the student a dollar, and they go on chatting as the student makes the bill into a peacock.

Shortly, the lawyer asks, "So—why should we hire you?" and the student responds, pointing to the peacock, "Well, I got a dollar out of *you* and I don't even work for you—yet."

He got a call back—and an offer.

* * * SMART HUMAN TRICK * * *

A student at one school put on his resume "Declared myself eligible for the NBA Draft as a high school senior." As he explains, "I didn't actually play basketball, but I researched it and found that you don't *have* to. *Anybody* can declare themselves eligible for the NBA Draft." It turns out that he'd done a number of inventive things like this. Employers who received his resume *loved* it.

* * * SMART HUMAN TRICK * * *

On a student's resume: "World's biggest Phil Mickelson fan." The student reports, "It brought golf into almost every interview, and lawyers love golf. It worked great."

There are seven categories of hobbies and interests that will goose up your resume value. They are:

- **Hobbies that suggest future rainmaking potential.** The classic one, of course, is golf. Some employers go so far as to suggest that golf should be a required class in law school; some employers even teach their new lawyers how to play! But it's not the only sport that counts. Tennis would play the same role. And it doesn't have to be a sport. For instance, if you take part in Toastmasters—the nationwide organization that sharpens your off-the-cuff speaking skills—it would show the same rainmaking potential.

Hobbies that show your involvement in the community also suggest rainmaking potential. Volunteering for Habitat for Humanity projects, for instance, selling raffle tickets for a church fair . . . they're not just good things to do, they're good for your resume!

- **Hobbies that reflect activities the employer or a significant client takes part in.** If you were interviewing as a Supreme Court clerk for the late Chief Justice Rehnquist, you'd have been smart to include tennis on your resume—because he played a doubles match with his clerks every week. Similarly, if you know through your research or mutual contacts that your employer has a softball team or is seriously into fly fishing or whatever, and that activity is one of your hobbies—it shows before you even meet the employer that you'd "fit in." Absolutely put it on your resume!

- **Hobbies that reflect positive personal characteristics, like self-discipline, leadership, teamwork.** Some people would tell you that these are the *only* hobbies to include, but that would be way too restrictive for most employers. Nonetheless, hobbies and interests that reflect well on your character are definite resume material. By way of example, team sports, being a competitive swimmer or a black belt in karate, a marathoner, captain of a team—all belong on your resume. One student had jiu jitsu and aikido on her resume. Just fine, although as one career counselor dryly notes, "I'd avoid anything with swords and knives."

- **"Brainiac" hobbies.** Chess. Bridge. SuDoku. Crossword puzzles. A software engineer/law student used "Collecting calculators." You know. Smart stuff. (PS: Connect the dots and word search puzzles don't qualify.)

  Note that there are competitions you can take part in (and mention on your resume), that suggest braininess without requiring it. For instance, the U.S. Crossword Puzzle Championships (anybody can take part—trust me. I've done it), or the U.S. Memory Championships.

- **Hobbies in which you've excelled.** Mastering or excelling in a hobby—for instance, playing an instrument or sport—turns a hobby into an accomplishment. It addresses your ability to succeed and reflects well on your motivation and determination and reliability.

- **Hobbies that reflect community service.** If you don't have a "community service" or "volunteer experience" section on your resume, absolutely include your community service in your hobbies. If you were a fundraiser, if you helped out at the church or temple tag sales, if you were a Big Brother/Big Sister volunteer, you were a "baby cuddler" at the hospital, you were a literacy volunteer—here's where it goes.

- **Hobbies and interests that provide conversational fodder.** This is the biggest, loosest, and I'd argue, most useful category of hobbies and interests. Villanova's Elaine Petrossian, who worked at a large law firm for years, says "Hobbies on student resumes really made a difference for me when I went in with no knowledge of a hobby and no interest in it, but the student explained it and made it interesting. If you can do *that,* it shows how articulate you are."

  Whether you've traveled, you're a bungee jumper, sky diver, potter, salsa dancer, scuba diver, champion clog dancer, excellent cook, raising sea monkeys—put it down! State-fair-ribbon-winning baker, riding horses and show jumping, playing water polo, it goes on your resume. A student at one school I visited had "Trapeze" in his hobby section—he'd learned it at Club Med—and he got a ton of interviews from it. Another student was a "seat warmer" at award shows. (When celebrities get up to hit the head during the Oscars, Emmys and so on, the show producers don't want empty seats on camera, so they have "seat warmers" slide in for the duration.) Needless to say, that generated a lot of curiosity among employers. Yet another student listed "virtual monkeys" as his hobby, and garnered questions about it.

The list goes on. Flotsaming. Wine making. Beer making. Clerk at cat shows. Irish step dance instructor. Henna painting (which is not permanent, just quirky and interesting).

And by the way, **you don't have to have a lot of experience in a hobby in order to include it. If you're learning to do something and you say so, great.** "Learning to fish." Fine. If you've scuba dived or sky dived once or twice, then in my book, it's your hobby. A student at one school I visited asked, "I used to race yachts, but I haven't since I started law school" (he was a Second Year). He felt bad about including it on his resume because he hadn't done it recently, but really—how often are you going to get a chance to race yachts in law school? I asked him if he'd feel comfortable talking about it in an interview and if he'd be prepared to do it again, and he answered "yes" to both questions. Couple that with the fact that when you're racing yachts you're going to be meeting lots of wealthy people—read, potential clients—and you've got a great resume item!

As this discussion suggests, **of any section on your resume, this is the one where your personality can really shine.** Through what you list you can let the employer know how serious or light-hearted you are. One student listed that he had "been a finalist in the Publishers Clearing House Sweepstakes five years in a row" ... as has, incidentally, *anyone* with a mailing address. Employers just ate it up.

A student in Michigan listed "Did Fantasy Baseball weekend at Tiger Stadium" as a hobby. Unusual and interesting, and a great conversational opener.

At one Midwestern School the SBA President had on his resume "Know all the dialogue from 'The Blues Brothers' by heart." He said it generated lots of lively conversation.

At another Midwestern school a student even mentioned that he'd "Had the opportunity to chat with Supreme Court Justice Alito at a reception." It gave him the chance to talk about how he'd done it—by offering to drive the judge for whom he was clerking down to Washington—and talk about his clerkship . . . the best thing on his resume!

Remember that in all of these cases, the hobby of interest was fuel for conversation in an interview. Be prepared to talk about the hobby and even demonstrate it. One student said in his hobby section that he could "Juggle five balls with moderate success." Again, a winner. Walking into one interview, the interviewer said "Catch!" and threw him a ball (which he caught, incidentally). It went over very well. Another student who listed "singing" as her hobby told me that she was asked more than once to sing in an interview. "I had a thirty-second clip of my best song ready. I belted it out. If you ask me to sing, I'm ready to bring it!"

Whenever your hobby comes up in an interview, be prepared to work it around to a work-related skill *or* ask a question as a follow-up. A hobby or interest, no matter how otherwise captivating, does your resume no good if it leaves you in the lurch at an interview.

The recruiting coordinator at one East Coast firm told me about a student who had "Japanese pop culture" on his resume as an interest. "Nothing wrong with that," she said, "But when pressed, it turns out all he meant was he liked to watch Japanese TV. He couldn't understand Japanese so he didn't know what was going on, but he liked it. I ask you: Why, *why* would we want to hire someone who likes to watch Japanese TV with the sound turned off?"

Sue Gainen echoes this by pointing out that "Every word of your resume is fair game. Expect to be grilled about what you write." A student at one Northeastern school put politics and public policy as interests on her resume, and was asked about her views in an interview. Her response: "I think FEMA should be abolished." As the interviewer commented, "She probably should have anticipated that I would know at least as much about the issue as she did. She really didn't have a well-reasoned viewpoint, just a kind of talk-radio knee-jerk response. It didn't show her off to her greatest advantage."

So much for the hobbies and interests that help you. Let's talk about **hobbies and interests to avoid including on your resume.**

Before you read this list, you need to remember the following: **If a hobby defines you and is such an important part of you that leaving it off would be like losing a limb, then include it.** I can't think of a hobby off hand that would qualify, but if you feel that strongly about it, you won't be able to leave it out of the office anyway. So they might as well know about it up front. It might cut you out of some jobs, but you might be willing to take that risk. Furthermore, **no hobby, no matter how inappropriate for the general employer population, is out of place** *if you know the employer does the same thing.* If the employer has a pierced eye brow, a serpent tongue, and a dumb-bell through his one-eyed trouser monster—albeit I'm not sure how you'd find that out in the normal course of researching an employer—body piercing is clearly *apropos* on your resume for that particular employer!

- **Body piercing, tattooing.** You think I'm joking. They've all actually appeared on law student resumes. But not yours! I'm on the fence about paintball. It's OK with some people, but makes others think of classified ads for mercenaries in *Soldier of Fortune* magazine. Proceed at your own risk with that one.

- **Astrology.** It makes you look stupid. I'm not saying it *is* stupid. And I'm not saying *I* think it's stupid—not to your face, anyway. But every employer told me the same thing. So even if you spend an hour a day working on your star chart—don't mention it on your resume!

- **Anything gross.** Taxidermy? No. "Spider collector and breeder." Ewww! "Won a raw egg eating contest by eating thirty in two minutes." Yuk! "Donating blood." Incredibly admirable but not a hobby! "Cryogenic sperm donor" to show "that I'm healthy and hardy." No! Taking rubbings of gravestones? No! No! No! You don't want them to be think-ing of the movie *Psycho* when they look at your resume. One employer received a resume with the following hobby sec-tion: "Gastronomy: sheep spinal cord, rat, stir-friend pigs' large intestines, 'fragrant meat' (dog), bitter melon and salty duck eggs, pigs' feet, raw crab, fermented poi, opihi." The employer commented, "I didn't want to know. *I did not want to know.*"

- **Anything mundane.** Reading, cooking, "enjoy sports," spending time with spouse and kids. Well, yay. The part about spending time with your family is vital and admirable, but it's not really a hobby, which is why it doesn't belong on your resume. And reading and cooking—nothing wrong with them on your resume, but spice them up! Do you like a particular kind of book—political biography, science fiction? One student wrote "Cheesy detective novels" on her resume with great success. What *kind* of cooking do you like to do—are you a champion candy maker, have you won a chili-cook off, do you specialize in a certain kind of ethnic cuisine? *Which* sports do you enjoy watching—or doing? (Incidental-ly, sex is not a sport, and it doesn't belong on your resume.)

- **Anything that makes you look lazy.** Computer games, shopping, TV, surfing the web—please! You may spend a lot of time with your Nintendo Game Cube—I personally think that Donkey Konga is a gift from God—but it doesn't go on your resume.

If you're particularly interested in a specific type of film, that would be OK. For instance, if you're a big fan of French films or Hayao Miyazaki or Ingmar Bergman, go ahead and list it. If you've made films—like those guys who recreated *Raiders of the Lost Ark* shot-for-shot—that's entirely different. That's not lazy. That's cool.

- **Anything that makes you look irresponsible or unreliable.** Clubbing—that's the big one. And I mean night clubbing, not anything violent. It may be that your principal activity outside of class is finding new and exotic places to get hammered, but it doesn't belong on your resume.

* * * CAREER LIMITING MOVE * * *

Law student from Colorado has several hobbies listed on his resume, and they're all casino games. An employer who received his resume said, "You got the impression this guy spent all of his time in Vegas."

Incidentally, "blogging" fits this description. If you have a blog on a hobby, describe it. But as one recruiting coordinator points out "When we see 'blogging' on a resume, we're terrified the student will blog about us and say things that reflect badly on the firm."

- **Anything titillating.** Winning wet T-shirt contests. Pole dancing (which some women do as exercise. Really.). In interviews, you want to be gender-neutral. If you put anything titillating on your resume, you will be defined by it—and not in a good way. "Hey—are we going to interview the pole dancer?" Not!

- **Anything—for lack of a better word—"precious."** Collecting Hummel figurines. Collecting Holly Hobbies. As a rule of thumb, anything that smacks of the Franklin Mint or Hallmark or dolls won't enhance you in employers' eyes.

- **Anything inexplicable.** One student had "goats" on his resume. Which means ... what, exactly? "I have a valid passport." Ohhhh-kay. "Speaking in tongues." A *hobby?*

- **Anything you are forbidden from discussing.** Everything on your resume is interview fodder. If you belong to a secret society you can't talk about—like the Freemasons—consider including it *only* if you're sending it to a fellow mason or someone you know is familiar with it. Otherwise, you'll have an uncomfortable interview moment when you say, "I'm afraid I can't discuss it."

- **Anything that you *don't really do*.** You may think, "I don't have any good 'resume' hobbies. I'll just make one up!" Don't do it! You'll get busted. The karma police will get you. Remember: Only include a hobby/interest if you can discuss it intelligently. "Classical pianist." Really? "Chopsticks" is not a classic.

One student who listed "Shakespeare" on his resume took it off after his first interview, when the interviewer asked "Which play is your favourite?" If you don't have a good resume hobby, take one up right now, if you're that concerned about it. But don't lie about hobbies on your resume!

* * * CAREER LIMITING MOVE * * *

Law student, relaxing in his apartment, gets a call from an employer. "I got your resume, and I'd like to interview you tomorrow morning," the employer began. "Are you available?" The law student responded, "Absolutely." "Good," the employer responded. "From your resume, I see you play golf. I want to get out and play nine holes tomorrow morning at my club. Pick me up at my office at nine"—and he gave the student the address.

When the student hangs up the phone, his roommate notices that he looks suddenly pale. "What's the matter?" asks the roommate.

"Dude," says the law student, "This employer wants me to meet him for a round of golf tomorrow morning." "What's the matter with *that?*" asks roommate.

"I don't play golf," responds the student.

It turns out that he put "golf" on his resume, meaning that he liked to watch it on TV—not that he actually *played* it. He doesn't! He begs the roommate—who *is* a golfer—to show him how to play it, right now.

The student shows up the following morning at the employer's office, feeling relatively confident. His confidence dissolves when they get to the club. On the very first hole, he hacks wildly at the ball, digging up divots right and left. The employer is furious that he's been lied to. He insists that the law student immediately take him back to the office.

But wait—there's more. On the way back to the office, the law student's car gets a flat—and the law student doesn't know how to change it. The employer, in his golf whites, has to get out of the car and change the student's tire.

* * * CAREER LIMITING MOVE * * *

In order to make a general interest in classical music sound more important, a student puts it on his resume as an interest in "17th Century baroque opera." He gets an interview with a partner at a firm . . . who happens to be a 17th Century baroque opera buff. The partner starts asking the student about it. "What's your favorite?"

The student responds, "Oh, it's so hard to choose just one . . ." but it's obvious fairly quickly the student knows nothing about it.

* * * CAREER LIMITING MOVE * * *

Students at a Southern law school—we'll call it Magnolia University—were putting on their resume, "Editor, Magnolia University blog." As their Career Services Director pointed out, "There *is* no official law school blog here. These students did their own blog and gave it the university's name. There's stuff on there that reflects badly on the school, and would definitely *never* appear on the school's official blog. We had to call them in and tell them, 'you're not the editor of the law school blog. You have a blog of your own, and you can say that. You can't tell employers you're something you're not.' "

I keep making this point, but it's worth repeating: **No hobby is inappropriate if the employer shares it.** There is an old story in politics—I seem to remember the individuals involved being then-presidential candidate John F. Kennedy and former president Harry Truman. JFK had received reports that people were uncomfortable with Truman's use of profanity while stumping for JFK. As JFK gingerly brought up the topic, Truman kept interrupting him: JFK would gingerly begin, "Mr. President, we need to talk about—"Truman would interrupt, "You're running a damn fine campaign, young man," and so on—until Truman mentioned that he'd recently scored a huge financial contribution to the Kennedy campaign, to which Kennedy replied: "The hell you say!"

The watchword here is: the better you research employers, the more people you talk to—the more likely you are to find the offbeat hobby that you share.

* * * SMART HUMAN TRICK * * *

Law student, heavily involved in synchronized swimming in college. Her Career Services Director and all of her friends beg her to leave it off her resume, because—well, you know. Everybody knows it's a sport that requires tremendous athleticism and self-discipline, but it does have that fingernails-on-a-blackboard reputation.

She ignores the advice and keeps it on her resume. Smart thing, too. It turns out that the wife of the managing partner at her dream employer is a synchronized swimming coach—and listing "synchronized swimming" on her resume is what gets her the interview.

* * * SMART HUMAN TRICK * * *

Law student sends her resume to all of the large law firms in a city on the East Coast. She lists as her hobby "Buffy the Vampire Slayer." This becomes a source of much amusement at law firms to whom she sends her resume. In fact, at a monthly lunch meeting of law firm recruiting coordinators in the city, one of the recruiting coordinators mentions, "Hey, did you all get Buffy the Vampire Slayer's resume?" The rest of the people at the table laugh, wondering if anybody would ever interview her.

All except for one woman, that is. She says, "Actually—Buffy is going to be one of our summer associates." It turns out that the hiring partner at the firm is also a huge Buffy fan—and when he sees this on the student's resume, he insists that she be brought in for an interview.

* * * SMART HUMAN TRICK * * *

Law student lists "Trekkie" as her hobby on her resume—much to the dismay of her Career Services Director, who points out that when people see it, they're likely to expect her to show up in costume, ready for a Star Trek convention. But the law student insists on keeping it.

As it turns out, the student is interested in pursuing Equine Law, and sends her resume to a number of firms with the specialty—including one that happens to represent one of the stars of Star Trek.

She gets the interview—and the job.

11. Other Information Section.

We won't reinvent the wheel here. Go back to your "Other Information" worksheet, and—**looking at the rest of your resume in its entirety—see if there's something about you that merits a mention to your target employers, yet doesn't fit in anywhere else.**

D. Handling Highly-Charged Resume Items: What to Do if You're a Lesbian Rifle-Toting Beauty-Pageant-Winning Hooters Girl

Well! I think the title of this section gives a broad hint to what we're talking about here: Namely, controversial items like politics, gay and lesbian issues, religion—you get the idea.

SQUASHING THREE-DIMENSIONAL YOU ONTO TWO-DIMENSIONAL PAPER   339

Now, I want to address something right up front: *Should* these be controversial? Of course not. I'd love to live in a society where they weren't. But in America, right now, they are. So let's spend a few minutes talking about how to address them on your resume. Depending on your wording, some employers will reject you out of hand simply because of a highly-charged resume item. As Willamette's Diane Reynolds says, "As a rule of thumb, employers think, if it's on the resume, it's in the office. If you're involved in a charged activity, employers figure you will bring it into the office." And if they feel uncomfortable with that, they may not even be willing to interview you.

At this point, you may be outraged. "Kimm, how dare you suggest that I take something that's so important to me *off* my resume? It's who I am!" I'm down with that. But look past that for a moment, because we need to discuss how different kinds of highly-charged items might be perceived by employers. I'll give you several alternatives for handling them on your resume. The decision on whether to leave highly-charged items on your resume is up to you, but if you *do* leave them on, I want you to know what you're up against.

On the other hand, it may be that you have highly charged items on your resume and you don't even realize it! That was the case with me. It was only when I talked to the very wise Career Services Directors for the first edition of this book that I realized that two items on my resume were controversial. I wonder, looking back, how many interviews I lost because of them! One of the items was that I did advance work for the Jimmy Carter presidential campaign when I was in high school. You know. Jimmy Carter. *A Democrat.* The other was my Law Review note topic, of all things; I wrote about legal liability for sexually-transmitted diseases. *I* thought it was really interesting, but really—having the word "sex," in any of its forms—sexual, sexually, sex bomb, sex-o-matic—isn't resume material! So this section may put you on notice that things that seem perfectly reasonable to you may in fact be controversial to potential employers.

With that in mind, let's talk about highly-charged resume items. First of all, let's talk about exactly what they *are*. I've separated them into seven broad categories, and highlighted potential problems with each:

1. CATEGORIES OF "CHARGED" RESUME ITEMS AND THE POTENTIAL PROBLEMS THEY CREATE

• Religion.

What's the problem here? Well, if you're heavily involved in one church, say, the Catholic church, and the partners at a firm you're applying to are all Jewish or Protestant or Scientologists or you name it, they may feel like you won't fit in.

One student had on her resume as a hobby "Converting people to Christianity." You can imagine how well this played with employers of other religions! But it doesn't have to be *that* heavy-handed to raise the spirituality issue—it can be as simple as teaching Sunday School, acting as a fraternity chaplain, or listing "prayer" as a hobby.

• Politics.

The problem here is the same as for religion. You may be a big supporter of the Democratic party, but I'm not creating any headlines by telling you that many lawyers are Republicans.

• Gay and Lesbian Issues.

The gay marriage debate of the last few years has brought into sharp focus how controversial homosexuality is. If you are gay, I'm not telling you anything you don't already—heartbreakingly—know. But what you may not realize is that homosexuality may be suggested on your resume in insidious ways, even if you don't bring it up explicitly.

One Career Services Director told me about a male student who had been heavily involved in the theater before he went to law school. He was reluctant to put it on his resume because in the past people had assumed that his theater experience meant he was gay. (I have a close friend, a former Alvin Ailey dancer, who deals with that same perception all the time.) This student decided to keep the theater experience on his resume, and wound up—wouldn't you know it—catching the attention of an employer who was also interested in theater.

So homosexuality may be implied on your resume in a variety of ways. For staunchly conservative employers, that's an issue.

• Fraternities/Sororities

Awrrright! Party on, Dude! OK. Perhaps that's not fair. I'll grant you that the image of college fraternities and sororities has evolved a bit from their "Animal House" days: their civic involvement has become more pronounced. But the image "raw" fraternity/sorority involvement suggests is doing a lot of partying and socializing, which in point of fact would make you a great rainmaker, but nonetheless is looked upon askance by legal employers.

• Gun Issues (in the form of belonging to the NRA or being an avid hunter)

If you include NRA membership or hunting on your resume, be aware of the specter of militias that it may suggest to employers—and also be aware that hunting is a controversial activity, especially among younger and female employers.

•Women's Issues (like abortion or battered women's shelters)

If you mention either pro-choice or pro-life activities on your resume, be aware that you'll likely alienate any employer whose beliefs differ from yours. And involvement in women's issues like battered women's shelters suggests a kind of feminism that may make conservative employers uncomfortable.

- **Drugs (I'm not talking about drug usage—but rather, drug issues, like legalizing marijuana)**

"I didn't inhale." The reaction to then-candidate Bill Clinton's answer to the question, "Did you ever smoke marijuana?" tells you everything you need to know about what conservative employers think about drug usage—although, of course, just about everybody who's been to college in the last thirty years has at least *tried* drugs. If the word "marijuana" shows up on your resume—even as an advocate of legalizing medical marijuana—you raise the image to buttoned-down employers that you're a stoner.

- **Beauty Pageants and Modeling**

Obviously there's nothing wrong with being . . . well, a hottie. But there *are* issues to discuss.

One involves the idea of "lookism." Putting beauty pageants or modeling on your resume will signal to employers that you're a babe. The impact that will have—depends. Taking into account that recruiting coordinators are usually women, and assistants to lawyers open their mail and they too are usually women—it's likely to be a woman who sees your resume first. She may not like the idea of raging hormones in the office.

Does that mean you've got to leave beauty pageants and/or modeling off your resume? Not at all.

Let's look at beauty pageants first. Pretty much everyone agrees that if you made it to a sufficiently high level—you won at least a state-level pageant—it goes on your resume. Anything lower than that . . . you may want to check with Career Services to see how beauty pageants play in your geographic area. As a rule of thumb they are viewed more favorably in the South than in the Northeast and Northwest. So if you're looking for a job in Texas, Miss Lima Bean, we all salute you. In New York City . . . maybe not.

If you took part in "kiddy" beauty pageants—absolutely off your resume. Too controversial.

Let's turn to modeling. Unlike beauty pageants, modeling is a job. Although it brings the whole "physical attraction" issue onto your resume, most experts agree that you'll certainly get interviews you wouldn't have nailed otherwise. You should especially include it if leaving it off would create a chronological gap on your resume. If you *do* include it, be sure to have a "canned" line or two to address it in interviews, to get on and off the subject quickly. (If may have helped you get the interview—but it doesn't say anything about the job you'll do, so it shouldn't take up much interview time!)

Modeling on your resume needs to be worded carefully. Runway modeling is fine "as is." If you were a clothing model, be general in your description—the word "lingerie" should never appear on your resume. Ever. If you were a nude model—for art classes or photographs—the word "nude" gets the same treatment as "lingerie."

Obviously this advice so far is all aimed at women. If you're a man and you were a model—sigh. There's no issue. Go ahead and include it on your resume ... however with the same description warnings as for women. No "lingerie," and no "nude."

2. FIVE ALTERNATIVES FOR HANDLING HIGHLY-CHARGED ITEMS

A. DAMN THE TORPEDOES! INCLUDE THE HIGHLY-CHARGED ITEM ON EVERY RESUME YOU SEND

What happens if you just include the highly-charged item, in its full glory, in every resume you send out? Well, as Tammy Willcox says, "Don't expect everybody to be thrilled by it." And Sophie Sparrow points out that "Although you'll be screened out of some interviews, maybe you don't *want* to work for an employer who'd screen you out on that basis." That's the real crux of the issue: You'll be screened out of a number of jobs. But if the highly-charged item is something that's very important to you, then you should keep it on your resume, and I'd applaud you for that.

However ... what makes this a stickier proposition is that it might not be the whole office that shares the view of the person reviewing your resume. That person may be the only homophobic atheist in the joint, but if they're the first one to see your resume listing your GLAAD membership and your role as youth leader at the church camp, your odds of getting an interview aren't promising.

It also may be that working with you would enlighten people at the office. Maybe their issue with Methodists or Democrats or gay people is just that they've never really known any. I'm not suggesting that you have to be a trailblazer, but it may also be that you like the idea of helping people to understand your point of view—which you'll never get a chance to do if they screen you out on the basis of your resume.

Ideally, if you do your research well, you won't be sending your resume to employers who aren't a good "match" for you. There's no single highly-charged resume item that's a negative for *every* employer. No matter what religion you are, what your hobbies are, what your sexual orientation is—there are plenty of employers who will embrace you. A student at a Georgia school who'd been a lobbyist for a national right to life movement had gone through contacts there to find a sympathetic firm, rather than trying to hide his political work somehow. I *completely* applaud that approach.

Incidentally, I don't mean to suggest that you only have two choices when it comes to highly-charged items: keep them on or take them off. The next two solutions offer a kind of "middle ground."

B. INCLUDE THE HIGHLY-CHARGED ITEM ON EVERY RESUME YOU SEND, BUT *ONLY* IF THE ITEM PROVIDES YOU WITH TRANSFERABLE SKILLS

William and Mary's Rob Kaplan suggests that you only include highly-charged items on your resume if they give you something an employer will find useful. Sheer membership in certain clubs or fraternities or political parties doesn't say anything about what you can *do*. But if your role in those groups went beyond signing up, then you're stepping into territory that might be useful to employers—and make it worth talking about.

By way of example, let's say you spent a year working for a presidential campaign, as I did. It just so happens my candidate was a Democrat, Jimmy Carter, and as I've mentioned before—lawyers are more likely to be Republicans than Democrats. Anyway, I did what's called "advance" work for the campaign; that is, I researched sites for rallies and speeches, I negotiated with hotel managers concerning accommodations for the press corps, and I dealt with the news media. Well, I took a lot of skills from that that an employer would be interested in, *regardless* of whether my candidate was a Democrat or a Republican. I had to be organized, and I had to learn to negotiate, and I had to learn to deal with all kinds of problems on the spot, as well as handling all kinds of prickly personalities. Those transferable skills would be valuable on a resume. But let's say instead that all I did was to stuff pamphlets in mail slots or take messages on the phone. There's not a lot transferable there. Now volunteering in and of itself is a positive attribute in the eyes of employers, but when you counter that with the highly-charged nature of politics, you may decide it's not worth mentioning. As Gail Cutter says, "The litmus test I always use for highly-charged items is this: Was the value of the experience more important than the potential downside of a controversial name?"

This also applies to fraternities. As Kathleen Brady advises, if you mention your fraternity, mention your involvement in civic work. For instance, did your fraternity raise money for charity? Fundraising is an activity that employers view very favorably, and so you should definitely include it. But if your fraternity involvement consisted of hearty and enthusiastic participation in the ice-shot slalom course at frat parties, then that's not a transferable skill worth mentioning!

In fact, even *with* transferable skills, you still have to be aware that you'll turn off some employers. With my Jimmy Carter experience, I found that employers were evenly split. Some said, "Wow! That's really interesting!" and put aside any partisan politics. Others responded with a sneer, "You worked for *Jimmy Carter?*" And of course I have to assume that at least some of the employers who never responded to my resume viewed it negatively! So if you do consider including your transferable skills from a highly-charged activity on your resume, be aware that it's a balance; there are *still* some employers who will get stuck on the item, and ignore the skills!

C. Include a "Euphemized" Version of the Highly-Charged Item

Here's a happy hybrid between including your highly-charged item and leaving it off your resume entirely: Keep the transferable skills, and 'de-fang' the controversial element. For instance, for politics, you'd say that you have experience working on political campaigns doing the following functions: canvassing, organizing fundraisers, and so on. Or for a controversial issue, you could say that you have been involved in advocacy and you've met with politicians, helped run awareness campaigns, and so forth. In other words, you're sufficiently general that you're not throwing a controversial tag on the activity, but you're specific enough to show the transferable skills you gained from it.

Now, based on conversations I've had with students, you'll have one of two reactions to this approach: You'll either embrace it as a way to get skills you want to show off onto your resume without running afoul of any employers—or you'll think it's a weenie way out. If it works for you, use it, but remember: at some point you'll have to come clean about it if it's on your resume, because inevitably someone in an interview will ask you, "This political work you did—who did you work for?" and you'll tell them.

"So why, Kimmbo," you're asking, "Shouldn't I just name names in the first place?" Aah, it's because timing is everything. There's a big difference between putting something controversial on a piece of paper that people see *before* they see you—and meeting them and having them feel comfortable about working with you before you explain what it is. Once they're comfortable with you, they'll be able to put anything you tell them in perspective.

D. HAVE DIFFERENT RESUMES FOR DIFFERENT EMPLOYERS

I've told you before that you should anticipate having a wardrobe of resumes, so that you can send different resumes to different employers. Well, there's no reason in the world that you can't put your highly-charged item on some resumes, and leave it off of others. Remember: a resume is a marketing piece. It's not a confessional. So if you research employers to whom you send your resume—and you're going to do that, right?—there's no reason to send a resume to any given employer that won't appeal to them.

One of the happier aspects of highly-charged resume items is that they cut both ways. Whereas there will be some employers who will screen you *out* because of those items, there are other employers who will take a definite interest in you *because* of them. For instance, involvement in liberal politics, volunteering at a battered women's shelter, and marching in Washington on behalf of abortion rights would all be *huge* plusses for liberal employers like the ACLU, whereas for a conservative, white-shoe law firm, these kinds of activities would make you about as welcome as Lyme disease.

You can generally sniff out an employer's attitude about many issues by looking at their web site or resume; they'll often list civic involvement. Also, if you look at the profiles of individual lawyers at the firm, you'll see by the nature of the things they include how the employer views different kinds of activities. For instance, if a prominent lawyer in the firm is a member of the board of trustees of a fraternity, then clearly fraternity involvement is not a negative there. If a photograph of a partner at the firm shows him sitting at his desk with a stuffed moose head on the wall behind him, then hunting will not be a resume activity that will make him shudder. You get the idea!

There are actually situations where your highly-charged item should not just be included on your resume, but actually *highlighted*. That's where you use your contacts through that activity to reach potential employers. For instance, if your rabbi or priest refers you to another member of the church or temple for a potential job, then your religious affiliation is going to be an important part of your resume. Same goes if the intermediary is someone at your gun club or one who serves on the national board with you of the Tappa Kegga Brew fraternity, or—you get the idea. In fact, you'll find that if the highly-charged activity is something that's very dear to you, this is probably the best way to find a job—because with shared interests you're likely to be much happier with an employer than if you felt you were "hiding" something.

If you have difficulty figuring out if a particular employer will respond positively to a charged item, ask at your Career Services Office about it. Part of what Career Services people do is to keep their finger on the pulse of the legal community, and they'll be able to give you insights into how different kinds of activities will "play" in the area.

So—consider sending different resumes to different employers. It takes more time to come up with several resumes than just one, but if it helps you nail a job you love with an employer who shares your values, it's worth it!

E. LEAVE THE HIGHLY-CHARGED ITEM OFF YOUR RESUME ENTIRELY

You may want to bite the bullet and leave the highly-charged item off your resume entirely. Does this sound hypocritical? It shouldn't. Remember, all we're talking about here is whether you put something *on your resume*. That's it. If you leave the charged item *off* your resume, that may help you get your foot in the door with an employer who may otherwise have rejected you out of hand. You can *always* bring up the issue in an interview and deal with it there, where you can handle the employer's objections in person. Once people have met you and decided they like *you*, it goes a very long way toward dealing with *any* issue. If you have a crusading spirit, it may appeal to you to change people's minds about something dear to you. It depends how *you* feel about it. I have a friend who's been a law school administrator at several law schools. He happens to be gay. He is vehemently opposed to putting anything on his resume that would suggest his sexual orientation, and in fact never brings it up until after he has accepted an offer, at which point he'll say, "By the way, don't be expecting me to bring *Marcia* to the office Christmas party." It works for him!

There's actually an easy question to ask yourself to determine if you should leave charged items off your resume: Would it bother you to work in an office where everybody else was openly hostile to your point of view? If people are anti-fraternity, it probably wouldn't bother you at all. If you're a Democrat and they're all Republicans, you may like the idea of spirited debate, and may be open to the fact that not everybody has seen the light. Ha ha. Sorry. I couldn't help it. But if you're gay and you're in an office where rude comments are made about "homos," or you're Jewish and the Protestant-dominated office is rife with anti-Semitic feeling—well. We can all see that that's an entirely different issue. But the fact remains: You're the only one who knows for sure what works for you.

E. How to Handle References (Psst: They Can Help Give You a Killer Resume)

Traditionally speaking, there are only two considerations when it comes to references on your resume. Either:

List them;

  Or

Don't.

We'll go through the pluses and minuses of each alternative, as well as talk about how you choose references in the first place. But the real cherry on top here is how you can use references to make your resume really shine! We'll save that for last. First, let's talk about . . .

1. How Many References Do You Need?

Three to five. That was easy.

2. Choosing References: Who Should They Be?

When a prospective employer is interested in hiring you, they want to know what it will be like to work with you. They'll want to know what kind of colleague you make and the quality of your work. And that's what ought to direct your choice of references: **People who know what it's like to work with you and/or the quality of your work product.**

That makes your best references people you've worked for or your professors, legal or undergrad. The people you've worked for needn't be people who paid you; clinical professors, volunteer experience supervisors are great. If you volunteer for the bar association—gosh, I hope you do—a prominent bar member familiar with what you've done would be a great reference. If you volunteer anywhere else—a political campaign, for example—your supervisor there can attest to qualities about you that would be very valuable to legal employers: your community involvement, communication skills, motivation, time management, and so on.

And of course with professors, your best choices would be—no surprise here—those whose classes you aced, ones for whom you were a research assistant, and ones who advised organizations in which you were heavily involved (e.g., Law Review, Moot Court).

If you're a 1L and you volunteer heavily in a particular class and have gotten to know the professor, (s)he'd also be a potential reference, even though you haven't taken an exam yet.

A. BEFORE YOU NAME *ANYONE* AS A REFERENCE, BE SURE YOU KNOW WHAT THEY'RE GOING TO SAY ABOUT YOU!

Most of us are pretty coy when it comes to references. "Oh, I trust you," is the general tone of the exchange. *You can't be so cavalier about something as important as a reference!* You have to treat references the way litigators treat witnesses: that is, you never ask a question when you don't know what the answer's going to be. When you're looking for a job, a reference can be the difference between an offer and a "See ya." You *have* to know what they're going to say, if not word for word, at least generally. Remember: if a reference is listed on your resume, a potential employer is very likely to call him/her, perhaps even *before* they decide to interview you. If references are not going to say strong positives about you—for instance, if they're going to damn you with faint praise—they're useless as references in the first place.

You may be wondering, "Exactly how am I supposed to ask, Kimmbo? 'Gee–what are you going to say about me?'" No. Well, not exactly. You're going to be more artful than that. What you want to say is, "I want to make sure that when I talk about the work I did for you (or the committee we served on together, or whatever) that we're on the same page, and what I'm saying reflects accurately what *you're* going to say." You're really asking the same thing—"What are you going to say about me?"—but you're doing so tactfully. And tact is a very good thing.

* * * CAREER LIMITING MOVE * * *

Male law student has about the worst experience he can at a law firm: he's falsely accused of sexual harassment. He is asked to leave the firm, and works hard to find lawyers for whom he worked who will say good things about him to potential employers. One in particular offers to help him out; we'll call the reference Lawyer Joe.

The student goes on a few interviews, all of which seem promising, but he gets no offers. After one of them, he gets a call from the interviewer, who says: "Listen—a word of advice. You may want to reconsider Lawyer Joe as your reference." Law student probes a little further and finds out that when potential employers ask Lawyer Joe why the law student left the firm, Lawyer Joe hems and haws, and says, "... well, it *wasn't* sexual harassment ..." which of course made employers think: that's exactly what it was!

B. THE BEST WAY TO CONTROL THE CONTENT OF REFERENCE LETTERS IS TO *WRITE THEM YOURSELF*

I don't mean "without telling the employer," of course. But you'll find that most references would love to be saved the hassle of writing a reference letter for you, and will welcome it if you write a (truthful) letter about yourself for them to sign. Many references will actually ask you to do this for them.

If so, don't be toxically modest. Have an out-of-body experience and imagine that it's your best friend you're writing about, not yourself. What would you say if you were trying to sell them to someone? You obviously don't want to slip into delusions of grandeur, but remember: when an employer is looking at this reference, it may well be the deciding factor in you getting an offer. Don't let modesty get in the way!

If you feel uncomfortable writing about yourself, go to your Career Services Office for help. They've written reference letters out the ying-yang. As Connecticut's Michelle Hoff advises, "It's important to have reference letters worded appropriately. Just tell your CSO what you've done, and they'll help you write them."

C. PROMINENT PEOPLE AS REFERENCES

Here's the situation. Maybe you have a family friend who is a celebrity. Maybe your boyfriend or girlfriend's father is a judge. He knows you and likes you. Won't his name attract attention on your resume?

Sure—but **they won't help you as a reference unless they have enough familiarity with you in a professional sense to say something positive about you.** The mere fact that they know you doesn't cut the mustard! One law student insisted on putting the comedian Jerry Lewis down on her resume. Lewis, it turned out, was a family friend. The student felt—rightly—that it would attract attention to her resume. It did, but it didn't translate into more interest in her, *because it didn't say anything about what she could do!*

I know this from harsh personal experience. A law school boyfriend of mine had a father who was a very prominent local attorney. The father very kindly offered to be a reference for me. That lasted for exactly one interview! Here's what happened. I was interviewing with a judge, and he said, "Oh, I see that Brumfety—Brumf is one of your references," and I proudly said, "Yes, he is."

Judge: "But I don't see on your resume that you worked for his law firm. Did you?"

Me, reddening: "Well, no."

"Then how is he familiar with your work?" sez Judge.

"He's not," I say.

"Then how do you *know* him?" he asks.

Me, swallowing hard: "He's my boyfriend's father."

End of interview.

Now, I could have salvaged my boyfriend's father as a reference if I had—well, not been such a chucklehead, for a start. I *could* have said to him, "I appreciate your willingness to act as a reference for me, but I'd feel better about it if you were familiar with some of what I've done," and talked with him about activities I'd been involved with, maybe let him see something I'd written—so he *could* comment intelligently on what he thought of me as a potential employee. Now, it still wouldn't have been *perfect,* because he was hardly objective. But it would have been better than what I did!

D. CLERGYMEN AND FAMILY MEMBERS AS REFERENCES: ONLY IF YOU'VE WORKED FOR THEM PROFESSIONALLY

As Diane Reynolds points out, a clergyman or a family member as a reference is a no-no. Not only are they not familiar with your work, but they're hardly going to be objective about you. You know this from the newspapers. Every time someone is arrested for a particularly heinous crime, their mother will inevitably say, "Not my Johnny! He's a *good* boy!"

3. SHOULD YOU INCLUDE YOUR REFERENCES ON YOUR RESUME, OR LEAVE THEM OFF?

If you've got room on your resume for the names, addresses, phone numbers and perhaps e-mails of your references, most Career Services Directors would encourage you to include them. This is particularly useful, as Diane Reynolds points out, if you're applying to out-of-town law firms, and the reference in question is from the town where you're applying for a job.

Susan Benson suggests that you include even more than contact information; she encourages you to include a line about how the reference knows you, e.g., "supervised my summer clerkship with Jekyll & Hyde."

What's the benefit of including names of references on your resume? As Kentucky's Drusilla Bakert notes, "You'll find that a lot of people will know your references. They may pick your resume simply because of that!"

If you *do* include your references on your resume, warn them first. Especially if you're sending out a lot of resumes, you're asking a big favor of your references to say nice things about you over and over again. Gird them for the responsibility!

And as I mentioned just a minute ago, make sure you know what they're going to say about you. If it's not strong positives, they shouldn't appear on your resume—in fact, they shouldn't be your references at all!

There are times when even very positive references shouldn't appear on your resume. There are two situations where this applies: First, **your resume runs over one page only if you include your references**; and Second, there is a downside to the references you have, e.g., **they're controversial**, like far-left or far-right wing politicians.

It's pretty important to keep your resume down to one page in length, unless you've got a truly extensive career before law school, or otherwise have tons of relevant information to share. So, if you find yourself toward the bottom of the page and you haven't got room for your references, leave them off!

If you do leave your references off your resume, be sure that you have a separate page with their names and contact information listed, and how they know you.

4. FORMATTING REFERENCES

- **If you put references on a separate page:**
- **List your header information—name, address, phone, and e-mail—at the top, just in case your reference page gets separated from your resume.**
- **Under your header information, center the word "References."**
- **List the name, address, and phone number of each reference. Under the contact information, include a short description of your connection with the reference**: "Former professor," "Taught my Contracts and UCC Classes," "Work/study supervisor," "Former employer," "Supervisor for 2004 Summer Associate Position," "Three Classes Taken With Professor X, including Constitutional Law Principles," "Brain chip mind controller."

5. STATING "REFERENCES AVAILABLE ON REQUEST"—NOT!

I know, I know, I know—every resume book you get has resumes that have this line at the bottom. On resumes for legal employers, don't do it. Why? *It doesn't do you any good.* Legal employers aren't stupid. If you don't mention references, any potential employer will assume that you have them—everybody can dig up *somebody* who can say something good about them! Can you imagine this conversation with an employer? Employer: "I see you don't list references on your resume. Can I have them?" You: "No." What are you? In the Federal Witness Protection Program? So either list the references on your resume, or have them available for employers. The "References Available On Request" line doesn't help you, and it takes up valuable resume space.

6. Consider Including Actual Reference Letters *With* Your Resume!

I've mentioned this idea a couple of times before, and probably will again before you're done with this book. I keep hitting you over the head with it because I think it's a *really* great idea.

If you're skipping around and you haven't read about this yet, here's what you do: You get reference letters from your references, addressed to "To Whom It May Concern" or "To Potential Employers Of [Your Name]". Then you buy some two-pocket folders, and when you send your materials to employers, you put your resume in the left-hand pocket, and your reference letters on the right. Now, you know I am not big on resume gimmicks, but this isn't a gimmick—and it *does* make perfect sense. What employers most want to know is: are you going to do a good job? Are they going to want to work with you? Prior employers telling them *"Hell* yes!" before they know anything else about you is the *perfect* way to convey that message!

Incidentally, here's why you put the reference letters on the right. You may have noticed that when you read magazines, particularly toward the front of the magazine you'll go nuts because it seems like every page is an ad. The reason it seems that way is that advertisers know that you look at the right hand page first—so that's where they insist on putting their ads. The editorial content is invariably on the left.

Well, when you send out reference letters and resumes, take advantage of the same phenomenon—put the thing you want employers to see *first*—the letters saying you walk on water—on the right-hand side.

The first student who gave me this idea was a charming student at Nova Southeastern. He had no grades to speak of, but he'd clearly done great work for a couple of employers. His letters were outstanding, and he sent them, in the format I've just told you about, with every resume. I asked him how they worked for him, and he smiled and said he'd received an interview from every employer he'd sent them to. Well! That'll do!

The only time you might not want to follow this advice is when you're sending your resume to the recruiting coordinator at a very large law firm. They only want to see your resume. But if you've targeted large firms exclusively, you'll want to go to Chapter 23 which focuses on that topic.

7. Reference Checking Services ... Why Spend the Dough?

There are services that'll charge you to check what people are saying about you. You don't have to whip out a credit card to accomplish the same thing; just have the CSO or a friend (posing as a potential employer) call on your behalf if you're at all concerned about what an employer will say.

8. BE AWARE THAT PROSPECTIVE EMPLOYERS MAY CALL YOUR PRIOR EMPLOYERS WHETHER OR NOT YOU LIST THEM AS REFERENCES.

On top of *that*, they won't ask you first. I've said it before: anything on your resume is fair game. Know before you send it out what people will say about you!

9. GIVE EACH OF YOUR REFERENCES A CURRENT COPY OF YOUR RESUME SO THEY CAN BETTER REPRESENT YOU

F. REORGANIZING YOUR RESUME TO SUIT DIFFERENT TYPES OF EMPLOYERS

In a *Wall Street Journal* article about wacky business cards, there was a mention of Deborah Blackwell, an Executive Vice President at Disney in charge of Disney's Soapnet Channel. She had bright orange business cards with a narrative that said: "For years, Deborah has led a double life. Soapnet GM by day, slinky, sophisticated cat burglar by night. We're not saying she's a crazy kleptomaniac or anything, but that crystal on her finger isn't cubic zirconia, all right?"

She told the *Journal* that the card conveyed instantly the nature of the channel: soap operas. But she *also* had a traditional corporate-issued business card as well! She pointed out that the orange cards weren't appropriate for "more serious business negotiations."

I open this section with that story for an obvious reason: There's no "one-size-fits-all" resume any more than there's a ubiquitous business card! What gets you an interview at one employer will land in the circular file at another. So if you're looking at different kinds of jobs, you'll use your worksheets to develop a wardrobe of resumes accentuating different elements of your education and experience, "pimping" it with new experiences where necessary.

In Section C–2 of this chapter, I talked about the importance of "focusing" your resumes. What we'll do here is take that one step further, and go through an example of reorganizing a set of experiences to suit different kinds of employers.

Let's say that you're a 2L, and you've got a few items to choose from in crafting your resume:

- A research paper that you wrote on a securities issue for the local bar association, which was published in their magazine.
- Six CLEs that you've taken, three on advocacy, one on ethics, one on family law, and one on securities law.
- Two volunteer experiences as a summer camp counselor at The Hole in The Wall Gang Camp, a camp for children facing life-threatening illnesses.
- A clinical program at school where you represented indigents in landlord-tenant issues.

- You ran your own Internet business in college, which financed 75% of your college education.

- Membership in the Phi Alpha Delta Law Fraternity, where you worked on fundraisers for charity, raising $9,000.

- Membership in the state bar association, and attendance at local bar association meetings and functions revolving around family law.

- A volunteer judicial externship after 1L, for a state court trial-level judge.

- An avid interest in windsurfing.

- Conversational ability in Spanish.

Let's say that your grades are mediocre, and you went straight from college to law school, so you have no prior careers.

How would we organize your resume?

It depends on who's getting it!

On top of researching what different general types of employers want, you'd do as much "individualized" research as you can. The employer's web site at the bare minimum. Beyond that, you could talk to upper-classmen or graduates who are familiar with the employer. Career Services. And if you get tidbits from any of these sources, you'd modify your resume accordingly. For instance, if you found out that the lawyer receiving your resume belongs to Phi Alpha Delta, your legal fraternity, you'd go into more detail about it. If you found out that the lawyer had an unusual hobby that you share, even if you might otherwise leave that hobby off your resume—include it! Points of commonality are great to include on your resume.

With that in mind, let's say you only had time for the employers' web sites, and you got general information about what they look for. Let's take a look at what you'd emphasize—and de-emphasize—on your resume for three different kinds of legal employers. (We'll discuss resumes for Non–Traditional Employers in Chapter 31.)

A. FAMILY LAW PRACTITIONERS (AT SMALL FIRMS)

In your law school education section, under activities you'd mention your fraternity involvement *specifically* to get the fundraising information on your resume; fundraising screams "rainmaking potential" to legal employers, and that's a huge plus.

In the activities section you'd also mention your bar association involvement.

After your law school education, you'd list "Additional Legal Education," and you'd list five of the six CLEs you've taken, in this order: Family law, advocacy, and ethics. You want them to see the family law CLE first, and you don't necessarily want to tell them about the securities law CLE; it's got nothing to do with what they do.

After that, you'd list "Legal Experience," and mention your judicial externship with the judge. You would not say that it was done on a volunteer basis; a legal job is a legal job! You'd offer some detail on the kinds of issues you researched.

In that section you'd also mention your involvement with the family law section of the local bar association.

Under that, you'd mention your "Other Experience," and talk about your painting business in college. You'd talk about the fact that you founded it, ran it, and how much of your education you funded with it.

Under that, you'd have a "Publications" section, and mention your article for the bar association on the securities issue.

Under that, you'd put "Skills," and mention your conversational Spanish fluency.

Finally, under "Hobbies and Interests," you'd mention your windsurfing.

Incidentally, you'd want to include both the terms "family law" and "domestic relations" on your resume, in case either you a) respond to an electronic job posting, or b) your target employers scan your resume. In either case, they're likely to do a "key word" search, and you want to make sure that any relevant "key words" they search appear on your resume!

Notice overall what we did here: We organized your resume so that what a family law practitioner would be most interested in—your sincere enthusiasm for family law, your fundraising ability, and your advocacy skills—are moved up on your resume. You don't want employers hunting around on your resume for what's relevant to them. You want to make their lives *easy* by highlighting why they ought to interview you!

B. LARGE LAW FIRMS

How would your resume be different?

For a start, you wouldn't mention your grades. Large law firms only want great credentials, and although you're a great person, your grades are mediocre. So they stay off. If you *do* have a strong upward trend or excellent grades in certain classes, you'd include those, but otherwise, you wouldn't mention grades at all.

Under activities, you'd list your fraternity experience and fundraising. Fundraising addresses your people skills and your eventual rainmaking ability, and law firms of any size want those. You'd also mention your membership in the state bar and the fact that you attend local bar association meetings, but you wouldn't mention the family law focus; large law firms don't practice family law, so it won't be relevant to them.

Under Additional Legal Education, you'd mention the securities, advocacy, and ethics CLEs you've taken, in that order. You'd leave off the family law CLE because it's not relevant to a large firm.

Under Experience, you'd first mention your judicial externship. You wouldn't say that you weren't paid, because it's not relevant! However, the experience itself is invaluable. Working for a judge addresses your research and writing skills, which are directly relevant to large law firms. You'd go into detail about the kinds of research and writing you did, to illuminate not just what you learned but the importance you place on the experience.

You'd also mention your computer business in college, but you'd want to consider *not* mentioning that you started and ran it. Attorneys at large law firms have told me that entrepreneurship is a mixed bag for large employers; they might think you'd chafe at not being the boss. But certainly stating that you were involved with the business and funded three-quarters of your college education would be appropriate.

In a skills section, you'd mention your Spanish ability.

Under Hobbies/Interests, you'd mention your windsurfing, as well as your volunteering at the Hole In The Wall Gang Camp. They both provide insights into the kind of person you are, and provide interesting information for the employer to discuss with you in an interview.

c. PUBLIC INTEREST EMPLOYERS

Let's take a third possibility, that you're interested in a public interest job. Maybe you're going to be a child advocate. How would your resume change?

For your law school section, you probably still wouldn't mention your grades. While it's true that public interest employers aren't as grade conscious as large law firms—*no one* is as grades conscious as large law firms!—your grades don't help you, so there's no point in mentioning them. You'd mention your Phi Alpha Delta experience as a fundraiser. You'd also mention your bar association membership, and the fact that you attend meetings involving family law.

In your "Additional Legal Education" section, you'd mention the family law CLE, the advocacy CLEs, and the ethics CLE, in that order. You'd leave off the securities law CLE, since it's not relevant.

Your next section would be "Volunteer experience," where you'd mention your judicial externship and your summers at The Hole In The Wall Gang Camp. They address both your familiarity with the courtroom setting as well as your dedication to working with children, both directly relevant to the job you want. Notice that here, it's fine to mention that your judicial externship was on a volunteer basis. You wouldn't otherwise draw attention to the non-paid status of your work, but when you have a section called "Volunteer experience," that's the only place it can go; putting it under any other experience heading would be misleading, and *nothing* on your resume can be false or misleading!

Your next section would be "Work Experience" or just "Professional Experience," where you'd list your computer business. Here, it would be fine to say that you founded and ran it, and that it financed much of your college education.

In "Skills," you'd mention your Spanish ability.

In "Hobbies and Interests," you'd mention your windsurfing, and you might also mention writing, and that you've been published in the local bar association magazine. There's no point in going into the topic, because it's not relevant to a public interest employer. (Be prepared to talk about it in an interview, of course; everything on your resume is fair game in an interview!)

d. SOME UNIVERSAL TRUTHS ABOUT RESUMES FOR DIFFERENT EMPLOYERS . . .

Notice a couple of things about all three of the resumes we created: the judicial externship is prominent. The best job to get after 1L is to work for a judge, hands down. It's translatable to all legal settings, and it's something you'll really enjoy.

Also on all of them: You haven't lied. You *never, ever, ever* lie on your resume, not even marginally. If you aren't happy with your grades, don't include them. If you can understand Spanish but you can't read it, you say "conversational fluency." You'll get busted sooner or later if you fib, and your reputation can't recover from it! What we have done is to edit, to be selective about what we include on your resume, and that's fine. It's a snapshot of your relevant credentials . . . not an expose!

G. KEEP TRACK OF WHO GETS WHICH RESUME!

You're keeping a correspondence file anyway; make sure that file notes which resumes have gone to which employers. There's a good reason for this: **if you wind up interviewing with an employer and take a copy of your resume with you, and/or you resend them your resume a few months or years down the road, you want to make sure they get consistent resumes**, mentioning the same experiences (updated as necessary).

* * * CAREER LIMITING MOVE * * *

Student sends out a number of resumes, including his summer job working at a firm that represents tobacco companies. After he sends out the resumes, he thinks the better of including the tobacco representation in his job description, and removes it.

An employer subsequently calls him for an interview, and he takes a copy of the revised resume with him. During the interview, the employer asks if he has a copy of his resume, and he produces it. The employer studies it for a moment, and says, "This resume is different than the one you sent. What's missing?"

The student responds, "I worked on some tobacco litigation. I just figured I didn't want to mention on my resume that I worked for the Devil."

He's joking, but he reports, "The employer's face immediately turned dark. It turns out that they had just taken on a tobacco company as a client, and the very thing that got me the interview was the fact that I mentioned the tobacco work. I think I would have gotten the interview without it, but the fact that I changed my resume . . . it killed my chances."

H. RESUMES IN RESPONSE TO JOB POSTINGS

When you respond to a job posting, it's likely that the employer is going to scan your resume electronically for key words. (We cover electronic and scannable resumes in Appendices D and E.) What you want to do is to make a T-chart, with the name of the job at the top, and on the left hand column of the "T," a listing of the particular requirements the job posting lists. On the right column of the "T," opposite every requirement of the job posting, list element(s) of your background that address that requirement.

We've already talked about how you reorganize your resume to push toward the top the information most relevant to the target employer(s). When it comes to rewording your individual resume entries for a particular job posting, include as many of the key words in the posting itself as you can. If, for instance, the posting is for a domestic relations firm and you talk about your summer job at a small firm which practiced family law, change the term to domestic relations.

If your resume is wanting for experience the employer calls for, remember, as we discussed in the last chapter, it's still worth responding, because the "perfect" candidate might not send in a resume.

Also, if you've got a *little* bit of time, there are quick fixes you can undertake to plump up your resume.

Which leads us to the next section . . .

I. PIMP MY RESUME: HOW TO GET GREAT STUFF ON YOUR RESUME *RIGHT NOW*

At one law school I visited, a law student raised her hand with one of the more amusing questions anyone's ever asked me:

"You know everything you talk about for people's resumes?" she said. "I don't have any of it. Nothing. I didn't do anything in college. I never had a job. I traveled in the summer. I'm a 3L. I've never had a law job. I've never done any activities in law school. I'm *lazy,* OK? So what am I supposed to put on my resume?"

Now, that's about the most extreme example of Sahara-like resume aridity that I've ever come across. At least she had a sense of humor about it. You're not that bad. And even if that's not your issue—if you have stuff for your resume, but it's all "menial" jobs, or it's all experience unrelated to law, or you got fired from every job you've ever had (which was me), it really is the same issue, namely: you can only put so much lipstick on a pig. If you are just seriously lacking in good resume content, even the world's most magical type font, silkiest paper and kick-butt format won't help you.

What do you need to do?

You need to pimp your resume.

Oooh, it's so *easy.* I don't care how bad you think your resume is now. Give me a few weeks—not full time weeks, I mean, but a few hours here and there—and we can whip that bad boy into shape like *that.* (I'm snapping my fingers.)

The principle behind the plan is the one I explained at the very beginning of this chapter: namely, viewing your resume as real estate. You've got an acre in which to make your pitch. You want to make sure that the bulk of that acre is taken up with things of immediate interest to the employer, right? So let's say you have eight years of experience working for a jute factory. And you go out today and volunteer for a project with the local bar association, researching an issue in criminal defense work because that's what you want to do. Now, on your resume, those eight years at the jute factory and the bar association project can each take up three lines on your resume—*even though one of them took eight years, and the other took two weeks.* Doesn't matter. They've got the same acreage on your resume. They have the same visual impact. In fact, if you list the bar association project *first,* it's got *more* impact!

So the good news here is: You're not a prisoner of what you have (or haven't) done. Let's talk about what you can do right now to pimp your resume!

1. TAKE CLEs, DAMMIT!

I sound like a broken record with continuing legal education classes, or CLEs, I know, but they're so great for you in so many ways. I can't tell you how many students I've talked to who've nailed great jobs through CLEs, whether it's through meeting potential employers at CLEs—or listing them on their resume, and getting their foot in the door that way.

Here's what you need to know about CLEs:

First of all, if you don't know it already, you should know that practicing lawyers have to take CLEs to maintain their license to practice law. The requirement varies from state to state but every state demands them.

Secondly, you need to know that CLEs are given everywhere. I don't care if you go to law school in Moose Breath; CLEs are given everywhere there are lawyers (or nearby). They're given on-line constantly; I get e-mails on a daily basis from the Practicing Law Institute and West's Legal Ed Center, to name two.

Third—they give CLEs on everything. Everything. I don't care if you want litigation, transactional, international, sports, entertainment, dog law, you name it, they give CLEs on it. So you can easily match your interests.

Fourth—CLEs are given at convenient times. Remember, practicing attorneys take them, so they *have* to be given at times where lawyers can work them into their schedule.

Fifth—CLEs are very time effective. Generally only a couple of hours, maybe an evening or a Saturday morning . . . in other words, time you could easily fart away without even noticing it.

Sixth—and I saved the best for last—as a law student, you typically get in for free or on scholarship. Practicing attorneys pay out the ying-yang for CLEs—it's a great business—but you don't. Now, CLE providers may not tell you this up front, certainly not for very popular programs. But there are two keys to nailing a great deal: First of all, call early; scholarships can be snapped up quickly. Second, be persistent. I know students who've been told "no" on their first phone call, only to call back and be told "yes." Also, if you run into a recalcitrant CLE provider, keep in mind that having you in the room doesn't cost the CLE provider one red cent. All of their costs are fixed. If you volunteer to stand at the back, and tell them you don't need the written materials, it costs them absolutely nothing to have you there. That's an argument that's been successful for students on many occasions!

To help pay for CLEs you simply can't get into for free, ask at Career Services or the local bar association for local attorneys who sponsor law students; as one attorney told me, "I pay for law students to take CLEs all the time. It's a write-off for me, and I need all the write-offs I can get!"

Now—how do you find CLEs? Three good sources: Your Career Services Office will often have them listed, as will your local bar association. The Practicing Law Institute gives them nationwide; you can find them on-line at www.pli.edu. They're awesome to law students.

Here's what you do with CLEs on your resume. List them directly below your law school education, under the heading "Additional Legal Education." As I explained in the sample resume at the beginning of this chapter, go into detail about the CLEs you take; the name, who and where given, and a general summary of what you learned.

If this isn't the mos def resume item you can drum up in a hurry, I don't know what is. You can take the lamest resume and make it shine with CLEs. Why? Because they speak so well of you. They reek of enthusiasm, and if you have to reek of something, enthusiasm's the thing of which to reek. On top of that, they suggest you have the practical skills to hit the ground running—an outstanding trait that will help get you jobs requiring experience that you may not otherwise have! They also speak to your networking ability. Oooh. Networking.

On top of all of that, they can mask all kinds of resume flaws. No experience? No problem. Huge prior career in something unrelated to law? It gets shoved down on your resume, making room for laser-targeted CLEs. Long gaps in your experience? Same thing.

Have I convinced you yet? Good. As soon as you put this book down, get after those CLEs!

* * * SMART HUMAN TRICK * * *

Male law student, just starting his third year. Very interested in estate law. He makes a point of going to every CLE involving estate law that's given locally during his third year. He winds up attending eight of them, and they're listed prominently on his resume.

Not only does he nail a job with the help of the CLEs, but the employer who hires him says he was essentially a second-year associate, because all of the CLEs he'd attended gave him practical skills and made him very familiar with the issues he'd be facing!

2. JOIN THE STATE BAR ASSOCIATION, AND VOLUNTEER LOCALLY ON A PROJECT

Honestly. How much does it cost to join the bar association as a student? Ten bucks? Twenty? In other words, not much more than a venti soy chai latte, right? Come on.

And it's really worth it. Apart from anything else, it shows your sincere interest in staying in the state to practice law. So putting it on your resume by itself is a plus.

But to really pimp your resume, volunteer on a project for the local bar association. If it's large enough to have sections, contact either the Young Lawyers' Section or a section covering a specialty that interests you. Tell them you're interested in becoming involved and volunteer to help out on something; if your time is limited, and I'm sure it is, tell them that—but again state that you'd like to help out. Whether they have you research an issue, help out with an event, no matter what it is—it's resume fodder. And it won't take you very long!

If you go to school in a sufficiently large city, the local bar association will have a volunteer lawyers program to help the needy. It gets you experience straight away, gives you resume fodder, offers the chance to meet potential employers—and you're doing a really nice thing for people who really need it.

If you don't know which state you intend to settle in after law school, join the bar associations in the states that are contenders. Again: it's cheap! And remember: if you join more than one state's bar as a student, *just put down the employer's home state bar on the resume you send them.* Listing the entire eastern seaboard of the United States, from Maine to Florida, won't give employers the warm jollies about you. Showing *their* particular state will!

Incidentally, joining an out-of-state bar association doesn't stop you from volunteering on a project. With the help of the Internet, there are always projects you can do remotely. Certainly you can research issues from anywhere in the country. And getting that local experience—local from the employer's perspective, anyway—is a real plus.

3.   DO A PROJECT FOR PSLAWNET.ORG.

If you don't know about pslawnet.org, you're in for a treat. It hooks you up with all kinds of great projects with a public interest bent. And by the way, when we talk about 'public interest' here, we're talking about a very broad swath of projects, from working with state attorneys generals' offices to advocacy groups.

The way you get projects is to go to the pslawnet.org web site. You plug in your interests, and look for projects that interest you. The projects, by the way, range in time commitment from several months down to about a week. Your grades are not an issue; the only qualification you have to meet is essentially that you have to show a sincere interest in the project you want to do.

Now, is this as quick as CLEs or bar association projects? Nope. But it's not a long-term commitment, either—and it's something you're likely to enjoy, and on top of that, it'll give you great experience and great contacts—and it will look great on your resume.

4.   WRITE SOMETHING! LAW REVIEW ISN'T THE ONLY GAME IN TOWN, YOU KNOW . . .

When we think about publications in law school, we think about scholarly journals. Scholarly journals that take a year. Right? Well, you can get publications on your resume *way* faster than that!

Here's what you need to know: every legal publication *outside* of the scholarly ones is crying out for content. Bar association publications (state and local), specialty publications, law-related web sites—they all need words. If you like to write, this is your golden—and quick—ticket.

Here's what you do. You go to your Career Services Office, and ask to be hooked up with an alum who practices in a specialty that interests you. (It doesn't have to be the only specialty that interests you; and if you don't know what you want to do, just pick a specialty that sounds interesting right now.) When you contact that alum, you're going to ask them a very enticing question: *"What issue would you like to read more about?"* When a practitioner hears that question, they're really hearing this: *Free research.* And I don't have to tell you how attractive *that* is!

Once you have a topic, you get on line and research the status of it. You may even interview a professor or some other expert about it. You draft up a one-page article on the issue. We're not talking about a weighty tome; something short and sweet.

Then you contact the editors of the kinds of publications I just mentioned, and you say, "I just wrote an article on an issue of interest to your readers." Tell them how you got the issue. And I *promise* you that you'll quickly find a taker.

Now, what do you get out of this? In the activities chapter, Chapter 10, I go into the myriad of benefits you get from this kind of activity— the contacts, the writing sample, and so on. But for our purposes here, it's a great resume item. Why? It gets a publication on your resume in a fraction of the time a scholarly journal would take. It proves your writing ability—a great skill for so many legal employers. And on top of that, it proves your enthusiasm for what you want to do—and I can't emphasize enough how important *that* is.

If for some reason you don't publish it, you can still use it on your resume. Call a section "Writing Experience" and you can include unpublished works as well as published ones.

An article published or not, also gives you **something to send to employers other than your resume and a cover letter.** What you may want to consider doing is taking your article, making copies of it, and sending it to potential employers as a kind of FYI, saying, "I just wrote this article, and I know you practice in this area. I thought you might find it useful." Include your name and contact information, and see where it goes. You wouldn't be the first law student to nail a great job this way!

5. CHECK WITH CAREER SERVICES FOR LOCAL ATTORNEYS/PROFESSORS WHO NEED SHORT-TERM HELP RIGHT NOW

Small firms don't hire on a regular basis; you know that. And many times, small employers will need help for a short-term project, but don't want to commit to a full-time employee. Well! That kind of opportunity has your name all over it!

Check with your Career Services Director or on-line listings to see what's available. The key here is to *check daily*. When small employers need help, they typically need it right now. They don't have the luxury of forecasting hiring needs several months or years down the road. So you have to jump when they need help. And there may be small employers in town who routinely rotate law students through the office. Again—that gets experience on your resume quickly.

The same may be true for professors at school; your Career Services Director may know about professors who have projects with short-term research needs.

Whether it's for a small firm or a professor, legal experience is legal experience—and it earns a privileged spot on your resume!

6. TAKE AN IMMEDIATE, ACTIVE ROLE IN A RELEVANT LAW SCHOOL ORGANIZATION; AND IF THERE ISN'T ONE, START ONE

Join the sports law society if you want to be a sports lawyer? Well, duh. But you'd be surprised how many students don't take this simple step, and if you haven't—do so immediately. And do more than that. Ask to get actively involved, so you can put something more than just "member" on your resume. For instance, get involved in seeking outside speakers, helping with the club's website or e-newsletter—and if they don't have those things, chip in to create them. And then, of course, make sure that you put on your resume what you're doing.

Remember, no matter when you get involved in an organization during the school year, it can go on your resume. And if you joined *last week* and immediately started trolling for speakers, you can still put on your resume that you seek outside speakers for the organization— because you do.

If your school doesn't have an organization that focuses on a specialty that interests you—or a nontraditional students' club if you want a nontraditional job—start one! E-mail lets you solicit members cost-free, and having meetings doesn't require a budget. I've talked with students who've started clubs, web sites, newsletters, and even solicited speakers and run CLEs on campus. I realize that we're stepping into the realm of activities as opposed to generating resume content—and I talk about that in excruciating detail in Chapter 10—but nonetheless, these are all ideas you can put to work in a hurry, and get them on your resume right away.

7. IF YOU'RE APPLYING FOR OUT OF TOWN JOBS, GET A CELL PHONE AND MAILING ADDRESS FROM YOUR TARGET CITY

Why, I could write a whole chapter about nailing out-of-town jobs. And whaddya know—I did. It's Chapter 17. For right now, let's focus on pimping your resume for out-of-town jobs.

Now, what's going on in the mind of an employer in another city when they see your resume? "If you're not from here and you didn't go to school here, how do we know you'll accept an offer if we make you one—and if you accept it, how do we know you'll stay?"

Joining the employer's state bar association helps answer that question, and I've already addressed that. Getting a cell phone with that city's area code and getting a local mailing address (through Mailboxes USA) cements the idea that you're serious about working there. Is it deceptive? No. It says: I'm committed to practicing where you are. And that's a huge positive.

8. DEVELOP AN INTERESTING HOBBY *RIGHT NOW*

Just because you don't have a "standing" hobby that's outstanding on your resume, doesn't mean you can't start one *today*. I've told you before that an interesting hobby can make your resume stand out from the pack, and give you great interview fodder. There's no law that says that hobby had to be in place before law school.

Remember: You legitimately have to *do* these things to consider them hobbies; you can't just list them and hope against hope that you won't be "found out." But once you've done them even once, you can list them as hobbies. And if an interviewer asks you about it, you can honestly say, "As a matter of fact, it's a new hobby for me. Here's what I like about it . . ."

Here are a few ideas to get you going:

- Geocaching—that is, GPS scavenger hunts. Very *au courant*.

- Barbecue judge. The Kansas City Barbecue Society is always looking for people to judge barbecue contests, and you take a very brief class to qualify. Go to the KCBS's web site to learn more.

- Ultimate frisbee. It's easy, you can do it at pretty much any park and it sounds cool.

- Kickball. The sport for people who can't play sports. The main activity of my youth, it is now fashionable again. It takes about five minutes to pick up and it's fun, fun, fun.

- Skydiving/parasailing. If you've done it once, in my book, it's your hobby, and it sounds exotic.

- Try out for game shows. Even if you don't make it onto the show, saying that you tried out will be interesting!

- Be a mystery shopper. You actually get paid to go to stores and rate their service, cleanliness, and so on. If you love to shop anyway, this is a great way to get an "unmentionable" hobby onto your resume. It doesn't pay a lot but you get free goodies, and it's all freelance. To find opportunities, go to the Mystery Shopping Providers Association website, www.mysteryshop.org. You can see more of what it's like on the mystery shopper message board at volition.com (a web site about getting free stuff). Also, be aware there are scammers in the field; don't ever pay for an assignment. *You* get paid. The mysteryshop website is a good way to separate the wheat from the chaff.

- Start a relevant website or blog, with information and links of interest to your target employers. I talk more about this in Chapter 10.

J.   Traditional Resume Items That You Should *Not* Include in Your Resume

You've probably read a lot more resume books than I have, and it may be that from them you've picked up some bad habits—at least when it comes to law-related resumes. Interestingly, resume items and sections that work for jobs in the "mass market" tend to rub lawyers the wrong way. I heard this from just about every employer and Career Services person. So: if you're sending resumes to law-related employers, don't include the following:

1.   AN OBJECTIVE LINE

You've seen these, right? A line at the top of the resume that says something like, "Objective: a permanent associate position with a forward-looking law firm focusing on environmental law."

Well—leave it out. Not just that particular line, of course, but any objective line. Why? Here's how lawyers react to it: "If you're sending me your resume, I'll assume that your objective is to get a job with me." It just states the obvious—or worse, it states something the lawyer *doesn't* do—"Seeking a position in criminal defense," and the employer doesn't have a criminal defense practice. Every legal employer has seen resumes like that, and it leads, naturally, to immediate rejection.

You don't need an objective line anyway. If you do as I suggest throughout this chapter, starting with researching the employer and focusing your resume appropriately, it's not necessary to have an objective line; you let your text speak for itself!

2.   A "PERSONAL" SECTION

Date of Birth, marital status, SSN, height/weight—no!

You see these once in a while, a section on a resume that says "Married, two children, excellent health." Lawyers will think, "I'm not allowed to *ask* you for this kind of information—why are you volunteering it?"

Here's the thing. If you want to let an employer know 'personal' information about you because it'll help your cause—for instance, you're seeking a job in a particular city because your spouse has accepted a permanent position there—then say it in your cover letter. Or put an "Other Information" section on your resume. When it comes to children, I don't disagree that as a woman, stating that you already have children and have balanced law school and family is a real plus. But if—and this is *very* controversial—you were to mention it on your resume at all, I'd have an "Other Information" section saying something about having gone to law school full-time while raising a family—I'd highlight it separately.

How about age or date of birth? Very touchy, especially if you're in—or approaching—middle-age. Now I personally find it *rawther* amusing that employers view applicants as "over the hill" when they've only got about half a century left to live. But as Sophie Sparrow points out, "If you're in your 40s or 50s, you may want to leave off the date you graduated from college. That's because your age alone may screen you out of some jobs."

Does that suck? Sure. Should it be that way? No. Are there ways to show employers that you've got great experience and that your maturity—at least, chronological maturity, I'm not passing judgment on your personality!—is a plus? Absolutely. And we discuss all of those issues elsewhere. (We deal with resumes for people with substantial prior careers in Chapter 22.) And you'll find appropriate resumes in Resumes #2 and #6, in Appendix B at the end of this chapter.) All I'm saying here is: Age and date of birth on your resume are a no-no.

* * * CAREER LIMITING MOVE * * *

On a student resume: "Willing to work long hours because I am single and childless."

3. A "SUMMARY OF QUALITIES" SECTION

Some resumes feature a "summary of qualities" section, and it will include things like "Talented, spirited, independent thinker." Don't include it for legal employers. As Sophie Sparrow points out, "That's a subjective evaluation, and that's the kind of thing that lawyers like to do for themselves." On top of that, it takes up a bunch of space that would be better used for other things (see "Pimp Your Resume" directly above). It also tends to be excruciating to create. So don't bother, for legal employers.

For non-traditional employers, it's a different story. Other industries *do* use them—so we'll discuss them in the Alternative Careers, Chapter 31.

4. A LINE THAT SAYS, "REFERENCES AVAILABLE UPON REQUEST"

As we discussed a few minutes ago, on your resume you either include full contact information for your references, include the actual letters of reference themselves, or leave references off your resume entirely. Lawyers will *assume* that you have references if you don't mention them. It doesn't do you any good to say that you've got references, and it takes up space. Don't do it!

5. SCHOOLS THAT ADMITTED YOU

What "might have been" is irrelevant. If you turned down Harvard because Barney's School of Law gave you a full scholarship, so be it. You state the full scholarship to Barney's, but you leave out Harvard.

6. LSAT SCORE

Nope! No matter how it makes you look like a brainiac, it cannot be included.

K. BEFORE YOU SEND OUT EVEN ONE RESUME ... TAKE IT TO YOUR CAREER SERVICES OFFICE FOR REVIEW

Every possible resume gaffe can be arrested before it ever makes it to an employer, if you take the simple prophylactic step of showing your resume to your Career Services Office before you shoot it out. It's not just typos the CSO will spot; they'll catch the subtle mistakes that might torpedo your job opportunities.

For instance, there was a student at one Midwestern school who had been a business major with chemistry and biology minors in undergrad. He did the premed track but washed out in organic chemistry. On his resume he had "completed premed track" on his resume, and sent out a few resumes without success before he visited his CSO for advice. As a counselor pointed out to him, "Mentioning the premed track hurts you. It questions your judgment and raises the issue of, 'Are you going to bail out of law, as well?' The chem and biology minors is good enough." When he made this minor change on his resume, he started getting interviews.

So visit the CSO before you send out resumes. It'll pay off!

* * * SMART HUMAN TRICK * * *

Before sending out her resume, a female law student takes it to her Career Services Office for review. A counselor suggests she reword the following phrase:

"Spent year off from college in missionary position."

L.   FAQS: BUT MY PROBLEM IS . . . HANDLING THE MAJOR RESUME ISSUES

I remember seeing a resume book in a bookstore a few years ago. As I flipped through it, I was greatly amused to find that each of the sample resumes included things like stellar work experience and degrees from Ivy League Schools. Well, duh. It's not hard to have a great resume when you've got great credentials and no 'skeletons.' But I rarely meet law students who fit that description, and gosh knows I wasn't that law student myself. Almost all of us have resume 'issues.'

The good news is this. There's no resume issue that's insurmountable. Either it's fixable on your resume, or it's possible to send out a letter without sending a resume with it (I talk about that in Chapter 8 on Correspondence).

Let's talk about the most common resume problems, and their solutions!

1.   PRIOR JOBS THAT ARE NAUGHTY OR CONTROVERSIAL.

Hooters Girl. Chippendale. Playboy bunny. Phone sex operator. Ticket scalper. You know who you are. And you know—or should know—the reaction your job title will get if it appears on your resume. "Hey, Andrea!" the office conversation will go. "Are we going to interview the Hooters Girl?" "Did we make the Chippendale an offer?" "Hey, did you hear that so-and-so used to be a Playboy bunny?" You want your outstanding work product and attitude to stand out when you start—not a naughty label!

How do you handle it on your resume? Note up front that men and women are viewed differently in the context of "naughty" jobs. Being a former *female* stripper is a very different animal than having been a *male* stripper. I know of at least one male student who'd been a stripper, and he got dozens of job interviews because of it (and some offers—*job* offers—as well). Nonetheless, I'd still counsel that you "soften" naughty jobs on your resume, male or female. You want to be defined by your professional qualities, not by your ability to dance wearing a marble pouch.

You can euphemize naughty jobs in one of several ways:

a. Mention the name of the corporation rather than the restaurant/magazine/club

Inevitably, the name of the corporation that owns the place where you used to work has a different name than the joint itself. State that name on your resume: "Worked in a Hughes Corporation Restaurant . . ." *and be sure to state how much of your education you funded by working there.* (One upside of 'naughty' jobs is they do tend to pay exceptionally well!) One of two things will happen: Either an employer will recognize the name (unlikely, unless they worked there too!) and will appreciate your discretion, a valuable lawyer trait; or they *won't* recognize it, and you're off the hook.

b. Don't Mention the Employer Name at All.

Mention, in narrative form, that you worked in a restaurant/telecommunications business/any generic description, describe your work similarly euphemistically ("waited tables," "acted"), talk about how much of your education you funded, and that's that. No need to mention that when you waited tables, you were wearing a bunny tail. The ticket scalper, by the way, referred to himself as a "nontraditional ticket reallocation specialist."

Remember, when you've got non-law-related experience, the most important element of your experience is the transferable skills. The name of the joint doesn't add anything to the equation, so consider leaving it off entirely!

Now, with either one of these solutions, will they ask you in an interview for the name of the place where you worked? Sure. You *have* to be comfortable discussing *everything* on your resume. But at that point, they won't have pre-judged you, and they'll see that you look entirely professional. You've already got your foot in the door. And mentioning your prior work, along with a line like, "I didn't mention it by name on my resume because although it was a great experience, I didn't want to be defined by it"—well, how does *that* say anything negative about you?

* * * SMART HUMAN TRICK * * *

Male law student, acted as an accountant for an internet porn purveyor for several years before law school. Mentioned the innocent-sounding name of the company on his resume, along with a couple of lines talking about his specific, finance-oriented duties and accomplishments.

He prepared for interviews knowing that employers would ask what the company did. So he rehearsed an answer in which he was honest and matter-of-fact, an attitude that said to employers: "You shouldn't have a problem with it."

And employers *didn't* have a problem with it. His approach worked, and he quickly nailed down a job.

* * * SMART HUMAN TRICK * * *

Female law student. Worked her way through law school as a Jell-o shots girl at a nightclub ... hauling in *a thousand bucks a night* in tips! On her resume, she stated that she worked for a restaurant and funded her entire education. Now, it's true that the joint also served food, so it was, in fact, a restaurant!

She wanted a public interest job. On interviews, when asked specifically where she worked, she'd tell the truth, adding: "I was very interested in graduating without debt so I could pursue my dream to go into public interest work."

It worked. She got a job.

2. A LOT OF PART-TIME JOBS DURING UNDERGRAD

You don't want a bunch of short-term gigs to dominate our resume. You may want to try a summary description like this:

> *"Continually employed in a variety of jobs including landscaper and rodeo clown to finance 100% of undergraduate education."*

> Or this:

> *"Additional part-time and summer employment from 20**–20** includes positions as camp counselor, lifeguard and retail sales associate."*

3. MY RESUME IS TOO LONG. HOW DO I MAKE IT SHORTER?

You just don't want a resume that goes on longer than two pages. It wears out employers who want a quick snapshot of what you're like, not a family album.

We go into great detail about resumes for people with prior careers in the Second Career, Chapter 22.

In the meantime, here are some tips for shortening your resume:

- Put your header information on two lines, like this:

HERMAN MUNSTER
1313 Mockingbird Lane   Chicago, IL 13130   (666)666–6666   hmunster@aol.com

---

- Narrow the margins, but not beyond ¾" so that if the employer reproduces your resume, information will not be cut off;
- Use a compact type font in a small-ish size, like 11–point Times or New Roman;

- Put dates in parens at the end of job descriptions;

- Make sure you've taken out all descriptions and activities that are irrelevant to the employers you're targeting;

- Fully describe 2–3 positions most supportive of your career direction and summarize the remaining work unless exceptionally meaningful;

- For college activities, list only those particularly significant, show leadership, community involvement *or* are activities the employer shares;

- Combine skills and interests sections, for example:

  Fluent in French.

  Proficient in LEXIS/NEXIS, Westlaw, PowerPoint.

  Interests include kayaking, hot air ballooning, and cutting-edge environmental issues.

- Consider giving a narrative paragraph to experiences that are not as important to the employers you're targeting:

  From 20**–20**, worked in a variety of positions including ...

  Other experience includes working as a waitress, counselor at Camp Granada, research assistant, and interior house painter (Part time, Summer/School years 2002–2004).

- Have subcategories. If you've had, say, five jobs in restaurants in two years, have a subcategory that reads:

  Restaurants, 2004–2005

  > *Worked in several high-volume food service operations. Gained skills in customer service and cash management.*

4.   Gaps in Your Chronology, Major and Minor

If you sailed straight through college into law school, then you've got the classic gap-free resume. But based on a lot of the students I've talked to, that description doesn't fit lots of people. Maybe you took time away from the paid work force to raise kids (if so, I address that separately under #5, directly below). Maybe you took time off to hitchhike around the country or go to Tibet with a yak and a mystic to find yourself. Or maybe you've faced a serious illness, spent time in jail, or been in a mental institution. I've heard them all. And dissimilar though they are, they raise the same issue for our purposes here: they create a gap in the chronology of your resume. How do you handle it? Here are some ideas:

- a.   **Whatever you do, don't organize your resume so that there's an obvious chronological gap.** If your resume shows that your last job ended two years before you started law school, employers' imaginations will run wild with those intervening two years. Were you a soldier of fortune? Were you institutionalized? Were you comatose? They won't stop with the benign explanations because they'll assume if there *is* a benign explanation, you'd have put it on your resume. So don't leave an obvious chronological gap.

Consider using a functional resume, which minimizes the impact of gaps. See Resume #6 in Appendix B.

b. **Don't "stretch" dates to cover the gap.** It may be tempting to add a couple of months—or years, I guess—to your tenure at other jobs to mask the gap. Don't even *think* about it. You never know how you might be smoked out. It might be when a prospective employer calls your prior employer. No matter when you are found out, it's fraud plain and simple. There are always other options for handling a resume gap!

c. **If your "gap" time was spent traveling—as is true for many students—you'll be pleasantly surprised to find that that's a perfectly acceptable resume item.** And there's a logical reason why. If you were an employer, what would you rather have: a student who's already traveled the world to 'find themselves,' and gotten that out of their systems—or someone who's going to be itching to do so *after* they start to work for you, and you invest in training them? As Boston University's Betsy Armour suggests, "All you need to do is create a category that says something like 'Life Experience.' Under that, put 'traveling in Europe, living on a kibbutz'—whatever you did. It gives an employer a window into who you are!" Deanne Coe Kursh echoes that: "It's important for an employer to see a complete chronology. It really doesn't matter what you did—*say* it! 'I traveled,' 'I decided my life's path'—there's nothing wrong with that. Students tend to think they have a lot more negatives than they really have!" I've heard them all. The student who was a ski bum for seven months. The most extreme story about this that any student has *ever* told me was a guy who had, under "Other Information," "Spent five years on the beach in Mexico." It apparently hadn't hurt him in his job search . . . and it generated lots of curiosity!

I can't talk about taking time away from school to travel without telling a story that still makes me laugh. At one of my *Guerrilla Tactics* seminars at a law school in the Midwest a few years ago, I chatted with students as they were filing in to the auditorium. Out of the corner of my eye, I noticed a guy walk up to the front row for a seat. He was handsome, had a great smile . . . and he was a dwarf. Now, I'm no giantess myself—I'm 5'1"— but I have to tell you, I spent the entire seminar thinking about this guy, because I was so convinced that when question and answer time came, he'd ask me a question related to his dwarfism, and I was trying to formulate a strategy in my head while I talked.

Well, question and answer time came and went, and although he hung around, he didn't ask me anything. Afterwards, a few students hung around to talk in a small group, and he joined us.

"I have a question for you," he said. *Uh oh,* I thought. *Here it comes.* "I took a year off after college to hitchhike around the country. How should I put that on my resume?" It took me a moment to realize that he hadn't asked me the question I was so anticipating. But then I stumbled over my words, because ordinarily I would say "Oh, you want to talk about how it was a growing experience ..." and I was horribly self-conscious about offending him! I think I finally stammered out something along the lines of talking about how the experience enriched him, which states he'd visited, and encouraged him to have a couple of brief, amusing stories to tell for interview purposes, so that the entire interview wouldn't be taken up with this one, very interesting experience. He smiled and nodded and seemed happy with the answer. But boy, did I sweat it out!

d.   **If the gap was relatively short—a few months to a year— artful dating on your resume can avoid making it seem like a gap.** Let's look at common situations law students have asked me about:

1.   **Taking the summer after First Year off.**

You know, it used to be that this was no big deal. When are you going to get a summer off any time soon? Today, the conventional wisdom is that you really need to get something on your resume after First Year to be competitive (we talk about this in the Birds and Bees chapter, Chapter 10). But let's say you didn't do anything. What should you do about your resume?

Don't worry about it! Just **make sure that you have some law-related activities during the school year to beef up your resume** (if you want some quick tips, look at "Pimp Your Resume" earlier in this chapter. Then, in interviews, when employers ask you "What did you do during the summer?" You can say you spent it with family or—well, whatever you did—but *immediately* follow up by saying, "But as you can see, as a 2L I have—" and then talk about what you've done to prove your desire to acquire skills and prove your enthusiasm.

2.   **A gap represented by time you spent looking for a job OR a job that you quit very quickly because it just didn't work out.**

Neither one of these are things you want on your resume; not explicitly, anyway. If you worked a job for two months and found out that the boss was a crook or a harasser or just a garden-variety jerk, do you really want to spend half of an interview talking about something that has no reflection on you or your skills? Nope. So *leave them off.* And with your time descriptions on your resume, you're going to be artful.

Let's say, for instance, that you started a summer job in May, and you left in July, and found something else immediately. On your resume you'd simply list that July–August job as:

Summer 20**.

Or let's say that you left a job in March of 2004 (that you'd started in September 2002) and it took you six months to find another one, which you started in September of 2004. On your resume, you could say:

2002–2004 Job One

2004–Present Job Two

I could go on like this, but you get the point. **If being honest but more vague about timing eliminates a gap you'd otherwise have to explain—do it!**

3. Taking a year off between college and law school.

In other countries—well, England, anyway—it's a time-honored traditional to take a year off between high school and college. We don't build those kinds of hiatuses into our American schedules—it's the whole productivity thing—but we should. If you were wise enough to take a year before law school to do *anything*, go ahead and mention it on your resume. Just make sure that it's interesting and suggests some kind of personal growth experience.

One student I talked to spent his year off as a semi driver, "to see how other people live." He listed it that way on his resume, and said that employers responded very favourably to it!

e. **If your gap time involved institutionalization, trust me, you're far from alone.** I used to tell a story about a law student with a prison record in my *Guerrilla Tactics* seminar at law schools, and I can't tell you how many times someone would sidle up to me afterwards, after all the other students had left, and say, "You know that story you told about the student who'd been in jail . . . ?"

Before you apply for any job, there's a non-resume-related issue to resolve, and that is whether or not your state bar will admit you. For jobs that require bar passage, the employer deserves to have you resolve that issue up front.

When it comes to your resume, I need scarcely tell you that you just can't go anywhere near institutionalization on your resume *unless it's directly related to the job for which you're applying*. Remember that story I told early in this chapter about the former prisoner who wanted to be a prisoners' rights advocate? That's the kind of job I'm talking about. Criminal defense work? That would qualify also. But there aren't many others that would.

For all of those other jobs, **either send a resume listing your prison job(s) without identifying the location** (e.g.,

"Groundskeeper, State of Connecticut, 1998–9"), **or send a functional resume** (like Resume #6 in Appendix B at the end of this chapter), leaving the dates off your work experience—or don't send a resume at all. Instead, send a letter containing the experience you *do* want to share. I discuss that strategy in detail in Chapter 7 on Correspondence.

Incidentally, in the Interview Chapter, Chapter 9, I talk about having an answer prepared to deal with your institutionalization, and I implore you to read that before you go on any interviews. The bottom line is this: You came to law school to reinvent yourself, and you *can* do it. You just need to do it strategically!

f. If you were in rehab ...

Well, look at it this way. If you go into Entertainment Law, you'll have a lot in common with many celebrity clients.

Seriously: Handle rehab in two ways:

- List the job(s) you had in rehab, if any; I understand that some rehab programs have you work at the same time.

- Send a letter without a resume, as I talked about in Chapter 7.

g. If your gap time involved caring for an ill family member, don't feel that you have to leave that off your resume. In the "Other information" section at the bottom of your resume you can simply state that from X date to X date you were caring for an ill family member, and that the situation has now resolved itself (you don't have to state how; it's nobody's business). Employers aren't going to have a problem with that, because let's face it: life intrudes. And if you do run into an employer who scorns your choice—honestly, would you want to work for them?

If you feel uncomfortable with this approach, then you can always send a 'functional formatted' resume (like Resume #6 in Appendix B), leaving off dates of work. Or you can take the approach I discuss in Chapter 7 on correspondence, and send a letter without a resume, so you can avoid the issue entirely—at least until you've had a chance to meet the employer and possibly receive an offer, when you'll feel much more comfortable discussing it.

h. Your own illness.

It happens. I talked with one student with a two-year gap on his resume because of an on-the-job injury. He's fine now, but ... two years is too long a gap to ignore.

Here's the problem. Any whiff of personal medical issues, even ones that are resolved, suggests to private employers that their medical insurance costs will skyrocket. If you're applying to private employers, then, **you're probably best off sending a letter without a resume** (as discussed in Chapter 8).

If you do send a resume, use a functional resume to minimize the impact of the gap.

Also, if you did anything related to your illness that gives you transferable skills—e.g., taking part in fundraisers—you can always mention those.

5. THE MOMMY THING

Excuse me while I step up onto my soapbox for a moment. There. *Raising children is work, dammit!* Nothing infuriates me more than hearing people talk about raising a family as "taking time off," or hearing a full-time mother being asked if she "works." (Actually, some things *do* infuriate me that much. Like having airport security confiscate my tweezers. What am I going to do? Storm the cockpit and pluck the pilot's eyebrows?) But you get my point.

There are four things you'll want to do if you've spent some time doing unpaid child-rearing:

a. No full-time parent sits at home eating bon-bons. **Think long and hard about all of the unpaid jobs you've done as a parent.** My sister-in-law Ellie, who has spent the last fifteen years raising my wonderful nieces and nephew, has tons of experience working with the PTA, organizing fundraisers, running scout troops, writing newsletters, taking part in community functions, and so forth. All of those involve transferable skills that would be useful to lawyers, and they should be treated like jobs on your resume. So talk about functions you've organized, what you've written, how much money you've raised. If you've been involved in civic groups, say so—that's got rainmaking potential written all over it, and we know what a plus *that* is for lawyers. Don't undervalue your experience just because you weren't paid for it!

b. Raising children is a full-time job, even if you have a paid full-time job or go to school at the same time. So **even though it falls into the category of personal information that an employer technically can't ask you about, I'd encourage you to include it on your resume.** Texas Tech's Kay Fletcher points out that "Employers are so worried that you'll go to work for them, get married, have children and quit. If you already *have* kids, you've proven that you know how to juggle commitments." Florida's Ann Skalaski echoes that, saying that already having children "Is a plus for employers. It means that you won't be having them on the employer's time!"

* * * CAREER LIMITING MOVE * * *

Female law student, top quarter of her class. The only thing on her resume is her GPA and class rank—no mention of extracurriculars. She got no bites from on-campus employers, and none from resumes she sent out. Employers feel she is 'one-dimensional.'

In desperation, she goes to her Career Services Office. It turns out there was a sizable item she's left off her resume: she has three children, all under the age of 6, and she is taking care of them at school while her husband operates his family's business some 300 miles away!

c. **Pick up the book "If You've Raised Kids, You Can Manage Anything," by Ann Crittenden.** Her thesis is great: basically, that the skills required to manage six-year-olds are directly applicable to managing people. A great book with great advice.

d. As a sneak preview of Chapter 10 on The Birds and Bees of Great Jobs, as you write your resume, think about all of the people with whom you've come in contact through your children—everyone from teachers to school administrators to pediatricians to other parents on the soccer or football or tennis team. Your first job out of law school is far more likely to come through one of them than from your resume. You've got a huge advantage over most students in the sense that you have an incredibly well-developed network of contacts.

The bottom line here is: having children can enrich your resume, not just your life!

* * * SMART HUMAN TRICK * * *

Female law student, in the "Other Information" section of her resume, mentions "During college, worked full-time, raised my daughter, and attended school at night." This entry is cited favourably by every employer with whom she interviews.

6. I'm Only a 1L and/or I Have Nothing to Put on My Resume . . .

One of the most common questions I get is from 1Ls, moaning that they have nothing to put on their resumes. Not true! Now, it *is* true that you don't have law school grades, and for on-campus interview employers, we know those are the Holy Grail. And if you do have grades, you only have them for your first semester, which are just about the most meaningless grades in law school—because so many people are figuring out the whole law school exam format that first semester.

Employers don't expect a lengthy tome of a resume from 1Ls. They realize you're unlikely to have much experience. So: what do you do to stand out?

a. **Stylistically:**

- Use 12–point type, and use a large font like Helvetica or Arial;
- Use 1" margins. Any larger than that looks odd.
- Add lines between sections of your resume if necessary.
- "Spread out" your header information. Put your name in 14–point type. Leave a line between your name and your address. Put your phone and e-mail addresses on their own lines.

b. **Make the most out of your college grades and highlights from your college career.** Make sure you focus on activities that show leadership, initiative, personality, responsibility, interests, energy, and anything that involved researching or writing, activities that stress your interpersonal skills, community participation, or suggest rainmaking potential like fundraising or team sports.

c. **Use "Experience" instead "Employment" as a section title.** That way, you can include community service, volunteer work, and "work-tinged" college activities like being on a faculty search committee.

d. **Don't overlook volunteer work you've done.** Treat it on your resume like a real job, and focus again on the transferable skills. Remember: the mere fact that you were willing to volunteer says good things about you to lawyers.

e. **Remember that no job, no matter how menial you consider it, shows your willingness to work.** As Tony Waller points out, "If you worked at Burger King, you worked in a high-stress, high-volume restaurant without getting fired, which is something. If you waited tables or dealt with the public in any other job, you had to think quickly on your feet—very valuable for lawyers. Also, you were willing to go to school and work at the same time." You should include a calculation of how much of your education you helped fund with it. Lawyers eat that stuff up.

f. **Be sure to include your LEXIS/NEXIS and Westlaw skills.** Some employers say "All students have them, it's not necessary to mention," but on balance, especially if you're looking for resume material, it makes sense to state them. You might be sending your resume to a lawyer who doesn't see many resumes, and may not know that computer skills are ubiquitous among law students. Those employers themselves are unlikely to have those skills and so knowing your way around LEXIS/NEXIS and Westlaw may be very valuable to them!

g. **Make sure you include interesting hobbies on your resume.**

h. **Pimp your resume** (as I described a few pages ago, in Topic I) with law school activities you can join right now, and with bar association memberships you can gather immediately.

7. HELP! THEY WANT MY TRANSCRIPT!

If you've got a brilliant set of grades, then hey—go ahead and plaster the world with your transcript. But you're reading this section because you've got the transcript that most of us have: it's in the bottom 90%, perhaps with overall OK grades, or perhaps with hills and valleys—some good performances and some ... ugh. You envision some interviews where the employer will go grade-for-grade through your transcript, asking "So what happened in Contracts Class? What happened in Torts? What happened in Con Law? What happened in . . ." Arrgghh!

How do you avoid this? Two things to do:

a. To the extent you possibly can, avoid having your transcript precede you to an employer.

I've pointed out before that if an employer sees you before they hear or see anything that has to be explained about you, they can put said item in perspective. When it's your transcript we're talking about, it's hyper important to hold out as long as you can. If they ask for it, offer to bring it with you to the interview.

b. If they insist on seeing it ahead of time, tell them that you're happy to provide it, but you "look forward to discussing it with you." Also, you can always include an explanatory note with your transcript.

You don't want to go into too much detail, but if you've got a grade (or two) that shoots your transcript, by all means include a short explanation.

c. Remember: 90% of employers were not in the top 10% of their class, either.

It's so easy to sit at home and visualize employers you're contacting as being Law Review, top 10%, Ivy League. Fortunately for all of us, that's not most of them. Odds are the people who see your transcript did no better—and perhaps a lot worse—than you. Don't freak yourself out about your grades!

(Incidentally, if you *are* freaked out about your grades, take a look at Chapter 13.)

* * * CAREER LIMITING MOVE * * *

Female law student, attends a school that allows space on transcripts for law students to provide an explanation if they want. She has one bad semester and three others that are fine. On her transcript, she includes the following explanation: "My poor performance second semester first year is due to my suffering from irritable bowel syndrome. I am happy to report it is all behind me now (no pun intended)."

* * * CAREER LIMITING MOVE * * *

Student who both goes through a headhunter and directly mails resumes to employers. The headhunter got a transcript directly from the registrar at the student's school, and that transcript reflects student's true grades, which are C's.

On the transcript that the student sends herself, the grades are magically converted to A's.

Perhaps predictably, one employer gets a transcript both from the headhunter as well as from the student herself. She doesn't just lose the job opportunity … the firm informs the DA's office, which threatens the student with fraud charges.

8. **PRIOR JOBS THAT WENT AWRY—AND THE FEAR THAT THOSE EMPLOYERS WILL GAB . . .**

Listen—there's no prior experience that defines you. No matter what happened in a prior job—or several of them—you came to law school to redefine yourself. And that's what you should do. But how do you keep those skeletons in the closet?

Here's the rub: If it's on your resume, it's fair game. Potential employers will call your prior employers regardless of whether you expressly list them as "references." If they find out that you sued your prior employer, you were caught stealing, and you had a bad attitude—yipes. That'll sting big time.

How to avoid it?

a. **Don't jump to the conclusion that a prior employer views you badly.**

On many occasions law students have nervously told me that they knew their old boss was going to trash their job chances. Nine times out of ten, the experience they told me about was incredibly minor; it loomed large for *them* but the old boss wouldn't even remember it! One student had been a stock analyst before law school. He'd only picked four bad stocks since he was 18. One of those stocks was a tip he'd given to his boss, who lost a thousand bucks on the investment. This student didn't know how to contact the old boss as a reference, worrying about the lost money. This was at a particularly turbulent point in the stock market, and I told him, "A *thousand* bucks? In a crappy stock market? It's probably the best investment he had!" I told him to ignore it and give the boss a call. He did, and sure enough, the guy had only nice things to say—the thousand dollar loss was a non-event.

So don't assume the worst. Be prepared—with all of the advice below—but don't jump in figuring they'll diss you.

b. **Put your head in the lion's mouth—and talk to your *bete noir* before you list them on your resume.**

Tell them, "I'm in law school and I'm applying for jobs. Obviously my experience with you is on my resume, and employers may call you about me. I need to know that we're on the same page in what we tell them." If you *did* screw up on a prior job, and the former employer just won't cut you a break, don't include the job on your resume, as I discuss shortly.

c. **Get a letter of recommendation from someone there who is willing to say good things about you, and send it with your resume.**

When you ask someone you worked for to give you a letter of reference they're unlikely to write something negative. Whether it's your most obvious supervisor or not, there's *someone* in a senior role who's likely to say something positive. If you get a letter from *that* person and send it with your resume, you make it unlikely that your target employers will call anyone else at the prior employer. If they call *anyone,* they're likely to call the person who wrote the letter.

d. **Knock the job off your resume, at least explicitly. List the employer generically.**

"Worked for large food manufacturer," "Worked for prominent local attorney," and so on. If the bad experience was one of a series of otherwise *good* experiences, you can "functionalize" that part of your resume. There was one student at an Arizona school who'd taught ESL at several places; all but one experience had been positive. He wanted to get another employer to lie and say he'd worked for them for the months he'd worked at the "evil" employer. Dangerous idea! It's bad enough to lie on your resume without recruiting an accomplice! Instead, here's how we fixed it. He worded that section of his resume: "Taught ESL 2001–2004 for several employers, including ..." and listed all but the negative one.

You need to be prepared to discuss the "generic" employer in an interview, of course. But then the employer will have *met* you, and they'll be able to put your negative experience in context.

e. **If the gig was so short it won't leave an obvious chronological gap on your resume, delete it. I'm talking about jobs of up to a few months.**

I talked with one student who'd spent two weeks at a law firm. She thought she'd be doing research and writing, and they were using her as a receptionist, with no sign of intending to give her any substantive work. She quit. She wondered how to word it on her resume. The short answer: Don't word it at all!

Another student, this one in the Pacific Northwest, had worked at a company as an accountant for three months before law school. He got fired because he refused to break the law for his boss. "This guy is *really* bad news," said the student. "He'd lie about me in a *heartbeat* to anyone who calls." I told him to get a straw man to call just to see what this guy says, and if it's *that* bad, then delete the job from the resume. Three months isn't long enough to create a gap.

Remember: Your resume is not a confessional. It's necessarily selective or it would be your autobiography!

f.   Don't send a resume at all; send a letter, as I suggest in Chapter 7 on Correspondence. If you worked for the employer for a while and you know that they'll tear you a new one to anyone who'll listen, don't give them the opportunity. If you had a series of unfortunate jobs—don't put yourself in the situation of getting rejected before you have a chance to explain. I talked with one student who had lost three jobs in one year. I asked why, and she said, ''Well, the first lawyer smoked too much and I complained about it so he fired me. The second lawyer had awful hygiene and tried to disguise it with this disgusting cologne. I couldn't stand it so I quit ...'' before she could go on I told her to send a letter instead of a resume, highlighting her skills and experience without naming these employers.

g.   You're familiar with my exhortations about lying on resumes. I want to point out that **none of this is lying. What it *is* is presenting the best possible you. And that's what your resume is supposed to do!**

   Furthermore, **if the employer requires that you fill out a form listing "all prior employment ..." none of the rules I've just given you apply. You have to fill it out honestly, without leaving out any employer, regardless how short your tenure was and why you left.** You'll have to formulate answers to address what you learned from each job, focusing on skills you can bring forward and lessons you learned. And remember: Nobody's got a flawless background; we've all got skeletons in our work closet of varying scariness. No matter how bad you think your mistakes have been, they look worse to you than they will to anyone else!

9.   A RESUME THAT SCREAMS AN INTEREST IN SOMETHING OTHER THAN WHAT YOUR TARGET EMPLOYERS DO.

Quick. You're a tax attorney, and you get a resume from a student who's president of the Sports Law society, organized a Sports Career Day at school, attended an ABA forum on Sports Law, and wrote a journal note about drug testing at sports events.

Is this student interested in working for you?

Maybe ... *but not according to that resume!*

I talked to one student in upstate New York with tons of public interest experience. She was truly interested in divorce law, but she said ''Nobody believes me. They think I'll bail out as soon as there's a public interest opening.''

It may well be that you've developed an honest interest in something recently ... so your resume as it stands doesn't reflect it. Or maybe you've got a dream you're efforting, but in the meantime you've got to do something you like less.

In that instance, you immediately take as many CLEs in your "target specialty" as you can, and list them on your resume. Join the Bar Association subsection for that specialty and put it on your resume. If there's a club at school for it—join. In Chapter 10 on "Birds and Bees of Great Jobs," there are tons of non-resume oriented things you can do to get your foot in the door just about anywhere, but you see my point: You want to "frontload" your resume with relevant information, starting now.

Remember: Resumes are about real estate. Make sure your prime real estate, toward the top of your resume, has information that will say to the employer, "I want to do—and *can* do—what you do."

10. YOU'VE GOT SOMETHING FASCINATING IN YOUR BACKGROUND, AND EMPLOYERS CAN'T TALK ABOUT ANYTHING ELSE WHEN THEY MEET YOU.

Maybe you competed in the Olympics. Maybe you were Miss America. Maybe you worked for a celebrity. At UNLV, students seem to have *tons* of interesting jobs. One student there had been a clown and was dressing strippers at a casino show to put herself through school. (That's not an oxymoron, "dressing strippers," by the way—they have to have something to take off!)

Employers may be so intrigued they can't talk about anything else, like, oh, your relevant skills.

I talked to one student in California who'd worked for President Reagan for three years. She'd also spent a summer working on a toxic torts conference. She moaned, "All employers want to talk about is Reagan, not the conference or any other experience I've had. I'm so frustrated, I want to take the Reagan experience off my resume!"

In a word: don't! The fascinating thing on your resume is very possibly what's getting you interviews in the first place. As we discuss in the Interviewing chapter, Chapter 9, **have a sparkling anecdote to tell—throw the interviewer a bone—and follow up with a question of your own**. Just don't ever yield to the temptation to delete something fascinating from your resume! Remember: You may have told a story a thousand times, but this particular employer has never heard it. They'll probably tell it to their friends and family. Be grateful to have something that so intrigues them!

11. I HAVE MY OWN BLOG/WEBSITE. SHOULD I INCLUDE A LINK TO IT ON MY RESUME?

It depends.

Remember that everything you send an employer—and everything they can find about you on the Internet—reflects on you professionally, the work product you produce and the kind of colleague you'd make.

If your website reflects your resume and includes *only* information appropriate for employers—no nude or semi-nude photos, partying references, etc.—**OK**. Also—proper grammar and no typos.

If your blog focuses on an appropriate hobby or law, fine. A student at Columbia had a blog called snakesonablog when the movie "Snakes On A Plane" was coming out. Very funny, great conversational fodder, absolutely harmless. Blogs focused on hobbies—sure. But if your blog/website includes rants about your professors, classes, or—Heaven forfend—your current employers—absolutely not. In fact, password protect it so employers can't see it, whether or not you list it on your resume. No employer wants a whiner and malcontent in the office, and they don't know you so they can't put your rant in the context of your personality.

We talk in great detail about blogs and websites in the Internet chapter, Chapter 11.

* * * CAREER LIMITING MOVE * * *

Male student sends his resume to a large law firm in California. The recruiting coordinator and hiring partner look it over. They notice that he has a link to his personal website listed at the top, and the recruiting coordinator says, "Want to take a look at it?"

"Sure," responds hiring partner.

They go to the guy's web site, and there, at the top, is the line:

"Scroll down to see my enlarged testicle."

Eyes wide, they stare at each other for a moment, before quickly scrolling down the website. Sure enough, there is an x-ray of an enlarged testicle, with the explanation that it had been caused in a tae kwon do incident.

Next to the x-ray were the words: "Testicle appears smaller than actual size."

Mortified, the hiring partner asks: "Were we supposed to *see* this?"

The recruiting coordinator responds: "Why not? He put the web address on his resume!"

Needless to say: No interview.

M.   THE FIFTEEN RESUME COMMANDMENTS

Did you see Mel Brooks' movie "The History Of The World, Part I?" It's all hilarious, but everybody's favorite scene is where Moses stands on the rock, holding three stone tablets, and looks skyward saying "Lord, take these fifteen—" he drops one of the tablets, which smashes on the ground. "Ten! These ten commandments ..." Ha ha. If you haven't seen it, you should.

So much for frivolity. If you flipped to this section first, you're not off the hook, you know. I haven't been blowing smoke for the last several dozen pages. They're *full* of useful tips. But the fact remains, no resume should go to an employer violating any of the following resume commandments:

1. THOU SHALT REMEMBER THAT THY RESUME IS A MARKETING PIECE, DAGNABBIT

Remember: the whole point of having a resume is to encourage employers to bring you in for an interview, by showing them that you can do for them what they want you to do, based on things you've done in the past—be they volunteer or paid, part-time or full-time, law related or not—and even if all your experience shows is your willingness to work hard and your enthusiasm for what they do.

Tailor your content and organize it accordingly!

2. THOU SHALT RESEARCH THY PROSPECTIVE EMPLOYERS FIRST

It's impossible to know how to organize your resume, and what to include on it and in what level of detail, without knowing what your target employers look for. The needs of a large urban law firm versus a two-person practice in a small town versus a public interest employer versus a non-traditional employer—are radically different, and your resume must be slanted accordingly. You can't do that without visiting employer web sites, talking to Career Services, talking with alums or upper classmen.

3. THOU SHALT SUFFER THY RESUME UNTO EMPLOYERS IN SMALL NUMBERS

You wouldn't respond positively to a marriage proposal that came to you in the mail addressed to "Occupant." Employers feel the same way about mass mailers, whether via snail mail or e-mail. You will get far more positive responses if you send out well-researched, targeted resumes to ten employers at a time than you will sending out five hundred identical resumes to diverse employers.

4. THOU SHALT FOCUS ON TRANSFERABLE SKILLS

Remember: Employers only care about what you've done to the extent that it reflects on what you can do for *them*. Don't expect employers to make the leap for you and figure out how your various job titles generated transferable skills. You've got to do it for them! As Georgetown's Marilyn Tucker advises, "You can't just say, 'researched and wrote memoranda on a variety of areas'—you have to be specific. Lisa Kellogg points out, "Tell them what *kind* of research you did. What kind of law? Was the research on-line? Also, if you tell them you 'wrote memos,' that's not specific enough! Were they motions you copied from a form book? Or were they summary judgment motions that require a lot of thought?" Experience you have counseling people, researching, negotiating, making presentations, organizing, fundraising—it's all directly relevant to what lawyers do, but you have to make it plain that you did it. Employers should look at your resume and have the reaction, "She did that *there,* so she should be able to do this *here."*

5. THOU SHALT FRONT-LOAD THY RELEVANT EXPERIENCE

All the experience you have—whether it's school-related activities, volunteer positions or paying jobs—is not created equal. For any given employer, make sure that you "rearrange" your experience—subdividing it into sections like 'related experience' and 'other experience' if need be—to make sure to showcase the elements of your background this particular employer will find most interesting.

On top of bumping the 'good stuff' up on your resume, be sure to go into more detail about it. Remember: the things any given employer most want to see about you should be given more real estate on your resume, and it should be choice real estate, which means: the further up, the better.

6. THOU SHALT QUANTIFY, QUANTIFY, QUANTIFY

The more specific you are about experiences that a prospective employer will value, the greater the possibility they'll believe you can 'hit the ground running'—and that's very valuable. Rob Kaplan gives the example of being president of your fraternity or sorority. "It's one thing to say, 'Oversaw budget, conducted weekly meetings.' You'll have a much bigger impact if you say, 'Served as chief officer of 115 member organization. Administered a $40,000 budget.' The reader gets a different sense of the level of responsibility you had if they know that it's a hundred members instead of 10, and a $40,000 budget versus $5,000."

7. THOU SHALT SMOTE FROM THINE RESUME ANYTHING NEGATIVE

Remember: It's a resume, not a confessional. Its purpose is to give employers an idea of what you can do for them based on things you've done in the past. By that I mean, *positive* things. I am definitely *not* saying to lie or mislead about your experience. But I *am* saying that you are not required to list every experience you've had on your resume. If your grades aren't up to snuff, don't list your GPA; highlight specific classes or work experiences that show you can do the work. A student at one school told me, "Career Services told me not to put grades on my resume, but I want to be honest—they'll eventually see them *anyway."* Well, yeah ... but there won't be an "eventually" if you don't get an interview *first!*

If you had a negative experience with a club/internship/job, either make sure the employer is on the same page with you about positives you pulled out of the experience, or knock it off your resume and consider sending a letter detailing what you have to offer, without sending a resume at all. A resume has *got* to consist of positives!

* * * CAREER LIMITING MOVES * * *

On resumes:

"I am not available to relocate right now due to multiple law suits against me."

"References available if absolutely necessary and taken with a grain of salt."

"Reason for leaving last job: It was a family-owned business and my father accused me of stealing."

8. THOU SHALT SPEW FORTH THY RESUME WITH FULL KNOWLEDGE OF WHAT EVERY EMPLOYER ON THY RESUME SHALT SAY ABOUT THOU, AND THOU SHALT WARN THY REFERENCES UP FRONT THAT THOU ART DISTRIBUTING THY RESUME

Remember: Your entire resume is fair game for employers. Once they receive your resume, they can—and might—call any employer you list on it, any professors you have whom they know, and *certainly* they can call your references without asking you first. So make sure you know what employers will say about you before you send out your resume; I realize that may mean talking with employers you'd rather see on a milk carton, but it's very important that you know what they're going to say. (Your very act of calling them, by the way—explaining you're in law school and looking for a job and you're just calling to align what you'll say about your experience with them with what *they'll* say—is often all it takes to make them say something on the positive side.)

Furthermore, warn your references that you'll be sending out resumes. Having people say wonderful things about you is a gift, and your references should be nurtured accordingly; it's just polite to let them know when the deluge is going to begin!

9. THOU SHALT CONFINE THY RESUME TO CONSERVATIVE PAPER, TYPE FONTS, AND INK COLORS

Legally Blond was a comedy—not a job search guide. That's why Elle could get away with a pink resume, and you can't. No neon green, no delicate watercolors, nothing except white. No ink color other than black. No color smiley-face adornments or other paraphernalia. And no "out there" type fonts; anything traditional will do just fine. Let the experience you list, and the way you describe it, make your resume memorable!

10. THOU SHALT HEW THY RESUME TO A SINGLE PAGE OR TWO

Unless you have either a great deal of experience before law school, or your experience is limited but it's *all* relevant to the employers you're contacting, keep your resume to a single page. Otherwise, go to two pages. The way you can tell is this: If you cut your resume to one page and you're leaving out information about yourself that will truly entice your target employers—then two pages are appropriate. But remember: As Diane Reynolds points out, "The more words there are on your resume, the less likely it will be read." So if you've got a ton of experience, prune dramatically!

11. Thou Shalt Conform Thy Resume to a Traditional Layout

You know that saying about how the only important thing is to be noticed? There's no such thing as bad publicity? Wrong-ola. You don't want to have the resume people will notice—and laugh at. So no folding up your resume to look like a court document. No round paper. No resumes on wine labels, match books, helium balloons. Use a traditional layout—like one of the ones in Appendix B at the end of this chapter—or one you get from your Career Services Office. And that's it. If your creativity needs a workout, try using it for marketing or advertising an activity in which you're involved, or work on fundraising for your school. Or maybe—just maybe—if your creative flair defines you, then joining a conservative profession like law is not for you, and you might want to consider a nontraditional career. But I'm going beyond my original point: with your resume—keep it traditional!

12. Thou Shalt Share Hobbies And Interests That Intrigue Employers, Not Scare Them

Trepanning, ferret legging, drinking your own urine for health, holding séances—do whatever you want to do for fun. Just don't list it on your resume, unless it's something that employers would find enjoyable discussing with you in an interview *or* you know for certain, ahead of time, that the employer engages in the same hobby. If you're not sure how employers will view your hobby because it's an outlier, check with your Career Services Office before firing off your resume to employers.

* * * CAREER LIMITING MOVE * * *

Law student enjoys container gardening; that is, growing plants in pots on her sun deck.

However, the wording on her resume conveys a somewhat different image. She lists as a hobby:

"Pot gardening."

13. To Thine Own Prospective Employers Be True: Thou Shalt Not Lie, Mislead, Nor Stretch the Truth

I went to law school. I know the temptation. I remember looking at my resume and thinking, "Kimmbo, if you're going to nail a job with this, you're going to have to flesh it out a little." And what happens then? It's innocent. All of a sudden "Yo quiero Taco Bell" turns into "Fluent in Spanish."

The problem? I don't care how obscure your lie is—I don't care if you put on your resume that you speak Urdu. I promise that you will walk into a legal office where the receptionist will greet you in Urdu. And when you're busted with a lie on your resume, the legal community that you thought was vast will shrink down to the person who busted you, and their best friend. You can't recover from that.

Deliberate lies are one thing. Most misrepresentations on resumes are innocent, but they're lies anyway. For instance, if your school calculates GPAs to three decimal points, then that's how it appears on your resume (if at all). No rounding up. If you're in the top 35% of your class, you're not in the "top third." No listing degrees that you never completed; if you took coursework toward a degree, say it. Be careful about listing as an honor something that is really an activity. Don't take full credit for a work project that was a joint effort.

And if you really do need more on your resume, read the section in this chapter called "Pimp Your Resume" to get great stuff on it in a hurry. Just don't lie. It's not worth it!

(Of course, this is not to say that credential inflation has never worked in other circumstances. In 1920, a European man placed a personal ad, describing himself as a "low-level civil employee" looking for a woman for immediate marriage. No takers. He changed his ad to read "mid-level civil employee," and snagged a wife. The product of that union: Pope Benedict XVI.)

* * * CAREER LIMITING MOVE * * *

Law student lists "Fluent in Swedish" on his resume. It turns out that the wife of a partner of a law firm he is visiting has traced her family tree to a small village near Stockholm. She had written to this village, and gotten a return letter in Swedish, which she couldn't read.

Her husband brings the letter to work, knowing that this guy is coming in for an interview. Without trying to put the guy on the spot, the partner points out what a coincidence it is that he speaks Swedish, because his wife received a letter in Swedish and she can't read it.

The partner hands the guy the letter. The guy looks at it blankly for a moment. He looks up at the partner, and says, "I made it up. I can't speak Swedish."

End of interview.

* * * CAREER LIMITING MOVE * * *

Law student spent his undergraduate career at a small school called Rhodes College. On his resume, in the education section, he has prominently listed, "RHODES SCHOLAR." Of course, he didn't mean the kind of Rhodes Scholarship that sends you to Oxford for a year; but he argued that he never *said* that, and so he wasn't lying. His Career Services Director pointed out that by separating his 'Rhodes Scholar' status from his college record on his resume, he was deliberately trying to mislead employers. He ultimately agreed.

* * * CAREER LIMITING MOVE * * *

Law student lists membership in the "PGA" on his resume. What he means is a student organization with that abbreviation, not the

Professional Golfers' Association. Employers, however, don't realize that, and assume he's a professional golfer.

14. Thou Shalt Not Leave Chronological Gaps on Thy Resume

Remember, if there's an obvious chronological gap on your resume, employers will assume the worst: Prison. Mental hospitalization. Federal Witness Protection Program.

If you took off time to travel or raise children, say it. If the gap is short—less than a year–word your timeline so that the gap is not obvious (for instance, instead of listing jobs as August 2004–January 2005 and then August 2005–May 2006, say "2004–5" for the first one and "2005–6" for the second). If the gap is extensive and something that hurts your image—like prison or mental hospitalization—either send a functional resume that doesn't mention dates, or don't send a resume at all; send a letter that highlights the experiences that make you look good.

15. Thou Shalt Leave the Proofreading of Thy Resume to a Source Greater Than Thyself: Thy Career Services Office

Research indicates that one out of three resumes goes out with typos on it. *One out of three.* (There was even a typo in one of the sample resumes in the first edition of this book!) Lawyers have a Freudian thing going on when it comes to typos. They figure, "If you can't get this very important document right, what happens when *I* give you work to do?"

How does it happen? Are we all so careless? Of course not. The problem is, by the time you send out your resume, you're not reading it—you're reading what you *think* is there, because you have it memorized. You just can't proofread your own stuff. As Phil Marshall points out, "We all know you *meant* to say you received an award for your *public* interest activities!"

Spell-checking obviously doesn't cut it, because it's so easy to misspell words as *other* words. I read a wonderful job search book that had this howler: "Once you have learned the basics about an employer, it is time to move on to illicit information about the people who work there." . . . presumably so you can blackmail them with it!

So before you send out your resume, go to Career Services and have them look it over for you. They'll catch typos and provide you with a bunch of other valuable advice. Don't go it alone!

* * * CAREER LIMITING MOVE * * *

Law student worked his way through college waiting tables in various restaurants. On his resume, however, his work experience appears as, "Worked my way through college in various *restraints.*"

* * * CAREER LIMITING MOVE * * *

Law student interned at the World Trade Organization. On her resume, she accidentally wrote "World Trade *Order.*" As one interviewer asked her, "What is this? Some kind of cult?"

*

Appendix A
Perfect Resume Checklist

Before you send a resume out, go through this checklist to make sure you've made the most of it!

Style issues overall:

_____ White paper (or light gray or cream, *if you insist*)

_____ Single type font throughout (in different sizes as appropriate)

_____ Size of type font: 10 to 12 point, name larger than body of resume

_____ Margins: 1" all around, slightly smaller to save space

_____ Length: One page if possible. Two pages for lots of relevant information/expertise. Important information not sacrificed for length

_____ Consistent use of abbreviations (JD, BS/BA)(Oct, Sept, Apr)

_____ No obvious gaps in chronology

_____ No photo

_____ No objective line (for legal employers)

_____ No "personal" section

_____ No "References available on request" line

_____ No mention of schools that admitted you

_____ No mention of LSAT score

_____ If you've sent this particular employer a resume before, the one you're sending now is consistent with the earlier one

_____ No typos

_____ Ain't no grammarical mistakes

Overall approach:

_____ Organize sections, use indents, bold, caps, underlines, and/or italics to draw the eye easily through

_____ Don't parse background excessively; balance number of sections to show off experience to greatest advantage without making resume "busy"

_____ No lies, exaggerations, nothing misleading

_____ Sufficient information to show capabilities/enthusiasm

Heading information:

_____ Name (nickname in parentheses *only* if difficult to pronounce)

_____ Current address (permanent address as well *only* for employers close to home)

_____ Phone number–no numbers transposed

_____ Phone number–at which most accessible

_____ Professional-sounding voice mail message on phone number listed

_____ E-mail address, spelled correctly and professional-sounding

_____ Name 1 or 2 points larger than body of resume

_____ No heading reading "Resume"

Education:

Law school:

_____ Full name, city, state

_____ Graduation date (anticipated or actual)

_____ GPA *if appropriate;* check with Career Services for cut-off

_____ GPA calculated as per school rules, to decimal point school calculates it

_____ Class rank *if appropriate;* check with Career Services

_____ Selected class performance *if appropriate* (excellent *and* relevant to employer)

_____ Honors and Awards, including selection criteria if relevant

_____ Activities (gauged to employer)

_____ Publications (if not included in their own section)

Additional Legal Education (if you've taken CLEs)

_____ Name, who taught/offered, brief description of coverage/skills learned

Undergraduate School

_____ Full name, city, state

_____ Graduation date

_____ GPA if appropriate

_____ Class rank if appropriate

_____ Honors and Awards

_____ Activities (if space permits and relevant to target employer(s))

Experience

_____ Divided into sections if appropriate to highlight experience most relevant to target employer(s)

_____ Know what prior employer(s) will say

_____ Includes "key words" relevant to target employer(s)

_____ Includes relevant volunteer experience(s)

_____ Descriptions start with action verbs. No introductory phrases

_____ Current tense used for current positions, past tense for old ones

_____ Employer names or titles first, depending on which is most impressive. Consistent use of employer/title order.

_____ Remove "a," "an," and "the" to make concise

_____ No "puffery," unsupported statements

_____ Descriptions long enough to make skills/accomplishments understandable and show relevance

_____ Focus on accomplishments and transferable skills

_____ Use quantifiers where possible

_____ Dates at end of descriptions to de-emphasize

_____ Includes how much of your education you funded with job (if appropriate)

Additional sections as appropriate:

_____ Publications

_____ Licenses

_____ Professional Affiliations

_____ Skills

_____ Languages

_____ Bar Memberships

_____ Other/Additional Information

Hobbies and Interests

_____ Accomplishes one of the following: Suggests future rainmaking potential, forms connection because employer/significant client shares hobby/interest, reflects positive personal characteristics, makes you look like a brainiac, provides conversational fodder

_____ Nothing inappropriate; check with Career Services

Researching target employer(s)

_____ Visited employer's website

_____ Conducted as much additional research as feasible: consulted Career Services, alums/upperclassmen, etc.

_____ Know what qualities/skills this employer (or type of employer) looks for

_____ Qualities/skills sought by employer(s) appear higher on page, in more detail

Appendix B
Great Sample Resumes
to Use as Models

The following resume samples incorporate the advice I've given you in this chapter. They're all concise, yet they highlight the person's accomplishments and transferable skills. I encourage you to flip through these and use one that you like the most as a model for you own resume.

Keep in mind that because this book is smaller than the standard 8½ "x11" size of a resume, the type size on these resumes is much smaller than you will use. Stay with a font between 10 and 12 points in size, so that your resume is easily readable!

Resume #1

A results-oriented resume with insightful descriptions of activities and experience.

Scarlett O'Hara

1 Peachtree Road   Altanta, Georgia   (404)555-1212

EDUCATION   Case Western Reserve University School of Law
                                                        Cleveland, Ohio
                JD expected 20**

                Emory University
                BA 20** Major: theater, Minor: Mathematics
                Financed 50% of undergraduate expenses through summer and
                part-time employment.

ACTIVITIES   **Zeta Zeta Zeta**: Theater Fraternity President, 20**. During
                tenure, increased membership over 200% and average monthly
                philanthropy hours from 5 to 25 through conception and imple-
                mentation of traveling play program for local inner-city high
                schools. Previous offices held: Chairperson, costume design
                group; Cochairperson, publicity and scheduling. Member, 20**-
                **.

                The Fiddle-Dee-Dee News: Features Editor, 20**, for stu-
                dent-run weekly magazine distributed communitywide. Ex-
                panded column and reviews regarding local nightlife to include
                activities for readers of all ages, helping to increase nonschool
                community circulation by 20% in 2 years.

                Have appeared in principal and supporting roles in numerous
                school and community plays, including dramas, comedies, and
                musicals. Received favorable reviews in local newspapers.

EXPERIENCE   **Cuyahoga County Auditor's Office**
                                                        Cleveland, Ohio
                Clerk, summers and school breaks, 20 **-**. Rotated through
                every department during first summer; developed ability to
                substitute with minimal training for most clerical staff during
                vacations. Received excellent reviews each summer; noted for
                flexibility, attention to detail in repetitive tasks, organizational
                skills, reliability on very short notice, and ability to learn
                quickly.
                Undergraduate Admissions Office, Emory University
                                                        Atlanta, Georgia
                Work Study Student, 20**-**. Employed 15–20 hours per week
                during school year. Learned basic office procedures and cus-
                tomer service techniques. Given increasing responsibility in
                drafting correspondence and speaking directly with prospective
                students and their parents.

REFERENCES   Professor Rory Schach   Sally E. Fingerhoofen
                (professor in several under-   (direct supervisor)
                Graduate courses)   Office Manager
                Theater Department Emory   Cuyahoga County
                University, Bldg. 3-D   Auditor's Office 1
                55 Noname Plaza   Breathalizer Place
                Atlanta, Georgia 12345   Cleveland, Ohio 67890
                (404) 555-1234   (216) 555-6666

Resume #2

This resume saves space by combining all similar positions in a career of substantial length into one description. The unusual name/address arrangement at the top is another way you can save space. You may want to consider this approach if you've got a lot of prelaw school work experience. (Also, note that this student highlights her interest in health law by including her relevant coursework.)

Melanie Hamilton

12345 Carpetbagger Way   Daytona, Ohio 54321   (516) 555–5555

Education

Case Western Reserve University School of   Cleveland, Ohio
Law
Anticipated date of graduation: 20**
GPA: 3.21/4
Relevant Courses: Health Care Controversies (interdisciplinary law/ medicine seminar); Health Care Advanced Research Seminar; Health Law; Health Law Clinic (one semester involving representation of indigent clients in litigation and transactional matters).
Mock Trial Competition: will participate, 20**-** Advocacy Program: ranked in top 15% in oral component of moot court competition, 20**-**
Health matrix: The Journal of Law-Medicine: Editor on student-run, scholarly journal, 20**-**; Associate Editor, 20**-**; Staff Member, 20**-**.

University of Maryland School of Nursing   Baltimore, Maryland
Date of graduation: 20**; BSN, *summa cum laude*
Inducted into six honorary societies

Legal Experience

Larry, Curly, and Moe, LPA   Cleveland, Ohio
Law Clerk for eight-attorney firm specializing in medical malpractice defense. Conduct research into recent trends in malpractice cases involving obstetrical actions in high-risk pregnancies. Receive exposure to court procedures through attendance at pretrials, medication hearings, and one trial. Regularly discuss cases and other issues and legal points with supervisors. May 20**-present

Professional Nursing Experience

Bay General Hospital, Intensive Care Unit. February 20**-July **
Baltimore, Maryland
Mideast General Hospital, Pediatric Intensive Care Unit. 20**-**
Milan, Ohio
Cleveland Clinic, Palliative Care Unit. 20**-** Cleveland, Ohio
Liberty Services Corporation, Coronary Step-down Unit. 20**-** Liberty, New York
In addition to providing intensive and palliative care to patients, advised doctors of daily changes in status and counseled families under great stress. Acted as patient advocate in many situations; used creativity, resourcefulness and diplomacy in acquired special services for patients and families, whose resources were limited. Regularly worked 12-to-14-hour shifts, occasionally around the clock, in situations requiring ability to make complex life and death decisions and handle continuing and ever-changing stress. Position required advanced and continually updated knowledge of medical procedures, pharmaceutical applications, and ethics.

Personal Interests
Competitive Masters swimmer, brown belt in karate.

Resume #3

This resume shows how you can highlight your legal experience by placing it in a separate section above nonlegal experience. Note how a typical temporary clerical position can be treated to maximum effect! Also, notice how first and second year grades are separated to emphasize a strong upward trend in grades.

Rhett Butler
120 Cavalry Charge Run
Cleveland, Ohio 44106
(216) 555–5555

EDUCATION

Case Western Reserve University School of Law, Cleveland, Ohio

Expected Graduation: 20**

Second year GPA: 3.42/4.00; First Year GPA 2.97;

Cumulative GPA 3.20

Appellate Advocacy Program: 12/75 overall rank in moot court competition.

Academic Scholarship, renewable for 3 years.

Black Law Students Association, Secretary: directed production of first regional handbook for all members.

Ohio State University, Columbus, Ohio

BA History, *cum laude,* 20**

GPA 3.78/4

President's Scholarship: four-time honoree for ranking in to 5% of class.

Student of the Year, History Department: selected by faculty.

LEGAL EXPERIENCE

Winken, Blinken & Nod, Cleveland, Ohio

Law Clerk, Summer 20**. Drafted briefs for all stages of trial and appellate and preparing clients for testimony at depositions and arbitration hearings of one case. Assisted as second chair at one trial, involving client's right to credit information in denied credit case.

Samson & Delilah Co., LPA, Washington, D.C.

Law Clerk, Summer 20**. Coauthorized brief in opposition to consolidation of plaintiffs of class action suit. Drafted *amicus curiae* brief submitted to U.S. Court of Appeals, regarding urea-formaldehyde. Received exposure to product liability and medical malpractice issues, as well as estate planning and probate law.

OTHER EXPERIENCE

Stride for Ohio, Ohio State University, Columbus, Ohio

Program Coordinator, 20**-**; High School Tutor 20**. Conceived and coordinated comprehensive tutoring/mentoring program for local disadvantaged high school juniors and seniors. Trained 55 fellow undergraduates to work with over 150 students. Personally visited five area high school principals; received 100% participation. Received Governor's Recognition Award in only second academic year of operation. Maintained less than 1% dropout rate throughout 2 years of stewardship.

Corporate Connection Temporaries, Beachwood, Ohio

Temporary Secretary, Data Processor, Inventory Control Clerk, etc. 20**-
**. Eliminated need for school loans through variety of short-term
positions. Developed ability to use a wide range of word and data
processing, spreadsheet and database programs with little or no training. Was regularly asked to return to same firms to fill subsequent
needs.

Resume #4

In this resume, the student highlights honors by placing them in a separate section immediately below education. Note how part-time and summer employment is accounted for, without long descriptions or even employer names, job titles, or dates—at the bottom of the resume.

12345 Twelve Oaks Place
Cleveland, Ohio 44106
(216) 555–1212

ASHLEY HAMILTON

ACADEMIC SUMMARY

20**   Candidate for JD
Case Western Reserve University School of Law,
Cleveland, Ohio
GPA 3.02/4

20**   BA Political Science
Georgetown University, Washington, DC
GPA 3.56/4
Relevant course outside major: accounting, finance,
micro and macro economics

HONORS

Case Western Reserve Law Review
- Note for publication, Spring 20**, entitled "A constitutional Energy Policy: an Examination of Some of the Current Issues."

George R. Wistle International Scholar Award
- Selected through merit competition to spend junior year at the Sorbonne, Paris, France.
- All courses were conducted at the graduate level and in French; Courses included European Common Market Economics and Politics, American Economics (from a European viewpoint).

EXPERIENCE

Summer   Phyfe & Drumm, Akron, Ohio
20** to   - As sole clerk, perform wide range of tasks for
Present   five attorney general civil practice.
- Draft pleadings and discovery; working with increasing independence.
- Permitted extensive client contact, including initial interviews and preparation of clients for testimony at depositions, arbitration hearings, and trials.
- Assist at trial, providing cross-examination points in case which was decided in client's favor.
- Developing manual and computerized research skills. Earned a substantial portion of undergraduate living expenses through part-time and summer service and clerical positions.

HOBBIES & INTERESTS

Speak French fluently. Have traveled Europe extensively, and had travel memoirs published in local newspapers. Hobbies include platform tennis and Level 5 whitewater rafting.

Resume # 5

This resume is interesting in that it uses a functional approach within each position description, even though the overall approach is the standard reverse chronological format.

INDIA WILKES

123 Musket Hill Drive   Cleveland, Ohio 44106   (216) 555–5555

EDUCATION
CASE WESTERN RESERVE UNIVERSITY, Cleveland, Ohio
School of Law. J.D. expected   May 20**
        Associate, Journal of International Law: will write note of publishable
        quality for Spring 20**, in the area of consolidation of patent applica-
        tions in international research projects.
UNIVERSITY OF VERMONT, Burlington, Vermont
M.S., Systems Engineering   20**
        Concentrations: optimization theory, robotics
B.S., Systems Engineering   20**
        Concentrations: systems analysis, electronic circuits

EXPERIENCE
Summer Associate, Intellectual Property Department   Summer 20**
JACKSON, COBERG, HOCHMANN & PHIPPS, Los Angeles, California
        Writing—drafting responses and amendments to office actions and
        Appeals board decisions, complaints of patent infringement, trade-
        mark applications. Corresponded directly with several clients on spe-
        cific technical matters.
        Research—employed Lexis, Westlaw, and Dialog to research a wide
        range of trademark and patent issues.

Systems Engineer, Consumer Credit Division   20**-**
TRW, INC., Los Angeles, California
        Technical Knowledge—completed high school profile project under
        budget (5.5%) and ahead of schedule (12%), by applying innovative
        solutions to software needs. Design is now used by company centers
        worldwide.
        Communication—originated and coordinated "Brown Bag Lunch Te-
        chie" series, still in practice, for clerical and professional employees
        who wish to augment their computer skills. Attendance grew from 22
        to 145 and led to significantly increased use of computers in all daily
        operations, with little need for extra training time and no change of
        manpower.

HOBBIES & PERSONAL INTERESTS

Have preformed in community theater musical comedies. Enjoy writing computer
games, playing golf and tennis.

Resume #6

This resume uses the functional approach, which you may want to consider if you've got an extensive career before law school. What it does is stress the transferability of experience, rather than focus on position titles, dates, and employer names—none of which would be terribly relevant to a legal employer. It captures only the most important achievements of a lengthy past career.

Pittypat Hamilton

Permanent Address
1234 Omystars Lane
Centreville, Ohio 44449
(614) 555–5555

Current Address
123 Flame Way
Cleveland, Ohio 44106
(216) 555–5555

Education

Case Western Reserve University School of Law, Cleveland, Ohio

20**—J.D. expected

American Institute of Banking, Cleveland, Ohio

20**—Certificate of Completion

Kent State University, Kent, Ohio

20**—B.S., Mathematics, Economics

Business Development

Increased branch deposit levels 19% in a $12 million branch office during each of the last 3 years of operation. Managed $5.5 million portfolio, achieving zero loan default during last 24 months. Increased commercial loans outstanding by 45% in same period. Outsold entire district in cash management products during last 3 years. Exceeded first year sales goal by record amount (first of 752 rookie agents nationwide).

Administration & Management

Managed nine person branch office achieving zero employee turnover through two mergers within a 6-year period. Cut hours of part-time staff by 33% through efficient scheduling without reducing banking hours or customer service. Trained staff in cross-selling techniques to market bank products and service.

Budgeting

Exceeded budgeted goals in deposits, commercial, consumer and real estate loans every year, consistently above district's average increases. Kept non-interest income on target while keeping non-interest expense below budget during same period.

Experience

Vice President—Trust Bank of Ohio, Centreville, Ohio (20**-**)

Assistant Vice President—Trust Bank of Ohio, Outerville, Ohio (20**-**)

Loan Officer—Homeowners Finance Corporation, Upperville, Ohio (20**-**)

Insurance Representative—Acme Life & Casualty Company, Centreville, Ohio (20**-**)

Community Leadership

Director, Centreville Chamber of Commerce (20**-**)

Trustee, Centreville Community Improvement Council, a United Way agency (20**-present)

Resume #7

This resume emphasizes an upward trend in grades, and co-and extracurricular activities. Note the interesting personal information included at the bottom of the resume.

Frank Kennedy

Permanent Address	Campus Address
1234 Miniball Road	1234 Main Street
Highland Park, Ohio 44444	Cleveland, Ohio 44106
(614) 555–5555	(216) 555–5555

EDUCATION

20**   J.D. candidate
              Case Western Reserve University School of Law; Cleveland, Ohio
              G.P.A.: Fourth semester 3.21/4.00   Third semester 2.97
                       Second semester 2.64   First semester 2.39
              Cumulative 2.82
20**   B.A.   Major: English   Minor: History
              Case Western Reserve University School of Law, Cleveland, Ohio
              G.P.A.: Major 3.52/4.00   Overall: 3.36

ACADEMIC ACTIVITES

Spring to 20**   **Craven Moot Court Competition**, Team Member. One of four
                 selected participate in national competition involving constitutional
                 issue.
20**-**   **Dean Dunmore Moot Court Competition**, Competitor. Ranked
                 8/75, overall score in competition portion of Appellate Advocacy
                 program. Advanced to national competition the following year.
20**-**   **National Handicapped Law Students Association**, Treasurer.
                 Helped found local chapter in order to raise campus awareness of a
                 group's special needs. Helped to lobby successfully for escorts in
                 campus vehicles, better equipped public facilities in law school, and
                 electronic system for rapid library stacks assistance.

EXPERIENCE

Summer 20**   Judge Edwin Smythe, U.S. District Court, Northern District of
              Ohio; Summer Extern. Drafted bench memoranda for a variety of
              civil lawsuits. Assisted Judge with status calls, pretrial conferences,
              settlement negotiations, evidentiary and sentencing hearings. Reg-
              ularly discussed issues with Judge and law clerks; gained insight
              into judicial decision-making and court process; improved written
              and oral communications through detailed critiques.
Summer 20**   Professor Albert E. Jones, Case Western Reserve University School
              of Law; Cleveland, Ohio; Research Assistant. Analyzed legislative
              history and recent developments of the Civil Rights Restoration Act
              of 1987 and the Americans with Disabilities Act of 1989, for law
              review article on the rights of the disabled. Researched judicial and
              administrative law, as well as congressional action and social
              policy. Drafted two sections of article.

ADDITIONAL INFORMATION

Childhood spent in France and Germany, leading to native fluency in both
national languages. Highly skilled in computer programs and applications, including word processing and spreadsheet software. Gaining proficiency in Lexis
and Westlaw.

Resume #8

This resume has an unusual, albeit still conservative, visual arrangement. Notice the wording that emphasizes reasons for holding positions, rather than recitations of duties.

Belle Watling

Permanent Address:	*Campus Address*:
1234 Demimondaine Place	123 Bustier Avenue
Centreville, Ohio 44444	Cleveland, Ohio 44444
(614) 555–5555	(216) 555–5555

EDUCATION

Case Western Reserve University	Cleveland, Ohio
School of Law	Expected Graduation: 20**
GPA	2.86/4.00
Activities	Journal of International Law
	CWRU Jazz Ensemble: tenor saxophone
University of Toronto	Toronto, Ontario, Canada
BA	20**
Major	Political Science, concentration in international relations
GPA	3.3/4.0
Honors	Dean's List, 4 semesters
	Varsity hockey and lacrosse
Activities	UT Jazz Quartet: tenor saxophone

EXPERIENCE

Cuyahoga County Prosecutor's Office	Cleveland, Ohio
Intern	Followed cases through several stages, attending trials and hearings, processing documents, observing client meetings and participating in investigations. Gained knowledge of legal process, skill in researching and preparing legal memoranda and interest in prosecution.
Summer 20**	
Dasher, Dancer, Prancer & Vixen	New York, NY
Docket Clerk	In preparation for law school, volunteered 20 hours per week to gain exposure to lawyers in practice. Concurrently worked as a waitress 35 hours per week.
Summer 20**	
Olive Garden Restaurant	Toronto, Ontario, Canada
Server	Financed undergraduate education without incurring loans after first year. Employed throughout all 4 years, during term, working 15–30 hours per week.
20**-**	

Special Skills

Computers	Westlaw and Lexis research and database applications
Languages	French: proficient in speaking and writing
	German: trained in reading

Appendix C
My Favorite All-Time Resume

OK, I couldn't resist including the resume I've always wanted to send out, but never have. I'm not including it here for any reason other than to give you a couple of yuks. (By the way, if you read through it and don't get it, you'll want to focus a little more closely on the last line of the resume.)

Kimm Alayne Walton
1313 Mockingbird Lane
jobgoddess@aol.com

EDUCATION   Harvard University School of Law
      Boston, Massachusetts   JD expected 20**
Harvard University School of Medicine
      Boston, Massachusetts   MD expected 20**
Yale University
      New Haven, Connecticut   BA and BS, 20**
      Joint major, Macromolecular Chemistry and Economics

ACTIVITIES   *Harvard Law Review,* President.
Manage 50-person staff and budget of $10 million. Simultaneously authoring law review note on admissibility of DNA evidence; U.S. Supreme Court requested prepublication copy, and will cite the article in the case *United States v. Block.*

Yale Crew, participant.
Led crew to NCAA championship. Took part in 2004 Olympic Games in Athens, winning a gold medal for the United States.

Have appeared in local and national theatrical productions, earning a Tony for performance in "Hi There, Gorgeous." Adopted seven handicapped Asian children. On visit to Mexico, deciphered ancient Mayan scripts on tablets at Chichen Itza, leading to discovery of ancient cures for cancer. Discovery expected to lead to cures for variety of modern cancer-related diseases.

EXPERIENCE   Microsoft Corporation
Codeveloped software program as silent partner, which formed basis for multibillion dollar software company. Surrendered stock to partner in 199*, earning a profit of $745 million.

Harvard laboratory for Advanced Medical Research
Summer intern, 200*. Researched molecular changes caused by aging. Discovered link between diet and aging. Patented research, which is expected to lead to increasing human life expectancy worldwide by 20 years.

HOBBIES &   Founder and President, Pathological Liars Club of the United
INTERESTS   States. Currently have 4.5 billion members and an annual budget of a billion dollars. Institutionalization expected imminently.

Appendix D
Internet Resumes

When you're sending resumes to employers electronically, in two very basic ways you're going to have to modify your paper resume:

1) You have to change them stylistically so that being transmitted electronically doesn't turn them to gibberish;

2) You have to focus even more intently on key words relevant to the employer, since they will unquestionably use programs to scan your resume for those key words.

Let's tackle each of those issues individually.

1. Style issues: making your resume readable electronically.

Here are the key elements you need to remember about the set-up of your resume:

a. Use only 12– or 14–point type, no larger or smaller.

b. Use a simple, sans serif font, like Courier, Times, or Arial.

c. As Emory's Carolyn Bregman advises, *don't* put your information in tables; it doesn't look attractive and it's difficult to read.

d. Eliminate all of the following common stylistic devices:

- Graphics
- Columns
- Boldface
- Italics
- Highlighting
- Underlines
- Lines both horizontal and vertical to separate sections
- Headers or footers
- Superscripts or subscripts
- Parentheses
- Brackets
- Slash marks
- Dashes
- Hyphens
- Tabs (use the space bar to move text away from the left margin)
  And ironically . . .

- No bullets! (Use either a plus sign or asterisk instead)

To replace them, use:

- All caps to highlight your name, section names (Experience, Education, etc.), and either your job titles or your employer names (depending on which you want to highlight—just be consistent, and use all caps all the way through for one or the other);
- Equals signs all the way across to replace page-width lines to separate sections;
- Plus signs or asterisks to replace bullets;
- Ellipses (. . .) after job titles and/or employer names

To take your "paper" resume and create an e-resume from it . . .

- Open the file containing your resume.
- Choose "Save as" and click on either text only, plain text, or ASCII.
- Close the file.
- Reopen the file. If any of the stylistic devices listed above (e.g., bullets, lines) remain, delete them and replace them with the ones on the acceptable list, above.
- Make your resume no more than 65 characters in width.
- If you haven't used it already, change to a sans serif font like Courier, Times, or Arial.
- Put all of your contact information on separate lines: name, address, phone, e-mail.
- Use the space bar to create indents.
- Use all caps to distinguish section headings, e.g.: EDUCATION, EXPERIENCE, HOBBIES AND INTERESTS, SKILLS.
- Make the key word adjustments as outlined below.
- Save the document, and close it.
- Reopen the document and see how it looks.
- E-mail it to a friend who uses a different internet service provider, to see how it translates. E-mail it in the body of your e-mail rather than as an attachment (and incidentally, do the same thing when you send your resume to employers).

* * * CAREER LIMITING MOVE * * *

Female student e-mails her resume to several large employers in the same city. She has a bulleted list of qualifications, not realizing that via e-mail the bullets translate as "kissing lips."

To make matters worse, one of her bulleted points is "Works well with people." As one employer comments: "When you see someone saying that they 'work well with people' and there's a kissing symbol next to it, you naturally wonder: Just *how* well? . . .''

Key word focus.

In the body of this chapter we discussed the importance of incorporating into your resume the key words relevant to your target employers. In an e-resume, they are that much more crucial. Employers will unquestionably use electronic word search programs to search your resume for the background they seek. How do you make it through this initial search?

Research, research, research.

If you are responding to a job posting, it will inevitably say that some elements are "required" and others are "desired" or "preferred." *The 'required' elements must appear on your resume;* whether those key words are in your education or experience or the names/descriptions of CLEs you've taken—I told you CLEs would be useful for this!—make sure they get on your resume.

This is particularly insidious if you have the right experience, but you word it differently than the target employer does. For instance, if they seek people with patent law experience and you include in your summer clerkship experience "intellectual property," the employer's key word search won't find your very relevant experience!

3.   E-mailing your resume to employers.

Consider sending your resume by snail mail as well as e-mailing it. That way, if there's a glitch in the transmission, you'll be certain the employer will receive your materials.

4.   Sample e-resume.

I've taken James T. Kirk's resume from earlier in this chapter, and converted it to "e-resume-eze." It ain't pretty, but it's perfectly internet compatible.

James T. Kirk
1 Wrathokhan Road
Enterprise, USA
888 555 5555
jtkirk@federationsol.edu

EDUCATION

———

FEDERATION SCHOOL OF LAW
JD expected 2***
GPA 3.02
Class Rank 55 out of 168
Space Law A minus
* * * Activities * * *

+ Space Law Club

Responsible for seeking out and contacting new speakers for the club's monthly meetings.

Edit the club's web site, featuring articles of interest drawn from scholarly and popular publications.

+ Phi Alpha Delta Law Fraternity

Organized "Meet the Lawyer" Day, bringing students together with practitioners in forty legal specialties. Event was attended by four hundred law students.

TRIBBLE UNIVERSITY
BA 2***

Major Physics

Minor Film

Financed 60% of undergraduate expenses through summer and part-time employment.

ADDITIONAL LEGAL EDUCATION

———

+ Space: The Final Legal Frontier," Continuing Legal Education Program, September 2***, offered by the Space Law Institute. Learned to draft complaints related to fallen satellite parts.

+ "Space Can't Take It Any Longer!—Legal Issues Involving Space 'Junk'," Continuing Legal Education Program, September 2***, offered by State Bar Association.

+ "Private Space Flights, Disclaimers and Liability Issues," Continuing Legal Education Program, October 2***, offered by Vulcan & Vulcan.

+ "Space Law ... Where Is It Going?" Continuing Legal Education Program, October 2***, offered by Space Law Institute.

LEGAL EXPERIENCE

———

PROFESSOR SPOCK ...

Research Assistant, 2***-* school year.

Researched issues involving cloning for upcoming textbook on patent law. Used LEXIS/NEXIS and Westlaw databases on a daily basis.

LAW FIRM OF BONES AND SCOTT ... Four-person patent law
    firm

Summer 2***

Interviewed clients, researched issues and wrote memoranda involving the patentability of inventions, performed patent searches.

OTHER EXPERIENCE

——

Piggly Wiggly Grocery Store ...
Summers 2*** through 2***

Packed meat for display and sale. Named "Employee Of The Month" seven times.

HOBBIES

——

Geocaching, reading science fiction novels

*

Appendix E
Scannable Resumes

The information in this section appears courtesy of Duquesne University School of Law.

A "scannable" resume is just what it sounds like: a resume capable of being scanned into a database.

This is not a resume you'll need if you're only applying to traditional legal employers. If you are applying to large companies, it's a good idea to have both a "traditional" paper resume, as we've discussed throughout this chapter, as well as a "scannable" one. You wouldn't send out the scannable version if an employer didn't ask for it . . . but some do.

Larger companies sometimes request scannable resumes for a few reasons, including:

- Having a computer scan resumes for key words is faster than eyeballing them;

- Employers with offices around the country can have a central database for applicants to every office;

- It's more efficient to store resumes on the computer rather than filing them;

- A single resume database can be used for virtually all applicants (whether lawyers, paralegals or assistants);

- The database can be used over a long period of time, so candidates for new positions can be identified and readily retrieved when future opportunities open up, saving the cost of new advertising or hiring a headhunter;

- It's a cheaper way to recruit.

A scannable resume differs from a traditional resume in that it has to optimize the computer's ability to read it.

Here's what you need to know about making your resume easily scannable:

- Follow all of the advice in Appendix D for Internet Resumes; all of those stylistic devices apply to scannable resumes, as well, as do the rules on key words. If an employer scans your resume into a database, they're planning to do a key word search on it.

- Use white paper only. Any other colour risks reducing the contrast between the type and the background, making it harder for the scanner to read.

- Use standard-sized paper. That's what most scanners are calibrated to handle; any other size requires special handling, which will alienate employers!

- Use only one side of each sheet of paper, if your resume spans more than one page.

- Use 12– or 14–point type, which ensures readability without being overpowering.

- Laser print (rather than ink-jet print) your resume; it will look crisper and reproduce better.

- Use a "clean," easily-scannable sans serif font, like Courier, Times or Arial.

- No handwritten comments on your resumes! (You wouldn't do it anyway. You *can't* do it for scannable resumes.)

- Leave margins of at least ¾" on all sides of your resume. Words closer to the edges of the page risk being cut off.

- If you have more than one page, ensure your name is on the top of each page. Scanners usually require pages to be separated before being scanned; having your name on each page guarantees your resume won't be confused with someone else's.

- Number each page of your resume, in case it gets jumbled while being scanned.

- If you have a resume of more than one page, attach the pages with paper clips rather than staples. Employers have to remove staples in order to scan resumes, and that extra work is guaranteed to torque them off.

- Don't fold your resume. Folded papers are difficult to scan and make more work for the employer–a no-no. Send your resume flat in a large envelope.

Appendix F
Words and Phrases to Avoid on Your Resume

French fries	Shafted
Northbound	Menial
Marijuana	Spank/spanked/spanking
Arrest	Least likely to succeed
Harassment	Terminated for cause
Parole	Laughably
Beer	Asked to leave
Nude	Rehab
Passion	Mediocre
Sperm donor	Never proven
Unfortunately	Accidentally
Hooters	Personality conflict
Academic Probation	Regrettable

Shout outs for materials excerpted in this chapter to the following law schools: Case Western, Iowa, New England, Tulane, Florida State, Vanderbilt, Syracuse, Connecticut, Gonzaga, Emory, Harvard, and California Western.

Chapter Nine
Interviewing: "The Secrets That Turn Interviews Into Offers"

Interviewer: Why did you leave your last job?

Interviewee: They told me I have incredibly poor judgment. So I sued them.

　　—The comic strip "Dilbert."

Appendices:

APPENDIX A: Extreme interview makeover: putting the principles in this chapter to the test.

APPENDIX B: Sample in-house interview evaluation forms.

APPENDIX C: The famous "three question" interview.

Related Topics:

Job Fairs—Chapter 10

Informational Interviews—Chapter 10

───────

Congratulations! You got your foot in the door. Maybe you got an on-campus interview. Maybe you sent the employer a great resume. Maybe you had blackmail photos. It doesn't much matter. Now you're faced with turning that interview into an offer, and in this chapter, Auntie

Kimmbo will teach you how to do just that. We'll go through your prep work—yes, yes, yes, I know how busy you are, and I won't wear you out with it. I'll tell you what to wear. We'll talk about the questions you should ask, and what questions you should *never* ask. I'll show you how to answer killer questions with aplomb. I'll give you a 31–point "Charm Offensive"—that's an oxymoron, isn't it?—With tips on making the interview rock from start to finish.

We'll talk about follow-ups, on-campus interviews, call-backs and phone interviews. We'll talk about handling disasters—whether they're of your own making, or it's the interviewer who's at fault. The bottom line is this: if you do everything I tell you to do, you *will* turn interviews into job offers.

With that in mind—let's get going!

A. Interviewing Down to the Bones: What's *Really* Going on Here?

In a job interview, no matter what the interviewer asks you, there's really only one thing the interviewer is asking him/herself the entire time, and it's this:

Do I want to work with you?

OK. It's not the *only* question. They want to see a panoply of things your resume can't tell them, like:

- Enthusiasm: Do you seem to want to work for them?
- Do you have good judgment?
- What's your motivation?
- Are you tactful?
- How are your people skills?
- How smart are you?
- Do you have a positive, confident attitude?
- Will there be a "fit" between you, your colleagues and the employer's clients?

I guess you could say those all go into determining if they want to work with you. But no matter how you slice it, this aspect of job searching—the "personality" part—is something that I've found law students tend to undervalue dramatically. We all think, "If I just had that solid gold resume, I'd be da bomb." It's just not true. The recruiting coordinator at a prestigious Midwestern law firm told me about a student from a distinguished school, #1 in his class, who was completely obnoxious in his on-campus interview. The recruiting coordinator told the hiring partner glumly, "He's #1 in his class. I guess we *have* to bring him in." The hiring partner shot back: "No—we don't."

I'll tell you something that *is* true:

If employers like you and want to work with you, they'll often convince themselves *that you can do the work.*

You just can't overstate the importance of bringing the best, friendliest, most enthusiastic "you" to the table. I've seen this proven over and over again. I remember talking with the hiring partner at a large law firm in Texas, and he told me about a student he'd interviewed. The guy looked phenomenal on paper: Top of his class, Law Review, the whole nine yards. On top of that, this student had had two jobs. One of them was researching oil and gas leases. Now, I live in Connecticut—no oil and gas here!—but this partner explained, "In my book, that's one boring job."

This student's other job, however, had been working as a bouncer at the Playboy Mansion.

The hiring partner told me that the interview was going pretty well, and about halfway through, he picked up the student's resume, and said, "Listen, you know I have your resume here in front of me, and you know I can see the jobs you've had. I want to apologize up front. I know everybody asks you the same thing, and you must be tired of talking about it. But my curiosity is killing me. I just have to know: What's it like ... to research oil and gas leases?" He went on, "I'm there cackling over my own joke—you know he thinks I'm going to ask about the Playboy job—but I look over at him, and he's completely stone faced. Silent. So, I clear my throat, and I say, 'Let's talk about Law Review.' "

The hiring partner went on to tell me, "You know what? In that one moment, I decided, 'I don't like you.' I didn't care how good he looked on paper. I mean, here he had this high-risk item on his resume"—trust me, if the word 'Playboy' appears on your resume, one way or another every interviewer is going to bring it up—"I bring it up, I make a little joke about it, *I give him the chance to turn the interview into a conversation*—and he cuts me dead."

Personality counts. And it's not just in law, by the way. On a flight from South Carolina to Indiana I once sat next to a woman who did recruiting for a hospital. She said, "Recruiting is the same everywhere. Everybody looks for people, not credentials. A guy might be the world's most brilliant thoracic surgeon, but if he's a pain to work with, you won't take him. People get too hooked on their own credentials."

Now, I could tell you a million stories like this, but you see my point: **What you're *like* counts for more than what you *look* like on paper.**

So the interviewer sits there the whole time pondering whether they want to work with you. With that in mind—what do you have to do to prove that they *do?*

You *prepare for interviews,* that's how. You have to do some solid preparation before you start your very first interview, and then you have to do a fifteen minute "tune-up" before every interview. I can hear you groaning. But trust me—it's worth it!

B. BEING PREPARED TO *GET* THE INTERVIEW

The employer's impression of you is formed before you get the interview. There's your resume, of course. But beyond that, if they call to invite you for an "in-person" or phone interview or a call-back, your phone presentation *counts!*

As Minnesota's Victor Massaglia advises:

1. Keep your resume, cover letter, transcript and writing sample near the phone. That way, you can be ready if an employer calls and wants to talk to you "right now."

2. Check your voice-mail message, Dude. It should be, like, professional.

3. If you share a phone, tell everyone you live with that you're expecting employers to call. Ask them to take a message for you. Otherwise, use your cell phone for employers.

4. When you can see from caller I.D. that it's an employer calling, have a pen and paper ready before you answer. Get contact names, correct spellings, e-mail addresses, driving directions, and note the day/time of the interview.

5. Return calls to employers *the same day.*

Remember: In every communication, the employer is forming an impression of you!

C. THE FIVE KEYS TO PERFECT INTERVIEW PREPARATION

The only way to have an air of relaxed confidence—and that's the air you want, by the way—is to prep for interviews.

The great New York showman Florenz Zeigfeld used to dress his showgirls in very expensive French silk underwear. People asked Zeigfeld, "Why do you bother? Nobody sees their underwear!" and he responded, "Maybe—*but they know they're wearing it.*" Preparation is your French underwear. You'll know you did it, and apart from all of the other benefits it will give you—great questions to ask, great answers to supply—it'll give you interview chops.

You probably have two principal problems with the idea of doing prep work, if you're anything like the thousands of law students I've talked to. "I don't have any time!" you'll say. Well, I'm not going to wear you out. One solid lump of preparation before you interview at all, and then a little "employer-specific" part before every interview. That's it.

You might have another problem with prepping for interviews. You might say, "I don't want to prep for interviews. I don't want to sound canned. I want to be fresh!" No, you don't. *You want the job.* And that takes a bit of preparation. Preparation doesn't make you sound 'canned,' by the way. It makes you sound enthusiastic. And that's the principal feature you want to get across in interviews: Enthusiasm is reflected in body language, in the questions you come up with for the interviewer, the answers you give to the questions you get, that add up to showing the interviewer, "I really want this job—and I'll be good at it, because I've put thought into how I'll fit in."

There are five elements of perfect preparation. They are:

- Develop a flexible answer to "Tell me about yourself";
- Prep answers for difficult questions you're likely to get;
- Research the employer and the interviewer;
- Develop questions to ask;
- Practice!

Let's go through each of them in detail.

1. **STEP ONE: BEFORE YOU GO ON EVEN ONE INTERVIEW, DEVELOP YOUR INFOMERCIAL; THAT IS, THE ANSWER TO THE QUESTION, "TELL ME ABOUT YOURSELF." AND REMEMBER THAT YOU'LL HAVE TO MODIFY IT FOR DIFFERENT KINDS OF EMPLOYERS!**

    "How would I describe myself? Three words. Hard working, Alpha male. Jack hammer. Merciless, Insatiable."

    —Rainn Wilson as Dwight Schrute on *'The Office.'*

If you've ever looked at books on job interviews, you'll see that "Tell me about yourself" is considered one of the most difficult questions you can be asked. Most people consider it excruciating. On top of that, most interviewees answer it *wrong*. Why? Because "Tell me about yourself" is not an invitation to give a mini-autobiography. "Oh, I was born in London, I have three brothers and sisters ...." No. What we're going to do is reword "Tell me about yourself" to talk about what it *really* means ... how you can prepare for it ... and how, if you handle it correctly, you can impress the interviewer within the first couple of minutes of starting the interview. (That, after all, is when interviewers tend to ask you the question—it's a great opener.)

So—what does "Tell me about yourself" really mean? It's the following question in disguise:

Give me the reasons to hire you.

You're going to answer with a thirty-second "infomercial" that you've already prepared.

Your infomercial will have two elements: **The first element is three qualities that have two features in common: One is that these are qualities that you genuinely have, and the other is that they are important to the employer.** You'll know that from your research, which we discuss in step three, below. Of course, if it's a job posting, the skills the employer seeks will be listed in the posting for you!

The **other element is a hobby or interest that you have,** along the lines of hobbies and interests that we discussed when we talked about your resume in Chapter 8. The hobby or interest gives you a "third dimension," a snapshot of what you're like *outside* of work, and gives the interviewer some idea of you as a whole person instead of just as a worker bee.

Now, let's talk about those three work-related qualities, and how you choose what to talk about. We're actually going to work backwards. Get a piece of paper. Draw a line down the middle, to form two columns. On the left hand side, at the top, write the word "Accomplishments." Go through your background and pick out—duh—your accomplishments, the things you're most proud of. Wendy Werner advises that "Your list should include things like, 'I started this organization in college,' or 'I raised this money,' or 'I wrote best brief'—things like that." Lisa Abrams calls this list your "claim to fame."

By way of a memory aid, look back at the lists you developed for your resume, in Chapter 8. The accomplishments can spring from jobs, school projects, clubs, volunteer positions, hobbies. Maybe you've written something you're proud of, or you've acted in the theater, or you raised kids while you went to college, or worked full-time while you got your degree. Or you made the Dean's List in undergrad every semester. Maybe you've climbed Mount Kilimanjaro. Maybe you held down a job for two years when everyone else who'd held the position before you was canned within a month. Maybe you were head counselor at a summer camp and you were the first person who didn't have any kids go home early because they were homesick. There's an endless variety of accomplishments, and you need to come up with yours! **How many? You should come up with a short list of them, anywhere from half a dozen to a dozen**.

There are a couple of things to keep in mind as you come up with this list. One is to be sure you **don't undervalue yourself by overlooking the job-related skills you've gotten from non-law-related and volunteer jobs**. One Career Services Director told me about a law student who worked a summer for the corporate counsel for the Professional Golfers' Association. This student felt stigmatized by the fact that he didn't have law firm experience, but he *did* turn the experience to his advantage in interviews. He looked at that job and realized that his boss was a perfectionist, and that the main thing he learned working for him was how to minimize the burden he placed on his boss's time. That meant he learned how to organize questions, manage himself, and be succinct, so as to bother his boss as little as possible. Well, you can imagine that not only is that an excellent law-related skill to have, but it was sufficiently off the beaten track to make for interesting interviews!

I've heard a bunch of colorful examples like this. One student was able to turn to his advantage his experience as a hot dog salesman at Yankee Stadium for seven summers. Another student had put himself through college as a door-to-door Fuller Brush salesman!

As you develop your list, **choose accomplishments that are as colorful as possible.** There are two good reasons for this. One is that you'll be making the interviewer's life easier. Being an interviewer can be a *real* snooze fest. You'll be using your accomplishments as examples about yourself in the interview, and every interviewer appreciates an interesting interviewee!

Another plus is that interesting accomplishments make you memorable. Inevitably, you'll have lots of competition for jobs, and anything you can do that makes you stand out *in a positive way* is a plus! As Vanderbilt's Elizabeth Workman points out, "Students who can tell engaging, memorable stories are inevitably the most successful at interviewing."

Now, at the bottom of that list, there may be an additional item that's not really an accomplishment, but it may be very relevant to your job search. **If you are looking for a job that is not in the city where you're going to law school, write down your connection with that city/those cities.** And make it something concrete: a spouse who's accepted a full time job there, you're interested in a practice area that's thriving there, you're joining family members or you used to live there or you've lived in various cities and you like the idea of living in that particular city because ... well, you like small town life, or whatever it is—something that will make the employer believe you've got a solid interest in the city. Geography counts!

So! You've got your list of accomplishments. Now you write at the top of the right-hand column of your sheet of paper—opposite your "Accomplishments" column—the following words: "Transferable skills this accomplishment illustrates about me." We talked a lot about transferable skills in the Resumes chapter, Chapter 8. Basically, transferable skills facilitate this analogy for employers: "Because you did X in that situation you will be able to do Y for me." For instance, if you worked your way through college, you're a hard worker, making the employer think: "You'll work hard for me."

While employers are all different, and you'll want to factor in employer-specific skills/qualities you discover from your research, this list represents the skills/qualities that appeal to most legal employers:

Qualities of an ideal lawyer:

Energy (hard worker)

Follow-through

Ability to juggle multiple tasks and prioritize

Ability to pick up new information quickly

Ability to deal with time pressures and tight deadlines

Team player

Initiative

Motivation

Creativity/Imagination/Inventiveness

Self-confidence

Flexibility

Intelligence

Persuasiveness

Persistence

Attention to detail

Willingness to accept responsibility

Ability to handle stress

Goal-orientation

Enthusiasm

Skills of an ideal lawyer:

Problem solving

Legal analysis and reasoning

Legal research

Factual investigation

Communication (written and verbal)

Counseling

Negotiation

Organization and management of legal work (office procedures)

Recognizing and resolving ethical dilemmas

Keep in mind that the same accomplishment can illustrate several transferable skills about you. Let's say that you worked in a busy restaurant for thirty hours a week during college to pay your way through. Well, it not only says you're a hard worker—it *also* shows you've got excellent communication skills. Or let's say that you were a camp counselor during the summers in college. It proves your enthusiasm for working with children as well as your ability to communicate with them—an excellent trait for someone who wants to be a child advocate, for instance. It may also show your ability to be a team player, if you worked in concert with other counselors.

Or let's say you volunteer at the bar association during law school, and you've researched an issue in family law, a specialty you'd like to practice. It shows off not just your research and writing skills, but also your enthusiasm for the practice area. Or maybe you were part of the varsity field hockey team in college. Sports, of course, are great resume items; they show your ability to be a team player, your ability to handle criticism, and your discipline.

I could go on and on, but you're clever. You see what I'm talking about. So write down those transferable skills next to the appropriate accomplishments!

How do you turn this list into an infomercial? Based on research you do about the employers with whom you'll interview—we talk about Research in step 3 below, and we talked about it extensively in Chapter 6—**look at the qualities they look for in people they hire, and then from that list choose the three most important qualities that you share.**

I am not overstating the matter when I point out that this ain't rocket science. You probably know most of it off the top of your head. For instance, if you're looking at public-interest jobs, you want to stress your volunteer experience to prove your enthusiasm, and perhaps activities that have brought you into contact with the kinds of people you'd be serving.

If you want to be a litigator, experiences showing that you think quickly on your feet would be valuable. For a large law firm, research and writing skills are paramount. If you're talking about a small law firm, it would be important for you to talk about being able to hit the ground running, take responsibility, your counseling skills, your comfort in talking with people.

And remember, certain skills and qualities are important to *every* employer. Hard work, enthusiasm, self-discipline, and reliability—those are always plusses.

None of this diminishes the importance of choosing employer-specific skills and qualities that you learn through your research. By way of example, let's say that you want to work for a particular law firm. You get the inside skinny on it from an alum who works there. This is what (s)he tells you: "It's fairly conservative. Hard work is appreciated and expected. They put a high premium on detail. They like enthusiasm and the ability to take the lead. You can fall between the cracks if you don't increase your recognition. It's fairly political. You need to be able to take job development into your own hands; nobody spoon feeds you."

You probably already have some of those traits on your list.

Now, take your accomplishments and transferable skills, and reverse them. That is, **cite your job-related skills and then use your accomplishments as support for those skills. This is a matter of "show me—don't tell me."** For instance, let's use my waitressing experience in college. I'd say something like, "I'm a hard worker. I put myself through college by working full-time waiting tables while I was taking a full class load. I waited on 20,000 people in two years."

So you've got your job-related skills, with examples. Let's spend a moment on that personal hobby/interest/achievement. Remember, I've said that it's crucial for the interviewer to look at you as a *person*, a complete, flesh-and-blood being, rather than just another interviewee. Mentioning a personal hobby/interest/achievement in your infomercial will accomplish that.

Of course, be selective in what you choose to mention. Look for something that makes you proud. Have you written a children's book?

Climbed Ayers Rock? Raised a child while attending law school? Back-packed through Europe? Is there a sport you enjoy? A student at one law school mentioned that she was an ultimate Frisbee player. "It's unusu-al," she pointed out, "and it highlights my skills as a team player."

While you're thinking of these, you want to take into account the same 'controversial' issues we talked about in the resume chapter. That is, if you like to take part in beauty pageants or you're a hunter or you're heavily involved in Democratic politics, you're going to want to be selective about the interviews in which you mention them. And don't suggest or even *intimate* that you do anything irresponsible, unethical or illegal. "I like to party hard," "I download tunes" . . . not an image that's good for you.

This personal interest aspect of your infomercial—like the rest of it—is going to be fluid, because you need to be able to change it depending on the employer. You're not going to *lie*, but if you learn that the employer and/or interviewer has an interest or hobby that you share, *that's the hobby you're going to mention.* For instance, if you learn that the interviewer is a golfer, and you golf, that's the hobby you'll cite. If you learn that the employer has a softball team and you love softball, that's your interest. If you discover that the interviewer is a serious Trekkie and you've been to a few Star Trek conventions yourself, that's what you're going to bring up. Hell, if you learn that the interviewer stuffs and mounts moose heads and you've got a phat taxidermy collec-tion of your own, *mention it.* It doesn't matter how far out the hobby is—as long as it's not embarrassing or illegal—if you share it with the employer and/or interviewer, bingo. You want to forge a connection with the employer, and having a personal interest in common is a great way to do that.

In the absence of an employer-specific hobby or interest, you'll have one that you use in every interview.

Now, you put together your job-related skills and achieve-ments to back them up, your personal interest, and you stand in front of a mirror and memorize it.

Consider prefacing your "infomercial" with how you found out what the employer seeks:

"I understand from talking to alums who've worked for you that you look for . . ."

"I understand from former clerks, Your Honor, that you want . . ."

"I did a lot of research into your firm and from what I learned, you look for . . ."

"Your job posting suggested . . ."

You've done the research anyway. Show it off!

Talk about yourself until you can do it comfortably. At first you're going to either want to throw up or laugh. But the kind of calm self-confidence you want to project is what you see in presidential candidates and Miss America finalists. They've got to talk about what they bring to the table with a smile and without flinching, and so do you.

If you find it difficult to say good things about yourself, pretend you're talking about your best friend, or, as Washburn's Margann Bennett recommends, "Pretend you're representing a client." You wouldn't have difficulty saying good things about *them*.

This infomercial will serve you much of the time, but as we'll see when we get to Step Three on Research, you've got to be prepared to switch skills and personal interests in and out depending on what you find out about the employer. Employers are very different, and while some qualities—hard work, enthusiasm—are appropriate for all of them, others are not. Being a great team player isn't going to be important if you're expected to work on your own and be a self-starter. For instance, let's say that upperclassmen with experience at a particular firm tell you that one thing the partners hate is to be bothered with incessant questions; they like you to work on your own. Well, if that's something you think you're good at, an interview with that firm would be a great place to say, "I pride myself on my ability to work on my own initiative. I can organize my work and handle responsibility without taking up my boss's time." Boy—think how that would fly with an employer who doesn't like to be bothered very much!

By the same token, thinking quickly on your feet wouldn't be supremely important if you're going to do real estate closings, whereas it's crucial if you're going to be a prosecutor or any other kind of litigator. As Diane Reynolds points out, "If you're interviewing with a litigator, and you won prizes for debate, that's a strength he'll definitely want to hear about!"

Great research skills? Of prime importance at a large law firm, not so much if you're expected to spend most of your time counseling clients.

Perhaps you've helped out at a homeless shelter, and the aspect of that that you most appreciate is your ability to relate to people who are down on their luck. With a Legal Aid job, that would be extremely valuable; with a Wall Street firm, it wouldn't. And the geography quality—why you are attracted to working in a particular city—is only important for out-of-town interviews. So—you see the point! Memorize your infomercial, but be prepared to change it.

Now—**how is this infomercial going to help you? It's the obvious answer to the traditional interview opener, "Tell me about yourself."** If you formulate your infomercial as I've told you to do, and you say it with humble confidence, you'll get the reaction so many students have experienced. I call it the 'nodding' response. You'll notice the interviewer start to smile and nod, and that's body language for their thinking: "This kid's *got it*." From there on, it doesn't much matter what happens in the interview; they've already decided you're da bomb.

Incidentally, don't get the impression that your infomercial is a one-trick pony. It will bail you out of many, many situations that are traditionally considered interview killers, from "What are your strengths?" to "Why should we hire you?"

It will also help you out in situations that are designed to trap you. You will probably face interviewers who ask you a question like: "Well, we're interviewing for this job at [fill in law schools that outrank yours]—why should we hire *you?*" or a variant of that: "I just interviewed the person who's #1 in your class. Why should I hire *you* instead of *him/her?*" Now, what's your atavistic urge when the hair starts to rise on the back of your neck? It's to attack the competition. "Well, you won't want #1 in the class when you read her anonymous blog . . ." No! It's very key in any interview *never* to say *anything* negative about anyone or anything. No prior employer, no professor, no law school—yours or any other—and no classmate!

So, how do you answer? You say something like, "I can't tell you anything about X law school or Y student, but I can give you the reasons to hire me—" and you launch into your infomercial.

Your infomercial will also help you out in situations where you're faced with a crappy interviewer. Let's say you have one who just talks and talks and talks the whole time, or (s)he fumbles and doesn't really ask you anything relevant. In both cases, you want to ask the question: "Tell me—what do you look for in people you hire?" When they give you a quality or a couple of qualities, you'll say, "That's good to hear. Here's what you need to know about me—" and go into your infomercial, modified as necessary. And if you're wondering how to break in if the interviewer is talking non-stop, what you do is wait for them to take a breath, and say something like, "This is very interesting, but I'm curious: What do you look for in people you hire?" They tell you, and then, kerblammo—infomercial.

So you can see how important your infomercial is, and why it's worth spending some time developing it. Get to work!

* * * CAREER LIMITING MOVE * * *

In an on-campus interview, the interviewer asks a female student, "What makes you, *you?*" She responds, "I love to work on cars."

As the interviewer comments later, "OK answer I guess, but what does it have to do with my work? Problem-solving maybe. But she didn't say that. She didn't say *anything.* She was one of those rare people who's much better on paper than in person."

* * * CAREER LIMITING MOVE * * *

As part of his "tell me about yourself" pitch, law student tells interviewers, "I wrote onto Law Review." Because Law Review didn't appear on his resume, the student says, "This would always pique the interviewer's curiosity. I would explain that I entered the writing competition for Law Review, and wrote a draft of the whole thing.

When the results came out, it's obvious that I *would* have been chosen. But a week before the deadline, I was just too tired to go on with it, what with First Year and then the writing competition. So I didn't finish it or turn it in. But I would talk about it to show my initiative." After a couple of dozen fruitless interviews, the student reexamined his "Tell me about yourself" response, and came to his own horrifying conclusion: "It wasn't telling interviewers about my great writing skills. It was telling them I was *lazy.*"

* * * CAREER LIMITING MOVE * * *

In response to an interviewer asking "Tell me about yourself," law student responds: "Well, it's not on my resume or anything, but I have a criminal record ..."

* * * CAREER LIMITING MOVE * * *

Interviewer: "Tell me about yourself."

Law student: "I'll try anything. I don't really stick with anything, though. I'm kind of a dilettante."

2. STEP TWO: DEVELOP ANSWERS TO DIFFICULT QUESTIONS YOU KNOW YOU'RE GOING TO GET

You've probably heard the classic advice to litigators: Never ask a witness a question if you don't know what the answer is going to be. No surprises. Your approach to interviews should be the same: The interviewer shouldn't ever ask you a question that catches you off-guard. Not to put an evil motive on interviewers, but the fact is that a large part of the interviewing process is designed to knock you off your game, to encourage you to say something that will eliminate you from contention. Auntie Kimmbo, on the other hand, is going to make sure that never, ever happens to you. We'll prep you for every difficult question you can get, so that you're *never* caught flat-footed.

You've already got your "Tell me about yourself" answer in your hip pocket. Let's talk about how you handle others.

A. THE MOST IMPORTANT POINT TO REMEMBER ABOUT ANSWERING ANY QUESTION IS THAT IT HAS TO REFLECT THE REAL *YOU*

When my son Harry's friend Bobby was three, his parents, Pam and Bob, took him to Disney World. Because two-year-olds get into Disney for free and three-year-olds cost about a thousand dollars a day, Pam told Bobby: "For today, you're two."

Bobby responded indignantly, "No, I'm not. I'm *three.*"

Pam said, "Yeah, usually. But today, if anyone asks, you're two."

So they successfully got into Disney. They were wandering around, and Bobby saw Snow White. He ran over to hug her.

"How old are you, little boy?" Snow White asked him.

"Well," responded Bobby, "Usually, I'm three. But today—I'm two."

I tell you this story by way of saying this: You'll make yourself crazy if you try to make yourself into another person when you interview. Smart interviewing isn't about putting on a front, kissing the interviewer's butt, saying the "right" thing. It's about being yourself . . . but being the smart, professional, engaging you—not the "say whatever pops into your head" you.

Let's face it. You're not one-dimensional. You have many strengths, weaknesses, many stories that you could tell to illuminate just about any character trait. What this section is all about is making sure that the *best* you is the one the interviewer sees, that the stories you tell about yourself are the most vivid, memorable ones you can think of.

I provide a lot of suggestions for wording answers in this section. They're ones that students have actually used. But those are just designed as a jumping-off point, so you can come up with your own answers, ones that are truly *you*. If you really start yanking interviewers' chains, if you talk about loving practice areas you can't stand and being down with the idea of working long hours when you have no intention of doing it, at best you'll wind up with offers for jobs you hate. This book is about getting jobs you'll love. So make sure that the answers you give are *smart* reflections of how you really feel!

B. AVOID "YES" OR "NO" ANSWERS. USE EXAMPLES, STORIES FROM SCHOOL, ACTIVITIES, OR WORK TO ILLUSTRATE YOUR POINTS

As Sue Gainen advises, "The only time you should give a one-word answer is to the question 'Have you recently been indicted?' "

Otherwise, take advantage of answers to make points about yourself. If an interviewer asks you, "Do you have any experience doing X?" and you don't, you can answer "No" and leave it at that . . . or you can say, "Not in an office setting. But I took part in a clinical program/I volunteered at the Bar Association/I took a CLE . . ." and elaborate on it. If an employer asks, "We pride ourselves on our hard work. Are you willing to work hard?" you can say (ideally) "Yes" . . . or you can say, "I'm used to hard work. I worked thirty hours a week during college to put myself through school. In law school, I've done X and X and X along with my school work."

So remember: Don't just answer questions. Use examples to back up your answers!

C. REMEMBER TO MAKE YOUR ANSWERS MEATY AND REAL

"I love the law," "I want to help people," are what you'd expect to hear from a wind-up doll. Make sure your answers demonstrate a realistic view of practicing law and life in general.

D. MEMORIZE YOUR RESUME, AND BE VERY FAMILIAR WITH YOUR WRITING SAMPLE

Case Western's Debra Fink advises you to be congruous; that is, everything—your writing sample, your resume, your references, the answers you give in interviews—has to match. She also points out that *anything* on your resume is fair game for an interviewer; in fact, some interviewers just look down your resume and pull out things to ask you. It's not the most imaginative approach to interviewing, but then, most legal interviewers aren't professional interviewers. So, as Kentucky's Drusilla Bakert points out, "Expect to be asked about your resume! Be prepared to respond in particular to things like chronological gaps, any weird job, personal experiences, grades, foreign experiences, and foreign languages."

Seattle attorney Jonathan Dichter was a stand-up comedian before law school. He reports, "I *always* got a question about it. 'Tell me a joke,' or 'What was it like being a performer?' I would segue that into talking about my courtroom skills. Some interviewers even tried to tell me a joke. I always laughed . . . of course."

So—take a cold look at your resume, and go through it line by line, thinking about what *you'd* ask as an interviewer. Why did you choose X as your college major? (Particularly if it was unusual you'll be asked about it. One student was a sculpture major; he'd talk in interviews about how it taught him problem solving. "It's just that then I was looking at a hunk of granite; now I'm looking at complex sets of facts.") Why did you get those grades? How did you do in so-and-so class? What did you do in X job? Why didn't you go back to that employer? If you send your transcript before the interview, be similarly prepped to discuss everything negative on it—succinctly.

What you want to avoid are stumbles and even worse, contradictions. If you contradict something you have in your resume or writing sample—or you say you left your last employer on good terms, and that employer says you were led out in handcuffs—you've got a problem. That's why it's so important not to fib, not even to stretch the truth on your resume. Feel comfortable with everything on it. Mock interviews are particularly useful for this, to make sure you answer smoothly.

In addition, make sure you have a pretty good idea of what your references and any employers on your resume will say about you. If necessary, give them a call or e-mail before you start to interview, to give them a heads-up that you're about to talk to new employers who may contact them. And if you have *any* qualms at all about what they might say, *talk to them first*. Apart from anything else, they'll respect the fact you had the cojones to call and talk to them, which by itself is likely to ameliorate anything they'd say about you—especially when they find out you're looking to become a lawyer!

If you interview over a period of time, go back occasionally and reread your resume, and review your writing sample.

* * * CAREER LIMITING MOVE * * *

Law student with a very full resume, tons of activities.

Interviewer: "Did you really do all of this?"

Interviewee: "No, but it doesn't matter."

E. GOOGLE YOURSELF ... OR, AS PRESIDENT BUSH THE YOUNGER WOULD SAY, USE "THE GOOGLE"

You google employers; it's only fair that they google you. Of course, what this means is that you've got to be able to explain every single mention of yourself on-line. I've heard of interviewers who greet students by holding out a download mentioning the student, and saying, "How do you explain *this?*" Golden Gate's Susanne Aronowitz says that "Associates at firms are routinely asked to search MySpace and review profiles of potential candidates. You've got to be careful!"

MySpace, FaceBook, other social networking sites and blog entries that seemed hilarious at the time might not be so advantageous in an interview setting. While we go into depth about on-line profiles and blogs in detail in the Internet chapter, it's worth mentioning here that you should consider deleting anything unprofessional on-line, for the duration of your job search. This would include—by way of painful example—any rants about your school, professors, or current/prior employers, how hammered you got last night, blunt assessments of the physical attributes of your classmates, and the fact that you want to hump all the players in the World Cup.

In short: before you interview, google yourself—and be prepared to discuss what you find!

* * * SMART HUMAN TRICK * * *

Employer who googled every student, and found one guy who'd apparently created a web site with a name along the lines of "pimpsnwhores."

In the interview, the employer mentioned the web site. The student laughed, and said, "I created that web site as part of a college class. You're the only one who's found it and linked it to me. Here's what the project was about ..."

The employer said later, "His explanation was excellent—it really made him shine. What could have been a deal-breaker turned out to be evidence of his ability to think quickly on his feet."

F. THE THREE MOST DANGEROUS WORDS IN INTERVIEW ANSWERS

I should preface this by reminding you that I've talked with thousands of students, hundreds of Career Services experts and hiring attorneys, and in every single case, the following three words herald a truly awful interview answer: *"To be honest ..."*

Those words—and their close relative, "To tell you the truth"—often indicate that you're about to share something you should *never, ever say in an interview.* "To be honest . . . I'm not sure I want to be a lawyer." "To be honest . . . I really hated working for that guy." "To be honest . . . that professor is an idiot." "To be honest . . . I just need to pay my bills."

You may think that this advice is at odds with my perennial caution never to lie in any aspect of your job search. But they're perfectly consistent. What you're presenting in every case is *the best possible you.* And I'm telling you right now that the best possible you is tactful, discreet, and professional—and doesn't just blurt out whatever comes into your head. Why is this so important? Because it's what your clients and colleagues will expect, and it's what you expect from other people! Think about it. If you were a potential client for a firm, and you went to them to talk about your case, would you welcome being told, "Holy crap! Your case *stinks!*" No. You'd expect them at the very least to say, "Based on what you've told me, we've got some serious challenges in pursuing your claim/defense, and I'll explain them to you."

Answering interview questions honestly *but intelligently* is a harbinger of how you'll handle yourself in professional situations. So watch out for those words: "To be honest . . ."

G. DON'T FREAK YOURSELF OUT ABOUT QUESTIONS YOU'LL NEVER GET. INTERVIEWERS CAN'T SEE INSIDE YOUR HEAD!

I often talk to students who are absolutely mortified about dealing with questions no interviewer will ever ask. One student, who'd worked for an absolutely horrible employer for a month before quitting, did the wise thing by leaving the experience off his resume. He asked me, "How am I going to deal with the question: 'Do you have any legal experience that isn't on your resume?'" I've heard about thousands of interviews and I have never, ever heard this question being asked. I told him, even if they *did* ask it, you'd be perfectly justified in saying, "It was such a brief experience that it gave me virtually no skills to bring to another job, which is why I left it off my resume."

Another student was terrified that employers were trying to get her to admit to a "starter" marriage she had as a teenager. I asked her why she thought so, and she told me, "My husband had a last name that's very common in our state [I'll call it Simmons, and let's say the state is Alabama]. I kept the name when we divorced. In interviews, they're always asking me, 'Simmons. Are you related to . . .' They keep asking me and asking me. I need to know how to bring up my marriage, because I know that's what they're getting at." You can see as well as I can that they're not getting at anything of the sort—they're just asking a perfectly natural question. I told her to smile and say, "I'm an Alabama girl and I get asked that all the time. I'm not related to so-and-so. There are just too many of us." She was so self-conscious of this early marriage, she assumed people could see through her!

In section (j) immediately below, we talk about the strategy for answering dozens of difficult questions. In a nutshell you talk about why anything negative about you won't affect your performance for a future employer. Read: You spin it. Don't make yourself *crazy* thinking about questions that loom large to you—but are unlikely ever to pop into an interviewer's head!

H. YOU CAN'T CONTROL THE INTERVIEWER'S IRRATIONAL RESPONSE TO A GREAT ANSWER. NO SINGLE ANSWER APPEALS TO *EVERYBODY*

If you follow the advice in this chapter, you'll go into interviews flawlessly prepared. That doesn't mean that what you say will appeal to every interviewer you encounter. No single answer *could*. Some people are just three standard deviations from normal, and there's no way to anticipate them.

One student at a Midwestern school had been an anti-terrorism marine before law school. He went on a hundred missions successfully, which as he explained, "Meant I came back alive." He said interviewers always asked him what he did, and he'd say, "It's top secret. I could tell you—but I'd have to kill you." He'd say it smilingly, and he said most interviewers laughed. "But one guy— stone cold silence. Man, it was *painful*."

A student at another Midwestern school was asked the question, "Who's your hero?" Now, there's no correct answer to this question, and the student had a perfectly appropriate response. He said, "My mom. She was from another country, and when she moved here she had to learn a new language and a new culture, and it required a lot of courage. I really respect her for it." He told me, "The interviewer just immediately shut down. It was like, 'Thank you and goodbye.'"

Now, how do you explain *that?* Maybe the guy hates his mom. Maybe he's Norman Bates. Who the hell knows. But that's the point. You *can't* know. You do your best to prep for interviews, and if the interviewer turns out to be a pod person, it's not your problem!

I. THE KILLER STRATEGY FOR HANDLING QUESTIONS ABOUT *ANYTHING* IN YOUR BACKGROUND THAT YOU DON'T LIKE

Everybody—and I mean *everybody*—has something in their past that they're not particularly proud of. You may think that there are people who have shiningly perfect credentials. There aren't. I always thought, for instance, that students who are #1 in the class are bulletproof in interviews. Not! I talked with one student, top of his class at a very prestigious school, and you know the question he got on interviews? "All A's. Don't you think you're a bit of a perfectionist?" Arrghhh!

Now, we're going to talk about specific strategies that you use for all kinds of flaws, but they're all based on a single premise. It's one that you already appreciate, from another aspect of your life. Namely, those ads you see on television for prescription drugs. You know the ones I'm talking about, the controversial ones: "Ask your doctor about ..." My brother Keir and I love to watch those ads because we like to talk about the side effects. That's our favourite part. He's seen an ad I've never seen. It starts out with an irresistible pitch: "Do you feel uncomfortable around large groups of total strangers?" That's a good market, isn't it? As far as I can tell, it's every adult in the United States of America. So this ad goes on, "You may be suffering from social anxiety disorder." Oh, I see. Then it goes on to sing the praises of some drug—I don't know the name of it, I'll call it Shynox—it extols the benefits of Shynox, winding up with the following words: "Of course, Shynox is not for everybody. Side effects may include nausea, tremors, sweating ... and explosive, unpredictable bowel movements."

Now, I don't know how nervous you were *before* about meeting new people. But can you imagine? You're at a social event, you're introducing yourself to somebody new, "Hi, my name is ... oops!" and you have to run out of the joint, like Cinderella as the clock strikes twelve.

My brother said he must have seen that ad half a dozen times without hearing those words "explosive, unpredictable bowel movements." Why is that?

Because they don't want you to.

That's why they use that mellifluous voice, the soothing music. When you get to the side effects, you're not listening ... because you're thinking about talking to your doctor.

The same principle applies in interviews. It's not the Achilles heel you have that will kill you.

It's the way you talk about it.

You can overcome any, and I mean *any*, flaw in your background, on your resume, you name it—if you figure out the words to use ahead of time. And that's what we're going to do here! Although the specific words we use will differ in each individual situation, the basic approach we'll use is this: ***For any difficult question, look at the issue behind the question, and address that, succinctly.*** For instance, let's take the grades question. We're going to go into detail about it shortly, but for right now, let's look at the issue behind the question "What happened to your grades?" It's this: "Are you competent?" For the out-of-town job search question, the issues are, "If you aren't from here and you didn't go to school here, how we know you'll take an offer if we make you one, and if you *do* take it, how do we know you'll stay?"

In addressing the issue behind the question, remember that your answer should show something positive about you; at the very least, it should show what you learned from a negative experience. If it was a bad work experience, what did you learn about dealing with a difficult boss/situation? If it was bad grades, what did you learn about studying or interpreting questions? **Talking about what you learned from any bad thing you've done is the absolute best way to redeem yourself.**

Finally, after you address the issue, be prepared to turn around and ask the interviewer a question. Faced with difficult questions, a lot of law students tend to ramble. Interviewers know that by not immediately filling in conversational "gaps," the interviewee often will—with something they didn't mean to say. "Although I don't intend to go back to Attorney X's office after graduation, I learned a lot about researching legal issues and dealing with clients." *Silence from interviewer.* " . . . and anyway—he was really disorganized. He didn't give me any feedback." So stick with your prepared answer, and when it's complete, if the interviewer doesn't jump in, turn around and ask the interviewer a question (I give you a lot of possibilities in Step Four, below). Otherwise, you might find yourself floundering around for the entire interview over an issue you didn't want to talk about in the first place!

So that's the strategy. Let's go into details about how you handle difficult questions you might face.

J. FORMULATING GREAT ANSWERS TO THE MOST DIFFICULT QUESTIONS

I read an interview with the great chef Jacques Pepin. He was asked about how to overcome cooking disasters, and two of his major tips were: Think about the menu, and prep as much as possible ahead of time.

The same goes for answering difficult interview questions. Based on your background, school, grades and the particular employer, think about issues that might give you trouble—I give you a thorough list of the likely candidates in this section—and prep your answers.

I hear from interviewers all the time that they don't go into interviews with an agenda. They're not looking for blood in the water. They ask what they think is a perfectly normal question— "How are your grades?"—*and the look on the student's face tells them everything they need to know.* Shock. Horror. Um . . . um . . . um . . .

The way you deliver your answers is as important as what you say. Having an answer you feel comfortable with is the *best* way to ensure that you won't have the deer-frozen-in-headlights reaction. In this section, we'll formulate those answers, so you can relax in interviews—and show interviewers the best possible you!

1. HOW ARE YOU?

Could a question be *easier?*

Hmm.

The principal point to remember is that in an interview, "How are you?" is merely a conversational opener. A nicety. **The *only* thing to convey in response is a pleasant smile, a firm handshake, and an indication of honest enthusiasm.**

"Fine thanks—and you?"

"Great!"

"Delighted to be here."

You can make up your own, but you see the idea: It's *not* an opportunity to talk about how you are—or convey anything other than enthusiasm.

No-nos:

"OK, I guess."

"Actually I'm not that good. I came down with the stomach flu last night and I was up all night with the Hershey squirts."

"You wouldn't believe the traffic on the way here! I was stuck between Exit 17 and 18 for an hour ..."

"Your stupid receptionist gave me the wrong directions ..."

"Exhausted!"

Just convey to the interviewer that you're happy to be there. After you answer, follow the interviewer's lead—either into pleasantries or the meat of the interview. It doesn't matter if a dam broke on your way to the interview and you had to swim the last five miles—"Fine, thanks" will do!

2. WHY AREN'T YOUR GRADES BETTER?

Grades, grades, grades. I hear about them occasionally ... maybe once or twice or ten thousand times a week. There's no question that we are absolutely grade obsessed. There's certainly a sense at most law schools that if you're not in the top ten percent of the class—and let's face it, ninety percent of us aren't—that there's no way to get a great job. I hear this issue broached in different ways. "Career Services doesn't do anything to help anyone but the top of the class," "Employers won't look at my resume because I'm not in the top ten percent," and so on.

Where does the obsession come from? We're not delusional. Look who gets on campus interviews. It's the top ten percent of the class, typically. And what do employers ask for in job postings? Top ten percent, top five percent, top whatever. We start getting the impression that grades are the only things that count. As Debra Fink points out, "This is a no-win question. If you're not #1 in the class, then you've got to say your grades don't indicate your ability. But if you *are* #1 in the class, then you'll be branded a perfectionist—and that's not good either!"

What makes this particular pony loaf stink even more is that we all know that your class is full of smart people—including you—and that while a job search for someone in the top 10% of the class and the 50th percentile of the class may be radically different, that huge GPA gulf can spring from a bad performance on one exam. What a rip!

I talk about handling the grades issue in detail in Chapter 13, "Help! My Grades Stink!" but for right now, let's just focus on how you deal with them in interviews. And we'll do that with the strategy I just taught you: We'll look at the issue behind the question.

The issue behind the grades question is, "Do you have the brainpower to do my work?" or even more succinctly, "Are you competent?" Well, of *course* you're competent. I don't care about your grades! But if the god of grades hasn't smiled on you, talk about what shows you *are* competent. More specifically . . .

a.   The Best Way to Respond.

This is, to some extent, circumstance-specific. If you *have* some tangible reason for your grades being below par—like a serious personal tragedy—say so. But word it *tactfully*. This is a situation rife with possibilities for TMI (Too Much Information). "I had to care for a sick relative who has since recovered" or "I had a health issue which is completely resolved"—wording like that is all you need—and follow it up with talking about your sterling performance otherwise, and follow *that* up with a question for the interviewer, to get you away from the topic.

But what if your bottom-90% performance isn't tied to a specific circumstance? Here's what you do: First of all, **acknowledge your grades, and acknowledge that you wish they were better** ("Look, my grades aren't what I wanted them to be, either!" "I didn't do well, and I'm not proud of it," "The grade god definitely didn't smile on me," "Boy, I'm sure glad I didn't have to take *that* report card home to Mom!"), **but go on to state that you don't think that your overall GPA is indicative of your abilities because** . . . and then pull out any of the positives you can from the following list. And note that when you do this, you're showing a sensitivity to the employer's underlying concern about your competence!

- Classes that you *did* excel in—particularly if they're ones that are relevant to the employer (e.g., Torts for an employer who does personal injury litigation, Crim for a prosecutor's office).

- Paper versus final exam courses—it helps to do better in paper courses, since writing ability is very important to legal employers.

- Clinics or academic-oriented extracurriculars in which you excelled. (As Sandy Mans points out, you can say something like, "I supplemented my class work with journal experience, where I learned ...")

- Work (paid or unpaid) experience where you've received great reviews.

- Certain tough profs for whom you performed well.

- The classic "upward trend in grades." Let's face it, the law school exam thing is tough. If it took you a semester or a year to figure it out before your grades improved, highlight that; employers care about what you're capable of doing for them, not what you did *then*.

- Show that it's just one or two classes that torpedoed you because you did particularly badly in them. But watch out! That draws attention to those problems, and you'll have to show that you did something about them, too— like talking to the professor, going back and looking at the exam and the material to see what you did wrong and correcting it, activities along those lines.

As Maureen Provost Ryan points out, "The key here is to stay positive! Don't make excuses. In fact, you can even say that! 'I don't want to make excuses about my grades. But what is indicative of my ability is ...'" and then move on to your list of positives. What you're doing when you pull out the positives, by the way, is to show that you are not defined by your grades! As George Washington's Laura Rowe Lane says, "Show that you're a well-rounded package, not a number with a decimal point!"

* * * SMART HUMAN TRICK * * *

Law student, dying to get into the prosecutor's office, goes on an interview there with a major obstacle to overcome: she has a D in Criminal Procedure. To make matters worse, the interviewer has her transcript.

The interviewer opens the interview by throwing her transcript at her, and saying, "How do you have the nerve to interview with my office when you have a D in Criminal Procedure?"

She responds, "I understand your concern. But I know Criminal Procedure inside and out. I knew everything that was tested on that exam. There were three equally-weighted questions. On one of them, the question itself asked for the result under the statutes. In class, we had always discussed the case law. So even though I knew the statutes, I automatically answered according to the case law. And I got it totally wrong. But I learned an important lesson: Read the instructions carefully! I'm never going to make *that* mistake again."

She gets the job.

* * * SMART HUMAN TRICK * * *

Student whose grades First Year were very good, except for a very low grade in Property. When asked about it by interviewers, he said, "I got bad exam-taking advice—from another professor, ironically. Before I took any exams, he told me to spend a third of my time outlining my answer and only then start to write. Well, I did that on my Property exam—and I only had time to write out two of the three questions. For the third one, I turned in my outline. I should have been writing from the start. And that's what I did in all my other classes, where I did fine."

b. Boners to Avoid.

1. Being thrown by the interviewer's attitude.

Remember: odds are 9 out of 10 that the interviewer was *also* not in the top 10% of his/her law school class (unless you're interviewing with a very large law firm). *Most* practicing attorneys, and some ultra-successful ones, weren't at the top of their class. If an interviewer puts you on the spot about your grades, it isn't necessarily because they're sneering down on you from Grade Olympus. They might just be grilling you to see how you respond to criticism, how you deal with having your feet held to the fire.

One student told me about an interview she had where the interviewer asked her about her grades, and before she could respond, he added, sarcastically, "Wait, don't tell me—your grades aren't indicative of your ability." She was momentarily thrown off, but she looked straight at him and said, "As a matter of fact—you're right. I'd be concerned about those grades if I were in your shoes, as well. But here's why you should hire me ..." and she went on to list her positives. She reported that the interviewer was completely taken aback by her confidence—and she wound up with a call-back interview!

2. Blaming the professor.

As Jose Bahamonde–Gonzalez advises, "Whatever you do, don't say, 'Oh, this prof's a jerk!'" Nobody wants to hire someone who puts the blame on someone else—even though it may be perfectly true that you got a rotten grade in Property because your professor was, in fact, a serious tool. *Mine* sure was! Instead, quickly acknowledge that you're not happy with your grade either, and *immediately* move to the positives. Making excuses doesn't encourage an employer to hire you—showing them what you can do for them, does!

3. Being coy.

Don't beat around the bush when you're asked about your grades. As Dave James recommends, avoid saying things like, "My grades are respectable," "I'm not in the top half." Come straight out with it!

4. Saying that law school exams don't prove anything.

We could argue this one until the proverbial cows come home, but it doesn't help you in interviews, for two reasons. For one thing, the interviewer isn't likely to have awesome grades, but if (s)he does—(s)he's probably going to disagree with you that "grades don't mean anything."

For another, it doesn't help you. Remember, whether it's by grades or by any other route, the interviewer is entitled to know why it is you'll be able to do the work. OK, maybe exams don't prove it—but it's up to you to bring to the table something that *does!*

5. Floundering.

Here's why prepping an answer to the grades question is so important. If you don't, you'll flop around like a fish in a boat, mumbling about "My grades don't define me," "I guess I should have studied more," and before you know it—your twenty minute interview is up and the interviewer still doesn't know why you can do the work. As Sandy Mans points out, "The worst thing to do is to hem and haw, and choke out, 'Well, I'm a C-range student ...' and trail off." Be comfortable with your grades, pull out the positives, and practice speaking with confidence about them. Remember: what matters is not so much what you've done, but your *attitude* about what you've done, the way you present it. You can't go back and change your grades, but you have complete control over the way you talk about them!

6. Highlighting a downward trend.

If you shot out of the starting gate at law school like a rocket and your grades have headed downhill since then, for gosh sakes, don't mention a trend at all! Instead, focus on journal experience or work experience—anything that shows your abilities and takes the focus off your grades!

7. Mentioning ongoing personal obligations.

When the factor that contributed to poor grades was a "one shot" event—the death of a relative, a divorce—you should mention it. But if it's an ongoing personal obligation that got in the way, like raising a family, be very careful. The specter you'll raise in the interviewer's mind is that you don't have enough time to do well in school, so you won't have time to do the employer's work, either. As Diane Reynolds advises, "Be sure to mention how many hours you *can* spend, like 60 hours a week," or say that you have live-in help now, or you've made other arrangements so you can dedicate yourself to your work as much as necessary.

8. Pretending you don't know what your grades are.

Interviewers always describe this to me as a real howler. "I'll be sitting there with a student, and I'll ask what his grades are like, and he'll look very thoughtful and say, 'You know, I really don't know,' as though he forgot to look or something!" Interviewers know as well as you do that you have your GPA and class rank tattooed on the inside of your eyelids. If they ask how you're doing and exam results have been posted, come clean, and highlight positives as necessary. Pretending you don't know is a weak fib!

3.   "WHAT'S YOUR GREATEST FLAW?"

This is the interview question where unwary interviewees go to die.

"What's your greatest flaw?" is possibly the most controversial question there is. Why? Because of the competing interests involved in the answer. On the one hand, you have honesty—and I've told you never to lie in interviews. But if your biggest weakness is your writing ability, or that you're lazy, or you think you're not too quick on the uptake, *you'd be a complete idiot to tell the truth!*

Instead, you have to view this question as the ultimate in interview game-playing. What the interviewer is really asking you is this: "Are you savvy enough to come up with an answer that doesn't torpedo you as a candidate for this job—yet is credible at the same time?" Stated another way: *"How well can you play this game?"* "What are you weaknesses?" is a lot easier to deal with if you look at it this way!

By the way—everyone knows this question sucks. So why do interviewers ask it? The answer isn't pretty. Remember, a large part of the interview process is not *choosing* candidates—it's *eliminating* them. One hiring partner even said, "How much easier can it get than asking someone what their flaw is, and having them tell you something that immediately eliminates them from contention?" Columbia's Ellen Wayne points out that "Once in a rare while a student will be honest and get tripped up, for instance, saying 'My writing skill isn't the best.' And the interviewer's mind will immediately go to that brief he's got to get out today. So it's a trap for the unwary!"

a. The best way to respond.

The all-time best response to this question comes from Rob Kaplan, who found it in a comic strip. The interviewer asks "What's your greatest flaw?" and the interviewee responds, "Lying in interviews." I *love* that, and it wouldn't hurt to lead off with it and then follow up with a more serious answer (if the interviewer isn't happy with the joke!). And for a *real* answer, the best response Career Services Counselors told me was this:

Highlight a past negative that you've corrected.

That is: choose something that's legitimately a flaw for you—but you've worked on it and overcome it.

Kathleen Brady gives this example: "Meeting deadlines. I never used to be able to do it. I did a lot of time management courses, and now I haven't missed any deadlines in law school." Another excellent possibility, courtesy of Maureen Provost Ryan and Sandy Mans, is "Shyness. I'm naturally shy. But I took steps to overcome it. I took on leadership positions while I was in college which forced me to do a lot of public speaking, and I joined the Debate Club, and I think I've licked it." A great advantage to the "shyness" idea, if it fits you, is that your very demeanor in the interview can bolster how well you've overcome it!

Deanna Coe Kursh suggests a similar one—public speaking. "I'm not a naturally gifted public speaker, but I recognize it and I get all the practice I can so that I can kick it." And Catholic's Amy Thompson volunteers this one: "I used to never be able to say 'no' to any project. In law school, I learned that between classes, Moot Court, and softball, I can't do everything. I can still do a lot, but I've learned to set priorities so that I don't drive myself crazy."

It's worth repeating that you can't just pick one of these that sounds good. They're examples meant to nudge your memory for things you've *genuinely* changed about yourself for the better.

Other than honesty, there's a strategic reason to use this approach. Namely: *if you name a flaw that you no longer have, it can't hurt you.* As we'll see with the "boners" list below, it's a mistake to think that there's an "innocent" flaw that won't hurt you in a law-related job. "I hate numbers" sounds good, but not when you realize that law is a business, and numbers are important. On top of that, answering with a flaw you've corrected leaves the interviewer without a follow-up. "Give me a flaw you haven't corrected?" Doesn't work, does it? Because you can legitimately answer, "I like to think there isn't any flaw about myself that I *haven't* worked on to improve." Hot damn, it's a good answer!

Now, it's not your *only* choice for an answer to the "flaw" question. **Humor often works**, like Rob Kaplan's "lying in interviews" gag. As Debra Fink says, "My favourite answer to this question is 'Chocolate. That's my weakness.'" She also says, "Company picnics. I just can't play softball!" A student at a law school in the Pacific Northwest would say, "I tend to add weight around the hips," and interviewers liked that. If you've got the kind of personality that can pull it off, humor can work for you. But remember, always have a more sober-sided answer available as a follow-up!

You could also use this answer to show off your comfort level with your credentials. For instance, if you're not happy with your grades, you can always smile and respond, "My grades!" Then you can explain, quickly, other experiences you've had that undercut your grades as a weakness—that is, job experience that shows you're competent, or specific classes in which you've excelled. Or, as Sophie Sparrow points out, you can say, "I haven't done as well as I wanted to, so I've been working with Professor X to correct that." Remember, you're not apologizing—but if you can confidently say that your grades are your weakness, briefly explain, and then quickly move on, you'll impress the interviewer with your honesty *and* your confidence.

If you have skimpy law-related experience on your resume, California Western's Lisa Kellogg points out that you can turn this to your advantage in answering the "flaw" question: **you can say that you don't have as much job experience as you'd like**—but clearly by looking for a job you're trying to remedy that. And you can even joke that with the interviewer's help, you can overcome your weakness!

You could also use a weakness the interviewer has already brought up. For instance, if the interviewer has already pointed out your grades or lack of experience or lack of paper classes or your lack of connections with the city where his/her firm is located, (s)he's dropped the answer to your "greatest weakness" squarely in your lap! You can just say, "As you've already pointed out, a weakness for me is ..." reiterate whatever the flaw is, and then explain what you've done (or what you're doing) to ameliorate it. That way, you're not exposing *another* flaw when you've already got one you can use!

* * * SMART HUMAN TRICK * * *

Female law student, petite, soft-spoken, and *very* youthful-looking. She wanted litigation and she knew her appearance worked against her. She said, "I know when interviewers look at me they think I look like a doll. On my first interview with a prosecutor's office, I came right out and said, 'I know how I come across. But I can surprise opposing counsel. Because I'm soft-spoken they have to lean in to listen to me. And because they underestimate me they under prepare, and it's easier for me to win."

She got the job.

* * * SMART HUMAN TRICK * * *

Interviewer asks law student the question, "If I called your last employer, what's the worst thing he would say about you?" Student responds, "He'd tell you that my worst flaw is that there was only one of me. He'd like a hundred people like me!"

The interviewer laughed. And P.S.: The student got the job.

b.   Boners to avoid.

1.   Turn a negative into a positive.

What's the traditional advice? Every time I'm asked about how to answer the "greatest flaw" question in my Guerrilla Tactics seminars, every law student in the room answers in unison: "Turn a negative into a positive." That is, choose a flaw that's really not a weakness at all. If you read job search books very much, you've seen this answer a hundred times. And we all know the answers they're talking about, right? "I'm a perfectionist," or "I'm a workaholic. I just don't know when to stop working. I don't go home until everything gets done." I love that. "I'm a workaholic. My grades stink and I'm not in any extracurriculars, but I'm a workaholic." No, I'm not. I'm *delusional.*

It's just a crappy, crappy answer, and here's why. For one thing, it's not true. Great interviewing isn't about lying; it's about presenting the best possible you. And the best possible you isn't a liar. On top of that, every interviewer knows it's a horse dung answer. Some interviewers will try and smoke you out by asking variations on the theme. I've heard interviewers ask, "Other than being a perfectionist or a workaholic—what's your greatest flaw?" Others ask, "What are your *three* greatest flaws?" They know that once you get past those two, workaholism and perfectionism, there *aren't* any others on the list. Number three will be the truth! "I steal office supplies."

Incidentally, I'm not suggesting that no one's ever tried to come up with a positive/negative other than perfectionism or workaholism. But the alternatives I've heard aren't any better. I talked to a charming young man at one law school, who told me that he'd interviewed with dozens of law firms with no success. I asked him if he noticed a point in the interviews where things seemed to go awry, and after thinking about it for a moment, he said, "I think it's when they ask that 'What's your greatest flaw?' question." I asked him what his response was, and he said, "Well, I take a negative and turn it into a positive, like you're supposed to. I say it's my passion. It makes me throw myself into what I'm doing, but then I forget about everything else." Horrified, I told him the advice I'd heard from employers: "Don't mention the word 'passion' in interviews! You're thinking about work, and they're thinking that you're a walking sexual harassment suit!" When he chose another flaw to talk about—one, of course, that he'd worked to overcome!—call-backs and offers came his way.

2. *Any* job-related skill.

Don't be an idiot and offer as a weakness anything even remotely like the following real-life examples:

"I don't like research."

"I can't write worth a damn." (At best, as Deanna Coe Kursh points out, you can say that other people are happy with your

writing, but you're not satisfied. Be careful—this is a loaded gun.)

"I'm always late."

"I procrastinate."

"I can't manage my time very well."

"I have trouble setting priorities."

"I can't say no."

"I really like to be home by 5:30 to watch the news."

"I'm a night owl—I don't get rolling until 11 a.m."

"I don't respond well to authority."

"I'm not motivated."

These all relate directly to your ability to thrive in most law-related jobs. As Diane Reynolds says, "You can't respond with *anything* that will stop you from functioning!" And Wendy Werner adds, tongue planted firmly in cheek, "It's important to 'lie' appropriately! You can't say you're stubborn or you've got a bad temper!" You may get an "A" for honesty, but with a large pool of prospective employees who *don't* have your skill-related flaw, you won't get the job, because you didn't play the game well!

Now notice that if any of these really are your flaws, you have two choices: work on them *right now* to overcome them, so that you can answer with the "I used to have this flaw . . ." *or* make sure that you look for jobs consistent with your weaknesses. For instance, if you hate research, interviewing for judicial clerkships is a really bad idea—where research is the coin of the realm. If you really insist on being home early every night, don't interview for jobs that require longer hours (read: large law firms). Contrary to popular belief, there are lots of law-related jobs that require a normal workday much of the time; most attorneys' general's office jobs, many prosecutors' offices, trusts and estates practices, many small law firms.

If you have that great a problem with authority, then consider hanging out your own shingle, or go into an office-sharing arrangement with a practitioner to get your feet wet.

You see my point. No matter how you go about it—don't answer with a job-related flaw!

3. "Stealth" job-related flaws.

These are a little trickier because it won't seem as obvious that they'll hurt your chances at getting a job. That's why I call them "stealth" flaws.

For instance, let's say you really don't like working with numbers, and that's why you went for your JD instead of an MBA. And you figure it's not job-related, so it's OK to mention it as a flaw. Gail Peshel cautions you to "Be careful! Saying you don't like working with numbers can infer that you don't like detail work, and that's what a lot of lawyers, especially new ones, have to do."

Or let's say that your problem is that you're bored with law school, or you hate your classes. Not directly job-related—but the interviewer could easily surmise that if you're bored with your schoolwork, you'll be bored with the employer's work, as well—so you won't do a good job of it.

Of course, as with everything to do with interviewing, the way you *present* the flaw determines how it will affect your chances. If you say that you're bored with law school because you can't wait to get your career underway, *that's* not going to hurt you—it shows your enthusiasm!

4. Arrogance.

Humour works. A humble "I've worked on this flaw" works. Refusing to answer—in any form—doesn't. "I don't have any flaws." R-r-r-right.

Similarly, saying "There's nothing for which you shouldn't hire me" is an in-your-face response that'll piss off the interviewer. *Tell* them about the flaw, and let them come to that conclusion *themselves*.

5. Anything that's an obvious lie.

Do you notice a theme developing with this "lying" business? I told you not to do it on cover letters, on your resume, and now in interviews. There's a big difference between presenting the best possible you, and lying. As Ann Skalaski says, "If your writing sample is awful and you say you're a perfectionist, the interviewer will *know* what your *real* flaw is—a lack of candor!" So don't choose as a weakness anything that's an obvious fib!

6. Mental illness or addictions.

Kathleen Brady says of the interview room that "This isn't therapy." An interview is not the place to talk about your drinking problem or your medicated schizophrenia. The problem with serious personal flaws is that they loom so large that the interviewer will be afraid that your personal problems will intrude on your work. On top of that, in an interview situation—where you've got twenty minutes to present the best you—is just not the place to get into very personal issues. Use this as a barometer: If you wouldn't mention it on a first date, don't mention it on an interview.

What about problems that bear on your job performance? I talked to a student at one law school who said she had Munchhausen Syndrome, such that she always looked bored. (I didn't think that's what Munchhausen Syndrome was, but that's what she said.)

She asked, "How do you converse when you have no social skills?" There are three things to remember about serious personal issues: One, don't interview for jobs where your problem is formidable. A person who always looks bored shouldn't be in a job that relies on heavy personal contact, like doing intake interviews at a legal aid office or counseling clients. Two, be prepared to talk about what you've done/can do to compensate for it. Three, do your research and find practitioners who've overcome the same issue. Trust me, no matter what's up with *you,* someone with the same challenge is doing what you want to do (and if you seek them out, by the way, they often make great mentors).

The bottom line is: choose a job-related flaw that you've worked on to overcome, and/or come up with a humorous answer, as we've discussed before. And undertake some mock interviews, asking specifically that the interviewer ask you the "greatest flaw" question, so you feel absolutely comfortable answering it.

7. Drawing a blank and saying nothing.

It worked for Dubya. Remember the press conference where President Bush was asked about any mistake he'd made, and he couldn't think of one? Well, he already had the job of his dreams. You don't. As Maureen Provost Ryan says, "The worst thing you can do when someone asks your weakness is to stop dead in your tracks, like a deer frozen in headlights." You have to come up with something.

* * * CAREER LIMITING MOVE * * *

Law student in an on-campus interview in the Pacific Northwest.

Interviewer: What's your greatest flaw?

Student: I pick my nose.

c. Once you've given your answer, ask the interviewer a question or shut up. *Don't fill the silence.*

The point behind having an answer prepared is that you not blurt out anything you didn't want to say.

I talked with one student in Kansas who'd interviewed for a library job she really wanted. She was depressed about it, and said, "The interviewer just sat there after I talked about my flaw. I was so nervous I blurted out, 'I have a learning disability.' I could see from the look on her face that I lost the job right there."

Don't be thrown from your game by silence. Answer succinctly, ask a question in response—and that's it.

4. WHAT ARE YOUR STRENGTHS?

A softball! In any one of its guises—the interviewer may ask, for instance, "If we called your last employer, what would they say your strengths were?"—the interviewer is really asking you, "What can you do for us—and what have you done that proves that?"

a. The Best Way To Respond.

You've already been there, done that. **The answer we talked about formulating for "Tell me about yourself" is tailor-made for "What are your strengths" as well.** Just leave off the personal hobby or interest and you've got your answer!

Incidentally, I have a personal story that involves this particular question. I somehow got an on-campus interview with a prestigious law firm while I was in school. I won't tell you who it was other than to say it was Jones Day. And they sent a big hoo-ha out to do the interviews. He might even have been their national hiring partner. He asked me, "What's your greatest strength?" Because I was a moron—and of course in many ways still am—I responded confidently, "My sense of humor." Ha ha. His face fell, and it was obvious that the interview was effectively over. So I asked, "Just out of curiosity—what do you think is the best strength a law student could have?" He brightened, and responded, "Judgment. Good judgment. Because if you have good judgment, it affects everything you do."

Needless to say, in every interview after that ... guess what my greatest strength was? The problem was, of course, that you have to have the record to back it up. If you took part in the International Beer Bong Championships rather than studying for finals in undergrad ... well. Judgment ain't your best trait, Babe!

b. A cautionary note about using "Sense of humour" as an asset ...

Although most employers will say they look for people with a sense of humour, and you might have a *wonderful* sense of humour, it's important to **couch it in professional terms** if you bring it up in an interview. That's because humour is a double-edged sword. You may be *le plus ultimate avec les bons* *mots,* or you may be the one more interested in cutting up than getting your work done. If you *do* use sense of humour, then, talk about how it's been useful in leavening tense situations. For instance, something like "One of my best traits is my sense of humor. In fact, I was elected class clown in high school, on the basis of a humor column I wrote for the high school paper. I've had a lot of jobs where I've worked with people who were very tense, and my sense of humor has always given me the ability to help calm them down." You see the point: you're showing how your sense of humour would be helpful in a work situation.

c. Boners to Avoid.

If job related strengths are the best, then logically the thing to avoid is strengths that won't do your prospective employer any good. For instance, as Laura Rowe Lane points out, "Don't say your strength is that you're patient. That doesn't really have anything to do with the law." Similarly, your proficiency with a particular audience—you're good with children, you've spent a lot of time volunteering with the elderly—isn't helpful to employers *who don't serve clients in those groups.*

* * * CAREER LIMITING MOVE * * *

Interviewer asks student, "What's your greatest strength?" and the student responds, "Working under pressure." Not bad, but he adds: "I *have* to be. I procrastinate so much I have to get everything done at the last minute!"

* * * CAREER LIMITING MOVE * * *

Interviewer: "What's your greatest achievement?"

Interviewee: "I acted as my own attorney and beat a felony rap."

* * * CAREER LIMITING MOVE * * *

Interviewer: "What's your best accomplishment?"

Interviewee: "Being found mentally fit to stand trial."

5. WHY SHOULD WE HIRE YOU?

Yet another twist on the "Tell me about yourself" theme. It's only slightly different, in the way that the interviewer is likely to use it. As Ann Skalaski points out, "It gives the interviewer ammo to take back to the hiring committee to make a pitch for you!" That makes it very important to you!

How to answer it? As Pam Malone recommends, "Answering this is a combination of 'can do' and 'will do' factors. You *can* do this job because of your experience, exposure, and abilities. And you *will* do it because of your willingness to work long hours, your thoroughness, and things like that.''

a. The best way to respond.

If they haven't asked you yet about your strengths or asked you the "Tell me about yourself" question, start with that answer (minus the hobby or interest). If they *have* already asked you about your strengths, then you can start your answer by saying, "Well, for one thing, the strengths I told you about before are a definite positive. But apart from that ..." and go into the elements I list below, for those that honestly apply to you. As you can see, these points strongly overlap with the kinds of elements you probably already have in your infomercial:

- You're willing to work hard.

- You'll be loyal to them because they gave you an opportunity.

- You're enthusiastic.

- You'll be committed to your work, because you've done your homework and you know theirs is the kind of practice you want to be associated with. (Of course, this means you have to have done that research first!)

- You're interested in building and developing clients (in other words, rainmaking), if the employer is a small to medium-sized private firm.

- You're easy to work with.

- You're willing to assume responsibility.

- You're diligent.

- Any experience you have that is directly transferable, e.g., research you did for a professor in an area of practice that the firm practices, a note or article you wrote on a similar area, or exposure to the same kind of client base through a clinic, internship, or prior work experience.

Debra Fink adds that if you can carry it off, once you've finished with your brief explanation of why they should hire you, smile, and add to your response something like, "I guess that leads naturally to the question—why should I work for you?"

* * * SMART HUMAN TRICK * * *

Interviewer: "Give me two reasons not to hire you."

Law student: "If I could give you two reasons not to hire me, I wouldn't be here wasting your time."

b.   Boners to avoid.

"Why should we hire you?" is a real hornet's nest, because there are several tempting ways to get stung if you get away from the idea of simply accentuating the positives you bring to the firm. Here's an idea of what you should avoid:

1.   Arrogance!

Arrogance is one of employers' prime complaints about law students. I'm sure you're *not* arrogant, but a clumsily-worded answer can give the impression that you *are*. What you want to do is to give confident answers that *imply* you're the best person for the job, without coming out and *saying* it. It's the difference between saying "I'll be loyal and committed to my work" and saying "I'm the best there is." The former works; the latter doesn't. As Ann Skalaski advises, "Temper your answer with humility! 'I know I don't know about practicing law, but here are the qualities I have that I hope will make me successful . . .' is the kind of tone you should aim for."

* * * CAREER LIMITING MOVE * * *

Law student in on-campus interview: "I don't care who else you're interviewing, I've got the best credentials for this job."

2.   Comparing yourself to other students.

This is a very ugly trait. I see it flare up occasionally when I visit law schools, and it makes otherwise attractive law students into real ogres. At one school I visited, there was a line of students waiting to talk to me after I gave a "Guerrilla Tactics" seminar. A guy at the end of the line was clearly impatient, rolling his eyes and making that clicking sound with his tongue as his classmates talked. As it happened, the woman in front of him—a classmate of his—was very reserved, and choked out her question for me very softly. As I was answering her, this guy cut in, and said to her, "Can you hurry it up? Some of us have *important* questions!" Can you feature it? Ironically, as it turned out, his question was, "I have so much more experience than these other students. I speak three languages. I've worked in other countries. I've got everything over them. But I keep going on interviews and I'm not getting jobs. Why?" Duh! I wonder!

The words "Compared to . . ." "More than . . ." just shouldn't ever show up in your interview patter. Putting down other people in interviews doesn't make you look better; it makes you look insecure.

Instead, focus on the specific, positive qualities you'll bring to the job—and let the interviewer draw the conclusion that you're the best person for it!

3.   Letting the employer feel like a name on a list.

While you will, of course, perform well for an employer who gives you a chance, don't make it sound like you're so desperate for a job that you'll take anything from anyone. Instead, as Jose Bahamonde-Gonzalez says, "Make them feel unique." There's a big difference between saying that you'll be loyal to them because, from your research about them, your skills are the kind of thing they've looked for in the past—and saying "I'll be loyal to anybody who gives me a job."

Remember—to the interviewer, the employer is the best place in the world to work (and if they don't feel that way, they *want* to feel that way!). If you bolster that idea, you're way ahead of the competition.

* * * CAREER LIMITING MOVE * * *

Interviewer: "Why should we hire you?"

Law student: "I'll be your slave."

6.   WHAT WILL YOU BE DOING 5 (OR 10) YEARS FROM NOW?

I know what you're thinking—"Well, excuse me while I pull out my tarot cards, so I can read my future and tell you." Virtually everybody acknowledges that it's a stupid question. As Tammy Willcox says, "No one admits that what they *really* want is to win the lottery and be sitting in the Caribbean drinking rum punch!" So, you may be wondering: Then why the heck does anybody ask it? Because there's a legitimate concern behind it. What they're really asking you is, "If we make you an offer, are you going to accept it, and are you committed to staying with us for the foreseeable future?" Remember, as a rule of thumb it takes an employer three years to earn back their investment in training you. So when they ask you what you intend to be doing 5 or 10 years from now, they're checking to see if you have any plans now *not* to be with them, then.

a.   The best way to respond.

I don't mean to sound glib, but to some extent your answer depends on what your plans *are* five or ten years from now. Here's what I mean. If you don't have anything that will *certainly, definitely* take you away from working for the employer in the next five years or so, you'll answer one way. And if you *do* have definite plans to leave them within that time— you've got another answer.

1. If you could *theoretically* be with the employer five or ten years from now . . .

If you're without-a-shadow-of-a-doubt certain of where you want to be five years from now, and you're interviewing with that particular kind of employer, you've been given a great gift. You can look the interviewer straight in the eye and say, "I'll tell you exactly what I want . . ."

But my hunch is, that's *not* you. Why? Of the thousands of law students who've talked to me, 99% of them have *no clue* where they'll be five or ten years from now. When I was in law school, *I* sure didn't. Welcome to the human race! It may be that you think you want to get your feet wet in law for a couple of years, and then do what you really want. Join the circus, run your own business, whatever. Or it could be you're thinking of starting a family, and want to devote yourself full-time to the world's most rewarding job. Or you want to leave a big-bucks large law firm and work in public interest. And as Tulsa's Jennifer Flexner points out, "Most people leave their first job after two years, no matter *what* they thought beforehand."

So it doesn't matter what you think you *might* be doing. Let's say that you wind up working with the employer you're interviewing with. If you turn out loving it, is anything concrete going to stop you from being there five years from now? If the answer is "no," then "The best answer is not necessarily the answer inside your soul," advises Nancy Krieger. Instead, you have to answer with something that meshes your natural uncertainty with what you could realistically see yourself doing.

Your answer has four elements:

a. Acknowledge that you don't know for sure;

This probably reflects exactly how you *do* feel, and there's nothing wrong with opening with it. As Teresa DeAndrado points out, "There's nothing wrong with saying that 'Life happens and no one can guarantee *what* will happen," or, as Jose Bahamonde—Gonzalez puts it, "It's OK to acknowledge that you don't know for sure, by saying something like, 'It's hard to make that forecast now because I'm just starting out,' as long as you go on to say something more definite, like 'Five years of practice in this specialty, and ideally with a firm like yours.' "

b. State that you intend to be where the employer is (with a couple of caveats);

For most private employers, geography is of prime importance. In fact, that's the principal issue with out-of-town job searches—"Why do you want to be here?" is on the top of the interviewer's mind. This is especially true for employers with one office, typically small to medium law firms. It's *pretty* important for large law firms, although they're more interested in knowing you want to join their particular practice.

So here are the rules of thumb:

- If you are looking for jobs in more than one city, that *may* come out in the interview, and so you *cannot* state that you want to be in any particular place. In that case, you *have* to stress that you want to be with a certain type of practice, and that you're geographically flexible.

- If you are looking for jobs in just one city, certainly state "I want to be a member of this community." It's a huge selling point for you!

- If you are looking for a public interest job or a very narrow specialty that is only practiced in a few places, then it's fine to stress that you really want to be doing this kind of work. For instance, if you want to do private international law, you're likely to be willing to work in the coastal cities where most international work is done (I know, I know, there's international law everywhere, but it's certainly concentrated on the East and West coasts). Similarly, if you want to do Intellectual Property, certain places like Silicon Valley are obvious targets.

If, on the other hand, you want to be a federal prosecutor, your desire to do that kind of work will trump your geographic commitment to any one city, since there's only one prosecutor's office in any one place and you're likely to be a little more flexible as a result. Also, there are federal agencies that expect you to "rotate" every few years, and a willingness to do that is a plus for you (but you'll know that from your research about the employer up front!)

c. Stress your career development at an employer *like* them;

As Diane Reynolds says, "Your answer has to be within the employer's ball park." So saying you want to be "working with a firm (or organization) like yours." If you're interviewing with a government agency, Lisa Kellogg advises you to say something like, "I plan on staying in the public sector."

You also want to mention career growth there. For a private firm, you want to talk about developing your expertise, gaining more responsibilities, and—in a small-to-medium firm, where client development is more immediate than at a large firm—you want to talk about building a clientele.

In a prosecutors' office, where you might start out prosecuting misdemeanors, they'd question your sanity if you said you wanted to go on doing that for five or ten years. It's just a springboard! You'd choose something more challenging, like, say, prosecuting complex litigation, or whatever else rings your chimes. Or you can talk about how you want to progress to new challenges. They'll eat that stuff up.

d.   Turn around and ask a related question.

Remember, asking the employer a question to follow up an answer is a great way to get yourself off the hot seat. Debra Fink advises that as soon as you're done with your answer, **ask " 'Of those who started with you five (or ten) years ago, what are they doing now?'** It tells you a lot about turnover!" Or, as Wendy Werner suggests, you can ask them, "Are you doing what you thought you'd be doing five (or ten) years ago?" This is another good comeback, as long as you don't ask it with an "in your face" tone of voice!

2.   If something will *definitely* prevent you from working for them five or ten years from now ...

You have a spouse in the military. Or your fiancé(e) is in medical school, and you'll have to follow him/her to a job when (s)he graduates. If you've got definite plans that mean you can't be working with the interviewer five or ten years from now ...

Remember: Things change. I can't tell you how many students have told me, "I thought we'd be moving ..." Med students fall in love with a city and get a residency in town after all. People leave the military. They get divorced. The short answer is, you don't *know* for sure where you'll be. As Hastings' Sari Zimmerman points out, "Five years is a *long* time." Furthermore, as SUNY Buffalo's Lisa Patterson advises, "80% of law school grads have left their first jobs within five years. You're highly unlikely to be there after five years no matter *what* you thought up front!"

So be discreet! It's perfectly fine to say what you intend to be doing *for the foreseeable future,* and then answer with the four elements we discussed above.

* * * CAREER LIMITING MOVE * * *

Summer clerk, large law firm on the West Coast. She blabs to all of her fellow summer clerks that she and her fiancé will be moving to New York when he finishes business school. Word gets back to the hiring partner at the firm.

No offer.

3. If you'll be available for no more than two years after graduation ...

Having talked with a lot of experts about this issue, two years seems to be the cutoff for "fessing up" about your future plans. That is, if your plans will take you away from the employer within two years ... say so.

I hear you, I hear you. "What are you, Kimmbo–*nuts?*" you're saying. "How the heck am I going to get a job if I tell them *that?*" Well, before you question my sanity any further, let me explain this advice.

For a start, if you don't tell them, you're lying—which will make you uncomfortable, if nothing else—and they're going to smoke you out soon enough. Let's play this scenario through to its logical end to see what I mean. You lie in the interview about your spouse in medical school, or you just don't say anything about it at all. You get the job. And within a month or so, there's a firm-wide cocktail party, spouses invited. You dutifully drag yours along, and at the party the two of you are chatting with a partner at the firm and his wife. The wife asks your spouse, "So—what do you do?"

"I'm in medical school, I'll be finishing up next year," responds spouse.

"Really?" sez partner's wife. "What specialty will you be going into?"

"Proctology," responds spouse.

Assuming that doesn't cut the conversation dead, partner cuts in, and asks, "Where will you be doing your residency?"

Spouse responds, "I have no idea. It could be anywhere in the country."

Oops.

Unless you intend that you and your spouse are going to live apart for a few years—and, truly, that's going to be hard for anyone to believe—it's immediately clear what you did: you hid a really important fact about yourself and your availability to work for the employer into the foreseeable future. To ladle it on even more: You expected them to pony up to train you—no small commitment—with no intention of allowing them a return on that investment. *And the minute they find out about your spouse's plans, they'll know immediately that you knew all along—and you deliberately misled them.* Not only will you have torpedoed your reputation at work, but you've destroyed any possibility of having them as mentors, references, and possible conduits for future jobs. You didn't just burn that bridge—you nuked it.

Let's look at the alternative. Instead of misleading employers, let's say that you include in your cover letter the fact that you're available for one or two years, and *perhaps* after that. As Tulsa's Vicky Jordan points out, "The best of all worlds would be if you move to a city where the employer has another office."

Certainly, there are going to be employers who'll say that if you're not available for a possible lifetime gig, forget it. *But there are many employers who won't say that.* Vicky Jordan advises that "Many employers, although they won't often come straight out and tell you, will find it a relief that they won't have to make a partnership decision about you. The fact that you're available for a set period of time is a plus." On top of that, you'll be living honestly. You'll be able to turn to people at this employer as mentors, references, and leads for your next position, wherever it is. And frankly, isn't that a better alternative than having to lie to people?

Furthermore, there are plenty of jobs, plenty of *great* jobs, that have a built-in time limit, and you should definitely look into those. Judicial clerkships—fabulous. Contract lawyering positions. Fellowships.

In fact, the whole "What do you plan to do ..." question is often only tough because you're uncomfortable with the truth. I talked to a student in Michigan who was looking for a job in Detroit. She said, "Why does *everybody* ask me, 'When are you going to quit and have kids?'" It turns out she was in her mid–30s and did, indeed, plan to quit in two years to have kids, take time off, and then come back to the law. She seemed greatly comforted by the idea of being honest with employers and looking for two-year gigs. She said, "I've just felt so dishonest. I know I haven't come across well because of it."

So don't look at your "limited time offer" as something to hide. Be honest about it. You'll still get a great job. And you'll feel a lot better about yourself!

b. Boners to avoid.

Mistakes students make in answering the "crystal ball" question tend to fall into three categories:

1. **Anything that suggests you're in for two years and then you'll bail out (if you've suggested you're available for the foreseeable future).**

... Although, as Maureen Provost Ryan points out, "Everybody knows that most people are out the door in two years!"

So you want to avoid saying things like, "I intend to have my own practice." What the employer hears is: "I intend to steal your clients." You'll also fumble the ball if you mention you intend to be in a city where the employer doesn't have an office. Or that you're using this job as a stepping stone into politics, or that you intend to be floating down the Amazon, or that you want to get training with this law firm before you save the world in a public interest job.

The watchword here: Don't say anything that suggests you have *concrete plans* to do something *other* than working for this employer!

2. **Anything too specific.**

This runs contrary to the advice you usually see in this book, doesn't it? After all, laser-targeting employers with specific research is really valuable. But when it comes to crystal-ball gazing, you've got to downshift and be less specific. So don't say anything like "Working for you," or even more boldly, "Doing your job." It comes across as flip and arrogant. Soften it a bit. Mary Obrzut suggests something like, "Working in a firm like yours, doing what you do, right here." Can you see the difference? It's general enough to be believable, while still indicating a sincere interest in working with the employer.

3. **Quality of life issues.**

Let's face it: the only way to be happy in your career is to create the right work/life balance. That's a great life philosophy, and a really crappy interview answer. Saying that you intend to balance work and family is an interview turn-off. Why? As Lisa Abrams explains, "The interviewer is interested in your commitment to the firm, so don't say anything like, 'I want to be working part-time.'" Remember: job searching is about showing the employer what's in it for them, so keep your answer on the "professional" side of your life!

* * * CAREER LIMITING MOVE * * *

In an interview with a San Francisco law firm, a young woman in response to the "where do you want to be five years from now?" question responded:

"I intend to be living with my husband, in Oregon, raising a family."

* * * CAREER LIMITING MOVE * * *

Interviewer from a high-powered law firm asks a law student, "What do you expect to be doing five years from now?" and hears in return: "I'm from Southern California, and we don't think past the weekend."

4. If it's not your dream job ...

You don't lie. But what you *do* is to talk about the skills you're looking forward to learning. Don't mention the things you don't think you'll like; focus exclusively on positives.

5. If they keep hammering you about it ...

It's probably because they question your sincerity. If you're interviewing for a job that is:

- At odds with your background;

- In a city with which you have no obvious connection;

- Way below your credentials (e.g., paralegal jobs)

... they'll be saying to themselves, "Is (s)he for real?" If you are—then stick to your guns!

I talked to a recent graduate of a West Coast law school who'd taken a temp job as a stop gap after graduation. It turns out she *loved* temping—she liked the flexibility, the reasonable hours, the swanky digs, the feeling that she wasn't tied down to anything permanently. She wanted to move to the East Coast and in a couple of interviews with temping outfits she felt that they didn't believe her goal was to stay a temp. I told her, "Stand your ground! You're telling the truth. Explain what you like, and if they're skeptical, stick to it anyway. You can always acknowledge their doubts and say, 'I know it's an unusual goal but it's how I really feel.' "

7. What Do You Know About Us?

Research strikes again! The research I implore you to do in preparation for interviews is going to bail you out of so many questions that most people consider difficult—including this one. If you've done your research—going to the employer's web site, googling them, asking Career Services and upperclassmen about them—you're going to rocket this question out of the park.

a. The best way to respond.

What you want to do is to smile, and say something initially that indicates your enthusiasm. Something humorous will do.

"Well—how much time do you have?" is a good one. "Just about everything except your astrological sign ..." I could go on, but you see the point. And **the things you want to mention about the employer are *things of which they're the most proud.*** You'll particularly find this in sections on employer web sites directed toward clients.

Also, if you've got good "humint"—that is, you've talked with Career Services/alumni/upperclassmen/practitioners and found out good things about this employer—dish! "I learned in talking with Jojo Phlebitz, who clerked with you last summer, that you ..." and so on. Showing that you've gone to the trouble of talking to people about an employer implicitly shows your level of enthusiasm for them!

Incidentally, if you're interviewing with an employer on whom you just couldn't find anything—you're responding to a job ad, it's a small employer in another city, all of your research avenues turned up dry—say that. "To tell you the truth, I did what I could to find out more about you"—and explain your research efforts—"with no luck." Then respond with what interested you about the posting: "In your posting, you mentioned practice area/city/qualifications, and that's why I'm here. I look forward to learning more from you." If you show that you made an effort to learn about them, you've accomplished all you need.

* * * SMART HUMAN TRICK * * *

Student interviewing for a summer legal intern job with a police department in a small town near her law school. The interviewer asks her "What do you know about our town?" As it turns out, as part of her interview preparation, she went to the town's chamber of commerce web site and knew everything about its history, back to the settlers who founded it! As she begins to rattle off this history, the interviewer sits back in his chair, and after a minute, says, "*I didn't know any of that—and I live there!*"

She gets the job.

b. Boners to avoid.

1. A blank stare.

That's what most employers expect. Or the functional equivalent of a blank stare: "Nothing—I was hoping you could tell me." The interviewer will think: "How much could you want this job if you didn't try to find out anything about us?" Don't let it happen to you!

* * * CAREER LIMITING MOVE * * *

Student in interview for a legal internship with a police department in a small town near her law school. The interviewer asks her, "What do you know about our town?" and she responds:

"Well—I drive through it on the way to school."

2.   Anything that reflects badly on the employer.

Let's face it: bad things sometimes happen to good employers. Layoffs. Scandals. Malpractice claims. There *is* a way to bring up media-worthy negatives, and I talk about it in the section on "Questions to ask." But when the employer asks, "What do you know about us?" that's not the time to say, "Well, of course, the huge layoff" or "I've been following the sexual harassment class action suit in the paper every day" or "I saw partner X doing the perp walk on TV last night."

3.   Anything that reflects badly on the person who told you the tidbit about the employer.

In the next chapter, on getting jobs through people, I stress the importance on the nurturing and care of your contacts. People who tell you the skinny on employers are helping you, even if—and sometimes *especially* if—what they say is negative. They can save you from a really crappy job, or at the very least, put you on notice of something to watch out for if you take the job.

This is all a lead-up to saying: *Don't trash your sources in an interview.* "Bobby Jo Bobijeau, your summer clerk from last year, told me you guys are a bunch of skirt-chasers." "My Career Services director told me that you tiptoe on the edge when it comes to ethics." "Your old associate, Phil Phlegmmer, told me you guys work your associates to death."

If someone tells you something negative about an employer, probe the veracity of what they're telling you—how do they know this is true? And if you satisfy yourself that it's true and you want the job anyway, *don't mention it in an interview!*

8.   WHY DO YOU WANT TO WORK FOR US?

Another research-dependent question! If you've been to the employer's web site, talked with Career Services about them, read summer evaluations, perhaps even talked with alums or upper-classmen who've worked there—this question's a no-brainer!

a.   The best way to respond.

As my lead-in suggests, **the best answer to this question is employer-specific, showing off your research**. As Lisa

Abrams points out, "Firms *love* to feel you think that they're special!" Maureen Provost Ryan echoes that, saying, "If you're sincere and you've identified this employer as a potential right spot for you, your enthusiasm will show. Talk about the nature of their practice and how exciting it would be to work for them. Visualize yourself actually working for the firm. Show your research and your response will ring with conviction!"

Remember: an employer doesn't want to hear you want an employer *like* them. They want to hear that you want *them* specifically.

With that in mind, here are some elements you might want to weave into your answer:

1. Location.

Remember the importance of geography! As Jose Bahamonde–Gonzalez advises, "It's especially important to explain why you want to be in the city where the employer is, if your resume doesn't show any connection with that city!"

2. The reputation of the employer, if you know it.

As Lisa Abrams suggests, it's great if you can say that in all of your research, "One name keeps coming up—XYZ law firm. I want to be a part of it!"

3. The type of practice.

You have to show a specific interest in the employer's focus. If it's a government agency or public interest employer or prosecutor's office, bring out what it is in your background that makes you interested in that particular kind of practice. The same goes for any private firm with one particular specialty.

If, on the other hand, you're talking about an employer with multiple practice areas—like a large law firm—Laura Rowe Lane recommends that you express your interest in being exposed to a variety of specialties. Stating a laser-focused interest in only one specialty is fraught with danger, for a couple of reasons. First of all, you'd have to be sure that it's a thriving practice area at the firm. Secondly, *unless your background undeniably and immutably directs you to one particular practice area,* the employer will want you to be flexible in making your choice. If you say, "I only want litigation," they're going to think, "You've never practiced law. You don't know what it's like. Where do you come off saying you won't try anything else?"

Now, obviously, there are exceptions where a laser-targeted focus makes sense. For instance, you're an M.D. and you say you want to do med mal defense. Or if you're a Ph.D. in a technical area and you want to do patent work—

well, duh. Sure. Or you've got extensive experience, perhaps as a paralegal before law school, in a particular specialty. But if you don't have anything in your background that explains and justifies a narrow focus, do yourself a favour, and keep your answer more general when you're talking with large law firms!

4. For private employers, a reflection on the size of the employer.

If it's a large law firm, Deanna Coe Kursh advises stressing that you're interested in getting good training, in getting some experience in different departments so you can serve clients better, and that you're open to new ideas and new challenges.

If it's a small firm with a broad practice base, Sandy Mans advises stressing things in your background that show you can take the initiative. "I'd like to work in a firm like yours because I've succeeded in these entrepreneurial environments in the past . . ."

5. Drop names if you have them.

That's Kathleen Brady's advice. So if you've heard something good about the firm from a former summer associate, or an alum who works there or is otherwise familiar with the practice, say so. If you feel uncomfortable dropping names, then you can always say you heard it "through the grapevine" at school.

6. Any sincere strokes to the employer's ego.

I know what you're thinking. There's no way you want to wear an ass turban in an interview. Well—get over it. Sincere compliments are a *really* good idea in interviews. Even if the employer has heard a compliment thousand times before, they've never heard it from *you*. I am reminded of a comment that Don Larsen once made. If you're a baseball fan, you probably recognize that name: Don Larsen is the only man who's ever pitched a perfect game in the World Series. He did it for the New York Yankees in 1956. He was once asked, "Don't you get tired of people asking you about that game?" and he responded, "No! Why would I?"

So if you've heard great things about the firm from other people or the media, *say* it. And cite the source to share the wealth. "Chet Checkmark, your summer clerk from last summer, said that his experience with you was fantastic." "I read your profile in *America's Greatest Places To Work With A Law Degree*." (Sorry. Shameless self-promotion.) "I read great things about you in Vault." "My Career Services Director, Ginette Genius, said she's only heard outstanding things about you from alums who've worked for you." Whatever it is, say it! As Kathleen Brady says, "Every firm wants to think it's the best in the world. It's always good to stroke their ego."

7.   Something quirky and humorous wouldn't hurt.

If you know something offbeat about the employer, mention it! "Who wouldn't want to be a member of the Maxx and Ruby undefeated softball team?" "Partner Wall-banger's portable margarita machine at firm events is legendary." Something the interviewer doesn't hear all the time is a plus—especially if you use it in conjunction with something about their work!

* * * SMART HUMAN TRICK * * *

Law student interviewing with a utility company in the Northeast. When asked why he wants the job, he responds, "The work sounds interesting to me, but on top of that ... your building has the best sledding hill in front of it. Whenever I drive by it I think, 'If I worked there, I'd be able to sled down it.' " The interviewer laughs and says, "I never thought about it, but now that you mention it—it *is* a great sledding hill!"

The student gets the job.

b.   Boners to avoid.

1.   Anything that smacks of "What's–In–It–For–Me?"

As Sandy Mans points out, "The employer doesn't care what's in it for you." Please, please, *please* don't respond with any of the following if you're asked why you want to work for "us":

- "The money."
- "I gotta pay the bills."
- "Because it would be a tremendous opportunity for me."
- "I'll get great training."
- "Your pro bono program."
- "Because I'm a veteran, and taking a federal government job will give me retirement credits."

Now, you and I both know that the reason you want the job is what's in it for you. That's how it *should* be—that's healthy self-interest! But this is a sales presentation. When you go to the grocery store, you don't see tag lines on products that say, "Buy this salsa so we can move to Bermuda!" "Gum Shredder Bran Cereal—try it, and I'll get a promotion!" No. They focus on what's in it for you.

Similarly, in an interview, you're focusing on what's in it for them. They've got something you want—a job. And in order to get it, you've got to keep a lid on responses like, "Because I gotta start *somewhere!*"

* * * CAREER LIMITING MOVE * * *

Law student in an interview with a government agency.

Interviewer: "Why do you want to work for the government?"

Student: "Because you work 9 to 5."

2.   Any comment that shows a lack of research.

Anything that makes the employer feel like a number, just another name on a list of employers who got your resume, does you no favours. Think about it: how would you feel if someone proposed marriage to you, and you asked, "Why do you want to marry me?" and they said, "I want to be married because ..." *That's* not what you want to hear. You want to hear what makes you so wonderful!

In interviews, as Maureen Provost Ryan points out, "You can never say, 'I've always wanted to work for a large firm.'" Firms are different, and they like to feel different. Similarly, "I'd take any job just to be in Honolulu," won't fly. "Because your firm is great" doesn't add anything to the mix. Telling an entertainment lawyer you want to work for him/her because you "love movies" or you "want to hang out with celebrities" isn't going to appeal to someone who wants to hear that you understand that the work involves contracts. Even a cursory visit to the employer's web site or your Career Services office will give you more specific insights than that!

* * * CAREER LIMITING MOVE * * *

When asked "Why do you want to work for us?" one student responded, "I have a friend who goes to school here, and he did research, and he said you were a good firm to work for. That's why I sent my resume."

Interviewer's response: "Really? What's your friend's name? I hope I get to interview *him.*"

3.   Anything that suggests a bad or strange motive.

* * * CAREER LIMITING MOVE * * *

In response to "Why do you want to work for us?" student answers: "To get back at my father. He's one of your rivals, and he's insisting that I get into his area of practice, so I'm interviewing with you to get back at him."

* * * CAREER LIMITING MOVE * * *

Law student from Nebraska, on an interview with an attorney from a Kansas City firm:

Attorney: Why do you want to work with us?

Student: I visited a psychic. She read my palm and told me: Kansas City.

4. Anything that suggests that the job isn't what you *really* want.

"Why do you want to work for us?" is really only a difficult question if you want to answer, "I don't." How do you handle it, and still be honest? Like the song says: accentuate the positive. Tell them things you like about this job. *Every* job, no matter how much you think you won't like it, will provide you with *some* useful skills. Whether it's research skills, working in a professional environment, sharpening your people skills ... geez, every job has *something* to acquit it! If there's honestly nothing there for you, don't interview for the job. But if there's even a little something ... say it—and leave out the negatives!

* * * CAREER LIMITING MOVE * * *

Interviewer: "Why do you want to work for us?"

Student: "To be honest, I'm not so sure I do."

5. "Lofty" answers.

You want to be careful about painting your answer exclusively with broad philosophical brushstrokes. "When I ponder the role of law in society ..." "When I look at Society's ills, I think about how I can best address them ..." As the partner at one law firm told me, "That's all well and good, but we've got *work* to do. OK, what motivates you is good, but show me that you understand what we've got going on in the trenches."

6. Bland answers.

Don't answer as though you're in a beauty pageant. As one criminal defense attorney commented, "When I ask students why they want to do my kind of work, I often get these canned responses like 'I believe everybody has a right to good counsel.' This isn't Miss America! Contrast that with one student who said, 'I think it'll be interesting and fun—it's the nasty stuff nobody wants to talk about.' *Him* we hired!"

9. IF YOU MAJORED IN X OR DID Y BEFORE LAW SCHOOL, WHY DON'T YOU WANT TO DO ... WHATEVER LOGICAL JOB RELATES TO THAT?

I hear this all the time. And when I was in law school, I *heard* it all the time, from employers. I was an accounting major, so they constantly asked me, "Why don't you want to do Tax?" The truth wasn't helpful, namely: I was the crappiest accounting major in the history of higher education. I did it only because my father badgered me into doing something "sensible." Well, yay. Wouldn't *that* have resonated with interviewers?

I see this happen most often with students who had technical majors in college. They're constantly asked, "Why not intellectual property?" Or nurses who don't want to go into Health Law. Or teachers who don't want Education Law.

No matter what your background is, law school is the chance to redefine yourself. **What's key in this answer is to display:**

a. **A firm understanding of what the employer does, and why you feel you would like it;**

b. **Transferable skills from your prior career/college major.** Analysis skills, attention to detail, problem-solving, I could name a million of them.

Notice that you're *not* badmouthing the specialty they're asking you about. "I'd sooner have red-hot bamboo shoots forced under my toenails than practice Tax Law." Inevitably they'll like the specialty you mention, and they'll question your judgment and discretion in dissing it.

* * * CAREER LIMITING MOVE * * *

Student with a biology major in college. He's interviewing with a law firm that specializes in trusts and estates. The interviewer asks him, "Why did you want law instead of medicine?"

The student responds, "I thought I could make more of a difference to society in law than with medicine . . ."

The interviewer later comments, "*More* of a difference writing wills than saving lives? I just couldn't get past that one."

A closely related question to "Why did you . . ." is "What good do you think X major will do you as a lawyer?" I've talked with law students who majored in everything under the sun. Casino Law. Sculpting. Video Game Development. The key to all of them is the same: that is, showing off your knowledge of what you want to do, and relating your college major to it. *Every* college major has skills transferable to lawyering. *Every one.* Whether it's people skills (Casino Law), problem solving (Sculpting), working as part of a team (Video Game Development) . . . it's just a matter of thinking about what you learned and how it will be useful to the employer. It's not what you did that counts—it's your reasoning in wanting to become a lawyer that makes the difference!

10.   WHY DID YOU GO TO LAW SCHOOL?

Well! Ironic, isn't it? Looking for a job is likely to make you ask yourself that very question! "Why the heck did I ever think *this* was a good idea?" you're saying. But let's talk for a moment about what you ought to say to interviewers!

a.   If law is your second or third or tenth career ...

Your answer is going to be very different than if you went straight from college to law school. Let's talk about it in the chapter that goes into detail about unique aspects of second career job searches. It's Chapter 22.

b.   If you haven't had another career ...

If you went pretty much straight from college to law school—as most law students do—the key thing to remember is that *your answer has to sound as though your decision to attend law school was well-reasoned.* And let's face it, at least part of the reason you went to law school *has* to involve logical thought! Maybe you were drawn to the positive aspects of a legal education; the intellectual challenge, the idea of pulling apart issues. Maybe you had a summer job or a life experience that exposed you to law.

It's also all right to start your answer with a quip. "I often ask myself that very question!" with a smile on your face is a fine way to lead in, as long as you follow it up with—you guessed it—a well-reasoned response.

Also, if the interview is going fairly well, you might want to wind up your answer by asking, "Just out of curiosity—why did *you* go to law school?" An open-ended question like this will help turn the interview into a conversation, and it gets you off the hot seat.

c.   Boners to avoid.

Since a good answer shows that your decision to go to law school was well-thought-out, you can probably tell what a bad answer is: **anything that shows a lack of thought**. That means that some answers that sound good at first, actually aren't. For instance, telling the interviewer, "My Uncle Pete was a lawyer, and I idolize him," or "I've wanted to be a lawyer for so long I don't even remember why" have a hidden flaw: They suggest that you've never thought about it, it was a knee-jerk reaction, or you made the decision in first grade when everybody was going to be a fireman or ballerina or dolphin trainer—and nobody had *any clue* what the real world of work is like!

Other boners to avoid include:

1. Anything that suggests law school was a default option.

"I couldn't get a job, man, so what else was I supposed to do?"

Now, interestingly enough, research suggests that only one-third of law students actually come to law school committed to a legal career. *One-third.* That means that if *you* were serious about it, you have two friends who weren't. And truth be told, if we were friends, I'd be one of them. I had no idea what I was going to do when I was a senior in college. I took the LSAT on a bet, and went to law school to avoid work. *But you can't say that in an interview.* I'm not telling you to lie, but I *am* telling you to be selective about what you say, and choose an aspect of law school that appealed to you *other* than the fact that it was a fall-back!

2. You did it for the money.

This, actually, is the most common answer I get when I talk to students. And why not? We all read—or at least, our parents do—those articles in the *Wall Street Journal* talking about the pots of dough that new associates at Manhattan law firms get. And that leads us all to think: Geez, if they're raking in the dead presidents, I want a piece of that! But the fact is, most legal jobs don't pay mad cheese—and if you say your motivation was money, any employer will question your dedication to the work itself.

3. Anything that suggests a bad motivation.

Amy Thompson warns you to avoid answers like "My parents wanted me to," since it doesn't show any enthusiasm on your part. Or even worse: "I was always good at arguing."

11. IF YOU WEREN'T GOING TO BE A LAWYER, WHAT WOULD YOU BE?

This is a really, really, nasty, tricky question. Here's why: *if you answer it promptly, the employer may eliminate you from contention.* Can you *believe* that?

Here's the thinking: If you're so quick to the trigger in naming an alternative, you probably don't want to be a lawyer. More than one law firm has *publicized* the fact that they ask this question in screening interviews for this precise purpose.

Of course, anybody with half a brain and any imagination at all could envision having more than one career. And it would be perfectly rational to think, "All I have to do is pick a career with skills related to law." But I'm telling you, it's a minefield. It's particularly important in this question to squash your natural instinct to come up with an intelligent, creative answer!

Instead, use something that's true and/or funny that doesn't involve other options, like:

- I'm so focused on law right now I haven't thought about anything else.

- I suppose if I thought about it for a while I could come up with something, but there isn't anything off the top of my head.

- Are you telling me this interview is going so badly I should consider not even being a *lawyer?*

- Nothing comes to mind. Just out of curiosity ... what would *you* be?

12. Why Did You Choose This School?

Aah. The "Be true to your school" question. And let's face it. It's virtually never asked of students who go to Harvard or Yale or Stanford. But if you go just about anywhere else, when it *is* asked, the look on the interviewer's face usually suggests they just smelled something bad. And it's almost *always* asked when you're looking for an out-of-town job (we handle that two questions from now), or you go to school in a city with several law schools, and yours isn't the one that *U.S. News & Wreck Your Life Magazine* ranked #1 in the city.

So, how do you handle it when your school is under attack?

a. The best way to answer.

The key here: *Stay positive*. Only make positive statements about your school. And if you can't do it without a straight face, practice in a mirror until you can. Remember: Part of what the interviewer is seeking when they ask you this question is your *judgment*. Did you make a wise decision—and will you do so when you work for them?

A family connection works—for instance, if an older relative or older sibling attended the school and had a great experience there, say it.

If that doesn't fit you, depending on what you can honestly compliment about your school, you've got a number of options for answering. You can stress:

- The interesting classes

- Profs that you like

- The size of the school

- The curriculum

- The writing programs
- The clinical program
- Successful alums

There are a couple of things to keep in mind about choosing options from this list. Number one, be prepared for follow-ups. For instance, if you say you like the curriculum, be prepared to say what you like about it. If you like the profs, be prepared to say which ones—and don't bad-mouth any you don't like!

Also notice that many of these options are things you couldn't possibly have known when you made your choice. That's OK. The interviewer won't notice, as long as you're cheerleading for your school. You can also ask at Career Services to see which aspects of your school are well-respected.

If you're really stuck, *look at how your law school sells itself.* See how you were suckered into—oops. Pardon me. How you were *encouraged* to attend. Go to the school's web site, look at the brochure, see what they brag about—and look at things you can honestly rave about, too.

Incidentally, for any aspect of the school that you mention, be sure that it jibes with the employer's practice. For instance, if you rave about your school's clinical program, that will be very useful if you're interviewing for a job where you're going to get litigation experience and client contact right away, like small firm/public interest/prosecutor's office/JAG corps.

A great way to finish your answer is to turn the question around on the interviewer. That is, ask—with a smile on your face—where the interviewer went to school. Even better, if you've done your research homework—which I have complete faith that you'll do—you already know where the interviewer went to law school, and you can say, "I know you went to Mental State Law School. What was your experience like there?"

b.   Boners to avoid.

The kinds of things you want to avoid saying are, depending on the mood you're in, often a little uncomfortably close to the truth. They include:

- "It was the best (or only) school I got into."
- "Yeah, you're right. It stinks."
- "I heard the social life here is *great!*"

My favourite answer to this question actually came from a classmate of mine from Hawaii. You may find it hard to believe, but there aren't many Hawaiians who wind up going to law school in Cleveland—and this lovely guy was pelted with this question on a constant basis for the first semester of law school. At one point, he pulled me aside and said, "Kimm, I just can't tell people the real reason I came here. I hadn't ever been to the mainland and I wanted to be in a place where I could ski. I thought Cleveland was close to Colorado. It wasn't until I sent in my deposit that I found out it's a thousand miles away!"

* * * SMART HUMAN TRICK * * *

Law student from a Midwestern law school with a challenging reputation. We'll call it Hay U. He goes on a call back interview with a large, prestigious Phoenix law firm, where he's talking with an associate who went to the University of Arizona. Two other associates walk in, pick up his resume, and start chuckling. One of them sneeringly asks him, "Why are you going to a dump like Hay U?" The student calmly responds, with "Let me tell you a couple of things about Hay U that you might not know ..." and he goes on to list some great programs and illustrious alums. They listen to him and leave.

The associate who's interviewing the student smiles at him, and says, "Good move. They went there, too."

He gets the job.

13. WHAT OTHER LAW SCHOOLS DID YOU GET INTO?

This question is sticky in three situations:

- It's an out-of-town interview, and you didn't go to a school in the employer's city even though you got in;

- You didn't go to the highest-ranking school you got into;

- You got into the interviewer's school and you didn't go there.

The best way to answer this question is with a variant on the "Why did you choose this school?" riff. That is, highlight the school's positive points.

You may also have other options that work well. For instance, if you chose a lower-ranked school because you got a great scholarship, *say it*. Wanting to go through law school with as little debt as possible is a really smart move. You can say, "I wanted as little debt as possible to give me the widest possible career choices."

Also, if you turned down a higher-ranked law school to go to one in the city where the employer is located, you're proving your dedication to the community, and *that's* a serious positive.

If you don't know where the interviewer went to school, be careful not to say *anything* negative about *any* law school!

14. THE OUT-OF-TOWN JOB SEARCH QUESTION: WHY DO YOU WANT TO WORK IN THIS CITY?

If you're looking for a job in a city other than where you're going to law school, you have a whole raft of issues to deal with. And that's why I've dedicated a whole chapter to this issue: It's in Chapter 17.

15. WHO ELSE ARE YOU INTERVIEWING WITH?

There's a hidden agenda with this question! As Debra Fink points out, "When the interviewer asks this question, the real question is: do you have ties here? Will you develop them here?" So it's essentially a question of *geography*.

With that in mind, what you should do is to **mention only other employers in the same city**—don't mention any other cities! Remember, I started this book by reminding you that a job search is not a confessional. You don't have any obligation to talk about every employer with whom you're interviewing! Say something like, "I'm interviewing with a few other firms/employers here in X, including . . ."

By the same token, you can't lie about the employers with whom you do have interviewers. Mention them by name. And before you get a chance to be led down a rabbit hole of questions like "Why did you choose them?" "Have you gotten interviews from any of them?" *immediately* follow up with adding, "But I'll tell you why I'm here talking to you . . ." *and talk about assets that your research has revealed about this employer.*

If you don't have any other interviews set up, don't answer "nobody." It makes you sound like a less attractive candidate. It's a twist on the whole dating principle that people are immediately more attractive if they're already taken. **If you don't have any other interviews, you can always say, "I'm in the process of setting up other interviews."** That's undoubtedly true!

Incidentally, if you do get an initial interview with an out-of-town employer, immediately call others from the same city and ask if you can meet with them on the same trip. The fact that you've got another employer on the hook will make them a great deal more likely to interview you—and it also gets the most bang for the buck out of the money you're spending on the trip!

16. WHAT KINDS OF POSITIONS ARE YOU LOOKING FOR?

Actually, this isn't all that tough. What you'll want to do is to pull out the features that reflect the job you're interviewing for. For instance, if it's with a small firm, you might want to talk about how you're looking for something where you'll be able to take on responsibility quickly, to develop clients, to be challenged by a diversity of projects, and that kind of thing. With a large law firm, perhaps you'll talk about enjoying the idea of an intellectual challenge. For a public interest employer, consider talking about your interest in helping a certain population. You see the point.

The real reason I included this question is that I have a great story about it. One student's response to this question was, "Anything where I don't have to wear a hairnet."!

* * * CAREER LIMITING MOVE * * *

Interviewer for large law firm: "What do you want to do?"

Law student: "I'm interested in commercial litigation."

Interviewer: "That's great. You realize we don't have a commercial litigation department."

End of interview.

* * * CAREER LIMITING MOVE * * *

Interviewer: "What kind of job are you looking for?"

Student: "Nothing too demanding. I just can't imagine doing more than required."

17.   Why Is There a Gap on Your Resume?

There are two kinds of gaps on your resume: Either you left off your GPA, or there are chronological gaps. Neither of these are interview killers, as long as you prepare your response ahead of time.

a.   The GPA gap.

We can dispense with the GPA issue quickly, because we've already discussed grades. If your GPA is low enough to leave off your resume—your Career Services Office can tell you what that point is for your school, since it varies from school to school—interviewers are very likely to ask you about your grades. This is a prime instance where *the way you say it* is crucial. As Drusilla Bakert advises, **"Just state what your GPA is—make it exact—and shut up."** Don't offer excuses or stumble over it, just come out and say it as though you were recounting your shoe size. Let's face it; you got the interview without them knowing your grades, and the fact that your GPA isn't on your resume kind of telegraphs that you didn't grade onto Law Review, doesn't it? So don't take up precious interview minutes by stumbling and bumbling over a simple number, of pretending that you "don't know exactly."

Now, if the interviewer's demeanor suggests that your GPA is a problem—their face drops, a friendly tone suddenly turns sour—you can always say, "I'm judging from your reaction that you're concerned about my grades. Is that true?" If the interviewer acknowledges it, then you jump into the "grades answer" we discussed a few minutes ago—you talk about what proves you can do their work.

There's a key caveat here: *you only ask that question and jump into your explanation if the interviewer's reaction suggests it's appropriate.* If the interviewer doesn't seem at all fazed by it and goes on to ask you more questions, then follow their lead and move on.

b. Chronological gaps.

Raising children. Voluminous non-law-related work experience. A job that went bad. Traveling. Jail. There are tons of reasons why you might have a chronological gap on your resume. Of course, you don't have one if you read Chapter 8 on Resumes, because I begged you not to send out resumes with gaps on them. But perhaps you already sent out a bunch of resumes before you read that chapter. If so, I *guarantee* you that interviewers will ask about the gap.

What's your strategy? It has two steps:

1. **State what you did.**

2. **Say that you didn't believe it contributed to your ability to work for this employer, and that's why you left it off your resume.**

If it was a job that went bad quickly, just explain matter-of-factly that you recognized quickly that the fit wasn't right, and rather than waste the employer's time and yours, you left.

Remember: All employers are truly interested in—and entitled to—is an explanation of how things you've done before will impact what you'll do for them. If the item in your background is negative, you have to reassure them why said experience will *not* impact your work for them.

No matter *what* you did during the "gap," state it succinctly and without grimacing. This is definitely an area where mock interviews can help you smooth your answer. If the look on your face and the tone of your voice suggest that it's not an issue, the interviewer will adopt your sense of confidence.

Incidentally, this is also a situation where it's a good idea to follow up with either a question to get you off the topic, or—if you haven't given it yet—your "tell me about yourself" answer. That is, you can say, "That may not be very relevant to whether I can do a good job for you—but I'll tell you what you *do* need to know about me ..." and go into your answer. Either way, you'll have overcome the "resume gap" obstacle with flying colors.

18.   WHY DIDN'T YOU GET AN OFFER FROM YOUR PRIOR EMPLOYER?

This is not just a tough question—it's a *killer*. In fact, it's so challenging that I've devoted a whole chapter to dealing with the problem of not getting an offer from your summer clerkship employer. It's Chapter 15. If you're in this predicament—read it!

19.   WHY DIDN'T YOU ACCEPT THE OFFER FROM YOUR LAST EMPLOYER?

Let's look at some of the potential reasons for turning down an offer. Maybe your last employers were jerks and you really don't want to work for them because of that. Maybe you didn't like the work, or the clients. Maybe you were under too much pressure. Maybe you're bored with that work, and you want to see what else is out there. Maybe the work's fine but the money is no good, and you want more. Maybe changed circumstances make the employer geographically undesirable. Those are all excellent reasons not to go back—but you can't say any of them!

There are, of course, reasons that you *can* mention. For instance, let's say that your prior employer specialized in a "sunset" practice, like asbestos litigation. With the business dwindling, even if you got an offer, you may not want to develop expertise in something that's going to go away. You'd *imply* that by saying something like, "What interests me about your work is that it's thriving, growing . . ." and in doing so implicitly suggest that your last gig was *not*.

The real key to this question is not to bad mouth your last employer under *any* circumstances. Remember the classic Seinfeld line: "Not that there's anything *wrong* with that . . ." It's entirely possible that the interviewer is familiar with your employer, and will know if they've got a reputation as jerks or for running a real sweatshop. **The way to answer tactfully is to mention positives about what you learned from working for the employer, ideally things that you'll be able to use for *this* employer. But then add that you were looking for something more—again, something the employer with whom you're currently interviewing offers.** For instance, let's say that you worked for Attorney Mark E. DeSade, a real bastard who worked you to death. You could say, "I learned a lot working for Attorney DeSade. I got a lot of responsibility and it was an intellectually challenging environment. But what attracted me to interviewing with you is that I understand that you offer . . ." and so on.

I talked to one student who'd clerked at an office that was entirely populated by Born Again Christians. That's great, if you're born again also. He said, "I just couldn't take the proselytizing. I don't know why it wasn't obvious to me in interviews, but I got there, and I felt like all they talked about was Jesus. It just wasn't me." They gave him a good reference, and in subsequent interviews he made a point of highlighting the research and writing skills he'd learned there—and he *also* made a point of asking, "Do you socialize with other attorneys in the office? Are there activities everyone takes part in together?" He says, "If I'd just asked that question when I interviewed at my old firm they would have told me, 'We pray together,' 'We do Bible study'—and I wouldn't have taken a job where I didn't fit in *at all.*"

What do you do if the look on your interviewer's face suggests that (s)he doesn't approve of your prior employer? Ignore it. Answer with "What I learned was . . ." and make it skills transferable to the job you're interviewing for. If your old firm had well-publicized ethical or fraud problems, talk about learning how to focus on your work and do the right thing in a challenging environment. If the employer was difficult or disorganized, you can acknowledge that by talking about how you learned to work for an employer who was difficult or disorganized! Don't take the bait and say something negative—"I can see from the look on your face that you think Attorney Shyster is a scumbag, too"—otherwise the interviewer will question your discretion.

20. IF YOU WANTED TO DO X KIND OF WORK, WHY DID YOU DO ACTIVITIES/INTERNSHIP/JOB [INVOLVING OTHER KINDS OF WORK]?

It seemed like a good idea at the time . . .

When my son Harry was born, I told everybody I was going to teach him how to talk like a pirate. No "mama" or "dada." I wanted him to say, "Arrgh, you scurvy wench, where's me grub?"

Of course, I didn't wind up *doing* that. I changed my mind.

Maybe you've had a change of heart over what you want to do with your law degree. You did a bunch of things related to one specialty, but now . . . you want something else. You changed your mind.

Welcome to the human race!

When you're asked about it, the interviewer is checking your *motivation* and judgment. That is, if you have a resume that screams one thing—sports, entertainment, international, public interest—and you're interviewing with personal injury outfit, they'll think—hmm. Do you really want this, or did you wash out of your dream job? Or did you try it and hate it, so you've changed your focus—and you might hate us, too?

In the Resume chapter I talked about "pimping" your resume to avoid this perception. But if you got the interview anyway, your answer just has to reassure the employer that you truly want to do what they do, that your research tells you you'll enjoy it and be good at it. Pull out what you learned, doing something else that will transfer to the employers you're targeting now. And remember: It's not an attack question. The employer has a legitimate concern, and you need to—and *can*—address it.

* * * SMART HUMAN TRICK * * *

Student who did an LLM in London for a year after graduating from law school. She didn't do it for the education but rather to satisfy her traveling jones. In interviews, she reports that "Every interviewer wanted to know why I did the LLM if I wasn't truly interested in the subject. I said, 'It wasn't for the academics. I knew I wanted to travel but also that I wanted to settle here permanently. I didn't want to waste your time applying for a job with you before I traveled. I thought learning more about the law was a good way to spend a year while I was away.' " She reports, "They nodded and all seemed satisfied with my answer. Which was a good thing, because it was the truth."

* * * SMART HUMAN TRICK * * *

Third year student interviewing with a prosecutor's office. The interviewer asks, "Why did you spend your summer with a large law firm if you want to be a prosecutor?"

The student responds, "Look at it this way. Isn't it amazing that somebody in the 40th percentile got *into* that firm? You need somebody with my persuasive ability!"

The student gets the job.

* * * SMART HUMAN TRICK * * *

Law student has a very specific goal: He wants to represent the defense in stockholder derivative suits. He takes a summer clerkship with a firm that represents *plaintiffs* in derivative suits because "It paid more money." He reports, "On top of that, they were a highly-respected firm. Everybody knows them. In interviews with defense firms, I always stress how my knowledge of how the other side thinks is very valuable. I compare it to Moot Court, where no matter which side you argue, you'll do the best if you know both sides. The interviewers like it. I'm getting callbacks. Of course, maybe they like it because I don't mention the money thing."

21. QUESTIONS ABOUT PRIOR JOBS THAT YOU CAN'T ANSWER BECAUSE THE WORK WAS CONFIDENTIAL

What if you worked for the CIA, or your work involved a security clearance, whether governmental or civilian? I've told you before about the student who was an anti-terrorism marine before law school. He couldn't say *anything* about his work!

The answer has two elements:

a) Pull out the transferable skills that you *can* discuss. For the marine, he knew how to think quickly and remain calm in a crisis, size up a situation quickly, communicate with people quickly and effectively.

b) If you can, tell an interesting anecdote. Everybody's curious about secret jobs. Satisfy their curiosity with an interesting story . . . and work it around to why you want *this* job—and why you'd be good at it!

22.   WHAT'S THE BIGGEST MISTAKE YOU EVER MADE? WHAT'S YOUR BIGGEST FAILURE?

In a nutshell: It's not what you *did*. It's what you *learned* from it.

As with many difficult questions, there's no reason that you can't open your answer with a quip. "Not being prepared to answer a question about the biggest mistake I ever made" might get you off the hook!

If not, use the following two-step approach:

a.   **Choose a relatively innocuous mistake related to work or school**—like choosing the wrong major in college and having to take extra classes when you realized your mistake. Avoid anything in your background that is truly serious: you were a crack addict, you did time for armed robbery. It's admirable that you overcame it, but you'll have to pick the interviewer up off the floor if you mention it!

b.   *Accentuate the steps you took to correct your mistake*. Your recovery is what says everything about you. "I'll tell you what I learned from that . . ." are *exceptionally* important words. You acknowledged the mistake, you took responsibility, the remedial steps you took . . . that's what your answer needs to focus on. You will *certainly* make mistakes as a lawyer—the interviewer and every other lawyer who ever lived has done so!—and how you correct your mistakes is the truly relevant point.

With the "greatest failure" question, if you can honestly say you view failures as merely obstacles to overcome, you can talk about what you did to recover from one. (And if you don't honestly feel that way—you should!)

23.   WHAT KIND OF SALARY ARE YOU LOOKING FOR?

While this question is common in certain other fields, it's not all that common in law.

Having said that, it's important to answer correctly. You don't want to undervalue yourself, but you don't want to give them a wildly inflated answer, either.

If you feel comfortable with it, and the interviewer is fairly laid back, you can always open humorously. "Well, I'm looking for a million dollars a year, but I don't think I'm likely to get it."

Whether you open with a joke or not, your best answer requires a bit of up-front research—which you're going to do, right?

a. **For large law firms, check their web site and/or NALP forms.** NALP is short for "National Association of Law Placement," and every large employer contributes to their guide to employers. It's at your Career Services Office. Check before you go into the interview to see how much they pay.

b. **For public interest employers,** check with your Career Services Office for salaries.

c. **For corporations/nontraditional employers,** go to Salary.com for salary information.

d. **For medium to small firms,** check statistics at your Career Services Office from NALP, or check them on-line at www.nalp.org. NALP does you an *enormous* favour by compiling very detailed salary statistics. They can tell you, based on geography, size of employer, and number of years out of school, a range of salaries that's normal for everywhere in the country.

Armed with this information, you can tell the employer one of two things. Either, "I saw on your web site what you offer new associates, and I'm happy with that," or, for a smaller employer, you can say, "I understand that the salary range for employers like you is between $50,000 and $60,000. That would be fine with me."

This works for a whole bunch of reasons. First of all, you're not skirting the issue entirely by saying you're "flexible." You're not pinning yourself to an exact figure. If the employer was thinking of paying you *less* than that range, you're putting them on notice of what they have to pay to be competitive. And best of all—you're showing that you researched the issue, and went into the interview with your eyes open. That's *always* a good thing!

Incidentally, if you're not happy with the dough but you took the interview anyway—you may be able to negotiate for more money. Accent on "may." I talk about this in detail in the chapter called "Off the Radar Screen: Special Tips For Nailing Jobs With Small Employers." It's in Chapter 18.

24. HOW DO YOU LIKE LAW SCHOOL?

Now, now. No swearing. The key here is not to be *completely* negative, even if you *hate* law school. If you like it, great—let your enthusiasm show! Maybe you don't like all of it, but you like the intellectual challenge, or you like stimulating conversations with your colleagues and professors—whatever. If you like some of it, stress the things you like *and don't mention the things you don't like.* "The professors are jerks," "All that work's a real drag, man"—just don't go there.

What if you really intensely dislike it—all of it? You can put a positive spin on that! Say something like, "Frankly, I can't wait to get out of school and start my career, and I'm frustrated with law school because it's holding me back from doing that!"

Remember: When an interviewer asks about what you're doing, they're evaluating your *judgment.* If you say you hate law school, you *chose* it. You're *there.* How does the interviewer know you'll like your job—and excel at it?

25. DO YOU KNOW X PERSON?

It could be a professor, someone at a former or current employer of yours, a fellow student. You're thinking, "Well, geez, Kimmbo—I don't know if I'd put that in the category of difficult question. I mean—either I know them or I don't."

You're right. But that's not what will hurt you. It's the way you *editorialize.* Most people find it impossible to just say "Yes" or "No" when they're asked if they know someone. They immediately jump in with an editorial comment. "Yes, I took Con Law with Professor Crapsey. What a snooze! I've never been so bored!" "Yes, I worked with Attorney Attaboy. He really tiptoed on the edge of ethics." "Yes, I do go to school with Tina Teton. Great body!" In any one of these situations, I promise you the response from the interviewer will be: "Really? Professor Crapsey is my father/Attorney Attaboy is my best friend/Tina Teton is my sister."

So here's the key to answering well. If you don't know the person in question, Just say, "No, I don't—why do you ask?" **If you *do* know them, *immediately* after you say "Yes," ask "How do you know so-and-so?" That way, you can frame your editorializing appropriately.** "Professor Crapsey—what an excellent and detailed grasp of the subject!" "Attorney Attaboy—he really goes the extra mile for his clients!" "Tina Teton—she's a lovely young woman." As you can see, you're *kind* of saying the same things. You're not lying. Remember the *Simpsons* episode where Marge was a real estate agent? Her mentor is showing her pictures of houses, and asks for her description. She looks at the first one and says, "It's *tiny!*" Her mentor corrects her: "Cozy!"

The second one is a wreck. Marge comments, "It's dilapidated!" Her mentor: "Rustic!"

The third house is on fire. Marge says, "Oh my God! That house is on fire!" And the mentor says, "Motivated seller!"

You get the idea.

* * * CAREER LIMITING MOVE * * *

Law student in interview with an interviewer from a state agency. Interview is going well, it's very comfortable and casual. Interviewer asks, "I see you worked at X. Do you know Ms. Y?" Student responds, "How could I miss her? She might consider washing her hair once in a while." The student notices that the interviewer's mood suddenly turns dark, as he comments, "Really? She's a close friend of mine."

Interview over.

26. WHAT'S THE MOST INTERESTING THING THAT'S NOT ON YOUR RESUME?

Your temptation may be to say, "I can tie cherry stems in knots with my tongue" . . . "I'm now a man, but I was born a woman," but it's not wise to yield to that temptation!

You have a bunch of choices. Did you do something unusual in your childhood? I split my childhood between England and the U.S. That would qualify. Did you have a "one-off" experience that didn't make it onto your resume? Did you climb Mt. Kilimanjaro, did you try out for a game show or a reality show? Really, anything is fine as long as it a) says something good or at least neutral about you, and b) it truly is *interesting*.

27. QUESTIONS RELATED TO PRIOR WORK THAT'S CONTROVERSIAL . . .

I've seen them all. Students who were strippers. Students who worked for internet porn providers. Students who were phone-sex operators. Heck, it doesn't have to be titillating. Maybe you were a lobbyist for a cause that's controversial, like legalizing marijuana, or either side of the abortion debate.

In the Resume chapter, we talked about the importance of "euphemizing" controversial work. In interviews, you're likely to be asked about whatever you "euphemized." Here's what you need to do:

a. Acknowledge that the interviewer's curiosity is legitimate. You're not under attack.

Remember, part of what the interviewer is judging is your *savoir faire*. If you show you can discuss even controversial topics with ease, you're saying a lot about your ability to deal with people in all kinds of situations.

b. Be perfectly matter-of-fact as you discuss the transferable skills you learned from the job.

I've told you over and over that every job has transferable skills. An ability to deal with people is one that virtually any job provides you. Lobbying gives you persuasion skills no matter what you lobbied *for*. You can come up with them yourself. But no matter what you say, remember that the interviewer will take a cue from the way you treat your prior job. If you treat it matter-of-factly, they will, too.

c. Come up with a quip and/or humorous anecdote to show your comfort with the topic.

The phone sex operator told interviewers, "I certainly learned how to give great phone," and then went into her answer about her (appropriately-described) communication skills *as well as* other, law-related jobs, and how they prepped her for the jobs she was interviewing for. She said it was never an issue after that.

d. Weave into your answer law-related experiences you've had and/or ask the interviewer a question.

You don't want the whole interview to be about your prior job. Give the interviewer your succinct answer, and move on to other topics!

28. IF YOU STATED AN INTEREST IN A PARTICULAR SPECIALTY IN YOUR COVER LETTER ...

Be *absolutely* up to date on the major issues involved in it. Lawfuel.com, law.com, Lexis/Nexis and Westlaw are sources that come to mind. The fact is, the interviewer will question your sincerity if you are unaware of a major issue in the specialty.

* * * CAREER LIMITING MOVE * * *

Law student sends employer a letter stating an interest in campaign finance law. She gets an interview.

The interviewer asks her, "What do you think of McCain–Feingold?"

Her response: "Of *what?*"

The interviewer says, "I wasn't trying to ambush her. But come on. How can you say you're interested in campaign finance and *not* know about *that?*"

29. WHAT MAKES YOU ANGRY?

A hornet's nest! Here's the trap: As Syracuse's Mary Harblin points out, "You really can't have anything make you angry at work. It's not productive. And it's very likely that you've never *gotten* angry at work. Instead, think about things that *frustrate* you and at the same time reflect well on you. Like coworkers who hold up the process, or people who don't meet deadlines and hold up others." You'd go on to talk about how you address those frustrations, how you communicate, and you'd choose solutions that make you look responsible and stable. Depending on how you feel about it, you could even talk about disliking it when coworkers disparage your employer. You'd have to be careful with that one; it has to be absolutely true, and you have to watch your delivery so you don't seem like a complete suck-up.

I'll give you an example of an episode I'd use from my life. When I waitressed my way through college, we were given twenty-minute breaks for lunch on weekends. If people with early lunches took longer breaks, it meant some wait staff didn't get a break at all. One woman, whom I'll call Alma, was a particularly egregious offender. There was a lot of grumbling about her. So one day, when she had overstayed her break by fifteen minutes, I ran into the lunch room and said in a panicked voice, "Alma! Come quick!" She bolted out of the chair and said, "What is it?" I responded: "I just wanted to make sure you weren't glued to the chair." I said it with a smile on my face, and she laughed along with everyone else in the break room. She never overstayed her break after that.

30.   WHAT WOULD YOU DO IF YOU WON THE LOTTERY?

Whoo-hoo! We know the traditional advice about answering this question, don't we? You're supposed to look the interviewer in the eye, and answer—without laughing—"I'd work for you anyway." Harvard's Mark Weber says, "When I was in practice, I used to love asking this question when I interviewed law students. I wanted to see if they'd lie to me. I mean, they knew as well as I did, if they won the lottery, there's *no way* they'd work for us. Because if *I* won the lottery, I wouldn't have done it, either!"

So—how do you respond? Snort and say, "Hell, I win the lottery, I'm *out* of here!" Pro-o-o-bably not.

The happy medium is to answer humorously, and then flip the question on the interviewer to get a conversation going. In other words, you can say things like:

- "How ironic that you asked—I actually *did* win the lottery, and here I am anyway."

- "Of course I would give it all away to charity. (Pause) Well . . . maybe not *all* of it."

- "That reminds me of an interview Joe DiMaggio did shortly before he died. An interviewer asked him how things would be different if he were playing today, with the salaries that baseball players command. DiMaggio responded that he would have walked up to [New York Yankees owner] George Steinbrenner and said, 'Hello, Partner.' "

- "Do you know something about the lottery ticket I just bought that *I* don't know?"
- "It depends how much I won. If it was a million, I'd pay off my student loans. Part of them, anyway."

Heck, you see what I'm saying. You can come up with cleverer stuff than me. But no matter how you answer humorously, finish up by turning the question around on the interviewer, and ask (with a smile), "OK—so what would *you* do if you won the lottery?" The answer is sure to provoke an interesting exchange between the two of you, and that's what you want interviews to be—great conversations!

31.   DO YOU HAVE X SKILL? (DRAFTING PLEADINGS, ETC.)

You might think, whatever they ask, either I can do it or I can't, I'll just tell them the truth.

You *could* do that. But here's a better route. If an employer asks if you know how to do *anything,* the best way to respond is: "I will."

Let's face it. You weren't born with any legal skills at all. Whatever you know how to do now, you've learned to do. And you're capable of learning anything else, as well. So if it's something you're interested in and it's at all feasible, tell them: "If that's what you need, I will." It shows your enthusiasm and your willingness to learn.

I've seen examples of this in other contexts a number of times. My two favourite stories come from show business. Lucille Ball, when she was first noodling around with doing *I Love Lucy,* was asked: "Can you play the banjo?" And she responded, "Give me two weeks, and I will."

Similarly, when Michael J. Fox was being considered for the movie *Back To The Future,* he was asked: "Do you know how to skateboard?"

"I will," he said.

So if an employer asks if you can do something—answer prospectively!

32.   QUESTIONS INVOLVING OTHER PEOPLE'S PERCEPTIONS OF YOU
. . .

These are *really* tough. "What would your last employer say about you?" A Career Services Director at one law school told me a particularly difficult version she'd heard from employers: "If I talked to ten of your classmates, what's the biggest misperception they would have of you?"

This is dangerous territory, because on the one hand you want to show a degree of awareness as to how you come across. "I don't know" is perilous, because you *should* be aware.

On the other hand, you don't want the misperception to be damaging to your image. "They think I'm shy," "They think I'm a huge partier," "They think I'm a know-it-all." "My old boss would say I talk on the phone too much," "I can't say because the judge imposed a gag order on all the parties."

When it comes to misunderstandings about you—whether it be a former employer, professor, classmates or anyone else—if you can say it honestly, say that you're pretty sure what people think of you is in line with the way you really are. If you truly have figured out that people misread you somehow, present it delicately. The way you talk about it depends on the nature of the misperception. If it's a positive misperception—people perceive you as more outgoing than you might naturally be, more confident—talk about steps you've taken to cultivate that perception and why it works for you. If it's a misperception you'd consider negative, talk about steps you've taken to correct it. "They might have said I was shy, but I have made a point of speaking up in class and taking part in extracurriculars to take care of it."

You don't want to brag, but you do want to say things that are both honest and reflect well on you. "I like to think that based on the work I did for Attorney Mazeltov, he'd say I think outside the box in solving problems. There was one situation where . . ." and then—as always—give a story to back up your point.

33. "Behavioral" Questions

The words "Tell me about" or "Describe a time when" herald behavioral questions. You might hear questions like:

- "Tell me about a time you failed to meet a deadline."
- "Tell me about a time you received harsh criticism."
- "Tell me about a really tough problem you solved creatively."
- "Tell me about a project you've done that completely absorbed you."
- "Tell me about a time when you made a bad decision."
- "Tell me about a time you disagreed with your boss."
- "Tell me about a time when you had to handle an angry customer."
- "Tell me about a time when you were faced with a difficult decision."
- "Tell me about a time when you worked well under pressure."

- "Tell me about a time when you overcame a major obstacle."
- "Tell me about a time when you had to tolerate an opinion that differed from yours."
- "Tell me about a time when you had to juggle multiple obligations."

There are many, many more, but these give you an idea of the kinds of "behavioral" questions interviewers might ask. The idea here, as you might imagine, is that what you *did* tells a lot about what you'll *do*.

Here are the keys to answering well:

a. **If the interviewer asks behavioral questions at all, expect them to be related to what you'll confront on the job.**

For instance, if you would have a lot of client contact immediately, you might be asked the "angry customer" question. If the situation is one that involves multi-tasking and time constraints, you might be asked the "working under pressure" and "juggled several projects" question. If you'll be working with a challenging boss, the interviewer might ask you the "disagreed with your boss" question.

b. **Since the questions tend to relate to job-oriented situations you might face, make sure that the stories you choose reflect skills and qualities the employer looks for.**

You're already ahead of the game in preparing for these questions, because in answer to your "Tell me about yourself question," you formulated examples to back up work-related qualities and skills you possess. Expand that list to cover a few more skills and qualities the employer seeks, and you've got most of your bases covered for behavioral questions.

c. **Notice that many of the questions are framed in the negative:** a time when you missed a deadline, received criticism, made a bad decision. In handling those, you should:

1. **Choose the example carefully; don't say anything that reflects badly on you as a potential employee.** So avoid mentioning a time you were fired, you were late repeatedly, you had recurring child care issues, where you wanted to leave your job early to get to your moonlighting gig, where you were accused of being lazy or stealing. As one hiring partner points out, "You want to be careful about showing bad judgment and a lack of planning." Another adds, "I hate to say it, but you can't be perfectly honest with this answer. If I ask

you the most embarrassing situation you've ever been in, it *can't* be *the* most embarrassing situation.''

2. ***Immediately* upon mentioning the negative, talk about what you learned from it and how you turned it around.** Remember: the interviewer is most interested in figuring out how you will behave in the future. If you learned from an experience, it's unlikely to repeat itself.

By way of an example, let's say you didn't receive an offer from your summer employer. You could use that as an obstacle. You'd talk about what you learned from the experience, and why you won't make the same mistake again.

With the criticism question, you'd want to reflect how you acted on the elements of the criticism that would improve your work. I told you in the "Overcoming Rejection" chapter, Chapter 5, about my hobby writing movie scripts. The first time I sent one of my movie scripts to an agent in Los Angeles, she sent it back immediately saying she couldn't be bothered to read past page ten. I was, of course, devastated, but when I went back and read the script myself, I realized that I'd made a common rookie mistake: My *story* started on page thirty. Everything before that was background! So I wrote back to her, and said that even though I'd found her criticism devastating at the time, I realized it was really the best advice I'd ever received about screenwriting. Gosh, I'm such a grown-up!

3. As Mary Harblin advise, **"Show that you reacted proactively.** If a problem involved someone else, show how you talked with the other person about it.'' Showing off your communication skills is a real plus.

4. **Don't insult the interviewer by answering with an example that doesn't reflect the question.** Your greatest obstacle can't be a B in Criminal Law. The disagreement with your boss can't be over which brand of coffee you have at the office. By the same token ...

5. **Don't be afraid to reword the question if you feel it's not terribly applicable to your background.** One student, when faced with the "serious obstacle" question, responded that he felt he'd been blessed, and compared to what some people had been through he hadn't faced any serious obstacles. If that's you, you could go on to say you've faced intellectual challenges and minor setbacks here and there, but none that would qualify as serious.

6. **Facing negative behavioral questions is one time in an interview when it's all right to say, "I'm**

afraid I just can't think of one in the moment." Or you can try to get the interviewer to reword the question. For instance, maybe you had a boss that other people viewed as difficult, but you didn't have a problem with him or her. You could ask if the interviewer would like to hear about how you handled that. For the angry customer, if you've never worked in a situation where you *had* customers, you can ask if you can talk about dealing with an angry teammate in a sport or on a school project, and how you overcame that.

7. **Don't say you've never missed a deadline, faced harsh criticism, and made a bad decision.** As Mary Harblin points out, "If you say you've never missed a deadline, you better have spent your career in the military. That's the only place it's believable."

8. **Mary Harblin advises you to "Avoid blaming other people irrationally."** For the deadline and criticism questions, for instance, be sure that you take responsibility appropriately. No employer wants a whiny buck-passer.

d. **Follow up your example with what you intend it to show about you.** "I tell you this story, because I like to think it shows that I . . ."

e. **You can also follow up with a question.** You can ask— *smiling*—"Are you telling me I'm likely to disagree with my supervisor if I work for you?" "Are you suggesting that the clients I deal with will probably be angry?" "If I work for you, should I expect some harsh criticism?"

34. HYPOTHETICAL QUESTIONS

Questions involving hypotheticals don't come up in every legal interview. They're rare in interviews with private law firms. But if you're looking for a position within a prosecutor's or public defender's office, or a judge, you're very likely to face hypotheticals. In judicial clerkship interviews they're more likely to involve your reasoning and philosophy, whereas with jobs that will quickly plunge you into client contact and the courtroom, you're more likely to face questions about what might happen during a day at work, like "You know your client is lying. What do you do?" or "You see another D.A. with drugs at a party. What do you do?" As Amy Thompson says, "For the public defender and D.A.'s offices, they *need* to see how you think and how resourceful you are. That's because they give you two weeks' prep, then you're out there!"

A student at a West Coast school told me about a typical experience: "I went to a public interest agency for an interview. They gave me a civil rights case two minutes before the interview and told me to read it. In the interview, they grilled me about the case, how I would argue each side, and so on. It was pretty nerve-wracking!"

Here's some advice about answering hypotheticals:

- **"Don't feel you need to be perfect,"** advises Jose Baha-monde–Gonzalez. "No one expects you to be familiar with all of the case law. What's much more important is for you to maintain a professional demeanor." In other words—don't let the question fluster you!

- **"Treat it like moot court,"** counsels Maureen Provost Ryan. "Take a viewpoint and argue the merits of the case. Expect some criticism, and if you get it, stick to your guns. If you don't, the interviewer will think you're weak. But if they come up with a good point, say so."

- **"It's OK to say that because you've only had a limited exposure to that area of the law, you're not certain what the answer should be,"** says Gail Peshel. But if you *don't* know the answer, **be sure that you come back with information about where you'd look to find it, how you'd research it**. You may also be able to deflect the question by analogizing it with a case you've analyzed be-fore. And you can *always* wind up by saying that you'd check with your supervisor/a more senior associate or clerk/the firm librarian (if the employer has one) for the next step. Employers don't expect you to reinvent the wheel, and stating that you'd be more efficient by relying on others is a positive!

- **"Whatever you do, don't hem and haw!"** advises Laura Rowe Lane. "Silence is OK." In fact, asking for a moment to think about it says *volumes* about your confidence! After you've taken a moment to think, either come back with an answer, or say, "I'm not familiar with it, but here's how I'd research it . . ."

- **Remember: Being able to say where you'd find an answer is just as valuable as coming up with one on the spot.** Don't risk a foolish answer if you're really not sure of yourself!

- **Assure the interviewer you would never answer a client question off the top of your head!** It may be that you AmJured the class that's the subject of a client's ques-tion. Or maybe you wrote a Law Review note about it six months ago. *It doesn't matter.* You *can't* answer questions in a snap. You might be wrong. So assure the interviewer you'd never do it!

* * * SMART HUMAN TRICK * * *

Female law student, interviewing with a prosecutor's office. The interviewer asks her, "You know about the three strikes rule. If the third crime was something petty, like stealing a piece of pizza, what would you do?" She said, "I couldn't tell from the way he asked it how he felt about it. I certainly had issues with it. I figured the best strategy was to dodge it; I said I'd consult with my colleagues to ensure a united front, that I'd need more facts, that I didn't think I could give a blanket response. He nodded and seemed satisfied with the answer."

- **Never, ever answer with anything unethical.** If the interviewer seems to be setting you up to take an unethical approach, *don't take the bait.* "I'd do whatever it takes to prevail" is the kind of answer designed to lead to a perp walk on the evening news. Don't *ever* step into unethical territory in an interview question!

35. WHO'S YOUR HERO?

You have three choices here: humor, a personal choice, or someone eminently "emulatable."

- **Humor**. Whenever I was asked this question in interviews, I'd answer "Ed McMahon"—you know, the guy from Publisher's Clearing House. I'd smile as I said it, and the interviewers always laughed.

- **A personal choice**. Parents, grandparents, someone who inspired you as a kid, a mentor. These are really a no-brainer.

- **A great legal mind or prior employer, a great historical figure or leader**. This would be an obvious professional choice.

No matter who you choose, here are things to keep in mind:

- **Make sure that you come up with a good reason for your choice**. What did this person do to inspire you?

- **Be sincere**. If you say "Chief Justice Marshall," you'd better have a rockin' reason, because it sounds like you're sucking up.

- **Don't worry about your answer sounding corny!** I talked to a student in Virginia who'd clerked for a judge, and he felt funny saying that this guy was his inspiration. I assured him that it wasn't corny at all, and even if you feel that way, it's perfectly fine to acknowledge that and say, "I know this sounds corny, but the judge I worked for really inspired me ..." Trust me. You'll sound just fine. And what employer doesn't want to hear that you chose an *employer* as your hero?

Depending on your rapport with the interviewer, you have an obvious follow-up, by asking the interviewer who his/her hero is. It could lead to an interesting conversation!

36.   "WHO *ARE* YOU?" QUESTIONS

This category of questions is a minefield. They don't solicit anything relevant to your ability to do the job, and they aren't a very viable way to find out something personal about you.

So why do people ask them? As Mary Obrzut points out, "They're getting at: Can you think on your feet? What if you get caught off guard?"

There's no way to give you a complete list of these questions, but this list gives you an idea of the kinds of questions some interviewers will ask you. If you have a clever response, great. Otherwise, **what's key with your answer is not the choice itself but your *reasoning*.** *Why* talk with that particular person? *Why* this kind of tree? The reasoning should reflect positive attributes about you and your good judgment. And you can always turn around and ask the interviewer the same question: "OK. Which historical figure would *you* like to talk to?"

Potential choices an interviewer might offer you include:

- "Who in history would you like to talk with?" (Let your imagination run wild!)
- "Are you a 'forest' person or a 'tree' person?" (I'd answer, "I don't know, but I assure you I'm not a Forrest *Gump* person.")
- "If you were a tree, what kind of tree would you be?" (A legendary Barbara Walters question.)
- "What's the last book you read?" (Have a decent book ready that you can discuss, even if it wasn't the last one you read. Or tell them—this book. Talk about impressing them with your preparation!)
- "What's the toughest decision you ever had to make?"
- "Which one of the Fruit of the Loom guys would you be?" (Seriously—an interviewer really asked this.)
- "If you could have been in any case in history, what would it be, would you be the plaintiff or defendant, and why?" (My favourite answer *ever* to this question was from a student in California, who was "absolutely stumped when the interviewer asked me this. I was so nervous that the only case I could think of was Marbury vs. Madison, the one we were studying in Con Law. It was hilarious. What made it so funny was that the parties themselves were absolutely irrelevant to the case, so there I am stumbling around about it being a landmark case, blah blah blah, and the interviewer

just wasn't buying it. I was so tempted to say that I'd like to be the defendant in the case of State vs. Me, where I'm on trial for killing the interviewer who'd ask me a question like that!")

- "If you were an animal, what kind of animal would you be?" (My favourite law student answer to this question is: "Certainly nothing in the rodent family.")

37. IF YOU ARE ASKED ABOUT ANYTHING YOU DELIBERATELY LEFT OFF YOUR RESUME . . .

We talked in the Resume chapter about how your resume is a marketing piece, designed to show the employer that you can do a great job for them based on what you've already done. It's by necessity edited; it's a resume, not an autobiography! So you might have left off brief, unfortunate work experiences, or classes you took for another degree, or a blog you write under a pseudonym, or . . . you name it.

What if the interviewer somehow finds out about it? **You say something along the lines of, "I didn't include it because I didn't think it contributed to my ability to work for you . . ." and explain why.**

What you're doing, of course, is to assure the interviewer that there aren't any serious flaws in your background that you're concealing from them. So your delivery is as important as your words. Speak matter-of-factly about the unimportance of what you excluded. Show that you're fine talking about it. If it's an unfortunate work experience, talk about the positives you *did* take from it. You can always wind up by talking about highlights from your resume that you thought *were* relevant.

K. DETERMINE, IN ADVANCE, HOW YOU'LL DEAL WITH ILLEGAL QUESTIONS

It's ironic, isn't it? The idea that illegal questions would come up in interviews for legal jobs—from people who are lawyers, for gosh sakes? But it happens, and fairly often, at that. In fact, a student in Florida was asked in an interview if she had children . . . and the interviewer was a female partner at an employment law firm!

What *is* an illegal question, exactly? It may not be what you think. It's a question that's asked of only a certain group of candidates, defined by race or gender or economic status, and it's a question that has nothing to do with your ability to do the work. In addition, the hiring decision has to be made on the basis of the information gleaned from the illegal question(s).

Of course, the most common type of illegal question involves asking women whether they're married and whether they have (or intend to have) children. Others include age and national origin.

It's important to come up with your strategy for dealing with illegal questions up front. I'll take you through your options so you can make a choice that works for you!

1. DON'T *ASSUME* AN EVIL MOTIVE!

You're not going to want to believe what I'm about to tell you: namely, most illegal questions are asked innocently. "But Kimmbo!" you're saying. "They're *lawyers!* They should *know* better!" Maybe so. But remember: they're not professional interviewers. As Jose Bahamonde–Gonzalez points out, "They're probably as ill-at-ease as you are, and may ask inappropriate questions as a result, just as a means of breaking the ice. After all, asking someone if they're married or if they have children would under any other circumstances just be friendly." I've mentioned to you before that the best interviews are conversations. In a conversation with someone new, you'd never feel constrained to talk only about work, current events and philosophical issues. You'd naturally migrate towards asking, "Are you married?"

One California firm sent out an interviewer to do on-campus interviews. He happened to be Jewish. He would ask Jewish interviewees questions like, "Do you keep a kosher home?" When confronted by the Career Services Director (who'd received dozens of complaints about these questions), the interviewer was flabbergasted, and responded, "What's the big problem? *I'm* Jewish!" He honestly didn't realize he'd offended anybody!

An illegal question may also be an inappropriate way of addressing a valid concern. Debra Fink explains, "If someone asks 'Are you married?' they may just be using a clumsy way of asking, 'Will you have to relocate?' Remember, a firm needs you to work for them for about three years to earn back their investment in training you, and they'll naturally be concerned if there's some impediment to your being able to remain within them into at least the foreseeable future."

I talked with a student at one school whose interview experience had been a real stumper. This student was a young *man* who'd been asked by an interviewer, "Are you married?" The student asked me, "Was he asking me if I'm gay?" I said I didn't think so, but the student and I both followed up with his Career Services Director, who called the employer to see what was going on. It turns out that it was a small law firm in a small town, and the interviewer explained, "I always ask students if they're married, because if they're not, they're unlikely to meet anybody here. There's no night life whatsoever—and they probably won't be happy!" As Mercer's Pat Bass points out, "That kind of question can get at issues like whether you've got roots there, your rainmaking potential. There's a lot to it."

I actually have experience with this issue from the interviewer's side of the desk. When I was in law school at Case Western, I was on the student committee that interviewed prospective professors. Now, if you're not familiar with Cleveland, you may find it hard to believe that there are a lot of people who don't want to live there. It's an undeserved reputation. Rock and Roll Hall of Fame! Rock and Roll Hall of Fame! But anyway, whenever we interviewed a potential prof, the question at the very front of our minds was, "Are you married?" We figured even if the interviewee him/herself was willing to move to Cleveland, *it was entirely possible that their spouse would say 'No way!'* We really wanted to know: Does your spouse's career make a move to Cleveland feasible? Might they even—heaven forefend—*like* the idea of it? But of course, we couldn't ask it . . . even though it was a very valid issue!

So—start off by assuming, as Desdemona did of Cassio that the interviewer erred of ignorance, not malice. With that in mind, you . . .

2. MAKE A CHOICE: EITHER REFUSE TO ANSWER, OR REWORD THE QUESTION TO ADDRESS A VALID ISSUE, AND ANSWER *THAT*

You always have the option of refusing to answer a question you find offensive. Remember, a question is only technically *illegal* if it's asked of a certain targeted group and it's the basis of the hiring decision. The problem is that in the moment you can't possibly know who else is being asked the same thing! You can, of course, ask, "Are you asking everybody that question?" but in asking that—or confronting the interviewer by responding "I'm not going to answer that" or "You can't ask that"—you've certainly cut off the possibility of getting a job with that employer. If you find those questions so offensive that you truly wouldn't want to work with anyone who would ask such a thing, then you've made the right decision.

But . . .

Remember: most of the time, the questions are innocent. On top of that, you may really want the job. That's why all of the Career Services people I've talked with agree that a better approach is this:

Reword the question to address a valid concern, and answer *that*. You're discreetly giving the interviewer the benefit of the doubt, and if they're truly not a jerk, they'll appreciate it. As Kathleen Brady points out, "It's important to be polite and remember your tone of voice when you reword questions. Remember—what you're looking for is the question behind the question. Respond to that."

For instance, if an interviewer asks, "Do you have kids?" you can respond with something like, "If you're concerned about how much of a commitment I can make to working for you, the answer is that I can devote as much time as necessary to my job." Or if the interviewer notices your engagement ring, and asks, "Do you intend to have children?" you could answer along the lines of, "That's sometime in the future. I understand the time commitment you expect from your new associates, and I wouldn't be wasting your time interviewing with you if I wasn't willing to make that commitment." Or you might be in the position to answer the way a student at a Tennessee school did: "My fiancé and I have already settled the issue: When and if we have children, he's going to be 'Mr. Mom.' In fact, it was his idea!"

You can preface your answer with a quip. "If you're asking me if I've done my part to ensure the continuation of the species, the answer is yes." Then give your more serious answer.

You might even answer the question and follow up by throwing it back at the interviewer. "Do *you* have children?" Comparing notes on parenthood is a great way to bond with anybody— including an interviewer!

Now, if you wind up with an offer and you accept it, you may well find out that the firm is stocked with offensive jerks and that you should never have answered the question in the first place. But at least at that point you've got a bit of work experience under your belt, and looking for job number two is a lot easier than nailing job number one!

3. IF YOU'RE MARRIED, BE PREPARED FOR THE QUESTION "WHAT DOES YOUR SPOUSE DO?"

It's not an appropriate interview question, but as I suggested in #2 above, the employer might have a legitimate concern that your spouse has career plans that would take you away from the employer. If you're comfortable with it, you can of course say what your spouse does; if not, it's perfectly appropriate to say something like, "The most important thing my wife/husband does is to support me in whatever I want to do with my law degree. That's why I'm talking to you!"

4. Report the incident to your Career Services Director.

If you think you've received a question that's not entirely innocent, be sure to report it to your Career Services Director. Even if it *is* innocent, you may want to say something—because even though you didn't find it offensive, some other student *might,* and you may want to save the interviewer any embarrassment.

Your Career Services Director will handle the issue sensitively, by the way. (S)he won't call the employer and challenge them, "You know what X said to me? She told me you've been asking illegal questions!" They won't rat you out, but they will make sure it doesn't happen again!

(Incidentally, for outrageous examples of illegal questions, check out the "Interviewers Hall of Shame" at the end of this chapter.)

3. STEP THREE: RESEARCH!

Research shows that 85% of interviewees don't do it: research. Mistake! You've got some research to do before every interview. Whether you're at the top of your class at a distinguished law school or you're trailing the crowd at Fred's Night YMCA Law School, it doesn't matter. You can't go into interviews cold and expect to impress the interviewer.

I hear you moaning, "But Kimm, I'm so *busy.*" I know, I know, I'm not going to wear you out. You're going to spend about fifteen finely-tuned minutes for every interview. And isn't a great job worth it?

A. HOW RESEARCH WILL HELP YOU

Let me count the ways ...

1. IT'S PROOF POSITIVE OF YOUR ENTHUSIASM

Throughout this book I've been hitting you over the head with the importance of showing honest enthusiasm for the employer. Nothing proves that more than knowing all you can about the employer and the interviewer, and showing it off during the interview. Think about it: how flattered would *you* be if someone came in to interview for a job with *you,* and they showed through their comments and questions that they'd gone to the trouble of finding out all they could about you. Wouldn't that tell you that they'd be a thorough and dedicated employee? True dat.

In fact, Notre Dame's Gail Peshel told me a story about a student who exemplified this. This student prepared for the firm he wanted as he'd prepare for a final exam. He did full on-line searches, talked to alums, and dug up all he could about the firm, especially the people he'd be interviewing with. When he got to the firm, the people he was supposed to talk with weren't there! But he'd researched the firm so thoroughly that he knew all about the people he *did* interview with, so he could ask them specifics about projects they were working on ... *even though he didn't know beforehand that he'd be talking with them!* Were they impressed? As Gail Peshel says, "Who *wouldn't* be?"

A partner at an eight-person firm talked about his all-time favourite on-campus interview. "We are all avid fly-fishermen at the firm. We routinely go fishing together on weekends. I mention sometimes in interviews that we all love to fly fish, and I get all kinds of reactions from students. Some of them say, 'Oh,' some of them express an interest in trying it, one woman even said, 'Is fly fishing a requirement of the job?' which I thought was funny. But there was this one student who somehow had found out about our fly fishing before the interview. He showed up in full fishing gear, holding a fishing rod, and he looked at me and said, "Let's go!" It was hilarious. He didn't have to say another word. I asked him back to the firm on the spot, and he wound up working for us."

* * * SMART HUMAN TRICK * * *

One female student at a Southern law school set her sights on practicing environmental law. There was one particular firm that she really wanted to work for. She read everything she could about the lawyers, and found that several of the associates were from her school. When she got an interview there, she took paperweights featuring a picture of the law school, and presented them to the alumni. They were impressed with her thoughtfulness . . . and she got the job.

2. YOU'LL COME UP WITH AWESOME QUESTIONS TO ASK

In the next section, we'll be talking about questions to ask during an interview. Hands down, the best questions spring from research about the employer. In fact, one of the bigger boners you can make is to ask questions you could easily have discovered from a bit of basic research ahead of time.

3. YOU'LL AVOID MAKING BONEHEADED COMMENTS

One of the biggest mistakes you can make is to lack even a basic knowledge of what the employer's practice areas are. If your law firm does criminal defense work, and you ask me which specialty I'm interested in, *it better be criminal defense!* If I say "environmental law"—well! How does that impress *you?*

As Kathleen Brady says, "Don't say you don't want to be a tax attorney to someone who's a tax attorney!" San Diego's Susan Benson adds, "Don't ask things like, "You practice insurance litigation? Really?"" And Florida's Ann Skalaski advises, "Don't say you're interested in Houston, Atlanta and Washington, if the firm doesn't have any offices there!"

Examples of this abound. A young woman, #1 in her class at a New England law school, wasn't getting any call-back interviews during on-campus interview season. It turns out she was telling all of the large law firms that she was interested in their domestic relations department. None of them had one. This one mistake completely shut her out!

Mistakes like these will immediately boot you off the potential employee island. A little homework and they're easily avoided.

* * * CAREER LIMITING MOVE * * *

A Second Year student at a school in the Pacific Northwest has an on-campus interview with a large law firm. She knows the firm has an environmental law section, but doesn't learn anything about their work beyond that. In the interview, she says, "I think it's so great that you do environmental work. I love it. My parents have always belonged to Greenpeace and I've been to tons of environmental protest rallies."

The interviewer comments afterwards, "She could have said it a lot simpler: 'I have no idea what you do.' "

4. YOU'LL LEARN MORE ABOUT WHY YOU WANT (OR DON'T WANT) TO WORK FOR THIS EMPLOYER

As you research particular employers, you'll sharpen your focus on what you want to do. Inevitably you'll react to things you learn by saying to yourself, "Hey—I love that!" or "I'm not down with that . . ."

That kind of self-assessment is always useful, because it gives you an idea of the kinds of employers you ought to target—and it tells you which traits you're looking for in an ideal employer. I've mentioned before the student from Georgia who sent out a mass mailer and got an interview with an outfit in Florida, which she described basically as "Kill the Manatees." She didn't know anything at all about them before the interview; she found when she got there was that they represented boat propeller manufacturers who opposed regulations designed to save the manatees. "Ugh," she said. "All overalls and mullets." Research can save you from that kind of mistake!

As Beth Kirch points out, "If you've got kids, you want to see if the employer is family-friendly. Their web site will often give it away. See how many of the women lawyers have kids. If they're involved in programs like sick child care, women's law initiatives, then they're for real."

5. YOU'LL BE A LOT MORE RELAXED AND CONFIDENT DURING YOUR INTERVIEW

There's no question about it: the more prepared you are, the more relaxed and confident you'll feel—and the better you'll interview. It will infuse everything you say and all of your nonverbal communication, too. That kind of self-assurance is very attractive to employers!

* * * SMART HUMAN TRICK * * *

Law student from a New England school has an on-campus interview with a small boutique firm from out-of-state. He researches the firm in depth, even finding the newspaper for the firm's town and scanning it for mentions of the firm.

Several of the firm's lawyers are in on the interview. At the end of the interview, one of the lawyers asks the student, "Do you have any more questions for us?"

He responds, "Yes. Did you find the guy who stole your vacuum cleaner?"

The lawyers are astonished. Their firm had been broken into and one of the minor things taken was their vacuum cleaner. "How on Earth did you know *that?*" one of them asks him. Needless to say, they're very impressed!

B. THE TWO THINGS YOU'LL RESEARCH—AND WHERE YOU'LL LOOK

You've got to dig up dirt on both the employer *and* the interviewer.

1. RESEARCHING THE EMPLOYER

For researching employers, check out Chapter 6. I've put all the information about employer research there, because it's so important in so many aspects of your job search, from cover letters to resumes to interviews.

However, when it comes to interviews, there are a couple of other items to keep in mind.

a. First, make sure you can pronounce the employer's name.

I've never seen a study about this, but I'll bet there's a direct correlation between having an unusual moniker and becoming a name partner at a huge prestigious law firm. Skadden? Arps? Flom? Cadwalader? Shook? I could go on, but you see my point.

It is absolutely crucial that you pronounce the employer's name correctly, no matter how unusual it is. For an on campus interview, ask at Career Services. For off-campus interviews, call the office, and listen to how it's pronounced by the receptionist. You can always say that you were calling specifically for that purpose. You won't look stupid—it's a wise move!

* * * CAREER LIMITING MOVE * * *

Student with middling credentials is dying to break into Entertainment Law. He gets an interview with a lawyer at a dream employer of his, Arista Records. He reports, "I'm sitting in this interview, and the guy gets a call from another law student. I could tell from his side of the conversation that this other student had it all—Ivy League degree, Law Review, everything. I figure, how am I going to compete with *this* guy?

"The lawyer gets off the phone, and he laughs derisively, points at the phone, and says, 'He's got no chance.' It turns out the guy had mispronounced the name of the label! It's AH-ris-ta, not ah-RIS-ta, the way he pronounced it.

"Thank God I got it right!"

b. Know the names of important people in the organization and any "breaking news" about the employer.

If you're interviewing with a prosecutor's office, *you better know the name of the prosecutor.* If the firm with whom you're interviewing merged with another firm *yesterday,* you better know about the merger and who it was with. Check the employer's website *immediately* before your interview to make sure you don't drop the ball!

* * * CAREER LIMITING MOVE * * *

The Bronx District Attorney's office conducted interviews at a New York law school. The interviewer started each interview with the following question:

"Who is the Bronx D.A.?"

Most students couldn't answer ... and their interviews ended immediately.

2. RESEARCHING THE INTERVIEWER

Researching the interviewer can help you out in a bunch of ways. It'll give you insights into questions you can ask. It lets you know where they're coming from in questions they ask you. And it can give you ideas about topics to bring up to turn the interview into a conversation—which is what you really want.

Some interviewers deny the importance of this kind of research, by the way. A lawyer on an interview panel at one law school said, "I don't believe in the idea of students looking up stuff in my background. It doesn't work."

The Career Services Director responded, "Interesting. By the way, I see you went to State College. So did I." They started chatting about it in front of the students. Then the Career Services Director smiled and said, "Do you still think personal stuff doesn't work?" The lawyer laughed and conceded the point!

Of course, at some point research becomes stalking. But the sources and methods we'll talk about here *work.* Watch the interviewer's reaction as you bring up things about their background to figure out their boundaries ... but err on the side of knowing *more* about the interviewer, not less!

a. Finding out the interviewer's identity.

I don't mean anything metaphysical here. What I'm talking about is finding out the interviewer's name. This is obviously only an issue for on-campus interviews, call-backs, and job fairs, where you typically don't know who the interviewer is ahead of time.

Here's how you solve this problem. For on-campus interviews, ask Career Services to call and determine the interviewer's identity (the idea here is to prevent the employer from getting twenty calls from students, all asking the same question). For job fairs, **give the employer a call the afternoon before your interview, and ask straight out who the interviewer will be.** If you hear "It could be one of a couple of people," "We're not sure yet," ask for names of the several people it might be. You can research three or four lawyers just about as quickly as you can research one. Then jot down notes on each potential interviewer (or enter notes into your Black-Berry, PDA, whatever), and then ask at Career Services (or at the job fair) before your interview for the name of the interviewer. That'll give you time to review your notes on the interviewer before your interview.

b.   Sources to use in researching the interviewer.

No surprise here: you use many of the same resources for interviewers as you do for their employers, namely:

1.   The employer's web site;
2.   Martindale/Hubbell;
3.   The employer's written materials at Career Services;
4.   Google;
5.   Students/alums who've worked with the interviewer;
6.   Students/alums who've worked in the same kind of job and might know what the interview will be like;
7.   MySpace, Facebook, and other social networking sites ... *with caution.* You can *only* use information that is professional or neutral, *nothing that could embarrass the interviewer and/or was clearly meant to be read by friends.*

c.   What to find out.

Among other things, you want to find out:

1.   Where are they from?
2.   Did they work before law school, and if so, where and doing what?
3.   Where did they go to college and law school?
4.   What were their significant activities in law school? (You know. Law Review.)
5.   What has been their career path since law school?
6.   Any significant hobbies?

If you want to dig even further, you could learn:

7. What have they written? If they've written articles, seek out those articles on-line and skim them. If they've written a Law Review note, shepardize it to see if it's been mentioned in a published opinion.

8. What major cases have they been involved with, especially recently? If you have time, review the cases;

9. If you talk to students/alums who've worked with them, ask what they're like (driven, laid-back, formal, casual), what they look for in people they interview, what to talk about and what to avoid talking about.

10. Their birthday!

* * * SMART HUMAN TRICK * * *

Student at a Virginia school found out before an off-campus interview that his interviewer would be celebrating his birthday on interview day.

At the last minute, the firm changed interviewers. After his interview, the student asked to stop by the original interviewer's office. He poked his head in the door and said, "Happy Birthday." The lawyer was very touched. On the way out, the lawyer's secretary told the student, "Good for you! *I* didn't even know it was his birthday!"

* * * SMART HUMAN TRICK * * *

A lawyer from a Midwest firm is scheduled to conduct on-campus interviews on his birthday. All day long, he conducts twenty-minute interviews, none of which are particularly memorable.

And no one mentions his birthday.

Until . . .

The last interview of the day. On the way out, the student turns and says, "By the way—Happy Birthday."

That student gets the only call-back interview.

* * * SMART HUMAN TRICK * * *

Student at a California school wanted to join the in-house counsel's office at a tech company. He got an interview with the general counsel, whom we'll call Biff. He talked with an alum that worked there and asked for advice about interviewing with Biff. The alum asked, "What's your ultimate goal when you talk to Biff?"

The student responded, "I want his job."

The alum: "Good. Tell him that! He loves to hear that kind of ambition."

The student commented, "I would never have said it if the alum hadn't told me to. I would have felt too brash. But it worked. I got the job."

* * * SMART HUMAN TRICK * * *

Law student, law school in Indiana. He's interviewing with a partner from a large New York firm. He calls an alum who works at the firm, and says, "I'm interviewing on-campus with partner Sven tomorrow. I'm really interested in the firm and I'd really appreciate your help. Any advice on what I should do?" The associate asks, "Dude—where did you go to college?" The student responds, "St. Olaf in Minnesota."

The associate says, "He went there, too. You've got to know the fight song. If you can sing it—you're in."

The student thanks him and calls his college roommate, who refreshes his memory for the song.

Sure enough, at the interview, Partner Sven says, "I see you went to St. Olaf. Can you sing the fight song?"

The student sings it, to the clapping accompaniment of the partner.

He gets a call-back interview.

* * * SMART HUMAN TRICK * * *

Law student researches her interviewer, reading his profile on the employer's web site. She finds that he wrote a Law Review note in law school, and she Shepardizes the note on-line to see if it's been mentioned anywhere. She finds out that a couple of judges have mentioned his note recently in their opinions. She downloads the two pages that mention his note, and slips the pages into her portfolio on the way into the interview.

At the beginning of the interview, while they are getting acquainted, she mentions, "By the way, I couldn't help noticing that you wrote a Law Review note in school. Did you realize that a couple of judges recently have mentioned your note in their opinions?"

He responds, "I had no idea."

She goes on, "I thought you might say that. I brought them with me." She hands him the two sheets, and reports: "He was so thrilled, after that, I could have thrown up on him, and I would still have gotten the job. He gets out his cell phone, he's calling his friends—I didn't even have to be in the room!"

Incidentally—she gets the job!

* * * SMART HUMAN TRICK * * *

Student with middling credentials at a Southern school. She manages to nail a couple of on-campus interviews. She reports: "I knew I was somewhere below what they normally go for credentials-wise. So I found out who the interviewers were going to be, and I sent them a letter ahead of time talking about how much I was looking forward to interviewing with them.

"Those letters really went over big. They both commented on them, and I think those letters really played a role in my getting call-backs at both firms."

* * * SMART HUMAN TRICK * * *

Student at a Texas school, has an on-campus interview with the Army JAG Corps. She does some research ahead of time. When she gets to the interview room, she knocks on the door, and calls out, "Permission to enter, Sergeant?" The interviewer responds, "Permission granted."

When she walks into the room, she can tell immediately that he's impressed. He asks her, "Do you have any military experience?"

She responds, "No, but I really want this job, so I found out as much as I could ahead of time."

She says afterwards, "This guy was so tickled with what I said, he gave me advice on what to say on subsequent interviews with everybody else in JAG."

* * * SMART HUMAN TRICK * * *

Law student has an on-campus interview with a litigator from a large firm. The morning of the interview, the student goes on-line and discovers that the lawyer had received a ruling from the 7th Circuit that very day. The student reads it.

At the interview, the student mentions, "I see you got a ruling from the 7th Circuit this morning." The interviewer says he hasn't had a chance to read it. The student responds, "Well, *I* have." He briefs the interviewer on it. Needless to say—the interviewer is incredibly impressed. The student gets a call-back.

* * * SMART HUMAN TRICK * * *

Student looks at his interviewer's profile on the firm website before an interview, and sees that the interviewer likes magic.

The student walks into the interview and says, "I understand you're interested in magic," and the interviewer responds warmly, "Yes."

The student responds, "Well, I'm wondering if you could do a little magic here and make a job appear."

The interviewer laughs. The student winds up with an offer.

* * * SMART HUMAN TRICK * * *

Student from Pittsburgh, driving for an interview with a Public Defender's Office in Kentucky. On the way, she phones a classmate and says, "Do me a favour, Dude. Here's the name of my interviewer. Go on-line and see what you find out about him."

The friend finds quickly that the interviewer just argued a case in front of the United States Supreme Court. The student mentions this in the interview and asks, "What was it like?"

The interviewer is absolutely thrilled. It turns out this student was the only one to mention the case. When the student goes on her second interview to meet others in the office, the interviewer introduces her with the line: "This is the student I told you about—the one who knew about the Supreme Court case."

3. RESEARCH OTHER PEOPLE AT THE EMPLOYER, WHILE YOU'RE RESEARCHING THE INTERVIEWER

Skimming everyone's biography is a good idea ... but if you're interviewing with the Justice Department or Baker and Mac-kenzie, that's clearly not possible! If instead you're interviewing with a smallish law firm, try it; or at a large employer, if you're interviewing with a particular practice area or department, research everyone in that section. Glance at where they went to school, any tidbits about their practice, any other highlights. In addition, as Tammy Willcox points out, "You want to see who you've got connections with. See if there's anyone from your law school, or your undergrad school. *They'll* mention it, and you'll be tripped up otherwise."

4. HOW YOU'LL USE WHAT YOU FIND OUT ABOUT THE INTERVIEWER

In the very next section, we'll talk about **questions to ask in an interview**—and that's the primary use of your research on the interviewer. But it will help you in other ways, as well. **It will stop you from giving embarrassing answers to questions**; for instance, if the interviewer asks why you didn't go to the local law school, before you respond, "Because I got into a much better one," it'd be helpful to know that the interviewer went there.

It will also give you an "exit strategy" for tough questions you're asked. If you're asked why your college major will be helpful practicing law, it's great if you can turn around and say, "I know you were a Biology major. How has that impacted your practice?'' or if you're on an out of town interview and the interview asks, "What makes you think you'll like it in X city?" what a great wind-up if you can say, "I know you're from Y and you went to Z to go to school. How did you wind up in X city?"

On top of that, **it's implicit evidence of your enthusiasm for working for the employer**. After all, you'd never go to the trouble of digging up information about the interviewer if you weren't truly interested in the job. And remember: enthusiasm is enticing to *every* employer!

* * * CAREER LIMITING MOVE * * *

Law student interviewing in a city we'll call Lillyville—which has a law school, Lillyville Law School.

She is scheduled to eat lunch with two associates. In the elevator on the way out of the office, one of them asks her, "You're from here, right? Why did you leave town to go to Prestige Law School?"

She responds, "Well, if I stayed *here,* my only option was Lillyville Law—and I wasn't going to go *there.*"

Oh, really? Because guess where the associates in the elevator went to law school . . .

Lillyville.

As one of them comments: "It wasn't so much that she went to Prestige—if I got in there, I would have gone, too—but in Lillyville there's a great likelihood that lawyers you meet went to Lillyville. Her whole attitude about it made you wonder how smart she really was."

5. "HELLO, TURD BLOSSOM." DON'T MENTION *ANYTHING* POTENTIALLY EMBARRASSING TO THE INTERVIEWER

In the course of your research—especially on social networking sites—you may discover potentially embarrassing information (or photos) featuring the interviewer. *For gosh sakes, don't mention it!* No interviewer needs to hear you utter the words, "Nice thong."

President Bush the Younger apparently nicknamed his advisor Karl Rove "Turd Blossom." You wouldn't walk into a job interview with Rove and say, "How's it hangin', Turd Blossom?"

Interviewers won't admire your research skills if you unearth something that embarrasses them. They'll question your tact and discretion . . . two very necessary skills for lawyers.

6. "NICE TO MEET YOU, MR. DUMBASS." THE MOST IMPORTANT ELEMENT OF YOUR INTERVIEW RESEARCH

If you aren't absolutely, positively sure how to pronounce the interviewer's name, resolve it *before* you set

foot in the interview room! For on-campus interviews, check with Career Services; off-campus, call the employer. You can even call off-hours and listen to the interviewer's voice mail to determine the pronunciation. I am English, and we Brits are the absolute *worst* for misleading names. My favourite is "Chalmonde-lay," which is inexplicably pronounced "Chumley."

Incidentally, I stole the "Mr. Dumbass" line from an old TV ad, where a guy is interviewing with someone named "Dumas" (which is pronounced Doo–MAH, by the way).

7. BE SENSITIVE TO THE INTERVIEWER'S DEMEANOR AS YOU SHARE WHAT YOU'VE LEARNED ABOUT THEM

I've mentioned before: At some point, researching becomes stalking. Note how the interviewer is taking what you say about them. Do they look surprised and delighted? Or do they look taken aback? One lawyer commented, "When I'm in an interview and the student knows every case I've argued, I feel like I've been stalked!"

A federal judge, interviewing a potential clerk, sat slack-jawed as she analyzed case after case that he had decided. His assistant, sitting in on the interview, commented, "Judge, she'll eat you alive."

If you get that kind of reaction, ramp back *immediately* and say something like, "I guess I let my enthusiasm carry me away," and let the interviewer take charge.

Also, try adding the source of your information to your comments and questions. "I saw in your firm profile ..." "Alum X who used to work for you ..." "I saw in a newspaper article ..." When they hear your legitimate sources, they won't think you're a potential bunny boiler!

4. STEP FOUR: DEVELOP QUESTIONS TO ASK (AND AVOID ASKING THE WRONG ONES)

Aha! When you think of questions in interviews, you think of what the interviewer will ask *you*—don't you? But the fact is, the questions *you* ask are just as important—if not more so. As Sandy Mans points out, "The questions you ask give you a real opportunity to distinguish yourself."

If you ask the right questions—and I'll show you how to do just that—you'll accomplish three important things:

- **You'll gather key information about the firm.**

    Well, duh! You're thinking. But it's easy to forget that interviews are a two way street. It shouldn't just be the interviewer figuring out if they want to work with you—you should be sitting there thinking, "Do I want to work with this firm?" Asking the right questions, and watching for how the interviewer responds—both verbally and in demeanor—can go a long way toward accomplishing that.

- **You'll turn the interview into a conversation.**

    I've told you already that the best interviews are conversations. Not only are they more pleasant, but when an interview is conversational, subconsciously the interviewer is thinking: this is what it would be like working with you.

- **You'll show off your research into the firm and the interviewer.**

    If you've gone to the trouble of researching the employer, for gosh sakes, show it off! Asking questions that relate to your research helps you do just that. Interviewers find these kinds of questions very impressive. Why? Well, remember the value of honest enthusiasm. If you ask questions that stem from your research of the employer, you're implicitly indicating your desire to work for them; you're showing that you "value your importance and that you're capable of making the right decisions for you," says Deanna Coe Kursh.

So intelligent question-posing is an extremely valuable interviewing skill, and that's what I'll teach you to do in this section. We'll discuss three principal topics: first, timing; second, great questions to ask; and third, questions to *avoid* asking.

A. TIMING: *WHEN TO ASK QUESTIONS*

The short answer is, as early and as often as the interviewer seems comfortable with it. Let the interviewer take the lead, but when an opportunity to ask a question comes up, take advantage. For instance, if you answer a question, you can always end your answer with a question for the interviewer. As Debra Fink points out, "If it gets to five minutes before the end of the interview, and the interviewer asks 'Do you have any questions for me?' it's too late!"

There's one special situation to note: **When you're on your first interview with a large law firm, ask the following question as soon as possible: "Which of the firm's practice areas would you say are growing the fastest?"** Why do you ask this early? Because it's likely at some point that the interviewer is going to ask you, "Which practice area are you interested in?" While it's perfectly acceptable and even wise to say that you're open to learning about the practice areas once you're there, if you want to show a specific interest in an area or two, those areas *have* to be ones in which the firm is thriving—because that's where they'll need associates!

It's important to be sensitive to how the interviewer wants the interview to go. See how they're responding to your questions; if they seem put-off or eager to get more information from you, back off. One student told me about an interview where she was asking question after question of the interviewer, and the interviewer finally snapped,

"Who's interviewing who?" The student commented, "She was obviously having a bad day, and I was just ignoring her whole demeanor. I did want to say, 'It's actually "Who's interviewing *whom*," ' but I didn't think that would help my case!"

For two other timing issues—what you do when the interviewer won't let you squeeze in a word, or what if the interviewer constantly fires questions at you—check out section M below, when we talk about handling interview disasters.

B. Prepare Yourself for the Possibility That The Interviewer's First Question Will Be, "So What Questions Do You Have?"

Usually the interviewer begins the questioning. But sometimes interviewers are tired or busy or don't want to carry the ball. Or they just try to put you on the spot to see how you handle stress. Or they're jerks.

Regardless of the motivation, be prepared to pick up the ball *immediately*. It doesn't happen often, but when it does, you want to be ready—and you will be, with the questions we discuss here!

C. Questions That Will Make You Into the Dream Interviewee

OK, here they are. I've lumped the questions you ought to ask into five categories. They are:

- Personalized questions designed to turn an interview into a conversation;
- Questions that show off your research into the firm and the interviewer;
- Carefully-worded questions about what your own job experience at the firm would be like (and I emphasize *carefully worded*, because you should ask this kind of question sparingly);
- Questions that depend on the size of the law firm and the age of the interviewer;
- Questions involving awkward 800–lb. gorillas—that is, bad news and scandals.

Before we go into detail about these questions, I want to warn you about a couple of things. One of them is this: I'm going to give you the questions that will impress the vast majority of interviewers. But as Susan Benson points out, "Certain interviewers dislike *any* particular question, even good questions!" So if you start asking a certain kind of question and you can see from the interviewer's response and body language that they aren't responding favourably, don't forge ahead; instead, back off, or ask a different kind of question. For instance, virtually everybody responds favourably to personalized questions. But let's say you've got a real tool who just doesn't want to talk about his/her experience with the employer (which in and of itself tells you something valuable about the place!). In that case, you'd back off and ask questions about the employer that you've developed as a result of your research.

My second warning to you comes courtesy of Diane Reynolds, who urges you to **make sure your questions don't sound canned or rehearsed.** Of course, the problem is that they *are* canned and rehearsed, and in order for you to interview confidently, they *have* to be! But they shouldn't sound that way. How do you accomplish that? I face this issue all the time myself, by the way. I've given seminars based on this book at law schools hundreds and hundreds of times. It's largely the same two-hour seminar over and over, although I change up stories here and there. Why doesn't it sound canned? *Because of the way I say it.* In interviews, by varying your tone, leaning forward, and smiling when you ask questions, you create the impression that you are truly interested in what the interviewer has to say in response.

It's also important to make sure that the wording is something that suits you. "If one were to initiate an employment relationship with your firm, what might one expect on a day-to-day basis?" probably isn't a question that will trip of your tongue. "What would a typical day be like for me?"—aah. Much better! You want to create the impression that you've never asked these questions before, even if you've asked them so many times you could answer them for yourself! You're helped in this regard by the fact that the questions I like the most—personalized questions focusing on the interviewer's personal experiences—really are unique to every interviewer, because no two people will have the same response.

With these warnings in mind, let's take a look at the kinds of questions you ought to ask during your interviews:

1. PERSONALIZED QUESTIONS DESIGNED TO TURN THE INTERVIEW INTO A CONVERSATION

These are the warm, human questions that go to the personal aspects of the job—the kinds of things that contribute so heavily to job satisfaction.

I am a huge fan of this kind of question. For one thing, they'll help you forge a rapport with the interviewer. For another, these are really the kinds of things you *should* be focusing on when you're looking at potential employers. That's because what will make you happy at work really has nothing to do with the name on the door. It's not even tied to the amount of money you make, although you may find that hard to believe! Instead, it's your day-to-day experience with the employer, how much you like the way you fill your time there and the people you work with, the people you serve. Former *Washington Post* editor Ben Bradlee once said that the purpose of biography is to answer one, simple question: *What was he like?* Well, the purpose of the personalized questions I encourage you to ask address an analogous issue: *What's the job like*? That simple, underlying question determines whether or not the job you're interviewing for really is your dream job!

These questions are slanted somewhat in favour of the typical interviewer, who is someone who's not very senior with the organization; for instance, in a firm, it'll typically be a junior or mid-level associate, or in any other organization, someone doing the work you'd expect to be doing in one or two or a few years' time. They wouldn't be appropriate for a human resources person, for instance, although for them you could modify some of these questions to make them appropriate (e.g., "What do people who do this job like the most about it?"). Incidentally, for questions specific to different sized employers and more experienced attorneys, look at topic 5 just below, "Questions that depend on the size of the firm and the experience of the interviewer."

With that mind, here are the kinds of questions you should ask:

a. **What do you like about your job?**

My absolute favourite interview question! Watch the interviewer's reaction before they have a chance to form any words, and listen to what they tell you.

For instance, let's say you want balance in your life—you have a family, or you intend to have a family, or you have hobbies you like to pursue, or you just like the idea of seeing daylight on a regular basis. You ask the interviewer what they like about their job and they respond, "We like to work hard and play hard"—a lot of them say that—"and we like to close the office early every Friday *at seven p.m.* and have a Happy Hour" (I've actually heard this answer from a firm!)

Now the interviewer can natter on about how "family friendly" the firm is, but if they consider Friday at seven p.m. "early," you know what they consider normal the rest of the time! And if long hours are a nonnegotiable for you, don't pursue the opportunity. You'll hate it, and just as importantly—they'll hate you.

b. **How did you choose the firm/agency/company?**

c. **What do you wish you'd known before you got here?**

d. **If you could change anything about your job, what would it be?**

e. **What do you find most challenging about being a lawyer?**

f. **When you go back to work/the office, what will you be working on?**

A junior associate at a large law firm urged me to recommend this question, and here's why. "No matter how crappy the law firm is, at some point *everybody's* going to work on *something* interesting. But it doesn't mean that the job is any good! If you want a real idea of what lawyers there do, ask the interviewer, 'What were you working on right before this interview? What are you going to do after I leave?' That'll give you a much better idea of what the work is really like!"

g. **What's the best thing that's happened to you working here?**

h. **What's the most interesting case/project you've worked on?**

i. **How is your job different than what you expected it to be?**

j. **If you were to stay for twenty years, why would you stay?**

Now, you can imagine how questions like these will jolt some life into even the most staid interviewer. As Nancy Krieger points out, "People love to talk about themselves. It also takes the pressure off you, as an interviewee!" These questions serve the dual purpose of showing your interest in the interviewer, as well as gaining valuable insights into how the employer operates and what you can expect if you work there.

Note that you can combine evidence of your research with personalized questions for the interviewer. "I saw in your profile on the firm web site that you clerked for a small firm during law school. This firm is huge. Did it differ at all from what you'd expected?" "I know the firm just merged with X firm. What has that been like for you?"

A couple of warnings. First, to reiterate what I warned you about earlier: don't make these questions *sound* memorized. Smile as you ask them. Don't speak in a monotone. Also, don't ask them in order; pay attention to the interviewer's response, and pick up the thematic threads to lead you to other questions.

* * * SMART HUMAN TRICK * * *

Law student in an on-campus interview with a utility company. Things were going all right when she asked the interviewer, "So— how do you like your job?" She reports, "His face fell. He looked at me, blinked a couple of times, and said, 'I hate it. It's tedious. I can't believe I'm still doing it.' I thought he was going to start crying!"

She got a second interview.

PS: She didn't take it.

2. QUESTIONS THAT SHOW OFF YOUR RESEARCH INTO THE EMPLOYER AND THE INTERVIEWER

Remember all of that homework I made you do? Going to the employer's web site, talking to Career Services, seeking out alums and upperclassmen? Well, you may find that your research unearths wonderful questions—and remember, a large part of the reason you do that homework in the first place is to show it off to the interviewer!

What kinds of questions can you ask based on your research? Sophie Sparrow advises that "You can **ask anything that's thoughtful and shows off your research,**" especially if it's **related to a practice area that interests you.** "For instance, 'I see that you've done a lot of mergers and acquisitions work. Will that continue?' " Or, as Amy Thompson says, "I read that you represented so-and-so. Do you do a lot of that kind of work?"

Amy Thompson also points out that **you can ask questions that tie the employer's practice to current events.** For instance, you can ask how they're prepping clients for a new law, or how they're handling a merger one of their clients is involved in.

Diane Reynolds adds that "**Good questions show that you know the firm and can translate that into a personal concern**. For example, what if the firm just added an environmental law department? You can ask how they made that decision, and whether there are other specialties they intend to add, and how they see those practice areas expanding in the future."

You can also show through your questions that you did more than google the firm—that you actually spoke to people about it. As Debra Fink points out, "If you found someone who's worked there before, and asked them what they did, you can use that in the interview! Say to the interviewer, ' "So-and-so said that he did X when he worked for you. That's exactly the kind of thing I want to do. Will I get the chance to do it?' Employers are always impressed if you've sought out someone who's worked for them!"

As you can see, these questions not only indicate that you've researched the firm; they also should elicit interesting responses! In addition, they show that your questions don't have to be profound. Just think about what you learn about the firm as you research, and ask the questions that spring to your mind as a result of that.

Of course, not *everything* you discover about a firm is fertile ground for questioning. Questions with a negative tone are dangerous, as I discuss below in "Questions involving awkward 800–lb. gorillas" and "Questions you should avoid like a pit viper."

Also, don't ask about topics you don't have the sophistication to discuss. For instance, one student asked an interviewer, "So, I see that you were head of the licensing executive council." The student had no idea what that was; he just dug up the tidbit in his research. As the interviewer said after the interview, "There was no way to have a meaningful conversation with this student about it, so there was no point in him asking it!" If you *do* want to ask about something beyond your "skill level," find a way to bring it back down to earth for you, so that you really can learn something useful. For instance, you could ask, "I see you were head of the licensing executive council. Did you start out in professional associations from the beginning of your practice?" *That* question would tell you something you could use.

* * * CAREER LIMITING MOVE * * *

Law student, former lobbyist, interviewing with a partner at a small law firm. In preparing for the interview, the student memorizes a list of questions from an interviewing handbook. He asks the partner, "Tell me about your training program."

The student reports later, "This guy took it the wrong way. He thought I meant I wanted to have someone lead me by the hand. It was a small firm and they couldn't do that.

"It really highlighted for me how stupid it is to take lists of questions out of context and use them. What was even stupider was that I didn't really care about the answer. Like I'm going to make a decision about who I want to work for based on their training program."

* * * SMART HUMAN TRICK * * *

Law student from Texas, has an interview at the offices of a very large law firm, which we'll call Foghorn & Leghorn. She finds out ahead of time from an alum that the firm is very proud of their support staff and services.

The first question she gets is, "Why Foghorn & Leghorn?"

She responds, "Frankly, even just being here I'm impressed with the fact that everything is done for you—librarians, copies, support work—so you're free just to be a lawyer."

They are very pleased with the answer.

She winds up with an offer.

3. THE QUESTION THAT GIVES YOU A CHANCE TO WHEEL OUT YOUR INFOMERCIAL

"What would the ideal candidate for this job look like?" or its analog "What do you look for in people you hire?" gives the interviewer a chance to describe the qualities the employer looks for ... and gives you a chance to say, "I'm glad to hear that. Here's what you need to know about me ..."

4. CAREFULLY-WORDED QUESTIONS ABOUT WHAT YOUR OWN JOB EXPERIENCE WITH THE EMPLOYER WOULD BE LIKE

The emphasis here is on "Carefully-worded"—because this kind of question is dangerous. Why? Well, remember that employers hire you based on what you can do for *them*—not what they can do for *you*. They pretty much assume that working for them would be a *great* gig for you! So any questions that involve what's in it for you have to be broached carefully so that they don't leave a bad impression on the interviewer.

Having said that, of course, your whole focus really is on what's in it for you! On top of that, if you *never* asked these kinds of questions, interviewers would find that kind of strange.

The kinds of questions to consider asking in this regard include:

a. **What would a typical day be like for me?** (One lawyer told me about her first job, which was working in the state attorney general's office in consumer protection. She said, "I hated it. The job was strictly research; no human contact. It was my own fault. If I'd just asked 'What would a typical day be like for me?' before I took the job I'd have known that ahead of time.")

b. **What kinds of cases/projects would I work on?**

c. **What makes a clerk/new associate/new lawyer really stand out?**

   In a second interview (I go into second interviews in more detail below), **you could go into more detail, with questions like:**

d. **How would I get feedback on my work?**

e. **How would my work be assigned?**

f. **Would I get to pick a department or would I be assigned?**

g. **Do associates ever change departments?**

   If your resume preceded you into the interview, you can also ask:

h. **What was it about my resume that got me this interview?**

The key here is that although these questions focus on you and what's in it for you, they suggest that you're sufficiently interested in the job that you *want* to know what it will be like.

Having said that, before you ask self-centered questions, be sure to read "Questions you should avoid like a pit viper," below. There's a fine line between healthy self-interest—and alienating the interviewer!

5. QUESTIONS THAT DEPEND ON THE SIZE OF THE LAW FIRM AND THE AGE OF THE INTERVIEWER

When I talked about personalized questions to ask, I told you that your typical first interview with an employer will be with a junior person, doing the work you'd likely be doing sooner rather than later. But that's not *always* the person with whom you'll be interviewing first. And, of course, you might be interviewing with different size employers. If you ask inappropriate questions based on either age or employer-size factors, it will seem as though you really haven't given this employer much thought—a pretty bad boo-boo. Here's how to avoid making that kind of mistake.

a. For interviewers of any experience level at large law firms:

As early as possible in the interview, ask the following question:

- **Which practice areas at the firm are growing the most rapidly?**

  I've mentioned this before, but it's worth highlighting, because it's a very important question. Why? Because it can bail you out when they ask you the following question, later in the interview: "Which practice areas are you interested in?" There are two ways to answer. The generic way is to say, "I'm open-minded. I'm interested in your firm because I understand you give summer clerks/new associates the opportunity to see . . ." and then go into what you know of their method for exposing you to different specialties.

  A great way to answer, using the answer they gave to *your* question about practice areas, is to say, "Of course I'm open-minded, but of the practice areas you mentioned I'd be most interested in . . ." and then name it. Here's why this is such a great answer. If a practice area is growing, that translates into needing more associates in that specialty. Answering with a practice area that's thriving greatly increases your chances of getting a job there. Conversely, answering with a practice area that's shrinking or static—and suggesting that you're not interested in anything else—won't help your case!

  A caveat: make sure that the answer you give really is something that interests you. Saying "Well, of the specialties you mentioned, I'd be most interested in dealing with nuclear waste law," when you either know nothing about it or just can't imagine ever doing it—well, I've told you not to lie, and winding up in a job you don't want is *not* a dream! It's fine to fall back on the generic "I'm open-minded . . ." response in that case.

b. For junior to mid-level associates at large law firms:

In addition to the "personalized" questions—what do you like about your job, and so on—you can add the following:

- Did you start off in your current practice area? If not, why did you switch? And was it difficult to switch?
- Who decides your 'to do' list?
- How do you get feedback on your work?
- Are there mentors? How does that work?

c. For senior partners at large or small firms.

Asking a more senior partner "What's your typical day?" is completely irrelevant to you. (S)he'll likely be hustling business for the firm, supervising younger lawyers and/or dealing directly with clients. And posing the question "Why did you choose this firm?" is likely to be answered with, "I founded it."

Instead, questions that would be appropriate include:

- **What qualities would an ideal new associate have?**
- **How has the practice changed over the last five years?**
- **How have your clients' needs changed over the last five years?**
- **Where do you see the partnership heading in the next five years?**
- **Who does your hair?**

   Just kidding.

Senior people have the perspective to answer these kinds of questions, and asking them reflects well on you! As Maureen Provost Ryan points out, "These kinds of questions show that you are thinking beyond your nose—you're thinking like a partner. You're tapping into the interviewer's own sense of the firm." And that's a real plus!

* * * SMART HUMAN TRICK * * *

Student asks a senior associate at a large firm: "People always say that most associates leave large firms within the first five years. You've stayed for ten. Why?"

Deadpan response: "Inertia."

d. For employers who don't routinely hire summer clerks/new associates.

Ask why the position is available.

If you're interviewing for a summer program or an internship, there's no need to ask this question. But otherwise, it can be *crucial*. As Sue Gainen points out, "If it's because somebody left recently, politely ask about the history of the position. One of our grads left a terrific job at another state's attorney general's office for a small firm doing what was for him the right mix of civil rights and employment law. What he didn't know—and didn't find out for a few weeks—was that there had been *11* associates in his position in the previous five years! He'd ended up working for a seriously loony lawyer with major professionalism—read, 'being investigated for corruption'—issues."

6.   QUESTIONS INVOLVING AWKWARD 800–LB. GORILLAS—THAT IS, BAD NEWS AND SCANDALS

What if you interview with an employer who either has a controversial practice—for instance, representing gun or tobacco companies—or is in the news, but not for a good reason? Perhaps some of the partners have broken away and started a rival law firm, stealing some of the firm's plum clients. Or maybe—as happened with the law firm of a partner I talked to—something scandalous has happened to one of the lawyers. At this guy's firm, one of the male partners was found, dead, in a no-tell motel room . . . wearing women's clothing. It was all over the news, as you might imagine!

Now, in any one of these situations, *the interviewer knows that you know about it, whatever it is.* In other words: it's an 800–lb. gorilla in the room. And the issue is: Do you bring it up? And if so—how?

You may be surprised by the answer. **Absolutely bring up bad news, controversies and scandals ... but do it discreetly.** This makes sense, when you think about it. As Nancy Krieger explains, "The interviewer will *expect* you to ask about it!" They'll have an answer prepared. And if you *don't* ask about something that has a large impact on the firm and your potential life there, the interviewer will question both your judgment and your desire to work for the firm.

But that begs the question: What do you say? "Hey, I saw partner x's chalk outline on the front page of the paper. Whoohoo! How are you guys ever going to live *that* one down?" You know better. Instead, **what you do is to ask about two relevant aspects of any scandal, bad news or controversy: one, its impact on people in the firm and how the firm is handling it, and two, how they address the issue with clients.** Those are both *very* sensitive ways to raise the subject.

Diane Reynolds uses as an example a large law firm that was all over the papers because of an acrimonious split in the firm.

The firm conducted on-campus interviews, and nobody asked about it. As she points out, "They *should* have asked, 'How has morale been affected by the split?'"

With the partner-in-the-rent-by-the-hour-joint, you'd ask the same question. "I couldn't help seeing the story about partner so-and-so. How are people at the firm dealing with it?"

What about a controversial practice? There's a very large law firm in Kansas that almost exclusively does defense work representing tobacco companies. It's a great employer, by all accounts. But what about the "merchants of death" aspect? I asked junior associates about how they handle it in on-campus interviews, and to a person they said: Nobody asks us about it. "It's really ridiculous," one of them commented to me. "I mean, it's what we do all the time. It's very interesting, exciting work. If students asked me about it, I'd tell them about my misgivings before I got here, and what it's really like. But they don't ever ask! It makes me wonder how much they know about what we do."

So, raise the issue, but raise it in a non-gossipy way, talking about its impact on the employer and clients. Trust me: Once you're there, you can take junior associates out for a beer, and they'll spill their guts with all the smack you'd possibly want to hear. But don't wallow in it before you get the job!

d.   Questions you should avoid like a pit viper!

You know the traditional advice about asking questions. You've heard it a million times. "There's no such thing as a stupid question." Ha! Ha ha! There's a *ton* of stupid questions. "Lassie was a dog, right?" The fact that there are so many stupid questions scares lots of people out of asking any questions *at all*. You already know that you *have* to ask questions, both to gather information and to show your enthusiasm for the job. So ... where do you draw the line between what you ask—and what you don't ask? Easy. Avoid questions in the following categories, and you'll be just fine:

- **The "What's in it for me?" questions.**
- **Questions with a negative tone.**
- **"Imponderables."**
- **Any question you could have answered yourself through basic research.**
- **Any question that shows you're clueless about what you've already covered in the interview.**
- **Questions involving potentially embarrassing details you learned about the interviewer from MySpace, Facebook, Watchme ... or any other source.**
- **The worst question boner of all: not having any questions!**

Let's take a look at each of these in detail.

1. Any questions that have a "What's–In–It–For–Me?" Flavor.

Don't ask *any* of these questions on an interview:

- **What are the hours? (It indicates an unwilling-ness to make a serious time commitment)**
- **What's expected of me?**
- **Tell me about your pro bono program.**
- **What billable hours do you expect?**
- **What's the benefits package like?**
- **How much vacation time will I get?**
- **What's the salary? (or the inexcusably offensive: "How much do you make?")**
- **What kind of secretarial support will I get?**
- **How many people besides me are you interview-ing?**
- **How long is the partnership track here?**
- **What's your policy on maternity leave?**

Why are these questions so poisonous in interviews? To be perfectly blunt, it's because the interviewer doesn't care what's in it for you. Remember, the employer only wants to know what's in it for *them*: whether they'll like working with you, whether they'll feel comfortable unleashing you in front of clients, how you're going to make money for them. That's what you've got to convey.

Now notice I'm not saying that these questions aren't important. They're *very* important. And I've told you before that being conscious of what's in it for you is the only way to nail a job you'll enjoy. What we're talking about is the appropriate setting for finding out what you really want to know. For many of these questions, simple research will answer them. Talking with Career Services, upperclassmen and alums familiar with the employer will fill in the blanks. And even if you're talking about an employer for whom that kind of research isn't possible, the "what's-in-it-for-me" questions are perfectly appropriate—*after* you've got an offer! What we're focusing on here is getting you to that enviable position. Don't ask these questions until you're there!

* * * CAREER LIMITING MOVE * * *

A prestigious law school is looking for a new member of the administration. They receive several hundred applications from all over the country. The name of a professor, Professor Wiggins, appears in the ad.

Professor Wiggins and his search committee narrow the candidates down to a couple of dozen, whom they intend to fly in for an interview. One of the candidates happens to call Professor Wiggins.

"I have a question for you," he says.

"What's that?" responds Professor Wiggins.

"Oh, I'm just curious about the salary."

Professor Wiggins tells him, and says, "Anything else?"

"No, that's all I wanted to know" sez candidate.

As Professor Wiggins comments later, "Here, he had the guy he'd assumed would be making the hiring decision, he could have asked me *anything,* and all he asked was the salary. We immediately removed him from contention because of that stupid phone call!"

2.   Questions with a negative tone.

Remember—the interviewer isn't on trial. If anyone is, it's *you.* So don't ask questions like:

- **Is this place a sweatshop?**
- **I've heard rumors about your firm. Are you not doing well?**
- **What *don't* you like about the firm?**
- **How many minority (or female) attorneys do you have?** (remember: tone counts. It's possible to ask this benignly, or, better yet, find out in your research so you don't have to ask the interviewer at all. Or wait for a call back, when you can look around and see for yourself what the firm composition is.)
- **How does your firm compare to X firm?**
- **I saw on the GreedyAssociates web site that you** . . .
- **You guys did really badly in the *American Lawyer* survey. What are you going to do about it?**
- **Why should I work for you when I can make twice as much money working for a big firm?**

It's possible you'd ask questions like these thinking that the interviewer will find your bluntness refreshing. They won't. They'll think you're a tactless, indiscreet jerk. Nobody wants to work with a social clod, or expose their clients to someone who might say, "What, are you kidding? You can't win in court with a claim like *that!*"

* * * CAREER LIMITING MOVE * * *

Female student interviewing in a small town down South. She is very conscious of the old-boy network in town. In an interview with a firm, she asks, "Do I really have a chance here, or is the old boy network going to keep me out?" The interviewer is offended.

As her Career Services Director reflects later, "She could have found this out other ways. She could have contacted female lawyers in the local bar association and ask for their advice, ask what they did about it. Just asking straight out like that can only be offensive."

You can find out the answer to virtually any question by asking in a discreet way. For instance, you can ask where the interviewer sees the firm heading in the next few years. You can ask what, if anything, the interviewer would change about his/her job. And when it comes to things like *American Lawyer,* they'll know that you've seen it. If you ask sympathetically, "You couldn't have been happy about *The American Lawyer* survey. How do you handle something like that?" I *promise* you they'll be well prepped to answer it.

When it comes to rumors, judged.com, greedyassociates.com—take all of that stuff with a grain of salt. Do your "humint" research—that is, human intelligence from Career Services and alums and upper classmen—and believe *that*. Remember, people who have an axe to grind are the first ones to take the coward's way out and diss their employers anonymously on line, ostensibly under the guise of "If I embarrass them publicly, they'll change." Talking smack behind your employer's back is no way to advance your career. I'm getting a little ahead of job searches here, but when it comes to dealing with things you don't like at work, handle it discreetly with people who are in a position to explain policies to you and make changes. You'll develop the reputation of being a stand-up person, and that will get you opportunities *forever*.

But back to interviews. No selfish questions. There's a time and place to find out all of that information—and an interview ain't it!

3. "Imponderables."

These are the questions that might sound good when you're thinking about them at home, but they're simply unanswerable. The two principle questions of this type are:

- **What's the culture of the firm?**
- **What's the firm atmosphere?**

As Sandy Mans points out, "How does the interviewer explain this? Anyway, it's something you can pick up for yourself if you get called back for an office interview, by looking for things like interaction between attorneys and support staff, and whether anybody's still there are 5 o'clock, or whether they leave as soon as possible."

So be sure that you only ask questions capable of meaningful responses.

4. Any question you could have answered yourself through simple research.

The hiring partner at a large Louisiana firm told me about his experience doing on-campus interviews. "The first thing I say to students is, 'Let me tell you a little bit about what we do.' That takes me a couple of minutes. I always wish that they'd cut me off and say, 'I know exactly what you do—that's why I'm here!' But they never do. We do labor law. Specifically, we represent management in negotiations with unions. After I explain it to students, I ask them: 'We're on the *management* side. Is that something you're comfortable with?' and they'll often say, 'I guess I could do that.'" His voice turned angry as he said, "I *guess* I could do that? I guess I could *lower* myself to it? Gee—thanks!"

The bottom line is this: If the interviewer has to tell you what they do, that's really bad news. In fact, if they have to tell you *anything* you could easily have gleaned from their web site or written materials at Career Services or a job posting, you've torpedoed your chances with the employer. So don't ask:

- How many attorneys do you have?
- What are your practice areas?
- In which cities do you have offices?

Remember: You've got about twenty minutes to convince the interviewer that they want to work with you. Don't waste even a minute of that time asking for information you could easily have found elsewhere!

5. Any question showing you're clueless about what you've already covered in the interview.

NALP's Pam Malone sums this up by saying: "Don't be brain dead!" Don't indicate to the interviewer that you've zoned out by asking something they've already covered in the interview. If you're not paying attention to what they're saying, how much could you possibly want the job? And just as bad: will you ignore what they have to say when they're giving you work assignments?

Now, in all fairness, it's possible you'll miss some of what the interviewer says if you're very nervous about the interview. In that case you probably memorized a list of questions, in order. Remember: it's important to keep your questions sounding informal, and to shift and modify what you ask as appropriate. Make sure you listen—really listen—so that you can delete any questions the interviewer has already answered.

6. **Questions involving potentially embarrassing details you learned about the interviewer from MySpace, Facebook, Watchme ... or any other source, for that matter.**

Employers often recruit their friendliest, most outgoing lawyers to conduct interviews. It's often easy to feel comfortable around them.

Sometimes ... *too* comfortable.

Remember: While you want to be friendly and establish a rapport with the interviewer, (s)he's *not* your friend. There's an invisible boundary you can't cross without the interviewer questioning your discretion and maturity, thinking "If you go over the line with *me*—how will you impress everybody else?"

I've mentioned before that if you hear about an innocent hobby, an accomplishment of the interviewer, a common hometown, school or former employer—by all means mention it where appropriate. "What's the view like from the top of Mount Kilimanjaro?" "Strange—you don't *look* like a chili cooking champion?" "What's it like to argue a Supreme Court case?"

All innocent stuff. And if you find it out from *any* source, on-line or human, fine.

Also—if you find you share a hobby and the interviewer asks about your hobbies, mention the one you share. You don't have to mention that you know they like the same thing. It'll be a great conversational booster.

But—anything potentially embarrassing, even if it wouldn't embarrass *you*—no!

"So ... you were a lingerie model."

"How did you explain your academic probation to employers?"

"What's it like in jail?"

Now, if it's information on their MySpace or FaceBook profile—you might be thinking, "If they're so sensitive about it, why not password protect it ... or not post it at all?" OK. It's stupid. But they've got a job! Don't *you* compound the foolishness by embarrassing them with their indiscretion.

* * * CAREER LIMITING MOVE * * *

Law student reads interviewer's MySpace profile, and figures she'll spice up the interview by bringing up what she found. The interview is going well when she says to the interviewer: "Nice photo on MySpace. I wish I had the body to wear that." End of interview.

7. "Insecurity" questions. "Do I have a shot?" "Am I in the running?"

You'll sometimes hear people recommend these questions as a way of teasing out how many other people are being interviewed for the job.

Don't ask. It doesn't matter how many people are being interviewed. It doesn't matter if there are two or 200.

Even worse, it really puts the interviewer on the spot. If you really want to ask a question along these lines, ask what the ideal candidate would have, and address anything you feel the interviewer hasn't seen in you so far in the interview. For instance, if they say "Excellent writing skills," you'd wheel out the evidence that you have those.

In short: You can get the same information without putting the interviewer's feet to the fire by asking if you're in the mix!

8. The worst possible question boner: Not having any questions at all!

Does this sound familiar? Toward the end of a job interview, the interviewer asks, "Do you have any questions for me?" and you respond brightly, "Oh, no. I think you've answered everything." It sure sounds familiar to me— because that's exactly what I used to do in interviews when I was in law school. I wish someone had told *me* what a huge mistake it is! As Jose Bahamonde-Gonzalez points out, "Asking questions is a chance to convey how interested you are in the job!" Lisa Abrams adds, "It doesn't matter if you've interviewed with five different lawyers in the same firm. Whatever you do, don't ever say 'All my questions have been answered.'"

Especially given the kinds of questions I've taught you, there's no reason ever to run out of questions for an interviewer. If you ask the personalized questions I like so much, you'll never get the same answer from any two attorneys, and there's no reason why you can't ask them of *every* interviewer. So don't ever fall into the trap of having no questions for the interviewer!

5.   STEP FIVE: PRACTICE, PRACTICE, PRACTICE

OK. You've done your detective work, and you've made up your infomercial and developed the questions you'll ask and answers to questions you'll get. The final step in preparing for interviews is *practice*. Why? Because interviewing is a lot like sex. You can read about it all you want, but you don't really know what it's about until you do it. As Albany's Sandy Mans points out, "Even students who interview well from the start in law school don't come by it naturally. They have practiced elsewhere, either through public speaking or student leadership positions."

So—how do you get interview practice? You ask for it at Career Services. Namely:

a.   Set up mock interviews through your Career Services Office. Every Career Services Director I know emphatically endorses mock interviews and bemoans the fact that so few student take advantage of them. I visit law schools routinely during mock interview sign-ups, and there will usually be many, many interview slots left unfilled. It's a sin. As Sophie Sparrow says, "It's important to be aware of how you come across, and you can only get that by doing mock interviews!"

Mock interviews are conducted either by Career Services personnel, professors, or local attorneys. Request a local attorney if it's at all possible, for a great, hidden reason: you wouldn't be the first "mock interviewee" to impress the interviewer so much that you're offered a job! Does that rock, or what? You go in for a mock interview and wind up with a job. (In fact, some people have done even better than that; I've heard of several law students who wound up marrying their mock interviewers. But I digress.)

No matter who conducts your mock interview, it's an invaluable tool for checking how you come across in an interview. Here's what you want to do:

1. **Ask up front for the interviewer to question you about topics you're nervous about.** Whether it's grades, a prior job, a resume gap—now's the time to get your patter down.

2. **Wear what you'd wear for a real interview, and get an assessment of your professional *raiment*.**

3. **Strike the right note between confidence and arrogance.** You want to come off as humbly confident about your abilities, yet grateful for the opportunity.

4. **Establish a rapport with the interviewer with "personalized" questions.** Since it's a "mock" interview and you can't, therefore, have researched the interviewer, stick with the "What do you like about your job?" "How did you choose your job?" "What would you change about it?" "What's a typical day like?" kind of question. (Of course, if you do have an opportunity to research the interviewer, all the better!)

5. **Have an open, enthusiastic demeanor.** Smile appropriately. Lean forward. Uncross your arms. Keep comfortable eye contact.

6. **Avoid nervous problems like hunched shoulders, a dropped voice, mumbling, fidgeting, and hemming and hawing.**

Also, **be sure to ask for a very blunt assessment of your interviewing skills.** Most people are very reluctant to criticize (although your law school experience may make that very hard to believe!). Tell the interviewer straight out not to spare your feelings, that you're here to improve, and the only way you can do that is with criticism. And, of course—be sure to thank the interviewer for their time!

Incidentally, many Career Services Offices will videotape your interview for you. If yours does, *definitely* take advantage of this service. You're likely to be very surprised—perhaps pleasantly!—by seeing yourself as others see you.

* * * CAREER LIMITING MOVES * * *

Reported by attorneys who conduct mock interviews at law schools:

- One student had the annoying habit of pushing spit between his front teeth with his tongue, and then sucking it back in—throughout the interview.

- A female student at one law school had a tremor in her voice that made her sound like she was crying. "I was afraid to ask her anything—I thought she would break," the interviewer commented.

- A male student at one law school was so nervous during the mock interview that he took a ball point pen from the interviewer's desk, started nibbling on the cap, and by the end of the interview, *he had eaten the whole thing.*

- A student blinked way too much. "I thought he was sending me messages in Morse Code," commented the interviewer.

- A student rolled her eyes up to the ceiling whenever she was thinking.

- A student twirled her long hair meditatively throughout the interview. The interviewer said, "I kept waiting for her to break into a chorus 'On The Good Ship Lollipop.' "

- A student continually bobbed his head during the interview. "I think he was trying to look agreeable," said the interviewer, "But all I could think of was he reminded me of a dashboard ornament."

- A student was "jumping out of his skin. He was bug-eyed and answering frantically. Thank God it wasn't a real interview for this poor guy. He needed to be medicated and then who knows, he'd probably be just fine."

* * * SMART HUMAN TRICK * * *

Alum from a California school agreed to do mock interviews for his alma mater. "I wasn't under any pressure," he reported, "Because I work for the state government, and my office never hires law students."

"So I'm interviewing these students, and it's all pretty predictable until this one guy, whose dynamite. Enthusiasm out the ying-yang. He was so amazing we actually *created* an internship for him!"

b.   What about using real employers for "practice"? That is—taking interviews with employers in whom you're not interested, just to practice your interviewing skills?

This is very, very controversial among Career Services people. And I'm on the fence myself. Here's the guidance on which most experts would agree:

1.   **If you wouldn't take work for a particular employer under *any* circumstances, don't take the interview.** For instance, if it's in a city that you just wouldn't live in even if red-hot bamboo shoots were forced under your toenails, don't interview for the job. Apart from anything else, faking enthusiasm for something in which you have *absolutely no* interest is excruciating; Charlie Gibson, as host of *Good Morning America,* said it's the most difficult aspect of his job. On top of that, it's not really fair to classmates (or fellow job fair attendees, or students from other schools) who may truly be interested in the job, but didn't get an interview slot because of you. As Josh Burstein points out, "It's not just about your own reputation. It's the reputation of your school and the students who come after you. Only interview for jobs you're serious about."

2.   **If you can't rule it out 100%—then what?**

   a.   **Remind yourself that there's no way to know exactly what a job is like—and whether you'll like it—until you've done it.** So be broad-minded about jobs you'll consider. It's easy to slip into a mind-set that's unnecessarily narrow. As Jose Bahamonde–Gonzalez says, "A lot of students think they want international law and nothing else. They don't realize that a lot of times it's just glorified corporate law, and once they're in it, they may not want it at all. And because they didn't interview for anything else, they passed up something they'd really love just because they had a narrow, unrealistic focus!"

   There are many students who poo-poo whole categories of jobs that I just *know* they'd enjoy. Two that come to mind are small law firms and the JAG Corps. Small firms get a bad rap due to lower starting pay, typically smaller town living, and a lack of perceived sophistication in the law they tackle. All unfair! As Pam Malone points out, "Normally, small firms give you *lots* of hands-on experience. And even if your starting pay is low, you get a lot more money, more quickly."

The JAG Corps is also a wonderful opportunity. I've talked with dozens of new grads who just love it. As Pam Malone explains, "It's got a lot of hidden assets, like loan repayment benefits, housing, and the fact you can get an L.L.M. for free. Also, the places you live are normally nice. The hours are good. There's not a lot of pressure. It's easy to network for your next move. It's great for women and minorities. And you get a lot of hands-on experience in many different practice areas." So be open-minded about jobs you'll consider. Research a broad range of employers. You don't know where your dream job may turn up!

b. Remember that your first job isn't going to be your only job. Even if the first job you interview for isn't your ultimate dream—trust me, general counsel at MTV doesn't go to a new law school graduate!—remember that your first job may *lead* directly to that job. As Amy Thompson points out, "You can't rule everything out while you wait for the perfect job."

c. Even if you don't want a particular job now, those same jobs may look entirely enticing down the road. As Pam Malone notes, "You don't know when you'll want to change careers. If you interview for jobs that don't particularly interest you while you're in law school, at least they give you a realistic frame of reference as to what's out there. When you want to change jobs, you just might remember that interview in a positive light!"

d. Remember that every interviewer you meet is a potential contact. Even if you don't want to work for them in particular, you may be able to keep in touch with them, and through them find an employer that really does make your heart race.

3. If you do take an interview with an employer who doesn't particularly ring your chimes—how do you handle it?

Taking into account all the positives of interviewing for an employer who doesn't initially interest you, **you prepare for the interview "as if."** What does that mean? **Do everything you would do if it really *was* a job that truly flipped your switch.** Do all of your research. Prep your questions to ask. Smile and project enthusiasm. Treat the interviewer with respect. In other words: Behave as if this is a real possibility for you. Because it *is*. As Maureen Provost Ryan points out, "You just can't assume that any job is beneath you before you check it out. Go on the interview, explore the job, treat it as a 'look-see.' Sometime fate hands you an opportunity you didn't expect!"

4. **Don't use an employer you *don't* want just to get to an employer you *do* want.**

If your sole intention in taking an interview is to get to someone else, don't do it. You know I'm all over the idea of making contacts, but if an interviewer shows up to interview you for a *job* the last thing they want is for you to say, "I just wanted to interview with you because you know X, and that's where I *really* want to work."

If you really want to get to the other person, you can always ask your "intermediary target" for a few minutes of their time at their convenience, and *then* ask them how best to approach that other employer. In other words: try to get some informal mentoring. For instance, if it's an on-campus interviewer, ask them as they break for lunch if they might have a couple of minutes at the end of the day, that you need their advice and would really appreciate it. *Then* you're being straight up, and they really might help you.

* * * CAREER LIMITING MOVE * * *

Law student in the Midwest, really wanted a job in sports. He found out that a firm interviewing on campus was sending its managing partner, and that the partner was good friends with a sports superstar's agent.

The student got an interview with the partner. The interview went well until the partner asked for questions and the student said, "I really wanted to talk to you because I'm hoping you can tell me how to get through to Agent X."

Interview over.

D. WHAT TO WEAR, WHAT TO WEAR ... SARTORIAL SPLENDOR

Research indicates that 90% of how people view us is nonverbal. In a nutshell: What you wear counts. *A lot.*

If you knew me, you'd know how ironic it is that *I'm* giving you wardrobe advice. I have absolutely no taste in clothes whatsoever. I actually won a gym membership in a Halloween costume contest once ... *and I wasn't wearing a costume.* Not deliberately, anyway.

Fortunately for both of us, I'm not your role model. But I've talked to lots of people who are very knowledgeable about what you ought to wear on interviews—and what to avoid!

1.   RULES OF THUMB FOR EVERYBODY

A. LOOK THE PART!

Remember that you're interviewing for professional jobs. People will look to you for your expertise, often in trying situations. When you're getting dressed for interviews, ask yourself: How would your parents want their lawyer to dress? If your liberty was at stake, what would you want *your* lawyer to look like? As Dave James advises, "Interviewers assume you look your best for interviews. If they think you didn't dress appropriately for the interview, they won't count on you setting a higher standard for the job!"

B. YOUR PERSONALITY SHOULD SHINE. YOUR SUIT SHOULDN'T

The idea in an interview is for them to remember you—not your outfit. Dressing memorably can actually hurt you.

I am reminded of a story about King Henry VIII of England. You know, the one with all the wives. When he was shopping around for wife #4, he solicited pictures of eligible European princesses. Of course, in those days, it wasn't a matter of e-mailing a digital photo. Instead, Hans Holbein, the renowned portrait painter, had to hire for Europe and paint portraits of these babes. The two principal contenders were a Swedish princess (I think her name was Christina, because they're virtually all named Christina), and the other was a German princess named Anne of Cleves. Now, in Christina's portrait, she dressed very simply in a black dress. All you really paid attention to was her face. Anne of Cleves, on the other hand, was showered in bling, and wore a magnificent gown. Her face was like a doily in the middle of a dessert buffet.

When King Henry got the portraits, he immediately chose Christina. Why? Because he knew that the way they were dressed told him everything he needed to know. Christina's simple outfit highlighted *her*. Anne's outfit *made up* for her. (As a postscript, Christina turned him down. Anne married him, and as it turns out, she was a real troll, just as he'd suspected. He soon divorced her.)

Incidentally, if you're thinking, man, Kimmbo, you really do your research—well, kinda. I actually read that story in a beer ad a few years ago. But it's *relevant!* In interviews, you don't want the interviewer to walk away thinking, "Holy cow, what an outfit!" Because you don't want them to call to borrow your clothes or get the name of your tailor. You want them to *hire you.* So—dress conservatively! As Susan Gainen advises, "If they remember what you wore, you did something wrong."

When you dress "professionally"—when you put on the uniform—you're implicitly telling the interviewer, "I'll fit in." And they really need to know that. If that bums you out, remember that we're only talking about what you wear on interviews. You can spend the rest of your time in belly shirts and scuba flippers, if you want. But when you're in front of employers, dress the part!

C. REMEMBER THAT YOU MAY BE ABLE TO DRESS MORE CASUALLY ONCE YOU ACTUALLY *HAVE* THE JOB. JEANS AND T-SHIRTS ARE *NEVER* APPROPRIATE INTERVIEW WEAR!

It may well be that you interview with an office that allows "business casual." Terrific. But even if you know that they dress less formally at work, don't dress that way for your interview. Why? It's largely a matter of respect. It shows you care enough about the job to get dressed up and make a good impression. So dust off that suit, at least for your interviews!

As Sue Gainen advises, "Jeans and T-shirts are appropriate interview attire if—and only if—1) you are meeting a lawyer at a coffee shop before or after her morning run, or 2) the suit you were wearing on the plane because you knew you had an early interview was taken from your body by force, your luggage was destroyed, and the only available clothing was what you could borrow from the air marshal."

D. DON'T GET WRAPPED UP IN THE MINUTIAE OF INTERVIEW WEAR

I'm going to give you the basics of interview dressing. Beyond what I tell you—don't waste time worrying about whether you wore *precisely* the right thing. You get the impression from some articles you read that a short-sleeved shirt can be the difference between "offer" and "no offer." But give interviewers a little more credit than *that!* As long as you stick with the basics, you're fine. As Lisa Abrams points out, "The most important thing about the interview is not whether you wear a peach or a white blouse, or carry a leather or vinyl portfolio. People just focus on those things because they're easy."

E. YOU SHOULD ENGAGE THE INTERVIEWER'S SENSES OF VISION AND HEARING—NOT SMELL

King Louis XVI of France took two baths *in his lifetime* ... and he was forced to take *those.*

Look what happened to *him.* Bathing is essential!

I probably don't have to tell you to shower the morning of the interview. And if you figure you don't normally need deodorant—you do today. If you *ever* sweat, interviewing will make you do it!

When it comes to cologne and perfume, the traditional advice is: don't overdo it. But I've found that people who *do* overdo it don't realize it. I have a very dear relative who has a "signature" perfume she always likes to wear. What she doesn't realize is that it's so overpowering that the children in my family call her "Pepe LePew" behind her back. I'm suggesting that if your perfume or cologne is too much, you don't realize it—and nobody's likely to tell you. So to be on the safe side: the day of your interview, don't wear cologne or perfume at all.

F. DRESS APPROPRIATELY FOR THE TYPE OF JOB AND ITS GEOGRAPHIC LOCATION

As you know, you can get a new suit for a couple of hundred dollars—or a couple of thousand. Where do you draw the line? It has as much to do with the type of employers you're interviewing with as it does with the elasticity of your credit! As Kathleen Brady points out, "On Wall Street, you need to wear the most expensive suit you can afford. But when you go to the D.A.'s office—drop the $800 Armani." So be sensitive to the general wealth of the employer *and* the clients you'll be dealing with when you're deciding on what to wear to your interview!

In addition, remember that if you need a good suit and your budget just won't allow it, the suit you buy doesn't have to be new. Go to the nicest neighborhood near your school or home and visit a consignment store or Goodwill. I have a friend who's a realtor, and she buys her suits exclusively at a Goodwill near where we live. But you'd never know. They're all exquisite designer suits, and nobody I know—and certainly no interviewer you meet!—will know they're last year's styles.

G. NO OBVIOUS PIERCINGS OR TATTOOS

Pierced ears for women are fine, but even then, don't put earrings in more than two holes.

Otherwise: no nose rings, eyebrow rings, tongue dumbbells, nose rings or studs, nothing visible.

If you have tattoos, dress strategically to cover them.

You might be thinking, "But it's *me*. It's who I am." As with any "visual" advice, you don't have to follow these rules ... but know up front that law is a pretty sober business, and there will be large swaths of employers who'll eliminate you from contention for petty issues like these.

H. NO MATTER WHAT YOU WEAR—BE COMFORTABLE!

Regardless of the culture of the employer or what the uniform ought to be, you *have* to wear something comfortable. If you don't, your discomfort will show, and that's far worse than any wardrobe *faux pas* you could make. As Jose Bahamonde–Gonzalez points out, the worst thing to do is to show up for an interview thinking, "I feel bad in this suit. I look like a grandmother. These flat shoes make my legs look fat"—which would be particularly awkward if you're a man. You need to be focusing on how you're going to impress the interviewer with what you say and how you behave—not how you look. So dress within the realm of professionalism, but make sure you feel comfortable.

I. IF YOUR RESEARCH DREDGES UP THE INTERVIEWER'S QUIRKY TASTE IN INTERVIEW ATTIRE, FOLLOW IT

Let's say that you learn that your particular interviewer eschews traditional professional wear, and likes to see interviewees wear something bolder. At one law school I visited, Career Services had recently hosted an interview panel, consisting of local attorneys. A female lawyer from a large firm commented, "I get so sick of looking out on a sea of gray and blue suits. I like it when a woman shows up in fire engine red." What does this tell you? That in an interview with *that particular interviewer, and that particular interviewer only,* wear something bright. You'll make a great impression. But in the absence of specific information like that, stick with the conservative wear I'm about to outline for you.

Incidentally, when I talk about an interviewer's taste in clothes, I'm not talking about what the interviewer wears to work, or what everybody in the office typically shows up wearing. Maybe the office norm is business casual. I've warned you before that that doesn't dictate your interview wardrobe: You wear a suit as a matter of respect, no matter what they wear to work, in the absence of specific guidance/intelligence otherwise.

J. USE COMMON SENSE WITH WHAT YOU HEAR ON INTERVIEW PANELS AT SCHOOL ABOUT INTERVIEW WEAR

I would encourage you to go to every single program your Career Services program puts on for you. And I would heed what the speakers say. But I'd be aware of this: They're giving you their opinions, and the guidance they give you may be—well, eccentric. This is particularly true for interview advice. You might hear a member of an interview panel tell you that it's all right for women to wear pant suits to interviews, and I admit that's a close call. But it's still wiser to wear a skirt suit, even though in most offices women could get away with pants at work. And the fire-engine red example I gave you in item (i) just above, where the interview panelist said female law students should wear bright colors to interviews—that translates as: "In interviews with *me,* wear bright colors." So be careful with interview advice you get from practitioners, and remember that what they tell you *they'd* like to see is not necessarily what you should wear for *every* interview.

Don't be shy about calling and asking the employer straight out what's appropriate. They're never offended. The Career Services Office at school can also tell you about most situations. Be particularly careful if you're told to dress "casually." Ask them *how* casual. Their interpretation of casual is probably a lot more formal than yours!

* * * CAREER LIMITING MOVE * * *

An attorney at a small firm on the West Coast reports, "We had one young lady coming in for an interview. She called and asked, 'How do people dress?' We told her, 'Fairly casual.' "

"She showed up in ripped jeans and flip-flops."

k. Don't Wear Buttons or Pins That Make Political Statements, Unless You Are Interviewing for an Advocacy Position That Reflects That Stance

If you're heavily involved in politics or feel strongly about a particular issue, you might have buttons and pins that reflect your views—either with candidates' names or pithy quotes. I saw a funny one once. "I'm not anti-Bush, I'm pro-intelligence."

Now, if you're a Republican, you can immediately see the problem with that pin. It's not funny to *you*.

Unless you are interviewing for an advocacy position, leave the buttons and pins off your interview wear. Even if the interviewer agrees with you, they'll question your judgment in wearing the button/pin in an interview situation. I talked with the hiring partner at one large firm who'd interviewed a female student. "The interview was fine until I noticed she was wearing a 'fetus feet' pin. It was hard to focus on anything else after that."

2. Rules of Thumb for Men

Here's the rundown:

- **Suit: Gray or blue.** Solid color or a conservative pin stripe. That's it. Good quality. Pressed. Nothing with a reversible vest. And in fact, no vest at all. And the only two breasts you take into an interview should be yours, not your suit's. No double-breasteds. Remember: You only need one good-quality suit for interviews. If need be, get one at a high-quality consignment store or at a Goodwill in a ritzy neighborhood.
- **Shirt: White.** Long-sleeved. Ironed. Tucked in.
- **Tie: Yes. Conservative.** Nothing with a battery.
- **Shoes should match your belt.**
- **Shoes should be darker than suit.**
- Moccasins are not interview shoes. Nor are flip-flops. Ditto bedroom slippers.
- **Socks—should match your pants or shoes.** *Not white.* Length: Sit down. Your skin shouldn't show.
- **Fly—zipped up.**
- **Hair and jewelry: Cut the ponytail and ditch the earring**, as well as jewelry in any other piercings. I've seen lots of guys who are hotties at law schools I visit who have both a ponytail and an earring. But when you're interviewing, take the least-risk alterna-

tive and get rid of the ponytail. You can always grow it back after interview season!

- **Bling—no.** A student at one school wore a hip-hop heavy watch chain with his interview suit. Interviewers *expressly* raised it as the reason for lost offers.

- **Facial hair:** It depends on the community. In most places, you're fine with a well-trimmed beard. No soul patch any time. Also, if you have a beard to cover acne or, I don't know, a vestigial twin, by all means don't shave it off.

3. RULES OF THUMB FOR WOMEN

As a general matter, Debra Fink suggests you rent the old Melanie Griffith movie "*Working Girl.*" She says, "If you want to be viewed as a professional, dress like Melanie Griffith *after* her transformation into a professional woman. If you want to be seen as a secretary, dress like her *before.* Wear a short suit, bleached hair, and too much makeup."

- **Suit: Conservative. Wool or wool blend.** Not linen; it wrinkles too easily. It doesn't have to be navy; just make it dark and *muted.* Jazz it up with a scarf or a pin if you like. And make sure the skirt is not tight. If it restricts the length of your normal walking stride, it's too tight.

- **Suit length:** Don't take your lead from TV shows about lawyers. They're supposed to be sexy. You're supposed to get a job. Real lawyers don't dress like that. Your skirt shouldn't be more than **an inch or two above the knee.** Remember: It's just for interviews!

- **Blouse: Conservative.** No prissy florals or animal prints. Any neckline is fine, but cleavage is not. And a jog bra is not a blouse.

- **Pantyhose:** Yes. **Flesh-colored.** And bring an extra pair, in case the pair you're wearing gets a run in it.

- **Shoes: Low to mid-heel.** No open heels or toes. No stilettos. The interviewer shouldn't wonder if you wear your shoes to your night job as a dominatrix. Shoes should be polished. And make sure the heels aren't worn; take them to a shoemaker if you have to. One interviewer told a Career Services Director that she'd been "so thrown off in an interview when the student had out-of-date, scuffed shoes on, that she was distracted the whole time." OK. The interviewer had issues. But you see the point.

- **Hair: No matter how long it is, make sure it's neat.** If it tends to be long and wild, pin it up or wear it in a ponytail for interviews. If you've got some wild streaks in it—I have bright red streaks in mine—put a temporary rinse in it for interviews.

- **Makeup: Subdued,** although it varies according to geography. You can get away with more in the South than you can anywhere else in the country.

- **Nails: No bright nail polish. No nail art.** Well-trimmed and neat.

- **Jewelry: No bling.** You can wear an interesting pin. Otherwise: Pearls and button earrings, that kind of thing. And no more than two studs in any one ear. And no visible piercings of any other kind.

- **To look older and be taken more seriously,** Boston University's Helen Long suggests wearing non-prescription clear glasses. "They give you visual *gravitas*," she advises.

4.   RULES OF RING FINGER FOR WOMEN

Ah, engagement rings. If you're engaged—and congratulations, by the way, marriage is wonderful—you have really two choices when it comes to wearing your ring to interviews:

- Take it off.

- Leave it on.

Here are the plusses and minuses of both.

Let's talk first about taking it off. Here's the very sound reasoning behind this advice: If you wear your engagement ring, the interviewer may subconsciously assume that if you're shortly getting married you'll be starting a family soon, and that will either divert you from your work—or you'll quit. If you take off your engagement ring, that can't be an issue.

Now, what are the downsides of this? There are two, it seems to me. One is that assuming that your interview goes well and you wind up with the job, they're going to know sooner rather than later that you're engaged. You'll put your ring back on. You'll talk about your fiancé and bring him to firm events. And the employer will quickly divine that you were engaged when you interviewed. Now, they may figure that you were savvy not to wear your ring during your interviews—or they'll figure that you misled them. That's a risk.

On top of that—and this is the sense that I get from most of the engaged students who ask me this question—it means you're going into interviews trying to hide something that's very important to you. Under every other circumstance you proudly wear your engagement ring. Many engaged women suggest to me that going into interviews "hiding" their engagement makes them very uncomfortable. And how well are you going to interview if you're uncomfortable? Not very!

Which leads us to Option B: **Wear your engagement ring.** I've already discussed the downside: interviewers will notice it, and may assume that you have impending wedding and baby plans that will interfere with your work. But you can combat that by having your patter on the matter ready to go, just as you would for any tough interview question. Essentially, what you'll want to do—whether the interviewer asks you about your ring (unlikely) or you see that they notice it (more likely) or whether they bring it up at all—is talk about how you're going to be getting married, but you don't have any plans to start a family immediately (if that's true) and even if you do, *you understand the time commitment working for them takes, you fully intend to undertake it, and you wouldn't be wasting their time interviewing if you felt any differently.* After all, your commitment to the job is a valid concern of theirs—and you can easily address it!

Now, all of this ignores the fact that law firms work out all kinds of ways to accommodate new mothers. It's not a matter of reality we're talking about here; it's an issue of perception. So do what makes you feel most comfortable!

5. THE "PURPLE SUIT" SYNDROME: IF YOU JUST CAN'T WEAR A PROFESSIONAL "UNIFORM," THINK TWICE ABOUT THE IMPACT YOUR CLOTHES WILL HAVE ON THE INTERVIEWER—AND WHETHER THIS IS THE CAREER FOR YOU . . .

Maybe you pride yourself too much on your individualism to be able to give up your funky clothes for an interview. Maybe you'd sooner sprout a third eye than wear a navy blue suit. Maybe you're so proud of your credentials and your savvy that you believe you can overcome any *outre* impression you create with your clothes. For instance, one student insisted on matching his ties to his socks. If he wore red socks, he wore red ties. He refused to give up this practice for his legal interviews. One Career Services Director has a name for this: the "Purple suit" syndrome, in honor of a female student who wore a bright purple suit on interviews.

What the "purple suit" syndrome says is this: If you've got a flamboyant personality that's reflected by a purple suit, you may insist on wearing a purple suit on the grounds that if the employer doesn't like the purple suit, they won't like you. If it means so much to you, go ahead and match your ties to your socks, or, for that matter, match your *hair* to your socks.

Here's the rub: No matter how much of a world-beating personality you have, no matter how blue-chip your credentials are, if you don't wear the uniform, there are employers who will reject you just because of your wardrobe. Now I'm not talking about whether your suit is the right shade of navy, or whether your blouse is cream instead of white. I'm talking about big, loud *wardrobe statements.* Sexy dresses, skintight suits, spike heels, multicolored fingernails or hair, multiple ear studs, that kind of thing. If it doesn't bother you that certain employers will reject you out of hand, wear whatever the heck you like. Thongs are fun. But do me a favour: If you've simply got to dress this way, reconsider whether you actually want to work for a conservative legal employer in the *first* place. Remember: Law is a serious business. People's wealth and sometimes liberty are at stake, and they want advice from someone who looks the part. Perhaps you should work somewhere with more flair—in the arts, for instance—where employers will appreciate and welcome your wardrobe individuality!

E. SHOW TIME! FROM THE NIGHT BEFORE YOUR INTERVIEW TO THE FIRST FIVE MINUTES

You're almost there. Let's talk about "interview eve" to the first impression you make on the interviewer.

1. THE NIGHT BEFORE YOUR INTERVIEW: THE FINAL TUNE-UP

Before you go to sleep, take a few minutes to prepare yourself mentally for the interview. Visualize yourself arriving with a confident, enthusiastic attitude. Review the answers to tough questions you're likely to face. Go over your infomercial. As Laura Rowe Lane points out, "Don't worry about sounding canned. You'll sound *comfortable.*" And if you're comfortable, you'll interview well!

Lay out your clothes. Make sure everything is clean and pressed. Listen to the news, scan the newspaper, and catch the headlines on-line to make sure you're up-to-date on what's going on in the world. And get to bed as early as you can. You want to be well-rested and refreshed!

2. THE DAY OF YOUR INTERVIEW: DON'T STUMBLE APPROACHING THE STARTING GATE!

It's almost "that time." What do you have to watch out for today?

A. IF YOU'RE SICK—RESCHEDULE

If you're ill, you can't have your game on. Call the employer, apologize, and ask to reschedule. Trust me. They'll appreciate that you didn't come in and sneeze all over them . . . or worse.

B. LAST MINUTE RESEARCH

As close to the interview as possible, take another quick look at the employer's web site, and check lawfuel.com, law.com, lexis/nexus or Westlaw and see if there's any significant late-breaking news relating to the employer, the interviewer, or their specialty. If you know something the interviewer doesn't know yet, you'll look like a *superstar.*

* * * SMART HUMAN TRICK * * *

Female student, a Third Year, had an interview with the SEC for an internship during the school year. She had prepped herself for the interview by researching the SEC, and she knew an important case was coming down the morning of the interview.

She read it as soon as it came out on Lexis/Nexis, both the majority opinion and the dissent.

During the interview, she mentioned, "I see the Nordstrand case came down."

The interviewer responded, "I didn't get a chance to see it yet."

The student said, "Really? Well, I thought the dissent was particularly interesting."

The interviewer stopped her, called in other lawyers in the office . . . and asked the student to tell all of them about the case. She did. When she finished, the interviewer asked her: "Would you be interested in our Honors Program?" (A *very* prestigious program, by the way.)

Would she? You bet!

c. WHAT TO TAKE WITH YOU

Easy. Bring:

- **An extra copy of your resume;**

Your transcript;

- **A copy of your writing sample;**
- **Copies of any references you have;**
- **A Tide pen;** (as Margann Bennett points out, "You wouldn't be the first student to spill coffee on his shirt on the way to the interview.")
- **A urine sample.**

Just kidding about the urine sample. I just wanted to see if you were paying attention. Anyway, bring everything (except the urine sample) even if you've sent copies of all of them ahead of time. It's easy for an employer to mislay papers, and you want to help them out if they have.

Incidentally, make sure the resume you bring with you is *identical* to the one they already have, unless you have some new grades/experience since you sent them a resume. If you thought twice about adding or deleting a prior job, it will trigger warning bells to the employer.

Carry everything in a slim portfolio, leather or a nice-looking vinyl or microfiber. Don't bring a backpack or book bag. Remember, the look you're aiming for here is professional. Don't remind the employer that you're a student!

Also, **if you're going to the employer's office or any location other than school, pick up a copy of *The Wall Street Journal* and take it with you.** I know this sounds petty, but look at it this way: If you're an employer and you show up late, what's going to impress you—seeing an interviewee reading the *Journal,* or seeing them reading a tabloid with the headline *Boy Locked In Refrigerator Eats Own Foot?* You see my point. Anyway, if there's a particularly interesting story in the *Journal*—there always is—it'll give you something to use to break the ice in the first few minutes of the interview.

D. CHECK YOUR LOOK IN THE MIRROR ON THE WAY OUT THE DOOR

A quick glance at yourself will capture any wardrobe *faux pas*.

* * * CAREER LIMITING MOVE * * *

A student has a day's worth of interviews at a law firm. At the end of the day, she catches her reflection in the glass door on the way out of the firm . . .

. . . and sees the price tag for her suit hanging down under her arm.

E. TIMING YOUR ARRIVAL

Aim to be five minutes early. No more, no less. If it's an on-campus interview, the timing is easy. If you're going to the employer's office or anywhere with which you're not familiar, build in a cushion of time in case you run into traffic or get lost. However, if you allowed *too* much time and you arrive way early, wander around outside or go to a nearby Starbucks—there's always a nearby Starbucks—so that you arrive no more than five minutes early.

* * * CAREER LIMITING MOVE * * *

Law student sets up an interview with an employer, a small firm. In a conversation before the interview, the interviewer asks: "Do you need directions to our offices? It can be confusing."

"No," responds law student confidently.

The time set for the interview comes and goes. No law student. Ten minutes later, the law student calls the interviewer, and the interviewer says, "Where are you?"

"I'm at the address you gave me," says the law student. "It's a bakery."

"You can't be at the right address, because *I'm here.*"

"So am *I!*" insists the student. "Are you sure you're not in this building?"

The interviewer, exasperated, says, "You're at 1100 Pacific Street?"

After a moment, the student responds: "I'm at 1100 Pacific *Avenue.*"

* * * YOU CAN'T MAKE THIS STUFF UP * * *

Two students have the first two interviews of the day with an on-campus interviewer. We'll call the employer Moon & Shine. The student with the first slot shows up a few minutes early. The student with the *second* slot shows up *way* early—before the first interview is even supposed to begin.

The two students don't know each other. "Are you here for Moon and Shine?" says one of them to the other, who interprets this to mean: *He's the interviewer*, and so he answers: "Yes." The student who asks the question takes this to mean, *He's the interviewer*. So: they each mistakenly believe the other is the interviewer! They walk into the interview room, and talk to each other for several minutes … before they realize that neither one of them is the interviewer!

F. IF YOU RECENTLY ATE SOMETHING RANK, SMOKED OR DRANK COFFEE—HAVE A BREATH MINT

Raw garlic and onions is probably not a great idea for a snack before an interview, but no matter *what* you put in your mouth, you can solve the problem with a breath mint.

G. DON'T BE LULLED INTO A FALSE SENSE OF SECURITY BY THE RECEPTIONIST OR SECRETARY!

That sweet little old blue-haired lady at the reception desk may be a wolf in disguise! I've heard countless stories, from hiring partners and Career Services people alike, about students who were careless about how they came across to the support staff … and paid the ultimate price of rejection *before the interview even began!* As Mary Obrzut warns, "Be conscious of the receptionist—even friendly questions may be meaningful. You have to assume that any answer to their questions will get back to the attorney you're interviewing with."

So for instance, if you're sweetly asked if you have children or where you live, assume that your answer is going straight to the interviewer. Similarly, as Amy Thompson warns, don't confess *anything* negative to the receptionist, like the fact that you really don't like this city, or you're only interviewing here because you have friends in town that you wanted to visit.

Also remember your *attitude*. The receptionist's opinion of you may carry great weight with the interviewer. As Tammy Willcox warns, "If you ignore the receptionist, you've shot yourself in the foot and you'll walk out of there bleeding! Attorneys rely on their secretaries *before* their associates!" On more than one occasion a student has lost a job opportunity because the receptionist rang the interviewer to say that the student was arrogant. So when it comes to receptionists and secretaries, follow Mary Obrzut's advice: "Be friendly—but be careful!"

* * * CAREER LIMITING MOVE * * *

Student from a distinguished law school, interviewing at a prestigious firm. He shows up a few minutes early, and the receptionist offers to show him around the office. He responds, "I'd rather have an attorney show me around, thank you."

* * * CAREER LIMITING MOVE * * *

Law student shows up at a large firm for a call-back interview. She introduces herself to the receptionist as "Amy Stillwell" (I've changed her name). The receptionist asks politely, "May I get you something to drink, Amy?" The student responds, "It's Ms. Stillwell."

3. HOW TO MAKE THE FIRST FEW MINUTES OF THE INTERVIEW WORK FOR YOU, NOT AGAINST YOU

You've got all of your ducks in a row. You've researched the employer and the interviewer. You've prepped questions and answers. You look great. You smell good. You have a right to feel confident, because you've done what you can do. It's time to meet the interviewer!

I can't overemphasize the importance of the first moments of the interview. Research suggests that interviewers make a decision about you within the first 40 seconds to four minutes of the interview. As Dave James points out, "Interviewers begin making judgments about you the moment they lay eyes on you." So first impressions count! Here's what you want to do:

- **If you are sitting down when you meet the interviewer (for instance, they come to get you in a lobby), stand up immediately. Never shake hands sitting down;**
- **Shake the interviewer's hand firmly (without crushing any bones, of course);**
- **Greet them** *by name*, **using "Mr." or "Ms."—don't call them by their first name unless/until they invite you to do so;**
- **Make eye contact;**
- **Smile; and**
- **Let the interviewer lead the conversation.**

Students often overlook the importance of handshakes. I've shaken thousands of hands at law schools around the country, and the majority of handshakes are fine; firm but comfortable. But the outliers are memorable. At one end of the spectrum are "wet fish" handshakes, where the person's hand just kind of hangs there in midair. At the other end are the ones that make you think the veins in your hand will pop, it's being crushed so hard. The thing to do is to shake hands with someone in your Career Services Office, and ask them straight out if your handshake is OK. You may think, "Geez, Kimmbo, isn't this kind of nitpicking?" I'm telling you, people *notice* handshakes. Make sure yours is OK!

Eye contact is another area where students I meet sometimes trip up. Particularly if you're either shy or from a culture where direct eye contact with someone is considered disrespectful, it may be difficult to look the interviewer in the eye when you meet. But it's *really* important. If you find yourself looking anywhere else when you meet someone, *practice* until you feel comfortable looking people in the eye. It's a small detail, but people notice if you're looking elsewhere.

The first thing the interviewer is likely to say, before you even sit down, is "How are you?" We discussed this question earlier. In a nutshell: answer with an enthusiastic "Fine, thanks," "Excited to be here"—something that conveys that you're looking forward to talking with the interviewer.

Let's talk for a moment about sitting down—something you're likely to do very early in the interview! If you're in a typical interview room situation, there are often only two chairs and the interviewer has put them where (s)he wants them. Take the seat (s)he gestures you toward. If the interview is in the attorney's office, there may be a small table with chairs in front of the desk. If the attorney comes around the desk to interview you sitting there, it tells you something, subconsciously, about the attorney's accessibility. They're not keeping a desk between you, which suggests a less formal, more relaxed relationship.

What about an interview in a conference room? Students occasionally ask me about how you choose a seat when there are twenty available! Experts say you want to sit in the seat 90 degrees from the interviewer. That is, you don't want to sit across the table from them, it's too "Citizen Kane"-ish. But you don't want to sit next to them either, because that's just ... weird. So the best is just around the corner.

In the first couple of minutes, the interviewer will usually engage in some small talk to break the ice. *Go along with whatever the interviewer wants!* Whatever you do, don't get caught up in the idea that you've got to hit the ground running because you've only got twenty minutes or so to make your pitch. If you do that, you'll get more and more nervous as the seconds tick by, thinking that you're running out of chances to explain why you're so qualified for the job. *Don't do it!* Let interviewers talk themselves into liking you, first. If they bring up sports, or the weather, or something in the news, go along with it. Keep up with current events for this very purpose. What you're doing is creating the indelible impression in the interviewer's mind that "I could work with this person." That's exactly how you want them to feel!

Of course, don't stake out an extreme position on any current event. If the interviewer at a Boston firm asks, "Did you see the Red Sox game last night?" You can't say, "The Red Sox suck, I'm a lifelong Yankees fan"—because if they're a Red Sox fan, you've alienated them needlessly. "Yes, I did," or "No, I didn't"—with a smile on your face, followed by "You a baseball fan?" is appropriate.

If they ask your view on anything, state it non-confrontationally, briefly and with a smile. "You a baseball fan?" They ask. If you're not, say something like, "I don't see many games, but how about you?"

rather than "It's a stupid waste of time watching a bunch of overpaid 'roid ragers.' "

Notice that you're not lying. You're not pretending to have opinions you don't have. You're just modulating what you *do* believe. If you wind up working with the interviewer, there'll be plenty of time for (ideally friendly) sports arguments!

When they lead into the body of the interview—after the small talk—take advantage of visual and verbal cues to see how comfortable the interviewer is ... which determines how much you'll have to carry the interview "ball." If the interviewer seems unsure, volunteer information about yourself and ask lots of questions. If the interviewer is assured and experienced, let them ask their questions, and add yours to the end of your answers.

F. THE CHARM OFFENSIVE: HOW TO BEHAVE THROUGHOUT THE INTERVIEW

Remember that the interviewer doesn't have laser vision to look into your soul. They can't divine how smart you are, how hard you work, what you're really like. All they have is what you present to them, in your words and behavior. Let's talk about some behaviors to manifest from beginning to end in your interviews!

1. GET WITH THE NEWS THROUGHOUT "INTERVIEW SEASON"

Keep up with the news every day. Scan the local newspaper, as well as *The Wall Street Journal* and *The New York Times*. Go to CNN.com, MSNBC.com, ABCNews.com, or your favourite news site. Scan lawfuel.com frequently for law-related news. Listen to NPR, *Morning Edition* in the morning and/or *All Things Considered* at night. Why? Because those are the things that lawyers look at and listen to. Interviewers will inevitably break the ice by talking about what's going on in the real world. If you say something like, "I don't have time to keep up with what's going on," you'll sound like you've got tunnel vision, and you'll put the interviewer on edge. I went to a football game at West Point once, and a cadet told me that they are required to read the front page of *The New York Times* and the front page of the Sports Section every day. You're not busier than cadets at West Point. It's a good habit to form!

Remember, part of what you're trying to do is to project the image that you're well-rounded, and knowing what's going on in the world is an excellent way to do it.

In addition, if you state an interest in a specialty in your cover letter to an employer, make sure you are up-to-date on developments in it! Lawfuel.com, law.com, Lexis/Nexis, Westlaw ... you can use any or all of them to make sure that you're *au courant* on what you say you want to do. If you're not and an interviewer calls you on it, they'll question your sincerity.

2. DON'T TRY TO SQUASH EVERYTHING YOU WANT THE INTERVIEWER TO KNOW ABOUT YOU INTO THE FIRST QUESTION

As Dave James advises, "Give interviewers a chance to ask what they want to know. If they go far afield, maybe your credentials are what they're looking for."

3. MAKE YOUR BODY LANGUAGE SPEAK FLUENT ENTHUSIASM

Did you know that dog handlers eat liver and garlic so that their voices keep their dogs' attention?

Well—enthusiasm is *your* liver and garlic. It's the way you draw in the interviewer!

I beat you over the head with the idea of showing enthusiasm at every juncture in your job search. Enthusiasm isn't just a function of what you say—it's how you say it. Studies show that in interviews, what counts the most is tone and body language, far outweighing the importance of the words used. At one law school, the #1 student in the class was unemployed. She had a hard time looking interviewers in the eye, she spoke very nervously, and she furrowed her brow in response to even casual questions.

Convey in your tone of voice and your body language that this is the job you want! Be sure to:

- **Sit up in your chair. No slouching!**
- **Lean forward slightly. It conveys both confidence and interest. Leaning back says you're either insecure or bored.**
- **Don't rest your elbows on the table or desk between you and the interviewer.**
- **Don't cross your arms. Hands comfortably on your lap, palms up, which conveys honesty. Gesture appropriately as you talk.**
- **Don't play with your hair, tug at your clothes, play with your jewelry, or fidget.**
- **Maintain *comfortable* eye contact. Staring at the interviewer is just as bad as constantly avoiding his/her gaze.**
- **No feet on the desk!**

You may also want to try a psychological tactic known as "mirroring." What happens when you "mirror" someone is that you pick up on their body language, and mirror it with your own. Facial expressions, eye movements, speech rate, tone of voice, breathing rate ... these are all things that are subject to "mirroring." If you think it sounds like too much to think about—I think it sounds that way!—it turns out that you often do it naturally. Researchers find that people "mirror" others all the time in social situations without even being aware of it. If you *are* aware of it, you can work mirroring to your advantage in an interview. What mirroring does is to create the subtle impression in the interviewer's mind that you're on the same wavelength. That kind of bonding leads to great interviews!

Does this sound butt-puckeringly manipulative to you? Do you just want to let "whatever happens, happen"? I'm down with that. After all, we all know that an air of unattainability is what works socially. And what I'm suggesting here is the direct opposite of that. *But it works.* In an interview, the fact is that the interviewer has something you want (or think you might): a job. Seeming enthusiastic about that job *does* put you in a one-down position, because you're implicitly saying, "Interviewer, you have the power to give me something I want, and that puts you in a better position than me." That's not to say that you shouldn't be confident in what you bring to the table, or that you shouldn't be a discerning interviewee—you should use the interview as an opportunity to decide which employer is right for you, as well. But the fact remains, you are at a social disadvantage because the interviewer has something you want. If that bothers you—acknowledge it, get over it, and show that you want the job! Remember: honest enthusiasm is very hard for an employer to resist. Do whatever feels comfortable to make sure they see that you're truly interested in the job!

4. YOUR ANSWERS ARE PREPARED. DON'T LET THEM SOUND THAT WAY

If you've ever seen me give the *Guerrilla Tactics* seminar, you probably guessed that I prepared the words ahead of time. But I try very hard to make it sound spontaneous.

In interviews, you've got to do the same thing. No interviewer wants to hear you speak robotically; if they did, they could have sent you interrogatories instead of interviewing you!

Be sure to modulate your tone, to wait for a moment when you hear a question before you answer, to follow the conversation without sticking to a script. When the interviewer asks you a question, don't say, "Oh–OK," and launch into your answer. Don't look around as though you're trying to remember what you wanted to say. Think about how you answer when your family members ask you questions, and aim for that kind of ease.

5. MAKE YOUR MESSAGE AND DELIVERY CONSISTENT

Dave James points out that when he was the hiring attorney for a City Attorney's office, "I had many applicants lethargically claim to be enthusiastic, meekly claim to be confident."

Don't undercut your message with the way you deliver it! Keep statements brief and avoid waffling words like, "I think," "I feel," "I hope." Don't repeat, which suggests you're not prepared: "I feel I'm qualified, truly qualified, for this job."

6. "PROFESSIONALIZE" YOUR VOCABULARY

If you're going to be a professional, it's important to *sound* like one in interviews. No matter what infuses your vocabulary outside of interviews, remember that when you're in the spotlight, you:

- Avoid describing things as "sweet";
- Minimize use of the word "like," as in, "So, I was, like . . .";
- Don't call the interviewer "Dude";
- Don't use the phrase "You know," as in, "Dude, I was, like, you know . . .";
- Don't use the words "and stuff," as in, "Dude, I was like, you know, down with that job, and stuff."
- No "kinda's," as in, "Dude, I'm kinda like, you know, bored with school, and stuff."
- No "sort of's," as in, "Dude, I'm kinda like, you know, bored with school. It's sort of, like, getting old, and stuff."
- Even if the interviewer uses it, no profanity . . . as in: "Dude, I'm kinda like, you know, bored with school. It's sort of, like, getting f* * *ing old, and stuff."

At first, you may be *very* self-conscious about avoiding terms that you use all the time in real life. But it gets easier. I remember when my little son Harry first started paying attention to words. I figured it was time to stop swearing, which essentially cut my vocabulary in half. It took a little while but I'm virtually dirty-word-free now.

If you have a hard time with this, practice with some mock interviews before you go on the "real thing."

* * * CAREER LIMITING MOVES * * *

From an employer's e-mail to the University of Minnesota Law School Career Services Office:

"OK, so you know when you're, like, interviewing someone? And like they seem totally qualified with like great experience and good grades and stuff, but like they're all 'like' this and 'like' that in the interview?

It's like totally annoying and pretty much impossible to hear any, like, good points they have, cuz like you just can't get past all the, you know, verbal ticks and extra words and stuff?

I like totally hate that.

. . . There were like *totally* people I would have otherwise hired but I was like 'that girl is going to sound like an idiot in court, no matter how well she writes exams.' It's like totally bumming me out, you know?"

7. FOCUS EXCLUSIVELY ON THE INTERVIEW

Pretend you're in a movie theater. Cell phones and Blackberries off! If you are expecting a very important phone call, set your phone on vibrate, and *don't mention it.*

Also: no taking notes. It's distracting to the person talking. You're better off "active listening," that is, looking at the interviewer as (s)he talks, nodding, smiling where appropriate, and adding "I'm listening" words like "Yes," "OK," "Mm-hmm."

* * * CAREER LIMITING MOVE * * *

Law student in an on-campus interview with an interviewer from a large law firm. A few minutes into the interview, the law student's cell phone rings. As the interviewer reports, "It's bad enough that it rang at all. The guy looked at the caller ID, and said, 'Excuse me.' So I figured, it's something important."

"It wasn't. It was a friend of his. While I'm sitting there, he made plans to go out drinking that night."

* * * CAREER LIMITING MOVE * * *

Law student in an on-campus interview. His cell phone rings. The interviewer reports: "The fact that his cell phone went off was pretty bad. But the real problem was his ring tone. It was a voice saying, 'Answer the f***ing phone'!"

8. DON'T MISTAKE ARROGANCE FOR SELF-CONFIDENCE!

I visit law schools all the time, and I rarely run into arrogant law students. I know they exist, but they obviously self-select out of seeing my *Guerrilla Tactics* seminar—because, of course, they know everything there is to know.

The problem with arrogance is this: people who are arrogant don't seem to realize it. They think they're just being "honest." "I'm the best, so why not say it?"

If you have great credentials and you're not getting either call-backs or offers, it may be an arrogance problem. What you want to watch for is this: Do you say things like "Writing comes easily to me ..." "I don't need training on ..." "Waste of time ..." Do you compare yourself to other students? Instead of saying "People I've worked for seem to really like my writing," do you say, "I'm the best writer in my class"?

* * * CAREER LIMITING MOVE * * *

Student from a very distinguished law school. He brings a bar chart to on-campus interviews, pointing out where he ranks compared to the rest of his classmates in every class.

Let other people speak for you; talk about yourself in terms of compliments you've received about your work from others. Consider including in your conversations with employers phrases like "I was fortunate enough to ..." "I've been lucky ..." "I was honored to ..." Humble confidence is the tone you're striving for!

To make sure you've got any potential arrogance problem licked, sign up for a mock interview or two, and ask the interviewer to be brutally honest with you. If you say, "I think there may be something about my interviewing style that is holding me back . . ." you're setting them up to help you find any flaws—including arrogance.

Having cautioned you against being arrogant in interviews, I must point out that every rule has an exception—the person who gets the job *because* they're arrogant!

There was a student at one law school who'd been a journalist before law school, and while he was waiting for an on-campus interview with a law firm, he took out a pen and edited the firm's brochure, correcting mistakes and tightening the language. Fine by itself, I guess—but he actually took his revisions into the interview, and handed them to the interviewer!

Now the vast majority of interviewers would be horrified by this kind of brash behavior. But as it turns out, this particular firm consisted of a bunch of young, aggressive litigators, and that kind of balls-out attitude was just what they wanted. The interviewer made him an offer on the spot.

But the fact remains: If you're playing the odds, employers are almost always turned off by arrogance. Speak humbly but confidently, and you'll be fine.

* * * CAREER LIMITING MOVE * * *

Second year student, absolutely brilliant, on a full scholarship at a prestigious school. In on-campus interviews, she tells the interviewers up front: "I hope you're ethical, because I won't talk to any firm that isn't."

9. AVOID "TOXIC MODESTY"

I've warned you about being arrogant. Being what Susan Gainen calls "toxically modest" is just as bad. Remember that the only way the interviewer is going to want to hire you is if they believe good things about you. Certainly your credentials can jolly them along, but in addition they're going to have to *hear* good things from you. These good things have to strike a middle note. On the one hand, they can't be arrogant. "I'm the only person for the job," "You need me," "Nobody has my credentials." Well, yippee. It might be true, but you shouldn't say it. But at the other end of the spectrum, an "Aw, shucks" approach to your eligibility is equally inappropriate. "Humble confidence" is the middle ground. In other words, you need to sell yourself, subtly.

Does that term—"sell yourself"—rub you the wrong way? It shouldn't. It's just a spin on the idea of being positive. To make this clear, imagine yourself walking into a car showroom. You've got at least some vague notion that you want to buy a car, otherwise you wouldn't be there. You stroll over to a car and a salesman walks up to you. You say, "Tell me about this car," and the salesman responds, "Well, it's pretty good for getting around, but the gas mileage stinks." You'd look at him as though he had lobsters crawling out of his ears, wouldn't you? That's because *when you're buying something, you're also being sold something—and you'll only be sold on positives.* Instead, what the car salesman is going to tell you is, "This is a great car!" and then back that up with a description of the car's positive features.

I had a hilarious experience in a pet store once. They had prairie dogs for sale—you know, like you see in the zoo. I didn't realize you could have a prairie dog as a house pet, and let me tell you, they were so-o-o cute.

So I asked the pet store guy, "Wow—do prairie dogs make good pets?"

"Sure," he sneered, "If you like rodents."

O-kay. I asked, "Do you keep them in a cage like a hamster, or let them run around?"

"Let them run around," he said. "Unless you value your furniture. They gnaw through everything. Fabric, wood, walls . . ."

Our conversation went on in this vein for a few minutes. To tell you the truth I only kept asking him questions because his attitude was so funny. I wonder if this guy ever sold *anything!*

In interviews, you're both the pet store guy and the prairie dog. The car and the salesman. Think about what you'd want to know about you if you were the interviewer. Volunteer positive information. As Marilyn Tucker points out, "Remember that the unspoken question on the floor throughout the interview is, 'Why should I be interested in you rather than the next person?' Don't wait for them to ask that question before you answer it for them, by showing them why they should be interested in you!"

Heck, you've done all of this preparation for the interview. You know everything about the employer you can possibly know, and you've rehearsed your questions and answers. *None* of that matters unless you show it off to the interviewer. So Sell! Sell! Sell!

10. DON'T GET ALL UP IN THE INTERVIEWER'S GRILL ABOUT ANYTHING YOU DISAPPROVE OF

You might disapprove of some aspect of the employer or the interviewer. Well, yay. Remember: it's tact that's golden, not silence. A job interview isn't the place for issues. If you don't want the job, don't take the interview! And if the interviewer says something that pisses you off, keep in mind that it's a reflection on them, not you. At the most, tell Career Services about it. They'll address it tactfully with the employer.

Remember: you're going to be joining a profession. You don't know who your colleagues will be down the road. Don't burn bridges when you don't have to!

* * * CAREER LIMITING MOVE * * *

Student interviewing with a prosecutor's office. "I'm willing to volunteer. You only pay $2,000 for the summer. That's essentially volunteering."

* * * CAREER LIMITING MOVE * * *

Student in an on-campus interview. She tells the interviewer, "I almost didn't take this interview, because I find your grade requirements arrogant."

11. DON'T ASSUME THE INTERVIEWER KNOWS YOUR QUALIFICATIONS AND CREDENTIALS. DON'T JUMP UGLY IF (S)HE MAKES A MISTAKE ABOUT YOU

Maybe your interviewer has had a chance to review your cover letter, resume, writing sample and transcript.

Maybe not.

Remember, lawyers make money when they're working on client matters. Recruiting is important, but it sometimes has to take a back seat to their client work. If the interviewer doesn't seem to know anything about you, don't be offended.

For instance, if you go to a school with "Washington" in the name, don't expect the interviewer to get your school right. Students at Washington University in St. Louis tell me that they routinely are asked how they like going to school in D.C.

Or maybe it's more simple. The interviewer confuses you with someone else, and starts talking about a job you didn't have or a school you didn't attend.

If this happens to you, clearly you have to correct the interviewer, but you want to be discreet about it. Smile, and couch your correction in terms like, "Actually, I didn't work for ... I worked for X. You must see an awful lot of resumes and got me confused with somebody else." "I go to the Washington University in *St. Louis.* Don't worry. People make that mistake all the time." Go on and either answer the question the interviewer would have asked if they had the facts right about you, or ask them a question—whichever smoothes over the mistake most quickly.

Correcting an interviewer's mistake about you is a way of showing off your people skills. Make sure you show that you are conversationally savvy!

12. DON'T VOLUNTEER YOUR FLAWS. INTERVIEWS AREN'T CONFESSIONALS!

Remember Nathan Hale? The famous American Revolution spy who was hanged by the British, after famously (and ostensibly) proclaiming, "I regret that I have but one life to give for my country"?

You probably don't know how he was caught in the first place. After successfully infiltrating enemy lines, he wound up at a tavern, having dinner with a British officer.

"I'm a spy," confided the Brit.

"Really?" said Hale. "Me, too!"

He was under arrest before the espresso arrived.

Sandy Mans points out that "If the interviewer doesn't ask about something that will expose a flaw, don't feel you have to state it yourself!" She says that students tend to give negative information because they're uncomfortable with talking about themselves, and so they discuss their weaknesses.

Remember, in your average interview, you've got only twenty minutes to convince the interviewer that you're the right person for the job. *Twenty lousy minutes.* Don't waste it talking about why they *shouldn't* hire you. As Mary Harblin says, "On a first date, you wouldn't point out a zit!"

Don't even casually mention negatives in the context of other answers. Don't mention them *at all*. "Well, I know I really don't have the credentials for this job, but ..." "I know you're really looking for someone with a lot more experience, but ..." "I don't really know about what you do, but ..." When you've got a sentence with a "but" in it, remove the statement before the word "but"—and explain why you're right for the job!

* * * CAREER LIMITING MOVE * * *

Interviewer: "Why did you go to law school?"

Interviewee: "When I was in jail, I had a lot of time to think about what I wanted to do with my life ..."

We've talked thoroughly about killer answers to tough interview questions. Remember: When an interviewer asks you point blank about a flaw, you address the issue *briefly,* explain why it won't impact your work performance, and move on. If they don't ask you about it—shut up about it!

The only time I would advise you to take a different approach is a *very* limited circumstance indeed. Namely, **when you know your grades are significantly below what the employer typically demands.** It makes my skin crawl even bringing this up, because I *never* want you to go into an interview, *not ever,* feeling as though you're not "good enough" for the job—because you *are* capable, *regardless* of your grades! But you may occasionally find yourself in an interview with an employer who demands grades you just don't have. Maybe you got your foot in the door through an acquaintance (good for you!) Maybe your school doesn't allow employers to prescreen, so that employers wind up interviewing students with GPAs they wouldn't typically consider. Such employers are normally large firms, because they're the ones who are typically credential hounds.

So—what do you do? Syracuse's Alex Epsilanty recommends that you "Bring up your grades to the interviewer—because you've got to turn everyone you talk to from that firm into your advocate." Take the bull by the horns and bring up your credentials even if the interviewer doesn't, explaining why you'd fit in even if your grades don't fit their usual criteria.

Don't use this wording exactly, but you want to say something like, "I know from talking with associates at your firm, as well as from my other research, that you typically only take students from the top 10% of the class. I can understand why you do that, and I acknowledge that I'm not in that part of the class, but I'd like to tell you why I'm confident I can do your work ..." and then go on to explain other factors that go into making you the ideal candidate—perhaps you wrote onto Law Review, or you've written other articles, or you've got great work experience (volunteer or paid), or stellar performance in certain classes that are important to the employer, or you've got the old standby, a "strong upward trend" in your grades. You see my point.

Is this always going to work? Nope. But I promise you, if the employer is one who typically only looks at students at the top of the class—well, their loss, but if that's what they do, it's not like they're going to ignore your grades. You can't take the attitude, "Well, if they didn't ask about my grades, I guess they don't care about them." If you have proof that they do, address the grades issue yourself, speaking with confidence about your abilities, and backing up your confidence with some kind of experience proving it.

You can't see me, but right now *I'm on my knees, begging you*— don't bring up any of your flaws in *any other* interview situation! If your grades are *slightly* below their usual standard—don't mention it. If you're interviewing with a medium to small firm, a government agency—don't bring it up. You're in an interview to sell, and that means focusing on your strengths!

13. DON'T ASSUME THAT YOU *CAN'T* GET THE JOB, OR ALTERNATIVELY: ASSUME THAT IF YOU GOT THE INTERVIEW, YOU'VE GOT A SHOT AT THE JOB!

You may occasionally find yourself in an interview for a job you think is beyond your reach. As I just discussed, you may have gotten the interview through a contact, with a prestigious firm that would never have interviewed you based on your paper credentials. Or maybe you lucked out and got an on-campus interview because the employer had to hold slots open for students who don't meet their traditional criteria. Whatever the reason, the bottom line is that you think you're in over your head.

Get over it!

I promise you, I *guarantee* you, there is no job you can't perform based on your paper credentials, no matter what the interviewer thinks going into the interview. I have talked to innumerable employers who've told me, "We weren't going to interview her ..." "He was our least-promising candidate ..." "We took a real chance ..." and they inevitably follow that up with: "But (s)he turned out to be a real star." Some employers have told me that *inevitably* their best lawyers are the ones who had to fight to get in the door.

The fact is, if you've researched the hell out of the employer, you've talked with everyone you can find who's worked there or knows about them, and you've done what you can by way of extracurriculars and work experience to show you're a star in spite of your grades, *then you can get that job.* No matter what employer you're talking about, *somebody's* worked there before who has worse grades than you. That is true of every employer in America. (If you're really concerned about your grades of course you should read the chapter called "Help! My Grades Stink!")

I've talked before about the importance of the words you use when you talk to yourself, championed by author Shad Helmstetter. There are really two basic ways you can look at "reach" interviews. You can tell yourself, "They never hire anyone with my grades, and they never will. This is a waste of time." Or you can say, "OK, they don't typically hire people who don't have great grades, but that doesn't mean they won't hire me. I've got my work cut out for me, but I *can*—and *will*—convince them I can do the work!" Same situation, two entirely different attitudes. Psyche yourself *into* the job, not *out* of it. As Teresa DeAndrado says, "If you got the interview, you have to assume that you have a chance at the job!"

14. DON'T BE DEFENSIVE OR APOLOGETIC

It's inevitable that some interviewer, sometime, will put you on the spot. You'll be asked about—well, fill in the blank with what torques you off. Less-than-stellar grades. No work experience. A home town that doesn't get good press. An undergrad or law school that ain't Harvard. Whatever you do, "Don't apologize, and don't be defensive!" says St. Johns' Maureen Provost Ryan. It's vital that you always maintain a positive spin on your abilities, your record, your character, your schools, everything. By all means, *explain.* "I didn't do well on my first year exams because, frankly, the style of law school exams caught me by surprise. But I've spoken with all of my first year professors, corrected the exam-taking flaws I had, and I'm confident my performance this semester will prove that I've overcome them." You've got to admit, that sounds a lot better than kvetching "I know my grades suck, and I don't know what happened. But I'm not stupid or anything."

So acknowledge whatever it is that makes you feel apologetic or defensive, but don't let those nasty reactions bubble to the surface. Smile, respond, and move on!

15. DON'T BE INTIMIDATED BY POWER

You know how Dorothy and her friends felt when they first saw the Wizard of Oz? You may find yourself in an interview sometime feeling exactly that way, shaking with intimidation. Maybe the interviewer is very prestigious, and/or wealthy and/or just an intimidating person, by dint of sheer force of will. How the heck do you interview well when the interviewer scares the hell out of you?

You gird yourself for battle, and remember: this isn't about how you feel. It's about what you *project*. I've talked with thousands of attorneys, some of whom make millions of dollars a year, and you know something? You'd be shocked how often they'll say that they are a lot *less* confident than they seem, but they know they have to put on a good show for clients and younger associates. You can't look inside a person's soul to see how they feel any more than they've got laser-vision into *yours*. Every interviewer with whom you ever speak will have faced exactly the same things as you: personal embarrassments, setbacks, self-doubts. So while you may respect the trappings of power—the expensive car, the corner office, the mega-salary, the Supreme Court victories—don't let the importance of the interviewer intimidate you. Be deferential, certainly, but that's true no matter how powerful you perceive the interviewer to be. Take a deep breath, and remember that even the most successful lawyers in the world need colleagues—why shouldn't you be one of them?

16. DON'T ASSUME YOU'RE UNDER ATTACK. IT MAY DELIBERATELY BE A "STRESS INTERVIEW"

Most of the time, interviewers will be at least relatively pleasant, and they'll seem genuinely engaged in what you have to say. But once in a while you'll face hostile questions, body language that says the interviewer couldn't be less interested in you, an environment that makes you say to yourself "Get me out of here!"

Relax. One of three things is going on. The interviewer may deliberately be putting you under pressure to see how you handle it. Especially for jobs that require you to be in court, the interviewer will want to see how you react when you face harsh questioning.

I had an experience like this myself. During the winter break of First Year, I interviewed with a tiny law firm in Greenwich, Connecticut. There were five partners, all of whom had been classmates at Yale Law School. Yeah. *That* Yale. So I'm sitting there with Case Western Reserve on my resume. One of the partners picks up my resume, and says, "So, how are you enjoying it at Chase?"

He didn't even get the name of my school right! I answered about how much I liked it—which I did. He went on and commented, "You know, we've never hired anybody from Chase before." *No kidding.*

I said, brightly, "Well, then, I should be a refreshing change for you."

They laughed. And incidentally—I got the job.

I remember one student I spoke with in the Pacific Northwest. She came to see me give a *Guerrilla Tactics* seminar, and afterwards she came up to talk to me. She was clearly very upset, so I quickly answered questions from other students so I could focus on her alone. She was sobbing as she said, "My dream is to be a prosecutor, but every time I get an interview, they tell me I'm not tough enough!" and she burst into tears.

Well-l-l . . .

A second possibility when you're up against it in an interview is that the interviewer is just a jerk. It happens. The proportion of jerks you meet when you're looking for a job is just the same as it is in the rest of your life. There aren't a ton of them, but they're out there. While employers generally try to send out their best and friendliest, it doesn't always work out that way.

A third possibility is that you perceive an attack where none exists. I talked to one student in the Midwest who was looking for a job in L.A. She said, "They don't believe I want California! They keep asking me, 'If you wanted to be out here, why did you go to school in Illinois?' " Another student, this one in Arizona, had clerked for a federal judge after 1L. She didn't have good grades, and she said, "They keep attacking me in interviews. They ask me, 'How did you get a federal clerkship with *those* grades?' "

Yet another student, this one in New England, said that when he went on an interview for an intellectual property position, the interviewer "Said to me, 'What was your thesis about?' What's he getting at? That his Ph.D. is better than mine?"

In each of these cases you can see that the attack the student perceived *wasn't really there.* (In the case of the Ph.D. guy, between you and me, he was a bit of a nut.) Remember: The employer has a legitimate concern about your skills and qualities, your judgment, your motivation, enthusiasm and sincerity, and they're going to ask questions that get at those issues. Those aren't attack questions; they're legitimate. A lawyer from an Oregon firm had an interview with a Second Year student, and asked her, "Why did you change careers?" He commented, "She took it as a criticism. I didn't mean it that way. I was just curious!" If you view questions like these as attacks, it may be because you aren't comfortable yet with the answers you give!

The key in any situation you perceive as an "attack" is to remain perfectly calm, and give the answers you've prepared. They're just *words* the interviewer is using. They only hurt as much as you *let* them. Use humor if you feel comfortable with it. You've thought about these issues. You know the best way to respond. Take a deep breath, ignore the barbs in the interviewer's voice, and plunge ahead.

17. DON'T BE OVERWHELMED BY WHAT YOU PERCEIVE AS YOUR ACHILLES' HEELS

Maureen Provost Ryan points out that "Students always have a problem with Achilles' heels—they worry about questions they'll be asked."

In this chapter, we analyzed the most common tough questions you might be asked and how you should handle them. And in your preparation, before your interview, you'll have done some self-assessment so that you are comfortable with yourself and what you bring to the table for the employer. Remember, no matter what flaw in your background you must overcome, it's got no predictive value as to how you will perform for the particular employer *unless you give that flaw power over you.* Talk to yourself over and over again in supportive terms, highlighting what you feel are your best traits. Tell yourself why it is that you'll do a terrific job. As Maureen Provost Ryan says, "View yourself as an irresistible candidate." And trust me—you'll start to believe it, and when you do, you won't have any Achilles' heels!

18.   NO LIES. NO EXAGGERATION. NO STRETCHING THE TRUTH

Remember: Interviewing is about showing the employer the best possible *you*. It's not a confessional—you don't let it all hang out—but it's genuinely *you*.

We all know what competition is like for plum jobs. And we also know what pressure often produces: the thought that if we just embellished the truth a little bit . . .

Don't do it! You'll get busted, sooner or later. For instance, Elizabeth Workman says "If you tell an employer they're your #1 choice, mean it. If you say it to every employer in town, they'll find out. People from different firms talk to each other."

Even if you *get* the job based on a lie, you can't keep it up throughout the time you work there. If you say in an interview that working routine long hours is fine with you but in actuality you have *no intention* of working past dinner time, who wins? Not you. Not the employer. If you exaggerate your experience at a prior employer, prospective employers will expect you to be able to do what you claim you did. Or they might talk to your former boss and you'll get busted that way.

It's important to stick with the truth—presented artfully. That's why I'm always encouraging to you talk enthusiastically about aspects of the employer for which you have genuine enthusiasm. For jobs and experiences that stunk, you pull out good—but true—aspects to talk about. For every negative experience you focus on what you learned from it. In short: you're not lying. But you *are* being tactful and discreet. And those qualities will serve you well!

* * * CAREER LIMITING MOVE * * *

Student interviewing with a medium-sized firm. The interviewer asks her, "Do you play softball?" She enthuses, "Softball? I *love* softball. Softball is my middle name. Why do you ask?" and the interviewer responds, predictably enough, "The firm has a team. We play every Friday."

She gets the job, and sure enough, soon afterwards the firm has a game—and the interviewer, citing her affection for softball, encourages her to play. She figures she can fake it, and agrees.

Before the game, everybody is warming up. She figures imitating everybody else is the safest bet. So she puts on a glove, and does some soft tosses with a colleague.

The game starts, and as luck would have it, she's the first one up. She picks up a bat and heads for home plate. As she stands there, she hears snickering. She turns to her bench, and asks what's so funny. The guy who interviewed her in the first place tells her, "When you bat, it's customary to take off the glove, first."

After that, her nickname at the firm is "Slugger."

19.   Don't Take Honesty to the Point of foolhardiness.

Oof. This is a very difficult topic to address. All of us—well, most of us—like to think we're honest. There's no question that it's important to be truthful in every aspect of your job search. But when you talk about attitude, or character strengths or flaws, likes and dislikes, you'd have to be a complete idiot to be blunt. Foolhardiness comes into play when honesty butts up against discretion.

Remember: You get to choose what you share. I am reminded of a Janet Jackson interview I once saw on TV. She had been secretly married to her manager for several years. The interviewer asked her, "How on Earth did you ever keep your marriage a secret?"

Her response: "I never told anybody."

Pretty obvious! Let's put this principle to work in an interview setting. Let's say you're interested in three different specialties—intellectual property, real estate, and criminal defense work. You'd be unique, by the way. And let's say that you're in an interview with an IP employer. The interviewer asks:

"So—what are you interested in doing?"

You could respond: "Intellectual property, real estate, and criminal defense." That's totally true. But put yourself in the shoes of the interviewer, who's going to think, "This student doesn't really know what (s)he wants to do. If we make him/her an offer, how do we know (s)he'll accept? And if (s)he worked with us, what if (s)he hates it and leaves?"

Let's go back and change the answer. Instead of saying all three specialties, you say: "Well, I'm really interested in intellectual property. That's why I'm here talking to you. I'll tell you what I like about it ..." Notice: you're *still* telling the truth. You *are* sincerely interested in IP. *But you aren't muddying the waters by talking about other specialties in which you're also interested.* To put it differently: you're being discreet. It's not talked about very much as a desirable trait in professionals, but trust me, *everybody* needs to be discreet. Displaying this trait in an interview is a head start on what you'll be doing throughout your professional life.

Let's look at another example. I talked with one woman at a Virginia law school who was a single mother of a four-year-old. She had two withdrawals on her transcript because her son had been sick and she had to bail out both times to take care of him. She didn't know how to handle it in interviews. I told her, "Tell employers that you have day care and back-up day care, that you understand the time commitment of the jobs you're applying for, and you know how important it is to live up to that commitment." She said, "But isn't that lying? I mean, if my son went into the hospital again, I would be at his bedside." I told her "Of course you would! So would the interviewer and everybody else with blood in their veins. But an interview isn't a confessional. Everybody knows 'life happens.' You don't have to bring it up in interviews."

* * * CAREER LIMITING MOVE * * *

Third Year Student at a Midwestern school.

Interviewer: "What are you doing during your last semester?"

Student: "I'm just hanging out and cleaning up barf. My girlfriend is pregnant."

20.   USE HUMOR CAREFULLY

In the section on generating answers to tough questions, I warned you about the idea of listing "sense of humor" as one of your assets. A sense of humor is a wonderful trait, but you don't want employers to think that you'll be too busy with whoopie cushions and hand buzzers to actually accomplish anything.

Ironically enough, employers often say that they look for a sense of humor in people they hire. What they mean is: *We want you to have our sense of humor.* And on top of that, they want you to be able to use that sense of humor to diffuse difficult situations.

In interviews, displaying your sense of humor is a delicate matter. I've told you about various situations where a quip makes sense to handle a touchy subject.

You hear examples of this in the media all the time.

Chief Justice John Roberts, an appellate lawyer before becoming a judge, once lost a U.S. Supreme Court case by a vote of 9–0. The client was apoplectic. *"How* could you lose *nine to nothing?"* he said.

"Because there were only nine justices," responded Roberts.

In 2006, Senator Barack Obama was asked by Larry King if he intended to run for President in 2008. Instead of jerking Larry around with "I really haven't thought about it," Obama responded, "You know, Larry, they say every United States Senator looks at himself in the mirror every morning and sees a President of the United States."

Of course one of the best known quipsters ever was President John Kennedy. There are entire books devoted to the humor he used in reaction to tough questions. On the campaign trail, for instance, presidential candidates are often criticized for their crowd estimates; they tend to wildly inflate how many people turn out to see them.

When Kennedy, a Catholic, was asked how he came up with his crowd estimates, he responded, "I tell Plucky [his press secretary] to count the nuns and multiply by a hundred."

When you're in interviews, gauge your humour to the interviewer. If the interviewer is very serious, don't try humor. If on the other hand the interviewer is more casual, try a quip to open a sensitive subject like bad grades, an unfortunate work experience, whatever.

Of course, it's always possible to take the humour beyond the interviewer's comfort level. I talked with one student who had a "gang interview" with several lawyers at a medium-sized firm. She said, "They were all joking around, and one of them said to me, laughing, 'What happens if we don't make you an offer?' and I shot back, 'I'll hunt you down and shoot you like the dogs you are.' All of a sudden: silence. None of them thought it was the least bit funny. The air completely went out of the interview. I knew my offer shriveled up right there."

If the interviewer tells jokes, the best response is laughter—not necessarily matching them joke for joke. But if you feel the need to respond, for gosh sakes, don't tell a joke that has any element that is racist, sexist, or offensive in any way. No sex. No ethnic jokes. You may be thinking, "There *aren't* any jokes like that. Not funny ones, anyway." I've actually searched hard for appropriate jokes, and I have one for you. (For more, go to my website, jobgoddess.net.)

Tiger Woods and Stevie Wonder are talking. Stevie mentions that he plays golf. Tiger, incredulous, asks: "How do you do *that?*" Stevie explains, "My caddy stands on the green, and when I tee off, I aim for his voice." Tiger asks, "Then how do you putt, once you're on the green?" Stevie shrugs and says, "My caddy stands at the hole, and again, I aim for his voice." Tiger still finds this hard to believe, and Stevie says, "Tell you what—why don't we play a few holes? In fact, to make it interesting, why don't we bet $10,000 a hole?" Tiger eagerly takes the offer, and asks when Stevie wants to play.

Stevie responds: "I'm easy. You pick the night."

21. AVOID TMI: TOO MUCH INFORMATION, OR: "WHEN DO I TELL THE EMPLOYER I'M LACTOSE INTOLERANT?"

The answer: Never.

I occasionally meet students who are having no luck interviewing, and I ask them: Is there a point in the interview when you feel the tide turning against you? Sometimes we can pin it down to one particular statement they make, when they share something about themselves that makes such an indelible image on the interviewer that the interviewer can't pay attention to anything else for the rest of the interview. Remember: you *control* what you say. Think about the images your words create!

I'll give you a few examples.

One female student had "Jekyll and Hyde" grades; that is, the first semester of first year had been a real disaster, but second semester—she'd been a brainiac. When interviewers asked her about the discrepancy, she'd say—in these very words—"I had an organ removed two weeks before finals first semester, and it interfered with my studying." You can see what was happening. As soon as she used those words "organ removed," the interviewer was thinking, "Gee, I wonder which organ? Spleen? Lungs? Stomach? Brain?" In other words: it was too much information! We worked on rewording it, so that she talked briefly about a nonrecurring medical problem, that her performance second semester showed her true ability, and so on. After she made this one simple change, she started getting call backs and offers.

There was another student who'd been a sheriff in Nevada for twenty years before attending law school. He'd make a point of telling interviewers, "I've seen brains splattered on the freeway. You can't give me anything I can't handle." While it made a good point about him, interviewers couldn't get past the "brains splattered on the freeway" imagery, and it hurt him. When he changed it to talking about "every situation you can imagine," he did a lot better.

Another student had faced clinical depression, and her grades see-sawed as a result. First year she'd done terribly, Second year she'd done exceptionally well, and Third year her grades were back in the tank. When an interviewer asked her about this, she said, "I suffer from depression. First year I wasn't medicated so my grades sucked. Second year, I was medicated, and I felt great and I *did* great. This year, I'm off meds again, so my grades aren't so good." The interviewer subsequently reflected, "What could I ask her? Could you please go back on your meds, and *stay* on them, if we hire you?"

Another student brought up in an interview his visit to Amsterdam's red light district. As Maslon's Dana Bartocci points out, "There's a difference between what you tell friends and what you say to employers."

Yet another student suffered from cystic fibrosis. Her prognosis was good, and the only thing she couldn't do was work herself ragged 80 hours a week. She was concerned about how to explain it to prospective employers. Her Career Services Director told her, "Don't! When they hear the words 'cystic fibrosis' they won't hear anything else you say. Don't interview for jobs that require long hours. That's it."

So when you're sharing information about yourself, be careful about the word pictures you create. Take a page from the movie *Dave*—if you haven't seen it, rent it, it's great—where the President of the United States has a debilitating stroke, and his press secretary describes it as a "minor circulatory problem of the head." Remember: interviews are for talking about what you bring the table, how you can help the employer accomplish their goals. Focus on that—and sanitize what you share about yourself!

* * * CAREER LIMITING MOVE * * *

On-campus interview. The interviewer asks the student, "How was your summer?"

The student responds, "It kind of sucked. My girlfriend moved in with me, we started fighting, and now she's pregnant."

* * * CAREER LIMITING MOVE * * *

Interviewer: "Where did you grow up?"

Law student: "Here. Actually, when I was a kid, my father tried to drown me."

* * * CAREER LIMITING MOVE * * *

An on-campus interview is just winding down.

Interviewer: "Have a good weekend."

Law student: "I hope so. I'm spending the weekend with a man I met on the Internet."

22. REMEMBER THAT INTERVIEWERS AREN'T PERFECT—HELP THEM OUT!

It's easy to get so wrapped up in prepping for your interview that you forget who's going to be on the other side of the desk—a living, breathing, and *flawed* human being. Because they're doing the interviewing, it's easy to cloak them with super powers they just don't have. One Career Services Director summed it up by saying "Most interviewers are *terrible!*" Another, more charitably, commented that "Most interviewers aren't very good at it. They're normally only doing the interviewing because their arm was twisted."

Remember: Lawyers are not trained interviewers. They didn't take a class in law school any more than *you* did. And that means you're likely to face at least a few mediocre-to-bad interviewers. What should you do? Help them out!

When they ask stupid questions—like the "Who *are* you?" questions I gave you earlier in this chapter—answer respectfully. Don't suggest that you're put off by the question. Use the question as a way to open up a conversation that elicits useful information from both of you. "Just out of curiosity—which historical figure would *you* want to have dinner with?"

In addition, *make sure* that you work in your "infomercial," the answer to the question "Tell me about yourself"—even if the interviewer doesn't ask it. You can always squeeze this in by asking the interviewer, "What qualities do you look for in people you hire?" Then when you hear them, you can follow up with, "I'm glad to hear that—" or "That's interesting—here's what you need to know about me—" and provide your answer. *Remember—no matter how lacking the interviewer is, your 'infomercial' must come out in the interview!*

In addition, pick up the slack by asking your "personalized" questions, the ones I encouraged you to ask, that get at the interviewer's experience with the employer. Again, this will give you an opportunity to work in information about yourself, as well as to turn the interview into a conversation—and take the heat off the interviewer!

If the interviewer goes beyond inept to making the interview disastrous—talking the whole time, making the job sound horrible, putting you on the spot—look at Topic M below, called "Disaster Strikes."

23.   IF THE INTERVIEWER MISPRONOUNCES YOUR NAME, CORRECT HIM/HER ONCE, *DISCREETLY*

Whether or not your name is difficult to pronounce, the interviewer may get it wrong. Correcting them is important, but you have to do it in a way that avoids embarrassing them.

You have a couple of choices. When you first meet the interviewer, when they mispronounce your name, say something like, "Actually, my name is pronounced Eye-gor. Don't worry—everybody gets it wrong."

I'm not wild about that, because the first impression it leaves with the interviewer is that you're correcting them.

Experts suggest that it's better to let it go, and then fairly early in the interview, in answer to a question, use your own name. "I'll tell you why I want to work for you. Last summer, I asked myself, 'Eye-gor, which classes have you really enjoyed the most?'" The interviewer will probably immediately say, "I'm sorry I got your name wrong!" and that gives you the chance to be magnanimous and say something like, "That's OK, everybody does," or "Don't worry about it."

Incidentally, sometimes your name reminds an interviewer of somebody else, and they can't shake the connection. There was a student at one school whose name was "Anona," and in an interview the interviewer kept calling her "Wynona." Well, we can all figure out why. He probably was trying to remember it by associating it with the singer Wynona Judd, and he just couldn't make the distinction. Whenever I go to the University of Miami Law School, the director, Marcy Cox, calls me Kimm Alan (instead of Alayne) Walton, because she associates my middle name with Annette Bening's character in *An American President*.

Honestly now: If someone mispronouncing your name is the worst thing that ever happens to you, you're in good shape. And look at it this way: When you get the job, you can always go back to the original interviewer and say, "Listen, it's *Eye-gore,* you freaking idiot."

Just kidding.

24.   REMEMBER THAT THE BEST INTERVIEWS ARE CONVERSATIONS. DON'T SUBDUE YOUR PERSONALITY . . . BE EASY TO TALK TO!

I've told you this before, but it bears repeating: the best interview is a casual give-and-take between you and the interviewer. After all, if you wind up working together, that's what you'll do—converse! As Dave James points out, "Too many students try to be inhibited and humorless in interviews."

How do you jolly the interview in the direction of a conversation? First of all, go with the flow in an interview. Don't stick to a rehearsed script. Sure, you've memorized the questions you intend to ask, and the answers you intend to give, but don't let those be engraved in stone. If the interviewer says something that sparks your interest, follow up on it! And if the interviewer answers one of your questions while (s)he's describing the employer, then delete that question from your list— otherwise, it will be obvious that you're not listening to what (s)he's saying. Good listening skills are crucial for lawyers—and lawyers-to-be!

In addition, as I've mentioned before, good conversations don't involve notes. **Don't bring in a written list of questions**. I know you're nervous, but go over a few of the "personalized" questions in your mind so that you know where to start. Do a couple of mock interviews if you're worried that you'll forget what you want to say. And practice your 'infomercial' in a mirror until you can say it comfortably.

Note-taking is a no-no as well. Students—typically if they've been reporters before law school!—often ask me if it's OK to jot down a few things during an interview. You can't do it, because it interferes with the conversational tone you want to strive for. Instead, pay attention to what the interviewer says, look at them while they talk, and speak confidently and comfortably yourself. It's easier than you think!

25.   IF SOMETHING IN YOUR BACKGROUND IS SO INTERESTING THAT INTERVIEWERS CAN'T TALK ABOUT ANYTHING ELSE . . .

You may have done something that seems so tremendously interesting that interviewers want to talk about nothing else. Maybe you were a bouncer at the Playboy Mansion. Maybe you worked for a celebrity or a movie studio. Maybe you were a finalist on a game show, or you appeared in a reality show. Whatever it is, interviewers can't seem to talk about anything else. In fact, it may be the very reason you got the interview in the first place!

A few things to remember:

a.   Grant them their curiosity. You may be sick to death of talking about whatever it is, but they've never heard it from you. Be understanding and acknowledge that it's a *positive* when people want to know about something you've done.

b.   Remember that the point of an interview is to show the potential employer what you can do for them. Talking exclusively about one thing you've already done probably won't achieve that. So what you want to do is:

c.   Throw them a bone. Have a favourite anecdote ready to go. Give them something they can repeat to their friends. One law student grew up on a farm. When interviewers were curious about it, she'd say, "I was the only kid at school who could name my lunch."

d. If it's feasible, weave transferable skills into your anecdote. So you would add to the farm gag, "I'll tell you one thing about growing up on a farm. You get up at five to milk the cows. There's *always* something that needs to be done. It really gave me a good work ethic."

e. Make sure the anecdote doesn't say anything negative about you.

You've got so many choices: you can choose stories that are funny, insightful, highlight a good quality. Just don't tell an anecdote that puts you in a negative light.

For instance, a student I talked to at one school was asked how he'd enjoyed his summer in Dallas. He told the following story: "I actually went to a protest rally by accident. I was just walking by it, and I got arrested for public drunkenness for having an open beer can. The great thing is, I defended myself and got off." Yay. Don't tell employers that one.

A student at another school, this one in New England, was asked whether she intended to return to Los Angeles, where she'd lived before law school. She responded: "Absolutely not. When I got my driver's license there, I was in line at DMV for two hours. When I was almost at the front of the line, the guy behind me started groping my butt. I called a guard over, and complained, and the guard said to me: "Do you want to go to the back of the line?" and I protested, "*He* should go." The guard shrugged and walked away. If I go back to LA, I'll have to renew my driver's license again. And I'm not going to put myself through *that*."

Don't tell that story *either*.

You've got a whole wardrobe of stories about yourself, in every setting. Make sure the ones you tell reflect well on you!

f. After the anecdote, have a question you're prepared to ask. Say something like, "I could talk about that all day, but I'm so interested to know about . . ." and take it from there.

* * * SMART HUMAN TRICK * * *

Law student who'd spent a year working for a city's mental health court. They did a lot of competency and conservatorship hearings. He was always asked about it in interviews, and he always told this story:

"There was a schizophrenic who was trying to get out of his conservatorship. The judge asked, 'Have you been taking your medication?'

'Yes, Your Honor.'

'Are you going to continue taking it?' asked the judge.

'Yes, Your Honor.'

'Have you been hearing voices?'

Just then, the bailiff's walkie-talkie went off, and a voice on it said, 'Murphy, you're needed at the West Entrance.'

There was dead silence in the courtroom.

The schizophrenic said, 'I heard *that.*' "

26.   DON'T GET *Too* COMFORTABLE IN THE INTERVIEW

If you're feeling comfortable with the interviewer, that's just great. But remember: It's still a professional setting. You're not buddies *yet.* So don't forget that you're not at home!

* * * CAREER LIMITING MOVE * * *

Male student, interviewing with a female attorney. She's impressed by his confidence, but her approval turns to disgust . . .

. . . when he puts his feet up on her desk!

* * * CAREER LIMITING MOVE * * *

Male attorney, interviewing a female law student. By his own admission, he's not very tidy, but he's somewhat shocked when the law student proceeds to spend the entire interview tidying up his desk.

* * * CAREER LIMITING MOVE * * *

Male student, call-back interview. In one of the interviews late in the day, he takes a can of chewing tobacco from a back pocket, dips . . . *and uses the attorney's empty coffee cup as a spittoon.*

* * * CAREER LIMITING MOVE * * *

Female law student, interviewing in an attorney's office with two attorneys. She's sitting on a couch next to one of the attorneys, whom we'll call "Dave." He asks her a question, and she responds, "Well, Dave . . ."

. . . with her hand on his knee.

27.   HANDLING "GANG" INTERVIEWS—THAT IS, MULTIPLE INTERVIEWERS IN THE SAME INTERVIEW

Generally, interviews will be one-on-one. Just you and the interviewer. But sometimes you'll find yourself with two, three, or—God forbid—a whole passel of interviewers facing you. How do you handle such an interview differently?

For a start, **when you answer a question from any one of the attorneys, make sure that you sweep *all* of them into your gaze as you respond.** And when you ask questions, make sure that you wind up asking at least one question of each of the attorneys. If you ask the "personalized" questions I strongly encourage you to ask, you can always ask the other(s), "Do you feel the same way?"

Of course, if you know in advance that you're going to face more than one interviewer, you'll have researched all of them. Be sure that you ask questions about their backgrounds. "Attorney X, I know that you wrote a law review note about X when you were in school. Did your research help you in practicing in X specialty?" As much as a single interviewer will be impressed that you researched him or her, the impression is magnified when you go to the same effort for *several* of them!

Other than on-campus interviews, where thank you notes aren't necessary—be sure to send a thank you to *every* lawyer who interviewed you. I know it's a pain, but it'll make you look really good. (At the end of the interview, be sure to get a business card from each of the interviewers to facilitate your thank yous.)

28. NO MATTER HOW BORED YOU ARE, DON'T LET THE INTERVIEWER KNOW IT!

Maybe you can't wait for the interview to end. Maybe you were out partying all night. Maybe you were studying till the wee hours. Maybe the interviewer is just a snooze. Regardless of the reason, you can't let on how much you want out of there!

No:

- **checking your watch;**
- **rolling your eyes;**
- **yawning or sighing.**

Sit up straight, look the interviewer in the eye, nod as appropriate, and remember: It's only twenty minutes. You've sat through boring law school lectures a *lot* longer than that!

29. REMEMBER THAT THE INTERVIEWER IS THE BOSS. FOLLOW THEIR LEAD

I've given you a lot of techniques for subtly directing the interview in the direction you want it to go, by asking open-ended questions and following up your answers with questions for the interviewer. But it's important to remember that in an interview, the interviewer is the boss.

I talked to one student at a Florida law school who had managed a Gap Store before law school. It turns out the interviewer had been a manager at The Limited. The interviewer asked her about her Gap experience, and they started talking about retail for a few minutes, until the interviewer said sternly, "We're not here to discuss retail. We're going to discuss law." The student says, "She was really abrupt about it. I felt like I did something wrong." I assured her she didn't, but still: If the interviewer wants to talk about *whatever* the interviewer wants to talk about, that's where you go. If the interviewer doesn't want to answer questions, you don't ask any. It's their show. Let them take the lead!

30. WIND-UP THE INTERVIEW ON AN "UP" NOTE!

Recognize these lines?

"Frankly, my dear, I don't give a damn."

"Louie, I think this is the beginning of a beautiful friendship."

"Nobody's perfect."

They are, respectively, the final lines of *Gone With The Wind, Casablanca,* and *Some Like It Hot.*

The last lines to movies tend to be memorable. And why is that? Because it's the image that lingers in your memory. Similarly, in an interview, you want to make sure that the last thing the interviewer hears from you leaves a good impression.

When you say your goodbye, do four things:

a. **Ask for a business card;**

b. **Ask about their timeline,** or when you'll be hearing from them;

c. **Smile, and extend your hand to shake hands (if the interviewer hasn't done so already);**

d. **Thank the interviewer for the interview, incorporating the interviewer's name:** something like, "I've really enjoyed meeting you, Mr./Ms. Amullmahay. Your practice sounds fascinating and I'd love to be a part of it." "Thank you for interviewing me. Talking with you just reinforced my interest in your firm/agency/organization." If the interview wasn't great, you don't want to characterize it as better than it was, but if you're still interested, you can always say, "Thank you for interviewing me. I learned a lot" . . . because that's always true!

31. REMEMBER THAT NO MATTER HOW *YOU* FEEL ABOUT THE JOB OR THE INTERVIEWER, YOUR SCHOOL'S REPUTATION IS AT STAKE IN THE IMAGE YOU CREATE FOR INTERVIEWERS

It is really important to remember that when you get on the interview bus, *there are a lot of other people in that bus with you.* Namely, your classmates, and everybody who attends your school after you. No matter how little you care about an employer, remember that you may have classmates who would love to work there . . . and their chances may be harmed if you do something thoughtless to the employer. It's not fair, but employers often judge schools by their interactions with individual students. Make sure that that works *for* your school, not against it.

A hiring partner told me about one incident where a student told a senior associate in on-campus interviews, "There's no need for you to get back to me. I'm not interested." The partner commented, "He just didn't get it. It's not just your reputation. It's the school. That kind of story gets around, and it reflects badly on your school."

So when you're tempted to get up in an employer's grill or treat them off-handedly, remember: be kind to your classmates, and behave accordingly!

G.   SPECIAL TIPS FOR ON-CAMPUS INTERVIEWS

Everything I've said in this chapter applies to on-campus interviews. A few special points are worth mentioning:

1.   Remember: no matter how much pressure you feel, the interviewer is under a lot more pressure than *you*.

"Oh, is that so, Kimmbo?" you may be saying. "Does the interviewer have student loan payments to worry about? Are *they* going to be unemployed if an interview doesn't work out?"

Well, no. You've got a point there. But here's the pressure you might not realize. Interviewers are putting their reputations on the line for students they recommend for call-back interviews. They're saying, "I think this person can do the work, and I think they'll fit in at the office." They face considerable downside risk. That is, if a student they recommend turns out to strike everyone else in the office as a real chucklehead, *the interviewer will never hear the end of it.* If the student winds up being hired and does a crappy job, a partner is likely to scream, "Who *hired* this moron?" As Sandy Mans points out, "Attorneys who do interviewing are under *tremendous* pressure to find the right person!"

With all of the research and preparation I've encouraged you to do, you're making it easy for interviewers to feel comfortable recommending you. That's what you *want* to have happen.

The flipside of the interview equation also creates pressure for interviewers, by the way. If you've got killer credentials and the employer really, really wants you on that basis alone—congratulations, by the way—the interviewer's going to look bad if you turn down a second interview with the employer. They'll be perceived as not "selling" you on the employer.

Just remember: you're not the only one who's got a lot on the line!

2.   Attend any information sessions/cocktail parties the employer holds before interview day.

Some employers hold these, particularly at schools where they're eager to recruit. If they hold an event—go. It shows your enthusiasm for the job! On top of that, make yourself known. Shake hands with the speaker/host and say you're looking forward to talking to them, and thank them for holding the event.

I saw this principle in action on a flight once. I was sitting across the aisle from a woman and her assistant. They were obviously going through resumes, and with each one, the woman was asking her assistant, "Do we know her? Do we know him?" When they took a break for a drink, it gave me the chance to ask what they were doing. The woman told me, "We're looking for new assistant editors, and we just interviewed on a college campus. We held an information session ahead of time. I'm only interested in talking to the students who cared enough to come to the information session." And this, mind you, was independent of *whatever* the resumes looked like!

Incidentally, if there is a change in generosity of an employer from year to year, it might be an indication that all is not well financially. I heard a memorable story about this at one distinguished East Coast law school. A Career Services Counselor told me, "This particular firm always held a lavish buffet for the interviewees the night before the interviews. It was always a "no expenses spared" bash. Then one year, they called and asked if they could scrap that in favor of a 'box lunch' kind of thing. So we did that. The next year, they wanted to economize even more. I said, 'You don't *have* to entertain them at all, you know,' and they said, 'No, no, no, we *want* to do it. Just out of curiosity: how much would we save if we took away the bags of chips?' I mean: *chips?* There was obviously something up. Sure enough, eighteen months later, they were out of business."

3. Don't apply for on-campus interviews for jobs you'd never take. You're not collecting shrunken heads. You're looking for a *job*.

Maybe you've got great credentials and employers just drool over the opportunity to interview you. Well, congratulations. Don't hog the interview schedule. You don't get a prize for gathering the most interviews. And while you might earn the envy of less transcriptically gifted classmates, they won't like or respect you for it.

So if you'd never work in any city other than the one where you're going to school, don't take interviews with out-of-town employers. If you won't work any more than a 40–hour workweek—I don't blame you—don't take interviews with employers who demand far more than that.

4. Pay special attention to who's coming on campus, and don't "front-load" all of your interviews.

Employers who get stuck with interview slots late in the on-campus "season" often lament the fact that students sometimes accept offers before the later interviews even start.

Scope out who's coming to campus before interview season starts. Research the employers, as I described in Chapter 6 and earlier in this chapter, to see who is really likely to fit you best. Whether they're coming in August or October, don't make a decision until you talk to them.

5. If you're waitlisted . . .

At some law schools, there's a waitlist for on-campus interviews. That is, if an interview slot opens up at the last minute, someone is chosen from the waitlist.

If your school waitlists and you wind up on the waitlist for an employer you're interested in, here's what you need to know.

Don't get your knickers all in a twist because you weren't preselected. As Josie Mitchell advises, "You're in a suit, you're interested in the employer, you've got nothing to do for that twenty minutes. So go in with the attitude, 'Why not?' Who knows what might happen? Every year at least one of our students from the wait list gets a call back, and many have been offered jobs."

Virtually every employer I talk with will describe a superstar in the office by saying, "He was far from our first choice ..." "We almost didn't talk to her ..." "If we hadn't met him in person at a bar association event ..." Heck, even *American Idol's* Simon Cowell gave Taylor Hicks a thumbs-down on his initial audition ... and he went on to win!

So don't resent the fact you weren't on the A-list. Low expectations are meant to be exceeded. Think how proud you'll be when you prove them wrong!

6. *Always* notify an employer (via the Career Services Office, if you like) if you're going to blow off an interview with them.

Whether you've accepted an offer elsewhere or for any other reason lost interest, *don't blow off employers without saying anything*. It's terribly unprofessional and it makes your school look really bad. Some employers actually stop interviewing at certain schools when they have a high "no-show" percentage. On top of that, you have no idea when this particular employer and/or interviewer might cross your path again. People move around *a lot*. You don't want the thing they remember about you is that you blew them off.

Just let Career Services know as soon as *you* know that you won't be attending an interview. It's the kind—and professional—thing to do.

7. Remember: on-campus interviews aren't the whole world. They're the tip of the job search iceberg.

Virtually every other chapter in this book addresses finding jobs that don't come on campus to find you. The vast majority of employers don't interview on campus; a job you'd love is out there waiting for you, but it's unlikely they're going to show up at OCI.

As Josie Mitchell advises, "Treat OCI as a back-up plan, not as your main job search tool." Not getting a job through OCI is meaningless. It doesn't mean you'll never find a job or even a great job—it's just that you didn't get one of *those* jobs, this particular way. There are a million ways to skin the job search cat!

8. What if you get lots of on-campus interviews and don't get any call-backs?

If you're interviewing for jobs that are not a "reach" with your credentials ... there's a hitch somewhere.

I'll tell you some of the more common causes of no-call-back-itis:

- You're interviewing for jobs you really don't want;
- You're answering a question with something that triggers a negative response in the interviewer;
- You've got a habit, verbal or non-verbal, that's throwing off the interviewer;
- You're not communicating, verbally and/or behaviorally, your interest in the job. If you answer questions monosyllabically, if you don't seem to know anything about employers, if you sigh or roll your eyes ... you're telling the employer 'I don't want to work for you.'
- If your school has a lottery system for OCI—where the employer doesn't get to choose who's interviewed—your paper credentials may be hurting you.

As a rule of thumb, Minnesota's Steve Marchese advises that "If you go on five on-campus interviews and after a couple of days you've had no call-back invitations, go to the Career Services Office and ask for help." Ask for mock interviews. Explain where in the interview you feel you're "losing" the interviewer. And if you're interviewing for jobs you don't really want ... that's a situation where interviewers really can smell blood in the water. I talked to a student at one school who had stellar credentials, but had no luck in on-campus interviews. As she explained, "I was a social worker before law school, and I'd specialized in working with the elderly. I really went to law school for elder law, which is practiced in my city only by sole practitioners and very small firms. I went on OCIs because everybody does. I knew it wasn't for me. I didn't get any call backs, and I guess I'm really not surprised."

Remember: job offers are like proposals of marriage. If employers feel you won't accept, they won't make you one. That's a matter of going back to Chapter 2 and figuring out what you really do want. Your enthusiasm will shine naturally when you go after jobs that really interest you.

The bottom line is this: inevitably there's an easy interview "fix" that'll set you right. Don't suffer in silence!

H. CALL–BACK INTERVIEWS

Congratulations! You crushed the initial interview. They invited you back. Now what? Let's go through everything you need to know about call-backs.

1. WHAT TO EXPECT

If you got a call-back, you've set the hook. There's no such thing as a "courtesy" call-back interview. The initial interviewer went back to the employer and said good things about you. What the employer will do with the call back is to introduce you to other people in the office, and they will ask themselves the same questions they had about you in the initial interview: Do they like you? Do they want to work with you? Will you fit in? *Do you seem to want the job?*

There are a variety of formats for call-backs, depending on the size and type of employer you're talking about. In most cases, you'll talk individually with between two and eight people in a row, for 20 to 30 minutes each; a call-back typically takes anywhere from a couple of hours to all day. Expect to talk to a variety of lawyers, from junior to senior. It may include a lunch and/or a dinner, and perhaps an activity from a cocktail party to sailing.

No matter what it entails, it's likely the last time you'll talk to the employer before they make a decision about you (although there are some employers—typically large companies, not law firms—that will take you through several rounds of interviews). They may make you an offer on the spot, but they may not. **The lack of an immediate response is not a rejection.** But because it's the last time you're likely to be able to influence them, it's vital that you make a good impression!

2. PREPARING FOR THE CALL-BACK

A. RESPOND *AS SOON AS POSSIBLE*

There are two reasons for this. First, the firm may be holding up other student offers waiting for your response. More selfishly, it's important to know that firms have occasionally cancelled call-backs once enough offers have been extended. You don't want to be caught out because you waited too long to respond.

B. IF YOU'VE RECONSIDERED, DECLINE THE CALL-BACK *GRACIOUSLY*

Maybe your dream employer coughed up an offer. Maybe your circumstances have changed, leaving this particular employer out of the running. Whatever the reason, if you wouldn't accept an offer from them, decline a call-back interview. There are a couple of reasons for this. One is that it's really not fair to the employer. Call-backs cost a lot of money for employers, both in actual cash money and in lawyer time. If you're not serious about potentially working for them, it's just not fair to put them through that expense. Also, they may have denied another student a call-back to offer you one. It's not fair to the other student, for whom this particular outfit might be a dream employer.

If you do decline the call back, do so *graciously.* "I've reconsidered and I really don't want you guys," is not gracious. "I really appreciate it, but my plans have taken me in a different direction/my circumstances have changed. I really appreciated meeting with Attorney so-and-so. Perhaps we'll have an opportunity to work together in future." And then send a thank-you note reiterating your message.

Now note that **turning down a call-back like this is only appropriate if *there are no circumstances under which you'd accept an offer.*** If you were just lukewarm on the interviewer or you're not sure you'd like the work or the city, give it a try! I can't tell you how many students went to visit a firm they weren't sold on, and wound up working there. Remember: Interviewing is as much about you deciding what you want as the employer deciding they want you. Keep an open mind!

C. THANK THE INITIAL INTERVIEWER

The first person you talked to at the employer is responsible for you getting your foot in the door. Call and thank them! A voice mail is fine if you can't get them, and even an e-mail does the trick (although it's not as "warm"). If you don't remember who it was because the interview was on-campus, go back to Career Services and find out. Tell the interviewer you appreciate the opportunity and you look forward to meeting their colleagues. Students rarely do this, and it will *blow them away.*

D. IF YOU WANT TO MEET WITH A PARTICULAR LAWYER OR DEPARTMENT, TELL THE RECRUITING COORDINATOR/OFFICE MANAGER/HIRING PARTNER

While you're planning your trip, mention any special requests you have to the person organizing your trip. It indicates, by the way, your enthusiasm for the firm and your familiarity with who they are and what they do—a real plus! They'll certainly accommodate you if they can.

E. FIND OUT WHO WILL BE INTERVIEWING YOU, AND RESEARCH THEM

You will probably be talking with several people at the call-back. The day before you leave, call the employer's recruiting coordinator (or other hiring person, if they don't have a recruiting coordinator, or even the initial interviewer) and ask who you'll be interviewing with. Go to the employer's web site and check their backgrounds: what their specialties are, how long they've been there, where they went to school, any other interesting tidbits. What you're doing is essentially a "mini-version" of your initial interview research into the interviewer.

Take notes on each interviewer and either put them on 3x5″ cards, in a small notebook, or on a BlackBerry—anything you can conveniently carry when you get to the employer.

F. ASK ABOUT WARDROBE AND ANY ACTIVITIES YOU'LL TAKE PART IN

Ask the person hosting you—the recruiting coordinator at a large firm, an office manager or partner at a smaller one—if you'll be doing anything that would require clothing other than a suit. If you're going sailing, you'll look like a major dork hanging out on deck in your navy blue suit!

G. ARRANGING TRAVEL

If it's an out-of-town callback—whoo hoo! Par-tay! Just kidding. Let's talk professionally about what you should do.

1. HAVE A CALENDAR SO YOU DON'T SCHEDULE INTERVIEWS THAT CLASH WITH OTHER COMMITMENTS

It's a good idea to have a "master calendar," either physically or on your computer or PDA, so that you don't plan a call-back when you have a major activity/deadline at school or work. If you have to reschedule because you weren't familiar with demands on your time, it'll make you look disorganized.

2. DON'T SCHEDULE TWO CALL-BACKS FOR ONE DAY. THEY'RE GRUELING

Well—aren't *you* the Prom Queen? Everybody wants you. But don't let them all have you on the same day.

It may be that you're going on more than one call-back in the same city, and they're with employers who do half-day call-backs. Spread out the interviews to at least two days. If not, you'll be talking gibberish and forgetting where you are by the end of the day!

3. DON'T TAKE THE LAST FLIGHT THAT WILL GET YOU THERE ON TIME

Here's a headline for you: air travel in America is unreliable, and getting worse. The *last* thing you can do is count on an on-time arrival. Trust me: I take more than a hundred flights a year, and it's rare for them to arrive on time! Instead, if your interview is a full day, take the second-to-last flight out the night before (if not earlier). That way, if there's something wrong with your flight, you'll still have one left as a back-up.

4. TAKE THE HOTEL, RENTAL CAR, AND AIRLINE TICKET THAT'S OFFERED TO YOU

No suites. No sports cars. No business class. No $28,000 lunches. (That actually happened, by the way—at an investment bank in New York. The bankers tried to *expense* it! It made all the local papers. And they're no longer bankers.)

Look at it this way: If you get the job, and you take it, they're going to be paying you many, many times the value of a stupid upgrade, and they'll be investing gobs of cash in training you. On top of that, these are people you'll be working with; don't trash your reputation before you even begin, by showing that you've got bad judgment. If you want to do it up, do it on your *own* dime.

* * * CAREER LIMITING MOVE * * *

Student from a distinguished East Coast law school. He's interviewing with a firm on the West Coast, which requires that he fly out on a Wednesday and return on Friday.

Because his girlfriend happens to be going to school in the city he's visiting, he decides to live it up. He requests a suite at the hotel. He upgrades his rental to a Jaguar X-type. He extends his stay through the weekend. And on the Friday night, he takes his girlfriend out to dinner and runs up a $400 alcohol tab.

He sends the tab for *the entire trip*, Wednesday through Sunday, to the employer.

5. DO *NOT* SET UP OTHER INTERVIEWS IN THE SAME TOWN ON THE EMPLOYER'S DIME

Here's the situation. You're interested in being in a particular city—let's say, Chicago. You send out a bunch of resumes. You get a call back from a firm called Grey Anatomie. You can't call firms you haven't heard from yet and say, "Hey—Grey Anatomie is flying me in. Can I set up an interview with you while I'm there?"

Don't get me wrong. I completely understand the temptation. Heck, you're going to be in town anyway, why not extend your visit by a day or two . . .

You just can't, can't, can't. If the call-back employer is paying your way, pretend it's a date. You wouldn't go on a date with someone and say, "While I'm here, would you mind if I see who else is at the bar?" (At least . . . I *hope* you wouldn't do that.)

It would really foul the well for you at the call-back employer if you express an interest in other employers. It would be just as bad to be sneaky about it. Let's say you tell them, "Hey, while I'm in town, would you mind if I stay an extra day to visit my Aunt Mabel?" Of course, you've got no Aunt Mabel, and you're using the time to troll for other jobs. Apart from the ethical aspect, here's why it's stupid: recruiting people are a gossipy bunch. They *talk*. They'll find out what you did, and *none* of them will hire you.

Do the stand-up thing. Stick with the one that brought you to the dance. You can always tell employers you haven't heard from that you are interviewing with Gray Anatomie, and you'd like to talk to them *at your own expense* (because remember, employers pay for call-backs, not initial "screening" interviews). You'll look desirable because someone else wants you. And you'll be doing the right thing.

6. IT MAKES YOU LOOK REALLY ENTHUSIASTIC ABOUT THE CITY IF YOU ASK TO EXTEND YOUR STAY OVER THE WEEKEND (OFFER TO PAY FOR THE EXTRA HOTEL STAY YOURSELF)

As Vanderbilt's Dorris Smith explains, it shows your enthusiasm for the employer's city if you ask to stay longer. Of course, you can always say, "I'd like to spend a little more time there, looking around. I'm willing to pay for the extra hotel night(s)"— perhaps not at the Ritz, of course! Or, if you have relatives, it's even better if you offer to stay with them—it shows your ties to the place.

7. ASK THE EMPLOYER FOR THEIR RECEIPT POLICY BEFORE YOU LEAVE

Most employers will ask for receipts for any expenses over $25. However, some employers won't reimburse *any* expense without a receipt. Find out ahead of time what kind of a paper trail is required.

Note that **some employers don't reimburse at all—typically government agencies and courts.**

8. FOR AN OUT-OF-TOWN CALL-BACK, IF YOU ARE MARRIED OR ENGAGED, ASK THE FIRM IF YOU MAY BRING YOUR SPOUSE/FIANCE(E)

Some firms will fly out a spouse. If your host doesn't offer, you can ask. They'll probably accommodate you. After all, it suggests that you're serious about the employer if you want your significant other to get familiar with the city!

A couple of things to keep in mind about this. First of all, *only* ask if you're married or engaged. A boyfriend/girlfriend doesn't qualify, no matter how serious you are.

Second, the fact that you're bringing a significant other with you doesn't mean they'll be with you all day! Instead, if the firm agrees to fly out your significant other, ask the recruiting coordinator for ideas about what (s)he should do while you interview.

Your significant other *will* be included in any non-interview activities, like dinner or a cocktail party. As a result, it's very important that your significant other dress (and behave) appropriately. You may be wearing your perfectly-tailored navy blue suits, but you'll look really bad if your significant other shows up at a partner's house wearing a "Kiss My Ass" T-shirt.

9. IF YOU ARE STAYING OVERNIGHT BEFORE YOUR INTERVIEWS, ASK THE RECRUITING COORDINATOR WHETHER TO BRING YOUR LUGGAGE TO THE FIRM OR LEAVE IT WITH THE BELLHOP AT THE HOTEL.

10. IF YOU ARE VISITING MULTIPLE EMPLOYERS ON THE SAME TRIP . . .

Good for you! Nothing makes you as attractive as being desired by someone else . . . socially *and* professionally. But when it comes to expenses, planning can be complicated when there's more than one name on your dance card.

Ask both (or all) employers ahead of time how they'd like it handled. Follow their guidance. Typically an even split works. And don't ever, *ever* try and roll each employer for the full cost of the trip. Trust me: Hiring people talk. You have no idea when your name will be mentioned in conversation, and if they find out that you rolled each of them for a whole trip instead of divvying up costs ... well. Your life's not long enough for your reputation to recover.

3. GETTING THERE: TRAVEL ISSUES

I travel all the time visiting law schools. Sometimes the travel goes more smoothly than others! Here's what you need to know:

a. Leave home earlier than you think you need to.

Don't make yourself crazy by figuring that the traffic will be fine, the taxi will arrive on time, the trains or buses will get there when they're supposed to. Allow at least half an hour more than you think you'll need.

If you're flying, get to the airport two hours ahead. I know that sounds excessive, but security lines are unpredictable.

b. Be sure you pack your 3x5″ cards about the employer (if you made "physical" notes).

Remember those 3x5″ cards I told you to write up about your interviewer? Make sure you pack them!

c. If you'll be taking taxis, carry cash ... more than you think you need.

d. Bring extra copies of your resume, writing sample, and references, in a professional-looking portfolio.

Yes, the employer should already have these. But if they misplace your paperwork and need extra copies, having them with you will make you look awesome.

* * * SMART HUMAN TRICK * * *

One student at a Florida law school made envelopes for each interviewer with her resume, writing sample and reference letters. She reports: "After I got my offer, the recruiting coordinator told me how impressed the lawyers were with those envelopes!"

e. Women: Wear low heels and carry your higher ones (if you intend to wear high heels), and carry an extra pair of pantyhose in your purse/briefcase.

Racing through an airport is impossible in high heels. And if you get a run in your stockings, you need a back-up pair. Princess Diana used to carry extra pantyhose, and you should, too.

f. Dress comfortably, and carry your bag onto the plane; don't check it as luggage.

Some people travel in their interview suits, but I wouldn't recommend it. Wear something comfortable. But if you do, *be sure* to carry on your bag! You wouldn't be the first student to lose their luggage in flight, and wind up interviewing in shorts and flip-flops!

g.   If the security line is longer than you anticipated, and you're afraid you'll miss your flight—go to the front and notify the security personnel of your situation.

I see this happen all the time at airports. Someone who doesn't travel a bunch underestimates how long it will take to get through security, and there they are in line—forty-five minutes from the security gate—and their flight is due to board in five minutes!

If you find yourself in a comparable situation, take charge. Go to the security person at the front of the line and explain that your flight is leaving soon. They'll ask for your boarding pass, but that's OK. They'll often shoot you right through security. Now, will you get a few dirty looks from people in line? Maybe. But if you've got a choice between missing your flight and enduring a couple of hairy eyeballs—choose the latter!

If the security people don't help you, go back to your airline's check-in counter and plead your case. They may have mercy and shepherd you through.

These options aren't guarantees—but it's worth doing anything you can to make your flight.

h.   Use the first stall in public restrooms.

This is only tangentially related to travel, but it's worth knowing. The most useful piece of advice I've ever heard about travel is that in public facilities like airports, always use the first stall—not the very last one. The reason is that virtually everybody walks past the first stall, so it's almost always the cleanest one. See? I'm always looking out for you.

i.   In hotels, collect the shampoos, soaps and lotions for charity.

You're *supposed* to take the little bottles of goodies, you know. Hotels expect it. It's not stealing. When you collect a few, donate them to homeless shelters, adult care centers, battered women's shelters . . . they all find those toiletries very, very useful.

* * * YOU CAN'T MAKE THIS STUFF UP * * *

Female law student, Midwestern law school. She gets very few call-back interviews. One of them is with an Atlanta law firm. She recalls, "I felt like such a grown-up. I was traveling a carry-on bag. I was wearing a suit. I was *it*, Baby.

I was sitting in the front row on the flight, and the bathroom was all the way at the back. When I got in there, I noticed that the soap was in little bars, in this gravity-fed dispenser. When I saw all those little bars of soap, I thought, 'Sweet! I'm not going to have to buy soap for the rest of law school!'

So I dispensed about twenty bars, and then I realized ... I don't have any pockets. I was wearing this belted suit. I didn't have a purse. So I had these handfuls of soap bars, and I had no idea how to sneak them back to my seat.

I finally figured out I could stuff them down my midriff, so they'd rest on the inside of my suit above my belt. I felt like a squirrel stuffing acorns in its cheeks. But they all fit.

I tried to walk back to my seat as nonchalantly as possible, but every few steps, a bar of soap would slide out. These businessmen on the flight glanced down at the ground, and saw this trail of soaps leading up the aisle.

I've never been so embarrassed in my life! For all that trouble, I wound up with about five teeny bars of soap."

4. IF THERE IS A MEAL THE NIGHT BEFORE ...

- If you're a woman, you can wear a conservative dress; men, a suit or sport coat and tie.
- Get back home/to the hotel *early*. You've got a big day in front of you. If the attorney(s) want(s) to take you out drinking, *graciously* decline. You wouldn't be the first student to show up hung over for a day of call-back interviews, because attorneys kept you out until three in the morning. Attorneys should know better, but they often don't. You've got to be the grown-up and piss on the campfire ... discreetly. "I'd love to, but can I take a rain check? You know, tomorrow's a big day. Have one for me."
- Keep the conversation lighter than you would for an interview. Ask about the firm's social life and the city (if you're out of town). Talk about current events. Ask your dining partners about themselves, how they wound up "here." Don't feel you have to wheel out your infomercial. Save the interview-y conversations for interview day!
- Ask the attorneys how to get to the firm, if it's not obvious. If it's out of town, ask how long a walk it is from your hotel, or if you need a cab. If you *do* need a cab, order one at the hotel the night before and confirm your order in the morning. Cab companies are notorious for blowing people off!

5. THE BIG DAY

A. EAT A GREAT BREAKFAST

Protein. Low carbs. I don't entirely buy the low carb thing that comes around every few years, but there's no question that a good protein-packed breakfast will give you the most, and the most lasting, energy for what's going to be a very long day. So go with an omelet, or bacon and eggs (hold the potatoes and toast), or even some fruit and yogurt. I know fruit and yogurt involve carbs, but basically what I'm telling you is, avoid pancakes, danishes, donuts, french toast—that kind of stuff.

And at breakfast—review your 3x5″ cards or BlackBerry info on your prospective interviewers!

B. HIT THE HEAD ONE LAST TIME

If possible, you don't want to show up, introduce yourself, and say, "Where's the bathroom?"

If you *do* have to visit the loo when you get to the employer—and there are no public johns nearby—tell the receptionist who you're visiting, and add, "But before that, can you direct me to a restroom?" You definitely don't want to meet your host or first interviewer and *then* immediately visit the restroom.

C. SHOW UP A FEW MINUTES EARLY

Try and show up between five and ten minutes early. If you're earlier than that, walk around outside or go to a nearby coffee shop to bide the time. If, God forbid, you're going to be late—call and alert them as soon as you realize it, so that they can work around you.

D. BE ESPECIALLY NICE TO THE RECEPTIONIST

I've mentioned before that the person sitting at the front desk when you enter an office often has a great deal of clout. Greet him/her warmly. If (s)he's not busy, engage in a little conversation. "I'm excited to be here. Have you lived in X city for very long?" and take it from there. Nothing negative; not how nervous you are, "I'm crossing my fingers this goes well," nothing like that.

* * * CAREER LIMITING MOVE * * *

Law student from Kansas, at a call-back interview in Austin. The receptionist asks, "Why Austin?"

The student responds, "Oh, I have no intention of working here. I just wanted to visit family."

E. OBSERVE ACTIVITIES AT THE RECEPTION DESK WHILE YOU WAIT FOR YOUR INTERVIEW

The reception area is often an employer's nerve center. Listen to the way people talk to each other and how the lawyers treat the receptionist when they stop by. It'll give you a sneak peek into the atmosphere of the firm.

F. IN EACH INTERVIEW . . .

As is true in every interview you do, you want the interview to be a conversation. You've already read the section on interviewing, and so you know how to play your part!

Remember those 3x5″ cards you made up on interviewers, or the information you loaded into your BlackBerry? Excuse yourself a couple of times during the day so you can hit the head and examine your notes. I know you think I'm hitting you over the head with those damned cards, but believe me, if you know *anything at all* about your interviewers, you are going to shine—because *nobody* goes to that kind of trouble!

Of course, call-backs are different from initial interviews in a few ways. Let's talk about them.

1. Questions to Ask

The best questions to ask are the "personalized" questions we discussed earlier in this chapter. The great thing about them is that you can ask them of everybody, and the answers will always be illuminating and different!

2. Remember: You Might Have Answered the Same Question a Thousand Times Before—But *This Interviewer* Hasn't Heard Your Answer!

"Why do you want to work here?" "How do you like _____ law school?" "On your resume, I noticed ..." Control your natural reaction when you've been asked the same question over and over again. No sighs, no rolling your eyes. Answer the question as though you've never heard it before. The last thing you want to do is to make interviewers feel like they're boring you. So treat each interviewer with the same respect and enthusiasm, no matter how "unoriginal" their questions are!

3. Be Careful About Bringing Up Information That You Glean From Photos and Decorations in the Lawyer's Office

As you glance around someone's office, you might see:

- Kid photos.
- Kid art.
- Trophies.
- Vacation photos.
- Diplomas and professional certificates.
- Professional artwork.

Any of these are distinct conversational "maybes." Many lawyers are rubbed the wrong way by having students ask them about family photos. After all, they can't ask you about *your* family.

But there are, of course, appropriate comments you can make. If a vacation photo features a place you've been—Macchu Picchu, the Sydney Opera House, the Eiffel Tower, no matter what it is— mentioning that you've also been there and asking how the lawyer liked it is fine. Similarly if you see in a photo that the interviewer is wearing a T-shirt with a school logo and you, a friend or family member went there—a quick comment is all right. With diplomas, you probably already know where the interviewer went to school, but if you didn't know before, asking about their school experience is safe conversation, especially if they ask you something about how you like *your* school.

They may have other professional certificates on the walls, as well—for instance, if they've argued a case before the U.S. Supreme Court or a state supreme court, they might have a certificate to prove it. You can always ask what that experience was like.

But remember: you've got twenty minutes to convince them they want to work with you. You don't want to take up the entire visit with a discussion of your mutual experience in the Galapagos!

* * * CAREER LIMITING MOVE * * *

Student on a call-back interview with a large law firm. Late in the day he is ushered into the office of a senior partner. The student glances at a formal portrait on the partner's desk, and comments, "Your daughter is beautiful."

The partner responds: "That's my wife."

4.   THANK EACH INTERVIEWER FOR MEETING WITH YOU

It's worth remembering that when a lawyer takes the time to interview you, what (s)he's *not* doing is working on client matters, and it's client work that generates money. That's not to say that they won't enjoy talking to you, but it's certainly time away from their prime function. At the very least, that merits a "thank you" when the interview is over!

5.   GET A BUSINESS CARD BEFORE YOU LEAVE THE OFFICE

Get into the practice of asking for business cards. At the end of the day, "debrief" yourself by jotting down notes about the interviewer on the back of the business card. You don't know if you might wind up working with them—and knowing something about them when you send thank you's and see them again at the office will make you look great!

6.   DON'T TAKE NOTES ON YOUR INTERVIEW SCHEDULE SHEET!

Some employers will give you a sheet that lists all the lawyers you'll be talking with during your call-back. Don't make the mistake of taking notes about them on that sheet! Use the lawyers' business cards or your own small notebook or cards (out of view of the lawyers, of course).

The reason for avoiding notes on the schedule is this: It's *very* likely that, during the day, interviewers will ask you, "So who else are you talking to?" and ask for your schedule. The last thing you want is to hand them a sheet with notations like "Tool," "Loser," "Not what *I* want to do!" written on it!

7. Ask Each Interviewer on The Way Out About Your *Next* Interviewer

In most call-back interviews, your last interviewer will walk you to your *next* one. A convenient topic of "bridging" conversation—between interviews—is to ask, "What is (your next interviewer) like?" "Tell me about X." It'll give you useful insights, as well as a potential topic of conversation with your next interviewer.

G. There Are Questions That You Only Need to Ask of One Person During the Day

You could even ask these questions of a recruiting coordinator or hiring partner:

- How would my work be assigned (if the website doesn't give it away, or you asked in the screening interview)?
- How would my department be determined (if the website doesn't say)?
- What would a typical day be like for me?
- How will I get feedback on my work?
- What kinds of cases would I work on?
- How does someone become a star? What makes them stand out?
- What's the client mix? (Your job security can turn on whether the firm has one very large client or a lot of smaller ones).
- Anybody here been indicted recently?

Just kidding.

H. Smoking Out the Hours You'll Be Expected to Work

You can't ask straight out about the hours you'll be expected to put in, because you'll (unfairly) sound lazy. And while you can—and should—ask about the kind of work you'll get, you may get a sanitized version of the truth. But asking in a roundabout way will often get you the down-low!

A great question to ask of junior associates is, "What is a typical day like for you?" You can also ask whether or not people at the office socialize during the week. If they work late, the answer will probably reveal that: "Oh, no, by the time we get out, we just want to get home," or "Sure, we get together for Happy Hours twice a week at the local watering hole." Also listen for indirect indications that you're expected to work long hours. For instance, if an interviewer talks about bringing doughnuts into work on Saturday mornings for everybody in the office, don't expect to keep your weekends to yourself. If people keep talking about the great restaurants that deliver to the office, expect to be there in the evenings. If they play sports together, or they mention outside activities they're involved in, their hours are probably more reasonable.

It goes without saying that if you see cots in some junior associates' offices, they aren't there to accommodate afternoon naps. They're there for all-nighters, and you proceed at your own risk!

* * * SMART HUMAN TRICK * * *

Student at a Southwestern school. He is at a call-back with a large firm. He's talking to two junior associates. One of them says, "Another great thing about the firm is that there's on-site day care. That way if you work late, you can go get your kid and come back to the office and go on working."

The student notes, "He's saying it like it's a positive. I'm thinking, 'Come *back* to work? *After* you get your kid?' So I asked him about it: "Is that a typical day for you?"

The guy answers, "Oh, yeah. I work from 7 a.m. to 11 at night."

The other junior associate cuts in, and snorts, "No way. That's not a typical day . . .

. . . I'm out of here by nine."

There are other ways of determining the hours. The most obvious is to ask at Career Services if they know, or if they can direct you to, alums who've worked there previously (current associates can't be asked directly).

Another way to determine hours requires a bit more work, but if it's something that worries you, it's worth it. If it's a firm near enough to your home for easy access, find a reason to stop by the office at 6:30 or 7 p.m. during the week, either to drop off a writing sample or an article you think might interest someone you've spoken with from there. If there are a lot of lights still on, and they tell you that they regularly quit work at 6 p.m., either it's a very unusual night or—what's more likely—6 p.m. is a goal they don't often meet.

No matter where the employer is located, you can call a junior associate with a question at 6:30 or 7 at night, at the office. If they're there to answer your question, you may want to casually ask what they're working on—if it's nothing out of the ordinary, then they're expected to be there at that time, and you will be expected to do the same.

There are also questions you can ask that will help you determine *exactly* the kinds of projects you can expect early in your career. I've mentioned before the associate who recommended, "You need to ask young associates, 'What are you working on today?' and not 'How many depositions have you taken?' or 'What have you gotten to do?' Ask them, *right now,* what they are working on. **Ask them, 'When I walk out of here, what are you going to be doing?'**" When they tell you, ask if that's a typical project for them; if they're juggling several projects at once, ask what else they're doing.

As other associates have told me, "Everybody is going to try to get you 'windshield time' somehow"—that is, time outside of the office—but it's what you do on a regular basis that determines how much you'll enjoy the job.

I. Clever Sleuthing: What to Observe, and Questions to Ask, to See If You're Really Going to Like the Place . . .

Students often ask me, "How do I know I'm really going to like a particular job?" It's easier than you think. The employer may have programmed answers to the most common questions, but they can't control the way they behave, the "standard operating procedures" in the office. Don't underestimate your powers of observation! When you are walking around the employer's digs, they'll be telling you how collegial they are, what a great atmosphere they have, how they aren't a sweatshop, how they want you to have a life, how family-friendly they are. (The Career Services Director at one distinguished law school told me about a meeting with the hiring partner of a prestigious local firm, who was complaining about the rumors flying around school that his firm was a sweatshop. "How are we going to put a stop to it?" he asked. She responded, "Stop being a sweatshop.")

Your eyes will go a long way toward telling you whether or not an employer is telling the truth. What should you look for? Consider the following:

1. Look and See Whether the Support Staff Looks Happy

I can't count the number of people who stress the importance of support staff. If you walk by the desks of administrative assistants, paralegals, researchers, and they all look happy, there's a good chance it's a good place to work. Why? For one thing, if the support staff is happy and treated well, it's likely that management's attitude is a magnanimous one toward associates, as well. And secondly, a happy support staff is more efficient and more helpful. When you start your job, you'll quickly find that there are tons of practical things to learn. The support staff already has that knowledge. If they're contented, they'll help you out in a million ways you couldn't have anticipated in school.

You can also watch to see whether or not you're introduced to support staffers as you're shown around the office. If you are, it's just more evidence that they are treated with respect, and you can expect to be, as well.

At one law firm, a student noted that "A partner who was showing me around was perfectly nice to *me*. But then we stopped at his secretary's desk, and he was so mean to her that he made her cry!"

2. LOOK TO SEE WHETHER OFFICE DOORS ARE PRIMARILY OPEN OR CLOSED

Open communication between senior and junior people is a key element of enjoyment for most new lawyers. You often hear people talk about an "open door" policy. This is one policy with a physical manifestation. As you walk around, look to see if people's doors actually are open. Take into account that if someone is working on a project where they can't be disturbed, they're going to have their door closed no matter how friendly an environment it is. But if the office doors are by and large open, that's a good sign.

3. IS THERE LAUGHTER IN THE HALLWAYS?

Everybody will tell you what a collegial place they work in. But if as you walk around you see a lot of long faces, they've got an interesting definition of "collegial." Great employers tend to have happy offices, and that means that people will feel free to stop in the hallways and chat—and laugh. If you notice this going on, you won't have to ask whether they're collegial or not. You've already seen it for yourself.

4. SEE HOW THEY REFER TO EACH OTHER

What you're looking for here is "Bart Simpson" or "Buffy Vampireslayer," as opposed to "Mr. Simpson" or "Ms. Vampires-layer." Junior lawyers at better employers often talk about everybody being on first name terms. If they do this off-hand as they show you around, that's a good sign.

You may also want to glance at name plates on offices. Some junior lawyers say that the fact that their name plates say "Bart Simpson" as opposed to "Mr. Simpson" is an indication of non-stuffiness that appeals to virtually everybody.

5. NOTICE WHAT KINDS OF THINGS DECORATE THE OFFICES

Many employers will tell you how family-friendly they are, and how they value the private lives of their employees. You can see if they're just blowing smoke up your—ahem—by looking at what decorates their offices.

At stuffy employers, you'll likely see wood-framed diplomas. At more relaxed employers, you'll see family photos, artwork by kids, sometimes little desk toys. If families really matter to them, those kinds of little touches are likely to be all over the place. You can tell what's important to people by looking at what surrounds them at work, and the extent to which *your* personality will be allowed to flourish as well.

6. LISTEN TO PATTER BETWEEN THE LAWYERS AT INTERVIEW MEALS

I go into interview meals in detail in Topic L below, but for right now, we're talking about what you can observe about the employer by paying attention to the interplay between lawyers at lunch, and listening to casual comments they make to you.

For a start, at any interview meal, encourage your host(s) to have a beer or a "drink" drink by asking them to order a drink before you. Trust me: they probably won't take much encouraging! You're going to have a non-alcoholic drink, but you want them to have a social lubricant to get them talking honestly.

Work into the conversation casual questions like "Is (name of firm) what you expected?" "What made you choose (firm)?" Especially if you're dining with more than one lawyer, they'll probably start dishing about people at the office as well as other employers—and you'll learn a lot more than you bargained for!

J. IF THE EMPLOYER IS YOUR FIRST CHOICE . . .

. . . say so, to an attorney you hit it off with, and/or the recruiting coordinator and/or hiring partner.

Enthusiasm is a huge positive. But make sure you save your "first choice" statement until you've forged a rapport with an interviewer. Otherwise you'll look like you're wearing an ass turban.

Incidentally: **don't tell more than one employer in a city that they're your first choice.** I've mentioned before that recruiting people talk. If you lie, you'll get busted.

* * * CAREER LIMITING MOVE * * *

The recruiting coordinators at large firms in a Midwestern city have lunch together once a month to compare notes. During interview season, they gossip about the law students they're hosting, because many of the students interview with more than one firm.

At lunch, the name of a particular student comes up. One of the recruiting coordinators mentions casually, "He told us we were his first choice."

Another recruiting coordinator pipes up, "He told us the same thing!"

And yet another recruiting coordinator: "You've got to be kidding me. He told us that, too."

Although he'd been a promising candidate, he got no offers from any of the firms in the city.

K. KEEP YOUR ENERGY UP ALL DAY

I have a friend who drove straight through from Connecticut to Florida for Spring Break, without stopping. I asked him, "How did you stay awake?"

He responded: "I popped windowpane acid."

I don't advise it.

But seriously, you *do* need to keep your attention from flagging as the day drags on. You've got to show just as much enthusiasm to your late afternoon interviewer as you did to the first one in the morning. So—what should you do? Accept the occasional caffeinated beverage that's offered to you, or ask for one. When you take your bathroom breaks, dab some cold water on your face and neck. At lunch, eat something light—salad and protein. No heavy pastas. Remember: It's just one day, and you've got a lot to gain!

Remember to show enthusiasm to every interviewer no matter when in the day you talk to them. If you exhibit exhaustion during the interview process they'll wonder if you have the stamina for the work. So when they ask you, "How's the call back process going?" Sari Zimmerman recommends that you never say, "I'm exhausted!" Make a comment about enjoying the conversations or meeting the people or learning more about the employer ... anything that's both true *and* positive.

L. Expect at Least One "Stress" Interview During the Day

It's exceptionally likely that at least one interviewer you face in a call-back will be *expressly* hard on you, to see how you react under stress. It's the good cop/bad cop thing. As I mentioned earlier in this chapter, the appropriate thing to do in response is to remain calm, and treat the situation like a Moot Court experience; view the slings and arrows as a test of your mental *cojones*. Don't cop a 'tude in return—and don't be offended!

M. Interview Meals

A big and important topic—so much so that I discuss it on its own. Look at Topic L, below.

N. If You're Interviewing for a Summer Clerkship and You'll Be Unavailable for More Than a Couple Of Days—e.g., a Honeymoon or Long-Standing Vacation—You've Got to Mention It *Sometime*

It happens. Life intrudes. While the employer will ideally want you for the entire summer program, a week or two away won't kill you. Heck, people *split* summers, and that involves a lot more time away than a simple week or two. (Of course, employers don't like split summers *either.*)

But the fact is, if you are getting married—mazel tov!—or you always vacation with your family for a set week or so, or there's a big celebration coming up that you really can't miss, mention it. **The consensus among experts is that you tell the employer when they make you an offer, *before* you accept.**

When they make you an offer, say something like, "I'd be delighted to accept. But before I do, there's something I think it's only fair to tell you. I'm going to be going on honeymoon the last two weeks of July/My family always rents a house on the Outer Banks for a week in August/you name it . . . which is very important to me." Then, the way you state your request for the time off is crucial. Two elements are necessary: Express your willingness to work extra hours or not get paid while you're gone, and drench your request in gratefulness. Tell them that you know you're asking them to go out on a limb for you and that they have no obligation to do so. Also point out that you wanted to be up-front about it, which is why you're bringing it up now.

Notice the timing. I'm telling you to spill the beans when you receive an offer. Why? You don't want to say anything during interviews, because you want to "set the hook" before you tell them you need time off. By the same token, telling them before they make you an offer is a stand-up thing to do. It's just not right to accept an offer without disclosing that you won't be available for part of the experience. As Michelle Hoff advises, "You have to take a long view of your career. You never know when you'll want to work with employers even if you don't work with them now. If you go back to them a year or two down the road, you want them to remember that you were honest with them. It means a lot to your reputation."

Incidentally—I'm only talking about holidays. **Religious observances shouldn't be mentioned**; employers will *assume* you'll take those.

On top of that, only use it for really serious obligations. As Michelle Hoff notes, "It's the strategy for obligations that are meaningful. Don't tell them 'I figure by August I'll be ready for a week off.' "

O. REMEMBER THAT THE RECRUITING COORDINATOR HAS A VOICE IN THE HIRING DELIBERATIONS

As Kay Fletcher points out, "Tell the recruiting coordinator things you wouldn't necessarily tell any of the lawyers. If you took medicine for a cold, tell him or her. That way if an attorney says you seemed tired and uninterested the recruiting coordinator can jump in and explain on your behalf."

Also, remember that even though recruiting coordinators will be extraordinarily nice to you, *they still work for the employer.* Don't say things to them that the employer shouldn't know. So many times I've heard recruiting coordinators talk about the 'true confessions' they've heard from students. "I'm only looking at this city because my boyfriend's going to clerk for a judge here" is the kind of thing you shouldn't tell *anybody.*

P. IF THERE ARE A FEW HOURS AFTER THE INTERVIEWS END AND BEFORE DINNER BEGINS . . .

Ask the recruiting coordinator for ideas about how to spend the time: landmarks, shops, museums that are interesting. As Kay Fletcher points out, "It proves your interest in the city."

Q. If the Interviews End and No Mention of Dinner Has Been Made, Don't Ask "Do You Have Any Dinner Plans for Me?"

It puts people on the spot! If they intend to host you for dinner, they'll let you know. Otherwise, you're on your own.

6. Following up

A. Send a Thank You Immediately to Lawyers Who Interviewed You, Dining Partners at Any Meal, the Host/Hostess at Any Event You Attended, and the Recruiting Coordinator/Office Manager Who Coordinated Your Visit

You are *really* not happy to see me telling you this. But you *have* to be gracious!

Ideally, no more than a day after you get home, send a thank-you for the interview. A call-back interview is a substantial investment of time for an employer, and often a significant outlay of cash, as well— so a thank you is definitely merited! And a thank you, incidentally, goes to every person with whom you interviewed—not just the "lead" or recruiting coordinator, with a note asking them to "Pass along my thanks to . . ." As Elizabeth Workman points out, "Recruiting coordinators say, 'Do they really expect me to go to every person they spoke with and say 'Thank you?' The few minutes you spend on those half-dozen notes makes a big difference!"

In addition, thank yous go to anyone you ate with and anyone who hosted you at their house. **Also, if you went to a lawyer's house, a thank you goes to their spouse.** It's an incredibly gracious thing to do, and it will not be overlooked.

I'd encourage you to take cards and stamps with you, and polish off thank yous at your hotel or on the way home . . . unless you're driving home, in which case writing thank yous would not be such a good idea. You'll be way too busy with your Blackberry and cell phone.

For what to say in your thank you, see topic J.

B. If the Call-Back Was "Casual," You Need Only Send a Thank You to Lawyers With Whom You Actually Interviewed

Especially at smaller employers, your call-backs may be informal. As Creighton's Shannon Kelly says, "You might talk with one person, another wanders in, you meet a third in the hallway. It's fine to send a thank you only to the lawyer with whom you met."

C. Send Your Expense Report Separately From Your Thank You

After you've sent your thank you, send your expense report. Don't combine the two; it looks bad. "Thank you, and by the way, here's what you owe me . . ." Of course, if you need guidance on how to format your expenses, and what kind of detail to include, call the recruiting coordinator or person who organized your trip for you.

c. Reimbursable vs. Nonreimbursable Expenses

Reimbursable expenses:

- Hotel (with reasonable tip for the maid, $2–5 depending on the cost of the room);
- Rental car and/or taxi and/or train to get to the employer and home;
- Mileage and tolls, if you drove—ask the employer for the rate they pay;
- Airfare;
- Meals (*reasonable* meals; if you did it up, only charge part of your meal to the employer. And no charging for friends! If you treat a friend, ask the waiter for *two* charge slips to separate the "chargeable" portion from the portion you eat. Pardon the pun.);
- Reasonable phone calls (if you use your cell phone, don't charge for phone calls at all).

Nonreimbursable expenses:

- Anything from the minibar—it works out to 50 cents per M & M!
- Alcohol;
- In-room movies;
- Entertainment;
- Extra night(s) in hotel or day(s) with rental car;
- Meals for friends;
- Dry cleaning.

* * * CAREER LIMITING MOVE * * *

Student from a New England school flies to California for a call-back. His hotel bill goes directly to the firm hosting him. The recruiting coordinator reports, "The hotel bill was pretty much in line with what I expected. However, as I glanced down it, I noticed that he had ordered two in-room movies. *Porn* movies! It wasn't the expense that was the problem, but where was this student's judgment? He knew we were getting the bill. Presumably he should have realized that it would be itemized. It was stupid, stupid, stupid."

* * * CAREER LIMITING MOVE * * *

Law student from a prestigious law school, flies to a call-back interview with a large firm. He's at the hotel for one night, and his room is billed directly to the firm. The recruiting coordinator is stunned when the bill comes in at $600—$400 more than the room itself should have cost. When she examines the bill more closely, she sees that *he emptied every single item from the mini-bar in the room!*

D. BE HONEST ABOUT YOUR EXPENSES

Don't jerk employers around about how much you really spent. If they hire you, they'll be showering you with doubloons. As Sue Gainen dryly notes, "Expenses should not be a source of income."

E. IF YOUR ONLY EXPENSES ARE TEENY, EAT THEM—DON'T CHARGE THE EMPLOYER

If you drove 25 miles to an interview, don't charge the employer for the mileage. If your parking and tolls are a grand total of ten bucks, don't charge it. If you stopped at McDonald's for a bite on the way home, don't send that bill.

I realize that money's tight in law school, but don't nickel and dime employers. They'll question your judgment. When they're investing time (which is money) in interviewing you and considering hiring and training you, don't cloud the picture with an expense reimbursement request for $8.67.

I.   TELEPHONE INTERVIEWS

Egads. *Telephone* interviews. To quote Dorothy Parker, "What fresh hell is this?" It's the worst of both worlds. You can't communicate "visually," which is how most information gets across. And you don't have the time to think between responses as you would if you communicated via e-mail.

But sometimes you have no choice; the interviewer is a long way away, it's an initial interview where they won't pay your way and you aren't going to spring for the trip either. So the telephone it is! Let's talk about how you make the best of it:

1. RECORD YOURSELF FIRST

Most of us have no idea how we sound. Record yourself answering the most common interview questions (choose some from the list earlier in this chapter). You'll undoubtedly notice how important it is to vary the tone of your voice. You may even catch some conversational "ticks," like using the word "like" too much, or hemming and hawing before you answer. You want to speak clearly, with a strong voice. If you talk very quickly—slow down!

You may even want to do a telephone mock interview with Career Services. That would be the best way to make sure that your telephone pitch is smooth!

2. PREPARE EXACTLY AS YOU WOULD FOR AN "IN-THE-FLESH" INTERVIEW

Do all the research you would do if you were interviewing in person. Prepare your infomercial tailored to this employer, and practice your answers. It may seem like an "interview lite," but it's still a *job* interview—and it deserves your full preparation!

In fact, you can do one better than "live" interviews, in the sense that you can write down everything you want to say, and everything you learn about the interviewer and the employer. After all, they can't see you!

3.   IF YOU'RE THE ONE WHO IS SUPPOSED TO INITIATE THE PHONE CALL, CALL THE *EXACT MINUTE* THE INTERVIEW IS SUPPOSED TO START

I told you in the "normal" interview section to turn up a few minutes early for interviews—largely to sweet-talk the receptionist. There's no point in doing that if you're phoning. Call exactly on time.

4.   DISABLE CALL-WAITING ON YOUR PHONE!

There's nothing more annoying than being put on hold when you're talking to someone. Under *no* circumstances should you put an interviewer on hold to take another call! Turn off your call-waiting. And if you somehow forget to do so, and someone else dials in while you're interviewing, ignore the other caller, and if the interviewer asks, "Do you have another call coming in?" say "I'm terribly sorry—please ignore it. You were/I was saying . . ."

5.   BE IN A QUIET PLACE!

Background noise can be terribly distracting in a telephone conversation. I should know. In one of the more boneheaded maneuvers I ever pulled looking for a job in law school, I actually interviewed for a judicial clerkship *on the pay phone at a Burger King!* The phone was near the drive-thru, so every time some joker pulled up to order lunch, you could hear in the background, "Uuhh .. gimme a Whopper, fries . . ." and on top of that, every couple of minutes, an operator came on the phone demanding "Deposit fifty cents more, please!" I don't have to tell you I didn't get the job. I probably also don't have to tell you that my hand was barely off the receiver when the rejection letter appeared in my mailbox.

So—go someplace quiet. If you're at school and the interview is on your cell phone, go to a private study room, or ask Career Services if you can use an interview room. You don't want any distractions!

* * * CAREER LIMITING MOVE * * *

Judge interviewing a potential clerk over the phone. The judge reports, "I knew this student was calling from his home. It was reasonably free of background noise, until I heard what I thought was him washing dishes. I thought that was odd, but then I heard an unmistakable sound.

"A toilet flushing."

6.   HAVE YOUR RESUME, WRITING SAMPLE, TRANSCRIPT, AND COVER LETTER HANDY

As Victor Massaglia points out, "You want to be able to talk about them," so have them at hand.

7.   Use Notes!

Remember I told you to write down everything you want to mention? What a great way to make sure that you don't miss anything! Make a list of key points you want to make about yourself and why you can do the job. Have your notes spread out in front of you when you call so that the interviewer can't hear you rustling paper. And don't *take* notes—a jotting here and there is OK, but you don't want to be distracted from what's being said. Writing while you talk may dampen the conversation, and the conversation is of paramount importance.

Also, if you're going to ask questions from notes, make sure that your questions sound natural. If you say, "By the way, Your Honor, I made note of the fact that in the case Mario Brothers v. Sonic that you cited the amicus curiae brief of . . ." well. You'll either sound like you're reading your questions . . . or you're a total tool.

8.   As the Interviewer Talks, Interject Short Comments to Let Them Know You're Listening

"I see," "That's interesting," "Yes." Nobody wants to talk into a void, and you certainly don't want them saying, "Are you still *there?*"

9.   Remember: All of Your Enthusiasm Has to Show in Your Voice

Expressing yourself enthusiastically without being able to use any physical cues is a real challenge. But make sure you speak animatedly. And *smile.* This may sound silly, but research suggests that a smile actually shows in your voice. It's worth trying, because you've got to be just as memorable as you would have been in person. Let your voice tell the interviewer, "I may not *be* there with you—but I definitely want to *work* with you!"

J.   Thank You Notes

Thank you notes are a kind of Catch–22. As Laura Rowe Lane points out, "A good one can't help you—but a bad one can hurt you!" I've talked with numerous recruiting coordinators who've pointed out how students *actually lost* offers based on bad thank you notes: misspelling the firm (or lawyer's) name, referring to something they didn't actually talk about, rotten grammar or spelling or typos.

On top of that, there are employers who don't like thank yous at all. An upstate New York employer told students that thank yous are "an annoying waste of paper."

But the vast majority of employers feel thank yous are important. In fact, I've talked with employers who *specifically* eliminated students from consideration because they didn't send a thank you. One employer commented, "If they couldn't be bothered to send a thank you, after we paid for their visit and took the time to talk with them, God only knows how they'd behave once they got here. We just don't want to work with people who are ungrateful." Another employer added, "We were interviewing for one new position, and of all the people we talked to, only *one* sent a thank you. It was a handwritten note. He got the job."

So to the timeworn question: Are thank yous really necessary? The answer is: Yep. **For every interview except an on-campus interview, you need to send a thank you. And at some law schools, thank yous are even appropriate for on-campus interviews; check with Career Services to see what's *de rigeur* at your school.** In fact, no matter *where* you go to school, if the on-campus interview was extraordinary, it merits a thank-you!

* * * SMART HUMAN TRICK * * *

Female student from a Southwestern school. She went on an out of town interview with a firm she just loved. When she got back, she went out of her way to get photos of a new renovation to her law school, and with her thank yous, she sent the photos to the alums she'd spoken with at the firm.

She got an offer.

* * * SMART HUMAN TRICK * * *

A student at a Colorado school was one of two finalists for a job. The other guy got it. In his thank you, the student was very gracious. He said, "I enjoyed the process. I was honored to be one of two considered . . ."

A few months later, the firm called. The other guy hadn't worked out. Would he still be interested?

So *ultimately* . . . he got the job.

Here's what you need to know about thank yous:

1.   A SNAIL-MAILED THANK YOU IS BETTER THAN AN E-MAIL THANK YOU, BUT E-MAIL IS A LOT BETTER THAN NOTHING

Gosh, isn't e-mail tempting? So easy. No looking for paper or card and envelope. No stamps. No going to the mailbox. But the very fact that you have to do those things when you "snail mail" a thank you is what makes it memorable. Employers know how little effort it takes to e-mail. Impress them with your thoughtfulness, and send a non-cyber thank you!

Of course, if you're just not going to send a card—or if you're going to delay so long that the benefit of the thank you is lost—most employers agree that e-mail is a lot better than nothing. Some say, "I don't want my e-mail loaded down with thank yours," but they're in the minority. On balance, you're wise to express your gratefulness.

2.   CONSIDER LAYING IN A STOCK OF CONSERVATIVE NOTE CARDS

The best would be note cards with pictures of your law school on the front. But anything conservative would do.

3. CONSIDER HAND-WRITING THE THANK YOU

Most experts say that a handwritten note or card is the best thank you, because it's the most personal. But if your handwriting looks like a lie detector print out, nobody's going to be insulted by a printed note.

4. HOW TO ADDRESS LAWYERS . . . THE "ESQUIRE" THING

Vanderbilt's Kathy Jernigan says that "Most recruiters are in favor of using 'Esquire' in lawyer correspondence." While there are people who aren't offended if it's missing, the least-risk alternative is to include it.

Kathy Jernigan explains how you handle it:

"On the envelope, you include the attorney's name, followed by Esquire. On the inside address, you include Esquire. Then you say, Dear Mr./Ms."

By way of example, let's say you're addressing correspondence to attorney Herman Munster. You'd address the envelope:

> Herman Munster, Esquire
> 1313 Mockingbird Lane
> Mysteryville, USA

On the inside, you'd repeat that address.

Then you'd write:

> Dear Mr. Munster:

Without including the "Esquire."

Incidentally, as Dorris Smith points out, "In business correspondence, you use a colon after the "Dear Mr./Ms. X" instead of a comma, even if you already know the person."

In addition, the inside greeting—the "Dear so-and-so"—should be in the same form you conducted the interview; that is, if you called them "Mr. Munster," write "Dear Mr. Munster." If the interviewer invited you to call them by their first name, then it's "Dear Herman."

5. CONTENT—PERSONALIZE IT!

Laura Rowe Lane suggests that you include a personal message if you can.

The following elements are mandatory:

- Thank them for their time;
- Reiterate your interest in the employer (saying something like, "Having met with you, I am even more excited about the idea of working for Snap, Crackle, and Popp").

If you can add any of the following, it will make your thank you truly stand out:

- Refer to something you talked about (e.g., "Thanks for the tips on using Excel");

- Remind them about what impressed them about you (e.g., "I'm glad you think my juggling experience is an asset");

- Include a *humble* line about why you think you'd be such a great employee (e.g., "Our conversation about the issues your clients are faced with reminded me very much of the research I did for Judge Glockenspiel");

- Follow up on an interest of the interviewer (e.g., "With your interest in Japanese cinema, I remembered one film you might particularly enjoy ...")

- If you talked about a hobby of mutual interest, a note about that would be great ("I look forward to talking with you about the Spring opera season.")

Obviously, you don't include *all* of these in a single thank you note, but you see the universe of options from which you can choose!

There is one major element to avoid: **Don't re-answer or re-explain something you think you got wrong. You'll only draw attention to it.** You said what you said. Only address issues for which you asked for additional time at the interview. If at any point you said, "Hmm. Can I get back to you on that?" the thank you note is the place to do it!

6.   Remember: Your Thank You Is Also a Writing Sample

Pay attention to the wording, grammar and punctuation just as you would for any writing sample the employer sees. No smiley face next to your name, no hearts to dot the i's, sloppiness, cross-outs, emoticons ... nothing unprofessional!

7.   For a Panel or Group Interview ...

Send a thank you to all of the interviewers.

8.   If You Interviewed With a Number of People Individually in the Same Office ...

... I used to think you could send one note to the person who organized your call-back. But I've been enlightened. As I mentioned in the call-back interview discussion, *everybody* **gets a thank you.**

Do you resent it? Well, think about what they're potentially offering you—a great gig. Training, mentoring, launching your career. Not only that, if they're on the fence about making you an offer, you don't know which interviewer's opinion will push you over the top. You want to make sure they're *all* on your side. And if a simple thank you note accomplishes that ... well!

* * * CAREER LIMITING MOVE * * *

Student who'd interviewed with several interviewers at the same office. She sent them all the same e-mail, and opened it, "Hey Gang."

9. IF YOU FORGET THE NAME OF SOMEONE WITH WHOM YOU INTERVIEWED . . .

You have two choices. Either go to the employer's web site, scroll down the list of attorneys and see if a name rings a bell—or call the main number at the employer, and throw yourself on the mercy of the receptionist. "The really outgoing guy with the blond hair, the one who's into paintball. I'm sending a thank you note, and I'm mortified I forgot his name." *Everybody* forgets names. It's much better to figure out someone's name than not thank them at all.

10. TIMING!

The sooner the better. Students have been known to FedEx thank yous the day after the interview. That's a bit over the top—not to mention expensive!—but you get the point. Get the thank you out within twenty-four hours if you can. Apart from anything else, the interview is still fresh in your mind, so it'll be the easiest time to bang out a personal note. Furthermore, they're unlikely to have made a decision about you by then, so your thank you can have some impact.

11. *SPELL THE NAMES RIGHT!*

The firm. The lawyer(s). Go to the web site, and if they don't have one, check Martindale/Hubbell or call and verify the spelling.

With the firm name, be sure that you get the commas right. Some firms use them to separate names, and some don't. And write the "trailing" letters accurately, whether they're P.C., L.L.C., and they are separated by periods or not. As Mary Harblin points out, "When you're a lawyer, if you file a lawsuit against a company and you leave off the 'Inc.,' you might be suing an entirely different entity. Details *matter*."

K. FOLLOWING UP AFTER THE INTERVIEW

Students often ask me what they should do to follow up. They want the employer to know that they're interested . . . but they don't want to seem like stalkers!

The fact is, when it comes to following up, employers are like snowflakes: no two are alike. Some will invite you for a second interview on the spot. Others might not call you for six months, and then let you know they're interested.

Some will never contact you at all. Schmucks.

1. ASK FOR A FOLLOW-UP STRATEGY DURING THE INTERVIEW.

The best way to deal with this is to do what I suggested in the "Questions" section; namely, **at the end of your interview, ask the interviewer when they plan on contacting students for call backs or offers.** Ask them whether you can contact them (or someone at their office) if you haven't heard either way by that time. Make a note of that deadline after your interview.

Wait a few days after the deadline, and if you haven't heard anything, call. No e-mail: phone call. You're not asking for their decision, you're just going to say something like, "I'm calling to follow up on an interview I had with Cornelius Rex at Shyster Law School three weeks ago." If you're polite—and you will be!—a call like this will never be considered overreaching.

2. IF YOU DIDN'T ASK FOR A DECISION DATE DURING THE INTERVIEW, WAIT TWO WEEKS

If you neglect to ask the interviewer when you can expect to hear something, Sandy Mans advises that you follow up with a phone call within two weeks to see what's going on. Again, this is just a friendly phone call to ask when you can expect a decision, and to ask if there's anything else you can provide: a writing sample, references, whatever.

3. IF THE INTERVIEWER TELLS YOU TO CALL BACK IN TWO WEEKS . . . THEN TWO WEEKS . . . THEN TWO WEEKS . . .

. . . and you just don't hear anything? One student told me about this experience, and that after three tries, the assistant to the hiring person wouldn't let him talk to her boss. The strategy here is to leave a voice mail for the hiring person when you know they won't be at work—late at night or early in the morning—saying something like, "I'm not pressuring you for a decision, but I wanted to reiterate my interest, and as soon as you can let me know, I'd appreciate it." Or you can try at 8 in the morning or 6 at night, when your "target" is likely to be in but the assistant isn't.

At some point, of course, you're going to come to the conclusion that this dog just won't hunt. But be persistent for at least a little while if you don't line something else up in the meantime. You never know when the next phone call is going to hit pay dirt!

4. IF THE INTERVIEWER LETS YOU KNOW THAT SEVERAL MONTHS WILL PASS BEFORE YOU HEAR ANYTHING . . .

Don't let them forget about you in the meantime! Every month or two, send an e-mail, card or letter reminding the interviewer of your continuing interest in the job. Update them with any new (good) grades, work-related experiences, achievements. Remember, with contact this infrequent you aren't being a pest—rather, you're showing that you're a potential employee with a great deal of interest in the employer, and great follow through!

5. GIFTS AREN'T NECESSARY

As Sari Zimmerman points out, "When employers get lavish gifts from students they start thinking, 'stalker candidate.' "

One student—I'll call her "Georgia Brown"—lobbying for a summer clerkship with a large, prestigious law firm, sent associates in her target department flashlights with a note wrapped around them reading, "Five reasons why Georgia Brown would light up your summer." Commented one of the associates: "It was weird."

6.   How to Get the Employer Interested in Hiring You—If You Think You're on the Bubble . . .

Here's the situation. You've interviewed and/or followed up with the employer, and you get the feeling that they like you . . . but things could go either way. It's a job you really want. What can you do to goose your chances?

My favourite tactic in this situation is one that you can only use for jobs you really, really want: **Contact your references, and ask them to call the employer for you.** Tell them, "I'm under consideration for this job, and it's a job I really want. Would you mind calling them and talking to them about me?" Give them all of the contact information. What you want them to say is something like, "I know you're considering so-and-so for a job. Here's why you should hire him/her . . ." This has worked a bunch of times for law students.

* * * SMART HUMAN TRICK * * *

Student with so-so grades, interviews with the county prosecutor's office. After the interview, she asks a couple of her professors to call the prosecutor's office with unsolicited recommendations for her. These calls push her over the top and she gets the job.

PS: It's the way she also gets her *next* job—as a federal district court judicial clerk!

* * * SMART HUMAN TRICK * * *

Law student who was interested in a very specific kind of contracting work, involving financing/leasing real estate deals in Asia. She was targeting a particular firm. She had worked for a developer in Japan and had, ironically, written a contract with this particular firm—on the other side!

The firm told her she was very close to getting the job. They asked her if she had done leasing agreements, and because she was nervous, she responded with only, "I'm familiar with those agreements." She said, "I just didn't think they would believe I wrote the contract!"

She called her old boss, and said to him, "This is a job I really want. Would you call them and tell them that I wrote the contract?" He readily agreed, and called the firm, saying essentially "She's great. You know, she wrote that contract you signed."

She got the job.

The caveats with this are ones you simply *must* follow. First of all, it has to be a job where the feedback you've gotten suggested you're in the running. "So-and-so really liked you, we're making our decisions now . . ." that kind of thing. And secondly, as I cautioned you earlier, it has to be a job you really want. You can't go running to your references to make phone calls to even half a dozen employers, because they won't want to be your references any more!

Having said that, when you do take this approach, it can make a huge difference. I've talked to employers who said it was the deciding factor in choosing a new hire. So, under the right circumstances—give it a try!

7. IF THE EMPLOYER OFFERS TO FORWARD YOUR RESUME TO OTHER EMPLOYERS BEFORE THEY'VE TOLD YOU THEIR DECISION ON YOU . . .

. . . **They've told you without *telling* you.** They're not going to hire you. ***But don't jump ugly about it.*** What they're saying is that they're willing to put their reputation on the line for you. They'll be saying something like, "We're not hiring him/her because of X, but (s)he's really impressive. You should talk to him/her."

It's not the time to play the petulant baby and say, "If you don't want me, I don't need *you*." The employer might be putting you onto a great gig. At least check it out—be grateful, and say thank you!

8. A GREAT EXIT STRATEGY IF THEY'RE STINGINGLY NEGATIVE . . .

Once in a while you'll run into an employer who is a real jerk. You'll call to follow up, and they'll be just awful. Rejection is bad enough without piling on humiliation. But some turds just can't help it. Instead of just saying "No," they'll laugh at you or sneer. Fools! What's really stupid is they don't know where you'll wind up. Hell, you could be a *judge*. So it's just stupid to alienate you.

If they *do*—you don't want to respond in kind or betray emotion. Take a deep breath, and pretend you've got another call coming in. "Oh—that's my other line. I've got to answer it. Thanks anyway." And hang up. No point in prolonging the pain!

L. INTERVIEW MEALS: IMPRESSING EMPLOYERS WHEN YOU STRAP ON THE FEED BAG*

If you dine as though you learned your manners at a hot dog eating contest, nobody's going to want to socialize with you—and they won't turn you loose in front of clients. Nobody expects you to be able to negotiate a 24-piece place setting of Queen Anne cutlery, or to wield an escargot utensil like a pro (remember Julia Roberts in *"Pretty Woman"*?), but you *do* have to have some modicum of good manners!

What I'll give you here is a very brief primer on common dining faux pas. Let's see what you need to know!

---

* This section is adapted from the truly fabulous book "What Law School Doesn't Teach You ... But You Really Need To Know," written by—well, me. The etiquette advice is largely from etiquette guru Sharon Abrahams, who runs seminars about business etiquette.

1. REMEMBER ABOVE ALL: WHEN YOU'RE EATING WITH EMPLOYERS, *YOU'RE STILL BEING INTERVIEWED.* DON'T LET YOUR GUARD DOWN!

The setting is casual. Your dining partners are lawyers close to your own age. They seem relaxed. Why not let your hair down, right?

Wrong. It's an interview in sheep's clothing. They're still "the employer," and you're still being judged. They may start dishing dirt on the employer, trading stories with each other (which is great "inside skinny" for you), but don't be lured into letting your guard down. As Sari Zimmerman points out, "You can be fine all day, but if you have wine when you're exhausted at the end of the day and you wind up with a lampshade on your head—no offer." Any story you tell that starts, "You wouldn't believe what I did . . ." is off-limits. So are dirty jokes. So are questions or comments that reflect badly on the employer. "I interviewed with so-and-so this morning. Is he always such a stiff?" "Why does everybody look so pasty? Do you guys work around the clock?" "An upperclassman at school told me [your firm] is a real sweatshop. Is that true?"

* * * CAREER LIMITING MOVE * * *

From law students during interview meals:

- "At least when I get out of law school, I won't have to work so hard."
- "I'm looking forward to making the big money."
- "I looked at working for the FBI but they do drug testing."
- "You guys don't do credit checks, right?"

2. AT THE SAME TIME . . . ENCOURAGE THE LAWYER(S) TO FORGET IT'S AN INTERVIEW. DON'T DISCOURAGE THEM FROM HAVING AN ALCOHOLIC BEVERAGE

You can learn things at interview meals that you typically can't learn anywhere else. The best way to do it? Don't let the fact that *you're* not drinking determine the mood of the table. To accomplish this, don't order your drink first. If the waiter asks you first, "What would you like to drink?" turn to your dining partner (or one of them) and say something like, "I'm not sure. What are you having?" or simply, "Why don't you go first?"

Alcohol isn't called a social lubricant for nothing. If the lawyers have a drink, they will often start telling you things that they had *no intention* of telling you, especially if you ask them questions like, "What's the firm's social life like?" "What's it like living in this city?" "Is working at the firm what you expected when you started?" and "When you were me—at an interview lunch/dinner like this!—what do you wish you'd asked about?" In other words: You want them to forget it's an interview lunch. But make sure *you're* always aware of it!

* * * SMART HUMAN TRICK * * *

Law student on a call-back with a large firm in New York. At lunch, the associates she was dining with had two scotches each. "These people who'd been fairly reserved turned into different people," she reports. "They were like, 'Don't take this job,' 'We work around the clock,' 'The work sucks.' I know they never would have told me that if they had been sober. I also figured it must be the truth."

3.   THE CARDINAL RULE OF INTERVIEW DINING: IF YOU CAN'T IDENTIFY IT, DON'T EAT IT OR TOUCH IT UNTIL YOU'VE SEEN SOMEONE *ELSE* TRY IT FIRST

An interview meal isn't the time to be adventurous in your food choices. Stick with what you know! If you see a bowl with a lemon floating in it sitting near your salad, it's not salad dressing. Don't drink it. It's a "finger bowl," designed to rinse your fingers before the next course. If you sit down and see a little plate with what looks like an embossed mint sitting on it, don't pick it up and pop it in your mouth. It's formed butter, and it's meant for your bread roll. Look around and see what other people do with something unfamiliar before you try it yourself!

* * * YOU CAN'T MAKE THIS STUFF UP * * *

Interview lunch. New York law firm, student from a small town in the Midwest. One partner and two associates take the student to an exquisite Chinese restaurant. The partner orders for the table. One of the dishes he orders is Mu Shu Chicken, a dish which is served with thin pancakes that look something like tortillas. When the dishes arrive, the waiter puts the Mu Shu pancakes next to the student. Mistaking them for face towels, she picks one up and dabs her face with it.

The lawyers, not wanting to embarrass her, do the same.

* * * YOU CAN'T MAKE THIS STUFF UP * * *

Interview lunch at a Japanese restaurant. The interviewee is a middle-aged law student who is almost completely bald. The student admits that he has never had Japanese food before. The lawyer orders him a platter of "cooked" sushi, which comes with a pyramid of wasabi, the hyper-hot green Japanese horseradish which is used *very* sparingly on sushi.

The student, mistaking the wasabi for mashed avocado, pops the whole thing in his mouth. As the lawyer reports, "I felt so sorry for the guy. He didn't want to admit that he'd made a mistake. So I sat there watching as he stoically tried not to show any pain, but his face turned red starting with his cheeks, and going all the way up to the top of his head."

4.   OK, ANOTHER CARDINAL RULE OF INTERVIEW DINING: IT'S NOT ABOUT THE FOOD. IT'S ABOUT THE *JOB*

That crucial piece of advice comes from Vanderbilt's Lisa Doster. What does this mean? It means that if you aren't sure how to handle *any* aspect of your meal, you err in favour of paying attention to the employer instead of the food, not eating something you're not sure about handling, excusing yourself from the table and going to the restroom to take care of anything stuck in your teeth. You'll eat plenty of meals in your life—perhaps even with this interviewer if you get the job!—but you have limited chances to make a great impression. Remember (pardon the analogy) on which side your bread is buttered!

5. CELL PHONES AND BLACKBERRIES OFF! (OR SET THEM ON VIBRATE, WHICH IS MORE FUN ANYWAY)

Do you remember the TV ad where the guy's cell phone rings during a grand pause in an opera, and he answers it, and the diva on stage throws a flaming spear through the phone to the wild applause of everyone in the audience? *Everybody* feels that way about cell phones. Unless you're a cardiologist, your wife's about to give birth, or the President of the United States is going to consult with you any minute about pushing the red button, turn *off* your cell phone when you sit down to eat.

If you set your cell phone or beeper on vibrate and it goes off during the meal, "Get up and excuse yourself," advises Sharon Abrahams. "Don't look at the Blackberry at the table, or—God forbid!—talk on the cell phone."

6. ORDERING THE FOOD. IT'S A MINEFIELD!

A. DON'T ORDER ANYTHING YOU'VE NEVER EATEN BEFORE JUST BECAUSE IT SOUNDS EXOTIC

Unless you are a *very* sophisticated and worldly diner—that is, you aren't easily grossed out—an interview meal is not the time to explore brave new culinary worlds. It might turn out to be something you hate—or can't figure out.

* * * EMBARRASSING MOMENT * * *

Summer clerk at a large Los Angeles law firm. The clerk had never tried artichokes before, and ordered one. "It came out on a plate and was arranged like a beautiful flower. I didn't know how to eat it. I didn't know you're supposed to eat the edible part off the leaf. Instead, I put a leaf in my mouth and chewed and chewed and chewed. I was dying. It was like a huge tumbleweed in my mouth. Finally, in desperation, I spit it into my napkin, dropped the napkin on the floor, and kicked it away from the table!"

* * * SMART HUMAN TRICK * * *

Student from a Southern law school, at an interview dinner. "Everybody else at the table ordered steak. To be different, I ordered something called 'steak tartare.' I didn't know what it was but I figured that it was a steak with tartar sauce, like on McDonald's fish sandwiches. I was wrong. It's *raw hamburger*. Even worse, it had a *raw egg* on top of it. I hadn't ever eaten anything other than well-done steak. But I could tell they were all looking at me, seeing how I was going to handle it."

"So I ate it. To tell you the truth, once you got past the texture, it really wasn't bad. The egg part was pretty gross, though."

B. Don't Order the Most Expensive Thing on the Menu

As Sharon Abrahams points out, "For an interview dinner, you use the same rule you'd use on a date: when it comes to the price of your entrée, don't read from right to left and order something because it's the most expensive thing on the menu!"

There's only one exception to this. If your host says, "Oh, you really should try the chateaubriand stuffed with foie gras in truffled 24–karat-gold sauce. It's delightful"—then you've got a free pass. Go ahead and order it!

* * * EMBARRASSING MOMENT * * *

Law student, toward the top of her law school class, gets numerous interviews and call-backs. Because she is on a limited budget at school, she figures that these interview meals are her opportunity to order the most extravagant items restaurants offer. "It got more and more ridiculous. Finally, at one restaurant I ordered the duck. I had never had duck before, but—it was the most expensive thing on the menu. So I ordered it."

"When they brought out the entrees, the lawyers all had normal-looking dishes. I had this *enormous* dish. I didn't know ducks got that huge. It was easily bigger than my head. I thought I would have a hard time seeing over it when people talked to me. What made it even worse was that I didn't even *like* it. I took one bite. Then I spent the rest of the meal kind of hacking it into smaller and smaller pieces and pushing it around on my plate."

"I was grateful to go home and go out with my boyfriend—and order chicken again."

C. Don't Order *Any* Food That Can Sabotage You

Foods on the banned list are pretty obvious. Sharon Abrahams calls these the foods that can "sabotage" you, like "French onion soup (the cheese strings are simply uncuttable), and anything you eat with your hands—corn on the cob, ribs, fried chicken, lobster, crab legs. And don't order a burger. As soon as you put a burger together to take a bite, whoosh! The burger flies out the other side. It's messy and greasy. Order your burger without a bun, and tell them you're on the Zone diet. Then eat it with a knife and fork."

You *can* order chicken on the bone, but when you get it you have to cut the chicken off the bone and eat it with a fork. "You can't pick up the chicken bones and eat the last gobbet of meat from them," says Sharon Abrahams.

* * * CAREER LIMITING MOVE * * *

Partners at a medium-sized law firm buy a table's worth of tickets for a dinner honoring a retiring judge. Several of the lawyers take along the three summer clerks. The food is Chinese, and it's served from a buffet. One of the summer clerks picks up a plate of Chinese ribs from the buffet and brings it back to the table. She eats the meat off the bone, and then—to the slack-jawed astonishment of her colleagues—she proceeds to eat the bones themselves, with a loud Crrunch! Crrunch! as she snaps off every bite.

d. If You Follow a Special Diet, Handle It *Discreetly*

As Sharon Abrahams recommends, "If you follow a diet that is kosher or vegetarian or you only eat plants that don't kill the plant they come from or you have allergies, call the waiter over and tell them *quietly* what your diet restrictions are. I'm allergic to wheat, so I can't have soy sauce, and I often have to mention that to the waiter. You *have* to take responsibility for your own food."

If you're ordering from a menu, it's simple enough to have your meal prepared specially. If the menu is catered, Sharon Abrahams suggests that you "Call ahead and ask for the menu. If you can't eat it, ask for 'just a salad' or whatever you *can* eat. They'll accommodate you."

* * * CAREER LIMITING MOVE * * *

Law student at an interview lunch. When the waiter comes to the table to take the order, she launches into a long list of allergies. "It was wild," comments one of her dining partners. "It was like she was allergic to everything except air. I mean, I understand the allergy thing, but the way she handled it made her seem so high-maintenance."

* * * CAREER LIMITING MOVE * * *

Student at an interview lunch. He and his dining partners are chatting pleasantly until the food arrives. When the student attempts to eat, he almost vomits. Naturally concerned, one of the associates asks him, "Are you OK?" and he responds, "I have a terrible case of acid reflux. Eating is almost impossible for me."

The associate comments afterwards, "We really liked the guy and felt really bad for him. But he should have told us ahead of time if he couldn't eat, or he needed some kind of special accommodations. We would have been fine with that. As it was, seeing the poor guy almost upchuck with every bite ... yuck."

E. ORDERING DRINKS AND WINE

When it comes to drinks with meals, "The days of the three-martini lunch are over," says Sharon Abrahams. "Getting drunk doesn't impress people. At lunch, don't drink at all. At dinner, if someone else wants to order wine, fine. You can have one glass, no more."

What if one of the lawyers asks if you want a drink at dinner, and they haven't ordered yet? As Georgetown's Beth Sherman advises, "Be careful. You can say, 'I haven't decided yet. Why don't you start?' If they order a drink, then you can, too—but remember to stop at one drink."

If they ask you to order the wine and you've never done that before, it can be embarrassing. Beth Sherman suggests that you say, "Thanks, I appreciate the compliment," and then ask the waiter for a wine recommendation. With that, you can get a consensus from the table about the wine everybody would like to drink.

* * * CAREER LIMITING MOVE * * *

Student on a call-back interview. She flies to the "interview city" and stays overnight the night before her interview. She interviews all day, and at the end of the interviews a partner and an associate from the firm, both male, offer to take her out for a drink before the partner drives her to the airport. She eagerly agrees.

At the bar, the two lawyers order a scotch. She orders a glass of red wine. The partner reports that "For every sip of scotch we took, she ordered another glass of red wine, and gulped it down. After the fourth glass, we started to get nervous."

She's clearly getting tipsy, but she doesn't stop drinking. The partner gently suggests that she stay at an airport hotel overnight, and take a flight home in the morning. She waves him off, insisting that she's fine. He reluctantly drives her to the airport. On the way, she yaks in his car. He insists that she stay in a hotel overnight, but she still refuses. He reluctantly loads her onto the plane, after she assures him she has a ride home at the other end.

The following day, he calls her to make sure that she got home all right. She says she did. After a little more conversation, the partner realizes: *She has no recollection of what happened the night before.*

* * * CAREER LIMITING MOVE * * *

Summer associate at a firm function at an Italian restaurant. He is sitting next to a partner at the firm and the partner's wife. He has too much red wine, and winds up whispering sweet nothings into the partner's wife's ear.

7. TIME TO CHOW!

A. WHICH IS MY BREAD PLATE? WHICH IS MY WATER GLASS?

This used to trip me up all the time. I'd sit down with people, we'd grab the bread plate we thought was ours—and someone would wind up without a plate while somebody on the other side of the table had two.

But I'm smarter now because of Sharon Abrahams. As she advises, the rule is, "Your bread plate is on your left, and your water glass is on your right." You can remember it with this: **Refreshment on the right, Loaf on the left.**

B. MUCH ADO ABOUT BREAD . . .

OK, I said you couldn't eat with your hands. But you'd look like a major dork if you used a knife and fork to eat a dinner roll.

Vanderbilt's Angela Chapman advises that you break off a bite-sized piece with your fingers, eat it, break off another one, and so on.

What if the bread arrives in a loaf, instead of individual rolls? You can't tear the loaf apart with your hands. You're not Cro Magnon Man. You're *civilized*. Instead, "Use the napkin that comes with the loaf to hold the loaf down with one hand," says Sharon Abrahams, "and cut off your slice." If the bread doesn't come with a napkin—you know, like at Outback Steakhouse—immediately ask the waiter to bring you one.

C. DON'T SALT YOUR FOOD BEFORE YOU TASTE IT

Supposedly it shows that you jump to conclusions. I find that hard to believe, but that's what experts on these things say.

D. CUTTING UP YOUR MEAT. DON'T MINCE THE WHOLE MEAL BEFORE YOU TAKE A BITE

Angela Chapman recommends that if you eat the American way, with your fork in your right and the knife in your left (as opposed to the European way, which is the reverse), you don't cut up a whole steak with your fork in your left hand before you transfer the fork to your right hand to eat. "You cut off one bite at a time, eat it, and then cut off the next one." It'll take you a little longer to eat, but that's probably better for your digestion anyway!

E. IT'S NOT A BIB, IT'S A NAPKIN. IT GOES IN YOUR LAP

F. IF MY DESSERT COMES IN A CHOCOLATE CUP, CAN I EAT THE CUP?

Of course. That's the best part! Otherwise they might as well serve your chocolate mousse in a baggie. Sharon Abrahams says that you should "Hold down the cup with one utensil and break it with another. If you don't hold it down, it'll fly! Then you stick the bites of cup to your spoon with a bit of the mousse."

8. THROUGHOUT THE MEAL: HOW TO SHOW PEOPLE YOU WERE RAISED IN A HOUSE WITH A TABLE, NOT A TROUGH

A. FOR EVERY COURSE, WAIT UNTIL EVERYONE IS SERVED BEFORE YOU DIG IN

If your dish arrives while someone else is waiting for theirs, don't strap on the feed bag just yet. Sit tight. It's up to the person (or people) still waiting to fire the starter's pistol and give you permission to begin. Don't chow until you get the green light from them.

B. No "Boarding House Reaches"—If You Want Something That's Not in Front of You, Ask That It Be Passed to You

A lawyer at one firm talked about being at lunch with a colleague who "reached across my plate for the butter. I could have bitten him, his arm was so close to my face. Even worse, he dropped his sleeve in my dish!"

C. Silverware—You Work Your Way From the Outside In

No matter how many forks, knives, and spoons are placed in front of you, the rule is always the same: the cutlery at the outside goes first, and you work your way inward, toward the plate, with every course. If you have any questions about which fork goes with what, discreetly ask the waiter.

* * * SMART HUMAN TRICK* * *

Associate at a very large firm in Washington, D.C. She is at dinner at a very fancy restaurant with partners and clients. She has eighteen pieces of cutlery in her place setting. *Eighteen*. She surreptitiously calls over the waiter, and says, "What the heck do I do with this?" as she gestures toward the cutlery. The waiter smiles, and says, "Barbara Bush asks the same thing."

D. No "Wandering Forks"

One lawyer told me about a lunch she'd had with the managing partner of her firm and a few other associates. "We all get our meals, and the next thing you know, the managing partner says, 'Hey yours looks good!' and stabs a piece of chicken on my plate. I had *no* idea how to react!"

E. No "Train Wreck in a Tunnel." If There's Food in Your Mouth, Your Lips Should Be Closed

As Sharon Abrahams says, "Chewing with your mouth open is OK if you're three years old and you have a stuffed nose. Otherwise, it's not OK." She adds that like much of good manners, "It's just common sense. If you talk with your mouth full, you can choke."

* * * CAREER LIMITING MOVE AND A SMART HUMAN TRICK ... * * *

Summer clerk at a large firm. He's brilliant, #1 in his law school class. At firm cocktail parties, he chews with his mouth open and spits partially-masticated bits of food at people. The managing partner calls in the recruiting coordinator and says, "We can't hire this guy. He's socially unacceptable." The recruiting coordinator gently raises the issue with the clerk, who takes it well. He goes out to "practice" dinners with friends, asking them to critique his manners. He cleans up his act, and winds up with an offer.

F. DON'T CHEW THE ICE

It's annoying, and besides it's supposed to show that you're sexually frustrated.

G. IF YOU'RE NOT SURE WHETHER THE OLIVES HAVE PITS, DON'T EAT THEM

Technically, you could discreetly spit the pit into your napkin. But you're better off not going there at all.

H. IF YOU'VE USED A FORK OR KNIFE, IT NEVER GOES BACK ON THE TABLE—ONLY ONTO THE PLATE

Sometimes you'll only be given one knife, and you use it for your salad. You'll need a knife for your main dish. What do you do? Don't put it back on the table, and for gosh sakes don't wipe it off with your napkin. Instead, just ask the waiter for another one.

I. NO ELBOWS ON THE TABLE

It looks bad. Really.

J. DON'T THROW YOUR WEIGHT AROUND WITH THE HELP. IT'LL MAKE YOU LOOK BAD

* * * CAREER LIMITING MOVE * * *

Summer associate sits in a restaurant with other summer clerks, attorneys and members of the Recruiting Department. He is extremely rude and demanding to the waiter. The incident is discussed extensively at the Employment Committee meeting when offer decisions are being made.

* * * CAREER LIMITING MOVE * * *

Summer clerk, dining with other summer clerks and two partners at a fancy restaurant. One of the partners, the managing partner of the firm, is getting flustered trying to attract the waiter's attention. The waiter is standing at a wait station some distance away.

The summer clerk stands up . . . and throws his fork at the waiter.

K. DISCUSSION TABOOS

Pop culture: Movies, best-selling books, all fine. Current events are fine. People tell you to avoid sex and politics—often wrapped up in the same headline!—but that creates too much of a conversational minefield. Just remember that if a controversial topic comes up and you disagree with your dining partner(s), it's not time for a throwdown. View it as an opportunity to learn how other people think. Don't try to convince them they're wrong . . . any more than they'll be able to convince *you.* Just say something like, "How interesting," "I see your point" (you *see* it, you don't necessarily *agree* with it), "You've given me something to think about"—those all get you off the hook gracefully.

Gross stories of any kind are also off-limits. This isn't the time to discuss that surgery special you saw on *The Discovery Channel,* or the road kill cookbook you just heard about—or anything disgusting you've ever eaten. When you're eating with your friends, heck, anything's fair game. But these are *interview* meals we're talking about, and you have to rein in your conversation topics accordingly.

* * * CAREER LIMITING MOVE * * *

Summer clerk at a large New York law firm, eating dinner with two other clerks and associates. "One of the other clerks starts talking about something called 'Wiggle fish' while we're looking at the menus. Someone asks him what it is, and he says, 'It's these little fish, and they're alive when you put them in your mouth. That's why they call them 'wiggle fish.' They don't die until you bite down on them.' I could see from the looks on the faces of the associates that they were grossed out. But the other clerk didn't notice. He goes on, 'That's *nothing.* I saw this movie 'Faces of Death,' where people are eating live monkey brains. They clamp this monkey's head through a hole in the middle of the table ...' I look over at the two associates. They're looking at this guy as though they're thinking, 'Have you lost your *mind?*' "

1. BALANCING DINING AND TALKING

A law student once asked me a great question about talking during interview meals. She said, "I never know what to do. I obviously can't eat when *I'm* talking or asking a question. But at the same time, I feel really awkward eating while the interviewer is talking. It seems rude to me. But if I don't eat when *I'm* talking and I don't eat when *they're* talking—when do I get to eat?"

Good question! Angela Chapman, who teaches etiquette dinners for law students, advises you to "Ask your question, take a small bite, and eat quickly as the interviewer answers." Wendy Werner adds, "You should plan on having at least a snack ahead of time. Don't plan on finishing your meal at the interview. The interview is the important part, not the meal."

M. IF YOU HAVE TO USE THE REST ROOM, SAY "EXCUSE ME"—AND THAT'S IT. YOU DON'T NEED TO ADD, "I'VE GOT TO DRAIN THE LIZARD," OR "I'VE GOT TO DROP THE KIDS OFF AT THE POOL"

Trust me. If you get up from the table in the middle of a meal and say, "Excuse me," nobody's going to think you had a sudden urge to juggle. You don't have to announce where you're going any more than you have to be specific about what you're going to do in there.

And especially if you don't know your fellow diners really well, avoid cute euphemisms. Remember Robert Wagner in *Austin Powers,* where he plays Dr. Evil's underling Number Two, and he's sitting in a casino at a blackjack table. He gets up and says, "Excuse me, I've got to go to the little boys' room." That was *supposed* to be funny. You don't want that image with employers!

Sharon Abrahams points out that it's much more polite if you hit the john before you sit down. If you do have to excuse yourself during the meal, "Leave your napkin on your chair if you're coming back, and on the table if it's at the end of the meal and you won't be returning to the table."

N. IF THERE ARE MEDICATIONS YOU HAVE TO TAKE IMMEDIATELY PRECEDING (OR WITH) MEALS, EXCUSE YOURSELF AND TAKE YOUR MEDS IN THE RESTROOM

* * * CAREER LIMITING MOVE * * *

Hiring partner at a medium-sized Chicago firm, commenting on an interview meal with a law student: "He took out this baggie with about a dozen kinds of pills in it. All different colors and sizes. He lined them up in front of him on his placemat, and he took them one by one. We were curious. Vitamins? Anti-psychotic medication? It was very distracting."

8. "CAN I HAVE A DOGGY BAG?" WHAT TO DO WHEN YOU'RE DONE EATING

A. WHEN YOU'RE DONE, PUT YOUR SILVERWARE SIDE BY SIDE ON YOUR PLATE TO INDICATE YOU'VE FINISHED. DON'T CRISSCROSS IT ON THE PLATE

* * * EMBARRASSING MOMENT ... * * *

Junior associate, on a business trip to London. She dines alone at a fine restaurant. Shortly after she begins to eat her entrée, she gets up to go to the restroom, leaving her knife and fork side by side on her nearly-full plate. She comes back to find her dinner cleared away. Because her cutlery was in the "all done" position, the waiter thought she was finished.

B. NO DOGGY BAGS. DARN!

I'm not suggesting that you clean your plate. At a lot of restaurants, the portions look like something Fred Flintstone would eat. But as the saying goes, you can't take it with you. It doesn't look professional.

* * * CAREER LIMITING MOVE * * *

Student at a call-back interview that involves a dinner. The portions are large and neither the student nor the lawyers finish their meals. As one of the lawyers reports, "I didn't really think anything of it when she asked for a doggy bag. I remember being a broke law student. But then she turns to me, points at the half-eaten chicken on my plate, says, 'Are you going to eat that?' and when I say no, she *picks up the chicken from my plate and puts it in her doggy bag!*"

c. THANK YOUR HOST!

Gratefulness is a huge positive. At the end of the meal, *always* remember to thank your host. If they're escorting you back to the firm after the meal, thank them again before you part company.

9. DISASTER STRIKES! WHAT TO DO WHEN SOMETHING GOES WRONG AT A MEAL

I won't go into the full panoply of interview meal disasters I've heard about. I'll just say that you wouldn't be the first person to perform the Heimlich maneuver on your interviewer/dining partner.

Here's how to handle the four most common dining disasters:

a. "EWW! I TOOKA A BITE, AND IT'S *DISGUSTING*"

Remember the movie *Big*, where Tom Hanks is a little boy in a grown man's body? He goes to a formal do, and tries caviar for the first time. He makes the "yuk!" face, grabs a napkin, and starts trying to zamboni the caviar off his tongue.

At an interview meal—don't do that. If you take a bite and it's gross, Sharon Abrahams says that "There are two rules. If it's something inedible, like bone, gristle, or a hunk of fat—you discreetly spit it into your napkin, and ask the waiter for a new napkin. If you don't like it, tough noogies." Swallow it quickly and chase it down with some water or a bite of bread to get rid of the taste.

A lawyer told me about an interview meal where the law student ordered a steak, and "obviously it wasn't the best steak in the world. I say 'obviously,' because the student kept finding gristle. He would masticate it for a moment, and then remove it from his mouth with his fingers and deposit it on a growing pile on the side of his plate. It was so disgusting, I couldn't pay attention to what he was saying."

b. "I DROPPED MY FORK!"

Easy. If you drop a piece of cutlery, just ask for another one. You never pick it up. And I mean you never *ever* pick it up, wipe it off, and continue eating with it. It's a lot quicker, but it's simply not done!

Not as though any of us have ever eaten anything off the floor. Heaven forbid. You're at home, the apple slips out of your hand, and you pick it up, wipe it on your shirt, and eat it. Right?

Pardon me while I digress. Every parent knows the five-second rule. You've heard it: If it's been on the floor less than five seconds, it's still edible. I remember once when my little niece Emily was three years old, and my brother Keir, sister-in-law Ellie, and Emmy and I were at the zoo. Toward the end of the afternoon, Emmy was at the end of her little string. She was whining for ice cream. Keir bought her a cone, just as the vendor was closing up shop. As Keir wheeled her away from the ice cream stand, she took one lick of the cone, and the scoop of ice cream went splat on the ground near her stroller. She started to scream. Keir looked around to make sure no one was watching, and made a snap judgment: he reached down and scooped up the ice cream with his hand. *From the ground. At the zoo.* And plopped it back into Emmy's cone. She happily finished it off.

Sorry. I just had to tell you that story. But the message for you is: At an interview meal, anything that hits the mat is off-limits!

c. "I Got Food Stuck in My Teeth" ... Or "The Lawyer Got Food Stuck in His/Her Teeth"

If it's food stuck in *your* teeth, Dorris Smith advises you "Not to draw attention to it." Excuse yourself, go to the restroom, and take care of it.

If the food is stuck in your dining partner's teeth, "You can't say anything about it," says Dorris Smith. "Just hope that it goes away." You can't say anything without potentially embarrassing the other person, so don't mention it.

d. "Oops! I Spilled It!"

Sharon Abrahams advises that if you spill something on yourself, you hail the waiter, ask for club soda, and excuse yourself to go to the restroom and wipe off your clothes.

If you spill something on someone else, apologize profusely, hail the waiter for club soda, and offer to pay the dry cleaning bill—in fact, insist on it. *Don't*, however, try to dab the spill off their clothes yourself. The stories are legion about embarrassed summer clerks trying to dab the spilled Coke from a female associate's chest or a male associate's lap. In those cases, the cure is worse than the disease!

* * * EMBARRASSING MOMENT * * *

Female law student, at an interview lunch with three lawyers from a firm. As she reports, "The junior associate sitting next to me was very quiet. Everybody else at the table was chatting away, but this guy said virtually nothing. He was very shy.

"Toward the end of the meal, I knocked over my glass of ice water. It landed squarely in this poor guy's lap. I thought he was going to jump out of his skin. I was mortified. He seemed uncomfortable enough, without me dropping ice in his lap!

"He was very gracious about it. Everybody handed over their napkins, and the waiter brought more. I kept apologizing all the way back to the firm.

"I guess he accepted my apology. Now we're married."

M. DISASTER STRIKES—HANDLING INTERVIEW MISHAPS WITH APLOMB!

Face it—at some point along the interview trail, you're going to encounter a disaster. It happens to everybody. It's easy to fall into the trap of believing that when disaster strikes, your chance at a job is shot. Far from it! **What determines your "offer viability" is not the disaster itself,** *but what you do in response to it.*

Ironically, having a disaster occur may wind up being a plus, because it gives you a chance to show off how well you handle the unexpected. I've heard over and over again about interviews where the worst possible things happened, and students felt that by handling the situation with a cool head, they actually looked better to the employer—and wound up with an offer they didn't think they'd get otherwise!

Let's look at a few specific examples and outline the strategies for handling them:

1. WARDROBE MALFUNCTIONS

Interview wardrobe malfunctions typically occur *before* the interview. That is, you arrive missing an important outfit element—or the whole outfit! Some wardrobe mishaps I've heard about:

- The student whose interview suit was in his luggage. He arrived safe and sound at the interview destination wearing a T-shirt and shorts. His suit didn't arrive at all.
- The student who stopped for a quick breakfast on his way to an interview. His grape juice wound up on his shirt.

Wardrobe malfunctions are, ironically enough, the easiest kind of interview disaster to deal with. All you have to do is—with great confidence—explain to the interviewer what happened, and say "I would ordinarily be tempted to cancel an interview in a situation like this, but I wanted to talk to you so much—I hope you can overlook what I'm wearing!" Trust me—they'll easily be able to overlook your lack of formal attire. And they'll respect your confidence!

* * * SMART HUMAN TRICK * * *

Female law student has an on-campus interview scheduled with the Army JAG. She walks to school, carrying her suit on a hanger. She arrives at school *sans* blouse—it fell out somewhere on the way there. Her initial temptation is to cancel her on-campus interview with the Army JAG, but her Career Services Director talks her out of it, convincing her to go through with the interview with her suit discreetly buttoned up.

She walks into the interview, and tells the interviewer what happened. He is so impressed with the moxie she showed in going through with the interview that she gets a call back interview—in fact, she's the only one from her school who gets one!

If a wardrobe malfunction occurs during the interview—you pop a button, a zipper gives—again, laugh it off. "That's the last time I buy a shirt from a street vendor," something like that. If it results in something visibly embarrassing—for instance, you're a woman and the popped button reveals your bra—button up your jacket. If you have a non-buttoning jacket, put on your coat and button it (if you brought one), or excuse yourself and get a safety pin from Career Services (if it's an on-campus interview) or the lawyer's assistant/receptionist (if it's an off-campus interview). *Everybody* will sympathize with you.

If it's a wardrobe malfunction that you don't realize until after the interview—pretend it never happened. One poor student got out of an on-campus interview, ran into a friend, and said, "Dude! I just had the greatest interview!" to which the friend replied, "Really?" and pointed to his fly. The student looked down, and realized that his fly had been open the entire interview, and worse yet, his shirt-tail was sticking out! But honestly: what can you do in that situation? The interviewer is unlikely to notice any wardrobe malfunction you have, and even if (s)he does, you'll be judged on how the conversation went. If you prepare for and conduct the interview as we've discussed, you'll be fine. And you'll be able to joke about it with the interviewer later on . . . when you're colleagues!

2. "BODILY" MALFUNCTIONS

Sometimes your mind is perfectly prepared for the interview—but your body isn't. Elizabeth Workman advises that you do what you can to avoid problems; be sure to eat something before an interview, to avoid a growling stomach.

But sometimes your body sabotages you, no matter how well prepared you are. I've heard of students having all kinds of nervous reactions to interviews; the one I often talk about in Guerrilla Tactics seminars is the student who got into an elevator with a partner from a large, prestigious firm. On the way up to the office, she threw up on him.

Hey—it happens.

As is true of any interview calamity, your recovery is everything. Apologize to the interviewer, reschedule the interview if necessary, make light of it—and you'll be fine!

* * * SMART HUMAN TRICK * * *

Female law student, in an interview with a partner from a law firm. As she reports, "The interview was going fine, when all of a sudden, I *farted*. And not a SBD (silent but deadly) one, either. It was loud and unmistakable, and it really stank up the room. Since there were only two of us in the room, I couldn't pretend it wasn't me. To make matters even worse, I momentarily forgot where I was, and said what everybody in my family says when they fart: 'Oops! Thunder on the poop deck!' The interviewer stared at me for a second, and I must have looked horrified. Then for whatever reason we both burst out laughing. Thank God by the time we finished laughing the smell was pretty much gone.

"I have to tell you, from that point on the interview actually went a whole lot better. I'd never recommend farting as a way to break the ice—but it worked for me!"

* * * SMART HUMAN TRICK * * *

Female law student, in an on-campus interview with a prestigious firm. She just got over an illness, and she feels fine. But apparently not *perfectly* fine, because during the interview, she suddenly ralphs and passes out.

Needless to say, the interview is over.

Heartbroken, she goes to her Career Services Director for advice. She says that she called her doctor, and asked what might have happened. The doctor explained, "Oh, that's a fairly common reaction to your medication. I guess I should have mentioned it."

No kidding.

The Career Services Director suggests that she write to the interviewer, explain what happened, and ask for another interview. She crafts a letter that begins:

"You will undoubtedly remember me, and our interview ..."

She goes on to explain about the medication. She apologizes and asks for another interview.

A few days later, the interviewer calls and invites her into the firm's office for an interview.

She winds up with an offer.

* * * CAREER LIMITING MOVE * * *

Female student, on-campus interview at a Texas law school. She belches and makes a face. She apologizes, "Sorry about that" ...

... but unfortunately, she doesn't leave it there. She goes on to say, "*That* was disgusting. You ever burp and get a bit of vomit in the back of your throat?" She goes on, "What would you call that? A 'vurp'? A 'bomit'?"

The interviewer reflects, "Not that it wasn't interesting in a disgusting kind of way, but in a *job* interview? She's got twenty minutes to talk with me and she's spending it talking about vomit!"

3. Meal Malfunctions

Drinking too much. Spilling something on one of the interviewers. Putting something in your mouth that turns out to be disgusting. Eating something and having a severe allergic reaction. There are a bunch of meal malfunctions that can occur—and I discussed them in Topic L, above, on interview meals.

4.   NO QUESTIONS FROM THE INTERVIEWER

It's not at all unusual to find yourself in an interview where the interviewer spends the entire time talking. Sometimes the interviewer will be so convinced that you won't know anything about the employer that they'll spend the whole time describing it to you. Maybe they'll talk about a hobby or an experience they've had and that takes up your entire interview slot. One interviewer spent an entire interview telling a law student about her wedding plans. Maybe the interviewer has predetermined that they're going to call you back (or *not* call you back) regardless of what you say, so they don't give you the chance to say anything at all.

No matter why it happens, you've *got* to squeeze a word in edgewise during the interview! Here's how to do it:

a.   If the interviewer is spending a lot of time describing the employer, at the first opportunity, politely interrupt the interviewer and say, "You know, I have a question about that," or, as Dorris Smith advises, "say 'You know, that very point reminds me of something I want to talk to you about ...'" and then take it from there, asking your questions. Trust me: the interviewer will be *delighted* that you took the initiative!

b.   If the interviewer spends the whole time talking about something else, listen politely for a few minutes, and when they come up for a breath, find a way to work the conversation back around to work. "It's so interesting hearing about your trip to Macchu Picchu. I'm wondering: was it difficult for you to rearrange your schedule at work while you were away?" Once you're back into the "work" groove, you'll have an opportunity to ask your questions—and get out your infomercial.

c.   Remember: If you only have time to ask one question during an interview, make it: "I'm curious—what do you look for in people you hire?" Work around to it as artfully as you can. And when you get the answer, respond, "That's great to hear. Here's what you need to know about me ..." and offer your infomercial, tailored, of course, to this particular employer!

d.   If you wind up at the end of the interviewer and you simply haven't had any luck trying to gently 'redirect' the conversation, ask the following question before you leave the interview: "It was so interesting hearing what you had to say, but I still have a bunch of questions for you. Is it all right if I call you, at your convenience?" You're at least alerting the interviewer to your interest in the employer, and gently pointing out that you didn't have much of a chance to talk.

I've never heard of a student asking this question who was told "No—you can't call me."

So—even if you don't get a chance to shine in the interview itself, you're keeping the door open to doing so, soon!

5.   THE INTERVIEW IS SUCH AN INTERESTING CONVERSATION ABOUT OTHER THINGS THAT WORK NEVER COMES UP

A law student in Vermont told me about a job fair interview she'd had. "The first thing the interviewer noticed on my resume was that I'd done Vista. He said, 'I always wanted to do that,' and he asked me a lot about it. Then we talked about Star Trek. Turns out we both love that. We never once talked about work! Is that a problem?"

Not really. It's only problematic in that the only skill you sold—albeit a valuable one—is your conversational skill.

That's not bad. Sometimes it would be just incredibly awkward and off-putting to bring up work if the interviewer is clearly enjoying talking with you about other things. Remember, the interviewer is the boss.

What you may want to try, at the end of the conversation, is to say something like, "It's been so interesting talking with you, but I realize we haven't discussed the work at all—or why you ought to hire me. Can I call you for ten minutes at your convenience so we can discuss that?" They may say, smiling, "Not necessary"—in which case, you've already nailed a favourable result—or they'll agree. Either way, you've made the point that you're enthusiastic and qualified!

6.   TOO MANY QUESTIONS FROM THE INTERVIEWER

Maybe you feel like you're constantly on the hot seat, with the interviewer firing question after question at you. It's exhausting and intimidating. You're sure you're going to say something wrong, the questions are coming so thick and fast. What do you do?

Easy. At the end of one of your answers, before the interviewer has a chance to fire *another* question at you, ask the interviewer an open-ended question. "That's pretty much what I did when I worked for Attorney so-and-so. I'm curious: I know your firm does a lot of litigation work. Can you tell me what you enjoy most about it/how you chose it/how it compares to what you expected?"

If you finish one of your own answers with a question in return—one that requires more than a "yes" or "no" answer—you've taken yourself off the hot seat. In addition, you've done what you can to turn the interview into a conversation. And that's the gold standard you're aiming for!

7.   THE INTERVIEWER CONTINUALLY ASKS YOU, "ANY MORE QUESTIONS? ANY MORE QUESTIONS?"

This is a curious kind of stress. You may feel as though you run through all of the questions we discussed earlier in this chapter, and you panic trying to think of others. On top of that, you might not have gotten the chance to say *anything* about yourself—and the interviewer has to hear good things about you to motivate them to hire you!

There are two ways to handle the situation when you get to the end of your questions. You can ask either: "What else can I tell you about myself?" or you can say, "I really want to work with you, and I'm sure I will think of other things to ask. May I call you when I think of them?" Either way, you're off the hook!

8.   THE INTERVIEWER IS CONSTANTLY INTERRUPTED BY PHONE CALLS

It's going to happen: despite an employer's best intentions, you'll wind up interviewing with someone who's in the middle of something big. They get interrupted every few minutes by phone calls, to the extent that it's impossible for them to focus on you.

Your initial reaction will probably be, "How rude!" But it doesn't help you to manifest that reaction in your words or your demeanor. Don't betray your irritation. Instead, the best way to handle it is to state, *politely*, "This is obviously a very busy time for you. Would you like to reschedule to a time when you'll be less busy? Or should I be talking to someone else in the office?" That way, you're giving them an out—while at the same time pointing out, very discreetly, that you're not getting the attention you need in order to be considered for a job!

9.   THE INTERVIEWER IS REALLY OBNOXIOUS

Man, I think I've heard them all. Interviewers who ask incredibly rude questions (one interviewer asked an ex-soldier: "So—what's it like to kill people?"). Interviewers who can't take their eyes off your chest (assuming you're a woman, and the interviewer is a man). Interviewers who pick their nose while you're talking. *Really*.

Here's what you have to do:

- The interviewer may be a jerk—or they *may* be goading you to see if you can take it. Either way, your strategy is the same: **Just take a deep breath, ignore the aggressive "sting," and answer the question as though it had been asked politely.**

  A student in Colorado told me about an interview with a lawyer who said, "Well, since you have all of these activities on your resume but not your GPA, I assume you're not in the top 5% of the class." OK—not the nicest way to ask, but it's really just the age-old grades question in a nasty guise. You respond with, "You're right. Here's why you should hire me anyway . . ."

  A student in South Carolina, an African–American, had an interview where the interviewer asked him, "How do you feel about the Confederate flag issue?" Gee–I wonder.

  Another student at Duquesne University in Pittsburgh, was sneeringly asked by an employer, "Doo-kweens," (it's pronounced 'Do-kane'). "Is that a tier one school?"

No matter what the interviewer asks, it's never the right time for Interview Smackdown. Instead, answer calmly. Make your case as though you were representing a client in court. Remember: If someone's trying to get your goat ... don't give it to them!

- If the interviewer isn't just trying to bait you and they really are a jerk, remind yourself that even though the interviewer is obnoxious, the other people in the office aren't necessarily equally rude. While it's true that employers typically try to send their most personable people to interview, sometimes they have to make do with whoever's available. Maybe the employer just doesn't realize how obnoxious the interviewer *is*. No matter what the explanation—don't judge the entire employer by the interviewer alone!

- Remember that nothing anyone says, let alone an interviewer, is a reflection on you. If someone is rude or obnoxious or has disgusting personal habits, say to yourself, "Isn't it a shame that this person has to go through life being ..." and fill in the blank with whatever unfortunate trait they bring to the table.

- If you're routinely asked an obnoxious question because of something in your background, come up with a flip answer for it. For instance, the ex-soldier student who was asked "What's it like to kill people?" responded, "Don't tempt me." Smiling, of course!

- If the interviewer's words or behavior suggest that they've written you off, see #12, below.

- If the interviewer's behaviour is truly over the top, don't take it on yourself to lecture them. Instead, if the interview was planned through your school, report the behaviour to your Career Services Director, who will handle it discreetly with the employer on your behalf.

  If it was an interview you set up for yourself, contact someone else in the firm, and be as discreet as possible as you describe the behaviour, couching it in terms of how it reflects on the firm. "I'm horrified to have to tell you this, but I'm interested in your firm and I'm sure you want to show it off at its best in interviews with students. Maybe nobody's ever told you, but ..." *attorney x mines for boogers in interviews*. If you embed your experience within general positive statements about the employer and concern for their reputation, your discretion will be appreciated—as well as your initiative!

10. THE INTERVIEWER SAYS NEGATIVE THINGS ABOUT THE EMPLOYER

Ironic, isn't it? The employer handpicks someone to put the best face on the work, and they come out and say, "Save yourself! Don't take this job!"

I've heard all kinds of amazing disses come from interviewer's mouths. "Don't work here. It's boring and you work around the clock. It's not worth it."

There are two things to remember if the interviewer takes this tack. **First, the fact that they're miserable might not mean you'll be miserable there, as well.** If they don't like the hours, it could be that they're at a point in their lives where they want to ratchet back. You, on the other hand, might feel you're willing to put in the hours to launch your career. Or maybe they didn't do the research they *should* have done up front, to make sure that they chose the right job. It might not be the right "fit" for them, but the job itself is fine.

You can ask questions that will probe this issue. Say things something like, "I'm sorry to hear that. I'm curious: Did you feel this way when you started? What do you wish you'd asked in interviews when you were considering X firm? What's changed about it, if anything? Looking back, what other choice would you have made?" And, if you ask it gently, "Why are you still there?" and "What do you think you'll do next?"

The other thing to remember is that when an interviewer tells you anything negative, take it very, very seriously. The mere fact that this is the person who's supposed to put the *best* face on the work suggests that anything less-than-positive that they say merits attention. You have several options: You can be blunt with Career Services about the negatives, and ask them straight out about whether the comments reflect what the job is like or whether it's just an issue with the interviewer.

By way of mentioning it to anyone other than Career Services, you've got to be more careful—because if you're interested in the employer, you don't want them to shoot the messenger! Take the issue the interviewer's negative comments create, and address it with other people who work there, or other people who are familiar with the employer. For instance, in an on-campus interview let's say you hear that the office is a "sweatshop," you can always ask other people there, "What's a typical day like for you?" "Do you socialize with your colleagues?" "If there's anything you could change about your job, what would it be?" If the original malcontent's views reflect the employer accurately, you'll get it from other people there, as well!

11. YOU MAKE A CONVERSATIONAL *FAUX PAS*

A few years ago, on a night when I couldn't sleep, I was blearily watching ESPN. It was around two in the morning and the announcer— I think it was Steve Levy—was reading the college football injury report. He got to one quarterback, and obviously meant to say that this guy was out with a bulging disk in his neck.

What came out, however, was "a bulging *dick* in his neck."

At first, I thought I was hearing things. But then I heard the camera crew howling with laughter in the background. Levy himself, however, was magnificent. If you didn't hear what he'd said, you'd never have realized from his reaction that he said it.

The fact is, mistakes happen. Things are going along swimmingly, and then you say something that brings the interview crashing down in shards around you. Depending on the nature of the faux pas, you may be able to recover very quickly.

What you want to do is to apologize immediately. Express your mortification, and ask the interviewer if they'd like to continue with the interview. If not, leave, and write a note to the interviewer *immediately* reiterating your mortification and assuring them you learned from your mistake. Remember: you're going to be in the same legal community in all likelihood, and you want to conduct "damage control" with people whenever possible!

By way of an example, there was one student who told me about an awful situation she'd just encountered in an interview. She was interviewing with a guy from a firm she really wanted to join, and the interview was going really well. Then he asked, "I see you go to Curly Joe Law School. Are you familiar with Professor Creampie?" The student responded, "Sure. Everybody knows her. You'd think she might want to shower occasionally." The interviewer's demeanor turned stony as he responded, "She's my wife."

Gulp.

The student said, "Even though the interview went on for a few minutes after that, it was clearly *over* for all intents and purposes. What should I do?" I repeated to her advice I'd heard: "Send a note expressing your embarrassment over what you said, and make your apology sincere. But also point out that you learned a very valuable lesson about being discreet and professional, and that you're sorry you had to learn it this way—but you're glad you learned it now." She did this, and reported back to me that when she subsequently saw the interviewer at an alumni event, he was—if not warm—at least cordial.

No matter what it is that you accidentally say in interviews, remember that life is a game of second chances. You'll have plenty of opportunities to redeem yourself, and no comment is a career killer. Apologize, and move on. You'll be fine!

12. THE INTERVIEW SEEMS TO BE GOING VERY, VERY BADLY

You're not going to hit it off with *everybody,* you know. No matter how skilled you are at *les bons mots*, at some point you'll be in an interview where the words between you and the interview will emerge from your mouths, hang suspended in mid-air, and crash to the ground. You just don't mesh. Maybe the interviewer has a bad attitude. Maybe they're angry about something. Maybe their spouse just left them. Maybe they just lost a big case. Maybe you remind them of someone they can't stand. Or maybe they're mad that they have to interview you at all. Or they think your credentials are so bad that it's a waste of time interviewing you. There could be ten thousand reasons why an interview might go badly—thank goodness it doesn't happen very often! But what should you do when it does?

For a start, don't blame yourself. As that list suggests, most reasons an interview goes south have nothing at all to do with you. People orbit in their own universes, and you're on the fringe. So the vast likelihood is that it's not you.

On top of that, don't jump to the conclusion that the interview is going as badly as you think it is. Some interviewers are just not skilled conversationalists. Maybe they're not "natural smilers." I can't tell you how many times I've given the *Guerrilla Tactics* seminar at law schools, and I've gazed out into the audience at certain students who just look like they'd rather bathe in boiling oil than hear one more word I say. Then when I'm done, they bound up to the stage, all smiles, praising the seminar and asking all kinds of questions. So sometimes it's just hard to tell. Don't jump to the conclusion that things aren't going well ...

... until you're sure. Then what? *Address it outright.* Maybe the interviewer is snarling questions at you, making flip comments about your credentials or your chances with the firm, or their facial expression just makes it perfectly obvious that they don't want to be talking to you. In that instance, say to them, "This interview obviously isn't going well. Is there something I could do to make a difference?" I call that the "Allen charge" question, the one that's designed to get an immediate result.

One of two things will happen. It's possible that the interviewer will say, "No," and then you smile, get up, and say, "Thank you for your time," and leave graciously. After all, if the interviewer has obviously, undeniably taken your candidacy off the table, why should you suffer the indignity of sitting there and being insulted? Asking straight out if it's worth going on with the interview is the straight-up and self-respectful thing to do!

But it's much more likely that you'll shock the interviewer into realizing that they're coming across less-than-positively, and they'll say, "Actually, I don't feel that way at all," or "I'm sorry—I'm distracted because ..." Either way, you'll impress the interviewer with your confidence, because it takes some serious cojones to ask a question like that straight out!

* * * SMART HUMAN TRICK * * *

Law student has a Ph.D. in etymology—the study of bugs, basically. As she reports, "My thesis was about how bugs with larger fat deposits seem to live longer than bugs without them. And the larger the fat deposits, the longer they live.

"As you can imagine, I worded my thesis very carefully on my resume, concerned that I might offend any employer with a weight problem. You really couldn't tell looking at it exactly *what* I'd researched. But I thought the important thing was that I had a Ph.D. at all.

"So I go on an interview with a firm, and I walk into the attorney's office, and sitting there is one of the largest human beings I have ever seen. This guy must have weighed several hundred pounds. I was *mortified* that he was going to question me about my Ph.D.

"Of course he did exactly that. 'This Ph.D. thesis—*what* was your hypothesis?' I put it scientifically so that it still wasn't obvious, and tried to bring up other topics. But he wouldn't let it go.

"Finally, I confessed, 'I said that bugs with more fat live longer.'

"He said, 'If I were a bug, what would you say about me?'

"I blurted out, 'I'd say you'd live forever.'

"I sat there, frozen. After what seemed like an eternity, he burst out laughing. So did I. It turns out he had figured out ahead of time what my thesis was about, and he just wanted to hear me say it.

"After that, the interview was great. I wound up with an offer."

N.   I CAN'T BELIEVE THEY DID IT: INEXPLICABLE INTERVIEW BEHAVIOR BY LAW STUDENTS

Every interviewer has stories about strange behaviour by interviewees. Most of the stories I've heard are cautionary tales that I've included as "Career limiting moves" throughout this chapter. But once in a while, you hear a story about something an interviewee did, and there's no moral to the story. It's just weird. Although they aren't instructive, I knew you'd enjoy reading them, so here they are:

* * * YOU CAN'T MAKE THIS STUFF UP * * *

Law student at an on-campus interview. He's Irish. So is the interviewer. They get into an argument about who's more Irish. It dissolves into a shouting match, which only ends when the law student stands up, drops trou, turns around, bends over . . .

. . . and shows off the shamrock tattoo on his ass.

* * * YOU CAN'T MAKE THIS STUFF UP * * *

Second career student in a call-back interview at a large law firm in Texas. He's interviewing with a female attorney. He comments, "You have lovely hands." She thanks him, and starts to ask him a question. He interrupts, "No, really. Your hands are small and beautiful. They look like the hands of a Philippine prostitute."

She is too shocked to comment, and he blithely goes on, talking about how he used to work in the Philippines, and he had a house maid who also "put out."

* * * YOU CAN'T MAKE THIS STUFF UP * * *

Student is applying for an internship at a city attorney's office. He is asked on a form, "Have you ever been convicted of a crime?"

He checks off, "Yes," and in the description box, he writes "Mr. Meanie."

The attorneys can't figure this out, until they talk to him and realize he meant "misdemeanor."

* * * YOU CAN'T MAKE THIS STUFF UP * * *

Student waiting for a call-back interview in the reception area at a firm. Out of the corner of her eye the receptionist notices him take out a nail clipper and start to clip his nails. He soon puts down the clippers, and starts biting his nails—and spitting the remnants onto the couch.

* * * YOU CAN'T MAKE THIS STUFF UP * * *

During a call-back interview, a student tells his first interviewer what a good time he had the night before, saying he was "out partying all night."

"I guess he had a really great time," comments the interviewer, "Because while I was talking, he fell asleep. I went back to work, and he slept until the recruiting coordinator came looking for him."

* * * YOU CAN'T MAKE THIS STUFF UP * * *

Student goes on a call-back interview with a law firm. The day goes great and he's really pumped when he leaves. As he's racing out of the building parking lot, he beats another car to the exit, and flips the other driver the bird.

As he does so, he notices who he's flipping off . . . it's the managing partner at the law firm where he just interviewed.

* * * YOU CAN'T MAKE THIS STUFF UP * * *

On-campus interview. Right after the student shakes hands with the interviewer, he asks the interviewer for a business card. The interviewer hands it over . . .

. . . and the student *licks* it. "Just wanted to see if it's engraved. Sweet!" he says.

* * * YOU CAN'T MAKE THIS STUFF UP * * *

Female law student, has a full day's worth of call-back interviews with a medium-sized law firm. She spends the day progressing up the "seniority ladder," interviewing with more and more senior attorneys—until her final interview of the day, with the firm's managing partner.

He starts off the interview by spending a couple of minutes talking, and as he does so, the student gets up—and starts jogging in place.

The managing partner's voice gradually trails off as he watches her, until he finally says, "What on Earth are you doing?"

She responds: "I've been sitting all day. I can't take it any more.

"My ass is killing me."

* * * YOU CAN'T MAKE THIS STUFF UP * * *

Law student is scheduled to interview with the hiring partner at a medium-sized firm, at lunchtime. The interview's going to take place at the firm's offices, which are located next to a public park.

The student shows up on time, and walks in carrying a brown paper lunch bag. As the interview begins, the hiring partner assumes that the student has his lunch in the bag. After all, it *is* lunchtime. But fairly soon into the interview, the hiring partner notices something strange: *the bag is moving.* As the interview progresses, he expects the student to make a comment about what's in the bag. But the student doesn't do so. Instead, he talks breezily about his work experience and what he's doing in school.

The entire time, the partner can't think anything except, *What's in the damn bag?*

At the end of the interview, the partner's curiosity overcomes him, and he asks: "I give up. What's in the bag?"

The student proceeds to open the bag calmly . . . and pull out a garter snake!

As the partner explains, "It seems that he had intended to bring his lunch to the interview, but as he was walking through the park, he spotted this snake. He took his lunch out of the bag and threw it away, and for some reason I'll never know, he decided to catch the snake . . . and bring it with him."

"I kind of liked the guy, but we've got our quota of weirdos here already."

O. INTERVIEWERS HALL OF SHAME.

In this chapter, I've focused largely on things students do in interviews. And there's a good reason for that: as my favourite radio shrink, Dr. Joy Brown, always says, the only behavior you can control is your own. You can't do anything about the interviewer.

That doesn't mean that interviewers don't do things that are bad or inappropriate or just plain weird. They do. Here are some of my favourite stories about just such behavior!

* * * YOU CAN'T MAKE THIS STUFF UP * * *

Law student shows up for an on-campus interview, and walks into the interview room expecting to see one interviewer. Instead, there are two. He's not taken aback, although he notices that "The seating is kind of weird. There's one lawyer sitting at the table across from the interviewee's chair. And the other guy is sitting back in the corner, right against the wall, like he was in a "time out" for being a bad boy or something. I go to introduce myself to the guy at the back, and the first guy says, 'Don't talk to him. Don't even look at him. Pretend he's not here. If you even look at him, the interview is over."

The student goes on to say, "I was completely weirded out. The natural thing to do when you're talking to two people is to look at both of them. It took every ounce of my self-control not to look at that other guy! I actually got a call back from these clowns, but I turned it down. If they played those kinds of mind games in the interview, I figured, what the heck are they going to do to me when I actually work there?"

* * * YOU CAN'T MAKE THIS STUFF UP * * *

Female law student in an interview with a litigator at a small firm.

"Are you willing to use your weapons in court?" he asks her.

She's puzzled, and asks for clarification. He says, "You know. Come on. Show a little leg, cleavage—your *weapons.*"

* * * YOU CAN'T MAKE THIS STUFF UP * * *

Call-back interview. A very attractive female law student is interviewing in a glassed-in conference room with a junior associate. She's facing a window; her back is to the hallway. She notices the associate looking over her shoulder and trying to stifle a laugh.

She turns just in time to see a junior associate shooting a moon.

* * * YOU CAN'T MAKE THIS STUFF UP * * *

Student interviewing for a law school administration job. It turns out that the administrator is a pole dancer at a strip club at night. She conducts the interview wearing her "evening clothes."

* * * YOU CAN'T MAKE THIS STUFF UP * * *

The disappearing interviewer ...

More than once, an interviewer has gotten up during an interview, said "Excuse me," left ... and never returned. One even said, "Excuse me, I've got to feed my meter," and never came back. In a panel interview, each lawyer in turn excused himself, saying "I've got to make a phone call," "I'll be right back" ... until the student was alone in the interview room.

* * * YOU CAN'T MAKE THIS STUFF UP * * *

Interviewer asks a student an open-ended question. As the student is giving his answer, the interviewer leans back, listens thoughtfully ... and starts picking his nose.

* * * YOU CAN'T MAKE THIS STUFF UP * * *

Call-back interview. Female student is invited to a cocktail party at a partner's house. She is talking with the partner, when he suddenly says, "I have to compliment you on your breasts. They're great." He turns and calls out, "Honey!"

His wife walks over, and he points to the student's chest, and says, "Check out her breasts. Aren't those the ones you want?"

The student reports, "It turns out she was going to get breast augmentation surgery, and they stood there calmly discussing how she ought to get a 'pair' like mine!"

* * * YOU CAN'T MAKE THIS STUFF UP * * *

Law student walks into an on-campus interview with an investment bank. The interviewer is sitting there, with a large pair of scissors on the table in front of him. The interviewer stands up, says his name without smiling, shakes hands with the interviewee, and after they both sit down ... the interviewer takes the scissors, reaches over, and calmly *snips the student's tie cleanly in half.* He says nothing. The student stares at him, waiting for some kind of reaction. Nothing. The student turns and walks out ...

... and sends the employer an invoice for the tie.

* * * YOU CAN'T MAKE THIS STUFF UP * * *

Law student goes to a firm for an interview, in October. The timing turns out to be relevant, because he is ushered into a conference room, where there are half a dozen attorneys facing him at a conference table. Sitting on the table near the "interview" chair is a pumpkin, and a knife. The student introduces himself, and the lead attorney looks at him and says, "Carve the pumpkin."

That's it. For the *entire interview.*

* * * YOU CAN'T MAKE THIS STUFF UP * * *

Student has a call-back interview with a federal agency. He is taken to lunch by one of the lawyers. Over lunch, the lawyer tells the student, "When I was a kid, my parents thought I was mentally retarded."

They walk back to the office. On the way, the interviewer says, "Excuse me, I gotta take a leak." He stops, unzips his fly, and pees on a wall.

* * * YOU CAN'T MAKE THIS STUFF UP * * *

Interviewer from a tax firm is scheduled for a day's worth of on-campus interviews at a Midwestern law school. Before the first interview begins, he gets a phone call telling him his wife has been in a car accident. Rather than cancel the interviews and/or reschedule or seek a replacement interviewer from his office, he carries out the interview schedule—but focuses exclusively on his wife's accident. He asks students questions like, "If I sue the other driver, what would my claim be?" "If they both ran a stop sign, who's liable?"

As one student reflected, "You couldn't help feeling sorry for him. I mean, his wife! But he shouldn't have been there. He was obviously so agitated he couldn't focus on us at all. He should have cancelled."

* * * YOU CAN'T MAKE THIS STUFF UP * * *

Female student, gets an interview with a local patent firm. Interview day turns out to be very snowy. Everything is closed. But because the student lives only half a mile from the firm, she walks there to leave a note, saying that she'd shown up.

It turns out that a senior partner is there after all. The student winds up with a long interview. During the interview, the student mentions that she's working on an article about a cutting-edge issue in intellectual property.

Two weeks later, the partner calls her and asks, "Can you bring a writing sample—that article you were working on?"

The student responds, "It's not even close to finished. I've got to check my sources, and—"

The partner cuts her off, and says, "That's OK. Just leave it here this afternoon."

Two days later, she gets a rejection from the firm.

* * * YOU CAN'T MAKE THIS STUFF UP * * *

Female law student. She responds to a job posting at school. The interviewer tells her to show up at 6 p.m. She says, "On their web site it said that the office closes at 5, so I thought that was a little strange."

She goes on the interview, and says, "It just got weirder and weirder. This guy had a stack of women's resumes, and for all the ones from my school, he'd pick up the resume, and say, 'What about her? What's she like?' "

She continues, "I come to find out, this guy isn't even a lawyer with the firm! He's a 3L from another law school in town who just happened to be clerking there. *The firm didn't know he was doing these interviews. They didn't even know about the job posting.*"

* * * YOU CAN'T MAKE THIS STUFF UP * * *

African–American female student, interviewing with a huge firm.

She asks, "What are you looking for in a new associate."

The interviewer answers: "A slave."

She shakes his hand and walks out.

* * * YOU CAN'T MAKE THIS STUFF UP * * *

Female law student interviewing with a male tax attorney, a partner in his firm, at his office. The attorney's office has a bathroom attached to it, with the door open.

At one point in the interview, the attorney asks the student, "Are you married?" She says "Yes," and he proceeds to rant about how his firm has had no luck hiring young married women, "They always say they're not going to have kids and then they do, and they go away on maternity leave and they never come back. It's a waste of time."

As if this wasn't bad enough, while he's raving on and on, he gets up from his desk, goes into the bathroom, stands in front of the toilet, and urinates ... *leaving the door open and talking the entire time.*

* * * YOU CAN'T MAKE THIS STUFF UP * * *

Female law student from a California school, on a call-back interview with a medium-sized Texas firm. One of the partners picks her up at the airport. To her consternation, he's crying. He explains that "Dave," the managing partner, "died today. Nobody's going to interview you. We're going to go to the country club. Everybody's there."

Because she doesn't have a car and she's pretty much at his mercy, she goes to the country club with him. There, several attorneys and their wives are gathered at a table, drinking and sobbing. The student sits quietly next to the partner who picked her up at the airport. After a little while, one of the attorneys stands up and says, "Let's go around the table and share our thoughts about Dave." The student is mortified as her "turn" approaches. At a complete loss for anything meaningful to say, she comments, "Judging from everything you've all said, Dave was clearly a wonderful guy ..."

She chokes out a few more comments, relieved when the attention turns to others at the table. Finally, after what seems like forever, the day is over, and the partner drives her back to the airport.

When he drops her off, he says, "I'm afraid you're not likely to get a job with us."

Shocked, she responds, "Why not?"

He answers earnestly, "You just didn't seem sincerely upset about Dave."

* * * YOU CAN'T MAKE THIS STUFF UP * * *

Student at a Midwestern law school. His first on-campus interview is with a prestigious West Coast firm. The student has a Middle Eastern name. Before the interview even starts, the student notices that on his resume the interviewer has written the word "No" next to his name.

It gets worse from there. The interviewer starts out by asking him, "Where are you from?" The student responds that he was born in Chicago, and the interviewer says, "No—where's your *family* from?" The student responds, "Iran," but goes on to reiterate that he was born in America and he is an American citizen.

The interviewer shakes his head and responds, "I'm not happy with your nuclear program." (This interview occurred at a time when the Iranian nuclear program was all over the news.) The student, increasingly uncomfortable, reiterates his "Americanness" and says "that nuclear program makes me nervous, too." The student asks the interviewer a question about the firm to change the subject, but the interviewer is having none of it. The interviewer says: "You know, you guys held my uncle hostage at the American Embassy."

After the interview (mercifully) ends, the student, dazed, goes to his Career Services Director, and says, "Is this normal? Can I expect this from every interview? Because if that's the case . . ."

She quickly reassures him that it's not just abnormal—it's never going to happen again. She calls the firm, reports the behavior . . . and needless to say, this particular lawyer's on-campus interviewing career is over!

* * * YOU CAN'T MAKE THIS STUFF UP * * *

Female student, in an interview with her dream employer. The interviewer asks her, "Tell me about yourself" and she goes into what she believes is a pithy, focused description of what she brings to the table. The interviewer apparently disagrees, because she looks over to notice that the interviewer is writing on her resume the words "Blah, Blah, Blah."

* * * YOU CAN'T MAKE THIS STUFF UP * * *

Law student attends a school that rents hotel suites nearby for on-campus interview season. A female law student reports, "I must admit that going to a hotel for a job interview kind of creeps me out in the first place. This one interviewer made it ten times worse. He answers the door, we shake hands, and it's only then that I notice the guy is wearing a shirt, tie . . . and boxer shorts! And he had on his socks, with those little sock suspenders."

"For a split second I was pretty sure I had the wrong room. But he knew who I was and seemed perfectly comfortable. I didn't know *what* to do. I went through with the interview but I was totally weirded out."

* * * YOU CAN'T MAKE THIS STUFF UP * * *

Male law student is the first interviewee of the day for an on-campus interviewer. He walks into the interview room, to find the interviewer sitting at a table, with a bowl of fresh apricots in front of him. The student naturally asks about the apricots, and the interviewer responds: "Oh, they're for you. Every time you say something stupid, you eat an apricot."

P.   THE JOB GODDESS'S COMMANDMENTS OF GREAT INTERVIEWING

1. Thou shalt prepare.
2. Thou shalt dress the part.
3. Thou shalt remember that the best interviews are conversations.
4. Thou shalt display thy best enthusiasm.
5. Thou shalt not lie.
6. Thou shalt ask questions that display thy research and enthusiasm.

7. Thou shalt have prepared answers for issues thou considers difficult.

8. Thou shalt remember that even the nicest people mayeth have a crappy day, and if they overwhelmeth you with meanness ... it's not you.

9. Thou shalt send thank you notes.

10. Thou shalt follow up.

Appendix A
Extreme Interview Makeover: Putting the Principles in This Chapter to the Test

We covered a lot of ground in this chapter. Let's see how they can radically change an interviewer's impression by doing a "makeover" of a crappy interview into a great one. Notice in each case that the student's credentials and experience are *identical* ... but the presentation is very different!

INTERVIEW #1: "BEFORE"

Interviewer: How are you today?

Interviewee: OK, I guess. Kind of nervous.

Interviewer: Do you know anything about our firm, Jekyll & Hyde?

Interviewee: Not really, Dude. Just what you put in your job posting.

Interviewer: Well, let me tell you about what we do. We have 25 attorneys. We do labor law—specifically, union-management negotiation and litigation.

Interviewee: No kidding?

Interviewer: Actually, it's even more specific than that. We only represent management, not unions. Would you have a problem going against unions?

Interviewee: Well ... in law school they're always talking about how everybody deserves representation, no matter how much you personally disagree with them. So, yeah, I guess I could do that.

Interviewer: I see from your resume that you don't mention your grades. How are you doing in school?

Interviewee: Well, um, like I'm not on Law Review, if that's what you mean.

Interviewer: What's your GPA?

Interviewee: I'm not sure exactly. Around, like, a 2.5.

Interviewer: Why haven't you done better?

Interviewee: I wish I knew. It's not like I didn't study. My professors were really unfair. And the competition at law school is really stiff.

Interviewer: I see that you clerked at Whipp, Lashe and Payne last summer. Did you get an offer from them?

Interviewee: If I did, I wouldn't be here!

Interviewer: What happened there?

Interviewee: I'm not sure. I think it was a personality clash. A lot of the lawyers I worked for didn't know what they wanted, so they couldn't appreciate the work I did.

Interviewer: Who else are you talking to?

Interviewee: Nobody. I've posted some resumes on-line and sent out a couple of mass mailers and I'm waiting for responses on them.

Interviewer: Where are you looking?

Interviewee: All over the place. I'll go anywhere to work. I'm not fussy.

Interviewer: What do you consider your greatest asset?

Interviewee: My people skills.

Interviewer: I see. Do you have any questions for me?

Interviewee: Not that I can think of. I think you've answered everything.

INTERVIEW #2: "AFTER"

Interviewer: How are you today?

Interviewee: Great, thanks. I've really been looking forward to talking with you.

Interviewer: Well, as you may know, we *were* going to post a job at your school next week. I was writing the ad when my partner, Ollie Holmes, stopped by and told me that he'd met you when he did a presentation at the bar association luncheon last week. He thought we ought to bring you in for an interview.

Interviewee: He made your practice sound really interesting. I couldn't wait to learn more about it. In fact, after his presentation, I got on-line and read the article you wrote in the State Bar Journal about negotiating benefits packages.

Interviewer: I guess I don't have to tell you what we do—representing management in negotiations with unions. You don't have a problem representing management, do you?

Interviewee: Absolutely not. I'd enjoy that. That's why I'm here.

Interviewer: I see from your resume that you don't mention your grades. How have you done in law school?

Interviewee: My GPA is 2.54. I know from talking to Mr. Holmes and others who've worked for you that you typically look for better grades than that. They also told me that labor law and trial tactics are the classes most closely related to what you do. I did great in both of those. I got an A-in Labor Law and an A in Trial Tactics. I was among the top four finalists in Moot Court. I like to think that I *am* really good at the skills you look for—and I'm willing to work hard to learn all of the things I *don't* know.

Interviewer: I see you clerked last summer for Whipp, Lash and Payne. Did you get an offer from them?

Interviewee: No, I didn't.

Interviewer: Why not?

Interviewee: Well, here's what happened. I worked on seven projects all summer. On the first two, I misunderstood exactly what the assigning attorneys were looking for. Frankly, I was afraid to ask questions because I was afraid of looking stupid. Needless to say, the research I did wasn't too useful to them, and they weren't very impressed with me. Fortunately, after those first two assignments, I read this great book, "What Law School Doesn't Teach You ... But You Really Need To Know," and I realized how stupid it was not to ask questions when I didn't have my assignments perfectly clear. After that, I made sure I corrected that mistake right away. All of the remaining projects I worked on went fine. In fact, all five of those attorneys have said they'd be willing to talk about my work, and I've written down their names and phone numbers for you. But those first two lawyers I worked for, they insisted I not get a permanent offer. That was a tough blow, but I learned an important lesson about making sure I know exactly what's expected of me.

Interviewer: If they had made you an offer, would you have taken it?

Interviewee: I would have considered it seriously, since they did something I like—litigation. That's what I like about your practice as well. Even if they'd made me an offer I would have interviewed with other employers as well, because I would want to make my first full-time job decision with my eyes open.

Interviewer: What are you doing now?

Interviewee: A number of things. I've been attending CLE's and bar association meetings on labor issues—as you know, that's where I met Mr. Holmes. Also, I've volunteered with the labor section of the local bar. In fact, I made a presentation last month at the labor section meeting. I interviewed negotiators for the Big Three auto makers, and made a presentation on what I learned. And to pay the bills, I've been waiting tables at Le Marmoset. If you've ever waited tables, you know there's no better way to hone your people skills than that!

Interviewer: I know what you mean. Do you have any questions for me?

Interviewee: Tons of them! For a start, I know you clerked for the state attorney general, specializing in economic crimes. What made you take a jump from doing that to practicing with Jekyll & Hyde?

. . .

Appendix B
Sample In-house Interview Evaluation Forms

Employers who regularly hire law students generally have evaluation forms for interviewers to fill out. As you can see, the criteria reflect many of the principles we discussed in this chapter!

(Samples courtesy of Emory Law School)

FORM #1:

ATTORNEY:

Please complete this form immediately after the interview and return it to the Recruitment Coordinator.

NAME OF STUDENT:

2nd Year Student _____   3rd Year Student _____   Other:

Date Interviewed:

Law School:

Length of Interview:

1. Circle the number that best describes the interviewee:

Personality	Strong				Weak	
Personable	1	2	3	4	5	abrasive
Enthusiastic	1	2	3	4	5	lifeless

Verbal Expression						
Articulate	1	2	3	4	5	difficult to understand
Quick to respond	1	2	3	4	5	undisciplined
Expresses organized thought	1	2	3	4	5	passive

Strongly favor	Favor	Acceptable	Opposed	Strongly Opposed
_____	_____	_____	_____	_____

2.   In which area(s) did the interviewee indicate an interest?

        Did not discuss

3.   Comments:

FORM #2:

INTERVIEWEE: ATTORNEY:

Please indicate your evaluation of applicant by checking the appropriate boxes below:

	Outstanding	Good	Average	Poor
Appearance	( )	( )	( )	( )
Personality/Demeanor	( )	( )	( )	( )
Self–Confidence	( )	( )	( )	( )
Maturity	( )	( )	( )	( )
Communication Skills/ Articulation of Views	( )	( )	( )	( )
Dedication to Work	( )	( )	( )	( )
Extracurricular Activities	( )	( )	( )	( )
Academic Achievements	( )	( )	( )	( )
Work Experience	( )	( )	( )	( )
Overall Impression	( )	( )	( )	( )

( ) Strong Candidate: Recommend for Immediate Hiring
( ) Good Candidate: Have No Reservations Regarding Hir-
                            ing
( ) Marginal Candidate: Have Reservations Regarding Hiring
                                 [please comment below]
( ) Weak Candidate: Should Not Be Considered Further for
                            Hiring
                                 [please comment below]

COMMENTS: *[If you checked either of the last two boxes above, you must comment]*

Do you think this person would accept an offer with this firm?

( ) Yes   ( ) Maybe   ( ) No

*

Appendix C
The Famous "Three Question" Interview

In 2005 or so, a test called "the cognitive reflection test" (CRT) got a lot of press. Apparently it was created by scientists at MIT to test job candidates' patience and decision-making.

While these questions seem simple, note this: of the first 3,000 students tested, more than half got the first question *wrong*.

For more on this test, visit http://mitsloan.mit.edu and search "on the ball: cognitive reflection test"

The three questions:

1. A bat and a ball cost $1.10 in total. The bat costs $1 more than the ball. How much does the ball cost?

2. If it takes five machines five minutes to make five widgets, how many minutes would it take 100 machines to make 100 widgets?

3. In a lake there is a patch of lily pads. Every day, the patch doubles in size. If it takes 48 days for the patch to cover the entire lake, how many days would it take for the patch to cover half the lake?

(Answers at bottom of page).

Five cents; five minutes; 47 days.

Shout-outs to the staff of the Vanderbilt Career Services Office for their help with this chapter: Elizabeth Workman, Dorris Smith, Lisa Doster, Kathy Jernigan, Angela Chapman, and Mary Griffin.

Chapter 10
The Birds and Bees of Great Jobs: Where Do Great Jobs Come From?

"We cannot live for ourselves alone. Our lives are connected by a thousand invisible threads, and along these sympathetic fibers, our actions run as causes and return as results."

Herman Melville

"I read somewhere that everybody on this planet is separated by only six other people. Six degrees of separation ... It's a profound thought ... How every person is a new door opening up into other worlds."

The character Ouisa Kettredge in John Guare's play "Six Degrees of Separation"

"Go out on a limb. That's where all the fruit is."

Mark Twain

"Wisdom becomes knowledge when it becomes your personal experience."

From a Yogi Tea bag tag

"Leap and a net will appear."

Seen on a bumper sticker

This is the most important chapter in this book. I've said that about other chapters, but this time I mean it. In this chapter we'll learn the skills that you'll use to nail down jobs for the rest of your life. You'll see how talking to people and taking part in activities will lead you to opportunities that other people don't even realize exist. You'll be happier, wealthier, and more successful than people who ignore the advice you'll find here.

What you'll do isn't foreign to what you've always done. You'll just look at conversations and activities through a different lens. As Georgia

State's Vickie Brown says, "You've done all of this before. People have turned you on to clubs and activities. You've probably even gotten jobs before because someone told you about them."

I've told you before that opportunities are "in the air." In this chapter, we'll see how saying and doing the right things can make those opportunities materialize.

* * * OVERHEARD AT A LAW SCHOOL CAREER SERVICES OFFICE * * *

Law student, to Career Services Director:

"No one ever got a job over a cup of coffee."

* * * FOUR LAW STUDENTS WHO FOUND GREAT JOBS OVER A CUP OF COFFEE * * *

- Student having a coffee at Starbucks. Two tables over, he overhears a conversation that is clearly a job interview. He says, "The interviewer was a lawyer with a small practice. The student was ... I don't want to sound mean, but there wasn't a lot going on there. He wasn't into it. I couldn't understand that because the lawyer made the job sound really good. When the student excused himself for a minute, I went over and said to the lawyer, 'Listen, I'm a law student and the job you're offering sounds great. Can I talk to you about it when you're done with this guy?" He said, "Sure."

   The lawyer quickly winds down the interview with the first student and talks to the second student. The student says, "I didn't even have a resume with me, but I told him basically what I'd done and what I wanted to do."

   "He made me an offer on the spot."

- Student gets the same drink at the same Starbucks every day on the way to law school. She develops a hi-how-are-you friendship with the barista. One day the barista asks her, "What are you going to do when you get out of school?" She mentions her interest in doing trusts and estates work, and the barista responds, "I think that's what my uncle does. You should talk to him." The barista gives the student her uncle's number, the student calls—and winds up with a job.

- A law student is having a drink at Starbucks with a friend. She and the friend have their resumes out, and they're working on them. She is interested in doing domestic relations work, and in the course of working on her resume she bounces ideas off her friend for wording her activities and experiences.

   A woman sitting at a table nearby walks over to her and says, "I couldn't help overhearing your conversation. I'm a lawyer. I handle a lot of divorces. I'd like to talk to you about working for me. Here's my card. Give me a call."

   The student calls, goes for an interview—and gets the job.

• Law student at Starbucks, having an informational interview with an alum from his school. He tells the alum a little about himself and his experiences to provide a context for his questions. A man sitting nearby walks over to him, introduces himself as a lawyer, and says, "If you're looking for a job, I'd like to talk to you about working for us." He gets the job.

What I'm *not* going to talk about in this chapter is networking. The word makes my skin crawl and I'll bet it does the same to you. I actually read a book about networking—I've mercifully forgotten the name of it—where the guy's whole strategy could be summed up like this: you're supposed to go to ten "professional" activities a month (in law, we're talking things like bar association activities, conferences, alumni cocktail receptions), go up to ten *complete strangers* at each activity, and say the words—*I'm not kidding here*—"Hi. My name is . . . I'm looking for a job. Let's talk about how you can help me."

Arrrgghhhh! *Shoot me. Shoot me now.*

The brilliant news is this: you don't have to do *anything* like that to nail great jobs. You will, however, have to talk to people. Most of the people you'll talk to are ones you know already. They're not job search resources. They're not "contacts." As Texas Tech's Kay Fletcher points out, "Even the word 'contacts' is awful. Do you go out for a beer with your 'contacts'? No. You go with friends. All 'contacts' are something *else,* too."

Of course, you'll have to talk with people you don't already know, as well. But I'll make it easy for you to meet them and break the ice. Face it: It's not like you never meet anybody new. Through your classes, your friends, your social activities, you meet people all the time. What you're going to do is change your focus a little bit in those conversations . . . as well as take on some new activities to position yourself for opportunities. Relax. I'm going to lead you by the hand through everything you should say, everything you should do. I promise you right now: you're actually going to *enjoy* this.

* * * POP QUIZ * * *

Would you recognize job opportunities when they arise?

Here's the set-up. You go to Career Services at school, tell a counselor what interests you, and (s)he gives you the contact information for five alums who do what you want to do. You send an e-mail to each one saying essentially, "I go to your alma mater. I want to do what you do. Do you have any job openings?"

Here's what happens:

a. One alum doesn't respond at all.

b. Two alums say they don't have any job openings.

c. Two alums say they don't have any job openings, but they have ideas for you.

Which situation(s)—if any—present potential job opportunities?

They all do.

There's no such thing as a dead end when it comes to seeking out jobs, because there's always the possibility of seeking advice from people, now or later—and advice leads to jobs.

Let's look at them individually.

(a). The alum who doesn't respond at all could be busy, could figure (s)he doesn't have any job openings, and since that's all you asked for, there's no point in responding.

Don't write people off so easily. You could e-mail this person two months from now and get an entirely different response.

(b). So what if they don't have any job openings? Whenever you get this response, you can always come back with a request for an "informational interview," where you ask questions designed to get advice that will help you break into the field, you say that you've researched it and you have a few questions you'd appreciate the answers to. We talk about informational interviews at length later in this chapter. The point is: a lack of job openings is in no way a dead end.

(c). I will personally come to your crib and spank you if you *ever, ever* fail to take alums up on an offer of advice! I'm going to wear you out with the statement *advice leads to jobs.* Whenever anyone is willing to share their expertise with you, take them up on it, and thank your lucky stars that people take such an interest in you.

P.S.: Don't ever send the e-mail in this quiz. Don't put people you don't know on the spot by asking for a job; ask for advice, for answers to specific strategy questions . . . in short, for the kind of help that leads to jobs.

A. HOW TO SMACK DOWN THAT LITTLE VOICE IN YOUR HEAD TELLING YOU THAT YOU *SERIOUSLY* DON'T WANT TO DO THIS

At this point, you may be saying: Why can't I just post my resume on-line? Why can't I just send letters? *Why do I have to do any of this?* Well—let's talk about it.

For a start, recognize where that little voice comes from, that voice making you wince at the thought of talking with people about jobs. I talk to so many students who echo the thoughts of one student: "I was really confident before law school. Now I'm afraid." Wendy Werner says that studying law makes people risk averse, because of the nature of the cases. Think about it: in all the cases you read, someone took a risk and got punished as a result. It's difficult to avoid internalizing that message.

Also, think about your classroom experience. As Beth Kirch points out, "Look at your law school classes. What happens when you raise your hand, when you stick your neck out? You get humiliated. At Career Services, we're saying, 'Get out there! Take a risk!' It's the total opposite of what your law school experience tells you is a good idea.''

So it's not you. It's the school you're in that makes you queasy about going out on a limb. But let's talk about why it's so very necessary.

1. NINE GREAT REASONS NOT TO RELY EXCLUSIVELY ON JOB ADS, MASS MAILERS, AND POSTING YOUR RESUME ON-LINE

A. JOB POSTINGS ARE ONLY THE LAST STEP IN A FOUR-STEP PROCESS OF CREATING JOBS. PEOPLE AND ACTIVITIES ARE THE BEST WAY TO SCOOP UP THOSE JOBS BEFORE THEY RIPEN INTO POSTINGS AND EVERYBODY ELSE IN THE WORLD COMPETES FOR THEM

It's easy to think that the Internet has every job in the world. It doesn't, for the simple reason that job openings have to "ripen" before they can be posted.

Before that, the birth of a job comes about this way:

- People don't even know they're looking for someone, but they're curious what's "out there";
- A general sense that adding at least one other person makes sense;
- There's a job available but it isn't advertised (at least, not yet);
- A formal job posting.

Even at that point, a lot of jobs will not get posted on line. As Lisa Kellogg says, "Students don't realize it, but it's *rare* for jobs to be advertised. Ads just aren't the way to get a job!" Amy Thompson echoes that: "Hardly *anything* is advertised!"

If that seems unbelievable to you, it's probably because you mistake where most of the jobs are. As Sandy Mans explains, "Sixty percent of law students go into private practice. Most of them go to small employers; that is, law firms with between two and ten lawyers." Those aren't the lawyers who interview on campus or even place ads.

So job ads are only the tip of the potential employer iceberg. In those first three steps of job creation, if you become known to the employer, you have the inside track on the job.

By way of a hypothetical, let's say that you go to Career Services and tell them that you're interested in working for a litigation firm. You ask for the name of an alum who's a litigator, so that you can learn more about it and get advice. You go and talk to the alum, who's very helpful. You thank him profusely and ask if you can leave your resume with him, in case he hears of anyone whom you might talk to. He agrees.

A few weeks later, alum is having a beer with a former classmate.

Alum: "How's work?"

Former Classmate: "We're swamped. I'm working around the clock. It's crazy."

Alum: "You thinking about hiring anyone?"

Former Classmate: "We really should. I guess I've been too busy to think about it."

Alum: "I just talked with a law student from Winky State. Really bright, really wants to litigate. You should talk to him/her ..."

Former Classmate: "Why not? Do you have his/her number?"

There are a million permutations on this theme, but you see how being a known quantity *in and of itself* can make all the difference. The activities we'll talk about in this chapter will accomplish exactly that.

* * * SMART HUMAN TRICK * * *

Law student at school in Florida. She cruises the Career Services web site and on-line sources every day, trolling for job postings. She goes to a local bar association lunch meeting. She reports, "I got those e-mails all the time, where they listed these lunches. I never went, but then I thought, it won't hurt me. Maybe there will be something.

"I got three leads from the lawyers at my table. And not *one* of those leads was posted *anywhere*."

B. PEOPLE DON'T GET INVESTED IN RESUMES. THEY GET INVESTED IN *PEOPLE*

I read a wonderful quote somewhere: "You're as successful as other people want you to be." Every person who's ever been successful at *anything* didn't do it alone. Sari Zimmerman calls the people who help you your "board of directors." Human beings are hard-wired to give advice, to be helpful. In order to tap into that, you've got to be a *person*, not a resume.

* * * SMART HUMAN TRICK * * *

Alum of a Midwestern school—we'll call it Wiki Law School—offers to help any students who ask. She gets frequent e-mails from students soliciting her help.

She attends a conference, and a student from her law school approaches her, telling her that "Will Connected, the Career Services Director at Wiki Law School, told me to seek you out for advice. I've been to several of these conferences, and when I noticed your name on the list of attendees, I thought I'd introduce myself."

The alum reports, "I help anyone who e-mails me. But the fact that she went to this conference, that she went out of her way to find me instead of just e-mail me ... she made an extra effort, and I made an extra effort for her."

c. Contact With People—Either Directly or Through a Mutual Contact—Is Statistically the Most Effective Way To Nail a Job

Most law students I talk to think on-campus interviews are where most jobs come from. I thought so, too, when I was in school.

Not even close.

Nationwide, only about 12% of law students get jobs through OCI. Four times as many—almost half—get jobs by either self-initiated contact with the employer or by a referral from a friend, relative, or family member.

If you think reaching out to people for jobs is icky, it only seems that way now because you haven't tried it yet. If you use the techniques you'll learn in this chapter, it'll be so pleasant you'll wonder why you've put it off so long.

Rob Kaplan says he receives many calls from grads who found jobs months after they graduated. Although they resisted the idea of initiating contact with employers while they were at school, they tell him, "I actually got my job that way. I wish I'd done it while I was still in school!"

* * * SMART HUMAN TRICK * * *

Law student in Miami, looking for a job in Seattle . . . making him about as geographically undesirable as you can be, at least in the continental United States. He doesn't know anybody in Seattle. He does one simple thing: He asks everybody he knows, personally, at school, at his part-time job, if they know anybody in Seattle, or know anyone who knows someone there.

With this one question, he generates a contact list with *two hundred names on it.*

Two hundred. Needless to say . . . he winds up with a job in Seattle.

d. You'll Get a Competitive Edge by Being Referred Directly to Employers. People Pay More Attention to What They Hear From People and What They See Themselves Than They Do to Resumes

As I mentioned before, in the CIA, they talk about "humint"— that is, human intelligence. Databases and satellites are fine, but the best information is rooted out by people, hearing it from someone's own mouth.

The same goes for careers. Employers will always prefer "humint" about applicants. Being a simple piece of paper can't compete. As Mary Obrzut points out, "Many law firms get two thousand applications for thirty summer jobs." Baker & McKenzie, the largest firm in the world, routinely gets more than ten thousand resumes for summer clerkships! As Maureen Provost Ryan advises, "You *have* to avoid the flood of resumes." You have to be more than a piece of paper to get a legal job just as lawyers themselves have to be more than a piece of paper to get clients. As Helen Long points out, "You don't pick a lawyer by them sending you a letter saying 'Can I be your lawyer?' You take advice from trusted people."

A student at one law school bemoaned on-line resume forms for governmental employers, which leave no room for creativity and not many characters to convey a message. "How," she asked, "am I supposed to get around *that?*" You can't, in the resume form, at least. But you can find alums that work at the agency and ask for advice and help, you can exhibit your enthusiasm . . . and you can remember that there is *always* a person making a decision somewhere. People can always be swayed with the opinions of people they know, with an honest show of enthusiasm.

Let's do a little creative visualization. Let's say that you're the hiring partner at a hotshot law firm, Scrooge & Marley. And you've got a stack of resumes on your desk, all neatly typed, all on 100% rag content bond paper, and you've got another hoard of resumes waiting for you on-line. You've got to find yourself an associate. Just at that moment, you get a call from your old friend Scott Farkle telling you that he met this law student at a CLE seminar, and he thinks the student would be great for your firm.

Now, what's going to have a greater impact on you? The fact that Student A's resume is embossed on gold leaf in that stack on your desk, or the fact that you've got a personal recommendation for Student B? You know as well as I do who's got the edge. Instead of resenting that, why not make it work for you? I'll show you exactly how to do it, and you'll see—it *will* give you an unbeatable competitive advantage!

* * * SMART HUMAN TRICK * * *

Law student at a southwestern law school. She wants a job in Mexico for the summer. She has mediocre grades, but she does speak Spanish. She tells her Career Services Director what she wants. The Career Services Director puts her in touch with companies near the law school that have plants in Mexico. She calls them. They invite her in for interviews—and she nails a job.

Incidentally—it's only *after* her interviews that she's asked for a resume, and even then it's a formality.

E. WHAT PEOPLE THINK OF YOU TRUMPS YOUR GRADES. IF THEY LIKE YOU AND WANT TO WORK WITH YOU, THEY'LL OFTEN CONVINCE *THEMSELVES* THAT YOU CAN DO THE WORK

At most law schools in America, on-campus interviews go to the "usual suspects" . . . namely, students in the top ten percent of the class. While there are sometimes sneaky ways to nail an on-campus interview (we talk about that at the end of this chapter), if you've got the people skills I'll teach you in this chapter, on-campus interviews will be irrelevant to you. There won't be employers who are off-limits to you, *regardless of whether they normally recruit only through on-campus interviews*. I know law students all over the country who've nailed unbelievable jobs even though their grades, to put it bluntly, stink. You don't hear about them very often at school, *because they keep quiet about it*. What they do isn't magic. It's a matter of talking to the right people and saying the right things. And we'll learn exactly how to do that!

* * * SMART HUMAN TRICK * * *

1L at a law school in the Pacific Northwest. He'd worked at a prosecutor's office before law school. He wanted to work at a U.S. Attorney's office in the summer after 1L. Problematically, the office *never* hired 1Ls ... and the 2Ls they hired had stellar law school credentials, Law Review and top grades. This student was at the bottom of his law school class.

The Assistant D.A. he worked with before law school called the U.S. Attorney's office and said, "Hiring him is not like hiring a student. It's like hiring a colleague. He's that good."

The student got the job.

f. The Answer to "How Many Resumes Will I Have to Send Out to Get a Job?" May Well Be Zero!

The time-honored way law students think they'll get a job in law is to send out a bajillion-piece mass mailer. Note, however, that the use of the word "honored" in this context is really misleading, because mass mailers are a butt-puckeringly bad way to find a job. You'll spend tons of time doing mail-merges on your computer, you'll spend hundreds of dollars on postage, and you'll generally wind up with zippo. On-line mass mailers and postings are just as bad. You'll get tons of rejections—when you hear from employers at all—and it's just depressing.

The fact is, for every hundred resumes you'd plan to send out, you're better off making even one contact. *One.* As Ann Skalaski points out, "Unless your resume is stellar and your mailings are personalized, you shouldn't send out stacks of letters." If you funnel your energies instead into people and activities, as I'll teach you to do in this chapter, you won't have to send out even one resume. When your friends ask you how many resumes you had to send out to get your job, you can tell them the truth: None!

g. The Skills You'll Use to *Become* a Lawyer Are the Same Ones You'll Actually Use to *Be* a Lawyer

Let's look down the road a moment and talk about the kinds of things you do when you're a lawyer. No matter where you work, you've got to deal with colleagues and superiors; you've got to impress them. Depending on your job, you'll deal with opposing counsel, judges, and court personnel. You have to deal with clients, sooner or later, which means you've got to be good at talking to them and gaining their confidence. And if you go into private practice, at some point you'll be expected to help enlarge the practice. How do you do that? Either by snagging new clients, or encouraging existing clients to use more of your services.

What does all of this scream at you? People skills, people skills, people skills. "EQ," as it's sometimes called. Even if you go into an alternative career, your success is going to depend on what people think of you, whether they want to work with you, whether they want to put other people on to you. Law Review doesn't give you that. Stellar grades don't either. Great people skills *do*. If you're good at meeting people, talking with them—everything we'll learn in this chapter—getting a job will just be a dress rehearsal for actually *performing* that job.

By way of example, one law student at a law school in New England volunteered at a lot of local bar association functions. When she interviewed with a firm, the senior partner was particularly impressed that she knew *tons* of people; it was much of the reason the firm made her an offer. So, if you have any qualms about working on your people skills, look at the long-term benefit you'll derive from it!

H. PERSONAL CONTACT IS VIRTUALLY THE ONLY WAY YOU'LL NAIL OTHER GREAT JOBS DOWN THE ROAD

There's a little game I like to play, and I'm going to let you in on it. It doesn't have anything to do with spanking, by the way. When I read articles about people, I always look for the paragraph about how they got into what they're doing now. You know something? It's never because of some on-campus interview. Inevitably, it's because they impressed somebody who was a classmate, or a colleague, or a superior, or a friend put them on to it. For instance, I remember reading an article in *The American Lawyer* a few years ago, about how lawyers involved with the 2000 Florida vote-counting fiasco— remember hanging chads?—got the gig. It was a flow chart, and it was really interesting. I would have reproduced it for you here, if I hadn't lost the article. But anyway! What it showed was that there was no call for resumes. There was no job posting. No on-campus interviews. Instead, it was because this one knew that one, who'd worked with another one, who'd served on a committee with the first guy—and on and on and on. It was amazing. And that article was just one example of what I'm talking about. Here's another one. In 2001, Senator Peter Fitzgerald of Illinois was looking for a new U.S. Attorney for Chicago (he had the right to recommend a candidate to the White House, as Illinois' senior Republican). He went to FBI head Louis Frieh and asked, "Who's the best assistant U.S. Attorney you know in the country?" Frieh told him it was Patrick Fitzgerald of the SDNY office. And, of course, Patrick Fitzgerald wound up with the job.

The fact is, every other job you get for the rest of your life is going to be through people, one way or another. As Rob Kaplan points out, "I'm always telling students that the reality is, once people graduate and change jobs, networking is the way you get those jobs. It's all based on your reputation and the contacts you have."

I talked with a really fascinating law student in upstate New York who exemplified this. She'd worked for the mayor of Los Angeles in press relations, and then at the White House with media corps. She said, "I did it all through people. Everyone who got those jobs did the same thing. We were always getting resumes from Harvard people with great grades. The people I worked for didn't care. My boss said, 'It's the first impression that counts.'"

A recruiting coordinator who conducts exit interviews at a very large firm said, "We get all of our associates by OCI, but when they leave us? It's *always* through someone else—not a job posting!"

That has some interesting ramifications for you, right now. Namely: If you don't have the credentials to get a bunch of on-campus interviews, if you're not at the top of your class . . . you may actually have an *advantage* over your credentially-gifted classmates. Why? As Gail Cutter explains, "On-campus interviewing actually does a lot of students a *disservice*. Because they can throw their resumes anywhere and get a job, they don't develop the skills they need to get jobs. They use it as a lottery, instead of thinking about how well a job will be suited to their needs." In fact, studies have shown that students who graduate in the *middle* third of the Harvard Business School wind up being much more successful than students who graduate in the *top* third, largely because of their skill, born of necessity, in making contacts.

So you may be massively pissed that jobs aren't dropping into your lap through OCI right now. But you'll be better off *forever* by developing the skills you'll learn in this chapter. You're just getting a head start!

i. Talking With People Can Give You Valuable Strategic Insights

Maybe you don't know if you need to get an additional degree to get into the specific job you want. Maybe you wonder how a study abroad program will play with particular employers. Maybe you don't know how to "spin" an element of your background. Maybe you don't have the grades to get into something, and you wonder if there's another way.

A student at one school said he wanted to work in non-proliferation, a teeny tiny specialty, and read an article that said that lawyers who do this are in a minute corner of the State Department. The article also said that they all have Ph.D.'s from diploma mills on-line. He wondered if he needed one, too. Who'd know that better than the people who are already there?

People who already do what you want to do can give you the skinny on just about anything you want to know. Whether we're talking about alums from your school, bar association section heads or even lawyers you read about, reaching out to people can have a significant impact on your career path. Maybe you don't really need an LL.M. after all, and you save yourself a lot of dough. Maybe there's a key "bridge" job that positions you for your dream job. Whatever the strategy, often the only way to find it out is to talk to people who do what you want!

Ideally I've convinced you why it's such a good idea to look at *people* as your primary means of nailing great jobs, now and for the rest of your career. But if I know you—and I like to think I do—you might be thinking, "Well, I can see that it's a good idea. But ... it still makes my skin crawl. It's not for me." There may be a few specific issues you've got going on. Let's talk about them ...

2. **ALL THE REASONS WHY YOU DON'T WANT TO TAKE THE PEOPLE AND ACTIVITIES ROUTE TO GREAT JOBS ... AND WHY ALL OF THOSE REASONS ARE STUPID**

- **"How am I supposed to get people to give me something when I'm not giving them anything in return?"**

    Here's the scenario. Let's say I have a friend who's a Career Services director who desperately needs a new counselor. I know a 3L at another school who'd be dynamite for the job. She's done all kinds of counseling activities in school and she's told me she wanted to get into it after graduation when she gave me a ride from the airport when I spoke at her school. I tell my friend the Career Services Director about her.

    Now: who's *not* getting something?

    The director is getting something because she's got a lead on a promising counselor. I'm getting something because I'm giving back to a Career Services director who's let me quote her in my books. And of course the 3L gets a job lead.

    Everybody wins.

    You may not be used to looking at job searching this way. You may think an employer is the one *giving* you something when they give you a job. But that's missing the point. When you're looking for a job, you're offering your talent, your hard work, your dedication and enthusiasm. Hell—the employer's going to be lucky to have you. Tell yourself that, over and over if you have to, until you believe it. Because it's true.

    Remember, even people who give you advice and put you on to *other* people are getting something in return. If you work out, the employer will be grateful to the contact for letting the employer know about you. But on top of that, they get a subtle but important kind of reward: the sense that they're "giving back." You hear successful people talk about this all the time. They've enjoyed the guidance and help of others, they've worked hard and risen up the ladder, and they want to lift people behind them. People like you.

Now, this suggests a crucial point that I'll address in more detail later in this chapter, namely: you *have* to manifest gratefulness to people who give you advice and contacts. You can't say "thank you" enough ways and too frequently. And you *must* let people know what happened as a result of their advice, their contacts. But the fact remains that helping you gives people the feeling that they're repaying the world for their own good fortune. (Just as you will do, by the way, when you're a success!)

So everybody wins in this game of getting job leads through people. Remind yourself of that as you seek opportunities. The fact is, if you tell yourself nobody will help you, that you've got nothing to offer, if you talk cynically to yourself, you'll sound cynical and beaten down. Nobody wants to work with *that* person.

I know from personal experience what a big difference appropriate self-talk can make ... especially when you're faced with something you *really* don't want to do! I've told you before that when I got out of law school, I wrote a line of legal study aids called *Law In A Flash*— that's right, the little flash cards in the yellow boxes—and I started a publishing house to publish them, because I couldn't find any "real" publisher to do it. (They thought the flash cards were childish, which, of course, they are.) As a freshly-minted law school graduate I had to try to rustle up a million dollars from investors. Now, if you thinking finding a job is tough, try begging for money sometime! It's brutal. I could have told myself, "There are millions of things these people can invest in. I don't have any background in business. There's no reason for them to believe me. I've been fired from every job I ever had. I've never written anything law-related before. My grades weren't great. They're never going to give me any money ..." Well, what good would *that* have done? My potential investors would have seen a beaten-down loser and would *never* have forked over the dough. But I talked the talk—to myself, and everyone else. I told myself, "This is a great idea. Law students are bored and intimidated by what they study, and these flash cards make it easy. I may never have had another good idea before, but *this* is a great idea. These investors—they're lucky to get in on something like this." I was defining myself by one huge positive. And I wasn't just getting something from them—I was giving them the opportunity to invest in something that stood to make them a lot of money.

Notice that redefining my task didn't change the essence of what I was doing: looking for money. But recasting it as a two-way street was absolutely essential to making it happen.

P.S.: Since you see *Law In A Flash* all over the place, you know the rest of the story. I raised the money.

Whether you're starting a business of your own or looking to work for somebody else, you see the point: don't undervalue what you're giving in return!

- **"I don't know anybody ..."**

I hear this from law students all the time. "I don't have anybody to tell, Kimmbo," they moan. "I don't know anybody!"

Number one: It's not true. You know tons of people.

Number two: It's not just who you know. It's who *they* know. And who you *get* to know.

It doesn't matter if you don't know any lawyers. You don't *have* to. As Ann Skalaski points out, "You may not know any lawyers, but you definitely know people who *do* know lawyers." Remember "The Six Degrees of Separation"? We're talking about people who are one or two degrees of separation from you. There are probably *thousands* of those, and among them I guarantee you are people who will be useful to your job search!

For another thing—what about your family? As Sophie Sparrow says, "You've always been by yourself? You were raised by wolves?" Of course not. You have parents, siblings, aunts, uncles, cousins. They're a great start, and they have a benefit that nobody else has— they implicitly have your best interests in mind. (Well—hopefully!)

On top of that, you have a social network. You have friends, teachers, classmates, barbers or hairdressers, dentists, you name it. Again: you may think, "What use are *they? They* don't know anybody!" The short response is: you don't know who they know. And trust me, you'll be surprised when you start to ask!

Finally, you need to remember that as useful as everyone you know can be, getting great jobs through people is not just a matter of talking to people "in place" in your life. It's not who you know. It's who you *get* to know, either through people or activities that I'll recommend to you.

Once you start following my advice in this chapter, you are going to be positively flabbergasted at how useful people seem to materialize. I have seen it happen thousands of times to law students. All they have to tell me is, "I didn't believe you when you said I'd find people ..." "All I did was start talking to this person at the dry cleaner ..." "You'll never believe where I found ..." and I know what's coming next!

- **"I don't like the idea of using people ..." or "I don't want to lean on my friends for jobs."**

Let's say we're friends, and I'm new in town. I need to find a dentist, a doctor, an insurance person. I want to know about the best restaurants. I need a good gourmet shop. And I ask you for your recommendations.

I have a question for you: am I using you? I don't think you'd look at it that way.

Let's try another one. Let's say that you and I went to college together, and I call you and say, "Listen, I know you're in law school. My cousin is a junior in college and he's thinking about going to your law school. Would you mind talking to him about it, which classes to take, which professors to take and which ones to avoid?" Would you be *insulted* by my phone call, or would you think—"Sure. I'll talk to him."

Again: are you being used? Notice in both situations, you're an expert. You've got knowledge I don't have, and I'm looking for the fruits of your wisdom.

The reason I took you through this little exercise is obvious: when you're talking to people about jobs, you're doing *exactly the same thing*. **The key is that *you aren't asking people for jobs*. You're asking for *advice*.** As Laura Rowe Lane says, "You aren't putting people on the spot! You're flattering them by asking what they do, for their perceptions." I've told you before that people are hard-wired to be helpful. They like to give advice. Giving advice is the coin of the realm for lawyers. Everyone likes to feel as though their opinions are worth hearing.

Now, this is all true only if you also *manifest gratefulness*. Later in this chapter, I'll talk to you about exactly what you say when you meet people and when they put you on to other people. It's crucial that at every step of the way, you express in words and behavior that you are grateful for the advice you get from others. Not only is it the right thing to do, but you never know when you'll want to ask them for *more* advice—and if you showed them gratitude the first time around, they'll be happy to do it!

* * * SMART HUMAN TRICK * * *

Female law student desperately wants to work for the EPA. She tries sending out cover letters and resumes, and gets nowhere. She wracks her brain for connections, and realizes that all she has is a guy she worked for as a mother's helper on Cape Cod when she was 12. She remembers that he was a big shot lawyer in Washington, but she doesn't know anything else about his job.

She's reluctant to contact him because she hasn't spoken to him in over ten years, and feels uncomfortable calling for a favor. Her Career Services Director convinces her to contact him anyway. She writes a letter that starts, "As you may remember ..." and recounts how they met. She then expresses her interest in working for the EPA and says that she'd welcome any advice from him.

As it turns out, he's *delighted* to help. He introduces her to his connections, and ... she nails her job at the EPA.

- **"The idea of talking to a bunch of strangers turns my stomach . . ."**

    I have good news for you. You don't *have* to talk to any strangers. Well, let me put that differently. You'll talk to some people you've never spoken with before. But you'll be talking to them because you know somebody they know, or you're taking part in some activity that brings you into contact with them. So they're not stone cold strangers.

    As you look through the activities I'll suggest to you later in this chapter, you'll see that some of my favourites involve volunteering at events where people you want to work with congregate (or at the very least, people who can put you *on* to those people). You'll find that if you have something to do, anything at all—whether it's handing out the name tags, pouring the punch, giving people rides from the airport, leading tours of your campus—whatever it is, if you have a role to play, it breaks the ice for you and makes people easy to talk to. You have a *purpose* in being there. Once you've volunteered at an event or two, you'll feel confident enough to engage new people in any circumstances.

    Furthermore, it's a mistake to think that nobody else feels as you do, that *everybody* else is comfortable at social events. They aren't. If you scan any crowd carefully, you'll see people standing at the edges, nursing a drink, looking uneasy. *Those* are people to engage, because they'll be grateful you did! Walk up, introduce yourself with a smile, shake hands, ask them what brings them to the event, and sooner or later ask "I'm here to learn more about what practicing law is really like. I'd love to hear about what you do." I promise you, you can do *that*. And once you do, it will open a whole new world of opportunities for you!

- **"I can't stand rejection."**

    Join the club. *Nobody* likes being rejected. As you know from reading Chapter 5, handling rejection is a *huge* issue in mounting any successful job search. Whenever you ask someone for help, advice or information, there's the inherent risk that the answer may be "no." That's what leads a whole ton of law students to far less effective, paper-and cyber-job searches. As Wendy Werner points out, "Students would like the job hunt to be less personal, 'my paper meets your paper.' So I'll send a paper and get a paper, and even if it's a rejection, it's a lot less painful than it would be in person." Amy Thompson adds, "Students are worried that people won't want to help them. It's like being rejected when you ask for a dance!"

    In this chapter we'll learn the approaches that will minimize the chance people will tell you "no." The key is that you'll be asking for *advice—not a job.* And you'll do it through mutual contacts and activities. As Amy Thompson says, "Put yourself in their shoes. If a friend of a friend asked you for advice about law school, you'd be happy to give it!" And Washington's Teresa DeAndrado adds, "You're not looking for a job. You're asking, 'I am interested in what you do. How should I go about it?' or 'What advice do you have?' or 'I'm trying to find out what classes I should take,' or 'I'd love to hear what you think of your job.' Then it's *flattering* for people to talk about themselves. Even their spouses' eyes will glaze over if they try to talk about work, so you're flattering them when you ask them about their work!"

When I talk to students about this approach, they'll often wrinkle up their noses and say, "But ... aren't they going to *know* what I *really* want is a job?" Maybe they will. *But you're not asking for one, so it's not an issue.* When you say to someone, "I'd love to learn more about what you do," they can hardly say, "Hey, wait just a minute— you want a *job*, don't you?" Not gonna happen. And even if they *do* the extremely unlikely thing and call you on it and say, "Are you looking for a job?" you'll have an answer ready: "Ultimately. But right now, I'd like to learn more about the market so I know how to position myself for an opportunity when it comes up. That's why I'm asking for your advice." So armed with the right responses, you're well protected from being put on the spot!

No matter how unlikely it is that you'll have people tell you "no" when you look for advice, I can't tell you it will *never* happen. Sure it will. People will be in the middle of a trial, bogged down with work or undergoing a personal issue. You might be willing to talk to just about anybody about your law school experience, but you probably wouldn't be so jolly about it during exam week! Or maybe you'll try to talk to people who are just crabby. There are a raft of reasons you might be told "no" that have nothing to do with you. How do you deal with those?

First of all, make sure you have more than one iron in the fire. That is, don't ask people for names, contact *one* person, and then sit by the phone or computer or mailbox waiting to hear from that single person. You want to have several possibilities open at any one time, so that you minimize the trauma to your feelings if and when some of them don't pan out.

Secondly, remember that this is not a matter of collecting shrunken heads or Easter eggs. You only need to wind up with *one job*. If one or ten or five hundred people are unhelpful, it doesn't matter, as long as you get a job, a *single* job, with an employer you really want to work for.

I talked to an international student at a Midwestern school, who had been a lawyer in Mexico. He sat next to a guy on an airplane, and when they started chatting it turned out that this guy was a lawyer. The student said, "Really? I'd love to practice in this country." The student said, "This guy immediately turned cold. He looked the other way. He got out the airline magazine and didn't say a word the rest of the flight." This student was terribly concerned that he'd done something offensive. Of course, you can see that his comment was innocuous. It wouldn't have killed this guy to murmur something encouraging. The fact that he *didn't* was a reflection on *him,* not the student. And it certainly didn't mean that the next person the student spoke to would be equally dismissive; in fact, a conversation with that person might be the key to a great job!

Finally—and most importantly—if you let the rejections you get stop you from contacting other people and taking part in other activities, you're giving those people a lot more power than they deserve. You're giving them the power to make you a failure, and they can't do that without your help. Instead, view occasional rejections as an inherent part of the process. Take a deep breath, and move on.

I speak from vast experience here. As I've mentioned before, the way I write my books is to contact experts, and then ask who else I should talk to. You see their names throughout my books. But for all of the people who talk to me, there are people who don't return my calls. Sometimes they *do* return my calls, and tell me point blank they won't talk to me. Now, if I gave up because of those rejections, if I focused on the people who *wouldn't* talk to me, you wouldn't be reading this book right now. Instead, I focused on the hundreds of people who *do* speak to me. And you know something? The people who didn't . . . maybe one day, they will. It's important not to solidify a negative impression of someone because you had one bad exchange. Give them the opportunity to change their mind about you, and you'll be presently surprised.

The bottom line is: you're just not so damned delicate that you can't take a few people telling you "no." Keep it in perspective. As Teresa DeAndrado points out, "The worst that'll happen is they'll blow you off. They can't take your birthday away!"

- **"I'm afraid of looking stupid."**

Anytime you're looking for a job, you're admitting that you don't have one—or at least, you don't have one you want. And that can make you feel stupid. It only compounds a feeling law school gives you in the first place! There's a clinical diagnosis for people who get through First Year unscathed, without feeling inadequate *somehow.* As Sophie Sparrow points out, "Law school makes people question the way they think. They go to law school, and they just don't get it. They don't understand the cases. They start to not trust their instincts." Pam Malone adds, "Most students have been successful *before* law school. But then in law school they're graded against a much higher caliber of students." That leaves law students, as Maureen Provost Ryan points out, "With no faith in themselves!" So you've been demoralized in school—why *wouldn't* you be wary of looking stupid when you have to make professional contacts?

It's important to remember two things: First of all, every single lawyer you talk to—heck, everybody you talk to in *any* position—was once you. They were once students who weren't sure what they were going to do with their careers. In a very basic sense, everybody can identify with you.

On top of that, the way you present yourself can eliminate the "I feel stupid" factor. As Sophie Sparrow points out, you can't approach people and say, "I'm out of work; I can't get a job." That's like wearing a "kick me" sign. Instead, characterize your endeavor as an educational experience; say, "I'm exploring a lot of options," because that's exactly what you *are* doing.

The people you choose to contact can also minimize the "duh" factor. One of the groups of people I encourage you to approach is your professors. *Nobody* has greater potential to make you feel stupid than a law school professor. When I meet them even today, I'm *still* somewhat cowed. But the key is to be selective in who you talk to, if you choose to approach your professors at all. Go to professors who gave you good grades, or profs whose classes you haven't taken yet. If you're a 1L and you don't have grades yet, go to professors in whose classes you feel comfortable (if there are any . . . there weren't for me!). The fact is, you may have professors who are really plugged into a specialty you're dying to enter, making them an obvious resource . . . and one to be exploited if you can get over the Wizard-of-Oz-ish demeanor!

So the mere fact that you're researching the job market doesn't make you look stupid. Every single employer in the world was in your shoes at one time or another. Don't let it hold you back from making the valuable connections you need to get a dream job!

- **"I don't have time to waste talking to people. I've got too much else to do, and I want to get a job *fast*."**

I hear this one all the time. "I just want a job. Isn't there an easier way?" Career Services Directors tell me about students who visit them, expecting the directors to open their secret drawer o' offers and hand them one.

I talked to a student at a New England school who said, "I'm a 2L. I want to spend the summer at a large firm in Palo Alto. I want at least two grand a week. My grades aren't great. I've got enough to do, so don't wear me out with stuff to do. What can I do that doesn't take any time?" I'm sure I said it more artfully than this, but honestly, the answer is: "nothing." It's a worn out adage but the fact is, anything worthwhile takes time. And there are few things more worthwhile than your career.

It's true that it takes longer to do "people"-oriented job search activities than it does to send out a bunch of resumes to employers, or post your resume on a website. But you know what? *It works better, and that's why I'm telling you to do it.* That's why *everybody* tells you to do it. You can easily send out hundreds and hundreds of resumes, and plaster the Internet with your resume, and not get one damn job out of it. On top of that, because it seems like you're doing such a lot, it'll seriously bum you out. I hear that all the time, too. When I ask students what they've done to find jobs, I'll often hear, "I've done *everything* . . . I've sent out *five hundred* resumes."

Trust me—that ain't everything. It isn't really anything. Because you are much more than a piece of paper. You're more complex, more interesting, and you have much more to bring to the table than any stinking resume could ever get across. If you're really going to nail great opportunities, *now and for the rest of your career,* you're going to do it through people. I promise you that. If you start doing the things I'm going to teach you in this chapter, you're always going to nail great jobs that other people don't even realize exist. You'll get opportunities before they're posted anywhere. In short, you'll be happier and more fulfilled in your career.

In the short term, does it mean a little more work, taking risks talking with people, taking advantage of what little extra time you have? Yep. But remember what they teach people in Alcoholics Anonymous: when people are tempted to have "just one," they should "look past the drink"—that is, look past the immediate gratification toward the long-term benefit. That's what's going on with getting great jobs through people and activities. You're looking past the short-term fix of sending out resumes toward the long-term benefit of a great career.

Now, that's not to say you shouldn't send out resumes. Go ahead. They're not mutually exclusive. (I tell you how to handle posted jobs in Chapter 7, and mail campaigns in Chapter 8.) But I'm imploring you to do everything in this chapter, as well—because ultimately, it's the skills you learn here that you'll be using, forever.

- **"I'm embarrassed about my grades . . ."**

  You may be worried about talking to people because your grades aren't great. If you're really hung up about your grades, check out Chapter 13 on grades. But here, let's discuss a few key points related to talking to people when you consider yourself "grade challenged."

  Remember from the outset that grades aren't everything, contrary to what the on-campus interview process would suggest. Only a tiny minority of students nationwide get their jobs through on-campus interviews. On top of that, keep in mind that ninety percent of practicing lawyers weren't in the top ten percent of *their* class, either. So the odds are 9 to 1 that any lawyer you talk to wasn't Law Review material. If you aren't, either, you've got great company!

  Instead, when you take part in activities and you meet people and talk to them, you're letting people see the best thing about you: *you,* and not your crappy grades. As Ann Skalaski points out, "Grades will never get you hired. People hire based on who they like."

  Before you meet people or take part in activities you *do* want to have a bit of patter to wheel out about your grades, something you feel comfortable saying that puts your grades in perspective. You're going to rehearse it until you can say it freely and with a smile on your face. Run your specific wording past your Career Services Director, but it could be something as simple as:

- "I've got a 2.5 GPA. Boy, am I glad I didn't have to show my mother *that* report card! But my interest in environmental law stems from my work on a Law Review article for Professor Phlebitz . . ."

- "I've got a B-minus average. It would be a lot better if I hadn't crashed and burned first semester! Since then, I've done a lot better, and I've taken a real interest in Tax Law because . . ."

As you can see, the idea is to have a couple lines to say, which accomplishes two things: First, you acknowledge your grades without being defensive or apologizing (a little humor doesn't hurt you here); and second, you immediately turn the conversation to where you want it to go—your career interests. If you do that smoothly, you'll *doubly* impress anyone you meet. Why? Because you'll display self-confidence, an important trait for any professional in any field, especially law. The fact is, nobody can make you feel bad about *anything* without your help. You have to be an active participant in that conspiracy for anyone to make you feel bad. "Yup, I'm shur stoopid, all right" . . . who does *that* help?

Remember, clients you'll have as a lawyer will never have an airtight case. You have to know how to handle their flaws. So if you can handle your own flaws with finesse, that augurs well for you when you actually practice law. The bottom line is: don't let bad grades hold you back from talking your way into your dream job!

- **"I resent the idea that I've got to go through this kind of hassle to find a job."**

  I know how you feel. I remember thinking when I was in law school, *"Man, I've done enough already. I've got education out the ying-yang. I'm paying a boatload of dough in tuition. I shouldn't have to do anything else to find a job!"*

  I was wrong. Those four words "I shouldn't have to . . ." are some of the most self-destructive words in the English language. As Lisa Abrams points out, "As a law student, you just can't have the attitude, 'I've paid my dues.'" Because the unfortunate fact is that you haven't. All that going to classes and doing your homework get you is a law degree. If you want to get the job of your dreams *with* that degree, you'll have to work for it, just as if you were taking an extra class called "Job Search 101." The bottom line is, as Cindy Rold says, "Nobody *owes* you anything!"

  Now, it's true that if you were President of the Harvard Law Review—or just about anybody else at Harvard, for that matter—you wouldn't have to do a lot to find a job. Employers would be drooling over the opportunity to talk with you. But you can't resent people who get the "low hanging fruit" of on-campus interviews. Look at it this way: whether it was getting into Harvard in the first place, or being at the top of the class anywhere else, those students did something that you and I didn't do. They earned it. And it means that their bare naked resumes will open doors for them in law school. You and I—we're the ones who have to do a little more to find our first job. That's the way it is.

Do I seem blasé about this? Perhaps. But resentment is such a stupid waste of your time. It can torpedo your entire job search if you let it. I've seen that happen over and over again with law students. I remember one in particular, who wailed, "I'm in the top sixteen percent of my class. I'm only *one percent* outside what they look at! I can't believe they wouldn't give me an interview!" This student simply couldn't get past one employer who'd refused her an on-campus interview. "Why? Why? Why?" She kept asking. Instead of devoting herself to pursuits that really would get her foot in the door—with that employer or anyone else!—she spent all of her time reliving the one truly unpleasant thing in her life. Where's the payoff in *that*?

I know from personal experience how poisonous resentment can be. I grew up with a serious weight problem. What the hell. I was a fat pant load. That was bad enough, but what made it worse was hearing over and over again that thin people made better eating choices, and that's why they were thin. This, as I'm watching my rail-thin sister eat deep-fried peanut butter and banana sandwiches. Grrr. Things only turned around for me when I read a diet book that offered a profound insight; it said, "OK, thin people can eat whatever they want, and you can't. So that's not fair. Now what?" It was only then that I realized that I could let resentment keep me fat forever, or I could bite the bullet—not the donut—eat less, and lose weight. It wasn't fair, but it was true.

So maybe you have to work a little harder to find a job than somebody with great paper credentials. Let's look for a moment at the bright side of this—and there's a *serious* silver lining.

Let's take a look a little down the road in your career. Even a year out of law school, let's say. You've started out in a job and you're ready to make a move to your second job. Now: how are you going to get that job? Let me give you a hint. *It's not going to be through on-campus interviews*. That's a limited-time offer. As soon as school is over, so is OCI. The *only* way you're going to get great opportunities down the road is to do what I'm going to teach you to do in this chapter. Every job you get for the rest of your life is likely to be through people and activities. (OK, you may use job postings and head hunters, but those rank a distant second.) You may be resentful of people who get jobs through on-campus interviews *now*, but if you take a long-term view, you'll see that you're honing the skills now that they'll have to develop at some point. Career Services Counselors at distinguished law schools often tell me that crunch time for their students comes two years after law school, when they've been at a large law firm and figure it's time for job number two. "They have *no idea* how to go about it, because they're used to employers coming to *them,*" is the refrain I hear over and over again. If you've already refined your abilities to talk with people and take advantage of activities, you're actually ahead of the game.

On top of that, having to put in a little effort to find a job actually means you'll make a better decision on your first gig. Here's why. OCI is just too damn easy. Employers show up, you interview, they call you back, you interview again, you get the job. You don't really have to *think* about what you'll enjoy, the kind of job that suits you. It fell into your lap, complete with massive paycheck, and you took it. But if you have to struggle a bit, you really get to think about what it is that you want to do. Again, this is not a benefit that's immediately obvious; it wouldn't have been to me, when I was in law school. But you'll actually wind up happier than if you took a brass ring dangled in front of you at school.

You can also make the whole process more enjoyable by viewing it as an opportunity to widen your circle of acquaintances and make new friends. You may be lukewarm on some of the people you meet— you may actively dislike a few of them—but you'll undoubtedly meet some people that you like very much. On top of that, you'll be forging valuable professional connections that you'll have forever. That's an incomparable asset!

So keep your eye on the prize: a great career. Once you've talked with people and taken part in activities and nailed that job, everything you had to do to get it will quickly fade in your mind. In fact, you'll be proud of the way you diligently pursued your dream!

- **"It goes against the whole idea of everything I learned as a kid, like 'be modest,' 'don't talk about yourself,' 'don't brag.' "**

Susan Gainen calls it "toxic modesty." The desire not to toot one's own horn can be overwhelming. And of course, nobody likes someone who's arrogant. But the fact is, when you're looking for a job, you have to be able to say good things about yourself. Kathleen Brady cites the Irish proverb, "If you don't toot your own horn, no music gets played." And Teresa DeAndrado points out, "You *have* to brag. You *have* to talk about yourself. You *have* to bother grownups and busy people." In other words—you have to forget a lot of what you learned as a kid!

The note you want to strike is one of humble confidence. When you point out things you've done, you can temper your accomplishments with "I was lucky enough to ..." "I know I have a lot to learn about being a lawyer, but I did ..." And you have to suggest that what you don't already know, you are capable of learning and doing.

The actor Michael J. Fox talked in an interview about his experience getting the lead role in the movie *Back to the Future*. As you may remember from the movie—and if you haven't seen it, rent it, it's awesome—skateboarding played a key role in a couple of scenes. In his first interview with the honchos making the movie, he was asked, "Can you skateboard?" and he said, "I will!" In other words: he *couldn't,* but he was damned well going to learn how!

There's no way around it: confidence stated appropriately is a necessity when you're looking for a job. I run into this all the time. When publishers ask me, "Do you think you could write a book about ..." the answer is always yes—even if I have *no clue* about the subject. Truth be told, when my publisher approached me to write the first edition of *this* book, what the heck did I know about finding a legal job? Or any job, for that matter? I didn't get invited back by my summer employer. I graduated from law school unemployed, and I wrote *Law In A Flash* and started my own company largely because nobody else would hire me. But I *did* know how to interview people, how to dig up useful information. In other words: I could honestly tell them that I could write a great book. And that's what they wanted to hear!

So set your childhood modesty aside when you're job-seeking. In order for people to want to help you, put you on to their friends, and ultimately hire you, they have to believe that you can do a great job. And they've got to hear it from *you.* It'll get easy almost immediately to say good things about yourself—when you see the great results it brings!

- **"What if they like me and want me to actually *work* with them? I'm terrified that I can't really do it, that I'm selling something I don't really have."**

  Join the club. Everybody feels that way to a greater or lesser extent, even the very most successful lawyers in the world. I routinely talk to law firm partners, making a tidy seven-figure income, who say "I'm scared half the time. I feel like I'm faking it." The key is they don't let anyone *see* the fear. And neither should you.

  It's natural to feel nervous about performing well. That adrenaline rush actually helps you do better. So acknowledge your nerves, recognize that everyone feels it, admit that you have a lot to learn— but be confident that you can, and will, master whatever you set your mind to.

- **"I want to do *concrete* things to find a job. Not just schmooze people ..."**

  Ironic, isn't it? Sending out five hundred resumes that nobody wants to see is considered *concrete* ... whereas, talking with people— showing off the very best thing about you, which is *you*— is considered a schmoozy waste of time. Hmm.

There's no denying that talking with people just doesn't have the "tangible" dimension that sending resumes and answering job postings does. As Rob Kaplan points out, it "just doesn't have the quantifiable quality that other elements of the job search have. If you bang out two hundred letters, you can feel them, you can touch them, you feel like you've *done* something ... whereas setting up an interview with a grad to talk about the job market in St. Louis doesn't give you that same feeling of accomplishment." And that's really at the heart of the problem, isn't it? Telling people (and yourself) that you've fired out 500 letters sounds so much more impressive than saying you've talked with ten lawyers and gone to a couple of CLEs, regardless of whether those two activities took the same amount of time. But remember—those ten conversations, those two CLEs will get you leagues closer to your goal than the 500 letters ever will!

So it's important to get past images and think about what really works, regardless of how it feels. If you don't believe that now ... you will, by the time you finish this chapter!

- **"I'm not going to be available to work for several months/a year/X period of time, so I shouldn't do anything yet."**

  I hear this all the time. I talked to one student in Florida in January who was graduating in May, taking the bar in July, and getting the results in November. He was moving to Illinois to work and wanted a small firm. That gave him a good ten months before he really needed a job, so he figured: why bother doing anything now?

  Ha ha. It's always smart to start the conversation now, to take advantage of activities, no matter *when* you'll be available. Remember: you're not applying for jobs, you're looking for advice and leads. You're practicing your people skills. Even if you're looking for small firms (which don't hire far in advance), you want people to know who you are and what you're interested in.

- **"I already have a job this summer. I don't need to talk to anybody."**

  Of course you're not going to look for a summer job if you already have one ... but you shouldn't shut yourself off from the world because of one summer gig.

  I talked to a 2L at one school, interested in family law, who was a member of the family law society at school. She helped put together a panel with a family court judge on it. A 3L who used to clerk for the judge encouraged her to do the same, but she said, "I already have a summer job. I don't need to talk to him."

  Wha-a-at? When you have the opportunity to talk to people about what you want to do, take advantage of it. Express your interest, ask questions, and in general take advantage of the strategies we discuss later in this chapter about informational interviewing. You never know when someone you talk to will be the key to your next great gig!

B. THE GOLDEN RULES OF FINDING JOBS THROUGH PEOPLE AND ACTIVITIES

I've talked with thousands of law school students about the principles in this chapter. When they don't have success as quickly as they'd like, they've typically made some fairly predictable mistakes.

In order to make the techniques you'll learn in this chapter maximally effective, keep the following rules in mind:

1. IF YOU'RE INTIMIDATED, START SMALL

One phone call. One e-mail. One conversation. One act of reaching out to someone Career Services puts you onto. You can manage *that*. *After* that, you can manage one more. And one more. But for right now, just come up with *one* thing you'll do.

This idea of taking tiny steps to accomplish goals is the Japanese concept of "Kaizen." There's a great book about this, called "One Small Step Can Change Your Life: The Kaizen Way," by Robert Mauer.

Mauer himself used Kaisen to lose weight. He didn't make big changes in his life. Instead, he decided to throw out the first french fry on his plate. Then it grew to two, then three, and bits of other food. It was easy. He wound up losing 45 pounds this way.

So don't tell yourself you have to find hundreds of people. Start with just one. It will lead to great things!

2. WHEN SOMEONE PUTS YOU ON TO SOMEONE ELSE, CALL. DON'T WRITE OR E-MAIL, UNLESS YOUR CONTACT TELLS YOU TO. YOU'RE MORE MEMORABLE THAT WAY

On the "hierarchy of memorability," you're least memorable on paper, more memorable on the phone, and most memorable in person. Wherever feasible, move up that scale! Alums your CSO recommends, friends of friends ... call, *unless* the person who put you onto them recommends an e-mail or letter. Advice specific to a person always trumps general principles about what works best.

If the idea of calling people makes you queasy, use this simple technique: leave a voice mail message "off hours" to say you'll be calling back later. Helen Long recommends that you script it so you'll find it easier, including something like:

- Your name
- Who told you to contact them/how you found them
- A short identifier (e.g., "2L at Case Western")
- That you'll be calling back later
- You're hoping for 10 minutes of their time at their convenience

- What you want, e.g., "I'm (looking to move to X) (very interested in practicing X law, like you)
- You'd really appreciate their advice about what you ought to be doing to better your chances, that you have specific questions for them
- That you'll be e-mailing them with your return e-mail address, if it's easier for them to communicate via e-mail
- Thank you!

Then call back. As Vickie Brown says, "I'll routinely hear from alums who say, 'Why don't the students just call me?'" It's much easier to say advice than write it. And you'll often get much blunter and more insightful advice than you could in an e-mail because a conversation can't be saved and forwarded the way an e-mail can.

Of course, if the person you're contacting prefers e-mail, then that's what you use. The *most* important thing is to follow their lead.

3.   DON'T ASK PEOPLE YOU DON'T KNOW TO CIRCULATE YOUR RESUME FOR YOU

When someone passes your resume on to someone else, they're vouching for you. They have to know you, at least a little bit, to feel comfortable doing that. With the activities you'll learn in this chapter, you'll give them that opportunity. Just don't make a resume circulation request your opening salvo.

4.   DRENCH YOUR COMMUNICATIONS WITH GRATEFULNESS

People are typically very helpful—but they aren't obligated to be that way. When anyone helps you in any way, thank them. And thank them in advance of their help: "I really appreciate your taking the time ..." "I'm very grateful ..." It means a lot, and it paves the way for future help.

5.   NEVER MEMORIALIZE ANGRY WORDS IN PRINT OR E-MAIL

If you're angry about *anything*—if you think someone has blown you off or done anything you don't like—*never, ever* e-mail them your thoughts. Give yourself a chance to cool off, and then if you absolutely *must* say something, call them instead of e-mailing them. Angry student e-mails have a way of making their way around the web. It's a reputation you don't want.

6.   RESPOND IMMEDIATELY TO E-MAILS; DON'T EXPECT THE SAME IN RETURN

Respond to e-mails the same day if you can, within twenty-four hours in any case, and if you have to be away from your e-mail, set up an auto response saying when you'll be back.

However—when you contact professionals, don't expect prompt e-mails from them. You have no idea when you contact them whether they're in the middle of a major project, away from their e-mail, or for any reason incommunicado. Give them at least two weeks to respond before you send an e-mail asking, "I just wanted to make sure you got my last e-mail . . ." and then repeat it, politely.

7. DON'T BLOW OFF MEETINGS

Maybe you changed your mind about meeting with someone. Maybe you nailed a job and you feel you don't need the meeting after all. Whatever the reason, *never, ever* stand up a professional. Call and reschedule or explain, and thank them for being willing to meet with you.

It's not just important for your own reputation—it's important for your school. You need to remember that when you venture out into the world, there are other people on the bus with you: all of the other students at your school. Employers often impute actions to other students from the same school, and you don't want to trash *everybody's* reputation because you decided to go to Happy Hour instead of meeting with that alum!

8. PEOPLE NEVER OFFER HELP WHEN THEY DON'T MEAN IT. *NEVER.* ALWAYS TAKE THEM UP ON IT

Nobody extends help to you because they feel they have to. They're never being polite when they say "Here's my card. Call me if I can help." You don't know when the next person you contact will have a great idea for you, will know someone who's hiring for your dream job, will give you a tip that changes your whole job search. Take them seriously!

9. WHEN PEOPLE GIVE YOU ADVICE YOU DON'T WANT, SAY "IT'S SOMETHING TO THINK ABOUT"

You'll hear great advice, bad advice, and everything in between. Don't jump ugly with people who tell you something that stinks on ice. The fact that they're telling you anything at all is a positive . . . and even if what they're telling you now ain't the best advice, they may come up with something later on that turns your life around.

On the other hand, you don't want to heartily endorse advice that stinks on ice.

Instead, take a middle ground. So when they tell you "Just wrap your resume around a rock and throw it through some windows," just answer with a stock response: "It's something to think about."

10. DON'T TURN OFF YOUR COMMON-SENSE-O-METER WHEN PEOPLE GIVE YOU ADVICE

This is a corollary of rule #9 above, that not all advice you'll get will be good. Don't take anyone's word as gospel. Remember that when anyone tells you *anything* the implied subtext is, "This is the world as I see it."

Much of the time the advice you get will be on-target, wise and helpful.

Occasionally, it will be butt-puckeringly bad.

I talked to a student from Seattle who was going to law school in New Jersey. He wanted to stay on the East Coast after graduation, and work for a large firm. A friend of his, a junior associate at such a firm, told him, "Dude, you're gonna have to lie. Tell firms that the reason you want to be here is that your parents are moving here. They won't believe you otherwise."

Now, this student goes to an East Coast law school, he'd gone to undergrad on the East Coast, and I asked him, "Let's start with the truth. Why did you really come here?" He said, "I stayed on the East Coast for law school because I really like the East Coast." I told him, "Then *say it*. It's a credibility issue. Your interest in the area is proven by the fact you stayed here for law school." The lie about his folks? Geez, how would he keep *that* up? He'd get busted somehow. In other words: The advice to lie was just awful (as it always is).

Another student, this one at a Southern school, had top-notch grades. Her issue was her—ahem—personality. She had a dour visage that really made people think she wasn't interested in what she claimed to want.

She went to a panel at school on large-firm hiring. Afterwards, she talked with one of the recruiters. The recruiter looked at her resume, and said dismissively, "With credentials like yours, send out five resumes. You'll get a job."

So the student sent out five resumes, got five interviews, and when they didn't turn into offers, she stopped in her tracks. She did *nothing* else . . . because this recruiter had assured her that all she'd have to do was send out five resumes. As her Career Services Director pointed out, "The recruiter couldn't possibly have known that this student's issue had nothing to do with her grades. They were great. She really needed to work on her interpersonal skills. But when she heard that 'five resume' advice, she latched onto it. And it was really, really bad advice."

So don't turn off your common-sense-o-meter when you ask people for advice. No matter how expert they might be, they could make a mistake. When it comes to career guidance, it's important to distinguish between the good, the bad, and the ugly. If you get advice that you think sounds suspect—it's completely at odds with what other people have told you, or it just doesn't comport with what you know of the field, the city, of people in general—bounce it off other people before you follow it.

11. GIVE BACK

If you're skeptical about people's good intentions, you're going to be pleasantly surprised by how helpful people can be (especially if you approach them correctly!). Remember that it's not a one-way street. Make yourself as helpful to others as they are to you. It's smart, it's strategic—and it's the right thing to do.

C. THE KEY TO FINDING GREAT JOBS FOREVER: THE "P.A. SYSTEM"

"Relationships are all there is. Everything in the universe only exists because it is in relationship to everything else. Nothing exists in isolation. We have to stop pretending we are individuals that can go it alone."
Margaret Wheatley

When you think of a P.A. system, you think of the public address system your high school had, right? Where they broadcast announcements during home room every day? Broadcasting is also the goal of the P.A. System you're going to learn here, although the "P" and the "A" stand for "people" and "activities." You're going to broadcast your interests, your enthusiasm, your availability, via people you know and meet, and activities in which you take part.

Everything in the world happens through people. When you watch the news, see how often a thread in the story relates to relationships. I'll give you just one example. When Watergate's "Deep Throat," W. Mark Feltt, outed himself, he did it through San Francisco lawyer John D. O'Connor. How did he choose O'Connor? It wasn't an ad in the Yellow Pages. As *The Washington Post* reported, O'Connor became acquainted with the Feltt family through Feltt's grandson, a classmate of O'Connor's daughter at college.

People, people, people.

I will give you dozens and dozens of ideas in this section—and I *know* that for the rest of your life, what you learn here is going to be your route to great jobs.

1. MANDATORY PREP WORK (RELAX. IT'S EASY)

Before you do *anything*—talk to anybody, take part in any career-related activity—do the following:

A. HAVE YOUR "PITCH" DOWN PAT

You have to be armed with a few readily-available "sound bytes" when you start talking to people and taking part in activities. Remember: you're going to be meeting professionals, and they'll be judging you as a professional. It's important to "sound" the part!

First of all, have your goal in mind. If you know what you want to do, or have it narrowed down to a few choices, practice a sound byte for your goal(s). "I took a great seminar in Family Law and I'm interested in learning more about what the practice is like ..." "I just wrote a journal piece about securities, and it really fired me up to get further involved ..." If you've got several different goals, you'll only mention the appropriate one in the setting; you don't tell a securities lawyer about your interest in family law!

You need to sound as though your choice is well-reasoned. Even a little research will accomplish that.

* * * SMART HUMAN TRICK * * *

At an alumni reception.

Alum: "What do you want to do when you get out?"

Student: "International Relations."

Alum: "That's interesting. I know a lot of people are interested in International Law, but I've never heard a student say International Relations."

Student: "Oh, I want International Law. But somebody told me to say International Relations because it sounds better. To be perfectly honest with you I'm not sure what it is."

If you don't know what you want to do—join the club, that's most of us!—no problem. Talking with people is a fantastic way to figure out what you'd like to do. When you talk with people, you'll say, "I'm trying to figure out what I'm going to do with my law degree, and I came to this today to learn more about X. I'd love to hear how you feel about the practice . . ." Talking with people is my all-time favourite way to make smart career choices, by the way. Be perfectly honest with people, tell them you're trying to figure out what you want to do by learning more about practice areas, and take it from there. It's a lot more fun that reading dry descriptions of practice areas—and a lot more realistic than your law school classes.

You're also going to need a brief introduction of yourself ready and rehearsed: "I'm Kimm Walton. I'm a Second Year at Case Western, and I work part-time for . . ." Then you talk about what got you interested in what the other person does, or launch into questions: "Tell me about what you do. How did you choose it? What do you like about it? . . ." and so on—the interview questions I recommended to you in Chapter 9.

It's also worth going back to the interview chapter to make sure you feel comfortable talking about anything you consider an Achilles' Heel. It's entirely possible that even casual conversations will involve questions about your grades, for instance— and if that makes you squirm, work on your answer before you talk to anybody.

Never, ever use "limiting words" in describing yourself. "I'm just . . ." "I'm only . . ." I hear this from students all the time. "I'm just a 1L." "I really haven't done anything . . ." I talked to one student who wanted to go into Tax Law with one of the big accounting firms, and when I asked her what she knew about it, she said, "Not much, really. I'm a bookkeeper and I talked with a few tax lawyers." Heck—that's more than a lot of people have done.

Another student, this one in Oregon, had done a ton of interesting things. One of them was to take the summer after First Year to live in an RV on the coast of Washington State, "Living on whatever I caught," and attempting to write a novel. "When I meet people, I tell them that I ran into a few snags with the novel and gave it up. As a matter of fact I try a lot of things, but I drop most of them." I told him: whatever you do, *don't* tell people that! He said, "But I graduated *summa cum laude*. I tell them that, too." That may be; but they won't forget the fact that you led with negatives. You can euphemize anything; "Running into a few snags" with a novel can become "I have a few loose ends to tie up." Like the plot, the characters ...

The fact is people will form their opinions of you based in part on what you say about yourself. You're not *just* an anything. You're a ton more educated than most of the world will ever be. Whatever you have or haven't done, you've got your dreams. So say things like, "Right now, I'm a 1L. I'm really interested in ..." "So far, I've done ..." without saying words that diminish who you are and what you've done.

B. KEEP CLOSE TRACK OF EVERY STEP YOU TAKE, EITHER WITH A PROGRAM LIKE MICROSOFT OUTLOOK OR WITH A CARD FILE, BINDER AND CALENDAR

When you are looking for a job, it's crucial that you document your search. There are at least two good reasons for this. For a start, if you quantify what you're doing—whom you're contacting, the activities in which you're taking part, when you've contacted people—it will help you keep track of exactly how much you've done. It's very easy to "inflate" your efforts; I hear this from Career Services Directors all the time, who'll tell me they give students a list of alums to contact. "I give them fifteen names, they'll contact two, not hear back from either one, and come back telling me it didn't work." When someone gives you a list of fifteen people to contact, *contact all of them before you go back to the well!* You'll be amazed at how many useful people you'll talk to, but if you don't keep accurate records, a couple of phone calls or e-mails will balloon in your mind. Keep track of everything!

On top of that, you need to keep track of when to contact and re-contact people, *when to send thank yous—very* important—and every scrap of information you learn about people you meet; their spouses' names, hobbies, children's names, accomplishments, and so on. It really doesn't take much effort, especially once you have your system in place.

For that system, you can go high-tech or low-tech. To keep track on your computer or PDA, you may already have a contacts program that you like. If not, try Microsoft Outlook. If you go low-tech, I'd recommend a simple 5x8″ file box and 5x8″ index cards to go in it. You can find them at any office supply store. You also want those alphabetical dividers, a three-ring binder and a three-hole punch. You may already have this stuff lying around!

When you start talking with people, and meeting new people through them and through activities, you want to keep track of *every single professional contact you make*. The information you want to record—with one file or card per person—should include:

- Name, address, phone, e-mail (typically from a business card);
- When and how you met them;
- Who referred you to them;
- Who they in turn referred you to;
- Any correspondence back and forth (keep your correspondence in the binder);
- Anything personal they've mentioned to you (e.g., interests, spouse's name, children's name(s), birthdays, anniversaries, vacation plans, accomplishments, anything that comes up);
- Salient points of your conversation(s) with them (e.g., what their specialty is, what they like or dislike about it).

You're thinking, "Do I *really* have to keep track of all of this stuff?" Mm hmm. You're establishing contacts you may have for a long time, maybe even your whole career. Ellen Sefton, Career Services Director at Florida Coastal, has a file system that keeps track of *every person she's met for the last fifteen years!* You can't think of professional contacts as people you pick up and discard. You'll want to know and remember everything about them that you can. Months may pass when you don't speak with them, and you don't want to forget anything about them in the meantime. There's no way to do that other than by writing it down! And that includes offhand stuff like birthdays and family names and interests. It may sound corny, but people are really impressed when you mention their children's names, or make reference to something that they may have told you months ago. (I know from personal experience how handy this kind of file is. I wish I had the memory people think I have—I do it all with index cards!).

So much for the card file and binder. You'll also want to maintain a calendar, virtual or literal, so that you can mark on it when you should contact people. For instance, if you send a letter or e-mail today saying that you're going to follow up with a phone call in two weeks, mark a date about 2½ weeks hence (leaving time for the letter to be delivered or the e-mail read), so that you're sure to remember to follow up promptly.

The point here is—don't pretend you're going to be able to remember everything in your head. Take great notes—and keep a calendar!

c. THE CARE AND FEEDING OF PEOPLE WHO HELP YOU OUT: IT'S A TWO WAY STREET, YOU KNOW!

When you're looking for a job, it's easy to suck up all the air in the room, figuring: "It's all about me"—who other people can put you on to, what opportunities they can tell you about. But remember: people tend to be healthily self-interested. Giving advice, helping students is something most people are very happy to do—but remember, as Gail Peshel says, that "It's a two way street!"

What does that mean? It has a couple of ramifications:

1. OFTEN, AND ENTHUSIASTICALLY, STATE YOUR GRATEFULNESS TO ANYBODY WHO HELPS YOU OUT

I can't tell you how many lawyers I talk to who will seethe, "This student called me for advice, and I spent half an hour talking to him, giving him names of people to contact. I told him to go ahead and use my name. And you know the little [fill in your favourite epithet] never even *thanked* me!"

I've told you often that most people like to be helpful. But if you don't express your gratitude, you can watch that benevolent spirit dry up like Death Valley. And it's got ugly ramifications. For one thing, you can't ever go back to the same person if you didn't thank them appropriately the first time around—and you'll often want to go back to the well for more help. On top of that, this person could well be your colleague for a lifetime. Don't take the risk of alienating them over something as simple as a thank you!

2. KEEP YOUR CONTACTS UP-TO-DATE ABOUT THE STATUS OF ANY ADVICE/CONTACT THEY GIVE YOU

Part of the reason professional people like to help students is they like to see the fruits of their advice. They want to know how you're progressing. So when somebody gives you an idea, a contact, an activity to pursue—*let them know how it turned out.* Again, there are at least two good reasons for doing so: For one thing, if you ever intend to go back to them for more help, you'll want at least some of your "interim" contact not to involve you asking for something. If every time you call you're asking "Can you help me ..." after a while they're going to get worn out. Don't get to the point where they ask you, "So whatever happened with the guy I told you to contact? ..." Keep them up to date! Just a simple note or e-mail is appropriate.

On top of that, if you're having trouble getting through to people your contacts put you on to, keeping in touch like this can have a hidden benefit: your contact might make contact for you. I often have students say to me, "My friend/professor/an alum told me to contact this guy. I left him a message two weeks ago, but I haven't heard anything. What should I do?" Other than not taking offense—people get busy, you know!—you can always go back to the original contact, *thank them for giving you the person's name,* and say, "I haven't had any luck getting through to him/her, but when I do, I'll let you know how it goes." That often prompts the contact to say, "I'll give him a call." So there can be a direct benefit to letting your contacts know what's going on!

3. WHEN YOU USE THEM AS A REFERENCE, LET THEM KNOW ANYTIME YOU SEND OUT A RESUME OR GO ON AN INTERVIEW

As Margann Bennett recommends, "If you're using people as references, let them know when you're sending resumes, and to whom. Also, let them know when and with whom you're interviewing. They might make a call on your behalf, recommending you. Also, once you interview, let them know how it went. Again, they might want to call the employer for you."

4. IF YOU LEARN ABOUT SOMETHING THAT COULD BE USEFUL TO PEOPLE WHO HELP YOU—OFFER IT!

Look at the people you know as a bank account. Sometimes you'll make withdrawals—asking for things—but you should also focus on deposits, on doings things for *them.*

It's never too early to get into the habit of giving back. As kind as people will be in helping you out, you should do the same in return!

It may involve a hobby the person is interested in, or a business contact that might be useful to them. For instance, let's say that you meet a lawyer named Gisela Werbezirk, who happens to mention that she's very interested in Thomas Jefferson. When you get home, you note on her card her interest in Jefferson. And the following month, lo and behold, you notice that *Civilizations* Magazine has an article about how Jefferson's original draft of the Declaration of Independence was actually modified by others. Well, make a copy and send it to Gisela, with a note mentioning that she might find it interesting in light of her interest in Jefferson.

The same goes for business opportunities you stumble onto that may benefit your contacts. For instance, if you have a friend moving to town and buying a house and one of your contacts is a real estate lawyer, recommend the lawyer to your friend. Or it may be that in your conversations with people and taking part in activities, you meet two people who really ought to know each other. Make the introduction. You'll be a hero to both of them!

Note that all of this reinforces the fact that you're becoming part of a professional community—you're not just wandering around with your metaphysical hand out. When you have the chance to return the favour . . . do it!

5. BE DISCREET ABOUT WHAT YOU DO WITH NEGATIVE INFORMATION

As a rule of thumb, if someone tells you something positive about someone else, be sure to repeat it—and attribute it. "Hermione Google said that she thought your firm is the best internet defamation defense firm in the city.''

On that same thumb, when you learn negative information, *handle it gingerly.*

Let's say a counselor at Career Services tells you that a firm has a questionable ethical reputation. If you interview with the firm, you can't even *intimate* that you heard that, and certainly not from Career Services! Talk to alums who've worked there, obviously do a Google/Lexis/Westlaw search to see what's been written about them—but don't ever, ever say, "I heard at Career Services that you've got ethical issues.''

It's as important to learn negatives about employers and markets as it is to hear positives. Make sure people feel comfortable sharing all kinds of information with you by protecting their images!

6. GIFTING THE PEOPLE WHO HELP YOU. HMM . . .

Maybe and maybe not. It's certainly not necessary and nobody expects you to give them a gift for helping you out. But small heartfelt tokens of appreciation? I've seen it work well.

For instance, once student got great help from an alum, and learned that the alum was an avid golfer, so the student sent her a set of golf tees with the law school's logo on them. It went over well. I've known students who've given helpful people Starbucks gift cards. Again, fine but not necessary.

A simple card with an honest sentiment means a lot. You can imagine how much it would mean to you to get a card saying something like, "Your confidence in me means a great deal to me. I'm honored to have your guidance and I hope someday, when I am successful, I can be as helpful to a student as you have been to me." Touching, eh? Of course, I poop this stuff out for a living. But you see the point: gratefulness doesn't *have* to include a gift.

7. IF SOMEONE SUDDENLY STOPS BEING HELPFUL . . .

. . . Ask them directly if you've done something wrong. Don't be defensive.

It's kind of unusual for someone to help you and then suddenly cut you off cold. There's got to be *something* behind it, and you should find out what it is.

I talked to a student at one school who had a very prominent mentor who invited her to professional meetings all the time. Suddenly the flow of invitations stopped, and she had no idea why. She was really mad about it.

Especially when you're going to be in the same legal community with somebody, it makes sense to sort out what happened. Just call—don't e-mail—and say something like "I hope I didn't offend

692   Guerrilla Tactics for Getting the Legal Job of Your Dreams

you in some way," and ask what happened. No matter what the reason, if the relationship can't be mended, thank them for the help they gave you, and wish them luck. Leave on an "up" note. You don't know when you'll run into them again.

D. Accept That Your Dream Job Might Not Fall in Your Lap With the First Contact You Make. It's Not a Magic Bullet. It's a Magic Winnebago

Ultimately, doing the things I'm going to tell you to do in this chapter is the most effective way to nail great opportunities.

But it's not instantaneous. As Washington's Elaine Bourne says, "You don't know *when* you'll get what you want." American's Matt Pascocello adds, "You can't 'microwave' relationships. Building contacts takes time. If a job comes out of a first meeting, it's just luck."

You'll inevitably face setbacks. There will be people who won't return your calls or respond to your e-mails. Hard as it is to believe, activities you attend may not all be overflowing with people begging to help you out. I talked to one student who went to a bar association meeting and said, "*Everybody* in the room was looking for a job!" You'll meet some people who are surly, busy, or just plain nether-bodily-orifices. A student in Georgia told me, "I went to a CLE, I met a lawyer and when I mentioned I'm a law student, he ran away. *Ran.*" It happens.

In other words: the personality distribution of contacts you make is the same as for any other population.

You may also face times where you feel like a plate of cinnamon buns, being passed from person to person to person. "I called this one who told me to talk to this one who put me on to this one . . ." and you'll find yourself thinking, *"Where's my job?"* Relax. It'll happen. It *always* does. As Susan Benson says, "It may seem like an eternity, but within a year you'll be sending out a business card. Time is a leveling factor. It doesn't matter how old you were when you learned to read, as long as you do now."

The fact is, you never know when the next phone call you make, the next person you talk to, the next event you attend is going to lead to the job of your dreams. It could be *tomorrow*. After all, you only need one job. Just make sure you have lots of irons in the fire—lots of people to talk to, lots of events you plan to attend, and of course your "traditional" job search activities, like sending resumes and using web sites. The bottom line is, you *are* going to find a job. In the meantime—be patient!

E. Keep Your Feet Moving!

The one sure way to keep yourself unemployed is to sit back and do nothing. It's *your* job search. Own it! Other people can help you—and they will—but honestly, nobody cares as much about your job search as you do. Don't let the time it takes to find a job harden into a bad attitude, because then you won't get *anything*. One Career Services Director told me about a survey she did of graduates who didn't have jobs yet. She got a note back from one of them saying, "I've been looking for a job for six months and have gotten nothing. What are you people getting paid for?" Well! Who's *that* going to help?

If you find yourself seriously bumming out, remember: there is therapy in taking action. Whether you contact more people, take part in activities, go to events—I'll give you tons of ideas—doing something, *anything*, will make you feel better than sitting at home, moping, eating cheese puffs, drinking beer and watching soap operas. If you've graduated, take a part-time volunteer job. Or temp work. Or better yet, take on a volunteer project for the local bar association, or take part in a pro bono project (we'll talk about these in detail later in this chapter). That will give you not only experience, but also some great job contacts! As Sandy Mans advises, "If you don't get your dream job right now, do *something*. Get *some* job. Don't sit at home waiting for your dream, because that only shows you're lazy."

The point is, your dream job won't come knocking on your door. You have to go out and get it!

F. START TODAY!

I know what you're thinking. "Yeah, I'll get around to it …." Don't fall into that trap.

I was at a dinner party once, and the woman sitting next to me asked, "So what do you do?" I told her I was writer, and she responded, "I'm a writer, too." I asked her what she'd written, and she said, "Oh, I have a book in my head."

I love that. A book in my head. Try finding *that* on Amazon.

There's an old Irish proverb that says, "You will never plow a field by turning it over in your mind." So start *today*. Do *something*. You've got your goal in mind, whether you have an idea of what you want to do—or you want to figure it out. You're comfortable with what you have to say about yourself and your credentials. As Ann Skalaski says, "The most difficult thing is picking up that first phone!"

G. WHAT TO SAY TO PEOPLE YOUR CONTACTS PUT YOU ONTO …

We talk about this in detail later in this chapter under Topic C, "Informational Interviewing."

2. THE "P" IN THE "P.A." SYSTEM: PEOPLE TO CONTACT

Remember, you've got two routes to your dream job: people and activities. We'll talk about people first. I'll take you through the different "categories" of people you'll be talking to. What you say to people in each category will be different; you can blurt out the fact that you're looking for a job to your aunts and uncles, but you wouldn't do the same thing with a person behind you in line at CVS!

It's important, when you're thinking of people to contact, that you remember two things: First of all, **don't write off anybody you know because you figure "they don't know anybody."** I've talked with thousands of law students, and based on their experiences, I can tell you this: You never know who the people you know, know. Not an elegant sentence, but you see the point! Your plumber might have an uncle or cousin who works at a great firm. The lady who helps you find a suit at the department store might have a daughter who's in a position to help you. Be diligent and thorough in your search!

Secondly, **don't assume that anybody knows you're looking for a job.** As Gail Peshel points out, "In fact, the perception is just the opposite; people *don't* think you're looking for a job if you don't say so." Laura Rowe Lane goes even further: "You can't assume [your Career Services Office] knows you're looking for a job. You can't assume they even know who you are!" So, no matter how obvious you think it is that you're in the market, say it anyway.

Third, remember what you're seeking: "informational interviews," which we'll discuss later in this chapter. While the people you tell about your career aspirations may know you're looking for a job—and may put you onto people with job openings—it's far more likely that they'll put you onto people who can help you with advice. That's the goal of an informational interview.

With those points in mind, let's go through everybody you should contact, in four principal categories: First, people you know well. Second, people you haven't seen in a while but who would still recognize you and/or your name. Third, people that you meet. And finally, "degrees of separation" people, that is, people that the first three categories put you on to. In each case, we'll talk about what you should talk about with them.

I encourage you to **get out a pad of paper, and as you read through the following pages, write down as many names as you can**. Put the list down for a couple of days, start to contact people on it, and add names as you think of them. The point is to make the list as complete as possible!

A. PEOPLE YOU SEE ROUTINELY AND KNOW WELL

For people you see on a regular basis and feel close to, **you can come straight out and tell them you're looking for a job.** You can say, in essence, "This is what I want. Who should I be talking to? What should I be doing? Do you have any ideas for me?" As Vickie Brown says, "If you wanted to score tickets to a game, you'd ask people you know. Jobs are the same."

There may be people in this first category with whom you don't feel comfortable being so bold. Maybe you sit next to the same person on the subway every day or order coffee from the same guy every morning, but you don't feel comfortable coming straight out and asking them for help. That's OK. **In *those* situations, you can be more subtle but equally effective**: You tell them that you're at that point in law school (they already probably know you're *there)* where you start looking at what you'll do with your degree, that you're interested in X, and if they think of anyone who could give you advice about it you'd appreciate it. If they ask you, "You're looking for a job, right?" you can always respond with something like, "That would be great. But I realize advice about how to break into X is very valuable, too." That way, you're not putting so much pressure on them.

Let's talk about who you should talk to!

1. YOUR CAREER SERVICES OFFICE AT SCHOOL

Well–duh. I can't tell you how many students tell me, "I'm not bothering with Career Services. They only help people in the top ten percent of my class." To quote Julia Roberts in *Pretty Woman:* Big mistake. I spent a whole chapter—Chapter 3—talking about how to make the most of your Career Services Office. But here, let's focus on the reasons why you should tell your Career Services Director what you want:

a. Don't assume that they know you're looking for a job.

A lot of students tell me, "Shouldn't it be *obvious* to them that I'm looking for a job?"

In a word: Nope. As Sari Zimmerman points out, "If a student doesn't tell us they're in the market for a job, we'll assume they *aren't,* that they've already found something."

Career Services will be right there for you—but only if they know that you're in the hunt!

b. They can put you on to all kinds of people you'd never have thought of on your own.

To put it simply, your Career Services Office is a resource-generating machine. It's their job to know *everybody.* If you tell them what you want, they can hook you up with alums in the specialty and/or geographic area, they can clue you into organizations you should contact and/or join, and they can put you on to activities where you'll meet useful people. But they can't do any of this if you don't tell them what you want!

c. They can put you on to jobs that come into Career Services on a random basis.

Here's a headline for you: most jobs don't come to your school through on-campus interviews. It just seems that way. On the contrary, every Career Services Director I talk to echoes the advice of Lisa Kellogg: "I get casual job requests from alums all the time. They'll want someone who's looking for environmental law, or someone who speaks a language like Mandarin Chinese. If a student lets me know they're looking, lets me know what their skills are, I'll know to call them when these jobs come in."

Michelle Hoff adds, "Employers call all the time, saying 'I don't want resumes, just tell me who . . .' and if students keep their profiles up to date with us, we can recommend them when we get those calls."

Timing is also crucial. Often when lawyers call, they need a clerk *today*. That's why you have to make your wishes known to Career Services *now*— so that when those opportunities come in, your Career Services director knows to contact you! Of course, they have to make the same listings available to everybody, but if you're diligent about visiting you might "luck out" and find something as it comes in.

It boils down to this: If your Career Services Office doesn't know who you are, and doesn't know that you're looking for a job, they won't be able to put you in contact with employers who may be looking for someone just like you!

d. Use summer clerkship reviews at Career Services to find students and alums to contact.

When you want the inside skinny on employers, there's nobody better than someone who's worked there—or works there now. George Washington's Sheila Driscoll recommends that you use summer clerkship evaluations to identify those students. "Some of the reviews are anonymous, but many of them aren't," she says. If you talk to students who've worked for an employer, you have a hidden benefit: employers often ask their current and former clerks for their opinions on student interviewees. If you make yourself known to these people, you may have a leg up on the competition.

2. YOUR FAMILY

Double duh. Nobody is more organically interested in your success than your family. You should absolutely let them know—if you haven't already!—what you're looking for. For all you know, you may have a third cousin you didn't even know existed—who does exactly what you want to do. It happened to a law student at a Midwestern school.

My hunch is that if your father is a partner at Skadden Arps, you've already thought of telling your family. But if you *haven't* told your folks, I'd guess there are a few of things that might be holding you back:

• **You're embarrassed that you have to ask.**

You wouldn't be the first person to think, "Gee, if I go to law school, jobs paying a kajillion dollars are going to fall into my lap." You may figure the *last* thing you want to do is to admit to your parents that you couldn't go it alone. The idea of turning to Mommy and Daddy for help may make your stomach turn.

To that all I can say is: Suck it up and ask. Your parents will have one of two reactions. Odds are they'll be delighted to help. You are, after all, the physical manifestation of their hopes and dreams ... at least, I sure *hope* so. Most parents are thrilled to be asked.

Their other, far less likely reaction is—"Gee. You went to law school. Why didn't jobs paying a kajillion dollars fall into your lap?" You can explain to them that while you know you will be successful, more than fifty percent of law students graduate without a job in hand. And more students get their jobs through personal referrals than any other way. You're just turning to them first because, well ... because you're the physical manifestation of their hopes and dreams. You probably won't use those words, but you see the point.

• **It's cheating.**

I hear this all the time from students. "My father is a judge/a politician/a very successful fill-in-the-blank. He keeps offering to help me out, but ..." and their voices trail off.

Take the help, dammit. Remember: nobody can really get you a job or make you a success. In her memoir, the legendary beauty Hedy Lamarr compared beauty to a fifty-yard head start in a running race. That's what help from influential parents is. *You're* the one who's got to go on the interview. *You're* the one who's got to do the work. If you wind up being a drooling idiot, *nobody's* going to keep you around. You ultimately are responsible for your success. But in the meantime ... parents who are in a position to help are manna from Heaven. Accept the help and thank your lucky stars!

• **You're worried they're going to pressure you into something you don't want to do.**

Particularly if you want to do something non-traditional—in which case, you'll want to read Chapter 31 about nontraditional careers—you may be worried about telling your parents what you want to do. Not that they wouldn't be delighted to hear that you want to be a juggler, mind you. (That's my favourite law student goal ever, I think!) But the fact is, the parents of many a law student have visions in their heads of Junior joining Bigg, Bigg and Bucks Law Firm, and wallowing in prestige and dineros. If you want to do anything else ... well, you may feel they'll be less than thrilled. One law school graduate, a Law Review member at an Ivy League school, told me about the day she told her parents she didn't think a large law firm would make her happy. "Happy!" her father steamed. "How can you not be happy on *a hundred thousand dollars a year?*"

You may similarly be concerned about how your parents will react to your dreams. If so: break it to them slowly. Explain to them how much you appreciate your law degree (particularly if they helped pay for it!), how the entire point of going to law school was to give yourself a career you'd enjoy. You could have dropped out of high school if you wanted to be miserable! Address their concerns, recognizing that they simply might not understand why you'd want to do something that's outside of their dream purview. But stick with it. Your folks love you, and they ultimately want you to be happy. They'll come around, even if it takes some time. And if you really have a hard time with them, enlist your Career Services Director to talk to them on your behalf—and you can always contact me, the Job Goddess, to back you up. Your folks wouldn't be the first ones I've e-mailed! (My e-mail address is jobgoddess@ aol.com)

- **Your parents aren't lawyers, and you figure they don't know anybody useful.**

  Students tell me this all the time. "My father is a plumber/my mom is a secretary/my parents own a convenience store ... *they can't help me.*" Sure they can. They've got friends, they've got a lawyer of their own, they know service people. And as I keep saying about everybody: *you don't know who they know.* Your parents are hard-wired to wrack their brains to help you. You may be amazed to find out who your parents know. So tell them what you're looking for!

- **You're worried the folks they put you onto won't take you seriously.**

  Maybe your folks' friends and colleagues know you a little *too* well—your partying habits and general *joie de vivre* may not lend you the gravitas associated with lawyers.

  Remember: images can change. Impress on them the activities you're doing in law school (with which they may not be familiar), your enthusiasm and seriousness about what you want to do. You'll change their minds. No reputation is engraved in stone.

- **Coach your folks on what to say.**

    You can come right out and tell your parents you're looking for a job. *You don't necessarily want them to say that to people they know.* Remember, it's just as useful to approach people for *advice,* and it's a lot less pressure on them. So encourage your parents to say, "Little Ricky is in law school, as you know. He's interested in being a maritime lawyer." And follow that up with either: "Can he call you? Would you mind talking to him, giving him some advice, telling him what it's like . . .?" or "Can you think of anyone he should be talking to, to find out more about it?" People are more likely to be helpful if they figure you're looking for advice, rather than just a job!

    * * * SMART HUMAN TRICK * * *

    Law student at a school in Ohio. A firm he wanted for the summer rejected him for an on-campus interview.

    His wife was a volunteer at Catholic Charities. A guy there was a lawyer . . . with her husband's dream firm. The wife and the lawyer started chatting about families. The wife mentioned her husband, and the lawyer asked, "What does he do?"

    "He's a law student," she replied.

    "Have him call me," said the lawyer.

    The student wound up working there.

    * * * SMART HUMAN TRICK * * *

    Law student dying to get into Sports Law, specifically motor racing. Her mother is a human resources person, and belongs to an association of human resources professionals. At an association lunch the mom mentions to the others at the table what her daughter wants to do. One of them turns out to be the human resources person for a nationally-known race track. She says, "Have your daughter call me." The daughter calls, and winds up with a summer internship at the track.

3. YOUR PARENTS' FRIENDS

You know. The people you call "Uncle" or "Aunt" even though you aren't technically related.

Your parents' friends have probably already offered to help you out. You may be reluctant to talk to them because they don't do what you want. As Sue Gainen recommends, "Unless the work they do is murder-for-hire, talk to them."

First of all, you don't know who they know. Everybody knows someone useful, including your parents' friends.

Secondly, if they are lawyers but simply not in a field that interests you, you can *always* learn something valuable from them. You can ask what characteristics are most important to successful lawyers, how they settled on what they wanted to do, questions like that. If they say, "Why don't you come to work for me?" You thank them profusely and tell them you appreciate it, you're in an information-gathering mode right now and you want to have an idea of as many specialties as you can before you settle on one. If you settle on something else, tell them, in your own words, you want to do this right now but you still appreciate their faith in you and who knows what will happen down the road.

The fact is, you don't want to alienate or insult your parents' friends. So let them help you!

4. YOUR CLASSMATES

"What, are you *kidding*, Kimmbo?" I can hear you shrieking. "They don't have jobs *either!*" Or you'll think: "We're all looking for the *same* jobs." Or maybe it's, "Who the heck are they going to know that I *don't?*"

Keep two things in mind: First of all, you and your classmates aren't as similar as you think. You're probably looking for different kinds of jobs and you're looking in different places. I've heard just about every goal on the planet from law students. So don't assume that everybody you know is looking for what *you're* looking for, and that they'll jealously guard their resources.

Secondly, remember, as Teresa DeAndrado points out, that "Your classmates are going to be your professional colleagues." You *should* be helpful to them, and they should be, to you. Classmates of mine from law school routinely forward business to each other. You might as well get into the practice of relying on your classmates, now! (The fact that you'll be professional colleagues also points out why it's sensible not to get *too* blasted at law school parties, and not to be too—ahem—profligate with your love life at school.)

The importance of making a good impression on your classmates was brought home to me a few months ago. I was riding the train home from Manhattan after speaking to new associates at a large firm there. The train was jammed with commuters. I sat next to a very handsome, distinguished looking man who was dozing off. As we left Grand Central Station, in one of his waking moments, I whispered: "Tell me which station is yours and I'll wake you up for it."

He found this sufficiently amusing that we started chatting. His name was Jeff Walker, and he said he'd been commuting into the city for many years, most of which he spent working for Donald Trump. "I was the second person he hired," he said. "I was the original 'Apprentice.'"

I naturally asked how he nailed *that* gig. He said he and Trump were classmates at military school. Walker went on to get a degree in architecture. When 'The Donald' started his building spree, he told his own architect, "I need a project manager, someone to look after my interests. I need someone tough, honest ..."

"I've got just the man for you," responded his architect. "Jeff Walker."

"Jeff Walker?" Trump responded. "Jeff Walker who went to the New York Military Academy?"

The architect said yes, and Trump responded, "He'd be perfect."

In other words: Walker got the gig because he'd impressed a classmate. The fact is, you have no idea the opportunities that may come your way via the kid in the next seat at class. You don't want them to think back in years to come and only remember you as the one upchucking at parties.

In terms of what you say to your classmates: the approach is going to be somewhat different than it would be for your Career Services Office, or professors, or alums ... because you see your classmates every day. What you want to do is to work your goal into conversations. Don't keep it a secret! "I'm looking for x type of law in x city, and man, do I have some work to do. I don't know where to start ..." What you want to do is, in the words of Henry Fonda in *Twelve Angry Men,* throw it out on the porch and see if a cat licks it up. You'll find more often than not that a classmate will say, "*I* know who you should talk to ... my father/mother/aunt/friend works at ..." and you've got a lead!

* * * SMART HUMAN TRICKS * * *

When I give *Guerrilla Tactics* seminars at law schools, afterwards students often line up to ask me questions, under the delusion that I might have something valuable to say. Of course I'm kidding.

They generally don't line up.

But the point is, inevitably other students waiting to speak to me come up with really useful ideas. Some of my favourite examples:

- At one law school in Nebraska, a student told me, "I'm tearing my hair out. I'm dying to get into sports, but my dream is so specific that I don't think I can get it. What I really want to do is work for the St. Louis Blues ..." Sure enough, a student standing behind him in line piped up: "The St. Louis Blues? My father does business with them all the time. You have to talk to him!"

- At a Texas school, a female student at my Guerrilla Tactics seminar moaned, "I want Sports Law and the problem is that there are no women in it." Another student piped up, "That's not true. There's a woman sports lawyer in town, she graduated from here, and she's always willing to help students. Call her."

- At a law school in Arizona, a student came up to me and said, "I know that you say that grades can't kill you, but *my* grades ..." I asked him how bad his grades really were, and he said, "I'm a Second Year, and I had to take Civil Procedure over again."

  Now, I know people have different opinions about Civ Pro, but for me personally, taking Civ Pro on an endless loop is my vision of Hell.

  So I asked him: "What do you want to do?" No matter what it was, I figured I knew someone with worse grades who'd already nailed a great job. He threw me a softball: "I want to go into politics. I don't know if I want to run for office or get involved in campaigns ..."

  The clouds parted! Do you think you need good grades for politics? Do you need *law school* for politics? Sure enough, a friend of his, standing behind him in line, looked at him and said, "I can't believe this is the first time I'm hearing this from you! My father is a political consultant. He manages ten campaigns a year. You could work for him!"

- At a school in Oregon, a student reports, "I got a judicial clerkship ... from a judge I didn't even approach!"

  "What happened is I applied for a clerkship with another judge in the same court. That judge decided to keep his clerk another year—a woman who'd graduated the year before me. He mentioned me to this woman, and she said, 'Oh, she's really terrific.' So the judge called another judge and said, 'My clerk says this student is great—you should talk to her.' That other judge called me in, and now I'm working for him."

- A student at a California school said his dream was to work for Intel. The student standing next to him said, "You're kidding. My parents both work there. Come over to my house for dinner."

- A woman at an Arizona school wanted to become a broadcast journalist, with her own law show. A classmate standing nearby said, "I worked at two radio stations before law school. You should start in radio to learn to read and write copy. I'll help you out if you want."

- A law student at a Southwestern school, interested in getting into politics in New Haven, Connecticut ... 2,500 miles away. A classmate pipes up, "My grandfather was the mayor of New Haven. We have a ton of contacts there. We can get together and talk about it."

- At a Midwestern school, a student raises her hand during the *Guerilla Tactics* seminar and says, "I want to do something related to animals. Is there such a thing as animal law?" Another student calls out, "There sure is. I know a 'dog lawyer' in Los Angeles. You should contact him."

- A student at a Southern law school mentioned that he wanted to use his German skills. A classmate said, "hey—I have a professor who's very interested in German law. You need to talk to him."

- At a law school in California, a 1L told me, "I'm dying to get into Entertainment Law." There's a specialty I never hear about ... and particularly *not* in California, as you might imagine;). It just so happened that I knew a student at his law school whom I call "Mr. Entertainment"—this guy knew all kinds of ways to nail a job in entertainment. I told this 1L to contact him, and I learned later what happened. "Mr. Entertainment" told him to go to television writers' conferences, with the explanation: "Law students never do that, and it's a great thing to do, because people don't realize that a lot of television writers are disgruntled former lawyers. You go, you mention you're in law school ... it's a great ice breaker."

  This 1L didn't have much faith in the advice, but he took it. He went to a television writers' conference in Los Angeles, and hung out near the bar. He got into a conversation with someone, and when they asked what he was doing and he said "law school," they responded, "Law school? Are you kidding? *I* went to law school ..."

  The upshot: from this one conference, he nailed a great summer job: interning on the set of *West Wing*.

5. YOUR CURRENT LEGAL EMPLOYER. THERE ARE DIFFERENT TACTICS FOR DIFFERENT SITUATIONS!

A. IF IT'S A LEGAL EMPLOYER AND THEY WANT YOU TO STAY THERE AFTER LAW SCHOOL—THEY ARE OFF-LIMITS FOR ADVICE ABOUT OTHER JOBS!

You knew this already. If your significant other wanted to marry you, you'd never say, "Well, thanks, but can you introduce me to . . .?" Employers have feelings, too. Don't talk about your job search with them.

B. IF IT'S A LEGAL EMPLOYER WHERE THERE'S NO CHANCE OF A PERMANENT GIG . . .

Absolutely ask for help. Say something like, "I really appreciate the opportunity to work here. I've learned a lot of valuable skills. What do you think I should do next? Who should I be talking to? If I wanted to use my skills in X where should I think about working?" If you've got a good relationship with them, you might even ask if they'll make a couple of calls to pave the way for you.

C. IF IT'S A LEGAL EMPLOYER AND THE SUBJECT OF A FULL-TIME JOB HASN'T COME UP YET, IF YOU WANT ONE . . .

Bring it up. Script your opening before you sit down with your boss, take a deep breath, and *ask*.

I often talk to 3Ls who are inching toward graduation, they've got a part-time gig at a law firm, and the subject of permanent jobs just hasn't come up. They feel uncomfortable bringing it up, and wonder whether they should.

In a word: Absolutely! I talked to one student who was one of almost two dozen externs at the D.A.'s office. There was *one* permanent opening. The student said, "I know the guy who'll do the selection, but I'm afraid of seeming too forward." As South Texas' Kim Cauthorn advises, "In that situation, you *have* to talk to that person. Sit down and say, 'I know there's one job. I want it. I need your advice about getting it.' You're not being too bold. You'll be expected to be assertive when you *have* the job. Show it in order to *get* the job."

So sit down with your boss and say something like, "I really enjoy working here. I've learned some very valuable skills and I appreciate the positive feedback I've gotten about my work. I'd like to continue full-time after graduation. Can we talk about it?"

Now, one of two things is going to happen. And then something after *that,* potentially.

The first possibility is that because you put a bug in their ear, they'll start thinking seriously about it and make you an offer. Or maybe they were going to anyway and you've just prompted them.

Or maybe they'll tell you "No." They like you but they just don't feel they have enough for you to do full-time/they can't support you/whatever. If *that* happens, don't be angry or resentful; take a deep breath and say, "I understand. You know that I have to start thinking about what I'll do after I graduate. Can you give me some people I should contact? Ideas for what I ought to do?" You may even ask them to make some calls on your behalf.

Now, here's the hidden benefit to taking this approach. I've seen it happen where law firms didn't think they could keep their part-time clerks after graduation, but when they started calling around to recommend their clerks to *other* employers, they realized, "Holy Cow. I don't want to lose this person!" and the very act of recommending the student to other people prompted them to make an offer of their own!

6. CO-WORKERS AND CUSTOMERS FROM ANY JOB YOU HAVE NOW, LAW-RELATED OR NOT

As long as it's no secret you're in law school and you're going to be changing jobs, people you know through current work are extra useful to you, because they know you when you've got your "game face" on; that is, they see you professionally.

When it comes to customers, if you've got the kind of job that brings you into frequent contact with the same customers over and over again, you probably talk with them more often than you do some of your friends. Work into the conversation what you're doing in school, and what you're looking for. If you feel uncomfortable about coming out and asking for help, you can always talk about the search you're doing through other people, and who *they've* put you on to. "I'm talking to everyone. I have a friend who actually found a lead through a guy behind him in line at a car wash! My mother's bridge partner put me on to ..." If your conversation partner is at least marginally savvy, they'll pick up the thread and say something like, "I wonder if I know anyone ..."

What if your job search is something you can't talk about? What if, for instance, you work for a law-related employer who wants (and expects) you to stay with them after law school? Then don't bring it up, even to people at work you consider friends. People at work are colleagues first, and friends second—unfortunately. You don't know who's got "staying power" until you leave the employer. But there are so many other categories of people to talk to, you're hardly hampered in your search. On top of that, make sure that you have contact information for people at work and frequent customers; you can always keep in touch with them and ask their advice *after* you leave the employer.

* * * SMART HUMAN TRICK * * *

Recent law school graduate can't nail a professional job right away, so he takes what he can get: a job working the cash register at Wal–Mart.

He makes a point of talking with people who come through his register line. One guy shows up fairly frequently, so their conversations get beyond "Hi, how are you?" It turns out this guy is running for state Attorney General. The grad asks to volunteer on his campaign, and helps out a lot.

The guy is elected Attorney General . . . and Mr. Wal-Mart gets a new job as well.

He's named Special Assistant to the State Attorney General.

* * * SMART HUMAN TRICK * * *

Law student in New York City, goes to school part-time and works as a conductor on the Long Island Railroad. He sees the same passengers all the time, and says, "A lot of them wear suits, so I figure there's a chance they're lawyers." He starts casually mentioning that he's in law school. He gets a job through one of his frequent passengers.

* * * SMART HUMAN TRICK * * *

Law student in the Southwest, works full time and goes to law school part time. He tells everyone at work that he wants to break into Entertainment Law. Two ladies in marketing tell him, "There's a guy in finance getting his MBA. A classmate of his is general counsel at a movie studio. You should talk to him."

The law student seeks out the finance guy, who gives him his classmate's number. The student calls the classmate, and winds up working at the studio.

7. YOUR PROFESSORS AT LAW SCHOOL

"Eeeuuuwww!!" you're probably thinking. "I don't want to talk to my *professors* about looking for a job!" I'm down with that. I would sooner have disemboweled myself than actually *talk* to some of my law school profs. I certainly wouldn't consider approaching professors you can't stand, or ones who scare the snot out of you.

But for professors you like, ones who teach classes you enjoy or have enjoyed, ones whose classes you've excelled in—absolutely! They can be useful to you in several ways.

Sandy Mans explains one way: **"Alumni sometimes call their old profs looking for talent,"** so if you let your **favourite professor(s) know what you're looking for, they can mention you when they get those calls.** This is *particularly* useful if you've got an overall mediocre GPA, but you were a rock star in that professor's class.

Professors are also often consultants for firms and companies. Josie Mitchell says, "Professors often know people they can contact on your behalf, which may lead to an externship or job." A student at a Northern California school got an interview at a high tech company's general counsel's office through a professor who consulted with them.

You should also consider getting from Career Services a list of alums who practice in an area that interests you, and then taking that list to profs you like to see whom they remember, and whom you should contact. As Debra Fink explains, "You can call those alumni and say something like, 'Professor Ignatz told me you might be particularly helpful,' or 'Your old law school prof, Professor Bungle, told me to give you a call ...'" That way you turn what might otherwise have been a cold call or a blah cover letter into something far more compelling.

Especially if you're a First Year, you haven't had a chance to take classes from a lot of professors whose specialties might really interest you. You can still lean on them for advice! Make a point of stopping by their office to introduce yourself, express your enthusiasm for their specialty, tell them you're going to be taking their class, and in the meantime you'd appreciate their advice. Trust me—law professors feast on sharing their expertise. They love to give advice. Give them that opportunity!

8. TEACHING ASSISTANTS AT LAW SCHOOL (LIKE WRITING INSTRUCTORS WHO ARE UPPERCLASSMEN)

Teaching assistants can be particularly useful to you because you know them pretty well, and they're likely to be close to your own age, which makes them easier to approach than professors. As Sophie Sparrow recommends, "Just go to them and ask them how they figured out what they wanted to do, and how they're going about getting there." It may turn out that they've got contacts they can put you on to, and since they're familiar with your work, their recommendations will carry some real weight.

9. JUDGES FOR MOOT COURT/CLIENT COUNSELING/ORAL ADVOCACY COMPETITIONS AT SCHOOL.

Judges for these kinds of competitions are often, well, judges. If not judges, lawyers. While you're showing off your lawyerly skills, why not seek advice from the people seeing them?

If you can, find out ahead of time who your judges will be, so you can figure out who to approach and flatter them by being able to say something about their background. "I know that you started your career with ..." "I know you worked on ..." "I think it's really interesting that you ..."

Particularly if a judge pays you a compliment, follow up with them! You can send them an e-mail saying something like, "I really appreciate your compliments at the Twinkie Law School Oral Advocacy Competition. I'd be honored to clerk for you after I graduate next year, and I'm hoping I can set up an interview at a mutually convenient time." You see the point. When someone already thinks favourably of you, you've got your foot halfway in the door.

10. ADVISORS TO LAW SCHOOL ACTIVITIES IN WHICH YOU'RE INVOLVED

If you come into contact with lawyers and/or judges through activities, by all means lean on them for advice. For instance, if you run the commencement committee, you'll probably talk to a number of potential sponsors and speakers. If you're on the moot court board and help run competitions, you'll speak to potential judges. You're perfectly positioned to ask for advice, and you'll stand out from the crowd because you've taken the initiative of getting involved in the activity.

* * * SMART HUMAN TRICK * * *

Student in the Pacific Northwest ran a moot court competition, writing the problem and recruiting all five judges. She asked all of them for career advice—which they all offered—and wound up clerking for one of them.

11. YOUR FRIENDS (INCLUDING BOYFRIENDS AND GIRLFRIENDS) OUTSIDE OF LAW SCHOOL

You don't live in a bubble. You've got friends outside of school. Even if you don't think they know anybody useful to you, let them know what you're looking for, and ask if they (or *their* families) know anyone you should talk to.

You may find that friends outside of law school will be surprised that you're asking for their help; lots of "civilians" believe that a law degree is an automatic ticket to jobs. (Let's not talk about what we ourselves thought before we started law school!) Explain to them that it's a great credential, but you still have to explore all of your options—and you'd appreciate their help.

* * * SMART HUMAN TRICK * * *

Law student, a 1L in Georgia. His girlfriend goes pumpkin picking in Florida. In the pumpkin patch, the girlfriend chats with a guy who turns out to be a partner at a law firm in Florida. She mentions that her boyfriend is a law student, and the lawyer says, "Why don't you have him send me his resume?" The girlfriend relates this to the law student, who sends a resume and sets up an interview over Christmas break. He gets a summer clerkship with the firm.

* * * SMART HUMAN TRICK * * *

1L law student wants to get into Entertainment Law. She goes to the ABA Entertainment Forum at the Grammys in Los Angeles, and takes her boyfriend with her. It takes place at the Beverly Hills Hotel. When they go to retrieve their car from the valet at the end of the conference, the line is a mile long. Her boyfriend says, "This is a waste of time. Let's go to the bar and have a drink, and wait until the line clears."

They go into the bar. She excuses herself to go to the ladies' room. Her boyfriend finds a seat at the bar, and finds himself sitting next to an instantly recognizable star and his manager. He starts chatting with them, and mentions that he's there because his girlfriend is a law student, and she went to the Entertainment Forum to try and get into Entertainment Law. The star and manager both tell him, "Tell her to give us a call," and give him their contact information.

12. NEIGHBORHOOD FRIENDS

If you've got friendly neighbors at home—lucky you—next time you're home and chatting, let those neighborhood friends in on your search. Inevitably they'll ask "How's law school going?" and that's your chance to talk about what you want.

13. EVERY PERSON WHOSE JOB BRINGS THEM INTO CONTACT WITH TONS OF PEOPLE—BANK TELLERS, DOCTORS, DENTISTS, INSURANCE AGENTS, HAIRDRESSERS, BARBERS, CHURCH OR TEMPLE SECRETARIES, PERSONAL TRAINERS, MANICURISTS . . .

Mentioning to your family's lawyer (or your own, if you have one) that you're looking for a legal job is a fairly obvious route to pursue. But every other service person in your life? Law students *rarely* tap these people as resources, even though they're a very fertile source of leads! Why? Because people in service jobs come in contact with more people than almost anybody else. So they're more likely to know lawyers, no matter how far removed their own profession is from practicing law. As Lisa Abrams points out, "My *hairdresser* knows more lawyers and judges than anyone!" Drusilla Bakert agrees: "Definitely call your family doctor, your barber. I had a student who got on the phone and started calling these kinds of contacts, and he had a job in two days."

So seek out service people you know, and say to them, "I know you talk with tons of people, so I'm hoping you'll be able to help me out. As you know, I'm in law school, and I'm looking for X. I'm wondering if you can think of anyone I should be talking to." You may be pleasantly surprised by the results!

* * * SMART HUMAN TRICK * * *

Female law student, trying desperately to get a job clerking for a particularly prestigious female judge. She tries everything she can to get through to this judge; no success.

The student goes to get her hair cut, and her hairdresser says to her, "So how's law school going?" The student responds, "I'm beating my head against a wall! I'm trying to get a job with Judge So-and-So, and I can't even talk to her. I—" The hairdresser cuts her off, and says, "Judge So-and-So? Are you kidding? Trixie—" she points to a manicurist along the wall—"does her nails!"

The student finishes getting her hair done, and goes over to Trixie and taps her on the shoulder. She says, "Is it true you do Judge so-and-so's nails?" Trixie says she does, and the student asks, "When does she come in?" Trixie responds, "She has a standing appointment Fridays, at noon."

The student turns to the manicurist in the next chair, and asks, "Are you available Fridays at noon?" The manicurist says she is, and the student urges, "Sign me up!"

The student shows up Friday at noon, and guess who's sitting in the next chair? Judge So-and-so. They get into a casual conversation, and the judge asks, "So . . . what do you do?"

The student responds, "I'm in law school . . . *how about you?*"

The judge responds, "I'm a judge."

Student: *"Really?* Wow. That must be great!"

In their ensuing casual Friday lunch meetings at the manicurists', the judge doesn't seem to notice that the student knows a lot about her. After a few weeks, the judge says, "Do you have a job yet? Would you consider working for me?"

Would she? Hmmm. OK!

* * * SMART HUMAN TRICK * * *

Law school graduate. Doesn't have a job. So what does he do during the day? Nothing. But he *does* know that today is garbage day, so he drags the garbage out to the curb. The garbage man pulls up, leans out of the truck, and asks him, "What are *you* doing home during the day?"

"I just got out of law school, I don't have a job . . ."

The garbage man says, "Really? I don't know if you realize this, but there's a guy down the street, he's a partner at a law firm. Why don't you go say hello, tell him I said so . . ."

What does the grad have to lose? So he dresses nicely, goes over, knocks on the lawyer's door, and says, "I know how crazy this sounds, but I just got out of law school, I'm looking around at what I'm going to do next, and the garbage man suggested I come and talk to you."

The lawyer says, "Oh, sure, Fred, he's a great guy! Come on in . . ." They talk. And the grad winds up working at the lawyer's firm . . . all because he talked to the *garbage man.*

* * * SMART HUMAN TRICK * * *

Student at a Nebraska law school. Her husband drives a tow truck, a flatbed used for fancy cars. She realizes that many people who can afford fancy cars are likely to be lawyers. She goes on a few "hook-ups" with him and chats with the customers as he hooks up their cars. Sure enough, some of them are lawyers. She tells them she's in law school and asks for business cards. She winds up working for one of them.

* * * SMART HUMAN TRICK * * *

Law student desperately wants to get into public interest work. She periodically chats with her mailman if she's home when the mail is delivered. It comes out that she's in law school, and the mailman says, "Really? My wife works for the city attorney's office." This student would *love* to work there, and says so. He shrugs and says, "Talk to my wife." She does ... and gets the job.

* * * SMART HUMAN TRICK * * *

Law student picking up her interview suit at the dry cleaner. The student comments, "Thanks. It looks great. It's my interview suit." The dry cleaner asks her what she's interviewing for, and she tells him she's in law school. He says, "No kidding. You know, Judge X brings his clothes here. He's a great guy. You should call him.

She does ... and winds up clerking for him.

14. REGULARS AT YOUR DELI, GYM, OR WATERING HOLE

If you regularly go for coffee to the same "Central Perk" type joint, if you go to the gym regularly, if you have a local bar where you often stop—for a nonalcoholic beverage, of course—you've probably made friends with people there. This is a form of friend-making with which I'm particularly familiar; I met my husband Henry, my best friend, and several members of my wedding party in a single Hip Hop class at the local YMCA.

The people you regularly see at places you frequent probably already know you're in law school. Casually bring up the fact that you're thinking about what you're going to be doing with your degree, and you're looking for people to talk to, for advice as much as anything else, and add something like, "If you think of anyone who might have some good advice for me, I'd appreciate it if you'd let me know."

15. PEOPLE YOU KNOW THROUGH RELIGIOUS ACTIVITIES

If you attend church or temple regularly, you know lots of people who do the same. Your religious leader is an obvious person to talk to; (s)he'll know lots of people who will respect his/her opinion. But that's not where you should stop. The church or temple secretary is a great resource; as Lisa Abrams says, "My mother-in-law is a church secretary. If I had a student call her, she'd have a list of thirty names to give them for information on *any* job!"

And, of course, there are other worshippers. For all you know, the lawyer you may work for next could be the person in the next pew!

* * * SMART HUMAN TRICK * * *

Law student at a Florida school. She goes to church when she returns home for Christmas break. A woman sitting next to her says, "We haven't seen you here in a while." The student says, "I went away to law school." The woman responds, "Really? My husband's a lawyer. You should talk to him."

The student does—and winds up working for him.

16. COMMUTING FRIENDS

There's a great silver lining to public transportation: you get to talk to people. If you regularly take a bus or train, you probably see the same people over and over again. And you may spend more time talking with them than with people you'd consider a lot closer to you. (In my part of the country—Connecticut—people routinely commute *two hours* to work in lower Manhattan. That's a lot of talk time!) So casually work into the conversation the fact that you're researching the legal market, and ask them if they can think of anyone you ought to talk to. Remember: Most people are happy to help, once you tell them what you want.

17. IF YOU HAVE KIDS, GROWN-UPS YOU KNOW THROUGH THEM AT SCHOOLS OR ACTIVITIES

If you've got kids, you routinely see teachers and other parents. Let them know what you're doing and what you want to do.

* * * SMART HUMAN TRICK * * *

Female law student, raising her young daughter alone. She holds political office and serves on the PTA. She's so busy that on her resume, as a hobby she puts "napping."

Her resume doesn't get results, but she starts telling the people she meets through her daughter's activities that she's in law school and she's looking into careers after school. One of her fellow PTA board members is a lawyer, and hires her.

* * * SMART HUMAN TRICK * * *

Law student is a dad. His ten-year-old son takes part in a soccer team. At a soccer game the law student chats with another dad, who turns out to be a lawyer. They set up a meeting—and the law student winds up with a job.

18. ANYONE ON YOUR HOLIDAY CARD LIST

If you know people well enough to send them holiday cards, there's no reason to keep them out of your job search. Drop them a note—*not* in the holiday card!—or call or e-mail them, letting them know you're researching jobs and would appreciate talking to anyone they know who could give you some advice.

19. FRIENDS YOU KNOW THROUGH SOCIAL NETWORKING WEB SITES

Whether it's Live Journal or any other site that engenders friendships, you may have found people on-line that you consider true friends. You'd help *them* out if you could ... so let them know what *you* want!

On top of that, the whole point of getting involved with social networking sites is to find new people to connect with. We go over this in great detail in Chapter 11 when we discuss the Internet, but the bottom line is: reach out to your social networking connections, and ask them for advice and/or if they know anyone you could approach for advice about breaking into what you want to do.

B. PEOPLE YOU DON'T SEE ROUTINELY, BUT WHO WOULD RECOGNIZE YOU OR YOUR NAME

Your "life closet" is full of people you once knew very well, but whose lives have taken them in different directions. You may feel reluctant to contact anybody on this list about looking for jobs, but there are two considerations you need to keep in mind.

First of all, put yourself in their shoes. If there was somebody you really liked but lost touch with, and they contacted you telling you they were considering law school and wanted your guidance on choosing which one to attend—would you be insulted? Of course not. If anything, quite the contrary—if you ran into them and learned that they'd been wondering about law school and *hadn't* called you, you might be hurt.

You'll find that as a rule of thumb people are delighted to reconnect. Take that chance!

Secondly—and law students ask me about this all the time— people are not insulted that you haven't kept up with them in the meantime. Really. Everybody understands that we all lead very busy lives, and time flies. You may wake up to find that someone you really like is the same person you haven't talked to in two or three years! Don't let that stop you from contacting them.

Third, remember that you're not asking for a *job*. You're not putting them on the spot. You're looking for *advice* about jobs. You're not putting pressure on them to hire you; you're just tapping into most people's natural tendency to be helpful.

Of course, make the contact more than just an opportunity to seek job help. You can always e-mail them first, remind them of how you know them (if you feel you need to), let them know you're in law school now, and you want to call up to say hello and ask their advice. Then when you talk, you tell them that you're at that point in law school where you start looking at what you'll do with your degree, you know they live in X or know about X or do X, that you're interested in X, and if they think of anyone who could give you advice about it you'd appreciate it, whether it's people to talk to, things to do or read or subscribe to.

Of course, if they ask you, "You're looking for a job, right?" you can always respond with something like, "Sure. But I'd really appreciate advice about what I should be doing." Again, you're not pressuring them ... but if they *do* know somebody who's hiring—great!

After you state your request, catch up with them in general. "I remember you were ... are you still into it?"

Be sure to state your appreciation for any advice they can offer, tell them you'll follow up in a month, and offer to help them in any way you can. You may think "Gee, I'm just in law school, what can I do?" but you never know ... you leave the door open in case they ever want to lean on *you*.

Also make sure that you aren't *too* subtle. About five years after law school, I got a call from a former classmate of mine, a really funny guy whom I'd known pretty well, but hadn't spoken with since graduation. He generally asked about how I was doing; he knew that I'd written *Law In A Flash* and started a publishing company. He said rhetorically, "I know *Law In A Flash* is everywhere, you must be doing really well with it." And he mentioned that he'd just started out as a stockbroker. We chatted for a few minutes and that was about it.

Later on, when I was telling one of my housemates about the conversation, he burst out laughing and said, "You idiot. Don't you get it? When you're a new stockbroker, you have to call everybody you know and try and get them to be customers!" Gee. It went right over *my* head. My law school buddy was so discreet about it that I totally missed that! He'd have been better off saying—after we caught up!—"Listen, Kimmbo, this is awkward, but I just got this job and I'm supposed to call *everybody* looking for business. Would you consider investing with our brokerage? Can I send you some information?"

So don't make your request so subtle that your audience misses it entirely!

Let's talk about the people who fit in this category.

i. Turn employers who reject you into informational interview targets.

Here's a group of people I'll bet you *never* would have thought to contact. Because you're thinking, "Geez, Kimmbo, why would I ever talk to people who *rejected* me? Good move!"

It's too easy to write off employers who reject you. But if they do something you really want to do, see if you can get *something* out of it by asking for an informational interview; that is, for guidance about what you ought to be doing to further your career objectives. (We talk about informational interviews extensively later in this chapter.) As Shannon Kelly says, "There's no downside to applying for jobs. If it doesn't work out, say thanks anyway—can I get some advice?"

In doing so, you've accomplished a couple of things. First of all, you've proven your enthusiasm for what they do. You wouldn't recontact them if you weren't sincere about what you want to do. An honest show of enthusiasm is a huge plus.

Secondly, you may get some really great advice on activities and events you ought to consider, other employers to approach, changes to your resume and/or interview style ... all kinds of things.

So don't view employers who reject you as a dead end!

* * * SMART HUMAN TRICK * * *

Reported by a 3L at a Midwestern law school: "I responded to a job posting for a large firm.

I got a rejection a few days later in which they stated they were firm on their experience requirement—which I didn't have.

I then asked if I could have an informational interview. The HR manager agreed.

During my visit, the HR manager scheduled a meeting with a senior partner who liked me and said they might consider modifying their experience requirement."

* * * SMART HUMAN TRICK * * *

From a law student in Arizona:

"An attorney I'd clerked with during the summer put me on to another attorney, whom I'll call Mr. Green. Mr. Green initially told me he didn't know much and his firm was not hiring.

A couple of months later, I asked him if he had time for a beer and could talk to me about the job market. He forwarded my information to his hiring partner, named Frank, and things progressed quickly.

First, I met with Frank on a 'social' meeting, as he called it. This was his way of screening me. After that, he asked me for an interview with all six lawyers in the firm's City X office."

ii. Interviewers you got along with from employers who've rejected you.

Along with employers who rejected you, consider individual lawyers at those firms with whom you really hit it off.

Here's the situation. You interview with a law firm, we'll call it Lower and Boome, and you really hit it off with one of the interviewers, Bambam Winneboso. Lower and Boome rejects you—*but that doesn't change the fact that you really got along well with Bambam.* He's probably disappointed that you didn't get the offer. So you call Bambam–an e-mail won't do!—and say, "I'm disappointed I'm not going to be working with you, because I really enjoyed our conversation. But you know me and you know what I can do. Who else should I be talking to? Do you have some advice for me?" If you feel uncomfortable coming right out and calling for that advice, you can e-mail or leave a voice-mail in off-hours *first*—to let them know you're going to call. In your e-mail or voice mail, you can say, "I really enjoyed our conversation, and even though I'm not going to be working with you, I'd truly appreciate your advice on what else I should be doing, who else I should be talking to."

One crucial point to keep in mind: *don't bad mouth the employer.* You can't say, "Gee, too bad you work with such a bunch of clowns." Just state your disappointment over not getting an offer, and *immediately* move on to how much you appreciated talking to them and how you'd like their advice. Remember: the legal community is small, and any interviewer's first loyalty is to their employer. Even if they goad you: "I can't believe how stupid they were not to hire you"—just brush it off with, "I appreciate your confidence in me." Don't take the bait!

So word your approach carefully. But do make the approach, if you've really hit it off with certain interviewers. I know lots of law students who've gotten great jobs this way!

Incidentally, this approach also works with interviewers from law schools that rejected you. It may be that you interviewed with alums from law schools that didn't appreciate your genius. It may also be that the school rejected you *despite* the interviewer's recommendation. If you got along with that person— contact them, just as you would an interviewer from an employer!

I talked with a law student at a Virginia school who wanted to go back and work in Mississippi, her home. She had interviewed for an Ivy League law school, and although she didn't get in, the interview had gone really well. During First Year, she recontacted the interviewer and asked for advice on what she ought to be doing to find something for the summer in Mississippi. He put her on to a couple of employers ... and she wound up with a job there.

* * * SMART HUMAN TRICK * * *

From a law student in Georgia:

"This Spring, I decided to write a few firms I interviewed with last semester and tell them I was still interested despite their initial rejection. I got an e-mail a few days later from a firm I interviewed with in October. I called the hiring partner and he said he was so glad I e-mailed him, because they were still looking for someone, and the only reason they didn't bother contacting me about the job was that they assumed I would have already accepted an offer from another firm by now."

iii.   Undergrad friends, classmates and/or roommates.

Depending on how long you took off between college and law school, your undergrad cronies are either very recent friends—or distant memories! In either case, it's worth contacting the people with whom you were close in undergraduate school.

If you feel awkward asking for help, remember what I've pointed out a few times now: You wouldn't be offended to hear from an undergrad friend looking at law schools, who wanted your advice about choosing one. People like being experts, and people who remember you fondly will be happy to talk with you and help you out!

What if you have a classmate from undergrad who's subsequently become famous? If they're someone who'd be a good contact, you might as well contact them. It's not like you're a stalker. They know you. Either they'll help you or they won't. Contacting them is the only alternative with a potentially positive outcome.

iv.   Undergrad professors and/or coaches.

The great thing about graduating from a college is that you're part of the "family" forever. Undergrad professors get calls from former students all the time! If there are professors you particularly liked and/or who taught classes related to what you want to get into, send them an e-mail telling them you're going to call to catch up and ask their advice. By the way, don't assume that professors don't know anybody outside of the school; that Ivory Tower thing is overplayed. Professors typically know a bunch of people. Tap into that network!

The same applies to coaches. If you took part in sports in undergrad, you had coaches who probably know tons of people. They know about your ability to be a team player and your self-discipline, which are qualities many employers seek. Particularly if you want to break into Sports Law, they can be a great bridge to people who can help you out.

* * * SMART HUMAN TRICK * * *

From a law school graduate in Kansas:

"The path that led me to law school began when I was getting a Masters in Journalism. I took a mandatory class in media law, and loved it. I established a friendship with the professor after I beat the curve on one of his exams. At some point in law school I kinda lost track of what had led me there to begin with, but after several fruitless months of job searching, I decided to get back to basics and try to find myself a job in the Communications Law field.

From the job board at school I learned about a set of fellowships available with a public interest organization in Washington, DC, an organization specializing in free press issues.

On nothing more than a hunch, I stopped by my alma mater one afternoon and ran into my old Media Law professor in the reading room. He told me he was a good friend of the organization's executive director, and that he would be happy to be a reference for me.

Needless to say, I dropped his name in my cover letter."

v.   High school friends and teachers.

The connecting thread for every school you ever attend—high school, college, law school—is that after you leave, you still "belong." It's still home. Contrary to the saying, you *can* go home again! Your schools, including your high school, expect you to lean on them from time to time. I've had a few situations where high school teachers of mine were the perfect experts to contact, and trust me—if they were happy to hear from *me*, juvenile delinquent that I was, your teachers will be *delighted* to hear from you!

When it comes to high school friends, there are two categories to think about: one is people you were genuinely close to, and the other is acquaintances who wound up in a position to help you, either because they live in a place you want to settle in or they've got a job that gives them contacts or ideas that might be useful to you.

If you think that just going to high school with someone isn't a significant enough commonality to justify contact, don't worry—it is. I routinely get e-mails from teachers and counselors from my high school asking, "I know you do this, would you mind helping out one of our students . . ." Because I have fond memories of my high school—well, *generally* fond—I'm happy to help. And you'll find that most people feel the way I do!

* * * SMART HUMAN TRICK * * *

Law student goes home for Christmas, and runs into an old high school buddy. They get to chatting because the buddy is thinking of attending law school. Shortly after that, the buddy goes on vacation to Los Angeles, and stops at a gym there to work out. He gets on a StairMaster, and on the StairMaster right next to his is a partner from a large Los Angeles law firm. They start chatting, hit it off, and the buddy mentions that he has a friend in law school who is looking for a job. The partner says, "Well, have him send me his resume."

The buddy passes along the partner's contact information to the law student. And the student winds up with a job there!

vi. Ex-legal employers.

Well–duh, you're thinking. Assuming that you left an employer on good terms, that employer can be a great resource—because you *know* that they know other lawyers! They went to law school so they've got their former classmates, they've got bar association connections—everything.

What about if that employer wants you back, and you don't want to work with them? That's certainly trickier. But presumably you were nice about it when you turned down their offer—right? If you stated how grateful you were for the experience they gave you, but you wanted to broaden your horizons as you start your career, then you might not want to write them off. You can always e-mail them and let them know that you'll be calling for their advice. That way, when you call, if they don't want to talk with you—they won't take the call and that will be that. But odds are they *will* talk to you. After all, most employers are conscious of the fact that whether you work together or not, you'll be professionals in the same community, and you never know what kinds of opportunities exist down the road for working together.

vii. Ex-non-law-related employers.

Don't overlook old non-law-related employers as a source of leads. Even though they aren't lawyers, they probably *know* lawyers. The most likely contact they'll have is the firm who represents them. Ann Skalaski points out that getting to law firms through their clients can be particularly effective.

viii. Co-workers and customers from old jobs.

When you think about old employers, don't confine yourself to thinking only about the boss—think of your former coworkers and customers, as well. Even if they're not lawyers, I harken back to the point I've made over and over again—you don't know who they know.

C. PEOPLE YOU MEET ... BOTH INTENTIONALLY AND UNEXPECTEDLY

1. PEOPLE YOU FIND ON-LINE

We'll cover this in "Cold e-mailing," Topic D(3)(a).

2. ALUMS OF YOUR LAW SCHOOL OR UNDERGRAD SCHOOL

You are the natural object of bounty for people who went to your school before you. Whether we're talking about law school or undergrad, alums or students just ahead of you in the food chain, contact them for advice!

Let's talk about alums first. Of course, you can do Lexis and Westlaw searches to identify the law school and undergrad school of virtually anybody. But if you want to be a bit more selective, **talk to Career Services about whom to contact in any given organization or city.** As is true of people in general, some alums will be more receptive to talking to you than others; Career Services can put you on to the most helpful alums!

Alums are particularly helpful if you're moving to another city, or you're trying to get into an organization for which your credentials are not a natural fit—either your GPA isn't what they typically look for, or it's a non-traditional job. When you're looking for a job out of town, you can tell alums that you're interested in moving there, that they must have faced the same issues as you when *they* first tried to go there, and you'd like their advice about what it's like practicing in that city, advice about breaking into the market, and anything you should be doing.

If, on the other hand, you're talking about getting into a particular organization, you want to skirt the human resources/recruiting people, and contact alums directly. State your enthusiasm for the organization, and ask their advice about what you might do to make yourself into a good candidate.

To the extent you can, ask them targeted questions, to show that you know something about them and you respect their time. Sue Gainen recommends that you ask questions like:

- "I know from Martindale Hubbell that you are a plaintiff's employment lawyer. Do you have ten minutes to talk to me about the market and the practice in X city?" "Do you think I should join the local ATLA chapter as a student?"

- "I know you're in a bankruptcy practice. I'm interested in debtor work, and I wonder if you might look at my resume and give me a quick heads up about the best debtor firms in X city?"

- "I know that you are in a business litigation practice in X city. Do you have ten minutes to talk to me about whether I should approach employers in your city looking to specialize in litigation, or should I present a more general business interest to prospective employers?"

Whenever you contact alums, what you'd ideally like is an informational interview which we'll discuss later in this chapter.

* * * SMART HUMAN TRICK * * *

Law student at a Massachusetts school. She wants to work for the SEC. She contacts two alums who work there. She reports, "I applied through central processing, but it's like a black hole. Who knows how long it might have taken, if ever? These two alums took me under their wing and shepherded me in."

* * * SMART HUMAN TRICK * * *

Law student from California. She's looking for jobs in Patent Law in Chicago. There's a firm that particularly interests her. They interview her, although they're looking for someone with a year's worth of experience. They like her, but reject her on grounds of lack of experience.

She stays in touch with an alum from her school who happens to be a junior associate there. He tells her that the firm's issue with new graduates is paying for the Patent Bar.

She contacts the hiring partner and volunteers to pay for the Patent Bar.

She gets the offer.

It's easy to overlook fellow undergraduate alums, but they can be great resources. There was a student at one New England school who wanted to get into intellectual property. He had a chemistry degree, and had been striking out with patent firms. He went back to his undergrad school and asked at alumni relations to ask about alums who'd gone onto law school with a "hard science" background like his. He got a list of names, and in researching them found that there were several who practiced at firms he'd like to join. He contacted them, and got a job through one of them.

3. UPPERCLASSMEN AT SCHOOL

Whether through friends or through your Career Services Office, reach out to upperclassmen. They can be extremely helpful. Whether you're looking at a particular employer, a type of work or even a part-time experience in school, don't overlook your (slightly) elders!

Here are three of the many ways they can help:

A. IF THEY'VE NAILED A JOB WITH AN EMPLOYER (OR EVEN INTERVIEWED WITH ONE) THAT INTERESTS YOU, THEY CAN GIVE YOU GREAT INSIGHTS INTO WHAT TO DO IN THE COVER LETTER/RESUME/INTERVIEW PROCESS

* * * SMART HUMAN TRICK * * *

From a student at a law school in upstate New York:

"I wanted to get a particularly prestigious fellowship in Washington, D.C. I knew from my research that it involved a detailed application and then a fairly arduous interview process. One of the interviews was supposed to last for several hours.

I mentioned it at the Career Services Office, and one of the counselors said, 'You should talk to student X. She got that fellowship last year.'

I contacted this student, and we got together to talk about it. She was amazing. She told me about the specific answers they look for on the application. With the interviews, she told me about some unusual questions and also how to frame my experience. She spent more than an hour 'coaching' me.

I sent in the application and got the interview. The whole process was exactly as she described it to me. I guess I don't even have to tell you that I got the fellowship."

B. If They've Had Success Nailing a Job in a Field That Interests You, They'll Often Share Their Secrets

Whether it's an event to attend, a web site, a particularly helpful mentor, students who've broken into a great gig will often clue you in on how they did it.

C. Many Part-Time and Summer Jobs Are "Passed Down" From Upperclassmen

Susanne Aronowitz calls these "Relayed jobs"—where current interns recruit their replacements, at the request of the employer.

Many employers don't want to read resumes and conduct rounds of interviews for jobs; they tell their current student workers, "Find me someone like you." Susan Gainen says, "Get to know upperclassmen through student groups, classes, peer mentorships." Making yourself known to these students is often the best—and only—way to nail these jobs.

4. People in "Affinity Groups"—Those With Whom You Share an Interest, or Ethnicity

Whether you're a woman, you're interested in a particular specialty, you're from a foreign country, or you belong to an ethnic group, consider seeking out lawyers and advocacy groups for those who are similarly situated.

Many schools and bar associations have women's law groups—you can reach out to the leader for advice. Many foreign countries have a joint chamber of commerce (German–American, Irish–American), which have been a source of great leads for foreign students. BLSA and Hispanic Law Societies–ditto.

Of course, people you reach out to are likely to ask you to get involved in the group, which itself is a good idea, too!

* * * SMART HUMAN TRICK * * *

Female law student at a Pennsylvania law school. She's Greek, and she wants to do immigration law in Philadelphia. She reports, "I went through Greek civic groups and talked to everyone who would talk to me about who I ought to contact. People were great. I got tons of names and got onto one immigration lawyer through a man who'd used the lawyer to get visas for his family. I wound up working for him."

5. IF YOU'RE SIGHT-OR HEARING-CHALLENGED, REACH OUT TO ADVOCACY ORGANIZATIONS AND RESEARCH TO FIND LAWYERS WHO FACE THE SAME CHALLENGE

I have met quite a few sight-and hearing-challenged students who find their job searches particularly frustrating. One hearing-challenged student in Kentucky told me, "I'm so frustrated in interviews by low expectations. I can lip read and speak very well, but people don't give me that chance."

Instead of approaching those who don't understand, seek out people who *do*. Lawyers who've overcome the same challenge as you are natural mentors. Write or e-mail or voice mail them telling them you respect what they've accomplished, you face the same challenge and you'd truly appreciate their advice and tips. If you have specific questions, ask them. But you get the point: reach out to people who *get it*.

6. PEOPLE YOU MEET THROUGH YOUR HOBBIES

Whether you're into trains or you're a private pilot or quilting or *whatever* it is, tell your fellow enthusiasts about what you're interested in doing, and ask for people to talk to.

* * * SMART HUMAN TRICK * * *

Law student who plays bagpipes as a hobby. He volunteers to play bagpipes at funerals. At one funeral, one of the mourners comes over to compliment him on his playing. They start to talk, and the mourner turns out to be a lawyer. When the student mentions he's in law school, the lawyer gives him his card and says, "Give me a call." Through the lawyer, the student meets another lawyer—and winds up working with him.

* * * SMART HUMAN TRICK * * *

Law student in the Midwest belongs to the Society for Creative Anachronisms. The group reenacts medieval times, in period costume. She discovers that several of the members are lawyers. She gets her 1L summer internship through one of them.

7. PRAY FOR JURY DUTY

What better way to have an excuse to be at the courthouse—and get the opportunity to talk to lawyers, clerks, judges? Most people in America dread jury duty. It's a golden opportunity for you!

* * * SMART HUMAN TRICK * * *

Law student at a law school in the South. He was called for jury duty, and chosen for a brief trial. He was a little confused about how much of his legal education to leave at the courthouse door. He sent a note to the judge, asking for advice.

At the end of the trial, the judge invited the student to extern for him the following semester.

8. PEOPLE YOU MEET THROUGH CASUAL CONTACT. TAKE OFF THE *% & #@!! I-POD!

I encourage you to play a little game that I play, whenever I read an article profiling somebody successful. Inevitably, there's a juncture where they got their next opportunity through casual contact. The fact is, the next person you talk to could be your key to nailing a great job!

I know a million stories about law students who've gotten incredible jobs through casual contact with strangers. Whether they're in line at the store, sitting on a plane or a train, sitting at the same table at a wedding, walking along the street, sitting at the next table at a restaurant . . . gosh, the world is full of people who are potentially your route to a wonderful job. While I don't expect you to be "on" 24/7, talking neurotically to *everybody,* I encourage you to make the effort to chat with strangers at least some of the time. This means *taking off that damned iPod!* I know it puts you into your own little world, but the problem with it is . . . it puts you into your own little world.

Please, please, please also take advantage of making human contact in situations where you could handle the transaction electronically. Don't always use the ATM; if your local bank is open, go inside to make a withdrawal or deposit. Talk with a teller instead of punching buttons on a machine. At the grocery store, don't always use the "automated" aisles; go to a human checker. You just don't know where casual contact will lead . . . but you have to make casual contact with *human beings* for it to lead *anywhere!*

Depending on the situation, there are tons of things you can talk about. When I talk with seatmates on airplanes, I'll generally start the conversation by asking if the city we're flying to is home for them. In other situations, I might compliment something about the person, or if they've got kids or pets with them, I say something genuinely complimentary about said *accoutrement.* In line at the movies, I'll ask what someone's heard or read about the movie. (I talk about 'how to talk with people' in more detail below.)

Now, people aren't always in the mood to chat, and I'm down with that. I'm not always Chatty Cathy myself. But as often as not, people want to talk. We're mostly hard-wired to enjoy it!

Apart from finding job leads, you'll find—as I have—that some of the most memorable conversations you'll have are with people you've never met before.

While it has nothing at all to do with finding a job, I have to share with you my personal favourite along these lines.

It happened on a flight from Dallas to Sacramento a couple of years ago. I had a window seat, and there was a very elderly couple sitting next to me. I noticed that they were holding hands and seemed very happy, which in and of itself was pretty touching. When they had trouble operating their cell phone, I offered mine as a way to start a conversation.

When I asked what was in Sacramento for them, the gentleman, Hal, told me that they were going there so that "Ida" could see his children. It turns out that they were *eighty-one year old newlyweds!!* Needless to say, this was an opening I wasn't going to miss! I asked how they'd met, and it turns out that they'd each been married to someone else, and the two couples had been friends. Her husband had died some years ago, and his wife had passed away six months before. They kept in contact, and friendship turned to love. It was just the most heartwarming story. When Ida excused herself during the flight, Hal told me, "I was married to my first wife for fifty-one years. When she died, I thought: I enjoyed being married so much the first time. Why not try it again?"

I took my first opportunity to get up, and raced over to tell a flight attendant about this remarkable couple. She told the captain. And next thing I knew, the pilot came onto the intercom to tell the passengers, "Ladies and Gentlemen, we have on board a newlywed couple, Hal and Ida. They're sitting in Seats 23B and C. Hal and Ida, wave so everybody can see you. Let's give them a round of applause!" People clapped politely, but as they turned around to see Hal and Ida waving, they realized that this was more than just another couple of newlyweds—and the applause became thunderous.

Later, as we were getting off the plane, it turns out that other passengers lingered to shake hands with Hal and Ida to congratulate them. It absolutely brought tears to my eyes.

So—Hal and Ida Wardell in Texas, shout-outs to you.

Aah. Touching, isn't it? Back to the world of job contacts. As I mentioned to you at the start of this section, I know a million stories about law students getting great job leads through casual contact. Here are some you'll enjoy!

* * * SMART HUMAN TRICK * * *

Law student in law school in the Midwest. She's interested in working in London. She goes home to New York for Christmas break, and goes to Talbot's to buy a suit. At Talbot's a clerk is very helpful to her, and they start chatting. The clerk asks what she needs a suit for, and the student says, "I'm in law school, and I'm getting it for interviews." The clerk asks where she's looking for a job, and the student says, "Well, my dream is to work in London . . ."

The clerk immediately brightens, and says, "My daughter lives there! She recruits attorneys for X"—and mentions an exceptionally prestigious American firm with a large presence in London. "You have to call her!" The clerk writes down her daughter's contact information, the law student contacts her—and winds up with a summer clerkship in London.

* * * SMART HUMAN TRICK * * *

Law student, interested in breaking into criminal defense work, takes his car to the car wash. It's the kind of car wash where you get out of the car and watch as it goes through. As he's watching his car get washed, he strikes up a conversation with the guy standing next to him, waiting for *his* car. It turns out that the guy is the most successful criminal defense lawyer in town. The student winds up working for him.

* * * SMART HUMAN TRICK * * *

Law student is also a mom. She's living in a new neighborhood with her husband and six-year-old daughter. She finds out through the grapevine that there's a very prestigious lawyer who lives down the block. She'd love to work for him.

Halloween comes around, and the law student takes her daughter out trick-or-treating. When they get to the lawyer's house, they knock—and the lawyer answers. When the lawyer hands the daughter candy, he says, "Here's your treat. Where's my trick?"

. . . the law student hands him her resume! He laughs. And she winds up with a job.

* * * SMART HUMAN TRICK * * *

Law student answers his cell phone while he's at a bar near campus, having a beer with some buddies. It's a wrong number. As he talks with the caller and tries to identify the mistake, they start talking. The caller says "It sounds like you're having a good time," and the law student remarks that he should be home studying. They take it from there.

It turns out that the caller is an investment banker. The law student mentions that he's in school, and the caller says, "What are you going to do when you get out?" The law student expresses an interest in corporate law, and the investment banker says, "Send your resume to my office. I'll pass it on to people I know." He gives the student his contact information ... and through the banker's friends, he gets a summer clerkship.

* * * SMART HUMAN TRICK * * *

Law student in New York, standing at a bus stop. She starts chatting with a guy in line behind her. It turns out that he's an attorney. She mentions she's interested in nonprofit health care. What do you know: he knows someone in the general counsel's office of a nationally-recognized non-profit health care institution ...

... and she winds up with a job there.

* * * SMART HUMAN TRICK * * *

Female student flying from Atlanta to Miami for an interview with a large law firm. She panics as the flight circles Miami, fearing she'll miss her interview. The guy in the next seat says, "You seem nervous." She tells him about her interview. Turns out, he's a partner at another large firm in town. He asks for her resume and interviews her informally on the plane. His firm calls her back, and she winds up with an offer from them—which she accepts.

* * * SMART HUMAN TRICK * * *

Student at an Ivy League law school. He'd had a terrible time getting into law school due to a learning disability that gave him a low LSAT. He applied to twenty top schools and got rejected by all of them.

He worked at Brooks Brothers to support himself while he tried to get into law school. When he helped customers, he sometimes shared his law school quest with them.

One of his customers turned out to have a husband who was a distinguished professor at an Ivy League law school. On top of that, she had a son with the same disability as this student. He talked to the professor, who pulled for him and wrote a letter to the dean pleading his case. After a two year campaign, he got in.

* * * SMART HUMAN TRICK * * *

Law student in line at a post office in Maryland. She starts chatting with the guy in front of her, who turns out to be the former Secretary of Transportation. They chat about law school, and he says, "Are you interested in a clerkship with the Department of Transportation?" She is, and he gives her his card and says, "Send me your resume. I can help."

* * * SMART HUMAN TRICK * * *

Law student in Northern California. She'd been a camp counselor after her freshman year in college. She is in the grocery store, when a little boy nearby points at her and calls out to his mom, "Mommy, Mommy, that's my counselor from camp!" He drags his mom over to her, and they introduce themselves. The student mentions she's in law school, and the woman says, "Call my husband—he's a lawyer."

* * * SMART HUMAN TRICK * * *

Law student from a school in Texas, playing blackjack at a casino in Las Vegas. He plays at one table for a few hours. He starts chatting with the guy next to him, who turns out to be a lawyer. The student winds up with a stack of chips—and a job.

* * * SMART HUMAN TRICK * * *

1L student at a Midwestern school, finishes his first semester exams and figures it's time to party. He heads for a bar near campus and takes a seat at the bar. He says, "I'm getting hammered, and I start talking to this woman sitting next to me. We're laughing, having a great time, when she mentions she's a lawyer. I ask her, 'Where do you work?' She tells me, and it turns out to be this firm I'm dying to work for.

"You've never seen anybody sober up so fast. I must have drunk a pitcher of ice water. I tell her how much I want to work there. I ask if I could give her my resume. She tells me, 'Sure. Bring it in. I'll introduce you around.' "

"To make a long story short—I'm working there now."

* * * SMART HUMAN TRICK * * *

Law student is out horseback riding. She stops at an intersection. A guy pulls up next to her on a horse. They chat. He turns out to be a lawyer ... and she winds up with a job at his firm.

* * * SMART HUMAN TRICK * * *

Student in Indiana, interested in working in Georgia. He's in line at a men's room at a bar near campus. He starts chatting with the guy in line behind him, who turns out to be a lawyer from, of all places, Georgia. They wind up playing a couple of games of pool. The lawyer says, "If you ever need any help, give me a call."

The student calls him—and winds up with a job at his firm.

* * * SMART HUMAN TRICK * * *

Female student in Virginia. She's in the laundry room of her apartment building, waiting for her laundry to dry. She's scoping out the local bar association newsletter for leads.

Another tenant walks in, sees what she's reading, and says "Are you a lawyer?"

"No," she responds. "I want to be one, though. I'm in law school."

It turns out the other tenant is a lawyer. She gives the student contact information for the hiring partner at her firm. The student winds up with a job there.

* * * SMART HUMAN TRICK * * *

Student at a New York law school, comes out of her last 1L exam depressed, convinced she'd done badly.

She goes to get her hair cut, moping about school, and her hairdresser says, "Don't feel bad. Here. This lady over here is a lawyer. Talk to her."

The lawyer assures the student that grades don't matter, and starts describing her own practice. They talk. The lawyer winds up asking the student to work for her for the summer.

* * * SMART HUMAN TRICK * * *

Law student at a Midwestern law school, flying home to the West Coast over Christmas break. In the terminal waiting for his flight, he strikes up a conversation with the guy sitting next to him. He says he's looking forward to getting home and playing some ice hockey. It turns out the guy is also an ice hockey player, and they talk about it. The guy asks him, "What kind of school are you going to?"

"Law school," sez student.

The guy mentions that his son's ice hockey coach is a really rich lawyer on the West Coast. The student says, "Would it be OK if I contacted him?" The guy says, "Sure. Use my name."

The student researches the lawyer on-line and finds that he's a partner at a medium sized firm specializing in insurance litigation—exactly what the student wants to do. He contacts the lawyer . . . and winds up with a job.

* * * SMART HUMAN TRICK * * *

Student at the barber, getting a haircut. He talks about law school with the barber. The guy getting a haircut in the next chair turns out to be a lawyer. They start to talk . . . and the student winds up with a job.

* * * SMART HUMAN TRICK * * *

Female student, picking up her interview suit at the dry cleaner. The cleaner compliments her suit, and they chat about her upcoming interview. Another customer in the store is a lawyer. He joins the conversation, and winds up giving the student his card and inviting her for an interview.

9. Count of Eavesdroppers in Public Places

Remember that laptop security TV ad with a guy on an airplane? He's sitting in a middle seat working on his laptop, and his two seatmates keep reading what he's working on.

We're all nosy. We're born eavesdroppers. In public places, that can work for you. If you're going to talk about your job search with your friends, why not do it at a café near school, instead of text messaging each other or talking over the phone? You never know who might be listening!

* * * SMART HUMAN TRICK * * *

Law student chatting with her mom about law school in a Barnes & Noble café. A man sitting nearby leans over and asks the student, "What are the elements of negligence?" Somewhat surprised, she tells him. He's a judge, and asks if she'd like to interview with him for a clerkship.

She gets the job.

* * * SMART HUMAN TRICK * * *

Student having dinner with his girlfriend at a swanky restaurant in Chicago. He's discussing an interview he had, talking enthusiastically about it. A man at the next table taps him on the shoulder, hands him a business card, and says, "Talk to me." It turns out that the man is a partner at one of Chicago's most prestigious law firms, and the student winds up with a summer clerkship there.

* * * SMART HUMAN TRICK * * *

Law student sitting in a Starbucks with a classmate. She's a 3L, and she tells her friend, "I want to practice when I get out, but I want to clear my head, first. I want to go to a retreat or something like that. I'm not sure what."

A student she doesn't know, sitting at a table next to herself, introduces himself and says, "You need to talk to this partner at the firm I clerked for this summer. He's a big believer in that. He took a retreat at a Buddhist temple and highly recommends it. Talk to him about it. Here's his number."

She calls the partner, gets his advice, and he says, "When you come back, give me a call and let's set up an interview."

She does, and winds up working there.

10. WEAR T-SHIRTS AND SWEATSHIRTS, CARRY BAGS, BACKPACKS, PORTFOLIOS, NOTEBOOKS, A KEYCHAIN WITH YOUR SCHOOL NAME OR LOGO ON IT ... BUT PERHAPS NOT ALL AT THE SAME TIME

You've probably got sweatshirts and T-shirts with your school's name on them. Whenever you wear or carry items featuring your school, you give people a chance to initiate contact with you ... and you never know when those conversations will turn into job leads, particularly because your conversation will open with a mention of law school.

I've frequently talked to students who had a person point to their school logo bag or shirt and say, "You go to X school? I went there," or "How do you like it?" Often these conversations turn into "What are you going to do when you graduate?" and there's your opening!

Of course, these conversations don't always go as planned. I was at the gym once and I saw a middle-aged guy wearing a Tufts University T-shirt. Because my husband went to Tufts, I happen to know that their mascot is Jumbo the Elephant. I don't remember the whole story of exactly why that is, but I do know that somehow Jumbo was stuffed after he died, and he burned up so that all they have left is the tail. Totally weird. But anyway, people who go to Tufts call themselves Jumbos. When I see people who went to school with my husband, they say, "Tell my fellow Jumbo I said hello."

So—back to the gym. I saunter over to this guy, and say, "So—you're a Jumbo." He does a double-take and says, "*Excuse* me?" I point to his shirt and say, "Your shirt—you went to Tufts. You're a Jumbo." He responds, "Oh! It's my son's T-shirt."

We look at each other for a moment and burst out laughing. I say, "Sir, for future reference—if a woman asks you if you're a Jumbo, the answer is, 'Why, yes I am!' "

11. CARRY LEGAL PUBLICATIONS, WITH THE NAME FACING OUTWARD

Whether you're talking about a law-related newspaper, bar association publication, *Student Lawyer* or *National Jurist*, consider carrying a folded-up copy under your arm so that people can see the name of the publication. As we just talked about for T-shirts and other logo wear, having a law-related publication gives people a "hook" on which to start a conversation with you. Of course, carrying a magazine with a title like *Horny Young Foot Doctors* might accomplish the same thing ... but you might wind up in conversations with people you'd rather not know.

D. PEOPLE YOU *ALMOST* MET

Here's the scenario. You go to the kinds of events and activities we talk about in topic 3, below, and you just can't find the person/people you went there to meet. Maybe they were constantly surrounded by people. Maybe you got distracted. Maybe you just couldn't find them. Are you out of luck?

Nope!

You actually may have a great opener for a follow-up note, along the lines of: "We almost met at the Phi Alpha Delta 'Meet The Judge' event last Friday night . . ."

It's attention-grabbing . . . and it shows you took the initiative to actually attend the event. As one law student described to me, "I sent a note like this to a lawyer who called me right away. He thought it was brilliant."

E. PEOPLE WHO'VE INSPIRED YOU

If someone inspired you to become a lawyer or pursue a particular specialty . . . let them know! Whether it's an author or teacher or a lawyer or anyone else, a heartfelt note saying, "I did this because you inspired me . . ." is wise to do for more than one reason. For a start, if people inspired you, they deserve to know it. It's good for your karma. On top of that, you can always ask their advice about pursuing your dream. After all, people are usually incredibly flattered to know that they provided your inspiration, and will often be willing to give you great advice. Try it!

F. PEOPLE WHO ENCOURAGED YOU TO GO TO LAW SCHOOL IN THE FIRST PLACE

Now, now. No calling them and saying, "So I did it. *Now* what, Smarty Pants?" Instead, say something positive about your experience, how you appreciate their encouragement, and tell them, "I'm thinking about what I'll do next . . ." and ask for their advice. They'll typically be flattered that their encouragement spurred you to action, and will be motivated to help you now.

G. PEOPLE YOU *SHOULDN'T* CONTACT

After giving you a complete run-down on people you *should* talk to—virtually everybody—I'd be remiss if I didn't point out that there are people you should *avoid* contacting. In most cases, this is fairly obvious—people you didn't (or don't) get along with. You know. Enemies. Former boyfriends/girlfriends who can't stand you, for instance. I dated a guy in undergrad who made the unfortunate mistake of proposing to me when my affections were largely elsewhere. After that, every time he saw me on campus, he went out of his way to walk over to me and sneer, "You are a complete zero." He did this so often that a friend made up a T-shirt for me that read "Complete Zero."

Obviously not a great job search resource, that poor guy.

But there's a whole different category of people you shouldn't touch, even though you may have been on very friendly terms. I'll call them "People who'd rather forget you're alive."

They are best illustrated by way of an example. At one law school I visited, a student hung around until everyone else left. It turns out that this guy was a coke dealer before law school and did time in da big house. He'd been completely rehabilitated. He said, "You know, listening to you talk about tellin' everyone you know what you want reminded me of something. When I was dealing, some of my best customers were lawyers. Some of them worked at really prestigious law firms. I know they'd remember me, and I'm thinking, I'd do what you said and call them . . ."

After my heart found its way back into my chest, I *begged* this guy not to call them. I told him, "That's not reaching out to acquaintances. That's *blackmail.*"

Somewhat along the same lines—but not quite—is the dilemma facing former bartenders. *Lots* of students have bartended and of course I recommend it in this chapter as a way to meet people. But calling on lawyers who were good customers at the gin joint? Hmm. That's a maybe. I've heard it work well, but you have to be careful not to reach out to people with a—ahem—overfondness for the sauce. Alcoholics will not want to be reminded of you. Proceed with caution.

When all someone knows of you is a less-than-savory nugget, they're not a good resource for you. Take the experience of a student in Texas. He's a staunch Republican, and runs the school's Federalist club. An alum, an international lawyer now living in Seattle, comes back to Texas to solicit volunteers for a Democratic presidential candidate. At an alumni reception that night, the student winds up sitting next to the lawyer, and the lawyer says, "So—are you going to volunteer?" The student hems and haws, "I'll try, I'll have to check my schedule . . ." when a professor of his sitting next to him says, "He'll never do it. He's a Republican."

It turns out the student is moving to Seattle, and really wants to do international work. The lawyer would be a great person to contact. He asks at Career Services about recontacting the lawyer, and his counselor tells him, "You can't. You might send an exploratory e-mail to feel him out, but you should probably write him off. He put you on the spot, and you lied." The counselor goes on, "But remember it's just one person. There are plenty of other fish in the ocean."

Easy to put firmly on the "Do not call" list are the following, all subjects of questions I've had from students:

- Former avid patrons of gentlemen's clubs;

- Former customers of escort services, gay or straight;

- Former phone-sex clients.

You get the idea. Most people are fair game ... emphasis on "most."

3. The "A" in the "P.A. System": Activities That Lead to Jobs

Don't get me wrong—telling people what you're after is extremely useful. But you've got to do more, if you want to fully explore your options. You've got to take part in activities if you want to make sure you're always plugged in to the best opportunities.

I'm going to give you a bazillion activities to consider. Whether you do any of these or come up with your own, **the activities you take on should have two qualities in common:**

First, they should involve people you want to work with or people who can put you on to them.

Second—and this is the one students tend to overlook—they should be activities you *enjoy.* If you try to convince yourself that the one thing you have to attend is something that makes your skin crawl, you'll come up with every excuse in the book to avoid it. The closer it gets, the busier *you'll* get, until you talk yourself out of going! So make sure that the activities you choose are ones you'll enjoy. **(As a rule of thumb, you can make any activity enjoyable by** *volunteering,* because having something to do breaks the ice for you. I'll go into more detail about this later on—but keep that in mind next time you're trepidatious about attending a bar association function, conference, or alumni cocktail reception.)

What I've done here is to group activities into **three categories: Writing, Volunteering, and Attending.** I've also included **a fourth category, which I call "Smoking out opportunities that other people miss."** They involve scanning publications and visiting web sites, recognizing great opportunities other students are likely to overlook.

Let's get started!

A. Writing Activities

Writing ability is something that many legal employers covet. The good news is, writing for Law Review and other journals at school is hardly the only way to prove you've got writing ability! There are many other more accessible, quicker opportunities to prove your writing chops. On top of showing that you can write, writing activities can be a great way to meet potential employers—or people who can put you on to them. Let's talk about the possibilities ...

1. Remember That *Every Legal Publication* (Outside of Scholarly Publications Like Law Reviews) Is Crying Out for Content—Write About an Issue or Profile a Lawyer.

This is one of my favourite all-time ways to get a great job. I've talked with so many students who've used it as a springboard into fabulous opportunities! As Marilyn Tucker points out, "Writing articles makes a *tremendous* difference for you. It not only gives you a great resume item, but it proves to employers that you really are interested in what you say you're interested in—and of course it proves you can write!"

It's easy to overlook is the fact that there are tons of legal publications, and they all need something to fill them up. Bar association publications, local, state and federal. Specialty newsletters. Law-related web sites like lawfuel.com. Alumni publications and student newspapers (I talk about those separately below).

There are two principal types of articles you can write: One involves a cutting-edge legal topic, and the other profiles a prominent practitioner. Let's talk about them separately.

A. ARTICLES ABOUT CUTTING-EDGE TOPICS

How do you find these topics? There are several possibilities. One is to **keep up with what's going on in the news.** Legal issues are in the headlines all the time. Another is to **ask a professor who teaches a subject that interests you**; (s)he'll be able to turn you on to issues that need more attention.

My *favourite* way to nail a topic is to **contact practitioners in the specialty—either on your own or through Career Services—and ask them a simple question: "What would you like to read more about?"** When a lawyer hears this, here's what they *really* hear: free research!

No matter where you find the topic, once you've nailed one down you get on-line and research the status of it. You may also interview a professor or two, or a practitioner who's an expert in the area, perhaps one who teaches CLEs about it. Generate a one-page article about the topic. It won't take you long—I promise.

Once you have your one-page article, approach editors of the publications that would be interested in it—as I mentioned before, bar association publications, school publications, law-related web sites—and tell them that you've got an article about a topic you know lawyers will be interested in learning more about. I *promise* you you'll find a home for your article.

Now: How does this help you? Apart from the fact that it gives you a great resume item *and* a killer writing sample, you get excellent contact with lawyers. And what do they know about you? That you have enthusiasm for what they do, and that you take the initiative. Inevitably, when a lawyer gives you a topic to write about or you interview them about their expertise, there'll be an opportunity in the conversation to mention how interested you are in what they do ... and that leads naturally to a conversation about how to break into it.

You may have two qualms about doing this. One is—why can't these lawyers just do this research themselves? Because 'professional reading' isn't a paying activity, that's why. Lawyers make money working on client matters, and background reading doesn't fit the bill. So you're doing them a favour.

You may also question your own expertise. "But Kimmbo," students have lamented to me, "I'm just a law student!" Ironically, you're *perfectly* positioned to handle these projects, because your research skills are absolutely fresh and up-to-date. Anyway, what's the difference between you and an "expert"? If you read up on an issue, then *you're* an expert.

The bottom line is, I've seen this article-writing work brilliantly for students. If you do it, you'll often find that it's the *only* thing you have to do to nail down a great job!

* * * SMART HUMAN TRICK * * *

Law student has a very specific goal: He's interested in the labor practice at a particular large law firm. He doesn't have the credentials they normally look for, and they won't interview him.

For his third year in law school, he makes a point of writing an article about a labor-related topic in the bar association newsletter every month. His name appears in the byline of every one of his articles.

In the Spring of Third Year, he gets a phone call from the head of the labor practice at his dream law firm. The lawyer says, "We're looking for a new associate in our department, and we see your name everywhere. You're clearly somebody we should be talking to."

He gets the job.

* * * SMART HUMAN TRICK * * *

Law student in Alabama, very interested in breaking into Homeland Security. He writes a few papers about the subject and posts them on-line.

He's Googled and cold-called by an official at the Governor's office in a nearby state, who offers him a job in Coastal Security consulting.

B. A PROFILE OF A PROMINENT PRACTITIONER

Law-related publications publish articles about prominent lawyers all the time. It's both instructive and inspirational to read about "how they did it." And if you're the one doing the interviewing and writing, it gives you direct contact with someone who could be a valuable contact for you.

You can find people to write about through Career Services, or by keeping your eye on what's going on in the legal world to see who's associated with prominent cases and issues.

For detailed advice on writing profiles, check out #4 below, where we talk about writing profiles for alumni publications and student newspapers—since the way you'll go about it is exactly the same.

2. LEGAL WRITING COMPETITIONS

So many students ignore these, even though you see posters at school about them all the time. I know *I* ignored them when I was in school at Case Western. "They must get thousands of entries!" I figured. "I can't win."

Well, I have since come to find out that most writing competitions get no more than three or four entries. *Three or four.* Some have to extend the deadline to get even *one!*

So don't blow off those competitions. If you're worried about the time commitment, you should remember that you don't need to schedule a huge chunk of time for them. Make a point of spending an extra half hour a day at the library after you finish studying. In tiny chunks you can accomplish a lot.

Legal fraternities like Phi Alpha Delta run writing competitions, as do many bar associations. A good resource is the ABA website: www.abanet.org/lsd/competitions/writing-contests/home. html.

When you do well in a writing competition, you've got natural contacts in the judges, whom you should approach for career advice. You can also send your writing entry to employers as an "FYI": "I know you practice dumpster diving law. I just won the Furniture Recycling Law Writing Competition, and I thought you might find my paper interesting ..." and then ask for an informational interview.

If you're *still* not convinced, you need to know that many of these competitions offer fairly sizable cash prizes. Swe-e-e-et.

3. TAKE ADVANTAGE OF YOUR SCHOOL'S WRITING REQUIREMENT (IF IT HAS ONE) TO CONTACT LAWYERS YOU'D LIKE TO WORK WITH

Many law schools have a writing requirement, and if *yours* does, it gives you a perfect opportunity to approach prospective employers in a nonthreatening way. Tammy Willcox advises that you call lawyers who practice in an area that interests you, explain that you have a school writing requirement to fulfill, and ask what they'd like to read about. They're likely to come up with topics for you, and they'll be not only flattered that you asked, but they'll also be impressed with your initiative. *And* it gives you a perfect opportunity to keep in touch with them—when you finish your writing project, you can send it to them, or, better yet, ask to hand-deliver it—and take advantage of the opportunity to talk about their practice.

So, if your school has a writing requirement, don't overlook its job search potential!

4. WRITE PROFILES FOR YOUR SCHOOL'S ALUMNI PUBLICATION OR SCHOOL NEWSPAPER—AND IF YOUR SCHOOL DOESN'T HAVE ONE, START ONE!

There's no better and more flattering way to talk with people than to tell them that you want to write an article about them. Writing such profiles is a great way to get your foot in the door with lawyers who might not otherwise be receptive to you. Think about it; when you offer to write a profile of someone, you're essentially telling them, "I want to spend half an hour hearing about how wonderful you are, how good you are at overcoming obstacles, what wisdom you'd like to pass along to other people . . ." There aren't a whole lot of people who aren't seduced by an offer like that. Your school's alumni publication and school newspaper are excellent opportunities for you to make contact with alums you'd like to work with!

As Gail Cutter suggests, use your Career Services Office to see which alums practice in areas that interest you. Research them as you would an interviewer; google them, check out their profile on their employer's web site or in Martindale Hubbell (on-line at Martindale.com). Then contact them and tell them that you'd like to write about them for the law school newspaper or alumni publication. Have a list of questions ready. You'll want to ask many of the same kinds of things that you'd ask in a job interview, ironically enough—how they chose their specialty, what they like about their job, what a typical day is like for them, what they wish they'd known before they started practice, what kinds of traits it takes to be successful in their work.

But you also have the benefit of being able to ask very valuable questions that you couldn't ask on an interview—like what kinds of advice they would offer to people who want to break into their field, what the downsides are. Of course, when the article is published, be sure you follow up with the person you profiled. And if you find you really would like to pursue a job with them or in their specialty, you've got the perfect calling card! You can say, "Having interviewed you, I'm really excited about what you do, and I'd like to break into it myself. How should I go about it?" Be sure that you also ask them who *else* you should talk to. The more contacts you make, the better off you are!

What if your school doesn't have a newspaper? Consider *starting* one—even if it's just on-line. Newsletters are inexpensive to publish and e-mailed ones are even cheaper, so it's not a hard sell for a Student Bar Association to support one. You'll, of course, still be able to interview people—after all, that's the point of this exercise—but you'll *also* have the feather in your cap of *starting* something, and initiative is a trait highly prized by employers!

5. APPROACH PARTNERS AND SENIOR ASSOCIATES AT FIRMS YOU'D LIKE TO WORK WITH AND VOLUNTEER TO HELP THEM WRITE ARTICLES AND SPEECHES

Here's the idea, courtesy of Tammy Willcox. It's based on the fact that partners and senior associates are encouraged to get their names in print and make speeches as a means of business development. They don't necessarily *want* to write these things and make these speeches.

That's where you come in.

Contact partners or senior associates who do what you want to do. You may even want to contact alums from your school. Say you'd like to do some research and writing involving what they do, and offer to volunteer on writing an article or helping with a speech. Ask for a topic. For articles, ask to share the byline, so that you get credit, too.

Not only is this a great way to get your foot in the door at a potential employer, but also to gain an informal mentor—and get a writing credit on your resume in a hurry!

6. WORK AS A RESEARCH ASSISTANT FOR A PROFESSOR

As Gail Cutter points out, "Professors have great connections! Students think professors are in an ivory tower, but they're not. Even if they don't practice law, they've got great contacts. And you'll get a great recommendation!"

If there are professors you feel comfortable enough to approach yourself, then go ahead and do that. Otherwise, ask your Career Services Director for guidance as to who's doing what. Either way, you'll get excellent research and writing experience, a potential introduction to employers—and you'll probably get paid, to boot!

* * * SMART HUMAN TRICK * * *

Female student, a 1L at a Southern law school. As she puts it, "My writing skills were terrible. *Terrible.* I went to a professor and explained my situation, and said, "I know I've got to do something about my writing because I won't get a job without it. Could I please research something for you?" He hesitated, and I said, 'It's free." That sealed the deal. I worked for him on a project and my writing really improved.

After that, when people asked me about my writing skills, I pointed out the work I'd done for this professor. I didn't mention that the whole reason I *did* that work is that I knew my writing was terrible.

I wound up volunteering on a children's issue with the local bar association. A fellow volunteer was a judge. We chatted and I mentioned my work for professor X. The judge asked me to work for him!

Can you believe it? Here I was all worked up about my writing skills . . . and now I'm working for a judge!"

7.   START A BRIEF WRITING SERVICE

There are many small law firms and sole practitioners who need writing help, but don't have enough work to keep an extra person busy on a part-or full-time basis. You can help fill that need on a freelance basis.

Now this might be a bit too much of a time commitment for you if you're still in school, but if you're a new graduate and you're looking for work, "It's a great way to make, and impress, new contacts," says Case Western's Debra Fink. For one thing, it shows great initiative. For another, it demonstrates your writing ability. And for a third, it helps you expand your web of contacts. If you'd like to pursue it, talk to your Career Services Director for the names of local alums and sole practitioners who might be able to use your services.

8.   WRITE A LAW REVIEW NOTE. YOU DON'T HAVE TO BE ON LAW REVIEW TO DO IT, YOU KNOW

I saved this one for last. Most people don't realize that writing—and, ideally publishing—a Law Review note doesn't require that you grade or write on to Law Review. You can just—well—*write one.*

Now, if you were to try this, I'd strongly suggest you solicit the advice and mentorship of a professor, because writing a Law Review note is an arduous process. It's like birthing an elephant. It takes a lot of time and a lot of detailed research. And then there's that damned blue book. But the fact is, I've known law students who've done it, and it's a way to get the magic "Law Review" credential on your resume without actually serving on the staff.

B.   VOLUNTEERING ACTIVITIES

I'm a huge fan of volunteering. Don't think of it as working without pay. Think of it as investing in your career.

The great news is that you can turn just about any event into one that you'll enjoy if you call ahead, find out who's organizing it, and volunteer to help out. Here's what you need to know:

- **Every activity you can think of requires volunteers**. Bar association functions, alumni functions, CLEs, conferences, you name it—they all require volunteers.

- No matter how reserved you are—and most of us consider ourselves shy—**volunteering makes it easy to talk to people**, because you have a *reason* for being there, a reason for speaking with people. Once the ice is broken, people are easy to talk to.

- **Volunteering takes something that's good for your career and turns it into a resume item**. You can put a section on your resume talking about the events with which you've helped out. What that creates in the minds of lawyers is that you're enthusiastic, and that you've got rainmaking potential—because taking part in activities and talking with people is a prime source of new clients for law firms. And if you've got rainmaking potential, you've got just about the most valuable skill there is!

Let's talk about some of the many volunteering opportunities there are. In this list, I'm sure you'll find something that appeals to you.

1.   WHAT TO ASK FOR WHEN YOU MEET PEOPLE THROUGH VOLUNTEERING . . .

It's important to know what to say to people—and more importantly, to know what to ask them for. We talk about this later in this chapter.

2.   THE TREASURE CHEST OF SECRET OPPORTUNITIES: VOLUNTEER AT YOUR CAREER SERVICES OFFICE

When I visit law schools—which is about a hundred times a year—I'm often staggered by how little regard some students pay their Career Services Office. A lot of times, when I ask students for directions to the CSO, they don't even know where it is!

I sing the praises of Career Services throughout this book. They can help you in a bunch of different ways, as I outlined in Chapter 3. But you can help yourself by helping *them*. Think about it. Everything that the CSO does—fielding job opportunities that come in from employers, setting up panels and seminars, finding on-campus speakers, running on-campus interview programs—is a ''secret'' opportunity to make valuable contact with employers. Here are a few ideas for making the most of these opportunities . . .

A. OFFER TO POST JOB LISTINGS THAT COME IN ON THE LAW SCHOOL'S CAREER SERVICES WEB SITE

I ask you: could there be a better way to get "dibs" on job listings than by offering to post them on-line? I mention elsewhere in this book the value of keeping up with on-line job postings on a very frequent basis, because the best opportunities come in at random and get snatched up quickly. Being the one who *posts* those opportunities is even better than that.

Incidentally, I've known Career Services Directors who make use of this tactic. When I visit law schools, I'll often be introduced to a new director—and when I ask what happened to the "old" one, I'll sometimes learn that a job posting came in, and it interested them—so they took it!

Why not get in on some of that action? You'll be doing Career Services a favour—and you'll get the inside skinny on the latest opportunities.

B. HELP SET UP PANELS AND RECEPTIONS BY ACTING AS A LIAISON WITH ALUMNI AND LOCAL PRACTITIONERS

In this role, you're the one who contacts alumni and local practitioners on behalf of Career Services to see if they can come and speak, take part in a panel, or attend a reception. This gives you an *excellent* opportunity to introduce yourself to potential employers without asking for a job. And, because you'll be working in Career Services, you'll have input on exactly who those speakers and reception guests will be—and of course, you'll propose ones whose practice areas interest you!

C. OFFER TO CONTACT EMPLOYERS TO TAKE PART IN 'CAREER DAY' FAIRS AND ACTIVITIES

Many law schools run "Career Days," where alums and local employers come on campus to talk about what they do, often in a combination of presentations and 'table talks,' where the lawyers man tables and students approach them for information.

For instance, the University of Minnesota runs an annual "Invitation to Career Day." As Minnesota's Sue Gainen says, "I have students call alums and local lawyers and ask, 'Can you come and talk to students for two hours about what you do?' It's *much* easier than asking for a job!"

D. OFFER TO BE A STUDENT ESCORT FOR THE ON-CAMPUS INTERVIEW PROCESS

Mind out of the gutter, please. We're not talking about *that* kind of escort!

In this role, you escort interviewers to the interview rooms, show them where coffee, restrooms and phones are, and generally make yourself helpful. As Kathleen Brady points out, "There are students who've gotten jobs by being escorts." It gives you a few minutes alone with the interviewer, and you're implicitly being shown in a positive light, because you're being helpful. And you're not under pressure, because you needn't say anything about wanting to meet with them while you escort them—it just gives you a chance to break the ice and chat with them casually. I would ask for a list the day before interviewers arrive, so you have an idea of whom you'll meet— and you can go to the employer's web site as well as google them to find out a little about them.

After you meet them, you can always follow up with a phone call or letter, which you'll open by stating that you met them at school. Assuming you made a good impression, it'll be much easier to ask for their help in either meeting with you or suggesting other people you should talk to.

* * * SMART HUMAN TRICK * * *

Law student at a law school in Indiana volunteers at Career Services, helping out wherever he's needed. One day, an interviewer from a large, prestigious St. Louis law firm is stranded at the school without a ride to the airport. The student reports, "I wasn't supposed to work that day, and I sure wasn't dressed for it—I was wearing a T-shirt and my 'Daisy Dukes.' But I offered to help out and give him a ride to the airport. On the way, we had a great conversation. If I had submitted a resume to this guy's firm, he never would have talked to me. I didn't have the grades. But because we hit it off, he asked me to come out to St. Louis and interview. I wound up working there!"

E. WORK ON OR CREATE A "JOB BANK," CALLING EMPLOYERS TO SEE IF THEY'LL BE ADDING LAW STUDENTS/NEW GRADUATES IN THE NEXT YEAR

There's no doubt about it, asking for a job is nerve-wracking—and that's why I give you so many ways to create an end-run around it. Working on or creating a "job bank" for your law school is a *great* way of doing so.

Here's the scoop. You and/or people at Career Services and/or your classmates call local employers—or any other fertile market for your school—and simply tell employers that you're calling on behalf of the school, and you're wondering if they're planning to add a law student and/or summer clerk and/or new associate within the next year. You can see the benefit here: you're learning about potential job opportunities before anybody else—but you're not asking for a job yourself!

If there are employers that particularly interest you, clearly those are the ones you'll call first. And it doesn't hurt to throw a little honest flattery into your conversation. "I think your work sounds interesting," that kind of thing. And if the tone of the conversation is friendly, there's no harm in saying that you'll be applying for the job yourself.

F. Work on, or Create, an "On Campus Informational Interviewing" Program

"On campus informational interviewing" is the brainchild of wonderful Beth Kirch of the University of Georgia. Here's how it works: It's set up just like on-campus interviews for jobs, where interviewers come in for a day, and students sign up for twenty-minute interview slots ahead of time.

The difference is this: students aren't getting jobs—they're getting advice. This has a couple of benefits. It doesn't put employers on the spot for hiring students; they're offering advice, which *everybody* likes to give, and it gives the employer good P.R. with the school and students. And it gives interviewing experience to students whose credentials might not otherwise qualify them for on-campus interviews. (Of course, students *do* sometimes wind up with call back interviews from the program—a happy fringe benefit!).

If you help set up such a program at your school, you'd be contacting employers—typically alums—and asking them to take part. Of course, because you're the one reaching out to them, you're making a natural contact—one that could easily help your job search.

G. Volunteer to Call Alums to See if They'll Take Part in Your School's Mentoring Program (if It Has one)

Many, if not most, law schools have mentoring programs, which match up students with alums who act as informal career advisors. (If your school doesn't have a mentoring program, I talk about setting one up below.) Calling alums to see if they'll be mentors is a non-intimidating way to break the ice and talk to them, and also to brush up your phone skills. Many alums are delighted to offer themselves as mentors; lawyers love to give advice! And, of course, if you're the first one to speak to them, you have not just your pick of mentors—but the opportunity to ask them for advice while you've got them on the phone.

H. Help Set up a "Speed Networking" Program at Your School

You've heard of speed dating, right? Like in the movies *Hitch* and *The Forty Year Old Virgin,* where people in bars talk to potential dates for a few minutes, a gong sounds, and they move on to the next person ... and so on.

Speed networking is a spin on that, which law schools are starting to tap into. As St. Thomas' Elizabeth Wefel explains it, students spend six minutes talking to an employer—not for a job, but for advice, as though they were meeting at a bar association function, CLE, or the like. Students are primed with interview questions on cards ahead of time if they want them, but you know all those questions from the interview chapter. At the end of the six minutes—bong!—on to the next employer.

There are twelve rounds or so, with a twenty minute break in the middle, and a mix and mingle before and after.

Students love it, and needless to say setting up a Speed Networking program involves a lot of useful people skills. So suggest the idea to Career Services, and if they already run a program like it, offer to help out in contacting practitioners to take part.

I. HELP SET UP A TABLE TALK EVENT WITH UPPERCLASSMEN DISCUSSING THEIR SUMMER EXPERIENCES

Students love to hear the experiences of students just ahead of them in law school. Some schools run an event where the upper classmen sit at tables around a room, and students walk up to talk to them about their experiences.

Helping to set up one of these events gives you a great opportunity to hear about a variety of specialties and settings ... and maybe get a lead on a great job.

J. HELP SET UP A "SHADOWING DAY" FOR STUDENTS TO SHADOW PRACTITIONERS

I've seen this at several schools, and it's just great. As Nebraska's Tasha Everman describes it, "We set up a schedule where all kinds of employers—judges, private practitioners, prosecutors, public interest lawyers—let students follow them around for a half-day or full day. Once they've agreed to do it, we make up a schedule sheet and students sign up to shadow the employer of their choice, first come, first served."

Obviously, shadowing attorneys is a great way to see if you'll like what they do—and get some great career advice from them. If you get in on setting up the shadowing schedule, you'll get "first dibs" at employers who interest you. And as is true of so many volunteering opportunities, it's a lot easier to call attorneys and ask for their participation than it is to ask for a job!

K. HELP SET UP A BROWN BAG LUNCH PROGRAM

These programs are informal lunchtime programs—as the name suggests—where attorneys chat with students about what they do. Fordham has one, and they call it "Career Pathways."

If you volunteer to help set this up, you call alums and local lawyers to see if they'll come in for lunch to chat casually with students about what they do. The students bring their own lunches, and you get Career Services to spring for the attorney's lunch. Of course, when you help set it up, you'll be choosing people to contact—and they'll be people whose jobs particularly interest you.

3. VOLUNTEER WITH THE ADMISSIONS OFFICE TO SHOW PROSPECTIVE STUDENTS AROUND CAMPUS

This is a really sneaky way to find a job, but it works. Here's what you need to know: Prospective students rarely come for campus tours alone. They bring their folks. And which profession are the parents most likely to be in? Ri-i-i-ight. Lawyers often beget lawyers. I can't tell you how many students I've talked with who nailed jobs through the parents of prospective students, just because they took them on a jolly tour of the facilities.

This works particularly well because you're showing a prospective student around school, you're at your gracious, most salesman-like best. Your people skills are front and center. You can always gently bring up the subject by asking the parents if they are lawyers, "Or will Michael/Emily be the first lawyer in the family?" If they're lawyers, you can ask what they do and take it from there—in between pointing out the Snidely Memorial Fountain and the Einstein Science Center, of course.

4. DO A PROJECT WITH PSLAWNET

If you haven't heard about PSLawNet (at pslawnet.org), you're in for a treat. It's a national program, started at NYU, that matches up law students with volunteer positions at more than a thousand public interest organizations nationwide ("public interest" is interpreted broadly, by the way; it's not just legal aid, but often prosecutor's offices, state attorneys generals' offices, nonprofits, and private firms with public interest or pro bono practices).

I could go on and on about what a great activity PSLawNet is, but here are a few of the benefits:

- The experience itself is invaluable. You do everything from representing clients, to taking part in administrative hearings, to research and writing.

- Beyond the experience itself are the contacts you make. PSLawNet jobs sometimes wind up in permanent jobs, and even when they don't, you make all kinds of contacts via the people you work with.

- The time commitment is light; 50 hours is the minimum, and you can knock that out in a week if you want to. As Sandy Mans points out, "You can do a couple of PSLawNet projects in the summer, and one over winter break." (That's three killer resume items!)

- Grades aren't an issue. As Sandy Mans points out, "There's no screening. You can always get a project with them." The only thing they do is a quick interview, to make sure that you are well matched to the project, that you're truly interested in it.

- PSLawNet gives you the chance to get legal experience on your resume. On top of the experience itself, the names of employers can be very valuable when you post your profile on sites like linkedin.com, where they can exponentially increase the people who contact you. (We talk about this in detail in the Internet chapter, Chapter 11.)

- If you ever feel disenchanted with the idea of practicing law, a PSLawNet project goes a long way toward getting you excited about it again, because you're really doing hands-on, practical, and in many cases, exciting stuff!

Now you may be thinking, "Swell, Kimmbo. I don't have any money as it is, and now you're telling me to take prime money-making time and use it *volunteering?*" In a word: Yep. As Mary Obrzut points out, "While you're doing PSLawNet, flip burgers at night. Bartend. Whatever!" The experience is that important.

Incidentally, if you take my advice and do a PSLawNet project—at least one—don't list it as "volunteer" or "unpaid" on your resume. We talked about this in the resume chapter, but it bears repeating: experience is experience.

Of course, our focus here is on the people aspect of activities in which you take part. Keep in touch with the people you work with on PSLawNet activities, and of course work into the conversation what your goals are. You can't have better contacts than people who are familiar with your work.

5. HELP OUT WITH YOUR SCHOOL'S SPEAKER'S BUREAU, AND IF YOUR SCHOOL DOESN'T HAVE ONE, START ONE

Most law schools have an organization that brings in off-campus speakers, a speaker's bureau. It's a tremendously useful organization to join. Here's why: It gives you great, nonthreatening contact with lawyers who might be very useful to your career. Whether you're the one doing outreach, to ask lawyers to speak at school, or you're the one who picks them up at the airport, meets them at school, tours them around campus, has lunch or dinner with them ... what a great opportunity to get "up close and personal" with lawyers who might otherwise be hard to reach.

If your school doesn't have a speaker's bureau, consider starting one. For a small budget from the Student Bar Association, you can set up all kinds of interesting lectures. You'll not only make great contacts, but you'll help your classmates, and you'll have a killer resume item that shows great initiative.

The way that you work your career goals into the mix is this: don't hit speakers over the head with the fact you're interested in doing what they do when you first talk to them. Instead, before you talk to them, you're going to have researched them and what they do. Ask a few intelligent questions when you talk to them, "I noticed you're involved in X case ..." "What was it like clerking for Judge so-and-so ..." "In law school, what got you interested in being ..." Then *after* they visit your school, call and tell them that you're very interested in what they do, and ask if you can meet with them to talk more about it. You wouldn't be the first law student to nail a dream job this way.

6. RUN, HELP TO RUN, OR START A CLUB AT SCHOOL FOCUSING ON THE SPECIALTY YOU WANT, OR SPECIAL CIRCUMSTANCES YOU'RE IN (E.G., SECOND CAREER STUDENTS OR 'MOMMY STUDENTS'), AN "AFFINITY" GROUP (REFLECTING YOUR ETHNICITY OR GENDER), AND BRING IN SPEAKERS

I see an awful lot of student resumes that list membership in various clubs, and—well, it's not *nothing*, but let's face it ... you can put a club on your resume without ever actually attending a single meeting, let alone taking a leadership role.

The real benefit of starting and/or running a club at school is that you're the one who gets contact with lawyers when you bring them in to speak. When you're contacting people in a role other than job seeker, you let them see a side of you that you want them to see—the enthusiastic initiative-taking leader. That puts you in a natural position to ask later for their advice about breaking into the specialty, or dealing with the particular issue that's the club's focus (e.g., balancing parenthood and work).

7. START A MENTORING PROGRAM AT YOUR SCHOOL, IF IT DOESN'T HAVE ONE ALREADY

Some law schools have mentoring programs that match up law students with advice-offering alumni. As we talk about shortly, it's a great idea to take advantage of such a program and hook up with a mentor ... if your school has such a program. If it doesn't have one, offer to help start one! What you do is to work with your Career Services office to contact alumni and determine their interest in becoming a mentor. The contact-making potential in such an activity is obvious; if you're the one contacting lawyers to determine their interest in being a mentor, you've got "first crack" at them, in terms of having a conversation about career interests. On top of that, you've got a great resume item, because it shows initiative in talking with people—a tremendous asset!

8. VOLUNTEER FOR POSITIONS AT LAW SCHOOL THAT GET YOU INTO CONTACT WITH ALUMS AND LAWYERS.

Every law school has them—volunteer positions with names like "liaison" or member of the "board of governors." Many times these positions go without any student being willing to fill them. *Big* mistake. Offering to serve in any capacity that gets you into regular contact with lawyers translates into an informal opportunity to sniff out career opportunities.

Whether it's acting as a liaison with a national fraternity or serving on the alumni board of governors, it's unlikely to be a significant time commitment. It goes on your resume, as evidence of your initiative and people skills. And of course, it could be your conduit to a great job.

* * * SMART HUMAN TRICK * * *

Second year student at a New England law school. For months, his school has been looking for someone to serve as the student representative on the Alumni Board of Governors. His Career Services Director twists his arm into taking it. He does—and winds up sitting next to an alum who happens to be general counsel for a major cable television network. They start chatting ... and he winds up with a summer internship at the network.

9. VOLUNTEER TO INTRODUCE SPEAKERS AT LAW SCHOOL EVENTS

When speakers come to your law school campus, *somebody* has to introduce them. Why don't you volunteer? The great thing is, when you introduce somebody, you can really lay it on. You can flatter them in a way that would probably make your skin crawl if you were speaking to them directly instead of to an audience. But trust me: as someone who's been introduced as a speaker more than a thousand times, you *always* like people to say nice things about you. I remember reading a quote that said, "We don't always like people we admire, but we always love people who admire us."

Introducing a speaker you'd like to work for or solicit career advice from gives you a chance to show off your eloquence and enthusiasm. I talked to one judge who said, "I spoke at a law school where a young lady had offered to introduce me. She had written the introduction herself, and by golly it was impressive.

She'd obviously done a lot of research on me. She was so impressive, I hired her."

10. Volunteer for the Local Bar Association

Very few students get involved with their local bar association. I know this, because when I speak at law schools around the country, local and state bar associations often sponsor me, and they *urge* me to talk up the bar association.

I know what you're thinking: "What am I going to do with a bunch of practitioners? I'm in *school.*"

The fact is, there are a bunch of time-effective ways to make great contacts, and get great experience, fast. Every bar association function needs volunteers. Whether you're working on the newsletter or membership committee, manning tables at bar committee functions, making phone calls, or as Gail Cutter suggests, joining a committee and asking the chairman if you can research something and report back on it—there are dozens of quick ways to help your career.

I just can't tell you how valuable it is to take part in the bar association while you're still in school, *especially* if you're going to be staying in the area when you graduate. I often talk with students who take this advice and almost immediately make contact with a lawyer who puts them on to a job. In Austin, Texas a couple of years ago, I talked with a student who'd seen me speak when she was at law school in Indiana. She transferred to the University of Texas, and stopped by to tell me that the first thing she'd done when she got to Austin was to join the Texas Bar Association, and she went to a local meeting. She told me, "I couldn't believe I was the only student there. I was talking to a few lawyers, and one of them asked me to come in for an interview. I'm working for the guy now."

If you're not going to be staying in the area, join the bar association for the state you intend to settle in, as well as the one you're in now. What are we talking—about ten bucks a pop? Two lattes at Starbucks and you've paid for your student membership in the bar. And the reason to join your "local" bar as well as your "destination" one is this—inevitably lawyers where you are now will know valuable people, no matter where you intend to settle. And getting experience taking part in bar association activities is an asset no matter where you get it. Of course, on school breaks, go to bar association functions in the city where you plan to settle, and volunteer there as well. It's a great way to get your feet wet and to get to know people in the city where you plan to wind up.

* * * SMART HUMAN TRICK * * *

Law student in North Carolina, planning on settling in Southern California. She calls the Bar Association for the city in

California and asks when their annual golf outing is going to be (most bar associations have such an event). When they tell her, she volunteers to help out. She gets a cheap airfare out to California, and they assign her the job of driving one of the golf carts for the day. As she reports, "I wound up driving around some of the most prestigious lawyers in the city. Between holes, we were chatting, and they asked me, 'So what are you up to?' and I told them that I'm in law school in North Carolina but I'm planning on relocating out here when I graduate, and I wanted to get familiar with the legal community."

"I wound up the day with a thick stack of business cards from lawyers who had *volunteered* to help me find a job! Through them, I nailed a great summer clerkship."

* * * SMART HUMAN TRICK * * *

Law student in the Pacific Northwest. He has mediocre grades. He offers to volunteer at the local bar association. They hold a raffle, and ask him to sell tickets. He meets lawyers who were volunteering on the raffle ... and one of them offers him a job.

* * * SMART HUMAN TRICK * * *

Local bar association has a charity golf tournament. They sell each hole for $250. A law student buys one. He stands at the hole, holding the flag with one hand—and a stack of resumes with the other.

Every time a lawyer sinks a putt, the law student hands him/her a resume.

He winds up with a job.

* * * SMART HUMAN TRICK * * *

Reports a law student from California:

"I was a nurse and went to law school at an on-line, unaccredited law school. If I wanted to practice anywhere but California, I'd have to practice for five years first—not an attractive prospect!

I joined the Illinois State Women's Bar Association, and volunteered to help them out on several functions. I met women lawyers both locally and from all over the state. I passed the California bar exam—what a horror—and I didn't want to have to take another state's bar, ever.

It turns out that one of my new friends through the bar association works at a firm focusing on federal administrative law, which means you can be licensed in any state. I wrote the supervising attorney a letter starting with 'X recommended that I contact you'—my friend—and made a point of working in how useful my nursing background would be to them. My resume was aimed at them. I was hauled in for three interviews, with hard questions I'd anticipated. I'm pretty sure I aced them.

Yesterday I was offered and accepted a job with them as an attorney. A great job—with great opportunities for advancement!''

11. CLEs (Continuing Legal Education Seminars)—Volunteer to Help Out With Them ... or Even Run Your Own!

We've talked about CLEs before—the continuing education classes that lawyers everywhere in America have to take to maintain their license to practice law. These CLEs are happy hunting grounds for law students!

Here are the basics you need to know:

- CLEs are given in every specialty you can imagine. Whether you're interested in patent law, sports, entertainment, transactional work, litigation, international, you name it ... there are CLEs offered on a frequent basis.

- They're given at convenient times. Since practicing attorneys have to take them, they're often given in the evenings and on weekends.

- They're brief. Many CLEs only last a couple of hours or so.

- I saved the best for last. Although practicing attorneys pay out the ying-yang for these classes, as a law student you can almost always get in for free, on scholarship, or for a very nominal fee. You can also ask at Career Services or the local bar association to see if any local attorneys are willing to sponsor law students for CLEs.

Shortly we'll talk about just attending CLEs, but right now we're talking about the step beyond that—helping to run them, or even running one of your own!

If you help out at a CLE, there are a bunch of things you can do. Even if you're doing something as simple as handing out the name tags or pouring the punch, you'll have a great avenue for meeting people, because the fact that you've got something to do "breaks the ice" for you. On top of that, if you find out who's attending the CLE up front, it gives you the opportunity to zero in on lawyers you'd like to talk to. Then if you're handing out name tags, for instance, and your "target lawyers" show up, you can tell them, "I'm glad you're here, I was looking forward to talking to you ..."

If you want to take some serious initiative, you can run your own CLE—or, ideally, with a few like-minded friends, to help spread out the effort. At some law schools, the students run CLEs routinely—I'm thinking specifically of Seattle University, where the students annually put on an Environmental Law CLE.

Here's how you do it. To start with, you choose a theme for the CLE, whether it's on a particular specialty or aspect of law firm management. (Check out the kinds of CLEs that are given by going to local bar associations or the Practicing Law Institute, at www.pli.edu). Then you need a sponsor, whether it's the state bar association or your student bar association, to provide the dough. The budget actually can be quite small, because there aren't a lot of expenses associated with CLEs, and attendees pay to come. You get accreditation through the state bar association, and again, from law students who've put them on, I understand this is not all that tricky, either. You solicit speakers, reserve space at law school, e-mail invitations to local attorneys. It's not your usual law school activity, but it does show tremendous initiative—and you'll really enjoy it!

* * * SMART HUMAN TRICK * * *

Law student with poor grades. His father is a lawyer who runs CLEs. The student starts helping out. He speaks with lawyers at the CLEs, and follows up with personalized letters talking about where they'd met. He'd say he was impressed with what they had to say, and he'd like to learn more.

He winds up with interviews at every high-powered law firm in the city.

* * * SMART HUMAN TRICK * * *

Reports a lawyer at a prestigious New York firm: "I went to a CLE. When I walked up to the registration desk to pick up my info packet, I gave the young woman sitting there my name. I was totally surprised by her response. 'Oh, Attorney So-and-So, I've been looking forward to meeting you. You work in complex litigation at X firm. You must work for partner X and partner Y.' I said I did, and she said, 'Were you involved in X case?' "

"She went on, and asked if she could talk to me about my work sometime during the conference."

"Here I was, just expecting my information packet, and she treated me like a rock star!"

"I have to tell you, she'd really done her research. I've never met such a go-getter. I wound up taking her résumé back to the firm, with a strong recommendation that we hire her for the summer . . . which we did."

12.   BARTEND AT ALUMNI COCKTAIL RECEPTIONS

Working as a bartender adds a whole new meaning to the phrase "break the ice"! If you hate the thought of *attending* receptions, here's the way to do an end-run around your discomfort—*work* the reception instead!

If you're worried about knowing how to mix drinks—don't be. As a former law school social director, I promise you, you don't have to know much beyond "Scotch and water." Any basic guide on mixology is all you need.

Kathleen Brady points out that this is an excellent way to chat with people. You can ask where they work, how they like it, and take it from there. (Of course, be sure to ask for business cards from the people who interest you, and follow up with a phone call or e-mail asking if you can meet them briefly at their convenience and talk more, that they whetted your appetite for what they do, and you'd like to know more about it!)

So bartending is a great way to make the most of law school receptions for alumni and practitioners. We've all been to happy hours, and everybody knows the most popular place at a happy hour is the bar—so if you're the one standing behind that bar, you're way ahead of the game!

13. VOLUNTEER AS AN EXTERN FOR A LOCAL JUDGE OR MAGISTRATE

It's important to remember that every judge and every magistrate in America has externs. While some of these are paid positions (and they're killer jobs, by the way), it's possible to volunteer, as well. If you spend even half a summer or work part-time for a judge for one semester, it'll do wonders for your job search in a whole variety of ways.

For one thing, you'll sharpen your research and writing skills, and just about every legal employer is interested in *that*. It looks fantastic on your resume.

For another, if you're not sure what you want to do with your law degree, a volunteer externship is a great place to start. It's the job I recommend more than any other for 1Ls who are unsure of what to do with their summer. Here's why: no matter which direction you decide to go, a judicial externship on your resume is the "universal solvent"—whether you go large firm or small, public interest or in-house—everybody respects judicial externships.

On top of that, you get to scope out the local legal community, and it helps you sort the wheat from the chaff. You see who's good and who's not, and you get the "courthouse skinny" on employers you ought to consider, and those to avoid.

It also tends to be an interesting and exciting job; you get a bird's eye view of the legal system at work, and lawyers who might otherwise snub you are *very* polite to you because you work for a judge. Especially after the grueling first year of law school, you *need* something to get you excited about being in law school—and working for a judge is just the tonic. (I also like the idea of working for prosecutors' offices and legal aid offices after First Year for just the same reason.)

Finally, you make excellent contacts. Can you imagine a better mentor than a judge who likes your work? Can you just see yourself sending out letters saying, "Judge X recommended that I contact you?" Or having a judge call an employer on your behalf? Awesome!

14. HELP OUT WITH CAMPAIGNS FOR CIRCUIT AND COUNTY JUDGES

Judges who have to be elected have to run campaigns—and for that, they need volunteers. As Attorney Nadia Ahmad points out, "Work on campaigns for judges, and you'll meet a *lot* of lawyers."

15. VOLUNTEER ON LAW SCHOOL FUNDRAISERS

If you worry that when you graduate from law school your dear alma mater may forget about you, fear not. They'll call you every few months to catch up . . . and ask for dough.

Now, "dialing for dollars" may not strike you as a great way to get a job—but it is. For a start, as Lisa Kellogg points out, it's a great way to network with alumni, especially if you give "great phone." After all, you're not calling for a job; you're calling about supporting the school. View it as an opportunity to update alumni on what's going on at school, not just to look for cheddar. Most people will be at least polite to you, and many of them will toss in a few samoleans. While you have them on the phone, there's nothing to stop you from saying, "Are you still with X and X firm? How do you like it there? I'm very interested in them . . ." or "Are you still practicing Aviation Law? I find that so interesting! I'd like to learn more . . ."

The other way fundraising for your school will help you is that when you have it on your resume, it shows employers that you have rainmaking potential—that is, the ability to bring in business. *Rainmaking is the greatest possible skill you can show a private employer.* If you are able to draw in clients, you will be happily—and wealthily—employed forever. The ability to get people to donate money is one of the few things you can do in law school that suggests with rainmaking ability. That's just one more reason why you should try it.

16. TAKE A NONPAYING JOB DOING *WHATEVER* YOUR DREAM JOB IS

There are services where you pay upwards of a thousand dollars to find volunteer positions at law firms for you.

Here's a news flash: you don't have to pay to get a volunteer job. **Those words, "I'm willing to volunteer to get the experience," are** *magic.*

If you're willing to work without pay, you would not *believe* the doors that will open for you. Now I'm not suggesting that you develop a taste for sleeping in your car and living on a steady diet of Kraft Macaroni & Cheese; you can do something else—like wait tables—for money. But in terms of getting experience, often you can get great gigs, opportunities you couldn't get any other way, if you're willing to volunteer. There are myriad great volunteer positions in sports, entertainment, public interest, you name it. And these jobs often turn into paying jobs when you've proven your value to the employer.

In Chapter 24 on "Glamour Jobs"—sports, entertainment, that kind of thing—I go into some detail about this. But volunteer positions aren't limited to those kinds of jobs. I've already talked about volunteering for judges, a great opportunity. You can also volunteer for all kinds of federal agencies—the Justice Department, the best possible place to take your law degree, takes volunteers all the time, as do the CIA, FBI, the National Parks Service ... you name the federal agency that interests you, it'll take law student volunteers. The same is true for state and local agencies, as well.

You can also volunteer at law firms and some companies, although some states' labor laws make it difficult for private employers to take on volunteers; your Career Services office will know if that's true in your state. If it's not barred by law, try it. There are at least three good reasons to do so. For one thing, a lot more doors will open for you when you mention the magic word "volunteer." Trust me. If you're not asking an employer to take a financial risk with you, there's not a whole lot to stop them from bringing you in!

In fact, one student I talked with got his foot in the door in just this way; the firm was a two-partner firm in Minnesota, and the partner he interviewed with was so tickled he'd be willing to volunteer that he hired the student on the spot. When the other partner walked into the room, the "hiring" partner introduced him to the student, and said, "Guess what? He's going to be working for us—for free!" The other partner responded, "You stingy bastard. Pay the kid!" As the student reported to me, "I walked out of there with a paying job—even though I was willing to work for free!"

Volunteering also helps you on the job in a subtle way; often, when employers aren't paying you, they tend to give you better work because they know you're giving them your time for free ... whereas when they *pay* you, they won't feel the slightest bit guilty about parking your butt in front of the copy machine for hours at a time! As one student described it to me, "I had friends in First Year who were so psyched to be getting summer jobs at these big firms, but really those jobs just sucked. They did photocopying, they ran errands, and they were bored. But I volunteered at the prosecutor's office and got the greatest experience. I came back to school so fired up about that job!"

The Honorable George Perez, Chief Judge of the Tax Court of Minnesota, echoes this: "I once told a judge I was so interested in clerking for her that I'd do it for free. She was shocked. 'You'd work for *free?*' Six months later, she called me and said, 'My clerk left unexpectedly. You're #1 on my list. I don't want to post this job. Come in for an interview so we can make sure it's a fit.' I got the job."

He goes on, "Being willing to volunteer does wonders for you. When clerks volunteer for me, I'll do anything for them. I'll make calls for them when they're looking for paid positions and give them a great reference. My record is perfect, by the way. When I make phone calls, my clerks get the job!"

Another reason to try volunteering is that it will get great experience onto your resume—experience that will not be listed as "volunteer," by the way. No matter where you get a volunteer job, just list it on your resume as you would for a paying job, without mentioning that you did it for free. It will easily eclipse anything on your resume that you consider a flaw.

Finally, volunteering is often the only way to break into ultra-desirable and competitive areas. Many public interest jobs go to students who were willing to volunteer there first; as Jane Reinhardt, director of Nassau County Legal Aid, says, "When we go to hire, the first people we consider are the ones with whom we're the most familiar. And those are people who've volunteered with us." The same is true for a lot of sports and entertainment jobs. The fact that you *start* doing something for free doesn't mean it will stay that way!

* * * SMART HUMAN TRICK * * *

Law student at a law school in Indiana, has mediocre grades. During Second Year she volunteers with the Justice Department, and during the summer after Second Year she volunteers with the Securities and Exchange Commission.

At the beginning of Third Year, she reports, "I was so nervous about my grades on my resume. I thought that as soon as employers saw them, they wouldn't look any further. But I sent out my resume and I got so many offers for interviews. All they wanted to talk about was my work experience at the Justice Department and the SEC. My grades never even came up!"

* * * SMART HUMAN TRICK * * *

Law student in Nebraska. During First Year, he applies to the Department of Justice in Washington, DC for a volunteer position over the summer.

He winds up spending the summer researching salvage issues involving a rather famous shipwreck: The Titanic. He says, "All of my friends thought I was crazy to take a volunteer job over the summer. But it was the greatest experience I could ever possibly have!"

17. Create a Web Site or an on-Line Newsletter on a Specialty That Interests You

You may think it's crazy to start a web site about a specialty. "Geez, I'm just in law school!" you're thinking. "What do *I* know about it?" Plenty, Weed Hopper. You're in a better position to keep your finger on the pulse of what's new than anybody else. You're in a "researching mode," and you're really comfortable with researching on-line—two things that are not true of a lot of lawyers.

I've talked with students who've started web sites on specialties they wanted to get into, and it's been a great entrée to jobs. They post articles and new cases relevant to the specialty and in some cases even e-mail newsletters to practitioners. They e-mail lawyers in their desired specialty announcements about the web sites, so the lawyers will visit. And of course they have information about themselves on the site, to entice possible employers.

Now, is this a bit of work? Of course. But if you're a Mac Daddy anyway, a web site like this establishes you as an expert in a specialty even while you're still in school!

* * * SMART HUMAN TRICK * * *

Law student, wanted to get into environmental law. He set up a web page where he summarized new cases. He sent letters to environmental lawyers telling them about it. As one of them reports, "It really made him stand out. It was a great way to establish expertise while he was still in school."

18. Volunteer at Conferences Involving the Specialty That Interests You

Professional conferences take place all the time; lawyers seem to take every opportunity to get out of the freakin' office! You can find out about these meetings on local, state and federal bar association web sites, as well as at Career Services at school.

What can you do at a conference? It's hard to count the activities I've heard about. Giving people rides from the airport. Giving guided tours of your city. Handing out name tags. Pouring punch. Summarizing the proceedings. Acting as a "gopher" for the organizers. There are a million things to do.

What you do is to contact whoever is organizing the conference, and offer your services. What you particularly want are activities that will get you in contact with attendees; stuffing goody bags or xeroxing for all or most of your time won't cut it. You can always finesse this by saying, "I'm happy to help out wherever needed, but I'm hoping that along with doing X I can do some things that will get me in contact with attendees, because I really want to talk with practitioners." That'll get you out of the back room!

* * * SMART HUMAN TRICK * * *

New law school graduate has his heart set on one, particular large law firm in Washington, DC. The only job he can get there is as a third shift proofreader, working from Midnight until 8 a.m.

In this job, the new grad reviews tons of documents, and he finds that the firm's telecommunications department is hyper busy—and he's really interested in what they do. So he keeps his eye on the local papers, and sees that there's going to be a telecommunications law conference taking place in DC. He calls and volunteers to help out, and he's assigned the job of summarizing all of the presentations at the conference.

His summaries are made into a booklet that goes to every telecommunications lawyer in the country ... including the head of the telecom department at his own firm. This particular partner is very impressed with the booklet, and he wants to talk to the lawyer who put it together. He buzzes his secretary, and mentions the byline on the booklet, asking, "Why does that name ring a bell?" She responds nonchalantly, "It's the kid in the basement." Stunned, he tells her, "Get him in here!"

The new grad comes in, and the partner points to the booklet and says, "*You* did *this*?" The new grad acknowledges it, and the partner asks, "How? Why?" The new grad tells him the story, and the partner shakes his head, and says, "Son, you don't belong in the basement." He brings the new grad up as a full associate, and the new grad reports: "Every other new associate here is from an Ivy League school, they're all Law Review. They look at me, I've got the best job here, they can't figure out how I got it ...

... and I'm not going to tell them."

* * * SMART HUMAN TRICK * * *

Third year law student, trying without avail to break into Aviation Law. He finds out on-line that there's going to be an Aviation Law conference three hundred miles away from his law school. He calls and volunteers to help out and the organizers ask what he wants to do. He says, "Well, I've got a car. I can give attendees rides from the airport." They go for that, and he winds up ferrying lawyers back and forth to and from the conference site. He reports, "The ride each way was about half an hour, when they were essentially my prisoners. It was a great chance to ask them about their jobs and to ask for advice about breaking into aviation law.

"I really didn't have to do anything else. I came away from that conference with tons of great contacts, and I got my job through one of them."

* * * SMART HUMAN TRICK * * *

Law student in school in Florida. As a First Year, she's dying to get into International Law. Her undergrad grades are mediocre, and law school hasn't started off on a promising note grades-wise, either.

She keeps her eye on the local papers to see if anything related to international law comes to town. Sure enough, she finds that there is going to be a meeting of the Organization of American States taking place near her city. She calls and volunteers to help out, and she's assigned the job of acting as a "gopher" for the person organizing the meeting.

In this capacity, she meets an awful lot of prominent people. She makes a point of bringing up in every conversation her interest in International Law as a career, and soliciting advice. One of them says, "Well, I can help you get to Washington for the summer. How would you like to work at the White House?" Not bad! At the White House for the summer, she again makes a point of talking about her career goals. One of the people she meets tells her, "I can help you out next summer . . .

"How would you like to work at the U.S. Embassy in Barbados?" And she winds up spending the summer there, helping out with legal issues. *In Barbados.*

* * * SMART HUMAN TRICK * * *

Law student, very interested in working in a zoo. Recognizing that there are law-related jobs everywhere—but completely clueless about what they might be in a zoo setting—she goes to the big yellow book of Trade Associations, looks up zoos, and contacts the zoo trade association. She finds out when their annual conference will be, and volunteers to help out. She winds up handing out literature at a table. At the conference, she learns that zoos all have risk managers, and that a law degree is very useful for that job.

Through the conference, she nails her summer job—working for a zoo risk manager.

* * * SMART HUMAN TRICK * * *

Law student, dying to work for the FBI. He finds out that a lawyer from the FBI is going to be a presenter at a criminal trial lawyers' association meeting locally. He calls and offers to give the FBI lawyer a ride from the airport to the meeting.

The student has lunch with the FBI guy, who offers to help the student. He tells him whom to talk to at the local FBI office, and offers to call on his behalf.

The student winds up with an internship there.

19. RUN A CONFERENCE ON CAREERS IN THE SPECIALTY THAT INTERESTS YOU, AND HAVE THE STATE OR LOCAL BAR ASSOCIATION SPONSOR YOU

What do bar associations do? They sponsor a lot of meetings. Of course, normally the meetings involved are ones they put on for themselves. But nothing stops *you* from getting sponsorship from the bar for a meeting of your own.

While this is a bit of work, you might consider running your own conference, focusing on careers in a specialty that interests you. A real test of your organizational abilities, it would require you—probably with the help of some willing classmates!—to reserve space, contact potential speakers, and advertise with posters and e-mails. The bar association kicks in for the expenses, which are really pretty minimal—especially since you won't feel compelled to serve caviar and champagne to the attendees.

I've heard of students doing this a few times, and it's worked out spectacularly well.

* * * SMART HUMAN TRICK * * *

Law student in the Midwest. She's hyper interested in Sports Law. She gets the state bar association to sponsor a weekend conference on Careers in Sports Law. She contacts every professional sports team in the state, and gets them to send a representative; she also gets sports lawyers to come and talk about what they do.

It's a great success—particularly for her! She is a hero to her classmates, who love the conference—and she enjoyed putting it together. Career-wise, she gets to talk to her dream employers without asking them for a job. And what do they know about her? That she is the kind of person who takes initiative in a big way. They get to see her in a leadership position. And when she calls again for advice about breaking into sports law, *they already know her and respect her.*

Now, again, I acknowledge that this isn't as easy as sending out a bunch of resumes. But it's a jillion times more effective, and more fun to boot!

20. VOLUNTEER TO WRITE MOTIONS FOR ATTORNEYS DOING PRO BONO WORK AT YOUR LAW SCHOOL'S CLINICAL PROGRAM (OR ASK FOR THEM AT THE LOCAL BAR ASSOCIATION)

This idea, courtesy of Santa Clara's Vicky Hubler, is a particularly great way to get concrete skills on your resume. Motion writing is the kind of practical skill that small to mid-sized employers covet, and it's easily attainable this way.

c. ACTIVITIES THAT INVOLVE "SHOWING UP"

Woody Allen once said that 80% of life is showing up. If you work it right, "showing up" can go a long way toward finding you a great job.

Of course, attendance in and of itself doesn't do a lot for your career. You're still going to have to talk to people, to work your career aspirations into the conversation and ask for advice. We talk about what to say shortly. But the activities I've outlined below give you the platform for such conversations.

1. CAREER DAYS AT SCHOOL

Well, duh. Obvious, but it has to be mentioned. Why? Because when I go to Career Days at law schools around the country, there are puh-lenty of unemployed students who don't show up. So I have to exhort you to go to the darned things.

Inevitably, Career Days involve some kind of "table talk." That is, lawyers from various practice settings will man tables with the idea of answering questions from any students who approach them. So: *approach them.* They *want* you to exhibit curiosity about what they do. That's why they're there.

I talked to one student in Minnesota who said, "I hate talking to people, but right after you told me to we had a Career Day at school. I walked up to the estate planning lady's desk and talked to her. She gave me her card and told me to call her. I didn't say anything but I'd sent her my resume a couple of times and never heard back. Talking to her was totally different."

It's important to remember that you don't have to say anything witty or unusually insightful when you talk to these people. Just an honest show of enthusiasm and/or curiosity fits the bill. "So—tell me what *this* is like . . ." "I'd love to know about your job . . ." "This looks interesting—tell me about it . . ." Questions along those lines work great.

Of course, if you know ahead of time which employers will attend *and* you call the day before to see who they're sending, you're way ahead of the game. You can research the employer and the lawyer; you'll really stand out by having that information at your fingertips. But even if you don't—showing up and talking to people is a great benefit to you.

2. ALUMNI RECEPTIONS

This was the career-building activity that used to tie my stomach in knots when I was in law school. When I *did* convince myself to go, I'd go with a few friends, hang out eating the free food and drinking the free drink with them for an hour, and then blow out of there—just as unemployed and uninformed as I was when I arrived. You could do the same thing ... but remember: I graduated without a job. Had I been a little smarter about those alumni receptions ... who knows?

You *are* going to be smarter about them. Do everything I suggest below about handling social situations. **Don't try and convince yourself that you don't have the time to go.** You've got a *little* to spare, and I talk to lawyers all the time who say, "It makes a huge impression when students attend these events."

And remember this: You are a natural object of bounty for people who attended your school before you did. They may be there primarily to visit with old law school chums, but they're at least *partly* in attendance because they *expect* law students to ask them for advice. Meet their expectations—and ask!

3. PHI ALPHA DELTA, AND OTHER LAW SCHOOL FRATERNITIES

If the idea of "fraternity" conjures up images of *Animal House,* you're not thinking about law school fraternities. At least—none that *I'm* familiar with!

There are at least three national law fraternities—Phi Alpha Delta (which is mine), Phi Delta Phi, and Delta Theta Phi.

The fraternities will help you out in a bunch of ways. First of all, they give you the opportunity to meet alums from law schools all over the country. If you're thinking of looking for a job in another city, they're an excellent resource. I know that at the Phi Alpha Delta national conferences there are thousands of lawyers and judges from everywhere in the country. It couldn't be happier hunting grounds for an eager job seeker.

PAD also holds writing competitions, has job listings, and great internships/externships for members. It runs exam review sessions and brings in speakers.

Fraternities also give you the chance to get involved in civic activities. These look particularly good on your resume, because they create the aura of "rainmaking"—the possibility that you'll be good at bringing in business for a law firm through your community activities.

Google them for more information. If your law school doesn't have a chapter, you can always start one of your own!

4. CONFERENCES INVOLVING TOPICS/SPECIALTIES THAT INTEREST YOU

I don't care how broad or narrow your interest is. Sports. Entertainment. Dog law. Aviation. Maritime law. Space law. There are conferences held about every possible specialty you can imagine. And my advice to you is to *go*. Obviously, what I'd really like you to do is to volunteer at these conferences, because then it's easier to talk to people. But even if you just attend, you're doing yourself a huge favour.

What you want to do is to **find out ahead of time who the speakers and attendees will be**; every conference will involve pre-registration, and you want to be friendly to the registration person/people so that you can cadge that list ahead of time. (For many conferences, the attendee list is freely available.) **Then check the list for potential employers**, google them, and keep your notes about them with you when you attend the conference. (A small note book or note cards are useful for this purpose.)

When you're ready to go, be sure to **take a handful of your resumes** in a portfolio that you carry. You may not need them—but you might. You should have them available, but not visible.

When you get to the conference, **get the schedule and see when your "speaker" targets will be speaking. Be sure to show up early to their presentations, and hang around afterwards.** Tell the speaker how interested you were to hear what they had to say because you're interested in doing what they do, you'd like their advice—either now or at their convenience—and be prepared to hand over your resume, if appropriate!

When it comes to attendees instead of speakers, be nice to the people at the registration desk, and tell them who you're looking for. They may be able to put you on to your "target." If not, look for a message board for attendees; there virtually always is one. Leave a note for the attorney in question, saying that you came to the conference hoping you'd meet them, you'd appreciate ten minutes of their time at their convenience, and leave your contact information (your cell phone number, for instance).

A note about expenses for a conference. A lot of professional conferences are very expensive; they're great moneymakers. Money might be tight for you (it is for almost *every* student), and even if you're doing all right, you probably don't have a grand to drop on a freaking conference. That's all right. Here's what you need to remember: the costs for the conference organizers are virtually all "fixed," not variable. That is, whether you attend or not isn't going to jack their costs up at all. Volunteer to help out, offer to forego the meals (which they *do* have to pay for individually), plead poverty—whatever it takes. And if the first person you talk to isn't cooperative, wait a day or so and call back to talk to someone else—or ideally the person organizing the conference. I know this works because I've done it myself. It's very hard to turn down a person who is honestly enthusiastic about what you're doing—and is just a little short of cash!

* * * SMART HUMAN TRICK * * *

Law student in Northern California. He wants to get into Education Law, and finds through a trade publication that there's going to be an Education Law conference 700 miles from his school. He drives down there—it takes him a very long day to make it—and reports, "It was a slog but it was so worth it. I was the only law student there. When I told the lawyers what I'd gone through to get there, they were really impressed. I got a handful of business cards . . . and a ton of opportunities."

5. Get a Mentor Through Your Career Services Office or the Local Bar Association

I'll bet your school has a mentoring program run by the CSO. Most of them do. And I'll bet you something else, too: it's terribly under-utilized. That's the case at the vast majority of law schools I visit. As Ellen Wayne points out, "Many alumni who volunteer to be mentors never get a single call! You *should* call them. Lawyers like to impart information—that's what they do!"

Lawyers who are willing to act as mentors for you are a tremendous asset. They can give you the inside skinny on the legal community, different types of practice, activities you should undertake and avoid. Remember: they signed up for this gig. If you're worried about talking to grown-ups who are going to be nasty to you—you *know* a mentor is going to be nice, because they *volunteered* to help out.

So take advantage of the mentoring program. Let your Career Services office know what your interests are (and where), so they can match you up with an appropriate alum. If you're not sure about your career interests, say that, too—they'll still find someone who can give you good advice. And who knows . . . you wouldn't be the first law student who winds up working for their mentor!

6. Shadow Attorneys

Shadow. Not stalk. What you do when you shadow an attorney is basically follow them around for a day or so, which gives you a snapshot of exactly what it's like to do what they do. While this is obviously a great way to meet people in your dream specialty, it's also an excellent way to figure out exactly what it is that you *want* to do. As I've said over and over again, the job you enjoy will be the one that involves people you enjoy working with, and the greatest possible percentage of activities that you like. Seeing first-hand what people do is the best possible way of figuring that out (next to doing it yourself).

The way that you find out about "shadow-able" employers is through your Career Services Office and/or the city bar association for the city where you want to practice law. It obviously involves taking a day away from your studies to follow a lawyer around, but truly: can you imagine a better reason to blow off class than *this?*

Here are specifics on handling your shadow day:

- **Make sure you have the directions down pat—you know, mapquest and google maps—and allow an extra pillow of time in case traffic and/or transit works against you.** If you're driving, ask the attorney where you should park. Plan to arrive ten minutes early; if you're earlier than that, walk around outside or sit in your car so that you get to the office a few minutes ahead of time.

- **Bring your resume, discreetly—in a portfolio.** You may or may not have an opportunity to whip it out, but you want it there just in case.

- Needless to say: **Google the person you'll shadow**, look at their profile at their employer's web site, ask at Career Services or the bar association to find out as much as possible about them.

- During the day, be sure to **collect business cards** not just from the person you're shadowing but also their associates.

- **At lunch, offer to pay for your own meal**. The attorney probably won't let you, but it's bad form to assume they're going to pay for you. It makes you look good if you offer.

- **At the end of the day—assuming it's gone well—leave your resume with the attorney**, saying, "Following you around like this has just reinforced that this is exactly what I want to do. May I leave my resume with you, in case you hear of anyone who may need someone like me?" I promise you they'll say "Yes." And of course, thank them profusely.

- **Afterwards—*immediately* afterwards—send a thank you**, not just to the person you shadowed, but also anyone else with whom you had significant contact.

Remember—when an attorney allows you to follow them around for a day, they're doing you a *huge* favour. That's not to suggest you shouldn't ask—you should—but you must indicate your gratefulness throughout!

7. ATTEND CLEs

Are you going to scream if I mention CLEs—continuing legal education seminars—even one more time? Sorry. I just *have* to!

In case you've been napping—or skipping around in this book, which is understandable—here's the scoop on CLEs. They're classes that lawyers have to take to maintain their licenses to practice law. Although you aren't a lawyer yet, you can *also* take CLEs, and I can't encourage you strongly enough to do so. They're given in virtually every specialty under the sun, so you'll definitely find something that interests you—and since many of these CLE classes are given at law schools, they're ultra convenient! Furthermore, they're typically free to students or involve a very nominal charge. Be sure to contact the CLE provider as soon as you find a CLE you'd like to take, however—the "scholarship spots" tend to go quickly, especially for popular topics.

If you go with a friend, don't sit together. As Gail Peshel suggests, "It's just too easy to talk to the people you came with otherwise!"

There are several excellent benefits to taking CLE classes, including:

- If you're not sure already, CLEs can help you figure out what you want to do.

    I mentioned this in Chapter 1 on figuring out your dream job, but it bears repeating: If you don't know what you want to do, CLEs are happy hunting grounds. Keep your eyes open at Career Services, your bar association's web site, and the Practicing Law Institute web site (www. pli.edu) for CLEs nearby. When you read about something in which you're even slightly interested . . . go! During breaks in the presentation, be honest with people around you, and say, "I'm still in school, I'm not sure what I want to do, but I came here today to learn more about this because it sounds interesting to me. *What do you like about it?*" Why is that such a great question? Because what you'll enjoy doing has nothing to do with the name on the door. It has to do with the people you work with, and the activities with which you fill your day. People who already do any particular thing are the best resource for finding what you'll enjoy! On top of that, they'll normally be happy to talk about it. People like talking about what they do. Furthermore, they'll identify with you, because remember: at some point, every lawyer in America was you, unsure of what *they* were going to do.

- You meet practitioners in an area that interests you.

    If you *do* know what you want to do, CLEs are a gold mine. As Gail Peshel points out, at coffee breaks or over lunch, you've got an excellent opportunity to talk with people doing exactly what you want to do—and better yet, you've got a built-in topic of conversation . . . the CLE you're both attending! Ask what they thought of the seminar, what other CLEs they'd recommend—and say that you're interested in the area of practice and you want to get more practical experience in it. As Debra Fink points out, "This really shows initiative!"

* * * SMART HUMAN TRICK * * *

Law student—we'll call her Essie See—interested in Securities Law. She attends a CLE about it. At check in, the person handing out name tags comments on the face that "You know, you're the only student here."

As the speaker begins his presentation, he remarks, "By the way, we have a law student joining us today. Essie See, why don't you stand up?" The student stands and waves to the crowd of lawyers there.

After the presentation, a number of lawyers approach Essie. Several of them offer business cards with an invitation to call and talk about jobs.

- You learn what's going on in the practice area.

    This kind of education is invaluable by itself. It may generate article ideas for you (if you're interested in writing), and it'll clue you in on what's on the minds of practitioners. You'll be able to go into interviews supremely confident, because you'll know how lawyers "talk among themselves."

- You get a *great* resume item.

    Debra Fink came up with one of my favourite all-time resume "boosters": adding a section called "Additional Legal Education" to your resume, directly under your law school education, where you list the CLEs you've taken.

    You can imagine the impact this has on employers. Let's say you want to be a litigator, and you take some CLEs on taking depositions and cross-examination. Think about how that will separate you from the pack! It shows dedication and enthusiasm aside from the sheer knowledge itself—and those are great assets to show employers.

- It's a great activity for "out-of-town" job searches.

    While I go into detail about "out of town" job searches in Chapter 17, it's worth noting here that CLEs are a great way to get your foot in the door in another city. During a time when you're going to be in that city anyway, find out ahead of time what CLEs are taking place, either through the local bar association there, www.pli.edu , or the Career Services office at a law school in that city (you can access them through "reciprocity" that your Career Services office will arrange for you). When you go to CLEs there, make a point of telling lawyers you meet that you're going to school in X city, but "I'm here because I'll be relocating here and I wanted to get to know the legal community." Trust me— when you've not just gone to a city on your own dime but actually taken the initiative of hunting down and attending CLEs there, you're going to be *very* impressive!

- The speaker might be a great "side-door" way to sneak into your dream employer.

  Here's the plan: You check out the web site of an employer you'd like to work for, and look to see if any of the partners are teaching CLEs sometime soon. (Lawyers often teach these things, you know.) If they *are,* be sure to attend that CLE, and take your resume and/or a business card with you. At the end of the presentation, go up to the partner, and say, "I was particularly interested to come and hear you speak. I'd really like the opportunity to work for your firm." Then, either hand over your resume (if it seems appropriate and/or (s)he asks for it), or give him/her your business card, and say, "I'll be sending you my resume. Here's my card."

  Can you imagine something that would distinguish you more from the competition than actually going to a CLE taught by a partner? It will certainly make a great impression!

* * * SMART HUMAN TRICK * * *

Student scopes out his dream employer's web site, and finds that one of the partners of the firm is teaching a CLE. He goes to the CLE, walks up to the partner afterwards, introduces himself, and hands over his resume, saying "I'm going to be applying for a job with your firm, so I was very interested in hearing you speak." He chats for a couple of minutes with the partner, who invites him in for an interview.

He gets the job.

* * * SMART HUMAN TRICK * * *

A 3L at a New York law school meets with a smallish firm. When he's asked for his salary expectations, he quotes large firm salaries and they respond, "Have a nice life."

Several months later, he goes to a CLE. It turns out that all of the members of this firm are also at the CLE, including a younger associate. The student goes to the associate and strikes up the acquaintance again. The associate says, "Hey, send me your resume." The student sends it, and winds up working there.

- CLEs will help you make it through initial screenings for on-line job postings ... where you might not have otherwise.

When you apply for jobs on-line, the employer will do a key word search of your resume. It's entirely possible that you don't have the legal experience to supply those key words ... but the names of CLEs *will* have them. You'll get your electronic "foot in the door" at employers who might otherwise not have considered you.

* * * SMART HUMAN TRICK * * *

Third year law student, in Oregon. He's very interested in Family Law, and he takes every CLE on the specialty that comes to town for the entire academic year—sixteen in all!

When he graduates, he is in hot demand among domestic relations lawyers in town. They know him from the CLEs, and on top of that, as his eventual employer points out, "With those CLEs, he's the equivalent of a second year associates!"

* * * SMART HUMAN TRICK * * *

First year law student, a mid-life career changer, has no luck convincing lawyers to interview her in her dream specialty: labor law. During the summer after her first year, she goes to eight CLEs on labor law while she works in a non-law-related summer job.

In the Fall of second year, she lists the eight CLEs directly under her law school education on her resume, and walks her resume into the offices of lawyers she'd like to work for. She marvels, "All of these lawyers who wouldn't look at my resume first year had their eyes bugging out of their heads when they saw what I'd done over the summer. I got interviews with all of them ... and I wound up working for one of them!"

* * * SMART HUMAN TRICK * * *

Law student transfers from a school in Michigan to a school in Arizona for her second year. As she reports, "I didn't know anybody in Arizona, and I figured that CLEs would be a good place to start. I had tried it in Indiana and it worked great. There was a CLE on litigation—a big one— at my new school, so I went. I met tons of lawyers and picked up a fist full of business cards, some of them from lawyers who asked me to come in and talk to them. It was fantastic. The thing that amazed me most of all was ...

... I was the only law student there."

* * * A PEEK AT A CLE SCHEDULE... * * *

On a visit to Lincoln, Nebraska, I picked up a schedule of CLEs being offered at the University of Nebraska for a single month.

I'm showing it to you for a few reasons. For a start, look at the variety of offerings. I'll bet there are talks about specialties you didn't even know existed.

Also, look at all of the gold mine of potential career advice you have here! The speakers at each event. The other attendees.

Furthermore, remember we're talking about a not-huge city, Lincoln, Nebraska. And just at CLEs offered *at the law school*. For just *one month*. No matter where you go to school, just *imagine* how many CLEs you can tap into!

February 22: "Top Ten Things You Need To Discuss With Your Client When Considering Mediation," featuring David Hubbard and Ann Meyer of the Mediation Center.

February 23: "Update on Coordination of Benefits in Workers' Compensation Cases and Other Topics," featuring Jill G. Schroeder, Baylor Evnen Law Firm.

March 6: "Employment Law and the Implications of *Roseland,*" featuring Susan K. Sapp, Cline Williams Law Firm.

March 7: "Discussion of Veteran's Issues: What's New" featuring John S. Berry, Berry Kelley Law.

March 13: "Employment Law—'Safe Harbor' Provisions When Your Prospective Employee's Name And SSN Don't Match, and Other Employment Hiring Issues," featuring Jerry L. Pigsley, Harding Schultz & Downs.

March 16: "Trust Accounts and Ethics" featuring Kent Frobish of the Nebraska Counsel for Discipline's Office.

8. TAKE PART IN MOCK INTERVIEWS THROUGH CAREER SERVICES

Virtually every law school's Career Services office offers mock interviews; that is, the opportunity for you to hone your interview skills without the pressure of a real job riding on the interview. The "interview practice" is only part of the reason to take part in mock interviews, however; a great fringe benefit is the fact that many schools bring in practitioners to do the mock interviewing ... and you know what *that* means! You get a terrific, and really sneaky, means to impress a potential employer/mentor/contact.

Gail Cutter points out that "Interviewers in mock interviews have been known to say, 'Great job! Send me your resume!' "

Gail Peshel recommends checking with Career Services to see if they use local attorneys for mock interviews, and if they do, "Research those interviewers as you would for any other interview." That's what you'd do for a real interview in order to impress the interviewer, so you'll want to do the same with a practice session.

9.   TAKE PART IN CLIENT COUNSELING COMPETITIONS ST SCHOOL

Why? For one thing, if you do well, it looks great on your resume. For another, the judges are generally lawyers.

Find out ahead of time who the judges will be. Approach the ones you'd like to work with (or whom might have advice for you). And, of course, if you impress them and they compliment you, that gives you a great opening to a follow up note or e-mail asking for advice.

10.   COLLECT BUSINESS CARDS FROM JUDGES AT ORAL ADVOCACY/MOOT COURT COMPETITIONS AT SCHOOL

As is true for client counseling competitions, the judges at oral advocacy/moot court competitions are usually judges or lawyers, often alums of your school. Find out who they'll be before the event occurs, so you'll know who to approach. Just walk up to them during a break or during a reception before or after the competition, introduce yourself, and say, "I know you do X. I'm so interested in it. Can I ask you about it? How I might position myself to break into it? . . ." the kinds of questions we've talked about so often before.

Even if you don't have the chance to find out who they are, there's no shame in walking up to them and asking about what they do, and asking your questions from there. The point is: When you've got living, breathing experts in the room with you . . . don't let the opportunity to talk to them go to waste!

11.   JOIN THE BAR ASSOCIATION *Now*—THE ABA STUDENT DIVISION AND YOUR STATE'S BAR—AS WELL AS ANY SUBGROUPS THAT APPLY TO YOU AND/OR YOUR INTERESTS. AND ATTEND MEETINGS!

It's a cryin' shame how few law students take advantage of the bar association. I'm telling you, they're sitting over there, sobbing into their beers because you just won't sign up. Perhaps I'm exaggerating. But really, every bar association I've ever seen would *love* more student members. Sign up *today*. And that's true even if you're planning to practice in another state when you graduate. Join the state bar for the state you're in now, *and* the one where you intend to practice. While you're at it, join the ABA.

It's not like it's expensive. It generally costs about as much as a decent lunch. It's *so* worth it.

Of course, joining by itself isn't enough. You have to *do* stuff with them. They run not just regular meetings for various specialties, but they run seminars on all kinds of topics, as well as special events and social gatherings. Florida State's Rosanna Catalano says "You have to shake a lot of hands and eat a lot of bad chicken and rice pilaf to get the job of your dreams." The ABA runs national conferences that are *really* useful. Locally, committees in different practice areas meet regularly, and put on programs on all sorts of topics, even some that will be directly applicable to you, like "Bridging the gap from law school to practice."

As well, there may be subgroups that fit you. The Young Lawyers' Division of many bar associations springs immediately to mind, but there are others, as well, including groups for different ethnic groups as well as women's groups (like the "Queen's Bench," the women's bar association in San Francisco, which is a *great* place to meet helpful people).

Make a point of going to the head of the section that most interests you and introducing yourself. Ask about the kinds of events you should be attending, tell them what you want to do, and thank them profusely for their advice. Of course, on top of simply attending events, if you want to volunteer that's even better. I've mentioned to you before that all of these programs and events need bodies to help set them up and run them, and that kind of volunteering is a great way to break the ice with people and make them view you favourably.

What happens when you start attending bar events? You will meet people who might have jobs available (or will know people who do). You'll get people thinking about you and where and how you might fit in; people might actually create opportunities for you. On top of all that, you'll be displaying honest enthusiasm for the profession. That *always* makes you look good.

12. ATTEND CHAMBER OF COMMERCE EVENTS IN THE CITY WHERE YOU WANT TO WORK

Attorneys often attend these events as a means of drumming up business. If you go, you're likely to be the only law student there ... and you'll have those potential employers to yourself.

13. ATTEND JUDICIAL RECEPTIONS SPONSORED BY BAR ASSOCIATIONS

14. GO TO "INNS OF COURT"

If you're interested in litigation, a judicial clerkship or government work, "Inns of Court" is an organization you need to know about!

As Mary Obrzut describes it, Inns of Court is a national program with branches in various cities that brings together practitioners and judges who meet monthly, where they hear presentations on topics like conflicts of interest, discovery rules, evidence changes—all kinds of litigation issues. Not only do you get a chance to learn some interesting and practical things, but you get a great opportunity to meet litigators, judges and legislators.

For more information about Inns of Court, check with your Career Services Director, or contact the American Inns of Court Foundation, www.innsofcourt.org.

15. Join Sports Teams Put Together by Law Firms or the Bar Association

If you're a semi-decent athlete, you've got a golden opportunity to meet people in the form of lawyers' sports teams. Many firms and bar associations have softball and basketball teams, and have league play as well as pick-up games. Ask your Career Services Office or the local bar association for advice about tracking down where such teams play, and give them a call—or just show up!—and ask to be included.

Now, if you're like *me,* someone who can't hit a basketball net with a bazooka, this isn't going to be a very fruitful route for meeting people. But if you *are* good, then you already know that taking part in sports, even pick-up games, is a great way to form a bond with people. And if those people happen to do something *you* want to do, you've created great contacts for yourself.

16. Seek Out and Take Part in Oral Advocacy Competitions Offered by the Local Bar Association

Oral advocacy competitions aren't confined to school, you know. Local bar associations often hold them. They're a great way to get your advocacy skills on your resume, but for our purposes here, they're a great way to meet helpful people—the lawyers who organize them as well as the competition judges.

* * * SMART HUMAN TRICK * * *

A law student in San Francisco takes part in the SFTLA trial contest, a four-hour oral argument. He reports, "I won the competition. It was a bit of work, but I got lots of business cards from the judges. They all told me to call."

17. Go to the Courthouse and Watch Trials

Take advantage of breaks from school to watch trials. It can help your career in a whole variety of ways (and on top of that, it's really interesting).

It gives you insight into what litigators, prosecutors, judges and judicial clerks do—so if you're trying to figure out your dream job, you get to see lawyers "in action."

It also gives you *excellent* interview fodder. You'll be able to drop into interviews comments about what you learned while watching trials. It shows a level of initiative and enthusiasm beyond what most students exhibit.

On top of that, the very experience itself can generate job leads. If you watch a criminal trial, make a point of walking up during breaks and introducing yourself to the prosecutor and judge. Tell them you came to see them work because you're in law school and you're interested in what they do. One prosecutor told me that when his office was interviewing for a new assistant DA, one candidate was someone he'd recognized as watching several trials. The prosecutor commented, "That really impressed me. Everyone says how much they want the job, but this guy had gone out of his way to show us."

Approaching a judge can seem intimidating, but when you're expressing your honest enthusiasm you've got nothing to fear. You'll be flattering the judge by watching him/her in action. Everyone appreciates an honest compliment!

Depending on the nature of the case, you've got another potential source of job leads in the other spectators. Let's say that you want to enter a particular specialty, and you know that a federal appellate court nearby is hearing arguments on an important case in that specialty. It's likely that lawyers in the specialty might be among the spectators. So during breaks, chat with your neighbors in the "pews." They may be more useful than you think!

* * * SMART HUMAN TRICK * * *

Law student in Texas. He wants a judicial clerkship. As part of his research, he shows up in person at the courthouse to watch the judges "in their natural environment."

He reports, "One of the judges had come to speak at my college. I went to her court and recognized her talking to some of her clerks in the hallway. I went up and introduced myself, and mentioned how her words had stuck with me.

"She was obviously touched. I wound up clerking for her."

* * * SMART HUMAN TRICK * * *

Law student in Washington DC has a very particular career goal: she wants to work with record companies. She keeps her eye on the US Supreme Court docket and sees there's a going to be a case involving internet downloading coming up for oral argument. She attends, and starts chatting with her neighbor in the gallery.

He turns out to be an entertainment lawyer who represents record companies . . . and she has a great job lead!

18. LISTEN TO VISITING SPEAKERS AND PANELS AT SCHOOL . . . AND BRING YOUR RESUME

If your school has a typical Career Services Office, it's a programming machine. You're probably deluged with e-mails about speakers, panels, workshops, receptions, you name it. If a presentation is at least marginally interesting to you, attend—and take your resume with you. Here's why: The only reason speakers visit your school is that they want to feel you're interested in what they have to say. When you attend, *particularly* if you ask questions, even more so if you walk up afterwards and introduce yourself . . . you're *showing* them that you appreciate their visit. As someone who speaks at law schools all the time, I can tell you from experience that that makes a *huge* impression!

I recommend that you bring your resume for a sneaky reason. If the speaker is someone you'd like to work with, you've got a great job lead. Here's what you do: You walk up to them afterwards, introduce yourself with a smile, tell them how interested you were in what they had to say, and continue, "I'd love to work for X. I've done (X in pursuit of that goal). May I ask your advice about what I should be doing and/or may I give you my resume?"

What do you do if the speaker is hyper-popular? Sports and entertainment attorneys are often crowded in by law students ten deep when they speak. A student at one school asked me, "How do I distinguish myself when *everybody* is just saying 'I want to work for you?' I don't want to seem like a *dork!*"

Good point. What will distinguish you is *research*. Google the speaker. Look at their (or their employer's) website. Do a Lexis/Nexis or Westlaw search and read a recent (and/or important) case they've argued. Research an important client of theirs. Dig for details. Most people won't. Ask about something in their background—obscure but not embarrassing—as a way to break the ice.

I've experienced this a few times from the speaker's perspective. One student I particularly remember asked, "Does your barbecued chicken recipe really work?" (My 'Starving Law Student' barbecue chicken recipe is buried in one of my books. And yes, it really does work!) This guy went on to ask me a job search question, but I was immediately struck by his research about me. It was a *great* conversational opener.

The way I learned the technique of approaching speakers makes for a funny story, by the way. A student at one school asked me, "How do I network my way into the CIA?" Great question! It's not like they broadcast the names of their employees. So I called the CIA and I asked *them* that question. Their answer: "We talk on campuses all the time about working for the CIA. If a student walks up afterwards with their resume, and expresses sincere enthusiasm in working for the agency, we'll often walk their resume to the person in Washington who makes call-back interview decisions." What better way to distinguish yourself from the Mongolian horde of applicants than *that?*

So—go listen to speakers at school. It may lead to great opportunities!

* * * SMART HUMAN TRICK * * *

A Southern law school. A student goes to hear a judge speak, largely because "They had free food, man." But the student is really enthused about what the judge has to say, and e-mails him a thank you. This launches a correspondence, which leads to the student clerking for the judge.

* * * SMART HUMAN TRICK * * *

A justice from the Kenyan Supreme Court is invited to speak to a consortium of law schools in Chicago. Hundreds of students from law schools in the city show up. Afterwards, one of them contacts the Kenyan Consulate to get the justice's e-mail address, and e-mails him a thank you. He mentions that he was so interested in the justice's comments because he's interested in working in Kenya.

One of the justice's clerks calls the student, and tells him the justice would like to interview him. He goes for an interview, and winds up with a clerkship.

19.   GO TO THE ABA MID-YEAR CONFERENCE

This is an annual conference held generally in February for a few days. The ABA is actively trying to increase student attendance at this national conference. As Vicky Hubler points out, "It has several programs aimed specifically at law students, like small firm panels. The speakers are all experts and very approachable." Because student attendance is historically not overwhelming, you'll often find yourself with little competition for speaking with people who can give you great advice. (To find out more about the conference, visit the ABA's web site, www.abanet.org.)

20.   EDUCATIONAL PANELS PUT ON BY FIRMS AND GOVERNMENTAL AGENCIES

Some law firms put on "dog and pony" shows for potential clients. They'll talk about their practice and sometimes focus on a particular issue of interest to the intended audience.

Of course, there's nothing wrong with *you* being a part of that audience, too! Keep your eye on law firm websites (check their press releases), the local newspaper, and postings at your local library to see when these presentations will occur. Take advantage of the opportunity to bring your resume, chat with lawyers from the firm, and generally impress them with your enthusiasm!

Governmental agencies also do public presentations, and you can use them exactly the same way.

* * * SMART HUMAN TRICK * * *

Law student in Nebraska. He's very interested in Patent Law, and sees that a Washington, DC-based patent firm—a very prestigious one—is doing a cross-country dog & pony show to solicit new clients.

He attends the presentation, and winds up sitting next to two lawyers from the firm. He starts talking with them, states his interest in working with them . . .

. . . and they walk him over to the managing partner to introduce him.

* * * SMART HUMAN TRICK * * *

Law student in Indiana, very interested in working in Election Law for the Justice Department. She sees that the person in charge of Election Law for the DOJ is going to come to town to head a panel for the public concerning Election Law.

She attends. When the panel is over, she walks up to the person in charge and introduces herself. She compliments him on the presentation, and states her interest in working there. He encourages her, and gives her some useful tips about applying.

D. FOLLOWING UP WITH PEOPLE YOU MEET

No matter what kind of "attendance" events you choose, follow-up is a key ingredient in the mix—and it's something that an awful lot of your classmates will overlook.

Re-contact people you meet, as soon as possible, asking to set up an "informational interview." We go over informational interviewing in depth in Topic E, below. In a nutshell, you want to research them on-line to learn more about them, and then e-mail or call them and say something like, "It was such a pleasure talking with you at X. I'd like to ask you some more questions about Y. I'm wondering if we can set up a fifteen minute informational interview at a time that's mutually convenient. I'd really appreciate it."

If you met them doing something "one-on-one," like a mentorship conversation, shadowing an attorney, or engaging in a mock interview, absolutely send a "thank you" note *the next day.* Here's what you need to keep in mind:

- A hand written note is best—preferably on your school's stationery or note card. A typed letter is next best. An e-mail will do in a pinch. The reason the e-mail isn't as good? It doesn't take as much effort, that's why. But it's a heck of a lot better than nothing.

- Thank the attorney for his/her time, and mention something specific to your conversation. "It was interesting hearing about your experience doing ..." "I was grateful for the opportunity to see ..." and go on to talk about how it's impacted your job search, if appropriate. "Talking with you made me realize I should attend/talk to/read ..."

In addition, if the attorney put you on to someone else, there'll be a follow-up to your follow-up. Namely: Keep them posted on what happened to the leads they gave you. This primes the pump so that when you want *more* advice, they won't feel like every time you contact them you're asking for something. Thanking them in between your requests keeps your contacts happy—and ready to give more!

E. SMOKING OUT OPPORTUNITIES OTHER PEOPLE MISS

As we learn throughout this book, there are opportunities *everywhere* ... especially if you look at everyday resources through a different lens.

Here are some ideas that have generated great job leads for students:

1. BAR ASSOCIATION ON-LINE CHAT ROOMS AND LISTSERVS

Some local bar associations run chat rooms and listservs for attorneys in various specialties. You can find a listing of excellent ones on-line at http://community.lawyers.com/chat/list.asp. While the prime audience for these chat rooms/listservs is practicing lawyers, it's worth checking them out for "accidental" job leads (and to learn more about specialties). As one student described it to me, "Most of the postings aren't useful to law students. But once in a while a lawyer will post something like, 'I really need help on this case. Does anybody know anyone who ...' and that's my chance to jump in!"

* * * SMART HUMAN TRICK * * *

Student at a Midwestern school. She wants to work in a town in Arizona. She goes onto the local lawyers' listserv. One of the lawyers has an open question about online research, and comments on how Lexis/Nexis and Westlaw have it sewn up.

The student posts a message talking about other forms of online research, and mentions that she's a law student. The lawyer e-mails her and asks her to talk to him when she comes to town.

She does ... and winds up with a job.

2. Read (or at Least Skim) Publications Including The Business Section of the Newspaper for the City Where You Want to Work, as Well As Federal, State and Local Bar Association Newsletters and Journals, and Alumni Magazines (for Both Law School and Your Undergrad school).

Job postings are a bit obvious. But there are lots of other, hidden job opportunities in newspapers and legal publications. Look for:

a. Changes in Law Firm Status: New Offices Opening, New Practice Areas and Firm Mergers

Whether they list job opportunities or not, these "status changes" often signal potential openings—making it an opportune time to contact them.

b. Conferences, Seminars, and Events Related to What You Want to Do

I've talked to so many students who glommed onto great events by reading about them. The student who wound up with a summer clerkship at the U.S. Embassy in Barbados because she went to a meeting of the Organization of American States—a meeting that she discovered in the local newspaper. The student who got referrals from Nelson Mandela—yes, *that* Nelson Mandela—because he noticed a newspaper article about an upcoming conference on trade with South Africa taking place in town, with Mandela as the featured speaker.

I've already hammered you to join the bar association. They run useful events all the time—the ABA has conferences that are excellent sources of leads in all kinds of glamorous fields.

The beauty of finding conferences and other events from publications is that you can tell from the headline whether you're interested, without having to read an entire article!

c. Law Firm Open Houses

I got this idea from a very savvy law student in Minnesota. He noticed in the local newspaper that a large law firm had just remodeled its offices, and it was holding an open house to celebrate. He was very interested in working for them. So he went to the open house, and made a point of introducing himself to lawyers there. While he was chatting with one of them, a law school professor of his walked up, and said to the lawyer, "This is one of my favourite students." The student wound up with a job!

d. Profiles of Lawyers Who Do What You Want to Do and/or Are Similarly Situated

You'll often read feature stories about people. When those people in question have a job you'd enjoy, these articles are a great opportunity to garner some very valuable advice.

What you do is to craft a letter to the person in question, saying something like, "I just read the article about you in X publication. I'm a 1L/2L/whatever student at X law school, and I'd love to follow in your footsteps. I've done (X in pursuit of this goal). May I talk with you for ten minutes, at your convenience, to get your advice about what I ought to be doing?" If you share something in common with them, make a point of saying so. For instance, I talked with a young Asian woman at a law school in Northern California, who felt she was being stereotyped as "meek" and therefore couldn't get her dream job, as a prosecutor. It turns out that a local bar association publication that very month profiled Asian women prosecutors in the city! The student got her foot in the door by sending one of them a note, saying she'd read the profile, she was very interested in working in the prosecutor's office, and as an Asian woman she faced some of the discrimination addressed in the article. She asked for advice ... and she got it. The prosecutor she contacted helped her a lot.

Now ... will *everybody* respond positively to you? Of course not. But we make a terrible mistake in life when we underestimate the value of honest flattery. And there's nothing more flattering than telling someone, "You inspire me."

* * * SMART HUMAN TRICK * * *

Missouri law student who's also a mom. She really wants to work part-time to balance her work and mothering duties. She reads in the local newspaper about how the prosecutor's office allows "job shares," where two people essentially split a single full-time job.

The article talks about two women with young children who have this arrangement. The student calls one of them and says, "I read the article about you. I'm a law student and a mom, too, and I'd love your advice about working part-time. Can I take you out to lunch?" The prosecutor accepts, and at lunch, the student reports, "We hit it off immediately. Lunch wasn't even over and she was already writing down names of people for me to call!"

* * * SMART HUMAN TRICK * * *

Law student in Alabama regularly skims his undergraduate alumni magazine, particularly the "Class Notes" section where alums send in their personal news. He sees that a lawyer at a firm he wants to work for, an alum of his undergrad school, has gotten married; the lawyer has his wedding announcement posted in the Class Notes.

The law student sends a congratulatory note, says how he found him, and asks for an informational interview. He gives his e-mail address. The lawyer e-mails him and offers to help. The student winds up with a summer clerkship at his firm.

E. ARTICLES WRITTEN ABOUT ISSUES IN SPECIALTIES THAT INTEREST YOU

Bar association publications are full of articles about topics in different specialties. You also periodically see them in general interest newspapers and magazines, as well.

When you read an article about an issue in a specialty that interests you, check the byline. It's almost always a lawyer who wrote the article. This gives you a great lead for advice about breaking into the specialty.

Here's what you do. Google the attorney, check Martindale Hubbell or Switchboard.com and find his/her address. Send a letter saying something along the lines of, "I just read the article you wrote in X publication. I found it very interesting, particularly because I'd like to work in X law when I graduate from law school. I've done (X in pursuit of this goal). I'd very much appreciate your advice on what else I ought to be doing to better my chances. May I talk with you for ten minutes, at your convenience ..." and so on. If they're too busy to talk, ask if you can get advice via e-mail (but remember: talking is a lot better!).

The reason this works so well is that writers *love* to be complimented on what they've written. As someone who's been a writer for a while now, I can tell you that when someone admires something you've written, you'll walk over broken glass to help them out!

F. ARTICLES IN NEWSPAPERS/MAGAZINES/LEGAL PUBLICATIONS, QUOTING LAWYERS WHO DO WHAT YOU WANT TO DO

When you read articles about issues in a specialty that interests you, inevitably the quoted sources will be experts in the field—professors and lawyers. Contact them! Say something like, "I read with great interest what you had to say about the law of space junk, because I'm very interested in practicing Space Law when I graduate from Fred's Night YMCA Law School. I've done (X in pursuit of this goal). I would greatly appreciate your advice on what else I should be doing. May I talk to you for ten minutes at your convenience ..." and so forth. Again, if they're too busy to talk, you can always correspond via e-mail for advice.

Because this is a route so few law students take in contacting lawyers, you will certainly stand out if you try it!

G. LAWYERS WHO SUCCESSFULLY ARGUED CASES YOU READ ABOUT IN NEWSPAPERS/LEGAL PUBLICATIONS

If you're interested in a specialty, you should certainly be keeping up with important cases focusing on it. When you read about them, if the prevailing lawyers aren't mentioned, go to Lexis/Nexis or Westlaw to see who they were. Contact them, saying something like, "I read your arguments in Moose v. Lodge with great interest because I am interested in practicing Elk Law when I graduate from Juicy Lucy School of Law. I've done (X in pursuit of this goal). I would very much appreciate your advice about breaking into the field. May I talk with you for ten minutes, at your convenience . . ."

As with so many of the approaches in this section, the novelty of how you found the lawyer works for you. Most students don't go to these lengths to get career advice from someone so perfectly positioned to give it . . . and you'll be noteworthy as a result!

3. READ CASES RELATED TO WHAT YOU WANT TO DO. LOOK TO SEE WHO REPRESENTED THE PARTIES, AND CONTACT THEM

This is a really, really flattering way to approach people. Let's say you're interested in doing "soft" Intellectual Property—trademarks and copyrights. So you keep up with cases involving Internet downloads. Read the opinions as they come down, and check to see who the lawyers are. Send an e-mail and say something along the lines of, "I just read the opinion in *Braindead Music vs. Perlman.* I was particularly interested in the arguments you made. I'm interested in breaking into the same kind of work when I graduate from law school. May I ask you a few questions about the field?" The fact that you complimented—*honestly* complimented—their work is a great lead-in to asking advice.

Incidentally—keeping up with new cases in your desired specialty is a great idea. It gives you interesting things to discuss with lawyers you meet, and it proves your enthusiasm for what you want to do.

F. "PAYING" OPPORTUNITIES THAT MAKE YOU VALUABLE CONTACTS AT THE SAME TIME

Every job has the potential to make you great contacts. Wherever you work, make a point of getting to know as many people as possible, both inside the office and in the community. Don't eat lunch alone. Accept offers of tickets to local legal functions. It doesn't just make your life more interesting . . . you never know when the next person you meet might be the key to your next opportunity!

There are some opportunities, however, that are often overlooked for their primary contact-building features. They include:

1. CLERKSHIPS AT LARGE LAW FIRMS *DURING THE SCHOOL YEAR*

Large law firms don't confine their student hiring to summer programs, you know. They hire clerks during the school year, as well . . . and the competition for the slots is *much* lower than it is during the summer. So even if you don't have the stellar grades large law firms normally require, you may be able to get your foot in the door. And even though they typically hire from their summer class, you wouldn't be the first "winter clerk" to wind up with a permanent offer. On top of that, you meet a ton of lawyers, all of whom know *other* lawyers at other firms. You can't overlook the contact-making potential of the job.

2.   TEMP/CONTRACT JOBS/"STAFF ATTORNEY" POSITIONS

Legal temp jobs are a no-brainer way to meet, and impress, potential permanent employers, as are staff attorney positions, where you're on a non-partnership track.

Often law firms will hire temps, also known as contract attorneys, for a big case or project. It's much easier to hire temps than to make the commitment to hiring "permanent" help.

Here are the basics you need to know:

- In terms of nailing jobs, check with Career Services and the local bar association for contract opportunities locally. Googling "temporary legal positions" and terms like it also works.

- You might not get a temp position on your first try. Experts say to *be persistent*. It pays off.

- You can contact employers directly to see if they have temp or contract attorney positions. Just ask something like, "Do you ever hire staff attorneys or know anyone who does, where I might get good experience?" This works particularly in a) markets that are growing, or b) the case of employers who aren't sure they need someone permanent.

- The bad news: firms are increasingly requiring that you pass the bar before you can temp for them, and if you move to another state, you generally have to take *that* state's bar, as well. The good news: another evolving aspect of temping is that it now generally offers health benefits and even 401Ks.

- Make yourself as useful as possible to the employer. Don't *ever* sit idle; when you see the need for extra help, offer your services! What you want to do is create the impression you're indispensable, to make the employer realize that they do need you permanently after all.

- Take advantage of the "usual suspects" for making contacts. Talk to as many people in the office as possible, don't eat lunch alone, and keep yourself active in the legal community, with the local bar association, while you're working.

It's important to note that virtually all temp agencies warn you not to talk to the employer about a permanent opportunity.

Ha ha.

They *have* to say that. What you want to do is to raise *subtly* the issue without putting the employer on the spot ... and at the same time solicit advice. Here's how.

When you work in *any* office, you'll normally make friends there, people you'll chat with more often than others. When that happens, take advantage of a casual conversation to ask something like, "This is the kind of place I'd love to work on a permanent basis. What do you think I ought to be doing? What would you do if you were me?" Or ask about other employers like them ... and perhaps whom you should talk to at that employer. If you're discreet about it, you won't make anyone uncomfortable, and you might nail a great job!

* * * SMART HUMAN TRICK * * *

Law student in Pacific Northwest whose dream is to work in the State Attorney General's office. She reports, "There was a hiring freeze, and they told me they just weren't going to hire anybody for a while. I thought I would temp in the meantime, and lo and behold a temp position opens up *in the State Attorney General's office!*"

"I took the temp job, and after I'd been there a few months, they gave me a permanent job. I don't know how they made it happen with the hiring freeze, and I don't care."

* * * SMART HUMAN TRICK * * *

Law student graduates from law school in Los Angeles, unable to find a permanent job, and takes a temp job as a result. She reports, "I really didn't know what I wanted to do, and I thought temping would buy me some time. It turns out I really love this job! The pay is excellent. The hours are reasonable, a lot more reasonable than the hours I see the associates working. And I feel like I'm free. I can leave whenever I want, go wherever I want. The offices are luxurious and I'm proud to be here. In school I never would have thought I enjoyed it. But I really, really do."

3. NON-LEGAL TEMP JOBS *IN BUILDINGS WITH LAW FIRMS*

Physical proximity to employers who interest you is a real benefit. Casual contact in the lobby, in hallways, on the elevator, in the building's café or newsstand ... you never know where those conversations may lead. As UNLV's Pavel Wonsowicz points out, "If you smoke, the days of smoke-free buildings mean you'll often find the same people huddled outside with a cigarette." If you see someone every day sneaking in a quick smoke, and they happen to be a lawyer ... you've got a built in conversation buddy.

* * * SMART HUMAN TRICK * * *

New graduate, southern California law school. Her dream firm wouldn't even look at her because of her grades.

She found out where their office was and took a job at the company in the office next door, acting as a temporary receptionist. She always wore a suit to work, always carried *Lawyers' Weekly* and *The Wall Street Journal,* and made a point of eating lunch at a cafeteria on the first floor which she knew was a mecca for lawyers at the firm.

In elevators, hallways, at the cafeteria, she routinely ran into the lawyers. When she ate lunch, she made a point of conspicuously reading law-related publications. A partner from the firm finally said, "From what you read, you must be a lawyer." She explained that's what she *wanted* to do but right now she was working a temp job as a receptionist next door. The lawyer said, "Well, you don't want *that.*" He got her an interview with the firm ... and they hired her.

4. WORKING AS A RESEARCH ASSISTANT FOR A PROFESSOR

"Great," you're thinking. "I get to meet a professor ... at my own school! Yippee!" Holster your cynicism there, Trigger. Your professors are often better connected than you think. Tell your professor-employer what kind of position you're looking for, and ask his/her advice about whom you ought to be talking to. Professors consult with firms, they often have a lot of former colleagues in practice, and they have tons of former students to draw from, as well.

It may well be that your research gives you the opportunity to make contacts of your own. Research, after all, doesn't have to mean burying your nose in books or on the Internet. There may be issues you research that involve talking with an expert, perhaps talking with a lawyer who argued a certain position in a certain case. You can't overlook those contacts for their future employment potential!

5. STARTING A BRIEF-WRITING SERVICE

A great way to make contacts, since outreach is at the core of the business. I described this in more detail earlier in this chapter, when we talked about writing activities.

6. JUDICIAL CLERKSHIPS

Working for a judge is in and of itself an awesome opportunity—it's a job most people love, and permanent clerkships are among the most coveted jobs in law. But as a traditional "temporary" clerk, you have myriad opportunities to make valuable contacts. The lawyers who argue cases before your judge, the prosecutors in criminal cases, other clerks and staff attorneys, fellow attendees at legal community events—any of these may be the key to your next great job.

While ethics hem in your job-searching activities as a clerk, there's no question that the people you get to know will be useful to you in your "next" life after clerking.

For more on judicial clerkships, see chapter 25.

4. WHAT TO SAY: TALKING TO PEOPLE YOU MEET AT EVENTS, HANDLING SOCIAL SITUATIONS . . . AND THE THREE THINGS TO ASK FOR

"I had a perfectly wonderful evening. This wasn't it."

Groucho Marx

Schmoozing. Brown-nosing. Kibbutzing. The idea of going to events with the goal in mind of helping your career raises all kinds of ugly images, doesn't it? But it shouldn't. What I'm going to teach you here is to make "professional socializing" easy and fun. The great news is this: Once you've done this a couple of times, you'll wonder why you ever wasted time with mass mailers. You'll feel comfortable with all kinds of people. And you'll be setting yourself up to nail great opportunities forever . . . because it's through conversations with live flesh-and-blood people that you'll find the best gigs for the rest of your life!

Here's what you need to remember:

A. IT'S NOT THE BATAAN DEATH MARCH. IT'S A GREAT OPPORTUNITY TO MEET PEOPLE YOU MIGHT ACTUALLY *LIKE*

Will Rogers used to say that a stranger is just a friend he hadn't met yet. I don't know if I'd go *that* far, but let's face it—the closest buds you have right now were once strangers to you. So you've had *some* experience talking to strangers. You're just going to polish those skills for the sake of your career! As Betsy Armour points out, "You've got to achieve a level of comfort with professional social situations at some point. You've got to start sooner or later. So you might as well start now."

B. DRESS *PRETTY* WELL

Wardrobe is one of the more difficult aspects of socializing. It's a "Three Bears" dilemma; that is, you don't want to be too dressed up—but you don't want to show up in your ripped jeans and flip-flops, either. What I'd do is to wear something *relatively* nice; for women, pants are fine, but make them neat. No tennis shoes. And a non-revealing blouse or sweater; no T-shirts. For men, again, either very neat jeans or dress pants. Collared shirt. No sneakers or sandals. What you're doing here is walking the middle ground; everybody knows you're a student, so nobody expects you to show up in a suit. But by the same token, you want people to view you as a potential colleague—so the "Eat Me" T-shirt doesn't create the image you want.

At one law school, the SBA president went to an event where the managing partner of a very prestigious firm was in attendance. The SBA president showed up unshaven, shirt half out, baseball cap on sideways. The partner commented afterwards, "Nice guy, but I couldn't trust him with clients if he dresses like *that.*"

Also—if you take a spouse or significant other to a professional event, remember that what they wear (and say) reflects on you. Prep them! If you're wearing a suit and your partner shows up in an outfit suitable for "Girls Gone Wild," you'll look bad.

* * * CAREER LIMITING MOVE * * *

Reported by an attorney in Missouri:

"I was at a local bar association function. I was chatting with a student, and one of the things that impressed me about him was that he had dressed up for the event. Usually when I see students they're wearing jeans and T-shirts. This young man had gone to the trouble of putting on nice trousers, a pressed white shirt, and a tie.

The tie seemed to have a small pattern on it. It was not until we had talked for a few minutes that I realized that the pattern on his tie was actually tiny, nude women!!!

I don't think I paid attention to a word he said after that."

c. IF THERE'S CHOW, GO EARLY IF YOU INTEND TO EAT

In other words: separate the "eating" and "meeting people" functions. The fact is, you can't balance a plate, glass, and shake hands at the same time, unless you're a contortionist with *Cirque de Soleil.*

Notice I'm not telling you to avoid food altogether. I remember law school. The whole idea is to get through without ever actually having to *buy* food. "Ukranian Securities Law Seminar ... full buffet! *I'm in!*"

So go early and eat all you want. Check in the mirror to see that you haven't got anything stuck in your teeth. And plunge ahead with the real purpose of the event: talking with people.

d. IF YOU'RE UNCOMFORTABLE ABOUT SOCIAL SITUATIONS, TRY A LITTLE CREATIVE VISUALIZATION

Most people consider themselves shy. While I give you lots of tips in this section about how to break into conversations and what to talk about, here's an exercise that can help a lot: visualize what you'd do if you *were* feeling confident about the event. Imagine how you'd carry yourself, how you'd look, what you'd say (I'll give you lots of tips about what to talk about in this section).

With that image in your mind, go to the event and act "as if"— that is, as though you really *are* confident. Remember: No one can see inside your head. They don't know how you feel. They hear what you say and see your demeanor. Act confidently and you'll feel confident!

E. IF YOU LIKE, SHOW UP WITH A BUDDY—BUT AGREE AHEAD OF TIME THAT YOUR WHOLE PURPOSE IN BEING THERE IS TO TALK TO OTHER PEOPLE, NOT EACH OTHER

If you're intimidated—and it's perfectly all right to feel that way at the beginning!—go with a friend. But for the duration—you're not hanging with each other. Look at it this way: you'll have lots to talk about on the way home. There's no point in going to professional social events—other than the free food—if you're not going to talk to new people.

F. IF YOU'RE LOOKING FOR SOMEONE IN PARTICULAR, GO OVER TO WHOEVER'S HOSTING THE EVENT AND ASK FOR HELP IN FINDING THEM AND/OR ASK TO BE INTRODUCED

If you are going to a social event or a conference or any other meeting with a particular "target" in mind, you might as well cut right to the chase. If you don't know what they look like, ask the person handing out name tags, checking you in, or hosting the event for an introduction. "I was looking forward to coming here, and I was really hoping to meet Attorney X . . . could you introduce me?" If they don't know the person, ask for someone who might. And if you strike out there, just go it alone and talk with whomever you meet. For instance, at a social event, you can go to the next item, and . . .

G. GET A DRINK, AND TALK TO PEOPLE IN LINE AROUND YOU

It's rare, verging on unheard of, for a social event involving attorneys *not* to have a bar. I was social director at law school, and even on my rinky-dink budget everybody expected *at least* scotch and beer (albeit not *together*).

A great way to "break the ice" is to belly up to the bar, and chat with other people waiting for a drink. Introduce yourself, smile, and shake hands. Any simple comment, "Interesting how the bar is always the most popular place at these events . . ." is all it takes. If it's an alumni event, you can ask the person what they do; at a conference, ask where they're from. I get into a lot more detail about what to say to strangers just below, but my point here is this: the bar's always crowded at social events, and it's a natural place to start a conversation with a stranger.

H. ABOUT THAT DRINK . . .

Notice I said drink. Not drink*s*. You're going to stop at one—two at the most. When you attend events that have a bar—alumni cocktail receptions, Happy Hours at conferences—it's easy to be seduced by that little voice in your head saying, "Awwrrrright. Par-tay!"

Ignore that little voice.

Hey, I remember law school. And I remember the temptation when the alcohol in question was free. But these professionally-oriented social events you're attending? They're for your *career.* Nobody's going to hire—or refer to other people—the person who belched the loudest after draining the beer bong. There's a quasi-German saying that's apt: "Ist der Beir in Manne, ist der Verstand in der Kanne," which translates as: Beer in the man, brains in the can.

Will the attorneys at the event stop at one drink? Probably not. *But they're already employed.* You're not going to match them drink for drink.

So—how do you handle the situation? It's easier than you think.

1. Nurse that drink for a *long* time. Don't think that anybody's counting what you drink. As St. Thomas' Vince Thomas says, "It may be the finest gin you ever had, but one is enough!" Abbie Willard agrees, saying, *"You* know your limits. You can have fun on one drink, without getting drunk."

2. If the alcohol is flowing *really* freely, and someone insists on bringing you another drink every few minutes, just take a sip out of the one in your hand, and when they're off retrieving another drink for you, surreptitiously ditch the one you have now. Put it on a table with other glasses, on a ledge, whatever. Nobody in the world is going to starve if you don't finish every drink you're handed.

3. Get your own drinks from the bar. And after the first one, make it sparkling water with a twist, which looks like a mixed drink.

4. If the action turns to doing shots, it's time to walk away. Don't make a big deal about it, but suddenly become interested in talking to someone else. You just can't keep a clear head with even one turn at the vodka slalom.

5. If the pressure gets too intense to drink—you're being badgered—then alternate. As Georgetown's Beth Sherman suggests, "Have a beer then a water then a soda then a beer. Control yourself!"

What if you don't drink at all? Remember that there's never been a social event—and there'll never be one—where *everybody* is drinking. Look around; the social pressure to drink isn't as unanimous as you think. Furthermore, what really bugs people who are drinking in a social situation is not that you're not drinking—it's the sense that you're silently admonishing them. So as Vickie Brown recommends, "You don't have to take part, but you *do* have to make them feel comfortable. Tell them, 'You go ahead!' in a hearty, encouraging voice. That'll alleviate the pressure on you!"

I. WHAT TO TALK ABOUT WITH PEOPLE YOU MEET ... AND WHAT TO AVOID TALKING ABOUT

Ultimately, you're there to seek career advice. But you need ways to spark lively conversations first. Let's talk about how to accomplish that.

1. ONGOING PREP WORK: GIVE YOURSELF INTERESTING THINGS TO TALK ABOUT

I was once at a bowling banquet for my husband's office bowling league. It was even worse than it sounds. We were sitting with just about the most uncharming couple you could possibly meet. This guy was railing on and on about how bored he was, about how the last bowling banquet he'd been to was so much better than this one, yadda yadda yadda ... until finally I said to him: "If *you're* bored, think how *we* feel hearing you complain about it?" I know it wasn't particularly "couth," but then ... I'd reached my limit.

I'm telling you that story for a reason. You, I, and everybody in the world has an obligation to be an interesting conversationalist. And the way to accomplish that is to **keep up with what's going on in the world**. Scan the headlines every day, either in the newspaper or on-line. Listen to National Public Radio's *All Things Considered* and *Morning Edition,* at least at the hour and half hour in the morning or at night. Scan the news weeklies at the library. Skim the front pages of *The Wall Street Journal* (especially the "middle column" with the human interest feature) and the front page and OpEd page of *The New York Times.* I love the financial page of *The New Yorker*—it's always thought-provoking.

And, of course, there's the satirical news website "The Onion," at theonion.com, which is just spit-milk-through-your-nose funny. A great source of conversational jump-starters.

Also, as I've advised you elsewhere, keep up with local and state bar association publications. You don't actually have to read them, but skim them for potentially interesting stories. The same goes for *The American Lawyer National Law Journal,* and lawfuel.com. The people you meet will read them, and you'll have that in common.

If this seems like a lot, what it really boils down to is ten to fifteen minutes a day. If that's all it takes to be a sparkling conversationalist, it's an investment worth making.

Of course, there are other published sources of conversation as well ... and time-effective ways to read them. For instance, if you're not familiar with the *Uncle John's Bathroom Reader* series, you're missing out on a source of fascinating information that's great fun to read when ... ahem, you've got little else to do. The articles—short, medium and long ones to fit every "visit"—cover everything from fascinating historical oddities to interesting people to ... oh, it's too broad to describe here. But pick one up. You'll find plenty to talk about.

Here's how you use what you learn in the news. When you meet someone new, you can always lead in by saying, "Did you hear they think they found water on Mars? I heard ..." "Have you heard about that movie, *The Chowderhead Gang?* I read ..." You'll find that most people will be tremendously relieved that you picked up the conversational ball, and will respond favorably.

2. WHAT YOU ASK FOR FROM PEOPLE YOU MEET. AND PSST: *IT'S NOT A JOB*

I talk to students all the time who say, "I've been to one (or two or three or four) things, and they didn't do me any good. I talked to these lawyers, but it didn't go anywhere." Without their even asking me, I can tell why: *Either they didn't ask for anything, so they didn't get anything ... or they asked for a job.*

All of the conversational openers in this section only help you if at some point in the conversation you work in a few appropriate requests. The fact is, when you meet people, you've got to ask for things *that people are typically very willing to give you*. While I cover this ground later in this chapter when we talk about "Informational Interviewing," it's important to remember it in a non-interviewing context, as well.

Now: what do you ask for? Not a job, interestingly enough. Asking people for a job puts them on the spot, and you don't want to do that. I talked to a student in Texas who said he'd tried making contact with a couple of people he'd found through people he knows, but the contacts "didn't go anywhere." It turns out that he'd led by saying "I'm looking for a job," and they immediately shut down. No surprise!

Instead, as Rob Kaplan advises, **you ask for three things that *lead* to jobs: Advice, Information, and Referrals. "AIR."**

How do you bring these up? In the natural course of conversation, you'll ask people what they do. Or they'll bring it up. Or they'll ask you about yourself. Those are all great openings for asking for AIR. "What you do sounds so interesting. I'd love to get into it. I've done x and x (toward that goal). If you were me, how would you go about breaking into it? What should I be doing? (Advice). Where can I find out more about it? (Information). If you were me, who would you be talking to? (Referrals)."

What if it's not what they do? Ask them anyway. You don't know who they know!

Now—why won't they be offended by this? Because people like to be asked for their advice, their opinions. Lawyers *love* to give advice—that's what they do for a living. Asking someone what they would do in your situation flatters them because it suggests you consider them an expert.

When you ask these questions, you might think that the person you're talking to can see right through you. Students often say to me, "Come on. They're going to *know* I'm looking for a job!" Maybe they will—but what can they do about it, if you don't ask for one? What are they going to do—stop the conversation, and say, "He-e-ey, wait a minute. Are you asking me for a *job?*" It just doesn't happen, because it's not what you've asked for.

You will be amazed by the responses you get to these questions, by the way. Students often report back to me that they get people saying "I'll call my friend for you ..." "Give my office a call ..." they get stacks of business cards, you name it. And all because they *asked for advice!*

Is it possible to "over-ask"? Absolutely. I recently heard a hilarious example at my son Harry's pre-school. A woman brought her daughter, whom I'll call Meredith, to school for her first day. The mom said to the teachers—whom she'd never met before— "By the way, Meredith ate a rock. If she has to take a dump, please hold a baggy under her butt and catch it so I can give it to the doctor."

As you might imagine, asking someone to corral feces in a bag is over-asking.

Over-asking is usually not the issue for law students I talk to. The vast majority of the time, students I meet don't ask for nearly as much as they could get, anxious as they are not to be told "no."

Over-asking is a delicate matter. You have to be sensitive to the verbal and non-verbal cues you get from people you meet in order to determine what the appropriate boundaries are. You may meet people whose gruff demeanor tells you that asking for even the most basic advice is risky. You'll meet other gregarious souls whose smiles and enthusiasm suggest that asking to move into their guest room wouldn't be too much! The key is to start with the basics—show enthusiasm for what they do, ask questions about them, ask for advice about what you should be doing, what they'd do if they were you ... and then watch for cues. If they say, "Gee, I really don't know," then continue your conversation about other topics. Trust me: for every person who *isn't* helpful, you'll meet ten who *are,* to some extent. So start small, ask for advice most people are happy to give ... and take it from there.

Very occasionally I'll meet a student who entirely innocently leans *way* too hard on people they meet. By way of example, I met a young woman at one law school whose nose was out of joint because she felt a lawyer she'd met had snubbed her. She went to an alumni dinner which she'd helped organize, and she wound up sitting on the dais next to a prominent alum whom she'd never met before. He was a state legislator. After chatting for a few minutes over appetizers, she told the alum she was applying for jobs in the State Attorney General's office, and asked the alum to act as a reference for her. He was evasive, said, "Well, good luck to you," abruptly changed the subject and shortly started talking to the person on his other side. She was offended and asked me why he'd behaved as he did. I told her—predictably enough—that she'd over-asked. "He doesn't know you or your work, so he can't put his reputation on the line as a reference for you," I said. Asking someone for advice is one thing; asking someone to vouch for you is something else entirely.

If she had instead asked him, "You might know something about this. I really want to work for the Attorney General's office. Could I get your advice?"—the result would have been entirely different. He may even have volunteered to make a call for her. But as it was . . .

A student at another law school had a similarly poor experience contacting alums. "You say it works," he said. "It doesn't! I tried." It turns out that his Career Services Director had given him the names of several alums to contact. He'd e-mailed them his resume, along with the simple request that they distribute his resume for him. Now, put yourself in the shoes of those alums. You don't know this student; an e-mail request tells you nothing about the kind of person he is. And he's asking you to do his mass-mailer for him!

Remember: Give people a chance to know you and like you so they'll *want* to help you. They can't get invested in you with an e-mail request. Talk. Listen. Ask questions. Take an interest . . . and let them come to the conclusion that you're someone whose aspirations deserve to be jollied along.

3. GOOGLE PEOPLE YOU KNOW WILL BE AT AN EVENT

For some of the activities in this chapter—like taking on a mentor, shadowing an attorney for a day, attending CLEs, doing mock interviews, or listening to speakers who come to your law school—you've got an obvious google target: the mentor, the CLE presenter, the mock interviewer, the speaker. But other kinds of "attendance" activities still give you an opportunity to google people, and a *great* way to open a conversation with them!

For instance, let's take alumni cocktail receptions. You can always go to the alumni affairs director at school or your Career Services Director, and ask who's likely to attend that you ought to seek out. Google that person/those people. Or, take the suggestion to watch trials at the local courthouse. Find out who the prosecutors are, and google them. Find out about people's backgrounds, to give you ideas to talk about with them. "I know you went to Santa

Clara Law School. How did you wind up here in Texas? ..." "I noticed you were involved in the case *Scrooge v. Marley*. I was curious ..." It's not a bad idea to jot down a few notes on people you're likely to run into, and carry those notes with you (inconspicuously, of course!). There's nothing more flattering to someone than knowing that you were so interested in meeting them that you learned something about them first.

As a caveat, remember to confine your questions/comments regarding what you've learned about someone to socially acceptable information. Their employer's web site, google, and other people are generally safe. Web sites like MySpace, Facebook, and other social networking sites are risky. Why? It verges on cyberstalking, and those sites are meant for friends of friends, not the whole world. You'll make people feel creepy if you ask "So—bad breakup with your girlfriend, huh?" or "How was that bachelor party in Vegas? Great pictures!" Tact and discretion are valuable skills for an attorney. Prove yours by hemming in what you mention to people.

4. Who to Approach if You Don't Have a Specific Person in Mind ... and Why a Loudmouth Friend Comes in Handy

If you're going to an alumni cocktail event or a conference, it may seem when you walk in as though everybody there knows everybody else. They're gathered in small groups, talking animatedly and laughing. And then there's ... *you*. And you don't know *anybody*.

If you're alone, here's what you do. Survey the crowd for a moment, and you'll notice something interesting. Not *everybody* is gathered in groups. **There will be people on the outskirts who look uncomfortable. Those are the people you approach.** They *need* someone to talk to! Walk up with a smile on your face, introduce yourself, and launch into one of the approaches I discuss in the next few pages. The fact that they're not talking with a lot of other people doesn't mean they're not worthwhile; some of the most influential lawyers are not social butterflies. Seek them out!

Another possibility is to **linger on the outskirts of a lively conversation.** If it's not about something unique to them, like reminiscing about something they all did together (or talking about plans for something they're going to do), gradually move closer. What will typically happen is that as you move closer, the people there will—without realizing it—make room for you. Then when there's an appropriate comment made, make your contribution. "You're going to Venice? I went there in college ..." "Wow—so did you ever get your suitcase back?" "Whatever wound up happening to that guy?" "Oh, I just saw that movie. I thought ..." Then after you've made your comment and they've responded, you can always introduce yourself. "By the way, my name is ..." and you're in. If a few minutes go by and there's no obvious entrée to the conversation, smile and walk away. No harm done.

Of course, **going to social events with a "loudmouth friend,"** as UC Davis' Mindy Baggish says, **can be a big help.** "Going with a loudmouth is a great way to talk to people you wouldn't approach yourself." They can break the ice, and then you take part with them in the ensuing conversation. If they only joined the conversation for your sake, they can always slip away gracefully.

Needless to say, walking up to groups of people is easier when there are two of you. And it has the benefit of being a learning experience. As Mindy Baggish points out, "Once you've seen your friend break into a conversation a few times, you'll feel a lot more comfortable doing it yourself."

5. THE SECRET OF CHARM: IT'S NOT WITTY REPARTEE!

A lot of us avoid talking to people at social events—and even going to them at all—for fear of not dredging up *les bons mots* when needed. We all know about legendary conversational openings lines, the ones that people never forget. For instance, when Prince Charles met his (eventual) wife Camilla, her opening line was, "My great grandmother and your great great grandfather were lovers. How about it?"

Of course, there *are* students who've come up with great openers. One student told me about walking up to a lawyer at a party and saying, "Everyone says you're an obnoxious son of a bitch. In my book, that makes you the most interesting person in the room. I just had to meet you." The student wound up working for the "obnoxious son of a bitch." But let's face it. Those kinds of openers are few and far between.

The good news is, you don't need them. What *do* you need?

You might have read Dale Carnegie's book *How to Win Friends and Influence People*. If you haven't, I'll summarize it for you in one sentence:

Get people to talk about themselves and they will love you.

The advertising guru David Ogilvy echoed this advice in talking about formulating ads people will read. A lot of experts say that ads require a lot of "white space." Ogilvy vehemently disagreed with this, arguing that he could get anybody to read a full page of tiny type. His secret? Give the page a headline reading, "This page is all about you."

People virtually universally like to talk about themselves. If you ask people about what brought them to the event you're attending, what they do, how they chose it, where they grew up

... unless they're in the federal witness protection program, they'll be delighted to chat. (My favourite answer to the "How did you choose your job?" question came from an Episcopalian priest sitting next to me on a plane: "Because God told me to.")

Of course, you don't want it to feel like an interrogation. When they tell you something about themselves, if you have that in common, say so. Or if they mention they just went on vacation to someplace exotic, you can comment on it and then talk about a favourite vacation of your own. After all, you don't want the conversation to be an interview; you're asking questions as a way of engendering a natural give-and-take.

6. *Never Underestimate the Value of Honest Flattery*

The thought of flattering people might make you feel slimy. Nobody wants to wear an ass turban. But there's a difference between paying an honest compliment and being a sleazy suck-up. When flattery is fake, it's disgusting. When it's honest ... that's a whole different story.

Everyone likes to hear that other people think of them what they think of themselves. Even the most successful people enjoy honest compliments. I remember reading an interview with Don Larsen—if you're a baseball fan, you may recognize him as being the only man ever to pitch a perfect game in the World Series—where he was asked, "Don't you get sick of talking about that game?" and he responded: "No. Why *would* I?"

So if you truly admire something someone's done, *tell* them so. "That couldn't have been easy. I really respect you for it ..." "How did you ever ...?" It sets you up to solicit advice from someone whose opinion you value!

* * * SMART HUMAN TRICK * * *

Law student in New York, interested in getting into International Law—specifically, he wants to work with South Africa. He keeps his eye on the local papers, and he notices there's going to be a conference on trade with South Africa taking place in Manhattan. He goes to it, and notices the keynote speaker standing alone for a couple of minutes. Appreciating the value of honest flattery, he walks up to this gentleman and says, "I've always wanted to work with South Africa. Hearing you speak has inspired me all the more. Can you give me some advice about it? Maybe the names of people I should contact?" He reports, "The guy was very gracious about it. He wrote down a few names for me, gave me some great advice." When asked who the speaker was, the student responds: "Nelson Mandela."

Now, *that's* a useful contact!

7. ASK QUESTIONS IN THE FORM OF "TELL ME ABOUT ..." RATHER THAN QUESTIONS THAT CAN BE ANSWERED "YES" OR "NO"

Asking questions that start with "Tell me about" can transform a dull answer into an interesting conversation.

I overheard a conversation at an airport that highlights this. A grandmotherly type was sitting next to a kid she didn't know. Here's their conversation, in its entirety:

"Are you in middle school?"

"Yes."

"Is it hard?"

"Yes."

"Are you reading?"

"Yes."

Wow. Fu-u-u-n, eh? Instead, ask people questions that are open ended: What's it like? Tell me about it? What did you do next? How did you handle it? Give people an opportunity to tell you stories instead of responding "Yes" or "No."

8. "DESERT ISLAND" QUESTIONS

Remember the episode of "The Office" (the American version, that is) where there was the office fire and everybody had to stand outside for a while? They all answered questions like, "Which five movies would you play if you were on a desert island," "Which five books would you take," those kinds of things.

Desert island questions make for great conversations. "If you could only eat one food for the rest of your life, what would it be?" "What would your dream vacation be?" You can comment on the other person's choices, share your own, ask about places they've enjoyed traveling to or talk about your own experiences ... it's just a great way to break the ice.

9. NEWS ITEMS

Avoid highly-charged items. The situation in the Middle East, a sexual harassment case that's made the news—no! But just about anything else is open season. Celebutante misbehavior? Sure. It's fun.

10. IF A CONTROVERSIAL TOPIC COMES UP, IT'S NOT TIME FOR A SMACK DOWN. TAKE A DEEP BREATH AND BITE YOUR TONGUE

In books about socializing, you often see the advice to avoid controversial topics, like sex, religion and politics. At the same time, you're supposed to talk about current events. Now, I ask you: how many headline stories are there that you can discuss that *don't* mention sex or religion or politics? Are you kidding me?

Here's what you *really* need to know. If a controversial topic comes up and it turns out that the person who's talking to you states a position that you disagree with, *don't feel that you have to convince them you're right.*

I am reminded of a story about President Kennedy. A friend of Kennedy's Undersecretary of the Navy, Red Fay, met with the president, pleading his case on a particular issue. When Kennedy came out supporting the *other* side, the friend railed at Fay, saying that Kennedy had misled him. When Fay reported this to Kennedy, the president responded, "Red, he mistook a warm smile and a friendly handshake for a firm show of support." Use the same tactic yourself; if someone else says something with which you don't agree, don't ask them to step outside.

It's not the time to proselytize *even if* the person you're talking to doesn't feel that way. Ask questions that get at that. "How did you decide to support Candidate Neocon?" "Were you raised in the Catholic church?" **View it as an education in seeing how other people think.** If they ask you if you agree with them, you can always say something like, "No, but you've given me something to think about," or "Not really, but I'm very interested in hearing what you have to say."

This came home to me on a flight from New York to Kansas City. The guy sitting next to me had been in New York to see a church choir; he was traveling with members of his church. You can see where this conversation was heading, but I didn't take the bait. I asked him about his job—he worked with computers—and he mentioned that he had a garage band and a website. After an hour or so, he asked me: "So, have you invited Jesus Christ into your life?"

Now, the truth is I like to think of myself as spiritual and I try behaving the way any deity would expect me to. So I basically mumbled something about being down with that. He went on, "All God asks is for you to believe in Him. He gave up His only Son for you . . ." I just let him talk, nodded, and didn't debate. I asked him more about his band, about how he feels about people downloading songs. It really was an interesting conversation, albeit it was interrupted every few minutes by his shaking his head and saying, "He gave up His only Son for you . . ." But if I had risen to the bait and argued with him about religion, it would have been miserable, neither one of us would have convinced the other, and I'd have alienated someone unnecessarily.

So don't freeze and don't jump ugly when controversial topics come up. Stay calm and make the conversation work for you!

In topic (k) below I talk about getting away from conversational duds. But for right now, remember: news is a great source of conversation, but not *controversial* news!

11. INOFFENSIVE SELF-REVELATION

Drop comments into the conversation that give the *other* person a chance to pick up the conversational ball. Margann Bennett recommends that you have three concrete things to say about yourself before you walk in. "While I was skiing in Aspen over Christmas break ..." "When I was growing up in France ..." "I just read this book about the spice trade—I had no idea how it dominated the world economy hundreds of years ago! It was amazing ..." "I visited this web site, geographyolympics.com, where you try to identify where countries are ..."

What you're doing is opening up the floor for the other person to say, "Aspen? What's it like?" "Where in France did you live? I went there ..." "The spice trade! That explains why ..." "I was the worst in geography at school ..."

It's important to note that *inoffensive* is the key word here. Places you've been, things you've read, non-pornographic movies you've seen ... it's all fair game. But physical ailments, complaints about school or work, issues with your significant other, negative comments about the event you're at, anything dealing with sex or alcohol consumption—it's off the table. When someone asks you "How are you?" or "How do you like school?" it's *still* not appropriate to launch into a litany of negatives. "How are you?" is the equivalent of "Hello," and that's why, even if you're carrying your head under your arm, the answer is "Fine." If you're asked about school, mention what you like about it—even if the only positive you can come up with is, "It's paving the way for me to get out and start my career, which is what I really want to do."

You can't complain about your professors (the person you're talking to may be related to them), the amount of work you've got (they're busier than you—trust me), the event you're at (they may know who organized it), or that you find law boring (gr-r-r-reat!). You can always get off the subject by turning around and asking them, "How did you like school?" or asking them about their work.

If you feel gypped because you can't be perfectly blunt, remember: you're not chatting with friends. You can bitch all you want and belch the alphabet around *them*, if you want. These are professional contacts, and even though you're not in an office setting, you want them to be subconsciously thinking about what it would be like to work with you, to have you represent them to clients. So put your most charming, professional face forward!

* * * CAREER LIMITING MOVE * * *

When asked "How are you?" at an alumni event, a law student responded, "Much better since my hepatitis cleared up."

* * * CAREER LIMITING MOVE * * *

Law student at a job fair meet-and-greet. He is chatting with a lawyer about his background, when he casually mentions, "My mother tried to kill me."

* * * CAREER LIMITING MOVE * * *

A Moot Court banquet. A lawyer introduces himself to a law student, saying, "Nice to meet you."

"On a good day," responds the student.

Apart from avoiding inappropriate sharing, be sure to "professionalize" your talking points. If someone asks you how you got onto a particular opportunity, say "mutual acquaintance," not "Dad." If you worry at all about how you'll come across, go to Career Services and bounce your anecdotes off of a counselor there before you try it in the "real world."

J. BE SENSITIVE TO VERBAL AND NON-VERBAL CUES ABOUT THE DIRECTION OF THE CONVERSATION

If the person you're talking to seems evasive when you ask questions—if they glance around, give one-word responses, shuffle uncomfortably—it's time to either change your approach or politely excuse yourself. If you're talking about something and they seem bored, ask a question. Being a great conversationalist means being aware of your audience.

* * * CAREER LIMITING MOVE * * *

A law student in New England went to a board meeting as the only student member on a panel of federal judges. Although the judges made several attempts to bring up topics they wanted to discuss, the student insisted on dominating the conversation. The lead judge became more and more bold with his signals for the student to shut up. The student told his Career Services Director afterwards, "I think I really impressed them with my persistence."

The lead judge subsequently told the Career Services Director, "He would *not shut up.* I did everything except slap him. I was *furious.*"

K. GETTING AWAY FROM DUDS

Your experience with social events so far—professional or not—tells you that the world is not exclusively populated by witty raconteurs. While most people have something interesting to say, you may occasionally wind up with someone who just doesn't have a conversational pulse.

Now, it's definitely true that everybody has *something* to say, if you dig far enough and ask enough questions. Everybody's interested in something, and it's a useful social skill to stick with conversations long enough to draw out even the shyest person.

But what if you try and launch a conversation with someone who just doesn't want to take the bait? Maybe they're preoccupied with work or a personal problem. Maybe they're just boring. We've all been around people who tell endless, pointless stories about people they know, calling these people by name when you have *no idea* who they are. "And then Greta called Susie into the office and said, 'Did you get the phone call about . . .' " Or they'll drone on and on about their genealogy. If genealogy is your hobby, I'm not dissing it, but I would caution you that unless you're descended from pirates, don't bring it up socially. There's nothing quite as boring as hearing about someone else's family tree! "Then my great-great grandfather on my mother's side apparently was a blacksmith in Poughkeepsie. His son, my great-grandfather . . ."

Or sometimes people just won't pick up the conversational thread you offer, and offer none of their own in return. When I chat with people on airplanes and they ask what I do, I usually tell them, "I write books, and I'm on a one hundred city book tour." This comment will generally open up a conversation about travel, careers, you name it. But sometimes, the person I'm talking to will say, "Oh"—and that's it. Now, saying to someone that you're on a hundred-city book tour ought to give them *something* to talk about, wouldn't you think? But sometimes—nada.

If you get stuck with a conversational dud at a social event, there's a very easy and effective way out—without insulting them. You simply smile and say, "Excuse me." You don't lie and say you're going to the rest room or to get another drink, in fact you don't offer any destination at all. Just "Excuse me," said *smilingly*. When you're socializing professionally, you've got to mine the most available ore. Don't linger all night with people who bore the snot out of you!

l. Collect Business Cards

Whether you're doing something that involves only one other person—like meeting a mentor or shadowing an attorney—or you're doing something that involves lots of people, like attending conferences and alumni receptions—get into the habit of collecting business cards. No matter how good your memory is, it will be difficult for you to remember the names of people you meet, and where they work. A business card does the trick.

Here's what you do with those cards. Immediately after the event where you met the card's owner, you "debrief" yourself, *on the back of the card*. That is, you write down everything you found out about them—colleagues, history, hobbies, family members, important dates coming up or just past, anything about their work. Everything. And then you keep the cards in a Rolodex or an album or something like it—Staples has all kinds of storage goodies for business cards. You store this information so that when you know you'll talk with them again, you can review what you learned the first time around, and casually mention anything appropriate—"Last time I talked to you, your son Johnny was doing a junior year abroad in Paris. Bring me up to date"—and you'll show off amazing people skills in doing so.

Talking about business cards naturally brings up a topic that students frequently ask me about, namely: **Do you need a card of your own while you're still in school? Nope.** Save your twenty bucks. Nobody expects you to have them. Now, you may be saying, "But what about when they give me their card? Or they ask me if I have one?" For a start, there's nothing awkward about a biz card only going in one direction. *I* don't have one, for gosh sakes. And on top of that, if they want your contact information, you can always ask for one of their cards and write your info on the back.

There's also a good strategic reason not to give people a business card, and it's this: It leaves the follow-up contact ball in your court. If you exchange business cards, then the attorney knows how to get a hold of you, and if they want to contact you, in theory they will. But if you don't have a card, and you collect theirs . . . *you're* in control. It gives you the opportunity to go home, google them, and then send them a follow-up letter asking for advice and stating an interest in what they do.

Having said all this, **there's no serious downside to having business cards made up.** You don't *have* to hand them out if you don't want to, after all. Just promise me that if you do get a business card, all it has on it is your contact information. *Please* don't get one of those cards where you put a "mini resume" on the back. For gosh sakes, you're too interesting to confine to a whole page—let alone a stinking little card!

M. FOLLOWING UP WITH PEOPLE WHO GIVE YOU THEIR BUSINESS CARDS

First of all: if people give you their card and say, "Call me," *call them.* **They** *mean* **it.** I've told you before—nobody offers to answer questions unless they *want* to. Don't ignore offers of help!

If they don't specifically offer help—here's how you contact them.

First of all, research them on-line, and then either e-mail or call them, remind them who you are and where you met, and ask for a fifteen minute informational interview at their convenience, saying you'd appreciate their advice. We talk about informational interviewing in Topic D, just below.

By the way, if you overindulged in alcoholic beverages at the event, don't draw attention to it in your follow up.

* * * CAREER LIMITING MOVE * * *

Law student at a national conference. He talked to a lawyer about other events worth attending. When the lawyer ran into him the next day, the student said, "Hey—sorry I was so wasted last night!"

The lawyer comments: "I actually thought we'd had a very interesting discussion. I had no idea he'd had too much to drink. It made me wonder: would he have been so interesting sober?"

On a related note: If people tell you to "keep in touch," see Topic E, below, on that very subject.

D. TALKING TO THE PEOPLE OTHER PEOPLE PUT YOU ONTO (AND THOSE YOU FIND YOURSELF): INFORMATIONAL INTERVIEWS

If you're diligent about talking to people and taking part in the activities we discuss in this chapter, you're going to have a lo-o-ot of informational interviews. That's the name given to the non-job-interview talks you have with anyone who's in a position to help you with your career goals.

Lewis and Clark's Lisa Lesage points out that informational interviews can help you in a multitude of ways. You can:

- Discover if a particular kind of job is something you really want to pursue;

- Learn the language and jargon associated with a practice area;

- Gain insight into how best to prepare yourself to enter this type of practice;

- Identify and cultivate relationships with people who've been successful doing what you want to do;

- Position yourself to be contacted when job openings occur;

- Build your self-confidence;

- Re-energize yourself by taking control of your situation and meeting with people who are content and satisfied.

It's very important to handle these conversations well. After all, you want to motivate the person in question to help you out. And on top of that, if someone else put you onto them, you've got that intermediary's reputation to think about. The last thing you need is for someone to call the person who gave you their name, and say, "Where did you find *this* chucklehead?"

Most importantly of all, you never know when an informational interview will result in an offer—even though it's not a *job* interview. As Albany's Joanne Casey says, "We've routinely had students talk to an attorney for advice, only to wind up being offered a call-back and a job. It's so important to impress the people you turn to for advice."

* * * SMART HUMAN TRICK * * *

New graduate of an East Coast law school. She sends a five-sentence e-mail to alums that practice family law in the city where she wants to live. The e-mail is nothing special; she asks for advice.

One alum writes back with some great advice. The new graduate writes back, thanking the alum profusely. They start an e-mail correspondence, which leads to a face to face meeting, which leads to a job offer.

Let's talk about how you handle informational interviews for maximum effect.

1. CONTACT THE PERSON AS SOON AS POSSIBLE AFTER YOU FIND OUT ABOUT THEM FROM SOMEONE ELSE

There are at least two good reasons to be hasty.

First, you want to nail a job as soon as possible, and the sooner you contact people the sooner you get your "career gears" in motion.

Second, you'll save the intermediary who gave you their name from any potential embarrassment. It often happens that if someone tells you to talk to someone else, they'll give that person a heads-up that you're going to call. If you don't do so promptly, you'll make them look bad.

On top of that you want to impress people who help you with your enthusiasm, which encourages them to help you more. If you casually blow off their suggestions on whom to contact, you're dissing them.

Of course, there are often great reasons for delay. Exams come to mind. When pursuing a lead just isn't practical, let your intermediary know: "Thanks for telling me about Attorney Flapdoodle. I intend to contact her [when], after [event]." If it's a month or two hence, so be it.

2. RESEARCH THE INTERVIEWEE BEFORE YOU CALL FOR AN INTERVIEW

Before you even call for an interview, find out all you can about the interviewee, just as you would for a job interview. An obvious place to start is the contact who put you on to them; ask that person for the kind of information you ought to seek, what the interviewee is like, anything special to mention or avoid mentioning.

If you've got the time, you can use the kinds of sources we discussed when we talked about researching interviewers in Chapter 9 on Interviewing. At the very least, check out the interviewee's profile on their employer's website, on Martindale Hubbell (www.martindale.com), and google them.

I suggest researching them *before* you contact them, because they may well say to you, "I've got a few minutes right now. What do you want to know?" You don't want to be caught off-guard. So do your research ahead of time!

The research is crucial because you don't want to waste the person's time with questions you could have answered yourself ahead of time. You'll have only a few minutes with the person. You don't want to ask them, "So where did you go to school?" "Was X your first job?" if all of that's covered online or your contact could have told you.

Also, it's a matter of respect ... and gaining their respect. They'll shut down and wonder about whether you're worth helping if you open with a question you could easily have ascertained ahead of time.

3. CONTACTING THE PERSON IN THE FIRST PLACE

A. COLD E-MAILING: CONTACTING PEOPLE YOU FIND YOURSELF

There's nothing that stops you from reaching out to anybody in the entire world. The Internet doesn't just put them at your fingertips ... it gives you a means of figuring out who to contact.

1. THE CATEGORIES OF PEOPLE YOU SEEK OUT:

a. People with whom you share a "mutuality."

Elaine Petrossian recommends that you contact people with whom you share something in common. They'll be more motivated to help you because of it.

The mutuality can be just about anything, including:

- Law school or undergraduate school (which you can determine with a Lexis/Nexis or Westlaw search ... or a painstaking Martindale/Hubbell search):
- Ethnicity (look for group memberships and languages spoken);
- A shared experience (similar job background or Peace Corps, a fraternity/sorority, a political campaign, and so on).

b. "Goal" targets: People who do what you want to do, or people you'd like to work for.

As I've mentioned before, the one thing of which you can be sure is that anyone who does what you want knows a lot of other people who do the same thing.

How do you find them? Many of the strategies we've talked about in this chapter work just great, including:

- Summer clerkship evaluations that are compiled by your Career Services Office;
- Career Services Counselors at school;
- People you've seen speak;
- Articles. Look for:
  - Attorneys profiled who do what you want to do;
  - Articles about practicing law that mention lawyers;
  - Articles about legal issues/cases that quote lawyers;
  - The journalists who write law-related articles;
  - Lawyers who write about cutting-edge issues;

- "The Top X Number of Lawyers In Y" articles.

2. HOW TO CONTACT THEM

By letter or e-mail, drop them a line.

If you share something in common, tell them how you found them, who you are (law student at X, for instance), what you have in common, and use that as a way of introducing the fact that you'd like some advice from them: "I know that you do X, and I'm really interested in learning more about it ..."

If they're geographically desirable, you might ask if you can meet with them for fifteen minutes, at their convenience, to get their advice. Assure them that you only want an informational interview and that you will *not* be asking for a job. And tell them that if it's more convenient for them to answer your questions by phone or e-mail, you completely understand. Give them your contact information, and end with a thank you.

Then: you wait. You can call to follow up in two weeks if you like, or send another e-mail, referring to your first one.

After that ... pick up with topic (c), below, "Contact 'hiccups'."

If they are "goal" targets, your approach has to be a little more subtle.

In your letter or e-mail, let them know:

- How you found them; ("I read about you in X publication ...") ("I noticed you quoted in the Sun Herald Picayune about the Y case ...")
- That you admire what they've done, were interested in hearing what they had to say, "You've given me a standard to aspire to," whatever fits the circumstance.

Then you can tell them that you're in law school, and you one day hope to do what they do (or whatever it is that you'd like to do). Tell them if they have five minutes to spare you'd appreciate advice about a couple of career questions you have. Promise them you're not asking them for a job. Give them your contact information, and thank them.

To tell you the truth, if your first communique ends with telling them about what you admire about them, you've done a great job. Virtually nobody ignores a "fan letter," especially lawyers who don't get many of them!

* * * SMART HUMAN TRICK * * *

Female law student, Midwestern law school. She sees an article in a legal publication about "The Fifty Best Women Lawyers In X," the city where she goes to school.

She makes a point of contacting the ones who do what she's interested in, congratulating them on making the list. She doesn't ask for anything; she just says, "You've given me a standard to aspire to."

Every single one of them responded to her. She reports, "They couldn't have been more gracious. A few of them said, 'If I can ever help you . . .' and you know I took them up on it!"

* * * SMART HUMAN TRICK * * *

Law student from Virginia, going to law school in California. She wants to go home to Virginia to practice. She searches on-line for lawyers who went to her undergrad school in Virginia. She checks to see who her college football team—we'll call them the slugs—are playing this weekend. Let's call the opponent the pirates. In the subject line of her e-mails to all five alums she writes, "I'll bet the slugs will pummel the pirates this weekend." She nails an informational interview with all five alums.

3. PICK UP THE REST OF YOUR STRATEGY STARTING WITH TOPIC (c), "CONTACT HICCUPS," BELOW.

B. CONTACTING PEOPLE OTHERS PUT YOU ONTO

1. Contact them by e-mail, letter or phone. If you call, leave a voice-mail (off-hours) or send an e-mail *first*, letting them know you'll be calling.

2. Always mention the name of your mutual acquaintance *first*, in order to form a bridge with your contact.

I've mentioned before that human beings are by nature risk-averse. If you lead with the name of someone the other person recognizes, it gives them comfort because someone else has already checked you out. So that name comes first.

Let's say a person named Ethelbald Grimmetz led me to you.

If I leave you a voice mail, I'd open with, "Hi. I'm Kimm Walton. Ethelbald Grimmetz recommended that I contact you."

If I send you an e-mail, I'd put Ethelbald Grimmetz's name in the subject line.

If I send you a letter, I'd open with the line, "Ethelbald Grimmetz recommended that I contact you."

3. Whether by E-Mail, Letter or Phone, Give a *Very* Brief Description of Who You Are

At this point, you've got your listener/reader hooked because you've mentioned the name of a mutual acquaintance. All you want to do is to add something to "place" you. "I'm a second year law student at Case Western, and I met Ethelbald when we went to a CLE seminar on the new discovery rules last week." Include a brief statement of your background or interest in the interviewer's field, location, whatever drew you to them. Make it short. A lengthy discourse about how your trek in the Himalayas had you sitting on a mountaintop contemplating what to do with your life . . . you'll wear them out.

4. State What You're Looking for. But Not Really

What you're *really* looking for is a job.

You're not going to say that, because doing so will put the person on the spot. It gives them a chance to say "We're not hiring." Click. As Gail Cutter points out, "If you ask them a question they can't answer, like 'Can you get me a job?' it makes you both feel bad." Maureen Provost Ryan adds, "You don't build rapport by asking for a job!"

If, instead, **you ask them for what they can *easily* give you—advice, information, and referrals about jobs that interest you, ways to break into the field**—you might get solid leads, *and* you've left the door open in case they *do* have a job opening. If they don't have one right now but one comes up, you've forged a relationship so that they'll think of you when the time comes.

There are a couple of ways to go. Shannon Kelly advises that "**You can start by sending specific requests, answers to specific questions, just to get the conversation started**." For instance, you could ask about how to spin something in your background, whether a certain course/clinical experience/CLE/activity would be helpful to breaking into what they do—really, anything. What you want is to get the career advice pipeline going. If they respond positively, you can always go on and request a face-to-face meeting.

As that last sentence suggests, **requesting a face-to-face meeting is the other alternative**. Ultimately, that's what you want: a meeting, in person, where you can get advice. **If that is geographically impossible (or inconvenient for the person), a phone meeting is the next best choice.**

As a means of getting that meeting, you want to say something about how you're interested in X type of practice, or practicing in X city, and that's why your mutual acquaintance Ethelbald Grimmetz recommended that you make the contact. You can say something like, "If your schedule permits, I'd like to set up an informational interview with you. I'd like to take you to lunch (or out for a cup of coffee, or 'I'd appreciate fifteen minutes of your time') at your convenience, to learn more about what you do. I'd really appreciate any advice you can give me."

As we've discussed before, this is looking for what Rob Kaplan calls AIR: Advice, Information, and Referrals. As he points out, nobody minds giving someone AIR!

Notice that you're not saying that you're *not* looking for a job. You can assure them that you won't be asking them for a job, because you won't; but it doesn't mean you're not in the market! As Debra Fink points out, "Don't say 'I'm not looking for a job, I'm only looking for advice ...' if you really *are* ultimately looking for a job. Because if you say that, you're shutting the door to a potential employer." If you don't mention it at all and a job opening comes up in the discussion, you haven't been dishonest.

So ask for a meeting, at their convenience. Make the time short—fifteen minutes is good—so they won't feel like they're blowing a whole morning or afternoon on it. And drench your request in gratefulness. Remember: most people are hard wired to be helpful, and the odds are overwhelmingly in your favour that they'll give you at least a few minutes.

5. CLOSE YOUR VOICE-MAIL, E-MAIL OR LETTER WITH A STATEMENT OF WHEN YOU'LL BE CALLING TO SCHEDULE A MEETING. AND FINISH WITH A SINCERE THANK YOU!

6. IF YOU LEAVE A VOICE-MAIL MESSAGE, CONSIDER FOLLOWING THIS BASIC FORMAT:

"Hi. My name is _____. X recommended that I contact you because of your expertise in _____/ you do _____/ you know about _____.

I'm a 1L/2L/3L/grad of X law school.

I'm interested in learning more about ...

I have a background in/I am interested in X because of Y. (Make this short—no more than thirty seconds, if that.)

I'd appreciate talking with you for fifteen minutes to learn more about what you do/seek your advice.

Again, my name is X. My phone number is X. That phone number: X. (Always say your number twice, and repeat your name at the end of your message so the person doesn't have to listen to it again.)

I look forward to speaking with you."

You may come up with wording that works better for you, and if so, by all means, use it! But you see the point here: Get across your message quickly, with the name of your contact in the lead. Ideally you'll be talking to this person very soon, and you'll have an opportunity to get into more detail about anything you want to mention!

7. DON'T SEND A RESUME AND DON'T OFFER TO SEND A RESUME; *ONLY* SEND A RESUME IF THE PERSON ASKS YOU FOR ONE

This is really a corollary of the idea that you're not looking for a *job* interview, you're looking for an *informational* interview. You don't have a lot of credibility if you say you're looking for information and then you send a resume with your e-mail or letter.

While it's not a big deal, you shouldn't even *offer* to send your resume. It may well be that the person is willing to give you a few minutes to answer questions, but reviewing your resume is a burden they're not willing to undertake. If you say "Can I send you my resume?" You're demanding more time, and there's no gracious way to say "No."

Instead, let them bring up the issue of your resume. If they ask for it, send it immediately.

If they don't, bring it with you to the interview, "under cover"—that is, in a portfolio or briefcase.

8. HAVE YOUR CALENDAR IN FRONT OF YOU WHEN YOU TALK TO THEM

As Tasha Everman recommends, "You need to be prepared to schedule a date and time, on the spot." Remember: they're doing you a favour. Don't make their life difficult by scrambling around for your schedule information, or worst yet, scheduling a meeting you can't really make.

c. CONTACT "HICCUPS"—HOW TO GET AROUND OBSTACLES WHEN THEY ARISE

1. WHAT IF THEY SAY NO?

Most people are happy to offer you advice. The emphasis here is on the word "most." Sometimes people won't be forthcoming. Maybe they're busy. They're having a bad day. A personal crisis. Maybe they're just a jerk.

If they just can't or won't help you, you've lost nothing. If they say "No," respond with, "That's all right. Can you refer me to someone else who might be able to help?" And if that still nets a zero, so be it. It doesn't reflect on you. Be gracious—say, "Thank you, anyway"—go to the next person on your list, take a deep breath, and forge ahead!

Don't under any circumstances respond in kind. *Especially* not by e-mail, which we have all learned lasts forever. Remember: This person may turn out to be a colleague. Maybe when they're having a good day they'll be very helpful to you. There's no point in burning professional bridges over minor slights. Take the high road and be nice and polite no matter how people treat you: it's the least risk alternative.

2. WHAT IF YOU TRY AND TRY AND JUST CAN'T GET THROUGH TO THEM?

Maybe you're diligent, you contact people and then call back when they tell you to. Maybe they tell you they're too busy to talk, or they don't respond at all. What should you do?

Step one is to tell the person who put you onto them that you're having trouble getting through. Maybe they'll tell you to keep trying; maybe they'll offer to try and contact the person themselves.

Step two: acknowledge that maybe now is not the best time for this person. Maybe they're truly incredibly busy or otherwise distracted. Don't jump ugly with them and don't be resentful; there are times in your own life when you're less than available.

Step three: When it's pretty obvious this dog won't hunt, send an acknowledgement that's polite: "I understand that this isn't the best time for us to talk. Thanks anyway. I hope we have an opportunity to meet in the future," words along those lines fit the bill. No angry words, and remember you're leaving the door open in case they really do wind up being open to helping you.

D. Send an E-Mail or Letter Thanking Them for Agreeing to Meet or Talk With You. Confirm the Date, Time, Place, and Purpose

E. If You Are Meeting Somewhere Unfamiliar, Get Directions!

Whether it's from Google maps, MapQuest or someone at the location (if it's a restaurant, say), make sure you have accurate directions as well as some notion of how long it'll take to get there. Aim to arrive comfortably early—ten or fifteen minutes.

F. Check Your Voice-Mail and E-Mail Right Before You Leave to Make Sure the Interviewer Hasn't Had a Change Of Plans, or Has Any Last-Minute Instructions

G. If You Don't Know the Person and You're Meeting in a Public Place, Ascertain How You'll Know Them

Tell them what you'll be wearing and some basic description of yourself. Also, if it's in a restaurant, be sure to tell the host(ess) that you're waiting for someone.

H. If You're Meeting at a Restaurant/Café, Offer to Pay

And remember to bring your wallet. The person may offer to pay—everybody remembers being a starving law student—and it's fine to take them up on it. But you should be willing to pay. After all, they're doing you a favour.

* * * CAREER LIMITING MOVE AFTER MOVE AFTER MOVE * * *

From a professional career consultant:

"Last week I had an informational interview lunch meeting with a law student we will call Bill. He was referred to me by a professor who is a good friend. Bill called, and we scheduled a lunch. I picked a place close to the university which he didn't know, but I gave him the restaurant's name and the street on which it was located. He called back in five minutes saying he needed to change the date, which I did. He said he would send me an e-mail to confirm. He never did. He did say that he might be a few minutes late as he was coming after class and sometimes class lasted a bit long.

"I went to the restaurant and waited. And waited. And waited. He was thirty minutes late. He came in and asked me if I was Sarah. (My name is Mary.) He didn't say his name. He then went to find the hostess. He came back again and asked if I was Sarah. I said no, but was he Bill? So I told him I was Mary, not Sarah. He apologized for being late, although he said he had called the restaurant and they had given him bad directions.

We sat down and he said, "Well, I guess you didn't get my e-mail if you aren't Sarah." I said I hadn't, and he went on, "If two wrongs don't make a right, what do three wrongs make?"

When the bill arrived—I promise I wasn't paying—he looked for his wallet, and realized he'd left it in his car. As he went out to get it he said, "I promise I didn't do it on purpose."

Throughout our meeting he told me what great communications skills he had. (Interesting, since he had just fouled up just about every line of communication he'd tried.) And at some point he said he was glad it wasn't a *real* interview. (Informational interviews *are* real interviews. I charge by the minute to see people, and this was a freebie.)

Soon afterward, I got an e-mail from him thanking me for my time, apologizing for his lateness, and indicating that he had "broken every cardinal sin regarding interviewing." And that the restaurant shouldn't go into the directions business.

I'm on the fence about how I feel about this guy. Maybe if I'd been a different person—more time-driven, more A-type—it would have been a disaster. But he did a pretty good job of poking fun at himself, and managed to pull himself at least slightly out of the fire.

4. THE DAY OF THE INTERVIEW . . .

Dress professionally, as though you were going to a job interview. Remember: You don't know where this interview will lead. You want the interviewer to look at you as a potential colleague and/or someone they'll feel comfortable recommending to other people. You don't accomplish that by showing up in a belly shirt and flip-flops.

Take a copy of your resume; tuck it discreetly into a portfolio, envelope-style purse or briefcase.

Show up no more than five minutes early, but don't be late!

As for a job interview, if there is a receptionist or assistant at your interviewee's office, be *very* nice to them. People take the opinions of their support staffers very seriously, and so you want to make a good impression.

5. When the Interview Starts . . .

When you meet your interviewee, they'll probably extend their hand to shake hands and say hello. If they don't, initiate the handshake, at the same time saying something like, "Thanks for taking the time to talk with me. I really appreciate it." (Remember, honest enthusiasm is irresistible. And if you're not enthusiastic about this interview, you shouldn't be here!)

6. Conducting the Interview—Questions to Ask

When you actually sit down to talk, remember that *you're* the interviewer. You're the one who's asking questions (although, of course, if the interviewee has questions for you, answer them!).

What kinds of questions should you ask? It depends, of course, where you are in your job search and what concerns you.

Part of the beauty of informational interviews is that you aren't expected to have the knowledge you'd have for a job interview. Gaining knowledge is the reason you're there! For instance, if you were interviewing a judge, you could ask what interning in his/her chambers would involve, whereas if you were interviewing for a clerkship you'd be expected to know that.

- **If you have specific questions about your credentials** . . . you can ask about how (and whether) to present items on your resume, whether to include certain activities/hobbies, and what else you might do to improve your chances of breaking into the field.

   If they do critique your credentials, for gosh sakes don't get defensive! Remember: You can't get better at *anything* if nobody tells you what you're doing wrong. If you agree with the criticism, say something like, "Yes, I can see that. Thanks."

   If you disagree with it, don't jump ugly. First, ask their rationale: "I'm curious about your thinking on that." Sometimes their reasoning will resound with you.

   If not, say something like, 'I see. Thanks.' Remember: You can always bounce their advice off someone else (like a career counselor at school). And you don't *have* to change *anything*. But if you're a P in the A when they say 'boo' to you, they won't want to help you.

- **You can ask questions you've dug up as a result of your research** . . . show off the fact that you know something about the interviewee. "I know that you took part in the Journal of Phlegm Reclamation Law at the Millard Fillmore Law School. Was it helpful to you? Do you think I ought to try it?" "You did an internship with the Spite Fence Project. What kinds of internships do you think would help me?"

- **You can ask about activities you should take part in, what you should read and subscribe to, organizations to join, events to attend.**

- **You can ask about what resources the professional organizations have to offer. Ask if the person you're talking to goes to meetings, and if you feel comfortable with them, ask if you can tag along.**

- **You can ask what kinds of experiences are helpful or necessary in the field, what kinds of people succeed in the field and what skills are necessary, what they look for in people they hire.**

- **You can ask for interviewing tips.**

- **You can ask geographical information—about the legal job market in the person's location, or where they think their specialty is thriving.**

- **You can address special concerns—e.g., if you're a woman, you might ask about women's advancement at an employer or type of employer, or ask about the employers who offer flex-time or part-time work.**

- **You can ask them about their background** ... ask questions that get at how they got where they are. How did they decide on a practice area? Did they do clerkships or internships during school, and do they think you should do them? How did they get their job at X? What classes did they find most useful? Which were a waste of time? Are there any CLEs they think you'd find useful?

- **You can ask about their feelings about their current job** ... What professional publications do they read? What do they wish they'd known about before they started working here? If they had to do anything else, what would their second choice be? What's a typical day/week like for them? What's the most interesting project they've worked on recently? What do they like best about their work? What do they wish they could change?

- **You can ask where they see the specialty going in the future.**

- **You can ask them the best piece of career advice they ever received.** Gee, it would be great if it was a book they read, and if that book happened to be ... sigh.

- **You can ask to call them back with other questions in future!**

7. **QUESTION CAVEATS**

   A. **DON'T ASK ABOUT ANYTHING YOU CAN'T DISCUSS INTELLIGENTLY**

   You may have found out something about the interviewee that involves highly technical knowledge. If you can't carry on a conversation about the issue, don't bring it up. "So, I saw that in the patent application you filed for the ossification gene, you stated that the liposomes on the site are subject to the exclusive licensing rights of your client. Can you tell me more about that?" A question like that doesn't help you much unless you're a techno-whiz, in which case you know I made all that stuff up.

B. DON'T HAVE A SET LIST OF QUESTIONS TO ASK; FOLLOW WHERE THE ANSWERS LEAD

Remember: you're not just here for information. You want to have a *conversation*. You want to impress the interviewee so that if they have a job opening or they know someone who has one, you're the person they'll think of first.

C. DON'T ASK A QUESTION FROM THIS LIST JUST BECAUSE YOU THINK IT'LL SOUND GOOD

The whole point of conducting informational interviews is to learn what you really want to learn. Ask those questions and those questions only!

D. BE CAREFUL HOW YOU PHRASE QUESTIONS

Be tactful. For instance, if you want to know about pay, ask discreetly: "What would a new associate/lawyer in this field expect to make?" Honestly, you can find out about pay a lot of ways other than bringing up the very sensitive subject with people. At Career Services at school, you'll find national statistics on pay for lawyers in all kinds of settings. And there's always Salaries.com.

Whatever you do, don't *ever* ask "How much do you make?" Students have done it, and it's *ugly*.

Similarly, for hours, you can ask, but don't betray emotion at the response. If they say they typically work from 7 a.m. to 9 p.m., don't say "Ouch!" or "You're kidding, right?"

E. IT'S OK TO TAKE NOTES

In a job interview, you'd never take notes. But when you're gathering information, it's fine. If you do take notes, however, don't get so wrapped up in writing that you ignore what the person is saying. Eye contact is important, as is active listening; nodding your head, saying "Yes," "I see," to let them know you're listening carefully.

8. DON'T FORGET THAT THEY MAY TURN OUT TO BE COLLEAGUES. NO TMI

Remember, these are *professional* acquaintances, not friends. Don't disclose things you wouldn't want colleagues to know. "I'm lazy," "I like to party . . ." Swell. Don't tell!

9. WHAT IF THEY DISCOURAGE YOU?

What if, contrary to the song, you *do* hear a discouraging word? I've talked with students who've had lawyers tell them dismissively, "Oh, you don't want to do *that!*"

When people try to talk you out of your dream, what's behind it? There are a number of potential reasons:

- They do it and they don't like it.

- They think, based on whatever they know of you, that you won't like it.

- Your goal is very difficult to attain and they don't want you to undergo those travails.

- They're testing your mettle to see if you've got the guts to stand up for yourself.

- They do it, they like it, but they're having a bad day/week/year.

There are others, but here in general is the strategy you use in the face of negatives:

a. **Don't immediately give up because someone tells you to.**

   You might love the job and you might be up to the challenge.

b. **Ask them *why* they're telling you what they're telling you.**

   "The hours are brutal," "Nobody's hiring in that," "People who do that are jerks," "That firm's a sweatshop," "It's boring."

   With specifics in hand you can dig deeper to see if it's still something you want, and even bounce the comment off other people to verify it.

c. **If your goal is still attractive to you, say so. "I appreciate your input, but it's still what I want. Can you help me?"**

d. **Remember: it's *your* life. Don't make someone's casual, negative comment your mantra.**

   I'm very sensitive to this. I've mentioned before that I created the *Law In A Flash* cards, and got three years of constant rejection and criticism of the idea before any bookstore bought it. I was convinced I was right, but virtually nobody else was. I'm not saying you should hold tenaciously to your dream for the sake of tenacity. Listen to what people tell you, even the negatives. But if you're still determined, hold on!

10. KEEP ONE EYE ON THE CLOCK

If you asked for fifteen minutes, when it gets within a few minutes of that deadline, say something like, "Look at the time! I said I'd only take up X minutes of your time, and that's a couple of minutes away."

That gives them an opportunity to say, "Oh, don't worry about that," or "OK." If the deadline is firm, you move to the two questions in #11 and #12, below. Either way, you've shown your courtesy. If they do have to stick to the deadline and you've got a lot more to ask, you can always ask for another meeting later on.

11.   THE SECOND-TO-LAST QUESTION YOU SHOULD ALWAYS ASK . . .

"Who else do you think I should be talking to? What else should I be doing?"

Remember, when you're making contact with people, you want to multiply those contacts. People can put you on to other people who put you on to other people . . . and you don't know when the next person you talk to will be the key to getting the job of your dreams.

If the person you're talking to gives you other names, make sure you write down the name(s) on the spot as well as any contact information the person gives you, to ensure you get it right. Ask the interviewee if you can say they referred you to these new contacts. Inevitably the answer will be "yes." And then you can open your first missive to *that* person with the seven magic words, "So-and-so recommended that I contact you . . ."

12.   THE LAST QUESTION YOU SHOULD ASK . . .

"May I leave you my resume, in case you come across some-one I should talk to?"

This is the excellent advice of Lisa Lesage. She advises that you ask for people to talk to, not just job openings. "Never say, 'If you know of someone who's hiring . . .' You want to leave it broader than that."

Assuming that the interview went well, it's appropriate to produce your resume at the end of the interview. After you've talked to a person, they're not going to be worried that you're actually going to hound them for a job. You've asked for advice, information, referrals, and assuming you had a good discussion, you've paved the way to leave your credentials.

Here's why this is such a good idea. Lawyers often tell me that they talk to law students they really like, but they don't have anything to offer them at the moment. Lisa Lesage says that "Lawyers talk to each other all of the time. When I was practicing, I'd have a file of resumes of people I'd talked to."

Maybe a few weeks will go by, and a lawyer you meet with will talk with a friend who'll say something about needing someone new at the office. At that point, the lawyer will say, "Oh, I just talked to a student you should meet." If you left your resume with them, they'll have your contact information at their fingertips. If you *didn't*, they may well forget your name!

So leave your resume with them, so that when they hear of something you ought to pursue, they'll know how to contact you.

13.   THANK THE INTERVIEWEE PROFUSELY FOR THEIR TIME

Remember—the interviewee's time is as valuable to them as yours is to you. Even a few minutes, even if it's over the phone, is a favour. Tell them how much you appreciate their advice, and that you'll keep them posted on your progress.

14. "DEBRIEF" YOURSELF

As soon as possible after the interview, jot down everything you want to remember from what the interviewee said. If they didn't say anything you found particularly useful, make a few cursory notes anyway, in case you ever have to refer back to the meeting for any reason. Keep a file of these notes, virtually or in a binder, including the kind of information I've told you before to maintain on people you meet:

- the name of the interviewee
- their position
- contact information
- who referred you to them
- when you met
- what was discussed
- any people they referred you to, and
- any subsequent action you took, like sending them a thank you note or contacting the people they referred you to.

15. SEND A THANK YOU ... AND IF YOU FORGOT TO BRING YOUR RESUME WITH YOU, SEND IT ALONG

For every informational interview you conduct, send a thank you note. It can be handwritten, if your handwriting is good. Note cards with a picture of your law school on the front work great. You can use an e-mail if you want, but it's not as memorable as a physical note.

In the note, mention any piece of advice you found particularly helpful, thank them for any referrals they gave you (and state whether or not you've contacted them, and if you haven't, when you *will* do so), and state that you'll be in touch again.

If you didn't bring your resume with you *and* the interview went well, send it with your thank you. As Lisa Lesage says, "Just include it and say that you'd appreciate their passing it along if they know of someone you should talk to."

George Washington University Law School uses the following simple example of an appropriate thank you note. (Don't copy it word for word; it's just here to give you an idea of what to say):

"Thank you so much for taking the time out of your busy schedule to meet with me yesterday. I appreciate the information and advice you gave me about the market for environmental attorneys in Houston. I will follow up with Mr. Smith as you suggested and I have already called for information about the Women's Bar Association. Again, thank you for your time."

16. PURSUE ANY NEW LEADS THE WAY YOU PURSUED THE FIRST ONE!

Just go back to square one, do your research, make your calls, and set up your interviews.

17. WHEN YOU SETTLE ON A JOB LET YOUR CONTACTS KNOW

Remember, when you make contacts, you're setting up a professional network you should maintain . . . and that means letting people know what's going on with you. Just a quick note to get your name back in front of them, stating what you've decided to do, and thanking them for their help, is pretty much all that's needed.

It's important to remember that great opportunities come about in unexpected ways. You'll switch jobs, probably many times, in your career. You don't know when someone you once met will be a colleague. So keep people thinking well of you.

18. REMEMBER THAT IT'S A TWO-WAY STREET: WHEN YOU HAVE ANYTHING OF INTEREST FOR PEOPLE WHO HELP YOU OUT, SEND IT ALONG

You may see an article on-line that involves a hobby or interest or professional goal of someone you've interviewed. Maybe you see their employer's name mentioned (in a positive way). Be as useful to the people you've met as they've been to you, and send them articles/links/information that will be useful to them. "I know your firm just started representing wineries. I heard from a friend of mine who's a wine merchant that a new winery is opening in the state. I thought you might be interested . . ." Making yourself useful to people is the very best way to keep them interested in what happens to you.

E. KEEPING IN TOUCH WITH PEOPLE

Students ask me about this all the time: "How do I keep in touch with people after I talked with them? I feel *stupid*. I don't know what to say."

Especially when people say "Keep in touch," you want to touch base every so often. How do you do it?

1. IF THEY'RE A POTENTIAL EMPLOYER, LET THEM KNOW EVERY TIME YOU GET NEW, GOOD GRADES OR EXPERIENCES, PAID OR VOLUNTEER, CLINICAL OR OFF-CAMPUS, OR IF YOU HAVE SUCCESS IN A COMPETITION OR ACTIVITY

They're not your parents. You're not sending your report card. But you do want to reiterate your interest in them when you have something new to bring to the table. Contacting them every four months or so doesn't put you on the ugh-not-him/her-again list by a long shot.

2. WHETHER THEY'RE A POTENTIAL EMPLOYER OR A HELPFUL CONTACT, FOCUS ON WHAT WILL BE OF INTEREST TO *THEM*

This outstanding advice comes courtesy of Andy Epstein, a lawyer and entrepreneur who's had a wild variety of experiences—and knows everything there is to know about dealing with people. His technique: "I keep any articles that will interest people I talk to. I clip or download the articles and send them along, *especially* if the people in question are mentioned or quoted. This works so much better for me than leaving a voice mail saying, 'Hi, just wanted to say hello.' You don't want people to think, 'This kid's just a *pest.*'"

F.   Job Fairs: How to Excel at Any Fair Without a Carousel

There are all kinds of job fairs: ones that are regional, ones that appeal to minorities, ones focusing on certain practice areas. Some are "by invitation only," that is, open only to students of certain schools. (If you're frozen out of one of these fairs, don't worry. Remember there are *always* ways to approach employers outside of job fairs.)

Perhaps the two most famous law career job fairs are the Equal Justice Works Fair (in Washington DC every Fall—a "must" for any student interested in public interest), and the Patent Law Program in Chicago every Spring—just the place to be if you're interested in Intellectual Property. (To find a complete run-down on the job fairs available to law students, check the website www.nalp.org/schools/fairlist.htm)

Employers like job fairs because they get to see students from several—sometimes many—schools in one place. Perhaps less obviously, employers get to test student enthusiasm for them. After all, if you make your way to a job fair to talk to an employer, you're probably pretty interested in working for them.

The fairs are typically free to attendees. Your only expense is for travel, but if the fair is far away and in a major city, that expense can be formidable. Check with your Career Services Office, because if enough students are interested in the same job fair, they'll often arrange for group travel at a discount. You can also road trip it with interested classmates.

Job fairs have various formats. Some of them have totally pre-screened interviews; that is, you submit your resume ahead of time and you're notified as to who wants to interview you at the fair. At others, you can sign up for interviews while you're there. Many feature presentations by speakers as well as "table talk"; that is, employers man tables and give informal informational interviews to student attendees.

Job fairs can be a great opportunity for you, if you know how to work them. Let's talk about it.

1.   Only Submit Your Credentials to Job Fairs And Employers You're Serious About

As Emory's Supria Kuppuswamy recommends, "Don't ever submit your materials simply to get 'a job'!" She points out that there are several good reasons for this:

- While you might think you can fool an employer into thinking you're sincerely interested in their geographical market or practice area, odds are they'll see through it;

- You'll hurt your school and other schools involved in the fair. If employers get a sense that students don't have sincere interest, they may decide not to participate in the fair again;

- You're taking away potential opportunities for another student who may have a strong interest in the market or employer. You wouldn't want them to do that to you;

- You're wasting time pursuing something that isn't a genuine interest. Plus, if an employer thinks you're wasting their time, you may have burned a bridge which may come back to haunt you later in your career.

Throughout this chapter we've learned dozens of ways to get to employers you genuinely want to work for. And with the plethora of job fairs out there, there are bound to be some that *will* genuinely interest you. Focus on those!

2. RESEARCH RESEARCH RESEARCH

I know I sound like a broken freaking record when it comes to research, but really, it's so easy on-line, there's no excuse not to do it. No recruiter is going to be thrilled to hear you ask, "So what do you guys do?" For employers you're targeting, be sure you do your research ahead of time. You can always take notes and tuck them discreetly into a pocket, bag or purse, and go over them in the restroom at the fair.

3. FOLLOW RULES *CAREFULLY*

Be sure that you are familiar with Job Fair requirements *before* you schedule interviews or send credentials. For instance, as Supria Kuppus-wamy points out, "Many job fairs have a rule that if you are selected for two or more interviews, you *must* attend the fair unless you have accepted a job offer. These rules are in place for a reason; namely, to ensure that the fair is well-attended and the employers get to see the candidates they want to see."

In addition, when it comes to sending credentials ahead of time, send *exactly* what the employers request *and no more*. If they want solely a resume, tailor that resume and *don't* send a cover letter. As Beth Kirch points out, "They get four FedEx boxes of resumes. There's a reason they ask for what they ask for." You can always expand your opportunities once you get to the Fair, as we discuss below; but ahead of time, send them what—and *only* what—they request.

* * * SMART HUMAN TRICK * * *

Law student at a Midwestern school reads about a diversity job fair down South. He diligently reads the promotional literature, and can't find a definition of 'diversity' anywhere in it. Reasoning that "geography can be a type of diversity," he registers for the job fair, figuring that "Our law school admits students based on geographical diversity, so maybe it will apply for this fair, too."

He signs up for an interview with an employer, and the first question the employer asks him is: "This is a diversity fair. What makes you diverse?" The student, at a loss, throws his hands up and says, "I am white, male, and straight as can be. From most perspectives I don't offer anything diverse, but I am from the Midwest. I hope you'll consider that!"

He gets the job.

4. Call the Employer the Day Before the Job Fair and Ask Whom They're Sending to the Fair. In Addition, Print Out the Martindale–Hubbell Information for All Lawyers at the Employer (or the Specific Office Represented) and Bring It to the Fair.

Whether it's the lawyers manning tables or lawyers conducting interviews, you want to know ahead of time who'll be there so you can research them. However, as Supria Kuppuswamy points out, "Even if interviewer names are provided in advance, they frequently change at the last minute."

"If you bring your laptop with you, you might have wireless access so you can do quick research on your interviewers. But you may not want to bring your laptop, and even if you do, you might not have wireless access. So go to www.martindale.com and print out a list of all of the attorneys at the particular employer or office to bring with you to the job fair, so you have some information on the attorneys with whom you may be interviewing in case of a last minute change."

5. Bring Many Copies of Your Resume

If there are going to be different types of employers at the fair, target your resume at the employers you're most interested in.

If it turns out that an employer who doesn't fit that category asks for your resume, you can always ask for their business card and tell them you'll send it to them immediately after the fair. That way, you can slant your resume as we discussed in the resume chapter before you send it to them.

6. Arrive Early

Job Fairs wear out employers. You want to catch them when they're still bright-eyed and bushy-tailed, to the extent they could ever be described thusly. So show up as close to the start time as you can. You won't look nerdy. It's not a party where you show up fashionably late. You'll look enthusiastic, and that's exactly what you want.

7. If the Fair Is Crowded, and You Don't Have One Target Employer You're Jonesing to See, Go to Employers Farthest From the Entrance Door First

Have you ever seen "The Unofficial Guide To Disney World?" It tells you how to hit every ride at Disney without waiting in line. It's awesome. The tip that's relevant to job fairs is to do things in a different order than most people do them. Most people will show up at a job fair and go to the table closest to them, and work their way around. To avoid crowds, do just the opposite: start further away and work your way back.

Of course, if you've got a target employer or two, make a beeline for them so that you're first in line.

8. HAVE YOUR "INFOMERCIAL" READY

A brief introduction, with your first and last name, school and year in school, and a brief description of a couple of relevant accomplishments, what you want to do, maybe an interesting hobby or achievement ("I rafted the Nile," whatever). You never know when someone will ask you, "Tell me about yourself."

9. IF EMPLOYERS WHO INTEREST YOU HOLD INFORMATION SESSIONS/RECEPTIONS AT JOB FAIRS—GO TO THEM

If you're at a job fair, I don't care how badly you want to hang out in the bar—go to receptions and information sessions held by employers who interest you, and make a point of introducing yourself to the lawyers from there. Make sure they hear your name. And in your subsequent interview, make a point of bringing up the fact that you attended, and if it's an information session, ask a question related to what you learned at the session.

Yep. It's that important.

* * * SMART HUMAN TRICK * * *

Two law students from a New England school attend a regional job fair. There's a presentation by a District Attorney at lunch time. While they had applied for interviews with the DA, they didn't get one. They went to the presentation anyway, introduced themselves, and asked outright for interviews during the afternoon session. He said, "Sure."

They were the only two students at the fair to receive call-backs.

10. IF EMPLOYERS HAVE "TABLE TALK" SO THAT YOU CAN TALK TO SOMEONE FROM THE OFFICE—BE ABSOLUTELY SURE TO TALK TO THEM

It's hard to overstate the importance of this. I talked to a prosecutor who regularly mans tables at job fairs, and he said, "It's always the same. I'm sitting there by myself. Students sneak up to the table and grab brochures, and then they run away as though I'm radioactive. I'm not asking for wit. Just ask me about my job, what I like about it. That's all. I'll talk. That's why I'm there!"

Beth Kirch adds, "Many employers use table talk as a screening mechanism. It proves student commitment."

Here's an added benefit to chatting with the "table talk" lawyers: more often than I can count, I've heard from students who didn't nail an interview with an employer at a job fair ... but they so impressed the "table talk" lawyer that they were offered an interview on the spot!

* * * SMART HUMAN TRICK * * *

Law student from a Pennsylvania school attends a job fair. He talks to the attorney manning the table for an employer that interests him. The attorney asks him, "Have you ever considered working for X firm?" (another firm with the same focus). The student responds, "Sure," and the attorney tells him, "Hold on a minute." The attorney takes out his cell phone and calls a friend who works for another employer, and says, "I'm talking to a student right now who would be perfect for you."

The student winds up with an interview with the other firm ... and a job.

11. IF YOU DON'T KNOW ABOUT THE EMPLOYER BUT YOU'RE CURIOUS, GRAB THEIR WRITTEN MATERIALS, GO AWAY AND READ THEM, AND COME BACK WITH INTELLIGENT QUESTIONS

12. DRESS, PREPARE, AND RESEARCH THE INTERVIEWS YOU GET JUST AS YOU WOULD FOR ANY INTERVIEW. AND SEND THANK YOUS!

It's a mistake to view a job fair interview as anything less than a full-blown job audition. Prepare just as you would for any other interview. And that means reading chapter 9 on Interviews!

Furthermore, make sure that you're physically up to the challenge. Don't drink too much, eat a high-protein diet, and make sure you're well rested so that you're at your best!

* * * CAREER LIMITING MOVE * * *

Student goes to a job fair, where she has a scheduled interview with her dream employer at 4 o'clock in the afternoon.

She says, "I wanted to get some practice in for that interview, so I went on six interviews in the two hours before. One at two o'clock, one at two twenty, and so on.

"By the time my 'real' interview came around, I was totally burnt. I couldn't talk. I just sat there. I was hyperventilating. The interviewer was so nice about it. But that was the whole interview. Me not being able to talk, and her consoling me."

13. IF YOU DON'T GET AN INTERVIEW WITH AN EMPLOYER YOU WANT ...

Don't give up! For a start, take advantage of the table talk and any receptions/interview sessions the employer holds. Have your best, most enthusiastic, well-researched game face on. You can always angle for an interview there, or try to set one up "off-site." If you impress them, of course they'll want to talk with you regardless of whether you nailed a job fair interview or not.

On top of that, make sure to check with them to see if there are any cancellations or no shows. I don't want to say that students are sometimes irresponsible about living up to their responsibilities to interviewers, but ... sometimes students are irresponsible about living up to their responsibilities to interviewers. They don't show, and they don't call.

Their loss is your gain. If you're there and the interviewer has an open interview spot, they might as well interview you.

Also, see if they'll talk to you over lunch or at the end of the day for a few minutes. If you get ten minutes with a lawyer from the employer's office, face-to-face, that's a damn good chance to make a great impression. And they'll be impressed by your enthusiasm!

14. Always Get Names of People You Talk With Who Are Manning the Tables

Ask for business cards. They may not have one; if they don't, jot down the name on their nametag.

15. Don't Forget That Sitting at the Tables Are *Human Beings*

Job fairs can be frustrating and overwhelming. The crowds of people, the plethora of employers, the grab for interview slots, the exhaustion. But when you break it down, what you're looking at is a series of simple conversations with individual people, each of whom has feelings, too. The same techniques that work in every situation: taking an interest in others, asking questions, showing enthusiasm—work at job fairs, too.

* * * SMART HUMAN TRICK * * *

Law student from Florida, at a job fair. She's standing in a long line to talk to the woman manning the table for the ACLU. The student watches the woman, who is clearly getting bored and tired. She wearily takes resumes from each student in line.

When the student gets to the front of the line, she tells the woman, "You must be really tired of this. I can understand that."

The woman immediately perks up. The student goes on, "But this is a job that I really, really want. I'm interested in gay rights"—the student had researched the woman ahead of time, and knew it was her specialty—"and I'll do anything. I'll volunteer. I really want it."

The woman says, "Give me your resume. Let me set it aside for special consideration ..."

The student gets the job.

16. Don't Overlook Other Attendees as Potential Lead Sources

Sure, they're looking for a job, too. But it could well be that they've stumbled on job leads they don't want—due to geography or anything else—that you'd love. If you don't chat, you'll never know!

17. Follow up

Within one day, e-mail the people you spoke to. In the e-mail:

- Remind them of who you are;
- Reiterate your enthusiasm for the employer;
- Reiterate why you think you're qualified;
- Thank them!

* * * YOU CAN'T MAKE THIS STUFF UP * * *

Two law students drive to an out-of-town job fair together. The fair is at a hotel.

They both get interviews with a firm they really want to join.

At the end of the day, they stop by the hotel bar for a drink. The law firm's interviewer is sitting at the bar. He invites them to join him for a drink.

So they have a few pops with the interviewer. The bar is shutting down, and the interviewer says, "How about we continue the party in my suite?"

They say, "OK," and go to the interviewer's suite. They have a few more drinks there.

The interviewer takes the phone book from his night stand, and starts flipping through it. He looks up at the students. "What do you say we wind up the evening with a couple of hookers? Two for me—one for each of you."

The students are horrified, and start mumbling about "Gee, it's late," "Thanks anyway," "We've got a long drive tomorrow ..."

The lawyer says, "Come on. Don't worry about it ... the firm will pay."

The students make a hasty exit.

P.S.: They both wind up with offers from the firm.

G. COLD CALLING ... AND OTHER STRATEGIES FOR PEOPLE WITH BRASS COJONES OR PEOPLE WHO CAN FAKE THEM)

You don't have to be born bold to exhibit *cojones,* you know. If you pick up the phone and call complete strangers, the people you call won't know whether you were born with nuts of steel ...

... or you're faking it.

Either way, if you undertake the strategies in this section, you'll never be unemployed. You'll latch onto gigs nobody else knows about. And you'll find that once you try these strategies, it's a lot easier than you thought.

Keep in mind that all of the strategies in this section are high risk. There's a substantial possibility that you'll get rejected with any given call or visit. But look at it this way: If you'd tell your friend to make that call . . . why don't you do it yourself?

And if you're the type who easily gets back up and dusts yourself off, or even *relishes* a challenge, you'll get opportunities your classmates only dream of.

* * * SMART HUMAN TRICK * * *

Law student from upstate New York, job hunting in Washington, DC. She was standing on a street corner waiting for the light to change. She looked down and noticed a business card lying on the sidewalk. She says, "Other people were walking on it, but I was curious. I picked it up, and saw that it was an attorney's business card.

"I looked him up on-line and realized that he was the kind of lawyer I wanted to work for. So I went to his office with his card. I explained to the secretary that I had found Attorney X's card on the sidewalk and wanted to return it to him. She was apparently amused by this, and let me talk to him. I gave him his card, told him how I found it, and told him that I'd taken the liberty of researching him and found that he did the kind of work I wanted to do. He interviewed me on the spot.

"I got the job."

* * * SMART HUMAN TRICK * * *

Law student, California law school. He stands at a busy intersection with a sign reading, "Law school graduate, will work for honest wages."

He got a job.

(This is Kimm speaking. I'm not necessarily *suggesting* this . . .)

1. COLD CALLING: WHOM TO CALL, AND HOW TO WARM THEM UP

A. CHOOSING YOUR TARGETS

There are two general ways to pick your prey: I'll call them "affinity" targets and "goal" targets. Notice that these mirror the categories of people we talked about when we discussed "Cold e-mailing"—it's just that your approach changes.

1. "AFFINITY" TARGETS: PEOPLE WITH WHOM YOU SHARE SOMETHING IN COMMON

The most obvious affinity target group is alums of your law school. Do a Lexis or Westlaw search or use an alumni database at school to find people. Of course, you'll probably want to narrow that list: you're not going to contact the thousands of people who went to your school before you! You can narrow it by specialty, by geography, by gender, by any other criterion that matters to you. The fact that you have something in common makes your targets more likely to both a) talk to and b) help you.

* * * SMART HUMAN TRICK * * *

Recent graduate, law school in California. He reports: "I didn't have a job and I didn't have any prospects. So I thought, what the hell. I got out Martindale/Hubbell and I went straight down the list of lawyers in Los Angeles, and every time I came to one that graduated from my law school, I picked up the phone and called them.

"I won't pretend that I wasn't nervous. Especially at first I was scared to death. I had a pretty simple pitch: 'I just graduated from X law school, I'm looking around for what I'm going to do next, I'd really appreciate any advice you can give me,' 'What would you do if you were me,' or 'I'm curious how you broke in to doing what you do.'

"I'd ask to set up a meeting at their convenience, but sometimes they just said, 'I've got a couple of minutes. Ask me your questions.'

"The thing that amazed me was that 75% of the people I called were willing to set up a meeting with me or talk to me on the spot. 75! Before I tried it I was absolutely convinced they would brush me off. It rarely happened. After a while it didn't even matter if somebody was rude, because I figured the next three people would help me out.

"I've made the most amazing contacts this way. People are a lot more helpful than I thought they'd be. And even when they're not, it doesn't matter. I've got a ton more people to contact!"

* * * SMART HUMAN TRICK * * *

German student, graduates from law school without a job. Her dream is Corporate International Law at a prestigious New York firm. She takes the Bar and passes it, and six months after graduation, she gets a lead on a New York firm from a friend. Before she contacts the person, she goes into the firm's database and looks for German speakers in the international department of the firm. She contacts them in German. They give her the inside skinny on the firm. By the time she talks to her contact, she knows what they need and are looking for.

She gets an offer . . . in International Law.

2. "GOAL" TARGETS: EMPLOYERS YOU'D LIKE TO PURSUE WHETHER YOU HAVE SOMETHING IN COMMON, OR NOT

You want to be in a particular city and/or a particular specialty. If it's a specialty you're looking for, do a Lexis or Westlaw search to identify your targets. If it's geography, you've got an even simpler research: the Yellow Pages. Do you know what proportion of job hunters in general find their job through the Yellow Pages? 69%! More than two-thirds. Yipes. And I didn't make that up. That statistic came from the book *What Color Is Your Parachute*. The author, Richard Bolles, reports that those jobs come about simply by people calling and asking, "Are you hiring?"

Particularly if you're looking for small law firms, mining the Yellow Pages can be very fertile territory. Those employers are unlikely to post job openings anywhere, *and*, incidentally, they're the place where you're most likely to be happy. Studies show that the happiest lawyers are in law firms with between one and four attorneys!

Regardless of your goal, use the appropriate resource to come up with a list of targets.

B. PREP WORK: WHAT TO DO BEFORE YOU APPROACH YOUR TARGETS

Cold calling doesn't mean you're cold when you call, you know. You need to warm up. Here's how.

1. RESEARCH

You can't avoid two sources: The employer's web site (if there is one), and Google. That's the absolute bare minimum.

If you want to go beyond that, you can use any of the resources in the Research chapter, Chapter 6. The more you learn, the better off you are. So do whatever research your schedule allows.

2. PRACTICE YOUR PITCH

When you use the strategies in this section, you're going to have a *very* limited window of opportunity when you talk to people. You've got to engage them immediately. That means that you can't be stumbling around for things to say. **There are two things to prep:**

Have your introduction down-pat. Make one that suits your personality, but remember, make it brief, and make it confident yet humble. You don't want to seem cocky especially when what you're doing is kind of cocky. Wording something like, "Hi, Miss Amullmahay. This is Kimm Walton. I appreciate you talking with me. I know how busy you must be, so I'll make it brief. I read an article about you in the Wisconsin Bar Journal. I found it very interesting because I'm interested in a career in environmental law. I'm a Second Year at Case Western Reserve Law School, and I'd appreciate the opportunity to talk with you. Whether you have any job openings or not, I'd appreciate your advice. I promise I won't take up more than fifteen minutes of your time."

That's no more than a minute. It's complimentary. It shows you've done some research, and it states what you want. Use your own words, but you see the point: Get to your point in a hurry!

The other element of pitch preparation is figuring out what you're going to ask of each target. Regardless of the fact you're being pretty bold, you can't ask for a job. You just can't. You can say: "Whether you have any job openings or not, I'd appreciate your advice about what I should do to break in." You can ask for advice: "What would you do if you were me? Anyone I should talk to? Activities I should take part in? Publications I should be reading?" You can ask them how they accomplished some element of their success that you're particularly interested in duplicating. (I routinely get inquiries from students who say, "I know you wrote *Law In A Flash*. I have this idea for a study aid and I'm curious ...") You can ask how to make the most of an accomplishment of your own, some element of your background: "I've got a Ph.D. in cardboard toilet roll recycling. I'm curious how I should pitch it ..."

C. Moving In For The Kill: Two Ways To Approach Your Targets

1. Approaching Your Targets By Phone

Giving great phone is a very important skill for a lawyer. You'll conduct a *lot* of business over the phone. Showing off your phone skills from the start is therefore a great benefit to you.

A. Make Your Life (Slightly) Easier By Leaving A Voice Mail Message Off-Hours

OK. This doesn't take the brass balls that you have. But it does make it easier on the person you're targeting if they know ahead of time that you're calling.

Call late at night or early in the morning, and leave a brief message stating your name, that you're a 1L/2L/3L/graduate at/of X law school, and that you'll be calling back later in the day seeking ten minutes' of their advice about careers. If you can work in something about them that your research dug up, use it here. Tell them how much you appreciate it and thank them in advance.

B. Getting Past The Person Who Answers The Phone

Secretary. Assistant. Whatever. The fact is, you can't talk to most professionals if their right-hand-person won't let you through. Here's how to work it:

1. Avoid the gatekeeper in the first place, by calling early or late.

As Debra Fink points out, if you call between 7:30 and 8:00 a.m., or between 5:30 and 6:00 p.m., you're likely to catch the person you want, and avoid his/her assistant altogether. Lawyers in every setting tend to work longer hours than their assistants, and when no one's around to answer their office phone, they're likely to do it themselves.

2. When you speak to a gatekeeper, adopt the tone and words of a colleague, not a job seeker.

When professionals call each other, they state their name and whom they're seeking in a confident tone of voice. Do the same thing yourself. Politely but firmly say, "This is Kimm Walton calling for Sarah Amullmahay." Use both the first and last names of the person you're calling.

The idea here is that if you speak with enough authority, the assistant may not question you, and simply put your call through.

3. If you're asked why you're calling, you're calling about correspondence. That's ultimately going to be true.

OK, let's say the assistant doesn't just roll over with your forceful approach. Let's go through some common options.

Assistant: Which firm are you with?

You: I'm representing myself.

Assistant: What are you calling in reference to?

(Assistants clearly like to end questions with a preposition)

You: I'm calling in reference to correspondence. Is Ms. Amullmahay available?

As Debra Fink advises, "Don't ever say it's a personal matter! For all you know, the attorney is having a personal crisis, and will be *very* angry with you for lying!"

Furthermore, you can't say you're looking for a job. It's the kiss of death. So if you say it regards correspondence, you can always tell the attorney that you're considering sending your resume, but you wanted to speak with them first. *That's* true.

If mentioning correspondence to the assistant doesn't work . . .

Assistant: Ms. Amullmahay is busy. She'll have to call you back.

You: I'm afraid I'm going to be in and out of class/work/home. I wouldn't want to miss Ms. Amullmahay's call. What's a good time to call back?"

(Notice two things: first of all, on your initial call, don't let them call you back. You want to be in control. Second, notice that you never ask *if* there is a good time to call; when you're going out on a limb, never ask anything that can be answered "no." Instead, offer choices.)

"Would it be better to call tomorrow toward noon, or just before the end of the day?"

If the assistant won't bite, just say you'll call back tomorrow.

Throughout this phone call, maintain a pleasant tone of voice. Smile. What you're doing is bordering on pushy. So keep your tone pleasant.

4. **Always get the gatekeeper's name.**

When you call again, you can refer to the gatekeeper by name. "Hello, Madge, this is Kimm Walton. We spoke yesterday." *Everybody* appreciates being called by name.

5. **On the second call, throw yourself on the gatekeeper's mercy.**

Make them your ally. You're already calling them by name. Say something like, "I'd really appreciate your help. I'm a 1L/2L/3L at X law school and I'm really interested in breaking into X law, just like Ms. Amullmahay's practice. I'll send my resume but I wanted to talk to her first for a few minutes and see if it's worthwhile sending it. I know how busy she must be, but I'd truly appreciate ten minutes of her time, at her convenience."

6. **If you call three times—either when the gatekeeper tells you to, or two days apart—and can't get through, leave a message for them to call you back.**

Just state your name, the advice you're seeking, and a brief statement of your circumstances, something in particular you know about them that's relevant, and state your appreciation for any advice they can give you. State again your appreciation of how busy they are, and say you look forward to hearing from them.

7. **If you leave a message and you don't get a return call in a week or so, consider sending a letter.**

Apologize for imposing, acknowledge that you know how busy they are, say "If your needs change, I hope you'll consider me ..." and include a resume and any great reference letters you have. Tell them you won't call again but you'd appreciate a call or e-mail if you could be of help to them or any other lawyers they know.

Remember: You never know when anybody might turn into a colleague. You want to leave them with a positive view of you.

8. **If at any time they hang up on you or demand that you not call back, follow #7 and send a letter. Don't jump ugly in return, either speaking or in writing.**

2.   APPROACHING YOUR TARGETS IN PERSON

Maybe you don't want to mess around with the phone. Maybe you want to cut right to the chase and visit in person. Great! There's probably no faster way of getting a job than to get out there and pound the pavement.

Most law students don't do it, frankly, because they can't work up the nerve for it. But if you can—bite the bullet and get out there! Career counselors applaud it. Attorneys respect it. And here's why: it's what a lot of *them* had to do to find a job.

If you plan it right, you can probably hit twenty law firms in a couple of days, and if you're interested in practicing in another city, that's a great way to make the most of your time. Wendy Werner says, "I had a law student who went to a city that had a high concentration of law firms in just a few high-rises. He researched the firms before he visited, and then he just cold-called. He walked from building to building, and he knocked off eight or ten law firms in each building. He asked to see the hiring partners, and if they didn't have time, he befriended the secretaries and asked when a good time to come back might be. Using this cold calling technique, he got a job in three days!"

Here's what you need to know about cold calling "in the flesh":

a.   In the post—9/11 world, it won't work in big cities.

Sad to say, you just can't do this in cities like New York. Almost every building has tight security at the door. But there aren't many cities that have this problem, and no suburbs do. So the vast majority of employers you're going to approach will, in fact, be approachable.

b.   Have your "papers" ready and waiting.

I don't mean to make you sound like an AKC puppy, but the fact that you're calling in person doesn't mean you're off the hook when it comes to having your resume and reference letters. Have them neat and available in a briefcase or portfolio, ready to be handed over on request. If you have a killer writing sample or your transcript is good, have those ready, too.

Of all times in your job search, this is one when you shouldn't obsess about your grades. The chutzpah you're showing is likely to trump any credentials concerns. And remember: Nine out of ten attorneys you approach weren't in the top ten percent of their class, either.

c. Look professional!

Wear a good suit, and have a portfolio or briefcase where you carry your papers.

What to say to the receptionist ...

Walk into the office confidently, and introduce yourself, with a smile, to the receptionist. "Hello. I'm Kimm Walton, and I'm here to see Tojo Johosevitz."

If the receptionist asks whether Johosevitz is expecting you, you have to be honest and say no, "But I was hoping I could speak with him for a just a few minutes."

You can even launch into a bit of your pitch, about researching the practice of environmental law, and you'd like a few minutes of the attorney's time if (s)he can spare them.

Remember: say all of this with a smile! Because you've taken the trouble to show up in person, it's likely that the person you're asking for will at least come out and say hello, at which time you can ask for a more convenient time to come and talk with them, if right now doesn't work.

If they won't speak with you, ask if there's someone else in the firm with whom you might speak.

If you run into a dead end, smile graciously, and leave.

I didn't promise you that every firm you'd approach was going to welcome you with open arms—right? But the fact is, it takes such guts to show up in person like that that it makes an impact on most employers. It shows the kind of drive, initiative, and confidence that's really prized in job applicants, and that's why, even though you run the risk of face-to-face rejections—the worst kind—you also face the greatest possibility of success.

* * * SMART HUMAN TRICK * * *

Law student, a 3L in Missouri. He has an unusual resume: mediocre grades, coupled with two summers working for federal district court judges. When asked how he nailed those two jobs with such average credentials, he says:

"I didn't do anything during the school year. I knew I wanted to work for judges, but I also figured my grades weren't going to get me there."

"I also figured that there would be students with really great credentials who *would* get offers from judges, but then they would reconsider getting high-paying jobs and they would bail out. Maybe that would be an opportunity for someone like me.

"Also, I was willing to work for nothing. I thought that would be very attractive.

"So both 1L and 2L, I waited until exams were over. Then I went and knocked on the doors of judges' chambers. I dressed well, I had my resume with me, I was really nice to anybody who would talk to me. I'd say, 'I realize how late this is, but I'm wondering if you need another student for the summer.' I made sure to mention that I was willing to work for free.

"Sure enough, I found judges whose 'first choices' had left them in the lurch. It wasn't so much that I was a great candidate. I was the *only* candidate. I was in the right place at the right time.

"That's how I did it."

3. WHY I DIDN'T MENTION E-MAIL

Because it takes no nuts to send e-mails. But cold e-mailing campaigns can work really well. Follow the advice on cold e-mailing we discussed earlier.

D. WHAT TO SAY ONCE YOU HAVE THEM ON THE PHONE . . . OR YOU'RE STANDING IN FRONT OF THEM

Thank them *immediately* for talking with you. Offer your brief pitch about yourself, and move into the questions you prepared ahead of time. At this point you're essentially in an informational interview, which we covered just a few pages ago.

E. BE PERSISTENT . . . BUT BACK OFF BEFORE THEY OBTAIN A RESTRAINING ORDER

As you can tell from the advice here, you've got to be able to get around "no's." You've got to be persistent. Cold calling just doesn't pay off otherwise.

Knowing when a target has become a dry hole is a matter of listening for cues. For some employers it'll be the first phone call; for others, it may take years. Take an interest in them, be helpful if you can with articles or news items that might be useful to them. Be sensitive to what you hear, and whether they're amused/unbothered by your persistence . . . or if their next call is going to be to the cops!

* * * SMART HUMAN TRICK * * *

Student flying cross-country. The guy sitting next to him on the plane is in business. He gives the student the name of a lawyer to contact, in the student's target city. We'll call the student Jeff, and the lawyer Lee Tigant.

Approach #1: Jeff calls Lee Tigant on the phone. He introduces himself and states what he's interested in. Lee Tigant asks him to send a resume. Jeff sends it.

Approach #2: No response. Jeff calls two weeks later to follow up. He leaves a message. Lee Tigant doesn't return the call.

Approach #3: Jeff calls again. He leaves another message. No response.

Approach #4: Jeff sends an e-mail. Lee Tigant e-mails back, saying that he's very busy and hasn't had a chance to review Jeff's resume.

Jeff assumes he's been brushed off. He stops calling.

A month later . . .

Approach #5: Jeff figures he'll e-mail one more time. The lawyer responds, asking him to send his resume. Again. Jeff e-mails it. Lee Tigant e-mails him back, saying "I'm impressed," and asks for an e-mailed writing sample. Jeff e-mails it. Lee Tigant does not respond.

Approach #6. Two weeks later, Jeff e-mails Lee Tigant asking if he needs any additional materials, and also to say that he will be in town for another interview in the event Lee Tigant wants to meet with him.

Lee Tigant calls, and says, "Let's arrange an interview."

Why?

"I'm really impressed with your persistence!"

F. PUTTING DEAD ENDS IN PERSPECTIVE

Simply put, cold calling is not for the faint of heart. You'll get hang ups. You'll get snarling rejections. You'll have lots of phone calls and e-mails unreturned. But as Debra Fink points out: "Look at yourself in the mirror afterwards—you may feel awful, but you won't be bleeding."

If you start feeling really bad about the rejections, go back to Chapter 5 on Rejections and read it. You'll feel a *lot* better. And remember: rejections come to an end. You'll get a job. And if you've got the nerve to use the strategies in this section, you'll have one sooner rather than later.

2. BEYOND COLD CALLING: JOB SEARCH STRATEGIES FOR THE STOUT OF HEART

Cold calling isn't the only job search strategy that requires nerves of steel. Here are others that take guts but work *great*.

A. MAKE PRESENTATIONS AT BAR ASSOCIATION MEETINGS.

Earlier in this chapter, I raved about the idea of contacting alums to find out what issues they'd like to read more about, writing an article about said issue, and getting it published in a bar association publication/law-related web site.

This takes that idea one step further. You take the research you've done, approach the head of the appropriate section of the local bar association, and offer to make a presentation to the members at the next breakfast/lunch meeting.

If the idea of public speaking doesn't curl your hair, it's a great way to get yourself in front of lawyers in a hurry; and to have them see you under very favourable circumstances, showing off your enthusiasm, your knowledge of issues they face as well as your presentation skills. It's a *great* strategy.

* * * SMART HUMAN TRICKS * * *

Law student, a 3L in South Carolina. He's had no luck nailing a job in his chosen specialty: criminal defense.

He contacts a prominent local criminal defense attorney, and asks him, "What issue would you like to be reading more about?" The attorney responds, "The admissibility of lie detector tests in South Carolina."

The student researches the issue, gets an article about it published in the local bar association newsletter, and on top of that, he approaches the head of the criminal defense section and says, "I just researched an issue I know your members are interested in. Can I make a ten-minute presentation about it at your next breakfast meeting?"

The guy says, "Sure," and the student gets up and gives his talk a couple of weeks later.

He reports: "The lawyers were great. They were very interested in what I had to say, and when I was done, some of them walked up to me and said, 'Here's my card. Give me a call.'

"I got a job through one of them. That presentation was the only thing I had to do."

B. MAKE PRESENTATIONS AT CIVIC GROUPS

Groups are always looking for speakers. I routinely get contacted by local groups of all kinds who want to hear about—well, the kind of stuff you're reading in this book.

Take advantage of that vacuum, and contact local church/civic groups offering to make a presentation about a legal issue and/or a big case in the news.

When you're on vacation from school, you probably often find yourself explaining important cases to your family and friends. This idea expands on that. You may not be a lawyer yet, but if you're very familiar with a case or issue in the news, you know more about it than any layperson—and probably more than a lot of lawyers. Share your expertise by making a presentation to a civic or church group.

Not only will it look great on your resume, but there will certainly be people in the audience who'll know lawyers. You can say straight out that the reason you're making the presentation is that you're interesting in practicing in X specialty when you get out of school. Your audience will probably take it from there and put you on to relevant lawyers.

c. IF YOU'RE INTERESTED IN CORPORATE COUNSEL'S OFFICES AT LARGE PUBLIC COMPANIES, GO TO ANNUAL MEETINGS

All of a company's grand poo-bahs attend its annual meeting. These are people who might never in a million years respond to your e-mail or letter—but they'll have no choice but to talk to you if you introduce yourself during a break at the meeting.

Dress well, have your game face on, and introduce yourself confidently. Say something along the lines of, "I know this is unconventional, but I'm here because I'm really interested in working in your general counsel's office. I'm a law student at X, and I [a little bit about you, any relevant work experience/abilities]. Can I send my resume to you or a colleague, and perhaps set up an interview?"

It takes nerve, but I've seen it work well—perhaps because it takes nerve!

* * * SMART HUMAN TRICK * * *

Student at a West Coast law school is absolutely obsessed with working for Disney. He takes every opportunity to meet with anybody with any connection to the company. He even finds out the CEO's birthday and sends him a birthday card!

But when it comes to getting a job, he's striking out. He can't even get an interview.

He finds out that Disney is holding a conference for its executives, which happens to fall during Spring Break of his second year in law school. He flies to the conference city, and hangs around the elevators at the conference hotel. When the CEO gets onto the elevator, the student follows him on, and makes a thirty-second pitch for a summer job.

His enthusiasm gets him the job.

d. EXTREME COLD CALLING: CALL THE PERSON AT THE TOP OF THE FOOD CHAIN

Normally when we think of cold-calling, we think of calling people who will potentially talk to us. We don't think of calling people at the top of the pyramid. But heck . . . when you're being nervy, why not?

I've talked with students who picked up the phone and called people they never in a million years thought would pick up the phone at the other end. But it *worked*.

Of course, you've got to have a compelling pitch and you've got to be ready to talk right now—but if you get through, who knows what can happen?

* * * SMART HUMAN TRICK * * *

Student in the Pacific Northwest. She wants to work at one of the Big Four accounting firms in New York City.

She gets on the phone and calls the hiring partner. He picks up the phone. She introduces herself, and says, "I'd like to work for you. I'd like your advice about what I ought to do to break in." He responded, "Why don't you send me your resume?"

She reports, "This guy had tons of people reporting to him. I figured there's *no way* he'd speak to me. But he did and to tell the truth he was pretty nice.

"So I sent him my resume. And I got the job."

Appendix
Sneaky Ways to Nail On-Campus Interviews

If you ever travel to Pittsburgh, you'll probably take U.S. Air, since it's a U.S. Air hub. If you do, you'll notice when you check in that the security checkpoint is behind you, downstairs. And it's usually mobbed.

If you look around, you'll notice a little sign that reads: "Alternate security checkpoint." And it has an arrow pointing to the left. If you ask the agent whether the sign is legit, (s)he'll tell you that it is, that the alternate checkpoint is fifty yards down a hallway, that nobody ever notices the sign and so there's never a line. And if you follow that path, you'll find a handful of TSA agents who are bored and happy to see you . . . and you'll save yourself about forty-five minutes of hassle getting through security.

My point in telling you this is that you don't have to follow the mob. Whether you're talking about airport security or employers, it's worth looking around for another way in.

If your dream employers are among the ones who interview on-campus—large law firms, government agencies—and you don't have the grades to get onto the interview schedule the traditional way, you need to use a bit of ingenuity to get your foot in the door. The techniques here range from the simple to the ballsy and outrageous, but they all have something in common: they've worked for other students.

1. Check your school's prescreening policy for on-campus interviews.

Here's the scoop. Schools vary in the way they handle on-campus interviews in terms of the latitude they give employers in choosing the students they'll interview.

For instance, let's say that Uptight & Starch wants to come to your campus to interview students, and they can fit 28 interviews into 2 days. Some schools give firms 100% prescreening; that is, they get to sift through the resumes submitted, and choose every single student they want to interview. In this case, Upright & Starch would get to pick all 28 interviewees.

Other schools let employers choose some percentage of the interviewees. For instance, at one northeastern school, firms get to pick 60% of the interviewees, so Upright & Starch would get to pick 17 of the 28 interviewees. The school's Career Services Office would pick the other 11.

You see where I'm going with this. If your Career Services Office chooses *any* of the interviewees, do everything you can to get one of those slots!

The policy on filling interview slots varies from school to school. For some, it's a straight lottery system; your resume is picked at random. Others have a wish list; that is, if you say that Upright & Starch is your #1 choice, you've got a good shot at getting one of those school-chosen slots.

Regardless of your school's policy on filling those slots, I'd go straight to your Career Services Director and beg for an interview slot, even though they're supposedly filled at random. A compelling argument would be to point out that because you're truly interested in Upright & Starch, you'll be more enthusiastic in the interview and you'll make the school look good. In any case, what have you got to lose? If your argument doesn't work, you've still got your random shot at being chosen. At best, your Career Services Director will reward your enthusiasm with an interview, or suggest other ways for you to get your foot in the door at Upright & Starch. The bottom line is, you're no worse off if you make the extra effort, even if there's no written policy that says it'll work.

Also, if your school has a lottery system and you don't make the cut, check to see if anyone has turned down a lottery pick. Students often do, sometimes out of a misplaced sense of pride. My advice to you is: an interview spot is an interview spot. Employers routinely tell me that they wind up hiring students they didn't even intend to interview. If your classmates don't realize that, step in and take that interview slot off their hands!

2. Find out who the prescreener at your dream firm is and contact them directly.

Resumes are prescreened by people. As soon as you see that a firm you want is going to be interviewing on-campus, call them and find out who does the prescreening. If they aren't willing to tell you directly, then go through your Career Services Office, find an alum who works there, and find out from the alum who does the prescreening.

When you've identified the prescreener, call them on the phone and ask for an on-campus interview. That's right. Call them. You can't e-mail them your resume or send it through the mail, because your resume will be thrown into the hopper with all of the other resumes they receive.

In this phone call, you've got to have all of your ducks in a row as to why this is your dream job, and why you're the ideal candidate for it even though you don't have the GPA you know they typically seek. Don't be defensive about your record, but don't be naïve about it, either; acknowledge it and move immediately to talking about why they should interview you.

Is this going to work every time? No. But sometimes it does, and it's pretty obvious why. You're exhibiting great enthusiasm, which is very compelling. And on top of that, taking the initiative to call the prescreener takes chutzpah—and that's admirable, as well.

Even if you don't get the interview, say "Thanks, anyway," and comment on how you hope that perhaps someday you'll get a chance to work with them. There's no reason to burn a bridge with this employer, when there are so very many ways to get your foot in the door.

3. Volunteer at Career Services to be an escort for on-campus interviewers.

We discussed this when we talked about volunteering at Career Services earlier in this chapter. If you're helping interviewers get settled, showing them around, you've got a few minutes of conversation time available. Dress appropriately—and use that time wisely!

4. Get an interview with the on-campus interviewer without getting an on-campus interview.

I'll bet you had to read that twice! Here's what I mean. It's entirely possible for you to meet with on-campus interviewers in completely novel ways, by taking into account the logistics of the interviewer's schedule. From the outset, I've got to tell you that it takes some major-league *cojones* to pull off this kind of thing, but if you've got 'em, by all means give it a try!

a. Prepare just as you would for any traditional interview.

Have your "infomercial" down-pat, just as we discussed in the interview chapter. Research the employer and the interviewer, and have great questions to ask. Show off in your questions the fact that you know and understand what they do. You can blend in some "informational interview" questions: How would I best position myself to work with you? What would you do if you were me? What activities should I be taking part in/publications should I be reading?

b. Suit up as though you've got an on-campus interview, and head for the Career Services Office.

Find out where your target employer will be interviewing. Then you have two choices.

1. **Hang out outside the interview room, waiting to see if any students are no-shows for their interviews.**

Blowing off on-campus interviews is a heinous no-no. It makes you and your school look really bad. But I guarantee you'll have classmates who'll ignore that advice and fail to show for an on-campus interview.

If and when that happens, there's your shot. The interviewer will probably come out looking for the phantom interviewee, and that's your chance to say, "(S)he's not here. But I am. I'm really interested in working with you. Can I talk to you for a few minutes?" Have your resume ready, and be prepped out the ying-yang. You're going to have to convince the interviewer why they should hire you even though they didn't even want to interview you! Having said that, this has worked for students more than once.

2. **Wait until the interviewer comes out for a break, and ask for a few minutes at the end of the day.**

This is another situation where an honest show of enthusiasm is absolutely vital. When the interviewer emerges to get a coffee or stretch his/her legs, jump in with your request: "I'm so interested in working for X, but I didn't get an on-campus interview. Would it be possible to talk with you for a few minutes after your last interview today?" Very, very few people will turn down a face-to-face request like this!

* * * SMART HUMAN TRICK * * *

Law student in Wisconsin. He's dying to work for Navy JAG. He applies for an on-campus interview, and doesn't get it.

He positions himself outside the interview room when the Navy JAG recruiter comes on-campus to interview. When the interviewer comes out for a lunch break, the student tells him, "I'm dying to get into Navy JAG. I didn't get an on-campus interview. Can you spare a few minutes at the end of the day to talk with me?" The recruiter says, "Sure."

The student shows up at the end of the day, and talks with the recruiter. During their conversation, the student says, "I'd really like to see what it's like to work with you. Can I shadow you for a day?"

The recruiter agrees. They set up a "shadowing day." The student goes and meets everyone the JAG recruiter works with. They all encourage him to apply for his commission. He does so, and he's rejected. He gets a call from the recruiter that day, who says, "Did you get it?" The student says, "No," and the recruiter says, "Don't worry. Nobody gets it the first time around. Try again in three months."

The student does—and he gets in.

3. Show up at the end of the day, and ask if you can walk with the interviewer to his/her car.

The interviewer has to get out of your school somehow, and it's going to take a few minutes. If you smile and politely ask if you can walk with them, they're unlikely to turn you down.

This strategy has resulted in call-backs for determined students, and you can see why—the nerve and enthusiasm it takes sets them *way* apart from the crowd, regardless of their grades!

c. If it's an out-of-town employer, make yourself useful to the weary traveling interviewer.

These tactics require a little more legwork ahead of time, but if you're willing to do it, the payoff can be big.

1. If you have a car, offer to give the interviewer a ride from and to the airport.

That gives you more time with the interviewer than *any* on-campus interviewee will get!

2. Find out when the interviewer is flying in. Put on your interview suit, and go and meet them at the airport. Hold up one of those limo driver name signs with their name on it, so you can identify them (if you don't feel comfortable picking them out of a crowd from their picture on the employer's web site).

Everybody who travels by plane has to walk through the airport, and most people who travel have to get their luggage. That leaves you, the enterprising student, with a window of opportunity in which to make your pitch. Sounds outrageous? Maybe. But it's resulted in interviews and offers more than once, and it could work for you!

5. Remember: On-campus interviews aren't the only way to get your foot in the door at any employer.

This chapter is redolent with ideas for meeting employers, for getting through to people who'd ignore your resume. On-campus interviews are just the tip of the iceberg. There's *always* a way to get yourself in front of employers you want to work for. Look at it this way: once you're working there, it doesn't matter *how* you got in. You're *there!*

Chapter 11
What the Internet Can— and Can't—Do for You

"What hath God wrought"

First telegraphic message, sent by Samuel Morse, May 24, 1844.

"I don't want to read your blog. Just tell *me how your day was."*

Caption to a Casey Shaw cartoon.

"You kids like to use the World Wide Interweb?"

John Michael Higgins as Corey Taft in *For Your Consideration*

Related topics: Note that useful web resources appear throughout this book. They don't all appear in this chapter.

Remember, way back in Chapter 2, we talked about how the secret of nailing great jobs is image and message control: being conscious of how employers see you and the way they get your message. (If you skipped over Chapter 2, I just saved you the trouble of reading it.)

The Internet gives you a powerful new realm for presenting yourself to employers, as well as finding people and information you couldn't find any other way, and connecting with people who can propel your career forward.

We're certainly moving toward a time where, as Vic Massaglia points out, "You can have a robust image on the web. You could have a blog with your resume on it, with links to the websites of prior employers. If you did well in an advocacy competition and it was videotaped, you could upload it to YouTube and have a link on your blog to it. How much better than *telling* an employer how good your advocacy skills are, would it be actually to *show* them?"

Of course, the Internet can also trash your reputation and delude you, as well. In this chapter, we'll talk about how to wring the most benefit from the Internet–and avoid the traps that snare the unwary!

Let's get started.

A. The Most Important Job Searching Principles to Remember

1. Employers Shouldn't Be Looking at Your Personal Stuff On-line ... but They Are. Imagine That Every E-mail, Social Networking Profile, Posting and Reference to you On-line is an Attachment to Your Resume ... Because it Might as Well Be

Employers will Google you. "They'll Google you when they get your resume. They'll Google you *again* at the end of a summer clerkship, before they make you a permanent offer," says Campbell's Keith Faulkner. Vic Massaglia adds that, "You have to anticipate that employers will look for digital dirt before they hire you."

You may be thinking, "What's on my FaceBook profile is for my friends. It's none of employers' business." True dat. But the fact is, whether you intended the naughty photos or drunken ramble solely for your friends or not, if it's accessible to employers and you send them your resume, they'll find it.

While you're job searching, **ego-surf at least once a week**. See yourself as employers can see you, and make sure that everything makes you look mature, discreet, professional (and if anything doesn't ... take advantage of the ideas in Topic E, below).

Check:

- Google (as well as meta search engines that cover virtually the entire Internet, like www.metacrawler.com and www.dogpile.com); on each search engine, check "images" "News" and "Newsgroup" directories;

- Blogs;

- Social networking sites;

- Forums and bulletin boards you frequent;

- IM accounts.

You know as well as I do what trouble careless e-mails and blogs have done to people. A recent survey of hiring personnel said half of them use the Internet to vet job applicants, and a third of those had revealed information that lost the applicant the job, everything from items that suggest questionable judgment to evidence of lawsuits against prior employers. What perhaps is even worse is that employers tend *not* to explain *why* they're rejecting people when the cause is something that showed up on-line.

The impact of on-line behavior is no different once you're on the job. People get dooced all the time for careless on-line behavior. A recent survey of large employers revealed that in the last twelve months a third of them had fired people for violating e-mail policies, forty percent had people on staff whose job it was to read other employees' e-mails, and half of them regularly checked the contents of e-mails sent by employees.

I collect newspaper stories about people who run into trouble on-line. Among my favourites:

- Remember the "astronaut love triangle" story? Where Astronaut Lisa Nowak apparently attacked her "love rival," Colleen Shipman, the other woman involved with fellow astronaut Bill Oefelein? It seems that Nowak found "steamy e-mails" between Shipman and Oefelein on Oefelein's computer.

  An exchange that apparently drove Nowak over the edge took place while Oefelein was piloting the space shuttle in December 2006. Shipman gave him a charm to take into space, and he e-mailed her a picture showing the charm floating in zero gravity. She replied that she couldn't see the charm, "pant, pant. It's like those erotic hidden picture games that they have at the bar . . . only you're fully clothed in the picture . . . But the thought of you without any clothes is pretty nice 'sigh'," she wrote.

  He responded, from the space shuttle: "I'm a boob. Apparently I can be a moron even when you are not physically with me. I imagine this doesn't surprise you anymore, this idiot you decided to like. You must really have me around your finger that I can't even function without you here and with you here I am slightly smarter than a slug. I don't know. Maybe, I should be a road kill scraper-upper. That shouldn't be too hard. I can scrape things up that don't move on the road like armadillos, after they've been discombobulated by sexy, hot bodies . . ."

  Memo to self: If I'm ever on the space shuttle, perhaps I should assume that maybe, just maybe, other people will be able to read my e-mails . . .

- A British secretary, dubbed "Bridget Jones" in the press, lost her job because of her blog. She wrote about work, but she didn't name the firm, she was anonymous, and in fact the only thing identifying her was a photo on the blog.

  It was pretty mild stuff. Among other things, she commented on her bosses' "plummy Oxbridge accents," and called them "very old school."

  She was accused of using office time to write her blog, and was fired as a result.

- John Green, a rising star at ABC News in 2006, crashed and burned when the Drudge Report posted confidential e-mails of Green's. One of them concerned a presidential debate in 2004, where Green said of President Bush, "Bush makes me sick." In another, he trashed former Secretary of State Madeline Albright, saying "Albright has Jew shame."

- Former Boeing CEO Harry Stonecipher had to resign when his affair with a colleague came to light . . . because of sexually explicit e-mails he sent her on the company's e-mail system.

- Henry Blodget, star Merrill Lynch analyst, was banned for life from the securities industry for praising stocks in public but deriding them as "dogs" in e-mails.

- A teacher in New York moonlighted as a pro wrestler. He called in sick when his wrestling conflicted with his school duties. He made it easier for investigators to track him down by saying on his web site, "I am a social studies teacher in my 'other life,'" and posting his wrestling schedule–so, for instance, when he had his mother call in sick for him, saying he was being treated for "flu-like symptoms," his web site showed he was touring Japan with the Zero One wrestling company.

  He resigned when investigators approached him.

- In 2006, *Slate* reproduced an e-mail that the actress Lindsay Lohan had allegedly sent to her friends and lawyers, ranting about her treatment in the tabloids. *The New York Post* described the e-mail as "rambling" and "semi-literate." It did not, perhaps, show her at her most intelligent, reading in part: "I am willing to release a politically/morally correct, fully adiquate [sic] letter to the press if any of you are willing to help. Simply to state my oppinions [sic] on how our society should be educated on for the better of our country. Our people. Also because I have such an impact on our younger generations, as well as generations older than me. Which we all know and can obviously see."

- After the Hurricane Katrina disaster, the FEMA director–Mike Brown, of 'You're doing a great job, Brownie' fame—was brought down in part by e-mails he'd sent during the disaster, showing him ruminating about how, for instance, his shirt looked on TV. (You can find the emails at www.melancon.house.gov.)

- The Mayor of Torrington, Connecticut, took down his MySpace profile when someone changed it to show his occupation as "male-bigalow," a reference to the movie *Deuce Bigalow: Male Gigolo*.

2. MAXIMIZE THE "MAGNETS" IN YOUR ON-LINE PRESENCE

When I say "magnets," I'm talking about the things about you that will connect you to other people. The music, books and movies that you like, for instance; it's possible to connect with people by putting in lots of items (as long as they're not questionable or titillating, of course).

I've already mentioned the idea of volunteering with PSLawNet or with *any* employer to be able to drop their name. Remember: every time the name of an employer appears on your profile on a site like LinkedIn or MySpace, it gives people another reason to connect with you; it acts as a "magnet," if you will. You never know when people you connect with on-line will be not just friends, but great contacts, as well.

3. THE INTERNET IS A GREAT JOB SEARCH RESOURCE. IT SHOULDN'T BE YOUR *ONLY* ONE

Your mind boggles when you see how many job postings there are on line, doesn't it? To bastardize an old saying, a million job postings here and a million there, and pretty soon you're talking about real opportunities.

While there's no downside to taking advantage of job postings on web sites, don't use them exclusively. Here's why. **Research suggests that the success rate of internet job searches if 4%.** *Four percent.* Those numbers are down around mass mailing territory, and can be just as depressing.

If all you do with the Internet is respond to job postings, you're essentially answering high tech classifieds. There's nothing wrong with that, but it shouldn't be the only arrow in your quiver. Vic Massaglia points out, "By the time a job gets posted on-line, thousands, perhaps millions of people see the same posting." You know you have to do more than that for a complete job search. So respond to postings on-line, but take advantage of other avenues, too, avenues that let employers get to know you, that let people start thinking about you before they even realize they're looking to hire anybody. You can do some useful "reaching out" to people on the web, but also make an effort to let potential employers see you, the person, not just you, the web presence—using the ways we discuss in Chapter 10, on *The Birds And Bees Of Great Jobs.* There are environments far more target-rich than the Internet!

Speaking of which . . .

4. NO COMPUTER BEATS THE 15–LB. NEURAL NETWORK CONNECTED TO YOUR NECK

You are now and will always be more impressive, and more memorable, in person than you could *ever* be on-line.

Remember the people aspect of job search. **Don't become a mouse potato.** For all that the Internet can do for you, it cuts out the 90% of communication that is non-verbal. It's confining in a way that even phone conversations are not.

You'll often find that the best thing you can do involves meeting people who get invested in your career; they give you advice and insights that lead you to great gigs. One reason it's so important is that law is a people business; not just clients but the people you work with, too. As Vic Massaglia says, "Someday you'll have to talk to clients, to sell. That's what practice is all about." The more often you let people interact with you, the more they'll envision what it would be like working with you . . . and that's exactly what you want.

5. THE WEB IS A GREAT WAY TO FIGURE OUT DIFFERENT PATHWAYS INTO EMPLOYERS

I'm always telling law students, no matter what you want to do, someone with your background has already done it . . . and there's no point in reinventing the wheel. Follow their example!

If you're curious about different ways of making your way into any particular job, here's how the web can help you: Look at profiles of attorneys who do what you want to do–whether via martindale.com or employer websites or any of the other myriad sources on-line–and look to see what *they* did to get where they are. For instance, if you're curious about whether you need an LLM for a particular kind of job, or you want intellectual property but you don't have a tech background, or you think your school isn't "good enough" for a particular employer . . . look and see what other people have done to get the same gig. I promise you, you'll find something reassuring, because there's no one set of credentials that are absolutely mandatory for any job. (You can always follow up by contacting the attorney(s) you find and saying, "I know that you did X, just as I did . . . I'd love your advice about how you got from there to . . .")

6. IF EMPLOYERS SEE YOU TALKING SMACK ON-LINE ABOUT YOUR SCHOOL, PROFS, CLASSES, CLASSMATES OR CURRENT WORK, THEY'LL ASSUME THAT IF THEY HIRE YOU, THEY'RE NEXT . . . AND THEY WON'T HIRE YOU

It's easy to think that rants about law school will be taken in context by employers, that they'll realize the comments were made with tongue planted firmly in cheek.

It would be great if that were true, but it's not. Employers are very sensitive about on-line postings. Part of it is concern about their own reputations, what you'll say about *them.* Another part of it has to do with the nature of the legal profession. It's *responsible.* People are trusting you with their fortunes and sometimes their liberty. It requires tact and discretion. A post on your MySpace profile saying, "Man, I got totally f* * *ed up this weekend" won't enhance your professional image.

* * * CAREER LIMITING MOVE * * *

From *The New York Times Magazine,* a question to "The Ethicist" columnist Randy Cohen:

> *"After I was scheduled for a job interview at a university, a member of the search committee Googled me and found my blog, where I refer to him (but not by name) as a belligerent jerk. He canceled the interview. It was impolitic to write what I did, but my believing him to be a jerk does not mean I would not be great at that job, and the rest of the committee might agree. Was it ethical of him to cancel the interview?"*

(This is Kimm talking: ethical or not, it was certainly *predictable.*)

7. ANONYMITY IS HARDER TO COME BY THAN YOU THINK. THE TERM "WEB PRIVACY" MAY WELL BE AN OXYMORON

Let's say you're smart and you post anonymously on-line. On sites like autoadmit.com, of course, you *have* to have a pseudonym. But if you blog, you do it with a fake name. You limit access to it. You post on message boards with an e-mail address that's not traceable to you. You set privacy settings on "high" on social networking sites.

But ... "Sites have no interest in privacy. Everything on-line is public information. You can have all the firewalls, all the security in the world. But if it's on-line, it's fair game," says Vic Massaglia.

Remember, no matter how careful you are, you can't stop other people from outing you. If *anybody* knows it's you, your anonymity is in jeopardy. And as one employer pointed out to me, "We look at those web sites, too. Contrary to popular belief, it's actually pretty easy to figure out who said what. They're not that mysterious."

* * * CAREER LIMITING MOVE * * *

Law student has a blog where he mildly chides his law school. "Nothing too bad, just gentle prodding," he points out. "But I'm not an idiot. I do it anonymously."

He is interviewing with a small litigation firm. After a couple of interviews, they seem very interested in him. "Suddenly," he says, "They go cold. I can't figure it out ... until I talk to one of my references. It turns out they talked to *her*, and she said, 'Have you read his blog?' They said no, and she said, 'Oh, you should, it's really funny ...' and told them where to find it."

"Now they're not returning my calls."

8. IF YOU CAN'T SAY SOMETHING NICE ... DON'T PUT IT ON-LINE. IN FACT, DON'T PUT IT IN WRITING AT ALL

Pop quiz: Do you remember what President Bush and Vice President Cheney said in their testimony to the 9/11 Commission? Did you *ever* know it?

The answer has to be "no," and here's why: *they insisted that their testimony take place in private, with no recording devices and no transcripts.* That's why you don't know what they said.

No matter what you think of President Bush's judgment otherwise, *that* was very smart. It also contains an important lesson: When you have something to say that might come back to smack you, *don't memorialize it in writing ... on the web or anywhere else.*

We spend a lot of time saying negative things. In fact, it's been proven that people bond over negatives more than positives. "Didn't that movie stink?" "What the heck did they do to that chicken dish?" "That speech—what was up with *that?*"

But when it comes to blasting people, don't ever, ever, *ever* do it on-line. Not in an e-mail. Not in a blog. Not on their (or your) social networking profile. *Nowhere.*

The simple fact is, you don't know when your words will come back to haunt you. Number one, you don't know who'll see it—or whom the recipient will forward it to. And you never know when your attitude about someone may change. I love what Katharine Hepburn said in the movie *The Philadelphia Story:* "The time to make up your mind about people is . . . never." You may turn around and decide someone's a real peach after all—but you've gravely threatened the possibility of a future truce if you tore them a new one on-line.

I'm not saying you shouldn't vent, complain, or even have a smack down with someone when they've done you wrong. Just don't do it on-line! Talk to them–ideally in person. Don't leave an on-line trail of negatives.

Abraham Lincoln had a useful policy. When anyone made him angry, he wrote them a letter. A really stinging letter. And let's face it, the man could *write*. Those letters must have been great. Nobody knows for sure, because *he never sent them*. The act of writing them excised the demons. He stashed the letters in a drawer, and they were only found after he died.

You don't need a drawer full of bile, but you see the point: vent your frustrations with people in ways that won't come back to bite you.

* * * CAREER LIMITING MOVE * * *

In 2006, an e-mail exchange was all over the Internet, and made it into publications like *Lawyers Weekly*. You might remember it. A criminal defense attorney had made a job offer to a young lawyer. She accepted, but then he told her he'd have to cut her pay because he'd decided to hire two people instead of one. Nothing untoward so far. They had a fairly nasty e-mail exchange after that, with her saying she decided not to work for the reduced pay (understandably), and him chiding her for refusing to talk to him about it, pointing out that he'd gone to the trouble of having business cards printed up for her, reformatting computers, and so forth.

Nobody would ever have heard about it if she hadn't followed up with an e-mail that said, "A real lawyer would have put the contract in writing and not exercised any such reliance until he did so. Again, thank you."

He shot back, in part, " . . . You need to realize that this is a very small legal community, especially the criminal defense bar. Do you really want to start pissing off more experienced lawyers at this early stage of your career?"

She e-mailed back–in its entirety–

"bla bla bla."

As *Lawyers Weekly* pointed out, "That sound that you hear is the sound of bridges burning."

9. NEVER POST PERSONAL INFORMATION ON-LINE

Your address, birthdate, phone number ... keep them off the web. Don't make yourself identity theft-able.

10. DON'T POST ANY CONFIDENTIAL WORK INFORMATION

If you post a writing sample, for instance, make sure all information that identifies the matter is redacted. If you're not sure what to remove, talk with your employer and/or your Career Services Office at school.

11. NO LIES—*ANYWHERE*

I've made the point elsewhere that you just can't lie about anything when you're looking for jobs. It's *particularly* true with the Internet. If you lie about your degrees, grades, jobs, *anything* ... it's just too easy to research you and bust you.

If you feel like you just don't look good enough to employers "as is," there are tons of ideas in this book for goosing your profile. Check out Chapter 7 on Resumes, the topic called "Pimp My Resume," and Chapter 10, on the Birds and Bees of Jobs, for ways to get noticed by employers for being the best possible you. And the best possible you isn't a liar!

* * * CAREER LIMITING MOVE * * *

Law firm gets a call from a client, a small company with a new Vice President, a guy with an M.B.A., a J.D. and an L.L.M. The client asks, "Can you check something out for us? This new guy tells us that we shouldn't withhold anything from his pay check, because as a Congressional Medal of Honor winner, he doesn't have to pay taxes."

A partner gives the issue to a summer clerk to research. The clerk comes back with her conclusions: "This man is definitely *not* a Congressional Medal of Honor winner. But there's something else you should know. This L.L.M. he says he has?"

The partner interrupts, "He doesn't have it."

The clerk responds, "More than that. The law school he claims he got it from ... he made it up. *The school doesn't exist.*"

B. SPECIFIC RULES FOR SPECIFIC SITUATIONS: E-MAILS, BLOGS, SOCIAL NETWORKING SITES

1. HANDLING YOUR E-MAILS WITH EMPLOYERS

E-mails with employers can make or break you. We covered e-mail correspondence in detail in Chapter 7 on "Correspondence" under Topic D, "E-mail Correspondence."

For "cold e-mailing" attorneys and setting up informational interviews ...

See Chapter 10, Topic D(3)(a) on "Cold e-mailing" and Topic D on "Informational Interviews," where we discuss those issues in detail.

2. HANDLING BLOGS AND PERSONAL WEB SITES

Handled appropriately, your own blog or web site can work wonders for your career. Handled inappropriately, of course, you can torpedo any chance you might have had.

A. IF YOU HAVE A BLOG THAT CAN BE TRACED TO YOU, MAKE THAT BLOG SHOW OFF THE BEST, MOST PROFESSIONAL YOU ... THE ONE YOU WANT EMPLOYERS TO SEE

The great thing about a blog is that it can be far greater in scope than any materials you'd send to an employer. You might want to include:

- "Highlights of my background."

  This *isn't* your resume, *unless you're only applying for one type of job with one size of employer in one geographic location.* The reason for this, as we discussed in Chapter 7 on Resumes, is that you want to tailor your resume for different kinds of employers, emphasizing and including items depending on the nature of the audience.

  If you have a "wardrobe of resumes" for different employers, use a "Highlights of my background" on your blog to encompass all of the elements that your various resumes have in common, awards you've received. Let's face it; your resume will be largely the same no matter *who* gets it. Those common elements are what you should include in your blog (cleansed of personal information like your address and phone number, as we'll discuss below).

- Offer "Resume available upon request."

  This covers employers who *do* want a resume from you. It gives you the opportunity to research them first, so you can decide how to fashion your resume appropriately.

- A writing sample.

- References.

- Video clips of stellar performances in moot court or other oral advocacy competitions.

B. CONSIDER CREATING A BLOG ABOUT THE SPECIALTY THAT INTERESTS YOU

In the "Birds and Bees" chapter—about activities that will help your career—I mention the idea of having a blog or web site that talks about issues in the specialty you want. This is an outstanding way to make yourself stand out to employers, in a totally positive light.

* * * SMART HUMAN TRICK * * *

Law student from New England, very interested in Environmental Law. He set up a web page to summarize new cases in the area. He sent letters to employers telling them about his web site. As one employer who received the letter commented, "It was a great way to establish his expertise."

Lawyers set up blogs like this all the time, by the way; for instance, Los Angeles employment lawyer Michael Fox runs the blog employerslawyer.com. Atlanta labor and employment attorney Julia Elgar runs a blog at www.hrheroblogs.com where she analyzes labor and employment issues raised by the hilarious TV show "The Office." *Really* great stuff.

If you run a blog or website where you compile new cases and provide links to relevant web sites and articles, you'll be proving your enthusiasm for–and familiarity with–your desired specialty, which is a tremendous plus in the minds of employers.

c. It's Fine to Have a Blog or Web Site About a Hobby or Interest

. . . unless, of course, you've got an 'out-there' interest. A blog about embalming techniques or turning road kill into jerky probably wouldn't do you any favours.

Having said that, there are plenty of lawyers who have blogs about their interests. Philafoodie.com is the blog of a Philadelphia securities lawyer, for instance. Or check out http://blogs.motorola.com/author/padmasreewarrior/

So if your hobby is not a shocker, go ahead and blog it. It can't hurt you. And it may attract potential employers who have the same hobby . . . or people who can put you onto them!

d. Routinely Search Your Name on Blogs to See What Other People are Saying About You

What other people write about you can have just as strong an effect on your image, good and bad, as things you say yourself. While employers might not put as much weight on other people's comments—after all, *you* don't have control over what they write—anything written about you contributes to your image.

Make sure your friends and on-line correspondents know that you're looking for a job, and ask them to be careful about what they say about you, perhaps even giving you an untraceable nickname so employers can't trace their postings to you.

* * * A CAUTIONARY TALE * * *

From a law student at the University of Minnesota:

"[Unnamed Federal Agency] is truly 'big brother.' My friend has a blog where he posted some stories from our recent Vegas trip (there is no way they could have found it with a simple Google search of my name). At the end of the interview they showed me that they had printed out the blog.

"It was quite a surprise (at least the stories weren't that bad, and they certainly weren't criminal). I was really embarrassed by the fact they found them though, but they assured me they wouldn't affect whether I was hired (mostly because I didn't write them), they just wanted to point out that I need to be careful if I worked there. It taught me a real lesson. I have to be very careful about what might be posted on the Internet that has my name somewhere on it."

E. IF YOU LIKE TO BE OUTRAGEOUS—AS MANY OF US DO—AT THE VERY LEAST PASSWORD PROTECT YOUR BLOG AND/OR WEB SITE, OR SHUT IT DOWN WHILE YOU'RE LOOKING FOR WORK, OR CREATE A MEAT PUPPET AND LET YOUR FINGERS RUN WILD

Let's face it: you're not going to say the same things to employers that you're going to say to friends. To make sure the two never meet, password protect anything you don't want employers to see. That's no guarantee that an employer won't be able to find it; you never know when someone will rat you out and post the password. But it's a whole lot better than nothing.

And for gosh sakes, don't put your web site/blog address on your resume if the content isn't appropriate for employers!

* * * CAREER LIMITING MOVE * * *

Recruiting coordinator at a large Texas firm is skimming resumes from law students. The firm's hiring partner comes in, and reads them over her shoulder.

The resume of one law student mentions a web address for his website. The hiring partner says, "I've never seen a student web site. Let's take a look."

The recruiting coordinator finds it. At the very top of the page is the line: "Scroll down to see my enlarged testicle."

The hiring partner and recruiting coordinator stare at each other. They quickly scroll down ... and sure enough, there is an x-ray of a testicle. Next to it, the student explains that he had a tae kwan do accident, and adds: "Testicle appears smaller than actual size."

The recruiting coordinator reports, "We were mortified. The hiring partner says, 'Gee, I don't think we were supposed to see this,' and I told him, 'Then he shouldn't have put the web page address on his resume!' "

F. IF YOU SAY SOMETHING EMPLOYERS DON'T LIKE, IT'S NOT A FREE SPEECH THING

You hear this argument a lot. "I'm allowed to say whatever I want; they can't hold it against me." Of course you're free to say anything (other than 'Fire' in a crowded theater). By the same token, employers are free not to hire you. I'd never tell you not to blog, not to have your own web page. Just be conscious of the image you're creating, be aware of the need to be tactful and discreet ... or password protect what you write!

3. HANDLING SOCIAL NETWORKING SITES

A. ABSOLUTELY TAKE ADVANTAGE OF LINKEDIN (AND BUSINESS NETWORKING SITES LIKE IT)

If you're not familiar with LinkedIn, this is how it works: You upload a profile that's a bare-boned listing of schools you've attended and organizations you've been associated with. People find you because they share those schools/organizations. As Vic Massaglia points out, "It's as good as 'passive networking' can get."

Incidentally, as we discuss in Chapter 10 on "The Birds and Bees of Jobs," **this is a *great* reason to consider volunteering activities like PSLawNet, judicial externships, clinics and the like; they get employers on your resume, they go onto your LinkedIn profile, and exponentially increase your opportunities**.

B. YOUR OWN PROFILE

The very words "social networking" suggests that you post a profile for your *friends,* not potential employers. But problematically—employers are taking a peek, too. Either password protect what you post, or make sure that you don't mention anything you wouldn't want an employer to see. As Beth Kirch points out, "If your profile basically documents your partying, employers are going to say, 'It's a judgment thing.'"

* * *CAREER LIMITING MOVES* * *

Career faux pas on social networking profiles are legion. Among them include:

- Female students posing nude (or topless or scantily-clad)
- Students holding a beer bottle and a joint
- Female students with beer cans lodged between their breasts
- Listing hobbies like "Club hopping" and "Posing for calendars"
- Making comments like "Law school sucks" "My professors are a**holes"

C. CHECK YOUR PROFILE OFTEN TO DELETE ANY INAPPROPRIATE COMMENTS PEOPLE ADD ABOUT YOU

While employers are generally understanding about the fact that you have no control over what other people say about you, there's no putting the djinni back in the bottle if they read comments that question your judgment or maturity. Make sure you sweep your profile often to make sure nothing "untoward" appears about you.

* * * CAREER LIMITING MOVE * * *

Midwestern law school, stellar student. He has a MySpace profile. His resume is on it. A friend posts the question, "Have you smoked pot?" to which the student responds, "Not today."

D. SEARCH YOUR NAME TO SEE WHO ELSE IS TALKING ABOUT YOU

As is true for blogs, see who else mentions you on their profiles. Negatives said by other people can affect your job search, too. Let your friends know that you're looking for a job, and you've got to be careful about what appears about you on-line as a result.

E. REMEMBER THAT IF YOU ONLY USE YOUR FIRST NAME IN YOUR PROFILES BUT YOUR FRIENDS POST COMMENTS USING YOUR FULL NAME, THOSE COMMENTS ARE SEARCHABLE

F. LOOKING AT EMPLOYER/INTERVIEWER PROFILES

"If they're looking at me, Kimmbo," you're saying, "Isn't it only fair for me to check *them* out?" Fair or not, you may find information you can't use.

I am reminded of a girlfriend I used to have. Her name was Lianna, and she was absolutely a nutter. She had a boyfriend she didn't trust, and she was always rifling through his stuff looking for evidence that he was cheating on her. Sure enough, she called me one day and said, "He's out of town. I went to his apartment and went through his desk. In one of the drawers he had a bunch of receipts. I found one for a fancy restaurant. It had two entrees on it ... and I didn't go there with him. What should I say to him?"

I told her what you would have told her, namely: You can't say *anything* about it, because *you shouldn't have been looking through his desk*. She always did that, by the way; asked me for advice about things she just shouldn't have done in the first place.

When it comes to employers and interviewers, if you can't resist the temptation to look at their social networking profiles, take into account that if they list personal information, *that information wasn't meant for you*. You can't mention it in letters, e-mails, or interviews. If the profiles mention both personal and professional information, you can bring up the professional stuff without mentioning where you found it. Remember: the two of you aren't friends ... yet. Don't put them on the spot by bringing up items they didn't expect you to see.

G. REMEMBER THAT *YOU DON'T OWN THE INFORMATION ON SOCIAL NETWORKING SITES; THE SITES DO.*

In the fine print they will tell you that they can use your information any way they want. Yipes!

C.   RESPONDING TO ON-LINE JOB POSTINGS

We cover this in the Resume chapter, Chapter 8, Topic I.

D.   DOS AND DON'TS OF POSTING
YOUR RESUME ON-LINE

In the "web resources" section at the end of this chapter, we cover lots of web sites that allow you to post your resume.

Wow. Talk about tempting. Just upload your resume onto a web site, sit back, have a cold one, and wait for employers to find *you*. Geez. It's even easier than on-campus interviews!

The experts I consulted about on-line resume posting were pretty uniformly cautious about it. Their issues fall into four general categories.

One, it's a mistake to think that it's the route most employers will take to find new people. Legal employers in particular don't lack for resumes and people approaching *them;* they don't have to go to sites that aggregate resumes to find promising new hires. As Vic Massaglia points out, "If you figure that 4% of jobs come through on-line job postings, an even smaller percentage comes through employers scouring posted resumes." Statistics suggest it's fewer than one in a thousand.

On top of that, if you post your resume on-line, it can tend to have a dampening effect on anything else you might do to find a job. "Why go to bar association functions," you could rationally say to yourself, "when my resume is doing everything for me?" I remember talking to a guy on an airplane once; he was looking for a job, and he lamented, "I've done everything. I've posted *five hundred* resumes on-line." In the universe of job search techniques, this guy was doing almost nothing; he felt terrible because he felt like the whole world was looking at his resume, and nobody wanted him. That couldn't be further from the truth!

Third, and worst from a strategic standpoint, is that if you post your resume on-line it's engraved in stone. Vic Massaglia points out that "You can't customize it. Where are the employers? What do they do? For instance, if you're looking in different cities, sometimes you'll want to say where you from and sometimes you won't. A posted resume stops you from making that change."

The fourth and perhaps most damning problem has to do with what happens to your resume when you post it on-line. Vic Massaglia advises that "You don't control your data. Would you stand on the Sears Tower and throw your resume out? No. You might get jobs you hate. And your resume might get into the hands of people you'd rather avoid." In 2006 *The New York Times* described a study that had been done by the World Privacy Forum. The Forum had posted hundreds of resumes on job sites, and followed them for a year to see what happened. Many were stolen; some were subject to identity theft. Other resume posters found that they were interviewed by employment consultants, who pitched services costing as much as $10,000.

If you *do* post your resume on-line, here's what you need to know:

1. DON'T LET ON-LINE POSTING BE THE *ONLY* THING YOU DO TO FIND A JOB

I'm begging you, no matter *where* you post your resume, do things that let people see you and get invested in you, as well. You'll find employers before they've even firmed up their plans to hire someone new.

2. TO THE EXTENT POSSIBLE, SCRUB YOUR RESUME OF IDENTIFYING INFORMATION

Use a post-office box of Mailboxes USA as your return address. Set up an e-mail account just for your resume. Consider a separate cell phone account as your telephone number.

Ideally you wouldn't put your photo or your Social Security Number on your resume *anyway*, so I scarcely need warn you about leaving them off an internet resume!

E. CLEANING UP YOUR WEB IMAGE

It's fine to say "Be aware of how you look on-line," but what if you don't like what you see?

It's one thing to have posts of your own that you're not particularly proud of. We'll cover that. But what if someone else smacks you on-line? We're all potentially victims of any yutz who wants to say anything they want about us on-line. Maybe you had a nasty breakup and your ex is harassing you on line. It could be anything.

What—if anything—can you do about it?

1. CREATE YOUR OWN BLOG TO STATE THE TRUTH AND DEFEND YOURSELF

Students have asked me periodically about dealing with really thorny Internet issues, like "What do I do if someone with my same name has a bunch of awful stuff about them on-line? When I get Googled, people think they're reading about *me*." Or students who've had relationships end badly, and their ex trashes them on-line.

What to do? One option is: fight back! If you have a blog, it'll show up in a Google search; you can even put it on your resume. Include on the blog highlights from your background–we talked about that earlier–and address the issue that's bugging you. "Please note that X is slandering me," or "Please note that there is someone out there with my name; the questionable material you find on-line are about that person, not me." (I had an issue like this once. Someone with my name had a terrible credit history, and every time I applied for a credit card I got falsely tarred with that person's baggage, even though we obviously had different Social Security numbers!)

You may wonder: If you bring up these issues yourself, are you drawing employers' attention to something they might not have noticed otherwise? Probably not. It's fair to assume that a growing number of employers will Google you, and if you plead your case in that context, you're being smart. As Vic Massaglia points out, "Employers appreciate a high level of self-awareness."

2. CONSIDER USING A SERVICE TO CLEANSE YOUR WEB IMAGE

Three that I've heard good things about include reputationdefender.com, zoominfo.com and naymz.com. You need to know that they're not free; they're businesses. A service like reputationdefender, for instance, offers "tiers" of services. At the lowest level, they'll troll the web periodically to find what's posted about you. For an increased fee, they'll try to help remove offending material from the source. Be aware that there are some things that can't be removed; court records and articles in major publications, for instance. But they're worth a look if you want to "sanitize" your web image.

3. IF IT'S YOUR OWN STUFF THAT'S THE PROBLEM, DISMANTLE ANY OFFENDING BLOGS/WEB PAGES, OR AT THE VERY LEAST PASSWORD PROTECT THEM STARTING RIGHT NOW

4. IF YOUR FRIENDS WRITE WARTS-AND-ALL POSTINGS THAT INVOLVE YOU, ASK THEM TO GIVE YOU AN UNPREDICTABLE NICKNAME SO EMPLOYERS WON'T BE ABLE TO IDENTIFY YOU

5. TRY TO PREVAIL ON THE OFFENDING POSTER TO REMOVE WHAT HURTS YOU

If someone posts something nasty about you, it may well be that if you explain how the post is affecting your job search, they'll remove it. This is really the easiest way to clean up your web image, because if the offending material is taken down, Google will remove any reference to it (in fact, the *only* time Google will play ball is if a web site's administrator removes the material first).

I have experience with this. A few years ago there was a guy who had a name very similar to mine, and when people looked for me on-line, they sometimes found him. It didn't much matter until once when a law school contacted him, thinking they'd contacted me, and set up a *Guerrilla Tactics* seminar at their school! I obviously didn't know anything about it, and when I didn't show, the school called my publisher and threw a fit. My editor in turn went ballistic, and wanted to track this guy down and tear him a new one. They were threatening legal action, all kinds of hellfire and damnation. I said, "Listen. This guy was just joking. I can't imagine he really wanted to hurt me. He thought it was harmless. If you explain to him the trouble he caused and tell him that if he knew me he certainly wouldn't want to do this to me, I'm sure he won't do it again."

It worked. Appealing to people's better nature is often the best way to resolve conflicts—including internet issues!

*** SMART HUMAN TRICK ***

Law student was editor of his college newspaper. When he was a senior, the paper ran an April Fool's edition, which had a profile of him accusing him of doing all kinds of crazy, lewd things.

Unbeknownst to him, the newspaper is Google-able. Employers who Google him see the profile, and don't realize that it's a joke.

The student prevails on his college to remove the archived newspaper article from its website. He contacts Google, and Google removes the reference. Problem solved.

6. POST YOUR OWN REBUTTAL

As Kurt Opsahl, an attorney for the Electronic Frontier Foundation, told *The Washington Post,* nothing stops you from posting something in response to what's posted about you. At least that way you've got your point-of-view out there, as well.

7. THERE'S ALWAYS LITIGATION . . .

. . . If you really, really want to take it that far. Kurt Opsahl points out that cyber-writers can be sued for defamation, and judges can force web site hosts to disclose a user's identifying information. Furthermore, even the threat of litigation generally jollies web site operators into removing the offending material.

8. WHAT IF SOMEONE HAS THE SAME NAME AS YOU, AND WHEN EMPLOYERS GOOGLE YOU, THEY FIND STUFF ON *THAT* LOSER? . . .

If you don't have a blog already, start one and make it plain that you're the law student. Lots of people have the same name. If employers haven't run into this before, they will, soon. A blog of your own, identifying you as *you,* will do the trick.

F.   IF YOU'RE BUSTED, AND AN EMPLOYER SEES WHAT YOU DIDN'T WANT THEM TO SEE . . .

Employ the following magic words: "I learned an important lesson."

A lot of mistakes that students make on the Internet are what I'd call rookie mistakes. If you're posting stuff for your friends, who'd think an employer would bother to take a look? That's not a fatal character flaw. It's thoughtless at best. If you tell them the truth–that you learned an important lesson about being discreet on-line–you'll go a long way toward revivifying your reputation.

G.   A Compendium of Web Resources
for Every Job Search Situation

As you know, the web is like a flu virus, constantly mutating. Here are some useful sites for a whole variety of job search purposes. I'll list more as I learn about them on my website, www.jobgoddess.net. (And if you find out about a great one–please share!)

The first site to visit, and visit often:

Your Career Services website at school. It will have information tailored specifically to your location and will have resources unavailable to anyone but you and your classmates. You'll probably have services like Symplicity that offer all kinds of research tools. Your school's web site will also have job postings that are absolutely this-minute fresh, from employers themselves. Take advantage of it!

If you're considering an out-of-town job search, go to the web site for the school that's located in–or closest to–the city you're targeting. Law school career web sites generally have a whole bunch of geographically-oriented links that are available to everyone.

Threshold resources:

Lexis/Nexis and Westlaw. Your school pays a ton of money for them, so refer to them often. Whether for researching employers, law-related news, finding attorneys through any one of a ton of identifiers, you can't beat Lexis and Westlaw.

Blogs on law school job search topics:

http://blog.lib.umn.edu/lawcso/vocare/ (my favourite, from the University of Minnesota)

Legal job openings:

Two caveats:

Many on-line job postings seek "laterals"; that is, attorneys with a year or two's worth of experience. Don't bum yourself out as you read them. Consider them an educational opportunity–and a chance to see what you'll be eligible for before you know it! (We talk about getting around the experience requirement in Chapter 8 on Resumes.)

Also, note that many career counselors have warned me that with some web sites more than others, there's an issue of "freshness"; you have no idea how fresh job postings are when they're not on your school's web site. So if you don't have success with them, it might very well be that the jobs have already been filled by the time you see the posting!

www.myspace.com click on jobs and search: legal intern. *Lots* of current listings)

www.attorneyjobs.com/ (subscription required; job opportunities domestically and abroad, job search tips, seminars, legal news)

www.alm.com (The National Law Journal)

www.ncsl.org/public/joblegis.htm (job vacancies writing legislation for states, listed by the National Conference of State Legislatures)

www.emplawyernet.com (subscription required; your school may entitle you to a discount)

www.lawjobs.com (revised daily—employment listings from more than twenty publications like the National Law Journal, New York Law Journal, and many others)

www.lawmatch.com (subscription required)

www.lawcrossings.com (subscription required)

www.vault.com/find-a-job_jsp (can search for jobs matching geographical, specialty, and level of experience criteria)

www.legalmojo.com

http://careers.lawinfo.com/ (resume posting service)

www.jobsfed.com *(Federal Jobs Digest, searchable by position type)

www.ihirelegal.com

www.legalemploy.com (Legal Employment Search Site; links to many legal employment sites, no listings on this site)

www.careers.findlaw.com (FindLaw for Legal Professionals; also contains links to other employment sites)

www.summerclerk.com (on-line databases and ability to apply directly to employers)

www.legalstaff.com (positions around the country, can set up free 'career agent service' that notifies you of job postings matching your criteria)

www.jdpost.com (legal job opportunities, summer and permanent)

On-line versions of legal publications:

Check Lexis/Nexis and Westlaw for numerous legal publications on-line. Also check:

www.law.com (The National Law Journal)

http://careers.findlaw.com (newsletters on specialties)

www.abanet.org (the American Bar Association)

www.abanet.org/buslaw (ABA Business Law Today)

www.bna.com (BNA's Corporate Counsel Weekly)

www.nbew.com (National Business Employment Weekly)

www.sec.gov/news.shtml (SEC News Digest)

www.natjurist.com/ (The National Jurist Magazine home page; has articles on job search)

www.studentlawyer.com (The ABA's Student Lawyer Magazine)

www.jdmag.com/ (J.D. Magazine–The Law Students Survival Guide)

www.jdjungle.com (J.D. Jungle)

Social networking sites and resources:

http://en.wikipedia.org/wiki/List_of_social_networking_websites (more social networking sites than you could believe ever possibly exist)

www.socialseeker.com

www.mashable.com/?p=1524

www.socialnetworkingconference.com/

Law news:

Numerous websites offer news; the legal research sites listed above are good resources. Also check out:

www.lawfuel.com (see "press releases" for expanding practices)

www.jurist.law.pitt.edu (law news from students at the University of Pittsburgh Law School)

www.law.com

www.palidan.com (legal, judicial, litigation and legislative news, as well as career resources by state)

www.abcnews.go.com/US/LegalCenter/

News on organizations:

www.news.google.com

www.news.yahoo.com

National Professional Associations for Lawyers:

www.abanet.org (American Bar Association; links to special divisions and specialty practice areas; for Young Lawyers' division, go to www.abanet.org/yld/home.html)

www.nla.org (National Lawyers Association)

www.napaba.org (National Asian Pacific American Bar Association)

www.fedbar.org (Federal Bar Association)

www.lpba.org (Lawyer–Pilots Bar Association)

www.acca.com (American Corporate Counsel Association; visit www.acca.com/jobline for job opportunities with corporations)

www.afda.org (Association of Federal Defense Attorneys)

www.abanet.org/dch/committee.cfm?com=CL320000 (ABA Committee on Commerce in Cyberspace) www.actec.org/ (American College of Trust & Estate Counsel)

www.atlanet.org (Association of Trial Lawyers of America)

www.nacua.org (National Association of College and University Attorneys)

www.aaml.org (American Academy of Matrimonial Lawyers)

www.naela.com (National Academy of Elder Law Attorneys)

www.nsclc.org (National Senior Citizens Law Center)

www.healthlawyers.org (American Health Lawyers Association)

www.innsofcourt.org (American Inns of Court; see also Chapter 10 on People and Activities)

www.aipla.org (American Intellectual Property Law Association)

www.iaba.org (Inter–American Bar Association; international lawyers)

www.nlgla.org (National Lesbian and Gay Law Association)

www.napp.org (National Association of Patent Practitioners)

www.aplf.org (Association of Patent Law Firms)

www.nationalbar.org (National Bar Association for African–Americans; also check www.cbacareers.com for Crimson & Brown's minority career placement database)

www.clia.org (Commercial Law League of America)

www.corporatebar.org (Corporate Bar Association)

www.fedbar.org/ (Federal Bar Association)

www.fedjudge.org/ (Federal Magistrate Judges Association)

www.firstamendmentlawyers.org/ (First Amendment Lawyers Association)

www.nobc.org (National Organization of Bar Counsel)

www.abanet.org/rppt/home.html (ABA Section on Real Property, Probate and Trust)

www.aaepa.com (American Academy of Estate Planning)

Legal headhunters:

www.nalsc.org (National Association of Legal Search Consultants)

Continuing Legal Education:

Check local bar association websites and your Career Services Office website for CLEs offered locally. Also check out:

www.pli.edu (Practicing Lawyer's Institute; gives CLEs nationwide, with scholarships for law students)

www.westlegaledcenter.com (on-line CLEs)

www.cce-mcle.com (Center for Continuing Legal Education)

www.lawjobs.com (on-line CLEs from American Lawyer Media)

To find lawyers:

www.martindale.com and www.lawyers.com (Martindale–Hubbell; the comprehensive web site of attorneys practicing throughout the United States, with contact information)

www.findlaw.com (for small firms, key in any town and specialty)

www.directory.findlaw.com (data on law firms and attorneys by geography and specialty, including corporate counsel and government lawyers)

www.eattorney.com

Job sites to learn more about legal and law-related fields (often with job openings):

www.attorneyjobs.com (you can access this via www.lawschool.westlaw.com)

www.hg.org/employment.html (lots of information; can post resumes here and ask for automatic e-mail notification when positions you're interested in are posted)

www.law.com (includes American Lawyer lists of largest and richest law firms)

http://community.lawyers.com/messageboards/list.asp#channel17 (message boards on various specialties)

www.nalpfoundation.org/webmodules/archive/gallery.asp

www.lcp.com (part of Westlaw, has many lists of law-related Internet directories, libraries, and research sources)

www.palidan.com (has directory of 100+ practice areas)

www.lawguru.com (free answers to legal questions from attorneys; see Q & A to see questions people ask of their lawyers in various specialties)

www.lawresearch.com (Internet law library; all kinds of information about firms, government agencies, associations)

www.research.lawyers.com (firms by practice area all over the country, with links to their web pages)

www.library.lawschool.cornell.edu/guides/ (Cornell Law Library)

www.lawnewsnetwork.com (from American Lawyer Media; compiles legal magazines and publications)

www.legalemploy.com *(many links to websites for law-related jobs)

www.law.indiana.edu/ (Indiana Law Library's site; one of the country's largest, offering many reference tools)

www.skyradionetwork.com/lawyers.cfm (profiles of lawyers and interviews about issues in topics like criminal defense, construction litigation, class actions, entertainment law) www.vault.com (Vault Reports, on specialties not just in law but other fields as well)

www.abanet.org/yld/careerinfo.html (American Bar Association young lawyers' division career information)

www.abanet.org/careercounsel (American Bar Association large collection of career information and advice)

www.lawschool.com (West's Employment Research links)

www.prosecutor.info (contact information for district attorneys and state attorneys general nationwide)

www.counsel.com ('Counsel Connect,' from the publishers of American Lawyer; offers links to articles, legal seminars)

www.newslink.org (American Journalism Review's on-line jobs database; has communications law openings)

www.law.cornell.edu/topics (Cornell Legal Information Institute)

www.lawforum.net

www.lawinfo.com/

www.lawmall.com

www.lawcrawler.com

How to sound like a really deep thinker:

www.cspan.org (features Q & A with Supreme Court Justices)

www.newyorker.com (type "Jeffrey Toobin" in the search box. He's the CNN legal analyst and New Yorker staff writer, who writes incredibly insightful articles about legal issues. The fact that he's also a major hottie . . . well, maybe that's just me talking)

Federal Government sources:

www.nalp.org/jobseekers/fedempl.pdf (NALP's Legal Employment Opportunities Guide)

www.usajobs.opm.gov (gateway to federal government jobs)

www.fedworld.gov/jobs/jobsearch.html (FedWorld Federal Jobs Search; can search abstracts of federal job openings)

www.usajobs.opm.gov/b5a.htm (Chart of governmental pay grades)

www.jobweb.org/search/jobs/fjapply.htm (Information on federal job applications)

www.usdoj.gov/oarm (justice department vacancies, as well as intern and volunteer opportunities)

www.usdoj.gov/usao/offices/index.html (Listings of US Attorney's Offices Nationwide)

www.govtjob.net (federal government job postings)

www.whitehouse.gov (the White House; incidentally, whitehouse.com is a porn site) www.senate.gov (U.S. Senate)

www.house.gov (U.S. House of Representatives)

Army jag: www.goarmy.com/jag/ (army JAG corps)

www.jag.navy.mil (Navy JAG Corps)

http://hqja.jag.af.mil/ (Air Force JAG Corps)

http://sja.hqmc.usmc.mil/ (Marine JAG Corps)

http://uscg.mil/legal/ (US Coast Guard Legal Division)

www.nps.gov (National Park Service)

www.nlrb.gov (National Labor Relations Board)

www.opic.gov/ (Overseas Private Investment Corporation)

www.rrb.gov (railroad Retirement Board)

www.nlada.org/Jobs (Legal Aid and Public Defender job postings)

www.cia.gov (Central Intelligence Agency)

www.occ.treas.gov/ (Comptroller of the Currency)

www.epa.gov/epahome (Environmental Protection Agency)

www.fcc.gov/jobs (Federal Communications Commission)

www.atf.treas.gov (Bureau of Alcohol, Tobacco, Firearms and Explosives)

www.usda.gov (Department of Agriculture)

www.doc.gov (Department of Commerce)

www.defenselink.mil/ (Department of Defense)

www.energy.gov (Department of Energy)

www.doi.gov (Department of the Interior)

www.dot.gov (Department of Transportation)

www.fec.gov (Federal Election Commission)

www.ftc.gov/ (Federal Trade Commission)

www.irs.ustreas.gov (Internal Revenue Service)

www.usajobs.opm.gov/b3.htm (Presidential Management Intern Program)

www.sec.gov (Securities and Exchange Commission)

www.ustreas.gov (Department of Treasury)

www.va.gov (Department of Veterans Affairs)

www.eeoc.gov (Equal Employment Opportunity Commission)

www.fca.gov (Farm Credit Administration)

www.fbi.gov (Federal Bureau of Investigation)

www.fdic.gov (Federal Deposit Insurance Corporation)

www.usitc.gov (International Trade Commission)

www.nasa.gov (National Aeronautics and Space Administration)

www.whitehouse.gov/omb/ (Office of Management and Budget)

www.opm.gov (Office of Personnel Management)

www.pbgc.gov (Pension Benefit Guaranty Corporation)

www.usps.gov (U.S. Postal Service)

www.sbaonline.sba.gov (Small Business Administration)

www.si.edu (Smithsonian Institution)

www.ssa.gov (Social Security Administration)

www.os.dhhs.gov (Department of Health and Human Services)

www.hud.gov (Department of Housing and Urban Development)

www.state.gov (Department of State)

www.uspto.gov (U.S. Patent and Trademark Office)

www.epo.co.at/epo (European Patent Office)

www.loc.gov/crsinfo (Congressional Research Service)

Courts sources:

www.uscourts.gov (Federal Judiciary homepage; includes Law Clerk Hiring Plan)

www.ncsconline.org (National Center for State Courts)

www.courts.com (lists new appointments to the federal bench; need i.d. and password from Career Services to enter)

www.courts.net (courts directory information)

www.vermontlaw.edu/career (Guide to State Judicial Clerkships; contact your Career Services Office for access and password information)

https://lawclerks.ao.uscourts.gov (Federal Law Clerk Information System; federal judical clerkship jobs)

www.judicialclerkships.com (advice on judicial clerkships, including a forum for exchanging information with law clerks)

www.uscourts.gov/vacancies/judgevacancy.htm (federal judiciary vacancies)

www.law.yale.edu/outside/scr/library/nom/index.asp (database of federal judiciary nominations and confirmations)

www.law.emory.edu/fedcircuit (Contact information and court opinions for the Federal Circuit court)

www.oalj.dol.gov (homepage for Office of Administrative Law Judges)

www.ustaxct.gov (homepage for U.S. Tax Court)

www.law.gwu.edu/fedcl (opinions of judges and special masters of the U.S.Court of Federal Claims) www.judiciary.senate.gov (homepage of Senate Judiciary Committee; has up-to-date information on federal bench appointments and confirmations)

www.fjc.gov (links to a database of federal judge biographies)

https://oscar.symplicity.com/ (this site posts federal judicial clerk positions and allows for the opportunity o apply on line for those positions)

State and local sources:

www.abanet.org/careercounsel/statebar.html (nationwide links to state and local bar associations)

www.findlaw.com (Nationwide links to bar associations and regional resources)

www.statelocalgov.net/index.cfm (links to state and municipal government sites)

www.statejobs.com (links to state specific sites with links to public and private sector employers in each state)

www.statelocalgov.net (state and local government jobs)

www.prosecutor.info (state prosecutor jobs)

Job openings in general: the major job sites:

www.jobcentral.com

www.jobster.com (from Facebook)

www.craigslist.org (click on city and review openings)

www.monster.com

www.jobsearch.org

www.hotjobs.com (from Yahoo; information on career, field, location, keyword)

http://careers.yahoo.com (includes salary negotiation advice)

www.careerbuilder.com (includes on-line job fairs and international opportunities)

www.ajb.dni.us (America's Job Bank; listings through state employment service offices)

www.employmentguide.com

www.flipdog.com (includes resume posting)

www.career.com (includes resume posting)

http://207.21.203.96/index.html (jobs at US companies, government at every level, as well as in Canada)

Sole practitioner guidance:

www.myshingle.com (outstanding, comprehensive site)

Alternative careers:

You can review openings and see descriptions on the major job sites listed above. Also check out:

www.careerjournal.com (The Wall Street Journal's on-line career source; excellent articles on a variety of career issues)

www.about.com/careers/ (see "Need a new career?")

www.jobmonkey.com ("the coolest jobs on Earth")

www.adr.org (American Arbitration Association)

www.ecojobs.com (environmental jobs)

www.bls.gov/oco/ocoiab.htm (The government's occupation outlook handbook; lists hundreds of popular careers)

www.rileyguide.com/network.html

www.careers-in-finance.com (job listings, recommended resources, and links)

www.careersingovernment.com (information, resources, job listings in public sector domestically and abroad)

www.coolworks.com/blogs/

www.agora.stm.it/politic/ (database of politically-oriented organizations)

www.academemploy.com (Academic Employment Network)

www.accountingjobs.com (Accounting and Finance Jobs)

Legal Publishing:

www.cch.com/ (CCH)

www.lexisnexis.com/careers/ (Lexis)

http://west.thomson.com/careers/ (West Group)

www.riahome.com/about/careers.asp (RIA)

www.aspenpublishers.com (Aspen)

www.cch.com (Commerce Clearing House)

www.bender.com (Matthew Bender)

www.bna.com (Bureau of National Affairs)

Legal employers who have recently won awards:

www.lawfuel.com/awards.asp (and "Law stars" on home page)

Live chats with lawyers in various specialties:

Check local bar association websites for listservs and chat rooms. Also try:

http://community.lawyers.com/chat/list.asp

Researching companies:

Apart from the major job search sites that have voluminous information about companies, try:

www.hoovers.com (comprehensive corporate research site; remember to add the "s" to "hoover," or you wind up at the hoover vacuum cleaner website)

www.wetfeet.com (corporate/industry research reports, including job opportunities with corporations)

www.vault.com

www.ziggs.com (profiles of people across companies; can create your own profile)

www.jobsearch.about.com

www.bigbook.com (on-line Yellow Pages)

www.selectory.com

www.jobstar.org/hidden/coinfo.php

www.commerce.net (Commerce Net)

www.state.de.us/dedo/index.html (Delaware Economic Development Office)

www.ectw.com (Enterpreneurs on the Web)

www.sbaer.uca.edu (Small Business Advancement National Center)

www.jobdig.com

www.robinsblog.com

http://www.businessweek.com/careers/index.html (this site will allow you to search a variety of different companies that are considered among the best for entry level positions)

www.ipl.org/div/aon (trade associations)

www.forbes.com (useful for basics on large private companies)

www.wsrn.com (Wall Street Research Cnet)

www.companysleuth.com (e-mails you every news story about the company you choose)

Sports and Entertainment jobs:

www.abanet.org/forums/entsports/home.html (The American Bar Association Forum on the Entertainment and Sports Industries)

http://www.sportslaw.org/ (The Sports Lawyers Association)

www.cnn.com/jobs (CNN)

www.showbizjobs.com (entertainment law jobs)

International jobs:

www.cils.org (International Law Internships available from the Center for International Studies) www.pslawnet.org (post-graduate international fellowship opportunities from PSLawNet)

www.washlaw.edu (useful links for international jobs)

www.jobsite.co.uk (Permanent and contract jobs in Europe and elsewhere)

http://www.cit.uscourts.gov/ (homepage for U.S. Court of International Trade; lists job openings)

www.state.gov/index.html (The United States Foreign Service)

www.abanet.org/ceeli (Central European and Eurasian Law Initiative; internship and fellowship opportunities)

www.italyun.org (homepage of the Permanent Mission of Italy to the U.N.; has vacancies in international organizations)

www.oas.org (Organization of American States; has international fellowships and employment opportunities)

www.worldbank.org (Homepage of the World Bank; has job openings both permanent and summer)

www.overseasjobs.com (Newspaper service for international recruiting; subscribe for access to thousands of jobs internationally)

www.abanet.org/intlaw (homepage of ABA Section of International Law and Practice; has activities and resources)

www.abanet.org/liaison/home.html (American Bar Association International Liaison Office; has information on ABA international meetings and programs)

www.ilsa.org (International Law Students Association; has information on conferences, memberships, scholarships, and links to other useful sites)

http://asil.intracommunities.org/jobs and www.asil.org (on-line jobs board for opportunities in international law, from interns to full-time)

http://www.rileyguide.com/internat.html (The Riley Guide International Job Search Page; can subscribe to career forum, post resume)

www.asil.org (American Society of International Law; has international law employment opportunities)

www.uscib.org (U.S. Council for International Business)

www.foreignrelations.org (Council on Foreign Relations; policy-oriented job openings)

www.derechos.org (Compilation of websites and contact information for international organizations and NGOs)

www.embassy.org (the Electronic Embassy)

www.overseasjobs.com (Overseas Jobs Express)

www.studyabroad.com (study abroad programs)

Summer jobs/internships:

Many sites that list job openings also have summer opportunities.

www.myspace.com (search: legal intern)

www.internshipusa.com

www.law.arizona.edu/career/honorshandbook.cfm (Government Honors and Internship Handbook; descriptions of federal government positions for summer and after graduation; contact your Career Services Office for passwords).

www.twc.edu (Washington Center for Internships & Academic Seminars)

www.summerclerk.com

www.home.sprynet.com/ear2ground/ear2/jlint.htm (links to legal internships, judicial clerkships and fellowships)

Fellowships:

www.iie.org/fulbright (Fulbright Fellowships)

Skadden fellows.

Funding:

www.fdncenter.org (Grant Writing & Funding Resources)

www.finaid.org (Scholarship Databases and Student Lenders)

www.pslawnet.org (includes summer funding sources)

Figuring out what you want to do:

www.abanet.org/careercounsel (Q & A on job search, hundreds of attorney profiles in different practice areas and alternative careers, and a vast archive of resources)

http://profdev.lp.findlaw.com (articles on finding out if law is right for you)

www.decisionbooks.com (on-line career assessments and career consultant locator)

www.grownupcamps.com (fantasy camps)

www.careerexplorer.net

www.careertest.us (career and personality testing)

www.careerlaunch.net (self-assessment)

www.collegeboard.net

www.review.com/career (self-assessment from Princeton Review)

www.listz.com (discussion groups in various industries)

www.topica.com (discussion groups in various industries)

www.egroups.com (discussion groups in various industries)

www.industryinsite.com

www.vault.com (message boards)

www.factiva.com (research employers/industries)

www.coach.net/personal.html (Professional career coaching from Coaching for Success)

Sites that direct you to other useful jobs sites:

http://www.law.vill.edu/studentservices/careerstrategy/docs/internet resources.rtf (particularly useful; this site has nine pages worth of links to guide you through your career search)

www.alllaw.com (links to law-related associations, job listings, and legal news)

www.fastsearch.com (provides on-line access to top law libraries around the country)

www.abanet.org/lawlink/associations.html (Legal Association internet sites, state and federal court sites)

www.abanet.org/yld/career.html (Career-related website links, from the ABA's Young Lawyers Division)

www.myjobsearch.com/employers/emerging/html (links to publications listing growing companies and organizations)

www.rileyguide.com (comprehensive guidance on internet job searches)

http://jobsearch.about.com/od/topjobsdb/a/topjobsites.htm

www.lawoffice.com (offers links to legal-related job openings)

www.jobslawinfo.com (16,000 + links to law-related resources)

www.job-hunt.org (Guide to on-line career and job hunting resources as well as professional associations)

www.home.sprynet.com/% 25ear2ground (Index to websites that post job openings in all settings)

www.IMprofile.com (links to blogs)

Search engines:

Other than the obvious Google and Yahoo and Ask, check out:

www.looksmart.com

www.zeal.com

Metasearch engines:

Search engines that virtually examine the entire internet:

www.metacrawler.com

www.dogpile.com

Salary info:

www.nalp.org/research/index.php (Employment and salary statistics for lawyers, courtesy of the National Association of Law Placement)

www.lawjobs.com (job listings, temporary jobs, directory of legal recruiters, employer lists, on-line CLEs, National Law Journal's 'What Lawyers Earn' survey)

www.infirmation.com (compares salaries at law firms up to eighth year)

www.salaries.com (salaries in general)

www.affiliates.com *(salary info from The Affiliates, a legal staffing organization)

www.careers.findlaw.com *(Look under 'Candidate Resources,' then 'Other Resources' for 'Salary Charts'; compares salaries in cities nationwide)

www.jobsmart.org (links to hundreds of salary surveys, categorized by profession)

www.ilrg.com

www.homefair.com/homefair/cmr/salcalc.html (salary comparisons for different geographic locations)

www.homefair.com/homefair/cmr/ataxes.html (state income tax rates)

Also, search for results of the state or local government's recent audits on-line, advises Georgia State Research Librarian Kreig Kitts. "It will tell you how much employees in certain departments are making. In Georgia, for instance, you can learn the salaries of everyone in the state Law Department, Department of Revenue, or the Judicial Branch by visiting https://www.audits.state.ga.us/esa/index.html."

Debt management, loan repayment, and loan options:

http://www.salliemae.com/content/tools/calculators/repayment/index.html (repayment estimator)

Public Interest:

www.equaljusticeworks.org (Fellowships, employment opportunities and career development)

www.law.harvard.edu/students/opia (Harvard University Office of Public Interest Advising; also includes links to other sites)

www.pslawnet.org (Public Service Law Network, an awesome resource for volunteer opportunities; includes internships, fellowships and post-graduate opportunities; search by geography and interest; also includes information about funding)

www.abanet.org/legalservices/probono.html (ABA site addressing virtually everything about pro bono) www.guidestar.org (for a free registration, you see basic information on nonprofits, as well as the nonprofit's finances, history, and some salary history)

www.nonprofitjobs.org (nonprofit job listings)

www.opportunityknocks.org (can register to receive e-mail alerts on openings)

www.law.umich.edu/currentstudents/PublicService/toolkit.htm (public interest job listings)

www.aclu.org (The American Civil Liberties Union)

www.hrw.org (Human Rights Watch)

http://www.naacpldf.org/ (NAACP Legal Defense & Education Fund)

www.publiccounsel.org (Public Counsel Law Center)

www.essential.org/ (National Association of Public Interest Law; links to public interest sites)

www.nlada.org/ (National Legal Aid and Defender Association; links to defender and litigation services as well as job openings nationwide)

www.eco.org (Environmental careers, legal and not-law-related)

www.ejobs.org (Environmental opportunities, law-related, in the U.S. and Canada)

www.fairhousing.com/ (Fair Housing resources: click on 'job listings' for openings)

www.acinet.org (Canadian Justice System: Public interest organizations in Canada)

www.oneworld.net (One World Jobs: international jobs with over a hundred organizations, helping people and the environment; has internships for law students)

www.undp.org/jobs (United Nations Development Program: Job opportunities worldwide)

http://www.foundationcenter.org/ (Foundation Center: comprehensive information about grants, fundraising, and philanthropic organizations)

http://philanthropy.com/jobs (Lists many job opportunities in nonprofit; can sign up for free notification of jobs in areas that interest you)

www.afj.org (Alliance for Justice; association of public interest organizations; describes internship and fellowship opportunities)

www.un.org (The United Nations home page; for permanent job opportunities, go to www.jobs.un.org/Galaxy/Release3/vacancy/vacancy.aspx or www.un.org/Dept/OHRM/index.html)

www.opajobs.com (Opportunities in public affairs–requires Career Services Office subscription at your school)

www.bazelon.org (legal advocacy center for the mentally handi-capped; information on community activities and job openings)

www.flaginc.org/ (nonprofit center for legal services to family farm-ers)

www.consumerlaw.org/ (National Consumer Law Center; has some job openings)

www.youthlaw.org (National Center for Youth Law; includes some job openings)

www.healthlaw.org (National Health Law Program; national public interest law firm; has links to career advice and job openings) www.abanet.org/ceeli (Central European and Eurasian Law Initiative; in-ternship and fellowship opportunities)

www.abanet.org/elderly (ABA Commission on Legal Problems of the Elderly)

http://www.nclej.org/ (Welfare Law Center; includes fellowship and other job opportunities)

www.lawyerscomm.org/ (Lawyers' Committee for Civil Rights Under Law)

http://www.un.org/Depts/OHRM/sds/internsh/index.htm (Internships with grad students at the U.N.)

www.naela.org (National Association of Elder Law Attorneys)

www.seniorlaw.com (SeniorLaw home page)

www.nvlsp.org (National Veterans Legal Services Program)

www.idealist.org (resource for employment opportunities with 20,-000+ nonprofits worldwide, has links to other sites and a career center)

http://www.usaid.gov/careers/ (USAID; humanitarian aid organiza-tion; has a resume bank)

www.amnesty-usa.org (Amnesty International; has links to U.S.-based employment opportunities, paid and volunteer)

www.care.org/jobs/index.html (Care USA; has employment possibili-ties domestically and internationally)

www.hri.org (Human Rights Internet; click on "Job Board" and then "Human Rights Job Sites" for links to job boards at related sites)

www.hrusa.org (Human Rights USA Resources Center; has informa-tion on careers, fellowships and internships. Click on "What's New")

www.ICRC.org/ (International Red Cross; has information on volun-teer relief efforts as well as job listings)

Writing competitions:

www.law.lclark.edu/dept/lawac/writing.html

http://www.law.duq.edu/career/students.html (The Common Plea link will take you to a bulletin posted by the Duquesne University School of Law listing, among other things, various writing competitions from across the country)

Removing negative stuff about you from the web:

www.Zoominfo.com

www.Reputationdefender.com

www.Naymz.com

www.google.com/remove.html (advice for webmasters about removing content from the google search engine index)

Women's Interest:

www.advancingwomen.com

Gossip about employers:

Remember, these comments are *unfiltered*, and you don't know the bias of the poster. But they're fun.

www.autoadmit.com (also known as www.xoxohth.com)

www.judged.com

www.greedyassociates.com

www.vault.com

Legal Employment Agencies links:

www.legalrecruiter.com (recruiting search and placement resource)

Social networking sites:

Other than the obvious ones–MySpace, Friendster, Facebook . .

http://en.wikipedia.org/wiki/List_of_social_networking_websites (more social networking sites than you could believe ever possibly exist)

www.linkedin.com (you create a profile and people find you; it's "passive" job searching but often effective; for guidance on creating an effective profile, visit http://jobsearch.about.com/od/networking/a/linkedin.htm

www.livejournal.com

www.xanga.com

www.socialseeker.com

www.mashable.com/?p=1524

www.socialnetworkingconference.com/

Researching places (especially valuable for out-of-town employers):

www.2chambers.com (chambers of commerce)

Cost of living calculators:

As Georgia State Reference Librarian Kreig Kitts points out, "Not sure how much more to ask when moving to a more (or less) expensive city? These calculators are useful for estimating how much you might ask when moving cities. So if you need to make 30% more in City B than you do in City A for the same standard of living, you'll know that 10% increase you're being offered might not be worth it!"

http://cgi.money.cnn.com/tools/costofliving/costofliving.html

http://swz.salary.com/costoflivingwizard/layoutscripts/coll_start.asp

http://www.cityrating.com/costofliving.asp

On-line job search advice:

www.jan.wvu.edu (Job Accommodation Network offers a free consulting service with information for the disabled)

www.findlawjob.com (a fee-based service, will compile a list of legal employers matching your criteria; offers cover letter and resume advice)

www.eresumes.com (Rebecca Smith's information on electronic resumes and internet job searches)

Temporary legal employment agencies:

www.hirecounsel.com (HIRECounsel, with offices in New York, LA, Washington, Chicago, Houston, Stamford and Hartford)

www.johnleonard.com (John Leonard Employment Specialists, in the Northeast)

www.kellylawregistry.com (Global legal placement firm)

www.lawcorps.com (LawCorps–Boston, NY and Washington)

www.legalsupportpersonnel.com (Legal Support Personnel–New York)

www.lexolution.net (Lexolution–New York, New Jersey, Connecticut, Washington DC, Maryland and Virginia)

www.us.manpower.com (Manpower, with offices nationwide)

www.affiliates.com (Robert Half Legal, nationwide and Canada)

www.specialcounsel.com (Special Counsel, offices nationwide)

www.stonelegal.com (Stone Legal Resources Group, worldwide)

www.strategicworkforce.com (Strategic Workforce Solutions, in New York, New Jersey, Connecticut, Chicago and London)

www.trakcompanies.com (Trak, Washington DC region)

www.updatelegal.com (Update Legal, offices nationwide)

(Thanks to Albany Law School for this list)

Connect with old school friends:

College websites will help you connect with fellow alums. Also try:

www.classmates.com

www.linkedin.com

Giggles:

http://anonymouslawyer.blogspot.com/ (Jeremy Blachman's fictional big firm lawyer; funny, especially if you like to take swipes at big law firms)

www.theonion.com (nothing to do with the law, but spit-milk-through-your-nose funny)

Shout-outs to Vic Massaglia of the University of Minnesota and Chris Borsani (Duquesne, '07) for their great help with this chapter.

Chapter 12
After the Offer . . .

Related issues—Negotiating for more money: Chapter 18, "Small Law Firms," Topic G

Congratulations! I'm so proud of you. To quote the actress Sally Field, they like you. They really like you.

Of course, there are still some issues to keep in mind. Let's talk about them.

* * * CAREER LIMITING MOVE * * *

Law student, California school. During his 2L summer, he clerks with a prestigious firm. The firm makes him an offer at the end of the summer, and he accepts it.

Thereafter, the firm learns from one of his classmates that this student hadn't attended class during the Spring Semester *at all*. He'd *completely* blown off law school. When the firm confronted him, he responded, "Gosh. I guess I thought you knew."

A. If It's Definitely What You Want— Accept It Right Away!

If this is your dream job and you're fine with the starting date, the dough, everything about it—there's no point in pussyfooting around. Career counselor Wendy Werner advises, "If you're clear on all aspects of the offer, accept!" As Debra Fink points out, this is a display of enthusiasm that any employer would appreciate. It will immediately add luster to your image, before you even set foot in the office.

When you do accept, make sure that you "follow up that you will need to see a written copy of the offer," advises Wendy Werner (see Topics D and E, below).

B. Don't Keep an Employer Dangling Very Long

As a rule of thumb, the amount of time you can wait before accepting an offer made to you depends on the nature of the employer. For judicial clerkships, it is customary to respond immediately. You really can't tell a judge, "Can I get back to you?"

For other employers, Debra Fink advises that you wait no more than 24 hours or so before responding. Joan King says "You have a day or two, no more." There are two reasons for this. One is that if you wait longer, they will question your enthusiasm. The second is that they may be keeping other students waiting pending your decision.

If you have issues to resolve before you accept, tell the employer in that first conversation (we discuss this in Topic C, immediately below). And if the employer isn't your first choice and you're waiting for other offers, see Topic F, below.

The fact remains: If it's a job you want and you don't have issues with it, accept ASAP.

C. If You Still Have Questions That Haven't Been Answered, Now's the Time to Ask Them

Remember the interview chapter, where we talked about issues you couldn't discuss before you had an offer? The "what's in it for me" issues, like benefits and pay? Well, when they've proposed to you job-wise, now's the time to ask. (The *way* you ask is something we'll get into in a minute.)

Depending on the size and nature of the employer, and what they told you as part of the offer, some of the issues that may concern you are:

- Pay (and when you can expect increases);
- Benefits;
- Pro bono policy;
- Latitude in choosing your own projects;
- What their billable hours requirements (and averages) are;
- Whether or not attorneys are expected to work late evenings and/or on weekends;
- Whether attorneys are expected to meet clients on weekends;
- What kinds of community activities attorneys are expected to take part in;
- There may, of course, be other questions specific to your circumstances (like what the lawyers at the employer do about day care, part time policies, etc.). As Wendy Werner points out, "What you

are trying to get to are some firm culture issues that go beyond what you've learned in the interview process, or through policies you've read. For instance, when they say a policy is indicated on a 'case by case' basis, you want to know what that means in practice."

When it comes to asking these questions, you've got to be tactful. Remember: You may well be working with these people, and you need to be mindful of what they think of you. If you say things like, "Listen, I've got some issues I've got to resolve before I give you my answer. You don't expect me to come in on weekends, right? I don't have to bring in any business, right?" you're going to ruffle their feathers needlessly.

Instead, ask if you can set up a meeting—over lunch or dinner, even, if that's geographically feasible—where you can discuss "a few details" about the job before you accept. State your enthusiasm for the employer; say something like, "I'm really interested in working with you. I'd like to get the answers to a few minor questions so that I'm sure we're on the same page," something non-confrontational like that.

If the employer is large, you may ask whether you can speak to one or two of the junior attorneys so that you can get some questions answered. They will undoubtedly comply. You can get at issues like hours and billables tactfully, by asking, for instance, "What's a typical week like for you? When do you come in, when do you leave? Is that typical? Tell me about the pro bono you do. Is that what most associates do? . . ." you get the idea.

The bottom line is this: It's hyper important that the "fit" between you and the employer be right. The employer doesn't want you to get there, be miserable and quit the first week, any more than *you* do. Resolve the issues that are on your mind before you accept!

D. When You Accept the Offer, *Get It in Writing*

Whether you had issues with the offer or not, as soon as you've decided to accept the offer, *ask for it in writing*. I can't tell you how many law students have come a cropper by hastily accepting an offer, only to discover when they arrived that the job as described to them verbally bore *no resemblance* to what they encountered.

Of course, you don't want to start your work life on an adversarial basis. But it's perfectly fair to say, "Just to make sure we're completely in agreement, could I have the offer in writing?" Or you can take it on yourself, write down the terms of the agreement, and send it as part of a note confirming your acceptance. You'd say something like, "I am delighted to accept your offer of employment. As per our conversation, I understand that we agree on the following: . . ." Finish up by reiterating how happy/excited/pleased to be joining the practice.

If you think this is a little "in your face," that you should just trust the employer . . . well. You're going to be a lawyer. Trust, but verify.

After all, an employer who's being honest with you won't mind seeing the terms of employment in writing. If someone hotly refuses to confirm their offer in writing, you have to question seriously whether they intend to live up to it.

E. WHAT IF YOU LIKE THE EMPLOYER, BUT YOU'RE NOT WILD ABOUT THE MONEY THEY'RE OFFERING?

It *may* be possible to negotiate for more, but that depends on the nature of the employer. If it's the government, there's no negotiating. Large companies: ditto. Large law firms: what, are you crazy? They already pay mad cheez. If you ask for more, that's probably grounds for justifiable homicide.

Small firms, on the other hand ... there, you've got a chance to squeeze out more dough. Because this is an issue specific to small employers, we discuss it in the chapter dedicated to small law firms, Chapter 18.

F. WHAT IF THE OFFER COMES FROM AN EMPLOYER WHO'S NOT YOUR FIRST CHOICE?

This is a really, really difficult situation, and what you should do depends on a few variables, namely: who else you have on the line, how close they are to making a decision, and how you really feel about the offer you just got. You're the only one ultimately in the position to weigh the competing factors.

Let's look at a few situations:

1. YOU GET AN OFFER FROM AN EMPLOYER, YOU'VE INTERVIEWED WITH OTHERS YOU LIKE MORE, AND YOU HAVEN'T HEARD BACK FROM THEM

You're actually in a really, really great position ... because you've got leverage with the employers who are considering you. You know how when you're single, people always look better when they're dating somebody else? The same goes for employers. When someone *else* wants you, you're automatically a more attractive candidate.

This is what you do. Thank the "offering employer" profusely for their offer, say that it's a serious decision to make and you hope they'll give you a week to decide. You can't really ask for more than a week. Then immediately contact the employer at the top of your wish list, and say something like, "I'm calling to let you know that I have received an offer that I'm seriously considering. However, with what I know about your organization, I might be more interested in working with you." This may speed up the decision-making process. And the *worst* that can happen is that you've got it on record that you have a clear interest in your dream employer, so that you can pursue them some time down the road. Wendy Werner counsels that "Remember, too, that it is not a good idea to 'name names.' Even if the employer you are most interested in asks you who else has made you an offer, you want this process to remain on the up and up; and you certainly don't want to play into firm rivalries. If asked, remember to demur for the sake of confidentiality."

Incidentally—this has to be a phone call, *not* an e-mail. E-mail can be forwarded *anywhere*. You don't want a record of the conversation.

2. YOU GET AN OFFER FROM AN EMPLOYER, AND ALTHOUGH YOU'RE INTERESTED IN OTHER EMPLOYERS MORE, YOU DON'T HAVE ANY "IN PROCESS"; YOU HAVEN'T INTERVIEWED WITH THEM AND THEY AREN'T CONSIDERING YOU FOR AN OFFER . . . YET

It depends how quickly you can, and are willing to, jump on those other employers. There's no downside to asking the "offering employer" for a week to make a decision; as I advised above, thank them profusely for their offer, tell them it's a serious decision and you'd appreciate a week to think about it. They'll probably give you that. Then let your fingers do the walking . . . *fast*. You've got to get onto those other employers immediately.

Either talk to a trusted advisor/mentor/professor and ask for employers to contact, or call candidates yourself, introduce yourself, and say, "I just received an offer from an employer in town. While I am very interested in working with them, I would appreciate the opportunity to talk with you because it might be an even better fit. Can we set up an interview?" I realize this is a rather ballsy approach, but you don't have much time to waste. If you've got to tie up another offer in a week, you don't have time to waste with anything other than a fast phone campaign.

Option (b) is to avoid looking a gift horse in the mouth, and to say to yourself, "OK, this might not be my dream employer. But I like it well enough, and it's going to be a good place to get my feet wet. I know that if I do a great job here, it'll line me up for great opportunities in future. And hey—maybe it'll turn out to be even better than I thought."

I talk all the time to students who take a job they're not so excited about, only to find that the gig is really awesome. Remember: your first job isn't a life sentence. A couple of years there, an apprenticeship really, and you can step into something else you might like even more. You don't die when you take a job, you know; you keep your eyes open, you stay involved in the community, and before you know it, other gigs come into view. And anyway, if your first job turns out to be *truly* awful, nobody's nailing your feet to the floor. You can always quit. You know how to get jobs. You did it at least once already.

So sometimes the best option is to just take what's offered to you, and make the best of it . . . which can be great!

3. YOU DON'T HAVE ANYONE ELSE IN MIND, BUT YOU REALLY DON'T LOVE THIS PARTICULAR JOINT

I talk with a lo-o-ot of students in this position. They don't have a firm idea of exactly what they want, but they're pretty sure they don't want what they've been offered.

Depending on your circumstances, the pressure to take an offer can be pretty immense. Some people will tell you that *every* first job sucks (they're wrong, by the way). There will be people saying, "You're lucky to have an offer at all." There's that looming student loan debt ... there's the fear of never getting anything else ...

Let me take a load of your mind: *Don't accept the offer.* Don't ever, ever jump at the first job that's offered to you out of fear that you'll never get another offer, if you think you'll be miserable working there. I realize that there's balance involved, in that you do have to get some legal experience under your belt, even if the job in question is not your first choice. But, I don't under *any* circumstances think it makes sense to work somewhere that makes you very unhappy. You'd be better off waitering in a restaurant on weekend nights, and volunteering with the bar association or attending CLEs or doing *whatever* interests you during the week, any of the activities we discussed in Chapter 10 on the "Birds and Bees of Jobs." When you do things you enjoy, you naturally shine and attract people to you. Life's too short to do things you just hate. So if the job you've been offered turns your stomach, turn it down. If you keep your feet moving in a strategic way, something better will definitely show up.

G.   ONCE YOU'VE ACCEPTED AN OFFER ... DON'T SHOP AROUND!

One of the absolutely, positively worst things you can do during your job search is to accept an offer and then renege on it. Don't even *think* about interviewing once you've accepted an offer! As Debra Fink says, "Few stories run through the legal grapevine faster than those about lawyers who renege on an accepted offer. Once you accept, there's *no* graceful way to back out!"

Ann Skalaski says that this most often happens when a student isn't sure they're going to get an offer from their dream employer, so they accept an offer from someone else—and then, sure enough, they *do* get an offer from their employer of choice. She says, "I always tell students in this predicament, think about how *you'd* feel if a firm that made you an offer called your Career Services Office and said, 'We've found a better student. Can we interview them?' You wouldn't want them to do that, so you shouldn't do it to them! It's just unethical!"

She adds that it's important to remember that "The value of your professional reputation begins in law school, with your classmates. If they know that you've done something like this, they'll remember it later on. And remember, your classmates may refer business to you later on. That guy you have a beer with could wind up being a judge!''

On top of that, it reflects really badly on your school. Employers often think that if you renege on an offer, it must be because your law school trains you to think that's OK. You may well be trashing the opportunities of your classmates with this employer. And even if you don't want the gig, it's not really fair to walk all over other people's chances, as well.

But . . .

What if your feelings are extreme, and you're seriously, seriously bummed out about accepting? What if the thought of working for this outfit makes you queasy? Here's something you might not have thought about: no employer wants a miserable new employee. They want you to be psyched about working with them, not just to show up and go through the motions. There's a steep learning curve in law, and your head has to be in the game for you to be useful to them. So if you've got really serious doubts about the job—if you just can't under any circumstances get your brain around the idea of working for them, even though you accepted the offer—call (or visit in person, if it's possible), and explain that you made a terrible mistake, that you want to reject the offer after all. Drench your comments in ruefulness; say that if they insist, you of course will live up to your obligations. It's *possible* they'll tell you to resolve your doubts; employers have been known to behave that way. On the other hand, of course, they may tell you to go . . . you know. It's a risk you take if you attempt to renege. If they do that, you've got to stay calm, say you understand, and apologize. Send a follow-up note apologizing again.

The downside of even *suggesting* you don't want to follow through on your obligations is so serious it's not even worth doing unless you are really, *really* mortified about the possibility of working there. Otherwise . . . suck it up and give it a try. As I mentioned above, you can always keep your eyes open for other gigs, and make a jump in a year or two. It'll pass in a heartbeat.

In short: take a deep breath before you accept a job offer. It's a whole lot easier to ask an employer for a few days to think it over than it is to wriggle out of something you agreed to do. Don't accept offers for jobs you don't intend to undertake!

* * * CAREER LIMITING MOVE * * *

A 1L at a California law school nails a paid summer internship with the in-house counsel's office of a prestigious international company.

Two weeks before the internship is to begin, the student calls the general counsel, and says, "Listen. I've accepted an internship this summer with a judge. Sorry."

The general counsel is so furious he calls the law student's dean at the law school, ranting, "I will *never* hire one of your students again. *Not ever.*"

Remember that employers you reject now may wind up being colleagues down the road. Don't burn bridges with thoughtless words and behavior.

H. REMEMBER THAT NO MATTER *HOW* YOU FEEL ABOUT THE EMPLOYER, YOU ARE GOING TO *DRENCH* YOUR *COMMUNICATIONS IN GRATEFULNESS*

I don't care how you really feel about an offer. And I don't care if the employer is Torquemada the Grand Inquisitor, and they're so crappy they can't hold onto anybody for more than two weeks at a time. As Washington's Josie Mitchell advises, "Don't burn bridges! Be courteous when you decline offers." You're *still* going to be gracious, you're still going to say you're honored they made you the offer, and you're going to say that perhaps you'll have the opportunity to work together in future. You don't know where you'll wind up or where *they'll* wind up. Law is a tight community, and you don't know when they'll become a colleague . . . or a judge. So never, *ever* say anything negative, even if you don't want to accept the offer.

* * * CAREER LIMITING MOVE * * *

Note: This is Kimm talking. This is one of my favourite all-time job search stories.

A 3L, from a very prestigious East Coast law school. He interviews with a large, prestigious Florida law firm, and he receives an offer.

Two weeks later, the hiring partner receives the following letter from him, in pertinent part:

"Dear Attorney X:

Thank you for your offer of permanent employment with your firm.

After careful consideration, I have decided that my career would be best served if I took my first job with a real law firm in a real city. I have decided to work with X firm in Boston . . ."

[The letter goes on in this vein, "It was an agonizing decision for me," "I have always been known for my excellent judgment," and so on . . . for two pages.]

The letter winds up with:

"But of course none of us knows what the future brings, and if my plans change, rest assured that I will once again consider your firm."

As the hiring partner points out, "*Consider* our firm? *Consider* it? Like you'll get the chance! This guy was the subject of derisive laughter at our firm for *months* afterwards."

Appendix: It's not what you say . . .

You've probably seen this e-mail exchange before; it flew around the Internet, and I mentioned it in Chapter 11, the Internet chapter. It's between a lawyer with a criminal defense practice (whom I'll imaginatively call "Lawyer"), and a student (whom I'll call, gee, "Student.")

The relevant background is that Lawyer had placed an ad for an associate on Craigslist. Student received an offer and accepted it. A start date had been set, but then Lawyer apparently decided to hire another associate, which necessitated reducing Student's starting salary.

Now, with a cut salary, there's no question that Student was well within her rights to change her mind. It's the way she went about it that got her into trouble . . . and exemplifies the classic advice that if you've got something negative to say, *say it—don't write it.*

Here's what transpired:

From: Student

Friday night, 9:23PM

Subject: Thank you

Dear Attorney X,

At this time, I am writing to inform you that I will not be accepting your offer.

After careful consideration, I have come to the conclusion that the pay you are offering would neither fulfill me nor support the lifestyle I am living in light of the work I would be doing for you. I have decided instead to work for myself, and reap 100% of the benefits that I sew [*sic*].

Thank you for the interviews.

From: Lawyer

Monday, 12:15PM

Subject: RE: Thank you

Student—

Given that you had two interviews, were offered and accepted the job (indeed you had a definite start date), I am surprised that you chose an e-mail and a 9:30PM voicemail message to convey this information to me. It smacks of immaturity and is quite unprofessional. Indeed, I did rely upon your acceptance by ordering stationery and business cards with your name, reformatting a computer and setting up both internal and external e-mails for you here at the office. While I do not quarrel with your reasoning, I am extremely disappointed with the way this played out. I sincerely wish you the best of luck in your future endeavors.

From: Student

Monday, 4:01 PM

Subject: RE: Thank you

A real lawyer would have put the contract into writing and not exercised any such reliance until he did so.

Again, thank you.

From: Lawyer

Monday, 4:18PM

Subject: RE: Thank you

Thank you for the refresher course on contracts. This is not a bar exam question. You need to realize that this is a very small legal community, especially the criminal defense bar. Do you really want to start pissing off more experienced lawyers at this early stage of your career?

From: Student

Monday, 4:29 PM

Subject: RE: Thank you

bla bla bla

Shout-out to Wendy Werner for her help with this chapter.

Chapter 13
"Help! My Grades Stink!"

"The C students run the world."

Harry Truman

"To those of you who received honours, awards and distinctions, I say well done. And to the C students, I say you, too, can be President of the United States."

President George W. Bush at the 2001 Yale graduation

"If only I were in the top 10% of my class . . ."

I hear that lament everywhere. Nothing can put a damper on your ambition faster than a less-than-great GPA. If the god of grades hasn't smiled on you, remember this simple sentiment:

To hell with your grades.

That's right. They only loom large now because you're in school, and *everybody* focuses on them. In this chapter we'll talk about how to deal with your grades so that you're on the same footing as everyone else. As we'll see, there's nothing—*nothing*—that's out of your reach just because your grades ain't great. Remember way back in the beginning of the book, when I talked about the keys to great jobs—image and message control, taking initiative, displaying enthusiasm—well, I didn't mention grades there, and there's a good reason for that. No matter what your grades are like, there's a way to nail a job you'll love.

If you don't believe that, it's because your mind has been poisoned by the evil atmosphere of law school. It's incredible how, as soon as the very first grade comes out, people are immediately typecast by their grades. People in the top 10% of the class are "smart," and their classmates are branded according to rank all the way down the food chain to the bottom of the class. Few things in law school broke my heart as much as seeing classmates who'd entered law school bursting with enthusiasm, full of hopes and dreams, having their spirit broken by a couple of bad grades

894

First Year. It was cruel and it was largely unnecessary. And do you know why? Because your ability to be a great lawyer is much more a reflection of the qualities you brought to law school, the enthusiasm you'll bring to your job, than it is on how you performed on a single three-hour exam for each class. You just don't feel that way because you're in the thick of law school right now. So, much of my task in this chapter is to work on how you feel about those grades, and how you can come to grips with discussing them without feeling defensive or defeatist. I *promise* you, you *can* get the job of your dreams, *regardless* of how bad your grades are. I know this, because no matter what job you want, I know someone with worse grades than you who already has it. If you don't believe me now, you will by the time this chapter is over.

Here are just a few stories to illustrate the point:

- Do you recognize the name "Alfred P. Murrah"? The Oklahoma City Federal Building that was bombed in 1995 was named after him. When I spoke at an Oklahoma law school shortly after that, I asked, "Who was Alfred P. Murrah, anyway?" The Career Services Director told me the following story: "He was a federal appellate judge who served for a long time. Very few people realize that he was named to the bench when he was 29—one of the youngest people ever to have that distinction. What almost nobody knows about him is this: He graduated from law school last in his class."

- A student at a New England law school had had great grades undergrad, but bombed in law school. He took Bankruptcy Second Year, and loved it. He volunteered for a bankruptcy judge, and in that role met several prominent local bankruptcy attorneys. One of them referred him to another lawyer who had just gotten a huge bankruptcy client, and needed a clerk. The lawyer hired this guy over the phone, telling him that although he didn't have the credentials the firm normally looked for, they'd hire him for this one project and if he did a good job, they'd give him a good recommendation for his next job.

  Well, he worked on the project, and did so well that at the end of the summer they made him a permanent offer. A year later, he was hired away by a prestigious firm that had a policy of only hiring students in the top 5% of their class!

- Law student at a Midwestern law school, in the bottom 5% of the class. Desperate for a job, he took a low-paying job with the state department of insurance. Through that, he made contacts at a small insurance company, and got a job there as in-house counsel. Unbeknownst to him when he took the job, the small company was planning to merge with an enormous, well-known insurance company, and when the merger went through, he became assistant general counsel, with a six-figure salary.

- Law student in the Northeast, a 1L with awful grades. He had read "Barbarians at the Gate," and dreamed of doing corporate acquisitions–something that only huge firms, hiring top students from prestigious schools, get to do. He was bereft at the prospect of not pursuing his dream, but the Career Services Director talked him into considering clerking for a small firm that did corporate work. He was sure that he would not enjoy working for *anyone* if he didn't have a chance of being in the *Wall Street Journal*. Lo and behold, he found he loved the work as opposed to the trappings of a huge firm. He was made an offer to be an associate after he graduated, and he gladly jumped on it.

- Western law school. The Career Services Director runs a panel that features alumni in very important positions in Washington, D.C. One of the panel members is a guy who heads a governmental agency–an extraordinarily good job! After the panel is over, one of the law professors in the audience pulls the Career Services Director aside, gestures toward the guy from the agency, and whispers to her, "Can you believe it? We didn't think he'd make it through law school!"

- My own law school roommate is a prime example of trumping bad grades. I was no Einstein, but she was the worst law student on the face of the planet. I don't remember her ever doing a shred of homework throughout law school. She'd go out drinking every night, wake up at five minutes to nine every morning, run her hands through her hair, and show up, disheveled and hung-over, for our 9 o'clock class. She only got one answer right when she was called on in class for the entire time we were in law school, and that's only because she happened to have her *Gilbert's* outline open to the right page. And at the end of the semester, she used that as a basis for trying to argue her grade up a notch! She went to the professor and said, "Come on. Aren't you going to give me any credit for class participation?" He looked at her in disbelief, and said, "You want half a grade, you got it. D! D-plus! What's the difference?"

Well, as it turned out, she married a Libyan immigrant when we were 3Ls, and he had a lot of friends with immigration problems. So, after she passed the Bar, she set up a sole practice focusing on immigration law, and she was hyper successful. Everything she lacked in terms of studiousness, she made up for with people skills–but her ultimate success would have been hard for *anyone* to predict when we were in school!

As these anecdotes show, it's *always* possible to overcome bad grades and land a dream job. Let's go step-by-step and talk about how you do it.

A.   BEAT THE MOST SERIOUS EFFECT OF BAD GRADES: THEIR EFFECT ON YOUR SELF WORTH

The worst thing about getting bad grades in law school is how they make you feel about yourself. Especially if you were a good student in undergrad, law school may be the first time in your life that you've ever had bad grades. As Sophie Sparrow says, "If you're used to outward forms of validation in the form of good grades, it's hard to feel validated when your grades are awful." Florida's Ann Skalaski echoes that, saying, "it's tough to be in the bottom half of the class when you've never been there before."

The most important thing to do when you've got bad grades is to keep them in perspective. Grades aren't a permanent condition. They don't indicate what you're capable of accomplishing. They're a snapshot of what you did under a highly stressful, books-closed four-hour marathon. They're not the entire picture of you. As Drusilla Bakert says, "Law school destroys your perspective. It trains you to focus, not to look at the Universe." But if your grades are bad, it's *very* important to get your perspective back; step away and look at that Universe. How do bad grades fit in? They show that sitting in a room taking a four-hour final exam isn't your best skill. *And that's it*. As Career Consultant Wendy Werner points out, "Great. Let's move on. You'll never have to do *that* again." Once you're out of law school, you never have to do anything resembling a four-hour closed-book exam (well, outside of the bar exam, anyway). So all bad grades really do is show that you're not very good at doing something that you'll never have to do for the rest of your life. That's really not so bad, is it?

You also have to consider that your grades are not a reflection on what kind of lawyer you'll be. As Ann Skalaski points out, "You have to think about what you thought would make you a good lawyer *before* you had grades. Whatever it is that you thought is *still* true." If you have great people skills, or you're a skillful negotiator, or you research well– all of that is still true, and all of those things will have a far greater impact on your success as a lawyer than any stupid grades you might get. As Drusilla Bakert says, "Students have this big misconception that grades are everything. They aren't! Few students appreciate the importance of personality, of relating to people. It's easier to get disillusioned about grades, but it's important to remember that law is a *people* business."

Another thing to remember about grades is this: It's an issue with a very short shelf-life. As Oklahoma City's Carol Kinser points out, "What do you call the person who graduated at the top of the law school class? Lawyer. What do you call the person who graduated at the bottom? Lawyer." It's only pathetic losers who talk about their grades when they've been out of law school more than a couple of years or so. Once you've gotten your feet wet with your first job, you'll be defined by what you do, not how you did in school.

Finally, remember what great grades do for you: as Sue Gainen points out, "Great grades don't get you jobs. They get you *interviews*." I talk to students every year, students with amazing credentials, who can't get jobs. There are a whole variety of reasons that might happen, but trust me, if your only issue is a lacking GPA, you're a lot better off than someone who looks great on paper but has the personality of a troll. Grades you can get around, as we'll discuss throughout this chapter. A really crappy personality? Years of therapy and heartache.

So don't let yourself be depressed about your grades. They're a reflection on how you performed in a four-hour timeframe on an exam, and that's it. They don't determine your worth, your potential success, or any other facet of your life—and anyone who tries to make you feel differently is insecure enough not to want to face the truth.

B. REMEMBER THAT ENTHUSIASM IS THE EQUIVALENT OF HAVING GREAT CREDENTIALS

Enthusiasm is so-o-o important to employers that I dedicated a whole chapter to it, Chapter 4.

Now, I'm not talking about being a goofy suck-up. There are other ways to show enthusiasm. The fact is, knowing about an employer, researching them, having intelligent questions to ask, talking with people who work there for advice, taking CLEs about what they do, maybe even volunteering for them—it makes you an absolute standout regardless of how you look on paper. It makes you look a *whole* lot better than the student with great credentials who couldn't give a rat's patootie about the employer and professes complete ignorance about them.

Employers make this point to me all the time. So often I'll hear an employer say, "We had this student approach us. We'd never have taken her based on her resume . . . but she turned out to be a superstar." I was at a job fair talking to a recruiter for the SEC, who said, "Students think they have to have a financial background to work for us. They don't. They *do* have to show a love for the SEC, to be familiar with the sections, to know what we do outside of enforcement. We'll take that over better grades any day."

* * * SMART HUMAN TRICK * * *

Midwestern student whose dream is to work for a City Attorney's office. She doesn't have the grades to get in, but she offers to work for free for the summer. They take her on, and as her supervisor reports, "She was amazing. She did all the work we assigned her, but she also spent several hours a day walking around the offices, asking the attorneys if they needed any extra help. She'd stay late if she hadn't completed her assigned work. She was our best prospect, by far."

C. RECOGNIZE WHY GRADES LOOM SO LARGE IN LAW SCHOOL: ON-CAMPUS INTERVIEWS

I can hear what you're saying. "Kimmbo, how can you argue that grades don't matter? Look at on-campus interviews. They only take students with great grades!"

I hear you. And it's true that the interview schedule at most law schools is laden with the same students over and over again, the ones at the top of the class. The same often goes for job postings, where employers ask for people in the top 5%—10%—top you-name-it of the class. That starts to make you think, "Geez, *no* employer wants anybody who doesn't have top grades!"

It's simply not true. On-campus interviews get disproportionate attention just because they're so visible. Everybody knows about them. But as I've pointed out several times before, they're just the tip of the iceberg. The vast majority of legal employers don't interview on-campus; in fact, most legal jobs aren't advertised anywhere at all ,and that's why it's so important for you to do everything we talked about in Chapter 10, talking with people and taking part in activities. OK, so if your grades stink, you probably won't be spending a lot of time showing up at school in a suit for on-campus interviews. You're going to have to be a bit more creative than that. It ain't no thing, for at least two reasons: First, the vast majority of your classmates are in the same boat, no matter where in the class they are. Secondly, those jobs available through on-campus interviews may be prestigious and high-paying, but if you skip ahead to Chapter 23 where I talk about getting jobs with large law firms (the bulk of on-campus interviewers), you'll quickly find that many people don't particularly enjoy those jobs. Sure, they're prestigious, but you're an unusual bird if you can be happy very long working phenomenal hours in a highly-politicized setting. Thirdly, there are a million ways to skin the large law firm cat; there's always a way to plot a course that will lead you into just about any job, at a large law firm or anywhere else. Again, we talk about that in Chapter 23.

Most importantly, not getting jobs through on-campus interviews is a blessing in disguise. If you've got to take the initiative to find a job— whether it's talking with people, taking part in activities, no matter what it is—you're doing the same things you're going to be doing for the rest of your life to nail great jobs. I've told you before that when you get out of law school you're likely to have at least a dozen jobs in your lifetime. After your first job, you can't call school and say, "All-righty-o! I'm read for job number two. When does OCI start?" Students who had to get creative the first time around are actually far better positioned to get great jobs after that. You may not believe me now, but I've seen this happen a thousand times, and when you've been out of law school a couple of years, you'll see the same phenomenon yourself. In the meantime, trust me: OCI isn't the end of the world. And the fact that it typically requires great grades is *no* reflection on the job market in general.

D. ACKNOWLEDGE THAT MOST OF THE PEOPLE YOU INTERVIEW WITH WEREN'T ON LAW REVIEW, EITHER

If you've got bad grades, it's easy to put yourself into a party of one, believing that every potential legal interviewer must have done much better than you in law school. Carol Kinser advises, "Repeat after me: 90% of the class will not graduate in the top 10%!" As Wendy Werner points out, "At least 50% of practicing lawyers were in the bottom half of the class. You have *many* peers out there!" Diane Reynolds adds, "Lawyers tend to hire from the part of the class they were in. If you're a nice and articulate person, you'll be fine." And Susan Benson says, "Many attorneys embrace the fact that they themselves weren't stellar students–and they embrace students who are like they were."

Carol Kinser points out that "I had an employer recently call in with a job posting. He requested that the hiring criteria section state that he was only interested in students at the bottom of the class, because that's where he ranked in law school. He said to me, 'Don't those A students realize that they're being interviewed by lawyers who were C students?' "

So as you contact people, make sure you don't look at everyone as being a better student than you are. They may not have been. Instead, you want to derive confidence from other sources. Which leads me conveniently to . . .

E.   REMEMBER THAT THERE ARE TONS OF GREAT JOBS WITH EMPLOYERS WHO ARE NOT GRADE-OBSESSED

Large law firms are the major grade culprits; they demand stellar grades. To that I say: So what? Latham and Watkins' Skip Horne points out, "Most—and I stress most—legal employers could give a hoot about your grades. They'd rather know how you are going to contribute to their practice, be it small, large, corporate, litigation, public interest, you name it." As Fordham's Suzanne Endrizzi points out, "There are 370 law firms with 100+ lawyers . . . and 48,000 with fewer than that." Stop focusing on the tiny minority of jobs that demand what you *don't* have . . . and pay attention to the Mongolian hordes that *do*.

If your grades are poor, and you've got your heart set on being a U.S. Supreme Court clerk or waltzing into a large law firm clerkship, then it's time to face the music. Unless you've got really juicy photographs of a Supreme Court justice or similar blackmail materials on an influential partner at a large law firm, it's not likely to happen. Not right away, anyway. Given that—why waste time applying for jobs that are heavily grade-oriented? As Susanne Aronowitz says, "The universe of jobs is divided into 'unrequited employers' and employers who want you. If you don't have great grades, you can go after the 'unrequited employers' who won't take your credentials or go after the employers who do. Focus your energy on the employers who want you—there are a lot more of *them!*"

Small to medium-sized law firms, especially those with a non-corporate law focus, public interest employers, most government employers, state agencies, those all tend to be jobs that are not focused on grades. As Ann Skalaski points out, "It's just not about credentials. The hidden message from most legal employers is, 'Will you stay? Will you bring in clients?' " That's got nothing to do with your grades. Ellen Wayne adds, "Small firm practitioners are only really concerned with two things: How much do I have to pay? And, How much do I have to train them?" Grades are a secondary concern.

A real plum of a part-time job you can get regardless of your grades is a volunteer externship with a judge. As Ellen Wayne explains, "You'll be more savvy. You'll see how lawyers negotiate, you'll see the process–and best of all, judges are great references." As she points out, state court judges frequently have no permanent clerks, so anything you can do for them is great. (We talk about judicial clerkships and externships in Chapter 25.)

There are many other jobs you can go after if your grades aren't great, but that's a start. The point is: don't make yourself feel worse about your credentials by banging your head against brick walls in the form of employers who will refuse to look past your grades. There are *many* employers who will welcome the assets you *do* bring to the table. Focus your efforts on them!

F. If Your Dream Employer(s) Demand(s) Outstanding Grades, Look for a "Side Door" That Will Get You In

OK. I just told you to avoid going after jobs where killer credentials are a "must have." What do you do if you really want one of those jobs? If corporate work at Huge, Huge and Large is your dream? Or you want to clerk for a federal judge? *Of course* it's possible. I don't care about your grades. It's your *timeline* and your *point of entry* that will change. What you want to do is to look at your first job as an "apprenticeship," or graduate work in law if you prefer, that sets you up to get the job of your dreams.

Let's take the large law firm dream. If you don't have the grades to nail an on-campus interview right now, there are a bunch of ways to circumvent that process. As we discuss in the Large Firm chapter, Chapter 23, they include:

- Clerking for a large firm during the school year, when the grade pressure is considerably reduced but you still have an opportunity to prove your chops;
- Establishing your own expertise in one of their specialties through publications;
- Developing a useful expertise elsewhere (e.g., at a state or federal agency);
- Doing a state court clerkship, then a federal court clerkship, then lateraling over to a large firm.

Or let's look at the federal court clerkship. I can't tell you how many students have made it into that outstanding position by starting with a lower court clerkship, one with less grade pressure. The fact is, once you prove yourself working for a judge, they'll be happy to pick up the phone and recommend you to their brethren on the bench. Another option is to volunteer for a federal judge. They take volunteers, and if you prove yourself in that role, you're in the catbird seat when it comes to paid clerkships.

Let's take another example: In-house counsel positions. Those virtually always go to lateral hires. Inevitably, a lawyer will develop a specialty in a private firm and then move over to an in-house position once (s)he's developed a particular expertise.

You see the point. It's not where you start; it's where you end up. I've talked to students who've moved into killer jobs from the most unlikely beginnings. I told you a bunch of these stories in Chapter 10. As Ann Skalaski points out, "Look at where jobs can lead. People with great jobs didn't necessarily start there!" Drusilla Bakert adds, "You have to think of your career as a continuum. You won't live or die with your first job. Have limited expectations for your first job, because you'll wind up with what you like within five years after graduation."

So if you're resentful that the world isn't your oyster coming right out of law school, cool your heels. If you use the skills we learned in Chapter 10 on people and activities, you'll be able to parlay any job you get into a dream job. You'll keep your eyes open, you'll keep expanding the number of people who know you, and if you do a good job at whatever you do, you'll be able to turn it into other opportunities. If on the other hand you let resentment poison your outlook, you'll have no one to blame but yourself when things don't break your way. So make the most of your grades and your experience, and accept the best job you can find. Like so many other law school graduates before you, you can turn that first job into your dream job!

G.   STOP FOCUSING EXCLUSIVELY ON IMPROVING YOUR GRADES

You may be horrified to hear this. "OMG, Kimmbo!" you're saying. "I've *got* to get my GPA up, or I'll *never* get a job!" Relax, OK? I'm not saying you should never crack a book for the rest of law school. What I *am* saying is that you have to *diversify* your experience to shift the focus away from your grades. I talked to a student at one school who had poor-to-middling grades, and was president of four organizations at school. His dream was to get into litigation, and he wondered if he shouldn't quit the organizations to focus on his grades. You already know the answer: as plugged in as he was to the legal community through the organizations, he was far better off using the people-and-activities route to nail a job, than to can activities that polished his people skills just to try–and not necessarily succeed–at raising his GPA a fraction.

Of course, when it comes to poor exam performance, it's worth figuring out what went wrong. Go back and look over your exams–

there's something that's a joy to anticipate, of course–and compare them with the professor's model answer to see where you went wrong. Perhaps there was a simple hitch in your test-taking, and once you fix it, you'll do fine.

What I want you to do is to avoid the thinking that goes, "If I just study harder, I'll do better." I'll bet you dollars to doughnuts that your grades weren't the result of you not studying enough. I've never spoken with a law student who'd done poorly, and found that it was because they weren't diligent in their studies. Quite the contrary; some of the students with the worst grades are the ones who put in the most hours. It's just that they didn't use that time as productively as they might have. Don't compound the error by doubling the amount of time you spend on your studies.

(Incidentally, I met a tutor who charges law students thousands of dollars to help them with their grades. I asked her what the secret was, and she said, 'Here's all it is. You read the section of an outline before you study the material in class. It doesn't matter if it's Gilbert's or Emanuel's or whatever. Then for each case you're assigned, you read the canned brief. Then you read the case and highlight the parts that were in the outline and the canned brief. Then you reread the canned brief. Then before the exam you do Law In A Flash. That's it.')

The short message is: You don't have to work around the clock to improve your grades, and burning the midnight oil probably won't help anyway. Spend that time doing other things that can enhance your image in the minds of employers, the kinds of things we discussed in Chapter 10 on 'The Birds and Bees of Great Jobs.'

H. Take a Good, Hard Look at Your Performance in Law School . . . and Ask Yourself Whether You're Using Your Grades as a Means of Self-Sabotage

This is a tough issue. It involves looking at your motivation for attending law school in the first place, and asking yourself whether it's something you really wanted to do (and *still* want) . . . or is something else driving you. Did you do it to avoid taking a job in something that didn't thrill you? Did you do it to please somebody else like, oh, Mommy and Daddy? Did you do it because you couldn't think of anything better to do?

You may find, after some serious thinking, that the reason you've done poorly in law school is that you've been sabotaging yourself, that you really don't want to be a lawyer, and that by getting poor grades, you've subconsciously tried to destroy it as an alternative. If that's the case, get thee to Career Services, and talk with a counselor about it. One of two things will be true: either you're not familiar with law-related jobs that you would truly love (and be motivated to work toward), or it's time to consider an alternative career (we discuss those in Chapter 31), or even whether you want to finish law school at all. You can bomb at law and be perfectly successful otherwise, you know. It happens all the time. Remember the writer/director Billy Wilder? He was forced to go to a high school for problem students. He wound up as a law student at the University of Vienna, where he lasted three months before he crapped out. He went on to win six Academy Awards for directing and screen-writing.

The bottom line is: law school isn't prison. You hold the keys to your freedom. It's an expensive path made all the more costly if you don't really want to do it. If you go do some thinking and come to the conclusion that it really *is* what you want, there's always a way to get it regardless of what your grades are like. If your heart *isn't* in it … it's time to think about Plan B!

I.   EMPLOY "WEAPONS OF MASS DISTRACTION" TO CONVINCE EMPLOYERS YOU CAN DO THEIR WORK

If you're going to convince employers to hire you in spite of your grades, you're going to take their minds *off* your grades and *onto* your abilities. As Skip Horne points out, "You have a lot more going for you than just what your transcript might reveal. To be honest, unless you have a perfect GPA, everyone could do better. Don't focus on the negative. Start highlighting all of the positives about yourself as a job candidate."

Reframing the issue is something that works in every setting, not just grades. Take the '96 Olympics, for example. Billy Payne, who brought the '96 Olympics to Atlanta, faced a formidable obstacle: the '84 Olympics had been in the U.S., in Los Angeles. The Olympic Committee would be highly reluctant to send the Olympics back to the same country so soon.

Payne came up with an ingenious solution. He determined that all of Europe would fit into the U.S. East of the Mississippi. So he argued that the U.S. should be considered differently between the East and West Coast. Obviously, it worked.

What about magic? You know how magic works, right? While the magician is encouraging you to look at his left hand, he's sneaking a dove out of his sleeve with his right hand.

When you're trying to get employers to look past your grades, you're going to use a perfectly appropriate sleight of hand. You're going to reframe the issue, and get them to focus on what's great about you, what you can really do–and not those grades!

1.   REDIRECT EMPLOYERS' ATTENTION FROM YOUR GRADES TO YOUR WORK EXPERIENCE, VOLUNTEER OR PAID

McGeorge's Dave James points out, "Grades are just a proxy for success. They're a predictor, that you'll probably be a good lawyer. Since that's what they're thinking, that's their premise; you have to come up with some other predictor of being a good lawyer, like practical work experience. 'I can't point to my grades, but I can point to ... I've been a law clerk/done an internship with this agency/done this clinical experience ... I have supervisors who will vouch for me and tell you I've done a great job, I've turned out the quality product you have every right to expect. I've demonstrated the intangibles as well: work ethic, team player, attention to detail, perseverance ...' "

He continues, "When I was a hiring attorney for the City Attorney's office in San Diego, I had an applicant tell me, 'I'm a hands-on learner.' I've quoted him thousands of times. If you can go in and say, 'I'm a hands-on learner. On exams I don't do so well, but in the real world I perform every bit as well. My practical experience is a record of success. My supervisors can attest to that, that I've enjoyed the success you want."

"If you can't give employers predictors of success in the form of grades, give them other predictors that are just as cogent, just as predictive of great performance. The fact is, nothing predicts future success like past success, in any forum."

2. SHOW EMPLOYERS YOU CAN DO THE WORK-DON'T JUST TELL THEM

It's fine to say that grades are not indicative of your abilities. But that's not the entire equation. *Something* has to show employers that you can do the work, and if it's not your grades, it's up to you to fill in the blanks and give them *something* to give them confidence in your skills.

In Chapter 10, we talked about all kinds of activities to show employers you can do the work. There are dozens and dozens of them, including volunteering doing anything it is that you'd like to get paid to do, writing articles for bar publications, volunteering to draft motions and pleadings for lawyers doing pro bono work. The bottom line is, you want to be able to tell any employer, "My grades may not show you what I can do, but I'll tell you what *does* ..."

* * * SMART HUMAN TRICK * * *

Midwestern law student, a 3L. He's dying for a federal district court clerkship. The judge he targets scoffs at him, saying, "Your grades are terrible. And I'd never hire anyone from your school anyway. If you want, you can volunteer, but I'll tell you right now it won't go anywhere."

The student says, "Fine, I'll volunteer." The judge asks him to write a memo about a case. The student does so, and reports, "The judge called me after he got a chance to read my memo, and he said, 'This memo is the finest piece of work I've ever received from any of my clerks. If you're still interested in working for me after graduation, the job is yours."

3. TAKE PART IN EXTRACURRICULARS THAT WILL MAKE YOU SHINE

Think about the aspects of law school that you like (and please don't say "lunch"). As Wendy Werner points out, "People with poor grades typically like the practical aspects of law school–clinical skills more than writing skills, and trial litigation more than tax issues. They're typically interested in solving people's problems and arguing before a judge." If that's true for you, go after extracurriculars that involve people. Go for a part-time job at legal services or the public defender's office. Take moot court and trial advocacy. Take part in the client counseling competition at school. Look for pro bono positions, like with PSLawNet–as Lisa Kellogg points out, "They'll pay attention to what you want–for instance, whether you want trial experience, or you want to do research."

If you like to write, consider volunteering for a judge or writing articles for bar publications or volunteering to research and write about an issue for the local bar association in a specialty that interests you.

The point is, you should focus on getting experience that is not tied to your classes. You want to be fully-rounded, so that when the issue of grades comes up, you can handle it gracefully and guide your questioner to aspects of your experience that are more positive–and that means choosing extracurricular wisely.

These activities will have the added benefit of bolstering your self-esteem. Give yourself a chance to shine by putting your skills to work!

4. COME UP WITH PATTER ABOUT YOUR GRADES THAT MAKES YOU FEEL COMFORTABLE TALKING ABOUT THEM

Remember the central premise of this book: image and message control. What you say, what you do, determines how people feel about you. A great example of this is airline pilots. You ever notice that they never admit to *anything* serious? You're sitting in your seat at the gate, and the pilot comes on and says, "Sorry for the delay, folks, we've got a little last minute paperwork to take care of"–and you look out the window and see someone duct-taping the wings onto the plane. "Folks, we can expect a little chop on the way up," which translates into, "The turbulence is going to shake your eyeballs out of their sockets." But they have to sound calm and reassuring, and they *do*.

The fact is, nobody can see inside *your* head and see how *you* feel about *anything*. They can only see the manifestation of your feelings in your words and behavior. When it comes to grades, it's essential that you come up with words that make you feel comfortable and seem confident. The simple fact is that people will react to you by taking the cue from you about how you feel about yourself. I'm not saying you'll ever feel thrilled about having less-than-stellar grades, but you can certainly present an air of confident nonchalance about them.

Step one is to come up with *some* explanation for your grades. As Diane Reynolds says, "Make your explanation positive and short."

- **If it was a one-semester problem, point that out.** As Diane Reynolds recommends, you can say something like, 'I was thrown for a loop. But I've taken tutoring, and I've got it under control. Not only that, I did great in Property . . .'"

    Jose Bahamonde–Gonzalez points out that you can say, "Getting used to law school was tough, but I assure you that after that initial shock, I found my weaknesses, and I've addressed them, and I'm better now."

- If it was a one-semester (or one year) illness, be somewhat oblique about it—this is a situation where you don't want to pull out X-rays—but say something like, "I had a one-time non-recurring medical issue that impacted my performance, but it's not going to happen again, and since then I've done much better . . ."

    One student I talked to had a great response to the grades issue. She had gotten an F in Moot Court, because she was on pain killers when she wrote her brief. It was pure gobbledygook. She said, "When employers ask me about it, I say, 'I was on drugs'—and then explain what happened. Then I go on and tell them why I *can* do the work. It always goes over well."

- **If your grades are consistently sub par,** Wendy Werner suggests that you **keep it simple and say something like, "My best skills aren't taking law school exams."**

- **Don't ever blame the professor or suggest you haven't thought about the issue.** As Jose Bahamonde–Gonzalez points out, "You can't say, 'Oh, this professor's a jerk.'" That may well be true, but you can't *say* it. You also can't shrug and say, "I don't know how it happened. Beats me." Grades may not show what you can do, but you *do* have to show at least some concern about them.

- As I pointed out in the Interview chapter, **a little self-deprecating humor doesn't hurt.** "Thank goodness I didn't have to show my parents *that* report card," anything like that is a good lead-in; it makes you feel comfortable and sets your audience at ease, too.

Step two is to talk about what you *do* have to offer, your "weapons of mass distraction." As Cindy Rold advises, "Think of what else you have to offer! You can say, 'I didn't do well in law school because I don't take law school exams well, but I'll be a great lawyer because . . .' and have other things to show for it." *That's* where your volunteering and extracurriculars come in. They'll take the "sting" out of your grades by giving you something to be proud of.

By the way, don't overlook your nonlegal experience as a source of great skills. As Tammy Willcox points out, "It's important to look for what the attorney is looking for. For instance, a public defender will look for students with poise, confidence, and those who are quick on their feet. So let's say you managed an 800–seat restaurant. You'd want to tell that employer, 'I can think on my feet, and make split-second decisions.'" Or let's say that you have experience as a nanny. Ann Skalaski points out, "You'd want to focus on your strong interpersonal skills. You'd say, 'I establish relationships easily and gain people's confidence quickly, as indicated by these people trusting me with their children.'" There are endless variations on this theme, but you get the point–it's not just legal experience that gives you the kinds of skills that legal employers look for.

Step Three is to ask for a mock interview at Career Services, and request that the interviewer brings up the grades issue. As Suzanne Endrizzi points out, you've got to feel comfortable in an interview setting talking about your grades. Going through mock interviews is a great way to make sure that your wording is smooth and presented confidently.

J. DON'T SUFFER ALONE—TALK TO CAREER SERVICES

"What's the point?" I hear you saying. "My Career Services Office only helps students in the top ten percent." No matter where you go to school, that is so completely *not* true. It sometimes seem that way because on-campus interviews focus on the students at the top of the class, but as we discussed in Chapter 3, your Career Services Office is so much more than an OCI shop. As one Career Services Director told me, "Students don't understand that we identify with them. We weren't on law review either!"

Your CSO can help you polish your patter about your grades, with suggested wording and mock interviews.

They'll have the inside scoop on employers who ignore grades. As Drusilla Bakert says, "I talk to employers all the time. I know the employers who want a litigator regardless of their GPA, who'll take people because they have common sense." South Carolina's Phyllis Burkhard adds, "I've had employers tell me specifically that 'We do no research, we only counsel, we negotiate, we tell juries stories. If we have to do research or briefs, we subcontract that out.' If a student comes to me and tells me they don't have great grades, that they hate writing, I'll be able to direct them to an employer like that."

Finally, your CSO will be able to help you, one-on-one, overcome the blow to your self-esteem that results from poor grades.

The bottom line? Don't suffer alone. You can always turn to people whose job it is to help you find the job you want!

K. YOU WON'T WANT TO BELIEVE THIS . . . BUT IF OCI JOBS DON'T FALL IN YOUR LAP, IN THE LONG RUN YOU'LL BE A *LOT* BETTER OFF

This is a dirty little secret of job search. If it's more difficult for you to find jobs *now,* you'll ultimately be happier than if jobs *did* drop off the trees and land on you.

What you're looking at is taking short-term pain in return for long-term gain. The reason is that outside of your first job, *every other job* you get for the rest of your life *cannot* come about through OCI. That only works when you're a student, and you've got the right credentials for it. Once you graduate, it doesn't matter if you were #1 in your class and you were the entire editorial staff of Law Review–you'll have to rely on other techniques to get your next gig. What will that mean? Correspondence. Talking to people. Taking part in activities. In other words, everything I hammered you over the head with earlier in this book. If you've already got those skills under your belt, you're so-o-o much better off.

On top of that, you're likely to do better on the job once you're there. The interpersonal skills it takes to land a job when you can't rely on your grades are the very same skills that will make you shine in the workplace. I've had more than one recruiting coordinator point out to me that their very best associates were the ones who had to struggle to get the job in the first place. "They're more enthusiastic, they work harder, they're more aware of how they're coming across," is the refrain I often hear.

So if you have to work a little harder to get that first job, it may not be obvious in the moment–but you've developed skills that will serve you well your entire life.

L. DON'T OVERLOOK EVERYTHING ELSE IN THIS BOOK!

The whole idea of nailing great jobs without great grades is part of the fundamental premise of this book. After speaking with thousands of students and career professionals around the country, I believe it more than ever. What I hope you'll take away from this chapter is the feeling that although you've got a little extra touch-up work to do because of your grades, you've got essentially the same job search ahead of you as any other law student. You're only stigmatized by your grades to the extend you let yourself be defined by them. Otherwise, go out, talk to people, send letters, take part in activities, do all the things I outline in this book to pursue the job of your dreams–because it *is* within your grasp!

*

Appendix

If Your Grades Are Only Low Because Your School Has a Low Curve, Consider a Couple of Options ...

May I be the first one to offer my condolences? I completely understand the whole academic integrity thing—and I agree with it—but job-search-wise, it still sucks. You may actually have perfectly good credentials ... they just don't look that way when stacked up against law schools that have an A-curve.

Three things to consider:

Ask your Career Services Office if they have printed materials to send with your resume. Some law schools have written explanations of the grading system specifically directed at employers. Take advantage of those.

Put your class rank on your resume *instead of* your GPA. After all, grades are only relevant in comparison to your classmates. If your class rank is good and it's just the GPA itself that doesn't stack up well against schools with grade inflation, your class rank will accomplish what you want.

Ask your Career Services Office for other advice about how students before you have handled the issue. No matter where you go to school, you're not the first student ever. Other students have faced the same issue, and they're all employed now, so your school has clearly learned to work with it. Don't reinvent the wheel. Ask what your predecessors have done. Whether they've got alums at employers that interest you and should be your targets, or they'll call on your behalf, solicit help from your school. After all—the low curve was their idea!

Chapter 14
I Go to Not-Harvard. How Do I Make up for My School?

Unless you go to an elite law school—and let's face it, the vast majority of us don't—there's often a nagging little voice in your head that says, *"Things would be so much different for me if I went to ..."*

My goal in this chapter is to convince you that no matter *where* you go to law school, whether it's an OK joint like my alma mater—Case Western—or Barney's Night YMCA Law School and Deli, the world really is your oyster. Your school will only hold you back if you convince yourself that it will. I didn't go to Harvard, and things have worked out pretty well for me. They will for you, too.

A.   THE TEN–POINT MINDSET

Overcoming Harvard envy is a matter of wrapping your mind around ten simple points. Here they are.

1.   PEOPLE DON'T HIRE SCHOOLS. THEY HIRE PEOPLE

As Latham and Watkins' Skip Horne puts it, "You can be at a so-called fourth tier school and have first tier credentials." He advises that you "Take advantage of every opportunity that comes your way, from academics to extracurriculars to clerkships, and focus on creating the most well-rounded job search candidate you possibly can." Nothing stops you from being a great job candidate, no matter *where* you go to school.

On top of that, in Chapter 10 we hammered home the importance of getting people invested in *you*. If you give people an opportunity to know you, through volunteering, activities and organizations, they'll get to like you and from that naturally springs thoughts of helping you out, giving you good advice, putting you on to people.

That entire approach is undergirded by the principle that people hire people. They don't hire resumes. They don't even hire schools.

I can't tell you how many times I've talked to students who told me they were the first one from their school ever to be hired by a particular employer. One charming young man I talked to told me about a judge he'd approached. The judge told him dismissively, "I've never hired a clerk from your school and I never will. You can go ahead and volunteer if you want but nothing will come of it." This student went ahead and volunteered, and wrote a memo for the judge that blew him away. The judge told him, "This memo is superior to anything any clerk from any school has ever written for me." He hired the student on the spot ... *in spite* of his earlier guarantee that he'd "never" hire anyone from there!

So do the things we talked about in Chapter 10. If you run into people who claim they'd never hire anyone from your school, remember: if they're impressed with you, they'll hire you ... no matter *what* they thought before!

2. REMEMBER: YOU *ARE* YOUR SCHOOL

In a very real sense, your school is a collection of all the students who've ever gone there. When you have contact with anyone in the legal community, their opinion of your school is at least in part influenced by what they think of *you*. Someone who might previously have not given your school a second thought might change their minds entirely because you impress them.

You can prove this yourself. Go through the NALP Guide to Law Firms—it has profiles of the largest law firms in the country—and look at the entry that tells you where each firm conducts on-campus interviews. You'll see the usual suspects, the distinguished schools, but then you'll often see an "outlier," a school much further down in the published rankings and/or thousands of miles away from the firm. I've talked with recruiting coordinators at these firms about this and the story is almost always the same: they hired one, just *one* student from a school where they'd never considered recruiting before, and they were so impressed with that student that they went back for more.

So as Susanne Aronowitz advises, "Bloom where you're planted." You can impress people no matter what their preconceived notions of your school are.

3. *NEVER* JUMP IN WHEN PEOPLE DISS YOUR SCHOOL. HAVE POSITIVES MEMORIZED THAT YOU CAN WHEEL OUT WHENEVER THE SUBJECT COMES UP

Gee, here's a headline for you: people can be jerks. When you mention where you go to law school, there will be people who'll sneer. I remember before I even started law school at Case Western, I was at a party and met friends of friends. When they asked me what I did and I mentioned I was about to start law school at Case, one of the guys said, "I wouldn't even bother going to law school if I didn't go to Harvard."

Bite me. Bite me hard.

The key thing to remember is *never, ever, ever* to agree with people who diss your school. As Skip Horne puts it, "You should never apologize for the law school that you chose to attend. If you're going to sit in a job interview and bad-mouth your educational institution, just think about the impression you're leaving with the interviewer, who probably wonders whether you'd do the same about your employer!"

Don't *ever* hang your head in shame. As Susanne Aronowitz says, "Don't hide behind your school. Don't blame your school for admitting you." Instead, she advises you to "**have positive qualities about your school at your fingertips.**" If you can't think of them off the top of your head, go to your school's web site and look at what they say about it. They paid marketing people a *lot* of money to write that stuff; take advantage of it!

Maybe your school has an outstanding reputation in a particular specialty. Or maybe you have professors who are excellent teachers or are great mentors or you have the opportunity to meet with them frequently (which is something that's not true of many elite schools). You can *always* honestly say that your school has alums who've been very successful in a variety of settings, because that's true of *every* school. Susanne Aronowitz tells you that "No matter where you go to school, you can take your degree and succeed *anywhere.*" Don't let the ignorant, stray comments of other people convince you otherwise!

People's words are just their opinions. Those opinions aren't necessarily right, and they certainly aren't engraved in stone. I've mentioned before the experience I had interviewing for jobs over Christmas break of 1L. I came home to Connecticut from Cleveland to talk with small law firms. I interviewed at one joint in Greenwich, a small firm with five partners who'd all been classmates at Yale Law School. I'm talking with these guys, and one of them picks up my resume and says, "So how are you enjoying yourself at Chase?" *Chase.* He didn't even get the name right! I told him I was enjoying it very much, and he went on and said, "We've never hired anybody from Chase before."

I answered brightly, "Well, then, I should be a refreshing change for you." They all laughed, and incidentally, I got the job.

Incidentally, before you go on any interview, review the answer to Question #12 ("Why did you choose this school?") in the interview chapter. In a nutshell: when someone gets all up in your grill about your school—stand up for it!

* * * SMART HUMAN TRICK * * *

Law student from a third tier school, sends a letter to a judge. He hand writes across the top of the letter, *"This is not from a Harvard Law Review student"*

The judge loves it, brings him in for an interview, and hires him.

(This is Kimm talking. As much as I love this story and the point it makes, it's probably not an approach that would work very often.)

4. You're Learning the Same Law as Students Do at Every Law School in the Country—Including Harvard

You already know that I created the study aid *Law In A Flash,* the flash cards in yellow boxes. Every law school bookstore in the country bought it, and that means just one thing: they all teach the same law. I didn't have a different set of flash cards for the Ivies. The bar exam doesn't differentiate between law schools. *It's all the same.* Whether you go to Harvard or Moe's Double–Wide Law School, you're studying the same cases, with the same case books, learning the same principles. If you watch *Judge Judy,* you'll apply the same thought process to resolving the issues that your brethren at distinguished schools would employ.

So don't put yourself in a one-down position assuming that people at elite schools are learning something you're not. It's all the same law.

5. *Every* School Has Illustrious Alums

If you talk to the alumni relations person at your law school, you'll learn that students who preceded you have done virtually everything: every setting, every specialty, alternative careers you might never even have considered. When people tell you that your school stops you from working in certain settings, they're talking out of their hat. I talked to a student at a third-tier school who said he wanted to work for the State Department, but his friends had discouraged him telling him "You have to go to Harvard to get in." Of course not! The way people talk about Harvard you'd think they graduate a hundred thousand law students a year. They don't. There isn't any possible way that every "prestigious" job is taken up by a student from an elite school. There just aren't enough of those students, for a start!

So if you think your school is holding you back, go in and ask what people before you have done with their degrees. You're in for a pleasant surprise.

6. Don't Listen When Lawyers Tell You "We Only Hire From Harvard"

Re-e-eally? A student at one law school told me about a lunch she had with a lawyer from one of the biggest law firms in the country, a joint with 1,000+ attorneys, who told her "We only hire from Harvard." Anyone who says that about a sizable employer is blowing smoke up your—*ahem.* You can prove this yourself. Go to Martindale Hubbell (or the employer's own web site) and look at the backgrounds of the attorneys. The whole "only Harvard" thing just isn't true.

When people tell you this, don't challenge them. Change the subject. Ask them about their practice, how they chose what they do, talk about current events, *anything* else. Just don't take those kinds of idiotic comments seriously!

Incidentally, **if you work during the school year (or for a summer) for an employer who then claims that they don't hire anyone from your school, there's something else going on.** Getting your foot in the door is the hard part. Once you're there, it's your work that does the talking. So if you work somewhere and they *subsequently* claim they can't invite you back because of your school ... it's just not true. They knew where you went when they hired you the first time. As one Career Services Director pointed out to me, "I had this happen to a student; he worked at an elite firm in Washington, DC for the summer, and at the end of the summer the attorneys told him they were happy with his work, but they weren't going to invite him back for the next summer because they only took 2Ls from the top 25 schools. I thought that was suspicious, and I called one of the attorneys he'd worked for, curious about this explanation. When pressed, the guy said, 'Frankly, he just didn't have the skills we're looking for.' The whole thing about our school was something they viewed as a kind way to break it to him."

So if you get this explanation from an employer, don't blame it on your school. Press until you find out what's *really* going on. Whatever it is, you can work on it and fix it ... but only if you know what it is!

7. RELY ON ALUMS. THEY'VE DEALT WITH THE SAME LAW SCHOOL ISSUES YOU FACE

If you do a mailer to employers in your target city and you send letters exclusively to people who went to distinguished schools, you're not preaching to the choir. Tap into the population whose down with what you're facing, namely: alums from your school.

Whether you're looking to move to a particular city or you're looking at a specialty or practice setting, go to Career Services and identify alums who fit those criteria. Contact them (as we talked about in Chapter 10) and solicit their advice. You can always say, "Since you also went to school here, you must have faced the same issues I'm facing with ..."

You are the natural object of bounty for people who went to your school before you. People are hard-wired to be helpful, particularly to those with whom they share something in common. Contact alums and see for yourself!

8. IF YOUR LAW SCHOOL HAS "CONCENTRATIONS," AND YOU PURSUE ONE, TOUT THAT

It may well be that your law school offers concentrations in certain practice areas, like health law, financial services, litigation, public sector law, international law, you name it. As the Career Services Director at one law school points out, "You can sell those concentrations! For instance, you can tell an employer, 'I'm applying to you because of my interest in Securities. I'm in this concentration. Our law school has dedicated a lot more resources to this concentration than most law schools. For instance, we have more classes, more professors, and more adjuncts focusing on this area. OK, I realize my law school is not a brand name, but we have an emphasis in this niche, which is world-class.'"

9. The Big Differences Between the Elite Law Schools and Every Other School . . . and How You Can Overcome Them

There's no question that attending an elite law school has benefits. Let's talk about the significant ones when it comes to job searches.

A. Tons of On-Campus Interviews

The number of firms who interview at elite law schools is staggering. Hundreds and hundreds of them. They compete over early time slots, worried that students will have opted for other firms before they have a chance to talk to them. Firms will court Career Services personnel at the elite schools, asking what they can do to lure more students. It's enough to make you sick.

Now if your school has employers who'll interview only a tiny segment of the student population—which is the case at most law schools—you probably think it would be great to have all of those firms come on campus. And it *would* be a lot easier to get jobs that way—at least right now. But in the long run, on-campus interviews are meaningless. No firm hires exclusively through OCI. There are always other ways to get in, as we discuss in Chapter 23 on Large Firms. The point is: tons of OCI doesn't determine your career.

B. Powerful Alums

There's no question that the halls of power are heavily littered with the alums of elite schools. But there are other lawyers there, too, from lots of other schools. While it would be great to be able to tap into an alumni network rife with powerful people, it doesn't mean you can't get through just because you didn't go to the same law schools. Using the techniques we talked about in Chapter 10, you can get to know just about anybody. What the name of your school won't do for you, your actions can.

C. Classmates Who'll Move Into Powerful Positions

Sure, if the smelly kid sitting next to you in Contracts class turns out to be Senior Partner so-and-so, General Counsel so-and-so, even *President* so-and-so, you've got a leg up in the job market because you can get them on the phone. But getting great jobs isn't a matter of who you know. It's a matter of who you *get* to know. I realize that I sound like a broken record when I harken back to Chapter 10 about finding jobs through people and activities, but honestly: whether you went to law school with someone or you meet them when you serve on the board of a local civic group with them, *it doesn't matter.* You're not a resume anymore; you're a person, and once you're a person, people are much more likely to help you nail great gigs. Anything that classmates can do for you, people you meet *outside* of school can do, too.

10.   ABUNDANT ON-CAMPUS INTERVIEWS DON'T HELP STUDENTS AT ELITE LAW SCHOOLS IN THE LONG RUN

Having to work harder to find a job than students at elite law schools has an enormous, hidden benefit. It has an analogy in the credit card industry, interestingly enough.

Some years ago, Congress passed credit card protection laws, such that consumers didn't have to pay contested credit card charges. Needless to say, the credit card companies squealed like stuck pigs at the prospect of having to pick up these charges. Then–Senator William Proxmire told them, "This is going to be good for you," even though in the short term it would cost them more.

He was right. Credit card protection laws are generally viewed as responsible for the explosive growth of the credit card business.

What was at work? A short term hardship in return for a long-term benefit. When you go to not-Harvard and you have to work a little harder to find a job, you're actually a lot better off for the rest of your career. The skills you use to nail a job *now* are the ones you'll use to get great jobs throughout your career: thinking hard about what it is that you really enjoy, fashioning a targeted resume and cover letter, taking part in the right activities, reaching out to strangers ... they'll benefit you forever.

Students at elite law schools, who *don't* have to do anything other than rely on on-campus interviews, don't develop those crucial skills. As a Career Services counselor at an elite school describes it, "The issues our students have with finding jobs aren't obvious while they're still in school. That's easy for them. They have problems once they've been out of school for two years, and they find themselves working at a large law firm in a job they can't stand anymore. They'll call and say, '*Now* what?' We ask them what they want to do, and they say, 'I want to do the best thing.' They're so used to being overachievers, they don't know how to ask themselves the hard questions, 'what do I really want?' They're used to grabbing the brass ring, doing the things that everybody else tells them they ought to want. When that leads them to something miserable, they don't know where to go next. The idea of contacting people for informational interviews, all those things that other students had to do in school, they're at a complete loss."

So not having offers from prestigious law firms fall into your lap in law school is, in a very real sense, a benefit to you in the long run. Stop viewing your job search as a hassle, and view it as an education, as a means of picking up skills you'll always use—because it is!

B.   WHAT IF YOUR SCHOOL IS UNACCREDITED?

If you go to—or you're considering—an unaccredited school, you've essentially got one additional issue to deal with, and that's the question people will inevitably ask you: "Why would you ever go to an unaccredited law school?" I've spoken at a bunch of unaccredited schools, from ones that were provisionally accredited by the ABA, to ones that were accredited by their state, to ones that had no accreditation of any kind. I even spoke in a law school once that was essentially in a concrete bunker at the end of a runway of a major airport. Every time a plane took off on that runway, I had to stop talking; you couldn't hear a thing!

There are actually a few reasons to consider an unaccredited degree, and they're the reasons you'd use to explain your choice to a prospective employer:

1. **THERE ARE BENEFITS TO NON-ABA ACCREDITED SCHOOLS THAT THEIR ACCREDITED BRETHREN DON'T SHARE**

These benefits include:

- A very practical education. Because classes are usually taught by local lawyers, you hear a lot of hands-on advice about being a lawyer.

- Unaccredited schools are usually cheaper and a lot more flexible than accredited law schools.

- You may be tied to a city, for professional or personal reasons, that doesn't have an accredited law school, so an unaccredited school is your only choice.

2. **IF YOUR SCHOOL IS STATE- OR PROVISIONALLY-ACCREDITED AND YOU INTEND TO STAY IN THAT STATE, SAY SO**

Students at schools that are "state accredited" typically have to take a "baby bar" after First Year to determine if they will be eligible for the regular state bar when they graduate. If you go to a state accredited school and you intend to remain in-state, for all intents and purposes you're at an accredited school. (And, of course, once you've practiced for a few years, you're eligible for reciprocity with other state bars, so the lack of accreditation quickly becomes a moot point.)

3. **IF YOUR SCHOOL ISN'T PROVISIONALLY OR STATE ACCREDITED AND NEVER WILL BE, REMEMBER THAT A LAW DEGREE OF ANY KIND IS A BENEFIT IN MANY "ALTERNATIVE CAREERS"**

There are various careers—we discuss them in Chapter 31 on Alternative Careers—where a law degree is helpful but not mandatory. In those careers, a degree from an unaccredited school has the same benefits as any other law degree. Whether you want to go into real estate development, the medical profession, or you want to go into a law firm administrative position like recruiting coordinator, marketing director or executive assistant, a law degree is a real plus. If you can get it cheaply and on a flexible schedule—why not?

Chapter 15
I Didn't Get an Offer From My Summer Employer

. . .

"Whatever has happened to you, it has already happened. The important question is, how are you going to handle it? In other words, 'Now What?' "

Jon Kabat–Zinn

If there's a law school equivalent of the Scarlet Letter, it goes to students who get dinged by their summer clerkship employers. Not getting invited back is an undeniable stigma, and if it happens to you, I feel for you.

Because it happened to me.

I won't go into detail here, except to tell you that I clerked for an enormous, prestigious law firm. At the end of the summer, the firm extended offers of permanent employment to 21 of the 22 clerks in my office.

I was number 22.

That came up in interviews once in a while after that, let me tell you. It came up with my parents over the dinner table for the next five years straight.

No matter what kind of employer you worked for over the summer, if you got rejected, your feelings were probably like mine. Shock. Disbelief. Embarrassment. Man oh man, was I *embarrassed*.

The simple fact is this: You *will* come back, and you'll nail a great job. You need to know how to put the experience in perspective, how to take what you need to learn from it, and how to present it to the world of employers.

A. STEP ONE: CATCH YOUR BREATH, AND TAKE A BREAK FROM YOUR JOB SEARCH

Don't tell yourself that you have to get right back up on the job search horse the day after your summer employer rejects you. As Pam Malone says, "It's devastating not to get an offer after your summer clerkship," and Betsy Armour adds, "People who don't get offers are usually heartbroken. They have to go through a grieving process."

So don't deny the enormous emotional impact of the rejection. Give yourself a few days when you don't try to explain the situation to *anyone*. If anybody asks about it, thank them for their concern but tell them you're not ready to talk about it just yet. Take a deep breath, regroup, maybe vent with a close friend or a counselor in Career Services.

Then, when you've got your emotions under control, it's time for a little detective work ...

B. STEP TWO: FIGURE OUT WHAT HAPPENED

Sometimes, sure, it's completely obvious why you didn't get an offer.

Of the more common and/or memorable situations I've heard about, maybe:

- You got hammered at a firm event and: Mooned your colleagues/made a pass at a partner's wife/threatened to knife your supervisor/slugged a client/stripped down to your underpants and jumped into the river/posed naked for a men's magazine and posted a link to it on your MySpace profile/took off your panties and pantyhose in front of your colleagues because "they were driving me crazy";
- You hired a stripper for a breakfast meeting;
- You left assignments incomplete at the end of the summer;
- You messed up a project (or more than one).

While it's possible you know exactly what sucked your offer into deep space, it may well be that you have *no clue* what happened. You finished the summer expecting them to slap you on the back and say, "We can't wait to see you again!" and then ...

Nothing.

I've talked with many, many students who didn't get offers from their summer employer, and inevitably when I ask them "What happened?" they'll answer "I really don't know ..." or they'll have an answer that couldn't *possibly* explain the situation. People will mumble, "I guess it was a personality conflict," or they'll describe an incident that just doesn't seem all that bad.

I remember talking to one student in California who said he hadn't gotten an offer from his employer because of a single comment that he made. He worked with another clerk for a small law firm, and the other clerk took a week's vacation in the middle of the summer. The boss noticed that this clerk was doing all the work for a few days, and commented, smiling, "Why is it that you're doing all the work?" and the clerk responded, similarly light-heartedly, "Because I guess [the other clerk] is a slacker." When the other clerk got an offer and this student didn't, he combed back over the entire summer and said, "It must have been that. I can't think of anything else. He liked all of my work."

Well—I ask you. Does that really seem as though it could explain a rejection? *Really?*

If you aren't *absolutely, positively sure* what happened, you're going to have to talk to the employer and ask them straight out why you didn't get an offer.

Now, I know how much you dread this. On a scale of difficulty from 1 to 10, almost everything in this book hovers around a 1. This is closer to 10, and there's nothing I can do to make it easier for you, except to say that you only have to do it once. John F. Kennedy said he could tolerate any pain if he knew for certain it would end, and finding out why you were rejected is a pain that you'll only have to endure once. As Rob Kaplan points out, "It's painful, but you *have* to get a clear explanation of why you *didn't* get an offer." Once you have that information, we'll talk in Topic C below how to use that information to your advantage with prospective employers.

The conversation with your former employer—finding out why you didn't get an offer—can be difficult, and it requires some preparation.

The most important point to remember is that you *cannot* let emotion enter into the conversation. Do some square breathing exercises, rehearse what you'll say, do whatever it takes to be perfectly calm when you call. (Incidentally, this *does* have to be a phone call; it can't be an e-mail or a voice-mail message.)

Who should you call? Depending on the size of the employer, you may have a few options. If possible, call someone in a position of authority with whom you got along. Inevitably, there will have been *someone* you liked, and they're the obvious target.

No matter who you call, Rob Kaplan recommends that you say something like, "While I'm disappointed, it's not to challenge your decision—but I have to get information to move forward. I want to be sure that what prospective employers hear from me is consistent with what they hear from you." **You're seeking *information*— that's all.** What you want is to find out which of four general categories your rejection falls into: Bad economics, a personality conflict, a brain-fart judgment issue, or self-sabotage (we'll discuss those in Topic C, below).

What if the person you call is really abusive, or rude, or unhelpful? Don't scream back. With a zen-like calm—feigned, if necessary—say something like, "I hear how angry/disappointed you are, but we are going to be members of the same legal community. I don't have the intention of saying anything negative about you, and I'm hoping in this discussion we can come to some compromise over what you'll say about me." Offer to draft a letter from the employer that you can include with your credentials, so that nobody has to speak to him/her.

If this is the first ugly confrontation you've ever had, it might take tremendous self-control to continue it. Just stay calm, and look past the conversation. Keep your goal in focus: *Getting this employer not to bad mouth you to future employers.* You'll probably find—as so many students have in the past—that your very willingness to *talk* to this person will make them think more positively of you. Throughout your career you'll have to make phone calls you dread; we all do. Getting this experience out of the way will make it so much easier for you next time you have to have a conversation you'd rather avoid!

C. CATEGORIZING YOUR REJECTION AND PULLING OUT THE POSITIVES FOR FUTURE EMPLOYERS

Whether it's a result of a conversation with your prior employer, or you knew immediately after you were arrested for theft of an office computer that you wouldn't be invited back, the fact that you didn't get an offer can be explained to your advantage.

Let's look at the four categories of rejections separately.

1. THE FOUR GENERAL REASONS FOR "NON-OFFERS":

A. BAD ECONOMICS

There are a few possibilities:

- Maybe you took the job knowing they wouldn't be making any offers.

- Or maybe there was the possibility of an offer at the end of the summer, and *nobody* got one.

- Or maybe they had a number of clerks and only had the budget/work available to hire a small fraction of the group.

If there was no possibility of an offer, you just tell future employers that you took the job knowing it wouldn't result in an offer, but it was experience you really wanted, and you learned ... and then list the skills that will be valuable to the employer you're addressing.

If *nobody* got an offer because the employer didn't have the budget or work, again, it's not a reflection on you or your performance. Stress the experience you got and the skills you learned, and leave it there.

The only one that creates an issue is the last option: they could only afford to hire a few of the summer people, and you didn't make the cut. Whether it's one out of three, two out of seven, no matter what the ratio is, it's an issue ... and we'll talk about it under #2, directly below.

B. A PERSONALITY CONFLICT

This is the one I hear most often, and with good reason: you may be the most agreeable person on the planet, but there are always going to be people with whom you just don't get along, no matter how hard you try. If you had a personality conflict with someone important in the office, it just doesn't matter how good your work was; you didn't get an offer because of the personality clash.

Regardless of how common it is, a personality conflict is an issue that can hurt your job search. We'll talk about handling it under #2, directly below.

C. A BRAIN-FART JUDGMENT ISSUE

Hey, it happens. It's certainly what happened to me, and it's what torpedoed my chances with my summer firm. Maybe the same thing happened to you. You innocently did something socially inept, and offended someone at work. Or you messed up a project, maybe by misinterpreting what you were being asked for or missing something crucial in your research. Or maybe you missed deadlines. Of course, before your *next* job, you're going to read my book *What Law School Doesn't Teach You* ... where we address all of these issues. But for now, let's just acknowledge that you had a failure of judgment, and it tanked your offer. We'll address how you overcome it when we get to #2, directly below.

D. SELF-SABOTAGE

Oooh. Here's a possibility I'll bet you haven't thought about. Self-sabotage.

Whenever students tell me that they didn't get an offer from their summer employer, the question I ask them before they have a chance to think about it is this:

"Did you like it there? Did you want the job?"

You may be surprised to find out that the majority of students answer with a startled, "Now you mention it—no."

There's a strong possibility you fit this description. Think back over your summer. Did you really like it there? Did you like the people? Is this what you could see devoting your life to for the next few years at least? If the answer is "no," then I'll guarantee you one of two things happened: Either you, perhaps entirely subconsciously, performed poorly so that you wouldn't be faced with an offer you really didn't want. Or you conveyed, through your words and behavior, the fact that you didn't like it. In a very important way job offers are just like marriage proposals: If the "offeror" thinks the answer's going to be no, they won't make the offer.

I can't *tell* you how many employers have described clerks to me with words like, "She didn't seem to like it," "He told the secretary he didn't want to be here," "She was sort of apathetic," "He didn't make an effort to get to know anybody." These all boil down to: You didn't seem to want it, they figured you wouldn't accept it if it was offered to you, so why bother?

No matter what form your self-sabotage took, you need to examine your motives. Did you take the job to impress someone else, parents or a spouse or friends? Or did you think you'd like it, but you really didn't know what it was all about?

No matter how you sabotaged yourself, remember this: Not getting jobs you don't want is the Universe working out just fine. It wounds your ego—it certainly did mine—but if in your heart you didn't want the job, you learned a really valuable lesson about not pouring your efforts into things you don't want. You discovered that you're not the kind of person who can perform well or pretend to like something that doesn't appeal to you. That's just you, and that's just fine. Go back to Chapter 2, figure out what you really *do* want—and pursue it!

2. Pulling Out the Positives From the Job

A. If It Was an Economic Issue . . .

Ask for a letter of recommendation and/or a superior's willingness to talk to potential future employers on your behalf.

Whether they had no intention to hire anyone permanently or they hired some people but not you, you have to have people who'll say good things about you.

If the employer hired only a few people and claim it was for economic reasons, ask the decision-maker directly what it was distinguished those who got offers. If it was a matter of "better work product" or "they seemed to want it more," then you've really got the personality/work issues we discuss below. If it was "they had a lot more relevant experience" or "with their background in X they'll be able to bring in clients," you've got the basis of a valid explanation for future employers.

B. If It Was a Work-Related Issue . . .

There are a few steps to take.

First, get positive reviews from anyone at the job who will provide them. It's unlikely that you fell down on every project or for every person you worked for. There's somebody with something positive to say about your work, and lean on them to be a reference for you. Whether it's in the form of a letter (good) or a willingness to talk to potential employers (better), a former colleague's agreeing to stand up for you can go a long way towards ameliorating the lack of an offer.

Second, if it was a matter of sloppy research or writing, volunteer on a writing project to prove that you can do it well. In Chapter 10 on the Birds and Bees of Jobs, I list a ton of writing opportunities. Whether it's for a clinical program at school or for a professor or for an alum or for the local bar association, do a brief piece of work that will show your skills at their best, so you can honestly tell any future employers, "I'm capable of turning in excellent work, as you can see from . . ."

c. If It Was a Personality Issue . . .

You can never, ever say it was a personality conflict. If you *do,* the person you're talking to will *immediately* assume that *you're* the one with the personality problem. It's totally unfair, but it's human nature. They figure you're the problem child and if they hire you, you'll disrupt their office, too.

No matter the source of the personality clash, take from the experience what you'd do differently in working with a similar person in future. Think *hard* about how you'd go about finding a way to work harmoniously with the person who flummoxed you. Did you ever see the Dustin Hoffman movie *Tootsie?* (If you haven't, rent it! It's phenomenal, maybe the best comedy ever.) Dustin Hoffman plays an out-of-work actor who dresses up as a woman to get a job on a soap opera. The reason he's had such a hard time getting a job is that he always challenges directors. But on the soap opera, when the director tells him that if he's got changes to suggest he should tell the director first, he responds, "Yes, I can see that." He bites his lip rather than jumping ugly, and he thrives as a result.

Sucking it up and getting along with people with whom you'd never be buds is just part of the grown-up working world. Expressing enthusiasm and gratefulness is an integral part of any job. It took me a long, long time to learn that. I got fired from every job I ever had until I got out of law school, and then I started my own company so I *couldn't* be fired. I always said things that I shouldn't have said. I really shot myself in the foot over and over again. Don't make my mistake. The sooner you learn to be tactful, to present your views in non-confrontational ways, to deflect other people's anger instead of responding to it, the easier your work life will be, and the more opportunities you'll have. You'll have the power that comes from having options, from being the one who decides whether you stay or go. Does it suck that you can't say whatever pops into your head? Su-u-ure. But it's necessary.

If you don't have a lot of relevant work experience outside of the employer who didn't invite you back, consider volunteering on a bar association project or with PSLawNet or any

of the other volunteering activities in Chapter 10 on "The Bird and Bees of Jobs." That way, you can always point to successes with other lawyers as a means of showing that you deal well with people in work-related situations.

D. Get Your Explanation Down Pat . . . Including the Six Magic Words to Overcome *Any* Prior Work-Based Issue

Whether you didn't get an offer that everybody else at work got, or you messed up your work or you pissed off somebody important, you are always, always, always going to use six words to open your explanation when the topic comes up:

"I learned a really valuable lesson."

That's it. *I learned a really valuable lesson.* Where do you take it from there? Your explanation has four elements:

1. **It is not defensive;**

2. **It is clear and concise;**

3. **It doesn't bad mouth the former employer (a *big* no-no);**

4. **It concludes on an "up" note; for instance, your willingness to offer references from your last job who *will* say good things about you, and/or work product that shows you off advantageously.**

As we discuss throughout this book, image and message control is all-important. It's not what happened to you or what you've done that determines your opportunities, it's the image and message you create for employers. While not getting an offer from a prior employer is a thorny issue, putting together an honest and credible analysis of the issue is absolutely crucial.

Not being defensive in your answer is a necessary element of showing your confidence about your skills. Remember: If you didn't get an offer from a prior employer it's natural for any future employer to question why. They're not suggesting you're incompetent or weird, they just want to know *why*. If the shoe were on the other foot, admit it: *you'd* be curious. So acknowledge their curiosity and don't be defensive.

Also, don't rattle on. A short explanation bespeaks a solid grasp of what happened and what you've done to overcome it. Going on and on will start to make the person you're talking to think, "Why can't (s)he get to the point . . ."

Not bad-mouthing the former employer can be *incredibly* difficult, especially if the person you're talking to goads you with, "I heard [the person you worked for] is a real shyster/jerk/monster . . ." Remember: a knowing smile can replace the most damning words. You can always smile and say something like, "I understand Attorney X has that reputation, but I did learn some valuable skills working for him . . ."

When you put all of this together, consider the image created by answers like these:

> *"Of the eight projects I worked on all summer, I had one project involving Estate Tax implications that the partner in question wasn't pleased with. I analyzed where I slipped up, spoke with the Estate Tax professor at school about it, and I'm confident that both my knowledge of the area and my research skills are exactly where they should be. In fact, I can direct you to other partners from the firm where I worked, and they can tell you about the quality of my work ..."*

> *"My former employer could only afford to hire two of the eight summer clerks, and unfortunately I wasn't one of those two. I was naturally concerned about it, but it turns out that both of them had a lot more work experience than the rest of us, and that's why they got offers. But if you have any doubts about my abilities, I have letters of recommendation from all of the attorneys I worked for at the firm, and they'll be able to vouch for the quality of my work."*

> *"My supervisor was very busy, and always gave me assignments on the fly. On one of them, I mistakenly believed I had all the relevant facts. To make a long story short, I didn't, and the two weeks I spent on that project were wasted. Although the rest of my work for the summer was very favourably received and earned excellent reviews, that one project led to my not getting an offer. I learned a really valuable lesson: verify the facts with the assigning attorney before doing <u>anything</u> else."*

> *"My work was excellent, and I would have undoubtedly received an offer if my boss had not been an incompetent, vicious, bile-spewing viper."*

> Just kidding.

What does all of this tell you? Handling a rejection from a former employer is a lot like overcoming any pitfall in your job credentials, like poor grades or a lack of work experience. The most important thing about it is the spin you put on it. If you can speak with confidence about the perceived flaw, the person you're talking to will adopt your sense of confidence. Practice until you feel good about what you're saying!

E.   Consider Getting Short-Term, Positive Work Experience Under Your Belt Before You Look for Your Next "Serious" Gig

Whether you're back in school full-time or not, consider balancing out your negative experience with a positive one, right now. Ask at Career Services for any professors who are looking for immediate research help, or small local firms (or sole practitioners) who could use an extra set of hands right now, or contact the local bar association and offer to work on a project. What I'm trying to say is: Consider doing *something* that you can point to as a positive, recent, law-related experience. That way, when you talk to employers, you can always contrast your experience at your "non-offer" employer with what you just did (or are doing now). It'll make you feel better about yourself, and it'll take the "sting" out of your summer rejection.

F. DON'T EVEN *THINK* ABOUT LYING ABOUT GETTING AN OFFER!

This is a *huge* boner. I've seen law students do it, and I understand the temptation: it's so much easier to avoid doing all of the work I'm telling you to do, and simply lie to future employers about receiving an offer.

Please, please, *please* don't do it. As Gail Cutter points out, "The legal community is *very* small, no matter how large it seems!" The odds that you'll be caught in your lie are very much against you. And if you *do* get caught, no matter *when* it is, there's the possibility you'll be dismissed immediately from your new gig. It's just not worth it. Bite the bullet, and do the work!

G. REMEMBER THAT IN THE LONG ROAD OF YOUR CAREER, NOT GETTING A SUMMER OFFER IS JUST A SPEED BUMP

If you just got rejected by your summer employer, it's *huge*. I remember the feeling. I felt like I was wearing a major "L" on my forehead, and everyone could see what a loser I felt like I was. Trust me: it's a fleeting emotion. If the worst career hurdle you ever face is not getting an offer from a summer employer, you're leading a happy life. I promise you that the hurt you feel right now will fade, and given time, you'll be able to put the rejection in perspective. If you have bad feelings toward your former employer, put that energy to use to benefit yourself.

Look at it this way: what emotion would you like to invoke in your former employer? If you wallow in misery, if you stop doing things to improve yourself and your resume and you don't pursue other jobs, your former employer's reaction will be: "Geez, thank goodness we didn't keep *that* loser! Thank God we dodged *that* bullet!"

But if you dust yourself off and follow the advice in this book and nail a great gig despite your rejection, the old employer's reaction will be: "Hmm. Maybe we let a really good one get away." Isn't that how you *want* them to feel?

So give yourself a few days to grieve, and then take the steps I've outlined here. Do some of the activities in Chapter 10 on "The Birds and Bees of Great Jobs." I promise you that no matter how badly your last job turned out, you can still nail a job you'll love.

Chapter 16
"I Go to a Distinguished School ..."

If you want to destroy a man, give him what he wishes for.

Anonymous

Note: When I use the term "counselor" in this chapter, I mean "current or former career counselor at an elite law school." I didn't want to write it out every time ... and you don't want to read it every time.

In many ways every job search is the same, no matter where you go to school.

But let's face it—when you're "institutionally gifted," when your law school tops the US News survey year after year, you've got a somewhat different set of issues than the student who goes to Fred's Gaseteria and School of Law. As one counselor comments, "At many schools, when you tell Career Services you got an offer, the response is, 'Congratulations.' Here, it's 'Let's talk about it.' "

So—let's talk about it! Let's discuss the issues that are unique to prestigious schools.

A.   FIGURING OUT WHAT YOU REALLY WANT
... FROM A MULTITUDE OF CHOICES

One of the greatest advantages of going to a prestigious law school is that your selection of employers is vast. In the breakfast bar of legal careers, you've got the champagne buffet.

Of course, that raises its own issue, namely: how do you pick? You can't work for everyone. You can't even interview with everyone. How do you narrow down the choices? There are a few principles to keep in mind.

1. Clear Your Mind of the Obstacles to Making the Right Choice for You

a. It's Time to Make Choices Based on What You *Want—Not* on Keeping Your Options Open

Here's a headline for you: *you don't have to maximize your options any more.* Every choice you've made until now has done that for you. You went to the best college, the best law school. As one counselor points out, "Don't approach employers that way!"

Why the temptation? It's partially the problem of being faced with too many choices. It's stress-inducing to try and opt for a single path, and when you make the choice that maximizes your options, you're essentially making a non-decision. You're putting off the fateful day when you have to say, "This is what I really *want*."

The hiring partner at a large law firm pointed out that "Students from prestigious schools often come here planning their next move. They're not fully invested in *this* job. You can see it. They're trying to build a resume; they're coasting, doing what they need to do to get by. They're not building a skill set, a talent. They're not cultivating relationships or learning about different practices and figuring out what they want. They're never fully engaged."

A counselor adds, laughing, "It's an attitude like, 'I'll marry for looks this time. I'll marry for love next time around.'" Another points out, "I get the question from 3Ls, 'How long do I have to stay at the firm before I leave?' I tell them, 'You haven't even *worked* yet!'"

Yet another explains, "The more that you're invested and engaged in learning at a place regardless of whether it's a 'big name' or not, where you get a good experience, get mentored by first rate people, look forward to going to work, *that's* what's so important. So that when future employers ask you what you did for two years, you're enthused about it and you can talk about the skill set you're taking away ... as opposed to going to a top firm and not growing, doing work that's not really interesting and exciting to you.

"Who do you think an interviewer will be more interested in? The person who's engaged and excited about their work, or the person who's been doing discovery and planning their exit strategy?"

This isn't to say you don't give *any* thought to your second move. As I've pointed out before, when you get out of law school, on average you're likely to have twelve different jobs. *Twelve.* It does make sense to have a long-range plan. But that long-range plan shouldn't be to have as many options as possible. As a counselor puts it, "With every choice you make you're opening some doors and closing others. Give thought to what you see yourself doing next, *not* a firm's generic reputation, figuring that that will necessarily provide better opportunities down the road. Depending on what you want to do, that's not necessarily true."

B. MAKE YOUR CHOICE FOCUSING ON WHAT MAKES YOU HAPPY, *NOT* WHAT SOCIETY WOULD TELL YOU IS THE "BEST" EMPLOYER

This is so-o-o difficult. As a career counselor at one elite school puts it, "For our students, every decision that's been best for them is what Society would say is the objective best. Often they confuse external prestige with their internal 'best.'"

What happens if you fall into this trap? You take a job with a name firm because everybody tells you it's a great firm, it's prestigious and sexy, and it's mentioned in the *Wall Street Journal* all the time. That carries you for a little while. But sooner rather than later, your core values will come into play. If you find you're doing something at odds with what's really important to you, you shouldn't spend even one more minute doing it.

1. THE BEST EMPLOYER IS THE ONE YOU MOST ENJOY WORKING FOR

There are lists out the ying-yang of firms considered the "top." What's really misleading is that many, many times, "top" means "biggest"; when you see rankings of top firms, they mean *most lawyers* or *most revenue* or the most of some other objective measure. They don't mean "top" in terms of "best employers."

The fact is, *your* best employer might be a guy with a glassed-in office at a discount store.

I'm kidding.

But you see the point. It's the way you fill your day that counts, not the name on the door. A former associate at a very large law firm commented, "I thought going to this firm would open any door I wanted. I worked on so many discovery issues, just slogging through mountains and mountains of paper. Then I would talk to classmates at other places, who were actually *doing* things. I thought, 'What's this getting me? I hate it. I'm not learning anything. They could train a chimpanzee to do this work. After a while the thrill of telling people the name of my firm, that wore off pretty fast."

Whether your "happy place" has a thousand lawyers with Ivy League degrees or not, no employer is great if you don't enjoy working there. That's why you've worked so hard and excelled; to live the happiest life, right? So keep the focus where it belongs: on the employer that most gives you the life you want to live.

2. NO MATTER WHERE YOU PRACTICE, THE VAST MAJORITY OF PEOPLE WON'T HAVE HEARD OF IT ANYWAY

As one counselor puts it, "If you came to this law school because you got in, because it's prestigious, you need to recognize that at the end of the day, most people won't even know who your firm is no matter where you go. The biggest firms in the country, the most prestigious ones? Most people haven't heard of them. Your classmates, sure, *they* know. But when you go to look at your second job, people will ask you, 'Tell me what you've done,' which is so much more important than 'Tell me where you were.' "

c. The Difficulty of Choosing an Employer Other Than a Large Law Firm . . .

There's *enormous* pressure on you to go to a large law firm, isn't there? Who largely populates on the on-campus interview schedule? Who funds all of the lavish receptions? Who would students at every other law school in the country *kill* to work for? The large law firms that are all over you, "like flies on a rib roast," in the words of Randy Quaid in *National Lampoon's Vacation.*

Of course, there are other pressures as well. You might have the student loan issue—so many of us do—that makes you feel that an employer less willing to shower you with doubloons and pieces of eight is simply not an option.

And then there's the "one time only" issue. As the student at one prestigious law school put it, "If I don't go to Skadden or Cleary or O'Melveny *now,* when am I ever going to get the chance again?"

If you've broached the possibility of a non-large-firm goal with anyone at school, their reaction might have convinced you that you're crazy to consider anything else. A student at a very prestigious school sought me out at a conference once, and said, "Listen. I think there's something wrong with me. What I think I want to do . . . my Career Services Office won't talk to me about it. They won't even acknowledge the question."

Needless to say, he had *my* attention. I asked him, "So . . . what is it that you want?"

In a hushed voice—the kind you might reserve for confessing a lurid interest in farm animals—he said, "I think I'm interested in personal injury work."

I laughed, and said, "Are you *kidding* me? I'll tell you what's going on. Your school produces partners at big-name firms, judges, U.S. Supreme Court clerks, law professors and presidents. They've probably never had anybody like you walk in." I wound up recommending that he get reciprocity with another law school, one that's not ranked in the top ten, telling him, "They'll be happy to talk to you. They'll put you onto alums who'll give you advice. Trust me . . . you might really enjoy it. A lot of people do!"

So recognize up front that if you think you might want something other than a large law firm, you're going to face resistance. As one counselor describes it, "I use the analogy of a river current when I talk to students. I tell them, I know where you'll end up, if you just slip into this current, you'll end up at a big firm in New York City or DC, Chicago, LA, that's where the current is going. There's nothing wrong with that. But that's not the only thing you can do. It's the path of least resistance and the most popular. But there are a lot of things you can do and places you can go ... but you've got to swim upstream. It'll be more work, but you can do it. You can enjoy it and be really successful. But a lot of people choose not to swim against the stream, and they won't understand it when you *do*."

Remember that people take their cue from *your* attitude. If you seem really jazzed about what you want to do, if you've made the choice that's right for you, people will come around.

2.   WITH THE OBSTACLES OUT OF THE WAY ... HOW TO DECIDE

In a nutshell: Do your homework!

Figuring out what you want is *work*. It's like an annoying one-credit class that you can't avoid. You can't find a list that will tell you what you'll like, "There's no *U.S. News* ranking for whether you'll enjoy a job," as one counselor points out.

Of course, the result is a job you'll relish, so it's all worth it.

A.   DO THE TOUCHY-FEELY SELF-ASSESSMENT THING, THROUGH CAREER SERVICES AT SCHOOL AND/OR CHAPTER 2, "FIGURING OUT WHAT THE HECK YOUR DREAM JOB IS"

The $64,000 question is this: *What's important to you?* This question, ironically, may be more difficult for you to answer than for students who attend less prestigious schools. Here's why: Particularly if you've never worked before, it may be difficult to distinguish between what's really important to you, and what you've internalized that's important to other people.

For instance, if you've always gone to prestigious schools, it would be easy to assume that prestige is one of your core values. But that may not be the case.

As we talked about at length in Chapter 2, the difficult element of self-assessment comes in realizing that no job is wonderful in every respect. On the Discovery Channel show *Flip That House*—of course, you might not have time for that kind of stuff—there's a designer who pointed out, "When you're renovating a house, there are three factors: Time, quality, and price. If you want it done quickly and well, it'll be expensive. If you want it done well and cheaply, it'll take a long time." I'd go on, but you're smart, you see what I mean. It's all about choices. About compromise.

The same principle applies to jobs. When someone else is paying your way, you won't find reasonable hours, a huge check, prestige, entrepreneurial creativity and enjoyable, challenging work all at the same place. It doesn't exist. So what you have to do, whether through

Chapter 2 or through self-assessment tests at Career Services is to figure out what your "must-haves" are.

By way of an example, a 3L at one prestigious school e-mailed me with the question, "I want to be in New York. I have a lot of hobbies and outside interests, and it's really important for me to have a life outside of work." That's a valuable piece of information, because it immediately eliminates the reality of new associate life at any of the big name New York firms!

If you don't do the homework, the downside risk is taking a job and wasting perhaps years doing something you abhor. There's nothing that stops you from jumping at the most prestigious offer you get. Everybody will applaud you. But you could well find out that you *can't stand* what you wind up doing.

A counselor pointed out to me that, "We don't have problems with our students. Not while they're still in school, anyway. They target a city, they interview with large firms, and they accept an offer.

Our issues all come about a year or two later. We'll get calls from alums who say, 'I hate this job. I *hate* it.' When we ask them what they want, they say, 'I want the best.' They're so used to grabbing for the brass rang, and being really *good* at it, that they've never taken a step back to think about what they really like to do. We have to tell them, there is no way you will ever find a job you truly enjoy, that you're suited for, if you don't do the internal piece first."

So do the hard work, first. Figure out what's really important to you, and what's expendable. It's the only way to make smart decisions about your career.

B. Will a Large Law Firm Make You Happy?

A huge topic, and one we cover at length in Chapter 23.

C. Take Advantage of Programming at School

Your Career Services Office will put on dozens and dozens of programs, featuring speakers talking about different kinds of practice areas, different business areas, and different types of settings. They often feature free food, and if you're like me, there's no reason to go through law school *ever* having to pay for a meal if you plan your programming correctly.

Seriously . . . it's easy to blow off programming. Don't do it. As author Daniel Gilbert points out in *Stumbling On Happiness*— it's a great book, read it if you haven't already—the only way to really know if you'll enjoy something is to talk to someone who does it. Programming at school gives you that opportunity, and you don't have to step outside of school to get it.

So keep an eye on what's coming to school. Attend everything that strikes you as being even remotely interesting. And if you have specific questions, go up afterwards and talk to the speaker, or follow up with them with an e-mail afterwards (complimenting their speech, of course).

Incidentally, if you wind up being really interested in the subject of a speaker's talk, let them know. It's a great and simple way to make valuable contacts, and get in on opportunities that might have been a stretch otherwise.

D. RESOURCES AT CAREER SERVICES, INCLUDING CONTACT WITH THE TREASURE CHEST OF INSIDE SKINNY: ALUMS

We've already talked about self-assessment tools; your Career Services Office can hook you up with those. They can also do you a ton of other favours.

The most valuable thing Career Services can do for you is to put you onto alums who've done just about everything, whether you're talking about being in a certain city, or working for a given employer, or in a given practice. As one counselor put it, "You want tax? We can find an alum in the city you want. That alum will talk to you about the practice area and the firms in the city that are known for it. We can do that for any city, any practice area, if you just ask."

Conversations with people doing in a given job is the best window into whether you'll enjoy it. Without even trying, you'll think, "That sounds great," or "I don't think I could put up with that ..." On top of that, people will give you *much* better information when they talk to you than when they e-mail you or fill out a survey. They'll be more candid and they'll respond to specific issues that concern you, and that's what you want.

Career Services can also provide you with reviews written by upperclassmen and alums. These can be quite blunt and therefore helpful. Especially if the "reviewer" includes their name, you can contact them and ask questions about their former employer.

Career Services stocks published surveys of large law firms as well. A caveat: as one career counselor puts it, "Take them with a large grain of salt. A lot of information you want won't be in them; you'll only get the employer's spin that way." Furthermore, "Remember that surveys depend on voluntarily participation. Nobody is sent to jail if they don't contribute." The people who tend to contribute most often to surveys are those on the fringes, people who have strong feelings one way or the other. They may not represent the vast majority of people in any given setting, which skews the results. But surveys can be illuminating, and they're often great fun to read.

E. GET ON-LINE AND SEE WHAT ALUMS HAVE DONE WITH THEIR DEGREES FROM YOUR SCHOOL ...

A great source of inspiration is the experience of alums. You'll come across jobs you didn't realize existed. As one counselor advises, "For a couple of days, do a couple of basic searches and see in small and mid-sized firms where the alums are, and see what cool things they're doing in your target city. There'll be places you've never heard of, firms that don't always come to mind. There are smart people in all of these different places. Be more of a contrarian!"

f. Read News Articles About the Profession

There is a constant stream of interesting articles about different aspects of practicing law. Take advantage of all of that research. Lawfuel.com, Lexis/Nexis and Westlaw, news.google.com ... skim them regularly to see what strikes your fancy.

g. Informational Interviews With Lawyers, Whether They Went to Your School or Not

As you probably already know, in informational interviews, as the name suggests, you're soliciting information rather than a job. When you're trying to figure out what you want to do, informational interviews can be a revelation. We talk all about information interviewing, from nailing them to questions to ask, in Chapter 10. As I've mentioned before, hearing what someone does, from the person who does it, is the single best way to figure out if you'll enjoy it.

h. Clinical and Mandatory Pro Bono Experiences

Use clinics and mandatory pro bono at school to explore your career options.

As to clinics, one counselor points out, "Whether it's a transactional or litigation clinic, it's like another summer program. Not taking advantage of the clinics is a huge mistake."

For mandatory pro bono, "If you're going to do it anyway, be strategic. Think outside the box. Focus on anything that interests you: an issue, an organization. Try something you wouldn't ordinarily do, so that you're gathering data points."

i. Your 1L Summer

If you're not sure what you want to do, change it up for your 1L summer. As one counselor advises, "Most students go to a large law firm for their first summer. Do something different! Do something in the public sector. Work abroad. Do something you'd never have thought of doing, because it'll be eye opening. You can always go to a large firm for your 2L summer if you want. You don't have to do it 1L as well.

Think about what might appeal to you as a career. If you think you might want to teach, work for a professor. If not—don't. Look at the summer as a way to help you make a career decision."

B. HOW TO DISTINGUISH BETWEEN LARGE FIRMS

As you know, large law firms are the most common employers of students from prestigious law schools. But of course, large law firms aren't all alike, and, as one counselor points out, "Students ask me all the time, 'What's the difference? How do I pick?' It's not like there's a U.S. News ranking called 'The law firm that will make you happy!'" "It's difficult to have a bunch of options and not be able to distinguish between them," in the words of another counselor.

"Students think that the firms are pretty much the same, but they're not," says a partner at one large law firm. "One firm might make you miserable, where another would be your dream employer."

This is perfectly illustrated by the experience of one counselor. "I got a call one morning from an alum at a large Chicago firm," she reports. "She was whispering, and she said, 'I'm under my desk calling you. I *hate* this place. I work for such *jerks*. You *have* to get me out of here!'" The counselor goes on, "That afternoon, I got another call, this one from an alum at the very same firm. He sounded fantastic, and he said, 'I just wanted to say thanks for turning me on to this firm. These people are great. I love it here.'" The counselor laughs, saying, "*Very same firm*. The two alums were in different departments, on different floors, with very different experiences. You'd think it was opposite sides of the planet."

What does all of this point to? The fact that **you need to *research* firms before you accept an offer from any one of them.** As one counselor points out, "I'm constantly surprised by how little research our students do. They say, 'I can't differentiate, so why shouldn't I choose the one with the most bucks?' It's a huge mistake. It just takes being *proactive*."

You needn't interview with a firm *at all* to learn whether it's the right place for you ... although, of course, you can do some of the research we'll talk about when you interview. But no matter when you do it, you *have* to do it if you're going to find the right place for you. As the recruiting coordinator at one large firm puts it, "The happiest people here are the ones who researched the firm ahead of time and chose it specifically."

Let's talk about the research you need to do, and the resources at your disposal.

1. RESOURCES

You're perfectly positioned to find out anything you need to know about any large firm in America.

A. YOU HAVE TO GO *BEYOND* WHAT FIRMS TELL YOU ABOUT THEMSELVES

As the hiring partner at one large firm points out, "Every firm says they're collegial. They all say there'll be a work/life balance, that there's a 'no a**hole policy.' I ask you: What *idiot* would not put their best foot forward?" A counselor adds, "The twenty minutes on campus and two hours at a firm are just not enough." Another points out that, "Law firms know all the tricks. They spend a ton of money on their web sites, they have in-house blogs, and they craft their images very carefully. You have to work *around* the 'firm spin' to find the truth."

B. RESOURCES AT—AND THROUGH—CAREER SERVICES

There is not a prestigious law school in America that doesn't have an awesome Career Services Office. Rely on yours to help you choose the right firm.

1. ALUMS TO TALK TO

Use Career Services to find the names of alums who can give you the inside skinny. As one counselor advises, "You can only really understand what's true about a firm by talking to people familiar with it." You want alums that fit one of these criteria: They work at the firm now, they *used* to work there, or they work at other firms in town. *Don't rely on the opinion of people who only summered at a firm.* The experience of permanent associates is very different than summer associates!

Don't overlook associates at other firms in the same city for an objective opinion. As one counselor says, "If a student comes to us and says, 'I want tax in X city,' we'll find that student alums in X city to talk about the practice area and firms that are known for it."

2. PROGRAMS TO ATTEND

Your CSO will put on *tons* of programs that will give you insights into what individual firms are like. Be sure to attend **programs that feature headhunters from the city(ies) you're targeting.** Headhunters will be *very* familiar with all of the large firms in any given market; that makes them a very useful resource. If you have questions that go beyond their discussion during the program, hang around afterwards and ask them then.

Also, keep an eye out for **panel discussions by lawyers in the city/practice area you're considering.** Again, research can't get easier than going to a program at school featuring people with the inside information you need. And if it turns out that one of the panel members is from a firm that truly interests you, walk up and introduce yourself afterwards. It never hurts to impress an insider with your enthusiasm; it jump-starts your reputation at work before you even arrive!

c. ONLINE RESOURCES

There are a bunch of resources that you'll find useful. Among the ones I heard the most about:

Use law firm websites and Lexis/Nexis and Westlaw to find alums from your school at firms that interest you. (You can get this same information at Career Services, where they'll be able to direct you to specific alums to contact.)

For news about firms:

> Blogs like www.abovethelaw.com and firm-sanctioned blogs by associates.
>
> www.lawfuel.com
>
> Articles in the news in LEXIS and Westlaw
>
> www.news.google.com

And, of course, the "gossip" sites. Take them with a grain of salt because they're unfiltered, but they can still provide useful tidbits:

> www.autoadmit.com (also known as www.xoxohth.com)
>
> www.judged.com
>
> www.greedyassociates.com
>
> www.vault.com

2. INFORMATION YOU NEED TO DIG UP

a. YOU NEED TO LOOK PAST "GENERIC PRESTIGE" TO A FIRM'S PRESTIGE IN THE AREA THAT INTERESTS YOU

As one counselor points out, "Unfortunately, a lot of students pick their firm the same way they picked their law school: just take the most prestigious one you get into." Another adds, "You can't tell students, 'Don't think about prestige.' It's *generic* prestige that's the problem. If you want IP litigation, the 'best' firm that doesn't have that strength won't help you!"

As the former associate at a large firm adds, "All of the big firms will have corporate and litigation practices. But they're not all the same. There's still something that makes each of them unique, and you want to find it. Maybe you want IPOs, or biotech, M & A, no matter what it is, use your resources to figure out what their strengths are. If they do IPOs and you want litigation, it might not be the best place for you."

b. FIND OUT WHAT WORKING AT THE FIRM IS LIKE ON A DAY-TO-DAY BASIS

In Chapter 9 on Interviews, I talked about the importance of determining what your working hours at an employer will be like. When you talk to alums who work at a firm that interests you, ask them specifically: What do you like about what you do? What would you change about it if you could? What do you wish you'd known when you started? How did you choose the firm? Your specialty? Who else did you consider and why did you choose this firm over those? Listen carefully to how other people made their decisions, what was important to them, and weigh that against what counts for *you*. (In fact, if you're having a hard time figuring out what your priorities *are,* talking to people about theirs can actually help you determine yours!)

c. Find Out the Pay Structure

As one counselor advises, "You need to understand the culture of the firm. Part of that is to understand the compensation system. It'll tell you a lot about culture. How do partners divide the profits? Is it a lockstep system, eat what you kill, modified lockstep? Or is it what's called a 'black box,' where nobody knows the formula? Or is it perfectly open? There are plusses and minuses to each."

To find this out, you can "Ask partners directly, when you go on a callback with the firm. You can also research it ahead of time by talking to associates who are alums from your school. No matter how you find it out, it's critical. If you understand the compensation, you'll understand the culture of the firm."

d. Look for Comings and Goings at the Firm

You want to determine the flow of partners and clients. As the partner at one large firm points out, "It's staggering to me that students don't do this. Their financial future depends on it."

How do you find this out? The Internet is actually a great resource for this kind of information. Check blogs, www.lawfuel.com, Lexis/Nexis and Westlaw. Search for specific law firm names and see what kinds of articles appear. They'll almost always disclose major events at large firms. As one counselor points out, "The Brobeck meltdown is a great example of an easily-researchable disaster in waiting. The AmLaw rankings showed an abnormally high 'profit per partner' number. Students who only paid attention to that number flocked to Brobeck, figuring they were doing great. But articles on-line showed that partners were abandoning the firm left and right. *That's* why the profits per partner were so high; the pie was being split among fewer people. It was just way out of whack."

"A year later . . . Brobeck was gone."

3. If You Can't Choose Among Your Offers From Large Law Firms . . . It May Be That You Don't Want *Any* of them

Because you *can* get the most prestigious jobs, it doesn't mean you have to *take* them. As one counselor points out, "I often have students come in when they're juggling half a dozen offers from prestigious firms. They'll say to me, 'I just can't pick.' It took me a long time to figure out that when they're really stymied, it probably means: 'I don't really want to do this at all.' "

So if you do the research we just talked about and you're still in a quandary, go back to Step One and figure out what you really want to do. It may be that you really don't want a large law firm at all!

4. IF YOU JUST CAN'T DECIDE, A JUDICIAL CLERKSHIP CAN BUY YOU TIME ... AND A PHENOMENAL EXPERIENCE

One way to put off making a choice of firms is to opt for a judicial clerkship. While we talk extensively about judicial clerkships in Chapter 25, it's worth pointing out here that because you go to a prestigious law school, a judicial clerkship is a particularly viable option for you.

The reasons to pursue a judicial clerkship are summarized by a counselor who points out, "It's just a year or two of your life, and the benefits are tremendous. Having a judge as a recommender for the rest of your life is awesome. And if you want to be a litigator, it's a year where you hone your writing/analysis skills, see a range of styles, see what to do and what *not* to do, and see how people present arguments. The prestige is great. It gives you a better understanding of the legal system. If you do go to a firm afterwards, you go in the same 'class' as your classmates; you avoid the drudgery of the first year or two. You get a 'signing bonus' at firms for having completed a federal clerkship. And best of all, for most alums, it's their best work experience."

I'd recommend a judicial clerkship to you even if you weren't having trouble figuring out which firm you'd like to work for. But if you *are* having trouble deciding ... a judicial clerkship is a *very* viable option!

C. REGARDLESS OF YOUR SCHOOL, YOUR CLASS RANK MAY LIMIT YOUR CHOICES

It may well be that you're getting a Harvard or a Stamford or a Yale or an NYU or a fill-in-the-blank prestigious degree ... but that degree doesn't guarantee you entrée to any employer in the country. Your class rank still counts. That may be absolutely impossible for you to get your mind around, but it's the truth.

As one counselor points out, "One of the most challenging counseling situations we face is when students come in and say, 'I want a judicial clerkship and I'm only willing to go to Los Angeles and New York.' If their grades are in the lower half of the class, we have to tell them: You won't get the clerkships in the choice cities. You'll have to look elsewhere. It makes them *furious.*"

What should you do if your grades aren't stellar? For a start, take a look at Chapter 13, "Help! My Grades Stink!" While you're in a much better boat than people with mediocre grades at less-distinguished schools, you still might have to go the extra mile to get the gigs you want.

For instance, consider the following, which are mentioned in greater detail in Chapter 13:

1. Tracking programs offered by the Career Services Office, and attending the ones where the speaker(s) is/are from your target employer(s). Make a point of introducing yourself afterwards (or during a reception connected with the event). State your enthusiasm for the employer and say you'd look forward to talking with them about working with them. As I pointed out way back in Chapter 4, there is almost nothing more attractive to employers than genuine enthusiasm.

2. Taking advantage of your mandatory paper requirement (if your school has one) to make yourself known to lawyers at firms and in specialties you're targeting. Ask them for cutting edge topics, and develop an informal mentoring relationship. Having an insider pulling for you can make all the difference.

3. Talking with alums at employers that interest you, and soliciting their advice and help in getting your foot in the door.

I could go on and on with ideas along these lines, but you see the point: if your GPA doesn't get you where you want to go, letting people see you and get invested in you ... will.

D. Not Every Employer Will Drool Over Your School

1. Legal Careers With Employers That Are Outside the "Large Law Firm" Paradigm

Here's the deal. When you go to a prestigious school, large law firms that are the dream of law students everywhere are the coin of the realm. Problematically, the further your goals fall *outside* of that model ... *the more difficult it will be for you to convince employers that you're serious about them.*

You may find this impossible to believe. After all: wouldn't *anybody* welcome a student with an elite law school education? The answer is: No. They'll have a hard time believing you. As the recruiting attorney at a very desirable public interest employer stated, "When I see an elite resume, I ask myself, 'What gives?' I'll scrutinize it. I'll be skeptical."

A recruiter for a city attorney's office adds, "When we get a Harvard resume, it isn't the right profile. We don't get many elite law school resumes, and we wonder: what's the real story here?"

"The irony is that students from elite schools think they'll get a favourable reception wherever they apply. Yes, if they apply to the U.S. Supreme Court, the Department of Justice, they'll be taken seriously. But if they apply for the Legal Aid Society or somewhere outside the profile of where those students typically go, they have to expect to get more than cursory scrutiny."

The result is that **if you seek a career with a non-large-firm employer, you're going to have a more 'traditional' job search.**

That is, you can't rely on on-campus interviews to get you what you want. Sort of stinks, doesn't it? As one counselor puts it, "There's a lot of resentment among students when they have to seek out employers outside of on-campus interviews." Another adds, "When we have students who want small firms, government jobs, public interest work, anything that's law-related—they're frustrated that they just can't stroll in and say, 'Where's the long list of employers with my criteria and where do I sign up to interview with them?'"

What you need to realize is that on-campus interviews are about as "unreal" as job searches get. Outside of the minority of employers who interview on campus—and the minority of schools at which they interview—job searches involve reaching out to employers with a targeted pitch.

How do you do it?

A. Front-Load Your Resume and Cover Letters With Items Addressing Your Target Employer

As one counselor explains it, "You can get away with a generic cover letter and resume when you're targeting big firms. They're just looking for 'gold stars,' and you have those. But further away from that large firm paradigm, you have to be more specific and direct with your letter and resume. Your package for a public interest employer can't be the same one you'd present to a large firm. Outside of large law firms, you have to show why you're committed." Joining appropriate bar association sections and school organizations, attending relevant CLEs, taking advantage of summers, clinics and papers to address your interests . . . those all breathe credibility into your materials. Talk to your Career Services Office counselors as well as alums who do what you want to do, and ask their advice about activities you should take part in to enhance your credentials.

In short: look at yourself as your target employer would look at you. Ask: Do my credentials show that I'm truly interested in this career? If you believe it—they'll believe it!

B. Anticipate Interview Questions About Your Motives

Just as you have to target your materials to your target employer, you need to prepare for interview questions about your motives. As we discussed in Chapter 9, the Interview chapter, one of the most important questions you need to anticipate is: "Why do you want to work for us?" It needs to show your understanding of the work and your enthusiasm for it. As one assistant district attorney points out, "I just love it when I talk to a student from an elite school, somebody who's on Law Review. I like to ask: 'What do those great credentials teach you about negotiating a plea bargain with a child molester?' They'll look at me, shocked. But they better have an answer!"

c. Target Employers With the Strategies in Chapter 10

If you're looking for employers who don't interview on-campus, you're going to have the job search that just about every other law student in America has. That shouldn't depress you; you'll learn job search strategies that you'll use to nail great gigs the rest of your life. You'll find them in Chapter 10, "The Birds and Bees of Great Jobs."

2. "Alternative" Careers

We talk all about Alternative Careers in Chapter 31. I mention that right up front, because as is true for the "non-large-firm" employers we just discussed, an elite law school degree won't give you a leg up in alternative careers. They're certainly within your reach, but you'll have to do the work any other law student would do to state your case.

Let's say, for instance, that you want to break into management consulting, a common alternative career for law students. Let's say you like the idea of counseling companies on strategy. And let's say that you were an English major in undergrad. As the recruiting coordinator at a major consultancy points out, "I'd ask you: Why should I hire you when I can go to Wharton, to Kellogg, in fact to any elite business school and hire anybody I want? What makes you *more* appealing with your legal background than people who are trained specifically in business? You might say you bring a unique perspective to the table—I hear that a lot—but you're still not trained in any of this."

Instead, as one counselor points out, "**You've got to do things to look the part**. For instance, take some courses at your university's business school. Do a *lot* of informational interviewing with alums who are consultants. Be engaged, interested, enthusiastic, and make your actions match your words."

Another alternative is to view the first couple of years out of law school as a way to build a skill set that will carry you into your dream job. For instance, let's say you want to break into private equity. As one counselor advises, "Look at the firms that represent the players. It's all about relationships. You work for a firm that represents the private equity firms you want to work for. If you're working with the people doing what you want to do, you might be working from a legal angle instead of the angle you really want, but you're in the game now. You're developing a network, working with people who do it. Look at the client base of firms you want to work for. Look at the people you can meet. Look at the firm that'll give you the most possibilities. It'll be your springboard, it'll give you tangible skills, it'll give you a network of relationships that will take you in-house because now you've got some training under your belt. You know what you're doing now as opposed to being raw potential. You've got judgment because you've got *experience*. You can go in-house, go to the business side, and go to a client. It's all possible."

E. Because You Often *May* Be Able Get Away With Bad Behavior, It Doesn't Mean You *Can* ... or That You *Should*

When I talk to attorneys and recruiting coordinators about elite law schools, I am deluged with stories of behavior that pisses them off. Among them:

- The student who extended his visit to a firm on the opposite coast to include a long weekend at an exclusive hotel ... and upped his midsized rental car to a Jag.

- Many students who've chosen to empty the minibar in their hotel room on a callback interview ... to the tune of hundreds of dollars.

- The student who told a firm in another city that he was seriously considered them, but he wanted to meet with more associates before he made a decision. The firm's recruiting coordinator bought his plane tickets, reserved a private room at an exclusive restaurant, ordered a buffet and recruited several associates to attend. Two days before the student's anticipated visit, the recruiting coordinator called the student to confirm the plans, and the student responded casually, "Oh, I guess I should have called you. I accepted an offer with another firm."

- The student who was invited to a call-back interview which included a dinner. He accepted, and said, "By the way, for dinner ... I want a tall thin blonde as a date." The firm complied.

- A firm's prospective summer associate had a wife who was going to give birth a month before his summer clerkship started. He called the firm and begged to be allowed to clerk during the Spring semester so he could get benefits to cover the birth. The firm agreed. The wife had the baby. Before the student's summer clerkship began, he bowed out and joined a rival firm in town.

- Students who requested that their employers pay not just to move their household belongings to an out-of-town destination, but also request payment to move their boat ... and their horse.

Before you ask for something outrageous just because you figure you can get away with it, I beg you to consider the following:

1. You might get away with it, but you'll start off with a reputation as a troublemaker.

As the recruiting coordinator at one prestigious firm points out, "We get outrageous requests from students at elite schools. The firm might go along, but these students don't know what they're doing to their reputations. They're coming in with a strike against them. People start rooting against you. And when you're a new associate, trust me, you need all the help you can get. It just makes sense, when you're getting a very generous package anyway, to remember to be nice to everybody ... and don't ask for more!"

2. You might not be able to get away with it after all.

The hiring partner at a large firm points out, "Contrary to popular belief, you can't get away with everything. We might be really predisposed to hire you because you have stellar credentials, but if you're a jerk, we won't take you. We don't call back every person we see at elite schools. Interviewers sometimes come back and say, 'We saw a bunch of duds.' We still want good people. We don't want to work with jerks. And we don't have to."

F. Arrogance ... and "Prestige Envy"

Here's the irony. Although you've got a lot to be arrogant about— let's face it, most law students in America would kill to go to your school—the arrogance thing is largely a myth, a creation of people who *don't* go to elite schools. I've spoken at elite schools a few times, and I've yet to meet an arrogant student. (I've met lots of arrogant students elsewhere, but *never* at an elite school.) This is echoed by a counselor who says, "Our students really aren't arrogant. It's more folklore. It's not the truth. They're respectful and appreciative. I *expected* them to be arrogant before I got here. Oh sure, there's an arrogant student here and there, but it's largely non-existent."

A counselor from another school echoes that, saying, "For most part, students feel grateful for the opportunities."

But the fact is, it exists in the minds of many people who aren't associated with elite schools, and if you're not aware of "prestige envy," it can really hurt you.

* * * CAREER LIMITING MOVE * * *

Second year student, elite law school. He goes to a call-back interview with a large firm, bringing with him two bar charts. One of them shows how his school ranks against other law schools in the country. The other shows how he ranks in his classes compared to his classmates.

* * * CAREER LIMITING MOVE * * *

Two summer associates, elite schools, Midwestern firm. The firm has an "Ask me anything" lunch with the managing partner every Friday. At one lunch, one of the associates asks the managing partner, "We have a question for you. We can make twice as much money if we go to a firm in New York. Why should we stay here?"

As one of the other summer associates reports, "You should have seen the managing partner. I thought his head was going to explode. Using some choice language, he basically said: 'If I was going to pay you what you're worth, you'd pay *me* for the first two years, *then* I'd give you a hundred and fifty grand a year.'"

"It was just about the worst thing they could have said. I guess they didn't realize that 'Ask me anything' doesn't really mean 'Ask me *anything*.'"

1.   IT'S NOT AN ISSUE AT LARGE FIRMS ON THE COASTS; OUTSIDE OF THOSE EMPLOYERS ... BEWARE

Before you start working with an employer, check the backgrounds of the other clerks and the junior associates. If you see a lot of "non-elite" law schools, expect to face "prestige envy." As a student from an elite school pointed out, "I went to a large Chicago firm, and there was a definite mark against me because of my school. They assumed I had an attitude from the get-go."

2.   ASSUME THAT EVERYONE KNOWS WHERE YOU GO TO LAW SCHOOL AND *DON'T MENTION IT*

Remember: people who aren't from elite schools will expect you to be arrogant, to look for opportunities to brag about your school. I heard from more than one recruiting coordinator, "So you went to a prestigious school. Bully for you. Shut up about it already." My advice to you is: don't give them what they're expecting.

A hiring partner at a large law firm told me about a Harvard student who was a summer clerk at his firm. He said, "This guy was very sensitive to the whole 'Harvard envy' thing. When we had a social event, with people bringing their significant others, I overheard a conversation he had with another clerk's wife. She didn't realize he was a summer clerk, and she asked him, 'What do you do?' He responded, 'I go to graduate school.' She asked, 'What are you studying?' and he said, 'Law.' She asked, 'Where do you go to school?' and he responded 'Boston.' It was only when she asked him which law school that he mentioned Harvard. This really reflected the guy's whole attitude; he was conscious that people would treat him differently if he told them where he went to school, so he always avoided mentioning it until his back was against the wall."

3.   DON'T GIVE ANYBODY A *REASON* TO THINK YOU'RE ARROGANT

Expect to go the extra mile to show you've got to prove yourself as an attorney just like anybody else. As one hiring partner advises, "You need to be aware that people have a chip on their shoulder, an axe to grind. If you're talking to anyone, you don't know who you're dealing with. Don't give them a reason to prove their hypothesis. You've got to work harder to be more polite, more respectful, and do good work. The job isn't going to fall into your lap. Getting the offer won't fall into your lap. If people don't want to work with you, it doesn't matter where you go to school ... you won't get an offer."

The recruiting coordinator at one large firm says, "You really do have to be aware that we're *expecting* you to be arrogant. Don't fulfill our expectations. We invited one student from an elite school to lunch, he accepted, and then didn't show up. We had another one who *did* show up, but then put the firm down! We asked him, 'Do you want to represent X type of company?' and he actually said, 'No, maybe I don't.'

We hear this kind of thing, we just chalk it up to, 'Oh, this student is from X elite school, what do you expect?' "

4. Remember That the Presumption That You're Really Smart Will Take You Only So Far

This is really a matter of what you do once you have a job than it is a job search matter—which means it belongs in my book *What Law School Doesn't Teach You ...* rather than here—but I'll mention it anyway.

When you walk into an employer with an elite degree, "You have a presumption you wouldn't have anywhere else," says the hiring partner at a large law firm. "It's a presumption in your favor. But if you start making mistakes, if you turn in bad work, people will start asking, 'How did you get into that school?' We want you to work out. That's why we came to school to recruit you. But we're not stupid. If we hire you after you've messed up, we get what we deserve. We won't let that happen."

Having an elite education is the equivalent of a 'free pass' on *Wheel of Fortune*. It'll get you through one mistake. After that ... mistakes count. Don't test this hypothesis! Be a pleasure to work with and turn in good work. You'll get great opportunities ... and you'll put the lie to the whole arrogance myth!

G. Just Because You Can Get Your Foot in the Door, It Doesn't Guarantee You the Choicest Positions and Assignments. How to Make Yourself Stand Out to Employers ...

Having the career you want and deserve is more than just getting a position at the employer you want. You need to make sure that you make a stellar impression on people you want to work with. After all, there will be a huge variety of jobs and assignments at any employer you choose. What you say and do has everything to do with the nature of the opportunities you get.

You can start this process even *before* you join a firm after graduation. For instance, as one counselor points out, "While you're a summer associate, see what practice areas you're drawn to. Go to one of the attorneys you enjoy working with and ask, 'What are some of the biggest issues you're dealing with? Are there any novel issues, any cases of first impression?' When you get back to school, use that as the basis for a 3L paper. Then tell the attorney, 'I'm going to write this paper,' and work with him/her to turn it into an article. You can get it published in any one of a variety of law-related publications."

"Now you've got credibility. First of all, this person will be blown away by your enthusiasm. On top of that you've got some cool work product, whether you go to that firm or another one after graduation. You'll know more about the subject than most people. You'll pave your way into the specific practice area you want."

H. WHEN YOU GET THE INTERVIEWS BUT YOU'RE NOT GETTING THE OFFERS . . .

The first thing to know is, you're not alone. As a counselor points out, "Every year there are students who don't get offers. I talk with people in Career Services at other elite schools. They all have the same results. The idea that everybody at an elite school gets a job through OCI is simply not true."

A counselor at another school echoes that, saying, "There's an assumption that because you go here it'll be easy for you to get a job through on-campus interviews. But there are people every year who strike out in OCI. More than a few. They're horribly embarrassed. They assumed they could walk in anywhere."

While not getting a job through OCI at a non-elite school is the norm, at an elite school it can be much more painful. There is both internal and external pressure on you. You don't know what's wrong, and other people wonder what's wrong with *you*.

Let's talk about the common culprits of "OCI failure," and address some simple solutions.

1. IT MAY WELL BE THAT EMPLOYERS YOU INTERVIEW WITH DON'T BELIEVE YOU WANT THEM

This is probably the #1 reason students at elite schools don't get offers. Simply put: your credentials don't speak for themselves. Employers *have* to believe that you are sincerely interested in working for them. If they don't believe it, they won't make you an offer.

So when you interview, make sure:

- You research the employer ahead of time, so you can talk intelligently about your enthusiasm for working for them (see Chapter 6 on Research);

- You state an honest interest in the city where they're located; be able to explain your desire to be there and show a familiarity with where you'd live (speak to a realtor or alum from there ahead of time if you don't know);

- If you want to split a summer, you've got an even greater challenge. You need an exceptionally compelling reason for not being able to choose between the employers, *especially* if they're in two different cities;

- Don't feel silly stating your interest in the employer. "I'd really enjoy working with you because . . .";

- Make sure your focus is crystallized. If you're looking at employers in four cities, you're going to have a hard time convincing *any* of them that you have a sincere interest in them;

- Follow all the rest of the advice about interviewing in the Interviewing chapter, Chapter 9.

2. Your School Might Not Be as Strong in Your Target Market as You Think It Is

It's easy to think that because you go to an elite school, every employer in the country will have an equal respect for it. Not so. As one counselor explains, "The assumption that you can go anywhere with your degree may not be accurate. Your school will be stronger in some markets than others. Prestigious schools have the same out-of-town issues as other schools. For instance, if your school isn't in the Bay area, firms there will assume you just want to vacation there, that you're not truly interested in working for them. You need to show a connection."

3. Try Mock Interviews to Find Any Simple Flaws and Fix Them

Did you have to interview to get into law school? Nope. You did it on your credentials. Which means it may be that while you look great on paper, your conversational skills in an interview setting could use some work. I almost always find that when law students strike out at on-campus interviews, it's because they're making a simple mistake, in something they say or a behavior that they don't even realize they exhibit. Once they sort it out, the call-backs and offers start to flow.

It's important to remember that even if you feel terribly uncomfortable interviewing for jobs, your discomfort isn't a permanent condition. Great interviewing skills can be learned. There are lots of people who start out uncomfortable chatting with strangers, and become incredibly good at it. President Kennedy's friend Red Fay recounted in his memoir an experience that is relevant. He reported that when he helped Kennedy with his first congressional campaign, Kennedy asked him to spend a few hours essentially babysitting a relative. Fay agreed, and found the experience excruciating. He said that this young man was unbearably shy. He didn't say anything, and any time Fay tried to engage him in conversation, even one-word answers seemed like a strain. Fay went on to say that after this one experience, he could never imagine ever willingly being around the young man again.

The young man was Robert Kennedy, who as we all know went on to become one of the most eloquent people in America, and Fay said he spent many a delightful weekend with Kennedy and his family.

You're a lot more eloquent than the young Robert Kennedy no matter how uncomfortable you feel conversationally. If you feel you need practice, reach out to your Career Services Office. They'll rehearse with you and set up mock interviews so that you can practice until you feel perfectly comfortable with the whole interview process.

4. If You Don't Get a Job Through OCI, Don't Let Your Anger Stand in the Way of Your Getting a Job Some Other Way

When you've got a prestigious education, it's easy to tell yourself, "I shouldn't have to do anything outside of OCI to get a job ..." "I shouldn't have to compromise ..."

Do yourself a favour and don't go there. It won't do you any good. As Malachy McCourt famously said, "Resentment is like taking poison and waiting for the other person to die." It doesn't get you one step closer to your goals.

Instead, recognize that OCI is a mere speed bump on the road to a dream job. If you have to do a little more than your classmates to get there, so be it. You'll be developing skills that will benefit you for a lifetime. Which leads us naturally to . . .

5. OCI ISN'T THE ONLY WAY TO GET INTO EMPLOYERS WHO INTERVIEW ON CAMPUS . . .

Every employer who hires through OCI also hires *outside* of it. Consider contacting alums, especially partners, at firms you're targeting. State your interest in the firm compellingly, and ask for their advice about what you ought to do to achieve your goal. Look at Chapter 10, The Birds and Bees of Jobs, for ideas about targeting and contacting employers that interest you. Look at other jobs that lead to the jobs you want. Remember: Whether OCI works out for you or not, there are *many* doors that lead into employers.

6. NO MATTER WHAT YOU LOOK LIKE ON PAPER, WHEN EMPLOYERS INTERVIEW YOU, THEY WANT TO HAVE AN INTERESTING *CONVERSATION*. GIVE THEM ONE

You're smart and you're interesting. Make sure that's the face that interviewers see. If you walk into interviews thinking, "I go to [fill-in-the-blank] school, it's up to you to impress me . . ." you've got it backwards. Be your most charming self!

* * * SMART HUMAN TRICK * * *

Hiring partner at a large law firm, interviewing on-campus at a prestigious law school. She reports, "All day, I was so bored I couldn't stand it. I interviewed student after student who had the same bland aspect. They all talked about Law Review, what they were looking for in a firm, not one of them was somebody I could even remotely see myself working with . . .

. . . Until the last guy. He was the last interview of the day. I glanced at his resume and noticed that he wrote that he could do perfect imitations of both Elvises–Costello and Presley. I asked him, 'Is this true?' He said it was, and I said, 'Show me.' God bless him, he got up and did, in fact, do perfect imitations of both Elvises.

That was the whole interview. I offered him a call-back on the spot. And PS: He was the only one that day who got one."

I. THANK YOUR LUCKY STARS FOR THE JOB SEARCH PROBLEMS YOU HAVE

As we've discussed throughout this chapter, there are job search issues you face when you go to an elite law school. They're perhaps not issues any other law student would appreciate; as one counselor points out, "I get the evil eye when I talk about the hardships of students here." You can't expect students from any other law school to appreciate how difficult it can be to choose from among prestigious employers, for instance.

In spite of those job search issues, don't ever forget that in your degree, you've got an asset to treasure the rest of your life. Whether you worked really hard to get in or you were lucky enough to be born in the deep end of the intelligence gene pool, you accomplished something that most of us didn't. Any job search issues you have are temporary; your degree is forever. As one counselor puts it, "At the end of the day, always recognize that you're in a very, very fortunate position."

Chapter 17
I Want to Be Not Here: Advice for Out–of–Town Job Searches

I hear this lament everywhere. Some schools are in small towns; you just have to move elsewhere to find work. But the desire to move isn't limited to small towns. Even in *Hawaii,* there are a fair number of students who want to leave and work on the mainland.

If you're interested in working somewhere other than the city where you go to law school, you're looking at a very do-able task. Let's talk about it.

A. WHAT'S THE ISSUE?

In a word: credibility. To put words to employers' fears: "If you're not from here and you didn't go to school here, how do we know you'll take an offer if we make you one...and if you take it, how do we know you'll stay?" They figure you're doing a mail merge with every law firm in the country, starting your letter with, "I'm seeking employment in Los Angeles/New York/Chicago/Miami..." and just plugging in the employer's city, with no real intention of settling there.

It's unlikely that employers you approach will have a prejudice against your school. As one employer described it to me, "We don't have anything against students from law schools in other states. We don't know anything about the schools at all. We don't have any basis for judging them."

B. MAKING YOURSELF "AWAY-FRIENDLY"

1. GO TO CAREER SERVICES AND DIG UP ALUMS WHO PRACTICE LAW IN THE CITY WHERE YOU WANT TO BE...AND DON'T STOP THERE IN FINDING LOCAL PEOPLE TO CONTACT

Your first line of attack is people who've trudged the path before you. You want contact information for alums in your target city. If it's a big city like New York and your school has a ton of alums there, ask your Career Services personnel for the names of alums who are likely to be the most helpful.

You'll want to pursue two avenues with these alums. First, contact them—e-mail is fine, a phone message off-hours works as well—telling them who you are, that you're looking to move to X city, you know they must have faced the same issues as you with an out-of-town job search, and tell them you'll be calling for advice (if there are specific activities and/or organizations you want to know about, ask about them).

If your law school has no alums in the city you're targeting, consider contacting your college's alumni relations director to find out if you have undergrad colleagues there. If they aren't lawyers they might not be able to offer much advice about the legal community, but they might be able to direct you to friends locally who can.

Remember that your professors might provide useful out-of-town contacts as well. Check profiles of your law school professors on your law school's website to see what they've done before, where they're from, where they went to school...and you can also ask at Career Services to see if they know any professors who've got ties to the city you're targeting.

Also, remember that people you know where you are now might know people in the city you're targeting. Ask your friends if they know anyone there whom you might contact.

In Chapter 10 on "The Birds and Bees of Great Jobs..." I told you the story about the Miami student who was targeting Seattle, and by telling everyone he knew in Miami what he wanted to do, he generated a list of *two hundred* people to contact in Seattle. *Two hundred!* So ask around. You don't know who you'll find!

2.   TARGET EMPLOYERS WHO'VE HIRED LAW STUDENTS FROM A LAW SCHOOL *LIKE* YOURS...EVEN IF THEY'VE NEVER HIRED ANYBODY FROM YOUR OWN SCHOOL

Law students often lament the fact that employers in other cities seem totally ignorant about their school. One great strategy is to argue by analogy. That is, look at schools in or near the city that are similar to yours; regional schools with perhaps similar programs and local reputations. Tell them, "I know you hire from X local school. If you like them, you'll like me, because my school is just like it." In doing so you'll convert an *unknown* quantity into a *known* quantity. As one career counselor points out, "Avoid talking about your school in a vacuum. Identify schools you know the employer can relate to, and talk about how your school is similar...and they'll be similarly pleased with you."

* * * SMART HUMAN TRICK * * *

Law student from a Midwestern law school, wants to work at a large law firm in Los Angeles. He researches the firm and finds that they've never hired anyone from his school. The student reports: "When I started interviewing out here nobody had ever heard of my school. So I targeted a specialty–education law–and this firm has it. I looked at everyone in the education department here, and found that they hired a lot of people from Loyola. I said to myself, well, my school is like a Midwestern Loyola. Loyola has an evening program, a good presence regionally, a lot of district attorneys and elected officials, the best grads at the best firms, just like *my* school. So when I interviewed and talked about my school, I said, "I realize my school may be unfamiliar to you, but I know you went to Loyola and you hire a lot of Loyola people. Let me assure you if you like Loyola, you'll like my school. There's a great commonality between Loyola here in L.A. and the kind of school we have in the Midwest at my school."

"I got the job."

3.   Save up Money for a Trip to Your Target City and Plan One Over a Break . . . or Make a Break of Your Own

Nothing convinces people that you're serious about moving to a city more than making your way there at your own expense. As Georgetown's Marilyn Tucker points out, "You're not likely to get a job in another city until you go there and pound the pavement!" North Carolina's Brian Lewis adds, "If they like what they see on your resume and know you'll be in town, their reaction might be, 'Let's see this person. What do we have to lose?' " It may be a lot more comfortable to stay at school and try to do everything via the internet, but it's not *nearly* as effective.

Whether it's a week's break from school, or you take a couple of days off school for the purpose, there's little you can do for an out-of-town job search that's more effective than actually going to your target city.

Before you go, do a few things:

- Tell the alums/attorneys you identified in Step 1, above, when you'll be there, and ask if you can take them out for a cup of coffee, at their convenience, and get fifteen minutes' worth of their advice. Look to the section on "Informational Interviewing" in Chapter 10, for questions to ask if you're stumped. And drink decaf; you're going to be drinking a lot of coffee.

- Contact the local bar association (or check out their web site) and ask what events, if any, are taking place while you're in town. If there's anything relevant to you—a general meeting, a young lawyers' division meeting, meetings in the specialty/ies you want to enter, ask to attend and/or volunteer.

- Check the local bar association's web site for any CLEs taking place while you're there that are relevant to your goals. If so, ask to attend. (See more about CLEs in Chapter 10.)

- If there are employers you've targeted without an intermediary contact, Oregon's Jane Steckbeck advises that you send them a letter saying "I will be in X city from Y date to Z date, and would be pleased to interview with you during my visit. I will call in the next week or so to see if we can schedule an interview at your convenience." This is a bit softer than saying "I will call in the next week to set up an interview," but some recruiters bristle at the bolder language–and you don't want them to do that! The very fact that you're there under your own steam puts you way ahead of the curve, because it speaks to your honest interest in the location.

4. See if Your Career Services Office Conducts Any "Away Interview" Programs for the City/Cities You're Targeting

It may well be that the city you're targeting has attracted so many students from your school—or employers from there are so interested in them!—that your CSO runs interview trips to the city or conducts regional interview programs. If so, it's a cost-effective way to visit employers (and it's a lot more fun to travel with other people). Check with your CSO for availability.

5. Get "Reciprocity" Through Your Career Services Office With a Law School in or Near Your Target City, and Check Local Classifieds

"Reciprocity" works this way: You ask your Career Services Office to request reciprocity from X Law School. Your CSO contacts that school's CSO and makes the request on your behalf. Assuming they agree—and schools usually do, although it's not by any means universal—you have access to certain of that school's Career Services facilities. What's offered, again, varies from school to school. Some of them will allow you to use the materials in their offices, some will give you access to on-line job postings, it's really all over the map. Of course, it doesn't hurt to be nice and polite when you contact them, because it's human nature to be more helpful to people who are nice.

6. Keep up With Local News by Scanning Local Newspapers On-line

This will help you in a couple of ways. For a start, you might see news of a firm opening a branch in your target city, or a law firm merger, or other news that suggests there might be job openings to pursue.

But on top of that, you want to be able to talk comfortably with lawyers from there about the city. If you can drop into a job or informational interview something like, "How have people been responding to the scandal in City Hall?" you'll create the indelible impression that you must be serious about moving there, because you wouldn't keep up with local news if you weren't!

7. Check Out the Local Bar Association's Website for Listservs and Message Boards

A great way to keep up with what's going on in the legal community is to see what lawyers say on the local bar association web site. It's a great way of making contact with attorneys from your target city without ever leaving home.

* * * SMART HUMAN TRICK * * *

Law student in St. Louis, wants to work in a city in Virginia. She gets onto the Virginia City's lawyers' listserv. One of the lawyers has an open question about online research. The student offers her advice about research alternatives, and mentions her law school. A Virginia lawyer who reads her response asks her to come in for an interview when she's in town.

8. CONSIDER DOING A VISITING SEMESTER IN (OR NEAR) THE CITY WHERE YOU WANT TO BE

If you're still fairly new to law school, this is a possibility to consider. As Tammy Willcox points out, "Doing a visiting semester at a school shows your commitment to the city." And she goes on to point out that it gives you other benefits, as well:

- It's easier to do a visiting semester than it is to transfer; your grades don't have to be nearly as good.

- You'll get another Career Services office on your side, and all of the opportunities that go along with that.

But the main benefit is certainly that it shows you really are interested in working in that particular city.

9. SPEND YOUR LAW SCHOOL SUMMERS WORKING IN YOUR TARGET CITY, IF AT ALL POSSIBLE

Again: it's a credibility issue. You're going to have a hard time convincing employers in Washington, D.C. that you want to work there if you're a 3L in Chicago and you've spent both summers in St. Louis. As Stetson's Cathy Fitch points out, "It's so much easier to leave town if you start strategizing as a First Year."

Here are a couple of thoughts about this:

- If a paying gig doesn't come your way in your target city, consider volunteering for a legal employer part-time, and doing something else for dough. As we discussed in Chapter 10, being willing to volunteer opens up a lot of exciting doors for you. Nobody cares what you do for money—as long as it's not illegal—if you're getting legal experience, too.

- If the summer thing just doesn't work for you, consider volunteering for the city's bar association, for a section that interests you, from school. You can research an issue from anywhere, and it gets you local contact on your resume. You can also take CLEs on-line from anywhere. In #14, below, we talk about resume issues for out-of-town job searches, and you'll want to do all of those things. Remember: it's a credibility issue. If you didn't spend summers in your target city, you have to make up for it somehow.

10. Consider Doing a Post-Graduate Judicial Clerkship as a Means of Breaking Into a Legal Community

Judicial clerkships are awesome in so many respects, *including* the fact that they are a great way to get your feet wet in another city. They give you an opportunity to get to know who the players are in the legal community, so that when you are ready to go into practice, you know who to approach...and who to avoid.

We talk in detail about judicial clerkships in Chapter 25.

11. Remember That Geography Isn't Important for Some Jobs

Geography is *usually* really important to employers. But not always. For instance, if you want to work in certain narrow specialties, there are going to be areas of the country that are no-brainers. If you wanted to do Internet Law, nobody would question your desire to be in Silicon Valley. If you wanted to do private International Law, again nobody would question your goal of relocating to the East or West Coast (although there's international work everywhere, it's certainly concentrated on the coasts). If you wanted Entertainment, L.A. and New York make the most sense.

The same rule applies for certain government jobs. For employers like U.S. Attorneys' offices and certain other federal agencies, as Albany's Sandy Mans points out, you're better off getting your feet wet in a rural area (where the job competition isn't so fierce), and then using that as leverage to get to the city where you want to be. Before you make a move like this, however, check with your Career Services Office to see if the specific type of job you want fits this description. There's no point doing a tour of duty in the boonies when it's your dream to be in Chicago, if it's not going to benefit your career!

12. For Hyper-Desirable Cities, Try for Neighboring Towns and Suburbs

It sometimes makes sense to broaden your geographic targets. For instance, let's say you want to be in San Francisco. Who wouldn't? Because it's so desirable, I've talked to students who took jobs "over the bridges" in Oakland and Marin County. They could live in San Francisco, party in San Francisco, make contacts for their *next* job in San Francisco...it's just that their first business card didn't say "San Francisco."

The competition for jobs just *outside* of desirable cities is a *lot* lower. It's a very smart way to get where you want to be.

13. Cover Letter Issues

Of course, follow the advice in Chapter 7 about correspondence. But on top of that, to address the out-of-town job search issue, Brian Lewis recommends that you "Be definite, not tentative, when stating your interest in the employer's city. Try starting your cover letter, 'Upon my graduation from law school in May, I will be relocating to New York.'

(Or better yet, if it's true, '...returning to New York.') Not 'I'm thinking about moving to...' or 'I'm exploring opportunities in...'"

14. RESUME ISSUES

- **Join the appropriate state's bar association and consider volunteering, even from a distance.**

    If you haven't done so already, join your target city's state bar association *today*. It costs so little while you're in law school, and it's an important credibility issue.

    Joining the bar association gets you on mailing lists. Scan the publications you get to keep up with local legal news and spot potential employers and job opportunities.

    Also, consider volunteering for the city bar; contact the head of the section for a specialty that interests you, and offer to research an issue. Again, this gives you valuable resume fodder (as well as excellent contacts!).

- **Get a cell phone number with the area code of the city where you want to be, and list that number on your resume.**

    Law students who've done this say it works really well. You can get a cell phone with any area code; if you list a "local" phone number on your resume, it's just another indication that you're serious about living in that city.

- **Consider an "other information" section to describe your connection to the city.**

    If it's not obvious why you want to be in a particular city, consider putting a section called "Other Information" at the bottom of your resume, explaining your connection. "Intending to join family members in Iowa City after graduation," for instance.

    While this is the kind of information you'd expect to mention in a cover letter—and should—it's often the case that your resume and cover letter will be separated once they get to an employer. You don't want your resume to get into the hands of a decision maker who looks at it and says, "Why the heck does this student want to live *here?*"

- **If you're looking at a few cities, only mention geography-related information relevant to the target employer.**

    If you're still undecided about where you want to live and you're thinking of New York, Chicago and L.A., for gosh sakes don't put on every resume, "Member of New York, Illinois and California bar associations, law student division." Don't list three different cell phone numbers, with area codes 312, 212, and 213. As we discussed in the Resume chapter, your resume is not a confessional. You want to mention things on a resume for a particular employer only the things that make you more attractive to that employer. So mention activities related to their city/state, and not others!

If you're specifically asked where else you're looking, of course you can't lie. Be honest, but immediately follow up with *what interests you particularly about the city where this particular employer is.* "I'm considering New York and Los Angeles as well, Mr. Chicago, but what interests me particularly about being in Chicago is that my family lived here for two years while I was in high school, and I really liked..."

15. INTERVIEW ISSUES

The big question you have to prepare for is, "If you wanted to work *here,* why did you go to law school *there?*" A corollary is, "Why do you want to work here?"

As I stated at the beginning of this chapter, the issue behind both of these questions is credibility: are you sincere about your desire to be in City A if you went to law school in City B? Here's how you handle it:

- If you went to a school much more highly esteemed than a local law school, say something positive about your school without dissing the local school, something like, "I thought Haryaleford was a great opportunity. But what I like about the idea of living and working here is..."

- If your desire to be in City A is a decision of fairly recent vintage, say so. You can say you didn't know where you wanted to settle when you started law school, but you were drawn to the idea of living in City A because...and give your reason.

   I talked to a student at a law school in Massachusetts who had grown up in Boston, gone to law school in Texas for a year "to do something different," got homesick and came back to Massachusetts. Now she was back, she realized all the things she liked about Texas, and wanted to go back *there!* A strange path perhaps, but she *had* lived in Texas and her explanation was genuine.

- About that reason for settling in City A: It has to be something concrete and credible.

  - If you have family members there, use them; say that you're joining family who live in the city.

  - If you are a "trailing spouse"—that is, you have a spouse or fiancé(e) who has taken a job there—that works, too, although you'd then have to explain that your significant other isn't going to be transferred elsewhere any time soon.

  - If you spent some or all of your childhood there, that's a good reason to want to go back.

  - If there are other things about the city you like, if you say you visited friends or vacationed there and just knew it was where you wanted to settle down, you can use that, too, but then you have to research the legal community and the city in general, keep up with local news, and be able to talk credibly about where you'd like to live, the neighborhoods you're considering. *Do not* ever tell an employer "Dude, I spent Spring Break here, and it *rocks!*" As the hiring partner at a large firm in one desirable coastal city commented dryly, "We know how nice the beaches here are, thank you."

- If you are interested in a practice area that is particularly vibrant in your target area *and the employer you're talking to has that specialty,* say so. Being willing to move to pursue a particular dream is great.

- If you're looking at small employers in small towns, you don't have to explain that you've always wanted to work in East Cornstalk; employers there probably won't believe you. But saying you feel comfortable with small town life because...and then providing a credible reason will do the trick.

* * * CAREER LIMITING MOVE * * *

Law student in Colorado, interviewing with a Washington, DC law firm.

Interviewer: "Why do you want to be in DC?"

Law student: "It's an exciting city."

Interviewer: "We agree, but that doesn't say why *you* want to be here."

16. TALK WITH A LOCAL REALTOR ABOUT SPECIFIC NEIGHBORHOODS WHERE YOU'D LIVE

Here's a headline for you: realtors are *always* willing to talk to you, if you say "I'm thinking of living in...." They'll clue you into the neighborhoods that would suit your circumstances. This will benefit you in a few ways. Whether you're talking about casual talks with alums, bar association functions, informational interviews or job interviews, being able to drop comments like, "I'm looking at living in Booger Town. What do you think of it?" will make you sound serious about living there.

17. READ CHAMBER OF COMMERCE AND REALTOR WEBSITES TO GET FAMILIAR WITH THE AREA

Yet another way of crushing the "credibility" question. Chambers of Commerce will tell you more about a city than people who live there probably know. Realtor websites will often show off the best elements of a city, as a means of luring you to live there. Those all give you items to wheel out when potential employers ask you why you want to live there.

C. Don't Ever, Ever Lie About Your Connection With a City

Students ask me sometimes, "Gee—wouldn't it just be easier to say I've got family there?" A student at one school told me that a *lawyer at a large law firm* had actually encouraged him to lie about it, telling him he wouldn't be "believable" otherwise.

As is true in every aspect of your job search, don't ever, ever lie to employers. You'll get busted, and your reputation can't recover. If they can't trust you, they won't hire you. If you do the things I've advised you to do in this chapter, you'll overcome the credibility issue no matter *where* you want to practice. Lying your way into a job just isn't the way to go. And even if you did lie and get away with it in the short term, what are you going to do once you have the job? *Hire people* to pose as relatives? Pretend they're in the witness protection program? It's a lie you can't maintain, so it's not worth offering it in the first place.

* * * CAREER LIMITING MOVE * * *

Law student in the Midwest, applies to law firms in several cities in Texas. He tells each one, "My wife just accepted a position in..." and plugs in the name of each city.

Unbeknownst to him, several of the firms he contacts are actually branch offices of the same firm; they just go by different names. One of the branches brings him in for an interview, and subsequently, when recruiting coordinators at the different offices are comparing notes, his name comes up. "He told us his wife is moving here," said one of them. "What!" said another. "He told us the *same thing!*"

It turns out they had all received the letter from this particular student. When one of them confronted him with his lie, he responded, "We intend to move to Texas, and my wife is a nurse so she could work anywhere, so I figured it's not *really* a lie."

The firm disagreed. No offer.

Chapter 18
Small Law Firms

Related issues:

    Resumes: Chapter 8

    Correspondence: Chapter 7

    Interviews: Chapter 9

    The Birds and Bees of Great Jobs: Chapter 10

Other resources: Read Donna Gerson's excellent book, "Choosing Small, Choosing Smart."

It's entirely likely that small law firms have flown below your career radar in law school. It's the large law firms and government entities that get most of the attention, because they interview on campus, and in the case of large law firms ... they're the ones who pay the mad cheese.

But the fact is, you're likely to be much happier in a small law firm than a big one. Professor Grayson at the University of Washington conducted a survey that showed that the happiest lawyers are at firms with 1–4 lawyers. Most lawyers will tell you that small firm life is the best, and even my paltry experience bears that out. Between my 1L summer work at a five-person firm and my 2L summer clerkship at a major firm, the small firm was better in every way (except pay!).

Happiness issues aside, a small firm is most likely where you'll wind up. More than 75% of attorneys in private practice go to firms with fewer than fifty lawyers (compared to the 12% who go to firms with a hundred lawyers or more). So it's a happy coincidence that the small firm atmosphere happens to be one that most people enjoy!

In this chapter, here's what we'll be covering:

- First, we'll talk about the "nature of the beast"; what kinds of small firms there are, what it's like to work at a small firm, and how they hire;

- We'll talk about 101 ways to find job openings at small firms;

- We'll move on to talking about nailing small firm jobs, from pimping your resume to interviews and getting around the "one to three years' experience" requirement;

- We'll wind up by discussing how you negotiate an employment package with a small employer, including how you bargain for more dough!

Now you'll notice that some of the techniques we discuss will arise in multiple settings. Taking CLEs (Continuing Legal Education seminars), for instance—they're a great way to find small firms, nail opportunities that haven't hardened into job postings, and pimp your resume. But hey—if one activity can help you in so many ways, it deserves more than one mention!

Before we get started, it's important to remember to be organized in your search. You're going to be researching, contacting, and following up with lots of people. **Keep detailed notes on everything you do—copies of letters and e-mails, notes on phone calls, contact information on everyone. You need to have a calendar for follow-ups and for interviews.** And keep those notes—you never know when you'll want to contact people again in the future!

A. THE NATURE OF THE BEAST

1. HOW BIG IS A SMALL FIRM, ANYWAY?

It's a fluid concept. As a rule of thumb, a small firm in a large city has up to 50 attorneys; in a mid-sized city, up to 25 attorneys; in a small town, up to 5. However, these are rough estimates. Compared to some mega-firms, with 1,000+ attorneys, almost every law firm is "small"!

2. THE DIFFERENT TYPES OF SMALL FIRMS

If you think of a guy in a glass cube in the middle of K–Mart when you think of a small law firm, you're in for a pleasant surprise! There are four basic kinds of small law firms:

a) **"Boutiques." Boutiques are small firms that focus on a particular specialty (or two).** They tend to do very sophisticated, cutting-edge work in their specialty, they tend to have a national practice, and they are often spin-offs from large firms. Most entertainment practices, for instance, are boutiques; it's much rarer for big entertainment practices to be part of a large firm. Other common boutique focuses include intellectual property, family law, estate planning, and criminal defense.

b) **Small firms in large cities.** These firms may be spin-offs from larger firms, and like boutiques, may have a national practice. They generally have between 2–50 attorneys. Because of their location, they are plugged into the way large firms hire and tend to hire more formally than small firms in smaller cities and rural areas. So they may use headhunters, and they may advertise openings in the classified section of legal newspapers (and their accompanying web sites).

c) **Small firms in smaller cities.** These will tend to be general practice firms, handling the gamut of problems from real estate to family law to the issues small businesses face. They generally have 2–25 attorneys. The practice will tend to be regional.

d) **Small firms in rural areas.** Like small firms in smaller cities, you'll find a general practice in these firms, but they will tend to be even broader. They generally have 2–5 attorneys. They'll do local government work, criminal work, real estate, family law, wills and trusts and everything else that "walks in the door."

3. THE DIFFERENCE SIZE MAKES: WHAT IT'S LIKE TO WORK AT A SMALL FIRM

When it comes to work environment, size matters! Your working life will be considerably different than it would be in a large organization. Among the differences:

a) **Autonomy**: You'll have a lot more in a small shop, simply because small firms don't have the personnel to fill several layers of management. That gives you more control over what you do. You might be able to take a case from start to finish; at a large firm, you're lucky to even see the inside of a courtroom when you're a junior attorney.

While some people feel more comfortable in the cocoon-like environment of a larger organization, many people like the idea of having more direct control over what they do and having more opportunities for entrepreneurship. That's a tremendous plus for small firms.

b) **Hands-on experience and client contact**: You'll get hands-on experience quickly. Again, without a cadre of lawyers ahead of you on the food chain, you'll find yourself thrown into responsible situations—taking depositions, handling cases, dealing directly with clients—*much* sooner in a small firm; in fact, in most cases, immediately. While that can be terrifying, it's exhilarating, too, and it makes you feel like a "real lawyer." Contrast this with large law firms, where clients are often names on a sheet of paper early on.

Immediate client contact makes it vital that you appreciate the emotional content of the work before you apply for jobs. Depending on the nature of the practice, you may be helping people with very emotional issues. Tax and real estate aren't particularly fraught with emotions, but with specialties like family law, criminal defense work, bankruptcy ... you'll be counseling people at critical junctures in their lives. Many junior lawyers I talk to find that very rewarding; I talked to one junior criminal defense lawyer who said, "It's very altruistic. These people have the worst odds. They need help. They need someone to speak for them."

So when you talk to people to research the practices you're considering, be sure to learn about the counseling aspect of the work.

c) **Training**: The amount and quality of training you'll get is likely to depend on how the small firm was created. If it was a spin-off from a large firm, it's likely that the partners will offer the kind of training they themselves got—that is, they'll put a priority on training. If *not*—that is, if the firm sprang full-formed from the imagination of one or a few of the partners—training is a wild card. You're more likely to "learn by doing" with in-house mentors to help you. As the partner at one small firm put it, "The reason large firms have training programs is that their new associates don't get a chance to *do* anything otherwise. They'd never get a chance to argue a motion if they didn't do it by 'pretend'!"

d) **Rainmaking**: You'll probably be expected to bring in business fairly quickly, because typically with small firms, you "eat what you kill." Generally, mommy and daddy birds are going to stop stuffing worms in your beak more quickly than they would at a large firm. If you're the kind of person who was actively involved in extracurriculars at law school, if you're gregarious, if you're a "joiner," and/or if you have strong ties to the community, rainmaking might *sound* intimidating, but trust me: it'll be a lot easier for you than it seems! Clients are often generated by taking part in community activities and getting to know people that way, not doing a "hard sell" on them. But if you're by nature very reserved and shudder at the thought of community involvement, a small firm that expects you to "get out there" might not be your ideal environment. (We talk a lot more about Rainmaking in Topic D, below.)

e) **Money**: If you start at a small firm you're likely to rake in fewer dead presidents at the start than you would at Huge, Huge and Large. That can be an issue if you've got substantial student loan debt. However, as we discuss in the chapter on public interest jobs, Chapter 26, you can always renegotiate student loan payments to take the job you really want.

Nonetheless, money is one of the issues that draws some students away from small firms. The reason large law firms are such prize catches in law school is not because most law students envy the life style; my hunch would be that most students don't have any idea what the life style *is!* (I sure didn't in law school.) Instead, it's the buckets of doubloons that are heaped on new associates that make large firms so attractive.

In the chapter on large law firms (Chapter 23) I talk about why this is risky decision-making. But here, I want to point out something interesting to you: while you'll start out making somewhat less money, *it won't stay that way*. Statistics from the National Association of Law Placement show that within five years of graduation, the pay of associates at small and large law firms are only ten percent apart. (That's because associates at large law firms experience what's called "compression"—that is, their salaries rise very slowly.)

The fact is, some of the highest-paid lawyers in America are at small law firms, not large ones. As Keith Faulkner points out, "Some small firms will offer you thirty or forty thousand plus 25% of what you bring in. You can make *big* money."

As we discuss throughout this chapter, rainmaking isn't as scary as it sounds. And once you demonstrate an ability to generate business, you'll always be happily employed. Later on in this chapter I talk about negotiating for more dough, to help ameliorate the sting of lower starting pay. But there's no getting around it: coming out of the starting gate, associates at large firms tend to make a lot more money than associates at small firms.

f) Specializing: Unless you go to a boutique, you'll generally start out as more of a "generalist" at a small firm. The reason for this is that most small firms have general practices, and with relatively few lawyers, each lawyer has to wear more than one hat. That's great if you like the idea of variety, and you don't want to be pigeonholed.

You'll undoubtedly develop more of an expertise in some things than others—as one small firm lawyer commented, "Even at a tiny firm, you wind up specializing at least a bit, because *some* lawyer in town is known as the best this or the best that"—but you're expected to be flexible at the beginning. Don't let this intimidate you. As the associate at one small firm points out, "I'm routinely called on to handle cases involving a dozen or so different specialties. It sounds like a lot, but it's really not. The firm wouldn't like me to admit this, but truth be told, most law is pretty easy to figure out."

g) Specialties available: There are specialties that are the virtually exclusive purview of small firms. Family law, for instance, just isn't a specialty you'll find at a large firm. Entertainment law is rarely found at large firms.

On the other hand, mergers and acquisitions, antitrust and complex torts are found at large firms and almost nowhere else (except boutiques). Large bankruptcies go to large firms; personal bankruptcy, small firms.

So the specialty that attracts you most may determine the size of the employers you approach.

h) Ability to "build out" a specialty for the firm: What if you go to a firm and you want to practice in a specialty—like entertainment, family law, whatever—that the firm doesn't have? At a small firm, you may well have the chance to develop it yourself. At a large firm, by contrast, you'd have virtually no ability as a junior lawyer to impact the expansion of the practice. I've talked with students who went to small firms, and after they'd proven themselves for a little while, successfully convinced the firm to let them start exploring the specialty themselves, developing a clientele. How exciting is *that?*

One student clerked during school for a lawyer with an entertainment practice. The lawyer mostly represented computer game people, and a model or two. The student specifically wanted to represent models, and went to the lawyer with the idea that she stay with the practice but focus on expanding the model representation practice. The lawyer agreed, and she stayed with him full-time after graduation.

i) **"Non-legal work" distractions**: "Non-legal" work—not "illegal" work!—differs in small and large firms.

At a small firm, you'll do more hands-on administrative tasks than you would at a large law firm. When you're at a large firm, you're supported by a battalion of word processors, librarians, supply room clerks, runners, mail room clerks, copy people, you name it. Obviously a small firm isn't going to foot the bill for that kind of support, so you'll spend more time doing things like handling your own paperwork and figuring out how to get papers served. That's not necessarily a negative, but when you're trying to solve a legal problem, it can be a distraction.

On the other hand, small firms don't have a hoard of non-billable distractions that large firms do. Large organizations are rife with committees and report requirements—"bureaucratic b.s.," as one large firm associate put it—that pose a huge drag on your time. Small firms don't have those kinds of distractions—communication is simpler and more direct.

j) **Small pond, big fish**: Every attorney in the firm has a significant impact on your environment. That can be good (if you like everybody) and bad (if you don't). At a large firm, you can much more easily avoid difficult personalities than you can in a small shop.

k) **Hours**: While it's hard to generalize, as a rule of thumb, hours are more livable at small firms than large ones. Lawyers often cite "quality of life" issues for joining small firms.

A major caveat when it comes to hours is that depending on the specialty you practice and the individual project you're working on, you might work long hours. If you're a litigator and you're in a trial, you'll work long hours. And certain specialties demand more time at work on a routine basis. For instance, a former associate at a small firm commented, "We did complex litigation, and we worked around the clock. There were only eight of us there, but it was too much stress and the hours were too long."

Check back to the Interviewing chapter, Chapter 9, and the section "Smoking out the hours you'll be expected to work" to figure out the hours any employer will expect you to put in.

k) Clientele: Boutiques may have a national focus, but otherwise, the clients of small firms are usually individuals and small companies, generally in same city or neighborhood as the firm. That's why they tend to prefer people with local connections.

l) Partnership track: At small firms, it's a lot shorter than for large firms; at some small firms, you're eligible for partnership within three or four years! That means you get a slice of the profits (and of course have a commensurate responsibility for bringing in business).

4.   HOW SMALL FIRMS DO THEIR HIRING

They hire any time and all the time, as the need arises. Comparatively few small firms hire on a routine basis, the way large law firms do. Small firms often call Career Services Offices with a plea for help *right now*. As one Career Services Director says, "I got a call just yesterday from a guy who said, 'I inherited my father's business, I need two people *right now!*"

Contrast this with large firms. Large law firms tend to hire the way salmon spawn—on a routine basis, through on-campus interview programs, where they make offers before Christmas for positions that will be there the following summer.

The on-campus-interview dog doesn't typically hunt for small firms. For one thing, on campus interviews require people and time. For a four-person shop, it doesn't make sense for 25% of the attorney firepower to travel around to law school campuses to goose that total up to five. When small firms interview on campus at all, they do so in the Spring rather than the Fall, and even then the small firms who take part tend only to be the small firms in larger cities, not the ones in smaller towns or rural areas. The good news about this is that it's never too late to start your small firm job hunt. Whether it's April, or second semester of Third Year, or after graduation—there's no bad time to get going.

Another reason OCI doesn't work for small firms is that small firms often hire "by the seat of the pants"—that is, when the need arises. As Mark Brickson of the University of North Dakota advises, "Some smaller firms advertise and basically interview all comers until they find the right person. Sometimes this can last for months. Other firms need somebody right now!" As this suggests, small firms aren't swayed by graduation and bar exam schedules, and that's a reality you've got to face if you're interested in the small firm market.

It's also important to recognize that hiring a new person is a significant decision for a small firm. They'll often require a bit of persuading (which I'll teach you to do in the section called "What Small Firms Look For In People They Hire"). As one small firm practitioner told me, "What students don't understand is that for a small firm, hiring a new associate is like a marriage. In fact, in some ways it's *more* than a marriage, because you spend more time with your colleagues than you do at home." Furthermore, "Taking on a new person is a big commitment in terms of making sure you have the work to keep them busy, and that you'll continue doing so into the future, and that you have the money to pay them. Small firms look very coldly at their expenses—rent, support staff, all kinds of overheads, and then determine if they can budget in a new person. It can be an agonizing decision."

B. 101 WAYS TO FIND JOB OPENINGS WITH SMALL LAW FIRMS

Not 101, really. I didn't actually count them. 101 is just such a nice number. But the fact is, there are *many* ways to skin the law firm cat. Job postings are the most obvious. I'll give you a bunch of resources to track down even the most elusive postings.

We'll also talk about how to use the more active routes to finding a great small firm to work for. The fact is, an actual job posting is only the very last stage of a four-stage process of job creation. If you get in on the first three stages, there won't ever be a job posting for the position you scooped ... you'll get it before anybody else even realizes it exists!

But I'm getting ahead of myself. Let's spend a little time talking about job postings, and all the resources you can muster to find the ones that other people might miss.

1. JOB POSTINGS: HOW TO FIND THEM, HOW TO RESPOND TO THEM

An obvious place to start looking for small firms is to find small firms who are looking for *you*— even if they don't realize it yet! Let's talk about how you find job postings, and then how you respond to them.

A. THE LOW-HANGING FRUIT ...

1. **Check your Career Service Office's job postings *on a daily basis.*** Small firm openings come up randomly; they're not confined to certain seasons. If you check the postings daily, you won't miss any.

2. **Check with your Career Services Office to see if your school has a small firm job fair or takes part in one with other law schools.**

   Sometimes small law firms aren't willing to visit individual schools, but they will come to regional fairs, where they can see students from many schools at once.

   If you do find a job fair, follow the advice in Chapter 10 on job fairs.

3.   **Scour local newspaper classifieds, which are virtually all listed on-line.**

4.   **If you're interested in small firms in a different geographic area than where you go to law school, get "reciprocity" with a law school where you want to practice.** They may have fresh listings on-line that aren't found in the job bulletins they publish. (To get reciprocity, you have to go to your own Career Services Director and have them send a letter on your behalf to the school whose listings you want to access. Not every school takes part in reciprocity, but a lot of them do.)

5.   **Check with the local bar association for the area where you want to practice to see if they list job openings; some bar associations do.**

6.   **Check with the bar association in the area where you want to practice to see if there are any local Spring job fairs.** Small firms sometimes make an appearance at these.

7.   **Check Craigslist on-line if the city you're targeting has it;** many employers post job openings on it.

B.   **Responding to Job Postings**

1.   **Respond to postings even if you don't have all of the qualifications they list.**

It's very easy to think "They're looking for experience I don't have yet ..." or "They want grades higher than mine ..." and then pass over the posting. It's a mistake to reject yourself before you even contact the employer! Here's why. When employers create job postings, they're listing the attributes of the ideal candidate. They may not expect to get all of those attributes, and even if they do ... the "dream candidate" may not apply!

Obviously, you want to do your very best to fit yourself into the qualifications. If your grades overall aren't up to snuff, highlight classes where you have done well, and expressly point out other situations where you *have* excelled (like clinical programs, other jobs, extracurriculars like moot court or journals).

In addition, follow the advice below in section C on pimping your resume for small firms.

2.   **If the posting doesn't list the name of the employer (i.e. it's a "blind ad")** ...

You want your cover letter and resume to mirror the qualifications requested in the ad. Use the buzz words from the listing, and make sure that your resume is organized so that the elements of most interest to the employer are listed first. You can't, of course, lie about what you've done, or just include lists of random words without any context (yes, students have tried it) ... but to the extent you can, offer descriptions of activities and jobs you *have* done fully enough to include the relevant words.

3.   If the job posting *does* list the name of the employer ...

You're far better off than you are in the "blind ad" situation. That's because you can research the employer *and* you can perhaps take other steps to enhance your chances.

When you know the employer, you can research them via any of the methods listed in Chapter 6 on Research; you can check them out on-line, you can ask at Career Services about them, you can check with anyone you know in the legal community for information about them.

Furthermore, you may be able to do more than just send in a resume and cover letter. *If the employer expressly states that application materials must be submitted in one particular way—e.g., on-line—then follow their instructions precisely*. If, however, they don't impose such limitations, **if you *possibly* can, drop your materials off in person.** Wear a suit, walk into the office with a confident smile on your face, and tell the person who greets you that you're there responding to the job posting, and you thought you'd drop off your resume and cover letter in person.

Why does this make a difference? Two reasons. I've mentioned to you before the "hierarchy of memorability"—you're least memorable on paper, next most memorable on the phone, and most memorable in person. You want to goose yourself up that pyramid whenever you can. Dropping off your materials in person vaults you to the top of it!

On top of that, it may well be that you'll get an interview on the spot. You wouldn't be the first law student to hear a receptionist say, "Well, while you're here, why don't I see if Attorney so-and-so can talk to you ..." This is why the "charm offensive" with the person who greets you is so important!

Whether the posting lists limitations on the way you apply or not, **you can make yourself more memorable by leaving a voice mail message late at night or early in the morning— that is, when nobody will be in the office—stating your name and that you just wanted to let them know to expect your materials, and that you're very interested in the position.** This voice mail technique works better than an e-mail (which people can easily ignore) and obviously signals your enthusiasm more effectively than just sending your letter and resume!

c.   Sneaky Ways of Finding Openings at Small Firms ... Including Scooping up The Ones That Haven't Ripened Into Job Postings Yet

I mentioned earlier in this chapter the fact that job postings are the culminating, fourth step of the job creation process. The first three steps are: People don't even know they're looking for someone, but they're curious what's "out there"; A general sense that adding at least one other person makes sense; There's a job available but it isn't advertised (at least, not yet). It's only *after* that that a job posting comes into being. If you can get to employers in the first three stages, you've obviously got the jump on any student who sits back and waits for a job posting!

There are many small employers that never, ever post job openings. *Ever*. The only way to get them is through talking with people and taking part in activities. As an attorney at one small firm pointed out, "Do students think we get business by sending out letters? We don't. We have to *talk* to people."

Now this requires more work than scanning job postings—sometimes a *lot* more work. But many of these methods do more than giving you the chance to scope out good employers; they let employers get to know you. Those are both tremendous benefits when it comes to actually nailing a job.

1. CALL SMALL FIRMS AND ASK STRAIGHT OUT IF THEY'RE HIRING

Well, gee. I thought I'd start with the most obvious strategy, first. Use any of the sources we discuss in Item 3, below, on "Targeted mailers," and call the firms directly. If you give great phone, this can work particularly well for you. (Of course, even if they're hiring, you'd want to turn around and research them before you apply for a job; we talk about that in detail under Item 3 when we talk about targeted mailers.)

2. THROUGH YOUR CAREER SERVICES OFFICE, FIND UPPER CLASS-MEN OR RECENT ALUMS WHO'VE WORKED FOR SMALL FIRMS IN THE GEOGRAPHIC AREA WHERE YOU WANT TO PRACTICE

There are two reasons for this.

First, they will know other lawyers in the community, and may have a good feel for who might need a new person. When you introduce yourself to them—by phone or e-mail or letter—what you're looking for is advice about small firms in town, and tell them that you'll be calling to follow up.

Second, when it comes to part-time and summer jobs at small firms, law students often don't realize that many of these jobs are "handed down" from student to student, and employers pay a lot of attention to the opinions of their student workers. The employer's attitude is, "We don't want to read resumes and interview people; find someone like you."

For "handed down" jobs, to follow up, ask the alum/upperclassman for the name of the person you should contact. Of course, before you contact that person, pick your contact's brain about the employer, the job, and what you ought to say to them! It may also be that if you impress the alum, they will walk your application to the person doing the hiring, and perhaps even put in a good word for you. I need scarcely stress to you how important this can be—so be suitably enthusiastic and grateful when you talk to that alum!

3. AS WE DISCUSSED IN CHAPTER 10, BROADCAST YOUR GOAL TO EVERYONE YOU KNOW: FRIENDS, FAMILY MEMBERS, AND SO ON

You don't know when the next person you talk to will have a great lead for you ... that you never would have discovered if you hadn't mentioned your goal!

* * * SMART HUMAN TRICK * * *

Student in Oregon, very focused on practicing land use in a small Oregon town we'll call Pinetrees. He volunteers on a community advisory group for the first two years of law school, dealing with planning for a wilderness area.

He mentions his goal to a classmate, who says, "Hey—I just read an article about a land use attorney in Pinetrees. You should read it."

The student reads the article and writes to the attorney, expressing an interest in his firm. It turns out that the attorney had been passively seeking an associate, but wanted to find someone very dedicated. He arranges to meet the student at an environmental law conference at the law school, and makes him on offer on the spot.

4. CHECK LOCAL BAR ASSOCIATION CHAT ROOMS FOR THE GEOGRAPHIC AREA YOU'RE TARGETING

Some bar associations have them, and when they do, attorneys will often casually mention that "We're looking for someone to do ..." There's your opportunity to jump in and offer your services.

5. VOLUNTEER AT YOUR CAREER SERVICES OFFICE TO DO A PHONE SURVEY OF SMALL FIRMS, TO CREATE A "JOB BANK"

When you do this, you aren't calling law firms to look for a job for yourself; you're checking to see if they anticipate having any openings for law students/new graduates in the foreseeable future.

How do you follow up? Send a note to the attorney with whom you spoke—a snail-mail note, not an e-mail—and attach your resume. In the note, say something like, "I was delighted to hear that you anticipate hiring a law student next summer, because I would like to be that student!" You'll have a chance to research the employer, and tailor your resume appropriately.

6. VOLUNTEER AT CAREER SERVICES TO HELP RUN A SMALL FIRM RECEPTION

There can be a table set-up, where attorneys sit, so students can bring their resumes and ask questions. It's not a job fair, so attorneys aren't under pressure to do any hiring.

You can help contact small firms to send representatives; that way, you're reaching out on behalf of the school ... but coincidentally getting to talk to lawyers who might be potential employers.

7. CHECK THE BUSINESS AND LEGAL SECTIONS OF THE LOCAL NEWSPAPER FOR THE GEOGRAPHIC AREA WHERE YOU WANT TO PRACTICE, AS WELL AS THE LEGAL TRADE PAPER FOR THE AREA (IF THERE IS ONE) AND LOCAL BAR ASSOCIATION PUBLICATIONS

You're looking for two things: "transitions"—that is, new firms opening, firms opening up a new branch in town, firms splitting up. Transitions often create job openings, even if they aren't listed as such.

You're also looking for articles about small law firms and/or profiles of practitioners at small firms. Following up on articles can produce great results.

8. INTRODUCE YOURSELF TO THE HEAD OF THE SMALL FIRM PRACTICE SECTION OF THE LOCAL BAR ASSOCIATION

Nobody is more plugged into "who's who" among small firms. If you give a brief background, say that you're planning on settling in the community and that you'd appreciate it if (s)he kept you in mind when talking with other firms in town—and offer your resume—you're off to a good start. At the same time, volunteer to help out with the bar association, whether on committees or projects or events or whatever. Being generous with your time will encourage other people to be generous with their advice!

9. GO TO COURTHOUSE, AND WATCH LAWYERS WORK

It's impressive because it takes initiative and proves your good judgment and enthusiasm. Introduce yourself to lawyers at the courthouse, and barring that, mention your courthouse visit in your cover letter. It will distinguish you from the mass of students who send a "blind" mass mailer!

10. TAKE ADVANTAGE OF "SHADOWING" PROGRAMS OFFERED BY LOCAL BAR ASSOCIATIONS

Many bar associations give students and new graduates a chance to see legal practice "close up" by following a lawyer around for a few hours or even an entire day. Request a practitioner with a small firm. Not only will this give you a chance to meet that particular lawyer, but you'll have a chance to get some insights into the practice, who else you ought to be talking to, what activities you should be taking part in ... in other words, don't overlook the informational interview aspects of the experience!

11. THROUGH CAREER SERVICES, FIND ALUMS FROM YOUR LAW SCHOOL WHO ARE JUDICIAL CLERKS IN THE AREA

Introduce yourself to them, by phone or in person, say that you're moving to town and you'd really appreciate their guidance on lawyers who seem both good—and busy. Lawyers who are busy probably need another set of hands, whether they realize it or not!

12. CONSULT YOUR LAW SCHOOL PROFESSORS

If you're staying near law school, or you have professors who are familiar with the community where you want to practice, they can be a great resource. Professors typically have "non-ivory-tower" lives before (and sometimes during!) their teaching experience, and can be an excellent resource—particularly if you've done well in their classes or are otherwise friendly with them.

On top of that, as Toledo's Heather Karns points out, "Small firms hit up professors and deans; they ask, 'Send me your best students.'" So if you make yourself known to your professors, you'll be at the front of their minds when they get these calls.

13. JOIN INNS OF COURT

You may not be familiar with Inns of Court—most students aren't—but it's a fantastic organization and can be a real boon to your career. What it is a nationwide organization of lawyers and judges (law students are welcome) who get together on a monthly basis, where they eat a meal and hear presentations typically on litigation-oriented topics like conflicts of interest, discovery rules, evidence changes. Some branches also focus on non-litigation topics like tax, family law, administrative law, and so on. But the point is, you get to learn some interesting things, as well as having a fantastic opportunity to meet litigators, judges, and legislators. It's a perfect chance to let people know what your goals are, and ask for advice about whom you should be talking to!

You can find Inns of Court on-line at www.innsofcourt.org.

14. ATTEND CLEs IN THE CITY WHERE YOU WANT TO PRACTICE

I realize that if I mention CLEs (Continuing Legal Education seminars) one more time in this book I'll have to pay royalties on the name, but really ... they're so good for your career in so many ways! If you attend a CLE about any aspect of small firm practice in the city where you want to be, you're going to be surrounded by lawyers who do what you want to do. Introduce yourself to other attendees during breaks, say that you're interested in joining the community, and ask their advice on what you ought to be doing. (In Chapter 10 we talk about CLEs in detail.)

15. VOLUNTEER FOR LAW-RELATED ACTIVITIES IN THE COMMUNITY, LIKE BAR ASSOCIATION FUNCTIONS OR CLE PROGRAMS (OR EVEN JUST ATTEND THOSE KINDS OF FUNCTIONS)

I discuss these in detail in Chapter 10.

16.   IF YOU'RE LOOKING FOR A SMALL FIRM IN (OR NEAR) YOUR LAW SCHOOL—AND THE CITY IS LARGE—CONSIDER TAKING PART IN A VOLUNTEER LAWYER PROGRAM

These programs involve pro bono work on matters like family law, landlord/tenant, immigration, and AIDS-related issues. Apart from doing a really nice thing for people who truly need help, these programs can be a real boon to your career. You'll get to meet and work with attorneys in the city, they'll get to meet you and see the quality of your work—and you'll have valuable contacts to rely on for ideas about firms to whom you should reach out.

17.   DO A TRIAL-LEVEL JUDICIAL CLERKSHIP IN THE GEOGRAPHIC AREA WHERE YOU WANT TO FIND SMALL FIRM WORK

Many, many experts recommended this idea to me. As both a means of ascertaining firms you'd like to work for *and* getting a "jump" on jobs that haven't firmed up as postings yet, it's an excellent strategy. Lawyers get a chance to see you, and start thinking to themselves, "Hmm, (s)he'd be good to have on board . . ."

You also get the ear of your judge, who (in most cases) will take a paternal/maternal interest in your well being and guide you toward good firms. On top of that, you get a great resume builder—everybody likes to see judicial clerkships. And if you're worried about grades, don't be. Especially for lower state courts, grades are not the factor they are for federal court clerkships. You still need good writing skills, but you can prove that in a variety of ways (non-law-review journal experience, moot court, researching for a prof, independent writing projects, articles for bar publications, etc.) other than law review.

18.   DO FREELANCE PROJECTS FOR A FEW MONTHS, BEFORE TYING YOURSELF DOWN TO A PARTICULAR EMPLOYER

Many small firms have projects they need done, but don't feel the need to hire a "whole person" right now. I've known a number of people who've done freelance brief writing for a living, and it gives you a great insight into what it's like to work with a variety of lawyers. When job openings with them do open up, you're first in line because they're already familiar with you and the quality of your work. (Among other ways of promoting yourself, you can advertise yourself in the classifieds or on local bar association web sites and in local bar publications, offering freelance services. You can also talk to people at the local bar association and ask for leads that way.)

19.   YOU CAN DO SOME LEGAL TEMPING

This isn't an option in every city, but in many it is, and again it's a good way to get hands-on experience at a number of different employers before you choose one. When a small firm needs a temp (or a freelancer or contract lawyer, for that matter), they often really need a new permanent associate—they just haven't realized it yet. Acting "as if" you were already an associate is a great way to convince them that they need the real thing!

20.   CONSIDER DOING WHAT'S CALLED "CONTRACT" WORK

Contract work is similar to temping and freelancing, but it's done for one employer and typically for one project. You'd liken being a contract lawyer to being an independent contractor or consultant. You don't work for the firm as an associate, but you work *with* them. You're paid on an hourly basis, and you're generally responsible for your own medical, disability and malpractice coverage (although your hourly rate will normally reflect that).

The good thing about contract work is that, first of all, it's easier to nail than a full-time permanent position, because it's less of a commitment for the employer; secondly, it gives you the benefit of seeing what an employer is really like without taking on a "permanent" position; and third, it has the potential to ripen into a permanent position, because the employer may decide they really need you there—and they know you contribute quality work.

Note that **contract work is rarely advertised. Employers hire by word of mouth or via unsolicited resumes.**

21.   HELP RUN A "SMALL FIRM MANAGEMENT" CLE FOR YOUR LAW SCHOOL ... OR PROPOSE IT TO YOUR CAREER SERVICES OFFICE

Pepperdine Law School was the first law school to run one of these, as far as I know. It's a tremendously clever idea, and here's how it works: The CLE is oriented toward issues facing lawyers at small firms: marketing and so forth. Student volunteers—like you—reach out to potential speakers, and market the CLE to potential attendees. At Pepperdine, the Career Services Director made one of the presentations, concerning—no surprise here!—incorporating law students into small firm practice. Students were encouraged to research the attendees, and were assigned to lunch tables with them. It was stressed to the students that this was a learning experience, not a forum for hitting up lawyers for jobs! But let's be realistic; when you have lunch with a practitioner, you've researched them, you have intelligent questions to ask ... you don't have to hand over a resume to get them thinking about you as a potential associate, or to think of advice for you about how you might become one for somebody else!

2.   RECOGNIZE THAT THE VERY BEST WAY TO GET A PERMANENT JOB AT A SMALL FIRM IS TO WORK THERE PART-TIME DURING LAW SCHOOL

As Ellen Wayne points out, "When it comes to small firms, it's easier to talk your way into a permanent job if you've worked there part-time.

That's because the difference between supporting someone at 20 hours a week and 40 hours a week—which is the difference between part-time and full-time—is a much easier decision for a small firm to make than it is to go from zero to full-time.''

3. TARGETED MAILERS, INCLUDING FINDING WHAT'S "OUT THERE"; LOCATING SMALL FIRMS ... AND SEPARATING THE GOOD FROM THE BAD

As we discussed in the Chapter 6 on Correspondence, targeted mailers can work. *Targeted* is the key; **plan on sending no more than 25 letters at a time. You can't adequately research more employers at one time than that.**

It's important to note that mailers of any kind to small law firms are not a "high return" activity, because their hiring is so sporadic. As one small firm lawyer commented, "There's no point in sending me a resume. What are the odds I'll have a job when you contact me?" However, you may luck out if you send letters to a number of employers. Of course, it shouldn't be your only approach. Responding to job postings and finding job openings through people should also be arrows in your job search quiver!

Let's talk about how you find small employers in the first place. Since they don't come on-campus to find *you,* you've got to be a bit more intrepid.

A. RESOURCES FOR FINDING SMALL FIRMS

Here are resources for finding small law firms all over the country:

1. **The yellow pages, under "Attorneys," either in hard copy or on-line at yellowpages.com or switchboard.com. Duh.** I thought I'd start with the most obvious source first.

2. **Contact the local bar association and ask for a directory of law firms in the geographic area where you want to practice.** www.palidan.com/statebar.htm lists all bar associations, from international to local. Other organizations you may want to contact include the National Employment Lawyers Association (NELA) and the National Lawyers Guild (NLG), which primarily consist of small firms. They have web sites, accept student members, and share membership lists.

   As John Marshall's Laurel Hajek points out, "Area bar directories and suburban bar association directories are great. They have all the information you need. Many small firm won't pay to be in Martindale Hubbell. For instance, a criminal defense lawyer in a rural area won't pay for MarHub but (s)he'll certainly pay for bar directory listings.''

3. Lexis/Nexis and Westlaw.

Both services have many ways to find and parse small employers.

In Lexis, you can search case files by employer name or attorney name to see cases they've handled. In addition, the legal news file will tell you if an employer or lawyer has been mentioned in publications like *American Lawyer* and *The National Law Journal*.

Westlaw has directories of individual attorneys and organizations, searchable by firm, size, location, practice area and law school attended. (You can also find virtually every practicing attorney in America in The West Legal Directory, at www.findlaw.com and on Westlaw at www.lawschool.westlaw.com.

4. **Consider bar associations based on gender, ethnicity and so forth.** Some even have membership directories which may be useful to you. Find them through www.abanet.org.

5. **Go to American Lawyer Media's homepage at** www.americanlawyermedia.com, publications and services link, scroll down to directories link for info on small firms.

6. **Check with your Career Services Office for useful directories, like those published by The Legal Directories Publishing Companies** (which puts out directories by state). Lawyers Diary and Manual in Newark, New Jersey, publishes annual directories for several states. California has the Parker Directory of California Attorneys. You get the idea; check with Career Services.

B. SEPARATING THE GOOD EMPLOYERS FROM THE NOT-SO-GOOD ONES ... RESEARCH!

When you have a large, undifferentiated mass of employers, you need to do some weeding out. After all, you want a job you'll enjoy ... not just *any* job! After all, if you're working in a three-person office where the other two people are bloody bollocky pig-dogs (in the words of Edwina of *Absolutely Fabulous)* you're going to be miserable. While you should certainly keep your eyes and ears open to sniff out a loser of a firm during the interview process, there *are* methods for doing a preliminary separation of the "wheat from the chaff" before you contact firms at all. They include:

1. **Talk with your Career Services Director and Counselors.** Because they're exceptionally well plugged-in, they'll often be able to give you scuttlebutt about all kinds of employers, and can often steer you toward the sterling employers— and help you avoid the stinkers.

2. **Look at Nexis on Lexis/Nexis to see if the firm has been in the news.**

   Check not just the firm name but the individual attorneys, as well.

3. **Through your Career Services Office or alumni relations director, find the names of alumni practicing law in the place where you want to live.**

   Contact those alums and solicit their advice about firms you ought to consider. Contact them by voice mail, not e-mail—and talk with them, don't carry on an e-mail correspondence unless they insist on it. When you are soliciting advice, people are much more forthcoming *talking* with you than *writing* to you.

   If possible, get together with them in person (invite them for a cup of coffee, and drink decaf, because you'll be drinking a *lot* of coffee!). The more they feel comfortable with you, the more open and helpful they are likely to be. If your law school doesn't have any alums where you want to live, go back to your undergrad career services/alumni relations person and see if anyone from your college went on to practice law in that location.

4. **While you're talking with your Career Services Office, see if there are any alums of your school who are judicial clerks in the place(s) where you want to practice.**

   Contact them and ask them about lawyers from the small firms in town; they'll know the quality of their work, and be able to steer you to quality employers.

5. **Talk to any local contacts you have**.

   Lawyers and judges are obviously best, but anyone you know in a community will have a lawyer of their own, and that lawyer is a good place to start. The key here is that you need people who'll be straight with you, and not just tell you good things about *everybody*. You want to know who does good work, and who's ethical and honorable. One young lawyer told me about his experience looking for work with a small firm. He talked with local lawyers for their suggestions, and when he mentioned one lawyer whom he'd heard was nice, the feedback he got was "He's a very nice guy, but he does terrible work." Useful information, that.

6. **Check with your Career Services Office to see if they have clerkship evaluation binders.**

   Most do, where prior clerks offer their insights into employers. You can also contact these former clerks for more "inside skinny." They may well tell you things directly that they wouldn't put in writing. They may also be familiar with other employers in the same community.

7. **Headhunters.**

   Although headhunters aren't a fertile source of jobs for you if you're still in school or newly graduated—they kick in once you've been out a year or two or three—they *will* be useful as a source of information. They can give you both general and specific information about the legal market in a given city, and/or practice area, and—if you're nice to them—some of what they've heard on the down-low about individual firms.

To get this information, be sure to express your gratefulness—"I know you only work with lawyers with experience, but I'd be so grateful for your expertise. I *will* have experience sooner rather than later, and I hope we can work together then . . ." and so on.

8. You don't have to rely on what other people think about potential employers. Go to the local courthouse and watch lawyers at work!

Lawyers who go to court don't work in secret, you know. There's nothing that stops you from going to the local courthouse to see them in their "natural habitat." By the way, doing this gives you a great line for your cover letters: "I took the opportunity to watch you argue X case in X court, and I was very impressed with your work. I'd enjoy the opportunity . . ."

If you are suitably "plucky," you can take advantage of breaks in the proceedings—or after the proceedings are over—to introduce yourself to lawyers, compliment them appropriately, and say that you'll be sending your materials.

9. Researching firms when all of your sources come up empty.

If you just can find anything about a firm other than its name, a little detective work with the phone can often get you useful information. Call them, and say "I'm looking for a law firm"—without giving your name—and ask the person who answers the phone about how many attorneys are there, the nature of the practice, how long they've been in business, and so on. They'll assume you might be a potential client. Don't mention your interest in a job!

c. TIMING YOUR TARGETED MAILERS

As a rule of thumb, if you're looking for a summer job with a small firm, consider contacting people over Christmas Break and throughout the Spring Semester. For small firms that routinely hire summer clerks, contact them over Christmas Break.

For permanent jobs, start mailing Spring Semester of your third year, although small firms may not hire until post-graduation or post-bar. But these are generalizations: As Creighton's Shannon Kelly points out, "It's not like small firms have an HR department. They often don't think about hiring. **Even if they have a clerk, that person could quit next week. Go ahead and send your materials."**

C. NAILING SMALL FIRM JOBS, FROM PIMPING YOUR RESUME TO COVER LETTERS TO INTERVIEWS TO FOLLOW-UPS . . . AND GETTING AROUND THE "ONE TO THREE YEARS' EXPERIENCE" REQUIREMENT

Once you've identified your targets, it's time to nail that job! Let's talk about every aspect of your job offensive:

a) Composing Your Resume For Small Firms.

In Chapter 8 on Resumes, we talked in detail about the importance of "customizing" your resume for different types of employers. That is, you present yourself differently depending on the employer to whom you're sending your resume.

When it comes to small firms . . . what do you need to stress about yourself? And perhaps more importantly, what can you do, starting now, to enhance your resume for small firms? When you take into account what it's like to work at a small firm—increased autonomy, immediate hands-on experience, "generalizing" rather than "specializing" (except for boutiques), spartan support staff— you can easily tease out the skills and qualities you'll want to demonstrate to small firms.

Note what's not on this list: *grades*. As Gail Peshel points out, "Smaller employers are more concerned with whether you'll stay or leave—geographic ties and rainmaking skills are much more important to them than grades are!" I talked to a student at one school who responded to a job posting for a small firm. He was all ready to wheel out his credentials and answer some tough questions. He called and introduced himself, and the lawyer asked only one question: "When can you start?" The lawyer didn't even ask about the student's grades at all! It turns out this attorney was not only a great employer, but the president of the local bar association! The student reports, "Through him I met everybody in town. It was awesome."

Of course, if your grades are good, include them on your resume. If you've excelled in certain classes, mention them. But don't get hung up on your grades!

So . . . if not grades, what *should* you stress about yourself?

a. **Self-starter:** You can't expect a lot of hand-holding in a small firm. Are you good at seeing what needs doing and doing it? What have you done elsewhere, in a legal or any other setting that demonstrates this?

b. **Ability to work without close supervision:** There just aren't the layers of management available in a small firm to provide close supervision. Have you worked in situations before where you were largely responsible for your own time?

c. **Direct work experience:** If you've got it, flaunt it. If you've worked for another small firm, it's the greatest indicator of your understanding of the work environment and ability to perform in it.

d. **Community involvement:** Except for boutiques, small firms expect you to "get out there" sooner rather than later.

There are two aspects to this. One is to show your connection to the employer's geographic area. Obviously if you grew up there or went to college or law school there, that's a plus.

If your connection to the community isn't obvious from your resume, you'll mention it in your cover letter (e.g., your spouse got a job there, you lived there through high school) and even at the bottom of your resume, if you have room, in a section called "Other Information".

What if you're talking about firms in small towns or rural areas where you have no connection? Not a problem. Most students who've nailed these jobs didn't have those connections either, and truth be told, how many people are going to have a personal connection to "Hooterville"? (The small town in "Green Acres," not the titty restaurant.) If you have any background with small towns, make sure that is highlighted in your resume. Otherwise, state in your cover letter why a small town or rural setting is appealing to you.

The other aspect of community involvement is your willingness and ideally demonstrated ability to take part in community activities. Remember: Letting people get to know you is the way legal business is often generated. So if you take part in extracurriculars at school, highlight those on your resume. Any voluntary activities in the community—fantastic.

Incidentally: This is not an issue for boutiques, which tend to have a national focus. In this sense they are large firms in small firm clothing.

* * * SMART HUMAN TRICK * * *

Law student in Minnesota, wants to go to a small farming community. He takes his work experience off his resume thinking it's irrelevant; he had worked for a family farm as a hired hand.

His Career Services Director convinced him to put the experience back on, telling him, "It's really relevant! Who's going to understand more about legal problems facing farmers than you? You'll talk their language."

What the student believed was a negative was a real plus. He put the experience back on his resume . . . and got a job.

e.   "Generalist" vs. "Specialist."

Small firms tend to have several practice areas, rather than a single focus. There are exceptions to this, of course; boutiques are focused narrowly, and some other small firms have a practice largely dedicated to a single practice area, like real estate. In those cases, you'll target your resume appropriately, as we discussed in Chapter 8.

But for your more common "generalized" small firm, you're better off not showing them a resume laser-focused on one specialty. For instance, if you're looking at a small firm that does real estate, some family law and civil litigation you're not going to send a resume that screams sports law or intellectual property!

What if you *do* have a resume that's focused on one particular interest of yours? There are two things to remember. First of all, you don't have to list everything you've done on your resume, not every club membership or extracurricular. On top of that, you'd be wise to focus on the roles you've played in your focused activities, because those roles may be very valuable to small firms. Maybe you found speakers for the entertainment law club, or you handled the budget or ran the web site or publication. Those activities reflect qualities that will be useful for small firms, and you should highlight them even if the particular specialty itself isn't relevant.

Let's talk for a moment about boutiques, because again, they're specialists and not generalists. If you apply to them, anything you can bring to the table relating to their specialty should be highlighted on your resume, including:

- excellent grades in relevant law school class(es);
- CLEs you've taken on the specialty;
- Writing experience on the specialty, whether for a scholarly journal or on a "freelance" basis for a bar publication or a web site;
- Clinical/externship experience related to it;
- Extracurriculars related to the specialty;
- Bar association committee membership related to it.

f.   Advocacy skills, for most small firms.

For most small firms and for boutiques that specialize in litigation, you'll need to show your advocacy skills. How have you done on oral arguments/moot court in school? Have you successfully taken part in client counseling competitions? Do you have clinical/externship advocacy experience? Were you a debater in high school and/or college? Have you used your advocacy skills for other employers—or for yourself? These are all experiences that should be highlighted on your resume.

g.   Work ethic.

Of course, every employer of every size and stripe wants to see a strong work ethic. But it's worth emphasizing here. So if you've worked your way through school, be sure to mention the hours you've worked and the percentage of your education you've funded. And if you've had other responsibilities that put an added burden on your time, again—mention them, so that your work ethic is obvious to employers who see your resume.

h.   Communication skills.

In small firms, you get client contact almost immediately. Therefore, your ability to communicate well is of vital importance.

Your written communication skills are one aspect of this, but your experience with people is perhaps more important. In this respect, jobs we often consider "menial"—waiting tables, working retail—are very valuable. (On my law school resume, I always mentioned that I waited tables in college, and that I served 20,000 people in two years. It always got favorable comment from employers.)

Of course, work experience isn't the only way to show communication skills. So are:

- Clinical programs;
- Extracurriculars;
- "Teamwork" (e.g., sports teams);
- Volunteer activities involving counseling, coaching . . . talking in general!
- Student Bar Association involvement.

i.   Ability to work under pressure and meet deadlines.

Remember: Law is a client-and deadline-driven business. Showing you've handled pressure working in other environments is a plus.

j. Detail-orientation.

Because you don't have a battery of support staffers at a small firm to check and recheck your work, it has to be perfect.

k. Research and writing skills (of secondary importance to most small firms).

While research and writing won't take up as much of your early career at a small firm as it would at a large one, it's still necessary that you show you have those skills. It is *particularly* important to exhibit 'practical' writing skills; showing you wrote motions for a clinical program or at another small firm is more valuable than a scholarly piece.

1. PIMPING YOUR RESUME: ACTIVITIES YOU CAN TAKE PART IN STARTING NOW TO UP YOUR OPPORTUNITIES WITH SMALL FIRMS . . .

As we saw in the "Resumes" chapter, Chapter 8, resumes aren't just a matter of what's "in place" already. You can do things starting right now that will enhance your resume for small employers, including:

i. Small-firm oriented CLEs.

I go into CLEs—Continuing Legal Education seminars—as a resume-enhancing tool in Chapter 8 on Resumes. They're so great for two principal reasons: the people you meet when you take them, and the resume bling they provide. They prove your sincere enthusiasm *and* your familiarity with issues facing practitioners.

ii. Volunteer with legal aid or legal services, or with Volunteer Lawyers Programs at your local bar association.

For most small "generalist" firms, getting hands-on experience with clients is an outstanding plus. Every legal aid and legal services office takes volunteers. If you can spare a few hours for it, you'll not just be performing a valuable service—you'll be pimping your resume as well!

iii. Join the bar association for the geographic area where you want to practice, and join the small firm practice section.

I've exhorted you before to join the bar association *now*, before you leave school, when it's really cheap. It doesn't hurt you to join more than one state's bar if you're not sure where you're going to practice. (Of course, don't list every bar association membership on your resume! If all you do is join the bar, so that you've got a "naked membership" with no involvement, only list the membership for the state where the employer you're contacting is located. But if you've participated in activities and projects with the bar, that goes on your resume no matter where it was.)

Along with joining the state bar, if you know the city or town where you'll be when you graduate, join that bar association and get involved. Even if it's from a distance, you can help out with a project. Be sure to mention your involvement on your resume.

iv. Get a cell phone with the appropriate area code.

A minor detail, but it makes a difference! It proves your dedication to the geographic area.

v. Take part in litigation skills contests.

Bar associations, legal fraternities and other organizations run litigation contests frequently. Because your ability to think on your feet and communicate well is so prized by small firms, doing well in competitions like this can make a big difference for you—and apart from anything else, the judges of such competitions are lawyers and judges, who can be valuable contacts!

vi. Write articles directed at small-firm practice for bar association publications.

If you write an article about some aspect of small firm practice, list it prominently on your resume under "Publications." It'll prove not just your ability to write but your enthusiasm for—and knowledge of—what your target audience does.

b) Getting around the "one to three years' experience" requirement.

If you've looked at postings for small firms, you may have noticed a depressing fact: most of them ask for one to three years' worth of experience. If you're still in law school (or you just graduated), this may lead to a lot of teeth-gnashing. "How," you may seethe, "am I supposed to get one to three years of work experience if no one will hire me in the first place?!?"

Relax, Weed Hopper. There are requirements . . . and then there are *requirements*. Remember: when employers write job ads, they're describing their "ideal" candidate. In many cases the "ideal" candidate doesn't apply . . . leaving the job to someone who doesn't have all the stated credentials . . . but all the potential!

There are two ways to enhance your resume to snag one of these jobs?

a. Show off what you've already got to its absolute best advantage.

As Lisa Lesage points out, "When attorneys say they want one to three years of experience, what they really want is someone who knows the ropes. Jobs you have during law school can easily give you that." She advises you to "Look at all the law-related work you've done, no matter what it is, and disgorge a line or two on every single thing. Don't simply say that you 'researched issues' or 'drafted memoranda and motions.' Instead, be very specific. Say that you drafted a motion for summary judgment in a 1983 case concerning privilege. Or that you prepared a deposition for a Title 7 case involving sexual harassment." For non-legal jobs you've had, be similarly specific so that you can pull out the skills that you can transfer to the legal job you want. Lisa Lesage advises that, "If you managed a restaurant before law school, don't just leave it at that. How many people did you manage? Did you handle budgets, or scheduling, or any other activities that would be similar in any setting?"

So you see the point—squeeze your experience *hard* to render every bit of advantage it can give you on your resume!

b. Those damn CLEs again . . .

I know, I know, you've heard it before: take CLEs. But when it comes to getting around the one-to-three-years'-experience bugbear, CLEs can save the day.

Here's the thing. Experience gets you several advantages— familiarity with the practice of law, with the issues the employer faces, a knowledge of the players in the community if you're in the same city, perhaps a book of business if you're in the same general location, and hands-on knowledge of working with clients.

While you can't rub a magic lantern and djinni up a book of biz, you *can* "simulate" the others—if you attend enough CLEs!

c) Correspondence.

a. Who to write to?

Your best option: A person someone told you to contact. See why I encouraged you to take part in all of those activities? Whether it's someone you know through law school or a legal fraternity or a bar association function or a seminar or CLE or anything else, the best possible letter starts with the seven magic words: *"So-and-so recommended that I contact you."*

A "still good" target for your letter is an attorney with whom you have something in common: whether (s)he is an alum of your law school or your undergrad school or you have something else in common (for instance, an unusual college major or work experience or home town).

A third alternative is, well—anybody at the firm. Montana's Mark Brickson recommends that you **contact the firm by phone to see to whom to address your letter: hiring partner, office manager, administrative assistant, secretary—and make sure you get the spelling of the job title and the person's name *exactly* right**. There's no shame in asking for or verifying a spelling—but getting it wrong in a letter is unforgivable!

If a phone call doesn't get you the appropriate target, just write to any lawyer on the letterhead. Heck—you tried.

b. What to mention?

The key element here is to *customize* your letters to the greatest extent possible. No firm wants to think that they're entry #123,509 in a mail merge! As I mention in the correspondence chapter, you get more bang for your buck by sending ten customized letters that take you half an hour each than from a one hundred-piece mass mailer that takes you the same amount of time.

So ... how do you customize your letters for small firms? Easy:

1. No addressing letters to "Hiring Partner," and no stating that you want to be a "summer associate"; small firms don't have summer associates.

2. If you were able to garner information about the firm from your research, mention it. Whether it's information on-line (from Lexis/Nexis and Westlaw searches of case law, jury verdicts, newspapers and periodicals, from the firm's web site, from Martindale–Hubbell, bar association membership directories or even the Yellow Pages about practice areas), complimentary comments about the employer from other people (your Career Services Director, professors, judges, other lawyers in the community, alums/upperclassmen who've worked there), whatever— show off the fact you chose them for a reason!

3. State an interest in the firm's practice area(s) or practice in general.

For a boutique, highlight your interest in their specialty(ies).

4. Weave in how what you've done will help them accomplish what they need, including rainmaking activities. For boutiques, rainmaking wouldn't apply.

5. Describe specific skills that will be useful to them. If you've handled litigation, as part of a clinical program or another job, for instance, say so to small firms that litigate.

6. If you're willing to work on a temporary, part-time, and/or contract basis, say so! Say something like, "While I am most interested in a permanent position, I would be willing to work on a temporary, part-time, or contract basis." Once you're there and you've proven yourself, you never know when that gig will turn into something

992   Guerrilla Tactics for Getting the Legal Job of Your Dreams

permanent and full-time. And if nothing else, it'll buy you time to talk to other employers.

7. If it's an out-of-town firm, emphasize your interest in the geographic area. A family or "historical" tie is good (e.g., you spent all/part of your childhood there). But any other reason for wanting to be there also works— whether it's because the type of practice you want to join is thriving there, or you like the type of community in which the employer is located for a particular reason (for instance, the employer is in a small town and you want to be there because you grew up in a small town and feel comfortable in a non-urban environment).

8. Again, for an out-of-town employer, mention in the letter a time period when you'll be in the area. You're more likely to get an interview if the firm doesn't have to cover the cost of a trip for you. It also shows your enthusiasm for working for the employer. If you don't intend to be in the employer's city at a time specific, you can always state in the letter that you're willing to come to City X at your own expense to meet with the employer and at mutually convenient time.

9. If you've joined the bar association for the state where the employer is located, mention it!

10. Look at the firm's web site, ads or written materials to get a general idea of the tone you should use. For instance, if a firm says on its web site, "We support dads in their efforts to maintain their parental rights," you'd want to focus on that particular aspect of family law in your letter, and stress your counseling skills.

11. Make sure your materials are absolutely, completely error-free. Students often think it's less important to be letter-perfect in materials they send to small firms because small firms are more casual. In fact, it's a *bigger* deal because there's nobody at a small firm to double-check your work!

* * * CAREER LIMITING MOVE * * *

Law student sends a targeted mailer to small firms in a town he's targeting. He includes the following paragraph:

"If hired, I could attract criminal clients to your firm. I frequent local bars and come into contact with a number of people who get in trouble with DWI, juvenile crimes, and minor traffic offenses. I could give them my business card and bring them in as clients."

As one employer who receives the letter comments, "Great. You hang out with a bunch of losers."

c) Follow-up calls ...

Following up is *crucial*. Don't consider your correspondence complete without it! Particularly if you put a line in your letter that you intend to follow up, you're unlikely to get to the next step with an employer if you don't make that phone call. And conversely, if you *do* follow up well, you might turn what would have been a rejection into an interview!

Here's what you need to know about following up.

1. It's a follow-up *call*. Not an e-mail.

You just hate me right now, because you don't want to call employers. E-mail is so much easier. But it's also far, far less effective, because it doesn't show the initiative of a phone call ... and it's too easy to ignore. So bite the bullet and make the call. Trust me: after the first one, it gets a lot easier!

2. Prep yourself before you call.

Don't call "cold," or you'll really be putting yourself on the spot. The advantage to a phone call is that you can have notes in front of you relating to what you want to say. Be prepared to talk about your qualifications and interests. It may be that you'll be asked to do a "de facto interview" over the phone!

3. When to call ...

Call two weeks after you send your materials.

4. What to say ...

Unlike large law firms and institutional employers, you aren't calling to see if they got your materials! This is *very* important, says legal consultant Wendy Werner. "What students don't realize is that attorneys at small firms have desks piled high with work. If you call and say, 'Gee, did you get my resume?' that puts all the pressure on the employer. You're asking them to go through piles of papers. You're asking them to *work*. And they won't like it. Instead, ask "I sent my resume to you two weeks ago. Can you tell me if you're interviewing?" or, if you're responding to a posting, "Can you tell me if you've made your decision?"

From there, it depends almost entirely on the reaction you get. You have to anticipate that the lawyer or administrator that you talk to is busy; they're at the office because they have work to do and clients to serve, and reviewing resumes isn't job #1. You can even acknowledge that you know the person you're calling is busy, that you're very interested in working with them and would greatly appreciate the opportunity to schedule an interview. If you can squeeze it in, mention a line or two about why you'd be so great for the job. If they insist they're too busy, you can even joke that if they're too busy to interview you, then they really do need your help! And, of course, offer to call back at a more convenient time.

In any case, your goal in the phone call is to move to the next step: an interview. Keep your focus on that prize!

5.   What to do with a "no."

Remember that "no" never really means "no." At the worst, it means "Not right now." Circumstances change, needs change. More business comes in. People move on. They get abducted by aliens. As the National Association for Law Placement points out, "A no in February may be a yes in April." So if someone tells you flat-out "no," reiterate your interest and state that you'll be contacting them again in a few months to see if things have changed.

In addition, even when it's a no, if it's an employer you're truly interested in, follow up with a letter. State your interest in the employer, your disappointment that you won't be working with them, your suitability for the job, and wind up by saying, "If your needs change, I hope you will reconsider me." You wouldn't be the first student to turn a rejection into an acceptance with an ultra-gracious follow-up letter!

Furthermore, you may be able to turn the employer into a useful conduit for other employers. You can always politely ask, "I appreciate that you don't need me right now, but could you perhaps give me advice on who else I should be talking to/what activities I ought to get involved in?" You can always try to turn a rejection into an opportunity for an informational interview.

d) Interviews.

Interviewing for a small firm position is in every important way just like any other interview—which is why you need to read the interviewing chapter, Chapter 9, if you haven't done so already. But because small firms are unique in some ways, certain aspects of your approach need to be stressed.

a.   Prepping for small firm interviews.

If it's an out-of-town interview, visit the relevant chamber of commerce website for information about the place; talk with a realtor about where you'd live as a young professional; review the local newspaper for several days before the interview, so you're familiar with what's going on in town. All of this will make you shine compared to the vast majority of students who'll go to the interview "blind."

Also, remember to look the part. If the interview is in a small town, don't look too "urban"—avoid expensive suits. I'm not suggesting that you stop at Goodwill for your interview wear, but Armani isn't going to go over well in Hooterville.

b. For out-of-town interviews, researching the interviewer can be particularly helpful.

You always want to research the interviewer—but for small firms in other cities, it can be particularly helpful. Here's why: there's a substantial chance that the interviewer isn't from there, either! That gives you the opportunity to say, "I know you're from X" or "I know you went to X college/law school . . ." and follow up with: "How did you wind up in X city? How did you choose X firm? How did you settle in?" And you can weave into that conversation how you'd do the same kinds of things.

c. What they're looking for . . .

Be prepared to discuss these elements of your background and abilities:

- Involvement in activities;
- People skills—the ability to converse easily with people and therefore deal with clients;
- The ability to juggle competing interests;
- Listening skills;
- Eagerness to work;
- Bar association affiliation and activities.
- Connection with and/or interest in the community.
- While people skills and activities suggest rainmaking potential, we discuss rainmaking separately in Topic D, below.

d. "Fit" is more crucial than in any other setting.

In large organizations, you don't have to get along with everyone. The jerks are fairly easy to avoid. But in a small firm . . . well, if you constitute 10% of the personnel, you can't run *or* hide. So the elusive personality fit is crucial! The best way to accomplish this? To the extent possible—relax! Imagine that a mutual acquaintance has told you, "Hey, you should really meet X. I think you two would have a lot to talk about." You're not facing the firing squad—you're having a *conversation*. Remember, fit works both ways: You want to be comfortable with the people you work with just as they want to be comfortable with you. So take a deep breath, relax, and let your natural personality shine!

e. Remember, *every* member of a small team is crucial.

It's always important to be pleasant to everyone you meet when you interview. In a small setting, it's even more crucial. Be nice to receptionists and assistants—they're more powerful than you think, and certainly at the start of your career, they know more about "lawyering" at that firm than you do! More than one lawyer has pointed out to me that it's easier to replace associates than it is to replace a great secretary.

They've got juice, so make sure you're appropriately pleasant and respectful.

f. Set your resent-o-meter on "low" for illegal questions.

You're more likely to get questions that smack of illegality in small firms than in many other settings. Are you married? Do you have children? Those kinds of queries are not uncommon.

I urge you not to jump to the conclusion that the interviewer is being rude or inappropriate! Particularly if the interview is out of town *or* the employer is in a small town, the employer could have justifiable concerns about your willingness/ability to settle there . . . and whether you'd be happy there if you did.

I'll never forget a student who'd interviewed with a small firm in a small town, and the interviewer had asked him "Are you married?" The student was stunned by the question—and I was surprised, too, since male students rarely if ever are asked that question! The student asked me, "Was he asking because he thinks I'm gay?" A follow up revealed this: The interviewer said that because the town they're in is small, any student settling there without being married would be unlikely to meet any suitable "prospects." They were concerned about whether he'd be happy there. Well! That's a far cry from questioning someone's sexual orientation.

Similarly, if the interviewer asks if your spouse would be willing to move—again, if you've got no obvious connection to the town, that's a valid concern. No firm wants to make you an offer you won't accept, and if your spouse wouldn't move there even if you forced red-hot bamboo shoots under his/her nails . . . there's no point in making you an offer!

The thing to do is to address the valid concern behind the inappropriate question, and not the question itself if it makes you uncomfortable. For instance: "If you're worried that I'll feel comfortable in Yak Falls, I wouldn't be wasting your time if I hadn't researched it and felt confident I'd be happy here." "If you're worried that I wouldn't accept an offer because of anyone else's relocation issues, I promise you that's not the case." "If I wasn't willing to be here for the foreseeable future, I wouldn't be wasting your time with this interview."

What they're entitled to know is: if the fit is right, would you consider an offer, and would you stay for the foreseeable future? You can, of course, just *answer* the question. "My husband grew up here/in a small town/has a job lined up here." "My wife is excited about relocating." "We're in the federal witness protection program, and so the further away we get, the better."

I'm just kidding about that last one. But you see my point: focus on the employer's valid concern, and address it in a way that's comfortable to you!

g. For non-boutiques, have an answer prepared for the question, "What do you plan to do to bring in business?"

We talk about proving rainmaking potential just below, in Topic D. For right now, let's just talk about the "business development" interview question that you might face in interviews with small firms.

As Jane Steckbeck points out, "It will not impress employers to hear you say, 'I'll join the local bar and go to monthly meetings.' They want to see that you've put more thought into it than that. There are all kinds of things you can do. By way of a few suggestions:

- Investigate your area Chamber of Commerce and be ready to identify specific programs or initiatives in which you plan to get involved. For instance, in Eugene, the Chamber holds a monthly 'Business after Hours' session in which business owners, government leaders, lawyers and so on gather to hang out, have a drink, and share information. This is a prime opportunity for new lawyers to get in the know, meet people, and potentially develop business. Some Chambers offer special leadership programs to participants who apply and are selected. These programs are designed to train people in the community to become leaders. These programs introduce participants to government players, educators, nonprofits, travel centers (airports), news media leaders. Such programs are great for developing not just leadership skills, but meeting people who may become clients.

- Plan to attend Chamber-sponsored lectures, breakfasts, and the like.

- If you're a woman, find out if your target has an active Women's Business Network, investigate it, then plan to join. These are women business owners who meet monthly to network and collaborate. In Eugene, membership is by invitation only, through sponsorship by another member, so it pays to get to know members!

- Be involved in local political party activities. It isn't necessary to become a political activist, just participate in meetings and planning.

- If you love a particular sport, continue to play in an adult league and/or coach a kid's team and/or get on the Board of Directors of a children's sports organization.

- Plan to get involved with other organizations, like a Symphony Board, local Red Cross, child advocacy groups, the YMCA, on a board level.

Of course there are many others, and you'd tailor your own plan to your own personality and tastes. Simply being able to articulate a plan shows small firms that you've given thought to how to become a rainmaker, and this goes a long way in an interview!"

h. Following up after an interview.

You'll find that small firm decision making is generally informal; as one small firm lawyer said, "We talk to you, we like you, you just show up for work the next day."

Of course, the particular hiring method for any individual small firm might be more involved with that.

If, after an interview, you really want the job, follow the advice in Chapter 9 on Interviews, specifically the section entitled "Following Up." Make a point of ingratiating yourself with the secretary or office manager (secretaries have much more power than most people realize). Ask what else you can do, if you can provide any other materials, and encourage them to call your references.

D. SHOWING YOUR RAINMAKING POTENTIAL ... TO FIRMS WHO WILL APPRECIATE IT!

Ah, rainmaking. Rainmaking—getting and keeping clients—is at the very heart of private practice. And why is that? Because law firms are *businesses*. They're highly-sophisticated, metaphysical hot dog vendors. Of course, they don't sell hot dogs ... they sell advice. But they do *sell*. And that's true of every law firm in America, from sole practices to the mega-firms.

While nobody expects you to "rainmake" early in your career at a large law firm—it would be kind of weird if you were in a position to bring in General Motors as a client as a first year associate!—at small law firms (other than boutiques), it's much closer to the beginning of your career. And that means that if you can show small firms your potential to rainmake, you're much more likely to nail an offer from them. As Debra Fink says, "So much depends on your ability to *get* the work, not *do* the work. You're worth so much more! It's the only sure way to ensure that you won't be laid off."

If you're cringing at this point—don't! The good news is that you can create the impression that you can be a rainmaker in the mind of the employer. This involves two steps: First, drawing attention to aspects of your background that suggest rainmaking potential. (You may think you haven't done anything that fits that description. I can pretty much guarantee you that you'll be pleasantly surprised!). And second, we'll talk about things you can do starting right now that suggest rainmaking chops. Finally, we'll talk about how you go about broaching rainmaking potential to employers. It's important to be subtle about it, because you don't want to come off sounding cocky! But let's start with something more mundane. Let's talk about exactly what rainmaking ability *is*.

a) Rainmaking ability: What the heck is it, anyway?

The ability to draw clients to a firm is a lot more than having a rich, influential Daddy and Mommy. As Marilyn Tucker advises, rainmaking is a skill you can *learn*. It involves making contacts, getting people to like and trust you, your ability to deal with people comfortably and enthusiasm. In short, it's being a "people" person . . . which you probably are already!

Ironically, many of the activities we talk about in Chapter 10, on people and activities, are the same kinds of activities that suggest rainmaking potential. So if you're comfortable with the idea of being proactive—or you've *made* yourself comfortable with it!—Congratulations. You're a fledgling rainmaker.

b) Finding the hidden rainmaking potential in your background and making the most of it!

As Rob Kaplan says, "If you ask most students about client development skills, their first reaction is, 'I don't have that!'" But you probably have *many* activities in your background that show rainmaking potential. You just haven't looked at them that way. I'm down with that, because as a law student, I did a bunch of things that reeked of rainmaking potential. I just didn't realize it. I was heavily into fundraising, for a start. I could squeeze money out of just about anybody. But when it came to putting that on my resume, I was squeamish. I thought, "What law firm is going to care about whether I can get fifty bucks from an alum?" Little did I know then that *that* skill was a lot more important than any of the stuff that *did* make it on to my resume! What was true for me is probably true for you, too . . . you've done things that suggest rainmaking, and you've probably downplayed them.

You aren't going to anymore! Let's talk about rainmaking potential from two perspectives: the kind of rainmaking that springs from your activities, and the kind that results from your family and your roots.

a. Rainmaking ability implied by your activities.

OK—it's time to get out paper and pencil and make a list of everything you've done that suggests you can be a rainmaker. As Wendy Werner suggests, "What you're looking for with rainmaking potential is anything that suggests you can meet people and generate business." So wrack your brain for any activities that are people-oriented, suggest that you're amiable, that you make friends and contacts easily. Like:

- You've started your own business (even if it was a part-time or summer business, like sealing driveways);

- You've run a business;

- You've sold or marketed anything, from publications to cars;

- You've had a prior career that connected you to a group of potential clients (e.g., you sold commercial real estate, or you were involved in healthcare management, or you were a teacher in a community);

- You've taken part in volunteer activities (whether it was charitable or coaching sports or *anything*);

- You've held a leadership role in any job or extracurricular;

- You've taken part in fundraising activities, for school or any other organization;

- You've taken part in United Way drives;

- You've participated in client mediation workshops in law school;

- You've taken part in moot court and/or client counseling in law school;

- You've taken an active role in the local bar association;

- You've been involved in civic activities (like Little League or the PTA or serving on local boards);

- You've played social sports like golf or softball;

- You've belonged to a country club;

- You've taken part in the Peace Corps;

- You've been involved in church or temple activities.

I could go on, but you see the common thread running through these activities—they involve *people*.

Once you've made a list of activities, hang on to it, because just below we'll talk about how you broach rainmaking potential to employers. And what if your list is empty? Take heart! We'll talk about activities you can do starting right now that will create that rainmaking aura!

b. Rainmaking ability implied by your family and roots.

If your last name is DuPont or Rockefeller or Kennedy, then chances are you don't need to be reading this section about how to make hay out of your family name. But odds are that your connections are a little bit more subtle than that. Perhaps, for instance:

- Your family is firmly rooted in the community, in that your parent(s) either hold positions of prestige (e.g., president of a bank or superintendent of schools), or they are extremely well-connected through community service, or are otherwise socially prominent. (P.S.: It doesn't hurt to be rich.)

- You went to a prestigious local private or Catholic school.

I'll give you a personal example. My father is a biotech venture capitalist of some renown. He's quoted in *The Wall Street Journal*, *Fortune Magazine* and that kind of publication all the time. At least, so they tell me. I'm a *New York Post* kind of girl, myself. But anyway, that's the kind of rainmaking potential I'm talking about here. It's the kind that makes employers scratch their heads and say, "Hmm, it probably wouldn't hurt to have this kid's name on the ol' letterhead."

If you do have this kind of rainmaking ability, it probably makes you a bit queasy to think about using it. It makes *me* queasy thinking about it. After all, nobody likes to think about getting ahead on Mommy and Daddy's coattails. But you know what? I've talked to too many law students, tens of thousands of them, to believe you ought to let any advantage lay unexploited. If you're a member of the lucky sperm club, for gosh sakes use it. As Susan Benson points out, "It's not name-dropping. It's rainmaking. It shows that you understand *business.*"

The fact is, ultimately it *is* about you. Having lucky lineage is like getting a fifty-yard advantage in a foot race. It's a benefit at the outset but ultimately your success depends on you, how you get along with people, and the quality of your work. For me, it sure didn't stop my summer clerkship employer from bouncing me unceremoniously at the end of the summer! Also, think about it from your parents' perspective. One of the peripheral benefits of success is the impact it has on people you care about. For your parents . . . that's you. Giving you a head start is part of what motivated them in the first place. So if you have this kind of rainmaking potential, view it as what it is: manna from Heaven.

But as with the other kind of rainmaking ability, the self-generated kind, you've got to be careful about how you broach it to employers. In fact, with *this* kind of rainmaking ability you've got to be *particularly* careful, because if it backfires you'll come off as a snotty little rich kid whom employers will disdain. Just below, in "Broaching the topic of rainmaking," we'll cover how you bring it up.

c) Things you can do *starting right now* to suggest rainmaking ability.

It's never too late to prove your rainmaking potential! As the list of rainmaking activities I offered a minute ago suggest, there are an awful lot of things you can still do, whether it's bar association involvement, fundraising participation ... it doesn't matter that you haven't done these things for years. And it doesn't even matter that what's *motivating* you is the desire to get rainmaking potential onto your resume. The fact that you're doing them *at all* is what counts.

d) Broaching the topic of rainmaking to potential employers.

Now that you've got something—or some things—to prove your rainmaking ability ... what do you do with them? Rainmaking isn't one of those things you can list on your resume as a skill—not overtly, anyway. And you can't put it in a cover letter, either. In point of fact, you can't even use the word when you make contacts. In any of these contexts you'll come off as arrogant.

"Geez, Kimmbo," you're thinking. "If I can't ever *talk* about it, what's the use of *having* it?" Relax. You *can* talk about it; it's just that you've got to be subtle about it, that's all. Let's look at how you go about bringing up rainmaking ability in a variety of contexts: when you take part in activities that put you in contact with potential employers, when you send cover letters and resumes, and when you interview.

a. Activities that put you in contact with potential employers.

Bar association functions, alumni receptions, conferences, CLEs ... as I urged you in Chapter 10 on people and activities, letting people see you is so much more effective than a resume can ever be.

Ironically, taking part in activities like these *in and of itself* suggests your rainmaking potential, because you're putting yourself out there. Most clients find their lawyers through word-of-mouth or by meeting them casually. As Woody Allen said, 80% of success is showing up. So you've already accomplished a lot when you do exactly that—show up!

Having said that, you want to make the "best you" shine at these activities. For instance, do simple things like smile, initiate conversations, collect business cards. As Marilyn Tucker says, "Rainmaking is all about personality. Be outgoing! You don't need to be Miss Congeniality, but students who show little enthusiasm or energy, and wait to be drawn out, aren't going to be seen as a client draw. Employers look at what their potential clients will see!" Pam Malone adds, "It's attitude. It's implying, 'I'll go above and beyond'—a 'can-do' attitude." Nancy Krieger chips in, "You need to be personable. That's more important than grades. Employers look for people who are *likable*."

So keep your finger on the pulse of what's going on in your community. No matter how much you think you're buried in schoolwork, you need to avoid tunnel vision. Keep up with the news, have interesting things to say, and show curiosity about other people and what interests them. Be the kind of person you enjoy being around. And when potential employers see you, they'll look at you through the eyes of their clients—and they'll be impressed with what they see!

b. Cover letters.

As is true in so many other settings, you can't mention the word "rainmaking" in cover letters. The most you could do, according to Diane Reynolds, is to say that you believe you have client development ability, and then back it up with something in your background that shows you've generated business before. (If you don't have anything to back it up, then don't mention it.) For instance, maybe you've done some fundraising successfully. In your cover letter, you could say that you particularly look forward to client development, because you've enjoyed people-oriented activities like fundraising at law school.

c. Resumes.

Resumes are a matter of "show me don't tell me." As Wendy Werner points out, you'll of course want to include any experience you have in running or starting a business, or in fundraising—anything that says you can meet people and generate revenue. In fact, any of the activities we talked about above is appropriate for your resume, and they all suggest that you have rainmaking potential.

In this context, be sure that you don't leave out any non-law-oriented activities that suggest rainmaking potential! That's a common trap, because law students often think that such activities have no bearing on their ability to be a good lawyer. Taking part in law school fundraisers and phone-a-thons? It absolutely goes on your resume!

* * * SMART HUMAN TRICK * * *

Law student whose life before law school included selling cars. He wants to work for a small firm, and he very much doesn't want to include his car shilling on his resume. His Career Services Director knows he's interviewing with small firms that require new associates to do some rainmaking. She convinces him to put his car selling experience on his resume.

He nails the job.

You will also want to include hobbies that suggest rainmaking potential. As Diane Reynolds points out, golf is the traditional rainmaker, so if you golf, on your resume it goes!

Family-connection based rainmaking potential is harder to squeeze in, but Susan Benson encourages you to find *any* way to mention it on your resume. For instance, if your last name is Bagelschlauf, and you spent the summer loading cement bags at the $50 million Bagelschlauf Construction Company, she said, "Don't be too proud to mention it!" So you see the theme here: you never use the word "rainmaking" per se, but you mention everything that goes into indicating that you have rainmaking potential.

d. Interviews.

Interviews are where your rainmaking potential is most likely to bear fruit. When you're interviewing with a small law firm, your rainmaking potential is going to be an issue on their minds, even though they're unlikely to mention anything about it. They'll be looking at you at least in part through the lens of potential clients. Are you likable? (Of course you are.) Will people feel comfortable around you? (Of course they will!)

The way to convey a "people-person" orientation in an interview involves all of the skills we talked about in the Interviewing chapter. Lean slightly forward in your chair during the interview to show enthusiasm. Maintain eye contact with the interview. Smile—when it's appropriate, of course! Don't speak in a monotone—convey the enthusiasm you feel for the job. Show with your words and your demeanor that you're happy to be there and grateful for the opportunity to meet with the interviewer. Take part in a mock interview at school—ideally videotaped—to see what you need to polish. As Pam Malone says, "Rainmaking ability often shows *implicitly* in interviews!"

An interview also gives you the opportunity to bring up items in your background that suggest rainmaking potential. As Wendy Werner points out, "If your dad owns a local bank, I would find a way to squeeze that into the interview, even if you're not asked about it." Amy Thompson similarly encourages you to "play up community ties, civic activities like Little League or PTA, to show you're well-connected. And address it *expressly.*"

But be careful to bring these items up in a matter-of-fact tone; if you sound like you're bragging, or that you have the ability to deliver tons of legal business just on the basis of who Mommy and Daddy are, you'll turn the interviewer off. You can always bring up connections in reference to something else; for instance, you can say, "I've always been interested in commercial law, because my father owns a bank and I've taken an interest in what he does," or "My interest in copyright law came about because my mother is president of a publishing company," or "I worked at Northstar Construction during the summers in college because I was interested in learning more about the family business." That way, you're not hitting the interviewer over the head with your connections, but you *are* making them known. And that's important! Remember, a face-to-face interviewer is your opportunity to make yourself shine in the eyes of the employer. Since rainmaking is a skill that's highly prized by legal employers, an interview is *definitely* the time to show off your rainmaking potential!

What about the situation where you're interviewing for a job in a city where you've never lived? It's more difficult to establish your rainmaking ability, but as Rob Kaplan points out, it's not impossible. He suggests that you "Turn your lack of contacts in the city on its head. You can say something like, "I've lived in a number of places, and I've always been able to establish contacts and feel comfortable in the community. I want to do that here, too.'" Turning a negative into a positive is a tired cliché, but in a situation where you're the new kid in town, you *can* use it to show that you can develop clients even though you don't have any roots in the community.

4.   The Bottom Line on Rainmaking ...

If you're looking for jobs with small firms, sooner or later you're going to be expected to bring in business ... and it's probably sooner. As Debra Fink points out, "Law *is* sales! When you practice law, you're going into your own business. And the key to your job security is your clientele—so a lot depends on your ability to *get* work, not *do* work. You can't be a good lawyer without clients!"

There are many, many practicing lawyers who as law students *never* thought they could generate business ... and today have a thriving and very lucrative practice.

E.   MONEY, MONEY, MONEY: NEGOTIATING MONEY AND TERMS OF EMPLOYMENT WITH SMALL LAW FIRMS

1.   PILING ON THE MAD CHEESE ...

If small law firms are such an enjoyable environment for most people, why do law students squirm so much at taking jobs with them? To bastardize a phrase, It's The Money, Stupid. As we discussed at the outset of this chapter, small law firms do start you at a lower salary than large law firms. A *much* lower salary. So much lower that you might be tempted to say, "I can't afford to work for a small firm."

Before you cut out a large and promising segment of the job market, let's talk for a moment about it, shall we? Consider the following:

a. Starting pay is meaningless

Well, not *meaningless* perhaps … but not totally meaningful, either, because it says nothing about your long-term earning potential.

In addition, if you look at listings of the highest-paid lawyers in America, they're rarely with large firms. You need look no further than Temple Law School in Philadelphia for proof of this. Excuse me—I mean the Beasley School of Law. Temple changed its name due to a gift of stunning largesse from its generous alum … a PI lawyer who founded his own firm.

So don't view the starting pay as any indication of your salary potential. You can do very handsomely, quite quickly.

b. What do you need to know to stack up more dead presidents? I've got a simple, five-point plan for you.

Step One: Knowledge is Power.

You need to know as much as you can about what the market will bear. The National Association for Law Placement puts out very comprehensive statistics (you'll find them at your Career Services Office) that tell you how much different kinds of law firms pay, in different geographic areas, not just as starting pay but several years out into the future, as well.

Why is this important? Two reasons. For one thing, if you find that the range for a small firm in the area where you're going to live is $50–60,000, and you want $100,000, unless you've got some very clear, very incriminating Polaroids, you're probably not going to get it. On the other hand, you might learn that the employer you're considering is offering you something at the low end of the scale. If so, there's wiggle room. You've got negotiating power before you ever enter the room.

Step Two: Don't *assume* that they're trying to spank you with a crappy pay package.

Remember: Small firms don't hire all the time, so they may not be familiar with the going rate for new associates. They may know the going rate, and not be in a position to offer it. Or they may only know that they're really busy and they need a new pair of hands … and they're scared to death about the ability to cover you if they don't bring in the business they're expecting.

On top of that, what you expect and what *they* made starting out are probably vastly different. Even twenty years ago, attorneys at large law firms—that's right, *large* law firms—started at about thirty thousand dollars a year. *Thirty thousand. At big, prestigious law firms.* It may entirely be true that an offer that seems low to you seems perfectly reasonable to them.

I mention this to you because starting off from a position of "How dare you?" isn't a helpful negotiating stance. Far better to assume ignorance than malice, and take it from there!

Step Three: Recognize that in the absence of other consider-ations (which we're going to talk about in a minute), you have limited negotiating power as a new lawyer.

When you are talking about a small-ish law firm looking at *you*, the untested lawyer, here's what they're seeing: "It will take you four hours to do a memo that years down the road you'll be able to knock out in twenty minutes. Much of your early time is written down or written off," says Carolyn Bregman. Quinnipiac's Diane Ballou adds that "When you start, you don't know anything. They can't send you out alone, you have to tag along, and they can't charge for you. And if you're going to work for just one person, bringing you in is a quantum leap no matter *how* much you get."

So don't get your knickers in a twist because you've got a J.D. That does not, however, mean you can't squeeze more dough out of the employer. Which leads me to ...

Step Four: Don't let the employer trap you into naming a figure first.

It may be that a small firm makes you an offer and asks you to name your price. The best advice? *Don't name your price ... at least, don't go first.* There are some employers who'll put you on the spot to assess your expectations. Instead, turn it back on them—*nicely*—by saying, "I imag-ine you have a range in mind of what you expect to pay. Can you tell me what that is?" If they continue to ask you for your price, give *them* a range instead of a single figure, with the bottom end of the range being the very least you'd accept.

Of course, when you're naming a range, you're facing a "Three Bears" kind of problem. That is, if you state a salary that's too high, you might price yourself out of the job. If you name a salary that's too low, the employer will question whether you understand the demands of the job or whether you have the skills that would justify a fair market salary.

You can get around these problems with advance prep. If you've done your homework and you know what the range in the geographic area is, you can name that range and say, "I understand that for firms your size in this area, the range is $50,000–60,000 a year to start, and I'd be happy with that," or "I'd expect the higher end of that because ..." and list the reasons why you're worth it, either due to experience or due to your willingness to expand the position based on your skills.

Step Five: If you want more, offer more ... or make it seem like you're not *asking* for more. Three negotiating stances that *work*.

Let's say that a small firm, Cassidy and Sundance, offers you $55,000 a year to start, which is bang in the middle of the range for the geographic area. If you want more, you've got three options for going after it: You can bring more to the table, you can ask for "non-dollar-figure" compensation, or you can negotiate up-front for down-the-road increases.

Before we discuss what these are, remember that asking for more money is not without risk. The firm may be open to your ideas, with the thought in mind that they want you to be happy working for them. Or they might be resentful that you brought it up at all. Make your approach *gentle* and watch for signals telling you to negotiate further— or retreat. And *always, always, always* stress to them that you are *grateful for the opportunity* to work with them, the money issue aside.

So—let's talk about the options for squeezing out more pay:

a. **If your issue with your pay is that you've got big student loan bills, your opening stance with the employer should be *telling them about your student loan debt*.** You don't need to be glued to the headlines to realize that law school tuition has increased astronomically over the last decade or two. It's a sin how much you spend on your law school education ... or, more likely, borrow for it. It's entirely possible that employers who make you offers have *no idea* how much your debt load is ... and will be sympathetic to you if you tell them. I've had a number of students tell me that when they told their potential employers that they were looking at $900–a-month student loan payments, the employers were open to paying them more ... sometimes in the form of paying the student loan providers directly.

The fact is, if you've got huge student loan debts, asking for more money doesn't make you selfish ... it might make the difference between your ability to accept an offer or not. So mention it!

b) **Think about what else you can offer the employer.** There are many possibilities, including:

- Consider negotiating for a cut of the business you bring in. This is a particularly easy sell, because if you don't bring in more business, you don't make more money. It's a no-lose proposition for the employer. And if you're concerned about whether you can actually bring in clients ... relax. You'll get involved in community activities, get on lists at the courthouse, do things you'll enjoy doing anyway, and the clients will accumulate that way. As you develop a reputation, as people get to know you, it gets easier and easier. And developing a ''book of business'' of your own, incidentally, means you'll *always* be happily employed, because you'll always be valuable.

- Offer to write a firm newsletter, on paper or on-line, as a means of gaining publicity, clients, and keeping the firm visible.

- Offer to give seminars to a key audience for the firm, be it the elderly (for estate planning work), investment clubs (for tax work), at the library (for a whole variety of practice areas), and the like.

- Offer to set up and maintain a firm home page, if you've got that kind of skill.

Any one of these would be a viable option for earning more money. What you want to be careful about is any work you do on the side. One lawyer told me about a woman who was doing contract work (that is, freelance lawyering) for several small firms. One of them made her an offer to join them as an associate. She wasn't thrilled with the offer, but took it anyway—and maintained some of her contract work. The firm found out, and the managing partner went nuts and fired her. So be aware that if you'd rather do extra work elsewhere than negotiate for more money from your employer, you need to be up-front about it and get the employer's OK first. Obviously you can do things like tutoring law students and bar examinees, and there are other kinds of freelance work—like web page design, database management, and so forth—that are unlikely to offend any law firm employer or potentially violate conflict of interest rules. In fact, telling them about it might shame them into paying you more, out of guilt that you've got to moonlight to pay your bills!

c. "Non-dollar-figure" compensation.

This is a bit of a misnomer, because what you're really asking for here does have a monetary value. But since you're not saying, "I want another $5,000," it doesn't seem like it. It's like going to a casino and betting with chips instead of money. You might plonk down a black hundred-dollar chip at the blackjack table without any hesitation, whereas you'd never put down a hundred-dollar bill. When you negotiate for non-dollar-figure compensation, you're relying on the same psychological principle. You can ask for things like:

- Insurance—medical, dental, life, disability (alternatively, if they're offering you insurance and your spouse's/partner's policy covers you, ask for the money they'd have spent on it to cover you);
- Malpractice insurance;
- If you haven't taken the bar yet, a bar review course;
- Professional fees (like bar membership);
- CLEs;
- Tuition reimbursement;
- Moving expenses, if applicable;
- Bonuses and/or fee sharing (for work you bring in);
- Profit sharing;
- Paid sick leave;
- Holidays, vacations, personal days;
- Paid parking;
- Reimbursement for car expenses, if you're expected to travel in your own car;
- Paid lunches;
- A 401K plan or other retirement options.

You get the idea—you're asking for a better package in non-monetary terms to soften the blow.

d. Negotiating now for down-the-road increases.

If the prospects for getting a higher salary look dim—or you try and strike out—consider negotiating for fixed-period increases in the future. You can say straight out, "I understand your position now and I respect it, and I'll work hard to prove myself to you. Can we revisit this issue shortly in the future? ..." Diane Ballou suggests that "You can ask for a reevaluation at three months, six months, nine months, with a chance to make more money then." As she points out, "This gives them a chance to get to know you and like you and need you, and your chances will be better as a result."

Actually your chances of nailing a big raise are *much* better if you can bite the bullet and negotiate after you've worked with them for at least a few months. Especially in small organizations, they may quickly find that they can't remember how they functioned without you, and that gives you leverage that you didn't have at the outset. You'll also be able to say that you progressed with your work product, your writing skills, and perhaps your business development ability.

2. WHAT IF YOUR BID FOR MORE SCRATCH FAILS?

Trying to negotiate for more money at the outset is *fraught* with risk. You may alienate an employer who otherwise would have been willing to welcome you with open arms, but now feels that you are selfish and ungrateful. And you may be resentful that they don't value your time more than your paltry salary suggests. What do you do? *Fuhgedduhbad-it. Pretend you never asked in the first place.* You've got to approach your job with enthusiasm, an air of appreciation and an obvious desire to learn, no matter *how* much money you make. How do you do that? Remember a phrase that is common to screenwriters: show them, don't tell them. You can say all you want about how much you're worth and how much they ought to pay you. But *showing* them, with great quality work and enthusiasm, will drive home the point better than the best negotiations up-front ever could.

I know this from personal experience. The first book contract I ever got was to ghost-write a book on biotechnology. They offered me $10,000 for *six months'* work. Six months! I was seething. On the inside, that is. I didn't have any choice. I could have told them 'til the cows came home that I was a talented writer, that I was worth a lot more ... but I hadn't done anything to prove it. I'd never published a damn thing. So I bit the bullet and took the job, and the book I wrote? They made three million dollars on it. *Three million.* As soon as it was an obvious success, they came back and offered me three thousand bucks *a week* to do more projects for them. My point is this: rest assured that you'll have plenty of opportunities to ask for more money once you've given an employer the chance to discover for themselves how indispensable you are! View your first few months as a learning experience (which they are), as the opportunity to build up "career capital" (which they are)—and the "apprenticeship" that sets you up for a great future—which they are!

3.   NEGOTIATING TERMS OF EMPLOYMENT

For large employers, where hiring is routine, the terms of employment are pretty routine, as well—salary, reviews, raises, and so forth are cookie-cutter. Not so for small firms and sole practitioners! Because they are less structured than large firms, the issues of importance to you may be ones that don't arise naturally in the course of your interviews and conversations. As soon as you've received an offer, and before you begin work, it's important to make sure that you reduce to an agreement every important aspect of your working relationship. As one lawyer explained it to me, "It's better to work out these issues while things are still great between you. You don't want to wait until there's a disagreement to resolve an issue, because it can get really ugly."

Also, remember to get this agreement *in writing*. It doesn't have to be a formal contract, but it should at least be a letter or memorandum memorializing your conversation about these issues. *It can't be simply a handshake deal!*

* * * SMART HUMAN TRICK * * *

New graduate, Midwestern law school. She receives an offer from a sole practitioner. It sounds to her like a good deal. She asks the lawyer to put the agreement in writing, and she reports: "He says to me—no lie—'If you make me write it down, it won't be as good. You have to trust me.' Can you believe it? I'm thinking, would you really want somebody working for you who's stupid enough to believe *that*?"

She turned him down.

It is important to remember: *these are not interview questions. This negotiation only takes place once you have a firm offer in hand*! Bringing up these issues when you're still "a-courtin' " will turn off even the most ardent employer!

Once you have your offer in hand, here are the general issues you want to resolve: (This list is courtesy of The Catholic University of America School of Law)

  a.   Job title:

       ☐ Law Clerk until bar passage

       ☐ Associate implies you will work toward partnership

       ☐ Attorney

       ☐ Contract Attorney

      Has certain implications, namely:

        • usually paid on an hourly basis

- not hired with a sense of permanence, although the contract arrangement may last for years
- receive an hourly rate; earnings can be comparable to annual salary of associate at the same level
- need to be careful how you represent your position to clients/the outside world.

b. Salary:

☐ Starting salary or hourly wage

☐ Will there be an increase after you pass the bar exam?

If so, how much will it be?

If you don't pass the bar exam right out of the gate, what will the compensation consequences be—if any?

☐ Date or frequency of payment

☐ Salary or performance review after what period(s) of time—three months, six months—and how often thereafter?

☐ Will salary increases be predetermined? If not,

  ☐ How will pay increases be determined?

  ☐ When will any such raises become effective?

☐ Annual raises:

  ☐ Standard or performance-based?

  ☐ When do annual increases go into effect?

c. Start date:

d. Hours/Billable Requirements:

☐ Is there a set minimum of billable hours that must be achieved?

☐ In accounting for billable hours, does the firm use hours actually worked or hours actually billed to the client?

☐ If there is not a predetermined billable hour requirement for an attorney at your level, how will your requirement be determined?

☐ How many hours per week can you expect to work on average?

☐ Is there flexibility? Examples of scenarios of flexibility:

- How is leaving early for an appointment viewed?
- If you have children, how will needs to leave when their needs arise (sicknesses, parent/teacher meetings) be dealt with?
- Can time missed be made up on another day?

- Is the atmosphere such that as long as the work gets done your supervisor(s) will not be overly concerned with the way you structure your work day?

- Is working from home or telecommuting an option?

☐ Are weekend hours mandatory? Are they typical?

e. Assignment:

☐ Which department/division/areas of practice will you be working in?

☐ Will you receive assignments from a single attorney or multiple attorneys?

f. Training/Supervision:

☐ What kind of training is provided for new attorneys? Small firms usually do not have a formal training program. That makes opportunities for training outside of the firm very important, such as CLEs and bar association courses.

☐ Is there reimbursement/budget for training for CLE courses? How many courses will the firm cover each year?

☐ Who will supervise your work on a daily basis?

☐ Is there anyone within the firm who will act as a mentor?

☐ What type of schedule does the firm have for periodic meetings between senior counsel and the associate to discuss cases and/or trial strategy?

g. Compensation Issues:

☐ What will your billing rate be?

☐ When your rate increases, will you benefit from the increased revenue?

☐ How are hourly matters vs. contingent fee cases handled?

(Some contingency fee firms have a monthly bonus system in place, depending on intake)

☐ How are fees generated by your clients to be distributed? (Which percentage to you, which percentage to the employer?)

☐ What portion of the fees generated on work you originate and service you provide do you receive?

☐ What portion of the fees generated on work you generate, with service provided by someone else, do you receive?

Sample formulas: after expenses—

- Profit would be split 35% to the person originating the business and 65% to those doing the work on the matter, divided pro rata by hours spent; or

- 15% to the person originating the business and 85% to the person doing the work

Another option: you receive a percentage of gross production over some minimum threshold amount.

☐ If fees are discounted for any reason, there should be equitable distribution of the discount, so neither employer nor employee is affected disproportionately. Adjustments should be allocated based on relative time value among all timekeepers on the matter.

☐ If you are <u>not</u> salaried ... be sure to obtain a <u>written agreement</u> on the compensation formula and other conditions of employment. (The ABA has model agreements available.)

☐ How will the firm define "your clients." How do referrals work?

- If the client is referred to the firm in general, what percentage do you receive, in general?

- If the client is referred directly to you, do you get a larger percentage of the profit?

☐ Define expenses.

- How are expenses allocated to your percentage of the profits?

- Who bears the costs up front?

h. Benefits:

☐ Vacation:

- How much do you get, and when are you eligible (that is, how long do you have to work before you can take vacation days)?

- How much vacation time do attorneys at the firm <u>actually</u> take?

☐ How many sick days are you entitled to?

☐ Insurance issues: Who pays?

- Health (medical, dental, vision)
    - If you have health insurance through a spouse/partner but the firm provides it for attorneys, can you receive the pay instead?

- Disability

- Life

- Malpractice

☐ 401(k) plan/profit sharing plan participation:

- How much can you contribute?

- What is the employer's contribution?

- On what date do you become eligible?
- Who is responsible for administering either the profit sharing plan or the 401(k)?
- When are statements sent to each participant?
- What is the vesting schedule for any profit sharing and/or employer contribution to the 401(k)?
- Who is responsible for the investments of the monies in either the 401(k) or profit sharing?

☐ What is the maternity/paternity leave policy?

☐ Who pays Bar dues/Associations fees?

☐ Who pays fees for conferences?

☐ What other perks are available, such as:

- Lap top computer (or loan to purchase one)
- Cell phone/Blackberry
- Business development expense account
- Car allowance

i. Bonuses:

☐ <u>Always</u> get this in writing, along with the compensation plan.

☐ How are bonuses determined?

☐ Who determines bonuses?

☐ When is the bonus distributed?

j. If you are moving to a different city to work ...

☐ Is there a moving or relocation reimbursement?

k. Bar Examination:

☐ Will you be reimbursed for bar exam expenses?

- bar review course
- cost of examination
- cost of MPRE if not previously taken

☐ How much time off will be allowed for studying prior to the bar exam?

☐ Will you lose your job if you fail the bar on the first attempt?

- If you retake the bar, how much time off will you be given for studying?
- Will the firm pay for fees for a second bar exam?

☐ Will the firm pay for fees to waive into another jurisdiction?

☐ Will the firm pay for an announcement of your joining the firm?

- Announcement in legal publication(s)

- Mailing of announcement

l. Office Administration:

☐ Are resources like computer, facsimile, support staff, postage, telephone, copies, stationary, and business cards available to you and paid for by the firm?

☐ If there is a secretary for your use, will you have to share him/her with other attorneys, and if so, how many other attorneys?

☐ Support services:

- Ask for a breakdown of who will be responsible for support services, like billing, filing, and general administrative work.

☐ Maintenance of library and resources:

- Is there a budget for the purchase of additional resources you may need?

☐ Do you have access to productivity reports (if they are generated)?

☐ Do you have access to client bills (for those clients for whom you have worked) and the receivables (for that client). This may not be an issue when employed on a salary-only basis, but would become relevant if your compensation is based on a percentage of receivables.

m. Future Plans:

☐ Set out long range goals.

- How often will you revisit the compensation/benefit structure?

- If you have been assured you can "flesh out" a new practice area, what kind of support will you receive for this?

☐ Distribution of income

☐ Will your salary decrease as you generate cases and fees and will you receive a portion of receivables instead?

☐ Partnership time table—when and under what circumstances can you expect to be invited into the partnership?

- Will the firm name be changed to include yours?

n. Overall:

☐ Research the firm and for whom you will be working.

- Be sure you are comfortable with the people and the atmosphere of the firm.

- Discuss the firm with previous law clerks, previous associates, and/or your Career Services Office and other contacts in the legal community.

In this chapter: Special shout-outs to Santa Clara University, NALP, The Catholic University of America, Albany Law School.

Chapter 19
Going Solo From the Start

Other resources: Jay Foonberg's excellent classic book, "How to Start and Build a Law Practice."

If you think about it, it's a bit out-of-place to have a chapter about solo practice in a job search book. Why? Because it's not a search. You don't have to send yourself a resume and cover letter. You don't have to interview yourself. You want the job, you got it. As Suffolk's Mary Karen Rogers points out, "Listen, law is one of those professions when you get out, you pass the bar, you always have that option. You can always go into business for yourself." Of course, you need the right personality— we'll discuss that in Topic A—but let's face it: the best way to ensure you'll get along with your boss is to be one. While being self-employed has its own built-in stresses, it certainly has one benefit: Nobody can fire you.

What we'll do in this brief chapter is to figure out if it's the right choice for you, and a few tips on getting started.

A. SOLO PRACTICE: IS IT RIGHT FOR YOU?

I talked with a lot of Career Services counselors, and asked the question: Who thrives in solo practice? As California Western's Lou Helmuth points out, "It's not a great 'default' option. There are people who say, 'I couldn't find another job, so I opened up my own practice.' When that's the case, you're talking about a lack of research (both in terms of understanding yourself and the job opportunities), you weren't sufficiently creative about pursuing options, you didn't prepare well enough for interviews and meetings, you didn't follow through effectively"—in other words, you slipped up on the skills we've learned throughout this book. Don't ever think opening your own business is the easy way out! Lou Helmuth says, "For the right kind of person it's a *great* option."

The kinds of elements that I heard over and over again describing the perfect solo practitioner were:

- You don't need monetary security.

    If you need a steady paycheck from Day One, solo practice shouldn't be your immediate goal. Especially in the beginning, your pay will be uneven; Duquesne's Ella Kwisnek says, "At first, money will be more 'out' than 'in.'" As Lou Helmuth points out, "You need a financial cushion when you start out, to cover your loans and daily living expenses, as well as the fairy nominal expenses of a new solo office, until current receivables will pay in sufficient proportion to cover those expenses. That could well be a year or more."

    In Topic C, below, we talk about ways to break into solo practice without hanging out your own shingle. But the fact remains: When you're writing your own paycheck, it can vary.

- You've always preferred running your own gigs.

    If you've preferred to run your own businesses, you've clearly got the entrepreneurial spirit a solo practitioner requires. Sari Zimmerman puts it another way: your core motivator has to be autonomy and independence. If that's what drives you more than anything else, more than security, stability, prestige or any other motivator—you're likely to be happy. As Dave James points out, "There are some people who know they have to work for wages. Others want to work for themselves and be their own bosses, and they don't want to be at someone else's beck and call." Maybe you sealed driveways or made doll clothes or ran your own landscaping gig, while other people got jobs in retail stores and restaurants. If you're comfortable as the boss, that's an indicator you'd enjoy solo practice.

- You feel comfortable selling and marketing.

    As your own boss, you'll spend a substantial amount of time attracting business. While this doesn't mean hard selling, it does require that you be visible in the community. In Chapter 18 on Small Firms, we discussed rainmaking.

- You have outstanding people skills.

    In every aspect of solo practice—from attracting business to handling court personnel and other lawyers to developing mentors to counseling clients—your people skills need to be stellar.

You need to have a high threshold of pain when it comes to rejection.

As Wendy Werner points out, "When you reach out to people to form alliances, you'll face rejection. A lot of it. You have to be able to tolerate it to succeed in solo practice."

- You have to feel comfortable as your own collection agency.

    Wendy Werner advises that "As a solo practitioner you've got to be dogged about collecting on your bills. Of course, it helps to have clear agreements up front. The ABA has sample forms you can use. But the fact remains, you need to collect money from people."

● You are absolutely driven.

As Ella Kwisnek points out, "If you go into practice for yourself, it'll be your life. It's not just doing the work. You're running a business, managing a staff."

● You are self-motivating.

If you need a lot of ego-stroking, solo practice won't give it to you. You have to be your own motivator.

● You have a built in potential client pool because of something else you've done/someone in your life.

If your father is a real estate developer or your spouse is a doctor or you're married to an immigrant with lots of friends with visa problems or you're a second career person who's been a community leader for years, it certainly "jump starts" your solo practice to have clients in the wings. It's not necessary, but it's helpful.

Self-assessment quiz: is solo practice right for you?

A number of counselors I talked to recommended that if you're considering solo practice, you should take self-assessment tests to determine if it's the right fit for you. Based on everything they told me, I thought I would save you some time with a one question self-assessment quiz to determine if you're suited to solo practice.

Question One.

Do you have brass nuts?

a) Yes

b) No

Scoring:

Give yourself one point for every "a)" answer you chose.

Analysis:

If you scored 1: Go solo.

If you scored 0: Don't go solo.

Facetious, yes. But you see the point: If you're going to go solo, you've got to have *tons* of confidence, both in approaching people and in earning their trust and respect.

B.   What You Can Do While You're Still in School to "Pave the Way" to Solo Practice

1.   Develop Practical Skills

Understanding the ins and outs of courts, drafting motions, pleadings and briefs...these are the kinds of skills to get under your belt while you're still in school.

Consider:

- Clinical programs at school;

- Volunteering with local pro bono programs;

- Working for a solo practitioner or small firm during the summer and/or part time during the school year;

- Volunteering with a public defender's office;

- If your state allows it, becoming a "certified intern" as a 3L; it'll give you a chance to get to know judges and get familiar with court-appointed work;

- Letting Career Services know that you want to do project work for solo practitioners or small firms; sometimes lawyers and firms will need help because they are only briefly overwhelmed;

- Posting on local bar association web sites your interest in helping with drafting motions and pleadings for lawyers, as well as making it known on listservs serving the local bar.

Another possibility is to do a volunteer judicial clerkship for a trial-level state court judge locally. You'll get to know everybody at the courthouse—a huge plus—and you'll see from an insider's point of view what works and what doesn't work, both in terms of pleadings, arguments and styles.

2.   LEARN ABOUT BUSINESS

If your law school offers a course on law practice management—some do—take it. Bar associations also offer seminars on opening our own firm; make sure you seek them out and attend. Dave James encourages you to "Learn all you can about the business side."

3.   GET TO KNOW USEFUL PEOPLE

If you start a solo practice directly out of school, you'll need to have useful people "in place." Get to know them while you're still in school. Two main categories include mentors and court personnel.

To find mentors, get involved in the local bar association, specifically the solo practice section. Volunteer on projects and make yourself useful. Let people know that you plan to go into solo practice when you get out. Through your activities, lawyers will take an interest in you and you'll develop mentor relationships.

Getting to know court personnel is also useful. Especially if you're going to get on court lists for court-appointed counsel, you need to be known to judges. As Ella Kwisnek points out, "You want judges to know who you are so that they'll think of you when assignments become available. It's not enough just to be a name on a list."

* * * SMART HUMAN TRICK * * *

3L, New England law school. He became a certified intern with the public defender's office, with the goal in mind of starting his own practice when he graduated.

Through the internship, he got to know judges at the local courthouse. When he got on court-appointed counsel lists after passing the bar, he was a "known quantity."

C. YOUR FIRST STEPS IN SOLO PRACTICE . . .

For a start, give yourself some breathing room in terms of how long it'll take to make a go of solo practice. Wendy Werner recommends that you "give yourself three years. Make a three year commitment to starting your own practice. That's how long it generally takes."

In the meantime, take advantage of all of the help you can get. Consider:

- "Let everyone in the legal community know that you've opened your shop," advises Lou Helmuth.
- Remember that small potatoes for an experienced lawyer may be a perfect gig for you right now. "Arrange to meet with more experienced lawyers, inquiring if it would be alright with them if you refer cases in their area of practice to them, which are 'too much for you to handle' when you're starting out," suggests Lou Helmuth. Surely they'll say yes. Whether that ever happens is unknown! But in exchange, they might be willing to refer you some smaller cases where they can't economically represent the client. You, on the other hand, may well be able to take the case, provide excellent representation, and though you don't get your full hourly rate you might still make several hundred or a thousand dollars. Not bad for your first case, eh?
- Seattle attorney Jonathan Dichter advises that you take advantage of search engines to get clients. "Make sure that if a potential client does a basic search, your name comes up first. Any web advertising company can help you. For instance, if I wanted to represent DUI clients in Everett County, I'd want any web search for 'Everett DUI attorney' to turn up my name first."
- Along the same lines, make sure you have a killer website. For guidance, search the web sites of other solo practitioners to get inspiration for yours.
- Get on court lists for assignments. Ella Kwisnek suggests you also be sure to "network to get assignments. You'll have the benefit of getting an hourly rate paid by the court, so you'll assure yourself of some income."
- Find a mentor through the solo practice section of the local bar association. There's a steep learning curve when you start, and having someone to call with simple questions can be an enormous benefit.

- Check and see whether a university or municipality nearby has a "small business development center" to help you develop a business plan. These centers are typically non-profit.

- Talk with LEXIS/NEXIS and Westlaw about discounts. On top of that, discuss with law librarians about which services are free, and which are the best.

- Be a frequent visitor to the local bar association's list serv. Most bar associations have them, and you'll get a lot of great general advice there.

- Google professional conferences for solo practitioners, and go! Many states have solo practice conferences that are exceptionally useful, both for the information offered and the contacts you'll make.

D. GETTING YOUR OWN PRACTICE WITHOUT HAVING TO START YOUR OWN PRACTICE

Renting office space and hanging out your own shingle isn't the only way to start your practice. You can ease your way in via a number of methods, including:

1. Consider joining an office suite of solo practitioners who each have a different focus.

Dave James suggest that you "Consider finding a group of lawyers who help one another. There might be one person in the suite who focuses on criminal law, one on immigration, one does wills and trusts, and someone else does corporations. It's very common. It's a tried and true way to open your own business." Talk with people in the local bar association's small practice section for leads.

Dave James recommends that you "Get your solo practice a jump-start financially by taking overflow work from the other attorneys. For instance you can make court appearances for the criminal lawyer, take on work from the immigration lawyer. If you've got somebody who can toss you work when they're overloaded, you'll be able to keep the lights turned on while you ramp up your own practice."

2. Get into an office sharing arrangement.

Ella Kwisnek recommends that you look for another lawyer with whom to share an office. This way, you both cut your overheads while you get your business going. Find a potential office-share partner by talking to people in the small practice section of the local bar, and/or posting a notice on the local bar association's web site or list serv.

One attorney who did this told about her experience: "I talked with people in the local bar association, and looked for people who were getting older, working a little less. I found a mentor and did an office share, taking overflow from him and doing public defense conflict work. When he got a case he didn't like, he'd say to the client, 'I don't have the time or the ability, talk to...' and he'd refer them to me. It worked out great."

3. **Find an attorney who is retiring and take over his/her practice.**

As Ella Kwisnek points out, "Attorneys sometimes advertise that they're retiring."

Even if they don't, there are at least three ways to find a retiring attorney.

One, go to local bar association meetings, make a point of introducing yourself to people, and tell everyone whose ear you can bend exactly what it is that you want.

Along the same lines, if you want to do litigation, go to the local courthouse whenever you can. Introduce yourself to the court clerk, bailiffs, judges, and tell them what you're looking for. After all, they'll know every trial attorney, and will certainly be able to identify the ones who are golf course bound. On top of that, they'll be a great resource for weeding out the good eggs from the bad ones, since they've seen local lawyers operate first hand!

A third, and less direct method, is to go to your Career Services Office at school and tell counselors your goal. Most law students don't appreciate what a gold mine their Career Services Office really are; they do so much more than organize on-campus interviews.

Another possibility is to look up solo practitioners in the Yellow Pages, either the actual book or on-line. When you find them, look them up in Martindale—Hubbell (on-line at www. martindale.com). Look at their graduation dates, and when you find ones that are thirty years ago, you've got a potential target audience for letters.

Yet another possibility is to get on-line, go to a chat room or enroll in a LISTSERV for the local bar association. Wait for an opportune moment, and pitch your services to members who suggest they're approaching retirement.

You may also consider a reverse job ad, in law-related publications, stating that you're looking for a practice. Emphasize your willingness and desire to work hard.

The bottom line is this: there are a bunch of ways to take over the practice of a retiring attorney...and it's simpler than hanging out your own shingle!

4. Consider working for a very small firm to start out.

Ella Kwisnek suggests that "working for a small firm gives you a chance to get your feet wet, to get the seasoning you need to build confidence." As we talk about in Chapter 18, the benefit of working for a small firm is that you get a lot of hands-on responsibility right away. You'll learn your way around the court-house and the legal community on someone else's dime, and you'll see close-up how to run a legal business. If you're jonesing for your own gig but it doesn't have to be "right now," a bit of experience with a small firm makes a lot of sense.

E. EXCELLENT WEB RESOURCES

I've mentioned elsewhere in this section the value of LISTSERVS on local bar association websites. While we cover web resources extensively in Chapter 11, here are two that are particular relevant to solo practice:

www.Myshingle.com—just first rate. You could learn everything you need to know with this site alone. Available to everybody.

www.abanet.org/genpractice/lawstudents/index.html—an outstanding website with newsletters, tons of resources. Open to both practitioners and students.

Chapter 20
Coming to America: Job Search Advice for International LL.M.s

I've met a lot of international LL.M.s at law schools around the country. They've inevitably got fascinating backgrounds ... and a real challenge finding jobs in this country.

In this chapter, I'll give you a bunch of ideas for your American job search. Whether you want to stay for a year or the rest of your life, I think you'll find the advice here will get you off on the right foot.

What we'll do here is to discuss the basic elements of your job search, including:

- The obstacles between you and a great job in the U.S.;
- Likely targets;
- The best way to find employers the employers you want (and who'll want you back);
- Cover letter, resume and interview advice.

Let's get started! Vamanos! Andiamo!

A. WHAT'S STANDING BETWEEN YOU AND A GREAT JOB IN THE U.S.?

There's no question that your job search is going to be different than it is for a run-of-the-mill American J.D. Let's talk about what you need to know.

1. According to Harvard's April Stockfleet, "The first thing you need to know is that as an international LL.M., you're a luxury

item to employers. If the economy is great, law firms can afford a Porsche. You're a Porsche. If they can barely handle the J.D.s they have, they'll take the bus. While LL.M.s are seen as a necessity in some industries, that's not universally true." It's crucial that you take a hard look at your skills and credentials so you can tell employers exactly what you can do for them, be it expertise in a body of law that's useful to them or their clients, or that they have a client base with dealings in your country and they need your familiarity with handling those.

2. It may be difficult, and it may *stink*, but you've got to realize that you're starting fresh in the United States. No matter what you accomplished back home–and I've spoken with some *phenomenally* successful International LL.M.s–the slate is wiped clean here in America. This has a number of ramifications that are difficult to accept:

   a. You'll get rejections that are inexplicable with your credentials.

   It may be painfully obvious to you that with everything you've done, you'd be valuable to American employers. Don't expect them to see that right away. It's like the Dan Ackroyd/Eddie Murphy movie *Trading Places*. Dan Ackroyd is an executive down on his luck, and he tries to pawn a very expensive watch. The pawnbroker offers him $50, and he says, "$50? This is a Roche Foucauld. It can tell the time simultaneously in London, Paris, Rome and Gstaad." The pawnbroker responds, "In Philadelphia, it's fifty bucks." When you look in the mirror, *you* see an experienced lawyer. *American employers* see a law student. Of course, there are a bunch of ways to convince American employers of your value, and we talk about how to accomplish that in the remainder of this chapter. But you can't expect them to take a quick glance at your resume and *get it*.

   Also, you *can't* let rejection affect your behavior. I devoted a whole chapter to dealing with rejection, Chapter 5, because it's such an important topic. As one career counselor points out, "You can't let your resentment show. You'll make enemies."

   b. You'll have a whale of a time explaining what you've done.

   You may already have noticed that Americans are—ahem—somewhat ethnocentric. They don't know barristers from solicitors. As Hastings' Sari Zimmerman advises, "Your role is essentially that of a translator. You've got to translate the significance of your experience to legal employers." You've got to be patient in explaining what you've done, and do so *with humility*. Use words like, "I was fortunate enough to ..." "I was lucky to ..." Let your accomplishments speak for themselves. The tone you want to strike is confident ... yet humble.

    c.   If you betray frustration with Americans and with your job search, that fact *alone* will stop you from getting a job.

It's impossible to overstate the following fact: People want to work with people they like. If you're angry, if you're belittling, if you're just venting your frustration, *you will alienate employers unnecessarily.* Remember: it's nobody's fault if a great job doesn't fall into your lap. It doesn't do that for most American students, either. You don't know when the next person you talk to will be the key that opens the door to a great job for you. You want to make sure you have your "game face" on; the friendliest, most enthusiastic you.

This was brought painfully home to me in an exchange with an International LL.M. at a law school down South. After I give my *Guerrilla Tactics* seminar at law schools, students often line up to talk to me individually. That's my favourite part of the seminar. At this particular school, the last two people in line were a very shy young woman and a *very* impatient looking man. It was everything the young woman could do to choke out her question for me; her voice was very slow and hesitating. The man, standing just behind her, kept making that "huffing" noise with his nose, tapping his foot, rolling his eyes, and betraying in every way how fed up he was with having to wait.

When she was halfway through her question, he cut in and said—and I'm quoting him *exactly*—"Will you hurry it up so people with important questions have a chance to talk?"

Can you *imagine?* I thought this young woman was going to melt onto the floor with embarrassment. I signaled for him to step down, and took her a few feet away so she could finish her question. When I'd spoken to her, I went back to the man and before I had a chance to say anything, he thrust his laptop at me and said, "Look at this. I'm a lawyer from X. I'm here for my LL.M. I speak five languages. My resume is far superior to any of these law students. But I am not getting a job. What's the matter with these employers?"

Well, I don't know what the matter was with those employers, but it's pretty obvious what was up with *him*. This guy couldn't see the value of personality. It trumps anything that appears on your resume! The fact is, if employers meet you and like you and want to work with you, they'll convince themselves that you can do their work. Let them see the *best* of you so that can happen!

3.   The whole visa thing. We're not going to get into the vagaries of visas here—the rules change periodically, and the deadlines are complicated—but it does add a level of difficulty in nailing a job in the U.S. You've likely only got a year after graduation to work

in the U.S. unless you can convince an employer to apply for an H1–B visa to keep you longer (which does happen).

On top of that, if you want to stay permanently, there are only a few states where you can sit for the bar exam (states differ; check with your target state's board of bar examiners web site to see their requirements).

Here's the impact the visa issue has on your job search. Large law firms, which have experience with international LL.M.s, will not consider it a big deal. The paperwork and the money are fairly routine for them. *Small* law firms, on the other hand, may have issues with it. The way to deal with it is this: Don't bring it up at all with large firms with a history of hiring international LL.M.s. For other employers, when you've had an interview and it seems like they'll likely make you an offer, offer to take the burden yourself, saying something like, "I'll deal with an immigration lawyer and pay any associated fees with getting an H1–B visa."

The key with this approach is not to sound desperate, but rather practical about the added burden on an employer of obtaining a visa.

Incidentally, it's up to you to know your visa status! Rely on your law school's international office for help in ascertaining it. The recruiting coordinator at one large law firm commented, "It's amazing how many times we'll have foreign LL.M.s say casually, 'Oh, my visa permit expired.' It's a *huge* deal. Take personal responsibility for it!"

4. The whole language thing. As one career counselor points out, "Your biggest test is this: Can you speak English?" Another adds, "If your English isn't good, you're going to have a *very* tough time getting a job here. Do whatever you have to do to improve your conversational skills. Don't hang around exclusively with classmates from your country. Get out and take advantage of every opportunity to speak English."

5. Set your expectations so that your experience in America meets or exceeds them. If you're looking for an education on the legal market in America, to enhance your English, to learn the U.S. legal system, you're going to be very happy. If you figure large law firms are just waiting to hear from you and shower you with cash . . . you're going to face some tough sledding. If you definitely want to stay here forever, it's going to be considerably easier for you to do that with a J.D. than an LL.M. Apart from anything else, a J.D. allows you to take the bar exam in every state. So maybe consider staying for a J.D. (your law school *may* allow you to convert your LL.M. credits to their J.D. program). You may be thinking, "Oh, no, not another *three years!*" But if you want to stay here for the rest of your life, it's worth it.

6. Law firms aren't charities. They aren't interested in giving you a three-month vacation so you can go home and get a promotion. You *have* to focus on *what's in it for them*. Think about how the considerable assets you bring to the table will benefit the employer, and articulate that. You don't have to do this by yourself, by the way. If need be, ask at Career Services for some alums you can talk to for "informational interviews"—that is, interviews with the goal of obtaining information, not a job—and tell them about your background and ask how you can frame it for employers. As one career counselor points out, "Think about how an employer can make money on you!"

7. Be aware of what your school's Career Services Office can (and will) do for you. It's possible you never dealt with a CSO back home, so it's important to know what you can ask for and expect. View them as your sherpa; as one career counselor puts it, "We'll help you climb the mountain, but you have to climb it yourself." You can expect to learn about alums that might be helpful to you, conferences, seminars and activities in which to take part, resume reviews, mock interviews, and all kinds of counseling. They won't write your resume for you, however, and it's not their job to set up a slate of interviews for you. They'll make your resume available to employers who come on campus to interview (and are interested in talking to LL.M.s), but that's an entirely different animal than setting up interview for you! Of course, as is true in every aspect of life, if you're pleasant to people in the CSO, they'll be more helpful to you than if you treat them badly. It's human nature. Be respectful and grateful and you'll get great and invaluable advice.

8. Remember that it's a small world. If you haven't told your employer back home that you're looking for a job in the U.S., they might hear about it through potential employers you contact here. As one counselor points out, "You might get a phone call from your home employer saying, 'Hey! You're looking for a *job?*'" Be sure that you have your ducks in a row before you contact employers here. Break it to them gently, if need be, saying something about how your working in the U.S. for a year (or the length of your visa) will be useful to them.

B. TARGETING EMPLOYERS WHO ARE MOST LIKELY TO HIRE INTERNATIONAL LL.M.s

New York City isn't called the center of the Universe for nothing. It's the most likely target for LL.M.'s because it's home to the big firms who can most use international skills. Of course, it's not the *only* place, but it's a prime target.

To find specific employers anywhere in the U.S. who hire international LL.M.s, check with your Career Services Office for alums of the program to see where they've gone; contact them and ask them about their employer and other firms with which they're familiar. In addition, you can do a Google search on-line, with a search that reads: "formerly foreign associate & [firm name]." You'll see how long LL.M.s stayed with the firm, whether it was short term or long term, and what they did afterwards.

You might also consider going in-house with corporations, whether in New York or anywhere else. Large companies with business interests and offices abroad are good targets. Utilize a book at Career Services called "The Directory of Corporate Counsel," or use Martindale–Hubbell on-line (www.martindale.com). If you look up large companies, you'll see that their general counsel's office will include people from different countries. If you see people from your country, contact them.

There's also the possibility of "alternative careers"; that is, non-lawyer jobs. Management consulting and investment banking—both very lucrative careers, by the way—come to mind, and they are areas that LL.M.s have successfully targeted before. To learn more about them, check at Career Services for books focusing on them.

C. THE BEST WAY TO FIND THE EMPLOYERS YOU WANT (AND WHO'LL WANT YOU BACK)

1. As we discussed in Chapter 10, the key to nailing great jobs is people and activities; that is, the people you get to know and the activities in which you take part. Go back and look at Chapter 10 for ideas on what to say to people and activities to target.

2. Keep up with the legal press, read newspapers on-line, and visit web sites of law firms and companies you're interested in. See if they're growing in areas related to your expertise and home country. For instance, as one California law firm administrator points out, "We're desperate for patent people. We'd take foreign LL.M.s with a technical background in a heartbeat."

3. Take advantage your unique knowledge of the legal system and legal issues at home! No matter where you're from, there are American lawyers who need to know what you know. This can pave the way to an American job. There are two routes to consider:

    a. Write articles for bar publications about legal issues involving your country.

    As we discussed in Chapter 10, law-related publications like bar association magazines and newsletters always need content. Take advantage of that fact by writing about what you know. Tips for lawyers doing business deals involving your country, advice for handling claims or clients with issues there ... you've got a wealth of knowledge to share. Write articles and offer them for publication. You'll get publications on your resume—that's a plus—but more importantly, with your name in the byline, you'll get exposure to attorneys who are interested in what you know. You can even send copies of the article(s) you write to attorneys you'd like to work for, stating simply that you thought they might be interested in what you had to say. You can go on and express an interest in what they do and ask them for advice about breaking into it. It's a great, non-aggressive way to find potential employers.

b. Make presentations at the local bar association (or the city bar association for your target city) about legal issues involving your country.

If your English is good and public speaking doesn't freak you out, this is a great way to get exposure to potential employers. You need to know that bar associations have speakers at meetings all the time. Taking the ideas we discussed for writing articles just now, consider offering to make a presentation at a breakfast or lunch meeting. It doesn't matter that you're a student! Talk to the head of the international section of the local bar (or any other section your expertise applies to). You'll find if you make presentations like this, attorneys will come to *you* with their business cards.

When it comes to reaching out to people on-line, you've got advantages that American students don't have, in that you have a built-in commonality with American lawyers from your country. No matter *where* you're from, you're not the first to come here! This is what you do:

a. Go to Lexis/Nexis or Westlaw or Martindale–Hubbell (at www.martindale.com) and look for:

1. Your law school back home (or other law schools in your country);

2. Languages spoken; As SUNY Buffalo's Lisa Patterson points out, "a lawyer who speaks your native language is a potential contact";

3. In Nexis, type in your home country and "partner." As April Stockfleet points out, "Every time your country comes up in the context of a business deal involving a law firm partner, you'll find that story. Look for the names of the lawyers involved."

b. If you read an article in a law-related publication about a field you want to get into, e-mail the attorney who wrote it, compliment them, and tell them you'd appreciate their career advice.

* * * SMART HUMAN TRICK * * *

International LL.M. from China. She reads American newspapers every day, scouring them for stories involving business deals impacting China. She reads about how IBM is selling its ThinkPad division to a Chinese company, LeNovo. She contacts everyone associated with the deal; the lawyers, the in-house counsel's offices, the financial services advisors, everyone.

She winds up with a job.

c. Contact the joint Chamber of Commerce for your country and the U.S. Most countries have a joint chamber of commerce like this; the British–American Chamber of Commerce, French, German, you name it. I've talked to International LL.M.s who've made great contacts through these organizations. (You'll find them on-line; they're mostly located in Washington, D.C.)

d. Look at specific practice areas in firms (or lawyers who represent clients from your home country), or lawyers who have clients with business dealings there. Golden Gate's Susanne Aronowitz says, "Target lawyers whose client base is such that your background and cultural base is a benefit to them." In those situations, contact the lawyers directly; they'll be most attuned to how you'd be valuable to the firm (although you can "cc" the recruiting coordinator as a courtesy). In these letters you can ask for a job, by the way, and not simply advice, which is what you solicit from most people you contact, as we discuss next . . .

e. When you've found your 'targets,' send an e-mail asking for advice. Say something like, "I'm new to America, I'm starting an LL.M. degree at X school. I'm trying to break into the American legal market, and I'm wondering if you can spare a few minutes to share some advice over the phone." Tell them that you want *advice* from them, not a job (advice leads to jobs, but it doesn't put people on the spot). You can say something like, "I know you're from Fredonia as well. You must have faced some of the same hurdles as me," or "I know you deal with cases/clients with a Fredonian connection. I would truly appreciate any advice you can give me, any activities I can take part in that will help me find a job here." Attach your resume to the e-mail *but say that you're doing so for background, so that they know something about you when they talk to you.* As one career counselor points out, "It will show where you've worked, what you've done, so that they know you're serious and that you're worth talking to. If you don't send a resume, the lawyer is likely to say to him/herself, 'What the . . . I don't have time to ask for a resume.'"

In addition, send a copy of your U.S. transcript if you have one yet.

You might also consider leaving a voice-mail message off-hours (or ask the attorney's assistant for their voice mail). Leave a message both in your native language and partially in English, asking for advice as we discussed above.

I realize that depending on where you're from, it might be horrifyingly forward to contact people like this. In America, it's absolutely acceptable—and you *need* to do it if you want to exploit your options here!

f. Realize that no matter how helpful people can be, your job search is your own.

Be sure not to pin all of your job aspirations on one single lawyer. As one international lawyer in New York commented, "I had one LL.M. student who made me feel like I was his sole lifeline in America. I wanted to help, but I just didn't want that much responsibility."

Cast your net widely. Ask as many people as you can for advice. And when people help you, be sure to thank them profusely and keep them apprised of how your search is going. When they have more advice for you, they'll offer it.

g. If you don't hear back from people you e-mail . . .

As one career counselor points out, "You want to be persistent *but not* a pest. You *have* to stop before they take out a restraining order on you!"

Persistence applies to your job search in general, *not* to any single person. With anyone you contact, follow the "three strikes" rule. That is, contact them three times, and if you don't hear back, write them off. Don't assume that they're trying to insult you. They might be busy, they might be in the middle of a personal crisis, or they might not have any good ideas for you. Think about your own life; there are times when you'd be open to helping other people, and times when you wouldn't. It doesn't mean you'll never meet this person or get any advice from him/her. You'll get great advice from tons and tons of people; if this particular person didn't work out at this one moment in time, so be it.

5. Sign up for lots of bar association activities and conferences. While J.D.'s should do this—and I *strongly* encourage it in Chapter 10—they often don't, and that makes these events a great opportunity for you. As one career counselor points out, "When you go, hang out with the 'old' people, not your friends." The more senior attorneys will be a great source of advice. Ask them for it! (Incidentally, while some of these events can be expensive, ask for the law student rate; it's typically nominal.)

6. If you want to work in New York City or any other city where you don't go to school, make a point of getting there *in person*.

Follow the advice in Chapter 17, on out-of-town job searches. Specifically, find people in your target city ahead of time—either through Career Services at school or via the internet—who are from your country or otherwise connected to it.

If you contact people and you don't hear back, it's no big deal. Contact them once more when you get to the city, and blame your e-mail system at school. "My e-mail may not have gotten through to you ..." If you don't hear then, write them off. "You can't badger people to death," as one career counselor puts it.

7.   Go to LL.M. job fairs.

Your law school probably participates in one in New York City every January, and there are others as well (ask at your CSO for those available to you). For advice on handling job fairs, see Chapter 10.

8.   At social events on campus and elsewhere ...

You'll have opportunities to go to receptions for attorneys and alumni, seminars, conferences, and all kinds of events where you'll rub elbows not just with lawyers but also J.D.s. You should take advantage of these events, but you need to know how to utilize them for maximum effect.

   a.   Check out the advice on handling social events in Chapter 10. What applies to American students applies to you, as well.

   b.   Have an opening line ready. Don't say, "I'm an LL.M." As a career counselor points out, "Your LL.M. is not your most attractive asset. Don't wear it on your forehead." Instead, say, "I'm studying at X Law School," or "I'm studying corporate law and I'm enjoying it."

   c.   Remember that most Americans have little experience with foreigners. Don't be condescending when Americans you meet are ignorant about your country. As one career counselor points out, "We live in a self-centered country that's self-sufficient." You can't be shocked if you meet Americans who've never left the country (remind yourself that all of Europe would fit in the United States *east of the Mississippi River!)* Avoid making comments like, "I can't believe you've never been to ..." *"You* only speak *English?"* Don't be offended if Americans don't know where your country is, or confuse it with another country. As one career counselor laughs, "Don't be surprised if you meet people who think Sweden and Switzerland are the same place."

      Instead of being resentful, be generous and magnanimous when Americans ask dumb questions about your country. If you're from Australia, they *will* ask you if you have a pet kangaroo. If you're from England, they'll ask if you've met the Queen. Have a funny answer ready to go. "Yes, we did have a pet kangaroo, until we ate him." Remember that people in your country have funny ideas about Americans, too!

d. April Stockfleet advises that "You want to be assertive but not aggressive in situations where you can meet attorneys." Don't elbow J.D.'s out of the way to talk to important people! As a law school career counselor adds, "Attorneys are looking to see if you'll play nicely at work. Even if they *do* hire you, they'll have more J.D.s than LL.M.s. If they think you can't get along without throwing your weight around, they won't take a chance on you." Adds another counselor, "They *want* J.D.s. If you chase J.D.s away, you've shot yourself in the foot!"

April Stockfleet offers an outstanding way to combat this problem. "Walk up to an attorney with a couple of shy friends who are J.D.s. Say to the attorney, 'Thanks for coming on campus. We enjoyed hearing your speech. These are my friends Cindy and Rob. I'm Annabella. We'd love to hear more about your practice.'"

e. View fellow students as colleagues, not competitors. As one career counselor points out, "Your classmates can help you if you're nice to them! Hang out with them. Part of the LL.M. experience isn't just to put an extra line on your resume, but to learn about Americans and American culture. You can't do that if you hang out exclusively with students from your country. Get to know Americans."

f. Ask your American classmates outright to tell you if you've done something "culturally weird." As one career counselor advises, "You don't want them pointing it out in front of other people. But your American friends are an excellent source of advice about what's culturally acceptable, and what's not. They won't criticize you if you don't ask for criticism. Tell them, 'If I say something or do something inappropriate, if we're talking one on one, let me know. If we're around other people, let me know afterwards.' The only way to fit in culturally is to have people *tell* you."

g. Remember that "Americans aren't like the 'Americans' you see on TV!" says one career counselor. "Not law students, anyway!" For instance, " 'Girls Gone Wild' is not a documentary." Be friendly, but respectful.

h. You *have* to talk to people; as we discussed in Chapter 10, you have to ask questions of strangers, take an interest in people you've never met. I talked to an international LL.M. at one school who said, "The problem with everything you say is that I'm not interested in other people. I'm not curious. I don't care about them and I don't like them." That's as may be. *You have to talk to them anyway*. In America, that's the way it works. If you're naturally shy, look at Chapter 27 for specific tips. But the fact remains: if you're not interested in people, *pretend* you are! People won't take an interest in you unless you show an interest in them, as well.

D. COVER LETTER, RESUME, WRITING SAMPLE AND INTERVIEW ADVICE

1. Overall: be honest about what you want, and it's got to be more specific than "A job in America." If you chase what you think American employers are after, you'll wind up with jobs you don't want . . . and you may talk your way out of a job you'll really like.

2. According to one career counselor, "Sell to your strengths. If you're from a part of the world where U.S. interests are thriving, you'll be valuable to U.S. employers because of that. If you're Chinese or Indian, there's a big market for your skills simply because of that. It's also true for some European countries, like Germany. *Business* is the key."

3. Cover letters

A cover letter may well be the first contact you have with an employer, so it's crucial to get it right. As a jumping-off point, read the chapter on Correspondence, Chapter 7, which will tell you everything you need to know about constructing great cover letters.

One of the most important elements of cover letter writing is to make sure your letters are personalized; no employer wants to feel they're getting a letter you've sent to a hundred other employers as well! While you'll reuse much of the same material from letter to letter, make sure each letter you send addresses that employer in particular.

In addition, as Susanne Aronowitz puts it, "You can't rely on your credentials to speak for themselves. You have to focus on what you can contribute to an employer."

In the Appendix at the end of this chapter I've included two sample cover letters, courtesy of Emory University. *Don't copy them,* but use them as inspiration for writing your own letters.

4. "Americanizing" a foreign resume.

Resumes for American employers may be very different from the ones you'd use back home. For a complete run-down on writing an "American style" Resume, see Chapter 8. Here, we'll focus on issues unique to converting foreign resumes to ones for the U.S. market:

a. *If possible,* keep your resume to one page. And I mean in normal, twelve-point type; you can't reduce your font size to five points to squash everything in! Instead, it needs to be edited down. If you have trouble boiling it down, remember that your resume isn't an autobiography; it's a starting point for information that will be fleshed out in a job interview. There is some advice in this section about editing your resume, but if you need further help, take your resume to your Career Services Office.

b. Make your resume uniquely your own. Don't copy samples; whether in this book or at Career Services, they're there for inspiration. Review a few before you formulate your own.

c. A question that international LL.M.s ask me a lot has to do with their names; that is, if you've got a name that's difficult for Americans to pronounce, what do you do about it? This is a *very* difficult question, and the answer to it has a lot to do with your feelings about the matter. As one career counselor points out, "In an ideal world, everyone could pronounce your name. But it may be a stumbling block. You have to decide: do you want a job, or do you want to preserve your strong cultural identity?" You may want to consider having an American nickname on your resume, which you put in parenthesis, like this:

Nihau (Nick) Chen

As a career counselor points out, "Nobody is going to freak out if the nickname on your resume doesn't match your passport."

If you do choose a nickname, run it past your American friends first to make sure it doesn't have any connotations that will hurt you. One international LL.M. chose the nickname "Cher," for instance. You don't want it to sound Hollywood, or outdated, or otherwise inappropriate ("Lolita" would be inadvisable.)

A related issue is what to do if your name doesn't disclose your gender. One solution is to take part in activities that are gender-specific, and put them on your resume (e.g., joining the Women's Bar Association). You also can choose a more gender-specific nickname. (I'm familiar with this problem personally; with the first name "Kimm" I've often had people assume in correspondence that I'm a man. So I use my middle name "Alayne" as well, and that generally does the trick.)

d. Items to leave out of your resume:

- No photos.
- No date of birth.
- No statement of your health or marital/family status.
- No LSAT score.
- No statement that you're "single, young and healthy and willing and able to work long hours."
- Leave out your primary/elementary school, high school, additional coursework and training, your seminar, your thesis topic and professor ... unless you get specific advice about a specific job stating that this information is relevant to the employer!

e. Just because Microsoft makes funny bullets doesn't mean you have to use them. Use the kind of bullets you see in this book; namely, plain ones.

f. Only include your visa status if you are a permanent resident or U.S. citizen.

g. Assume that no matter how well known your university or employer is back home, Americans know *nothing* about it. *Nothing*.

h. Make no assumptions about geography. List both city and country for your school(s) and employer(s). For instance, it's Mexico City, *Mexico*.

i. For your undergraduate university, use the academic rankings of world universities that you'll find on-line. A good source is www.chinalawprofblog.com; there are others, as well.

j. Put your "undergraduate" degree in your native language, with its American equivalent (if appropriate) in brackets.

k. Be sure to put down your class rank in law school.

l. Include any courses you've taken in English. If you did a pre-LL.M. course in U.S. Legal English or took an intensive English course, say so!

* * * SMART HUMAN TRICK * * *

LL.M. student from South America. He attended an English boarding school and an American college in his home country. On his resume, he wrote: "Entire schooling in English."

m. Make sure that you "translate" your law degree from back home into its American equivalent, if possible. (For instance, in some countries an LL.M. is the equivalent of an American J.D.)

n. Include information in parentheses to translate your work experiences into something meaningful for an American audience; e.g. "Fredonian Ministry of Business Affairs (equivalent to U.S. Department of Commerce)."

o. Include any honors and awards you've received. Put them under the appropriate heading (corresponding with the applicable school and/or job).

p. You need to describe the work you've done at your prior employers, to the extent it shows what you're capable of doing for employers you're targeting, the "transferable skills" we discussed in Chapter 8. (This will mean descriptions that are much *longer* than they are in Japanese resumes, where there is virtually no description of the work done and the employer's name says it all; and descriptions will be much *shorter* than they are in a "curriculum vitae" from many other countries. It's not enough to say, for instance, "I set up this program."

Instead you have to describe the program, when you set it up, and specifically what you did.)

q. Avoid abbreviations; spell out phrases and names.

r. Don't say your home country firm was "the most prestigious" or "the preeminent ..." Instead, use descriptions that you find on websites like www.legal500.com and www.iflr1000. com, or include rankings in publications (e.g., "#1 firm in Asian Lawyer Magazine.")

s. Include your employers' web addresses. That way, American employers can check them out.

t. If you passed the bar exam back home, *say so* on your resume, and be prepared to produce your bar passage certification. In addition, make a point of stating your country's bar exam pass rate on your resume. In many countries, the bar exam is much tougher than it is in America; Japan, Korea and China all have a miniscule pass rate, for instance. You can find your home country's bar passage rate in a book called "The International Directory of Lawyer Qualifications," published by NALP. You'll find it at your law school's Career Services Office.

u. If your home country law firm was a correspondent firm for a U.S. or international firm, say so. Put in brackets, for instance, [correspondent law firm for Baker & McKenzie].

v. If the name of your law firm back home makes it look like a sole practice, talk with your Career Services Office here in America about wording that makes it plain how prestigious the employer was. (In some countries, firms that are very prestigious have names that would make an American employer think it's a one-person shop.)

w. Be aware that jobs you think of as mediocre back home might be very prestigious in America. For instance, in many countries government work is not esteemed and clerkships are nothing to comment on. In this country, just the opposite is true ... so the good news is that a job that wouldn't have won you kudos at home may well be very impressive to American employers.

x. In terms of choosing which language in which to send your resume:

• As a rule of thumb, if you're sending it to a U.S. firm, just send it in English in the American format.

• If you're sending it to the foreign office of a U.S. firm, you can submit it to the foreign office in that language *and* the U.S. headquarters in English.

y. Include a "hobbies and interests" section. American employers like to see your "third dimension." If you've got something "extra" to show off, this is the place to do it; International

LL.M.'s have been known to be Olympic athletes, chess champions, concert pianists, national polo players, you name it. But you don't have to have been a hero back home! Any interest that makes you—well—*interesting* will do, whether it's an interest in "smelly cheese" or Ancient Greek. (For guidance, see Chapter 8.)

z. If you were a transactional lawyer in your home country, include a "deal sheet" with your resume listing the transactions you handled, including the *value* of those deals (*as long as it's ethical to disclose them in your home country*); If you were a litigator, include a list of cases you took part in. While this will make your resume longer than the standard U.S. "one page" limit, that's all right.

aa. Don't include names of clients or the *specific* nature of a case or deal that would violate attorney-client confidentiality rules. You can always say something like, "patent case involving a multinational corporation" or "high-profile licensing matter." Remember, your judgment as well as your experience is at issue!

5. Writing samples.

You need to know that American employers will probably request a writing sample. We talk about choosing an appropriate one in Chapter 7 on Correspondence. In particular, be sure that if your writing sample was edited by someone else (a professor or journal editor), you include a cover sheet stating that.

6. Interviews.

Read Chapter 9 on Interviews, for complete guidance on preparing for American interviews. Beyond that:

a. Ask your career advisor ahead of time whether your clothes are appropriate for interviewing. A hiring partner at one large firm says, "I often interview LL.M.s whose clothes are just not quite right. A double-breasted suit might be appropriate at home, but not here. Same for three-piece suits on men. And on women, colorful suits and mini-skirts? Absolutely not." As April Stockfleet says, "Don't take your interview suit standards from Hollywood! In the movie *Legally Blonde,* don't dress like Elle Woods. Dress like her serious friend."

It may be a good idea to bring interview suits with you from home. They may be a lot less expensive there. Even if you do have to buy interview wear here, remember that you only need *one* good interview suit—you don't need a wardrobe.

b. Be aware that employers will assess your English speaking ability in an interview. There are a couple of points to note: First, speaking softly does not make your English better. Mumbling doesn't help. If your English isn't perfect, speak confidently and clearly anyway.

Second, as April Stockfleet points out, "Remember that many Americans are not used to speaking with people with foreign accents and are therefore on a 'satellite delay.' So, if you speak with an accent, give them two seconds to understand what you've said. Americans tend to speak more slowly. If you speak more slowly, it will improve your accent and help you get over the 'satellite delay.'"

c. Don't bring up negatives about yourself. An interview is a chance to show off the best possible you. I talked with a Russian LL.M. at one school, who said she was a slower writer than others, but after a little while she could bring herself up to speed. She said she'd brought this up in interviews and she wondered if that was a good idea. I told her, "Don't say it. If you say you're a *little* slower, they'll assume you're *really* slow!" Work hard to make sure your skills are where they need to be, but remember: there's no perfect candidate for any job. Talk about experiences you've had where employers were happy with you, and realize that everybody has skills and qualities that are less than stellar.

d. Follow the interviewer's lead. You'll generally find that the interviewer will spend the first few minutes with pleasantries. Don't get nervous; don't think they're not taking you seriously; and don't try to change the subject! They'll get around to the "meat" of the interview soon enough.

In addition, don't demand a response date. There's a big difference between saying "Can you give me an idea of your time frame for making a decision?" which is perfectly fine, and saying, "When will you call me?" or even worse, "When do I start?"

e. Realize that interviews in America tend to be much more extensive than they are in other countries, *especially* call-back or "second round" interviews. In other countries, it's not unusual to talk to one partner and that's it, you get an offer. In this country, you can't expect a decision to be made at the interview, and it's perfectly acceptable to ask the employer's time frame on making a decision.

F. Body language issues: It's not just what you say that counts. It's how you behave. A few pointers from counselors who've interviewed International LL.M.s frequently:

1. Eye contact: Americans do more of it than most people. Looking down is a sign of respect in other cultures; in America, subservience in an interview is not a positive.

2. Lean in a little bit to show interest, but "Don't sit on their lap," advises one counselor. "Imagine there's a small table between you and that you're leaning on the table."

3. For gosh sakes, smile! As April Stockfleet points out, "In your country, people may assume you're stupid if you smile as much as Americans do, but the fact is, Americans smile. It's not always because they're happy, or friendly, or they just thought of something funny. It's often because they don't know what else to do. It's a default expression. When no other facial expression is appropriate, just smile." This is *so* important. Americans often think that Europeans look harsh because they don't smile in repose.

4. Don't cross your arms. It'll make you look defensive.

g. Be sure to ask your Career Services Office for a "mock interview" after you've read Chapter 9. Tell the mock interviewer that you want criticism on your interviewing style, from cultural differences in mannerisms to answers to questions to questions you ask the interviewer.

* * * CAREER LIMITING MOVE * * *

Female International LL.M., asks of a female interviewer: "Where did you buy that handbag?"

E. CULTURAL ISSUES . . .

You've probably noticed already that American social mores are a *leetle bit different* than the way things work back home. I'm aware of it, since I grew up in England. Even though we speak the same language, things are *very* different in America!

One significant difference comes up every time English relatives visit us here. I remember having a teenage English girl stay with us. She went to the grocery store with me, and looked quizzical as I chatted with the produce guy, the cashier, the grocery bagger. On the way out of the store, she asked me, "How do you know those people?" I told her, "I don't know them." She looked horrified, and said, "But you were *talking* to them!" In England, it's simply not done. You don't talk to people until you're introduced by a mutual acquaintance. My grandparents lived next door to a lady named Chirie Self for *twenty years,* in a semi-detached house, without saying hello because nobody introduced them. *Nobody.* They were so relieved when they finally found a mutual acquaintance to make the introductions, and after that, they became fast friends.

Your culture may have similar differences. On top of the socializing tips in Topic C, above, law school career counselors share the following advice:

1. "One of the common problems I see is that students have heard that 'Americans like a good firm handshake,'" says April Stockfleet. "I've had students almost break my hand. There's an idea that it shows how aggressive and powerful you are. *Please* don't shake hands that way! Practice your handshake with counselors at your Career Services Office on American friends before you go

to interviews or attend social events. It's not a tennis racket or a power struggle, you're not arm wrestling. It's just a 'hello'!"

2. Another career counselor points out that "It's not OK to ask people how much money they make." If you need to know salaries before you apply for a job, look at salary statistics in Career Services or on www.nalpdirectory.com—they'll have them for every type of law firm job in the country—or check web sites like www.salary.com.

3. It's perfectly acceptable to ask people what they do. You can even ask, "So what keeps you busy?" It's an easy jumping-off point for a conversation, and no American is offended by it (whereas in England, asking what people do for a living is a *real* no-no).

4. You have to aim for the golden mean in talking with people who can help you—alums, lawyers who do what you want to do, anyone at all. On the one hand, you have to be willing to ask for advice. Americans are very open to offering advice as a general rule, and you'll miss a lot of great opportunities if you don't ask.

    On the other hand, "You can't attach yourself like a barnacle to a single lawyer," says one career counselor. "Don't make one person your lifeline."

    (For advice on what to say to people who can help you, see Topic C, above.)

Appendix
Sample Cover Letters for International LL.M. Students

Great cover letters can make a huge difference in your job search. That's why we spent a whole chapter, Chapter 6, talking about them!

These sample cover letters will give you ideas about how to word your own letters. *A really serious caveat: do not copy these letters.* I always think twice about including sample letters in my books, conscious of the fact that no matter what I say, students will copy them. Employers find it hilarious to get cover letters from different students worded identically, and trust me, it's not a positive kind of hilarity. So use these excellent letters for inspiration only!

Another caveat: the best letters of all start with seven magic words: "So-and-so recommended that I contact you." Where possible, always open your letters with the name of a mutual contact. The letters here are for situations where you can't find such an intermediary.

Letters adapted from a handout from Emory University School of Law.

Cover Letter #1:

> 1313 Mockingbird Lane
> Anytown, USA 00001
>
> (800) 555–1212
> February 14, 20___

Fred Flintstone, Esq.
Flintstone & Rubble
2 Boulder Drive
Bedrock, Indiana 20222

Dear Mr. Flintstone:

I am a Venezuelan attorney presently attending Emory University School of Law and I will receive a Master of Laws Degree (LL.M.) in May

20___. The LL.M. degree has provided me with the opportunity to study international corporate law in great depth. I am interested in applying to Flintstone & Rubble for an internship following the completion of my studies in May. I am particularly interested in your firm because of its relationship with Escritorio Juridico Tavil y Associados and I believe I would be able to help service your clients with an interest in Venezuela.

I received my degree from the Universidad Catolica Andres Bello where I graduated with honors for the highest grades in several of my classes. My academic course work as well as my position as a foreign associate with the firm Wilmer, Cutler & Pickering in Washington, D.C., have provided me with a substantive background in corporate and commercial law.

Throughout the pursuit of my law degree in Venezuela, I held legal positions which often required as many as thirty hours of work each week. Those positions enabled me to attain, while still in school, the practical experience one ordinarily only receives years after graduation from law school. I look forward to putting that experience to work on your firm's behalf.

I have enclosed a resume and writing sample for your consideration. I would be pleased to speak with you about the needs of your firm during the coming year. I will be in Bedrock from December 23 to January 8 and would appreciate meeting with you during that period. You can reach me at the address and phone number listed above. I look forward to hearing from you.

Sincerely,
Ignacio Molina

Cover Letter Sample #2:

> James Bond
> 1 Aston Martin Square
> Emfive, Ohio 50505
> (216) 555–1212
>
> November 30, 20 ____

Francisco Scaramanga, Esq.
Scaramanga & Goldfinger
3 Avenue of the Americas
New York, NY 20120

Dear Mr. Scaramanga:

I am a Swiss lawyer presently attending Emory University School of Law as a Fulbright Scholar, and expect to receive an LL.M. with a focus in Corporate Law in May 20____. I am interested in applying to Scaramanga & Goldfinger for an internship after my studies this May. My student visa provides up to a year of practical training in the United States, and therefore I am primarily interested in an internship for that period of time, but might also be interested in staying there on a long-term basis. Scaramanga & Goldfinger drew my attention because of the firm's reputation in the area of corporate and international financial transactions.

I received my Law Degree from the 007 School of Law, ranked the #2 private university in Switzerland by *European Business Week Magazine,* where I graduated with honors. My academic course work as well as my professional experience have provided me with a substantive background in corporate and commercial law. As an associate at Drax & Partners, I participated in all aspects of complex commercial litigation matters, and gained substantial experience in dealing with international clients. Recently, I co-authored an article entitled "Personal Liability Issues for Corporate Directors of Multinational Corporations," with a partner from each of Drax's Zurich and Paris offices.

Enclosed please find a copy of my resume and an outline of my transactional experience for your review. I would welcome the opportunity to meet with you to discuss my qualifications and your hiring criteria in greater detail. I look forward to hearing from you soon.

> Very truly yours,
>
> James Bond

Shout-outs for extensive advice in this chapter to April Stockfleet of Harvard and Mary Maher of Northwestern.

Chapter 21
Students of the Night: How Do I Get a Job When I'm Working Full-Time?

Related topics: Second Careers, Chapter 22

If you go to school at night and work during the day . . . gosh. I stand in awe of you. I don't know how you fit everything in. Maybe you don't. And if you jettison anything from your schedule . . . it's usually your job search.

Of course, you can't avoid it entirely. There are issues you have to face. Let's talk about them.

A. DO EMPLOYERS HAVE A PREJUDICE AGAINST EVENING STUDENTS?

In a word: no. As a partner at one very distinguished law firm pointed out, "It makes no difference to us. We go on the basis of academic track record, evening or day."

The fact is, as one Career Services Director points out, "Evening student credentials are often *better* than day student credentials." Career Counselor Wendy Werner adds, "Integrated ranking systems show that evening students are consistently superior."

If you perceive a prejudice against you, it may be that employers have another issue that's not so obvious. Depending on when you start your legal job search, they may perceive that you're not serious about making a switch. If you're currently in a position that pays you better than a starting associate position, they may question whether you'll really trade (temporarily) down. Because you're probably a bit older than the average law student, they may have issues with whether or not you'll take direction from managers younger than you (we address this issue in the Second Career chapter, Chapter 22).

So don't jump to the conclusion that employers have something against you. Do what we discuss in this chapter and throughout this book, and you'll be happily employed as a lawyer before you know it.

B.   "When Do I Make the Jump?" Figuring Out How to Get Legal Experience During Law School—And When

Legal experience while you're in school is really, really important. It's as true for evening students as it is for day students. As one Career Counselor describes it, "It proves your commitment and increases your marketability. You get practical skills." Duquesne's Ella Kwisnek adds, "There's no getting around it: employers like a look-see before they hire people."

What's the issue? As Akron's Jay Levine points out, "It's a trade-off; what enables you to attend law school—your job—precludes you from accruing a lot of work experience." The Esquire Group's Gina Sauer adds, "There's a whole spectrum of options to choose from. You may perfectly justifiably say, 'I can't afford to quit my full-time job with benefits to take a part-time, $10/hour clerking job.' But look at what that clerking job offers you: a chance to prove to a prospective employer that you can write, research and analyze. There are ways to prove that without going cold turkey and quitting your full-time job. Think of it as a spectrum. On one end is continuing with your full-time, non-legal job and keeping your fingers crossed that somehow you'll get an attorney position when you graduate; on the other end is quitting your current job for a clerking job. In between there are a whole lot of ideas that will add substance to your resume, and the closer you can get to the clerking experience, the better off you are." We'll discuss those options below.

No matter how you cut it, though, getting legal experience while you're still in school is paramount. As one career counselor points out, "If you really fancy yourself changing careers, at some point you're going to have to take the plunge *before* you graduate. I tell my evening students, 'Nobody made you go to law school. Don't tell me that you can't get away to get some legal experience, because if you expect to be a lawyer, you're going to have to make a break with the past and commit to this new degree. Whether it's taking four weeks off in the summer and getting some experience somewhere, taking a leave of absence, whatever it is, dedicate some time to your future!'"

Let's talk about your options.

1.   Clerking for a Firm Full-Time While You Attend School at Night. You Can Start Anytime After First Year ... If You Can Stomach the Pay Cut

There's nothing that stops you from seeking a full-time, year-round day job in law while you're still in school. You can start anytime after

First Year. This gives you the benefit of seeing law practice from the inside. You'll get great practical skills. You'll be able to put in perspective what you're learning at night.

On top of that, if you clerk full-time during the school year for one employer, you can try out *other* employers during the summer. Let's say you start a full-time clerking gig after your first year in law school. That gives you your summers after Second and Third year to play with, which would let you graduate with experience with *three* different legal employers. If you can do that—you rock!

Of course, the downside is the probable pay cut you'd suffer from your current job. If you've got fixed obligations like a mortgage and/or a family to support, it's not feasible, and there are other options we'll discuss in this topic that will make more sense for you.

* * * SMART HUMAN TRICK * * *

Law student, East Coast law school. He starts in a full-time day program. After First Semester, he realizes that his grades are not going to get him into his dream job: a high-powered large Chicago law firm.

He transfers to the evening program at a Chicago law school. He applies for a full-time clerking position at the firm, and gets it. As he says, "I knew with my law school grades that getting into the firm through their summer associate program would not be open to me. I also researched them and found that the competition for their full-time clerking positions was much lower. After I worked with them for two years, they made me a permanent offer."

2.   ALTERNATING WORK WITH LEGAL EXPERIENCE IN THE SUMMER

In the traditional job-search mode, law students work with an employer the summer after their second year, get an offer at the end of the summer, and return to the employer full-time after graduation.

If you can eke out a summer, or most or part of a summer (the traditional summer program lasts fourteen weeks), **it makes sense that it be the summer after your third year of law school.** That way, your summer employer would be considering you for the following year, just like they do for day students. If you can work both Second and Third Year summers, great. If you want to work after First Year? You don't have much coursework completed by then, but if you're willing to volunteer to get some experience, it's out there for you.

"Great Kimmbo," you're thinking. "How am I supposed to find that much time to take off during the summer?" You know your job better than I do, but there may be the possibility of:

- Pooling vacation time. South Texas' Kim Cauthorn advises, "Stock up personal days, vacation days, whatever you can."

- Negotiating an "extended vacation" with your employer, so you can spend 4–8 weeks with a legal employer. As San Francisco's Jacqueline Ortega points out, "Evening students who combine vacation, unpaid leave and work schedule adjustments to gain legal experience find it's an exhausting summer . . . but well worth it to show employers their creativity and commitment to work hard—excellent selling points in a job search!''

- Taking an unpaid leave of absence.

If you're able to take more than one chunk of time to work full-time for a legal employer, unless you're laser-focused on what you want to do, try different types of employers in different settings. Trying something for yourself is the very best way to determine if you'll enjoy it . . . and a job that didn't particularly appeal to you up front may wind up being something you truly love.

3. WORKING FOR A FEW MONTHS AS A LAW CLERK AFTER GRADUATION (AND BEFORE BAR RESULTS COME OUT)

Once you graduate, you can't practice law until you pass the Bar. You might want to consider taking that time to get formal legal experience. It will give you a few months, which is plenty of time to expose legal employers to what you can do. While studying for the Bar will take up a sizable amount of time, you more than anybody are good at juggling multiple responsibilities!

4. KEEPING YOUR FULL-TIME GIG THROUGHOUT SCHOOL: UTILIZING VACATIONS, WEEKENDS, AND THAT 25th HOUR EVERY DAY WHEN YOU'RE SITTING AROUND WITH NOTHING TO DO

There are two categories we'll consider: jobs and projects.

A. JOBS

There are a couple of options to consider. **One is to utilize a vacation and do a PSLawNet project.** We discuss these in Chapter 10 in more detail. In a nutshell, PSLawNet projects last at least fifty hours—you can do one in a week—and cover a broad spectrum of public interest jobs, from working to state's attorneys generals to traditional advocacy organizations. The great thing about PSLawNet is that you get hands-on experience and it's got no grade requirements; if you're sincere about your desire to do the work, you get the job. For more information, go to www.pslawnet.org.

Another option is to **check with your Career Services Office and ask if there are employers who are willing to work specifically with evening students, realizing that the time commitment has to be very small.** As Cleveland State's Jayne Geneva points out, "There are 'evening friendly' externships and judicial clerkships. Particularly if the judge in question went to evening school, they may be amenable to working with you."

On top of that, Gina Sauer points out that "You may be able to shave off just enough hours from your full-time job to allow you to take on a clerkship that requires only a few hours a week." I talked to a student at one law school who worked for a solo practitioner five hours a week, for instance. If your schedule is at all flexible and you can work around an afternoon or morning, you can get some legal experience while you're still working full-time.

You might also consider **doing Saturday intake for a legal services office,** which is particularly useful if you want to get into public interest.

Another possibility is to **take advantage of clinics at school.** If they're amenable to your schedule, clinics give you the opportunity to get practical, hands-on experience while you're still a student. Employers view clinics very favourably as a result. Check with your school's clinical program to see what's amenable with your schedule.

Yet another possibility is to be a faculty research assistant. As Jayne Geneva explains, "Much of that work can be done any time. It gives you a chance to build a strong rapport with a professor who'll be a great reference. You'll get experience at the same time that can help you land a job after school."

B. PROJECTS

If you can't scrape out a few hours on a routine basis but you can squeeze in projects here and there, here are some ideas for you:

- **Take CLEs**. Continuing Legal Education Seminars. We discuss them in detail in Chapter 10. They're great in so many ways: resume fodder, exposure to issues facing lawyers in specialties you want to practice, and the opportunity most importantly to meet people who do what you want to do. Best of all, they're typically brief; a few hours and you're done.

- If you just can't appear "live" at a CLE, consider taking them on-line. The West Legal Education Center (westlegaledcenter.com) and the Practicing Law Institute (pli.edu) both offer on-line CLEs. While you don't get the very valuable "meet and greet" opportunities that live CLEs give you, you still get the other benefits.

- **Write an article for a bar association publication or law-related website**. We discuss this idea in detail in Chapter 10. It's a fairly simple matter to get a cutting-edge issue from an alum of your school, a practitioner you know or a professor, and writing a brief article about the status of the issue will take you very little time. It has the benefit of giving you a publication on your resume, providing you with a great writing sample, and giving you an "FYI" to send to employers you want to target. It also has flexibility; you can write it in whatever time you can squeeze in.

- **Volunteer to research an issue for the local bar association.** Contact the head of the section that interests you, and volunteer your services. Again, because writing can be squeezed into time you *do* have, this is an attractive option. On top of that it gives you a chance to get to know someone who's very well-connected, and that certainly improves your job prospects.

- **If your company has a legal department, volunteer to work on a project for them**. Many, many evening students have paved their way into the legal department at work this way. As Dave James says, "Go over to the legal department and say, 'Listen, can you toss me a project?' and do it on your own time. 'Give me a research assignment, I'll work at night, on weekends, mornings to get it done." There's nothing like giving someone the opportunity to see your legal skills at work ... not to mention your work ethic.

- **Do a journal article or note or research paper for academic credit on a subject that interests you**. Instead of taking a class for credit, working on a project like this gives you the opportunity to develop expertise in a specialty that intrigues you.

- **Volunteer for attorneys or professors.** Check with Career Services to see if there are local attorneys or professors who need "spot" help. Many times there won't be enough to keep someone busy on a regular basis, but there's a need for an extra brain for a few hours. There's no reason that brain can't be yours.

C. JOB SEARCH STRATEGIES

In some ways, your job search is just like it is for day students. There are four basic categories to consider: On-campus interviews, job postings, targeted mailers, and finally people and activities. Let's talk about each of them as they relate to you.

A. MAKE A REGULAR APPOINTMENT TO WORK ON YOUR JOB SEARCH

You already employ great time management skills. Make time to squeeze in one more obligation: your job search. As one career counselor points out, "Pretend it's a one-credit class that you're taking. If you set up a specific time every week to work on looking for a job, whether it's talking with potential employers, contacts, working on your resume or polishing your interview answers, you'll take the pressure off the rest of your time."

B. USE YOUR CAREER SERVICES OFFICE!

A common gripe I hear from evening students is that they feel ignored by Career Services at school. Nothing could be further from the truth. As one Career Services Director explains, "It's very, very hard to reach evening students on an institutional basis. We can't get attorneys to do programs late at night when evening classes are over, and evening students have a hard time making it to programs at four or five in the afternoon. We're willing to talk to them whenever it's convenient for them, and we can of course work by e-mail with them."

I know from personal experience that when law schools bring me in to speak to evening students, my *Guerrilla Tactics* program tends to be very sparsely attended. Aside from the damage it does to my ego, it doesn't make sense for Career Services to put on programs for a largely empty room.

That doesn't mean they don't stand ready to help you in any way you need it. From helping to polish your resume, giving you mock job interviews, helping you figure out what you want to do and giving you names of people to contact for advice, they're a wealth of information. Susanne Aronowitz advises you to "Work with your CSO on when and where to apply." **Make a point of talking to someone at Career Services at least once a semester,** if not more often.

c. ON-CAMPUS INTERVIEWS

There's no reason why you shouldn't take part in on-campus interviews on the same basis as day students. Of course, on-campus interviews comprise only a tiny segment of the employer community—mostly large law firms—and they typically demand stellar grades for those interviews. But, if you want those jobs and you've got those grades, that's an option.

If you just can't make it to on-campus interviews because of work obligations, remember that that's not the only door into those employers. **Many employers will do a "resume collection" at school.** Submit your resume for those employers. In addition, see topic (G), below, where we talk about other means to get to employers, through people and activities.

d. JOB POSTINGS

Not every job is posted, even on-line. But you should check your Career Service Office's web site on a frequent basis, at least twice a week, to see what's being posted. We talk about how to fashion your resume to respond to job postings in Chapter 8 on Resumes.

e. TARGETED MAILERS

A mail campaign can be an effective job search tool, and it's got the advantage of being flexible. We talk about mailers in Chapter 7 on Correspondence.

A particular target you should consider is **lawyers who went to an evening program themselves.** Through your Career Services Office, identify "evening alums" from your school. Check them out in Martindale Hubbell or a school alumni directory and see which ones practice in areas that interest you. In your cover letter, be sure to mention that you have night school in common. Of *any* attorney, people who went through evening programs themselves will appreciate your work ethic!

Another target is **employers who've hired students with backgrounds like yours.** Do a LEXIS or Westlaw search, or search a school-based database, to see who's hired evening students in the past. They've proven they're open to hiring evening students, and that makes them good targets.

f. Never, *Ever* Send Letters on Your Current Employer's Letterhead!

It's a terrible career limiting move. You're contacting employers on a personal basis, not as a representative of your employer. Sometimes students have suggested this to me as a means of making sure the employer pays attention to their letter. Well, it *will* get attention—but not the kind of attention you want.

Remember: it's not the name of your employer that'll get you the job. It's the experience you gained there that'll be useful to a legal employer!

g. People and Activities

There's no getting around the fact that reaching out to people, whether they're people you know or get to know or you meet them through activities, is the premier way to nail jobs.

Among the sources that make the most sense for you, because of your unique situation and limited time:

1. Skim Chapter 10 for Ideas

Of course I would encourage you to *read* chapter 10, because it's brimming with ideas for nailing great jobs. But if you do nothing else, skim the "Quick Fix" for people to talk to and activities to take part in. You'll find something that resonates with you. Take advantage of it!

2. Tell People You Work With What You Want to Do, And Ask if They Know Anyone You Ought to Be Talking to

Assuming that your work friends know that you're in law school and that sooner or later you're going to jump, your colleagues can be fertile job search sources, even if they aren't lawyers and you figure they couldn't possibly know anyone who could help you. They know you and they know your work ethic, and that's a huge plus. Just tell them that you're looking for advice about what you ought to be doing to get familiar with the legal community, for instance.

* * * SMART HUMAN TRICK * * *

Evening student, works full-time at a large company. He mentions to two nice ladies in HR that he's going to night school and he wonders if they know anybody who can help him learn more about Entertainment Law. One of them says, "There's a guy who's getting his MBA, he did a project with a film studio. You should talk to him." The student looks up the MBA, talks to him, and the MBA hooks him up with the person he worked for at the film studio. The evening student winds up working there after graduation.

3. TALK TO LAWYERS WHO SERVE YOUR CURRENT EMPLOYER

Duquesne's Ella Kwisnek points out that lawyers who work essentially for *you* are a great resource. Ask them for advice about what you ought to be doing to pursue your goals, and if you're interested in what they do, pursue the possibility of working with them. As Ella Kwisnek says, "If you've got the right connections and experience you can wait until after the Bar to switch jobs."

4. WHEN YOU CONDUCT INFORMATIONAL INTERVIEWS WITH PEOPLE, BE SURE TO ASK HOW TO "SPIN" YOUR BACKGROUND

For instance, ask "Will my background in X be useful if I want to work in Y setting? How would you advise that I market that background?" Hearing from people in a specialty how to position yourself is the best way to ensure that you'll attract the employers you want.

5. SUBSCRIBE TO THE EVENING STUDENT LISTSERV IF YOUR SCHOOL HAS ONE; IF THEY DON'T, ASK THAT THEY START ONE

Some law schools have a listserv directed specifically at evening students. It's a great place to pick up job hunting tips and share questions and successes.

6. GO TO ANY CAREER SERVICES OFFICE PROGRAMMING YOU CAN POSSIBLY ATTEND

While I realize work may prevent you from attending the programs you'd like to see, try to squeeze them in on a lunch hour or right before school if you possibly can. There are a bunch of great reasons for this. Not only will the information be helpful, but meeting speakers at programs is a great way to stand out. Walk up to them afterwards, introduce yourself, tell them how much you enjoyed their speech (assuming you did!), and offer your resume or ask if you can speak to them further for more advice. Try to set up an informational interview if you can. Many students have nailed job opportunities in just this way.

7. LEAN ON YOUR PROFESSORS

Contrary to their ivory tower reputation, law professors can be a great source of advice and contacts. They often maintain substantial networks in the legal community. Be sure to lean on them for help.

8. CONTESTS

While I talk about these in Chapter 10, I wanted to mention them here because I think they're particularly useful when you're dealing with a restricted time schedule.

- **Take part in writing competitions.** They are a *great* way to get the attention of employers (and earn a little extra scratch, by the way; the cash prizes are normally nothing to sneeze at). They have the benefit of flexibility; you write when you have the time.

- **Take part in oral advocacy competitions, whether Moot Court** or any sponsored by bar associations or legal fraternities. Depending on your schedule, Moot Court competitions might be a stretch. But there are many other oral advocacy competitions offered, as well; check with Career Services to learn about the ones in your area. Winning one of these competitions will be a boost to your resume *and* bring you to the attention of employers.

* * * SMART HUMAN TRICK * * *

4th year evening student, California law school. He has a technical background. He tries to find a permanent job, to no avail. He takes part in an Intellectual Property writing competition sponsored by the local bar association, and wins it. One of the judges tells him, "If you're looking for a job, talk to me." The student does so, and winds up with a very prestigious IP firm as a result.

9. LAW SCHOOL ORGANIZATIONS FOCUSING ON SPECIALTIES THAT INTEREST YOU

You might not be able to attend many meetings if any at all, but organizations will give you the opportunity to learn who the players are in your chosen field, and you can always contact them for advice outside of formal organization functions.

10. CONTACT THE HEAD OF THE LOCAL BAR ASSOCIATION SECTION THAT COVERS THE SPECIALTY YOU WANT

Call and introduce yourself. The best thing to do is to volunteer for a project (which we've already discussed), but even explaining your situation and asking for advice about what you ought to be doing to propel your career goals will help you. Better than talking on the phone is meeting for a cup of coffee if you can *possibly* squeeze it into your schedule, since you're more memorable in person than over the phone (or via e-mail).

D. WHEN EMPLOYERS LOOK: TIMING DIFFERENT TYPES OF JOB SEARCHES

While there are no hard-and-fast rules, and I encourage you to conduct informational interviews and ask around *all* the time, here are some general guidelines on when different types of employers hire. Remember: Err on the side of being too early rather than too late, and check with Career Services to verify when employers in your target market hire:

1. **SUMMER POSITIONS**
    - **Large law firms (50+ attorneys), medium firms (20–50 attorneys), federal and state agencies, corporations, some public interest organizations: Fall.**
    - **Everyone else (most small firms): Spring.**

Note: If you're going to work for one summer only, make it the summer after Third Year, when employers will make permanent hiring decisions for the following year.

2. **LAW CLERKS DURING THE ACADEMIC YEAR, BOTH PART-TIME AND FULL-TIME:**
    - **Large law firms: Early August through late September. Same for government agencies, associations, and public interest organizations.**
    - **For smaller firms (<20 lawyers): Whenever the need arises; start trying early in the academic year.**

Note that if you're going to clerk full-time, some employers recommend waiting until Third Year in order to have enough coursework under your belt to be useful.

3. **PERMANENT JOBS:**
    By and large, **same schedule as summer positions.**
    Note, however:
    - **Government honors programs: September of your final year.**
    - **Many small firms, some corporations and government agencies: post graduation,** *after the bar exam,* **from late August through early November.**
    - **Career Fair Registrations: as early as September of your final year.**

E. FIGURING OUT WHAT YOU WANT TO DO . . .

This process is no different for you than it is for any other law student . . . you just have more job experience on which to draw information about what you like and what you don't like. Read Chapter 2, where we go over this in detail.

F. RESUME ISSUES

Your status as an evening student isn't really an issue; you'll do the same things to highlight marketable skills and tailor your resume for specific employers as you would in a day program. The real issue tends to be how you characterize a prior career; we discuss that in Chapter 22.

If you're worried that your resume is sparse because of your work commitments, consider the activities we talk about in Chapter 8 on Resumes, specifically the section called "Pimp My Resume."

G. INTERVIEW ISSUES

Whether it's a job interview or an informational interview, there are certain unique issues that might come up. While you should read Chapter 9 on Interviews for advice common to all law students, expect to deal with the following issues and questions:

1. Remember that you have assets day students don't have ... make the most of them!

As Career Counselor Wendy Werner points out, "Use your experience in the interview process! You can say something like, 'If I come to work for you, I'll have one job. Right now, I have two. When you talk about somebody being able to bill hours or be efficient, this is how I've demonstrated that the last few years ...' No day student can compete with that."

2. "Why did you choose the evening division?"

As is often the case, it's important to look at the issue(s) behind the question you're being asked. The issues undergirding this question could include:

- a question over your commitment to practicing law, and the thought that you might not make the jump at all;
- a mistaken impression by the interviewer that the evening division is easier to get into than the day division, so you're not as qualified;
- Worries about how much money you're going to need starting out in law, and a concern that an offer you receive might not stack up favourably against what you make now.

With those issues in mind, you can understand the elements your answer has to include:

- The source of your interest in law (and it has to be something *other than* making more money; you need to comment on the nature of the work and what drew you to it; the best answer would build on skills you've developed in other settings).

- You have to comment on your commitment to being a lawyer and your enthusiasm about getting started, perhaps a comment about how "you've heard" from administrators at school that the evening division is at least as/more competitive than the day division (assuming that that's true!), and that you've researched this employer, you understand the nature of the business including how much it pays and you wouldn't be wasting the employer's time otherwise.

3. "Why aren't you involved in Law Review/Journal/more activities?"

I know what you're tempted to say. "Are you freaking *kidding* me??" Maybe they're just testing you to see if that's how you'll respond. Don't take the bait!

Instead, explain your schedule calmly to the interviewer, explain why you've made the choices you've made, and *especially* be sure to highlight any activities you *are* involved in, law related or not, including community activities. (Remember: law is a business. Community involvement is a code word for "rainmaking potential.")

If the interviewer mentions Law Review or Journal in particular, an underlying issue is your ability to write. Whether it's in law school, through a related activity like a clinic, bar project or competition, or any other part of your life that gave you the opportunity to develop your writing skill, mention it.

4. "Why haven't you worked in a legal job before?"

Obviously if you *have* made time for clerkships or internships, you won't get this question. You're only likely to get it if you're seeking permanent jobs as a fourth year and you haven't had time to get any significant legal experience.

There are two issues behind this question: One is whether or not you "get it," since you haven't been exposed to legal employers before, and the other is whether you're truly committed to practicing law.

With those in mind, your answer should include transferable skills from any jobs you've held before. We discuss those in detail in the Resume chapter, Chapter 8. In addition, don't be afraid to tell the employer why you haven't gotten any legal experience. As a career counselor at one law school points out, "It's almost always an economic issue, and there's nothing wrong with that." Explain that you've had to work full time and that precluded you from getting legal experience. If this is the case, explain *particularly* your ability to pick up new skills quickly—and experiences you have proving that— and that you've spoken with enough people about this kind of work that you feel you understand what will be expected of you.

5. **"What in your prior education/experience will benefit you in practicing law?"**

This is a chance to really shine, because you have a benefit that many students don't have; students who go straight through college to full-time law school have a much harder time with this question that you do. Just focus on your transferable skills! Go back to the Resume chapter, Chapter 8, and review the skills you bring to legal employers.

It's very important to remember that you can't assume *anybody* knows what you've done just by the job titles. You have to pull out the specific skills that those experiences provided you.

6. **"What are your salary expectations/How much money do you make now?"**

While most lawyers won't be ballsy enough to ask you straight out how much you make, it's been known to happen. No matter how it's asked, here's the issue behind the question: the interviewer is concerned that if you make more now than you will starting out with the employer, you'll expect more than other applicants.

The way to deal with this question is to do salary research at two websites: www.nalp.org and www.salaries.com. At the NALP website especially you will find specific guidance about how much legal employers pay, both upon graduation and for years into the future, and what the range is in different locations for different sized employers. Armed with this information, you can tell the interviewer with complete confidence something along the lines of, "I know I'm starting out in something new and that entails a temporary salary cut. I'm comfortable with that. I'm interested in the long-term, and to me salary is a short-term factor." Remember that if the employer is small, you may have the chance to negotiate for more money; we talk about that in detail in Chapter 18 on small firms.

7. **Questions we discuss in Chapter 22 on Second Careers:**

"Are you willing to be a first year associate and/or start all over again?"

"How do you feel about a supervisor younger than you?"

"Why did you go to law school?"

"What are your transferrable skills?"

H. Recognize That the Hardest Employer to Target May Be the One You Have Now

I often talk to evening students who are interested in becoming lawyers for their current employer. While it works sometimes, it's worth knowing that particularly if you're in a support position now—a paralegal, an executive assistant—it will be difficult to go straight from your current gig to a lawyer position.

I know, I know, that's awfully unfair. After all, who's more familiar with your professionalism and work ethic than your current employer? And you feel comfortable there. You know everyone, and they know you.

And that's the problem.

As one career counselor pointed out to me, "It's sometimes impossible for employers to change their vision of you. They're used to you providing supporting documents or making appointments, and now you expect them to view you as a lawyer. It's not that they don't want to, it's just that they can't get their minds around the change."

While there are things you can do to help change your image, like dressing more like a lawyer and less like what you are now and volunteering for legal research projects, you may find it a lot easier to earn your "chops" for a couple of years somewhere else and then lateral back into your current employer. With even a short gap, it'll give them a chance to look at you through a different lens.

I. DON'T WAIT *Too* LONG AFTER GRADUATION TO FIND A NEW JOB!

A the old saying goes, strike while the iron is hot. For you, the iron is hot while you're still in law school. The longer you wait after graduation to make the jump, the less convinced any legal employer will be that you're serious about it, and the staler your skills will be.

If it's a money issue, as soon as school is over, start taking on volunteer projects for the bar association, go to CLEs, and otherwise keep your toes in the water until you do feel comfortable changing jobs. But I can't stress strongly enough: Change jobs as soon as you can!

* * * STUPID HUMAN TRICK * * *

Evening student, a paralegal at a large East Coast law firm. His grades are mediocre, and when he interviews with legal employers, the best he can do is a job paying half what he's making as a paralegal, to start.

Five years after graduation, he realizes that if he'd taken a lawyer job on graduation, his salary by now would have far surpassed what he's making as a paralegal. As he reports: "This job search is murder. No law firm believes that I really want to be a lawyer at this point. I've actually had lawyers tell me, 'That was a stupid decision.' I can't argue with that."

J. RECOGNIZE THAT LAW SCHOOL MAY MAKE YOU REALIZE HOW MUCH YOU LOVE YOUR CURRENT JOB AFTER ALL . . .

OK. It can be expensive. And it can take a lot of time. But there's no law that says that you *have* to use your law degree. You may well find that spending four years in law school, around law students and professors, reading cases and talking with practitioners, all makes you realize, "Hey. I've got it pretty good!"

If that's the case, there's nothing wrong with that. You're a much better educated whatever-you-were-before, and as my mother always used to tell me, nobody can take your education away from you.

* * * SMART HUMAN TRICK * * *

Law student in Ohio. He's in his fifties, and he works as a systems analyst for a federal agency. He contemplates going to work for a prosecutor's office and then lateraling back into his agency, but he just can't work up the motivation to do it.

Then one day it dawns on him . . .

"I figured out: the reason I'm not leaving is that I really don't *want* to leave. A lot of days I've got nothing to do but surf the web. I *like* that."

"So I've decided, I'll take the bar, go to bar association activities, sit in on court case on vacations, read Supreme Court cases . . . and keep my job."

Chapter 22
Second (or Third or Fourth or Fifth) Career People (Including Returning– to–Paid–Work Moms)

"You can't turn back the clock, but you can wind it up again"

> —Bonnie Prudden

"It's better to be at the bottom of a ladder you want to climb than halfway up one you don't."

> —Martin Freeman as Tim Canterbury in the BBC version of "The Office"

"It's never too late to be what you might have been."

> —George Eliot

"Ancora imparo (I am still learning)."

> —Michelangelo, at age 87

"You may have noticed ..."

That's the way the question normally starts. *"... that I'm not exactly twenty-three years old."*

When I give the *Guerrilla Tactics* job search seminar at law schools, second career students often have questions: Is it true that employers don't want older students? What am I supposed to say about my prior career? *Where's my job?*

Relax. No matter how "chronologically enhanced" you are, employers want you. As a partner at one of the country's most prestigious firms commented, "Second career? That's a huge plus."

People in every field have done remarkable things regardless of their age. People a lot older than *you* have taken on new gigs with spectacular results. For instance, the architect Frank Lloyd Wright wrote his autobiography at age 65, with his career largely regarded as over. Several years later, he was on a roll ... designing, among other things, the greatest private home of the 20th century, Fallingwater.

And then there's George Washington. He came out of retirement at age 57 for a promising gig ... President of the United States.

Age may not be just a state of mind, but it's no impediment to getting a great new career. In this chapter, we'll talk about resolving all the issues that go into nailing your dream job ... whether you graduated from college last year or forty years ago.

A. BENEFITS YOU BRING TO EMPLOYERS BECAUSE YOU'VE WORKED BEFORE, AND YOU'VE GOT A FEW EXTRA YEARS UNDER YOUR BELT

● **You "get it" when it comes to the working world.**

One of the biggest complaints employers have about twentysomething new lawyers is that they don't understand the nature of the professional world. If you've worked before, you understand professional etiquette, how to dress, how to behave. Depending on your background, you might have handled a leadership role and know how to deal with support staff. You may have worked long hours, so you won't be fazed by that if an employer requires it. You might have learned how to handle a tough boss. In other words, a lot of issues that would trip up a new lawyer who went straight from college to law school won't knock you off your game.

● **You've developed contacts that could be helpful to you in finding a legal job.**

Your prior experience gave you a chance to meet people. You may think, "Those chuckleheads? They don't know *any* lawyers." Don't write them off so fast! As we discuss in detail in Chapter 10, you don't know who other people know. When you start asking around, you'll be surprised how many useful people spring out of the woodwork.

● **You've got skills transferable to a legal employer.**

No matter *what* you've done—even if you've been a full-time mom for the last howevermany years—you've developed skills that will be useful to a legal employer. We talk about those in detail, below.

B. CHALLENGES THAT ARE UNIQUE TO SECOND CAREER STUDENTS

You've got benefits "first time careerists" don't have ... but you've got issues they don't have, as well. Let's talk about them.

1. AGEISM

If you took two years off between college and law school, this isn't an issue. But if you've got a decade or more on your law school classmates, you may find ageism rearing its ugly head when you go to look for jobs. Interviewers may be flat out insulting. There's even a nickname for the problem: The "Vampire Syndrome," as in: the relentless quest for new blood.

As Career Counselor Wendy Werner says, "Ageism is definitely there. When people *don't* want to hire you, they'll think of every reason to avoid it. But there are plenty of people who do want you. You can't control bias. You can only control your attitude. Nobody wants to hire an angry person."

Remember: everybody gets a job. The second careerists who are the most successful at it include in their job search arsenal:

- Researching jobs and knowing what's expected of them, so that when they're asked "Are you willing to start over?" the answer can be a hearty "Yes!" with the research to back it up;

- Stressing their willingness and ability to take direction from—and work with—people who may be a lot younger than they are;

- Knowing the starting salary of jobs they target (ask Career Services for statistics), and expressing their willingness to work with that;

- Confronting the issue head-on as soon as they perceive it's a problem, saying that they look forward to learning from people with more legal experience than they have;

- Making sure that their appearance is up-to-date, from hair to professional wardrobe;

- Making a point of conveying their feeling that although they have a lot of experience, they know they have a lot to learn as a lawyer;

- Explaining that their new career in law builds on things they liked/learned in their prior career, without dissing what they used to do;

- Setting their resent-o-meter on high. They respond to insults with humor.

What I've seen happen much more often than ageism is a matter of second career students not getting jobs they really don't want. If an employer perceives you won't like the job, they won't hire you. Let's take large law firms, because they're the ones students most often accuse of ageism. Now, I have spoken a number of times at large law firms, and when I look out at a sea of new associates, either there are some second career students out there ... or there are twenty-five year olds who've lived a *very* hard life. Large firms *do* hire older students; as the partner at one very prestigious firm told me, "It's a plus. If they've got the stellar credentials we're looking for, we prefer to take them."

If you find that's not the case, ask yourself: Do you have a strong tolerance for bureaucracy? Do you mind spending long hours researching week after week after week? Second career students often say to me, "Large law firms don't want me, it's my age," Inevitably, when I talk to them about life at large law firms (See Chapter 23), they'll say, "I don't want that." And I'll respond, "Then that's the Universe working out: You're not getting jobs you don't want."

If you do want a large law firm job, you've got to make it plain to them that you understand the life and the demands, that you've talked with people who do it, that you're used to hard work and you're not intimidated by it. If they don't ask you about it, *tell them anyway,* because they might be assuming you won't do it and so don't ask you about it.

The bottom line is: your age won't keep you out of *any* job, if you appreciate the employer's concerns and address them directly.

2. YOU MIGHT MAKE LESS—A *LOT* LESS—STARTING OVER AS A LAWYER THAN YOU DID IN YOUR LAST JOB

At least half of the second career students I meet tell me that they came to law school "to make more money." The cold reality is that depending on how you fared financially in your last career, a new lawyer's salary can represent a real shave and a haircut. It's not uncommon to start as a lawyer making under fifty grand a year. Of course, there's lots of potential to make a *lot* more money than that, but in the short term you might find legal salaries startlingly low.

3. YOU'LL HAVE TO EXPLAIN YOUR CAREER SWITCH. OVER AND OVER AND OVER AGAIN

Here's the problem. Employers will assume one of two things. Either you were terrible at what you did before (in which case they don't want you), *or* they assume you were good at it, and you're a job hopper and/or crazy to leave that gig.

As we'll explore in more detail later on in this chapter, you need a ready answer for the inevitable questions about your career switch. Essentially, as we'll find out, it's got to have at its heart building on elements you liked in other job(s) you've had. It has to be honest and you have to say it with confidence. But the fact remains: you will have to explain why you changed your mind. As Santa Clara's Alex Bullaria points out, "It's not a criticism. Don't imagine attacks where they don't exist!"

C. SPECIFIC STRATEGIES FOR EVERY ASPECT OF YOUR JOB SEARCH

Chapters One through Twelve apply to everyone seeking a job, whether they've had no work experience or forty years of it. Deciding what you want to do, correspondence, resumes, interviews, finding great gigs through people and activities ... it's largely the same. Here, we'll talk about aspects of your job search that are unique to you because of your prior work. As Career Consultant Kathleen Brady points out, "Planning a career change is like solving a business problem. You have to define objectives, develop strategies, monitor progress and take corrective action when needed."

1. FIGURING OUT WHAT YOUR DREAM JOB IS

All the strategies in the world won't help you if you don't know what you want to do. Here are some pointers:

A. GO BACK AND READ CHAPTER 2

Everything that applies to decision-making as a first-time careerist applies to you, as well.

B. THERE ARE SPECIALTIES THAT ARE OBVIOUS TARGETS DEPENDING ON YOUR BACKGROUND. THEY'LL BE THE EASIEST TO BREAK INTO

Of course, it's not all about aiming for the easiest target ... but that doesn't hurt. As McGeorge's Dave James points out, "The easiest job to get is the one you already have." And you may really enjoy utilizing your existing expertise.

As The Esquire Group's Gina Sauer points out, among the more common "switches" for second career people are:

Old Career: Advertising/Public Relations

Legal specialty: Trademark or entertainment law

Old Career: Government

Legal specialty: Municipal Law

Old Career: Accounting

Legal Specialty: Tax Law, Mergers and Acquisitions, Family Law

Old Career: Engineering

Legal specialty: Patent law, Product Liability, Mass Torts (e.g., plane crashes)

Old Career: Human Resources

Legal specialty: Employment Law, Labor Law, Employment Benefits Law

Old Career: Real Estate

Legal specialty: Real Estate Law, Landlord/Tenant, Environmental

Old Career: Doctor, nurse, hospital administrator

Legal specialty: Personal injury, Product Liability, Medical Malpractice

You can probably fill in the blanks on your own prior career with even a cursory glance at the specialties we talked about in Chapter 2, and by skimming Lisa Abrams' excellent book *The Official Guide To Legal Specialties.*

The bottom line is, your most obvious target builds on what you already know!

c. IF YOU'RE DEAD SET AGAINST PRACTICING IN A SPECIALTY RELATED TO YOUR PRIOR CAREER ... CONSIDER GIVING IT A BRIEF TRY DURING LAW SCHOOL ANYWAY

If you were involved in technology before law school, it's a no-brainer to go into intellectual property law. If you were a doctor or a nurse, health law or med mal is an obvious choice. If your background is in accounting, tax law beckons you.

And it may well be that you want *nothing more* than to *avoid* what you did before. You may think, "I came to law school *specifically* to get away from that!" I hear you. But remember: if you have a background related to a practice area, it's not just a lot easier to get a job, but you'll enter the field feeling a lot more confident because you know the jargon and understand the field. Also, being a lawyer in a related field may be *entirely different* than you expected it to be. You might love the area from a different perspective.

So for a semester or even part of a summer, consider giving the "obvious" choice a try. You wouldn't be the first second career law student to do an about-face in their career choice as a result!

d. REMEMBER THAT YOU'VE GOT TO BALANCE YOUR GOALS, JUST LIKE ANY LAW STUDENT

In Chapter 2, we talked about how the principal compromise you have to make in practicing law is balancing time against money. That is, the more money you want to start out making, the longer hours you'll put in, because you're selling time. You're the only one who can make the decision about how much you'll trade work/life balance for higher pay.

Note, however, that this is a *short term issue*. While the starting pay in small firms can be less than half that at large firms, your pay will rocket up much faster until it's on a par with large firms within a few years. In addition, if you're good at bringing in business to a small firm, you can negotiate a cut of what you attract, and your pay can increase dramatically that way.

But the fact remains: as a rule of thumb, it's time or money.

e. TALK TO PEOPLE WHO DO WHAT YOU THINK YOU MIGHT LIKE TO DO

The single best way to figure out what you want is to talk to people who do things that interest you, listen to their experiences, and see how those lives measure up to your vision for your own life. Don't be embarrassed about asking questions; people are happy to talk about what they do.

Whether it's alums of your school (whom you'll find through Career Services), lawyers you find through CLEs or conferences or lawyers you know from your prior career or personal life, *ask* people what they like about what they do, what they'd change about it, how they got started. Listen for themes. Ask pointed questions about issues that are important to you. You'll identify what you want, and you'll have a good time figuring it out.

F. RECOGNIZE WHERE YOU'RE LIKELY TO BE HAPPIEST

No single job suits everyone, of course. Yet interestingly enough, Professor Grayson of the University of Washington Law School conducted a survey of second career attorneys, and found that they were happiest in small suburban firms where they took the part of counselors. It turns out that when clients look at a forty-year-old lawyer, they assume the lawyer's been practicing a while ... and that's what they want.

At small firms, you'll have more autonomy, you'll have a better work/life balance than at a large firm, and you'll be able to progress quickly through the ranks, particularly if you bring in business. In fact, "If you have a forceful personality and you bring a book of business, it's possible to come in as a partner," reports one career counselor. The small firm setting tends to be a happier environment for all kinds of law school graduates, but *particularly* second career people.

Having said that, there are other environments you might especially like, depending on what motivated you to go to law school. Many second career students enjoy judicial clerkships. These positions typically provide very reasonable hours, they're intellectually stimulating, they offer decent pay ... and when you look for a job afterwards, you've got an edge. Other second career students aim for public interest. The opportunity to "give back" is very rewarding (and p.s.: public interest employers are militantly anti-ageist).

G. REALIZE THAT YOUR BEST GIG MAY BE ONE YOU CREATE FOR YOURSELF

It may well be that your dream job is one that you create out of whole cloth. After all, you've got a unique set of credentials. Why not think creatively?

I talked to one student who'd been a pediatrician before law school, and he intended to offer high-net-worth people a 24–hour medical and legal service when he graduated from law school.

Whether you start a consulting business or an Internet business or any kind of business at all, being your own boss is something many people enjoy. Remember: one great reason to go to law school is to reinvent yourself. If you've got the financial means to do it, let your imagination run wild!

H. THINK ABOUT A JUDICIAL CLERKSHIP

I've talked with more than one judge who considered a prior career a plus for their law clerks. "There are many times where I'll want someone with a different world view, a function of a different career," commented one judge.

I talk all about judicial clerkships in Chapter 25, and I can tell you, they're a *great* way to break into just about anything you want ... on top of being stimulating jobs in and of themselves. Think about it!

I. CONSIDER ALTERNATIVE CAREERS

We talk about these in more detail in Chapter 31, but recognize that "Alternative careers are great options for second-career students," according to The Esquire Group's Gina Sauer. "For a start, take a look at industries tangential to the industry you were in. If you were in insurance before, you know hospitals and medical people. Take a look at the Federal Reports Book "600 Things To Do With A Law Degree." Your experience + your law degree = one of those 600 careers! Also, take a look at your skill set. Look at what you did on a daily basis. That will be useful in a lot of alternative careers."

2. "SPINNING" YOUR PRIOR CAREER TO POTENTIAL EMPLOYERS

A large part of nailing great jobs is knowing how to present your background to potential employers. Having work experience in any capacity is a huge asset. Let's talk about how to "spin" it!

A. DON'T BE MARRIED TO JOB TITLES

When you send your resume to legal employers, assume that you're describing your former employer(s) to a savvy high schooler: someone who knows nothing about what you did. Talk about responsibilities and achievements, and stay away from relying on your job title(s) to convey what you bring to the table.

B. PULL OUT TRANSFERABLE SKILLS

We've talked about the concept of "transferable skills" before; that is, what you've learned in one area as it applies to another area. No matter what job you've had, you learned things that are relevant to the practice of law.

For instance, let's say you were a school teacher. I've talked to many former teachers who made the jump to law, and they were stumped about how to pitch it to legal employers. As Quinnipiac's Diane Ballou, herself a former teacher, explains, teaching is an excellent background for law. She lists some of the best assets it gives you: "Experience standing in front of people, which makes you good on your feet, an excellent skill for lawyers. Furthermore, since teachers don't have anyone looking over their shoulder most of the time, you're good at working independently. And apart from writing and verbal skills that all legal employers covet, you're good at explaining things to people. That means you'll be good at reducing complex legal ideas to a level clients can understand."

1.   SKILLS AND QUALITIES DESIRABLE TO LEGAL EMPLOYERS

"It's fine to talk about transferable skills, Kimmbo," you may be thinking. "But how the heck do *I* know what legal employers want?"

While it will be somewhat dependent on the specific employer, there are certain skills and qualities that are generally attractive to them. It's a great idea to find lawyers who do what you want to do (through Career Services or the bar association, for instance) and conduct informational interviews to hone in on what they look for in people they hire.

Use this list as a guide to the accomplishments and activities to detail on your resume, because they indicate your "lawyerlike" skills. (The list was adapted from a Hastings College of Law publication.) Also, as Akron's Jay Levine points out, "Don't forget to talk about the transferability of 'real world' skills like exercising good judgment."

Skills:

- Problem solving
- Analysis
- Research
- Factual investigation
- Communication
- Counseling
- Negotiation
- Advocating
- Advising
- Writing
- Editing
- Lobbying
- Researching
- Selling
- Public speaking

Qualities desirable for lawyers:

- Energy
- Initiative
- Motivation
- Follow-through
- Ability to juggle multiple tasks and prioritize
- Ability to pick up new information quickly
- Ability to deal with time pressures and tight deadlines

- Ability to work well in a team
- Creativity

2. IF YOU'RE HAVING TROUBLE PULLING OUT TRANSLATABLE SKILLS, FLIP IT-ASK YOURSELF ABOUT WHAT SOMEONE WOULD NEED TO DO YOUR PRIOR JOB FOR A MONTH

If you're stumped, a great way to figure out your transferable skills is to turn the tables, and describe what someone would need to be able to do if they wanted to do *your* job for a month. What skills would they need? What knowledge would they have to have? What talents and abilities? What personality would help them deal with the culture and the people?

You'll find inevitably that in trying to explain it *this* way, it'll be a lot easier to see what *you* learned on the job.

C. IF YOU'VE WORKED WITH LAWYERS AS A CLIENT, HIGHLIGHT THAT

As Wendy Werner advises, "If you've been in business, you want to say 'I've been a client, I know what it's like to be on the client side. This helps me understand how clients think, what they expect, and how to talk to them in lay terms.'"

D. DON'T UNDERVALUE WHAT YOU'VE DONE

When most of us think about what we've done, we don't think much of it. "I did it, how big a deal can it be?" For a legal employer, it may be a very big deal. Based on the transferable skills we just discussed, look hard at what you've done to pull out the transferable skills.

E. DON'T OVERVALUE YOUR PRIOR WORK EXPERIENCE, EITHER; YOU'RE NEVER REALLY "OVERQUALIFIED"

Remember: when you're starting out fresh in law, you may be an incredibly accomplished "something else ..." but you aren't an experienced lawyer. There isn't any way that you're overqualified when you haven't practiced law.

Instead, what's really going on is that you may be so qualified in something else that lawyers will have a hard time believing that you do, indeed, want to start all over again. In this situation: *Say it.* Come right out and say "I know I have a lot to learn ..." "I know everything there is to know about X but when it comes to being a lawyer ..." Let them know that *you* know where you stand. One successful job seeker, a scientist who was now looking to become a patent attorney, truly had outstanding credentials—but what got him his job was his humility. He said, "I realize I have these accomplishments, but I had to present them differently in speaking to lawyers."

I talked to a woman at one law school who'd been heavily involved in non-profit management. She was convinced that she came off as overqualified. She told me, "I *know* I've got a lot to learn—" I stopped her and said, "Then *say* so!" Employers need to hear it.

Another law student at another school, this one on the East Coast, told me that he wasn't getting jobs he was applying for, only because "I'm too qualified." I asked him what kind of jobs he was applying for, and he said, "A few firms. Skadden Arps, Sherman and Stearling . . ." he went on like this for a moment before I stopped him, and said, "What have you done that makes you overqualified for *them?*" We're talking, after all, about some of the most prestigious law firms in the country! He said, "I was a lawyer in Brazil for ten years." Now, that *would* be useful experience for the right employer, but this guy—with middling law school grades—wasn't spinning it that way. He just *assumed* that his experience would carry him on a sedan chair into any American firm.

Take your experience and view it through the lens of transferable skills. Talk with other people who've made the transition to law from your prior career. And take a realistic view of how it helps you with your new career. It's an asset . . . but you have to present it correctly.

On a related note: what do you do if employers keep telling you you're overqualified? It can happen. I talked with a student at one law school who had a Masters in Public Policy from an Ivy League School. She wanted a clerk's job with the state as a way to hobnob with employers doing what she ultimately wanted to do, environmental law. It was a good plan, but she kept hearing, "You're overqualified for that job." It really bothered her, until she started responding, "I appreciate the implied compliment, but the point of *having* qualifications is to have options to do what I want." When she said this, doors started opening for her.

F. BE AWARE OF STEREOTYPES ASSOCIATED WITH YOUR PRIOR CAREER

"Sometimes the problem is that a legal employer will understand your prior career all too well!" says North Carolina's Brian Lewis. He uses as an example former elementary school teachers, "particularly in the area of litigation or complex transactional work. The problem for former teachers is that everybody had teachers and thinks they know what they're like and what they do. They think back fondly to Miss Crabtree, their meek and mid second-grade teacher who taught spelling and simple arithmetic to docile students."

If you know about a stereotype associated with your prior career, you're much of the way towards defeating it. You can acknowledge it outright, for a start, and say something like, "I know you remember your elementary school teachers, and you maybe you can't see them as litigators. Here's what makes me different . . ." and talk about your legal training, experiences you've had in activities at school as well as internships, externships, and other law-related experiences. You'll change the employer's mind about you!

3. MAKE YOUR RESUME SING

A. READ CHAPTER 8

We went over Resumes in great detail in that chapter.

B. GET THEE TO CAREER SERVICES

Because your prior career presents additional issues in formulating your resume, lean on your Career Services Office for help in refining it. They'll be familiar with the specific types of employers you're targeting, and will help you ensure that your resume has the right focus.

C. LENGTH ISSUES . . .

We've all heard the "one page resume" mandate. That's not a hard and fast rule. The watchword is *relevancy*. If you have a lot of relevant experience, past gigs that give you transferable skills, go ahead and use two pages. "It's when you're detailing your responsibilities as a grocery store cashier that the two pages is a no-no," says one career counselor.

In each entry, gauge the detail you include with two principles in mind:

1) Include enough detail to make the description understandable to a layperson, focusing on transferable skills and knowledge;

2) If your targeted job is related to your prior work—e.g., tech work for an IP position—more detail is appropriate.

D. "LEGALIZE" YOUR EXPERIENCE

Take out jargon from your resume, and don't rely on job titles to convey what you're capable of doing. As Golden Gate's Susanne Aronowitz advises, "You can't send a resume as a senior marketing executive to lawyers and expect them to 'get' what you can do."

E. FOCUS ON YOUR TRANSFERABLE SKILLS

We just talked about the importance of "spinning" your prior career appropriately, by pulling out transferable skills from your old jobs. On your resume, be *explicit* about the related activities you had in your last job, using "legal" terms. Represented, counseled, taught, negotiated . . . use words with which lawyers can identify. Translate duties or tasks into skills they require if the experience isn't directly relevant. As Dave James points out, "The ultimate inquiry is, 'what do the lawyers do at the employer that's receiving this resume?' Everything they do that you've done, you highlight on your resume."

A law firm administrator who used to be in the Army said, "Your resume isn't a historical document. It's a persuasive piece. In the military, I recruited doctors. That's relevant to my job. I also did funeral details. That I didn't put on my resume, because it's immaterial."

The bottom line is: your resume can't be too long if it focuses on skills legal employers want you to have!

* * * SMART HUMAN TRICK * * *

Second career student at an East Coast law school. He spent ten years before law school as a professional musician, playing with a band that toured local nightclubs. He went to law school to become a litigator, and "to get a regular paycheck, man." He had difficulty getting employers to take him seriously until he changed his resume. Where it had read solely, "Year X to Year Y, professional musician," he included details like:

- Negotiated contracts with club owners on behalf of the band

- Routinely performed in front of groups of a hundred people or more

- Created band's web site and handled all public relations.

His new resume generated considerable interest, and helped him land a job with a small firm . . . as a litigator.

F. BE AS CONCISE AS YOU POSSIBLY CAN

Dave James points out that "Legal employers aren't as interested in what you've done in the past as you think they should be."

He goes on, "I've seen resumes from people in the banking industry who'll have resume entries saying 'First I was a teller, then a bank branch manager, then vice president of so-and-so bank . . .' Every entry should be roughly proportional in size to its importance to the employer you're sending it to. When you have a two-page resume and a full second page is devoted to a previous career, that's too much. They don't care that you were a computer specialist or teacher to that extent. I've been on the hiring side, and that resume screams to me that there's an inflated view of the significance of that previous career. Employers don't want to bring you in if you're living in the past."

"Instead, collapse your experience by putting titles and firms together. Instead of a separate entry with a blurb for each job, put them all together.

"So instead of 'Teller: First National Bank, Administrative Assistant: Second National Bank, Vice President: Third National Bank,' and so on, have inclusive dates from the start of the teller job to the end of the vice president job. Do a collective blurb that shows your progression. That collapses what could have taken three-quarters of a page into an inch and a half. And that inch and a half is now proportional to the significance of that experience."

Remember that lawyers won't devote much time to skimming your resume. Make sure that it's as "punchy" as possible!

g. For Gosh Sakes, if You Brought in Business or Otherwise Quantifiably Contributed to Your Prior Employer's Bottom Line or You've Raised Money for Any Community Organization, *Say So on Your Resume* ... *and Provide Numbers*

Law is a business. If you're going to go into private practice, sooner or later you'll be expected to bring in clients. If you've proven that you're persuasive by improving the financial situation of a prior employer, *say so*. If you're a champion fundraiser, *say so*. It screams "rainmaking potential" to legal employers, and there is nothing—*nothing*—more valuable to them.

You don't, incidentally, use the word "rainmaking." Just describe what you did—"Increased revenues by 200%, bringing in $3 million in business from new clients"—and let your results speak for themselves.

h. If You Have Resume Laden With Experience in a Field You Don't Want to Go Into After Law School, "Front Load" Your Experience Section With CLEs on What Interests You

We talked about this trick in the Resume chapter. Basically what you do is to view your resume as real estate, giving the "prime" real estate—toward the top—to activities related to what you want to do next. CLEs (continuing legal education seminars) are tailor-made for this; they take very little time and they inescapably indicate your interest in a particular specialty.

You can go even further and provide a narrative paragraph on your prior career, without giving each employer or experience a separate section. This will further "collapse" it down so that it is less prominent to employers.

And, of course, go to Career Services and let them fine tune your resume for you!

* * * SMART HUMAN TRICK * * *

Female student in Alabama. She'd done a lot of work with domestic violence before law school, but reported, "I don't want to go into public interest work or family law. I want to do Bankruptcy."

She started attending all of the Bankruptcy CLEs she could find. Furthermore, in interviews she pointed out to employers that her core skill was being able to counsel people in extreme situations.

She found a job with a small firm, specializing in bankruptcy.

i. Consider Sending a Letter Without a Resume

We discussed this heretical concept in the Resume chapter, Chapter 7. Briefly put: If your resume doesn't help you for *any* reason, don't lie on it, don't leave gaps ... just don't send it. Send a letter instead, where you discuss your experience in a way that helps you, focusing on the skills you bring forward and your law school experience, without having to discuss what *doesn't* help you.

Here are a few situations that merit letters without resumes:

- I talked with one law student who'd been a funeral home director for several years before law school. I couldn't help it; I got that "Ewww" look on my face. He looked at me and said, "That's how *everybody* reacts when I tell them!" What we did is to talk about what he'd done as director; he'd run a business, he'd had lots of people contact (*live* people, I mean); he'd counseled people and been heavily involved in the community. Beetlejuice Beetlejuice Beetlejuice. So he had many transferable skills, it's just that it didn't do him a lot of good to be specific about where he'd worked. He couldn't avoid it on a resume . . . but he *could,* in letters.

- Another student had a very different set of facts, but the same issue. "What do I do if I've had eight jobs in eight years and my review is always that I'm a pain in the ass?" she said. I could see what she meant; when her Career Services Director got up to introduce me, this student *heckled the director.* Different circumstances, same advice: don't send that resume!

- Yet another law student had had several careers: Masseuse, artist's model, hospital administrator and psychotherapist. With a background in jobs requiring various states of *deshabille,* her experience was best summarized in a letter.

- Another student had five different graduate degrees—*five*—and had most recently taught Greek history at the college level. He said, "I realize my resume makes me sound like a professional student—and a geek." He was concerned about sending out a C.V. with all of his degrees and jobs. A letter rather than a resume fit the bill.

As a rule of thumb, once you've met people, you can tell them just about anything in person because they can see *you* and they can put what you're telling them in context. You can modify your presentation as the reaction of your audience warrants. You don't have that kind of control when you send written materials.

So if you have something in your background that doesn't help you, consider sending a letter . . . and bringing your resume with you when you get an interview.

J. DON'T *EVER* SEND OUT A RESUME WITH A TIME GAP ON IT

We cover this issue in detail in Chapter 7. The bottom line is, whether you took time off to raise children or you were out of the job market for any other reason, employers will fill gaps on your resume in the worst possible way. Don't let that happen!

k. Never Include Lies or Misleading Descriptions of Prior Jobs

Don't inflate your experience. You have no idea when or how you might get busted, and there's no way to repair your reputation if you do.

If you're worried about a gap in your resume, explain it or send a letter instead of a resume. If you think your experience isn't impressive enough, take part in some activities right now—like CLEs, volunteering for the bar association, writing a piece for a bar publication—to goose up your credentials. Just don't lie!

* * * CAREER LIMITING MOVE * * *

Reported by an employer: "We interviewed a second career student who had on her resume, 'Created pipeline for $10 million in new business." We told her we were very impressed with her ability to bring in that much business, and she said, 'Oh, I didn't bring it in. I created a pipeline that was *capable* of it.' I suppose it wasn't a lie *per se,* but it was *very* misleading."

l. If You've Got a Whale of a Lot of Experience, Consider Sending a Functional Resume

We talk about these in Chapter 7. Essentially, a functional resume gives you the opportunity to lump together similar experiences so that they don't take up page after page of resume space. **Consider summarizing non-legal employment in a succinct paragraph or under a single descriptive heading with names of employers, titles, and dates of employment. Less important or older experience can also appear without descriptions, to save space.**

No matter how long and illustrious your career has been, and regardless of whether a lengthy C.V. would impress employers in your prior field, you just *can't* send it to legal employers. They won't read it and so it doesn't do you any good! Work with your Career Services Office to pare it down to no more than two pages or so.

I remember meeting a second career student at one law school, a real rocket scientist. I mean it. She had been a rocket scientist for twenty years before attending law school. She had spoken at numerous conferences and had tons and tons of publications. She proudly handed me her resume, which was the size of a small phone book, and said proudly, "What do you think of *this?*" I turned it over, looked at her and said, "Tell me three things you've done that would help me as an attorney." She stood there thinking for a minute, and then named three very useful things she'd done. I told her, "Great. Summarize all this experience on one page, mention how many publications you've had without naming them, and put the three things you told me about at the top of your resume, just below your education."

4. INTERVIEW ISSUES

A. READ CHAPTER 9

That's the Interviewing chapter. While there are interview issues that don't apply to "straight-through" law students that we'll discuss here, that chapter is perfectly applicable to you.

B. RESEARCH, RESEARCH, RESEARCH

Going into an interview well-versed on the employer, its practices, and you show off that research in the interview, you'll find that interviewers will look past your age and focus on what you're saying. A survey conducted by *Fortune Magazine* showed that if interviewers felt that older workers had conducted detailed research and came to the interview with an understanding of the business, their age was not a factor.

C. LOOK THE PART

And by "the part," I mean "eager new lawyer." Executive coach Tom Massey was quoted in *Fortune Magazine* saying, "I see people in their 70s who are vibrant, energetic, and in great demand. I also see 'old' 50–year-olds who are burnt out."

So ... exercise. Sleep well. Eat stuff that's good for you. Get a good haircut and dress professionally yet up-to-date. Nothing dowdy. You know ... advice that's good for anyone of any age. It's particularly important for you, in conveying the image that will get you the jobs you want!

D. RECOGNIZE THAT IF YOU'RE A 1L AND ON-CAMPUS INTERVIEW EMPLOYERS AREN'T INTERVIEWING 1LS, THEY WON'T MAKE AN EXCEPTION AND INTERVIEW YOU

This is a source of a great deal of frustration for second career students. "But I'm a mechanical engineer. You'll be doing them a favor!" As one career counselor points out, "That may be true, but we didn't create the rules. Anyway, you're not at a disadvantage. There are many options for talking to employers beyond OCI. Use those!"

E. ANTICIPATE BEHAVIOR AND WORDS THAT BORDER ON INSULTING

Your resume might make it perfectly plain that you didn't graduate from college last year, or even three years ago. Don't expect employers to read that closely, however. You may find yourself greeting interviewers who seem stunned that you're not in your early twenties. As one second career student commented to me, "It was readily apparent in several interviews that the resume readers didn't realize that a person with twenty years of work experience must be older than 25!"

Another talked about how "One interviewer greeted me with the words, 'You look much too important to be a law student.'"

Others have been told flat out, "I didn't think you'd be so old."

If you run into this kind of treatment, don't engage. It's not an invitation to a smackdown. Even if this person is a turd, it doesn't necessarily reflect the attitude of the employer in general. You'll have other opportunities to address the tactless behavior (for instance, bring it up with your Career Services Office). If you can come up with a quip in the moment to address the question, use it. You can always say, smiling, "I have no idea how to respond to that."

F. SPEAK RESPECTFULLY TO THE INTERVIEWER *EVEN IF* (S)HE'S CONSIDERABLY YOUNGER THAN YOU

You may be somewhat older and a *lot* more accomplished than the interviewer. It doesn't matter. Call them "Ms." and "Mr." until they tell you to address them by their first names. The last thing they want is the feeling that you'll upend the hierarchy at work; taking charge of the interview will do exactly that.

I know how much this stinks, by the way. As one career counselor points out, "Second career students *hate* the idea of showing respect in interviews. But that's your place on the structure. It's a political game. There are consequences in not playing it."

Remember: you always have the option of going into solo practice or joining a small shop as more of a peer than an underling. If you bristle at authority, that's probably the right choice for you.

G. HAVE "SOUND BYTES" PREPARED

There are a few elements you should have formulated and memorized:

1. Be prepared to discuss your background *even if the interviewer doesn't ask you about it*. Talk about the major transferable skills you have.

2. Have a line ready to wheel out if the issue of your age comes up.

   You can explain how being a little older is an advantage. Career Counselor Wendy Werner advises using lines like, "When I go to a meeting with a client, nobody's going to wonder how long ago I graduated. They'll think I've been out fifteen years. That's to your advantage."

   Another option is humor. It's inappropriate for an interviewer to raise the issue at all, but if they do, responding humorously will keep the job opportunity alive for you. A computer programmer who wanted to be a tax attorney, for instance, would tell legal employers that "I'm good at explaining things people don't want to know" . . . clearly a useful skill for a tax attorney!

* * * SMART HUMAN TRICK * * *

Female law student, late 30s, has an on-campus interview.

Interviewer questions her dedication to law as a career, and she responds: "You're lucky to have me. I'm old enough to be President of the United States."

She gets the call back . . . and the job.

* * * CAREER LIMITING MOVE * * *

Female law student, mid 50s. In an interview, she tells the employer, "If you hire me, you get a diversity 'two-fer.' A woman . . . *and* an old person."

H. STUDY THE INTERVIEWER'S DEMEANOR TO DETERMINE WHICH ELEMENTS OF YOUR BACKGROUND TO MENTION

If, for instance, the interviewer seems concerned about your willingness to work long hours, talk about the hours you worked in a prior job (if they were long), or the hours you put in balancing work and school (if you're an evening student). If those don't fit the bill, talk about how much time you spend on studying and taking part in law school activities (if that fits the bill).

If you've run your own shop or you've been a supervisor and the interviewer seems concerned about your willingness to be part of a team, bring out situations where you've worked with others, even if it's just as part of a study group at school where you've, say, divvied up responsibilities for creating study outlines, or a student activity where you've worked with others.

I. HAVE ANSWERS TO TOUGH QUESTIONS READY TO GO

There are certain questions that are tougher for you than a "straight-through" law student. It's important to have answers planned and rehearsed to confront these questions.

1. "WHY LAW SCHOOL?"

There are a whole host of reasons why you might have gone to law school. Whether or not you're blunt about it when you're asked is another matter entirely. Second career students have offered many career-limiting responses to this question, including:

- "I took the LSAT on a dare."
- "I've always been good at arguing."
- "I really like John Grisham books."
- "I'm doing it to get back at my former husband. He hates lawyers."
- "I want to make more money."

There are a few things to remember in formulating a response to the "Why law?" question.

First of all, remember that you're not under attack. In the interviewer's shoes, you'd be naturally curious about that prior career, too.

The two keys to a great answer are "Stressing a long-term interest in the law, and pulling the transferable skills from your prior career," according to Quinnipiac's Diane Ballou.

Let's take the long-term-interest element first. What this does is to dispel the notion that you're jumping into the law blind. Stress any experience you've had that exposed you to what you'd *really* do as a lawyer. For instance, the career of a relative or an acquaintance, experience you have dealing with lawyers of your prior employer, a relevant clinic, volunteer work, or even informational interviews with attorneys would qualify. Watching old *Perry Mason* reruns *wouldn't*.

We already discussed transferable skills. What you'd do in preparation for any particular interview is to look at that employer's particular practice, at what you'd do starting out there, and pull out your most relevant experiences. They might be skills specific to your former job, or specific to a practice (e.g., stockbroker to securities lawyer), or general (time management, counseling, selling).

Incidentally, if your old field 'dried up,' it's fine to mention that. Maybe you were in a sunset industry. Making a jump from it is fine to mention to employers. You'd still have to explain why you specifically chose law as opposed to any other field, of course. But if your old job was fading away, that's nothing to hide.

I talked to one student who'd been a manager of nuclear power plant construction. He loved it, but when nuclear power plants stopped being built (although of course that could always change . . .), he had to make a move. When employers asked him about it, he said, "It was like being an astronaut and having NASA eliminate manned space missions." Completely understandable . . . particularly coupled with a stated enthusiasm for law and an explanation of what he learned in the experience that would make him a great lawyer.

If you left your prior career for multiple reasons, remember that interviews aren't confessionals: mention the reasons that help your job chances, and don't mention others.

I've stressed over and over again that you should never lie to employers. But you don't have to be candid to the point of foolhardiness, either.

I talked with one student who'd been a restaurant manager for several years, but left when he contracted cancer and couldn't physically do the work anymore. He had since conquered the disease, but when he described his reason for turning to law, he said "I had ongoing health issues." I asked him, "Would you have eventually gone to law school, anyway, or would you have stayed in restaurants?" and he responded, "Oh, no, I was always interested in law. I would have gone one way or another." I told him to focus on that, and not to discuss the health issues.

Another student had been a financial analyst for several years before law school. Now she wanted to go into Tax Law, and when interviewers asked her why she had left her prior field, she said, "I hated what I was doing." She wasn't getting any call back interviews, and argued, "Well, I'm telling them the truth." That's as may be, but remember: you chose your prior career as well, and presumably you went into them figuring you'd like them. I asked her, "Would it be fair to say that you enjoyed the aspects of financial analysis that would carry over to a tax practice?" She responded, "Of course," and I said, "Then focus on those, and don't mention what you hated!"

In finessing this kind of answer, it's important to feel comfortable with what you say. Your Career Services Office will set up mock interviews for you at your request, and those interviews can help you with the wording you'll use for "real" interviews.

* * * CAREER LIMITING MOVE * * *

Interviewer: "Why did you go to law school?"

Second career student: "A channeler told me to get out of investment banking."

2. "AFTER DOING SOMETHING SO INTERESTING, WHY WOULD YOU WANT TO BE A LAWYER?"

... which doesn't say a lot about how the interviewer feels about his/her job, does it? There are other ways interviewers ask this question, by the way. One interviewer asked a student with a particularly glittering background, "Why the *hell* did you go to law school?"

Here's the problem: If your last gig sounds really glamorous or otherwise fun, legal employers will question your sanity in choosing law. I talked to one woman at a Midwestern law school who'd spent ten years in politics. She had been press secretary for a number of politicians, and had spent her 2L summer working in the governor's press office. She lamented, "I'm number five in my class, and I can't get a job." I asked her, "These jobs you're interviewing for—do you really *want* them?" She said matter-of-factly, "No. What I *really* want is to work with fashion houses. Or Court TV." Well! Here she'd had this really glamorous career, and what she wanted was *another* glamorous career. Employers can't read your mind, but they know when you don't really want to do what they do. *That's* pretty obvious! So job one is to make sure that you're only interviewing for positions that truly interest you. You can't—and shouldn't—fake enthusiasm. If you don't think there's anything that interests you, go back to Chapter 2, and treat your job search as an education about the vast array of jobs out there, before you start searching for any particular one.

Other students have had equally amazing prior gigs. A student at a New York law school had represented Jordan—the country, not the basketball player—in front of international tribunals, arguing that they had acted in accordance with UN guidelines on torture. Another student had started writing a newspaper column at the age of 16, and had published hundreds of feature articles since then.

If you *are* enthusiastic about jobs you're interviewing for, address the glamour issue head on. Tell interviewers straight out, "It *was* very interesting, but I'll tell you why I'm drawn to what you do . . ." and tell them the truth about why your goal is what it is. If your "plea" includes the fact that you've talked with people who do it, that you've had the chance to volunteer or take a clinic or shadow someone, that you've heard a lot about it at bar association functions or CLEs . . . they'll believe you. They'll *have* to, because you're telling the truth, and—more importantly—it'll *sound* that way!

3. "HOW WILL YOU FEEL WITH A SUPERVISOR YOUNGER THAN YOU?"

This is a *very* important issue for legal employers. They're terrified that you'll come in, upset the apple cart, and start telling your younger supervisors, "Let me tell you something, you little whipper snapper . . ."

Instead, as Gina Sauer recommends, "You need to provide specific examples of your ability to work with younger people. 'I've worked with people of different ages/levels/experience, I'm a team player, and I have experience on a project where . . .'" Let your experiences speak for you.

You could also say with a smile, "In terms of experience, I'm younger than you are," and then give your examples.

4. SALARY QUESTIONS . . .

While salary questions are unusual in interviews for legal jobs, they're more likely to come up for you, because employers will be concerned that your money expectations will be high. As Sue Gainen says, "You can't tell an employer, 'But I need to make this much . . .'"

Knowledge is power. Before you interview for any job, research the approximate salary range. You'll find the statistics for legal jobs all over the country at www.nalp.org and at your Career

Services Office; for alternative careers, check www.salary.com. Then when the salary issue comes up, you can say, "I understand from research that firms like yours offer between X and X." If you want more than that, look at Chapter 18, Topic E on negotiating for more money ... but you'd wait until you received an offer for that. You wouldn't bring it up in an interview!

Notice what this kind of answer does for you. It means for a start that you don't have to discuss how much you made in your prior career. And it suggests your familiarity with the employer, which is a huge plus. On top of that, if they were anticipating offering you *less* than the market rate ... they can't anymore!

5. "ARE YOU WILLING TO BE A FIRST YEAR ASSOCIATE AND/OR START ALL OVER AGAIN?"

Of course, only say "yes" if that's the truth! If not, don't take interviews with employers who expect it of you.

If you *are* willing to start anew, your answer has to convey not just your willingness but your *enthusiasm* for it! You can even say, "I wouldn't be here wasting your time if I *wasn't* looking forward to it," and then fill out your explanation with proof that you've spoken with people/done research so you know what to expect. In other words, back up your enthusiasm with knowledge.

Incidentally, it's all right if you're also nervous about starting over. That's natural. But the employer doesn't have to hear it.

You can also point out that you don't view it entirely as starting over again, because you expect to build on the skills you learned doing X ... but make a point of saying that you know you've got a lot to learn, and you look forward to it.

6. "WHAT ARE YOUR TRANSFERABLE SKILLS?"

Well! I think we've talked *this* to death. Just be prepared to discuss the skills that are most applicable to this employer.

J. DON'T SPANK EMPLOYERS

I've talked with a lot of second career students who have the feeling that lawyers are whiners. They'll tell me, in that Popeye voice, "Arrghh, these lawyers, they don't know what stress is!" "You want to talk about *pressure?* In my old job, I carried ice blocks at three in the morning with my teeth ..." "Working on a whaling ship, now that's a job for a real man!" I'm just kidding about those last two, but you see my point. It's entirely possible that what you did before involved a lot more responsibility, stress and pressure than being a lawyer *ever* would.

But you can't say that. Lawyers think they've got high-pressure jobs, so play along. It may well be a walk in the park compared to what you've done, but being condescending won't get you the gigs you want. You *can* say, "I'm used to working under pressure ..." and then describe what you did. But that's a far sight from saying, "Pressure? *You* have no idea what pressure *is!*"

5.   FIND "UNPOSTED" JOBS THROUGH PEOPLE AND ACTIVITIES

As we discussed in detail in Chapter 10, people and activities are the key to nailing great jobs. You've probably already gotten jobs that way. I'd encourage you to read that chapter, making a list of people to contact and things to do. In particular, consider:

- Recontacting any attorneys you've worked with in any capacity, no matter how long it's been. You can always e-mail them first to let them know you'll be calling. A woman at a West Coast school had been a wine distributor, and wanted to get into tax law with her law degree. She went to her old clients and asked them who their tax attorneys were; they put her onto their lawyers, and she contacted the lawyers saying, "Your client X told me to contact you." As she reports, "Contacting lawyers through their clients *guarantees* that they'll talk to you. They want to keep the clients!"

- Taking part in a "Students Older Than Average" group at school (or encouraging your school to start one if it doesn't exist). Some law schools have these groups, and second career students report that they're very helpful not just in making contacts but in feeling less isolated in school.

- Contacting former employers and co-workers.

A.   WHEREVER YOU CAN, GET INTO EMPLOYERS THROUGH YOUR CONTACTS RATHER THAN THROUGH THE RECRUITING COORDINATOR/HIRING PERSON

If your work or community activities have brought you into contact with lawyers you'd like to work with, use that route to get your foot in the door. Here's why. If you go through a formal hiring person, they'll judge you strictly on the basis of your law school credentials (read: grades). If you bring a lot of other things to the table, you're best off making your case through someone you know. As the recruiting coordinator at one large firm pointed out, "If we have partners who tell us to bring in someone for an interview, we do it. We don't have a choice."

B.   IF YOU'RE A "PERSON OF A CERTAIN AGE," MAKE SURE THAT WHEN YOU VOLUNTEER PEOPLE DON'T ASSUME YOU'VE RETIRED

A student in upstate New York, in her 60s, found that when she volunteered for legal organizations they just assumed that she'd retired, and she was helping out for fun. She started telling people she volunteered with, "I'm volunteering because I want to be a lawyer!" People were surprised, but when she made it plain she was there to get her foot in the door, they helped her out.

D.   IF YOU WERE IN THE MILITARY . . .

Well—thanks for stepping up to the plate, for a start.

With a military background, you've got a few issues to consider:

1.   TRANSLATING MILITARY EXPERIENCE INTO "CIVILIANESE"

Your first, most important task is to make your military experience comprehensible to legal employers. As a rule of thumb, if your title was anything other than "Chairman of the Joint Chiefs of Staff," assume lawyers won't know what you did if you don't explain it to them. "X–4 Officer on Flux Capacitor Transmogrification Program, responsible for WY Velocity Vector Group" is Greek to legal employers.

How do you yank out your transferable skills? As Career Counselor Amy Mallow advises, "You have to go beyond your title, and look at the skills you learned that would be applicable in a civilian environment. For instance, let's say that you've had to work as a member of a group to accomplish tasks. That proven ability to be a team player is valuable to many legal employers. Also, look at what you've done and identify if you've had to organize projects, juggle conflicting responsibilities, create a budget, or train people—things like that. Those are skills that will generate interest in you from civilian employers."

It pays to practice this. Pretend you're talking to a civilian you want to work for, and you have to give that person the reasons to hire you. You've got to make the connection for them; think about what it is you'd do if you worked for this employer, and how your experience translates into the ability to do—or quickly learn—those tasks.

Use wording like "In the army, I did X, and this shows that I can do Y for you." Saying that you've attained the rank of, say, Captain, isn't by itself meaningful to civilians. But if it required you to supervise increasing numbers of people, that reflects leadership, a skill that's valuable to legal employers. You'd want to go even further and state the number of people you've supervised. Numbers are something that anyone can grasp, while saying you led a "platoon" or a "company" isn't.

Also highlight any technical skills you've learned that would be relevant to the kind of career you're after. For instance, if your military work involved using computers, that's a skill many employers covet. Or perhaps your experience gave you scientific knowledge that would be useful to an intellectual property practice. Or maybe you've become familiar with an industry that forms the client base for a certain specialty. Whatever your experience is, it might give you a particular expertise that you can easily sell to appropriate civilian employers.

2.   REMEMBER THE CHARACTER TRAITS THAT MILITARY EXPERIENCE INHERENTLY SUGGESTS

Leadership, integrity, respect for authority, the ability to hit the ground running and learn tasks quickly . . . those are all qualities that naturally flow from military experience. Sprinkle them into your correspondence and interviews when you want to stress how your military experience will help you in civilian jobs.

3.   EXPECT SOME INTERVIEWERS TO BE JERKS

You don't need me to tell you that some people have a negative view of the military. You might even interview with them. A law student who was a former soldier was actually asked by an interviewer, "Did you kill people?"

If this happens to you, shrug off the insult, and say something like, "I'll tell you what I learned that will be useful to you . . ." and leave it at that. Remember: no single interviewer reflects everybody at an employer. You may be talking to the only idiot in the place. If you like, report the matter to your Career Services Office. But in the moment, take the high road.

4.   TAKE ADVANTAGE OF ON-LINE RESOURCES AIMED AT FORMER MILITARY PERSONNEL

There are job boards on line that focus expressly on ex-military people. While they are job boards for *all* job seekers, it's worth giving them a look-see to see what they offer, and at the very least give you organizations that seek people with a military background:

www.military.com

www.recruitmilitary.com

www.vetjobs.com

5.   REACH OUT TO ATTORNEYS AT EMPLOYERS WHO HAVE A MILITARY BACKGROUND THEMSELVES

Law students with a military background often overlook an obvious source of tremendous help: lawyers with the same background.

When you're doing targeted mailings (Chapter 7) or seeking out lawyers for informational interviews (Chapter 10), make a point of doing a LEXIS or Westlaw search for attorneys with military backgrounds, or when you're targeting a particular employer, look at the attorney profiles on the employer's web site. Amy Mallow also recommends that you "Contact the Pentagon and ask them for databases and profiles that show you the same thing."

While there are other points of commonality you can use—for instance, choosing attorneys who are alums of your school—the military gives you just one more reason to target a particular attorney for advice.

6.   IF YOUR MILITARY EXPERIENCE GAVE YOU TECHNICAL EXPERTISE, REACH OUT TO LEGAL EMPLOYERS IN SPECIALTIES THAT WOULD FIND IT VALUABLE

Your Career Services Office at school can direct you to those employers, or you can do a LEXIS or Westlaw search yourself.

When you contact these employers, make sure your resume reflects your technical expertise *immediately* after your legal education, at the very top of your experience section. Remember: you always want to front-load your resume with the information most relevant to the employer who's receiving that resume. So highlight your technical expertise for employers who will value it by listing it *first*.

E.   If You're a Returning-to-Paid-Work Mom ...

May I tell you first of all how much I resent it when people ask moms if they've been "working"? Ha! Motherhood is a 24–7 job. A *job*. Just because you don't get paid for it doesn't make it less of a career.

There. I'll get down off my soapbox now.

Let's talk about transitioning back into the paid work force if you've taken time off to mom ...

1.   Take Advantage of the Advice in Chapter 10

If you sit with a pad of paper and a pen and skim the headings in Chapter 10, you'll see that you have a wealth of resources for getting back into paid work. From people to activities to flexible gigs to part-time jobs, it's all there.

2.   Talk About What You're Looking for With Everyone You've Met Because of Your Kids

Face it: you've met tons of people because of your kids. From teachers to other parents to administrators to coaches ... the list is long.

As we discussed in Chapter 10, it's important to let people know what you're interested in doing. Don't ask them for jobs; tell them you're in school (if they don't already know) and ask if there's anyone they can suggest that you talk to for advice, any activities in which you ought to take part.

I've talked with so many returning-to-paid-work moms who've found great jobs just this way!

3.   Look at Doing Contract Work

We talked about contract work in Chapter 10; it's basically project-oriented temporary work for law firms. It's easier to get than a permanent gig because employers are only making a short-term decision about you. *Nonetheless,* it gets your feet wet and it gets you a resume item, as well as exposure to employers.

4.   Volunteer for the Bar Association

I suggest this for everybody, not just moms, but really—it's a great way to meet people and gets leads on jobs before they ripen into job postings. Make a point of joining, introducing yourself to the head of the practice that most interests you, and volunteering for research projects and/or events.

5. RESUME ISSUES

A. NO TIME GAPS!

Whether it's with community activities, committee work, helping with your kids' school . . . you can't leave time gaps on your resume. Nobody can. Employers fill them in in the worst possible way. Institutionalization. Prison. Federal Witness Protection Program. If you had periods of time where you raised your kids without taking part in any activities, say so. Raising children is a perfectly appropriate resume item. The point remains: no gaps!

B. PUT ON YOUR RESUME ANY COMMUNITY ACTIVITIES IN WHICH YOU'VE BEEN INVOLVED, *PARTICULARLY* FUNDRAISERS

We've all seen those reports in the newspapers around Mother's Day every year, where they calculate that if a mom was paid for everything she did, she'd earn in excess of $100,000 a year. Right. In our dreams. While you can't put down "chauffeur, nurse, tutor . . ." and so forth on your resume, be *sure* that you list any community, fundraising, and leadership activities in which you've taken part. Mention numbers where you can; amounts of money raised, budgets managed, and numbers of attendees at functions you ran. They all suggest rainmaking potential, and there's nothing more valuable to private employers than that.

C. GO TO CLES AND CONFERENCES TO GET PROFESSIONAL ITEMS ON YOUR RESUME, AND TO MEET PEOPLE

Especially when you feel you've got a somewhat sparse resume, CLEs—continuing legal education seminars—are a great way to get relevant information on your resume in a hurry. We talk about CLEs in detail in Chapter 10.

6. DON'T BE SHY ABOUT CONDUCTING INFORMATIONAL INTERVIEWS WITH YOUR SPOUSE'S FRIENDS AND COLLEAGUES, AND ANY OTHER LAWYERS YOU KNOW

One of the most difficult things to do is to change the way people think of you. If they're used to thinking of you as Henry's wife and Harry's mommy, the thought of you as a lawyer-in-training can be challenging.

A great way to get around this is to conduct formal informational interviews with people who know you through your spouse or through the community. Tell them you're thinking about what to do with your law degree and you'd like to meet them for fifteen minutes, maybe over a cup of coffee, to pick their brain for ideas. It's a better idea to do this as a regular interview than just to chat about it at a party or a soccer game, because an informational interview will automatically put you more in the role of a student.

7. INTERVIEW ISSUES

A. BE CAREFUL ABOUT HOW YOU BRING UP YOUR FULL-TIME-MOMMY DECISION

You don't want to say anything that suggests that being a full-time mom is superior to being a working mom. If you're interviewing with a woman, she might well have made a different decision than you, and probably still considers herself a good mom. And if you're interviewing with a man, he might well be married to a working mom. Instead, just say that it's the decision you made, and now you're interested in working with this employer because ... and get them *off* the mommy issue!

B. DRAW ANALOGIES USING WORK YOU DID ON COMMITTEES AND FUNDRAISERS AND COMMUNITY ACTIVITIES ... NOT IN YOUR MOMMY ROLE

There's no question that managing children has a lot of parallels with managing people in the workplace. In fact, there's a whole book about that very topic: *If you've raised children you can manage anybody.* But in interviews, you don't want to talk about how handling squabbles between your twins makes you good at resolving conflict. As one career counselor points out, "That might be accurate, but it won't carry a lot of sway with an interviewer."

Instead, draw analogies from your "grown-up" activities. For instance, you could point out that by running a school fair you utilized your management skills, because you had a crew of fifty people and a budget of $50,000. Or you emceed your kids' school's annual fundraiser to hone your public speaking skills. Whatever it is, you see the point: use activities that aren't mom-oriented to show off the transferable skills you bring to the job.

* * * SMART HUMAN TRICK ... EVENTUALLY * * *

From a new alum in his mid–40's to his law school career counselor:

"My streak of interviews without offers has continued for the several months since I contacted you last. Clearly, there is something seriously wrong with me as a person that I am not getting, and which makes me so objectionable that nobody will hire me.

I am at the point where my wife has ordered me to seek professional help. You have been great but you have done all you can. Can you recommend some kind of professional service I could use?

Thanks again. I appreciate your help."

An e-mail to the same counselor a month later:

"I finally got hired. I don't know if this made the difference but I dealt aggressively with the age issue. I also dressed like a Republican, and got a fresh hair cut."

Who knows?"

Chapter 23
Large Law Firms: Are They for You? ... and if They Are, How Do You Get in Without Stellar Credentials?

"There is no fortress so strong that money will not take it."

        Cicero

From a Dilbert comic strip:

Dogbert: "Welcome to Dogbert's seminar on work-life balance. First, review this list of your priorities:

Family

Job

Exercise

Vacation

Must-dos

Medical

Eating

Hygiene

Sleep

Romance

Holidays

"You have time for three things. Work and holidays are two. You get to pick the third."

Funny, isn't it? Everyone comes to law school with a different dream, but then Second Year comes around, and–bang! Everybody wants to go to a large law firm. It's like salmon spawning. It happened to me. If it hasn't happened to you yet . . . it probably will.

Here's the rub. The two rubs, actually. No matter how alluring they seem, working at a large law firm may not be your dream job. I'm not talking about the paycheck—that's certainly a dream!—I'm talking about the day-to-day existence. Maybe it's for you, and maybe not. In this chapter, we'll see how important it is not to fall prey to misleading descriptives. It's easy to assume that the employer who pays the most is the "best." It's easy to see a published list of "top law firms" and assume that means "best place to work," rather than "largest" or "most revenue," which is what they measure. Size itself doesn't make an employer good or bad. Depending on what you're like and what you want out of a job, you might enjoy large firms. *Your* "top" employer is the one that suits you best, regardless of how many lawyers work there and the swag the firm brings in. We'll spend the first half of this chapter figuring out if a large law firm really is your "top" employer.

The other rub is that even if it *is* the right setting for you, you may not have the credentials to make large law firms roll out the red carpet for you and sprinkle peony petals before your feet. The vast majority of us don't have solid gold credentials. So, the last half of this chapter addresses ways to get into large firms if you don't have the GPA chops to go in through the front door.

Let's get started.

A. Is a Large Firm the Right Place for You?

There's a cottage industry built around slamming large law firm life. Books, blogs, movies—some of them really funny—they all suggest that life at large law firms is just awful. The comments I've heard from many career counselors and law firm lawyers and administrators certainly reflect that:

> *"Most people are miserable at large law firms!"*

> *"Most people shouldn't be associates at large firms. It's an awful fit."*

> *"After a couple of years with a large firm most people look in the mirror and say, 'I want to be happy.' "*

> *"Law students don't know what it's like at a large law firm! Their sense is it's like the 1950s, when every girl wanted to be a stewardess. They think it's exciting, sexy, adventurous, and prestigious. The truth is that it's really hard to succeed."*

> *"There's this misconception that working for a large firm means glamour, excitement, great deals, interesting clients, travel. The truth is that they'll spend four years in the library. They get lied to a lot!"*

"Look at large firm people a few years down the road. They look like they've had the life beaten out of them."

Yikes. On top of that, large firms have pretty deadly attrition statistics. Studies variously say that half of associates at large firms are gone after three years; after five years, the "see ya" rate rises to 70%.

So that's the bad news. But there's another side to the story.

"A lot of people who are unhappy at large law firms probably shouldn't have been there in the first place," commented one attorney development administrator at a large law firm. "I'd say that of the ones who leave, a third shouldn't ever have been there; a third find a better job because of their large firm experience; and another third make a jump because their life circumstances change, they get married, they have kids, they want more time."

And those statistics on attrition are only relevant if you compare them to workers in general. According to a 2006 study by salary.com, at any given time almost two-thirds—62%—of people said they would be looking for a new job within three months. *Half* had already posted their resumes on line. (Incidentally: If you're working, it's really, really *stoopid* to post your resume on line, unless you don't care if your employer sees it.)

So you could reasonably argue that associates at large law firms are at least as happy as anybody else. As a partner at one large, prestigious firm puts it, "Most people at law firms are happy most of the time. It's unusual to find that everybody's happy every day. Especially in law, especially at large firms, there are significant demands. Hours can be very grueling. Circumstances can be difficult. Deadlines can be difficult. If you're a litigator, there's the contentiousness in terms of dealing with opposing counsel, the frustrations with judges not understanding or disagreeing with your position, but of course that's not unique to large firms. But it can make life as a lawyer at times quite difficult, and sometimes generally challenging. However, the fact is, most lawyers are generally happy in that they find their work fulfilling, challenging, interesting. It's not boring."

The key element in determining if you'll be happy at a large firm? **Research, both into what you want and what large firms are like ... and due diligence about the nature of the firm(s) you're considering.** I'll provide you a good start in this chapter, and you should without question check out resources like the AMLAW 100 and AMLAW 200 from *The American Lawyer* (they're at your CSO), but when you're talking about any particular employer, there's no getting around the fact that you need to talk to people there—several times, in depth, and not just the people thrown in front of you when you're being wooed—as well as people who used to work there or are otherwise familiar with the firm. As a law firm partner says, "The best source of information is to talk to people who've graduated a year or two ago.

Let's face it; many firms actively recruit top law students, they're wined and dined, and given a great presentation. Meanwhile there can be tendency to lock up ogres in the dungeon until students have signed on! The best way to do due diligence is to go outside formal recruitment process and talk to alums at law schools. That's how I found this firm. I got some pretty blunt assessments, good and bad, in a way that a formal interview process can't cover."

Another partner at another firm adds, "Firms often try to pass themselves off as something they're not. Some like to sound like they're Navy SEALS, as though it creates some kind of mystique ... but they really aren't that tough. Others market themselves as humane, but in reality are something less than that."

A recruiting coordinator at a large firm laughs, "We have a kind of code. We have some lawyers here who are serious a**holes, but in front of students, we characterize them as 'smart and aggressive.' " A hiring partner at another firm notes, "Every firm says they're collegial, there'll be a balance, there's a no-a**hole policy. What idiot will not put their best foot forward?"

You'll find that firms have different personalities. At some of them, if you get so drunk at a firm function that you yak in the potted palm, you'll be ostracized. At others, it's like, "Hey! Sandy's in the club!" Also, firms have strengths in different areas. If you want a particular specialty, you need to research firms to see who's strongest in your target practice area. Keep an eye on the legal press on-line, look at firm websites to see what they accentuate, and ask around. And keep an open mind; don't let a couple of anecdotes form your opinion of a large firm in general.

So there's a bit of homework you'll have to do when you close this book. We'll talk here about the nature of large law firms in general, and also the upsides and downsides of starting your career with a large firm.

* * * SMART HUMAN TRICK * * *

Law student, considering one particular large firm. During his interviews, he is told the firm's hours are "on a par" with others. He asks to meet with junior associates, and talks with one over lunch. During the meal, the associate mentions casually, "I get the best service from West research attorneys at 2 a.m."

1. HOW LARGE LAW FIRMS WORK

When you think of large firms, your perception probably goes to the prestige, the classy offices, the fabulous salaries, the front-page clients. You probably haven't given much thought to what makes them *run*. As a jumping off point, it makes sense to explain to you *exactly* how large firms function.

At its heart, a large law is just like a hot dog stand. They're both businesses. A law firm has a product that it sells for money. Like every business, it makes more money by doing one of two things: either by increasing its sales or decreasing its expenses.

When you're talking about products law firms produce, you're talking about *billable hours*. You've heard *that* before! Basically, a "billable hour" is time that's directly attributable to a client, so the time you spend researching, or talking with a client, or writing memoranda or briefs or contracts, or appearing in court, that's *billable* time. Time that you spend on administrative matters, or breaks, or lunch, or recruiting new associates, training, continuing legal education, pro bono work, professional reading, surfing the web—that doesn't count. All that counts are billable hours, hours directly attributable to a client. So to get back to my point about a law firm's product, the more of its product it sells to its clients, the more money it makes. And that means that the more billable hours a law firm's attorneys spend on a client's work, the more money the firm makes.

It's also important to know who *makes* that extra money. As with any business, the profits go to the owners. In law firms, that means the equity partners. As you probably already know, law firms have two, basic levels of attorneys: partners and associates. Equity partners own the firm. So if it's more profitable, they make more money. (There is another class of partner called "non-equity partner." As the name suggests, those partners do not own the firm. "Why," I asked one law firm administrator, "Do they call them partners, then?" "So they can say 'I'm a partner at so-and-so at parties,'" she laughed. "Hey—it works. They stay.")

The other class of people at law firms are associates, who are salaried employees. No matter how much the firm makes, associates get their salaries. They don't partake in the profits of the firm, although in many large firms, they do get bonuses (however there need not be any direct relation between those bonuses and the firm's profits).

Pretty simple so far. I'm telling you all this by way of background, because this structure has important ramifications for you if you join a large firm.

2.   THE UPSIDES AND DOWNSIDES OF LARGE LAW FIRM PRACTICE. WHETHER IT WORKS FOR YOU DEPENDS ON WHAT DRIVES YOU . . . AND WHAT YOU CAN TOLERATE

You may be absolutely, brilliantly happy at a large law firm. It all depends on what's important to you, what your life circumstances are like. You're the only one who can tell not just what you want and don't want, but how intensely you feel about any particular facet of a job. In this section, we'll figure out if the large law firm thing will work for you.

A couple of notes up front.

These upsides and downsides are categorized according to how most people I talked to felt about them. That doesn't mean you'll feel the same way. Long hours are a negative for most people; you may enjoy being consumed by your work.

A second point: these are all from the perspective of a junior associate. Not a summer clerk; summer clerkships are meaningless. They don't call them "summer partners" for nothing. And they're not from a partner's perspective, either. A firm is a very different animal when bringing in business is your principal goal.

With that in mind, let's look at the plusses and minuses of large law firms:

A. THE UPSIDES OF LARGE LAW FIRM LIFE

When I asked counselors, lawyers and administrators "Who's happy at a large law firm?" I got some humorous answers. "The psychos." "Nobody." "The huge egos."

But when they were being serious, the phrases I heard over and over again were:

"Students who are driven"

"Students who thrive on intellectual challenges"

"Students who like the opportunity to be a piece of very big-name, sexy issues"

"People who don't care about controlling their schedule"

"Students who recognize they have to pay their dues."

"People who are competitive"

"Students who are driven by prestige"

"People who value the professional development aspect of getting a large law firm credential"

"Students who want to 'mature' for a couple of years before they make a longer-term decision"

"People who have a work-hard, play-hard mentality"

"The person who likes the opposite of what most people like! If your work is your life, you'll be successful there."

Let's take a look at the upsides I heard the most:

1. MAD CHEESE

There's no getting around it. The starting pay law firms offer—comfortably into six figures—is greater than any other single category of legal employer. If money has always been a prime motivator for you, large law firms are a sensible target.

Money can be an *enormous* motivation if you're like most law students and live life pretty close to the vest economically. One hiring partner at a large firm told me, "Law school is the last time poverty is fashionable." Who's not sick of instant macaroni and cheese and 50 cent draft beers? On top of that, you've probably racked up a whopping great pile of student loan debt, and you may be facing substantial student loan payments as a result. As one law school career counselor pointed out, "For some students, their student loan debts mean that with a large firm income, after they've made their loan payments, they're living on just an average salary."

The plan of many a law student is to go to a large firm for two or three years, pay off most of their debt, and then go on to what they "really want to do," virtually debt-free. There's certainly merit to that plan.

But let's take another look at the money issue ...

First of all, are you *sure* that money is a core motivator for you? If you've never had it, the bling might seem tempting, but it may not make you as happy as you think it will. Research suggests that happiness *does* increase as income rises ... *up to $50,000 a year!* After that, it's not a factor. Rather, it's always the *next* $10,000 that people feel will make them happy. We're hard-wired *not* to be satisfied with what we've got, and that certainly applies to money. I read a great quote once that said, "Is a man with $16 million happier than a man with $15 million?" Maybe .. but not because of the extra dough.

Secondly, notice that I said large firms have the highest starting pay. They are *not* the sole province of huge earning potential, however. You can make piles of dead presidents in other jobs as well. There are alternative careers like investment banking, where the money is obscene. In law, there's personal injury work and specialties like it, which is *very* lucrative and only practiced by small law firms.

Furthermore, although small firms start you off with much lower pay than large firms, your salary will grow much more quickly. Large firms suffer from what's called "compression"— that is, the salaries stay relatively flat because of the high starting rate. At a small law firm, you can soon catch up with and even surpass what you would have made at a large law firm. On average, small law firm and large law firm salaries are only 10% apart after five years.

While the potential of enormous dough isn't there for government jobs, if you look at what you make on an hour-for-hour basis, it's a lot closer than you think. There are some absolutely fabulous government gigs—the Justice Department, state attorney general offices, federal agencies—that are not just great jobs but typically have *very* reasonable hours. If you work half the hours for a lot less pay, on an hourly basis you may not be losing out.

But of course, you can't work two government jobs. And if money is a big motivator for you, that augers well for your happiness at a large law firm.

2. Prestige

Prestige and money together are the strongest motivators for working at a large law firm. If you're driven by both of them, large law firms are an obvious target. When people ask you where you work (or where you're going to work), who *doesn't* want to mention an employer that makes their jaws drop?

"Some people just like being at the top of their game," reports a senior associate at a very large law firm. "Let's face it. If you're a baker, where do you want to see your stuff? At fabulous weddings . . . or in some grocery store in New Jersey?"

It's worth sharing a few words of caution about prestige.

For a start, if it's the only thing keeping you going, you need to know that it wears thin *very* quickly. After all, prestige is something that really only works for you when you tell other people where you work, or you see your firm's name in the paper. Your happiness is a function of your life on a day-to-day basis. If you're doing something you don't like, you'll begin to resent it very quickly, whether it's prestigious or not. As one Career Services Director told me, "I don't want to break anyone's dreams, but if all you want is the right office, the right corner, the right view— then you really don't want to be a lawyer." Think about what it is that you're going to be *doing,* not the sound of the firm's name as it rolls off your tongue. After all, it's your *life* we're talking about!

Another point to consider: Large firms aren't the only place where you can find prestige. *Many* Career Services Directors, as well as practicing attorneys, point out that small "boutique" firms, which are recognized for a particular specialty, carry all the prestige of large firms. Your Career Services Director, alums, local attorneys, and upperclassmen can tell you who these firms are in your city. It's worth doing a little bit of digging to find them. Also, there are a lot of people—me included—who think some really choice jobs are elsewhere. The Justice Department, judicial clerkships, prosecutors' offices, and a whole ton of public interest gigs, renowned small firms—the list goes on and on. Prestige is a matter of perspective.

You also want to be careful about the desire for prestige masking other issues you have. It may be, for instance, that you went to an OK college and an OK law school, and working for a large firm would be the first time anybody would *ever* be impressed with what you do. "It was *so* seductive," reports one student from a second-tier law school. "Everybody knew the firm I clerked for. As soon as I mentioned its name, I was automatically cloaked with intelligence, prestige, success, all of which had never been associated with *me* before. It made me ignore what the whole job was like, and for me it kind of sucked."

Finally, you want to distinguish between your internal desire for prestige and *external* pressure to choose the most prestigious option. That little voice you hear—egging you on to take the firm with the sexy name—may not be your own.

For instance, you may be choosing the prestigious option to please your parents. A former associate for a very large firm said, "My parents wanted me to go to law school in the first place. They helped pay for it. I knew how proud they would be to be able to say, 'My daughter works at . . .' " As one Career Services Director adds, "If your parents want you to work at a 'name' firm, they're only responding to a media thing. They probably only know the splashy names they see on TV or read about in the paper."

3. PURE CHALLENGE

If you thrive on challenge, a large law firm can be intoxicating. You've got challenges in terms of the amount of work you're expected to do, the billables you're expected to rack up, the deadlines, the kinds of legal questions you have to resolve. As one recruiting coordinator reports, "People who are classic Type A personalities thrive in this environment. They're not happy unless they're under a lot of pressure."

4. SEXY CLIENTS/SOPHISTICATED WORK

If you get juiced by the idea of seeing the names of your firm's clients in the media, a large firm is a smart target. As one associate at a large firm reports, "When you're at a firm like mine, it's where the top companies send their work. If Disney merges, where are they going to go? We'll be at the top of their list." Another adds, "There's something cool about doing work for companies whose names you see in the Wall Street Journal every day."

I talked with a venture capitalist about the law firm who represented his firm, and I asked: "Why don't you use a smaller firm? You could get the same work done, probably for less money." He laughed and said, "You don't understand. We're talking about deals for hundreds of millions of dollars. The investors and investment bankers we deal with expect to see certain names on the law firm letterhead. There are very few of them. Uncle Joe's law firm might well do work that is just as good if not superior, but we could never hire them."

The "sophisticated work" aspect is more of a puzzler. You probably can't define it, even though you've heard it over and over again. I asked tons of lawyers, counselors and administrators for their definition, and they were all over the map:

"Cutting edge issues"

"Intellectually challenging work"

"An established practice with big-name clients"

"A variety of issues, not just slip-and-fall cases"

One recruiting coordinator came right out and said, "Frankly, I don't know what it is—all I know is that *every* law firm says that's what it does!"

Having said that, there are sound reasons to seek a "sophisticated practice" at a large law firm.

For instance, it may be that your dream is to work for certain heavyweights in a particular department of a large firm, people who are real stars in the field. In that case, that firm is an obvious target.

Or let's say you've done some soul-searching, and you're intellectually drawn to particular specialties that can only be handled by large firms. For instance, securities issues, cutting-edge corporate deals, M & A, complex corporate litigation–those kinds of practices can really only be handled by large firms. As one Career Services Director pointed out, "There's a difference between saying you want a certain kind of practice and saying you want to work at a large law firm. If you want a certain type of clientele that goes to large firms, that's a good reason to opt for a large firm. But if you just want to be a litigator, you can do that anywhere." A law firm administrator commented, "There are people who just have a passion for the kind of work we do. There are associates who just love the idea of taking new companies public. It's not just money. It's not just something they fell into. They have a genuine passion for it."

If you don't have such laser-targeted goals, however, it's a mistake to assume that large law firms are the only ones that do sophisticated work. As one Career Services Director points out, "Some solo practitioners change the face of the law!" A recruiting coordinator suggests that you can find very sophisticated work being done by "boutique" firms whose lawyers have broken away from a larger firm. There are many, many environments with "sophisticated work"—government agencies, judicial clerkships, employers of every stripe—so if it's just generically challenging work you want, you can find that in *many* places!

Finally, keep in mind that it doesn't matter if your employer does sophisticated work—what counts is whether *you get to do any of it*. As one recruiting coordinator points out, "You have to ask yourself, what does it mean to *you* if your firm has a sophisticated practice? How does it impact *you?*"

It's possible to get trapped for years in tedious document reviews and other discovery issues, writing memos and briefs on tiny aspects of huge cases. (It's also possible to avoid that, if you lobby for yourself effectively. That's really more appropriate for another book like, oh, my book *What Law School Doesn't Teach You ... But You Really Need To Know.)*

So that's it: if sexy clients motivate you, large firms make sense. And sophisticated work? If you're selective about it, you'll find that at large firms, too.

5. EXCELLENT RESOURCES

Everyone who's happy at large law firms raves about the outstanding resources. "There's nothing for me to do here except *think,*" said one large law firm associate. "There are support staffers for everything. We have state-of-the-art computer equipment. The minute a new gadget comes out, we get it. The research materials are unbeatable. The librarians, the databases we can tap into, the training, I could not be more impressed."

There's no way any other kind of legal employer can compete with that. Some lawyers at other settings would sniff that "Large firms need great training programs because the junior associates don't actually get to *do* anything," but the fact remains: If great resources are important to you, you'll like large law firms.

6. BRILLIANT MENTORS AND ROLE MODELS

While you can find brilliant lawyers and role models in many settings, there's no question that many of them congregate in large law firms, where they are the "marquee" names. One junior associate reported to me the experience of "Sitting in the office of a lawyer I'd read about for years, we were chatting about strategy on a case he was handling and he read me a brief he wrote. It was like music. I felt so privileged to be there." Another junior associate reports that, "It's a tremendous benefit to see great lawyers at work. You get to observe without plunging in."

The existence of great mentors and role models varies from firm to firm; the research I encouraged you to do at the start of this section will help you identify which *specific* firm(s) has/have the people you'd most like to work with.

7. A CREDENTIAL THAT CAN OPEN OTHER DOORS

If you think about going to a large law firm for a couple of years and then doing what you really want to do, you're not alone. A lot of students have that same idea, and it's not an unsound strategy. As one former associate with a large firm reports, "It's ironic. When small or medium firms look for laterals, they take associates from large firms ... even though those people won't have done as much litigation!"

Another benefit of working for a large firm: you may figure you can pay down a lot of student loan debt for a couple of years, and then take a lower-paying job you enjoy more. It's difficult to maintain that kind of discipline; a lot of associates find that the way they reward themselves for grueling hours or unsatisfying work is to splurge. "Nobody needs an $800 trenchcoat," said one associate. "But I'd been working around the clock, and what the hell, what's the money for?" Nonetheless, if you're careful with your money, you can pay off much if not all of your debt. That's a tremendous benefit.

You may, however, find yourself with "velvet handcuffs." Particularly if you buy an expensive home, a pricey car, and you get used to dining in fine restaurants, it can be hard to ratchet back to living like—well, like the rest of us live. It's easy to become addicted to the fine things that a large salary can buy you. Again, it takes discipline to avoid the temptations.

Furthermore, it's *very* difficult to maintain your enthusiasm for work you don't enjoy. It depends on how much you dislike it and what your "threshold of pain" is. Remember: working for a large law firm requires dedication, and the firm needs to feel you want to be there in order to keep you. It's one thing to be lukewarm about a job when you start; it's another to actively dislike it and just feel as though you're selling yourself for the dough. You don't deserve that—and neither does the firm!

You may, of course, wind up finding that you enjoy it, no matter what you thought coming in. It's a great idea to go in with an open mind, figuring that you'll determine what you want to do next when the opportunity presents itself (and trust me, it will, whether in the form of a headhunter or a departing partner). If you wind up loving it—well, that's life working out just fine.

B. THE DOWNSIDES OF WORKING AT A LARGE LAW FIRM

Of course, there are negatives to working for a large law firm just as there are downsides to working for *any* employer. As I pointed out in Chapter One, there are great jobs, but there are no *perfect* jobs. I heard an interview with an astronaut—who's got to have just about the best possible gig there could be—who said that his job is enjoyable about one day a week. The rest is taken up with tedious meetings and functions. So, being an astronaut is fun *20% of the time.* The key with any job is to take the one that offers you the most of what you like, and the least of what you don't. Keep that in mind as we talk about the less-than-attractive aspects of large firm practice.

1. THE HOURS

Have you ever been the Franklin Roosevelt Library in Hyde Park, New York? There's one exhibit I particularly enjoy. It talks about Roosevelt's stint at a large law firm in New York in the early 1900s. What's so hysterical about it is the caption that accompanies a photo of the young lawyer Roosevelt. It talks about how, while he was a lawyer, he regularly went to the symphony, he sailed, he played bridge a couple of times a week ... on and on and on.

Ha! Ha ha! Old FDR would get the shock of a lifetime if he came back and started at a large firm *today!* While it's true that the hours ease up as you progress up the ranks at large firms, when you start out, they're pretty grueling.

In defense of large firms, they're not the only professional setting that requires a dramatic time commitment. Talk to any investment bankers you know, and see whether they're home in time to watch the five o'clock news. Ha ha! As a rule of thumb, here's the math you need to know: huge opening salary = long hours.

It's a dues-paying issue, plain and simple. The *Wall Street Journal* ran an article about professionals who were rockers on the side, and they included partners at large New York firms. One of them, Bruce Meyer at Weil Gotshal, a guitarist in two cover bands, was quoted as saying that playing in the bands "Is a function of the additional time and money that comes from a successful career."

So there's a light at the end of the tunnel. But when you start out, "hours" isn't really quite the right way to talk about the time commitment being a new associate at a large firm takes. Nights, or weekends, or holidays, might come closer. Sometimes, the truly horrendous hours you have to put in go by euphemisms like "dedication" or "hard work." The fact is, *time* is the largest sacrifice you make when you work for a large law firm. There is *no way* to avoid it.

Don't believe me? Well, all you have to do is look a little deeper into how law firms make money to see where the enormous time commitment comes from. The enormous salaries that you associate with large firms—easily into six figures—don't come from a money tree. Let's say you go to a firm paying you $175,000 to start. They have to pay you that salary whether you work 40 billable hours a week or 80. The difference is that the more you work, the more money the firm makes. Let's say that your time bills out at $250 an hour. Well, if you bill 40 hours a week, the firm pulls in roughly half a million dollars because of your efforts (this assumes you work 50 weeks). If you bill 80 hours a week, the firm pulls in another half a mil, and that *second* half mil is pure gravy. Sure, you'll get a bonus, and there's overhead associated with you, but you can see the point: *a large law firm is going to squeeze all the work out of you that it possibly can, because it will make more money if it does so.* One recruiting coordinator at a large firm described the situation to me this way: "It's kind of like

Amway. The more hours the law firm bills for its associates, the more money the partners make." A law firm administrator pointed out that "Of the money that's earned for each associate, roughly a third goes to the associate's salary, a third goes to overhead, and a third goes to the partners. The overhead and salary stay the same as the billables increase. That's why associates who bill more hours are so valued." A former large law firm associate adds, "It's the 'duh' factor. What did you think they were paying you all of this money for? Yes, you're fabulous, but the firm isn't going to value you the way your mom does. I had a colleague, he billed 250 hours a month, he was a *machine*. The partners loved this guy. They were always coming up to him, slapping him on the back, saying things like, 'Saw your numbers! You're the man!' He *was* a great guy, but all that matters is the numbers you generate. It's all about your ability to generate revenue. That's why they hire you. That's what they're about: revenue generation."

I would point out, as Seinfeld says, "... not that there's anything *wrong* with that." When you work for someone else it's natural for them to make money out of you. That's why they hire you in the first place; if they didn't think you were a moneymaker, it wouldn't make sense. But it's got serious ramifications for you. The quality of life issues that may be a primary focus for you will only concern an employer if they feel you won't join them or stay if those issues aren't addressed. Otherwise, they're interested in hours. And hours. And more hours on top of that. It's not unusual at large law firms to put in sixty to a hundred hours a week.

"But wait a minute," you're saying. "I've read the NALP forms. I've seen articles. I've seen the recommended billables for new associates. Sometimes it's 2000 or 2500 hours. That's 40 or 50 hours a week. I can handle that!"

Uuuhh ... not quite. For one thing, those published hours are sometimes fanciful. As one personnel Director at a large firm says, "Don't believe what you read. If a firm says that it requires 2,900 billable hours and that its associates work 3,000 hours a year to get that, that's just a flat out lie. It's more like 3,500 hours." As that quote implies, you're making a mistake if you confuse *billable* hours with *working* hours. There's a huge difference between the two.

Remember, when I defined billable hours for you a few minutes ago, I said that they were hours that are attributable to a particular client's work. Things like document production, drafting memos or briefs, research, client meetings, court time, that all counts. *Working* hours are what you *normally* think of when you think about the number of hours you've got to put in; it's all the time you spend at the office. But the fact is, time that you can't bill doesn't count! So any time you spend chatting, getting a coffee, hitting the head, training, administrative tasks, recruiting, pro bono, keeping track of your billables—none of that is billable time! (Some firms count pro bono hours in your billable total, but trust me, it's not viewed the same way no matter *what* they tell you.) Even if you're really efficient, you'll find you have to work about ten hours for every eight billable hours you generate. So that means if a firm expects you to log 2,500 billable hours a year (which is low), you'll have to *work* about 3,125 hours, which puts you over 60 hours a week—if you work a full 52 week year, without a break. Compare that to government lawyers, who work a total of about 2,000 hours a year and don't have to worry about billables at all!

It's important also to note that firms justifiably try to downplay the billables issue. They'll say that a figure is a "goal" or "suggested," not mandatory, and that it's OK if you don't reach the number they provide. *Don't listen*. Associates laugh when I ask them about that. "Oh, *right*," they say. "If you don't meet the billables target on a monthly basis, they talk to you about it. It looks really, really bad."

What makes billable hours even more onerous is the record-keeping that goes along with it. Firms require that you keep very detailed logs of your time, because clients demand it; many clients hire auditors to see that they're being billed correctly, and the more detail you provide, the more justification the firm has for its bills. Many firms require that you break your time into tenths of hours, and you have to account for every one. That means that you have to keep track of every six minutes you spend at work, all day long.

If you don't appreciate how much time you waste, or how much of a pain it is to keep track of your time in six-minute increments, try this little experiment. For two days, keep a log of your time, from the moment you wake up until the moment you go to sleep. Break it into six-minute chunks. So, if you wash your face and brush your teeth for six minutes, that's one chunk. Keep track of classes, commuting, studying, work, chatting with colleagues, breaks, everything. It'll show you two things. One, it's amazing how little of your time is actually spent productively, even if you feel as though you work continuously from morning until night. And two, you'll see what an incredible pain in the neck it is to keep track of your time this way!

On top of the long hours and the record keeping is the problem of *unpredictability*. Many associates complain that they wouldn't mind the hours so very much if they could plan around them, but they often can't. As partners at large firms point out, this is not a function of the firms as much as it's a function of client needs. When clients pay huge money for representation, they expect 24/7 service. They expect matters handled on the spot. And that's what they get. As one Career Services Director points out, "Let's say you've spent a long time planning a vacation with your spouse, and the day before, a partner calls you and says, 'Too bad. Sorry. You've got to stay.' How will you react? I find that brings home *exactly* what the time commitment to a large firm means!" An associate at a large firm adds, "Working all night, I can take. It's not so much that as it is that you have to follow up by working all day *again*. When I hear students moan about how exhausting call-back interviews are, I think to myself, 'If a whole day of interviews wears you out, you can't possibly do this job.' "

Stories abound of associates being called on in the most outrageous situations. One associate told me about being called by her supervising partner with a question *while she was in the recovery room after giving birth!* A recruiting coordinator chimes in, "If you're working on a case, you don't know *when* you're going to be called on to pull an all-nighter. If it's Friday, Christmas is on Sunday, and you suddenly find out that you've got a brief due in court on Wednesday—goodbye Christmas!" A Career Services Director points out that "You *do* have to cancel vacations. It's the nature of the beast. If you want flexibility, don't go to a large firm. Because if you have huge clients like large firms have, they can yank your chain like smaller clients *can't*." A former associate with a large firm adds, "If you *weren't* busy, you were panicking about not making billables. It's feast or famine!"

Obviously, **the long hours are more of an issue for some people than others. There are three kinds of people who are fine with it. One is people who genuinely like to be consumed by their work.** I have to tell you that this isn't many people, but I've met students who truly relish the idea of devoting all of their faculties to their job, whether it's law school or a law firm. That kind of person *thrives* in a large firm. One law firm administrator laughs, "There genuinely are people for whom billable hours are not a burden. If you think, 'Oh, my God, it's so difficult to keep track of my time,' it's a problem. But there are associates who'll say to me, 'The time flew by, I can't believe I didn't even notice those 2,300 hours!' " As one recruiting coordinator points out, "If you weren't the kind of person who studied fifty hours a week in college, if you coasted on the least work, you won't suddenly be the type to work 80+ hours a week at a big firm."

Then there are students who acknowledge without malice that their job requires dedication. As one law firm administrator points out, "There are people who just aren't too concerned about work taking the priority. It's OK with them, they're not conflicted about wanting to get home. They'll say, 'For the next few weeks I won't be home and that's OK, it's my work, it's what I do.' "

I talked to a 3L who was joining one of the country's premier law firms. I asked how he felt about putting in long hours, and he shrugged and said, "I figure for the next three years, the firm owns me. It's all I'll do." That's a pretty healthy attitude. If you go in *assuming* that your job will take up most of your waking hours, you'll be pleasantly surprised when it doesn't.

Finally, there are people who consider racking up big billable hours an exciting challenge. As one law firm administrator comments, "There are people here who are not happy unless they're faced by constant challenges, in terms of work and deadlines. The demands of a 2,400 hour billable requirement keeps them constantly challenged."

And, of course, firms differ in the time commitment they require, and different practice areas have different time requirements. If you're working on an IPO, you're going to burn the midnight oil. If you do estates and trusts work, you'll work far more regular hours.

The only way to draw an accurate bead on the time demands of any particular firm or specialty within a firm is to talk to people familiar with it. You can't rely on people who are trying to recruit you; it's not in their best interest to tell you the truth. I talked to one former associate from a large firm in Louisiana, who said she'd left because she couldn't take the hours. She complained, "When I was a student, they lied to me. They flat out lied to me about the time commitment." I asked her, "Did you do any recruiting when you were with the firm?" She said she did, and I asked her, "Did you tell students the truth about the hours?" She responded immediately, "Of course not. That's not done."

Instead, talk to other associates at the firm, or former associates you identify through Career Services at school. If you can, meet with them in person, over lunch or even better over a drink after work, where they'll relax and be more likely to blab.

When you have an accurate read on what'll be demanded of you, you'll be able to make a decision about whether the hours are a deal-breaker. If you go ahead, you'll be going in with accurate expectations and your eyes open.

2.   THE POLITICS

If you're the kind of person who insists on being judged purely on the quality of your work, think twice about going to a large firm. Law school is a meritocracy. The working world is not. Sure, you've got to turn in excellent work. But your image counts, as well. As I often tell new associates, it's not how smart you are, it's how smart people *think* you are; it's not how hard you work, it's how hard people *think* you work. A *Harvard Business Review* article described the appropriate mindset at work as "prudent paranoia.'' The more people there are in the office, the more there is to be concerned about.

Of course, politics is not limited to the large law firm environment. It's present in every office setting. It's just more pronounced at large firms, where what people think of you can have an enormous impact on your success.

3. THE BUREAUCRACY

Any time you're part of a huge organization, you'll have to deal with bureaucracy. It's true whether you join the government, a large corporation ... or a large firm. Committees, formal procedures, layers of management—it's not something that many people relish. If you've had exposure to it and know your way around it, you're probably fine with it. If you're a free spirit and don't like to be shackled by red tape ... you'll have trouble with it.

4. THE NATURE OF THE WORK

Many students are lured to large firms by the thought of exciting, glamorous work for big-name clients. If you progress up the food chain at a large firm, it's definitely there. But for the first few years ... reality check time!

As one Career Services Director pointed out, ''A lot of students go to large firms thinking they'll be on the cutting edge of issues, that there will be no monotony or repetition. But there is a *lot* of repetition. There's nobody there to do the crummy work *for* you.'' Another stated that, ''For the first couple of years, you do the grunt work. After that, there's more intellectual stimulation, but for the first couple of years, there's not.'' An attorney at a large firm said, ''With a large firm, you just don't get the quality work right away. It's *very* routine.'' Another reported, ''Everyone says you get great experience here that you can take anywhere, but if you want to get client contact or be in court right away, you won't get that here.'' Adds another, ''In large firm private practice, you're not going to get to use a lot of your skills for a few years. You won't appear in court, you won't get client contact. Are you willing to forgo them for an employer to be named later?''

In defense of large firms, they do make an effort to take the chimp work off the plates of new associates. They increasingly dump it on the plates of paralegals and contract lawyers, for instance. And *everybody* gets to do something interesting at least once in a while; they're conscious of keeping their junior associates from quitting, and they know that involving them in exciting work at least now and then accomplishes that. They also provide interesting training programs to spice things up. Nonetheless, associates often complain about weeks spent on document reviews, checking different versions of a document for variances, tedious tasks of all kinds. As a rule of thumb, if a matter requires the attention of a lawyer and it's not very interesting, a *partner* isn't going to do it. A *senior associate* isn't going to do it. They've paid their dues. *You,* the junior associate, are going to do it.

Often, the work you associate with being a lawyer—being in court and interacting with clients—doesn't come about at a large firm for the first few years. Clients don't want to deal with junior associates; they're paying a lot of money, and they want senior people. As an attorney at a large firm told me, "The ones who get the 'face time' with clients are the partners, not the new associates." Another pointed out that, "You need to like the nature of the work, not the name of the client. Working at a large firm isn't about flying on the corporate jet, or having dinner with the CEO. The problem for new associates is that it's hard to see clients *at all!*"

Court time is similarly hard to come by. Being a litigator for the Justice Department or a small firm or the JAG Corps or a public interest employer means court time *immediately,* sometimes the first day you're there. There's a lot of pressure that comes with that, of course, but at least you're a courtroom lawyer. If you're a litigator at a large law firm, it may be years before you even get to stand up in court and argue a motion. You'll learn at the elbow of geniuses, and if you relish that idea, you'll like the setting.

5. THE LACK OF AUTONOMY

As one recruiting coordinator points out, "Something that comes as a real shock to students is that at large firms, you have no control over your own time." Coming from a school environment, where you essentially set your own hours outside of class, that may be very difficult to handle. As one former associate at a large firm reports, "People think, 'I know what it means to bill 2,400 hours because I work hard as a student.' But that's not really being honest. That's magical thinking. Because you think as a student, am I going to study from 1 to 5 p.m . . . .or 1 to 5 a.m.? It's not face time, it's whenever you get your work done. But as an associate at a large firm you're putting in face time to please partners, clients, it's completely different."

When you start out at a big firm, you have supervising attorneys who decide how you spend all of your time. You typically don't have a choice of assignments. You pretty much do what you're told, when you're told to do it. As one hiring partner told me, "You've got to be willing to work as a team player." That means that the good of the project takes precedence over anything *you* might want to do. Large law firms are no place for prima donnas! Furthermore, you *may* wind up in a specialty you don't enjoy, and, depending on the firm, it can be tough to make a switch (although almost any large firm would rather help you switch departments than lose you entirely). If you chafe at this kind of control, this may be a factor in your success—and happiness—at a large firm.

6. THE NATURE OF THE CLIENTS

I heard more sad stories about misconceptions over the nature of large firm clients than any other aspect of large firm practice. As one attorney at a large firm told me, "It's important to know who the clients *are.*"

Here's the problem. When you hear that a large law firm has a banking department, or an environmental law department, or a litigation department, you are going to make assumptions about what those departments do based on impressions you already have about different areas of practice. What you do at a large firm is basically spend all of your time rearranging the assets of the wealthy. You do mergers, acquisitions, and contracts for wealthy corporations and people. As one recruiting coordinator at a large firm said, "If you are a do-gooder or you want to make a difference, it's not for you!" She went on to point out that her firm's banking department basically handled foreclosures—that is, kicking people out of their houses. Another hiring partner told me, succinctly, "If you want to save the environment or march on Washington, don't go to a large firm!" While many of the best large firms have exemplary pro bono programs that feed your soul, you can't rely on your "paid" work to do so.

A Career Services Director told me the story of a top student who'd come to her office, saying that she was very interested in environmental work. She marched into Career Services, announcing, "I want to work for a large law firm, representing the environment." As the Director told me, "It was very sad. I asked this young woman, 'Exactly who is going to hire a large firm to represent the environment? Large law firms do environmental work from the *other* side. No family of rabbits is going to hop in and say, 'Please protect our habitat!' "

To be perfectly blunt, if you go to a large firm, you will often find yourself representing clients who are not on the side of cases with which you emotionally identify. If your firm represents tobacco companies, you make arguments for them. As one junior associate at such a firm pointed out, "If you feel as though tobacco companies are 'merchants of death,' this isn't the place for you. But if you feel as though people make their own decisions and take risks with their eyes open, then it's an interesting, exciting place to work. We're always prepared to answer questions about it when we do on-campus interviews. But students never ask us about it."

A former associate from a large firm recounts, "I left because I just didn't feel good about what I was doing. We did defense work on a cervical exam case, where the plaintiffs were women with cervical cancer. We'd have practice group meetings where they'd be high-fiving each other when they beat these women. They were psyched, and I was horrified."

Of course, many matters large firms handle are not fraught with emotion. Most business deals are neutral. But it's important to talk to people about the specific firms *you're* targeting, so that you can draw a bead on the clients and the kinds of projects you'll work on. You *must* be able to leave your emotions at the door if the firm(s) you're targeting don't represent clients whose positions you endorse. As one partner with a large firm points out, "If you view your work as an intellectual puzzle, as a challenge, you'll enjoy it here. If you get emotionally attached to the arguments you make, you won't. I think that's true at many firms. It's certainly true here."

3. DON'T BE DELUDED INTO THINKING LARGE LAW FIRMS ARE "MOST OF THE JOBS OUT THERE"

You may think you have to try for a large law firm job because there's very little else available. Wrong! As one Career Services Director points out, "Law students have this perception that large law firms are a majority of the market, but they're not—not by a long shot." Another adds that "Most students don't wind up at large law firm, but rather at firms with 2 to 10 attorneys."

So where does this misconception come from? On-campus interview programs. One Career Services Director comments, "Sometimes large firm interest is there just because large firms are so visible." Nationwide, large firms account for 70% of on-campus interviews! That's because large firms are virtually the only employers who can spare the horses to conduct on-campus interview programs, and they can plan their hiring needs sufficiently ahead of time for it. While small firms interview in the Spring Semester at law schools, and some governmental and public interest entities take part, on-campus interviews are dominated by large firms. Most other jobs require that you go out and find them ... which we talked about extensively in Chapter 10 of this book.

So check your motivations, and see if your interest in large law firms stems not from anything you'd do if you worked for them, but rather because you think they're the only game in town. They're not!

4. DON'T BE SEDUCED BY THE IDEA THAT "EVERYBODY WANTS A LARGE LAW FIRM JOB, SO THERE MUST BE SOMETHING TO IT"

Peer pressure is an *enormous* factor in creating a lust for large law firm jobs. It's perhaps *the* central factor. One Career Services Director told me about a student who was going to work for Legal Aid, and a classmate said to him, "You can't do that! You'll bring our class median salary down!" Another pointed out that "It's definitely true that the success model in law school means working for a large law firm, and that's it—since top students are the only ones who are seen as having access to those jobs."

You'll also get subtle pressure from your school to go to large firms. They want to hold you up as an example to incoming students as evidence of the kind of firms who'll hire students from your school. They want you to pave the way for other students behind you. And they want you to be sufficiently well-heeled to make generous donations to the school. So your peers won't be the only ones breathing down your neck to accept the large firm gig.

Pay attention to what *you* want. As one hiring partner said, "Have realistic expectations about the pay, the hours, the areas of law. Think about what you want to *do,* not what your parents or the student next to you wants!" *Think* about all the upsides and downsides we just discussed. Go in and talk with your Career Services people about it. Talk with any alums or upperclassmen or lawyers you know who are familiar with large firm practice, and see what *they* say. And, most importantly, think about what you really want. If you're not sure what you want, go back to Chapter 2 and read it, so you're sure you're making career decisions based on what's truly important to you. Because when it comes to choosing a job, the way you want to spend your life day after day is all that matters. Don't let other people's dreams for you color that decision!

5. WHAT IF YOUR MOTIVATION IS AVOIDING SCHMOOZING FOR CLIENTS?

What we're talking about here is client development, or what's more commonly called "rainmaking." Whether it's through community involvement or public speaking or actively soliciting clients, it's a function that most lawyers in private practice wind up performing. The deal is that if you're at a *small* firm, you're expected to start rainmaking pretty early on. If you become a solo practitioner, it's the *first* thing you do.

At a large firm, on the other hand, you aren't expected to "rainmake" until you approach partnership. As one large law firm partner told me, "If we have students who talk about rainmaking, it's a little queer."

So as a junior associate at a large firm, you're right that you wouldn't have to rainmake. But keep a couple of things in mind: If you plan to stay at a large firm for a while, you eventually *will* have to lure business. It's not really all that difficult and you're probably a lot better at it than you think. The fact remains, over time your duties will evolve from *doing* the work to *supervising* the work to *bringing in* the work.

Furthermore, large law firms are hardly the only place you don't have to bring in business. It's not an issue for all kinds of plum government jobs, from federal agencies to judicial clerkships to prosecutors' offices. Same for public interest employers. Many boutiques don't expect junior associates to rainmake. So if you think you have to go to a large firm to avoid rainmaking—think again!

B. GETTING THE LARGE FIRM JOB YOU'RE LUSTING AFTER IF YOU DON'T HAVE STELLAR CREDENTIALS

Have you ever been to the Pittsburgh Airport? If so, you were probably flying U.S. Air, since it's a U.S. Air hub. And if you checked in at the U.S. Air counter, you probably looked over a balcony behind you, down onto the security check-in area. The line is almost always massive.

But at the top of the stairs leading down to security, there's a tiny sign that says, "Alternative Security Checkpoint," and has an arrow pointing to the left, down a small hallway. I noticed that once, and asked an airline representative, "Is that sign for real?" She said it was, and I said, "How far away is it?" She shrugged and responded, "About fifty yards."

Now I was intrigued. "Is there a long line there?"

She responded, "Never."

So I asked, "Why don't people use it."

Her answer: *"Maybe because it's not right here."*

That was good enough for me. I grabbed my son Harry and went to the alternative security checkpoint, where we sailed right through.

I've told you this story before. I'm not retelling it by way of bolstering Pittsburgh tourism, but rather to point out: large law firms are the same way. There's more than one way in, and if you don't have stellar credentials, the alternatives are much better alternatives than the front door.

Two warnings up front: While all of these techniques have worked for other law students and they might well work for you, there are no guarantees. But you'll be doing so many interesting things in the meantime, I *do* guarantee you'll wind up with a gig you enjoy.

The other warning is this: This isn't easy. You'll get dissed a lot. You'll get rejected. You'll have to have a thick skin and stand up for yourself, doing what you have to do to prove how wonderful you are. If you're up to the challenge, I'll give you the ammunition you need!

Let's start out by talking about the traditional large law firm hiring model. You're not going to follow this model, but let's talk about it anyway.

Normally, large law firms interview law students in the Fall semester of their Second Year of law school, seeking summer clerks for the following summer. During that summer program, the firms will make decisions about whom they want to hire permanently. Those permanent offers typically go out at the end of the Summer, and by and large, unless you seriously drop the ball—like I did in *my* summer program— you'll get an offer.

Of course, that doesn't explain all large firm hiring. Firms also hire Third Years when they don't get everyone they want and need from their summer programs. And they even hire a few students after First Year, although that's normally reserved for students either from distinguished law schools or with a phenomenal undergraduate background. In addition, of course they hire "laterals"—attorneys with experience garnered elsewhere—and they hire clerks during the school year as well as in the summer.

That sounds pretty easy, doesn't it? It is. It's deceptively easy, if you've got great paper credentials. As a recruiting coordinator at one large law firm puts it, "The process is entirely bloodless. You send me your resume. I look at your school, I look at your GPA, and I look at a grid. For your school, we'll take GPAs over a given level. If you make it: Interview. If you don't: no interview. That's it."

I wish I could tell you there's more to it, and *occasionally* there is. If you bring to the table an amazing pre-law school background in a relevant field, large firms might give you a look-see in on-campus interviews. But you can't count on it.

None of this is meant to depress you, by the way. You're going to skirt the whole on-campus interviewing process. There are puh-lenty of ways to sneak into a large firm *outside* of OCI. In this section, I'll lead you through strategies that have worked for other students.

Before we talk about that, however, we've got a couple of threshold matters to discuss. First, you need to accept the fact that on paper, you're not the person large law firms are looking for. And second, you need to cast the credentials you *do* have in the best possible light.

Let's talk about those in a little more detail.

1. TWO CRUCIAL OPENING STEPS

A. DON'T RESENT THE "GRADES" OBSESSION OF LARGE LAW FIRMS

... And make no mistake about it; large law firms are laser-focused on grades. *Great* grades. Top-of-the-class grades. And Law Review. I've had the following conversation with more than one partner at large law firms:

Me: "Do you ever hire second career students?"

Partner: "Sure—if they have great grades."

Me: "Do you hire evening students?"

Partner: "Sure—if they have great grades."

Me: "Do you hire students with no legal experience?"

Partner: "Sure—if they have great grades."

I never ask the following question, but I'm tempted:

"Do you hire talking mules?"

We know what the answer would be ...

"Sure ... *if they have great grades.*"

Grades, grades, grades. We have at least two issues with that, don't we?

Issue one: Can't they *see* that there are students with lesser grades who are *equally likely* to be *great* lawyers?

Issue two: "If I have great grades *except one* that pulls my GPA down, isn't it *ridiculous* not to consider me?"

Let's talk about those issues. Let's address the question of whether there are great lawyers-in-waiting with less-than-stellar grades. The answer is, *of course there are, and large law firms know it. The Wall Street Journal* cited in a 2006 article that "Fancy schools, good grades and Law Review smarts don't necessarily translate into workplace success. But these markers are about the only differentiators law firms have." (Ha You'll disprove *that.*)

One hiring partner I spoke with was very up front about it, saying, "It's obviously true that there are people who would be excellent attorneys even though they have mediocre grades. But it's a fact of life that with the number of resumes we get and the number of students we interview, you've got to have great credentials to get in through on-campus interviews." Statistics for every large firm bear that out. Large firms typically get more than a hundred resumes for every spot they've got in their summer programs. *Over a hundred.* So you're talking about large law firms who demand great credentials, to paraphrase the punch line of an old joke, "Because they can." Furthermore, the hiring partner at a large firm pointed out that "It costs us more than three thousand dollars for each in-house full-day interview, and we don't take nine of ten people we call in. It's a huge expense. We just *can't* interview everybody!" Firms just don't have the time or the incentive to dip below the top of the class, *unless you provide them with one* ... which is what we'll learn to do in just a minute.

On top of that, some partners at law firms argue that the grades thing is a matter of morale. "Everybody who's already here has incredible credentials," the argument goes. "What are we going to say to *them* if we start admitting people who don't look good on paper? What will we tell our clients? We tell them we hire the best, that's how we justify our fees." Oh-kay.

They'll also make a pure candlepower argument. That is, the smartest law students tend to get the best grades. There's not a perfect correlation, but it probably exists. If you perform well on exam after exam after exam, you're probably good at thinking quickly and synthesizing sometimes disparate legal principles into an intelligent argument. Law Review similarly suggests that you can develop novel legal arguments to address issues that are difficult to resolve. You could argue that *none* of that is terribly relevant to the bulk of the work that new associates do ... and if large firms were really interested in hiring great lawyers, they'd conduct personality inventories to ensure that there was a good emotional "fit" for their new associates, such that they wouldn't leave after three years.

But perhaps that's just me talking.

Let's get back to that grades issue for a minute. One large firm even did a study to see if there was a correlation between lawyers who made it to partnership, and what their law school grades were like. The only sound predictor was *undergraduate* grades; law school grades bore no correlation with it at all.

The recruiting coordinator at another large firm acknowledged, "We've found that our best associates are often the ones who had to work the hardest to get in here. They're more enthusiastic, they work harder, they shine."

Does that change how large firms hire? Nope. Of course they want you if you're enthusiastic and a hard worker ... *if you've got great grades.*

The grades obsession is particularly absurd when you're talking about students who miss the cut because of a single crappy exam. I've talked to *so* many law students who say, "They take the top ten percent from my school. I'm in the top *eleven* percent. I would have been top ten if it hadn't been for my one bad grade in ..." fill in the blank. Crim. Civ Pro. Property. Contracts. One lawyer told me he'd seen a statistic that showed that a single bad grade in law school can cost a law student *two hundred thousand dollars in future earnings.* What kind of a stinking pile of pony loaf is *that?* One crappy grade? One former attorney at a large firm told me his rather incredible experience. After law school, he'd been a highly-esteemed staff attorney for his state's supreme court. He got glorious references from the justices. He applied for an associate position at a prestigious law firm. Now, let's look at what we've got: a former federal district court clerk *and* supreme court clerk with *fabulous* references ... and just one bad grade on his record, from *seven years ago,* in Criminal Law, when he was a First Year. His contact at the law firm said, "I'm really pulling for you, but I have to be honest with you: That grade in criminal law is going to make it tough." This attorney reports, "I was speechless. My grade in *Crim?* After all of my other grades *and* my clerkships? I didn't know what to say." As it turns out, the hiring committee was able to look past this major flaw and make him an offer.

If you're seething about the grade thing at this point, I hear you. But here's what you need to know: You've got to *accept* it. It is, in the words of former Defense Secretary Donald Rumsfeld, what it is. If you go to large law firms with the sole argument "Grades aren't everything," you'll lose. If you resent criticism of your grades, you'll lose. If you want to get up in the grill of anyone who sneers at your credentials, you'll lose.

Bitching about the grades thing accomplishes *nothing*. What you simply *have* to do is to let the lofty attitude roll off your back. You'll need to focus exclusively on things you do well and why you'd be a great associate (which is what we'll talk about in the next section) and ignore everything else. You have to muster all of your nerve, all of your talent, all of your chutzpah, all of your savvy, and forge ahead with the strategies I'm going to give you ... if you want that job!

B. Cast the Credentials You *Do* Have in the Best Possible Light

Before you approach large firms, you have got to go through your credentials with a fine-toothed comb and pull out every highlight you can possibly muster that addresses your ability to do great work, particularly in the area of research and writing. Just as we talked about when we discussed interviewing in Chapter 9, you have to be able to recite your strengths when you're seeking a gig with a large firm. You don't have the grades, so you've got to showcase what you *do* have.

Let's talk about reframing your GPA first. If any of the following apply to you, use them:

- If you had one lousy exam result that pulled down your GPA, figure out what your GPA would have been if you'd performed as well on that exam as you did on everything else ... and figure out why you dropped the ball on that exam.

- If you had a bad start but did well once you figured out the law school exam thing, point out your upward trend.

- If you had a one-time event that marred your performance First Year (a personal tragedy or illness), euphemize it but mention it. "A serious family tragedy occurred in my first semester. I'm fine now, but it dragged down my performance then." It's not an excuse—it's an explanation.

- If you've had to work full time to put yourself through school, say so.

- If you've done better in paper courses than exam courses, highlight that, since paper courses are analogous to the research that dominates a new associate's time at a large firm.

What if your grades are just mediocre and that's all there is to it? Maybe you can't legitimately say that a meteorite came through the ceiling of your apartment and destroyed your outlines the week before finals. It just means that you'll have to distinguish yourself some other way, namely, with work experience, be it work study or paid or pure volunteer work. Whether it's working as a research assistant for a professor or working for a firm or government agency or prosecutor's office or a judge, or you have a substantial prior career in a field relevant to a target firm's practice area, it's up to you to prove that, while your grades don't show it, you've got the skills a large law firm looks for. If you have references who can call and rave about you on your behalf, even better.

It's an uphill climb at large law firms if you don't have stellar credentials, but you can see the theme here: you've got the candle-power even though your grades don't show it.

By the way, be careful about highlighting entrepreneurial activities. If large firms think you won't be happy without being your own boss, they won't hire you. One student had his own company and had the idea to interview large firms to represent him, with the thought in mind that when he graduated they'd hire him as an associate. Another student, this one a woman, had her own real estate development firm with a staff of twenty. She figured her management and business skills would make her valuable to a large firm. While these students and others like them are really impressive, if you look at them as a large law firm would, you'd question: will they be dedicated to their work, with the distraction of their "side" businesses? Will they be happy or comfortable as subordinates? If you've got the same entrepreneurial bent, you need to look seriously at whether you really want a large law firm associateship. And if you *do,* talk about the skills you developed in business, downplaying your role as the boss!

On the flipside of that, what if you don't have *anything* in place to impress a large law firm? There are other options, things you can do starting right now. The bottom line is that there are many ways to substitute other activities for the grades you don't have. Let's talk about those activities now.

2. GETTING LARGE FIRMS TO NOTICE YOU FOR THE NON-GRADE ASSETS YOU CAN BRING TO THE TABLE ... WHILE YOU'RE STILL IN SCHOOL

On-campus interviews aren't the only way to make yourself known to large law firms, you know. There are two major ways to accomplish it while you're still in school: take part in activities that bring you into contact with attorneys from large firms, and get your foot in the door through people you know (or seek out).

Let's talk about them.

A. TAKE PART IN ACTIVITIES THAT BRING YOU INTO CONTACT WITH LARGE FIRM ATTORNEYS

A recruiting coordinator reports that, "If a partner tells us to bring in a student for an interview, we do it. It might be someone who would never have gotten in with their resume." What this highlights is the importance of finding ways to make yourself known—in a positive way!—to attorneys at large firms. The relevant activities can be found in Chapter 10. For example, writing and publishing articles, writing profiles of lawyers, taking part in writing contests, writing a Law Review note, volunteering at Career Services, helping out with your school's Speakers' Bureau, participating in your school's mentoring program, fundraising, volunteering for law school committees, joining the bar association and volunteering, going to CLEs, joining sports teams, and clerking during the school year for a large firm.

B. SHAKE THE TREES FOR PEOPLE WHO CAN HELP YOU GET YOUR FOOT IN THE DOOR . . . AT LEAST FOR AN INTERVIEW

The point of all of the activities we discussed in Chapter 10 is to get an interview with a large firm. There's another way to accomplish the same thing: through people you already know, or those you meet.

Many law students get *at least* an interview with a large law firm because someone with influence leans on the firm's recruiting coordinator to bring them in. While you've got to handle those interviews like a true master—we'll get to that in a minute—don't overlook the possibility that someone you know can help you get that first meeting.

You can't be squeamish about this, by the way. If you don't have the credentials large firms typically look for, you've got to use every arrow in your quiver to get them to look at you. And if that means leaning on connections . . . lean away!

It may be that you don't think you *have* any connections. Not true! There's **your Career Services office**, for the start. **They'll know people at the firm you're targeting and will probably know alums who got in without stellar credentials themselves.** You can always ask these alums for advice about what you ought to be doing to do the work they do, and as we've discussed so many times, advice leads to jobs.

There are also your **professors**. Ewww! you're thinking. Listen, I wouldn't go to the professor who gave you a C, but **if you've excelled in a professor's class or done top-notch research work for them, they'll help you.** Professors are a lot better connected in the legal community than most law students realize. Don't be surprised if they'll call a firm on your behalf and say something like, "This research assistant was a lifesaver; his/her grades don't represent his/her skills . . ." and that can get you an interview.

Also, **don't overlook speakers who come to your school.** There's hay to be made in going to listen to them speak. When they're done, walk up with your resume, state your enthusiasm for what they had to say, and tell them how interested you are in working with them. Ask if you can e-mail them to follow up. It takes a set of brass ones to do this, and you'd have to judge from the attorney's demeanor how approachable they are, but the fact remains that law students have gotten interviews this way.

Another fertile source of interview possibilities is **clients of large law firms.** If you know anyone who is represented by a large law firm—either individually or because of their work—tell them you'd like to work with the firm that represents them, and ask if you can talk to the lawyer who represents them. Trust me: when a client calls and says, "I've got a friend/nephew/neighbor/pen pal who's a law student and they're interested in working for you. Would you interview them?" The firm's not going to respond, "Hardy har har. No way!" They'll *at least* give you an interview. It's a customer service thing.

Beyond Career Services and professors and speakers and clients, maybe you don't realize that the people you know actually have connections that you can use. I've pointed out many times that you don't know who the people you know, know. As we talked about in Chapter 10, sometimes the unlikeliest people are your best conduit to people you want to talk to. Tell everybody what you're after. Fraternity brothers, sorority sisters, upperclassmen who think a lot of you and themselves get offers from large firms, people you meet casually—you never know whose good word will get you in the door!

* * * SMART HUMAN TRICK * * *

Law student applies three times to a large firm in New York. He's shot down every time. He goes home over Christmas break, and visits his girlfriend's family. Her great uncle is there, and the student mentions to the great uncle that he's looking for a job. The great uncle is a doctor; it turns out that he has a patient whose neighbor is a partner at this particular New York firm. By this circuitous route the student meets the partner and gets an interview. He's convinced it's a joke, but he goes ahead with the full-day interview . . . and walks out with an offer.

Now, it may be that you have connections and you *know* you have them, but you've shied away from using them because it makes you feel uncomfortable to think of "using" people. I strongly encourage you to reprogram your thinking so that you put this "connections" business in a more positive light. When you go through contacts to get your foot in the door at a large firm, all you're doing is asking the person they put you onto for *advice.* You can state your interest in doing what they do, but assure them you're not asking them for a job. Ask them questions about what they do, ask questions based on research you've done about them and the employer and their practice, tell them about your situation and ask for advice about what you should be doing to position yourself to do what they do, bounce specific activities you've done or are contemplating off them for their opinion. That's puh-lenty. If they help you get an interview with the firm, that's just great, but you can't go in expecting that. Remember: everybody likes to offer advice . . . nobody likes getting hit up for a job!

c. SEND YOUR CORRESPONDENCE TO ATTORNEYS WHO AREN'T DELUGED WITH RESUMES

Law students almost always send their materials to hiring partners or recruiting coordinators at large law firms. If you don't have stellar credentials, that's a mistake; we talked a few minutes ago about the "grades grid." Either they'll interview a student with your GPA, or they won't. But if you're more creative with your correspondence targets, you could well get an interview you'd have lost otherwise.

What you want to do is to target attorneys based on two criteria: 1) Attorneys with whom you share something in common, and 2) The department head of the practice area that interests you, to whom you pitch the impressive "non-GPA" elements of your background.

Let's look at the "commonality" group first. Look at attorney profiles on the employer's website and consider sending your materials to:

- Alums from your law school or, barring that, from your undergrad school;

- If you're from another country, attorneys who are from there, too;

- Attorneys who share another aspect of your background, whether it's military service or a fraternity or sorority or Peace Corps experience or anything along those lines.

When you contact them, go ahead and point out what you've got in common, that you'd like to work with them and you'd appreciate any advice or help they can give you in that regard. Tell them that you'll follow up, and then call them and take it from there. At the very least they're likely to give you some ideas, and that's great.

Let's look at the other group, the department heads. If you go this route you'll tailor your letter to address your interest in the specialty, back that up with some concrete evidence that you really are interested in it (course work, CLEs, extracurriculars), evidence that you'll be really good at it (this is a good place to highlight a prior career and/or writing experience), and you'll ask for an opportunity to meet with them. You might even want to consider sending a letter without a resume. This way, you'll avoid the possibility that the partner will ignore your letter and just forward your resume to the recruiting coordinator—which is what you wanted to avoid in the first place! If you really want to go balls-out, you might consider sending your letter (with or without resume) by an expedited service like FedEx so it really gets noticed. Hey—it's your money.

I have to caution you that you can't send letters to department heads of large law firms if you *don't* have anything to bring to the table other than mediocre grades. What you're doing when you take this route in essence saying, "I've got credentials that talk to my ability to do a *great job* for you, but they wouldn't be appreciated by your recruiting folks. That's why I'm contacting *you.*"

If you contact a department head this way, at the very least you've upped your chances of getting an interview because you've contacted someone most law students won't contact. That does two things: it makes you stand out due to lack of competition, and it shows your initiative by seeking them out. Initiative is a trait highly prized by lawyers. You wouldn't be the first law student to get a prize associate position at a law firm in just this way!

D.   CONSIDER LARGE FIRMS IN "LESS DESIRABLE" MARKETS

If a large firm is your goal and the geography is a secondary consideration—or you can *make* geography a secondary consideration!—you'll improve your chances of getting into a large firm as an associate.

I don't mean to suggest that credentials aren't important to large firms in smaller cities—they *are*. But the fact is, the large firms in less attractive markets aren't going to be able to lure the same students as ones in the glamorous markets like New York, LA, San Francisco, Boston, Seattle, Chicago, Miami, DC, and any other large, glamorous cities I've just insulted by leaving them off this list.

If you turn up your nose at the idea of going to a non-glamorous city, let me point out a couple of things: I've been to just about every city in America, and they *all* have something wonderful to offer. You'll be pleasantly surprised by just about any city you visit. On top of that, the money you make in a smaller city goes *so-o-o* much further than it does in a glamorous market. You'll be able to salt away a lot more dough and live a *much* better lifestyle in a less-glamorous city.

The bottom line is this: if you make yourself flexible geographically, you'll make it easier to break into a large firm. It's still not a cakewalk—but it's not so challenging.

E.   HANDLING THE "COURTESY INTERVIEWS" YOU GET

What's a "courtesy interview"? It looks like a job interview, it feels like a job interview, in every outward way it appear to be a job interview ... but they don't anticipate making you an offer. It's not that they won't—the whole purpose of this section is to talk about how you turn those interviews into offers—it's just that that's not the point of the interview. One hiring partner said, "We give courtesy interviews all the time. The resumes are red-flagged, with a note explaining their connection: 'Related to so-and-so.' "

The fact is, whenever you get an interview with an employer *in spite* of your credentials, it's an uphill climb. I don't say that to you to depress you, but rather to gird you for battle.

Let's talk about what you need to do.

1.   READ AND FOLLOW EVERY BIT OF ADVICE IN CHAPTER 9

You are going to have to have your game face on in a big way. As one partner at a large firm advises, "You need to impress everybody with how bright, enthusiastic and energetic you are.

We'd rather have a person with 10% more enthusiasm than a top ten student with no commitment. Being hungrier for the job is a point in your favor."

Do every bit of research and rehearsal called for in Chapter 9. Look hard at the backgrounds of the attorneys with whom you'll speak. See if there are indicia that they didn't have stellar grades; maybe they didn't go to Ivy League schools, maybe they weren't on Law Review, maybe they "worked their way up" to the firm from another job (we talk about that technique just below—it's a great way to break in). Skim the backgrounds of other associates to see who might have "snuck in" without great credentials; you won't be the first one, you know! That way, if anyone makes the argument to you, "We only hire from Harvard . . ." or "We only take Law Review . . ." you have the ammunition to say, "I know you demand people with excellent credentials, but I'm sure there are associates here who do excellent work and didn't come in with the grades you generally demand. Let me tell you why I think I fit in that category . . ." (You wouldn't want to name the associates you found; that would be too 'in-your-face' and you don't know *how* they got their job. But it's good support to know that not everybody at a firm fits the "great credentials" mold.)

Also, have a mock interview through Career Services, so that you can practice your explanation of why this particular law firm should hire you.

On top of that . . .

2.   EXPLODE YOUR OWN LAND MINES. BRING UP YOUR CREDENTIALS WITH EVERY LAWYER WITH WHOM YOU MEET, AND TELL THEM WHY THEY SHOULD HIRE YOU ANYWAY

This is completely the opposite of the advice that I gave you in Chapter 9. I told you there that you don't bring up negatives. The *only* time to bring up your grades is in this situation: you're interviewing for a job that's a serious stretch with your credentials. An associate at a large firm who'd talked her way in with mediocre credentials said, "The most important piece of advice I can offer is that you have to turn every lawyer you talk to into your advocate. You have to market your abilities to *all* of them, so that they go to the hiring committee with a recommendation that they hire you. You need *everybody* pulling for you."

You can even acknowledge that you realize this is a courtesy interview, and that you're here to prove that you should be a part of the organization. As one hiring partner advises, "Come out and say, 'I know I'm not in the part of the class you normally take,' and work it in with positives." Whether you're selling job experience before law school or any of the skills and activities we talked about earlier in this chapter, make sure you make your pitch to each person who interviews you. A partner at a large firm advises,

"Students often undersell work experience. It costs a mint to train associates. If you can hit the ground running, if you understand client service, it *counts.*"

What you *cannot* assume is that if they don't bring up your GPA, it's not an issue. I've heard this happen a million times. One student told me, "My uncle got me an interview with this great firm. I talked to four attorneys. My grades never even came up! I guess they didn't mind." I asked him if he got an offer, and he said, "No. That's what I can't figure out. The interview went really well ..." What he didn't realize, and what's so easy to overlook, is that if an interview is a "courtesy" interview, they'll talk to you with no real expectation of making you an offer. Your grades don't come up because there's no point; they don't expect you to justify your grades because they don't expect to work with you. Doesn't that suck? But if you *know* it, you can *combat* it. Whether they anticipated making you an offer or not, if you have a sufficiently convincing case for why they should, they just might. As one hiring partner puts it, "If they like you, you make a connection, even if they don't hire you they might pass your name on to someone else who will." Be prepared!

3. Don't Fence Yourself in Regarding Specialties (Unless You're Truly Laser-Focused and Won't Do Anything Else)

The smartest thing to do regarding specialties is to research the firm up front to see which of its practice areas are thriving, where it's growing. Ask around and skim the firm's web site and the legal press for clues. Of the growing specialties, if you can focus on one that truly interests you, great. Ask your CSO or talk to alums about it to learn more. Then, if you're asked what you want to do, you can say something like, "From what I know, what most attracts me is X." It does have to be a genuine interest, but it doesn't have to be your *only* one, of course.

Why go to this kind of trouble? Because a thriving practice is where a firm is most likely to need extra hands. What you *don't* want to do is just pick a specialty at random, or worse, lie.

* * * CAREER LIMITING MOVE * * *

Law student interviews with a large firm. A partner asks him what he wants to practice, and the student responds reflexively, "International," even though, as the student later confesses, "I don't really know anything about it."

The partner responds, "Great. We don't need anybody for that. When there's an opening, it's yours."

4. Be Ultra-Nice to Support Staffers

Here's the scoop. Recruiting coordinators *hate* setting up courtesy interviews. "It's a pain in the a** to rearrange schedules for an interview that's not going go anywhere," they grouse.

Defang them by expressing your gratefulness. Come straight out and say you realize how much work it is to schedule an interview like this, and that you really appreciate it. *No* students ever say thank you for courtesy interviews. Make yourself stand out by being the one who does!

3. **Go in Through the Side Door: Intermediate Steps After Graduation That'll Position You for a Large Firm Job a Couple of Years From Now**

"Kimmbo!" I hear you shrieking. "I don't want to *wait* for a large firm! I want it *now!*" I know, I know. But here's the thing: let's say that I told you, "I found an LLM program, where if you spend two more years in school getting a master's degree, you can walk into a large law firm."

Would you do it?

Most students to whom I ask this question answer with a resounding "Yes." I'll bet you would, too. So my question is this: If you'd be willing to spend not just two years but also *cash money* to get into a large law firm, why not do the things I'm about to recommend to you?

As one law firm administrator says, "The dirty little secret of our hiring is that our lateral resumes are never as good as the ones we get for summer clerkships. We will hire people with a couple of years' experience whom we never would have *looked* at if they applied for our summer program. We just hired a woman who'd gone to a third-tier law school, failed the bar twice before she passed, worked as a contract attorney for a small firm, and then we hired her. We never would have hired her as a student. But she was in a practice area we wanted, and here she is."

Going in after a year or two or three or four has a kajillion benefits, including:

*   You get a chance to prove what you're arguing—that your work is a lot better than your grades;

*   You avoid the first few years at a large law firm, which everybody agrees are the *least* fun;

*   You typically go to a large law firm with your "class"; that is, you go in at the same level as people who graduated your year from law school;

*   You often have an enjoyable time somewhere else, working fewer hours and gaining some great skills.

To be perfectly honest with you, I don't think *anybody* should go straight from law school to a large law firm. A lot of large firms are starting to agree with me, and they *only* hire laterals—that is, people with experience elsewhere after law school.

How do you go about getting from law school to a large law firm if you don't take a direct route? You're essentially going to be "trading up." Tony Waller uses as an analogy the guy who traded a paper clip for a house. You've probably heard of him. He didn't exactly trade a paper clip straight for a house; he traded the paper clip for something else, he traded that for another thing, he wound up with a rare snow globe of the rock group Kiss, which he traded for a role in a movie, which he traded . . . for a house in Saskatchewan.

Your experience isn't a paper clip, and you're not jonesing for a house in Saskatchewan, but you see the analogy. You build from what you've got so that you position yourself for your dream gig.

A. LOOK AT THE PROFESSIONAL BACKGROUNDS OF LAWYERS AT FIRMS YOU'RE TARGETING

This should be your first line of attack, for reassurance if nothing else. If you look at the profiles of attorneys on any large firm web site, you'll see that they didn't all go to Harvard and they weren't all on Law Review. You'll see that at least some of them had other jobs after law school, first. Some of them will come over from government gigs, small law firms, judicial clerkships. Maybe they'll have a couple of prior jobs, say an assistant state's attorney and then an assistant U.S. Attorney.

What does this kind of information tell you? It tells you that if the firm has hired from a certain talent pool before, they'll do it again . . . and you'll also get ideas for specific "intermediate" jobs you'll enjoy.

B. JOBS OUTSIDE OF YOUR TARGET FIRMS THAT WILL PAVE THE WAY INSIDE

I've talked to associates who've had an enormous variety of experiences that led to their large firm positions. Among them are:

- Judicial clerkships (*very* fertile territory, especially federal court clerkships);

- Government jobs, including the Justice Department, U.S. Attorneys' offices, state prosecutors' offices, federal and state agencies, among others;

- Small and medium-sized firms, where they developed a specialty that was attractive to the large firm they eventually joined.

Note that you don't have to have just one job to lead to a large law firm. Let's look at the judicial clerkship route. Federal court clerkships are a stretch if you don't have great grades. But state court clerkships, with less competition, are far more accessible. So let's say you start with a state court clerkship, you do a great job there (of course!), and then you move up to a federal court clerkship, and *then* you lateral into a large firm. Talk about a great way to go. Judicial clerkships are awesome jobs. You'll enjoy yourself, you'll develop great lifelong mentors in your judge(s), and as if that weren't enough, *large firms pay signing bonuses to federal judicial clerks.* Can you imagine that? The firm that wouldn't have looked at you just a few short years ago will *pay* to get you. Sigh. That's life working out just right.

Note that what you're doing when you take this route is what we've talked about throughout this chapter: instead of just trying to tell a large firm you can do excellent work, you've *proven* it to them!

c. Non-Permanent-Associate Jobs *Inside* Your Target Firm That Can Give You a Boost

I left this for last, because although it can work, it's not a guarantee.

What you can do is to take a contract attorney or temp position as a lawyer with a large firm, and then attempt to roll it into a permanent gig. A temp agency can fix you up with those positions, and you can contact firms yourself to see if they hire contract attorneys. Most firms do.

Once you have the temporary position, you basically make yourself indispensable. Do an outstanding job on the work you're given. As one recruiting coordinator points out, "Staff attorneys and contract attorneys are sometimes undervalued unfairly as 'paper pushers'—but that's what permanent associates do, too!"

Keep up with the firm's press releases, see what's important to them. When you see anything in the media or on-line that you think would be useful to a partner or associate at the firm, download it or copy it and give it to them, saying why you thought it would be useful. Offer to co-write an article with a partner, as we discussed earlier in this chapter. If you work off hours or weekends, let any permanent lawyers in the office know you're there and tell them to let you know if they need help with anything. Get to know all the lawyers you can. As one hiring partner points out, "We bring in contract attorneys for big cases. They're here a year or two. If we like them, we keep them. It's like a long audition."

I've seen contract and temp lawyers work their way into a permanent gig. It's rare, but it happens. And in the meantime, you haven't lost anything. You're getting paid, you're working for a great firm, and it gives you the time and the opportunity to seek a full time gig, whether with this firm . . . or any other employer.

* * * SMART HUMAN TRICK * * *

New law school graduate has his heart set on one, particular large law firm in Washington, DC. The only job he can get there is as a third shift proofreader, working from Midnight until 8 a.m.

In this job, the new grad reviews tons of documents, and he finds that the firm's telecommunications department is hyper busy—and he's really interested in what they do. So he keeps his eye on the local papers, and sees that there's going to be a telecommunications law conference taking place in DC. He calls and volunteers to help out, and he's assigned the job of summarizing all of the presentations at the conference.

His summaries are made into a booklet that goes to every telecommunications lawyer in the country ... including the head of the telecom department at his own firm. This particular partner is very impressed with the booklet, and he wants to talk to the lawyer who put it together. He buzzes his secretary, and mentions the byline on the booklet, asking, "Why does that name ring a bell?" She responds nonchalantly, "It's the kid in the basement." Stunned, he tells her, "Get him in here!"

The new grad comes in, and the partner points to the booklet and says, "*You* did *this*?" The new grad acknowledges it, and the partner asks, "How? Why?" The new grad tells him the story, and the partner shakes his head, and says, "Son, you don't belong in the basement." He brings the new grad up as a full associate, and the new grad reports: "Every other new associate here is from an Ivy League school, they're all Law Review. They look at me, I've got the best job here, they can't figure out how I got it ...

... and I'm not going to tell them."

* * * SMART HUMAN TRICK * * *

Student at a New Jersey law school graduates in the bottom half of her class. She takes a contract lawyer position with a premier New York City firm. She's there for a year, in which she seriously impresses the firm with the quality of her work. When her project is complete, her supervisors put in a good word for her at *another* large New York firm—and she joins them as a full associate.

You'll notice that I didn't mention taking a paralegal position at a large firm after you graduate. There's a good reason for that. While it used to be true that you could go into a firm as a paralegal or legal secretary and become a lawyer, "you can't do it today," reports a hiring partner at one large firm. "Having said that, I suppose if you showed stupendous initiative, you were a viable member of the team, you showed extraordinary effort ... but still. Many firms are very suspect of paralegals with higher ambitions. It's hard to get around the title."

So try any of the other methods we talked about in this chapter. They might be your key to the job you want!

Chapter 24

Glamour Jobs: How to Nail Jobs in Sports, Entertainment, International . . .

"What draws you more: the wrapping . . . or the gift?"

   Poet Richard Lewis

"Being a celebrity is not so great a gig. You end up disappointing the people who thought you were what you never said you were."

   James Taylor

Sports, entertainment, international.

If I had to choose three specialties I'm asked about more than any other, this triumvirate qualifies. There's no question they've got the "It" factor.

In this chapter, we'll bounce around some ideas for breaking into these extremely attractive fields. We'll talk about some of the jobs, traditional and nontraditional, that are available. But we'll start off with something that's very important to remember . . .

A. AT THE HEART OF THE MATTER, NAILING THESE JOBS IS JUST LIKE NAILING ANY OTHER JOB

We spent the first twelve chapters of this book talking about every aspect of snaring the job of your dreams. It doesn't much matter what that dream is, whether it's Library Law or working for the NFL. As the song says, the fundamental things apply. You've got to:

- show enthusiasm;

- do your research;

- have a targeted resume;
- talk, talk, talk to people;
- take part in activities that will get you in touch with people in the field and provide resume fodder.

It's *so* much more important to talk to people than to, oh, use the web. You'll learn about opportunities you couldn't find any other way. I've seen it happen over and over again from students who've nailed unbelievably sexy opportunities.

I could go on, but you see the point: everything in the first twelve chapters is applicable here. The big difference is that there tends to be a lot more competition for these glamorous jobs. Regardless, if you do everything I taught you to do in the first part of the book, that won't matter. You'll *get* those jobs!

B. ENTERTAINMENT

Sports and entertainment are closely aligned. I guess you could say that all of sports *is* entertainment, although not all of entertainment is sports. A lot of what we'll learn here applies to a sports job search, as well.

1. WHAT IS "ENTERTAINMENT LAW," *REALLY*?

"Entertainment Law" is really an umbrella term. It covers a lot of traditional specialties. As one entertainment lawyer points out, "We're lawyers first. We don't think of ourselves as 'entertainment lawyers'— our business just happens to be in a sexy context." Another adds, "It's not all fun and no work. In all likelihood, when a movie premieres, you'll be cloistered away in your office reviewing documents, not on the red carpet smiling for the cameras."

With that in mind, let's talk about some of the practice areas that impact Entertainment:

- Intellectual property (licensing, copyrights, trademark, in other words, "soft" IP)
- Corporate/business transactions
- Tax
- Bankruptcy (One new graduate developed an expertise in bankruptcy, and when a major music company was buying lots of bankrupt music companies, they hired her).
- Labor and employment
- Franchise law
- Antitrust
- Business Litigation
- Constitutional/First Amendment (think: defamation)

- Immigration Law (what if members of the crew, talent aren't U.S. citizens?)

- Media law

- International law

- Finance

- Telecommunications

- Alternative dispute resolution

- Criminal law (hey, it happens)

- Insurance (for every major entertainment event, an insurance lawyer's advice is a must)

2.   WHERE THE JOBS ARE . . .

A.   IN-HOUSE COUNSEL AT ENTERTAINMENT COMPANIES

Every large entertainment company has an in-house counsel's office. Some of them are pretty large; Polygram and MCA have more lawyers in-house than the largest entertainment firms.

B.   FIRMS FOCUSING EXCLUSIVELY ON ENTERTAINMENT

Entertainment firms tend to differ from other law firms in several respects:

- They tend to be small. A ten-person firm is considered large.

- Because they bill by the value of the transaction to the client, not by the hour (as traditional firms do), and the clients rarely dispute fees, there is a *great* deal of money to be made.

- Entertainment firms prefer to hire "fresh" talent and train them, rather than hiring laterals.

- Partnership is harder to come by in these firms, but it doesn't matter, since senior associates can earn several hundred thousand dollars a year.

C.   FIRMS THAT HAVE AN ENTERTAINMENT PRACTICE, ALONG WITH OTHER SPECIALTIES

You know—large law firms.

D.   NON-TRADITIONAL JOBS IN ENTERTAINMENT

1.   Studio administration

2. Agenting

3. Trade associations

4. Nonprofit management

5. Lobbying on behalf of the entertainment industry

E. RESOURCES FOR FINDING ENTERTAINMENT EMPLOYERS

Your Career Services Office will have a lot of resources, including:

1. Pollstar: a monthly directory that lists all record companies, booking agencies, and management companies.

2. *Associations Yellow Book*

3. *Entertainment Law Careers* (by William Henslee)

4. *The Princeton Review Guide to America's Top Internships* (has quite a few in entertainment; although not specifically focused on law students and you may have to talk your way in, these are available to you).

5. *Careers in Communications and Entertainment*

6. *All You Need To Know About The Music Business*

On-line resources:

www.abanet.org/forums/entsports/home.html (The ABA's sports and entertainment forum)

www.stanford.edu/group/sesla/

www.besla.org (Black Entertainment & Sports Lawyers Association)

www.visualnet.com—entertainment job listings.

3. HOW TO NAIL JOBS IN EACH OF THE SETTINGS

A. IN-HOUSE COUNSEL'S OFFICES:

In terms of nailing one of these gigs: while they will hire summer interns, they don't hire lawyers fresh out of law school. They hire laterals. Your best bet for breaking in is to establish your expertise elsewhere, becoming a lawyer with the skills we listed in #1 just above, keeping your ear to the ground for entertainment opportunities, going to entertainment law functions and CLEs, and making the jump when opportunities arise.

B. FOR ENTERTAINMENT JOBS IN GENERAL: (WE'LL DISCUSS SPECIFIC SETTINGS IN A MINUTE)

We learned in Chapter 10 about the importance of people and activities. In Entertainment, it's impossible to overstate how important it is to talk, talk, talk. Nailing these opportunities is definitely a matter of who you get to know.

On top of that:

● Develop great skills. Entertainment lawyers don't entertain; they review contracts, negotiate deals, everything "normal" lawyers do. The better you are at those, the better an entertainment lawyer you'll be. And don't think that any skill set cuts you out of entertainment. As U.C. Davis' Mindy Baggish, a former entertainment lawyer herself, points out, "For as long as I can remember word on the street was that if you didn't come from a transactional background, you wouldn't be able to find a job in-house with a studio, that they didn't hire litigators. That's not true. In fact, there are several studios that hire former litigators to staff their in-house transactional/business departments. The thinking is that litigators have seen what can go wrong with a deal, and so they'll be able to draft deals that are foolproof."

- Consider working in cities where the entertainment industry is based, where movies are made and music is recorded: Los Angeles, New York, Nashville, and Orlando. There are, of course, entertainment-related jobs in other cities, as well—like Washington—but those cities are the "target-rich" environments.

- Ask at Career Services for names of alums who are in entertainment. Contact them for informational interviews (we discussed this kind of interview in Chapter 10).

- Keep an eye on your Career Service Office's job postings *every day*. You wouldn't believe how many entertainment-oriented gigs will come into your law school. If you don't notice them, it's because they're snatched up the day they're posted. Check *every day* to make sure none slip through your grasp.

- Look at activities in law school that involve participation by alumni, and see if there are alums you want to get to know. One student was asked repeatedly to be the student member on an alumni board at his law school. No student wanted the position. He took it, and wound up sitting next to an alum who was in-house counsel for a cable network. He wound up with a summer job at the network through her.

- Take CLEs about entertainment topics. Learn how business deals are done in the part of the industry that attracts you. (The people who teach CLEs also make great contacts, as do the other attendees.)

- Attend symposiums and conferences. Go to the ABA Forum on Sports and Entertainment. Volunteer at these events to be even more memorable.

- Educate yourself (via informational interviews) *before* you try to find a job. You'll sound a lot more credible to entertainment employers, and you'll be able to answer (and ask) questions intelligently.

- Ask at the Career Services Office at school or at the local bar association for "shadowing" opportunities. A great way to see what entertainment lawyers do, figure out if you'll enjoy it, and make valuable contacts is to follow them around for a day.

- Consider creating your own internship with an entertainment organization. Students have done this successfully. Give the organization an idea of what you'd like to do and emphasize that you will work for free. An extra pair of enthusiastic hands can't hurt!

- Join an entertainment law society at law school; get heavily involved in outreach; start one if your school doesn't have one.

- Remember that you might have contacts you don't even recognize as such. You might already know musicians or actors; maybe they were classmates of yours. You can talk to their agents, their lawyers, and if you're close enough friends, when you get a job as a lawyer they might *become* a client. Nothing makes you more valuable to a legal employer than bringing in clients of your own!

- Except for large law firms, expect to, offer to, and welcome volunteer opportunities. Your goal is to get your foot in the door *any way you can*. While there are a few paying jobs, you *have* to be willing to volunteer (and you may get school credit for your work). It doesn't matter if you take on a part-time job at the same time to pay your bills; waiting tables comes to mind, but you might be more creative than me. The point remains: many jobs that will get you started in entertainment are unpaid. Production companies, studios, entertainment unions, recording companies, non-profits catering to young talent ... they all hire volunteer interns. One student told me about an interview he had with an executive at a major film studio. The executive said, "I can't pay you, but I'll introduce you to everybody." Sold!

- Write articles about entertainment issues for bar publications; write profiles of entertainment lawyers ... a great way to meet people who might not have spoken to you otherwise!

- Join Lawyers for the Arts, the pro bono organization. Whether or not you want to work with the clients you'll represent, entertainment lawyers do their pro bono work that way, and you'll meet *them*. Also, Lawyers for the Arts conducts workshops and holds presentations, and you'll want to attend those not just to learn but to meet the other attendees.

- Run a conference on careers in entertainment. You can get sponsorship from your school, the alumni association or the local or state bar.

- Join the entertainment law section of the bar (if your city has one) while you're still a student. Go to events.

- Look up local non-profit agencies, and see who's on the board of directors. If there are people involved with entertainment *and* you're interested in the non-profit, consider volunteering for the board. As Mindy Baggish points out, "Many entertainment clients are devoted to specific causes. If you share their commitment, remember that common ground engenders relationships."

- Remember that if a client recommends that their lawyer talk with you, you'll get that interview. Attorneys don't turn down interview requests that come via clients. So if you know or can get to know an entertainment client, that's one way to get your foot in the door. (In terms of handling that interview, see Chapter 9 on Interviews.)

- Get familiar with the industry by reading the trade papers, like *Billboard* and *Variety*.

- Think about creating a blog on entertainment-related issues. In Chapter 11, we talked about the lawyer who writes about labor issues raised by the TV show *The Office*. If you come up with something clever, consider sending the link to employers you'd like to target.

- Persevere. There's a lot of competition, and a lot of rejection ... but *somebody* gets those jobs, and it might as well be you.

- Turn people who are close to you into your "scouts." It's more than who they know; it's who they *meet*. Tell them that when they meet anyone who can help your cause, they should tell the person about your interest in what they do, and ask if that person will talk to you and give you some advice about what you ought to be doing. I've seen this work a bunch of times. It's worked for me, as a matter of fact. I've mentioned before that I write screenplays for a hobby, and everyone I know knows that I'm always looking for a way to sell one of them. My father was sitting on a plane and started chatting with the guy next to him, and what do you know—the guy happened to be a movie director. Dad told him I write screenplays and asked if he'd talk to me. We've been in correspondence ever since. People are almost universally helpful ... give them a chance to be exactly that!

- When you volunteer or intern, make yourself indispensable. Work long hours. Be there when they need you.

- Be really nice to secretaries and receptionists. You'll be talking to them a lot.

- Exude enthusiasm. I've talked to many students who've successfully nailed fabulous entertainment internships and jobs, and to a person they said that their enthusiasm was what pushed them over the top. One student had applied for a clerkship with HBO Business Affairs. There were thousands of applicants, and seven finalists—of which she was one. "The seven of us had to videotape interviews," she said. "In mine I made a point of telling them how much I wanted the job, the people I had talked to, another internship I'd done in entertainment to learn more about it. I'm sure my enthusiasm got me the job!"

- For any particular internship, try to find people who've had the internship before. Go through Career Services, ask the internship provider for people who've done the internship before (which they may or may not provide), shake the trees to see if you can discover who they are. Ask them for advice about your application. (It's easier to do this by phone than via e-mail; you'll get better advice.) Also, if it's at all possible, drop off your credentials in person. You're more memorable in person than you are over the phone or by mail or e-mail.

C. **FIRMS DEDICATED EXCLUSIVELY TO ENTERTAINMENT LAW**

1. Timing: Don't wait until Third Year to send out resumes!

    The earlier you get involved, the better. Try for a clerkship after First Year.

2. Learn all you can about the business and the clientele. For instance, if you're going to be representing entertainers, be aware that you'll be on call every hour of every day. If your client gets arrested you've got to bail them out or figure out a way to get that done if they're on the other side of the world. You see what it is really like to be a star—namely, being under constant pressure to outdo your last success. That kind of pressure sometimes leads to, ahem unattractive behavior, sometimes including drug use and alcohol abuse (by your clients, not you). You, the lawyer, become psychiatrist as well as lawyer, and you have to deal with important issues for which you are unlikely to have any formal training.

3. Helpful backgrounds: Business (an MBA doesn't hurt) and/or accounting, with a great facility in English. It's important to be able to communicate well and be understood. As is true for athletes, performers may have a high intellectual level but they won't typically be well-educated, and so being an entertainment lawyer means communicating with people who have brains but not necessarily the academic background to go with it. Because entertainers can make huge amounts of money, there are important decisions to be made relating to that wealth, and entertainment lawyers have to be able to explain that business to them.

4. Activities:

    Attend all of the law-related entertainment functions that you can, and buttonhole the speakers—they expect it. Keep up with entertainment publications like *Variety* and *Billboard* to see what functions are taking place. Go to them, or even better, volunteer to help out.

5. Cover letters, resumes and interviews:

    Don't try to impress them with your knowledge of the entertainment business, because many entertainment lawyers are amused by the misconceptions of law students. Instead, stress that you are going to work your butt off to be the best clerk they've ever had. As many an entertainment lawyer says, "It's not about hanging out with stars. It's hard work! The first time you meet a star, that's great. After two years of traveling forty-eight hours a week, you're tired."

Interviews: minimize your interest in entertainment. As a lawyer for a major studio points out, "When people come to us looking for a job as a lawyer, they'll think it's helpful to have done films in college or to have worked in a production company. I'll interview people who will say, 'Oh, I love entertainment, I love the movies.' Actually a love of the entertainment business is suspicious. It makes you think that they want to do *entertainment,* not what we're doing. We're *lawyers.*"

D. LARGE FIRMS THAT HAVE AN ENTERTAINMENT PRACTICE

I've heard from many, many people that the *best* way to enter a large firm's entertainment practice is *not to aim for it overtly.* I know that sounds sneaky and manipulative, but large law firms are suspicious of students who only aim for their entertainment work. As UC Davis' Mindy Baggish, a former entertainment lawyer herself, points out, "Everybody in entertainment at large firms will tell you the same thing: Don't mention your desire to practice entertainment law in your cover letter or in interviews, *even if* the firm says it has an entertainment law practice."

Instead, what you want to do is get into the firm and then "lateral into" entertainment. Here's how you do it:

- "Let the firm know that you are committed to the practice of law generally," advises Mindy Baggish. "Because entertainment law is seen as the 'sexiest' practice, a lot of law students are interested in practicing it. What about all of the firm's other clients? The hiring committees have to have young attorneys to work with them."

- Get a solid grounding in a specialty that will involve entertainment clients. Once you've developed a specialty you can apply your skills to entertainment clients. If you do transactional work, you negotiate deals and negotiate contracts, it doesn't matter whether you're doing it for a plumbing company or a movie star—it's the same skill. If you litigate, drafting complaints and motions for any client is transferable to drafting complaints and motions for copyright and trademark violations. As Mindy Baggish points out, "Once you've worked on a matter that involves an entertainment client, doesn't that, by default, make you an entertainment lawyer?"

- Do your regular work and volunteer to take on extra projects for partners who handle entertainment clients. Make sure they know who you are. Make sure you're in the office when they're there, especially if they show up when there are few other associates around; let them know you're there and offer to help out. As often happens, you may find more and more of your time taken up with entertainment clients until it's the bulk of your schedule.

- Use your pro bono work to handle entertainment clients.

- Ask for work involving specialties that are useful in entertainment: trademark, copyright, publicity ... Whether you wind up with entertainment work at your current employer or not, it will set you up for an in-house gig with an entertainment company.

- Let people know the work you want, so that when they have overflow they'll give you projects.

E. NONTRADITIONAL JOBS

1. Studio executive jobs: Having a law degree is extremely useful. You typically break into management by acting as a lawyer for studios first, where you see how deals get done and you help facilitate those deals. It's a relatively small jump to actually being in a production role yourself.

2. Agenting: You either: (i) work your way up from the mail room (yes, it's a cliché, and yes, it still works); (ii) Interning; (iii) bringing in clients; or (iv) bringing in deals.

* * * SMART HUMAN TRICK ... AND CAREER LIMITING MOVE * * *

A tale of two students ... Query: which one will make it?

Female law student, going to law school in Florida. She explains that she wants to be an agent representing music groups after she graduates. In the meantime, she goes to nightclubs for "new talent" night every weekend (not a bad hobby), and when she sees promising groups, she introduces herself to them and says, "I'm not a lawyer yet, so I can't represent you right now. But you don't have any money, so you can't afford a lawyer anyway. In the meantime, when you get gigs, why don't we just talk about it informally, and I'll give you some friendly advice, you can use it if you want, or ignore it. But by the time I get out of school maybe you'll like me enough and trust me enough to represent you for real."

Student #2: Another female student, this one in New York City. She's very angry and very frustrated. She says, "I've talked to everybody I can talk to, and the best thing I've been offered is as a receptionist at a record company. A *receptionist!* And I've got a *law degree!*' When she's congratulated for breaking into entertainment— and she's told about the student in Florida—she responds, 'I'm not going to do *that*. I want to be *trained*.' "

Moral to the story: If you're relying on finding someone to take you under their wing and tutor you, don't pursue entertainment. It can happen, but it's very unlikely. Assertiveness pays. Creativity pays.

* * * SMART HUMAN TRICK * * *

Female law student in Tennessee. She did an internship with a music company in college, and reps new artists part-time while she's in law school. She helps review contracts and negotiate shows. She says, "I intend to join a large agency when I graduate. I want to go in with a built-in clientele. Maybe none of my artists will make it big, but they tell their friends about me, and then *they* come to me. *Somebody's* going to make it. I figure that anyone can draft contracts, but people who bring in business are golden. I'll be uniquely valuable."

3. **For nontraditional jobs of all kinds in entertainment:**

    Don't overlook internships. Many entertainment companies hire interns. Music companies, booking agencies, ICM, CAA, HBO, the Academy of Motion Picture Arts and Sciences, management companies, film companies, concert promoters ... there are tons of great internships available. They pay very little if anything, but they are a great way to break in. That's how Tony DiSanto, executive vice president of series development and programming at MTV, got his foot in the door. A great resource is *The Princeton Review Guide to America's Top Internships*.

4. **Online Resources:**

    Job openings in entertainment and media companies:

    www.entertainmentcareers.net

    www.showbizjobs.com

    www.ifcome.com

    Hieros Gamos (Art Law On The Web):

    www.hg.org/art.html

    Volunteer opportunities to help local artists:

    www.starvingartistslaw.com

    Villanova Sports & Entertainment Journal:

    www.law.villanova.edu/scholarlyresources/journals/sports andentlj/

4. Don't Forget That You Can Always Start Your Own Shop

One way to ensure you get the job you want is to create your own. While you're in school, take on internships, go to conferences and seminars, join Lawyers for the Arts, and learn all you can. Take some business classes if you're not familiar with business. Read profiles of people who've done what you want to do, and see how *they* did it; you don't have to reinvent the wheel.

It takes major *cojones* and a high threshold of pain to start your own gig. It's also tremendously exciting. If you've got the personality and the desire . . . think about it!

* * * SMART HUMAN TRICK * * *

Female law school graduate in Texas. She's got a hankering for entertainment, but she goes to a large firm where she does real estate work. She doesn't love it. A client tells her, "We'd like you to come in-house for us." She responds, "I really want to do entertainment-related work." They tell her, "Then set up your own office. Do our real estate work, it won't take up all your time, and you'll have time to generate entertainment clients."

She does exactly that. Within three years of graduation, she has her own firm, doing real estate . . . and entertainment.

C. Sports

Maybe you've been a sports nut all of your life. If you live and breathe sports—except for your law school studies, of course—you would probably give anything to break into sports law. And if you want the job, you'll probably *have* to!

Just kidding. I talk to law students all the time who've successfully nailed a job in sports. In this section, we'll talk about how you can do exactly that.

1. What *Is* Sports Law?

According to sports lawyer Jack Swarbrick, of JB Sports (a marketing and management company), sports for law school graduates breaks down to:

- Intellectual property ('soft' IP, in the form of trademarks and copyrights);

- Broadcasting rights;

- Event identities;

- Unique antitrust issues; and

- Traditional business associations issues (as in forming franchises, licensing, forming and negotiating agreements, and creating new event properties).

There are also issues involving sponsorships, labor law, due process (drug testing) . . . even insurance law! As Minnesota's Sue Gainen points out, "Insurance impacts everything. Every sports event, every facility needs insurance. Every sports figure needs workmen's comp. At every deal table, there has to be an insurance guy. It's not just auto cases!"

2. Remember: Even Dream Jobs Are Still *Jobs*. They Have Their Downsides as Well as Their Positives

I remember talking to a law student who recounted that he'd been at an NFL game, and spotted a college roommate sitting near the field at the fifty yard line. It turned out this guy had nailed an internship with ESPN, and he called out to this law student, "I have the best job in the world!" The student sighed and told me, "That's the job *I* want."

I'd hasten to point out that what he *wanted* was to sit at the fifty yard line at football games. Whether he wanted the *job* was another matter entirely!

It's hyper-important, with sports as with every other job that you *talk to as many people as possible to learn what jobs are really like, rather than fantasizing about them*. Every job has downsides. Every single one.

I read an interview with a guy, TY Votaw, who was the head of international affairs for the PGA. The headline for the article said it all: "The best job in the world." Well ... maybe. For one thing, the job involved traveling 200 days a year; that is, more than half the time. Votaw had children at home and mentioned how much he enjoyed spending time with them. Trust me, frequent travel isn't that much fun if you've got children you're missing. On top of that, the reporter commented on Votaw's opportunity to visit the best golf courses on the planet, and asked if there were any he was looking forward to playing. Votaw responded, "The dirty little secret is that when you're in the business of golf, you don't get to play as often as people who aren't in the business." Read: It's a *job*.

Make sure that what you're after is something you'll enjoy, not just that it's got the trappings of sports attached to it!

3. Traditional Sports Lawyering Jobs

If you're talking about traditional lawyering activities involving sports, you've got three basic possibilities:

- Working for a firm that does sports law, representing athletes, teams, leagues, and other related entities.

- Working for a team or a league as in-house counsel.

- Working for an entity that sponsors or invests in sports. As Jack Swarbrick describes it, "The Coca–Colas, the McDonalds, the John Hancocks of the world, these are companies that have investments in sports, and they need to protect these investments. These kinds of organizations need people to work on agreements and protect the marks associated with sports sponsorships."

4. Nontraditional Sports Careers

That is, nontraditional yet related to law. There are a million sports jobs that have nothing to do with law. If you've got the talent of Tiger Woods, for gosh sakes, *play*.

Furthermore, many of these jobs aren't ones you can nail coming out of school. The New York Yankees aren't going to invite you to manage the team. But a rookie league team? Sure, that's a near-term goal. Be willing to work for a team doing *anything,* sometimes for very little pay, and take it from there.

Let's talk about the nontraditional jobs that make sense:

- Jobs aligned with specific sports teams, including General Manager, Business Manager, Director of Minor League Operations, Marketing Director, or Traveling Secretary.

- Sports agenting/marketing.

- Director of a sports complex/stadium operations/sports event coordinating.

Since you may not be familiar with these jobs, let's talk about what they involve.

A. JOBS ALIGNED WITH PARTICULAR TEAMS

There are, of course, dozens of jobs with sports teams. Here are a few:

1. TEAM GENERAL MANAGER

Every professional sports team has a general manager. You're the sports equivalent of the president of a company, in that you handle the team's day-to-day activities, and you hire and fire people, among other duties. Depending on the size of the organization you're managing, you might also handle the team's publicity and marketing. You are also responsible for helping to put together a winning team, and so you have to stay up-to-date on your sport and who the prospects are. You also help negotiate salaries. In the smaller, lower-division teams, you might go by the title of "business manager" or, in baseball, "director of minor league operations."

2. BUSINESS MANAGER FOR A PROFESSIONAL SPORTS TEAM

All professional sports teams have a business manager. In this role, as the name suggests, you handle the business of the team. You solicit bids for any goods and services the team needs, help handle contracts, and deal with problems confronting the team and its members. You may also have to work with the stadium that hosts your team. You have to keep track of all of the bills associated with the team, and keep accurate records. You also work closely with the traveling secretary who handles the team's travel needs, helping to plan hotels, transportation, and everything associated with travel. As all of this suggests, the job is one with lots of varied responsibility.

3.   Marketing Director for a Professional Sports Team

You handle every aspect of marketing the team and its players. You create and implement marketing campaigns, create new markets, and handle licensing for the team's name and logo. Your duties may stretch from handling giveaways and contests at the stadium itself, to developing and handling personal appearances and press interviews for the athletes.

For bigger, higher-level teams, there are assistant marketing directors, and you typically move into the marketing director's role from the assistant position. For lower-level teams, you'd probably also have public relations duties, which would mean preparing brochures, newsletters, press releases, and handling trade shows.

4.   Traveling Secretary for a Professional Sports Team

This doesn't mean "secretary" as in, "Miss Snodgrass, take a letter." Instead, you handle all of the travel arrangements for the team, including chartering planes and buses and negotiating deals with hotels and restaurants. You handle operational details on the road and make sure that all of the athletes and other people associated with the team have their basic needs met. You also handle crises and problems that pop up on the road.

B.   Sports Agenting

Sports agenting is a tremendously cutthroat business, involving cultivating young athletes to let you represent them, and then getting those athletes (and sometimes coaches and other sports-related personalities) the best possible deals with their team and companies who want them to endorse products and services. Some agents also act as financial advisers, helping athletes handle their investments. As some sports agents have said to me, "I spend all day on the phone, looking for deals, making deals, closing deals. If you don't 'give great phone,' this is not the business for you."

C.   Sports Marketing

This term has a variety of meanings, but all of them revolve around one activity: selling. For instance, when you represent an athlete and you analyze that athlete's appeal and then try to encourage sponsors to hire your athlete to hawk their products, that's sports marketing. And it's also selling. Jack Swarbrick points out that sports marketing "involves many things that athlete clients will ask lawyers for beyond representing them in negotiating a contract, like packaging a sports event for presentation to a network."

D.   Sports Event Coordinating

The Olympics, the Kentucky Derby, the U.S. Open, and every other major sporting event ... they don't just happen. They are carefully planned. And the people who do that careful planning are sports event coordinators. In this role you either work for a facility, like a resort or stadium or arena, or you work for (or as) a sports promoter who handles different events at different locations.

E. FACILITIES-ORIENTED JOBS

There are a number of these. If you work for a particular facility, you might be a director of a sports complex or director of stadium operations (or any one of the people who work for them). You work with others, like public relations people, marketers, security people, to figure out what kinds of preparations are necessary. You may have to handle the media and set up related events like press conferences and cocktail parties or meals, and you may have to handle transportation and accommodation for athletes, officials, and other visitors. In addition, you have the preparations peculiar to each sport or event— for instance, track events will require special equipment, timers, and the like. And you will always have to troubleshoot problems that are sure to arise.

5. EVERYTHING WE DISCUSSED ABOUT BREAKING INTO ENTERTAINMENT APPLIES TO SPORTS, AS WELL. IN ADDITION, HERE ARE SOME DO'S AND DON'TS TO KEEP IN MIND

DO look broadly at the sports industry. Jack Swarbrick points out that "Sports isn't just being an agent." There are *many* administrative jobs, and if you love sports you'll find that not only will you enjoy those jobs, but you'll find that your law degree is a real plus!

DO "become a good lawyer first." Jack Swarbrick feels that you need good writing skills, good negotiating skills, you need to know how to draft agreements and solve problems.

DO realize that if you go to a large law firm, don't expect to go directly into sports. Instead, get a solid grounding in a specialty and keep your eyes open for serving sports clients. "Lateral" into it. You can do it with many, many specialties. For instance, you can start in employment litigation, represent nonprofits, and handle work for sports organizations in that capacity. Or you can work your specialty and volunteer for extra work from partners who handle sports clients. There are as many paths into sports at large law firms as there are sports lawyers.

DON'T rely on Martindale–Hubbell for firms that say they practice sports law, since those listings tend to include "Everyone who has ever had any involvement in sports" according to Jack Swarbrick, as opposed to a vigorous, growing practice now. Instead, "Talk to someone with an honest-to-God sports practice, and find out who's doing what through them. Or search Martindale–Hubbell or Lexis or Westlaw for litigation matters involving sports." Sports-oriented publications and law-oriented web sites, like www.lawfuel.com, would also help; look and see which lawyers are mentioned in conjunction with deals.

DO be flexible. Jack Swarbrick laughs that "90% of law careers are shaped completely by accident!" He got his own start in sports as a labor and litigation lawyer at Baker & Daniels in Indianapolis, representing traditional clients, Midwestern manufacturers. He had no ambition for sports law. However, one day the managing partner stopped him in a hallway and said, "Do you have any time? Call this guy. He's got a problem."

The managing partner handed him a slip of paper, and the 'guy' turned out to be involved with U.S.A. Gymnastics, which had just relocated to Indianapolis. When Swarbrick called him, he explained that they had a 14–year-old gymnast whose hometown in Texas wanted to sell bumper stickers to help pay for her training. They were worried about whether selling the bumper stickers would harm her eligibility. Swarbrick researched it, found that the bumper sticker sales wouldn't fly, and he set up systems to preserve her eligibility. That 14–year-old girl turned out to be Mary Lou Retton, whom you may know was a gold medalist in the 1984 Summer Olympics with an absolutely thrilling performance. Swarbrick says that "After that, other people in sports started calling me." As he advises, "Just follow your career wherever it goes. Don't ever say, 'I don't do that,' because you don't know where it might lead."

Another lawyer, this one in San Francisco, became in-house counsel for an NFL team this way: he handled bond issues for a major law firm. He got involved in a bond issue for a new ballpark, and because of it he delved into the politics of building a new stadium. As a result, he got to know all of the people involved with the team, and they invited him in-house.

DO meet as many people as you can. Attend conferences and seminars, but realize that it takes determination to get to the people you want to meet. In their own habitats, "Established presences have elaborate defense mechanisms," because they get contacted "all the time."

DO take classes in school involving issues that come up in sports: Sports law is an obvious target, but others aren't. Collective bargaining, labor law, tax, estate planning, alternative dispute resolution, family law, insurance ... as we've discussed before, all kinds of substantive areas touch on sports law.

DO consider directing intramural sports while you're still in school. As sports lawyer Chip Lipscomb recommends, "Organize the fields, the insurance, the schedule and the referees."

DO volunteer. According to Jack Swarbrick, "If you live in New York City, work your normal workweek as a lawyer and then volunteer at Madison Square Garden." Others have told me that you can volunteer while you're still in school, even if you're not in a big sports mecca. For instance, for intramural teams you can organize the fields, the insurance, the schedule and the referees. And of course you can volunteer for sports agents, teams, and leagues, as well.

DO recognize that when it comes to sports agenting, "No kid who can't read a freshman literature book is going to take a new law school graduate as their agent, unless they were college roommates." If you want to be an agent, there's nothing stopping you from volunteering for one during school, and then joining a firm as a sports lawyer and moving into agenting from there. "In order for sports agents to take you on permanently, you'll have to have a unique skill. For most agents, that means either a financial skill that they can sell—for instance, you have a CPA—or you have relationships, you know athletes."

DO be a good writer. "If you can't write clearly you can't think clearly," says Jack Swarbrick. A lot of sports work involves writing proposals, brochures, and other "plain language" literature. Notice that you don't need Law Review to prove your writing skills—you can write for sports-oriented newsletters and other publications.

DO be technologically sophisticated. "You need to know how to manage and manipulate databases," says Jack Swarbrick.

DO show that you're creative. Much of what goes on in sports-related careers doesn't have precedent, there aren't applicable case laws or statutes. Jack Swarbrick looks for people who show creativity "in virtually anything. For instance, maybe it wasn't so easy for you to get to law school in the first place—maybe you didn't have the money, maybe you had other obligations that made it difficult. Overcoming obstacles like that requires creativity."

DON'T bother with sports-related job fairs. "If you look at what's going on at these, it's all sellers and no buyers. They tend to be a waste of time."

DO whatever it takes to get your foot in the door. Once you're in, you can move around to other jobs. Take the example of Dave Dombrowski, general manager of the Detroit Tigers. Here's how he got his start: while he was in college, he interviewed the Chicago White Sox general manager as part of a paper on the general manager's role in baseball—who suggested that he job hunt at baseball's winter meetings in Honolulu. Dombrowski went there, and at the meetings he snagged a job interview with the White Sox. Dombrowski said he'd do "anything" to work with them—move cartons, shovel sidewalks, type, anything at all. He started, at $8,000 a year (!!), as an administrative assistant in the White Sox minor league and scouting department, doing everything from filing to making travel arrangements for spring training to operating the scoreboard to chauffeuring around the team's owner, Bill Veeck.

Within a year he moved up to assistant director of player development, and two years later he was director of player development. Then, at the age of 26, he became assistant general manager, then general manager of the Montreal Expos.

The moral of the story: it doesn't matter where you start.

DO check your ego at the door. The people you contact in the sports industry are not only very busy but very put upon. It's not the career for you if your feelings are easily hurt when a phone call or letter goes unanswered.

DON'T give up when you don't get a response. Follow up time and time again. "Not now" doesn't mean "not ever." Remember that especially for sports agents and people like them, their jobs require a great deal of self-confidence and assertiveness, and if you want to work with them, you're going to require the same skills *getting* the job as you would in *performing* the job. Michael Jordan's legendary agent David Falk got his first job by calling a sports agency every day for a month before they finally brought him in for an interview!

DO keep records of your contacts, and follow up with people you meet at conferences, seminars, and every other opportunity to meet people in the industry.

DO "aim where they aren't"; consider breaking in via sports that are not yet fully established. Every student thinks of football, baseball, hockey, basketball as targets. But sports like the X Games, skateboarding, snowboarding, up-and-coming women's sports, any sport you'd see on ESPN 2 off-hours ... the competition there won't be so fierce, and because many of these sports appeal to younger people, they've got great potential for growth. Sports agent Brian Balsbaugh is the premier agent for poker players. Yup. Poker. He got into it when he realized that with TV cameras focused on poker players, there was "real estate" on their shirts and hats that could be sold to sponsors. He'd been representing golfers, but quit immediately to focus on poker. Within a year he had snatched up all of the top poker players. The point is: no matter where you get your skills, be creative about where you'll apply them!

DO remember that you probably don't have to leave school to get your feet wet in sports. If you go to a school with a significant sports presence, there'll be an office that handles NCAA compliance. Look at working, doing work/study or volunteering for them.

DO write as much as you can for sports-oriented publications, or take advantage of *any* advantage to write about a sports-oriented theme (remember Dave Dombrowski and his college research paper on the role of general managers in baseball). You'll not only give yourself writing experience, proof of your writing skills, and a great resume item, but you'll have something to send people *other* than your resume—something that will actually help them!

DO keep in mind that you only get what you want through mutually beneficial relationships. Every person you contact in the sports industry knows what they can do for you—what can you do for *them?*

Often that means that you have to work for free (or very little) to start out, while you develop a marketable skill. The chief operating officer of the New Jersey Nets, in a radio interview, was asked how to get ahead in a professional sports team, and he answered: "Be willing to do *anything*." The old "up from the mail room" story *works* in professional sports.

DO take an active role in the Sports Law club at school, and if your school doesn't have one, start one. On top of that, if the club publishes a newsletter on Sports Law, write for it; if it doesn't have one, offer to create one.

DO consider creating your own internship with a professional team. The fact that an internship doesn't exist yet doesn't mean it never will ... or that the team wouldn't be receptive to the right pitch. Look at what other teams offer, and fashion one for a team you're targeting. Law students have done this, creating not just a great gig for themselves but a legacy for students from their school.

DO consider creating a blog or web site addressing sports issues. You can provide links to useful web resources and articles, and write your own commentary on sports issues. Send the link to employers you'd like to target.

DO what you'd do for any goal: tell everyone you know what you want. You don't know who they know ... or who they'll meet.

* * * SMART HUMAN TRICK * * *

Law student dying to get into Sports Law, specifically motor racing. Her mother is a human resources person, and belongs to an association of human resources professionals. At an association lunch the mom mentions to the others at the table what her daughter wants to do. One of them turns out to be the human resources person for a nationally-known race track. She says, "Have your daughter call me." The daughter calls, and winds up with a summer internship at the track.

DO tell your undergrad coaches about what you want to do, if you took part in sports in college. They probably know tons of people. They also know about your ability to be a team player and your self-discipline, which are qualities many employers seek.

DO consider running a "Careers In Sports Law" symposium at school. You can get sponsorship from your school or from the local or state bar association.

* * * SMART HUMAN TRICK * * *

Law student in the Midwest. She's hyper interested in Sports Law. She gets the state bar association to sponsor a weekend conference on Careers in Sports Law. She contacts every professional sports team in the state, and gets them to send a representative; she also gets sports lawyers to come and talk about what they do.

It's a great success—particularly for her! She is a hero to her classmates, who love the conference—and she enjoyed putting it together. Career-wise, she gets to talk to her dream employers without asking them for a job. And what do they know about her? That she is the kind of person who takes initiative in a big way. They get to see her in a leadership position. And when she calls again for advice about breaking into sports law, *they already know her and respect her.*

6.   GREAT SPORTS INTERNSHIPS

Anyone in sports will tell you that internships are a great way to get your foot in the door. Here are some to aim for:

- Professional sports leagues (like the NFL, NBA, MLB, NHL).
- Teams, both major and minor league.
- College athletic departments in Division I or Division II schools.
- The NCAA
- Corporations that sponsor leagues, teams and athletes
- News organizations that report on sports
- Sports marketing agencies
- Sports agents

Beyond those, you can intern in any number of areas—operations management, recruiting, marketing, and law.

To get information on specific internships, check the web sites of teams and organizations. If you strike out there, let your fingers do the walking; pick up the phone and call the organizations, talk to anyone who'll talk to you in human resources or even at the reception desk, and ask about internships, how to get more information, how and when to apply. Drench your communications in gratefulness. You'll find there's a tremendous benefit when it comes to digging up opportunities most people will never find if you take the simple step of *asking for advice, over the phone or in person.*

7.   RESOURCES: CONFERENCES, WEB SITES AND BOOKS

A. CONFERENCES

1.   Sports-oriented CLEs (we discuss CLEs in detail in Chapter 10). CLEs are not really conferences, but they are sports-directed and attract the employers you want to meet.

2.   The American Bar Association's "Forum on the Entertainment and Sports Industries," which runs yearly. It attracts some very high-profile speakers, making it worthwhile to attend (or even better, to volunteer for). For information, check out this web site: www.abanet.org/forums/entsports/home.html

B. WEB SITES

www.sportslaw.org (Sports Lawyers Association; law student memberships available)

www.nflpa.org (National Football League Players Association)

www.womensportsjobs.com

http://sportsworkers.com

http://womenssportsfoundation.org

www.majorleaguebaseball.com

www.marquette.edu/law(search "sports")

http://news.findlaw.com/legalnews/sports/sports_law

www.nfl.com

www.nba.com

www.ncaa.org

http://sports-law.blogspot.com/ (Sports Law Blog, with legal issues, commentary and links to other sports sites)

http://news.findlaw.com/legalnews/sports

www.hg.org/recr.html

www.jobsinsports.com (can search job databases and post resumes)

C. PERIODICALS

- Sportsguide of Princeton, NJ, publishes the "Sports Market Place" annually. It lists teams, associations, publications, broadcasters, promoters, and suppliers—really every sports resource you could want. It is also indexed by product, brand name, executive, and geographic area.

- The Sports Lawyers Association puts out a worthwhile electronic newsletter called "The Sports Lawyer." Look for information about it at www.sportslaw.org/

- Fitness Information Technology publishes the "Sports Marketing Quarterly." www.fitinfortech.com

- The Sports Business Daily gives you a daily insight into sponsorships, advertising, sports governing bodies, franchises, stadiums, and legal issues. You can reach them at: www.Sports businessdaily.com

D. BOOKS

Check at Career Services, where you'll find a lot of resources including books like:

- *The 50 Coolest Jobs in Sports,* by David Fischer.

- *How to Get a Job in Sports: The Guide to Finding the Right Sports Career,* by John Taylor.

- *Career Opportunities in the Sports Industry,* by Shelly Field.
- *How to Get a Job in Sports,* by Dale Ratermann & Mike Mullen.

D. INTERNATIONAL

1. WHAT IS IT?

If you love the idea of traveling to gorgeous cities, staying in the best hotels, eating at the finest restaurants in the world, you'll love ...

... *Vacations.*

Of course I'm being facetious, but you see my point. It's too easy to think, "Gee, I want to see the world, I'll be an international lawyer." You *may* get to travel as an international lawyer, but one of the problems with international law is that it encompasses so many things, it's impossible to say what an "international lawyer" does. You can spend your entire life sitting at a desk in the Midwest ... or you can be dodging bullets at refugee camps in the Middle East. In fact, one thing you want to avoid is ever telling an employer, "I want to do international law." Employers often tell me, "When I hear 'international law' from a student, I smile. I figure they don't have a *clue* what international law means."

Well! We're going to change all that! We'll talk about some of the more popular settings for international law, and we'll talk about how to break into the field. Having said that, it would be possible to write an entire book about this subject; a whole lot *have* been, as a matter of fact. We'll just dip our toes in the water. But I think you'll find that the techniques that we've used throughout this book—talking with alums and practitioners, attending activities, volunteering—will get you wherever you want to go.

As a threshold matter, beyond thinking 'International,' take away the label and answer a few questions:

- Do you want to live here, or abroad?
- If you want to live abroad, do you want to live in an established city, or are you OK in a refugee/unsettled situation?
- Do you want to represent individual clients (people or corporations) or do you want to work on policy and economic issues?
- Do you want to do transactional or litigation-oriented work?
- Do you want to make a bunch of money or do you want to help people?
- Are you sure you don't want to just *vacation* in exotic places?

The more you can focus on what you truly want, the easier your search will be. It may not be obvious to you; talk to counselors at Career Services, talk to alums who work in a variety of international law practices, here and abroad, to help figure it out. Of course, there are also great web resources, which we'll discuss throughout this section.

Two great "threshold" web resources are: www.internationalcenter. umich.edu (The University of Michigan Law School; general information about working abroad)

U.S. Foreign Service (both internships and permanent jobs world-wide): www.state.gov

2. TYPES OF INTERNATIONAL LAW

International law is something of an umbrella term, covering several distinct types of jobs, and many substantive areas, from litigation to corporate work to government relations and many more ... even family law! (What if someone goes abroad and marries a foreign citizen? When they divorce, there are issues of support, custody, asset division ... they're all impacted by international issues).

"International law" is typically broken down into two general categories. As American's Matt Pascocello explains it, those are public international law, and private international law.

A. PUBLIC INTERNATIONAL LAW

As Matt Pascocello defines it, public international law deals with "questions arising under treaties, boundary and territorial disputes, certain maritime claims, and questions of State responsibility. It's generally practiced by government agencies and non-governmental organizations (NGOs)."

The NGOs would include organizations like the World Bank, the United Nations, the International Monetary Fund, the Organization of American States, and the European Bank for Reconstruction and Development, and public interest organizations like Amnesty International.

The government agencies would include "the usual suspects," like the U.S. State Department, Department of Commerce, Overseas Private Investment Corporation, Office of the U.S. Trade Representative, the Department of Justice, and many more.

Notice that what we would generally consider public interest international jobs can be either public or private, but they tend to be NGOs.

B. PRIVATE INTERNATIONAL LAW

As Matt Pascocello points out, private international law is "everything else"; that is, everything that's not public international law. It involves representing private parties "where the issues are either country-specific or transnational, and involve the application of local law, foreign law, or international agreements and treaties."

Where do you find it? There are obvious and not-so-obvious players, including:

- international departments of large law firms;

- boutique firms specializing in areas like antidumping and customs laws;
- general counsel's offices of corporations with international interests;
- other specialties in large firms, where the clients represented or issues have an international aspect, like tax, labor, finance, corporate, M & A.

In "Breaking in," Topic 8, below, we talk about strategies for getting into these employers.

3. "Target Rich" Environments for Public International Law

Some organizations have more international work available than others. Here we'll talk about "target rich" environments. **Note that just about every federal government agency has *some* international work, from the SEC to the Department of the Treasury to the Federal Reserve Board (international banking). It makes sense to troll federal agency websites for internships and permanent jobs involving international issues, which just about every federal agency has. Because fewer students look there, the competition for those jobs is *considerably* lower.** *(This section adapted from a NALP presentation by Rob Kaplan, Beth Kirch, Paula Nailon, and updated by Alexiss Bogger)*

A. *Never Forget* That People Are Often the Key That Opens the Door to Opportunities

Don't peg your whole search on websites. Talk to your Career Services Office, professors, alums, practitioners you find—they often generate great ideas for you.

B. U.S. Government Organizations

- Arms Control and Disarmament Agency (http://dosfan.lib.uic.edu/acda/) (offers fellowships)
- Central Intelligence Agency (www.cia.gov) (hires summer clerks and new graduates)
- Department of Defense (www.dod.gov) (hires summer interns)
- Export–Import Bank of the United States (www.exim.gov) (hires summer interns)
- Office of the U.S. Trade Representative (www.ustr.gov) (hires interns during the year and during the summer)
- Overseas Private Investment Corporation (www.opic.gov) (has academic year and summer internships)
- U.S. Agency for International Development (www.usaid.gov) (internships available year-round)
- U.S. Army Corps of Engineers (www.usace.army.mil) (hires new graduates)

- State Department (www.state.gov) (both the Office of the Legal Adviser, which hires interns and new graduates, and the Foreign Service. Has interns and hires new graduates)

- U.S. International Trade Commission (www.usitc.gov)

- U.S. Trade and Development Agency (www.tda.gov)

- Department of Justice (www.usdoj.gov) (hires interns and new graduates) (the best targets, according to the Justice Department's Office of Attorney Recruitment and Management, include:

  - Antitrust;

  - Civil;

  - Criminal;

  - Foreign Claims Settlement Commission;

  - International Criminal Police Organization (Interpol);

  - Office of Intelligence Policy and Review

  - Immigration and Naturalization;

  - Office of International Affairs;

  - Executive Office of Immigration Review

c. INTERNATIONAL NON-PROFITS AND NGOS

1. See Chapter 26 on Public Interest Jobs for all kinds of public interest resources; many of them have international opportunities. Also, check with your Career Services Office for hard copy resources.

2. Note that once you have a target organization either from the list below or anywhere else, look for *people* in it, whether through the CSO at school, alums, professors, or anyone else. Talk to *somebody* about the organization before you seek a job there!

3. Depending on your interests, there are dozens and dozens of organizations that you can target. They include:

   a. Economic Development:

      - Asia–Pacific Economic Cooperation (www.apec.org/apec/about_apec.html)

      - Asian Development Bank (www.adb.org)

      - Center for Institutional Reform and the Informal Sector, Department of Economics, University of Maryland (IRIS)(www.iris.umd.edu)

      - European Bank for Reconstruction and Development (EBRD)(www.ebrd.com)

      - European Investment Bank (www.eib.org)

      - Financial Services Volunteer Corps (FSVC)(www.fsvc.org)

- Inter–American Development Bank (www.iadb.org)
- International Executive Services Corps (IESC)(www.iesc.org)
- International Monetary Fund (www.imf.org)
- Organization for Co–Operation and Development (OECD)(www.oecd.org)
- Village Banking (www.villagebanking.org)
- World Intellectual Property Organization (WIPO)(www.wipo.int)
- World Trade Organization (www.wto.org)

b.   Environmental:

- International Union for the Conservation of Nature and Natural Resources (www.iucn.org/wssd/)
- The Nature Conservancy (www.tnc.org)
- Winrock International (www.winrock.org)
- World Resource Institute (www.wri.org)
- World Wildlife Fund (www.worldwildlife.org)

c.   Human rights:

- Amnesty International (http://web.amnesty.org/jobs)
- Human Rights First (formerly Lawyers Committee for Human Rights) (www.humanrightsfirst.org)
- Human Rights Watch (www.hrw.org)
- InterAction (www.interaction.org)
- International Human Rights Law Group (www.lawgroup.org)
- Lawyers Without Borders (www.lawyerwithoutborders.org)
- World Organization for Human Rights USA (www.humanrightsusa.org)

d.   Immigration:

- International Catholic Migration Committee (www.icmc.net)
- International Organization for Migration (www.iom.ch)

Refugees:

- American Refugee Committee (www.archg.org)
- International Committee of the Red Cross (www.icrc.org)
- International Rescue Committee (www.theirc.org)

f.   Women's rights:

- Domestic violence resources (www.dvsheltertour.org/links.html#international) (contains links to international domestic violence resources)

- Sisterhood is Global Institute (www.sigi.org) (comprehensive list of international human rights organizations focusing on women's rights)
- Women's Groups (www.euronet.nl/fullmoon/womlist/countries) (list of women's organizations, organized by country)

g. United Nations: www.unsystem.org (has an alphabetical index to links to U.N. organizations and other sites; you can find UN vacancies using the Job Opportunities link).

h. Other focuses:

- American Jewish World Service (www.ajws.org)
- American Bar Association's Asia Law Initiative (www.abanet.org/aba-asia)
- American Bar Association's Section of Dispute Resolution (www.abanet.org/dispute/disputeinternship.html)
- American Bar Association's Section of International Law Internship Program (www.abanet.org/intlaw/intlinternship)
- CARE International (www.care.org)
- The Carter Center (www.cartercenter.org)
- Catholic Social Services (www.cssalaska.org)
- Colombo Plan (www.colombo-plan.org)
- Food for the Hungry International (www.fh.org)
- Freedom House (www.freedomhouse.org)
- International Food Policy Research Institute (www.ifpri.org)
- International Institute for the Unification of Private Law (www.unidroit.org/english/presentation/main.htm)
- International Republican Institute (www.iri.org)
- International Senior Lawyers Project advisor (www.islp.org)
- Korean Peninsula Energy Development Organization (www.kedo.org)
- Mercy Corps (www.mercycorps.org)
- National Democratic Institute (www.ndi.org)
- North Atlantic Treaty Organization (NATO)(www.nato.int)
- Organization of American States (www.oas.org)
- World Vision (www.worldvision.org)

4. "TARGET-RICH" PRIVATE INTERNATIONAL LAW RESOURCES

I know I sound like a broken record but it's important to remember that the *best* resource you have is the "human" one; talk to professors with international backgrounds or interests at school, as well as asking at Career Services for alums who live abroad/practice international law. You'll get better information from people than you *ever* will from web resources.

Having said that, here are some web resources to try:

For short-term opportunities with law firms worldwide:

www.abanet.org/intlaw/internprofiles.html (The ABA's International Section makes this list of openings available seasonally; you can't open it all the time. You can e-mail intlaw@abanet.org to find out when the next list will be available if you have trouble accessing it.)

For U.S. law firms with international practices: www.martindale.com (Martindale–Hubbell)

For job listings/internships in Europe: www.eurobrussels.com (updated daily use links on top left side of page to access jobs by sector, like law firms or NGOs)

For job listings in Asia: www.recruit-legal.com/jobsearch.asp

5. Internships Abroad

A summer internship in another country can be a life-changing experience. As University of San Francisco student Nate Sponsler reflected in the USF student newspaper on his summer in Kenya, "It reaffirmed what I have known for a long time but possibly had lost track of during my first year in law school: I am privileged just to have the opportunity to be in law school and my education will one day place me in a position to help those not so privileged."

Not bad for a summer job. It beats xeroxing.

Getting an internship abroad takes some work, but the opportunities are definitely there.

Here's a game plan for you to consider. (It's largely advice from Elizabeth Qually, an '06 George Washington Law grad, based on her own experience.)

A. Step One: Identify Target Countries

Elizabeth Qually points out that "If you have in mind a specific place due to prior experience or language abilities, you have some advantages because your search will be focused. However, if you simply have a vague idea of where you'd like to go, I highly recommend identifying 1–3 countries with which to start your search. Your search will naturally broaden, and you may end up somewhere you never expected, but a little focus in the beginning is always good."

"Where you start (and end up) needs to be governed by a few initial criteria and some preliminary research."

The criteria are:

- Safety
- Money
- Weather

- Language

As a general matter, a tremendously useful website is www.state.gov/r/pa/ei/bgn/, which gives you information about the land, people, languages, history, government, political conditions, economy, and foreign relations for each country listed. Also, you can post questions about living in any particular place on two websites, www.expatriates.com and www.craigslist.com (go to "travel" forum at bottom left of page).

Still, let's look at those four elements—safety, money, weather, and language—individually:

1. Safety

Helpful websites: CIA World Factbook: www.odci.gov; State Department: www.state.gov.

According to Elizabeth Qually: "I was unfamiliar with a lot of countries and had no idea of the political climate or safety level of each nation. Do this research first because even if you feel daring, U.S. Missions and private companies probably already pulled their offices out of highly unstable countries."

2. Money

Helpful website: www.LonelyPlanet.com

According to Elizabeth Qually: "Expanding your search beyond Europe to exotic places with far away names has two distinct advantages. First, there are many more opportunities—10,000 people want to work in France, but you may be the only one who applies to Swaziland. Second, it's cheaper. The developing world is significantly less expensive than Europe, and you can, in theory, save money despite the travel costs because the cost of living is so low. Lonely Planet and other travel guides offer a dollar to local currency exchange rate, and you can guesstimate living costs by their hotel and meal rates. In many developing nations, you can live on less than $10 a day."

3. Weather

Helpful website: www.LonelyPlanet.com

According to Elizabeth Qually: "My first choice was Delhi, India because I had lived there before. But it is 120 degrees—no exaggeration—there in the summer time, and I would be wearing a suit every day. It didn't put me off entirely, but beware.

Public interest NGO-type jobs probably won't have air-conditioned offices. Even if your office is air-conditioned, it might be very difficult to find an air-conditioned apartment or an air-conditioned reasonably-priced hotel. Air-conditioning is a real luxury in most developing nations. On the flip side, some places are very cold, some with snow, even in the summer (e.g., Bolivia), and hot water is a real luxury."

4. Language

Helpful website: CIA World Factbook, www.odci.gov

Elizabeth Qually says: "If you want to work in an NGO or anywhere domestic, you've got to speak the language. International firms and US and UN agencies will speak English in the office, and your high school French or Spanish can get you around town. But if you anticipate doing any domestic firm or public field work, you gotta speak the language pretty darn well. I initially limited my search to nations where the official language was English (e.g., in India, law firms work primarily in English)."

5. The Case for Developing Countries

Elizabeth Qually: "Students often overlook developing countries in favor of working at the Hague or in London. But developing countries offer some of the richest opportunities. Here are the pros:

- They are less popular, so the competition for the internships is scarce.

- The people who work in countries no one can find on a map are flattered that you're interested in the area they love, so they're more likely to work around your needs.

- They're cheap.

- Often, their law is just at its beginnings and a lot of new and exciting developments are occurring, little mini-revolutions: new constitutions, reconciliation tribunals, foreign direct investment, new industries, massive infrastructure projects, labor rights, and so on.

- The people are great.

- It's a real adventure! No McDonalds or television for the summer, but camel trek? Yes!"

B. Identify the Sector

There are three general choices: Private, public, and public interest/NGO.

1. Private Employers

A. Pros

1. This is the most flexible and responsive sector, so:
    - Most likely to recognize the value of free labor;
    - Have the least amount of restrictions about deadlines, security checks, and medical clearances;
    - Have the most resources to accommodate an intern;
    - Are the most willing to create an internship that didn't exist before;

- Can respond to inquiries as late as April.

2.   They have tons of money, so you're likely to have air-conditioned offices and working computers.

3.   As a rule of thumb, they are the easiest places in which to assimilate:

- International firms have American and British citizens working for them, so Western culture governs office norms;

- English is generally the operating language, so while you may speak Portuguese in the streets, you'll do your law in English.

4.   The work you do will definitely be law-related if you work in a firm. However, with other companies this is less certain (see below).

B.   CONS

1.   Money:

- You're not eligible for public interest grants or scholarships;

- You may have to bring five suits across the world, which is an expensive investment;

- It may be harder to live like a low-budget traveler in an international business climate;

- You'll be the only one in the office who doesn't have lots of money (unless, of course, you *brought* lots of money).

2.   You have to wear a suit. Not always, but often enough.

3.   Your contact with locals may be limited.

4.   It may not mesh with your goals; most people who want to go abroad want to work in foreign policy, human rights, that kind of stuff. They don't envision representing a private corporation.

2.   PUBLIC EMPLOYERS

A.   PROS

1.   They offer some amazing extraordinary opportunities: legislation, policy-making, constitutions, politics, human rights, and so on.

2.   They have *some* money:

- They'll often offer a modest stipend and/or housing;

- They probably have decent office infrastructure, although not as nice as a private firm;
- They're generally a little more organized and reliable than an NGO or a small firm.

3. You may be able to get public interest money, perhaps if you work for the UNDP or USAID.

4. You'll speak English in the office.

5. Elizabeth Qually points out that "I've found the people who work in foreign governments to be some of the nicest, most responsive people. They got really excited about my interest in their organization and country. When they couldn't help me (because there wasn't space or because of bureaucracy) they often directed me to NGOs and other organizations."

B. CONS

1. Public employers may be less equipped to deal with a *legal* intern and so your work might be more general. Often the legal counsel for a US agency just does ordinary legal work, in-house labor contracts, that kind of thing. No crazy-awesome treaty-writing there ...

2. The government is super-bureaucratic. Even when managers really want you to be there, often the paper-pushers in DC swill force them to work through red tape. You may want to expect:

- Horrible and endless applications; European organizations are the worst at this (the ILO, the UN);
- Security checks;
- Medical clearances.

Because of this, you often won't know if you got in, or if you've cleared all of the technicalities, until late April or even May. It's stressful.

3. You might not get public interest money after all.

3. PUBLIC INTEREST/NGOS

A. PROS

1. Meaningful work!

2. The least amount of red tape. In many cases you can just show up and volunteer your time.

3. You make the internship. If you like the idea of creating your own parameters, you can get really creative.

4. You can wear jeans! Or, at least, comfortable clothes.

5. You get real people contact. Offices are run primarily by nationals, not Americans and Europeans.

6. Scholarship Money and Grants Are Available for Public Interest.

B. CONS

1. They tend to be disorganized; ironically, the groups most in need of free labor are by far the least likely to get back to you in any kind of timely fashion. And once you have the job, there's a good chance that the scope of your responsibilities will be very vague and amorphous. It can be frustrating. (To avoid this, it's a good idea to create a work plan that outlines the purpose and goals of the internship. Outline what you want to accomplish and also what the organization's goal is in hiring you. Include when you'll start, what if any training you'll get, the hours, the location of the work and a tentative schedule of activities. Ask them to provide you with details of what they expect from you.)

2. They have no money, so:

● The offices can be uncomfortably cold or hot;

● There's a lack of infrastructure;

● While you might be interested in substantive, meaningful legal work, the reality is that most public interest groups spend a tremendous amount of time trying to raise money;

● The lack of money also means a lot less leverage with those in power. NGO input, and therefore yours, is the least likely to be put into action.

3. Reports Elizabeth Qually: "I ended up investing the least amount of time in NGOs just because the response return was so low and the insecurity was so high (an NGO might just be a shack and two people, for all I knew). But at the end of the day, this is what I really wanted to do and I was a little sad I didn't get the chance."

4. INTERNATIONAL TRIBUNALS AND FOREIGN COURTS

If you're interested in doing the equivalent of a judicial clerkship in a foreign country (they're often called 'internships' in other countries), get thee immediately to Yale Law School's web site. There you'll find "Opportunities with International Tribunals and Foreign Courts," which tells you everything you need to know, from identifying target courts to finding funding to getting your foot in the door (including talking to people like alums and professors with foreign experience. Some things never change.).

To see the guide, go to www.law.yale.edu, click on "alumni," then "Career Development," then "CDO Publications." Scroll down to "Clerkships" and click on "Opportunities with International Tribunals and Foreign Courts–Public Version."

C. Generate a List of Target Organizations (Plus Resources for Finding Them . . .)

1. Identifying Private Organizations Overseas

Elizabeth Qually advises that "The most obvious place to start in the private sector is with law firms. To find law firms that do a lot of work in your country/countries of choice, use this web site:

www.legal500.com/index.php.

(other useful sites: www.globalcounsel.com and www.iflr1000.com)

Legal500 will give you the lowdown on the legal system in more than 70 countries, tell you if foreign firms are allowed (often they are not), and what firms are working with and investing in different industries. It also has articles containing information on new legislation, developments and cases in specialist practice areas, written by the leading lawyers in each jurisdiction. It's an amazing site to help you really understand the legal market.

Also, consider contacting the U.S. Embassy and U.S. Chamber of Commerce for the foreign city/cities that interest(s) you.

If your target country doesn't allow international firms to set up shop, they force foreign businesses to partner with local firms. Legal500 will tell you a few of these partnerships, but to find domestic law firms that do multi-national work (or domestic work for that matter), there are two excellent resources:

www.martindale.com/xp/Martindale/home.xml   (Martindale Hubbell; just highlight the country, type in the city, and press "go.")

www.hg.org/index.html (Heiros Gamos; a comprehensive legal and government web site.)

By way of a caveat, note that unless the official language of the country is English, foreign firms are most likely to speak the local language, so your language skills better be almost native, enough to work in the law.

Incidentally, an oft-overlooked source of internships is the in-house counsel's office of non-legal companies. There is an endless list of commercial real estate companies, construction and engineering firms, health and medical organizations, high tech, and so on, all organizations with legal departments. Since I was interested in development, I ended up contacting some of the businesses with which USAID actually contracts to do work. They were incredibly receptive and I got one immediate offer.

A great resource for finding these companies:

http://jobline.acca.com/index.php (a searchable database of employment for in-house counsel)

Also, consider the ABA's list of short-term opportunities with law firms around the world. It's seasonal, from mid-spring to late-summer each year. www.abanet.org/intlaw/internprofiles.html. When you need to find out when the next list will be published, e-mail intlaw@abanet.org.

2.   IDENTIFYING PUBLIC ORGANIZATIONS OVERSEAS

For internship opportunities in general with international organizations overseas: www.wcl.american.edu/career/ (click on "job search skills & resources" then "International" under "resources")

Some programs to consider:

The International Trade Center (an internship offered jointly by The United Nations Conference on Trade and Development and the World Trade Organization): www.intracen.org.

The World Trade Organization (focus of internship is on multilateral trading): www.wto.org/english/thewto_e/vacan_e/intern_e.htm

The U.S. State Department (has both foreign and domestic internships; apply in the Fall): www.state.gov/m/dghr/hr/intern/

The United Nations (various international internships): www.un.org/Depts/OHRM/examin/internsh/welcome.htm

International Labour Organization (ILO)(has internships abroad in a number of fields, including labor law and labor relations, elimination of child labor): www.ilo.org/public/english/bureau/pers/vacancy/intern.htm

The World International Property Organization (WIPO)(Intellectual Property Focus): www.wipo.org.

The Public Service Law Network Worldwide (at PSLawNet; lists tons of public service internships both domestically and abroad): www.PSLawNet.org

The Center for International Legal Studies (can intern during the summer or for two months after graduation): www.cils.net

The United States Agency for International Development (USAID): www.usaid.gov

Elizabeth Qually points out that "The national governments of the countries to which you are applying have lots of offices and a lot of opportunity, so check out their government pages. The only roadblock is that some governments require security clearances and, hence, you must be a national. That was the case for me at the National Reconciliation Council in Ghana. But it's not the case everywhere. It's definitely worth investigating."

3. IDENTIFYING PUBLIC INTEREST ORGANIZATIONS OVERSEAS

There are web sites that list literally thousands of NGOs, charitable organizations, and public interest organizations. With this list, you'll find links that will take you just about everywhere:

- www.ngowatch.org (list of NGOs by issue and location)
- Internships–USA, human rights: www.internships-usa.com/humanrights/hrindex.htm (over 100 organizations seeking interns to assist them in the struggle for human rights throughout the world);
- Idealist: www.idealist.org (directory of nonprofit and volunteering resources on the web, with information provided by 20,000 organizations in 150 countries);
- Lawyers without Borders: www.lawyerswithoutborders.org/ (offers both international internships and jobs in the human rights community);
- Oneworld: www.oneworld.net/ (Dedicated to promoting human rights and sustainable development by harnessing the democratic potential of the Internet. Contains U.S. and International job listings.);
- PSLawNet: www.pslawnet.org (incredible job searching database and funding sources);
- Soros Foundations Network: www.soros.org (supports the development of open societies).

D. STEP FOUR: SEND OUT YOUR INQUIRIES

1. IN CONTACTING ORGANIZATIONS, KEEP TWO THINGS IN MIND

- Try to find the name of *someone* who may have some leverage (a manager, director, a partner)—the higher the person is in the organization, the more likely they can make things happen and the more likely they are to recognize your special contributions. Sometimes the individual will just direct you to the internship office. Others will make you go through it as a formality. But others will circumvent it altogether. It depends how much they want you and how willing they are to break the rules!

    Do's and Don'ts in contacting people:

    DO contact the specific person *in charge* of the particular office;

    DO follow up on all contacts that friends offer. Drop those names! "So-and-so recommended that I contact you ..."

DO mention common experiences you have with that person, if possible ("Oh, I see we both went to Stanford!"). It's often easy to find the backgrounds of people on-line.

DON'T just follow the "internships" or "employment" link on websites. Everybody does the same thing.

DON'T just contact the central office. Look at individual offices.

DON'T write "To whom it may concern." Find *names*.

- Keep track of your contacts. Elizabeth Qually recommends an Excel database for e-mail inquiries and lists, with the following headings:

  - Organization;
  - Country;
  - Sector;
  - E-mailed? Y/N
  - Response
  - Contact
  - Networked through . . .
  - E-mail address

As Elizabeth Qually points out, "This database was really helpful because sometimes people will contact you two months later, and you don't know what they're talking about or remember them. You can also keep track of who responds and who doesn't. I ended up listing and inquiring with more than 100 organizations."

2. TIMING

If you're going to write to a variety of organizations, hit them in this order:

a. Public Sector—they have the earliest and strictest deadlines, along with the longest and most laborious applications. Do these first.

b. Private Sector—Some of the contacts you make will direct you to an intern officer, and some of their programs start early . . . but there will still be a lot of open doors in March.

C. Public Interest—some NGOs and like organizations don't even know their needs until late in the year. Others take months and months to respond, so an early and persistent inquiry is a good idea. There is no hard and fast rule here, except don't stop trying when March rolls around.

3. What to Say

As is true in every inquiry, if you were put onto the person/organization by someone else, *mention that name first.* Otherwise, this is the note Elizabeth Qually sent out. Modify it as appropriate for your circumstances:

> *"Dear ___,*
>
> *As a first year law student at ___ Law School, I am inquiring about internship possibilities with ___ in ___. I will be able to provide my own funding and hence do not require a salary or transportation costs. [If, this is, in fact, true for you. Otherwise, leave it out.]*
>
> *While an undergraduate at ___ I studied ___, expanding my studies with ___ abroad in ___. Now I would love to return to ___.*
>
> *(Here, consider a personal note if you have it, e.g., "I really loved my time in X when I went abroad," or "I see you went to X as well," or "I got the name of your company investigating your finance project in Botswana," ...)*
>
> *If you have any intern positions available or any suggestions regarding local organizations or contacts, I would very much appreciate the direction. Attached, please find my resume as an MS Word document. If you have any questions or concerns, do not hesitate to contact me.*
>
> *Thank you very much for your time.*
>
> *Sincerely,*

As Elizabeth Qually says, "Be polite, be friendly, and follow up on your responses ASAP. I generally found people abroad to be responsive, even if they couldn't help me, and I swear, some of them, just by e-mail, feel like friends now. Cheesy, but true."

PS: Remember that if a job abroad doesn't work out, there's always a study abroad program!

E. Step Five: Verify All Details, and Create a Work Plan

Make sure that you verify with the organization all of the relevant aspects of your summer experience, including:

- Where you'll live;
- What (if anything) you'll get paid;
- Any resources you should bring with you.

Also, in the realm of "anything can happen," bring along a list of all related organizations in the region, as well as an independent research project (you can always do it as a side project). Learn what you need to learn about the culture of the country, if you don't know it already. Talk to people who've worked there already, find alums who are familiar with the area, ask on websites like craigslist.

Finally, create a work plan that sketches out the purpose and goals of the internship, covering basically what you hope to accomplish, whether it's a research and writing project, the opportunity to meet people in a certain community, observing the proceedings of international tribunals, and so forth. Share the plan with your host organization, and make sure you're on the same page.

Your work plan should include your starting and ending date, training period, hours, where you'll work and a tentative schedule of activities. Ask for at least one evaluation of your work, and ask them what they expect of your work. If you ascertain all of this up front, you'll help ensure that your international experience is as fulfilling as it can be.

And by the way . . . Bon Voyage!

A work plan takes a bit of work.

Step 1: Identify potential organizations to provide internship experience. Key sources: web sites, directories and guides on international law, profs, alumni, and other students. Profs of International Law often act as consultants for international orgs and have significant contacts in the field. Alumni practicing abroad.

Step 2: Evaluate internship opportunities they offer. International orgs can be a poor source of substantive work. One reason: a law degree here is an undergrad degree elsewhere. Also, if you speak a foreign language, you may wind up translating documents the whole time. To ensure you'll do something meaty, talk to people who've worked for the organization as an intern before. Ask at Career Services. Also, ask the organization directly what they've had interns do in the past.

Step 3: Start early. Summer internships—start in December. Do your research first. Applying for visas takes time. If you miss deadlines, try anyway. Maybe the deadlines in question are "soft."

Finally: Create a work plan that outlines the purpose and goals of the internship. Having a work plan for your host organization to review is a key component of the experience. It should outline what you hope to accomplish: e.g., complete a legal writing sample (based ideally on your own research), network with members of international community, observe proceedings in international tribunals, etc. It should also set forth the organization's goals in hiring you, e.g., obtain help with a large project.

Include the stating date, training period, hours, location of work and a tentative schedule of activities. Ask for a mid-summer and end-of-summer evaluation. Ask them to provide you with details about their expectations with respect to your work.

6. STUDY ABROAD PROGRAMS: SHOULD YOU DO ONE?

We all know what you want the answer to be! Here's the thing. I can't give you an *entirely* unqualified "yes." Employers generally say that they'd rather see you developing lawyerly skills here, whether on a paid or volunteer basis, than spending the summer on the French Riviera. Excuse me! Studying law in France!

Having said that, you can do both. Because summer abroad programs don't take up the whole summer, nothing stops you from working in the U.S. before or after your program; even if you have four weeks, you can get a volunteer gig with a judge or state or federal agency or a prosecutor's office or a public defender or ... you get the idea. Then you get the best of both worlds: study abroad *and* experience.

You can also take on a part-time legal job during law school as a 2L, so that when you interview and employers ask what you did over the summer, you can tell them ... and then explain that you're "getting legal experience now."

A study abroad program after your 1L year makes sense especially in the following situations:

- If you want to live and work in a particular country, do a summer abroad program there, and take advantage of the opportunity to intern there at the same time. You can either work part-time during the program, or stay a few weeks before or afterwards to work. In fact some study abroad programs *include* an internship, which is great.

- Even if you don't work in the country during your internship but you'd like to return, use the opportunity of being there to search for an employer. It's a lot easier to do when you're "on the ground."

- If you want or need to polish your language skills, going to a summer abroad program in a country to accomplish that makes sense;

- If you've never traveled abroad, it makes sense to broaden your horizons.

* * * SMART HUMAN TRICK * * *

Female law student goes on a summer abroad program in Europe. When she's not taking classes, she makes a point of searching for foreign law firms to work for. She goes to local legal functions and knocks on doors ... and ends the summer with offers to return from *two* local firms.

If you're on the fence about a summer abroad program, ask the program coordinator for the names and contact information of students who've taken part in the program in previous summers. Contact them and let them know you're contemplating the program, and ask what they thought of it, how it impacted their job search.

For a complete run-down on summer abroad programs, check *The National Jurist's* annual review of programs: www.nationaljurist.com/guides/abroad.html

The ABA also has a guide to study abroad programs: listed by country www.abanet.org/legaled/studyabroad/abroad.html

7. DOMESTIC OPPORTUNITIES IN INTERNATIONAL LAW

Maybe you're interested in doing international work here at home. There are lots of settings for it, both as a summer job and permanently. They include:

- U.S. firms with international law practices;
- The in-house counsel's offices of companies with international interests;
- The ABA Central and East European Law Initiative (CEELI)(has a legal analyst intern program in Washington, DC): www.abanet.org/ceeli/home.html
- The U.S. Foreign Service has domestic internships; they're a great opportunity. www.state.gov/index.html.

8. TIPS FOR BREAKING INTO INTERNATIONAL WORK . . .

We've already discussed summer internships and summer abroad programs. Here are some avenues that have worked for other students:

a. Follow the advice in Chapter 10, on people and activities. Everything there applies to international jobs, as well!

b. From a law student who'd been phenomenally successful in nailing international opportunities: "Don't apply for jobs; *dream* of jobs. Many international organizations will hire you even if they don't think they have any job openings. It's up to you to research them and tell them how you'll be useful to them. I've had half a dozen jobs overseas, and didn't apply for any of them. I made them up."

c. For identifying permanent employers in other countries, look at "Internships Abroad" Topic #5, above) for advice that's equally applicable to permanent jobs.

d. Work your goals into conversations. You never know when the next person you talk to may be able to help you!

e. Brush up your foreign languages. There are international jobs where a foreign language isn't *necessary*, but it's always at least helpful. (In your research into any internship or job, make the foreign language requirement one of your questions.)

f. Get published in relevant publications, like foreign trade journals, or write articles about international law issues in bar publications. We talked about the idea of writing articles in detail in Chapter 10.

g. Consider helping international lawyers write articles for publication. Partners at law firms are all under pressure to publish; if you write an article for (or with) them, you've got a co-authoring credit and an excellent contact.

h. Consider taking the foreign service exam. Ha! Ha ha! Easy for *me* to say. It's a killer. But the Foreign Service is a great career, and the foreign service exam is the way to break in. www.state.gov/index.html

i. Consider taking short-term election monitoring, supervising or registration positions. You can find opportunities at the following web sites: The U.S. State Department (www.state.gov), United Nations (www.un.org), Organization of American States (www.oas.org), Organization for Security and Cooperation in Europe (www.osce.org).

j. Join the bar association as a student, and join the International Law Section. Attend meetings, introduce yourself to people, and volunteer. (The ABA's International Law Section is at www.abanet.org/intlaw/home.html It has many useful programs, workshops, publications and meetings)

k. Join other relevant organizations, including:

   - The American Society of International Law: www.asil.org (has members worldwide. Sponsors programs, conferences, and other activities, and has useful publications)

   - The International Law Students Association: www.ilsa.org (has more than ten thousand law student and lawyer members worldwide. Sponsors moot court competitions, publications, conferences, programs, law student foreign exchanges.)

l. If you want to work do international work domestically, work for a multinational U.S company in the general counsel's office, or join a large firm with an international practice. Remember that while international work can arise anywhere in the country, it's most likely to be prominent in firms in New York, Washington, Los Angeles and San Francisco.

m. As American's Matt Pascocello advises, "It's a *lot* easier to look at what you like to do *independent* of the international component." That is, look at whether you like to do transactional work, litigation, labor, no matter what it is, and then plan to join a firm and segue into the international practice. As Minnesota's Sue Gainen points out, "They don't let 'baby lawyers' do international anyway." Once you've got the job, you make yourself useful to the lawyers with international work, offer to do projects on top of what you're assigned, and ease your way in.

* * * SMART HUMAN TRICK * * *

Law student, Southern law school. He wants to do international work. He joins a large law firm in Washington, D.C. for his 2L summer. He does corporate work, but he makes a point of talking with a partner who does international arbitrations. He helps him out with projects, and lets him know that if he gets an offer he wants to work with him.

He gets an offer, and starts his permanent career with the firm
. . . working on international arbitrations.

n. Don't overlook your professors as valuable resources. Check with
Career Services to see which professors have been involved with
international work, and take their classes (ideally) or at least talk
to them for their advice on what's out there and what you ought
to be doing to break into it. They'll be able to put you on to
people and organizations you might not have found any other
way.

o. If it's being abroad that matters to you first and law, second,
consider an alternative career. For instance, nothing stops you
from joining the Peace Corps when you graduate (www.
peacecorps.gov); law school graduates have done exactly that as a
kind of fellowship or judicial clerkship substitute. If you ever
want to get away to somewhere exotic before you "start your
career," the Peace Corps is a great way to do it.

p. Apply for jobs with companies that have branches in the foreign
country you want to live in, and aim for one of two likely
possibilities: either a division that researches business opportunities abroad, or in the in-house counsel's office, handling international affairs. (Note that this is a job that generally goes to
laterals, not new graduates, although it's been known to happen.)

q. Do a Lexis/Nexis or Westlaw search, or ask at Career Services, for
alums who do international work. Contact them for informational
interviews (we discuss informational interviews in Chapter 10).

r. Keep up with the news. Skim newspapers and legal publications,
particularly ones focusing on international issues. When you read
about someone who does something internationally that interests
you, e-mail them and tell them so!

s. Join your school's Speakers Bureau (if it has one) or volunteer
with Career Services to bring in speakers to talk about international law topics. If you're the one doing the inviting, you've got
access to a person who might give you great advice about breaking into international work.

t. Resume issues: Apart from the obvious—highlighting international law-oriented classes, activities, CLEs—consider doing the following as well: include any extensive foreign travel, any opportunity to spend time abroad working (the military, the Peace
Corps), your foreign language skills (and be precise; are you
conversational/fluent/can you read but not speak or vice versa?).
In addition, don't abbreviate anything: spell out the month in
dates on letters, spell out names of states, and avoid acronyms
(Bachelor of Science instead of "B.S."). If you've taught school,
include ages of children and not just grades. Remember also that
if you apply to foreign employers, conventions on resumes may be
different in their country; seek advice from alums who work

there. (For instance, European resumes regularly run to several pages.)

u. Interview issues: Everything we talked about in Chapter 9 on Interviews applies to international interviews; in addition, remember that questions that would be *verboten* in the U.S. are customary abroad, and cultural differences exist (Asians don't make eye contact as much as Americans do; Germans tend to smile less. Again, ask alums for advice about the specific country/ies involved.)

v. Go to work for a law firm with an office in the foreign country where you'd like to work. This seems kind of obvious, but it's not as fruitful a path as it could be. Before you go to work for a firm with a foreign office you covet, check the firm's web site and look at the backgrounds of the lawyers in your choice office. You may well find that all of the lawyers are "locals," and the firm doesn't put American associates there. Even if they do, foreign assignments are considered real plums; they don't go to new associates. (The best way to nail one of these assignments is to be very friendly to the people who know openings in the foreign office will be coming up, hiring partners and support staffers. But handling your job is the subject of another book, *What Law School Doesn't Teach You ... But You Really Need To Know.)*

w. Attend every international conference that comes anywhere near your city. Even better, volunteer. Go to hear every international speaker who comes to school. Keep your eye on your local newspapers, your Career Services website, and the local bar association website. Go to the speech, and make a point of going to up introduce yourself to the speaker afterwards. Tell them you enjoyed their speech, and ask their advice on working in their home country. And after they leave—send a thank you!

x. Make yourself useful to people who can help you out!

As I stressed in Chapter 10, it's so important to remember that help flows both ways. Often, making yourself useful to someone who can help you is a great way to turn them into an "organic mentor." You don't know where their advice will lead you!

* * * SMART HUMAN TRICK * * *

Law student at an East Coast law school. She finds out that there is a Council on International Relations that meets in her city. She contacts the head of the organization and offers to be a note-taker for meetings. As she reports, "I'm the only student who shows up. I've gotten to know all of these lawyers, who've given me great ideas."

* * * SMART HUMAN TRICK * * *

Law student in school in Florida. As a First Year, she's dying to get into International Law. Her undergrad grades are mediocre, and law school hasn't started off on a promising note grades-wise, either.

She keeps her eye on the local papers to see if anything related to international law comes to town. Sure enough, she finds that there is going to be a meeting of the Organization of American States taking place near her city. She calls and volunteers to help out, and she's assigned the job of acting as a "gopher" for the person organizing the meeting.

In this capacity, she meets an awful lot of prominent people. She makes a point of bringing up in every conversation her interest in International Law as a career, and soliciting advice. One of them says, "Well, I can help you get to Washington for the summer. How would you like to work at the White House?" Not bad! At the White House for the summer, she again makes a point of talking about her career goals. One of the people she meets tells her, "I can help you out next summer . . .

"How would you like to work at the U.S. Embassy in Barbados?" And she winds up spending the summer there, helping out with legal issues. *In Barbados.*

* * * SMART HUMAN TRICK * * *

In the first edition of *Guerrilla Tactics*, I wrote about J.T. Mann, from the University of Maine Law School, one of my favourite all-time law students. This guy is amazing. What I want to recount here is how he got his international internship:

"While J.T. was a student at Maine, he stayed in close contact with the Career Services Director, Tammy Willcox. He also got to know everyone he could, from his classmates all the way up to the Dean. One thing he let everybody know is that he could speak Spanish.

It turns out that a large insurance company in Maine wanted to do a joint venture with a Spanish company. They weren't happy with any of the chauffeuring services in Portland, so they called the dean of the law school and said they needed Spanish-speaking chauffeurs for the visiting bigwigs for a couple of days the following week. Since the dean knew J.T. spoke Spanish, he told J.T. about the opportunity. J.T. signed up, and was assigned to chauffeur for a day.

During the week before his chauffeuring day, J.T. brushed up on his Spanish. He dug up some Spanish music tapes he had. And he found out who he would be chauffeuring—it was going to be the president of the Spanish insurance company, his daughter, his chief financial officer, and his British banker. He did some research on the president of the company, learning his background and his American holdings.

When J.T. picked up his "fares," he just listened—at first. For the morning, he drove them from appointment to appointment. Then, after lunch, he asked them, in Spanish, if they'd like a tour of Portland. They said yes. He put in his Spanish music tapes, and drove them around, showing them the points of interest. They were delighted he spoke Spanish, and they loved the tapes. They talked to him, and the conversation strayed from business. He told the chief financial officer where he could get a good deal on golf clubs. He told the president's daughter about great places to shop. He dropped them off in the afternoon, knowing he'd be back to pick them up to drive them to dinner.

After he dropped them off, he went and bought a wide-angle photo of Portland. It turns out it was a rainy day, and although J.T. had said that Portland was a lovely city, it wasn't being shown off to its best advantage that day. When he picked them up for dinner, he presented them with the photograph. By the time they got to the restaurant, the president of the company insisted that J.T. join them for dinner. He did. During dinner, where J.T. was seated next to the president, they discussed all kinds of things. The president mentioned a city in Spain where his daughter was working, and J.T. mentioned that all he knew about it was that it was where Christopher Columbus had died. The president asked him how he could possibly know that, and J.T. Responded that it was because he had seen a wonderful painting of Columbus on his death bed, and it was in that city.

The president was very surprised, and said, "I know that painting. I *love* that painting." Then he looked at J.T. and said, "You should work for me."

So that summer he did. He went to Madrid, and lived in a company apartment with maid service. He did bits of everything for the insurance company, including some work in the legal department. He made himself as useful as he could be, and he wound up writing an article for a Spanish insurance industry magazine about his internship."

Shout outs for extensive advice in this chapter to Jack Swarbrick, Chip Lipscomb, Elizabeth Qually and Mindy Baggish.

Materials consulted for this chapter include handouts from George Washington University, American University, Catholic University, and NALP.

Chapter 25
Approaching the Bench: Judicial Clerkships

Other resources: Debra Straus's excellent book "Behind the Bench."

I've recommended judicial clerkships to law students more than any other kind of job. It's an awesome way to start your career. Most people look back on their judicial clerkship as the best professional experience they ever had. A clerkship gives you a "behind-the-scenes" view of the judicial system, an outstanding credential, often a great mentor, and a chance to think about what you want to do afterwards. And as the Valparaiso Law School booklet on judicial clerkship says, "Working for a good judge is like getting to work every day with the best senior partner in a law firm."

Sold yet?

You probably already know what a judicial clerkship is. Judicial clerkships are one- or two-year assignments (more typically two years) where you are essentially a research assistant either for a particular judge (an "elbow clerk") or, with a pool of clerks, for an entire court. Your duties vary depending on the judge and the court, but by and large you're reading and listening to parties' arguments about legal issues, researching these issues, and writing about them. (As we go into a little later on, your duties vary greatly depending on whether you're a trial or appellate clerk, so don't read too much into that basic description.) You can also get summer and school year jobs with judges, as I discuss in the "Early Preparation" section a little later on.

What makes judicial clerkships so great?

Thirteen Great Reasons to Consider a Judicial Clerkship.

1. **A judicial clerkship is an *excellent* credential, perhaps the best all-purpose credential you can get.** Whether you

want to go to a law firm (large firms pay a signing bonus for federal court clerks), a company, government agency, public interest organization, become a law professor—no matter what you want to do next—judicial clerkships are the "universal solvent."

    2.   One prospective federal district court clerk told me about his experience. He said he planned to do a mailer to large firms toward the end of his clerkship. One of the judge's current clerks said, "Don't be ridiculous. This summer I'll take you out to lunch with lawyers from all of the large firms." Wow.

For some prestigious fellowships—like the Office of the Solicitor General—a judicial clerkship is a virtual requirement. (Of course, specialty courts will tend to "brand" you; clerking for the Federal Court of Claims suggests an intellectual property bent that wouldn't much interest a rural small firm ... but a trial court clerkship would *definitely* impress any firm with a litigation practice, since it gives you an insight into how judges think, and litigators need to impress judges.)

2. **Judicial clerkships give you a chance to delay your permanent career decisions**. I can't tell you how many students tell me, "I just don't know what I want to do yet." Well, if you're really puzzled, why rush yourself? A judicial clerkship gives you a year or two before you make that jump into something more permanent. As one judicial clerk puts it, "This is great. It's a free ride." If you string two or more judicial clerkships together, I guess you could in theory put off a permanent decision until you retire! On top of that, your circumstances may mean you can't—or shouldn't—look for a permanent job right now. For instance, you've got a fiancé, spouse, or significant other in grad school or the military, and they'll be moving to a different city in a year or two, and you'll go with them. It would be both career-ically unwise, and not terribly ethical, to interview for permanent positions knowing you're going to be hitting the trail in a year or two. It's so much better to take a job with a natural ending that coincides with your life plans.

3. **The job is *very* intellectually stimulating**—Your judge will often look to you for creative ideas and use you as an intellectual sounding board. That's key, because ABA studies have shown that intellectual stimulation is the single most important determinant of job satisfaction. (Free pizza was a close second.)

4. **Judicial clerkships are frequently the great grade equalizer**. One student at a small Midwestern law school, ranked very last in his class, struck out finding any kind of law firm job in his chosen city, Boston. He took a clerkship with a city court in the Northeast, did well at that, and got into one of Boston's fifteen largest, most prestigious law firms immediately after his

clerkship. If you dropped the ball grades-wise in law school, you're gong to have some talking to do to convince a judge you've got the writing and research skills (s)he's looking for (we talk about pitching your credentials in a little bit). But especially for lower-level smaller courts, which are out of necessity less grade-sensitive but equally enjoyable to work for, you've got a chance to get into your ultimate dream job via a clerkship.

5. **Future potential to rack up stacks of dead presidents**. As I just mentioned, many large firms pay a bounty for federal judicial clerks, and on top of that, they'll pay judicial clerks the salary of a second- or third-year associate (depending on whether you do a one- or two-year clerkship) when you start. In other words, while many large firm associates have been cutting their teeth in a library cubicle, you've been having the fun—and admittedly lower pay—of a judicial clerkship ... but you come in to a large firm when things typically start to get interesting.

6. **Clerkships are an outstanding opportunity to hone your research and writing skills**. Virtually every legal employer values the ability to research and write, and everybody knows that judicial clerkships clean your clock on those basic skills.

7. **You'll get an outrageously useful recommendation and contact**. When it comes to looking for a job after your judicial clerkship, letters that begin with the words, "Judge Crater recommended that I contact you ..." are letters that are going to get *read* and they'll *always* earn a response.

8. **You have a real hand in determining justice**. As a judge's right-hand person, you have input into every case the judge decides, and may have a significant impact on the lives and fortunes of people involved in the case. That kind of meaningfulness is a far cry from being a research drone that never gets to write a full memo, let alone get anywhere near actual parties in a case. Couple that with the unique opportunity to peek behind the scenes of courts and you've got an unbeatable combination.

9. **You'll get exposed to a wide range of cases and issues**. This not only helps you make your long-term career choices, but it also makes you attractive to potential employers. You'll also get to know a bunch of potential employers and may, therefore, be able to avoid the whole sending-out-cover-letters-and-resumes grind entirely. It's also an ego boost. As one judicial clerk points out, "It's incredible how casual a lot of lawyers are. You wouldn't believe how many idiots you'll see. I figure, 'OK, I won't be disbarred, because if these jokers haven't been, I won't be.'"

10. **You'll typically work *much* more reasonable hours than first year associates in large law firms**. For instance, federal district court clerks work, on average, 40–to 60–hour weeks, and federal appellate clerks typically put in 40 to 50 hours a

week. Judges differ in their time demands, of course, but that's the norm.

11. **Not for nothing, lawyers who might otherwise sneer at a new lawyer will be kissing your butt just because of your connection to your judge**. I realize this isn't the kind of thing most polite people would mention, but let's face it, when you've just spent three years in law school being humiliated in class in front of your classmates, it's nice to think that there's a whole cadre of people who will feel compelled to treat you with respect!

12. **It gives you a chance to scope out a legal community for future employers**. *Especially* if you're looking to move to another city, a judicial clerkship will give you an unmatched opportunity to get familiar with judges, court personnel, lawyers, and the legal community in general. You'll get to see lawyers in their natural habitat, and separate the wheat from the chaff.

13. **You get to know your fellow clerks**, who are typically not just interesting people but also will be professional contacts down the road.

Am I suggesting that judicial clerkships are for *everybody* and that they're *always* wonderful? No, of course not. There are a few downsides to consider:

- If you hate to research and write, you're barking up the wrong job. No matter which court you go to, researching and writing is the hallmark of the job. If you don't like it and/or aren't good at it, look elsewhere.

- Not every judge is a brilliant mentor. The occasional judge goes so far as to be a lunatic. One of my all-time favorite stories involves a female judge. She was known for showing up in court in short skirts and holding a poodle on her lap *in court*. She was out driving when a state trooper following her car noticed that it was weaving. When he pulled her over and walked up to her window, she slurred, "Do you know who I am? I'm a (hiccup) goddamned judge!" When the trooper told her that didn't matter, she pulled out a gun, waved it at him, and warned him that if he gave her a ticket, she'd give him a .38—caliber vasectomy.

   Clerking for this judge would be undoubtedly be memorable . . . but for the wrong reasons. And while you can research judges to some extent up-front (we'll talk about that shortly), you can't assure you'll always pick a winner. And even if you *do* get a judge who's usually a sterling character, everybody hits a rough patch now and then. If you catch a judge in the middle of, say, a nasty divorce, you're unlikely to find the most benevolent mentor.

And if you *do* get a judge who's less than nurturing, there's little you can do about it. As one former judicial clerk told me, it's not as though you can look to other people in the office for a job recommendation. You're uniquely at the mercy of one person, so you've got to bite the bullet and do whatever is necessary to make sure that recommendation is a good one, even if you're working under very difficult conditions. In these circumstances it's important to console yourself with the fact that judicial clerkships have a definite end, and when the time comes, your misery will be over.

- You can't bail out on your clerkship if something better comes along in the meantime. It's like a prison sentence ... but not really. I've occasionally had judicial clerks tell me, "My clerkship is OK but I'm thinking one year is enough. I want to do something else the second year ..." The words "Too bad" come to mind, because you really, really can't leave a judge before your clerkship is over. Remember, at most it's a two-year commitment. Less than law school. There'll be plenty of opportunities when it's over, so make it as enjoyable you can, and stay!

- There's the money issue. You already know you won't make as much as you would at a large private firm, but you don't make that much *anywhere* else. Nonetheless, the pay for judicial clerkships is substantial, probably a lot more than you think, and you can generally defer student loan payments while you're clerking (check with your Career Services Office for details). The fact remains: While a judicial clerkship sets you up to make serious dough down the road, and many employers pay a "bounty" to former clerks, you won't haul in the mad cheese while you clerk. (For web sites disclosing current pay rates, see the Appendix at the end of this chapter.)

Regardless of their downsides, judicial clerkships are still my favorite job for law students.

In this chapter, here's what we'll do:

First, we'll talk about common misconceptions about judicial clerkships. I want to get this out of the way first, because I've got a strong suspicion that many, many law students who would *love* judicial clerkships self-select out without realizing a judicial clerkship is within their grasp. I don't want that to be you!

Second, we'll talk about early preparation—that is how to use law school opportunities to set yourself up for a judicial clerkship.

Third, we'll talk about the different kinds of clerkships there are, and part of that is discussing the general framework of courts in this country.

We'll then talk about other court-related jobs (like staff attorney-ships), and we'll follow that up with "a gold mine of frequently over-looked clerkship opportunities").

Then we'll look at what you an expect of different kinds of clerkships.

We'll follow that with discussing how to nail down the clerkship you want. I'll start out there with a simple checklist to follow and we'll talk in detail about every item on it. We'll talk about how you choose a court and a judge. After that, we'll talk about the elements of applications for judicial clerkships—everything from cover letters and resumes to han-dling offers and going to bat a second time if you don't get a nibble the first time around.

Phew! Let's get started!

A. COMMON MISCONCEPTIONS ABOUT JUDICIAL CLERKSHIPS ... LIKE 'MY GRADES AREN'T GOOD ENOUGH'

Misconception #1: "You've got to have great grades to get a judicial clerkship."

This is not *universally* true. Yes, the United States Supreme Court is kind of fussy about the grades thing. As a rule of thumb, the more prestigious the court, the more desirable the location, the better the paper credentials you need. Judges almost always ask for "top 10%" credentials in published sources, but as many court insiders point out, that's just a "scaring off" tactic. Judges rarely adhere to it in practice. I've talked with Career Services personnel at law schools who point out that there are *frequently* judicial clerks from the bottom half of the class!

Of course, great grades and Law Review don't hurt, because judges want sharp people with excellent research and writing skills. But the fact is that there are other ways to prove those skills beyond grades and journal experience, and beyond that, you never know what's going to ring a particular judge's chimes. One law student with awful grades got a *hundred* judicial clerkship interviews because he was an entrepreneur before law school and that piqued judges' interests. Another student nailed dozens of interviews because judges were interested in his prior career as a roadie for a rock band! Some judges may only want someone who's interesting in chambers. Maybe you'll go after a clerkship with a judge who doesn't care about grades overall, but *does* rely heavily on the opinion of a professor for whom you happened to excel, or for whom you were an stellar research assistant.

I've also talked to judges who point out that they prefer second career students, for their "different perspective" on the world.

It also makes sense to remember that competition for particular clerkships depends on how desirable the clerkship is perceived to be.

If you want to clerk for the U.S. Supreme Court, you've got to have solid gold credentials in every way. But let's set that goal aside for a moment. As a rule of thumb, appellate courts are extremely competitive *but* geography plays a *very* significant role in the competition for any particular court. For instance, appellate courts in less-populated areas are less competitive than, say, district court clerkships in Manhattan. Aiming for clerkships off the beaten track can get you gigs that would have been a stretch otherwise.

Also, senior judges, magistrate judges, and courts of special jurisdiction often receive fewer applicants.

If you don't have sterling conventional creds going for you, in your cover letter play up whatever you do have, be it a fascinating background or a sparkling personality. You never know what may spark a judge's interest!

* * * SMART HUMAN TRICK * * *

Law student at a Southern law school. He performed two federal court internships. He reports how he got them: "I went door to door and knocked! I introduced myself to secretaries and asked if the judges needed any extra help. One judge told me, 'My clerk is overwhelmed—here are a couple of projects to research.' "

"I'm proud to say that he was so pleased with my work on those, he invited me to stay on."

Misconception #2: "If you don't meet the strict deadlines for clerkships, you'll never get one."

I would never encourage you to blow off deadlines. However . . . .

While judges traditionally fill their permanent clerkships very early, circumstances do change. New clerkships are authorized, new judges are confirmed, or clerks don't show up or don't work out or drop out for health or maternity reasons or they're abducted by aliens.

The bottom line is, it pays to keep in touch with judges once in a while, dropping an e-mail to say hello and find out if anything has changed, and/or to check in late in the game to see if clerkships have opened up. One enterprising student in the Midwest did *two* federal district court clerkships during his two summers in law school, despite strictly mediocre grades. How did he get them? He just showed up at judges' chambers immediately after exams ended, was *exceptionally* polite and ingratiating with everyone he talked to, and asked if they needed an extra pair of hands. He said, "I knew that there would be students who would blow off judges in favor of law firms paying a lot of money." Admittedly he had to knock on a lot of doors and faced a lot of rejection; it was a *very* high-risk strategy. But the point is, clerkships aren't static. Unscheduled openings do occur, and if you strike out through traditional means, there are always opportunities "out there."

Misconception #3: "You've got to get a judicial clerkship, if at all, coming straight out of law school."

Not true! Judicial clerkships aren't the U.S. Olympic Gymnastics team—your opportunities don't end at a painfully early age. In fact, judges are increasingly interested in hiring clerks with post-graduation experience under their belts. It's not a prerequisite, but judges like grads who already have good work habits and perspective. So if you go out and get a few years' experience doing something else, it won't hurt your chances with a judge—it'll help you.

B. EARLY PREPARATION—HOW TO USE A LAW SCHOOL TO SET YOURSELF UP FOR A JUDICIAL CLERKSHIP . . . INCLUDING SUMMER INTERNSHIPS AND EXTERNSHIPS

What you do in law school can pave your way into a judicial clerkship. While some things—like getting great grades and taking part in writing competitions—are excellent ideas no matter what you're going after, others are unique to judicial clerkships. Let's talk about them.

1. GET GREAT GRADES AND DO LAW REVIEW. DUH

Great paper credentials are the most obvious stepping stone to a judicial clerkship, and if the god of grades smiles on you, nailing a judicial clerkships will be *much* easier. But whether or not that happens there are things to do to grease the wheels. Like . . .

2. DO AN INTERNSHIP OR EXTERNSHIP WITH A JUDGE

As we discuss in the "1L" chapter (Chapter 28), I firmly believe the best all-purpose summer job you can get after your first year in law school is an internship with a judge. They're often volunteer positions, which means waitering on weekends if you need cash, but it's so *worth* it. Judges routinely mention that it makes a tremendous impact on them when students are willing to volunteer to gain experience.

You can also get part-time jobs during the school year with judges. And then there are judicial externships, which are available to 2Ls and 3Ls during the school year with federal district courts and various state courts. You typically get class credit for those.

The best way to find out if a particular judge hires interns/externs is to *call the judge's chambers and ask their assistant*. If they do, you can ask a secretary/assistant or clerk what to include in your application package (which will often include a cover letter, resume, and writing sample; others may want transcripts and references).

While all judges differ, externs primarily research and write memos for the judge and clerks. They attend hearings, draft opinions, and help out administratively. In some cases, what externs do very much mirrors law clerks' duties; other times, they get more menial tasks.

No matter *what* you do, an internship or externship introduces you to working for judges ... and certainly gives you an excellent credential and reference for a post-graduate clerkship. And, of course, there's nothing that stops you from applying for clerkships to the very judges you interned or externed for!

Perhaps best of all, you should know that because there are often very few applicants for these positions, the competition is low and you can typically get in with more modest credentials.

Incidentally, Ellen Wayne has an excellent method for nailing volunteer judicial externships: "Sit in on an open court session in the town where you want to practice (which may mean using your school breaks for this purpose). Get a feel for the temperament of the judge, and when you find one you like, introduce yourself to the court's bailiff, drop off a resume, and say you'll follow up with a phone call. And if you're interested in a particular specialty, don't overlook the court for that specialty. For instance, if you like bankruptcy, go to bankruptcy court. If you like family law, go to domestic relations court. If the idea of volunteering bothers you, it shouldn't. Your future legal employer will only care that you got the experience; they won't care whether you got paid for it or not!"

Finally, a note on contacting judges: Make a point of saying you're willing to volunteer, that you want the experience so much you're willing to work for free. "If you don't say so explicitly," says one judge, "I'll think you assume you'll get paid."

3. CONSIDER TAKING A SEMINAR COURSE IN THE FALL OF YOUR SECOND YEAR

Why? You'll have to write a paper, and seminar papers are good writing samples. Also, it gives you a pretty obvious recommendation source—the professor who teaches the course, and will thus be very familiar with your writing.

4. CONSIDER ACTING AS A RESEARCH ASSISTANT FOR A PROFESSOR

Since research is such an important element of judicial clerkships, this kind of activity can be a real plus. In addition, judges tend to weigh letters of recommendation more heavily from professors you've worked for than professors whose classes you've taken.

5. TAKE CLASSES FROM PROFESSORS WHO ARE FORMER JUDICIAL CLERKS WITH COURTS AND JUDGES YOU WANT TO TARGET

As former judicial clerk Kristin Waller points out, "You want to forge personal relationships with professors who know judges. Taking their classes is a great way to do that."

6. TAKE PART IN WRITING COMPETITIONS

Writing competitions are a great, and horribly underutilized, way to prove your writing chops. You see posters for them all the time at school.

As I've mentioned before, they typically get stunningly few entries. I've talked with writing competition organizers who've told me, "We sometimes have to extend the deadline to get even *one* entry!"

So even if you don't think you're the world's greatest writer, try a writing competition. It's a great way to hone your skills, and the judges are sometimes—well—judges. No matter who's evaluating the entries, if you do well, it will go a long way toward proving to a judge that you've got the skills (s)he seeks.

By the way, if that's a little rumbling whine I hear in the distance, along the lines of, "But, Kimmbo, I don't have time . . ." sure you do. You just don't have big blocks of time, that's all. Just go to school an hour, one dinky hour, early for a couple of weeks (or stay an hour later), and do your contest entry then. Make a firm appointment with yourself for that time. You won't miss the time and it could pay huge dividends.

7. DO A CLINIC

Clinical professors know judges. That makes them great references, and also great sources of information about which judges to approach.

* * * SMART HUMAN TRICK * * *

Female student, Georgia law school. She learns through lawyers she talks to that the director of the prosecutorial clinic at school had been a prosecutor, and that he knew local judges. She took the clinic, and showed the director a list of judges she was targeting for clerkships. He told her, "Apply to this judge. Your personalities will mesh."

She reports, "I got him to write a letter of recommendation for me. My entire interview with the judge was about the director of the pros clinic. 'So, you know Director X,' he said. This guy's recommendation was pretty much all he needed. He made me an offer on the spot."

8. TAKE PART IN ADVOCACY COMPETITIONS

Bar associations, fraternities, all kinds of organizations hold advocacy competitions for law students. They frequently feature local judges as judges. If you do well, introduce yourself to the judges, collect business cards, and follow up with a thanks-and-nice-to-meet-you note to pave the way for a clerkship request.

9. CONSIDER WRITING A LAW REVIEW NOTE ON YOUR OWN. YOU DON'T HAVE TO BE ON LAW REVIEW TO DO IT, YOU KNOW

I'll bet you didn't know you could do this, did you? The fact is, I've known law students who took it upon themselves to write a Law Review note even though they didn't grade or write on to Law Review. Law Reviews publish notes regardless of whether the author is on staff, if the note in question is good enough.

Doing this would obviously make an enormous impression on a judge (or virtually any other research-and-writing-oriented employer, for that matter). Is it a lo-o-o-o-t of work? Yep. Does it require tremendous self-discipline? Yep. And a faculty mentor and an intimate knowledge of the blue book and ... and ... and ... Yep. But if you're so inclined, it's one way to increase your odds of getting a judicial clerkship.

10. TAKE PART IN INNS OF COURT

We discussed in Chapter 10 the value of the organization Inns of Court. Inns of Court is a national program with branches in various cities that brings together practitioners and judges who meet monthly, where they hear presentations on topics like conflicts of interest, discovery rules, evidence changes—all kinds of litigation issues. Not only do you get a chance to learn some interesting and practical things, but you get a great opportunity to meet litigators, judges and legislators. I've talked with students who've nailed *outstanding* opportunities through meeting judges at Inns of Court. You can learn more about it at www.innsofcourt.org.

11. HELP SET UP A "JUDGE SHADOWING DAY" FOR YOUR LAW SCHOOL

Do something that's nice for your classmates and good for you at the same time. You can do this under the auspices of Career Services or a school organization (my legal fraternity, Phi Alpha Delta, runs them). Contact judges and see if they'd be willing to have a student "shadow" for a day, and then advertise the opportunity to your classmates.

Among the judges you'll of course contact ones that you'd like to clerk for. It gives you an opportunity to get to know judges, it shows off your enthusiasm for a clerkship, and it introduces your classmates to a great job.

12. AFTER YOU RESEARCH JUDGES, SHOW UP IN PERSON IN THEIR COURTROOM

If you have the opportunity, watch your target judges "in action." You'll see how they interact with their clerks and with everyone else in court, which will give you an insight into their personalities and the kinds of bosses they'd make.

If you get the chance, introduce yourself to the judges during breaks in the proceedings. Tell them that you were very interested in seeing them at work because you'll be applying for a clerkship with them. It's nothing but flattering to take this kind of initiative, and it reflects well on you!

* * * SMART HUMAN TRICK * * *

Law student in Texas. He is interested in a state trial court clerkship. After researching his target judges, he goes to the courthouse. He'd heard one of his target judges speak on campus when he was in college. He remembered what she'd said. He went to her courtroom and recognized her standing outside in the hallway, talking with her clerks. He waited for a break in the conversation, walked up and introduced himself, mentioning how her words had stuck with him.

He wound up clerking for her.

13. TAKE ADVANTAGE OF EVERY OPPORTUNITY TO MEET JUDGES, WHETHER AT SCHOOL-SPONSORED EVENTS OR VIA PERSONAL CONTACTS

Judges, like all employers, want to work with people they like. Because judges have such close daily contact with their clerks, it's even more important for them than it is for most employers. So if you meet them under *any* circumstances and they take to you, you'll be able to nail a clerkship a whole lot easier.

Make a point of going to the kinds of events we discussed in Chapter 10, on people and activities. Ask at your Career Services Office for opportunities to meet judges, through speeches they give on-campus or other community functions. Take advantage of "judge shadowing days" set up by organizations like Phi Alpha Delta. Ask if people you know know any judges they can introduce you to. And, of course, never overlook the opportunities presented by casual conversation. You never know when the next person you talk to will be a judge.

C. WHAT'S OUT THERE? THE TONS AND TONS OF COURTS THAT EMPLOY JUDICIAL CLERKS

There are three general types of courts for which you can clerk: Federal Courts, State Courts, and—well—everything else (including specialty courts like federal claims courts, as well as administrative law judges. I'll discuss those opportunities in the section titled "A Gold Mine of Frequently Overlooked Clerkship Opportunities.")

1. FEDERAL COURTS

The federal court system offers a wealth of clerkship opportunities. There are thousands of federal judicial clerkships.

The federal court system is roughly divided into courts whose names you'll recognize, and some you won't. Let's talk about them:

a. **The three-level system.** Ideally, this will not be a revelation to you. The federal court system has three levels:

Ideally you know that the top court in the U.S. is the Supreme Court. If not, put down this book and go study!

The intermediate appellate courts are called Courts of Appeal. They are divided nationwide into circuits; there are twelve circuits, each covering a different geographic region.

At the lowest rung are the trial courts of general federal jurisdiction, which are called "District Courts." There are 89 districts encompassing the fifty states. (There are also District Courts for Washington, D.C., Puerto Rico, and territorial courts for Guam, the Northern Mariana Islands, and the Virgin Islands.)

To complicate matters, there are three kinds of judges at the District Court level: District Judges, Bankruptcy Court Judges, and Magistrate Judges.

District judges hear all matters over which the District Courts have jurisdiction, including civil cases arising under federal law, federal criminal prosecutions, admiralty and maritime cases, and cases between citizens of different states.

Bankruptcy court judges hear matters related to—surprise surprise—federal bankruptcy laws.

Magistrate judges assist the judges with their work, typically presiding over hearings and hearing motions. They sometimes also hear civil cases with the parties' consent, and they hear criminal misdemeanors.

b. Specialty courts.

The federal court system has four main specialized trial courts, two specialized appellate courts, and many administrative law judges in federal agencies. They all present clerkship opportunities. We discuss them in Topic F, below, in "A Gold Mine of Frequently Missed Clerkship Opportunities."

2. STATE COURTS

Let's take a look at state courts. The different states have different court structures, but as a general rule, you have a state supreme court (which in New York, as you may remember from civil procedure, is called the court of appeals, but in most states it's called the supreme court), underneath that you have state intermediate appellate courts (although not every state has an intermediate level), and under that you have state trial courts of general jurisdiction. States also typically have specialty courts and courts of limited jurisdiction, including municipal courts, probate courts, and criminal courts.

D. THE CLERKSHIP EXPERIENCE—THE NUTS AND BOLTS OF WHAT YOU DO AS A CLERK IN VARIOUS DIFFERENT KINDS OF COURTS

Of course, what you do as a clerk depends very much on the particular judge you work for. Some judges might want you to maintain their libraries in chambers, draft speeches and lectures for conferences and bar functions, and some may even expect you to do administrative work. Others will expect you to run personal errands. But there *are* generalizations that can reasonably be made. As a rule of a thumb, there is much more people contact at the trial level, and much more research in appellate courts. Trial courts, where you have to deal with parties (the litigant kind, not the beer-bong-and-vodka-slalom kind), witnesses, experts, and the rest of the cast of characters makes the setting lively, if not hectic. Appellate courts, by contrast, are more cerebral and some are downright monastic. Which you'll like better depends on your personality.

By and large, here are the tasks you can expect in different kinds of clerkships:

● Federal District Courts

You'll typically be involved in decision-making at every stage of the proceedings, including conferences, bench memos, pretrial motions, evidentiary hearings, and jury and non-jury trials in court. You can expect to prepare memos, attend oral arguments, attend or conduct settlement conferences, write draft versions of the judge's opinions and orders, prepare the judge's bench and organize exhibits keep records and handle administrative tasks like scheduling, review motions and make recommendations on them, and prepare trial memoranda for the judge (including a summary of the issues presented in a case). You might also handle calls from attorneys and schedule court appearances or meetings for attorneys. You might check cites, and you may run personal errands for the judge.

Although you'll provide written opinions, you'll have less time for in-depth research than appellate clerks do. Instead, you'll frequently have to research issues on-the-spot at trials.

While judges vary, district court clerks typically work 40 to 60 hours a week.

● Federal Courts of Appeals

In some ways, you'll find that a court of appeals clerkship is like an extension of law school, in that you can expect to research and write about issues presented on appeal. You'll handle fewer matters than trial-level clerks and you'll have more time, but the flipside of that is that there will be a higher level of expectation for the quality of your written opinions. You'll grow to appreciate compromise among a panel of judges, and you'll edit other clerks' draft opinions. While you'll have less contact with attorneys and factual documents than a trial-level clerk, you'll have more contact with other judges and staff.

Specifically, you can expect to help out with screening cases, drafting memoranda summarizing the parties' briefs, writing memos on key issues and rulings, helping prepare administratively for oral arguments, attending oral arguments, writing draft opinions including extensive research and analysis, and drafting dissents, concurrences, and rulings.

Although judges differ, appellate court clerks typically work between 40 and 50 hours per week.

● State trial courts

Right off the bat, remember that *most* legal disputes in this country are handled in state courts of general jurisdiction, which are the primary forums for contract disputes, torts, criminal prosecutions, divorce and custody matters, and probate of estates. It's worth noting that some of these courts assign particular judges on a rotating basis to specific areas, like family law or major felonies, and that would obviously impact your duties as a clerk for these judges.

It's a mistake to think that you won't deal with any issues of federal law at state trial courts. There are federal constitutional challenges to the admission of evidence at state criminal trials, challenges to state statutes, and many others as well.

Also, note that if a certain kind of economic activity dominates a state, you'll hear more of that kind of case. The most obvious example is Delaware, whose courts have historically been predominant in the area of corporate law.

As is true of any trial level clerkship, the experience is often exciting. You get a bird's eye view of the litigation process, from complaint and answer through discovery, pretrial motions, settlement conferences, jury selection, opening and closing arguments, witnesses, evidentiary objections and rulings, jury instructions or judicial fact-finding, and post-trial motions.

You have to be great at juggling multiple tasks, learning new areas of the law quickly, and you have to be very organized.

Apart from their other assets, state court clerkships give you the benefit of making local contacts for the future, getting an insider's view of the abilities and reputations of local lawyers, and getting inside knowledge of procedural issues in state courts.

- **State trial courts of special jurisdiction**

    Depending on the focus of the specialty court—they include, among others, probate courts and family courts—you will get an excellent grounding in the specialty, including getting to know the judges and lawyers in the area, as well as learning procedures and seeing what kinds of strategies and arguments work the best.

- **State appellate courts**

    Appellate clerks lead a calmer life than trial court clerks. As you know, when a case reaches an appellate court, the losing party at the trial level is arguing that the trial court erred in deciding particular issues of law. That's the focus of appellate courts. While appellate courts do hear emergency matters that require research and writing under time pressure, you generally get more time to contemplate, since the briefing and argument schedules are set well in advance and generally follow a preset monthly cycle. The record has been developed, the fact-finding is complete, the issues are framed, and the appellate court can consider them. The clerk's job in these courts is more than 90% research and writing.

    If you enjoy the idea that you don't have to deal with surprises, procedural posturing, or the raw elements of trial litigation, you'll like an appellate clerkship.

• State supreme courts

Similar to the experience you get at an appellate court, with an added element: state supreme courts are more likely to hear a higher percentage of cases involving really thorny, difficult issues of law. Many state supreme courts have large areas of discretionary jurisdiction; that is, the justices decide whether they want to hear the appeal to any given case. As a clerk, you might have a hand in that process. Also, some really important kinds of cases— like death penalty cases—are sometimes appealable directly to state supreme courts.

E. OTHER COURT-RELATED JOBS (INCLUDING STAFF ATTORNEYS)

Everything we've talked about until now has involved "elbow" clerks—that is, clerks for particular judges. There are many other kinds of clerk-related jobs at courts as well, and I've heard good things about all of these kinds of jobs.

For a start, there are "staff attorneys" in some courts. As a staff attorney, you're part of the court's central staff. You typically review cases for the entire court, write memos, and work with the judges on things like motions, pro se petitions, and cases decided without oral arguments. These jobs differ from judicial clerkships in that they're not associated with a particular judge, they're permanent, and they *generally* require experience (although a few don't). Federal circuit court staff attorney positions are sometimes for a fixed five-year term. Staff attorneyships are becoming increasingly popular, and they are real plum positions.

Staff attorneys typically work a very reasonable 40– to 50–hour week, and some courts even allow staff attorneys to "split" positions. For instance, two people each work a 25–hour week (a real boon to people with young children).

Staff attorney jobs sometimes mutate into elbow clerkships at the request of judges, either temporarily or permanently.

At the federal district court level, courts also employ "writ clerks" or "pro se clerks," who handle petitions from prisoners. (People who fill these positions may also be called staff attorneys.)

And then there are permanent law clerks. These *are* elbow clerks, but as the name suggests, the job is permanent rather than temporary. These are becoming increasingly popular with judges. These positions are *highly* sought after. I talked with one woman who'd been a judicial clerk, and then moved on to be a litigator with a large firm. She was in the middle of a trial when her judge called her to say that he'd been authorized to hire permanent clerks, and he wanted her to come back. She dropped everything—*in the middle of a trial!—* and zoomed back.

F.   A GOLD MINE OF FREQUENTLY-OVERLOOKED OPPORTUNITIES

When you think of clerkships, you probably think about just a few different kinds of clerkships. At least *I* do—federal district court, circuit courts, and of course the U.S. Supreme Court. On the state side, trial level, appellate, and state supreme courts. But the fact is, those are only part of the story—there are *tons* of often-ignored clerkship opportunities, and we'll talk about some of those here. First, we'll take a look at courts, and then we'll look at different types of judges.

1.   COURTS AND FEDERAL AGENCIES

A.   U.S. BANKRUPTCY COURT

As a clerk for the bankruptcy court, you primarily review and prepare the weekly calendar. Not many bankruptcy court opinions are written; instead, you focus on procedural and administrative matters. Every judicial district in the country has a bankruptcy court.

You'll find that this kind of clerkship is a great background for practicing either bankruptcy law (duh) or commercial law.

B.   U.S. COURT OF FEDERAL CLAIMS

This D.C.—based court handles cases where there are claims for monetary judgments from the United States. The claims it hears include, among others, government contract disputes, inverse condemnations, and Indian tribe claims. It doesn't handle criminal or tax cases. Its decisions can be appealed to the Court of Appeals for the Federal Circuit.

Clerks for the Federal Claims court sometimes travel with judges to other cities to hear cases.

C.   U.S. COURT OF INTERNATIONAL TRADE

As the name implies, it handles civil claims involving tariff conflicts and it hears appeals from the U.S. International Trade Commission (which investigates and rules on unfair practices in the import trade).

D.   U.S. COURT OF APPEALS FOR THE FEDERAL CIRCUIT

This court hears appeals from U.S. District Courts nationwide in cases involving patents and any disputes where the U.S. is a defendant. It also hears appeals from the U.S. Court of Federal Claims, the U.S. Court of Veterans Appeals, and the U.S. Court of International Trade.

This is a *particularly* great clerkship to pursue if you're interested in a career in intellectual property or international trade law.

E. U.S. Tax Court

This D.C.—based federal court adjudicates appeals between the IRS and taxpayers, involving income, estate, and gift taxes. It is actually an independent judicial body within the legislative branch of the government. This is a particularly attractive choice if you want to practice tax law.

F. Court of Appeals for the Armed Forces

As the name suggests, this court hears appeals from court martial convictions in all of the armed forces.

G. U.S. Court of Veterans Appeals

This court reviews decisions of regional Boards of Veterans Appeals on cases involving disputes over veterans' benefits.

H. U.S. Territorial Courts

If you want to perform a judicial clerkship and work on your tan at the same time, consider U.S. territorial courts in the U.S. Virgin Islands or Puerto Rico. There are also U.S. territorial courts in Guam and the Northern Mariana Islands. They all hire students from U.S. law schools.

I. Tribal Courts

In certain states (like Alaska) you can clerk for tribal courts. For more information, see the National American Indian Court Judges' Association website, at www.naicja.org.

J. Federal Agencies

If you have a specific area of interest, clerking for an administrative law judge who hears cases in that area is a *great* way to start your career. Apart from polishing your skills, you've got the prestige of a federal clerkship and a definite advantage on breaking into that agency as a lawyer when your clerkship is over.

Dozens of federal agencies have administrative law judges, and some of them hire clerks. The agencies that hire clerks include the Department of Agriculture, the Department of Energy, the Department of Justice (including the Executive Office for Immigration Review), the Department of Labor, the EPA, the NTSB, and others. Check with your Career Services Office, the Federal Administrative Law Judge Conference on-line at www.faljc.org, as well as agency web sites (listed in Chapter 11) for more information.

2. Categories of Judges

There are more judges than you can shake a stick at. Not that you *would,* mind you, because it would be disrespectful. The point is: there are many clerkship opportunities with judges in positions you might not have realized existed.

A. FEDERAL SENIOR JUDGES

These are judges who are semi-retired. They've lightened their caseloads but they haven't totally retired. The choicest senior judges to clerk for are former chief judges.

The benefits of working for these judges include the fact that they've spent a lot of time as lawyers and judges and can provide you with insights that a greenhorn judge might not have.

Also, the competition for clerkships is often less fierce than it is for "active" judges—and the workload is lighter. Furthermore, senior judges can typically pick and choose the cases they want to work on. They generally choose the most interesting cases, which means more interesting work for you, as their clerk.

B. ADMINISTRATIVE LAW JUDGES

There are many federal agencies that have administrative law judges. In all, there are over 1,000 administrative law judges in 28 different federal agencies. They hear cases pertinent to their particular agency. Not all of them hire clerks, but some do. The Federal Administrative Law Judge Conference on-line at www.faljc.org is a good source of information on opportunities.

C. U.S. MAGISTRATES

Magistrates are appointed by U.S. District Court Judges. They are judicial officers with limited statutory authority. Typically, they supervise pretrial (discovery) proceedings, conduct settlement negotiations, draft recommendations on motions, hold evidentiary hearings, and preside over civil trials. In criminal matters, they usually arraign defendants, hold detention hearings, and conduct misdemeanor trials. As an assistant to a U.S. Magistrate, your duties vary depending on your magistrate's responsibilities. However, because of their trial court focus, they're an obvious choice if you want to become a litigator.

D. JUDGES IN SMALL TOWNS AND LESS POPULATED STATES

Predictably enough, the most difficult clerkships to get are in the federal courts in cities like Boston, Chicago, New York, L.A., San Francisco, and Washington, D.C. But there is tons of judicial talent outside the large metropolitan areas. These judges get fewer applications and, hence, clerkships with them are somewhat easier to get. As one judge points out, "The Editor in Chief of the Yale Law Review isn't going to want to come to Kansas City."

Furthermore, for federal courts, federal law is the same everywhere. Clerkships in Midland, Texas can be just as valuable as geographically more sought-after postings, but they're *much* easier to get because there's less competition for them. If it's a clerkship you want, it doesn't pay to be a geographical snob!

E. NEWLY-APPOINTED JUDGES

The attraction here is that these clerkships are typically easier to get since they get fewer applications than "established" judges. One of the reasons for this is that there is no fixed calendar for judicial appointments, so applying to them often means missing the usual clerkship "rush."

To find out about these opportunities, check on-line at LEXIS and Westlaw and keep up with the legal press. If you find someone who has been nominated for a federal judgeship but hasn't been confirmed yet, send an application and *acknowledge in your cover letter* that you know they haven't yet been confirmed, but you want to clerk for them when they are. Request that they keep your application on file until they are actively considering clerks.

F. UNEXPECTED OPENINGS

As I've pointed out before, judicial clerks sometimes vaporize before their clerkships are over, for a variety of reasons. As with newly-appointed judges, these openings can come up at any time. The best way to get these is to check frequently with your Career Services Office at school and to keep your eye on relevant web sites (we cover them in Chapter 11). Career Services is a particularly fertile source because judges facing a sudden opening will often contact Career Services Offices for help.

G. HOW TO GET JUDICIAL CLERKSHIPS

According to the ABA's magazine *Student Lawyer,* most law students who successfully harpoon a judicial clerkship apply to at least 40 to 50 judges (although of course the ABA wouldn't use a word like "harpoon" in this context). So be prepared for a bit of work. Getting a judicial clerkship is a job in itself!

We won't discuss deadlines here, because they change pretty frequently. Check with your Career Services Office to see what the current deadlines for various clerkships are. As a rule of thumb, however, you need to know that they tend to be *very* early; it's not unusual to have deadlines for post-graduate clerkships occur in the Fall of *Second* Year—in other words, a year and a half ahead of time! So it pays to check with your CSO soon, like, today.

What I'm going to focus on here are the non-deadline elements of bagging a judicial clerkship—choosing a court, choosing a judge, and things you just have to know about cover letters, resumes, writing samples, letters of recommendation, interviewing, how to handle offers and acceptances, and how to try again if at first you don't succeed!

Let's start off with a checklist for pursuing judicial clerkships:

● Choose the judges and courts you want to approach;

● Find references and ask for letters of recommendation;

- Update your resume;
- Write cover letters;
- Mail applications to judges.

We'll talk about each element in detail.

1. IF YOU'VE GOT NO FIRM IDEA WHAT COURTS OR JUDGES YOU WANT, HAVE SOME CONVERSATIONS WITH FORMER CLERKS FIRST

When you're doing your initial recon, it makes sense to go to Career Services and get the names of alums who have just completed judicial clerkships. You can do this during the Summer if you like. Give them a call, and ask them about their experiences, what advice they have. You know from reading this book that the activity I recommend most is *talking to people*. It's your best, most interesting source of information.

2. CHOOSING A COURT

A. WHAT KIND OF EXPERIENCE DO YOU WANT?

If you prefer a more intellectual environment, you're better off with an appellate court. If you want more of an adrenaline rush, a more people-oriented experience, a trial court clerkship will make you happy.

B. DO YOU HAVE AN INTENDED PRACTICE AREA?

If so, that may make a certain court (or type of court) attractive.

A technical background and in interest in intellectual property would steer you to a clerkship in the Federal Circuit, which tries patent cases. If you're jonesing for a tax gig, the U.S. Tax Court would make sense. If you dream of being a professor, an appellate clerkship makes a lot of sense, where you'll do a lot of thinking and writing. If you dream of being a litigator, a trial court (or magistrate) clerkship will serve you better than an appellate position. If you want domestic relations, a family court makes sense. You get the picture.

C. WHERE DO YOU WANT TO SETTLE AFTER YOUR CLERKSHIP?

Here's the thing. You want to be as geographically flexible as possible in seeking a clerkship. Having said that, in terms of developing contacts and paving the way for your future career, you're best of doing a clerkship in the general area where you'd like to settle afterwards.

Note, incidentally, that just because a court is located in a certain city, it doesn't mean that the judge's office is there, *especially* for appellate courts. As you do your research, be sure to make a note of this if geography is an issue.

3. CHOOSING JUDGES

There are thousands of judges in America. You can't apply to all of them. (Well, I suppose you could, but it's not a time-effective search.) Let's talk about how you figure out your targets.

A. Use "Humint"!

I can't state this strongly enough: do not *ever* pursue a judicial clerkship if you can't find "human intelligence" *somewhere* on what the judge is like.

Your experience with any particular judge depends largely on how that judge delegates work and interacts with his/her clerks. Is (s)he combative or relaxed? Does (s)he put a lot of responsibility on clerks, or very little? Does (s)he prefer to discuss issues with clerks, or do clerks draft opinions for his/her review?

This kind of information is the exclusive province of people who are familiar with the judge. If they've clerked for the judge or are otherwise familiar with the judge, they'll have this information. You can find it by asking at Career Services for alums and/or professors who've clerked for particular judges. Often Career Services Offices maintain binders of surveys from former judicial clerks, which can offer snapshots of life with particular judges. Some schools maintain databases of alums who have clerked for judges. Take advantage of those resources!

As one former federal clerk points out, "There are at least two reasons to do this investigation up front. For one thing, once you take an interview, you're pretty much stuck. If the judge makes you an offer, you have to take it. And in that interview setting, no clerk within earshot of their judge is going to say 'Don't take this clerkship. Run, don't walk, away.' Even if the interview makes you believe you won't get along with the judge, if the judge thinks you *will,* you're stuck. That's why it's so important to know up front about what the judges are like, so you don't interview with someone you won't get along with.

Secondly, the nature of the job is that you are subject to the absolute power of one person. It's not like a law firm where there are other people for prospective employers to talk to. With a judge, it's only that judge's name on your resume. They won't call his secretary, they won't call other court personnel, they won't call other clerks—they'll call the judge. You have to stack the deck in your favor as much as you possibly can."

B. Find Judges With Whom You Have Something in Common

Look at judges' bios (check the resources in the Appendix at the end of this chapter) to see what they did before: their community activities, and so forth. You may have something in common that gives you an edge, whether it's a charitable activity or a common work experience (e.g., you summer clerked at their old law firm or you worked at a prosecutor's office and they're a former prosecutor).

* * * SMART HUMAN TRICK * * *

Female law student, researching federal judges. She learns from alums of her law school that one particular judge hires "cookie-cutter female Jews, he's seriously into Jewish causes." She reports, "That's great for me, because that's exactly who I am." She accentuates her Jewish community involvement on her resume, and at the interview when he questions her in Hebrew, she responds in Hebrew.

She gets the clerkship.

C. YOUR DUTIES WILL VARY DEPENDING ON THE JUDGE'S DUTIES

You'll have a different experience depending on whether your judge is a Chief Judge as opposed to a Senior Judge or a new appointee. Chief Judges will have more administrative responsibilities than other judges, and some of that administrative work may trickle down to you.

Working for Senior Judges—ones who are semi-retired—doesn't mean you'll have nothing to do. It depends on the judge. Some choose only cases in their areas of interest, or they prefer to travel around. Those appetites will obviously influence your work as a clerk.

If you work for a freshly-minted judge, on the other hand, you'll have an influence on setting up the chambers, and that's fun.

D. BEWARE OF MAKING CHOICES BASED ON POLITICAL ORIENTATION . . .

You may be tempted to target judges because you view them as being "liberal" or "conservative." Most experts consider this a mistake. Here's why:

- Most cases don't have a bright-line liberal/conservative distinction. It's not that relevant. As former judicial clerk Robert Shaw–Meadow points out dryly, "It is difficult to become too emotionally overwrought by the Federal Rules of Civil Procedure."

- You may get along really well with a judge who disagrees with you politically; it can be stimulating!

- Judges don't like to be chosen on that basis, since they want your support on every decision they make . . . not just ones that agree with your politics.

E. DON'T *EVER* APPLY TO A COURT AND/OR JUDGE WITH WHOM YOU DON'T SERIOUSLY WANT TO CLERK

Here's a rule of thumb: If you wouldn't accept an offer from a judge, don't apply for a clerkship with him/her.

For a start, you're paying your own traveling expenses, so blanketing the country with applications can get pricey. More importantly, you're not collecting shrunken heads, you know. You're dealing with *very influential people*. Don't even *think* about applying for judicial clerkships just to get the interview experience. Etiquette on accepting offers from judges is *very different* than it is for other kinds of employers. In short: you accept the first clerkship that's offered to you. So make sure that *every* one you apply for is an opportunity you honestly want. (We talk about finessing this issue with setting up the timing of your interviews and squeezing in a 24–hour window to make a decision later in this chapter.)

What this all adds up to is that you've got to do your detective work up front to ensure to the greatest extent possible that the clerkships you go for are the ones you want. Talk to everyone you can, and check out all of the web resources at your disposal (we talk about them in the Appendix to this chapter). Of course, there are going to be judges you'd prefer to work for more than others. But remember: a clerkship is a great experience, and the judge you wind up with will *still* provide you with a great experience. On top of that . . . nothing stops you from doing more than one judicial clerkship, so you always have another "bite at the apple" if you want it!

4. TIMING YOUR APPLICATIONS

You'd think this would be fairly straightforward. And it *would* be, if courts didn't change their minds every five minutes about their deadlines. To find out what the deadlines are right now, use two web resources:

- For federal courts, go to http://www.cadc.uscourts.gov/lawclerk/

- For state courts, use the Vermont Law School Guide to State Judicial Clerkship Procedures, available on-line at http://vermont law.edu/career (get the password from your Career Services Office, or check the hard copy version at the CSO).

For post-graduate clerkships, the deadline can be anywhere from Spring of 2L to Fall of 3L. Regardless of the deadline for your target courts, as a strategic matter **make a point of getting your application in as early as possible in the hiring process.**

5. MECHANICS OF APPLYING FOR FEDERAL CLERKSHIPS: OSCAR (ONLINE SYSTEM FOR CLERKSHIP APPLICATION AND REVIEW)

Traditionally, you apply for clerkships by mailing your materials to judges' chambers. That's still true of many courts. *However,* a growing number of federal judges are accepting applications electronically using OSCAR. You can find out more about it—including judges who are taking part—at the Federal Law Clerk Information System web site, https://lawclerks.ao.uscourts.gov/

6. COVER LETTERS, RESUMES, WRITING SAMPLES, LETTERS OF RECOMMENDATION, INTERVIEWING, FOLLOWING UP, HANDLING OFFERS AND ACCEPTANCES, AND HOW TO TRY AGAIN IF AT FIRST YOU DON'T SUCCEED!

We discussed all of this in exhaustive detail earlier in this book. All I'm going to do here is cover issues that are specific to judicial clerkships. You're not off the hook; go back and read those chapters!

A. Cover Letters

No matter what else your application includes, it will have a cover letter. Let's talk about how to formulate them.

While no source I've seen (or talked to) says what I'm about to tell you in so many words, it's pretty clear that the level of detail you should include depends to some extent on the paper credentials you're bringing to the table. For instance, a cover letter that states: *"I am writing to you to apply for the position of judicial clerk. I will be available any time after May 15th the year after next. I am #1 in my class at the Harvard Law School and will be President of the Harvard Law Review beginning next Fall. Thank you and good night."*

. . . would undoubtedly do the trick nicely all by itself.

But most of us aren't three standard deviations above the mean on the old poisson distribution of credentials. For the rest of us, as the Superior Court of Boston tells applicants, your cover letter gives you the chance to highlight your experience, interests, and individuality.

1. While We Discussed Cover Letters In Great Detail In Chapter 7, Here Are a Few Tips Specific to Composing Letters for Judicial Clerkships

a. To the extent you possibly can, personalize the letter to the judge and court. You don't want to feel like a number. Neither does a judge. Show off your research. "Having talked with local lawyers/alumni/former clerks . . ." tell them why you want to work for them *specifically.*

b. If you have specific intelligence about what a particular judge looks for in cover letters, follow that advice to the exclusion of everything else. A clerk for one federal district court judge reported that her judge often brought in students for interviews if their letters amused him. In a situation like *that,* you'd exhibit humor in a letter that wouldn't be appropriate otherwise!

c. If you have a tie to the geographic area, particularly if you're applying to a state court, say what it is! If you don't have a tie there, you need a sentence or two talking about how you're willing to relocate to gain the clerkship experience. Because you have to pay your own travel expenses, judges won't offer to interview students they don't perceive as serious candidates. Also, clearly state in your letter that you're willing to pay to come to town for an interview.

d. For specialized courts, it makes sense to include a sentence or two about any relevant experience in that field, and why you are interested in the court. You don't want a judge to feel you'll apply to anyone you'll think will take you.

e.   If you have relevant experience that doesn't appear on your resume, mention it. For instance, let's say you were asked to present a paper on a relevant topic at an upcoming conference. While that wouldn't appear on your resume, it should appear in your cover letter.

f.   If you have any direct experience with the judge, mention it. "You were on the panel that voted me Best Oralist in the Moot Court finals" or "I was a student in the Constitutional Law Seminar that you taught in the Fall of 20__." Use your judgment, however. An experience with the judge that starts "You were probably too drunk to remember . . ." would not be appropriate.

g.   As a matter of practical reality, judges are less inclined to interview out-of-state candidates, knowing that students have to foot the travel bill. State why you want to be there in your letter.

h.   Don't use official letterhead for your letter; whether it's a firm for whom you clerked during the summer, a business you own or work for, or anything else. You're not writing to the judge in your "official" capacity, and they'll find it inappropriate to see you "representing" an organization.

i.   Be aware that your cover letter is the judge's first exposure to you writing style. Make it clear and lively, and brief—no more than a page. And as is true for every written thing any employer sees *no typos*— double-check the spelling of the judge's name and have at least one other person read your letters. As one judge notes, "Spelling my name right—that's a real bridge-builder for me."

j.   Be aware that your personality will be gauged by what you write. One applicant wrote the line, "I relish the clash of superior minds." Puh-leez! As one former judicial clerk puts it, "I would read letters from students trying to figure out if their personality would fit with the judge's. There was one guy who sounded totally arrogant; he kept talking about his prestigious summer associate job. I just knew that he wouldn't get along with the judge, but he knew someone who knew the judge and so he got an interview. I interviewed him first and I'm telling you, it was like pulling teeth trying to talk to this guy. Pure torture. I knew it from the letter."

k.   Keep in mind that a current clerk will likely read your letter first, so don't say anything arrogant like, "I'll be the best clerk you've ever had."

l.   Don't blow smoke up judges' butts. As one judge points out, "You can't send me a letter saying, 'You're the best judge' or 'I've always wanted to work for you,' because I know you sent my neighbor the same thing."

m. No gimmicks! Don't include a short story in the body of your letter. No sending a scrap book about yourself. Yes, people have really done it.

n. No lies! As one judge points out, "Judges call people at your school to see if you're telling the truth."

o. In your first paragraph, include the date you will be available to start work.

p. If you've got an unusual reason for wanting a clerkship and you have definite plans for what you want to do with your career afterwards, say so. Otherwise, don't bother with them. Judges know how desirable clerkships are, and stating the obvious won't help your campaign.

q. Be enthusiastic but sincere. If you have an honest, particularized interest in working for this particular judge, if there's something you truly think is great about him or her, something that motivates you to want to work for him/her, go ahead and say it. But if you send a form letter to fifty judges all saying "It's been my lifelong dream to work for you," it's going to smack of sleaze.

r. What about if you have something you need to explain away—say, a semester's worth of bad grades? You have two options: The best is to get one of your references to mention the matter in their letter of reference. ("Ms. Tayk is a hard-working student who has an excellent analytical mind. Her grades have been solid in every semester except the spring of 20__ , in which she was injured in an automobile accident and had to miss five weeks of class. She made the tough decision to finish the semester as best she could, and did remarkably well under the circumstances.") If you've got an employer or professor who's sympathetic, that would work well. If not, you might want to mention the situation in your cover letter (show your cover letter to your Career Services Office before you send it to make sure you word it well!).

s. Remember the old screenwriter's adage "Show me, don't tell me." Don't say that you're "hard-working, a self-starter, with great research and writing skills." Instead, describe achievements that *show* what you've got. For instance, working thirty hours a week to finance your law school education shows hard work. A brief description of research for a journal or professor or a writing contest you won will show you like to research and write, and that you're good at it.

t. Be sure that you accurately state the judge's title in your letter, whether it's Chief Judge or Judge or Justice. "Yo Babe" won't cut it. Always be formal. "Dear Chief Justice Amullmahay:" is appropriate. If you just aren't sure, check with Career Services or call the judge's chambers and ask. You won't look stupid; you'll look respectful and detail-oriented, which are both positives.

u. On the envelope and inside address, the judge's name is always preceded by "The Hon.," "The Honorable," or "Honorable."

v. The preferred closing for letters to judges is "Respectfully." "Sincerely" is also common and acceptable. Avoid closings like "Hopefully," "With Fingers Crossed," or "Your Faithful Liege Man."

2. ANATOMY OF AN EFFECTIVE COVER LETTER FOR A JUDICIAL CLERKSHIP.

This format incorporates many of the tips we just discussed. (Adapted from The American University Washington College of Law.)

1. Appropriate (i.e. conservative) Letterhead <u>or</u>:

2. Street Address

City, State Zip

Date (spelled out)

3. Judge's form of address (see list after this letter)

Full name of the Court

Name of the Courthouse (if applicable)

Address

4. Dear Judge/Justice/appropriate salutation from list on next page:

5. **Opening Paragraph/Positioning Statement.** Include the following basic information: a) the position you are applying for by year; b) your status as a law student, and where you go to school; c) the name of any contact (former clerk, alum, professor, or other individual who knows the judge or court); and d) why you are interested in clerking for the judge or court (two or three sentences).

6. **Heart of the letter.** Highlight a few experiences from your resume by discussing the skills (research, writing, analysis, etc.) you developed and, if possible, how these positions increased your interest in obtaining a judicial clerkship. Obviously, if you worked as an extern/intern for a judge, this would be an ideal position to mention. Emphasize relevant honors, awards, and other accom-

plishments. Remember to merely *highlight* certain aspects of your resume, not *summarize* it.

7. **Closing paragraph.** Include the following information: a) items you are enclosing in your application packet (resume, transcript, writing sample, recommendations) and b) any dates you will be in the area for potential interviews, and your knowledge that you will foot the bill for the interview.

8. Sincerely/Respectfully,

Printed name

Enclosures

3. **JUDGES' TITLES, FORMS OF ADDRESS AND SALUTATIONS.**

It's important to get these *exactly* right.

a. Chief Justice of the U.S. Supreme Court:

Form of Address: The Chief Justice of the United States

Salutation: Dear Chief Justice (last name):

b. Associate Justice of the U.S. Supreme Court:

Form of Address: Associate Justice (full name)

Salutation: Dear Justice (last name):

c. Federal or state court judge

Form of Address: The Honorable (full name)

Salutation: Dear Judge (last name):

d. Justice of a State Supreme Court:

Form of Address: The Honorable (full name)

Dear Justice (last name):

e. Magistrate Judge, federal or state

Form of Address: The Honorable (full name)

Salutation: Dear Magistrate Judge (last name):

B. **RESUMES FOR JUDICIAL CLERKSHIPS**

While we discussed resumes out the ying-yang in Chapter 8, there are three unique elements that apply to resumes for judicial clerkships:

- Because you might be applying for clerkships at least a year in advance, by the time the clerkship starts you will have experience that you don't have now. For instance, you'll want to say "Will work this summer for the American Judicature Society," or "Appointed Notes Editor for the Journal of Wood Tick Law, for the academic year 20__–__" or "Prospective judicial clerk for Federal Circuit Judge Crater." This is important, because although whatever you're including is prospective experience *now,* it will be under your belt by the time you get to *this* judge.

- Include personal hobbies and interests. Most experts agree that it's a good idea *all* the time, but it's particularly helpful in resumes for judicial clerkships. Because judges work so closely with their clerks, they want to see that you're personable and well-rounded (assuming, of course, that you *are).*

    It may be that your research reveals that you have a common interest with a particular judge, like tennis or fly-fishing. If you're lucky enough to find that out, include that hobby on the resume that you send to that judge!

- If you've worked as a judicial intern or extern before, you need to be careful about how you word your experience. As a general rule:

    - Be *precise* in your title. If you were an intern/extern for a judge during the school year, don't say you were a "judicial clerk." These distinctions are taken very seriously!

    - If you did substantive work as opposed to filing or photocopying, describe what you did in general terms. For instance, you could say that you "performed the work of a law clerk, providing research assistance in connection with cases before the court."

    - Don't mention specific cases on which you worked.

    - Describe generally issues that you researched, e.g. First Amendment issues.

    - Don't claim credit for drafting opinions; remember that the opinion bears the judge's name no matter how much of it you wrote, so you shouldn't bag it for yourself.

- Transcripts

What can I say? Send it. An unofficial one is OK. Don't white out any grades.

3. WRITING SAMPLES

Because writing is the coin of the realm with judicial clerkships, judges really value writing samples. It's important to choose well! Your writing sample should be not just well-written but well-organized, demonstrating your legal research and analysis skills. Beyond that, there are two elements to address: length and type.

For length, judicial clerkship guru Debra Strauss says you want to stay below twenty pages. If your sample is a Law Review note or Journal piece, which is likely to be far longer than twenty pages, select your best excerpt, and set up the context on a cover page.

On the lower end of the sample length scale, seven to ten pages is fine. Five is too short. If your writing sample happens to be short, then send two of them—different ones, that is!—to fill out the page recommendation.

When it comes to type, take into account the *kind* of judicial clerkship you're applying for. If it's a trial level court like a federal district court, you're better off with something concrete, like a brief. An often-overlooked source of excellent writing samples for trial level courts is unedited law school exam essays—they show better than anything else your ability to write under pressure!

For an appellate court, something theoretical like a law review note is more appropriate. No matter what you choose, if it's writing that you did for a law firm, *always* check with the firm first to ensure that it's all right to use the particular piece of work as a sample. Assuming that it *is,* be sure to mark on the sample that you've OK'd it with the firm—say something like "Approved for Release"—and redact any client names or identifying facts. Judges will appreciate—and demand—your respect for confidentiality. It's a serious boo-boo to send a judge a writing sample that reveals something confidential!

No matter what kind of writing sample you choose, don't send something heavily edited by someone else, which covers just about every published Law Review note. Instead, send *your* draft of your Law Review or Journal note or a short excerpt of it.

Also, don't send a writing sample with a grade or a professor's comments on it, no matter how rapturous the praise.

Finally, if you've worked for a judge before, don't use as a writing sample an opinion that you wrote under the judge's supervision. Ironic, isn't it, since an opinion would be the best possible writing sample you could send a judge! However, a lot of judges view it as bad judgment and will use that basis alone to disqualify you from consideration. It doesn't matter if the judge you wrote it for heartily endorses your use of it; it's the opinion of the judge you're applying to that counts. If you believe the opinion you wrote is your finest work, you might ask the judge you wrote it for to mention it in their letter of recommendation ... assuming, of course, they think it's as good as you think it is.

4. LETTERS OF RECOMMENDATION

You're typically going to want two or three letters of recommendation, although different judges have different requirements, so check first. (If you are lucky enough to have more people who can say concrete, great things about your abilities, wonderful—there's no harm in sending four letters, sometimes even more. Some judges are impressed by an abundance of recommendations. But normally three letters is puh-lenty, and two are fine.)

Here are a few tips to keep in mind:

- When it comes to choosing references, as a rule of thumb, judges view faculty references more highly than employer references (although you shouldn't overlook sterling employer references—use both!). If you already worked for a judge, fabulous—there's one reference. If you use any other employer, be sure to use your supervising attorney. If you don't, judges will smell a rat.

- If you e-mail a recommendation letter request to a professor and you don't hear back, contact them in person. Stop by their office. Take a deep breath, and ask them about your request. Don't assume a failure to respond is a refusal! There could be a bunch of reasons they didn't respond that have nothing to do with a negative image of you. Having said that, if a professor agrees to write you a letter but doesn't seem entirely enthusiastic, reconsider using them as a reference. A vague, neutral letter does you more harm than good. (It's fine, by the way, to address this right out: "You don't seem entirely thrilled with the prospect of recommending me, and if so, let me know; I need strong recommendation letters and if you don't feel comfortable writing me one, I'll find people who do." It takes major *cojones*— or the ability to fake them—to say this to a professor, but because recommendation letters are so important to judges, it's a lot easier to address the issue with a professor than it is to lose a clerkship opportunity!)

- What if a professor is negative? Don't give up your judicial clerkship quest based on one lousy exchange! Instead go to Career Services for guidance. (Professors can be very wrong about you, you know. I was once turned down for a teaching assistant job in law school, because the professor said I didn't seem sincere about wanting to help law students. Go figure.)

- Request letters from professors as soon as your target judge list is firmed up. Professors get approached by a lot of students, and you want to make sure they have adequate time to write you a great letter. Furthermore, they may be conscious of not sending too many letters to any one judge, and you don't want to get frozen out.

- It's *far* better to use a professor with a familiarity with your work over one you perceive as having a "big name." A letter from a star professor who has *no clue* who you are does you no good at all. The more specific the letter, the more credible it will be. As one judicial clerk points out, "I read letters of recommendation all the time. You can *immediately* tell when the referrer doesn't really know the student. It's just a lot better to have a letter from a reference with a lesser reputation who really knows you well."

- If you possibly can, get a reference from someone the judge knows. You can "reverse engineer" this by asking professors which judges to approach for a clerkship, which judges they know; that way, you'll know that the judge knows that professor! It is impossible to overestimate the value of a recommendation from someone a judge knows and trusts. "So, you know Professor Hinklebottom. Great guy!"

- It's OK if you don't know professors personally; not many law students do! When you tell them you'd like them to write a recommendation letter for you, acknowledge that they don't know you and ask if they'll meet with you to get to know you better and learn about your career goals.

- It's a good idea to give your references a packet of information about you *before* they write your recommendation, so that the letter they write can encompass that information. Consider including your resume, your transcript, your writing sample, and the judges you've targeted (at least so far).

- If you got a great grade in one class and not so well in others, when you approach the "great grade" professor for a recommendation, don't try to hide the other grades. At best, the professor will look stupid by raving about your excellent credentials when the judge can see that your exams are only occasionally brilliant. At worst, the professor will find out and refuse to write you a recommendation at all because of your deception. It's just not worth it. Anyway, recommendation letters are a great place to explain away an occasionally spotty performance in law school . . . so be honest!

- Always be sure to show the professors you approach a list of the judges you're targeting. For one thing, they may know some of the judges and will want to write something more than a standard form letter to them. For another, if a lot of law students have asked to write a letter to a particular judge, they may feel they aren't the best recommender for that judge because their opinion will be diluted by the large number of letters they've already written.

- If a professor asks you if there's anything specific they want to say about you, they're trying to help you out. As I've already mentioned, letters of recommendation are a great place to "explain away" elements of your resume or transcript that are less than stellar. On top of that, you might have specific achievements you want to highlight. Go ahead and let the professor know that!

- Ideal recommendation letters include information on attributes like these:

- Intellectual ability;

- Research and writing skills;

- Recognition and ability to analyze legal issues;

- Oral presentation and advocacy skills;

- Time management skills;

- Ability to be a team player and get along with others;

- Ability to articulate and defend your positions;

- Ability to work well under pressure;

- Ability to respect and observe rules on confidentiality.

- Because a lukewarm or brief general recommendation can torpedo your chances, ask your "selectees" very frankly what they will say about you, and if you should choose someone else instead. In particular, tell your references any personal things about you that you do *not* want mentioned in the recommendation, like a pregnancy, a disability . . . or a blog. You need to know that recommenders frequently, *and totally innocently,* tank students' chances at clerkships by blabbing something inappropriate. For instance, if you've got a voice like Tweety Bird, a reference may mention that in your recommendation letter by way of ensuring that the judge isn't taken by surprise on meeting you. A revelation like that may well have the effect of eliminating you from contention altogether. So be up-front about anything personal you don't want revealed, and if the reference insists on including it, find other references.

- Don't let references use a form recommendation for you. Offer to draft the letter yourself if need be. As one judge points out, "Form recommendations from professors are meaningless. All they show is that the professor doesn't know the student."

- You want recommendations that show that you stick out from the crowd. If need be, as a first-year or freshly-minted second-year student, look to an undergrad professor who knows your work well. Judges realize that professors who teach First Years rarely get to know students well, so they don't expect raves from them.

- Make sure that your recommendation letters are personally addressed to judges, not "To whom it may concern . . ." Provide your recommenders with a diskette of judge contact information so that they can easily do a mail merge.

- Keep in mind also that glowing letters from your first-year legal research and writing instructor aren't the most convincing, because the way you perform on rote, mechanical writing exercises common to those classes doesn't indicate creativity or true critical analysis.

A few technicalities. When you ask for a reference, provide an envelope with the judge's name and address and a "re: your name" line on the outside, in case the letter gets separated from the rest of your application. Offer to word process letters and return them to your references for review and signature.

Concerning delivery, there are really only two ways to get letters to your judges: either you or your references send them. Having your references send letters directly to judges is a minefield, because if the letter gets to the judge either substantially before or after your application package, there's a serious risk of the recommendation being misplaced. If you've got an incomplete application package in the form of missing recommendations, you won't be considered for the clerkship. Yikes!

To avoid this, if you have any references who *insist* on sending their letter of recommendation directly to the judge, then be sure to needle them to send the recommendation at approximately the same time—ideally, the same day—you send your application.

A far better alternative is to send the letters yourself, along with your application. No chance of misplacing them that way! The way to overcome any hint of funny business is to have your references seal their letters of recommendation and sign their name across the seal on the back flap. It's well worth trying to get your recommenders to go along with this plan. Letters arriving before or after your application packet reaches the judge's chambers are frequently lost.

5. UPDATING YOUR APPLICATION AFTER YOU FIRE YOUR MATERIALS OFF TO JUDGES . . .

OK. So, you've been diligent and you've made your applications, and then you get a new semester's worth of grades, or you publish an article, or you win a prize, or you're appointed to the U.S. Supreme Court. Just kidding about that last one. But for any of the others, you want to send a letter to your target judges announcing your good news. Anything that ups your chances of an interview is worth mentioning!

6. INTERVIEWING

We talked in detail about interviewing in Chapter 9. Let's go over a few tidbits specific to interviewing with judges:

- For each clerkship, keep in mind that judges will typically interview between five and 25 candidates—so you need to stand out in a positive way!
- If you get an interview, you've got a serious shot at the job. It suggests the judge has already determined you're capable

of performing the role of clerk, and the interview largely determines if there's a personality fit between you and the judge and whether you'll adapt well to the judge's chambers. As one judge points out, "I want to know: are the applicants nice people? How do they think? I want to make sure I'm not hiring someone with two heads!"

- Interview formats vary; generally they last between thirty and ninety minutes. There is usually only one round of interviews, but some judges use more. Usually you meet with the judge's secretary/assistant first, then the judge, then the current clerks, although you might meet with them all at once. Remember: the moment you enter the courthouse, have your game face on. Anyone's opinion of you could count!

- Scheduling issues:

  - When you receive an interview offer for an out-of-town interview, call the offices of other judges in the area to whom you also applied. Let the judge's assistant know you'll be in the area interviewing with another judge, and ask if they'd be interested in interviewing you while you're there. (Incidentally, don't talk with the judge directly about this; it's an etiquette boo-boo! The judge's assistant will handle this kind of scheduling.) Debra Strauss advises that this kind of leveraging may pull your application out of the pile and get you an interview. Remember, judges won't reimburse you for your travel expenses, so you want to consolidate trips to the extent you can.

  - As we'll discuss in a minute, if you receive an offer from a judge, you pretty much have to accept it on the spot. What if the first judge who makes you an offer isn't your first choice? One potential option is to manipulate your schedule—although it's risky. If you try it, you rank the judges you're targeting. You try to schedule "less favored" judges on the late side of the judges' available dates. That way, you can ideally interview judges you prefer earlier on, and perhaps nail a clerkship with them first. *This is very risky because judges hire on a "rolling" basis; if they find the right person, they cancel remaining interviews.* If you try to rank judges like this you could lose out on *both* opportunities. The only truly safe bet is to apply only to judges you truly want to work for.

  - With earlier interviews with "preferred" judges, make sure to find out before you leave when they expect to make a decision. Make a note of the date, so that if you get calls for interviews with "less favored" judges, you can schedule those interviews for a date *after* your more favored judges make their decisions. That way you don't have to worry about scheduling or declining an interview with a judge you're not as wild about.

- To minimize the cost of out-of-town interviews, look into the possibility of video conferencing from school. Some judges have the ability to video conference, and that can give you an opportunity to interview with judges you'd otherwise have difficulty visiting.

- As with every interview, you need to research your prospective employer—in this case, the judge. You should find out if an alum or professor from your law school has ever clerked for this particular judge, or for this particular court, and find out everything you can. It would also be useful to talk to anyone you know who's a prosecutor or legal aid lawyer or who used to be one, since they'll know a lot of local judges.

What kinds of nuggets might you be able to dig up? You want to find out if there are any questions they routinely ask, or whether they look for certain attributes in their clerks which you can highlight about yourself.

Here are a couple of examples.

One judge pointed out that, "I tell interviewees that I'm ruthless on editing. The red ink flows freely. I ask them how they feel about seeing their work get hacked to pieces."

Another judge talks of seeking clerks with a lot of *chutzpah*. He only wants clerks who are willing to be open with him about their opinions. In interviews, he asks the following question to get at this trait: "What would you do in this situation? I've given you an opinion to draft and I've told you how I want the case to come out. You strongly disagree with me. What do you do?" He said that most students who haven't researched him give him the answer they think he wants—"Hey, you're the judge, if you want it to come out that way, I'll write it that way"—*even if that's not how they truly feel*. What he *really* wants is the student who'll say, "If you hire me, you're hiring me for my mind, and if I disagree with you, I don't care if your mind is made up. I'm going to tell you what I think." He told me that any student who takes the simple measure of calling his chambers first to talk to any of his current clerks would learn that about him. It often makes the difference between an offer and no offer.

One student told of researching judges, and learning from an alum that one of her target federal judges always asked the question, "What are the ten most important cases in American history, and why?" I ask you: how could you *possibly* answer that question without knowing it up front?

So you can see how important it is to research judges!

- Other kinds of research include Lexis/Nexis and Westlaw searches for the judge's recent opinions and articles (Note that some state trial court judges won't have any published opinions. Westlaw and Lexis have recent opinions for most judges. For articles about them, search Westlaw ALLNEWS for press releases mentioning them). Pay particular attention to dissents and concurrences, which will tell you a lot about the judge's philosophy and writing style. Not only that, but judges aren't immune to flattery. Taking the time to study the judge's writing shows that your interest in the judge is sincere and personalized. As one judge points out, "There's no ego hook like hearing the words, 'I read what you wrote in X case ...' "

- If you see that your target judge is making a public speaking appearance, make a point of going and introducing yourself. Talk about how interested you are in meeting with them. You can't *help* but stand out if you go to this kind of trouble.

- Be *thoroughly* familiar with your writing sample and any experiences you talk about on your resume. If the judge brings up any substantive legal issues at all, their most likely target will involve something you've written or worked on.

Once you're all prepped, what do you have to know about the actual interview itself? Here are a few things to keep in mind:

- Bring extra copies of your resume, transcript, and writing sample with you. And be punctual!

- You have to be conscious of what judges are looking for. They want a person whose judgment they can trust, whose abilities they can rely on, and perhaps most importantly, somebody they feel they will enjoy working with.

- Your words and demeanor have to ooze interest in the law. You don't have to be a bookish nerd, but on the other hand it's not a good idea to say that law school is a real snooze.

- Be aware that you may interview with a current clerk. You need to know that judges may view their clerks' opinions *very* seriously. As one judge points out, "If my clerk isn't happy, I'm not happy." As is true of interviewing with junior associates at law firms, don't be lulled into a false sense of security by the fact that the person who is interviewing you is very close to your age. They aren't your buddy. They are the judge's eyes and ears, so be eternally vigilant in what you say and do. No conspiratorial, "Hey, is it true that he's heavily into the sauce?" or "Jeez, the secretary seems like a real hard-a**. Is she like that all the time?"

- As is true in every interview—don't dis the help. Chambers are *notoriously* egalitarian. Even if the judge refers to his/her staff by first names, don't *you* do it unless expressly invited to do so by the person in question. Otherwise, it's Mr., or Mrs., or Miss, or Ms. And don't be arrogant! If you high-hat the judge's administrative assistant, it won't much matter if you consider yourself the second coming of John Marshall— you won't get an offer. Finally, don't let your guard down. Even if staffers assure you "We're really just here to answer any questions you might have, not to interview you," don't kid yourself—*they're there to interview you.* One judge even talked about a ruse he uses to get his secretary's impression. "When I bring in students for a second interview, I have my secretary tell them that I'm on the phone, and to have a seat. Then she talks to them for fifteen minutes, before she sends them in to me. Afterwards, I always ask her opinion of them. They don't even realize she interviewed them."

- Judges want to know your outside interests. Because they work closely with their clerks, they'll want to get a sense of your three-dimensionality. One judge told me a particularly funny story about this. I asked him how he'd chosen his most recent clerk, and he said, "I'm somewhat embarrassed to admit it, because it wasn't as though his grades were the best. And it wasn't as though his other experience was particularly stellar. What stood out during the interview was that he happened to mention that his hobby is Northern Italian cooking. For the rest of the interview, all I could envision was this guy preparing a meal for me and the other clerks. I'm quite sure he doesn't know what tipped the scales in his favor!"

There are a few unique aspects of clerkship interviews you need to keep in mind. As one former judicial clerk points out, "The one thing that was the same for every clerkship interview I had was that they were all *odd.*"

For a start, you have to be aware that judges are not trained interviewers. As one judicial clerk points out, "They don't know how to gauge abilities. They don't know what to ask. What it really comes down to is personality, personality, personality."

* * * SMART HUMAN TRICK * * *

Law student in Kansas, setting up an interview with a judge over the phone. After they've firmed up the details, the judge adds, "By the way, bring a six pack."

The law student reports, "I didn't know if he was joking or not. It was right at the end of the conversation. But I thought, what the heck. I like beer, too. So I took a six pack with me. When the judge saw it, he laughed out loud. We each had a beer during the interview. And incidentally, I got the clerkship."

On top of that, you have to be *very* conscious of an *exceptionally* important difference between interviews for judicial clerkships and any other kind of job interview: *judges frequently ask questions that would be a no-no anywhere else.* They'll ask you about your politics. They'll ask you about what your father does for a living. They'll ask you whatever they feel will help determine what makes you tick.

You may well find that the interview will involve a substantive legal discussion. After all, discussing legal issues is a common activity for judges and their clerks. Because they don't expect you to be able to discuss every legal topic in the Universe—lucky thing, that—they'll probably bring up something you've had a chance to think about.

No matter what happens in the interview, follow the judge's lead. They'll all have different styles. One clerk comments, "I interviewed with one judge who was a jokester, he was into sports, that's what *he* talked about. The very next interview—all business. 'Here's the position, this is what I expect you to do,' a very cut-to-the-chase kind of person." No matter which direction the judge takes the interview—follow it.

We could spend an entire chapter talking about answering interview questions, and—hey! We did that already! Go back and look at Chapter 9 for the philosophy of answering interview questions, and look at the answers to those questions, which of course a judge might ask you. In addition, consider the following questions that might come up in an interview with a judge:

- How did you choose your Law Review topic? How did you handle it?
- How would you approach a particular controversy in the news? (Judges love this one. Be sure that you follow the advice in Chapter 9 on Interviews, and keep up with the news during interview season);
- How would you handle (theoretical problem or issue)?
- What issues concern you the most?
- Who is your favorite jurist, and why?
- What is your least favorite U.S. Supreme Court holding?
- I see from your resume . . . (be *thoroughly* conversant with *every line* of it).
- Which other judges have you applied to, why, and who else you've interviewed with; (don't say something like "all the liberal judges" or "all of the conservative judges"; judges shy away from clerks with ideological axes to grind)? Assure the

judge that if (s)he makes you an offer, you'll take it. As one judge points out, "I ask this to see if I'll get a prompt answer when I make an offer."

- What do you intend to do after the clerkship?

- Why do you want *this* job? There are two key elements to address: stating why you want to clerk, and why you want *this* clerkship. While your answers should be your own, common reasons include wanting to advance your legal education, your interest in learning about the judicial process, or your desire to get a great background for being a litigator (good for a trial level clerkship) or a law professor (for whom judicial clerkships are almost *de rigueur*). Concerning this particular judge, your answer can reflect your research; "I've heard from prior clerks that ..." "I understand that people who clerk for you have the opportunity ..." "From your published opinions ..." "I made a point of coming to your courtroom to see you work ..."

- Do you think a one-year term is long enough to make the job worthwhile?

- How far do you think you've progressed in developing your writing skills—or—on a scale of 1 to 10, how do you rate your writing ability?

- Tell me about a time when you've had to juggle multiple tasks under tight deadlines? (This is especially popular with trial court judges)

- Do you like to write? (The answer better be a hearty "Yes." Prospective judicial clerks have torpedoed their chances with answers like "It is a love-hate relationship" and "I sometimes find it very frustrating" and "It's too lonely for me.")

- Can you work without close supervision?

- What judges have you particularly admired because of style, substance, or ideology?

- How important to you are the political views of the judge? (For reasons we discussed earlier in choosing judges based on political ideology, ideally you can honestly answer that they are not important.) One judge had a student tell him, "I believe most people are wrongly convicted." As the judge commented, "You can't do this job with that attitude."

- How conversant are you with the significant current decisions of the U.S. Supreme Court? Do you read *U.S. Law Week?* (A bit of a minefield. If you say "Yes," you may well be quizzed about a recent significant decision. You can always say that you try to be, law school studies permitting. And with *Law Week,* you can always note that if you *don't* read it, you can still download Supreme Court cases from the web.)

- Which newspapers do you read regularly?

- What was the last non-legal book that you've read?

- What qualities do you have that will make you a valuable law clerk? (As in any job interview and as we discussed in Chapter 9, this is a combination of your research into the judge and finding what (s)he values in clerks, and three traits that you genuinely have);

- Tell me about the courses (grades, professors) you have had in law school. (Highlights only! But if you learn in your research that the judge knows a professor of yours, mention that professor favorably);

- "I see you have experience advocating for X (e.g., prosecutor, public defender). Could you evaluate cases impartially for me?

- Do you prefer to work with others or independently?

- How would you handle a situation in which you and I disagreed about the proper resolution of an issue or case? (As one judge pointed out, "I ask students, 'If we ever disagree on a case and I write in opposition to your memo, will you be upset about it?' If there's even the slightest bit of hesitation, they won't work out. Some people think they're always right, that *they* should be the judge. That just won't work.")

- What are your interests outside of law school?

At the risk of making you shudder, your interview may even include a writing assignment. Some judges are known to give prospective clerks an issue to research and then turn them loose in the library to come up with an answer.

You should also have questions to ask. Your questions, naturally, should show your interest in, knowledge about, and enthusiasm for, the job. Ask about:

- the judge's opinions in cases you've read;

- how the judge resolved the issues;

- what a typical day is like for the judge's clerks;

- the judge's favorite case ever and what (s)he liked about it;

- the most challenging aspect of being a judge;

- contact with clerks that the judge has;

- the judge's most difficult decision ever and why;

- what the judge looks for in clerks;

- what the judge's clerk's primary responsibilities are;

- how they've found the transition from X work to being a judge, *if they're new to the bench;*
- the judge's favorite clerk ever and what stood out about him/her.
- "inside skinny"; you can ask "I understand that clerking involves X, but is there anything specific about the way your chambers operates that I should know?"

Tailor these questions to your own personality. For instance, with the "favorite clerk" question, if you've got a colorful imagination you would probably come up with something like, "If you were walking along and found a magic lantern, and a genie popped out and told you that you could have the perfect clerk, what would that clerk be like?"

If you read an interview with the judge in a legal publication, you can pick up the thread of those questions and follow up. It shows that you've done your research!

Also, if the judge asks you substantive legal questions, you might want to ask one of your own. You could, for instance, ask how the judge's decision in a given case might be affected by a subsequent Supreme Court ruling. There are two things to consider in asking this kind of question: One, don't ask questions about issues you can't discuss intelligently. It's the problem I always have in Paris. I can learn how to ask for something in French, but the problem is, they always *answer* in French, and then I'm sunk. So if you bring up a legal issue, make sure you have your feet under you first! Second, some judges don't like substantive interviews. That's why you wait for them to ask you a substantive question before you do the same in return.

You'll also probably interview with the judge's current clerk(s). You need to have questions for that situation, as well. You can ask:

- What's a typical day like for you?
- How much do you interact with the judge?
- What's the most challenging aspect of your job so far?
- How has this clerkship affected your career goals?
- What are the judge's greatest strengths and weaknesses?

The moral here is this: while interview length and structure vary form judge to judge and staff to staff, from a casual chat to the intellectual equivalent of a body cavity search, your approach should be the same: you've got to prepare yourself as best you can, dig up whatever information you can about the judge, and then go in, take a deep breath, smile, relax, and be your friendliest self! As one former judicial clerk points out, "Everything judges look for is a personality fit. Will this person fit in with the judge, with the other clerks? That's the main issue in the interview. If there's a fit, it'll be a great experience. If there isn't . . . you don't want the clerkship."

7. FOLLOW UP

Send a thank you note right away, to the judge, clerk(s), secretary/assistant, and anyone else you met with during the interview process. We talk about those in detail in Chapter 7 on Correspondence.

After that, if you don't hear anything for three weeks, call the current clerk or secretary—your choice—and say you're still interested, and ask when a decision will be made. This phone call might give you the chance for a casual chat, and if that comes up, take advantage of it! Judges tend to rely very heavily on the opinions of people who work for them, and any good word in your favor can only help your cause. Use the opportunity to restate your enthusiasm for the clerkship, and ask if there's anything further you can provide . . . and wind up by saying that you hope to get the chance to work with the person you're talking to.

Incidentally, if after interviewing you decide that you don't want the job, remove yourself—gracefully—from consideration right away. One student talked about interviewing with a judge who disdained domestic violence, saying that it was generally the woman's fault. The student said, "I worked at a battered women's shelter, and I just couldn't have disagreed with her more. The thought of working with this woman turned my stomach. Although I didn't say anything at the interview, as soon as I got home I called her secretary and asked that I be removed from consideration. Ugh."

8. HOW TO HANDLE OFFERS AND ACCEPTANCES

You need to know that if a judge is going to make you an offer, it's likely to be speedy—perhaps even at your interview—and there won't be much flexibility in response time. Some judges will make "exploding offers"—that is, they'll expect an immediate response. Others will give you twenty-four hours.

This poses a real dilemma for you, if you happen to get an offer from a judge who isn't your first choice. Why? Because judges talk. If you turn down one judge in a district or circuit, they'll pass that along and it will diminish your chances of getting offers from others. On top of that, it'll hurt your school's reputation.

What can you do about this? Not a whole lot. You *may* try to say that you have to check with your spouse (if you have one), or try another (valid) reason for delaying a day or so. You can always say how delighted you are to receive the offer, and you'd like to think about it overnight if that's all right with the judge. Promise you'll call tomorrow.

With that twenty-four hours, call the other judges you *haven't* heard from since you interviewed with them, tell them you've received an offer, tell them you're still interested in clerking for them and ask if they've made a decision. Either they'll tell you you're out of the running (hey—at least it's a resolution), or they may be prodded into making you an offer since they know it's now or never.

If they tell you they haven't made a decision yet but you're still in the running, you're out of luck, I'm afraid. Experts agree that it's a bad idea to turn down a judge when you have no concrete basis for doing so. Of course, you shouldn't apply for a clerkship with any judge you really wouldn't want to work for, but I've told you that already. Face it: a judicial clerkship with a judge you really like, even if (s)he's not your first choice, is still a really sweet gig.

Incidentally, when the happy day comes when you accept a clerkship offer, it's customary to withdraw all of your other applications immediately. If you've had other interviews, call those judges' chambers; if you haven't, a letter is appropriate. It's not an Easter egg hunt, you know—once you've got your clerkship, bow out of the game right away!

* * * CAREER LIMITING MOVE * * *

Student from an elite school, interviews with a federal judge and receives an offer on the spot. She responds, "I'm waiting for Judge so-and-so to get back to me. Can you wait 24 hours for a decision?"

The judge immediately withdraws the offer, contacts Judge so-and-so, who is also incensed and turns down the student, as well.

9. WHAT IF THE JUDGE IS ABDUCTED BY ALIENS AFTER YOU'VE ACCEPTED AN OFFER WITH HIM/HER?

I'm kidding. I doubt *that's* ever happened. But sometimes issues do come about after you've accepted an offer. Sometimes the judge is appointed to a higher court, and opts for hiring new clerks; sometimes the judge loses an election and has to go back to being an ice cream man; sometimes the judge retires, or . . . dies. *Then* what?

There are a couple of options. First, try to get some help from the judge (except in the case of death, in which case help is only available through a séance). Ask directly if the judge knows about other clerkship opportunities. After all, it's not your fault you're in this fix! Another option is to find out the identity of the judge's successor, and approach that person for a clerkship. You can also try the advice in 10, directly below, about other options.

10. HOW TO TRY AGAIN IF AT FIRST YOU DON'T SUCCEED

What if, despite your best intentions, you didn't make it the first time out of the gate. You didn't get a clerkship. Don't give up! There are a few steps that Debra Strauss advises you to take:

a. **Reevaluate your application and job search process**. Sit down with a counselor at Career Services and review what you did, painful as that might be, to see if there are any obvious glitches you can remedy. Ask for a mock interview if you think things fell apart at that stage. In other words, make sure everything you sent and said was as smooth as it can be.

b. **Consider other options and courts**. As you know from our discussion of courts and the on-line research materials at your disposal, there's no excuse for limiting your search.

c. **Research newly-confirmed judges**. There are new judges all the time, and they all need clerks. This "fresh meat" may prove to be fertile territory for you.

d. **Remember that some clerking vacancies open up late because people change their minds and opt out**. It's worth keeping an open mind, and making sure that your last contact with judges you really want to work for includes the line, "While of course I'm disappointed I'm not going to be working with you, if circumstances change I hope you'll consider me again." Do what you can, whether via someone in the judge's chambers whom you've befriended or through professors or Career Services, to keep your ears open for late-breaking possibilities.

*

Appendix
Web and Hard Copy Resources for Judicial Clerkships

Web resources for judicial clerkships:

Salaries: Federal courts: http://www.opm.gov; judicial clerks are paid on the JSP scale, which are equivalent to the GS scales.

State courts: http://www.vermontlaw.edu/career (get the password from your Career Services Office)

Contact information for all federal judges: Symplicity (available through your Career Services Office). Find the clerkship database under the tab CLERKSHIP.

Biographies of judges:

Legal Directory of Judges: Westlaw, WLD–JUDGE (all state and federal judges)

Court websites

Federal Judges Biographical Database: www.fjc.gov/history/home.nsf

Links to court web sites:

www.courts.net/index/html

www.ncsc.dui.us/courts/sites/courts.htm

Federal law clerk information system: https://lawclerks.ao.uscourts.gov/

Provides very detailed information about the clerkships each federal judge has available, application deadlines for each judge. *Note that not all federal judges post their openings on this system.* One helpful entry on this site is judges who do *not* hire clerks, which can be helpful in avoiding sending materials to judges who won't hire you no matter what.

State court websites, including some contact information for state court judges:

National Center for State Courts has links to many of them: www.ncs online.org

Federal and state clerkship opportunities:

Westlaw: WLD–Clerk database. *Caution: experts suggest this is not updated frequently, so it's not a comprehensive list)*

Judges who anticipate clerkship openings:

Lexis: CAREER; JCLERK. (Searchable by judge name, court, or by law school or undergraduate name)

Judicial vacancies and nominations: Great for getting clerkships in a hurry, since newly-appointed judges need clerks right away.

http://www.uscourts.gov/judicialvac.html (maintained by the Federal Judicial Center).

For finding new nominees:

http://www.law.umich.edu/currentstudents/careerservices/nomdb.htm (maintained by the University of Michigan Law School)

http://www.law.yale.edu/outside/scr/library/nom/index.asp   (maintained by Yale Law School)

For nominations and confirmations:

http://judiciary.senate.gov/nominations.cfm

For openings with new judges who post opportunities with the Federal Law Clerk Information System: http://www.uscourts.gov, click on "Employment," which takes you to OSCAR.

Hard copy resources for judicial clerkships:

Judicial Yellow Book (bios of all federal judges and state appellate judges)

Federal Yellow Book (for contact information for administrative law judges)

The American Bench (bios of all federal and state judges)

Almanac of the Federal Judiciary (federal judges, including media and attorney assessments of them)

BNA's Directory of State and Federal Courts, Judges and Clerks (includes state court structures)

NALP Federal and State Judicial Clerkship Directory (includes responses to clerkship questionnaires sent to federal and state judges. Listings include application procedures, current clerks, and other information.)

Federal-State Court Directory

In addition, let your fingers do the walking! Nothing stops you from calling judges' chambers for information.

Shout outs for materials excerpted in this chapter to the following law schools: George Washington, American, Hastings, University of Connecticut, Mercer, and Catholic.

Special thanks to Debra Strauss and Kristin Waller for their contributions to this chapter.

Chapter 26
Do the Right Thing: Public Interest

"Never doubt that a small group of people can change the world. In fact it's the only thing that ever has." Margaret Mead

"Be the change you wish to see in the world." Gandhi

"We make a living by what we get. We make a life by what we give." Winston Churchill

"If you want to lift yourself up, lift up someone else." Booker T. Washington

I don't have statistics to back it up, but my guess is that a public interest career would make more law students happy than anything else they could do with their law degree. I talk to law school graduates who do all kinds of things, and sometimes they have jobs they like very much, but the people who seem the most devoted to their careers are the public interest lawyers. Because there's a lower profit motive than there is with many kinds of jobs, people who go into public interest work tend to be more dedicated to what they're doing, and dedicated people are more likely to be happy. One public interest lawyer—a young woman who helped battered women in Africa—said to me, "All of the people I graduated from law school with question why they're doing what they're doing. They're all making so much more money than me. But I tell them, 'Represent one battered woman, and you'll never question what you're doing again. You'll realize why you went to law school in the first place. Your whole life makes sense.'"

I talked to a Legal Aid lawyer in her sixties, and asked her, "Do you ever think about retiring?"

She responded, "Hell, no! I figure I've got at least another thirty good years of work left in me."

I don't hear anybody, *anybody,* in any other area of the law talk that way!

Whether or not public interest will make *you* happy is, of course, another matter. In this chapter, we'll explore public interest, from talking about its benefits, to discussing the kinds of public interest jobs exist, to handling the money (or lack of money, more accurately) issue. We'll move on to talking about how you position yourself for a public interest career while you're still in school, and we'll wind up with talking about how you break into public interest work: cover letters, resumes, interviews, activities. In the Appendix at the end of this chapter, we'll talk about Fellowships.

Let's get started!

A. WHAT THE HECK *IS* "PUBLIC INTEREST," ANYWAY?

It's not as obvious as it seems! Who operates in the "public interest"? You could make that argument for a whole bunch of lawyers. As a general matter, you could call public interest the area that provides legal representation to people, groups, or interests that are historically underrepresented in our legal system. That's pretty broad, and it sweeps in lawyers who work for the government, since (in theory, anyway) everything the government does is in the public interest. There are a kajillion government jobs, and many of them are absolutely fantastic, whether working for federal agencies, the Justice Department, states attorneys' generals offices, city attorney offices, judges, or many others.

Other than government lawyers, you can break public interest jobs into a few general kinds of organizations:

- Non-profit organizations: There are two types: Issue-oriented groups (also called public interest law centers), and client-oriented groups.

    The issue-oriented groups often take cases in order to create legal policy and precedents that will affect people on a particular issue, like employment discrimination, housing, civil rights, and the environment. They may also do political lobbying, grass roots organizing, and similar activities.

    These organizations include the NOW Legal Defense and Education Fund, the National Center for Youth Law, EarthJustice, and the NAACP Legal Defense and Education Fund.

    Client-oriented groups, as the name suggests, target certain populations. Examples include Advocates for Children, the Gay Men's Health Crisis, and the Workplace Project.

- Legal Services/Legal Aid

    These are non-profit organizations whose primary mission is to provide free or low-cost representation to low-income clients.

The distinctions between the two organizations vary around the country. In some places the names are interchangeable. In others, one organization represents clients on civil matters (typically legal services) and the other covers criminal matters.

Legal services offices generally receive support from the Legal Services Corporation, a federally funded program that awards grants to organizations nationwide to provide legal services to low-income people. The practice areas generally include family law, consumer law, government benefits, bankruptcy, housing, and education law.

Some legal services agencies have a geographic focus, while others serve a particular group (e.g., the elderly, immigrants, the disabled).

- Criminal defense.

  In one guise or another, all states provide attorneys to criminal defendants who can't afford it. Some states employ attorneys themselves for this purpose; in other states, non-profits that contract with the state provide attorneys. Legal Aid is often the organization that provides these services.

  Depending on who employs them, the attorneys are either "public defenders" or "criminal defense legal aid attorneys."

- Public interest law firms.

  These are firms whose primary focus is not a profit motive; it is to help under-represented people or causes. Practice areas are varied; they may include plaintiff's side employment discrimination, unions, civil rights, criminal defense, environmental issues, disability rights, AIDS/HIV, lesbian/gay/transgender rights, prisoner rights, tenant advocacy, children and youth, and education law.

  These firms support their work through contingency and statutory attorney's fees. Clients are generally represented regardless of their ability to pay.

  Note that very few law firms are pure public interest firms. Every firm does *some* level of *pro bono* work.

B.   Why You Should Consider a Public Interest Job

There are a bunch of good reasons to think about public interest. They include:

- Of all career goals, this is one you're likely to "just know." If you're the perfect public interest candidate, you're motivated by the desire to be dedicated to a cause. The idea of shifting around money between large companies is anathema to you. You probably took part in community activities in college and perhaps even before. Your parents might have been activists. Many public interest lawyers "always knew" it's what they were drawn to. (That's not everyone, of course. Some public interest lawyers fall into it because they're inspired by a friend or classmate. But the 'I was born that way' model is more common.)

- "Psychic income." Fulfillment. Whatever you call it, it's the feeling you get from doing what you truly think is a good thing to do. You're representing the "good guys," you leave work feeling pumped about what you've done for other people. It's the hallmark of public interest lawyers. As a public defender says, "They don't call us 'the best lawyers money can't buy' for nothing."

- The ability to make a difference. In many public interest jobs you're working directly with people whose lives you impact in a major way.

- Autonomy. There tend to be few layers of management in public interest organizations, so you have a lot of control over your work.

- Immediate responsibility. In many public interest positions, you'll find yourself in court almost immediately. They don't have clients insisting on being represented by "partners" with years of experience under their belts. You get to appear in court "often in the first month," reports one public interest lawyer. "It's exhilarating, terrifying, exciting . . . you get trained, of course, but you get to use your skills immediately. I have classmates from law school at large firms who are lucky if they get to see the inside of a courtroom for the first five years. I'm there all the time."

- Opportunity to refine your lawyerly skills. There's no better way to get great skills than *using them constantly*. In public interest, you do exactly that.

- The hours are typically very reasonable. As we discuss in interviewing, below, it's a mistake to bring this up with public interest employers, but the fact remains that the life tends to be very manageable. If you're interested in work-life balance, if you have children or other outside-of-work responsibilities, it's a great alternative.

- The hours are often flexible. Part-time schedules are not uncommon. While lawyers in firms can work their way to a flexible or part-time schedule, it's the exception to the rule.

- Because there's no profit motive, you avoid ever having to bring in business *and* you often find your employer will be more receptive to your changing specialties; after all, they won't be losing money on you as you become efficient in another area.

- You're part of a like-minded community. Having colleagues who share your views and dedication makes your workplace a pleasure.

- Of course, there are downsides as well. They include:

- Money. Money. Money. While you might make more than you expect, there's no way the money competes with many private section legal jobs.

- The work can be emotionally draining. As one former public interest lawyer points out, "I got too involved with my clients' lives. They were often in such terrible straits that I found myself trying to take care of them, helping with their kids, their relationships. It can eat you alive if you're not the kind of person who can balance involvement in your work with a certain emotional distance."

- Fewer frills. You'll have a lean support staff, you won't have state of the art computers, and you'll often have low-cost offices. If you have to see mahogany hallways when you enter work, public interest isn't for you!

- It may not be where your sympathies lie. I had a roommate once who actually said, "I don't get all the sympathy for poor people. It's their own fault." Perhaps not a born public interest lawyer. It could well be that your core motivators don't mesh with public interest work; if your heart races at the thought of money and prestige, check out the chapter on large law firms, Chapter 23.

C.   COMMON MISCONCEPTIONS ABOUT PUBLIC INTEREST WORK

- **Public interest isn't the place you go to "find God."**

  Many students are drawn to public interest believing it's a calling. It's great to be drawn to work you find emotionally fulfilling, but remember, it's *work*. If you tell a public interest employer that you're interested in the work they do because you seek emotional and spiritual fulfillment, you perhaps aren't showing the knowledge of the practicalities of the job that will convince them to hire you.

- **"I can move over to public interest after I've spent a couple of years making big money."**

  You can, and people do, but it's not that easy. The reason is that you *have* to show your commitment to public interest work, and if you've been shuffling money around in corporate transactions for a couple of years, you're going to have a hard time proving that. If, instead, you've volunteered your time and learned some useful, practical skills in your practice, you're on the right track. Also, if you plead your case well—that you always wanted to do public interest, that you've had to work to pay off some student loan debt before you could take reduced pay, that you've paid off loans and lived frugally—you might strike a nerve.

- **"Public interest lawyers are a bunch of liberals."**

    No! Remember, public interest work involves representing causes, and some causes are ones you'd consider conservative, like right-to-life.

- **"Public interest work and *pro bono* work are the same thing."**

    Nope. Public interest work, as we've already learned, involves representing people, groups or interests historically underrepresented in our judicial system. *Pro bono* work is *volunteer* legal work that attorneys in any field do in an effort to serve the public interest. So all *pro bono* work is public interest, but public interest work isn't necessarily done on a *pro bono* basis.

D. WHAT'S OUT THERE: WEB RESOURCES

Two points up front: Of course use Lexis and Westlaw. On top of that, check local bar association web sites (via Google). They often provide directories of public interest employers. With that in mind, here are a bunch of other resources you'll find useful:

www.PSLawNet.org (As we discuss shortly, PSLawNet is a great source for opportunities in public interest, both in school and post-graduate.)

Harvard Law School Guides: www.law.harvard.edu/students/opia/planning/pig1.php. (The Harvard handbook called "Serving the Public: A Job Search Guide, Volume 1. Has more than 2,000 public interest/public sector employers. Searchable by focus and location.

www.pslawnet.org (NALP's *Federal Legal Employment Opportunities Guide;* describes federal jobs and has a comprehensive list of federal agency web sites.)

www.equaljusticeworks.org (home page for Equal Justice Works. Includes links to other public interest sites)

www.tlpj.org/search.cfm (web site for The Trial Lawyers for Public Justice. Has more than 2,000 lawyers' associations, online legal resources and public interest groups, including nonprofit resources and advocate contacts.)

www.nlg.org (home page for the National Lawyers Guild, an association of attorneys concerned with social justice. Has useful links to other organizations, as well.)

www.nlada.org (home page of National Legal Aid & Defender Association)

www.essential.org (listing of nonprofit organizations around the country; great resource for summer internships)

www.nonprofitjobs.org (job openings, legal and non-law-related, with nonprofits. Searchable by employer name, salary, type of work, location)

www.ptla.org/links.htm (legal services organizations)

www.ptla.org/international.htm (international legal services organizations)

www.loc.gov/rr/news/fedgov.html (Library of Congress' Internet Resource Page, with links to federal government branches)

www.just-advocates.com (Offers a list of private public interest law firms)

www.idealist.org (The home page of Idealist: Action Without Borders. Searchable job board for thousands of public interest jobs, both volunteer and paid.)

www.wclawyers.org/wclPublications.html (Washington Council of Lawyer's *Registry of Summer Public Interest Opportunities,* focusing on opportunities for law students looking for public interest work in DC.)

www.rcjobs.com (home page of Roll Call, a newspaper focused on Capitol Hill, which lists legal and policy jobs openings)

www.ecojobs.com (requires subscription; check with Career Services to see if your school has one. This site features current job openings in environmentally-oriented careers.)

www.internships-usa.com (requires school subscription; check with Career Services at school. This site has contact information for organizations that offer internships for students, in both legal and non-legal fields.)

www.ecoemploy.com (features environmentally-oriented job postings. Searchable by state and categories (e.g., government, firms, non-profits, companies).)

www.ejobs.org (environmental jobs and careers)

www.environmentalcareer.info (Environmental Career Center's home page. Has job postings with all kinds of organizations. Can post resumes here.)

www.eco.org (home page of the Environmental Careers Organization. Has a selection of paid internship opportunities with both governmental and private public interest employers.)

www.envirolink.org (features a directory of environmental organizations.)

www.sustainablebusiness.com/jobs (The "Green Dream Jobs" home page. Environmentally-oriented employers post job openings here. Also has links to other relevant websites.)

www.hcn.org/unclassifieds.jsp (The bi-weekly newspaper "High Country News." Has a national resource and public land focus for the Western part of the country. Environmental non-profits out West post job openings here.)

www.lta.org/resources/ltjobs.htm (job openings for non-profit land trusts and land conservancies, courtesy of The Land Trust Alliance.)

E.   Handling the Money Thing

"The only people who think money buys happiness don't have money."
   David Geffen

Money is an issue for public interest work. There's no way around it. You'll make a financial sacrifice to pursue work you find incredibly meaningful. But you know what? If it's what you want to do—*it's worth it.*

Money ain't everything. If you ever want to be miserable, take a job *just* because it pays a lot. That'll suck. As Orson Welles said in the classic movie *Citizen Kane,* "It's not hard to make a lot of money ... if money is all you want."

The fact is, you can have tons of fun on less dough. If you look at the greatest times of your life so far, I'll bet not one of them had to do with the most *expensive* time you had. Travel expert Arthur Frommer's credo is that the less money you spend when you travel, the more fun you'll have. I know one of my best trips so far was a few years ago, when I helped a girlfriend move from Connecticut to Vegas. We drove cross-country, with a vow never to spend more than $5 on a meal or $20 on a hotel. It was a *riot.* At the other end of the spectrum are friends of my parents. The assistant to one of these guys told me, "I'm setting up a trip to Egypt for [this guy and his wife] and another couple. You know what they do? They fly to a place, they get a limousine and a driver, and they drive around and look at the sights ... and they *never get out of the limo.* They look out through the windows, and then they go to the next place. It costs them a fortune ... but really!!" Money does *not* equal fun. Or happiness. Or anything other than, I don't know. More bling.

Nonetheless, there are a few do's and don'ts to keep in mind about the money issue:

- DO realize that you may make more in public interest than you think. Some public interest jobs pay a lot more than students tend to think. They also offer great benefits. In my state, Connecticut, public defenders are on *exactly the same pay scale* as prosecutors and judges, and it's pretty handsome, let me tell you. So don't assume you'll be poor as a church mouse if you pursue your public interest dream.

- DO see if your law school has a loan forgiveness program. Many do, so that students can pursue public interest jobs that would otherwise have been out of reach financially. Also check to see if the job you take will allow you to defer your student loan payments for at least a few years; that can give you the opportunity to allow your salary to grow a bit before you have to start making payments.

- DO create a budget to see how much money you really need. Be honest about your threshold of pain. You don't *need* anything. You don't need a new car, you don't need to live in a certain neighborhood, you don't need expensive clothes, and you don't have to eat at expensive restaurants. You may want to, and you may feel you deserve them (and maybe you do). But be aware that every lifestyle choice you make will impact the salary you can start with, and trust me on this one—a job that makes you happy is one of the greatest gifts you can give yourself. You can generate a budget with help from counselors at your Career Services Office. You may be surprised that if you see in black-and-white what your needs are, they may be lower than you think.

- DO minimize your law school borrowing. We've all heard about the $50 pizza; that is, that's how much it costs if you use student loan money to buy the pizza in the first place. There's also the $4,000 Starbucks cappuccino; that's how much it costs to pay back a $3–a-day weekday coffee habit.

- DO structure your repayment options in a way that's most palatable to you. If you want to spread out your payments over many years, that will dramatically lower your initial payments and allow you to take a much lower-paying job at the outset. But the flip side of that is while other people are buying houses and pursuing their post-student-loan financial lives you'll be soldiering on with loan payments. It all depends on what works best for you.

- DON'T overlook *any* scholarship possibilities. You may think your grades don't qualify you for scholarships, or you may only be familiar with a few of the ones you *can* get. Don't cheat yourself! Bar associations, special interest groups, and civic groups all have scholarships, as do many other organizations. I had a law school classmate with *strictly* mediocre grades who had much of his law school paid for by a scholarship for students of Ukrainian descent. His Ukrainian-ness had never been very obvious to me, but he laughed when he told me that to qualify you only needed to be one-eighth Ukrainian, and he was *that*. The point here: talk to your financial aid director at school to discover sources of obscure scholarships.

- DO remember that not all summer public interest jobs are volunteer. There are paid gigs, and even for ones that are unfunded, you can often get funding through a summer fellowship. We talk about that in the Appendix at the end of this chapter.

- DO take part in writing competitions. The prizes for these puppies are often *several thousand dollars*. As we discussed in Chapter 10 on activities, writing competitions are notoriously sparsely entered. Take half an hour a day to poop out an entry. The prolific 19th century novelist Anthony Trolloppe wrote dozens of books, while working full time at the British Post Office and raising approximately five dozen children, by writing early in the morning before he went to work. If you take a page from his book—pardon the pun—you can see that you can accomplish a lot with time you'll hardly miss. And it can help fund your dream.

- DO live cheap in school. You've probably heard the old chestnut, "Live like a lawyer while you're still a student, and you'll live like you're a student when you're a lawyer." Go to school functions that offer free food. I notice when I visit law school campuses to talk about *Guerrilla Tactics* that the attendance at my seminar doubles when there's a buffet offered, so clearly students are taking my advice on the free food gig. If you schedule it well, you might not have to buy groceries until you graduate! Also consider sharing an apartment, avoiding "gratuitous shopping" (my husband's term), buy clothes at consignment stores (that's what I *still* do), and cook cheap stuff. You'll be stunned how much money you can save making small changes in your life!

* * * SMART HUMAN TRICK * * *

Law school student at a New England law school. She desperately wants to break into public interest work, but her dream job pays $40,000 and her student loan payments will be too high for her to afford to take it. Heartbroken, she turns down the offer.

But then she comes up with a plan.

She goes to a major city and takes a temp job, working crazy hours to pay off as much of her debt in a hurry as she possibly could. Between September and December, she managed to pay off *forty thousand dollars* of debt. With her debt hacked back, she figures if she can make $50,000 a year she can make a go of it.

She reapproaches her dream employer and asks them if the job is still available. It is. She explains that she's whittled down her debt, and ask if there's any flexibility in the starting pay. They are able to increase it to $45,000, and she negotiates quarterly reviews of her work, with a potential of making a $5,000 raise after one year. That takes her to her $50,000 threshold . . . and she takes the job.

F. How To Position Yourself for a Public Interest Career While You're Still in School

1. Activities

- **Read Chapter 10 for a wide variety of activities applicable to all legal jobs, including public interest positions.** You'll get dozens of ideas there; in this section, we'll focus exclusively on public interest-oriented ideas.

- **You can't start early enough in building a public interest "campaign."** Because it's so important to demonstrate a commitment to a public interest career, the sooner you start the better. (In fact, you may already have valuable volunteer experience in college . . . or before.)

- **Clinical programs.**

    If you did only one thing to boost your public interest career, this would be it. Taking part in a clinical program has so many benefits, including:

    - The ability to see for yourself what public interest jobs are like. There's no better way to figure out if you'll like something than experiencing it yourself.

    - You'll get letters of recommendation from people whose opinions really count.

    - You hone the skills you'll use on the job. As San Francisco's Jacqueline Ortega points out, "Don't forget skills development! Most public interest agencies expect recent graduates to represent clients almost immediately and don't have large resources for training."

    - You'll meet people who can put you onto great opportunities when you graduate.

- As I have stated numerous times in this book, do a PSLawNet project. PSLawNet is an enormous database of public interest organizations, offering everything from short-term volunteer and paid internships to full-time jobs and pro bono activities. It is searchable by interest and location. You can complete a PSLawNet project in a week, and it provides you not just a resume item and skills, but also great contacts. I can't recommend PSLawNet highly enough. You'll find PSLawNet on-line at www.pslawnet.org.

- Ask at Career Services for names of alums with public interest jobs. Contact them for informational interviews. (We discuss informational interviews in Chapter 10.)

- Ask at Career Services to see if any professor is writing about a public interest topic. Ask the professor if you can be a research assistant.

- Write an article on a public interest topic and submit it for publication in a public interest-oriented publication.

- Serve on the board of directors of a community or nonprofit organization.

- Participate in school organizations that involve public interest events (e.g., bringing in speakers on public interest topics). You can also bring in speakers by volunteering at Career Services.

- Go to relevant Career Fairs, *especially* the "big one": the Equal Justice Works Annual Career Fair and Conference held in Washington, DC every Fall. It has incredible speakers and workshops and attracts hundreds of public interest employers. See www.equal justiceworks.org for more information.

    There are other conferences around the country, as well. New York has the Public Interest Legal Career Fair every Spring, which attracts upwards of 200 employers from around the country. It offers interviews for summer and full-time jobs, information tables, and panel presentations. Ask at your Career Services Office at school for information about it.

There's also the Robert M. Cover Public Interest Retreat open to students from around the country. It's held in March in New Hampshire under the auspices of Boston University. The Retreat gives you the chance to interact with public interest lawyers and like-minded students from everywhere. Contact your Career Services Office for more information.

- Go to every seminar and hear every public interest-related speaker you can. Talk with them afterwards, share your interest in public interest work, and ask for a business card.

- Join the National Lawyers Guild, a national public interest organization. www.nlg.org.

- Volunteer to work in the community on public interest projects that attract you. Best of all, volunteer to work with the organization you'd like to work for post-graduation; *many* people have broken into public interest law that way. As one public interest lawyer points out, "When positions open up, we hire people we know."

- Read newspapers, magazines and bar publications. When you read about people doing things that sound interesting to you, contact them for informational interviews.

- Go to conferences in your chosen area. Better yet, volunteer to help out; you'll meet tons of useful people who might put you onto opportunities.

- Consider a summer fellowship. Check with Career Services for funding opportunities available to you.

2. CLASS SELECTION

It depends on your specific public interest focus. While there's no particular focus that's necessary for many public interest careers, if you intend to go into policy or nonprofit management, experts suggest it helps to take classes in tax, labor law, corporations, antitrust and accounting.

If your school does have public interest-focused classes, take them and get to know the professors; professors often have contacts in the legal community and will put you onto them.

Also, if you find that a professor has a background in work that interests you, consider taking a class from that professor. If you do well, you'll have a great reference. Even if you don't take classes from these professors, seek them out and ask them about their work, state your interest in it, and ask for their advice about breaking into it.

G. Breaking Into Public Interest Work: Cover Letters, Resumes, Interviews and More

1. Be a "Known Quantity"

The activities we discussed earlier in this chapter, as well as the activities in Chapter 10, all let public interest employers see your dedication and your skills. They're the best possible way to get your foot in the door.

2. Research!

Through both people and on-line materials. The #1 beef public interest employers have with job seekers is feeling as though they're getting a generic letter. "I don't want to hear that you're interested in public interest work," says one employer. "I want to hear what you know about us, why you want *us.*"

3. Consider Creating Your Own Job

It may well be that the job you get is one you make up for yourself. There are a couple of options. You can come up with your own project and approach funding organizations to support you; in other words, create your own public interest organization! Another option is to think about organizations that interest you, and how you might provide services to their clients. You wouldn't be the first person to get into public interest work this way!

* * * SMART HUMAN TRICK * * *

Female law student targets the YMCA as an employer. She reports, "I knew that they wanted to help underprivileged people in the community. I offered to give legal advice to underprivileged women. I wrote up a proposal about how much it would cost and what I would do. They took me up on it!"

4. Keep an Open Mind

The precise job you thought you wanted might not open up, but something equally wonderful is out there for you. Get as broad experience as you can, via volunteering or part-time jobs, until things open up.

5. Consider Temping Until a Job You Want Opens up

Public interest jobs open up on a random basis. It may well be that your graduation doesn't coincide with an opening with the kind of organization(s) you're targeting. As Brooklyn's Joan King advises, "Hold on to your dream. Temp to pay the bills until a spot opens up."

* * * SMART HUMAN TRICK * * *

3L, California law school. He wants to work for a city office, but he has no luck. He contemplates interviewing with law firms instead, but decides to talk to a temp agency first. He takes on a few temporary positions for six months, keeping in touch with the hiring attorney of his choice employer in the meantime to let him know he's still interested in the job. When a position opens up, he gets the job.

6. Cover Letters

a. **Read Chapter 7 on Correspondence.** Everything there applies to public interest positions.

b. As is true for every cover letter, if someone referred you to the employer, mention that name *first*. ("Florence Nightingale of Nurses Without Borders recommended that I contact you ...")

c. Show a knowledge of, and *specific* interest in, the particular organization you're contacting. Tell them how the organization came to your attention. As one public interest lawyer comments, "I want to see why you want to do the work we do, not the experience you want to have!" Also, use the middle part of the letter to convey how your experiences and skills will benefit the employer.

d. Never address a letter to "Hiring Attorney" or "Sir or Madam." If you can't find the right name on-line, call the organization and ask who the addressee should be.

e. If your resume is business-oriented, your cover letter *must* explain why you're now looking at public interest.

f. Weave in relevant experience to prove your commitment to the organization's cause.

g. It's fine to tell a *brief* story about what drew you to the cause. Show your letter to your Career Services Office to make sure your story is told appropriately; you don't want to sound naïve about the work. As one public interest lawyer points out, "When I get a three-page cover letter that includes the line 'When I was sitting on a mountain top in Tibet, it suddenly struck me ...' I stop reading."

h. For volunteer positions, state your willingness to volunteer or that you've got an outside source of funding.

i. Don't mention class rank.

j. Don't refer to the employer as a "firm" (unless it is, in fact, a public interest law firm).

k. No puffery; don't make general statements about what an asset you would be to the organization.

l. As a general rule, keep the letter to one page *unless* you've got the experience to justify more.

m. Remember: your cover letter is the first writing sample an employer has. If they're going to trust you with writing briefs, they have to be comfortable with your letter!

7. **RESUMES**

a. The most important element of your resume is proving your commitment to what you want to do. Every facet of your experience that addresses it should move up on your resume. It need not be at the law school level; you can go back to college and beyond. For instance, if you want to be a child advocate, your summer camp counseling experience with children will be important, because it proves your commitment to working with children. If you've been politically involved, you can describe your political activities in a "political experience" section or include it with your community involvement. (Whether you mention candidates by name depends on whether the name helps your cause; if you're not sure, check with Career Services.) The same goes for volunteer work for religious organizations, which can be very relevant. Whether you mention the religious organization by name or make it more general depends, again, on your audience.

    If you *don't* have any "public-spirited" experience, that's OK. Get it starting now! Get involved in student groups and clinics to show your commitment.

b. If you have public interest-related experience, set it up in its own section, called "Public Interest Experience" or "Related Experience." This can include both volunteer and paid positions.

c. When you discuss your law school education, be sure that you highlight any clinical courses you've taken, any public interest-related substantive courses you've had, and any writing you've done on a public interest topic (you can separate this into a "Publications" section).

d. Highlight relevant skills learned in activities/jobs *outside* of public interest (counseling, advocating, brief-writing, and any other skills you learn about in researching the employer).

e. If you have fluency in other languages, highlight it with a "Languages" section on your resume. Language skill is particularly important in public interest work. Don't exaggerate your skills; if you're conversational, say it; if you can read it, say so. If you're fluent—of course, say that, too!

f. As is true of every legal resume, don't include an "Objective" or "Statement of goals" line.

8. **FOLLOW UP ON LETTERS**

Calling to follow up on a letter to an employer doesn't make you a pest. It shows your initiative, and that's a good thing. Unless a job posting specifically says No Phone Calls, call a week and a half or two after sending your resume and cover letter, say that you sent a letter on X date, and you're calling to follow up and see if you can set up an interview.

For more on follow ups, see Chapter 7 on Correspondence.

9. Interviews

a. **Read Chapter 9 on Interviews.** Everything in that chapter applies to public interest interviews, as well: research, questions to expect and to ask, and so on. The only note I would add has to do with wardrobe. Public interest lawyers have pointed out to me more than once that students tend to dress too casually for public interest interviews. Says one Legal Services lawyer, "Poor people want their lawyers to look like 'lawyers,' too." So dress the part: suit, neatly groomed hair, polished shoes. If you're convinced that that's *not* the way to dress for any particular interview, talk to someone at the office ahead of time for specific guidance on what to wear.

10. When You Receive a Job Offer . . .

Congratulations, incidentally! If you get an offer for the job you want the most, go ahead and accept, obviously. If it's not your first choice, here's what you do: thank them enthusiastically, tell them that you're very interested, and ask when they need an answer from you. You do *not* have to answer on the spot; most employers will give you a week or two.

Take this time to call your "higher" choices to let them know you received an offer, and ask them when they intend to make a decision. Hearing that someone else wants you will often jolly an employer into making you an offer, as well!

If you wind up turning down an offer, you need to remember that your reputation and that of your school is at stake. Do it politely, drench it with gratefulness for the offer, and do it by phone (at the very least). You can't e-mail it, and you can't leave a voice mail message; tell them you'll call back, and leave your phone number so they can call you. Turn down offers as soon as you know you won't accept them, to give them as much time as possible to find someone else. If you have to turn an offer down because you've gone through your budget in detail and you just can't afford it, tell them you hope that you'll have the opportunity to work with them in future.

And never, *ever* renege on an offer after you accept it. It's really, really bad for your reputation, and it hurts your school, too.

*

Appendix
Public Interest Fellowships

Summer Fellowships:

You can often fund a summer job in public interest with a summer fellowship. Some of these fellowships involve applying for a position first and then obtaining funding separately; others help place students, and still others will fund you with a particular agency. Plan early in the school year, and go to your Career Services Office to learn about funding opportunities specific to your school.

As a rule of thumb, you need to have a job in hand before you apply for fellowships to fund it. (Organizations understand the importance of funding, by the way, so they're all right with making their offers contingent on your ability to find funding somewhere else.)

To improve your chances of getting funding, consider the following:

- Make sure you show how the work you want to do will satisfy the funding entity's criteria. Explain your relevant professional and personal experience doing the work you want to do *or* serving the type of community you intend to serve.

- Be specific about what you intend to do. What kinds of activities will you undertake—research, providing training or service, providing technical assistance? What specific population will you serve?

- If you need to supply a budget, make it realistic. Research costs ahead of time.

- Have Career Services review your application.

Also, don't overlook less-obvious sources of funding. For instance, you can enter writing competitions for dough—the prizes are often very generous, and writing competitions normally get very few entrants. If you can write about a public interest topic or even the topic of your proposed fellowship, you're *way* ahead of the game. Check posters around school and ask at Career Services for upcoming writing competitions.

Post-graduate fellowships:

(This advice adapted from Hastings College of the Law)

Post-graduate fellowships give you a great opportunity to break into public interest work, and to work with public interest organizations who might not otherwise be able to afford to hire you or wouldn't consider an entry-level attorney. On top of that, you develop expertise in the area you choose, and you showcase your initiative and community involvement. Also, you get to meet people who will be very useful to you in your subsequent career.

A fellowship involves a financial grant to work for a year or two with a public interest/public sector organization (there are other organizations that host them as well, but we'll focus on the public interest/public sector ones). They are awarded for a whole variety of activities, including research, community activism, direct services, impact litigation, community economic development, and many, many others. It's kind of like "independent study" for grown-ups.

Fellowships often results in a permanent job with the sponsoring organization.

A. Types of fellowships:

There are several types. The two most common ones are fellowships that are funded by a third party, and fellowships that are funded by the host organization itself. There are others—for instance, academic fellowships that give you academic credit, international fellowships that allow for work abroad, "prestige" fellowships like the Fulbright and Rhodes, and law-firm-sponsored fellowships, where you typically work on *pro bono* matters. You can find out more about the others at Career Services. We'll confine our discussion to the first two. Let's talk about them separately:

1. **Fellowships funded by a Third Party a/k/a Project-based Fellowships:** This type of fellowship program consists of a student applicant, a sponsoring agency (e.g., Equal Justice Works, Skadden, Echoing Green), plus a host organization. A typical example of this type of fellowship would be an Equal Justice Works fellowship to fund a position and project at Communities for a Better Environment. These programs tend to have these characteristics in common:

   a. **You have to identify a host organization to host the work *and* a project to be funded.** The quality and credibility of the host organization are evaluated seriously by the funder, so it's important to choose selectively. It might be worthwhile to research organizations to find ones that have hosted fellows in the past; check also to see what kinds of projects have been funded at these organizations.

Specific factors a funding organization will look for in the host organization include: high quality staff and services, financial stability, and quality of training.

b. **You have to establish ties with the host organization before you submit your fellowship application.** You may even have interned there in the past. It's important to discuss your proposal closely with the host organization. Staff members there might even have suggestions for creating a truly unique proposal to meet a previously unfilled need, and will write letters of support for your project to include in the application. Proposals that would simply extend existing services are rarely funded.

c. **The term is usually more than a year,** typically two.

d. **You need to submit a formal application, which is pretty involved.** A project description, letters of support, a proposed budget ... you've got your work cut out for you. The funding organization will scrutinize your application closely to see how thorough it is and whether you've demonstrated ties to the community you propose to serve.

2. **Fellowships funded by the host organization:** Some fellowships are simply salaried positions at established organizations. It's like a one or two year contract lawyering position. There's no need to develop a program proposal or secure a sponsoring organization. Examples of these programs include the Hall & Associates Fellowship to work at their public interest firm, the Earthjustice Legal Defense Fund Fellowship, the Center for Reproductive Rights, and the Amnesty International Fellowship. The following characteristics tend to distinguish fellowships funded by a host organization:

a. **Generally no project proposal is involved; there is a preexisting program that the organization has designed.** It would behoove you, however, to research the organization and projects with which it's been involved. Check its website, and talk to Career Services, alums, and anyone they can put you onto.

b. **Candidates are evaluated on their commitment to, and "fit" with the organization, as well as demonstrated relevant past experience.** We talked about this in the body of this chapter.

c. **Generally the term of the fellowship is one to two years.**

d. **You submit standard job application materials, like a cover letter and resume.** The cover letter or personal statement should highlight those experiences that demonstrate a commitment to serve the organization, the targeted cause or the organization's client population.

e. **After the term of the fellowship is up, you pack your things and off you go** . . . unless a staff position opens up or the organization comes up with additional funding for you.

B. Nailing fellowships:

1. Start early!

While deadlines vary, it's never too early to get the fellowship wheels moving. Because you have to show a commitment to public interest, it'd be a good idea to get started, oh, say, *now*. (For deadlines on specific fellowships, check out www.pslawnet.org).

Let's talk about what you need to do:

a. **Research to figure out which kind of fellowship you want.**

Check out the resources listed below under "resources" . . . but that's not enough!

- Use "humint." Human intelligence. Talk to staff at sponsoring organizations *and* at the organizations you'd like to work for. Ask for guidance and suggestions, including current funding priorities and for current and former fellows to talk to.

- Go to Career Services and identify past fellowship recipients among alums from your school. Call them and ask for advice.

- Ask at Career Services for hard copy books of past successful fellowship applications.

- Read all available materials about the funding organizations you're considering. Pay careful attention to the purpose and goals of the funding organization and granting criteria (e.g., grades, experience, type of project, location of project, etc.). View that information as a job posting, and make sure that your application reflects it.

- Consider creating your own fellowship! Check out The Foundation Center Website (www.fdncenter.org) and The Idealist (www.idealist.org).

- Research past recipients and projects. The sponsoring organization will expect you to be familiar with what they've done before.

b. **The money issue:** Fellowships vary in what they pay. As a rule of thumb, they pay modestly to quite well, but the pay isn't the only thing to consider; they also generally offer benefits, and most of them will pay your student loans for the duration of your fellowship.

2. **Maintain a calendar with the differing deadline dates for your target fellowships noted clearly.** Fellowship

applications are involved; knowing when the deadlines are allows you to work backward and give yourself ample time to get all of the elements in order.

PSLawNet (www.pslawnet.org) also maintains a useful fellowship calendar. Consult it frequently to make sure you're on track.

3. **If your proposal involves a project, how to figure out what to do:**

There's a contemplating part to this, and a talking-and-research element. *(Adapted from Golden Gate University)*

a. **The contemplation questions** . . .

The more you know about yourself and your goals, the more easily you'll be able to convince a fellowship provider that you deserve it! Ask yourself:

- What kind of work would you like to do? Individually represent people? Build coalitions? Develop policy? Focus on impact litigation? Lobby?

- What measurable outcomes/goals would you like to achieve? Clients served, legislation proposed or enacted, advocates trained, specific changes to existing case law, coalition formed to address an issue?

- How is the project unique? What makes it necessary? How do you know the need exists?

- What in your background/interests makes you the person to do this project? What's your connection to it? How does it fit with your long-term career goals?

- Who do you want to work with? Who'll be good co-workers and/or mentors? Is there an organization that makes sense as a "partner"?

- Is your timeline realistic? Who do you need to develop relationships with to make your project succeed?

b. **The talking-and-research element** . . .

You don't have to do all the work yourself, you know. Make life easier by relying on other resources, like:

- Summaries of projects that fellowship sponsors have funded before.

- Look on-line at new developments in the area of the law that interests you, and read (or at least skim) any relevant law review articles.

- Talk with faculty members (like clinical professors and profs who teach public interest-related subjects) and practicing lawyers for ideas.

- Ask at Career Services for people you should talk to (like former fellowship recipients and public interest lawyers) for ideas.

4. **Writing your fellowship application.**

   a. **Read the application materials *extremely carefully* and follow the instructions to the letter!** You have to tailor each application to the particular requirements of the funding organization. Equal Justice Works, one of the largest providers of post-graduate fellowships, states that "One of the most common mistakes applicants make is failing to read carefully all of the application materials."

   b. **Make sure to convey your commitment to the cause.**

   c. **Show how your experiences make you well qualified to carry out your goals and action plan.** Think about your experiences broadly; as we discussed when we talked about Resumes for public interest positions, think about sharing experiences in college, both paid and unpaid work, professional *and* personal formulative experiences. That means that resumes for fellowships often exceed one page, and that's fine.

   d. **Read, reread, put it away and read it again.** Show your application to friends, faculty, family, Career Services, and staff at the host or sponsoring organization. You want to make sure your work is the best you have to offer.

   e. **If your application includes a program or project proposal:**

      1. **Make sure your proposal meets the funder's particular goals, preferences, objectives and requirements.** This is one of the most critical factors in a successful fellowship application. For instance, is the funder looking to support direct services or litigation? Does the funder prefer to sponsor unique projects? Projects that fill a gap in existing services? Urban programs? Rural programs? National projects? Community-based projects?

      2. **Think carefully about how you can demonstrate the importance, benefit, impact and value of the project you propose.** You'll need convincing evidence (rather than untested opinions) that the activities you propose will be effective. Pilot programs are particularly persuasive. In order to satisfy the funder about this, specifically outline the strategies you'll use to accomplish your objectives and the baseline you'll use for measuring the success of your project.

      3. **Be able to show that your project could not take place at the scope you propose *but for* the fund-**

ing you hope to receive. If you could do it for nothing, the funder won't be motivated to provide money for it.

4. **Look at prior successful proposals for guidance.** Identify them through the web resources we discuss below or through Career Services.

5. Specific components of fellowship applications.

As a rule of thumb, there are elements in common with any job application, and elements that are different. The "usual suspects" include a cover letter, resume, transcript, writing sample, and references.

Beyond that, bear in mind that the specific requirements of each fellowship will vary, and you need to follow the instructions for each. For instance, **fellowships that are mostly salary stipends usually require a personal statement rather than a lengthy independent project or program proposal. The following guidance is for most program or project proposals:**

a. **Abstract or summary:** As a general rule, you'll see this section only in lengthy proposals to third party funders. Similar to a summary of the argument, the abstract serves as an umbrella statement of your project and a summary of the entire proposal. It provides a brief statement of the problem or issue you hope to address and proposes your solution. It should also contain a brief statement about the host organization, including name, history, organizational structure, and purpose. Take that information from their web site.

b. **Introduction:** The introduction sets out the background of the project and what the project will accomplish in terms of target clients served, basic approach, and so on. Bear in mind that poorly stated goals or unrealistically ambitious goals will hurt your application. You'll want to state clearly the need your fellowship will address, and provide any facts or other evidence to support that need. Use compelling language in your application; be your own best advocate! As an example, Equal Justice Works in its application materials contrasts the following two proposals:

> **Not specific enough:** "I propose to work on consumer fraud issues in Los Angeles."

> **Just right:** "I propose to develop new litigation strategies to expose and stop home equity fraud against poor, disabled and elderly residents in Los Angeles."

When funders review the background for the project, they'll examine whether the application shows that you have a solid understanding of the legal and institutional problems facing the community you propose to serve. They also will need to see how your project fits into the structure of services already existing to serve the community.

c. **Program/project description:** This is the real nuts and bolts component of the application. This is the section the funders will rely on to determine the overall feasibility of your project in terms of goals, budgets, timetable, future financing and evaluation procedure.

- Explain exactly what you intend to do; as well as when, where and how you intend to do it. Describe the organizational structure and staff, facilities or other resources that will be part of your budget. In order to deal effectively with those issues, you'll need to provide a detailed time frame and concrete budget.

- You also might wish to discuss the prospects of future funding.

- Don't let the project description simply duplicate the information on your application form or in your letters of support. Funders say that applicants make a mistake by simply referring to the supporting documents for more information.

- It's often compelling if you can show how the Fellowship's initial support will be followed by institutional continuation of the project; funders like to know the ball won't be dropped when the fellowship ends.

d. **Letters of recommendation or support from the host organization:** The best letters are those that speak to your ability to carry out the project and the overall feasibility of your proposal. They will demonstrate the quality of your work and your personal strengths. Specific examples will be helpful.

In addition, try to have your references reflect the diversity of your experience (e.g., a letter from someone who can attest to your academic ability, a letter from a past work supervisor, and a letter from a clinical faculty member). To allow your references to comment directly on these subjects, give them a copy of your application as well as a resume if they aren't familiar with your relevant experience, or offer to sit down with them and talk about it.

Some funders request a letter from the host organization. In these letters, the funders are looking to see support for both you and your project. The most effective letters of support will evoke a spirit of cooperation and will indicate that you will receive effective training and supervision. There is generally no page limit for the letter of support from the host organization (which you usually write yourself), so some applicants use the support letter to amplify their project description or personal statement.

6. **Submit your proposal to more than one funding organization.** While they'll have somewhat different requirements, once you have your basic materials together it's easy to modify them for different organizations. You'll up your chances of being funded by approaching multiple funders.

7. **Consider locating your project away from the coasts to increase your chances of getting funded.** Equal Justice Works expressly encourages applications from people who want to work somewhere other than large coastal cities. Going to places that traditionally have had a hard time attracting attorneys is attractive to funding organizations. (Of course, if you've got a personal connection to a city, that improves your chances, no matter *where* the city is.)

C. Resources.

1. On-line:

-   PSLawNet (www.pslawnet.org); the fellowship corner provides a comprehensive list of fellowships, and deadlines for them. You can also get this in hard copy at Career Services.

-   Yale Law School's handbook for tips on fellowships: www.law.yale.edu/outside/pdf/Career_Development/cdo-FAT_public.pdf

-   Equal Justice Works (www.equaljusticeworks.org). Largest provider of post-graduate legal fellowships in America.

-   Public Interest Clearing House (www.pic.org), a wealth of information on fellowships and other public interest opportunities.

-   The Foundation Center (www.fdncenter.org), resource on private funding sources, with an emphasis on human services.

-   Echoing Green Foundation Fellowships (www.echoinggreen.org)

-   Skadden Fellowships (www.skadden.com)

-   Presidential Management Intern Program (www.pmi.opm.gov)

-   Georgetown University Law Center Clinical Fellowships (www.law.georgetown.edu/clinics/fellowships.html)

-   Ford Foundation Program Assistantships (www.fordfound.org)

-   Soros Foundation Fellowships (www.soros.org)

-   Idealist.org (www.idealist.org)

- Ashoka Fellowships for Social Entrepreneurs (www.ashoka. org/fellows/ashoka_fellow.cfm

- Center for Law in the Public Interest (www.clipi.org)

- Center for Reproductive Law and Policy (International Program Fellowship and Blackmun Fellowship) www.crlp.org/ ab_em_irrfellow.html and www.crlp.org/ab_em_black1.html

- Center for Human and Constitutional Rights (www.center forhumanrights.org)

- Earthjustice Legal Defense Fund (www.earthjustice.org)

- Environmental Law Institute (www.eli.org)

- Equal Rights Advocate Ruth Chance Fellowship (www.equal rights.org/about/rchance.asp)

- Fried Frank Fellowships (www.ffhsj.com/recruitment/ny_ fellowships.htm

- The John J. Gibbons Fellowship in Public Interest and Constitutional Law (www.gibbonslaw.com/gibbons/ community/fellowship.cfm)

- Human Rights Watch Fellowship (www.hrw.org/about/info/ fellows.html)

- Independence Foundation Public Interest Fellowship (www. independencefoundation.org/pdf/2002PFA.pdf)

- Institute for Current World Affairs (www.icwa.org)

- Juvenile Law Center Zubrow Fellowship (www.jlc.org/home/ work/fellowships.html)

- Lawyers Committee for Civil Rights Under the Law–George Lindsay Civil Rights Fellowship (www.lawyerscommittee.org/ jobs/aboutlccrul.html)

- Libel Defense Resource Center (www.ldrc.com/LDRC_Info/ ldrcjobs.html)

- National Consumer Law Center–Consumer Law Fellowship (www.nclc.org)

- Natural Resources Defense Council (www.nrdc.org.)

- Relman Civil Rights Fellowship (www.relmanlaw.com)

- Robert Bosch Foundation (www.cdsintl.org/fromusa/bosch. htm)

- Rockefeller Brothers Fund Fellowship in Nonprofit Law (www.law.nyu.edu/ncpl/main.html)

- U.S.AID Democracy Fellows (www.usaid.gov/about/ employment/fellows/fp_wldem.html)

2. Not on-line:

- People, people, people. More important than anything you can find on-line. Talk with Career Services, clinical professors, staff at any organizations with which you volunteer already for ideas about projects and advice about applications, as well as to find people who've successfully applied for fellowships before. Talk to *those* people about their experiences.

- Ask at Career Services to see if they have binders of successful proposals from alums. You'll find great inspiration in those.

- In hard copy: *The Harvard Law School Public Interest Job Search Guide.*

Shout outs for materials excerpted in this chapter: Fordham, Hamline, University of Minnesota, William Mitchell, Suffolk, Hastings, Golden Gate, Yale, Villanova

Chapter 27
Talking to Strangers
Freaks Me Out

. . .

Did you know that two-thirds of people consider themselves shy? I'm actually not sure that's the right number. But it's a *lot*. The fact is, most of us are intimidated by the thought of talking to strangers ... especially when the talk stems from your desire to get a job. In Chapter 10, when I talked about asking lawyers and alums for advice about your job search, we discussed how important it is to ask for things. If you're naturally a reserved person, that can be excruciating.

There's no question that extroverted people have an edge in their job searches. They interview well, they approach people with ease. Yet the irony is that shy people are often much better at work. Introverts focus better and concentrate more effectively than their more extroverted brethren. On top of that, you might be surprised to learn that most Fortune 500 CEOs are introverted. Research suggests that while extroverts have an edge getting into the first rung of management, when introverts do break through they progress better and more quickly. As recruiting coordinators tell me often, law firms *certainly* need introverted people.

All of this tells you that if you're shy ... take heart! Every Career Services Director I've talked to has told stories about shy students who overcame their natural reticence and wound up with great gigs. All it takes is a little more preparation, a little more rehearsing, and more measured steps than a more extroverted person. You'll wind up at the same place: your dream job.

Let's talk about what you need to keep in mind.

A. REMEMBER THAT NOBODY CAN SEE INSIDE YOUR HEAD. THEY CAN'T SEE HOW YOU FEEL. THEY ONLY SEE WHAT YOU MANIFEST IN YOUR WORDS AND BEHAVIOR

This is *the* most important thing to keep in mind. Because introverts are very self-aware, they tend to assume that their feelings are transparent. They're *not*. The best way I can illustrate this for you is with a story. My husband, Henry, is a classic introvert. He can easily go for long periods of time without saying anything, and at parties he's happy letting noisy people hold the floor.

A few years ago, Henry decided he wanted to get an MBA. He applied to a few schools, including NYU. You may already know that business schools often request an interview, and NYU did exactly that.

Henry was very nervous about the interview. He was worried that he'd tank his chances if it didn't go well. To ease his concerns, we ran a few mock interviews. I was the NYU admissions director, and he was, well, him. We went through everything from his opening handshake to questions he ought to anticipate to opportunities to wheel in relevant experience. We went over it a few times, until he felt comfortable with what he was going to say.

Interview day came. He went into Manhattan, and called me when it was over. He was laughing when he told me, "You won't believe what happened. I did everything we talked about. I couldn't believe the impact it had on her. She was nodding her head when I talked, and after a few minutes, she said, 'Mr. Reinhardt, we'd love to have you come in and observe a few classes, to meet our professors.' Then she said, 'Now I have to remind you that because you're not an admitted student, you won't be able to participate in the class discussions. Having only known you these few minutes, I know how hard it will be for you not to volunteer.'" We both laughed. My husband has *never* raised his hand to volunteer under *any* circumstances. But he handled this interview so confidently that the admissions director didn't realize that!

You see my point. It's not how you feel. It's what you *project*. A lot of what we'll be talking about will help you act more confidently, and you'll find that soon enough, you'll feel more confident, too.

B. KEEP IN MIND THAT MANY, MANY ATTORNEYS ONCE FELT EXACTLY AS YOU DO NOW

As Oklahoma City's Carol Kinser points out, "Many successful attorneys were nervous law students once. They will sympathize with you. Keep that in mind to take you over that initial outreach 'hurdle.' Try turning the tables. When you get to be a practicing attorney, if you received a call or an e-mail from a law student asking for some much-needed mentoring assistance, wouldn't you be happy to help ... recalling that you were once where they are now? In a heartbeat!"

So don't assume that those confident attorneys you see always felt that way. As Carol Kinser says, "There are lots of people out there willing to help. Once you get the ball rolling, who knows where it will take you?"

C. One Alternative Is to Take the Path of Least Resistance: Take Job Search Steps That Are Comfortable for You

It's not so important to use any one technique to nail a job. It's important to do *something*. Many times, if you perceive that nailing a great job will involve talking to strangers, it'll scare you into not doing anything at all. I talked to a student at one New England school, a shy fellow who'd sent resumes to a bunch of hiring partners of large firms, people he'd found in Martindale Hubbell. He was now faced with following up, and he said, "I just don't feel comfortable calling them." Geez—who *would?* It's not the place to start if you're naturally reticent!

There are *tons* of things you can do that you'll find pretty simple, no matter how shy you are. Let's talk about them.

1. Tell Counselors at Career Services That You're Shy, and Ask for the Most "Accessible" Alums to Contact

You won't be the first shy person to approach Career Services. You won't even be the one-hundredth. The advantage of telling Career Services is that they'll be able to hook you up with alums that'll put you at ease. It's their job to know everybody, and they will put you onto people who'll be easy to talk to. Heck, you may find yourself talking to an alum who is *also* shy, and can give you some pointers from personal experience on how to deal with it when you practice law!

Once you talk to those people, Wendy Werner points out that you'll move down the "food chain" to talk to people they put you onto. You'll find that the more you talk to people, the more comfortable you'll get.

2. E-Mail Is Tailor-Made for the "Contact-reticent"

If you're shy, don't put additional pressure on yourself by contacting people by phone. It's easier to do it by e-mail. As we discussed in Chapter 7 on Correspondence, you open wherever possible by saying "So and so recommended that I contact you." If you aren't contacting a person you found out about through someone else, you open by talking about how you *did* find them. Ask your question, and then tell them you'll be calling them to follow up and learn their answer.

If you approach people this way—an e-mail followed by a phone call— you'll be much more at your ease because they'll know who you are, why you're calling, and you won't be putting them on the spot.

3. Take Advantage of On-Line Message Boards and Chat Rooms

While I'd encourage you to step away from the computer as much as possible, there's no question that you can seek out people on-line. For instance, see whether the bar association for the city you're targeting has a chat room for attorneys. It's a good way to see what's going on in the community. Look at what attorneys are asking one another, and at an appropriate point, jump in with your own questions or comments.

4. GO TO SOCIAL EVENTS WITH BOLD FRIENDS

UC Davis's Mindy Baggish advises that you go to social events with a "loudmouth friend," the idea being that you tag along as your friend approaches people. Once your friend has broken into the conversation, your friend drifts away, you stay ... and you're part of the conversation. As Mindy Baggish points out, this gives you the added benefit of being able to observe your outgoing friend, and seeing what they say and do to meet new people.

5. REMEMBER THAT MANY PEOPLE FEEL AS YOU DO; SEEK THEM OUT WHEN YOU GO TO SOCIAL EVENTS

If you look around at *any* large social event, you'll notice that there are lots of people who feel just as you do. They're standing off to the sides, nursing a drink, looking down or around or shifting uncomfortably. Susanne Aronowitz recommends that you "Rescue other shy people! Look for people who are holding up the walls at social events. If you approach them and just say hello, introduce yourself, they'll be relieved that you took the lead."

6. LOOK FOR EVENTS THAT INVOLVE TALKING TO ONE OR TWO PEOPLE, NOT A WHOLE ROOMFUL

Susanne Aronowitz recommends that you choose activities that involve one-on-one contact, like dinners—where you're faced with talking to the people at your table as opposed to a hall full of strangers. She adds, "Have a few questions ready to ask people. A good one is 'So, what keeps you busy?' People can interpret it as they choose. Also, make sure you keep up with the news, read the paper; consider it research for social events, so that you'll always have something handy to talk about."

D. "OVER PREPARE" FOR INTERVIEWS

In Chapter 9, I gave you tons of advice about handling interviews, everything from research to questions to anticipate and answers to have prepared and memorized. If you're naturally introverted, do all of your prep work, but focus most intensely on practice, practice, practice. Rehearse your answers in front of a mirror. Request mock interviews; do more than one. The fact is, the more prepared you are, the less nervous you'll feel about interviews.

1. FOCUS EXTRA EFFORT ON FIRST IMPRESSIONS

If you're shy, when you meet people you'll have a tendency to look down, not to smile, to have a weak handshake. These can be particularly problematical, because research suggests that people draw conclusions about someone they meet within the first thirty to ninety seconds. You want that first impression to be favourable.

To overcome these issues, solicit the help of your Career Services Office or an understanding friend. Practice entering the room, greeting the person, and rehearsing the first thirty seconds of your conversation. Walk confidently; no slouching. Look the person in the eye. Smile. Develop a firm (but not bone-crushing) handshake. Have a couple of comments you feel comfortable making, whether it's "I've been looking forward to talking with you," "How is your day going so far?" "Can you believe this weather?" something to break the ice.

Remember: Nobody can see inside your head. If the first impression they make of you is that you're comfortable and confident, they'll hold that thought.

2.   IF THINGS DON'T GO WELL IN AN INTERVIEW, CONSIDER ADDRESSING THE SHYNESS ISSUE HEAD-ON

What if your shyness gets in the way of a great interview? Shy career counselors have told me that you should consider addressing the issue straight out. If you feel the interviewer hasn't made a favourable impression of you because you haven't put your best foot forward, consider saying something like, "I need to tell you something. I'm an introvert, and that makes job interviews a real challenge for me. But I think I can do a great job for you. Here's what you need to know about me ..." and then give them the infomercial you planned before the interview, the one I told you to construct in the interviewing chapter, Chapter 9.

One lawyer I talked to had tried this, and said, "It was a panel interview, the worst kind: five interviewers, and me. I could tell that they weren't interested in me, that I really hadn't come across very well at all. The interview was kind of trailing off. I really, really wanted the job. So I said, 'I'm shy and I know I'm not handling this interview well.' Even saying that, they really sat up and took notice. Then I said, 'I know I'm perfect for this job, and I want to tell you why.' I told them. That was toward the end of the interview. It turned the whole thing around. I got the job."

E.   TAKE PART IN ACTIVITIES THAT WILL HELP YOU "COME OUT OF YOUR SHELL"

Shyness isn't a disease. But there's no question that there are a lot of situations that are much easier if you're just a little outgoing.

Certain activities can jolly you towards feeling more comfortable talking with people.

1. NO MATTER WHICH ACTIVITIES YOU CHOOSE, REMEMBER THE VALUE OF ACTING "AS IF"

Before you take part in any activity or go to any social event, imagine in your mind how you'd handle it if you *were* comfortable with strangers. How would you walk in? What would you look like? What would you say? Then: act your fantasy.

Why is this so valuable? Because psychologists point out that behavior change often precedes and causes attitude change. If you act "as if" you feel confident, you'll start feeling that way. Shyness need not be a permanent condition. Before long, you won't remember a time when you didn't feel comfortable talking with strangers!

2. VOLUNTEER FOR ACTIVITIES THAT BY THEIR NATURE INVOLVE TALKING WITH PEOPLE

In Chapter 10 on the Birds and Bees of Great Jobs, we talked about dozens of activities to get you in touch with people who can propel your career. Go through those activities and find the ones with which you're comfortable. Whether you're handing out name tags at bar association events or writing profiles of prominent practitioners for a bar publication, you'll be talking with people because you have a role to play. You're *supposed* to be talking with them so there's no pressure to make small talk. You'll find that it's a lot easier to talk with people when you're "official."

3. MAKE A POINT OF ENGAGING IN SMALL TALK IN SITUATIONS WHERE IT DOESN'T MATTER

In the grocery check-out line. In line at a fast food joint. At the gas station. Waiting for a commuter train. Minnesota's Steve Marchant recommends that you "Practice talking with people in easy situations." Make a point of opening a conversation with the person in line behind you, on the platform next to you, at the next gas pump. You can bring up anything; a particularly friendly limo driver once said to me that he always opens with the weather "Because everybody has an opinion about it." In grocery stores, I always check out what the person in front of me is buying, and if they have an unusual ingredient I'll ask what they're going to make with it. Or if they're clearly having a party— they have ten bags of potato chips—I'll say something like, "Wow. You must really like potato chips." Or I'll check out their key ring, and if they have an unusual keychain, I'll ask about it.

Now you may think my little opening lines are lame, but I've noticed that more often than not, other people really like to chat, they like human contact, and they like other people to initiate it for them. This isn't always true, of course; sometimes people don't engage. But when that happens: who cares? I'm never going to see this person again. If they're in a bad mood or just not into talking, that's OK. It's great practice for situations where small talk *is* important, at job-related functions. If you practice in unimportant situations, you'll feel comfortable when small talk can break the ice with someone you really *do* want to talk to.

4.   TRY TAKING PART IN TOASTMASTERS

Toastmasters is a national organization *specifically* focused on making people feel more comfortable with their public speaking. You can find it on-line. They have chapters virtually everywhere. What happens is that you get together with the group and take turns speaking for five minutes, off the cuff, about a given topic.

People who've taken part in Toastmasters say it can have a dramatic effect on your speaking confidence. And remember: everybody in the group feels the same way you do. They're there expressly because they don't feel comfortable speaking in public. They'll sympathize with you and support you.

F.   CONSIDER THE POSSIBILITY THAT WHAT MAKES YOU RETICENT IS THAT YOU'RE NOT PURSUING JOBS YOU REALLY WANT

It's *hyper* difficult to feel comfortable with people when you feel fake. A reserved student at one law school said to me, "How am I supposed to keep up a charade of enthusiasm?" It's only a charade if you really don't want what you're going after. If you're confident and outgoing in some situations but you're reticent in others, maybe you need to try the suggestions we've already discussed . . . or maybe you need to reexamine your goals.

This was the case with a student in Oregon. She was working full-time in human resources at a company, and going to law school at night. She was *very* reserved. She said everyone told her she had to start getting experience, and she talked about trying to clerk with the in-house counsel's office at her company. Within a few minutes, she said, "What I really want to do is art fraud work." She went on to say that she'd found a three-month course on art fraud that was taking place in Europe, and she was dying to go. It turns out that her Career Services Director, standing nearby, chipped in that there was a professor at her school who had a background in art fraud cases, and also a local FBI agent who'd spoken about art fraud at the school. This student, who had previously been painfully shy, was suddenly all fired up and talking animatedly. In other words: it wasn't so much that she was shy—it's just that she couldn't fake enthusiasm for something she really didn't want.

So examine your motives and make sure you're pursuing what you really want to do. You'll find that will go a long way toward overcoming your concerns about talking with people about it.

G. Acknowledge—and Embrace—the Fact That You May Always Be Happier Talking With People One on One Than in Groups

No matter what you do, your personality is your personality. I've told you before that introverts are much better than extroverts in a bunch of situations. My introverted husband is far more observant than me, often picking up information in social situations that go over my head because I'm too busy blabbing.

If you spend the rest of your life doing better talking with people one-on-one, there is absolutely nothing wrong with that. Do what you have to do to make yourself comfortable in social situations, but embrace what makes you, you!

Chapter 28
"I'm A 1L. Where Do I Start?"

"1Ls make no mistakes, their errors are mere portals of discovery."
　　Anthony Bastone II

"Egads!" you're thinking. "Isn't First Year difficult *enough* without thinking about stupid *jobs?*"

Yep.

"I mean—graduation is *years* away."

True dat.

"So...I don't have to do anything but study...right?"

Well-l-l...

The sad truth is that your job search starts now. You might not have much to do *yet*, but the sooner you start at least thinking about career issues, the better off you are. In this chapter, we'll cover everything that you need to do career-wise as a 1L.

Don't worry. It's not tough. There will be puh-lenty of time left for studying and everything else in your life.

A.　To Work Your 1L Summer
... or Not to Work

You probably hear a lot of conflicting advice about this. The reason for the confusion is that the standards have evolved. It used to be that your 1L summer was a "free pass." You could do whatever you wanted.

Then dinosaurs stopped roaming the Earth, and things changed. Competition for jobs is stiffer now, and the feeling today is: You really should start building a resume during your 1L summer. As St. Thomas'

Elizabeth Wefel puts it, as a 1L your mission is to "Explore, engage, experience." Blowing it off can put you at a disadvantage.

As we'll discuss in this chapter, this view isn't a hard-and-fast rule. But it's a guideline, and if you possibly can, you should make an effort to nail some kind of gig for the summer.

B. Dispelling Some Myths About 1L Summer Jobs ...

"There are no summer jobs for 1Ls."

Not true. There are lots of jobs. There aren't lots of *large law firm jobs* for 1Ls. But your best experience 1L wouldn't be in that environment, anyway. We talk about a lot of possibilities in this chapter, and the bottom line is: if you want a great experience, it's out there waiting for you.

"Your first summer job typecasts you."

I've heard this *so-o-o* many times! I can't imagine anything further from the truth. You can always change course in law school (and even after that—people do it all the time). If you're terrified about how to characterize your 1L summer experience if you subsequently change your mind, that alone can convince you not to follow your dream. Go ahead and do what appeals to you most right now. In Chapters 8 (on Resumes) we talk all about how to "pimp" your resume if you've got experience in something other than what your target employers do. It's really not a big deal ... and certainly not a reason to skip over what you want to do this summer!

"If you're not at the top of the class, don't bother applying for jobs that ask for top 10% grades."

As we discuss in Chapter 7 on Correspondence, don't count yourself out of job postings and signing up for on-campus interviews because your grades don't match the credentials the employer seeks. When employers write up the credentials they want, they're portraying their dream candidate. That person may not respond to them, and on top of that, you may have something *else* to bring to the table that attracts their attention.

So, sure, you'll get a lot of rejections if you respond to ads/interviews when the grades sought are higher than yours; but you never know who *will* want to talk to you. And remember: you only need one job.

C. Some Preliminary Words About Timing ...

Below, I give you a timeline for doing everything in your 1L job search. But right up front, you need to know a couple of ground rules:

1. Before November 1, You Can't Use Your Career Services Office at School

OK. That means the CSO can't, technically anyway, speak to you. You can visit the CSO website, of course. And they almost certainly spoke to you at Orientation. And no one's going to check student IDs at campus presentations; I speak at law schools in October and I talk with plenty of 1Ls.

But the rule is there for a good reason. Your academic credentials are important. Getting used to the whole law school studying thing is a major undertaking. So the idea is to give you a couple of months before you start thinking about jobs.

2. BEFORE DECEMBER 1, LEGAL EMPLOYERS AREN'T SUPPOSED TO INTERVIEW 1LS OR CONSIDER THEM FOR EMPLOYMENT, ACCORDING TO GUIDELINES FROM THE NATIONAL ASSOCIATION OF LAW PLACEMENT

While nothing *stops* employers from considering you, of course—nobody's going to jail for it—you're best off not sending formal application materials to legal employers before that.

3. THESE RULES ARE NOT A HINDRANCE TO YOUR JOB OPPORTUNITIES!

You probably came into law school thinking about what you want to do when you get out. Nothing stops you from contemplating that issue, from talking with non-CSO people *anytime* for guidance and information. Heck, if you're at a Labor Day picnic before law school even starts and your folks introduce you to a federal judge, you'd be an *idiot* to say, "Sorry, Your Honor, I can't talk to you about your work right now." You're always on a fact-finding mission.

But the fact is, when it comes to a pedal-to-the-metal job search, you can accomplish *a lot* after these deadlines. You've got several months of law school before your summer starts. *Many* 1Ls don't nail their summer job until March or April. Nobody's going to snag an opportunity from under your nose if you wait until Winter Break to contact employers!

D.   FIGURING OUT WHAT TO DO WITH YOUR 1L SUMMER . . .

Man, I can't tell you how many ways I've heard First Years spend their summers. From obvious choices like law firms to corporations to clerking for African supreme courts to working in zoos to . . . you name it.

Here's some guidance on figuring out what *you* ought to do . . .

1. IF YOU CAME TO LAW SCHOOL WITH A DREAM IN MIND, NO MATTER HOW WILD-A** IT IS, USE YOUR 1L SUMMER TO TRY IT OUT!

I talked to a student at a law school in DC who'd taken the patent bar coming out of college, already held three patents of his own, and he wanted to spend his summer with a patent litigation firm talking about revamping the way patents are litigated, based on his own experience. "I don't really want to practice law," he said. "Should I even bother looking for this freakish summer job?"

Heck yes! Why not? If there was ever a summer for wild-eyed speculation, the summer after 1L is it.

"But Kimmbo!" you're thinking, "*How* am I going to nail it? What if I want something like sports or entertainment or..." Stop! Here's the key. There's *always* a way to get experience in anything you want...if you're willing to make sacrifices. All you need to know are six little words:

I'm willing to work for free.

Whether in cover letters or conversations, if you say those in conjunction with something like, say, "I'm so eager to gain experience doing what you do..." you will open just about any door. (I am reminded of a stand-up comedian who once said, "If you know three little words you'll never be poor: "Stick 'em up.")

Does that mean you have to make *no money* to do what you want? Of course not. There are some summer gigs that pay and furthermore, you can always split a summer—if you're working for free, employers tend to be pretty flexible about working around a paying gig, whether it's temping a couple of days a week, working at Starbucks, waiting tables or working as a Jell-O shots girl at a nightclub (it's been done). On top of that, depending on the job you aim for, there will be grant, work/study and fellowship money available. In short, don't turn down an opportunity because of the money angle. What you lose in money you will make up for in the richness of your experience.

Remember: the whole point of law school is to redefine your life, to set yourself up in a career you'll enjoy. The only way to know if you'll like something for sure is to try it for yourself. So if you've got a goal in mind, *do it,* for gosh sakes. If you love it as much as you thought you would, your summer will get your foot in the door. You'll meet people and get something valuable on your resume; nobody will care if you did it for free. It just shows how determined you are.

And if it turns out you don't love it...so what? Eliminating possibilities is a good use of a summer, too, and no matter what you do, you'll learn *something* useful to your next job. You'll be able to say to future potential employers, "I'll tell you what I learned: how to research employers ahead of time to figure out what will be a good fit for me. That's how I found you. And I'll tell you what I *did* enjoy about my summer—I learned X and X and X, and I understand from research that those are useful to you..."

So don't worry about your future job search. Dreams are great, and if you've got one, use your 1L summer to try it out!

2. IF YOU'RE NOT SURE WHAT YOU WANT TO DO ... JOIN THE CLUB!

Very few 1Ls really know what they want to do. I've mentioned before that only one in three law students comes to law school even convinced they want to be a lawyer *at all*. Why *should* you know? In fact, employers are more suspicious when 1Ls proclaim confidently what they want; "How the heck do *you* know what a utilities lawyer is?" is the kind of refrain I hear. So there's no shame in not knowing.

There are several options to consider:

- work for a judge;
- work for a district/state attorney's office/public defender's office (*particularly* useful if you think you want to litigate);
- work for a public interest organization;
- work for a government agency (federal, state, county, city);
- work for a law firm—large, medium, small, solo practice;
- work in a corporation's in-house counsel's office;
- work for a legal temp agency (in a variety of settings);
- work as a research assistant for a professor;
- work on something related to a hobby you love;
- go on a summer abroad program;
- attend summer school.

How do you choose among them? They've all got benefits. But if I had to choose one, I'd recommend **working for a trial-level judge, federal or state court, whether paid or volunteer.** Having talked with thousands of students about this, I'll summarize my reasoning from Chapter 25:

- It's a great background no matter what you decide to do. If you go to a firm, in-house, government agency, if you want to be a professor or anything else in law...everyone respects a judicial clerkship/internship.

- It makes everything you learn in law school fall into place. I don't know about you, but Civil Procedure still makes me go, "Huh?" But if you work for a judge, you see law in its "natural habitat." It's cool to see how the theory you learn comes to life.

- You'll have a great mentor and reference in the form of your judge. Most alums who worked for judges view the judge as their greatest advisor, and the experience of working for a judge—whether for a summer or in a post-graduate clerkship—as their best work experience.

- You'll polish your research and writing skills, the two skills more legal employers want than any other.

- You'll have a chance to check out lawyers and firms and hear reputations from an insider's point of view. This is a great help when you make decisions about where to work subsequently.

- You meet lo-o-ots of people, and as I point out all the time, people are the key to opportunities.

- Human conflict is exciting. All drama is based on it. That's why so many courtroom lawyers become novelists. If you want to see conflicts played out and resolved, working for a trial-level judge is the place to find it!

The reason I think trial level courts are preferable to appellate level, at least from a 1L summer perspective, is that they're more people-oriented and fast-paced. Appellate work is more writing-oriented. If you prefer a more solitary job, appellate work will be your gig.

Notice also that I mentioned that you might have to volunteer. Judges take volunteer clerks/interns all the time. It's such a valuable experience I recommend that you offer to do it for free. You can always talk to Career Services about grants and scholarships, or take on a part-time paying gig to earn some dough.

Having pointed out my favourite 1L summer job, I have to tell you that you can have a great experience in a whole variety of settings. Any one of the activities I listed above is an excellent way to spend your summer. Let's talk about a few more considerations in choosing between them.

As a rule of thumb, smaller law firms are easier to target for the summer than large law firms (unless you go to an elite law school). This shouldn't bum you out, because the hands-on experience you'll get is generally in inverse proportion to the size of the firm: the smaller the firm, the more "real work" you'll get, and I'd suggest that you'll enjoy that more. When I clerked at a five-person firm in Greenwich, Connecticut after 1L, I talked with clients, I sat in when one of the partners was a judge in small claims court, and I did research on really fascinating cases.

At government agencies you'll similarly get great experience. Whether it's the U.S. Department of Justice—a truly incredible employer—or a local city attorney's office, you'll get your hands dirty with real work.

* * * SMART HUMAN TRICK * * *

1L at a Midwestern law school. Instead of taking a paying job, he volunteers at the Federal Defenders Office. After the summer, he reports, "It was *such* a better opportunity than being the copy boy at a large firm! The first day I was there, I got a huge file and the words, 'Here's your case. It's going to be a landmark.' It could not have been a more exciting experience."

How about the hobby angle? Depending on the hobby and how much you love it, that's a viable option. You need to remember that law touches everything; you name it, and there's a law-related job associated with it. Serious oenophile (wine lover)? Law students have worked with lawyers who represent wineries and wine importers. Like animals? Law students have worked with zoo risk managers, who are lawyers. Like car racing? Law students have interned with NASCAR. If you *love* it, there's a summer job connected with it!

Working as a research assistant for a professor gives you the opportunity, obviously, to hone your research skills. If you have an idea of the specialty you want—from international to litigation to you-name-it—working for a professor who focuses on it is a great start to your career.

If you decide you want to do a judicial clerkship—wise move—a professor's recommendation is *huge*. Also, you'll also be in a relaxed and flexible environment.

How about "non-work," like a study abroad program or summer school? I talk about summer abroad programs in detail in the "glamorous careers" Chapter, 24, where we discussed International Law. In that context they make a lot of sense. If you don't intend to go into International, employers see summer programs for what they are: the chance to see something really interesting. It's not a career positive, but it's not a negative, either...and when's the next time you're going to have the chance to spend a couple of months abroad? If you do opt for a summer abroad, experts recommend that you spend the remaining weeks of your summer volunteering in a legal position to get some experience. At the very least, expect to take on a law-related job in the Fall when school starts, so you can tell employers that you're getting experience. (Since you'll have knocked out some credits, you'll have more time to play with.)

Summer school also gives you flexibility in the Fall when you return to school. As SMU's Karen Garland points out, "Wiping out credits frees you up Second Year." You'll have the time to take on a job that would be a stretch for your classmates, and the competition for school-year jobs is considerably lower than it is for summer gigs.

3. Can I Spend the Summer After 1L at a Large Firm?

It's a definite maybe. Some law students do. Here's what you have to know, and what large firms are unlikely to tell you directly.

Large firms hire 1Ls for their summer program largely as a matter of public relations. That is, they want those students to go back to their schools and rave about their experience, so that the firms can lure 2Ls. *That's* why, if you look at the summer program statistics for large firms in sources like the NALP Directory, you'll see that they hire 1Ls from the "usual suspects," distinguished schools like Harvard, Yale, Stamford, and the like. So I would tell you up front that if you don't go to one of those schools, it's a tough ticket—not an *impossible* ticket, but a very, very tough one. And what makes it tough has nothing to do with you personally, and whether or not they think they're wonderful, and regardless of whether you could do the work! You need to remember that whether or not you get a gig with a large firm after 1L, there are always ways to get your foot in the door, which is what we talk about in Chapter 23.

Before we do that, let's spend a moment talking about how you get into a large firm after 1L if you don't go to a distinguished school. You're going to have to dazzle them with what you *do* have, since you don't have much law school experience. You'll want to point to:

- An outstanding undergraduate record; if you went to a distinguished college or university, all the better (as Vermont's Abby Armstrong points out, "Make hay out of your undergrad. Being from a recognized undergrad school will help you be viewed as the cream of the crop.");

- Outstanding performance in Fall 1L classes, if you got any grades (note that you don't talk to large firms before December 1);
- Relevant work experience before law school (for instance, working in a law-related area or in a governmental agency related to a firm's practice or in an industry that's attractive to them).

You might have large firms interview 1Ls through Spring on-campus interviews; check with Career Services to see if that's available. If not, contact firms yourself, using the techniques we talked about in the Correspondence chapter (Chapter 7). Furthermore, remember that legal temp agencies will often give you the chance to get your foot in the door with large law firms. *These jobs tend not to be the most exciting,* but they do get a "big name" on your resume, and give you the chance to hobknob with people in an environment that attracts you.

Most importantly: don't feel as though your 1L summer defines you. If you get great experience anywhere, *that's* what counts.

4. WHAT IF A COMPLETELY NON-LAW-RELATED OPPORTUNITY COMES UP?

I've periodically had law students say to me, "I know I should work after 1L, but I have the chance to do this awesome..." and then they'll tell me about a once-in-a-lifetime opportunity. One student told me about a chance he had to build a house in Alaska, and "I'll never get this chance again."

Well for gosh sakes *do it!* Remember, there are lots of ways to make up for no work experience after 1L: taking a part-time job during your 2L year comes immediately to mind, or working in a bit of part-time volunteering in whatever time you can squeeze in during your 1L summer, or any of the activities we talked about in Chapter 10.

The fact remains, your life is more important than your job search. If something incredible comes your way, don't think twice about it. Do it.

5. DON'T TAKE A JOB YOU HATE JUST BECAUSE IT'S EASY TO GET

As Richmond's Bev Boone points out, "At the very least, split your summer. Doing something you hate will sour you on law school." There are so-o-o many fabulous opportunities, and so many ways to find and fund them. Don't bum yourself out with a job that doesn't excite you!

E. HOW TO FIND EMPLOYERS

There are three basic choices:
- Job postings/Spring OCI;
- Targeted mailers;
- Talking to people and taking part in activities.

If you've read Chapter 10, you know that the last option is my favourite; it'll put you onto the 75% of jobs that are never posted anywhere. (Targeted mailers will do that as well, but letting people see and talk to you "in the flesh" gets them invested in you more easily.)

Let's talk about each avenue separately.

1. RESPONDING TO JOB POSTINGS/SPRING ON-CAMPUS INTERVIEWS

There's a myth that often flies around law schools that there aren't any jobs for 1Ls. That's a stinking pile of pony loaf. There *are* jobs, and in fact more than a few will show up in the form of job postings from your Career Services Office and Spring on-campus interviews at school.

Starting in November of your First Year, make a point of checking your CSO's web site at least twice a week for new postings; if you can do it daily, even better (your CSO may also e-mail new postings to you). I've talked with so many 1Ls who nailed great summer jobs, some even in sports and entertainment, because they watched their Career Services postings like a hawk and jumped on those opportunities as soon as they came up.

Similarly, Spring OCI deserves your attention. While Fall OCI is populated by large institutional employers who are primarily interested in 2Ls, in the Spring you'll often find employers who are more diverse *and* interested in hiring 1Ls. Look over the list of who's coming to campus and submit your resume to the ones that interest you (we'll talk in a minute about that resume...and that interview).

Don't forget about diversity fellowships, if you're eligible. Ask at the CSO for details and deadlines.

2. TARGETED MAILERS

What's a targeted mailer? Basically, it's not a mass mailer. It's letters that are personalized to employers, so they feel you're truly interested in them, not just "a job."

Of course, problematically, you *are* interested primarily in "a job"! Your letters can't come across that way, and when we talk about cover letters, below, we'll talk about how to breathe life into them.

A. FINDING TARGETS

There are a bunch of ways to accomplish this. **The people and activities route, as I outline below, is my favourite way;** nobody's going to talk up a crappy employer to you, but those employers could well be listed in the Yellow Pages. Having said that, let's talk about other ways to dig them up:

- Ask at the CSO for hard copy resources and binders;
- Go to Chapter 6 for research resources and Chapter 11 for Internet resources;
- Use Lexis/Nexis and Westlaw, which have a wealth of employers (Westlaw's www.findlaw.com lists small to medium private employers);

- Use Martindale–Hubbell (at www.martindale.com) for larger private employers;
- Use the NALP Directory of Legal Employers (at www.nalp directory.com) for large employers; this directory helpfully tells you if the individual employers hire 1Ls;
- Use www.pslawnet.org for public interest, public sector and plaintiff-side private firm positions;
- Consider targeting smaller cities for 1L jobs. There is less competition outside the large cities. The quality of the experience is what you're after, not the name of the city. Even if you're jonesing for a big city, consider the small cities around it as a way to make yourself "geographically desirable."

B. TIMING (SEE ALSO TOPIC H, TIMELINE)

As a rule of thumb, you should consider finalizing your letter and resume over Thanksgiving, ready for sending to employers on December 1st, with an eye toward setting up interviews over Winter Break.

This isn't to say you can't do mailings Spring Semester; January through March are prime times to send out mailers as well, with an eye to interviews over Spring Break. And of course I've talked with students who successfully sent out mailers in April. But if you want to be ahead of the curve, the Thanksgiving/December timing is your best option.

C. NUMBERS

There's no magic number of letters that guarantee you a job. You never know when the next one you send will hit pay dirt. It's not unheard of for 1Ls to send 50–100 letters. Consider doing them in chunks of ten, which will make them more manageable. I wouldn't send more than a hundred because there's, oh, those pesky classes you have to go to and, you know, your life. It just gets too time-consuming to send out tons of personalized letters.

D. FOLLOW UP

Remember that sending out letters is meaningless unless you also follow up. If you talk to upperclassmen you'll find that many of them didn't nail opportunities with letters; it was following up on those letters that did the trick. (We talk all about following up in Chapter 7 on Correspondence.)

E. FINALLY, IT'S REALLY IMPORTANT TO KEEP TRACK OF YOUR CORRESPONDENCE

Create a database to keep track of your letters, and have a binder with copies of each letter in it. In the database, keep track of when each letter was sent, your follow up and results. You've *got* to be organized if you want to conduct a successful campaign!

3.   TALKING TO PEOPLE AND TAKING PART IN ACTIVITIES

Aah. The goose that lays the golden eggs. We covered this in detail in Chapter 10—the most important chapter in this book—but let's talk a little here about that goose as it relates specifically to you, as a 1L.

There's no question that the best gigs you'll get for the rest of your life will come through people. You'll learn about opportunities, get the inside skinny on employers, find out who to talk to and what they want to hear. Whether it's people that other people put you onto, people you work for, people you meet through activities, the flesh and blood you—not your resume—is the best thing you have going for you.

So make a point of doing the following:

- Check out the "summer clerkship" binders at your Career Services Office, where the experiences of prior students are gathered. When you see ones that look interesting, get in contact with the students/alums who submitted them. Talk to them about the experience and how they got the job. You'll get a wealth of personalized advice that way.

- Along the same vein, ask at the CSO about upperclassmen who had great 1L summer experiences; seek them out and talk to them about it. They'll probably give you tips for nailing the same gig, and it's not unheard of for employers to ask former summer workers for their input on whom to hire.

- Go to CSO presentations at school. Walk up and introduce yourself to speakers after their presentations, express your interest in what they do—enthusiasm is always a plus—and ask how to break into it for the summer.

- If you have a mentor through your CSO, *use that person*. They volunteered to be a mentor, so they're serious about helping you. Pick their brain for ideas about what you should do and who you should talk to; they may even make phone calls on your behalf (although you can't ask them to!).

- Check with your CSO and the local bar association about shadowing an attorney for a day. It gives you not just insight into what the job is like and intelligent answers to interview questions, but a great opportunity to meet someone who might be (or put you onto) a potential employer.

- Go to trials over breaks from school; introduce yourself to judges and prosecutors. You'll make a *tremendous* impression, because law students rarely take this step, and it speaks volumes to your enthusiasm.

- Try to go to three CLEs (continuing legal education seminars) in your Spring Semester. (We talk about CLEs in detail in Chapter

10.) They're a tremendous, and rarely used, means to nail great jobs.

- Remember that you are the natural object of bounty for alums from your law school. Whenever you can, contact lawyers who went to your school (instead of the recruiting person, if there is one). If you're looking out of town, contact alums from your school who are in your target city, and ask them for advice. If possible, go to the city during Winter or Spring Break, contact alums and tell them you'll be there, and invite them out to lunch/coffee to ask for advice.

* * * SMART HUMAN TRICK * * *

1L law student, Arizona. She wanted to be in New York for the summer. She e-mailed an alum from her school who was practicing at a large firm in New York. They had a brief e-mail correspondence when the student told the alum that she'd be in town for part of winter break. She invited the alum out for lunch.

At the lunch, the alum invited the student for a "courtesy interview," saying "Don't expect anything." The student went for the interview, was invited back the following day for a second interview . . . and got an offer the following week.

- If you've got some nerve, consider walking you credentials door-to-door to employers you've identified, when you're on a break from school. This won't work in cities with tight security like New York, where most buildings have limited access, but it'll work just about everywhere else. *Nobody* who uses this technique goes unemployed for very long. (We talk about it in detail in Chapter 10.)

- A phone campaign can also work wonders, if you "give great phone." Just call employers and express your interest in working for them for the summer, and ask if they ever hire 1Ls. You may get an interview on the spot, so be prepared! Again, because so many people send credentials, you'll stand out. Of course, some people will be rude and hang up on you. So what. Go to the next name on your list. You're not collecting Easter Eggs or shrunken heads. You only need one job!

- Talk to everyone you know—friends of parents, people your parents use like stockbrokers, bankers and accountants, your own friends and classmates and professors—about what you're looking for. You want scouts. You don't know who people know, or who they'll meet. When an employer is confronted with a faceless stack of resumes, even one comment from someone saying, "You should talk to *this* kid" can make you stand out.

* * * SMART HUMAN TRICK * * *

1L looking to work in a corporate in-house counsel's office for the summer. She sends some resumes to companies in her target city, and then mentions casually to a friend of her parents (FOP) what she's trying to do for the summer.

The FOP says, "Oh, did you send a resume to Acme Corporation?"

"I did," responds the student.

The FOP says, "I know the hiring attorney there. I'll call him."

The FOP does so, and says to the hiring attorney, "She's a really good kid. I've known the family for years. You should at least talk to her."

The attorney responds, "It's a good thing you called. I already put her resume on the reject pile. She doesn't have any experience. But if you think I should talk to her..."

The student gets the interview—and the job.

F.   COVER LETTERS, RESUMES, INTERVIEWS . . .

1.   OVERALL: SELL WHAT YOU'VE GOT!

Those are the words of Minnesota's Sue Gainen. "You've got energy, enthusiasm, curiosity. Employers respond to those. Make sure every aspect of your job search reflects them!"

2.   COVER LETTERS

If you do a targeted mailing, your cover letter will be the first glimpse of you an employer gets. It *counts*.

We discussed cover letters in detail in Chapter 7. We'll just cover a few specific tips here.

First of all, remember that the very best letters start with the words, "So-and-so recommended that I talk to you..." You get those through people and activities, and we already discussed that!

If it's a letter to an employer with whom you don't have a mutual acquaintance, your first and most important step is *research*. Remember, these are *targeted* letters; they're personalized to the employer.

Let's say you're looking at small firms in your home town (or a city where you want to be). Go to their websites (if they have them). Join the state bar and look in the local bar directory for information. Look at their ad in the Yellow Pages. Google them. Find out whatever you can. Then follow the advice in Chapter 7 about weaving together your research with what you bring to the table for them, be it a connection to the city where they are located (*very* important), highlights of law school so far, undergrad experiences, work experience or just your enthusiasm.

When I ran a successful mail campaign as a 1L, I wrote letters pointing out that I'd waited tables 30 hours a week to put myself through college, so I was a hard worker. I also added a line about how I knew it was difficult to make a decision on a law student with no legal experience, and that I exemplified what had once been said of Princess Diana, "She is only what she will become," but I hoped they would interview me because I was so eager to learn. I also said how much I enjoyed law school. It was a geeky and quirky letter, but it did reflect what I was like and hey—I got interviews from it and nailed a really great summer job, from attorneys who'd never hired a 1L before and had never even *heard* of my law school, Case Western.

While the part of your letter that addresses why you want a particular employer will change from letter to letter, most of it will be the same. Run your letters by counselors at your CSO before you send them to make sure they reflect *you* in the best, most positive light.

3. RESUMES

It can seem really tough to put together a resume as a 1L. If you're like most law students, you went straight through undergrad to law school. You may be wondering, "What the heck do *I* have for legal employers?" More than you think! (If you're a second career person, we talk about describing your prior experience on your resume in Chapter 22.)

We discuss handling a 1L resume in Chapter 8. If you read that, you'll make your resume sing—even if you've never had a law related job in your life!

4. INTERVIEWS

Whether it's a quick chat on the phone, an on-campus gig or an extensive office visit, you're unlikely to nail a summer job without an interview. We talked about interviews extensively in Chapter 9. Review it before you go on even one interview.

The most significant question you may get is, "What do you want to do?" There's no problem with being honest, or at least putting a good spin on honesty. No one expects you to have firm plans so early in your law school education. It's fine to say, "As a 1L, I just don't know yet, but here's what I've heard/learned/researched about you..."

G. WHAT IF NOTHING WORKS? . . .

Well! *Something* will work. But if time gets away from you or you go on some interviews and nothing pans out or if you're offered things that truly don't flip your switch...then what?

1. IF YOU HAVEN'T DONE SO ALREADY, TELL EMPLOYERS *DIRECTLY* THAT YOU'RE WILLING TO VOLUNTEER

Volunteering makes almost all jobs attainable. If you haven't considered it before, think about it now. I can't stress strongly enough that *nobody cares* if you volunteer; you don't put it on your resume. You just put down what you did. I talked with a student at a Midwestern law school, a 3L who had two amazing gigs on her resume; she'd worked for the SEC and the Justice Department for her summers. I said, "This is fantastic!" and she said, "But what about my grades?" Her experience had been so great I didn't even notice her grades! She had volunteered for the two jobs, but it didn't show on her resume. What showed was that she had two hyper-valuable job experiences.

On top of that, you'll often get better experience volunteering than you will being paid; employers know you don't have to be there, and they tend to give you better, meatier work as well.

So think about volunteering!

2.   REVISIT SOME EMPLOYERS WHO TURNED YOU DOWN OR NEVER GOT BACK TO YOU

As I've pointed out before, sometimes students wash out of summer programs. They decide to do something else, often something that pays more (or pays at all, if it's a volunteer gig). So it's always worth a follow-up call just to see if anything changed; if they don't have a job for you, they might have ideas of who else you should call.

If employers never got back to you at all, they might not have thought they'd need someone at the time; things might have changed.

Again: it doesn't hurt to revisit employers. Take a deep breath, sound eager, and make that phone call. I've told you a few times now: you only need one job. The next phone call you make could hit pay dirt!

3.   IT'S *NEVER* TOO LATE TO NAIL A SUMMER GIG. YOU NEVER KNOW WHEN SOMEONE WILL SUDDENLY DROP OUT OF THEIR SUMMER JOB

Whether it's April or even May, every year there are *some* jobs that open up. In Chapter 10 I told the story of the student who worked both summers in law school for federal district court judges. He had strictly mediocre credentials. He got the jobs by waiting until exams were over both summers, and then going and knocking on judges' chambers' doors, asking if they needed an extra pair of hands; he said he knew there'd be people who'd give up the (fantastic) jobs for paying positions. He was right.

I wouldn't *suggest* waiting until after exams to nail a job, but the point remains: things open up late.

4.   REMEMBER THAT THERE'S VIRTUALLY ALWAYS A PROFESSOR AT SCHOOL WHO NEEDS A RESEARCH ASSISTANT; IT'S A REALLY GOOD GIG (FOR REASONS WE DISCUSSED EARLIER) AND YOU CAN OFTEN NAIL IT IN SHORT ORDER

As we discussed earlier in this chapter, being a research assistant for a professor has a number of advantages. Only one of them is the fact that you can break into it at virtually any time. Ask at the Career Services Office for advice on which professor(s) to approach.

5. CONSIDER DOING WHATEVER YOU WANT FOR DOUGH, AND MAKE A POINT OF GOING TO AS MANY CLES AS YOU CAN OVER THE SUMMER

If you really want to pile on some dead presidents doing something non-law-related, consider taking some CLEs at the same time. Plan on doing as many as you can; as a law student you get in for free, or a very nominal price. CLEs give you the chance to learn more about a specialty (or specialties) that interest(s) you, talk to lawyers about what they do, ask for advice, and get something really fantastic on your resume. We talk all about CLEs in Chapter 10.

6. REMEMBER THAT EMPLOYERS WHO REJECTED YOU FOR *THIS* SUMMER CAN STILL BE USEFUL CONTACTS FOR 2L

Don't get all up in the grill of employers who reject you this summer. You've got another summer and post-graduation to think about as well...as well as two years in school when you could potentially work part-time. You don't know when a rejection now will turn into a "Welcome!" later. So if you feel you came close to a couple of jobs, keep in touch with those employers. Things can change!

7. IF YOU'VE HAD A BUNCH OF INTERVIEWS AND NO OFFERS, GO TO THE CSO FOR A MOCK INTERVIEW

It happens. You may be saying or doing something that turns off employers without realizing it. A simple fix is to request a mock interview with your CSO. They'll be able to zero in on exactly what's going on with your interviewing style.

8. ASK WHETHER YOU'RE APPLYING FOR JOBS YOU REALLY WANT

Maybe you're not getting summer jobs because you're not conveying enthusiasm to employers, and maybe that's because you don't want the jobs you're applying for. If that's the case, go back to Step One and figure out what you really want to do this summer. Maybe it'll take talking with people about what they do, *without* looking for a job, so that you can genuinely summon up enthusiasm for it. Whatever it takes, you need to know that employers can sense when you're just going through the motions. It's a waste of their time...and yours!

9. DON'T SUFFER ALONE. GO TO THE CSO

They're there to counsel you, remember? Tell them what's going on with you and ask their help. They'll come up with ideas for you that you'd never have dreamed up yourself ... and they'll make you feel a lot better.

H. A TIMELINE FOR FIRST YEAR: WHAT TO DO, WHEN

Here's a general run-down of when you should consider doing all of the things we talked about in this chapter. A major caveat: If your

Career Services Office gives you a *different* timeline, follow their guidance, not mine. They'll know in your specific market, and with the specific resources they provide you, how you ought to arrange your search.

In the absence of that: here's a plan for you.

1.   SEPTEMBER/OCTOBER

- Don't do *anything* except focus on getting used to law school. Your grades don't determine your career, but good grades sure make things a lot easier for you.

- Having said that: when you have a chance to meet lawyers socially or when interesting speakers come to town, take advantage of the situation. Ask lawyers how they got into what they do now; listen to speakers and if they do what you want to do, walk up afterwards and introduce yourself. You might as well get used to talking to lawyers. You're going to be doing a lot of it.

2.   NOVEMBER

- Per National Association of Law Placement (NALP) guidelines, you can officially talk to counselors in your Career Services Office as of November 1. Charge!

- If your CSO holds orientation sessions, *go*. Get familiar with the resources and the counselors.

- If your school has an on-line recruiting system, be sure to post your profile and make sure you understand how it works.

- If you haven't done so already, read Chapters 1 through 12 of this book. Or at least skim them. And read any other chapters that apply to you.

- Start to work on your resume and a general draft of a cover letter that you can modify for individual employers.

- Bring your resume and cover letter to your CSO for review.

- Start to think about what you want to do for the summer after 1L.

- Start to check your CSO's on-line postings for summer opportunities.

- If you can, finalize your resume, targeted mailing list and cover letters over Thanksgiving Break.

3.   DECEMBER/WINTER BREAK

- NALP guidelines ask interviewers not to interview or consider 1Ls for employment until December 1st.

- Before you send your materials to employers, have them reviewed by the CSO for grammatical and spelling errors.

- Send your materials with the goal of setting up interviews over Winter Break.

- If you intend to target large law firms, get your materials to them before Winter Break. (Check with your CSO to see if large firms interview at your school in the Spring, and if so, who.)

- Start your "people" campaign, especially over Winter Break; tell everyone you know what you want, and ask who you should be talking to. Contact the people they put you onto.

- Join the bar association for the state where you intend to wind up (and perhaps the one where you go to school). Skim publications that are sent to you for potential employers and ideas about what you'd like to do.

- Over Winter Break, you can accomplish a lot, other than decompressing from law school! You can:

  - Go to local bar association functions no matter where you are, and talk to lawyers about what they do for ideas about what you might like.

  - Use legal web sites or local newspapers to identify attorneys you might approach. Lawyers appear in the press all the time.

  - Conduct informational interviews (See Chapter 10) with people who do what you think you might like.

  - Polish off your resume and some cover letters, if you haven't done so already.

4. JANUARY/FEBRUARY

- Update your resume to reflect your grades first semester. Or not; if you didn't get good grades, ask at the CSO for the general grade cut-off at your school for putting your grades on your resume. If you did really well in any individual classes, include those individual results. And if you're seriously bummed about your grades, don't be. Read Chapter 13. Lots of successful lawyers stunk it up on law school exams.

- Continue checking job postings from Career Services.

- Ask at Career Services if there are any Spring Job Fairs you could/should attend; some Public Interest Career Fairs take place in the Spring. (Follow guidance on Job Fairs in Chapter 10.)

- Continue targeted mailers.

- Remember that small firms, agencies, and judges tend to hire in the Spring.

- Follow-up with phone calls to employers to whom you sent your resume.

- Go to CSO activities and workshops.

- If your school has it, participate in Spring OCI.

- Start checking the local bar association web site, www.pli.com, and other CLE providers for CLEs about specialties that interest you.

Where possible, attend these CLEs to learn more about the practice and to meet potential employers. Try and go to 3 CLEs this semester (and every ensuing semester in law school).

5. **MARCH**

    • Continue with targeted mailings and following up with employers. Try to arrange interviews over Spring Break. Again: remember that small firms, agencies, and judges tend to hire in the spring.

    • Follow up with employers you haven't heard from. You can't be shy about it. A simple phone call can often turn a non-response into an interview.

6. **APRIL**

    • Continue to attend school and bar activities, and talk to as many people as you can for advice.

    • Continue to check postings from the CSO and any e-mails they send you. There are employers every year who don't hire until April...for summer jobs!

    • Follow up with employers who turned you down earlier. You don't know how things might have changed; the person/people they expected for the summer might have washed out.

    • Finalize your summer plans, and if necessary find summer housing.

    • Tell your CSO about your summer plans and give the office your summer address.

Materials excerpted in this chapter include handouts from: Emory, Hastings, Florida State, and Tulane.

Chapter 29

It's 2nd Semester 3rd Year and I Don't Have a Job— What the Heck Am I Supposed to Do *Now?*

"I've been so much happier since I went back into denial."

Caption on a New Yorker Magazine cartoon

So ... graduation is looming, and you don't have a job nailed down yet. It is *so-o-o* not too late. In this very brief chapter, I'll address a few issues that might be holding you back.

1. REMEMBER THAT YOU'RE NOT ALONE

When you don't have a job in hand as a Third Year, you can feel very lonely. I did. You think, "Geez, everybody else here has a job!"

It's a mirage. As I've pointed out before, more than 50% of law students nationwide graduate from law school without a job in hand. It's just that people who don't have jobs tend to be quiet about it, and people who've nailed great gigs are noisy.

Remember that everybody finds a job. Everybody. Especially you. It's just a timing thing. You'll be happily employed before you know it.

2. HAVE AN ANSWER READY WHEN PEOPLE ASK YOU WHAT YOU'VE DONE AND/OR WHY YOU DON'T HAVE A JOB YET

Don't jump ugly when people ask you about the whole job thing; they can't read your mind and they don't know how you feel about it. It's just a question, for gosh sakes. You don't have to answer with the complete, unvarnished truth. "I screwed up my summer clerkship and I was the

1283

only one who didn't get a offer," would have been the complete truth in my case. Nobody needs to hear *that*.

Instead, answer with a general sense of what you're doing now. "I'm actually looking at a few options now ..." No matter what you're actually doing, that's true. Whether you're surfing the web for employers or sending letters or talking to people or you've got interviews scheduled, you're looking at a few options. Humor also works; if you have a funny line to say about your situation, use it. "I'm going to be doing graduate work in job search" works. *Whatever* you say, say it confidently, and people need never know that you're concerned about it.

3. GO BACK TO CHAPTER 10 ON PEOPLE AND ACTIVITIES. SKIM IT FOR IDEAS

You may figure it's too late to put into effect the "talking/taking part in activities" as we discussed in Chapter 10. I hear that all the time from 3Ls. "Everything you say sounds great but I've got no time left for it." I'd tell you that it's *never* too late. Anything you could do throughout law school you can do now. I talk to second semester 3Ls all the time who find that it's the *very next thing* they do that opens the door for them.

Among other things from Chapter 10 to consider:

- Volunteer to write motions and pleadings for lawyers doing pro bono work. It gets you more skills and gives lawyers the chance to see what you can do.

- Volunteer to research an issue for the practice section of the bar that interests you.

- Get a part-time job for the rest of school, even if it's just a couple of months, and even if it's on a volunteer basis. Again: you're getting more on your resume, learning more skills, meeting more people ... and you don't know who they know.

Honestly, the list of things that'll work for you is just endless. Last year, for instance, I talked to two young women at a law school in Georgia. They were both 3Ls and it was January. They had the same question: "We're going to graduate in May. We both want Sports Law. What can we do *now?*" I rattled off a few ideas from Chapter 10. One of the activities I recommended was attending sports-related CLEs. They wanted to move to Texas, and I suggested they go there and do the CLEs over Spring Break. One of the women rolled her eyes and said, "I don't have time for any of that stuff." The other said, "OK."

I got an e-mail a few weeks later from the woman who'd seemed game to try activities. She told me that she'd gone to Texas over break, she'd taken two Sports CLEs, and she said, "You have no idea how great those were. I met several sports lawyers. I told them I was moving to Texas and wanted to get involved in Sports Law. One of them offered me an interview. I'm going to be working for him!"

I don't know what happened to the other student, the one who didn't have time to do anything. But I *can* tell you that if you get yourself out there, great things happen. Don't ever think it's too late!

4. THINK MORE BROADLY

I often meet 3Ls who've created their own prisons and locked themselves in. It's easy to tell yourself, "I want X, and I'm not going to settle for anything else." Whether it's a large law firm or a job in a glamorous city like San Francisco or New York or L.A. or Washington, you may tell yourself that if you don't get precisely what you want, you won't take anything at all. As one Career Services Director commented, "3Ls tend to eliminate jobs and practice areas too easily!"

Here's the problem. Graduation is coming up, and you're going to have to do something. If you've got student loans, you're going to have to do something for dough. What I'd recommend doing is thinking more broadly, just for now, to get a start to your career. Look at a first job as a stepping stone to getting what you want, for positioning you for your dream job, as a kind of *de facto* LL.M. if you will.

For instance, as we discussed in the large law firms chapter, 23, there are all kinds of jobs you can take that will let you lateral into a large firm, whether it's working for a government agency or developing an expertise at a small law firm or a whole bunch of other "interim" gigs.

What about the glamorous city issue? There's no question that it's harder to get a job in a city that everybody else targets. What I'd recommend is thinking outside the box geographically. Remember that every big city has little satellite cities around it; you can live the big city life and have a reverse commute if you work nearby, and you'll be able to go to bar events and CLEs in the city so you can meet people who'll be useful in moving onto a job in the city itself.

5. WHAT IF YOU WORK FOR A LEGAL EMPLOYER NOW, AND THE SUBJECT OF PERMANENT EMPLOYMENT HASN'T COME UP YET? . . .

I've talked to a lot of students in this situation. They're plugging merrily along at a small firm or a government agency, they like what they're doing and would like to continue, graduation is looming . . . what do you do?

Bring up the topic yourself! This is how:

- Make the timing opportune; when you hand in a project your employer raves about or they otherwise compliment you or they're in a good mood because something great happened at work . . . pounce.

- Say something, in your words, along these lines: "I love working here and I've learned a lot, I hope I make a contribution. Graduation is coming up in May, and I really have to look at what I'm going to do next. Can we set up a meeting to talk about the possibility of my working here full-time after graduation?"

A couple of things might happen. They might be open to it, and if that's the case, great! If *not,* use that to your advantage, as well. Don't be defensive; say, "I understand. But as you know, I've got to do *something.* Can you give me some advice about who I should be talking to/would you mind talking to potential employers on my behalf once I contact them/would you put in a good word for me with lawyers you know?" Here's the benefit of this approach. Not only does it tap into a potential network of employers for you, but it also might make your current employer change his/her mind. They'll start thinking, "Hmm. I'm saying all these great things about this student. Maybe I don't want to lose him/her after all!"

The biggest obstacle is just bringing it up in the first place. Time it well, take a deep breath, and plunge in. Look at it this way. Right now, you don't have a permanent job. If you bring up the subject, one way or another, you will get one. It's the least risk alternative.

6. REMEMBER THAT THERE ARE PLENTY OF EMPLOYERS, *EXCELLENT* EMPLOYERS, WHO WON'T HIRE YOU UNTIL YOU GRADUATE . . . AND PASS THE BAR

Small law firms come to mind. Not only do they hire on an "as needed" instead of a fixed calendar basis, but they often need for you to be licensed to practice before they can bring you on. Many, many more law students work for small law firms than large ones, and truth be told they tend to be a happier work environment than large firms.

Other employers hire sporadically, as well. Public interest employers hire when they have an opening, and that could be anytime. So don't fool yourself into thinking that even close to a majority of employers like to have their ducks in a row before you graduate. It's just not true.

Having said that . . .

7. DON'T FOOL YOURSELF INTO THINKING IT JUST MAKES SENSE TO WAIT UNTIL AFTER YOU GRADUATE AND PASS THE BAR BEFORE YOU DO ANYTHING ABOUT JOBS

It may be that there are employers who won't hire you until after you pass the Bar, but that doesn't mean you should sit around with your thumbs up your butt career-wise until then!

Take advantage of the time you have left in school to do the activities we talked about in Chapter 10. Continue a targeted mailing campaign to employers (other than large law firms, who hire early). If there's an employer you're targeting (like a prosecutor's office) that won't make any offers until Bar results come in, volunteer for them in the meantime and if need be do something else part-time for pay.

Regardless of when an employer will hire you, it makes sense to do your prep work, take part in activities and meet with people ahead of time.

* * * SMART HUMAN TRICK * * *

Law student, Illinois school. She wants to go into public interest. She starts her search in April of her Third Year—*one month* before graduation.

She contacts an alum in Washington, DC, who works in public interest. The alum is very helpful and puts her onto the headquarters of a public interest organization in Virginia. She talks with a woman there who recommends her to the head of the organization. They conduct a phone interview with her, and she gets the job. She reports: "I can't believe I'm actually doing this in April. I never would have imagined it. But reaching out to people, it *works*."

8.   DON'T EVER TELL AN EMPLOYER *"I'LL TAKE ANYTHING"*

Trust me, I know how you feel. I *was* you. With graduation—and student loan payments—looming, there's the temptation to jump at any job at all. But as Tasha Everman says, "Don't look for the 'McJob'—'I'll take anything' sounds really bad."

As is true for any job search, employers need to feel that you're genuinely interested in working for them. We talked about this earlier in this book when we discussed enthusiasm, cover letters, resumes, and people and activities. There's no difference whether you're in your first semester of law school, or your last. The same attitude—"I'm interested in working for *you*"—has to prevail.

9.   LOOK AT JOB POSTINGS FROM THE CSO *EVERY DAY*

Some of the best opportunities will show up in the form of employers calling your CSO on a random basis. You never know when an employer you'd really enjoy working for will call your CSO *today*. Make a point of checking the job postings as often as possible, researching the employers who post and firing off your credentials as soon as possible.

10.   IF YOU'RE STALLING AT A CERTAIN POINT IN THE JOB SEARCH PROCESS

. . .

. . . Target exactly where things are going south. If you're sending letters or responding to postings and not getting interviews, have the CSO review your letters and resume. If you're getting interviews but no offers, have the CSO set up a mock interview for you to see what's going on.

No matter how far you're getting, make a point of going back and reading Chapter 5 on handling rejection. Rejection is a temporary situation but it can really dog your job search chances, because you start feeling so bad that you don't want to try anything else. It's *so* important to remember that the very next thing you do, the next person you talk to, might be your key to a great job. You can't give up, and that chapter will help you keep your chin up.

11.   DON'T SUFFER ALONE. GO TO YOUR CAREER SERVICES OFFICE

Again, I have to remind you that there are more students like you than there are students with offers in hand. Even if you *were* the only one, you shouldn't go it alone. Go to Career Services. Contrary to popular belief, they're not just interested in setting up on-campus interviews for people in the top 10% of the class. They're there to counsel and offer ideas and turn you on to opportunities you might not have found by yourself. Give them the chance to help you!

Chapter 30
I Graduated Without an Offer ... Where the Hell Is My Job?

"Sweet are the uses of adversity."
> William Shakespeare

"In three words I can sum up everything I have learned in life. It goes on."
> Robert Frost

You're out of law school, and you don't have a job. And that sucks.

I know, because I was you. I didn't have a job when I graduated. And that sucked, man.

In this chapter we're going to address this situation, and move you into the "employed" column as soon as possible. What you need to know up front is this: unemployment is not a permanent condition. Your obituary isn't going to read, "(S)he graduated from law school, and ... that was it." You're not going to spend the next sixty years flatlining. There's something great in store for you. There's actually a school of thought that says you can't be truly happy without being miserable and unemployed first! The fact is, your unemployment is immediate and concrete; what's in store for you is something you just don't know yet. You can't wrap your arms around it. And that's a very anxiety-producing situation.

Let's talk about it.

A.   What's Going on?

There are two ways to get to this point: Either you haven't looked for a job, or you *have* looked for one but what you've done hasn't worked.

If you've been searching, you may find it hard to believe that anybody *hasn't* been. It happens. I gave a job search seminar at one law school for unemployed graduates, and focused a lot on handling rejection, recharacterizing summer jobs gone bad, handling finances, and those kinds of issues. Two young women came up to me afterwards, and they were incredulous. They said, "You talk as though we should have done stuff before we graduated. We didn't. We planned from the beginning of law school that we'd go to class and take the summers off, and worry about getting a job after we graduated and passed the Bar."

Needless to say, I was a little taken aback. "You mean—you *never* did anything with a legal employer?"

"No," they sniffed.

I'm rarely at a loss for words, but I sure was then! I could have asked how they possibly overlooked everybody doing on-campus interviews and talking about their summer jobs, but ... what would have been the point?

So there's one option. If that's you, you've got to start doing what we'll talk about in Topic C *right now.*

But my hunch is you've done at least a few career-oriented things, and they haven't worked out as you intended. What we'll talk about in the rest of this chapter applies directly to you. The good news is this: no matter what *hasn't* worked before, we'll talk about a bunch of strategies that *will.* You'll be handing out business cards before you know it.

B. DON'T LET REJECTION DEFINE YOU

You're not going to want to believe this, but you're going to wind up a lot happier than colleagues who had jobs fall in their laps through OCI. Having to work to find a job means you have to put more thought into what you would enjoy doing, what your strengths and weaknesses are, you have to research and talk to more employers, and you'll make better decisions as a result. On top of that, your job search skills will benefit you forever. The skills you use to find *this* job will help you nail great gigs for the rest of your life. So no matter how bleak things look now, they're going to look a *lot* better, soon.

(For a lot more on dealing with rejection, see Chapter 5.)

* * * SMART HUMAN TRICK * * *

From an e-mail sent to me by a law school graduate:

> *"I started looking for a job in September of last year. I took a bunch of attorneys out to lunch, wrote letters, sent 'thank you' cards and basically followed the advice in your book to the letter. Nothing happened for seven months! Nobody called. The people who said they would call never did. There were many times when I came home to my wife and said, 'I think I*

might get a job with so-and-so'; it never happened. I got rejected again and again and again ...

One of the attorneys I went out to lunch with was a partner at a firm I'll call Joe and Blow. He was so impressed with me he called the #1 partner in front of me and told him to set up an interview with me. I was instructed to call the partner the next day. I did. The #1 partner said he would call me back right away; he never did. "Just another a**hole," I thought ...

... for the next seven months I did everything in your book. I also took on independent contractor work. Frankly, I was sick of your goddamn book and all the goddamn advice in it.

Then after seven months I got a call from #1 partner. He said, "Hi, this is so-and-so from Joe and Blow." You know what I felt? ANGER. I was pissed. This #*$& Q(was supposed to have called me months ago. I was totally sick and tired of getting absolutely no respect from these stinkin' attorneys. I said, "What can I do for you?" He responded, "Can we get together for lunch tomorrow?" I went to lunch, and we talked. I asked some tough questions, and was confident; I actually had a pretty good job in the contracting work, so I had nothing to lose.

He called me a week or two later and I went to lunch with him and the major client of the firm. A couple of weeks later, they hired me. They gave me the salary I requested and everything else I wanted! The added bonus: #1 partner and I get along great!"

C. HAVE WORDS PREPARED TO DESCRIBE YOUR SITUATION BEFORE YOU TALK TO ANYBODY ABOUT JOBS

I'm convinced that a lot of unemployed law school graduates hold themselves back from talking with people and going to law-related activities because they dread the question I dreaded:

"So ... what are you doing?"

It's *hyper* important to have a stock answer that you pull out for this question. I've got some ideas for you, but you'll probably come up with better ones of your own:

"I'm doing advanced graduate work in job search."

"You know those people who graduate knowing exactly what they're going to do next? I'm not one of them."

"You know how it is. You graduate, you've got your job in hand, your life laid out, and you know exactly what's coming. Well, *you* might know how it is. I don't."

If you don't betray anxiety about your situation, other people will take your lead. You see smart people doing this in the press all the time. I remember reading an interview with tennis player Andy Roddick, who was preparing for a tournament where he was likely to meet Roger Federer, one of the best tennis players ever, in a late round. At the time

Federer held an 11–1 record over Roddick in career meetings. When Roddick was asked about this, he responded, "Hey, nobody beats me twelve times in a row." What a great attitude! The fact is, people take their cue about how to treat you based on your own behavior. If you seem alright with what's going on, they'll feel alright about it, too. And people are much more likely to come up with ideas for you if they feel relaxed and comfortable.

D. DO *SOMETHING*. THERE IS MAGIC IN ACTION

You've probably done what we all do—gone around with a picture in your head of what your life would be like after graduation, the kind of job you'd get, the car you'd drive, your house, your salary. If things aren't shaking out like that immediately, it doesn't mean they're never going to happen. It only takes one phone call, attending one event, to get a job. It could be the next phone call you make, the next event you attend. It could be the 50th one. You never know. But if you don't make that call, you skip that event, you'll never know the opportunities you missed. Just do something. *One thing*. Immobility feeds on itself ... and so does action!

1. ACTIVITIES TO GET YOU IN TOUCH WITH POTENTIAL EMPLOYERS

While we go over these in detail in Chapter 10, here are a few ideas that have worked particularly well for recent graduates:

- Take part in sports teams with local lawyers (they're often sponsored by firms or bar associations);
- Volunteer doing whatever you want to do;
- Take advantage of informational interviews. As Golden Gate's Susanne Aronowitz points out, "Everybody identifies with you. If you say, 'Hey, I'm waiting for bar results, I'm trying to get information ...' people will talk to you."
- Don't overlook your fellow bar review students as contacts. Especially if they're from another state and already attorneys, they could put you onto a great gig.
- Don't skip the Yellow Pages as a source of potential employers. While there are firms who won't pay to be listed in Martindale–Hubbell, *everybody* is in the Yellow Pages.
- Skim bar association publications and the legal/business section of the newspaper for attorneys to contact.
- Check with the local bar association to see if they have a membership list you can access; it may even be on-line.
- Stay in touch with your former classmates who are now employed. Suck up your pride and let them know you're looking. Remember: most jobs are never posted *anywhere,* and the only way to find those openings is through people. If you have friends who are working, they may well get the inside skinny on jobs that you'd

never find out about any other way. Your friends from school know you and know what you're capable of doing. You're not looking for a handout; you're bringing something valuable to the table. Give them a call!

- Talk to headhunters in your target market. You don't have a "head to hunt" yet; they probably won't be useful helping you find a job. But they *will* be useful in telling you about the market, who's who, who you might contact yourself. After all, although you're not a great target for a headhunter before you nail your first gig, within a couple of years, you will be. It makes sense for them to be nice to you now, because they'll want you to contact them again in the years to come!

- Go back to employers who rejected you last semester or last year; it may well be that you've done something in the meantime that will make you more attractive to them.

* * * SMART HUMAN TRICK * * *

New graduate, Washington D.C. law school. She had contacted a law firm in the Fall semester of 3L, and got a form rejection. She does a seminar paper during Third Year, and since it concerns one of the firm's practice areas, she sends it to them after graduation. The partners are intrigued with the paper, and invite her for an interview.

She winds up with an offer.

* * * SMART HUMAN TRICK * * *

New law school graduate in the Midwest. She's taking Bar/Bri in Illinois, and she sits next to a guy who happens to be a lawyer from Texas, whose firm transferred him to its Chicago office. She asks him where he works, and he names a law firm she's dying to work for. Through him, she gets an interview ... and a job.

* * * SMART HUMAN TRICK * * *

3L, law school in New York. He meets with a small law firm; they like him and ask him about his salary expectations. He quotes a large law firm salary, and they respond, "Have a nice life."

Several months later, after graduation, he goes to a CLE. All of the members of the small firm are there, including a younger associate with whom he'd gotten along particularly well. He walks over and said hello, striking up their acquaintance again. The young associate asks, "What are you doing?" and the graduate responds, "Still looking at a few things ..." The associate says, "Send me your resume." The graduate does so ... and winds up with a job there.

* * * SMART HUMAN TRICK * * *

Recent graduate. He reports: "I didn't have a job and I didn't have any prospects. So I thought, what the hell. I got out Martindale/Hubbell and I went straight down the list of lawyers in Los Angeles, and every time I came to one that graduated from my law school, I picked up the phone and called them.

"I won't pretend that I wasn't nervous. Especially at first I was scared to death. I had a pretty simple pitch: 'I just graduated from X law school, I'm looking around for what I'm going to do next, I'd really appreciate any advice you can give me,' 'What would you do if you were me,' or 'I'm curious how you broke in to doing what you do.'

"I'd ask to set up a meeting at their convenience, but sometimes they just said, 'I've got a couple of minutes. Ask me your questions.'

"The thing that amazed me was that 75% of the people I called were willing to set up a meeting with me or talk to me on the spot. 75! Before I tried it I was absolutely convinced they would brush me off. It rarely happened. After a while it didn't even matter if somebody was rude, because I figured the next three people would help me out.

"I've made the most amazing contacts this way. People are a lot more helpful than I thought they'd be. And even when they're not, it doesn't matter. I've got a ton more people to contact!"

2. Maintain a Non-Demanding Job While You're Looking for a Full-Time "Permanent" Gig

You may find this ironic, but it's actually easier to look for a job while you're working. "How can that be?" you're wondering. Well, when your time is structured, you're actually more efficient than when you're totally free. My screenwriting mentor, Stewart Bronfeld, told me that when he was a producer-writer at NBC, when he needed a project done quickly he would always turn to someone who was busy. "*That* person knows how to manage his time," he said. So if you're worried a full-time gig will stop you from getting a great job—it won't!

It's important, of course, for the interim job to have the right attributes. The perfect job will have these features:

- It'll pay enough to meet your financial needs, at least at a minimal level; (if you can afford to volunteer, *fantastic)*
- It will provide enough time during the business day to arrange career interviews;

It can be part-time, second-shift or weekend work.

There are two types of "gap-fillers": jobs that are related to law, and jobs that aren't.

If you go for a job related to your dream gig, it should have the following attributes, it can do a lot for you that you may not even realize:

- It may give you a chance to meet people in your target practice;
- It might give you a chance to hone your legal skills;
- It might enhance your resume;
- It might give you a chance to get a bird's-eye view of a job you think you want, without making a long-term commitment to it.

What kinds of jobs are we talking about here? Project-oriented work for small firms or solo practitioners, legal temp jobs, legal assistant or paralegal work, and anything that shows up on your CSO's job postings on-line. If you let your CSO know that you're looking for temporary positions with legal employers, you may be surprised how many leads they'll have for you. The dirty little secret of job searching is that it's a lot easier for an employer to make a short-term commitment to you than a permanent one. (For listings of legal temping agencies, check out the *National Law Journal's* web site www.law.com.)

You can also do a post-graduate internship. According to Minnesota's Steve Marchese, "Consider a post-graduate internship, to last from August until January. It's a low-risk proposition for the employer, and a great experience for you."

Let's talk a moment about non-law-related "gap fillers." Its ideal attributes would include:

- Not requiring a long-term commitment;
- Not requiring any training (or very little);
- Easy to get;
- Low stress, so you can concentrate on your job search;
- Predictable hours, so that you can plan your job search and interviewing schedule with confidence.

Remember that no matter where you work, whether law-related or not, you can always do pro bono work while you're working. Especially if you want to break into public interest, keep volunteering until an opening occurs.

2. Don't Let Temporary Gigs Depress You. Contract Lawyering Is Actually a Career Some Attorneys Choose

Whether you're working as a contract lawyer or for a legal temp agency, *don't* let the idea that you're not in a "permanent" job get to you. Temporary jobs can lead to all sorts of amazing opportunities. Go to bar events, volunteer, remember that there's some great permanent gig waiting for you, you just haven't found it yet. A temporary job gives you the chance to pay your bills *and* look for a job, *and* you get legal experience on your resume. That's a great combination. On top of that, as one law school graduate points out, "I temped while I was looking for a permanent job, and I think it gave me a level of credibility that other applicants didn't have. I told employers, 'I'm currently working a temp gig, but I'm looking for something new.' "

If you take a temporary legal gig of any kind, there are three important items to consider:

a. Make sure time is flexible. You need time to look. Late shift is great.

b. The temp agency will tell you not to talk to lawyers at the office about jobs. Ha ha. Don't *ask* for a job, but you'd be foolish not to bring up the topic with questions along the lines of, "I really like this kind of work. If you were me, what would you do to break into it? What activities should I do? Who should I be talking to?"

c. Dress like a lawyer.

If you try doing temporary work, you may actually find that contract lawyering is something you want to pursue long-term. I've talked to a number of law school graduates who looked on it as a stop-gap, only to find that they enjoyed it so much they've stuck with it.

As a contract lawyer, you basically work as an independent contractor for firms, working either on projects or a set number of hours per week. Firms like it because they don't have to have a permanent slot for you; it's an easier decision to hire you when the work demands it. *Your* life on a day-to-day basis is largely what it would be if you were a permanent associate, and firms often keep their contract lawyers long-term. You get a very handsome hourly rate, but then again you basically have your own business, and have to pay taxes and account for your income that way. (For a discussion of this on-line, see www.myshingle.com.

When it comes to listing your contract work on your resume, you've got a couple of options. You can say that you were self-employed, which is accurate: You'd say, *The Law Office of [your name], Contract Attorney,* and then describe your contract positions and projects. If you work primarily for one firm, you can always ask them if you can call them your employer for purposes of your resume; saying that you worked for a particular firm is accurate even if you did it as an independent contractor. Just run it by them in advance to make sure they're fine with it!

E. MAKE YOURSELF A SCHEDULE, *AND STICK TO IT*

It's easy to suck up a ton of time and accomplish nothing. When you look at what you've tangibly done, you might find that the reason you're not finding a gig is that you're not really doing as much as you could be doing.

Instead, set up a schedule for yourself. Make a point of coming up with a number of items that you'll do every day, whether it's talk to five people, send out ten targeted mailers, contact the bar association for an activity to attend, schedule a CLE ... set yourself up with tangible goals so that you are using your time productively.

And keep track of the results! You'll be amazed at how your efforts will multiply; this person will put you onto that employer who'll suggest you take part in this activity ... you'll generate leads with each step you take. And all you need is for one of those leads to turn into a job!

F. TURN OFF YOUR COMPUTER. WELL—DON'T TURN IT OFF, MAYBE. BUT SPEND A LOT MORE TIME IGNORING IT

I know you won't really ignore the internet in your job search, and you shouldn't. But you should spend more time on the people-oriented activities we discuss in the rest of this chapter.

When you *are* on-line, look at the resources we discussed in Chapter 6 on Research, and Chapter 11 on the Internet.

G. FOCUS YOUR EFFORTS ON NO MORE THAN A COUPLE OF PRACTICE AREAS/SETTINGS

One of the things that may have hindered your job search so far is something that hurts a lot of law students: that is, difficulty confining yourself to a single goal (or maybe two). Maybe you like a whole lot of things. Maybe you're terrified of being "pigeonholed." Here's what you need to do: tell yourself that you're not making a lifetime decision. It's a preliminary decision, to be revisited over and over again. Do what appeals to you the most right now; if you find you love it, great. If you don't, you can always change course later on. In fact, some of the happiest people I know are "serial careerists," who change jobs every few years when something better comes along. If that winds up happening to you—fine! But for right now, pick something and focus on it.

H. YOUR COVER LETTERS

We cover these in detail in Chapter 7. Follow that advice. Pay special attention to two pieces of advice: First, if you possibly can, start your letters with the words, "So-and-so recommended that I contact you." That letter will get so much more attention than a letter that doesn't start with a mutual acquaintance.

On top of that, *always* address your letters to *somebody by name* in the organization. If you don't have a mutual acquaintance, call and ask for the name of the hiring person, or go on-line and choose an alum from your law school (or even undergraduate), or choose someone whose practice focuses on something that interests you. You *always* need a name—choose someone who has *something* in common with you or does something you're targeting.

As important as sending letters is following up. It's meaningless to send your credentials if you're not going to follow up afterwards. We discuss this as well in Chapter 7. It takes some nerve to make that call—but it's crucial!

I. Your Resume

Go back and read Chapter 8, where we discussed resumes in detail. In particular:

1. **Recast what you've got.** Are you milking your work and school experience for its maximum potential? It's possible that you're not seeing the possibilities in what you've done. I remember meeting a law school graduate in Nebraska in a particularly memorable way. After I gave the *Guerrilla Tactics* seminar at her school, she raised her hand during the Q & A session and said, "I graduated five years ago and I've never had a job." Well, after every student in the room had broken the sitting high jump record, I told her, "Let's chat afterwards and see what's going on."

   It turns out that she hadn't been sitting around watching TV and drinking beer for five years. She'd actually done a lot of law-related things, but because she hadn't done what she'd dreamed of—work at a large law firm—she characterized it as "nothing." She'd done some really interesting projects, like writing a legal handbook for ambulance drivers. When we talked about her experiences and how she ought to put them on her resume, she began to see that she had skills to bring to the table. Within a month, she was working at the local prosecutor's office, and couldn't have been happier.

2. **If your experience isn't helping you, get stuff on your resume in a hurry. "Pimp your resume," as we discussed in the Resume Chapter, Chapter 8.** Take advantage of CLEs, writing competitions, writing an article on an issue or a profile of a lawyer for the bar association ... there are a ton of things you can do *right now* to make your resume sing.

J. Interviews

Follow all of the advice in Chapter 9 on Interviews. Specifically, be prepared for what you'll say in response to "Tell me about yourself," and the killer: "Why don't you have a job yet?" The most important thing to remember about this question is that you have to get *immediately* past the precise question, and turn it into something that promotes you. You can say something like, "It would have been great to nail down a job before this, but I'll tell you what I bring to the table for you ..." and then talk about how you'll help the employer accomplish what they want. Humor also doesn't hurt, at least as an opening and if the interviewer's demeanor suggests they appreciate humor. You could try something like, "I like a challenge. I figure *anybody* can get a clerkship after Second Year and get an offer out of it. I wanted to challenge myself." You could then add, "But seriously. I can tell you why you ought to hire me ..."

What this will do is this: it will show that you're confident, which is really important. It will highlight how you'll help the employer, which is also crucial. And the interviewer won't even notice that you didn't really answer their question!

Remember: In interviews, the interviewer doesn't have laser vision. (S)he can't see how you feel; (s)he can only hear what you say and see how you conduct yourself. Euphemizing issues you don't want to discuss is smart strategy. I remember hearing an interview with someone from the State Department, who said they instruct people who work there never to say, "I made a mistake." Instead, they're to say they "lost control of the situation." (I'm not actually sure that's better, but it doesn't include the word 'mistake'!)

So read Chapter 9, and plan your strategy for tough questions you anticipate. You'll be shocked how well things will go when you have the words ready!

In addition, to practice those words, do a mock interview through Career Services. It doesn't matter that you've already graduated; they'll be happy to set one up for you.

K.   IF YOU GET FEEDBACK FROM EMPLOYERS THAT THEY'RE LOOKING FOR SOMETHING YOU DON'T HAVE . . .

Consider "pimping your resume," as we discussed earlier in this chapter; we talk about it in detail in Chapter 8. It's the idea of getting valuable elements on your resume in a hurry. For targeted skills, two of the best ideas involve, first, taking CLEs on relevant issues (you can find out about CLEs through any local bar association web site, and you can generally talk your way in for free by volunteering to help out and/or pleading poverty while you're looking for work. After all, their costs are all fixed; having you there doesn't make it a penny more expensive for them.) Second, consider volunteering for the bar association to get the skills/knowledge you need (or volunteering to help lawyers who do their pro bono work with your school's clinical program).

The bottom line is this: It's easy to cram practical skills onto your resume in a hurry, focused in any way that will make you more attractive to the employers you're targeting.

L.   "WHEN DO I GIVE UP ON MY DREAM? . . ."

I get asked this question a lot. My short answer is: never. You never give up on your dream. Whether or not you pursue it full-tilt right now . . . that's a different question. There are two issues at work, it seems to me:

1.   **What's your threshold of pain?** It may be that there are reasons you can hold out for a while. When I graduated from law

school and was pursuing my dream of running my own publishing company, I lived in my parents' basement while I created what became the *Law In A Flash* flash cards. I lived in that basement for *three years*. I cobbled together menial jobs that brought me twenty grand total for the entire three years, just enough to pay my student loans and little else. I didn't have a day off. I couldn't buy *anything*. And when people asked me what I was doing, their response was generally, "What are you? *Crazy?*" But because I didn't have any responsibilities and my parents were willing to sacrifice their basement, I had a pretty high threshold of pain. I was also aided by the fact that I was living five hundred miles away from my law school, so I didn't have to worry about running into my classmates. Having people ask you constantly what you're doing, or even worse, questioning your sanity, can make you nuts in and of itself. So I had the benefit of being able to disappear into my cave and write with no distractions!

You might not be in the same situation for a bunch of reasons. You might not be interested in making those financial sacrifices, and I understand that. So part of the equation is figuring out how much you can tolerate.

2. **Does it make sense to do something else to facilitate your dream, in the short term?** It may well be that if you get some work experience doing something that's not what you dreamed of, it will position you better to pursue your dream. For instance, in my case I could have gone to work for a small transactional firm that represented small businesses, to give me a better idea of how businesses are run, funded, and the issues they encounter. That would have made me a *much* smarter businesswoman from the get-go.

Depending on what *your* dream is, it may make sense to work for a couple of years and use that opportunity to take advantage of CLEs, bar association functions, and the ability to build a resume that laterals you into what you want.

The short answer is: while practicalities can dictate what you do right now, you never have to let go of your dream!

M. Necessity Often Breeds Creativity

When a job doesn't fall in your lap, you may come up with an idea that would never have dawned on you if you'd been gainfully employed. I *guarantee* you that if I'd graduated from law school with a job offer in hand, I'd never have dreamed up *Law In A Flash*. I wouldn't have had any reason to. Similarly, there might be something lurking in your mind that will only see the light of day because you're searching for something to do!

Throughout history, desperation has been fertile grounds for creativity. A couple of examples:

- At the 1904 world's fair in St. Louis, an ice cream vendor selling cups of ice cream had so many customers he ran out of cups. In desperation, he looked around to see if any nearby vendor might have spare containers. All he could find was a waffle concession. He quickly bought some waffles and began selling them wrapped around a scoop of ice cream. The substitute became even more popular than the original.

- Gerry Thomas, who invented the TV dinner, did so when he was a salesman for a frozen food company called Swanson. Swanson was stuck with an oversupply of turkeys being shuttled around in refrigerated railroad cars. Thomas hit upon the idea of selling frozen turkey dinners to use up the excess supply of turkeys.

You get the idea. Maybe there's something uniquely creative waiting for you ... and being unemployed when you graduate is the only way to seize it!

N. IF YOU'RE AT THE END OF YOUR ROPE ...

For gosh sakes, reach out to someone. Anyone. Being unemployed when you graduate is a situation that's as bad as you make it. If graduating without a legal job in hand is the worst thing that happens to you, you're doing damned well.

We've spent this entire chapter talking about solutions, and one of them will work for you. Maybe you have to try them over and over and over again, but *something* will work. If you're so depressed that you just can't get yourself motivated to try any of them anymore, it's time to call your school and talk to the Dean of Students. Trust me: you won't be the only depressed graduate they've ever helped. They're *there* to help you. You're still a member of the family. If you do nothing else ... make that call!

Materials excerpted in this chapter from The University of San Francisco, Hastings, and Golden Gate.

Shout-out to Matthew Pascocello of the American University Washington College of Law for his contributions to this chapter.

Chapter 31
I Want to Be a Not-Lawyer: Alternative Careers

"If you want perfect safety, you have to sit on the fence and watch the birds fly."

Orville Wright

Having a law degree doesn't force you to be a lawyer, you know. As entrepreneur Andy Epstein says, "It's law school—not *lawyer* school." The only important thing is for you to find a job that makes you happy, and it may well be one that doesn't put an "Esq." after your name.

After all, I'd be the worst person in the world to try and convince you that practicing law is what you really should be doing. I've got a law degree, and I've *never* been a lawyer. Your "best use" may similarly be outside the practice of law ... and as Northern Illinois' Mary Obrzut points out, "There are some jobs out there that'll really knock your socks off!"

* * * SMART HUMAN TRICK * * *

New graduate, elite West Coast law school. He takes a job with a very large, prestigious law firm in the Midwest, although his heart is not entirely in it.

Wanting a little something more in his life, he becomes a volunteer firefighter. He enjoys that so much, he gives up the law firm, and makes firefighting his career.

I keep a notebook of jobs that stand out in some respect. The entries include brewmaster at Anheuser Busch (you taste beer for a living); driver of the Oscar Mayer Weinermobile (typically people do it for a year after they graduate from school, like a judicial clerkship ... but not really); Travel and entertainment editor at Playboy Magazine; Scanning the newspapers of the world looking for "hot spots" for investment houses; Captain of the Q.E.2; movie location scout.

There isn't a reason you couldn't have any of those jobs with a law degree .. or any other job, for that matter. Because law touches everything, you can *always* make an argument that your law degree is useful somehow ... although the further you get from practicing law, the more of a stretch that is! Of course, it's far more likely that you want a gig that bears *some* relation to your degree (I list the popular targets in Appendix B at the end of this chapter).

Ironically, you'll find that this chapter isn't a radical departure from everything we've talked about. Why? Because almost everything I've told you to do applies whether you're looking for a job practicing law or whether you're looking to be a juggler or baseball manager or Barbie-doll-shaped cake maker or television news show host (like Tim Russert) or rancher or suitcase girl on *Deal or No Deal* (all jobs held by law school graduates, incidentally). You'll still have to do some thinking to decide exactly what you want ("not-law" doesn't cut it!). You'll still want to talk to people and take part in activities as your primary means of learning about jobs you think you want, and ways to get those jobs. The basic philosophy behind correspondence, and resumes, and interviewing is largely the same.

You *will,* however, find that there are certain elements of your search that will be a lot tougher. Deciding on what you want to do, if you don't narrow your universe to practicing law, is a lot tougher, just because there's so much more to choose from. As Career Counselor Kathleen Brady points out, "The good news is, you can do anything with a law degree. The bad news is ... you can do anything with a law degree." It's the difference between saying "Go out of the building through the red door," and "Go out of the building using any door *except* the red door."

You'll also have a credibility issue to overcome; convincing employers that you don't want to be a lawyer, when you've spent three years in law school, can be a challenge. (Of course, we'll talk about how to handle it in this chapter.)

But let's face it: there's difficult, and there's difficult. I remember visiting the Fort Worth Zoo, where they had a cheetah cub named Esmeralda. The sign in front of her enclosure said she was the product of a zoo-bred mother and the semen of a wild Namibian cheetah. And I thought to myself: now, collecting the semen of a wild Namibian cheetah. *That's* difficult. Nailing a nontraditional job with a J.D.? Comparatively not so tough, don't you agree?

So let's talk about it. Let's start out with ...

A. Smoking Out Why You Don't Want to Practice Law . . . and Discussing the Ramifications of That

You may think, offhand, that it's kind of silly to rehash why it is you don't want to practice law. Feelings are facts, you don't want it, and that's that, right? Well, not quite. There might be *some* kind of legal practice you'd love; you just don't know about it yet. As St. John's' Maureen Provost Ryan points out, "Most students who think they want out of the law wind up recommitted to it in a whole new way. Only 5% give it up all together!"

The reason it's worth starting your nontraditional search by figuring out whether you really don't want to practice is that, believe it or not, you give up a *lot* when you decide not to practice law. You don't have the prestige of being a lawyer, and you probably don't have the same money, either. Furthermore, if there's any tiny part of you that thinks you might want to practice law, it's a lot easier to practice for a year or two and then jump into something else, than it is to abandon law and then, a few years down the road, try and get back into it. Considerations like those lead to advice like this, from Illinois' Cindy Rold: "Before you become convinced you don't want to practice law, take some time to think about what it *really* is that you don't like!"

So the point of this section is to figure out whether a law career really isn't for you. What I'll do here is start with the seven most common reasons for not wanting to practice law. Then we'll talk about what you should do if you're not *completely* sure that practice isn't for you. And, finally, we'll talk about the ramifications of turning your back on practicing law, so that you know what you're in for.

1. So—Why Don't You Want to Practice Law? The Seven Most Common Reasons

a. You Don't Think You Can Get a Job Practicing Law, and Nontraditional Jobs Are Easier to Get

From the conversations I've had with career counselors around the country, this is the #1 reason law students want to turn their backs on law. If you did a lot of job searching before you picked up this book, it could be that you were so frustrated by the search that your mind transmogrified that frustration into a feeling that you just don't want to practice law, after all. "Surely," you may be saying to yourself, "it *must* be easier to get a nonlaw job! And self, stop calling me 'Shirley.'"

Now it may take a bit of soul searching for you to realize this is what's coloring your decision. The law school career counselors I've talked to say that they don't have to scratch the surface too far to find that this is what's motivating many students who come in saying they don't want to practice law.

So, at its roots, what we've got here is a fear that you won't be able to get a job practicing law, and a perception that nonlegal jobs are easier to get. Let's talk about each of those in turn.

1. "I DON'T HAVE THE GRADES TO GET A JOB PRACTICING LAW"

As Cal Western's Lisa Kellogg points out, "Grades make people think twice about practicing law; they get nervous about every decision." Albany's Sandy Mans adds, " 'I'm looking for something law-related' is a euphemism. It normally translates into: 'I'm not doing well in school, and I need to rethink it.' " Career Counselor Wendy Werner is even more blunt: "When students say, 'I want a nontraditional career,' it's usually a lie. They're afraid. They think they need to be open to other options. They're afraid of not getting what they want."

If you've read much of this book at all, you know I believe in your ability to get a job, regardless of your grades. Heck, there's a whole *chapter* about that issue, Chapter 13! Instead, it's much more likely that you've been spending your time on things that aren't terribly productive, like mass mailers or responding to job listings that don't match your credentials. If you follow the advice in Chapter 10 about finding jobs through people and activities, there's no question in my mind that you'll be happily employed before long. So don't let your fears concerning your grades convince you that practicing law is not for you!

2. "IT'LL BE EASIER TO GET JOBS OUTSIDE OF LAW"

Just the opposite, as Kentucky's Drusilla Bakert points out. Wendy Werner says, "Employers will ask, 'Why *don't* you want to use your degree?" Maryland's Jose Bahamonde–Gonzalez adds, "You have to convince employers outside the law that your desire to do something else is a *positive*— nobody wants to hire a failure!"

Before you consider turning your back on law because you think it'll be easier to get a job doing something else, remember that whatever you choose will be full of people who do have the background tailor-made for it! As Career Counselor Kathleen Brady points out, "What's nontraditional for you is *very* traditional for someone else." Now, it's true that there are some fields where a law degree has cachet, like real estate development, law firm administration and many corporate jobs, but even in fields like those you have to show a positive interest in them. It's not enough simply to be dissatisfied with the idea of practicing law.

So the bottom line on this particular motivation is: it's not valid. Don't be misled by the idea that it's easier to get a nonlegal job than a legal one.

B. YOU CAN'T IMAGINE WORKING WITH PEOPLE LIKE YOUR CLASSMATES AND/OR YOUR PROFESSORS

As Notre Dame's Gail Peshel points out, a lot of students who think they don't want to practice law are really reacting to a bad law school experience. It may be, as San Diego's Susan Benson says, that you just can't imagine going to work with your classmates! Or maybe you've been grilled by professors, and you figure *they're* jerks, and that if that's what lawyers are like, you want nothing to do with them.

I'm down with that. I remember my class at law school, and I'd rather eat slugs than have to work with one or two of my classmates. But it's a mistake to generalize your law school experience to practicing law. For one thing, even though there may be some real trolls in your class, there must be *some* classmates you like. When you look for a job with the plan we've discussed throughout this book, you'll gravitate toward organizations that are peopled with the kinds of personalities you *do* get along with. And when it comes to disliking your professors, it's important to remember that they're playing a role when they're in the classroom. Many professors who pride themselves on being really tough in class are actually pretty nice outside of it, and yes, I'm actually writing this with a straight face. So you have to remember the *context* when you think about professors you can't stand.

Furthermore, you've got no guarantee that any field you choose *outside* of law will be populated with people you like *more* than your classmates. There's no profession you'll ever find where you can honestly say, "Gee, I like every last one of these people."

So if you think you don't want to practice law because you don't like the atmosphere at school—don't give it up Read the topic, "What to Do if You're Not Absolutely, Positively Sure That You Don't Want To Practice Law," later in this chapter and try the techniques I talked about in Chapter 10 before you give up on the profession *entirely*.

C. YOU'VE HAD (OR ARE HAVING) A BAD WORK EXPERIENCE

As Michigan's Nancy Krieger points out, a rotten summer clerkship is a frequent reason students turn their interests away from practicing law. And Case Western's Debra Fink adds, "You may not hate the law, but just the place you're working—the firm, the politics, the people."

If you *are* having a miserable time at work, it's hard *not* to stereotype the rest of the practice of law the same way. I'm down with that, because it was a gruesome summer experience that convinced *me* I didn't want to practice law. I clerked at one of the biggest, most prestigious law firms in the country, and I was *miserable*. I thought to myself, "Working for a large law firm is what everybody wants to do. It's the best you can do in law. And if *that* makes me miserable, then I must not want to practice law at all."

If you've read much of this book, you can see the holes in my reasoning. For one thing, working at a large firm *isn't* "the best you can do in law"; it's a huge mistake to think it's the right working environment for even a substantial minority of law students, let alone *everybody*.

Furthermore, there's no single job that represents what "practicing law" is like. I got a hilarious e-mail from a woman a few years ago, who told me that she was transitioning out of another career and she'd gone to a career coach for guidance on what she ought to do next. She took a battery of personality tests, and they showed that she was analytical, enjoyed detail work, and so forth. She said to the career coach, "Gee. Doesn't this suggest I'd enjoy being a lawyer?" and the coach dismissively responded, "You don't want *that*. All lawyers do is argue, and they're all miserable." Ha! Ha ha!

The fact is, law jobs in different settings are so different they're entirely different careers. Your experience at a U.S. Attorney's office will be radically different from a Wall Street firm, which will be nothing like a corporate counsel's office or a public interest employer. Heck, your experience in different practice sections *of the same law firm* can be different as chalk and cheese. The only thing all of those jobs share is the title "practicing law." They've got different environments, very different kinds of people and enormously different responsibilities.

So if a bad work experience is convincing you that you don't want law, don't give it that halo effect! Instead, first consider some of the ideas in Topic 2, just ahead, before you turn your back on the law.

D. YOU'VE GOT OTHER INTERESTS, AND YOU JUST DON'T SEE HOW YOU'RE GOING TO MESH THOSE WITH PRACTICING LAW

It may be that you have some strong, driving interest, and you're not sure how you can put that together with practicing law. After all, when most people think about practicing law, they think about litigation. But there are *many, many* other options—jobs that blend *all kinds* of interests with the practice of law! Here are a few of the anecdotes I've heard from Career Services Counselors around the country:

- One student at a Southern law school was absolutely positive that he didn't want to practice law; he'd gone to acting school, and he didn't see how he could do anything related to that. Today, he's a lawyer with the Screen Actors' Guild.

- One student liked the idea of being a forest ranger; he wanted the outdoor life. He went into construction law, which gave him a lot of fresh air—*and* allowed him to keep the prestige (and the salary) of practicing law.

- A lawyer named David Musslewhite liked the idea of running a coffee house *and* being a lawyer, so he opened a combination coffee house/law office called "Legal Grounds" in Dallas, with the tag line "Friendly neighborhood law and coffeehouse."

- A student at a school in the Northeast was doing insurance defense litigation, and hated it. When he dug further into exactly what it is that turned him of, he found that he liked the technical aspects of the work, but he hated the litigation. He made contacts, and did some informational interviews to find out how he could keep what he liked about his job, and yet shed the aspects he *didn't* like. The job he found did just that, allowing him to assess potential liabilities without having anything to do with trial work: he's the risk manager at a zoo!

The Career Services Office at George Washington University compiled a list showing how a J.D. + experience in something else (paid or volunteer, or a hobby or another degree) have added up to a nontraditional career for its graduates. They include:

J.D. + volunteer fund raising = nonprofit management

J.D. + knowledge of insurance industry through insurance defense practice = risk management

J.D. + love of horses = lobbyist/legislative analyst for national equestrian association

J.D. + previous job as nurse = compliance officer for medical device company

J.D. + grassroots political experience = executive director of legislative commission

J.D. + lending training program with bank = bank vice president, loan review

J.D. + sales experience = regional sales coordinator, legal software company

J.D. + MBA and mediation classes = manager, employee relations

The point here is that no matter how unrelated to the law you think your interests are, there may be a way of blending the two so you'll have a job you really like. Go talk to your Career Services Counselors, and tell them your concerns, and solicit their help. They'll be able to open your eyes to a whole raft of practice options that I'll wager you never knew existed!

* * * YOU CAN'T MAKE THIS STUFF UP * * *

From a 2005 *Chicago Sun–Times* article:

Lawyer/porn star must have interesting business card

Criminal defense attorney Ronald S. Miller does more than file briefs—he also takes them off.

Miller has spent days in front of a judge and nights in front of a camera as Don Hollywood, a porn star. His wife, a former accountant, is also a porn star.

"My whole life, I've been one of those people who sees the wet paint sign, and has to go up and touch it to see if it's wet," said the 56–year-old Miller. "I want to experience everything, try everything."

He has appeared in more than 9 films in the past seven years.

Miller said he tells his clients about his night job and has had no trouble balancing the careers.

Ethics expert and attorney Arthur Margolis said Miller isn't breaking any rules moonlighting as a porn actor.

"There isn't anything more unethical about that than being an actor or a novelist or somebody who sells frozen yogurt," Margolis said. "The only thing you have to be careful of, as you would in any other industry, is you don't do anything criminal or unethical in the sense of dishonesty."

Diane Curtis, a spokeswoman for the California Bar Association, declined to comment on Miller's second career but said Wednesday the bar doesn't have a policy prohibiting such activity.

E. YOU THINK LAW IS BORING

Maybe you find your schoolwork boring and you're worried that if you practice law, that will be boring, too. After all, there *are* jobs that require you to do a lot of what you do in law school—research, write briefs, write memoranda, and so forth. (Ironically enough, it takes up much of your time if you're a new associate at a large law firm!) But that's not *all* of law, not by a long shot. As Northern Illinois' Mary Obrzut points out, "If you think law is boring, try a year with the state attorney's office or the public defender. It's exciting, and relatively easy to get, and it's great experience. It doesn't pay as much as other types of law, but you may find you really like it!"

In fact, there are a whole *lot* of law jobs that you'd find stimulating. The reason they may not be obvious to you is that the jobs everybody talks about—namely, big firm jobs—are heavy on research and writing, at least for the first few years. So talk to your career counselors at school, and state your concerns. They'll direct you to alums who do things you'll find exciting. Or make contacts of your own, as we talked about in Chapter 10. The point here is: Don't condemn the entire practice of law based on what you do in law school!

F. YOU DON'T LIKE THE ADVERSARIAL NATURE OF LAW, OR IT OTHERWISE DOESN'T APPEAL TO YOU EMOTIONALLY

If you don't like taking a strong position on one side of an argument, any job that requires that will make you miserable. There *are* areas of the law that aren't adversarial—for instance, trusts and estates and tax work are two areas that come to mind—but they may not be your cup of tea, either.

Or, as Wendy Werner points out, maybe you don't like the idea of billing your hours, as lawyers in private practice have to do; perhaps it's too intrusive, to "Big Brother"-esque for you.

Or maybe you never wanted to practice law in the first place; you just wanted better writing and analysis skills. A classmate of mine was motivated to go to law school because he was a newspaper reporter; his publisher wanted him to start reporting on legal matters and suggested that he go to law school for background.

Any of these motivations are valid reasons for not wanting to practice certain kinds of law. But as I've pointed out before in this section, it's impossible to lump all of legal practice into one brief description. It's not all adversarial, and there probably is something that would appeal to you emotionally. The problem with all of the motivations we discussed here is that knowing what it is that you *don't* like doesn't help you get a job doing something you *do* like. What you have to do is go through the exercises in Chapter 2 which help you isolate the elements you need for job satisfaction. And talk with people, people in lots of different jobs, to see what they like about what they do. Talk with your Career Services Counselors, and state your concerns about law. They'll have other ideas for you on jobs you ought to consider.

The bottom line here is that it may be true that you're not emotionally suited to practice law. As Maine's Tammy Willcox says, "Some people would wither and die with a law job!" Maybe that's you. But make sure you've researched it and determined that you really don't want it, before you turn your back on it!

G. The Whole Reason You Wanted a Law Degree in the First Place Is That You Thought You Could Do Anything With a Law Degree

You can do anything ... but not *because* of your law degree. As the Career Services Director at one law school points out, "You *can* do anything with a law degree ... as long as it involves practicing law." Susan Benson echoes that, adding, "The 'lawyer-as-surgeon' idea, that you can do anything with a law degree, is *nonsense*." As George Washington's Laura Rowe Lane says, "What a law degree *does* get you is respect in other things, but even then, only *certain* other things."

You can roughly slot jobs into three categories:

● Jobs where you need a law degree (or really should have one), like practicing law or being a judge.

● Jobs where a law degree is helpful, like real estate development, or managing a nonprofit organization, or being a law school administrator.

- Jobs where a law degree is no help at all, and instead you have to explain it away.

The closer a job is to traditional lawyering, the easier it'll be to break into. Of course, if you're willing to undergo more training, there really is nothing you can't do. Surgeon? Sure ... if you go to med school. Clown? Sure ... if you go to clown college.

2. What to Do if You're Not Absolutely, Positively Sure That You Don't Want to Practice Law ...

Good! If you're reading this, it means you didn't skip this section. That's a good thing, because there's a strong possibility that there's some way to practice law that will make you happy.

Here are some things to consider doing:

A. Consider Taking the Bar Exam

Ha. Ha ha. Easy for *me* to say. I didn't take it. But the fact is, just about every expert you talk to will tell you to take the bar exam even if you don't intend to practice. That's good advice, and here's why: As I discuss later in this chapter, it's *very* important to convince nonlegal employers that you're not choosing them because you couldn't make it in law. Willamette's Diane Reynolds says, "Taking the bar exam may sound heretical to some people, but you need it to validate that you're a lawyer and not a failure." On top of that, it adds credibility and luster to your credentials.

Furthermore, if you *do* decide after all that you want to practice law in a few years' time, then you've taken and passed the bar when it's easiest to do so; that is, when you graduate from school and everything is still relatively fresh in your mind.

So if you think there's a slight possibility you may want to practice law, taking the bar is a smart move.

B. *Consider* Biting the Bullet and Practicing for a Year or Two

If you think you want to do something other than practicing law, many law school career counselors suggest that you practice for a year or two anyway, and *then* try something else. There are several reasons for this:

- It will stop you from having regrets later on. As Franklin Pierce's Sophie Sparrow points out, "Practicing in a comfortable setting for a year or two before you try an alternative stops you from looking back and saying, 'I gave up. I should have persisted!'"

- The easiest time to practice, if you think you'll *ever* want to, is when you graduate from law school. As Florida's Ann Skalaski says, "At least *try* practice first, because it's hard to get back in without having a year or two under your belt."

- It will make you more marketable to nonlegal employers. As Drusilla Bakert points out, "The dirty little secret is that the vast majority of nontraditionals practiced law first!"

If none of those reasons resound with you, then don't bother practicing law at all. But if they *do,* then go practice at least briefly. Of course, it's *still* important to find a job you like; I'm not advising that you grit your teeth and do something you *hate* for a year or two. Which leads me directly to my third suggestion ...

c. TRY A LEGAL JOB THAT REQUIRES A LITTLE CREATIVITY AND EXCITEMENT!

If you think you don't want law, it may be because you're not broadening your horizons enough to cover types of practice that you might really enjoy. Jose Bahamonde–Gonzalez suggests "Getting some hands-on experience, like clerking for a judge, or working for a public defender." Ann Skalaski advises students who think they want out of the law to "consider the public sector—in-house counsel with schools, city attorney, county attorney—jobs like that." Gail Cutter tells law students with qualms about traditional practice to "Consider law experiences where there's more creativity—for instance, public interest work."

Another great way to get you juiced about law is to do a PSLaw-Net.project, which we talk about in detail in Chapter 10. It puts you into a volunteer public interest position, although public interest is defined broadly, everything from traditional advocacy to state attorneys' generals' offices. The gigs are relatively short, and they're a great way to meet a lot of people and do some very interesting stuff. They may even revive your interest in practicing law!

The bottom line is, you may not be excited about practicing law only because you haven't been exposed to types of practice you'd love.

d. CONSIDER TAKING TIME OFF FROM LAW SCHOOL

If you're still in law school, and you really think you don't want to have anything to do with practicing law, consider taking some time off. As Nancy Krieger says bluntly, "If what you really want to do is manage a bookstore, why go to law school?"

You may be horrified at the prospect of not finishing law school, but if you're really convinced you don't want to practice law *and* you don't want to do anything closely related to it, there's a solid argument to be made for at least taking a sabbatical from it. For one thing, you're spending a lot of *somebody's* money to go to law school, if not your own. For another, even if you are in school because you're putting off getting a job—that's why I went!—you can do that getting *any* graduate degree, and you might as well make it one that you like.

And there's always the fact that taking time off doesn't have the negative impact on employers you think it will. As I've pointed out before, employers would much rather that you got your doubts out of your system *before* you started working with them—not *afterwards!*

Finally, as Susan Benson points out, it's not as though you can't come back. The ABA gives you five years to finish law school. That means you've got two years to play with.

I've actually advised students to do this a bunch of times. I've had 1Ls come up to me and say things like, "Before law school I was trying to figure out if I wanted to be a singer/actress/pilot/whatever, and now I'm here, I think I really want to do the other thing ..." I always tell them: Give yourself a year. Pursue that dream for a full calendar year, and tell yourself that you'll make your decision on coming back when you've given it a shot. One of two things will happen: either the other dream will consume you and you won't want to come back, in which case you've made the right decision. Or it won't seem so grand once you're doing it, and law will suddenly look a whole lot rosier. You'll come back reinvigorated and eager to give law a try. Either way—you win!

E. PROCEED THROUGH THE REST OF THIS CHAPTER AS THOUGH YOU'RE SURE YOU *DON'T* WANT TO PRACTICE LAW

Here's the thing: a lot of what I'll advise you to do in this chapter applies whether you think you maybe kinda sorta want to practice law, or whether you're running screaming from it. That's because I'll show you how to pick out the attributes that are important to you for *any* job you pursue, and how to nail that job. After all the Holy Grail here is the job of your dreams, and if that means you don't want to practice law, that's OK. So pretend for right now that you don't want to practice. The decision-making process we'll talk about will help you determine what you really want to do, law-related or not.

3. IF YOU'RE CONVINCED YOU DON'T WANT TO PRACTICE LAW, BE AWARE OF THE TRADEOFFS THAT ENTAILS!

Before you decide conclusively not to practice law, you need to be aware of the tradeoffs that entails. These might not change your mind— they didn't change mine!—but you need to know about them before you make your decision.

A. NONLEGAL EMPLOYERS MAY NOT EMBRACE YOUR LAW DEGREE

Depending on the nontraditional job you choose, you may find that your law degree actually works *against* you. I discuss this in great detail in Topic E, later in this chapter. But for now, suffice it to say, in Wendy Werner's words, that "Nobody wants to be a default option!" Some employers will feel that they're only a fall-back position because you couldn't nail a legal job, and as soon as one opens up, you're history. Or they may hate lawyers. Some people, hard as it is to believe, do. Be prepared for a sneering response to your education from some quarters!

B. YOUR FAMILY AND FRIENDS MAY FEEL YOU'RE "WASTING" YOUR DEGREE

Don't expect everyone you know to be a thousand percent behind your decision not to practice law. I've been out of school for years and I think my father is still crying himself to sleep over the fact I turned my back on it.

If you go to a prestigious law school, if you do *anything* other than go to a large prestigious firm, you'll meet resistance. As a career counselor at an elite law school puts it, "For our students, anything other than a large, name firm is an alternative career!"

No matter where you go to school, you'll get this reaction even if you get into something closely related to law. As you know, I created the *Law In A Flash* flash cards. It would have been well nigh impossible to do that without a law degree, and I think it was a pretty sound way to use my education. But when I tell people about what I've done (and what I'm doing now), I'll occasionally get that "Tsk, tsk . . . aren't you sad you're wasting your degree?" *No . . . I'm sorry I have to explain myself to chuckleheads like you, however.* I don't actually say that. But you see my point: when you step away from the law, a lot of people, even those who love you, may question your decision.

C. YOU WON'T HAVE THE "TRAPPINGS" OF PRACTICING LAW; THE PRESTIGE AND, PERHAPS, THE MONEY

It may not seem like it from where you sit, but for a large segment of the population, being a lawyer carries a certain cachet. It is, after all, considered one of the "professions." When you turn your back on it, you jettison the prestige associated with it, too. You aren't a member of that exclusive little (well, big) club. You may be able to replace the prestige and the money by doing something else that has those some qualities, but you won't get them from your law degree.

This came home to me in a discussion I had with a student. He was contemplating designing video games (a really cool gig), and his question was: "Won't the other designers resent me because I'm a lawyer?" I responded, "But you won't be a lawyer. You'll be a very well-educated video game designer." He was a little taken aback by this. But the fact is, if you do something else, you're not a lawyer-in-other-clothing; you're a "something else."

B. STEP ONE: FIGURE OUT WHAT YOU REALLY WANT AND NEED

It goes without saying that you can't find a job you'll enjoy if you don't know enough about yourself to know what you'll find enjoyable. As Career Counselor Kathleen Brady points out, "There's power in passion." You need to figure out what motivates you in order to find the nontraditional gig that you'll enjoy the most. Hastings' Sari Zimmerman likes to use the career anchors, based on work of Edward Schine, to figure this out. There are several core motivators: autonomy and independence; managerial competence; technical competence; security and stability; entrepreneurial creativity; service or dedication to a cause; pure challenge; lifestyle (work/balance); financial rewards; prestige. While you probably want *all* of those things—who doesn't?—something will ring your chimes more than the others.

We covered all kinds of "discover yourself" exercises in Chapter 2. Go back and review that chapter for help. Furthermore, don't hesitate to take advantage of tests you can take at Career Services at school—there's Myers/Briggs, the Strong Interest Inventory, just a whole raft of them.

You can also take career questionnaires on-line at several sites. The College Board has one, at www.collegeboard.com (click on "careers"), as does The Princeton Review, at www.review.com (click on "careers" then "career quiz").

In addition, take a look at what you do *outside* of work and school to figure out what really motivates you. Kathleen Brady offers the example of a law student who says, " 'I want to pitch for the New York Yankees.' You have to ask, 'where does that come from?' A love of baseball. There are lots of nontraditional jobs that can spring from that. There are jobs with Major League Baseball, with the minor leagues, with independent baseball leagues, with fantasy camps. If it's a love of baseball that's the unifying thread, you research it and see where it leads you."

C.   Step Two: Figure Out What You Bring to the Table

Knowing what you can do for an employer is a necessary precursor to nailing a job with any organization. Employers don't want to know what you've done; they want to know what you're *capable* of doing for them, based, of course, on things you've done. **There are certain skills that come from attending law school,** and I list them in Appendix A at the end of this chapter. Be sure to utilize that list in ascertaining what you bring to employers!

Also, **take a sheet of blank paper and list the concrete sources of your skills and knowledge.** *(This form courtesy of George Washington University School of Law):*

Write down the following headings, and fill in each one:

Educational Background:

Undergraduate

☐ *Include undergraduate major, minor, or areas of concentration, as well as specific course work that is unique or that you particularly enjoyed.*

Post-graduate

☐ *Include any post-graduate degrees, including your J.D., as well as course work toward any uncompleted post-graduate degree.*

Additional training:

☐ *Include any special certifications or significant CLE study.*

Work Experience:

☐ *Include all nonlegal jobs or internships held prior to, during, or after law school.*

Volunteer Experience:

☐ *Include any and all volunteer work you have performed or positions you have held.*

Industry Knowledge:

☐ *Include industries, businesses or fields about which you have acquired some substantive knowledge. This does not necessarily mean you have to have worked in that industry; you can often acquire expertise through association, especially through your law practice experience. For instance, if you did insurance defense work, you already have a working knowledge of the insurance industry. If you are an employment lawyer, many of your clients are human resources professionals, and you understand basic human resources principles and procedures. If you had a prior career with an HMO, you probably understand how hospital administration operates through your daily contact with that industry.*

Personal Interests/Hobbies:

☐ *Don't limit yourself! You would be surprised to learn of the kinds of passions, combined with a law degree, that can lead to a nontraditional job Anything from horses to history to hiking is fair game.*

As this form suggests, your skills don't have to come from jobs and school; they can also come from your hobbies, your personal life. Before I was married I lived with a couple of guys, which sounds a lot naughtier than it really was. One of my roommates was a guy named Michael McGovern, whose hobby was photography. He'd had an ancestor who was a pioneering photographer. Mike's day job had nothing to do with photography, but he was absolutely passionate about it; he was familiar with the work of many early photographers. He rolled that knowledge into a job working as an archivist for a renowned photo archive, Bettman Archives.

As you compile your transferable skills, it's super important to **characterize your skills in terms of *verbs*.** "I *can* ..." as opposed to "I *am* ..." Stated another way, you have to talk about what you do, not what you are. Take law school itself. "I am a law student" doesn't tell an employer what you can do. "I research, I analyze, I advocate in Trial Advocacy class ..." *That's* "skills" talk.

When you say you have a skill, be able to summon an example to prove it. "I know how to write well. I wrote the orientation brochure for incoming law students at my law school, and I wrote an article for the local bar association newsletter on ..."

D. STEP THREE: FIGURING OUT WHAT'S OUT THERE

It's not enough to say "I hate law." You can't be a "not-lawyer." You have to be a *something*.

Problematically, there are zillions of jobs out there. More precisely, the federal government lists 30,000 job titles in this country. You can't research them all. But you can zero in on jobs you might enjoy more easily than you might think. Here are a few ideas:

1. PRELIMINARY TOOLS

a. Go to a major job site, like Monster or Career Builder, and just browse. As Minnesota's Sue Gainen recommends, "Make a note of anything that catches your attention." Kathleen Brady adds that "Those web sites let you look at jobs related to topics. You can see what you're drawn to and what you can eliminate by looking at job descriptions."

Fordham's Hilary Mantis also recommends that you check out classified sections of newspapers, which you can mostly find on-line. "Just look for whatever sounds interesting. Don't do any editing!"

As you check out these sources, pay *special* attention to the actual content of jobs, not just their titles. It's too easy to fall in love with a title. You don't live a title, you know; you live the content of the job. I'm painfully aware of this, being a writer. I meet lots of people who say they want to be writers; one lady I'll never forget actually told me she *was* a writer. Of course I asked her, "What kinds of things do you write?" and she responded, "Oh, I have a book in my head." I love that. I have a book in my head. Now some people who want to be writers really do enjoy writing, and let's face it, it's not as though it requires a formal degree. You got a pencil and a pad of paper, you're a writer. But I suspect a lot of people have feelings more akin to what Carrie Fisher (herself a really great writer) once said: "I like to *have written* a book." There's a big difference between wanting to see your name on the cover and wanting to fill those pages (which can often be a lonely pursuit).

Furthermore, remember that the setting can make the same job title into a very different experience. Let's take nursing (an easy one for me, because my mom's a nurse). Your job as a nurse is very different if you work in an emergency room, or a maternity ward, or as a private-duty nurse for an elderly person. And if you work for a doctor in private practice, a lot of what your job will entail depends on the personality of your boss and the responsibilities you're given. In all of these situations, you'll need different personality traits to thrive, and the environment will provide different kinds of benefits. So a job title like "nurse" doesn't really tell you whether you'll enjoy being a nurse in any particular setting.

b. Go to a web site like www.jobhunt.org. "It's a great resource if you have absolutely no idea what you want to do," advises Hilary Mantis.

c. "Don't eliminate yourself from anything based on a lack of experience in the field," recommends Kathleen Brady. "You might have a story to tell that resonates with those employers. Just get a feel for what appeals to you, first."

d. Look at materials geared toward college students. Kathleen Brady points out that "Sometimes a J.D. can substitute for elements of a traditional career path." In addition, looking at materials for college students will give you the buzzwords you need to know.

2. When You've Narrowed Down to a Few Industries or Topics That Intrigue You . . . Get Some "Humint"

You should never, ever make a career decision based on what you read. I realize that sounds ironic coming from an author, but really, this book is just a jumping-off point. You need real human contact to refine your goal.

Up front you need to know that people like to talk about what they do, and they're generally very open about discussing their careers. I've found this to be true 99% of the time. When you say to someone, "I'm trying to figure out what I want to do. What do you like about your job? What would you do if you were starting over again?" you'll be pleasantly surprised by how helpful people can be.

While Chapter 10 is full of ideas for meeting people (and they're virtually all applicable to a nontraditional job search), there are at least five routes I'd recommend specifically:

- Go and chat with counselors at Career Services, for several reasons: First, you'll be talking to a kindred spirit. Most career services counselors have law degrees, too. So they chose a nontraditional career themselves!

  For another thing, they'll know alums who both have unusual jobs *and* were successful in jumping into another career entirely. When you discuss with them what kinds of attributes you're looking for in a job, they can put you onto alums who do things you might enjoy. Those alums will be a great source of both advice and contacts.

  Finally, they can put you onto other kinds of research aids that will help you refine your nontraditional search even further. So pay them a visit!

- Contact the trade association for the industry that intrigues you, and talk to someone there about careers in the industry; also, ask for events that you can attend to learn more.

Part of the mission of trade associations is educating people about the industries they represent. Call, tell them you want to learn more about careers in the industry, and ask to talk to someone who can help you.

On top of that, ask for conferences and seminars they hold. Every industry has an analogue to bar association events. Those are a great way to get all kinds of helpful information, and make valuable contacts at the same time.

Some associations will offer short courses on the industry, which are well worth taking to learn the landscape and the lingo; some of these courses are even offered on-line. Also, ask whether the association runs or knows or message boards or chat rooms focusing on the industry; visit those to see what issues are hot and, again, to learn the buzz words. (You can always correspond with people who post, but be sure you read for a while before you ask questions.)

For advice about making the most of events—who to talk to, what to say—see Chapter 10.

* * * SMART HUMAN TRICK * * *

Law student wants to get into the beauty products business. She doesn't know much about it, but she finds out that a trade show is coming to a city nearby, and it would give her a great opportunity to learn about the business and meet people. Problematically, it's open only to people in the industry.

She calls the organization running the trade show, and talks to someone who seems helpful. The person tells her, "Listen. Just go and print up business cards saying you're an independent distributor. You can get into the show with that." The student says, "But I don't want to be a distributor," and the trade show rep responds, "I realize that. You're just using it to get into the show. Once you're in, you can talk to anyone you want."

● Informational interviewing.

As we've discussed before, informational interviewing involves seeking information from people rather than jobs. We discuss it in Chapter 10. It's a great way to figure out what you want to do. You find potential informational interviewees everywhere; asking people you know, through trade associations, by reading about them in industry magazines or on-line or in newspaper stories, by going to employer websites and looking for people with whom you share something in common. The best ones, of course, would be people who also have a law degree. (Incidentally, don't contact anyone until you've done some research on the industry. You don't want to waste people's time asking them questions you could have answered on your own.) E-mail them, explain who you are and what you're doing, and ask if they can speak to you for ten minutes at their convenience because you'd truly appreciate their advice. Again: you'll be surprised how many people will talk to you and give you some truly useful insights.

The kinds of questions you might consider asking include: *(adapted from the George Washington University School of Law)*

- Describe your job, your duties and responsibilities;
- What do you like the most about it? What do you like the least about it?
- What are your working conditions like—hours, autonomy, flexibility?
- What legal skills do you use the most? What other "nonlegal" skills do you use?
- Does [current employer] consider your law degree valuable? How do you know?
- What about your background or skills do you think got you this job?
- Is there room for advancement for a J.D. in your position?
- Do you know of positions like yours in other industries or fields?
- What other jobs do J.D.s hold in your company/office?
- How did you originally learn about your job? How did you find the job opening? How would I learn about openings?
- Are there any classes/seminars/conferences I would attend to better position myself for a job like yours?
- Is there anything you wish you'd known when you started in this job?
- If I wanted to apply to your company/organization in the future, to whom would I send my resume?
- Is there anyone else I should talk to?

Of course your questions will vary according to the research you do into the person and the job, and you'll add and delete questions depending on the answers you get.

- Shadowing.

  Through industry groups and trade associations and maybe through people you know, try to spend a morning or afternoon shadowing a person who does what you think you want to do. Seeing a job up-close and in person is a great way to see if you really would like it.

- Vocation vacations.

  There are businesses that'll set up a week or two's worth of doing just about any job in the world (one of them is www.vocation vacations.com). You could try one of those, or just go ahead and set up a volunteer gig yourself. There are employers in every field who'll give you a chance to spend a couple of weeks volunteering; mount a phone and e-mail campaign to find them. There's a body of thought that says that you can't truly know if you'll be happy doing something until you do it yourself. A "vocation vacation" gives you that opportunity!

Incidentally, it's important to negotiate your role before you volunteer. Working on a restaurant's reservations database won't tell you what working in a restaurant is like. Spending a week helping out on the line in the kitchen, will.

• Look at periodicals in the field.

"Remember that law touches everything," says Kathleen Brady. "You can look at a discussion of an issue in a periodical, and be able to say to yourself, 'They need me here.' "

• Check out Yahoo groups and bulletin boards to keep up with industry trends.

E.   STEP FOUR: PREP YOUR TOOL KIT

There are a few elements to discuss:

• You need what Kathleen Brady calls a "pitch statement," something to pique the interest of nontraditional employers;

• You need to tweak your resume;

• You need to prep for interviews;

• You need to figure out whom to contact . . . and how to approach them.

We'll discuss each of those below. But first, let's address a couple of threshold issues.

1.   IN EVERY ELEMENT OF YOUR SEARCH, KEEP YOUR EYE ON YOUR TRANSFERABLE SKILLS

I can't emphasize this strongly enough: if you're going to convince employers who aren't obvious targets that you're the right person to hire, you've got to make it crystal clear what you bring to the table. In every aspect of your job search—conversations, letters, resumes—explain why what you've got is relevant to them.

For instance, let's say that you want to get into some kind of social work. As Kathleen Brady points out, "Lawyers listen to *facts*. Social workers talk about *feelings*." So your law degree isn't going to be terribly appealing to potential social work employers *unless you explicitly tell them the specific skills you bring to them*. As an example, let's say that you took part in the Client Counseling competition, and you did really well in it. Let's say that you've taken clinics at law school, and as part of that you've counseled low-income people. And let's say that in your spare time you volunteered at a battered women's clinic. In all of these activities, you've both honed your ability to counsel, to listen to people's problems, and to help in solving them, *and* you've proven your enthusiasm for counseling. *That's* what you bring to social work—but it's only because you've pulled from what you've done the skills that you can offer!

Let's take another example. Let's say you wanted to get a job as a director of a nonprofit. You'd want to highlight leadership and fundraising experiences, and if you have it, proof of your commitment to the nonprofit's focus (through volunteer work and community service). You *wouldn't* highlight your research skills, because those aren't relevant to this kind of job.

Let's take a third example, something out on a limb, something I probably never would have discussed with you if I hadn't read an article about it in *The Wall Street Journal* this morning: Being a butler. Apparently there's been a resurgence in the butlering profession because of the explosion of wealth in America. Before you scoff, "Kimmbo, I'm not going to *buttle* for a living," you need to know that it often pays six figures *to start, and* you get free room and board, *and* the demand is enormous. You live in fabulous mansions and travel to exotic places. Depending on who you work for, you might get to hang with celebrities. Heck, you'll *live* with them. That's what a lot of students who profess an interest in Entertainment Law really want, it seems to me. No-o-ot a bad gig.

The job, which goes by the title "Household Manager" nowadays, requires that you:

- negotiate with vendors, like pool cleaners and home theater installers;
- be tech savvy (so you can set up spreadsheets);
- manage multimillion-dollar budgets;
- communicate with and manage other household staff;
- facilitate entertainment and travel arrangements.

You can see just how your law degree is useful! Negotiating with vendors, communicating with household staff—you're there. Multitasking all of these responsibilities—you've got it. You're probably tech savvy, too. On top of that, your law degree gives you a whole raft of useful knowledge. "Sir, may I point out that the Olympic-size swimming pool is known as an 'attractive nuisance.' If I may suggest a fence ..."

You might have engaged in extracurriculars that gives you the entertainment facilitation skill; I was social director in law school, for instance. As for the budget management, maybe you ran your own summer business in college, or maybe you were a business major. Perfect. Or you can take a class on it. Or you could always go to butler school to fill in the gaps; the Starkey International Institute for Household Management in Denver runs 8–week classes on it, according to the *Journal.*

Obviously, I'm not suggesting that you take your J.D. and buttle. But it does show how your law degree can be a launch pad into many diverse fields!

2. DON'T EXPECT NONTRADITIONAL EMPLOYERS TO EMBRACE YOUR LAW DEGREE

Some nontraditional employers are completely down with law students. Common alternative careers like law firm and law school administration positions? You don't have much to explain away. But beyond that . . . Gee, here's a headline for you: a lot of people don't like lawyers. You may be thinking to yourself, "Well, geez, Kimmbo, I'm not a lawyer, and I don't want to *be* one!" Aha, but you see, people who hear you've got a law degree *automatically* consider you a lawyer. I don't know why that is, but it is. I've been a writer ever since I graduated from law school, but some people still insist on calling me a lawyer, even though I've *never* practiced law! So, you have to be prepared for people to be put off by the idea that you're a "lawyer."

As one career counselor points out, "When students tell me they want to go into business, I tell them that business people don't *like* lawyers. They view them as impediments to doing deals! You have to overcome that image."

To combat the lawyer image problem, make it plain that you understand how they feel about lawyers, but you aren't one. Explain that you've done a lot of research and you understand what they do and want to do it yourself, *then* state what you *did* get from law school, and how it benefits what you want to do now. That takes the focus off of your being a lawyer, and puts it where it belongs . . . on what you want to do next!

3. DON'T GET ALL UP IN PEOPLE'S GRILLS ABOUT HOW SUPERIOR YOUR CREDENTIALS ARE

From the Mount Olympus of law, it's easy to sneer down on credentials you figure are less impressive than yours. But here's a set-up for you. Let's say you want to get a job working in America's Test Kitchen (which produces the most fabulous recipes you can possibly imagine; check out the magazines *Cook's Illustrated* and *Cook's Country*.) What they do is bring you in for a day to make a bunch of food, and they watch you. Then they tell you to develop a recipe.

Let's say that there are two candidates for the job. Let's say that you're a law student, and, what the hell, let's say you go to Harvard. And you're on Law Review. And let's say the *other* candidate has five years' worth of experience in a restaurant.

Guess who's going to get the job?

As San Diego's Susan Benson says, "Employers acknowledge that, yes, law students have skills—but they won't take that over people with experience in the field. You have to bring something else to the table as well!"

As Kathleen Brady puts it, "When you're applying for an HR job you can't say, 'I'm a lawyer and that's superior to an HR background.' The response will be, 'I'm in HR and I don't like you.'" Remember: you're on a level playing field in areas outside of law. You don't have an advantage. You need to make the most of what you *do* have in order to stand out!

4. Formulate Your "Pitch Statement"

You have to be able to tell employers *succinctly* both *why* you want to do what they do (given that you have a law degree), and *what* you can do for them.

The "why" has got to avoid two pitfalls: the perception employers will have that the only reason you're talking to them is that you couldn't get a legal job, and the thought that as soon as you *do* nail a legal job, you'll blow. You need to assure the employer in every forum—cover letters, interviews, contact of any kind—that this is a career goal you've actively chosen and that you've researched it, you're confident you want it, and you have no intention of leaving. As Sandy Mans points out, "No other employer wants someone who's just an unhappy lawyer!"

One of the advantages of gathering the "humint" we just discussed is that it gives you credibility when you turn around to seek jobs.

The "what you can do for them" is your transferable skills, made crystal clear. For instance, let's say you want to be a teacher, and you've done some trial work, whether it's in a clinical program or a summer job. You can say, "I take large complex ideas and break them down to manageable pieces." That's *exactly* what teachers do! If you have trouble doing this kind of translating, utilize your Career Services Office for help, or talk to the contacts you've made in your research phase.

5. Your Resume

To a large extent, everything we talked about in the resume chapter, Chapter 8, still applies. You have to focus on accomplishments, and you have to rearrange your resume to suit the needs of specific employers. It's just that you'll have to do research so that you know specifically what your nontraditional employers seek; rearrange your resume accordingly, or take classes in the field/attend conferences to get relevant material on your resume.

Drusilla Bakert offers the example of a law student applying for a corporate management position. She says, "If it's a position as assistant benefits director that you want, you'd want to emphasize on your resume that you've taken Labor Law and Trusts & Estates. That way, you're *showing* why you'll fit!"

Depending on the employers you target, your resume may change very little .. or a lot. For jobs closely related to law it won't change that much; but for employers further away from the law school orbit, you may find yourself actually *downplaying* your law degree!

Let's say you wanted to get a job in sales. You'd emphasize your fundraising experience in law school (assuming you have any, and if you don't, volunteer to call alums right now!). You'd also highlight your experiences making presentations in Moot Court and elsewhere. And of course, if you have any selling experience in any job you've had before, you'd accentuate that.

The bottom line is, it's very important to convey expressly to the employer, on your resume as well as in every other communication with them, that you've got the skills they want. You can't expect them to glean it through osmosis!

Hilary Mantis recommends that you have a heading on your resume with the focus of the nontraditional career you're after. "For instance, if you want to be a writer, have a section on your resume called 'Writing Experience,' and put *anything* you've got in that section, whether it was written for school or on a volunteer basis."

You may want to consider sending a functional resume, which we discuss in Chapter 8. Remember, with a functional resume, you're not listing positions you've held, but rather skills you have or functions you've performed. You'd have sections like "Research," "Writing," "Fundraising," "Public Speaking," and "Management"—tailored to your experience and the target employer, of course—and you'd summarize your experience in those areas. Taking into account that employers will generally spend no more than a minute and a half on your resume, the functional approach may be an effective way to minimize the impact of your law degree.

6. YOUR INTERVIEWS

The interviewing chapter, Chapter 9, applies to every kind of interview, including nontraditional ones. You're going to research employers just as you would law firms. When it comes to making up an infomercial about yourself, you'll just tailor it to the transferable skills you bring to this employer . . . just as you would with a legal employer.

When it comes to questions you ask, you'll largely ask the same ones you'd ask of a legal employer. That's because the questions I favor, the "What's it like?" ones, are designed to forge a bond with *any* interviewer.

When it comes to *answering* tough questions, many of the ones you get will be very much like the ones in the interviewing chapter. But because you don't have the educational background that's a natural lead-in to the job, you'll want to marshal everything you can from your law school experience, your extracurriculars, your work experience, and your undergrad schooling to show that you're the right candidate.

You have to expect question like:

a.   Why should we hire you? This is part of your "pitch," the infomercial you develop for every interview. Focus on the transferable skills you bring to the table, and make it plain that you've researched the employer and the industry so you understand what they want!

b. If you wanted to do this, why did you go to law school? (Your answer will have to involve an explanation that you went to law school to develop certain skills, or because you thought it would be useful in business, or a similar answer tailored to the particular employer; or because you were inspired by a particular alum or speaker or law school graduate you read about or met. It's your credibility that's at stake. You'd follow up by saying, "but my interest in X field is shown by my participation in X/volunteering with Y/classes in Z ..." so that you wind up on a positive note.)

c. What if a legal job opens up six months from now? (Your answer has to involve something that shows your sincere interest in this field, whether you say explicitly "I wouldn't be here wasting your time if I weren't serious about this field, as exhibited by my participation in/volunteering with/classes in ..." as above.)

7. Who to Approach ... and How to Approach Them

There are a whole bunch of promising routes into a nontraditional job you'll like. Apart from answering job postings, consider:

- Take the "people and activities" suggestions in Chapter 10, and adjust them as necessary to accommodate your non-traditional goal.

- Go to Career Services and ask for alums who do the nontraditional work you're interested in pursuing. They'll be excellent resources.

- Go back to the "humint" resources we talked about a few minutes ago, and look at them as potential sources of leads: trade associations, industry events, and so on.

- Get on subscription lists for industry publications. When you read about people who do what you want to do, contact them and ask their advice. Even better, volunteer to write profiles for these publications; it'll give you a great chance to talk to people who can become informal mentors to you.

F. When Do You Give up on Your Dream?

Oof. I get this question from students and graduates periodically. I guess my answer would be: never. You never give up on your dream. There are a few things to consider:

- For pursuing your dream right now, it depends on your circumstances and your threshold of pain. If you've got a mortgage to pay and a family to support, it might not make sense to be unemployed for a long period of time or take on a string of volunteering gigs or sink your life-savings into your perpetual motion machine research. And regardless of your circumstances, it depends on your threshold of pain. When I got out of law school, I was willing to live in my parents' basement, scrabble around for menial paying gigs to pay my student loans, and essentially live on nothing—about seven grand a year—to start my own publishing company (and create what became the study aid *Law In A Flash*). I'll never forget what my father told me when I first mentioned the idea of *Law In A Flash* to him: "It's a million to one shot, and I think you're crazy. You'll never be able to raise the money. Law students have never used flash cards. But if you're ever going to do this idiotic thing, you may as well do it *now,* when you've got nothing to lose." With encouragement like that, who *wouldn't* pursue their dream? But you see my point. Your circumstances—and what you're willing to put up with—determine how long you'll wait before you say "uncle."

- There's nothing that stops you from pursuing your dream *while* you do something else, whether it's practicing law or anything else you do for dough. If you want to start your own internet business, for instance, you can do that in your spare time. The writer Scott Turow wrote *Presumed Innocent* on the commuter train while he was practicing law in Chicago.

- You also have the option of practicing law and *then* moving into what you want to do, after you've had the opportunity to save some money and/or pay of student loan debt. Truth be told, I probably would have been wise to do some transactional work for a couple of years before I started *Law In A Flash,* learning about how businesses are started, funded, and run. You can always take a job in law that exposes you to the industry you'd like eventually to join.

G.   What if You Change Your Mind Years From Now and You Want to Practice Law *Then* . . .

Most career counselors recommend that if you have any thoughts of practicing law any time in your life, do it first, because it's easier.

That doesn't mean that doing things backwards—doing an alternative career *and then* practicing law—is by any means impossible.

As a rule of thumb, "The closer your immediate dream job is to a practice area or legal topic, the easier it is to go back," according to Arizona's Mary Birmingham. No matter what your "interim" job is, when you're ready to hop back into law, you'd have to explain exactly what it is you bring to the law firm table as a result of your experience. In some ways this is analogous to the issue second career students face (we discussed that in Chapter 22), it's just that your "first career" is after law school instead of before it. Mary Birmingham herself spent the first few years after law school working for a labor union, handling arbitrations and mediations. When she decided to try practicing law after all, she successfully sold herself to litigation firms as someone who knew how to present a position and represent clients. She points out that if your other experience has put you in the position of bringing in clients—making you the golden goose of law in the form of a rainmaker—that's a huge plus.

No matter *what* you do in the meantime, you can always pave your way back into law the way a lot of students get there in the first place: volunteering. As Arkansas/Little Rock's Dianna Kinsey reports, "Volunteering *does* work!" You'll get the skills and contacts you need if you're willing to donate a little time.

In addition, it's worth remembering the "5 o'clock club," which is essentially a career counseling organization where people meet weekly in cities around the country. There's a counselor present, and people form groups to talk about the career issues they're facing ... including transitioning. It's for manager-level people or above, which is why I'm telling you about it prospectively, for when you're ready to make your second (or third) move. (For more information, visit www.5oclockclub. com)

So if you're sure you don't want to practice law right now, your law degree is forever. It's not a "limited time offer."

* * * SMART HUMAN TRICK * * *

Law student graduates from school and moves a thousand miles away from school to accompany her husband. For nine years, she raises children. When she eventually decides to become a lawyer, her responses from employers can be summed up with: "Your degree is nine years old, you've never used it, and you're from a law school we've never heard of."

She keeps trying, and through bar association events meets a lawyer who expresses interest in hiring her but also is very doubtful. She tells him: "Let me volunteer for a month and prove to you what I can do." She does ... and he hires her. She becomes one of the employer's prized attorneys.

H. Recognize That at the End of the Day, the Whole Purpose of Attending Law School in the First Place Was to Make Yourself Happy

Here's something we often overlook: if you want to be miserable, you can drop out of high school and accomplish that. You've been in school for at least *two decades* when you graduate from law school. You deserve to be happy; you've sacrificed for it. And if the job that makes you happy has nothing whatsoever to do with law ... so be it!

*

Appendix A
The Transferable Skills Law School Gives You

(This list is adapted from the excellent book "The Road Not Taken," by Kathy Grant and Wendy Werner.)

- **Ability to analyze facts.**

  Problem-solving is the main skill you get from law school; from reading and briefing cases, Moot Court, any journals that you work on, and exams. This is a particularly useful skill when it comes to identifying business problems and creating solutions.

- **Ability to work in teams or groups.**

  If you've worked with other students in Moot Court, or in a trial skills program, or in a study group, you've got the transferable skill of teamwork; that is, the ability to divide responsibilities and come up with a cohesive outcome. This is useful in any enterprise that is project-oriented.

- **Ability to be a self-starter.**

  As a law student, most of what you do is independent study. Any work as a law clerk typically exposes you to working without supervision, as well. Every employer appreciates employees who are self-starters.

- **Risk awareness.**

  As a law student you learn to be aware of the potential risk involved in transactions, products, policies, and programs. (As I've pointed out elsewhere, law students are sometimes *too* aware of risks, and it paralyzes them in their job search!) As an employee, risk awareness is useful in alerting your employer to any risks they may be taking, and it is very useful in creating preventive policies, products, or programs.

- **Counseling (including the ability to establish rapport, to listen, to reflect concerns back to clients, to empathize, and to problem-solve).**

  If you've taken part in client counseling competitions, clinics, or classes that involve counseling clients, then you have these transferable skills. These skills are useful in almost any position involving client or coworker contact.

- **Familiarity with legal terminology.**

  Going to law school gives you the ability to read and understand documents that are Greek to laypeople—things like contracts, leases, and statutes. This skill is useful to employers in predicting the long-term impact legal documents may have on their organization. It also gives you the ability to communicate comfortably with people who work on legal matters.

- **Knowledge of specific topics (like insurance, health care, tax, criminal law, corporations).**

  Depending on your coursework, you've got a broad base of knowledge about a wide variety of areas. Especially if you can combine this knowledge with an undergraduate degree that focuses on a certain area (e.g., patent law with an undergrad technical major, or construction law with an undergrad architecture or civil engineering major), you are a potential employee with a lot of knowledge to offer an employer—and a strong background for learning more.

- **Strong motivation and the skills associated with it (working under pressure, ability to complete projects, ability to juggle multiple responsibilities).**

  In law school, you respond to an enormous amount of pressure while balancing a heavy workload. As a law student, you have to meet strict deadlines and juggle multiple responsibilities. Also, as a law student you are perceived as having a history of success as well as the ability to complete projects. These skills are all highly prized by employers.

- **Ability to think independently.**

  As a law student, you are encouraged to think independently about issues and problems, coming up with your own solutions to them. You are taught to go beyond looking for answers, and instead identify issues. For potential employers, this translates into creative thinking skills and an ability to see the whole picture.

- **Ability to negotiate.**

  If you've taken part in clinics, seminars, or classes that focus on negotiation, or any extracurriculars that require you to negotiate (for instance, as the business editor of a journal), then the ability to negotiate is a skill you bring to the table for potential employers. Your ability to negotiate will enable you to open the doors to new clients and new business, as well as to "close the deal."

- **Ability to persuade.**

Taking part in Moot Court, as well as brief writing in your legal writing program, and writing for a journal, gives you the ability to persuade. This is a useful skill for convincing clients, other managers, staff, or peers.

- **Ability to prepare effectively.**

Law school demands that you be always prepared so that you can respond quickly and accurately. This is a useful skill in businesses which must react and respond to new information and industry changes to stay profitable.

- **Ability to speak before an audience.**

Responding to questions in class, as well as taking part in Moot Court and any extracurriculars that require public speaking, will give you a valuable skill for employers. Ease in front of an audience is an asset in presenting facts, information, or business proposals.

- **Research skills.**

Much of the work you do in law school focuses on research, as do many extracurriculars and law clerking jobs. Research skills are a valuable asset for many employers who must rely on employees to dig up accurate and comprehensive information for them.

- **Writing ability.**

Your exams, legal writing program, Moot Court, and any journal experience give you the ability to write in a clear and precise manner. This skill gives you the edge in business communications. Good writing skills are *always* in high demand.

As we discussed in the body of the chapter, depending on your unique law school experience, you may have many more transferable skills. For instance, if you've done a lot of fundraising, then you've got interpersonal and business development skills that would be valuable to many employers. And your undergrad and work experiences and hobbies will give you even more skills. So go through what you've done, and take from your background the skills that you bring to future employers. I think you'll find that you're valuable to a wide variety of employers!

*

Appendix B
Popular Law-Related Jobs

These are great alternatives if you don't want to practice law, but you want to do something related to it. (Note that in Appendices C and D we'll discuss popular targets for J.D.'s as well: Appendix C covers opportunities with companies, and Appendix D, law school administration jobs.)

Note that these are *very* brief descriptions; I provide sources for learning more about each one.

Also, as is true for every other job we talk about in this book, your best option for breaking in often is through *people and activities.* Seek out people who do what you're interested in and take part in activities that get you in touch with them, as we hammered home in Chapter 10.

1. **Law school professor.**

You need strong academics to become a law school professor; look at the profiles of your own professors if you don't believe me. *However,* it is possible to lateral in from other jobs; I had a law school classmate who went to a medium-sized firm, ran an ACLU office, and then became a law professor. He's a strong writer but his grades were crappy. So it's possible.

You find openings in the *Chronicle of Higher Education,* which you can find on-line at www.chronicle.org, and the American Association of Law Schools, www.aals.org/services_recruitment.php

2. **Undergraduate professor.**

Areas related to law include legal history, political science, business law, communications law, and similar courses.

Check out The Chronicle of Higher Education, www.chronicle.org

3. **Public accounting.**

They hire J.D.'s for tax and consulting. The "Big Four" are Ernst & Young, PricewaterhouseCoopers (atrulyannoyingwaytowriteaname-don'tyouagree), KPMG, and Deloitte & Touche. Check out www.careers-in-accounting.com

1333

4. Court administration.

There are many jobs in courts outside of judicial clerk and judge. Check out The Federal Judicial Center (www.wfjc.gov), the National Center for State Courts (www.ncsconline.org).

5. Law firm administration (or consulting with law firms).

There are *tons* of "not-lawyer" jobs in law firms. They include personnel director, client services or marketing director, pro bono coordinator, diversity manager, business development manager, recruiting coordinator, attorney development manager. These jobs pay well and have excellent perks. As one attorney development manager at a large firm pointed out to me, "This job sure beats being a lawyer here."

Another job becoming increasingly available at law firms is Litigation Support Analyst Manager. Per Fordham's Hillary Mantis, "This involves e-discovery. You know that every e-mail you type is discoverable! It's a huge, growing field. If you've got good computer skills or intellectual property courses or you are very conversant with data bases, or you've got a computer programming background, you can get into it. In fact it's often a job you enter by temping first."

You may also sell your skills to a variety of firms as a consultant. For instance, you might offer marketing consultation to firms (if you have a marketing background), or build out law firm web sites or otherwise consult with them on web image, advertising, promotions and so on.

Check out The National Association of Law Placement, www.nalp.org; Association of Legal Administrators (www.alanet.org).

6. Bar association administration.

(With local bar associations, ABA committees or sections. Jobs include Public Relations, Director of Lawyers Assistance Programs, special project coordinator, and legal services project director.)

Check out The American Bar Association, www.abanet.org/career counsel/hrlegal.html. For state and local bar associations, use the portal at www.abanet.org/barserv/stlobar.html.

7. Law School Administration (See Appendix C).

8. Mediator/Arbitrator.

(Possible employers include national organizations, labor unions, large corporations, dispute resolution boards.)

Check out http://research.lawyers.com/Alternative–Dispute–Resolution. htm/, The American Arbitration Association (www.adr.org) , American Bar Association (www.abanet.org), Federal Mediation and Conciliation Service (www.fmcs.gov), Judicate (a really useful site, at www.judicate. com) .

9. Law Enforcement.

(FBI or CIA agent, hearing officer, human relations specialist, investigator)

Check out the FBI (www.fbi.gov), National Public Safety Information Bureau (www.safetysource.com), CIA (www.cia.gov).

10. Government.

(Some examples include the contracts office for government agencies at the federal, state or local level; international or interstate trade relations specialist; land use examiner; congressional staffer.)

Note that Capitol Hill teems with law school graduates, both in legal and nontraditional roles. Check out the *Federal Yellow Book* (from Leadership Directories; it's at Career Services) for targets. Caveat: This is an area where it's vitally important to get to know people as a means of getting your foot in the door.

11. Nonprofit management.

If you have a public interest bent, consider nonprofit management. There are other jobs at the executive level available to J.D.'s as well, "including grant writer and development director, staff attorney and director of planned giving," per Kathleen Brady. Use the web resources we talked about in the Public Interest chapter, Chapter 26, particularly the web site www.idealist.com, and also look at the *Chronicle of Philanthropy* (www.philanthropy.com) for openings. Also look at the web site for the American Society of Association Executives, www.asaecenter.org, which lists lots of jobs.

12. Business (See also Appendix C, for jobs in companies *outside* of the general counsel's office.).

Opportunities exist in a variety of areas, including financial planning, banking, insurance, management—the choices are virtually endless. As South Texas' Kim Cauthorn points out, "J.D.'s can do many jobs that traditionally called for MBA's."

Browse any of the major job search sites listed in Chapter 11, as well as www.wetfeet.com.

13. Journalism/communications.

(Possibilities include legal correspondent for a television or radio network, editor or writer for a legal magazine or newspaper, reporter on legal issues for any magazine or newspaper).

Check out The American Society of Newspaper Editors (www.asne.org), as well as www.khake.com (overview of dozens of journalism/broadcast media jobs).

14. Consultant.

You name it, and there's a consultant who focuses on it, from management to health care to compensation.

Management consulting consists essentially of going to large companies with a team of other consultants and offering advice on strategy and operations. It can encompass more, but that's the heart of it. Three blue-chip consulting firms that hire J.D.'s are McKinsey & Company (www.

mckinsey.com), Deloitte & Touche (www.deloitte.com), and Clark Consulting www.clarkconsulting.com.

Also check out: www.amcf.org (the web site for the Association of Management Consulting Firms), and www.managementconsultingnews. com (has a free e-mail newsletter).

15. Legal trainer/instructor.

(For state and local bar associations and independent continuing legal education (CLE) providers who conduct training programs and seminars for lawyers. Other possibilities include an instructor in a legal assistant or court reporter program, or director of a legal assistant program at a community college. Some background in educational programming is desirable.)

Check out ALI–ABA (www.ali-aba.org) ; Institute of Continuing Legal Education (www.icle.org) ; Practicing law Institute (www.pli.edu) ; National Institute for Trial Advocacy (www.nita.org).

16. Legal Research and Publishing.

(Research associate, legal research trainer/marketer for computer research vendor, editor for legal publishers)

An outstanding publisher to consider: Jones McClure, at www. jonesmclure.com.

Check out Aspen Publishers (www.aspenpublishers.com; a sentimental favorite of mine because they now own Law In A Flash, the study aid I created); Commerce Clearing House (www.cch.com); Thomson/West (my publisher; check out www.thomsoncareers.com); Matthew Bender (www. bender.com); the Bureau of National Affairs (www.bna.com).

17. Legal Search consultant.

(Assist law firms in locating experienced attorneys and merger candidates)

Check out The National Association of Legal Search Consultants (www. nalsc.org).

18. Healthcare/Risk Management.

(typically employed by hospitals or other healthcare providers; some practice, healthcare, or management experience is extremely beneficial).

Check out The American Association of Nurse Attorneys (www.taana. org); American Hospital Association (www.aha.org); American Medical Association (www.ama-assn.org).

19. Trial consultant.

(Aid in jury selection and other aspects of trial.)

Check out The American Society of Trial Consultants (www.astcweb. org).

20. Real estate development.

Check out www.realestatedeveloper.com, The Urban Land Institute at www.uli.org.

21. Trade associations.

Trade associations offer a myriad of lawyer and non-lawyer jobs you can target. I've heard just great things about working for them. For a start, it's a great way to mesh your interest in another industry with a law-related job, whether you're into skiing or biotech or fashion or *anything*. You get a broad perspective on an industry and there are a bunch of interesting things to do, whether it's researching and developing an expertise on issues that face the whole industry, conducting seminars for association members (do I hear 'travel opportunity'?), or lobbying.

Consult: *Yellow Book* of Associations (published by Leadership Directories; it's at Career Services), the directory of associations (www.marketingsource.com/associations/ (subscription required, but it can be really cheap); Yahoo trade association directory (http://dir.yahoo.com/Education/organiztions/Trade_Associations/.

22. Small businesses.

Most of the business world isn't huge companies with divisions with formal titles. Most businesses are small, and there are opportunities in management with these companies for J.D.s. Since they typically don't have in-house counsel, managers with a legal background are very useful. And in one of these roles, you get to wear several hats; you might get to do the marketing, negotiate with vendors and review contracts, meet with clients/customers, you name it.

To find these opportunities, among other things you should get out into the business community; get to know people at the local chamber of commerce, bankers, and check to see if your state makes enterprise loans to small businesses (the people who review those loan applications will know lots of small businesses). Also, keep up with the local business press, looking for companies to contact. Tell people you know—including lawyers, particularly those with a transactional practice—what you're looking for. Shake the trees for people who might know entrepreneurs!

23. Start your own business!

This one is close to my heart, because it's what I did. I can tell you from experience that a J.D. gives you a level of credibility with investors and vendors that would be hard to attain with any other education. It's *particularly* easy to start a business today, because of the Internet. There is a growing number of law school graduate/internet entrepreneurs. (For instance, the web site www.cuteasbuttons.com offers children's clothing, and it's the brainchild of a law school graduate.) With web sites, you make money either with Google's small text ads, with banner ads, and through "affiliate marketing," where you get paid for funneling customers to other sites. You can make a *very* handsome living this way.

You can run a business from anywhere, even out of your house. Beyond that there are office buildings designed for start-ups, where you pay only for the services you need (e.g., receptionist, computer experts), and there are even "virtual offices," where you have a phone number and address even though you're not physically there.

There are a million books on starting business; a good starting point on-line is www.sba.org, the federal government's Small Business Administration, with advice about starting your own business, and www.entrepreneur.com for articles about every aspect of starting a business.

Appendix C
Corporate Jobs for J.D.s
... Outside of the
General Counsel's Office

There are lots of options open to you if you want to be a not-lawyer at a company. As one corporate in-house lawyer points out, "There's a lot of fun stuff out there! Lawyers don't always get the glory. If your company does a deal and you, as the lawyer, do 90% of the negotiating, it's *still* the business guy who gets the credit. It's *fun* to be on the business side, where you can be more of a big-picture, strategy person."

To learn more about the kinds of jobs that exist in companies, check out a great website, www.wetfeet.com.

A great way to break into any corporate position is via an internship. Check out www.interships.wetfeet.com and www.internweb.com. You'll find that many business-side internships are offered to college students rather than grad students, but even in those cases it's worth giving them a try—law students have been known to snag them. Also, note that starting out in the in-house counsel's office gives you a springboard into other parts of the corporation. But we're focusing on nontraditional jobs here, so we'll set that aside for a moment.

In addition, Wake Forest's Bill Barrett recommends that you "Go over to a business school—if you have one on campus, that's convenient—and look at the job postings. With a J.D. you can make a credible argument for many of them." Also check and see which employers are showing up on campus to interview MBA's; it's worth sending them your credentials, as well. And, of course, you can check company web pages for openings they list themselves.

No matter how you plan to get your foot in the door, remember: you need to show a well-defined enthusiasm for these jobs; they can't be a default. Arm yourself with research and a knowledge of your transferable skills!

The jobs that J.D.'s often go into in companies include:

1. Mergers and acquisitions. This is perhaps the perfect leap for lawyers to make because law and M & A are so closely intertwined.

2. Risk management/insurance. With an understanding of risks and how to avoid them, a law background is perfect for risk management-oriented work.

3. Corporate finance, the treasurer's or comptroller's office: all options if you have a finance background (or get one).

4. Employee relations, labor relations, personnel administration.

5. Consumer awareness. A law background helps you to know what you can, and should, say.

6. Lobbying, which is an especially fertile option for businesses in aerospace, liquor, and tobacco—but many, many other industries and companies employ lobbyists, as well.

7. Regulatory Compliance (depending on the industry).

8. The traffic department—depending on the industry in question, this can involve supervising, organizing and analyzing transportation, and distribution and shipping procedures.

9. Public relations. A law degree helps here because with a knowledge of securities laws, you know what you can and can't say to shareholders.

Visit companies in Second Life (wwwsecondlife.com). Some of them are building a substantial presence there; you can get a perspective on what the companies are like and what kinds of careers they offer by sending your avatar there. Some have even started having job fairs on Second Life, although it'll be a little while before those become commonplace!

Appendix D
"And I Am Telling You, That I'm Not Going ..." Law School Administration Jobs

Advice in this section courtesy of Susan Gainen, University of Minnesota Law School.

Some people can't get out of law school fast enough. Others never want to leave. You may find it hard to believe, but people generally enjoy law school administration jobs (and their analogs in colleges.) That might be hard to believe because the law school personnel you see the most are professors, and let's face it, you wouldn't exactly characterize most law professors as Mr. Happy.

But the fact is, there are a ton of other administration jobs, as well. If you like the idea of working with students, a law school environment can be great for you.

Incidentally, you can find openings for these jobs, and learn more about them, through the bible of higher education, *The Chronicle of Higher Education* (www.chronicle.com). Also take a look at NALP's website, and search "lawyer to administrator" www//nalp.org.

Jobs to consider include:

- College/university attorney.

   OK. Technically this isn't an alternative career, because you get to be a lawyer. You're basically in-house counsel for a major corporation whose business happens to be education and research, and your job is much the same as an in-house counsel's gig: you conduct or manage litigation, draft contracts, and/or deal with

1341

environmental, employment, discrimination or intellectual property issues, among many others.

- Career Services director/counselor.

    Apart from anything else, this is the surest way to get quoted
    in books I write.

    Beyond that, this is a job where you get to wear at least six
    hats: counselor, teacher, lawyer, mother or father, nag, and cheer-
    leader. You have to be an active listener, understand adult learn-
    ing styles, juggle responsibilities, be a creative team leader, good
    delegator, and be able to figure out how to do more with less
    (Career Services budgets are notoriously, and criminally, small).
    But there's no question that when you have a student who nails a
    dream job and credits you for helping them get it, it's an incompa-
    rable rush.

    To find jobs, consult www.nalp.org (the National Association of
    Law Placement), and be sure to tell your Career Services Office at
    school what you want to do ... they may know about openings
    coming up at other schools. It doesn't hurt to volunteer at Career
    Services while you're in school, but I've told you that a million
    times already.

- Dean of Students.

    Perhaps the most emotionally challenging of all law school
    administration jobs, Deans of Students enforce academic rules and
    help students get through law school while maintaining their
    personal and family lives. As Dean of Students you often deal with
    students facing personal problems like disability, divorce, depres-
    sion, miscarriage, birth and bankruptcy. Obviously, to thrive in
    this job you have excellent listening skills, you have to like people
    and you have to be able to live with unpredictability.

- Director of International Programs.

    A law school might have two types of international programs:
    one which grants the LL.M. degree to international students, and
    the other which allows current students to study abroad for a
    summer or a semester. Sometimes law schools hire a director of
    international programs to handle these; other schools assign the
    duties to a tenured faculty member.

    In this job you admit LL.M. students, arrange visas, review
    immigration paperwork, teach courses for foreign students, and
    counsel international LL.M.s. This aspect of the job gives you a
    chance to get to know students who often have a fascinating
    background, and as one LL.M. director points out, "These are
    lovely people who could not be more grateful for any help you give
    them." The job also requires you to maintain contacts with
    foreign law schools with which your school has exchange pro-
    grams, choose the students who get to study abroad, and make

sure they get the appropriate academic credit for their work, among other duties.

- Director of Judicial Affairs.

Not *that* kind of affairs. The job's not that racy. Instead, the Director of Judicial Affairs administers the code of conduct for students, administering policy, helping create and revise policies, and helping to settle disputes about student conduct. Depending on the campus' philosophy of student affairs, the position can be considered an educational endeavor on the one hand, or punitive and corrections-oriented on the other.

- Director of public interest programs in (or near) a law school.

The number of law schools that have in-house public interest programs or counseling offices is growing. In this position you're essentially running a small business. If you have a public interest orientation as well as an interest in fundraising and development, you'll enjoy this job.

You'll find these positions in the *NALP Bulletin* (at Career Services or on-line at www.nalp.org).

- Public interest counselor.

Many law schools have full-or part-time public interest counselors as part of the Career Services Office or in a separate public interest advising office. The vision and commitment to public service required of those who work in public interest programs are a base-line requirement. It gives you the chance to counsel students on public interest careers, as well as talk with many public interest lawyers and employers.

- Athletic Department Compliance Offices

Because the National Collegiate Athletic Association (NCAA) seems to promulgate rules at the rate rabbits procreate, there are an increasing number of jobs for compliance officers in Division I and Division II schools' athletic departments. This job is a great jumping-off point for other sports oriented jobs, like working for the NCAA itself.

In this job, you monitor the NCAA and other conference rules, educate athletic department staffs, student athletes, parents and fans about these rules. Counseling students about the NCAA rules and the rule relating to turning professional include discussing how the rules apply and what a student athlete's different options might be in the process of considering a professional career.

In addition, compliance officers work with parents, Booster Clubs, and fans, keeping them up-to-date on the limitations and consequences of everyone's generosity, among other duties.

A good way to break into this job is to take an internship (paid or volunteer) with a compliance office during college or law school. Jobs are also posted at www.ncaa.org/news.

- Director of Admissions.

    As the Director of Admissions, you find, market to, evaluate, admit, and enroll students. Because law schools are largely tuition-driven, you also have to fill the class.

    In this job, you are often the first person a prospective student sees. You'll talk to and write to thousands of prospective students each year, and you'll deliver the school's message in person, by phone, by mail, and via the web. You have to be a good marketer, strategist, and politician ... and you have to be willing to undertake a fair amount of travel.

    Other than the *Chronicle of Higher Education,* you'll find listings for these jobs in the *AALS Bulletin* (American Association of Law Schools, on-line and at Career Services).

- Alumni Relations.

    Although tangentially related to fundraising, the primary function of alumni relations people is ensuring good communications between a school and its alumni.

    Most law schools publish alumni magazines at least twice a year; that's the responsibility of the alumni relations director, along with maintaining alumni records, scheduling reunions and homecoming events, and depending on the state, organizing continuing legal education seminars for alums. The director may also schedule dean's visits with other cities and communicate with other departments in the university and the law school. The director might also be the school's point person for media contacts and serve as liaison from the law school to university communications committees and alumni committees.

    Apart from the *Chronicle of Higher Education,* you'll find openings in the *Chronicle of Philanthropy* (at Career Services).

- Director of Student Legal Services.

    Student legal services offices basically function as a kind of "legal aid" office for students, making presentations and providing legal advice on a variety of issues ("How loud can my party be?" or "How do I handle a deadbeat roommate?"). Hundreds of schools have these offices, which provide both direct client service and education about the law.

    In general, in this job you do non-fee generating civil work and minor criminal work. The bulk of most caseloads is consumer counseling, tenants' rights, and family law. You also produce programs on all aspects of student life, from noise ordinance to debt management.

- Law Librarianships.

    Now, now. This isn't the "shhhh" kind of librarianship. While your focus is on collecting, preserving, managing and managing access to all kinds of information sources. You get to solve puzzles and problems, and often you get a chance to teach classes, often on legal research to First Years. There are roles for the most gregarious extroverts as well as traditional introverts.

Other than law school libraries, you can work in law firms, public law libraries, bar libraries, and corporate and government law libraries, including the Law Library section of the Library of Congress. Many state courts and state attorneys general have separate law libraries, as do many legislatures.

You do have to have both a J.D. and a Master's in Library Science to break in, so you'll need another degree. You can find job openings in the *Chronicle* as well as the American Association of Law Libraries web site (www.aall-net.org).

*

Appendix E
Other Resources, Web and Hard Copy

Web resources:

Chapter 11 gives you a ton of great resources. In particular, consider:

www.vault.com (information about companies, company-specific message boards, guides to non-legal careers like investment banking and consulting)

www.wetfeet.com (great job search resource, including company, career and industry profiles

www.rileyguide.com

www.acinet.org (click on "videos"—bet this isn't the first web site where you've done *that,* wink wink nudge nudge—and you'll find videos on 450 different careers)

www.bls.gov/oco (The Occupational Outlook Handbook)

Hard copy resources (check Career Services):

There are many more than this, but these are a good start:

Federal Reports, "600 non-traditional jobs for lawyers."

What Can You Do With A Law Degree? By Deborah Arron

Alternative Careers for Lawyers by Hillary Mantis

Breaking Traditions: Work Alternatives For Lawyers (ABA)

Searching for an Alternative: A Law Student's Guide to Finding Non-Legal Jobs (NALP Alternative Careers Committee)

In addition, check with Career Services for binders of alums from your school who've gone into nontraditional fields. You'll identify interesting gigs *and* you'll have someone useful to contact.

Materials excerpted in this chapter, courtesy of George Washington University.

Shout-outs for help with this chapter to Kathleen Brady, Hillary Mantis, and Susan Gainen.

Index

References are to Pages

INDEX

INDEX

†